Professional Meeting Management

Comprehensive Strategies for Meetings, Conventions and Events

Fifth Edition

EXECUTIVE EDITOR
Glen C. Ramsborg, PhD
Senior Director, Education
Professional Convention Management Association

LEAD EDITOR
Brian Miller, EdD
Assistant Professor
Hotel, Restaurant, and Institutional Management Program
University of Delaware

CONTENT EDITORS
Deborah Breiter, PhD
Professorship in Convention & Conference Management
Rosen College of Hospitality Management
University of Central Florida

B. J. Reed, EdD, CMP
Associate Professor and Chair
Department of Communication Technologies
University of Wisconsin—Platteville

Amanda Rushing, CMP
Director, Conferences and Meeting Services
American Society of Civil Engineers

KENDALL/HUNT PUBLISHING COMPANY
4050 Westmark Drive   Dubuque, Iowa 52002

The PCMA Education Foundation supports PCMA through fundraising and grant-giving by focusing on education and research that encourages the highest levels of professionalism in the meeting industry. As part of the Foundation's mission, we are proud to have assisted in the development and execution of the fifth edition of *Professional Meeting Management*. We are confident this newest edition will become an essential resource guide for all in the meetings profession.

John Patronski
Executive Vice President, Industry Development
GES Exposition Services
Chairman, PCMA Education Foundation Board of Trustees

The Convention Industry Council (CIC) has granted permission to use the Accepted Practices Exchange (APEX) Glossary of Terms. Throughout the text, the APEX terms are used unless a definition does not exist for the term. Additionally, other references to the contribution of CIC and APEX are noted throughout. All have been used with permission.

Every effort has been made to make attribution to previous contributors and materials in this book. PCMA will be pleased to rectify any omission to the source of information contained within this publication in future editions.

Front cover: Left and right photos courtesy of PCMA

Copyright © 1985, 1989, 1996, 2002, and 2006 by the Professional Convention Management Association

Perfect bound version:
ISBN 13: 978-0-7575-2666-4
ISBN 10: 0-7575-2666-7

Case bound version:
ISBN 13: 978-0-7575-2759-3
ISBN 10: 0-7575-2759-0

Printed in the United States of America
10 9 8 7 6 5 4 3 2 1

DEDICATION

Professional Meeting Management
Fifth Edition
is dedicated to

Barbara C. Nichols

Whose vision, ingenuity, and passion for education inspire us all.
Her ongoing work to improve our profession resonates
throughout the entire meetings and hospitality industry.

CONTENTS

Meeting Production

Legal and Ethical Considerations

LIST OF ILLUSTRATIONS

> Evolution requires us to continually refresh our competitive advantage, sometimes in dribs and drabs, sometimes in major cataclysms, but always with some part of our business portfolio at risk and in play. To innovate forever, in other words, is not an aspiration; it is a design specification. It is not a strategy, it is a requirement.
>
> —Geoffrey A. Moore, *Dealing with Darwin: How Great Companies Innovate at Every Phase of Their Evolution*

Though every professional association has its own mission, vision, goals, and strategic plan, we all share a common commitment: to connect our members to the knowledge, insight, and ideas they need in order to be successful. World-class meeting professionals create world-class meetings, and the Professional Convention Management Association (PCMA) is committed to providing the education and information to create those world-class meeting professionals. Professional development has been at the core of PCMA since the association's inception in 1957, and *Professional Meeting Management* is one of our flagship resources and one of the most tangible expressions of PCMA's role as a thought leader for the meetings industry.

Professional Meeting Management is a vital tool addressing the diverse needs of all meeting professionals. It is a comprehensive tool that has a place in the work of everyone contributing to the meetings industry. Each edition of meeting professionals at all levels—from the hospitality student preparing a class paper to the veteran meeting professional refreshing his/her knowledge about an individual topic—from the convention services manager double-checking an industry standard, to the university faculty member outlining course content.

Additionally, *Professional Meeting Management* has provided timeless information and contemporary content as well as standards that have stood the test of time—a wealth of information that all meeting professionals need in order to design and manage the myriad of meetings that occur around the world every single day. As part of its strategic plan, PCMA is fully committed to enhancing its role as the education and resource center for the meetings industry.

We speak a great deal about lifelong learning, almost as if it is an option that we can choose to pursue. In reality, however, such learning is mandatory, not optional. If we as a profession are to remain relevant, we must evolve and change. If you as a meeting professional want to remain effective, you must learn, grow, and evolve. As the famed philosopher and author, Mortimer D. Adler, once said, "The purpose of learning is growth, and our minds, unlike our bodies, can continue growing as we continue to live."[1]

---

[1] http://www.gotd.org/searchsearch2.phtml?keywords=growth. Retrieved April 3, 2006.

Though we seem to live in an era of disposability, some things still have permanence and an extended shelf-life. *Professional Meeting Management* is one of those things. It is not a perishable commodity, but rather a trusted friend that will stand the test of time. Look on the bookshelves of almost any meeting professional and no doubt you will find a well-used copy, one with frequently visited sections tagged and highlighted passages on most of the pages. We have no doubt that this fifth edition will claim the same space ... on your bookshelf and in your efforts to create world-class meetings. PCMA is here to support you in doing just that.

Deborah Sexton
President and CEO
Professional Convention Management Association
Chicago, Illinois

In a digital era in which our lives are becoming filled with PDFs, MP3s, podcasts, Google search results, and blogs, you hold in your hands one of the long-lasting forms of information and knowledge exchange: *a book*. Since the Gutenberg printing press swung into action in the 1450s (a bit before the first edition of *Professional Meeting Management*), the book form has been the primary source of on-demand information.

The book you are holding is not just any book. *Professional Meeting Management* is one of the "must have" resources for anyone working in the meetings industry. This is your professional search engine that connects you to the fundamentals of almost every aspect of effective meeting design and management.

THE EVER-EVOLVING MEETINGS PROFESSIONAL

The meeting manager has not been relegated to simply counting cups and saucers for coffee breaks for a long time. Although ensuring efficient logistics management is still a critical part of the job portfolio, it must now be augmented by competencies and knowledge associated with an increasingly diverse mix of topics and issues. In his provocative book, *A Whole New Mind*, author Daniel Pink suggests we are in the midst of a major shift in our economic focus,[1] a shift that has interesting implications for the meetings industry and for our professional development.

Pink notes that our economy has moved through several key stages or "ages": an Agricultural Age characterized by farmers, an Industrial Age characterized by factory workers, an Information Age characterized by knowledge workers, and the merging Conceptual Age, which he believes will be characterized by creators and empathizers. Pink asserts that in this conceptual age, qualities typically associated with right-brain thinkers (artistry, empathy, emotion) will take center stage and be of greater importance. Why? Because our economy has gotten about all the value it can out of the left-brain thinking (logical, precise, analytical) that has long been dominant.[1]

In many ways, the meetings industry (and the role of meeting managers and related professionals) have traveled a similar path. We are no longer just concerned with meeting a budget and having the right amount of food at social gatherings. We are also about trying to create memorable events that help people network with others, which builds their enthusiasm and connection. Having an accurate general session room diagram is the minimum expectation nowadays; designing a powerful learning environment is the new gold standard. Logistics may have been our foundation, but the focus on learning is our future.

---

[1]Pink, D.H. (2005). *A whole new mind: Moving from the information age to the conceptual age*. New York: Riverhead Hardcover.

THE EVER-EVOLVING PROFESSIONAL MEETING MANAGEMENT

Although what you are reading is the foreword to this edition, the edition itself looks *forward,* providing the information, tools, and tips you will need to meet the needs and expectations of meeting participants in our ever-changing profession and this emerging Conceptual Age. As with previous editions, it provides the content relevant to the myriad of daily decisions and activities in which you engage. The book is divided into three sections, each linked to one of the following fundamental questions:

1. **What is professional meeting management?**
2. **What is a professionally managed meeting?**
3. **What is a professional meeting manager?**

Section One expands the framework of professional meeting management, moving beyond event planning and logistics to the design and execution of meaningful learning experiences. It explores how meetings and conferences are the means through which many value propositions (or ends) are fulfilled. In many ways, it looks from the outside in, exploring meeting planning in the larger context in which it operates and the environmental trends that will continue to influence what we define professional meeting management to be in the future.

Section Two anchors this edition of *Professional Meeting Management* by offering more than 40 chapters written by industry leaders whose expertise and insight you will find to be invaluable in professionally managing a meeting, and represents an enhanced and updated version of the content found in previous *Professional Meeting Management* editions. Complementing its in-depth exploration of the critical components of meeting and conference design are two "bookend" sections, or extended essays of Sections One and Three.

To enhance your use and application of the information contained within the covers of this book, we have incorporated a variety of components into most of the chapters, including:

1. *Learner Outcomes*—provide a snapshot of the learning you can expect to possess after reading a chapter.
2. *Overview*—summarizes in a few paragraphs the chapter's content.
3. *Put It Into Practice*—contains a case study or best practice that offers practical application of chapter content.
4. *Put It Into Perspective*—provides examples connecting chapter content to the different types of meetings and different types of planners.
5. *Fast Facts*—interesting and useful facts that will provide further insight on a specific topic.
6. *Did You Know?*—poses questions or ideas that will spark your interest in the topic.
7. *Summary*—concludes each chapter by reviewing the key content connected to each of the stated learner outcomes.
8. *References*—attribution is as accurate as possible. Using text from previous editions makes it impossible to cite a source not previously cited.

9. *Key Terms*—as defined by Accepted Practices Exchange (APEX) format, are highlighted at the end of each chapter and many are defined in the book's glossary.

10. *Compelling Questions for Consideration*—are designed to further stimulate your thinking as you go about your work. It has been said that the answers we get depend on the questions we ask. By asking more provocative questions about designing learning experiences, we can generate more meaningful solutions.

Section Three, exploring what a professional meeting manager is, addresses the changing role of the meeting professional and the professional growth that will be required for meeting professionals to remain as valued partners in achieving organizational goals. It further highlights some of the critical future considerations for meeting professionals. This section looks from the inside out, moving from the insider role of a meetings professional to the world in which that professional will be operating.

Throughout this text, *meeting planner* refers to someone who handles at least some of the basic planning logistics for a meeting. A *meeting manager* is responsible for strategic decision making to guide the planning stages for that meeting. *Meeting professionals* refer to all of the many people who pull a meeting together—planners, managers, and suppliers across the industry.

So, whether you are in need of left-brain facts and figures or right-brain ideas and concepts, you will find what you are looking for in *Professional Meeting Management*, 5th edition. Since *PMM*'s first printing in 1985, it has been one of the most critical resources for the meetings professional. No doubt its important place in your resource library—and in your daily work—will continue.

Glen C. Ramsborg, PhD
Executive Editor
Senior Director, Education
Professional Convention Management Association
Chicago, Illinois

ACKNOWLEDGMENTS

The future belongs to the flexible, the creative, and those
with a talent for working well with other people.

—*Granville N. Toogood, "The Articulate Executive in Action"*

There are many, many people who have inspired, taught, influenced, and supported Professional Convention Management Association (PCMA) educational endeavors through the years. Whispering through the pages of this book are the words, ideas, and thoughts of individuals who have written the four previous editions of *Professional Meeting Management*. The impact of these individuals and their commitment to excellence continues within the pages of this new edition. A tribute to all who have gone before is chronicled in Appendix D.

The torch has been passed in this edition to more then 100 people who have had an active involvement in the enhancement of this edition.

The process began with an initial survey sent to the PCMA membership and a diverse group of faculty members in many of the colleges and universities throughout the country. To the more than 600 people who responded with thoughts and ideas, identifying needs, and general comments, a special thank you. Many new and innovative ideas have been incorporated.

As the process continued, a cross-section of individuals was identified to review each of the existing chapters. A minimum of three reviewers for each chapter made evaluative comments, which were invaluable to the chapter authors. The integrity of the content and state-of-the-art information is reflective of their combined efforts. Their names and the organizations they represent are listed in this section.

A new feature of this edition is the attribution of each chapter's contributor/ author, which addresses the professional needs of many of those involved. While content may not have been completely rewritten, all chapters have been edited and updated. Therefore, those who worked on the current chapters, which may have been partially written by former authors, are named. This change will also allow for easier recognition in future editions of those professionals who shaped the content of each chapter. A special thanks is extended to the contributors/authors who, on a tight schedule, more than met their responsibilities.

One of the goals that I set for this edition was to alter the focus of the meeting professional from a strictly tactical sense to a more strategic approach. Although this is an evolving process, in future editions this approach will be more fully realized. We must keep in mind that we are in the business of bringing people together to learn, to network, and to buy and sell.

The tactical needs and requirements remain a very critical component of meeting management. These references are represented as the most current and on the cutting edge. However, as business changes and evolves, the successful meeting professional must think about and develop strategic responsibility. Consequently, there are many factors that influence the success of the meeting professional. You will note that there are several new chapters in this edition that begin to address this strategic approach.

We put together a team of content editors to represent academia, practice, and innovation. Throughout the past year, as PCMA Senior Director of Education, I have met many people and have made many new friends, including Dr. Deborah Breiter, an esteemed educator at one of the country's largest universities. Her understanding of the needs of faculty and student, and of the body of knowledge for the profession, is visionary.

Dr. Brian Miller is the consummate educator and researcher. He has been a real asset to the team given his background on the hotel operations and facilities side of the business coupled with his teaching at the University of Delaware. His consulting has provided him a worldwide vision. He brings a unique mix of life experiences and perspective to this work.

Dr. B. J. Reed, CMP, has provided a unique perspective during this revision. Professionally, she has been involved on the supplier and meeting management sides of the industry and is also an educator at the University of Wisconsin—Platteville. She brings her background as a CMP as well as her expertise in grammar and punctuation as she reviewed much of the manuscript.

Amanda Rushing, CMP, brings the practical aspects of meeting management together in her quest to improve the quality and professionalism of the industry. She is able to look at the credentialing requirements and compare these requirements to "real-life" meeting management, but also, always strives to look beyond the traditional function of logistics and give feedback that holds a strategic perspective.

There are three individuals who have supported the addition of the web based Integrated Learning Systems, which provides faculty with educational resources to more effectively and efficiently integrate the use of the text in the classroom. In addition to Dr. Reed, Dr. Amanda Cecil, CMP, from Indiana University, Indianapolis, and William R. Host, CMP, from Roosevelt University, Chicago, have identified and coordinated these learning aides from many sources and have helped make this a useful tool for teaching. It has been a immense honor to work with such great people.

There is a host of other individuals that are involved in the publishing world. The folks at Kendall/Hunt Publishing have been terrific to work with. Philip Puckorius, a long-time acquaintance, has provided invaluable guidance and direction over the entire process. The manager of the project was Laurel Sutherland, who kept on top of the details and pushed and nudged, always at the right times, to keep everyone and everything on task. Sheri Hosek, project manager, provided the invaluable service of keeping track of manuscripts and managing the volumes of electronic files; and, to Kara McArthur, copy editor, and Terri Schiesl, compositor, who made us all look good. There are many others who, behind the scenes, are doing their jobs to make this all happen. Thanks to everyone for keeping us on track, on time, and within budget.

The cornerstone of PCMA is and always has been *education*. The support of the organization and the PCMA team has been incredible. A special thank you to PCMA President and CEO, Deborah Sexton, for her continued belief in the significant contribution this book makes to the industry; Sian Moynihan, Executive Vice President, Kelly Peacy, Vice President, Meetings and Events; Robert

Cowan, Chief Financial Officer; Sherrif Karamat, Chief Partner Relations Officer; Sandy Eitel, Director, Marketing and Communication; Michelle Russell, Editor, *Convene;* Lorena Fuentes, Senior Manager Meetings & Events; Megan Leek, CMP, Education Specialist; Connie Leahy, Education Specialist; Daris Nelson, Assistant, Executive Office; and, Julie Fawcett, Marketing Specialist, for their consultation, support, and encouragement. Each, in their own way, has contributed ideas and assistance to make this happen.

Last, but not least, I want to acknowledge PCMA Manager of Education Kristin Crane. She not only kept PCMA's education department on track and moving forward so that I could devote my time to this edition's revision process, but she also served as an enlightened sounding board. I could always count on her to provide clarity and her unique perspective—and to roll up her sleeves and dive into this project at a moment's notice.

A special acknowledgment of the Board of Trustees of the PCMA Education Foundation for providing grant monies to fund this revision. Their support of PCMA educational endeavors has always been generous and timely.

And, to my wife, Barbara, whose patience and understanding long ago passed my understanding. Thank you for your love and support throughout a project that has taken so many hours over the past months.

Glen C. Ramsborg

None of us is as smart as all of us.

—*Ken Blanchard, "One Minute Manager"*

The following list of individuals participated in the review process and in other ways contributed to this project. To all of them, we owe a debt of gratitude.

Catherine Anderson-Brown, CMP
CAB & Associates
Professor, Centennial College,
    Toronto, Canada

David Angeletti, CASE
Chief Marketing Officer
Conference Archives, Inc.

Kenneth F. Backman, PhD
Associate Professor
Department of Parks, Recreation
    and Tourism Management
Clemson University

Jeffrey Beck, PhD
Assistant Professor
The School of Hospitality
    Business
The Broad College of Business
Michigan State University

Bradley Beran, MBA, PhD
    Director, Hospitality and Food
    Service Management Program
Syracuse University

Vicky A. Betzig, CMP
President
Meetings Industry Consulting

Mary Jo Blythe, CMP
President
Masterplan, Inc. and Destination
    Innovators, Inc.

MaryAnne P. Bobrow, CAE,
    CMP
Managing Partner
Bobrow & Associates

Kathleen Mayer Bovello, CMP
President
Bovello & Associates

Deborah Breiter, PhD
Professor, Convention &
    Conference Management
Rosen College of Hospitality
    Management
University of Central Florida

Andréa Bright, CMP
Ontario Nurses' Association

David C. Brower, MBA
Instructor and
    Coordinator of Inter-
    Institutional Programs
State University of New York at
    Delhi

Chris Brown, CEM, CMP
Senior. Meeting, Exhibits and
    Trade Show Manager
Association Headquarters, Inc.

Michael Bruley
Vice President, Sales
    Administration
Freeman

LuAnn Buechler, CMP
Professional Meeting Consultant,
    LLC
Adjunct Professor
University of Wisconsin - Stout

Lori L. Burke, CMP
President
LLB Enterprises

Steve Call, MS, CTC
Director, Travel, Hotel and
    Tourism Management Degree
Ohio University

Ronald J. Cereola, JD, MBA
Assistant Professor
College of Business, Hospitality
    & Tourism Management
James Madison University

Bobbie Connolly, CMP
Member Services Coordinator
Alegent NPG Health-Link

Robert T. Cowan, CPA, CAE
Chief Financial Officer
Professional Convention
    Management Association

Jeffrey Cufaude
President/CEO
Idea Architects

Nancy Debrosse
Vice President, Marketing and
    Communications
Projection Presentation
    Technology

Andrea Doyle
Senior Writer, *Convene*
Professional Convention
    Management Association

Sari Edelstein, PhD, RD
Assistant Professor
Simmons College

Joan L. Eisenstodt
Chief Strategist
Eisenstodt Associates, LLC

Meg Fasy, CMP
Executive Director, Industry
    Relations
iBAHN

Jim Fausel, CMP, CMM
President
The Conference Connection

George G. Fenich PhD
Professor
School of Hotel, Restaurant, and
    Tourism Administration
University of New Orleans

Laurie Fitzgerald, CMP
Meetings Manager, Sales Support
Allstate Financial

Lesley A. Foster
Senior Conference Manager
National Association of Home
    Builders

Mary German, CMP
Director of Convention Services
Arlington Convention & Visitors
    Bureau

Paulette Cozzi Goedert
Barnes & Thornburg LLP

Ralph S. Goodman, CMP, CHME
President
RS Goodman & Associates

Diane E. Graham
Vice President, Member and
    Conference Services
American Association of Motor
    Vehicle Administrators

David Gudinas
Director of Events
Home Buyer Publications

Leslie Hettenbach, CMP
Meetings Manager
American Urological Association

Tyra W. Hilliard, JD, CMP
Associate Professor
University of Nevada, Las Vegas

William R. Host, CMP
Assistant Professor
Manfred Steinfeld School of
    Hospitality & Tourism
    Management
Roosevelt University

Jonathan Howe, Esq.
President and Senior Partner
Howe & Hutton, Ldt.

Dyanne Hughes, CMP
President
The Meetings Solution, Inc.

Elizabeth "Liz" Huh, CMP, CAE
Director, Meetings & Conferences
American Association of School
    Administrators

Laura Metcalf Jelenik
Associate Executive Director,
    Continuing Education,
    Meetings and Exhibitions
American Association of Oral and
    Maxillofacial Surgeons

Donald C. Jenkins, CASE
Account Executive
National Speakers Bureau

David L. Jones, PhD
Assistant Professor
College of Business, Department
    of Hospitality Management
San Francisco State University

Michelle W. Jones, CMP
Director, Member and Foundation
    Services
National Association of
    Independent Life Brokerage
    Agencies

Susan Katz
Director of Corporate Events
True Value Company

Shannon Kelley, CMP
Registration and Housing
    Manager
American Academy of Audiology

Kelly Landis
Conference Coordinator
Lippincott Williams & Wilkins

Michael Landry, PhD, MBA
Associate Professor of Marketing
Northeastern State University

Beatriz Leonardo, CMP
Director, Client Services
aNd Logistix Inc.

Curtis Love, PhD, CHE
Associate Professor
University of Nevada, Las Vegas

Sally Magallanes, CMP
Meeting Consultant

John McCarthy
President
Continental Air Transport Co.,
    Inc.

Michael T. McQuade, CMP
Director, Sales & Marketing
Washington State Convention &
    Trade Center

Chef David Miller
Instructor, Program Coordinator
College of Technology, School of
    Culinary Arts
Idaho State University

Timothy A. Moses
Director, Meetings and
    Conventions
American Academy of
    Dermatology

Monica Myhill, CMP
President
Meeting Returns

Kathleen Niesen, CMP
Education Manager
American Academy of
    Orthopaedic Surgeons

Brian D. Palmer, MBA
President
National Speakers Bureau

Susan Rawlins, CMP
International and Knowledge
    Development Manager
TAPPI

Naomi A. Romanchok, CMP
Adjunct Faculty
Northern Virginia Community
    College

Sylvia Rottman, DMCP
President
Great Events/TEAMS, Inc.

Keith A. Sexton-Patrick, CMP
Director of Convention Services
    and Destination Services
Mohegan Sun

Christine Shimasaki, CMP
Executive Vice President of Sales
    and Marketing
San Diego Convention & Visitors
    Bureau

James Spellos, CMP
President
Meetings U.

Camille Stern
Director of Administration
Convention Management Group,
    Inc.

Sandra Strick, PhD, CWE, CHE
School of Hotel, Restaurant, and
    Tourism Management
University of South Carolina

Valerie Sumner
Principal
VRS Meetings & Events Inc

Denise Suttle, CMP
Assistant Director of Convention
    Services
Albuquerque Convention &
    Visitors Bureau

Teri Tonioli, CMP
Vice President, North Central
    Region
Conferon Global Services, Inc.

Greg Van Dyke
Senior Vice President, Marketing
Audio Visual Services
    Corporation

Glory Wade
Conference Coordinator
Vanguard Integrity Professionals,
    Inc.

Heidi C. Welker
Vice President, Marketing
AVW-TELAV

Shari Wilson, CMP
Associate Division Manager,
    International Meetings
Rotary International

What Is Professional Meeting Management?

Meetings and conferences are serious business. They often are critical to organizational success, both in terms of the value delivered to members and stakeholders and the revenue generated for the bottom-line. This section highlights the strategic contribution of meetings to an organization's overall portfolio of services and the contemporary thinking and leadership required for meeting management to be valued by departments and senior executives in an organization.

CHAPTER 1

A Fresh Perspective

Jeffrey Cufaude
President and CEO
Idea Architects

Learner Outcomes

When the reader has completed reading this chapter, he/she should be able to . . .

1 Relate the concept of design to that of professional meeting management.

2 Differentiate between leadership and management.

3 Apply the six right-brain aptitudes to professional meeting management.

4 Contribute more value through personal effort as a result of increased professional capacity.

5 Generalize the present concepts of design, leadership, and management to the development of learning experiences and meeting management.

> The most common misperception is the word 'design.' People think of primarily pretty pictures or forms. They don't understand the depth to which design goes—not only in products, but in every aspect of our life. Whether it is the design of a program, a product or some form of communication, we are living in a world that's totally designed. Somebody made a decision about everything. And it was a design decision.
>
> *Sam Farber*
> *Founder, Copco Cookware,*
> *OXO Kitchen Tools, WOVO Serveware*

OVERVIEW

Successful individuals can simultaneously create the future while leading and managing the present. Doing so often requires rethinking how meeting managers do what they do and the very nature of the work itself. This introductory chapter is an invitation for you to reconsider what constitutes success for a professionally managed meeting—now and in the future—as well as to reexamine and enhance the value you contribute as a professional meeting manager.

CRAFTING THE LEARNING EXPERIENCE

When friends and colleagues ask you what you do for a living, "crafting the learning experience" might not be the occupational title that you share with them, but it is an apt descriptor. Todd Oldham designs furniture. Donna Karan designs clothing. Frank Gehry designs buildings. You design meetings and conferences that strive to be value-rich, powerful learning and community-building experiences.

Whether it is an annual meeting for tens of thousands of people or a one-day summit for a small group of high-level thinkers, what most individual events have in common is that they are about learning. People come to a meeting to obtain the information, knowledge, and insight that they need to accomplish their own goals and objectives. Your design efforts are a critical determinant of the value and learning individuals experience from an event.

Have you ever stopped at the grocery store to pick up a couple things, only to find your arms overloaded after a few minutes? It would be nice if handbaskets could be found in select locations throughout the store and not just at the entrance. That is the type of suggestion Paco Underhill, the generally recognized father of the science of shopping, would make to the storeowner. Underhill is the founder of Envirosell, a consulting firm that monitors shoppers' behaviors and habits. The lessons he and his colleagues have learned are captured nicely in *Why We Buy: The Science of Shopping*.[1] The challenge to the meeting manager is to embrace the concept and thought when designing and planning a meeting.

A DESIGNED EXPERIENCE

Shopping is a highly designed experience, perhaps now more so than ever before. When you walk into an individual store, the elements of the design surround you:

- The layout of the overall space
- The layout of individual departments and sections
- The signage directing you throughout the store
- The lighting
- The music (or lack of music) playing in the background
- The product displays
- The checkout stations
- And much, much more

Powerful Learning Experiences: Questions to Ponder

Think of a learning experience that you found to be compelling and very valuable.

1. What was the nature of the experience?
2. How did people interact?
3. What was the content and format?
4. What informal learning and interaction opportunities were offered?
5. Based on your experience, what would you say are the critical ingredients for a powerful learning experience?
6. How are those ingredients being incorporated into the experiences you design?

Put It Into Perspective

How to Think Like a Designer

- **Look for inspiration everywhere**. The opportunities for inspiration surround us if only you will take the time to notice them. Pay attention to store layouts whenever you shop. Take a stroll through an elementary or high school and see what is new with learning. When you are in a hotel or convention center look at how other groups are using the space.
- **Keep an idea file**. Whenever you see something that catches your interest—be it a cool marketing promotional brochure or a quote from a new book—toss it into an idea file that you can draw on the next time you have a learning experience to design.
- **Spend some time scanning**. Yes, you need to be able to execute room set ups and hotel contracts flawlessly, but you also need to get in touch with the broader disciplines that are woven throughout a successful learning experience: architecture, graphic design, marketing, technology, travel and leisure, food and nutrition, learning, and so on. Allocate a couple of hours each month to peruse web sites and periodicals that hold implications for meetings and conferences even if they are on the fringe of your daily efforts.
- **Pay attention.** Designers often seem to have bionic vision, noticing the little details and undercurrents or trends that pass others by. They obsessively analyze how consumers interact with products and environments in an effort to glean how things can be improved. You should do the same with your own meetings and conferences, trying to watch events and interactions unfold in real time but with the attention to detail that would allow you to replay every moment in slow motion.
- **Remember form and function.** A box. A stool. A bench. All fulfill the function of seating, but each takes a different form. When you are trying to enhance the design of your meetings and conferences, preserve the functions that are important and valued; but be willing to play with new forms.

All of these environmental cues subtly influence sales and customer satisfaction.

The interaction between the store and the customer (or a meeting participant and conference) is captured in a simple theory attributed to noted organizational development scholar Kurt Lewin:

$$B = f\,(p, e)$$

Behavior (B) is a function (f) of the person interacting with the environment. Change the players (p) in an environment (e) and different behaviors might emerge. Change the environment but keep the same players and you will again get different behaviors. Dramatic differences can result from what occurs in a meeting or conference environment. You do not always have a choice about who attends your meetings, but you do have the ability to influence their behavior toward your desired results with each choice you make about the various elements of the learning environment you create.[2]

What do you know about the people who are likely to attend your meeting or conference? Generate as descriptive a profile as you possibly can, including demographics, learning styles and preferences, social interaction preferences, service expectations, and so on. Then ask yourself what kind of environment needs to be created to increase the likelihood that you can achieve your desired results given what you know about the likely attendees.

What do you know about the environment of your meeting or conference? You do not always get to make all the choices that you might like about a meeting's environment. Given that reality, it can be instructive to generate a profile of all the "givens" of the environment for a meeting or conference. After doing so, ask yourself what attendee profile is the best target audience given the desired results and what is known about the learning environment.

"By focusing attention on a vision, the leader operates on the emotional and spiritual resources of the organization, on its values, commitment, and aspirations. The manager, by contrast, operates on the physical resources of the organization, on its capital, human skills, raw materials, and technology."[3]

But the meeting manager cannot design in isolation, and it is imperative to put the work of professional meeting management into a larger context: meetings generally are a means to an end, not an end in and of themselves. Whether it is organized for a corporation, association, or government enterprise, a meeting or conference is a container for value. Regardless of a meeting's size or scope or who is responsible for its management, it is meant to make something positive occur for the participants whose interest and attention it targets. Increasingly, meeting logistics and operations that are well-organized and efficiently executed are becoming a minimum expectation, not a value-added attribute. In other words, meeting managers will not accrue goodwill simply by designing a well-run meeting, but they will face criticism and concern for any miscues that participants assume simply should not occur.

What follows is a quick look at strategy as it relates to designing compelling learning experiences. The goals you set for any individual meeting or conference should support and advance the overall goals for professional development in your organization, which should in turn support and advance your organization's overall mission, vision, values, and goals. The design of an effective learning experience then requires being clear about the following things:

- Your organization's mission, vision, values, goals, and objectives
- The goals and objectives for professional development (all meetings and conferences)
- The desired results for the particular event you are designing

When you have clarity for these aspects of overall strategy, as you design each individual element of a learning experience you should find yourself thinking about how it can help advance the overall definition of success for professional development, as well as your organization's overall strategic plan. To put it in simpler terms, an interior designer does not define success simply as obtaining a great reading chair for you. The designer defines success as creating the overall look and feel you want for your home, then incorporating that look and feel into each individual room, and finally ensuring that each element in a room supports the overall lifestyle you desire.

As you make each of the hundreds of decisions that go into a successful learning experience, you have to ask yourself how your choices help advance these broader definitions of success. If your organization's vision is to be the industry's or profession's leading source of knowledge, how is your meeting going to help contribute to realizing that desired result? If one of your organization's goals is to be more customer-friendly, how will you weave outstanding customer service into each aspect of your conference operation?

What is the bottom-line? An individual meeting or conference is not simply an end in and of itself; it is a means to the larger end of your organization's overall mission and vision. The critical question: are you leveraging the potential of each and every component of a meeting or conference to achieve your desired strategic results (for the event, for professional development, and for your organization's overall vision)? Professional meeting management increasingly will be about applying the methodical mindset meeting managers use to determine room blocks and meal function guarantees to all of the elements of the learning experience. By reframing each element of a typical meeting or conference and exploring how it can be used to enhance learning, you can increase the potential value your attendees will obtain.

THE TRANSITION UNDERWAY

In many ways this requirement to deliver value beyond logistics parallels the economic evolution Daniel Pink outlines in his important book, *A Whole New Mind*. Pink notes that we are evolving from the Information or Knowledge Age into a Conceptual Age in which right-brain attributes represent the value-added opportunities.

Why? Because in so many instances, the efficiencies and operational enhancements derived from left-brain attributes like analysis and reason have been milked for all they can contribute. If the qualities we associate with professional meeting management do not expand beyond traditional logistics and merely doing things right, some of this work becomes a likely candidate for automation or for outsourcing to other countries. As Pink notes in his book, if a computer can do it faster or someone else can do it cheaper, that is the way that the work will be accomplished. If computer software programs can replace work previously done by accountants, and engineers in other countries can be retained at lower costs to do work according to U.S. specifications, it is not too difficult to imagine that significant portions of meeting management could be automated or moved overseas.[4]

For professional meeting management to remain relevant in the future, it will require even greater emphasis on meeting leadership and not just on management. Without overemphasizing semantic nuances, the work of organizational gurus like Peter Drucker and Warren Bennis[5] has long documented the commonly held distinctions between management and leadership. *Management* is about doing things right. *Leadership* is about doing the right thing.

With this distinction, management is about controlling the process and using primarily quantitative or objective metrics to determine success. The components of effective management are left-brain attributes derived from the qualities valued in a manufacturing or assembly-line economy: what systems should be used to produce the same product over and over again at the lowest cost possible?

An emphasis on leadership, in contrast, emerged with the dawn of the information or knowledge economy, when the products being built were not cars or electronics, but invention and new knowledge. As a result, leadership generally focuses more on mission and vision, organizational values, and teamwork and relationships.

Leadership addresses what choices should be made given the environment in which an organization operates and the results it hopes to achieve. *Management* addresses the practices and systems that can be used to achieve those results in a consistent high-quality manner.

If professional meeting management merely ensures efficient logistics for a conference program that offers content that is of little value to your members and stakeholders, obviously, it is a failure. Similarly, having the brightest minds gathered to speak about the most cutting-edge issues will not be successful if meeting operations are overlooked or poorly executed. Contemporary usage interchanges "management" and "leadership" almost without regard to the historical definitions just described. In addition, the job titles or classification individuals possess often are not aligned with this defined difference. As a result, call it what you will, but success in today's competitive, ever-changing environment requires individuals to embrace both disciplines. They must be able not only to determine what is the right thing to do, but also be able to flawlessly execute any chosen strategic direction.

PROFESSIONAL MEETING MANAGEMENT IN THE FUTURE

The following 11 meeting management capabilities and commitments are aligned to meet the expectations future meeting attendees likely will bring to the personal and professional development gatherings they choose to attend.

1. Incorporate technological advances and processes that simplify logistics for all parties involved, as well as enhance customization and personalization of the participants' experiences.

"There is a profound difference between management and leadership, and both are important. To manage means to bring about, to accomplish, to have charge of or responsibility for, to conduct. Leading is influencing, guiding in a direction, course, action, opinion. The distinction is crucial."[6]

2. Increase and more clearly demonstrate return on investment to the participants, their employer, and any sponsors, as well as the convener or host organization(s) for the meeting itself.

3. Be inclusive of an increasingly diverse mix of conference attendees and their needs, learning styles, and preferred formats for content delivery.

4. Lavish attention on all elements of the meeting to create a cumulative and integrated experience that delivers value seamlessly.

5. Expedite participants' connection to the people, ideas, and answers that most interest them.

6. Offer thoughtfully designed learning environments that are human scale and conducive not only to the delivery of information, but also to the facilitation of knowledge exchange, community-building, and accelerated learning.

7. Embody and exemplify the mission, vision, goals, and brand attributes of the meeting or conference host organization(s).

8. Help advance the profession or industry, as well as those affected by the work of the meeting participants, and not just the sponsoring organization's bottom-line.

9. Engage the highest quality faculty who are proficient in both the content areas they are addressing and in facilitation techniques that are appropriate for adult learners in general, and the meeting's target audience in particular.

10. Provide meaningful sponsorship and exhibition opportunities that facilitate the business that meeting participants and sponsors and exhibitors hope to transact.

11. Model best practices in customer service and customer relationship management.

OPPORTUNITY IS KNOCKING: ARE YOU READY TO ANSWER?

In *Simplicity*, author Bill Jensen reminds us that "Our greatest limit is our ability to make sense of, and connect everything demanding our attention ... [to] how we create clarity."[7] To fully embrace the 11 professional meeting management attributes outlined above will likely require meeting managers to rethink what matters most and what efforts need to be eliminated or, at minimum, relegated to the routine through better use of technology.

Writer and organizational behavior specialist Margaret Wheatley has suggested that "The things we fear most in organizations—fluctuations, disturbances, imbalances—are also the primary sources of creativity." Professional meeting management, like most professions and industries, is being confronted with remarkable disturbances and fluctuations in the work it includes and how that work is accomplished. Time will tell if meeting managers seize these imbalances and draw on them for creative inspiration to rethink their roles and to become even more valuable contributors in the future by designing innovative meetings and conferences.

A WHOLE NEW MIND: GETTING YOUR RIGHT BRAIN IN SHAPE

Success in the dawning Conceptual Age will belong to individuals and organizations that take a different approach to competitive advantage, according to author Dan Pink. "The left brain has made us rich, but now anyone can make and sell the basic product," he says.

Instead, success in the Conceptual Age will require adding more right-brain (what he calls "R-directed") aptitudes to complement our left-brain ("L-directed") reasoning. "We'll need to supplement our well-developed high-tech abilities with abilities that are high concept and high touch," asserts Pink.[8]

Six Right-Brain Aptitudes to Master

In his book, Pink identifies six right-brain aptitudes he believes offer competitive advantage when your products or services have eked out all the left-brain efficiency that is possible.

1. *Not just function but also design*—Learning experience implications: It should be a given that the registration materials, program booklet, and all other aspects of the meeting are functional. Value is added when each of these is intentionally designed to be more aesthetically pleasing. Pay more attention to sensory elements: visuals, sounds, and smells. And remember that part of effective design is what *does not* appear, the negative space. For meetings this means white space in your printed materials, silence and times for reflection in the individual sessions, and breaks and free time in the overall conference schedule.

2. *Not just argument but also story*—Learning experience implications: The end of "bullet point meeting marketing" may soon be upon us. Increasingly, making the case is tied not only to offering factual information, but also to being able to weave that information into a compelling narrative or story. Meeting marketing needs to tell the story of the learning experience people can expect and the experience itself needs to create opportunities for people to "share their story" with colleagues in an appropriate way.

3. *Not just focus but also symphony*—Learning experience implications: Participants need to not only dive deep into content related to their profession or industry but also to have opportunities to connect to ideas and content from disciplines that exist on the fringe. They need to complement specialist knowledge with generalist awareness. Meeting managers can facilitate this need with increased attention to:
   • cosponsorship and collaborative meeting efforts
   • a more strategic mix of session content
   • exposure to speakers and resources from outside the specific industry

4. *Not just logic but also empathy*—Learning experience implications: Technical expertise alone will not ensure individual success. But for many people, their academic preparation focused almost exclusively on skills related to their particular discipline and this focus is echoed in their professional meetings and conferences. Meetings and conferences increasingly need to offer learning opportunities in the "new" areas of technical expertise that all individuals need to possess regardless of their profession or industry: interpersonal communication, teamwork and group process, and meeting and workshop facilitation, and so on.

5. *Not just seriousness but also play*—Learning experience implications: People are time-starved, information-overloaded, and severely stressed out. While attending a professional meeting is not supposed to be a vacation, it can be an opportunity to help rejuvenate attendees so that they return to their work with more enthusiasm and energy. Fun and play are going to return as critical elements of meetings and conferences and the savvy meeting manager will identify small and large opportunities to make their learning experiences more spirited.

6. *Not just accumulation but also meaning*—Learning experience implications: People do not need more stuff. They need more useful and valuable stuff. In other words, more content is not necessarily the issue. Learning experiences should offer more analysis and insight into content to yield richer and deeper

---

Fast Facts

Six Right-Brain Aptitudes to Master

1. Not just function but also design
2. Not just argument but also story
3. Not just focus but also symphony
4. Not just logic but also empathy
5. Not just seriousness but also play
6. Not just accumulation but also meaning

meaning. In many cases, less will actually be more. Less time will be spent on sharing information and more time will be spent on making sense of the information that is shared. Session design and speakers or facilitators need to support participants' "meaning making" activities. And the more diverse your meeting participants are, the more diverse the meaning they need to make by connecting with the conference community as a whole, and also with other participants just like them. Finally, as individuals seek more overall meaning and purpose in their lives, they may increasingly be in search of mentoring, coaching, or career counseling at the meetings and conferences they attend.

"Everyone can develop high-concept and high-touch aptitudes, just as everyone can become literate and numerate," according to Pink. "R-directed attributes are fundamentally human attributes. We just haven't had to use them as much in the past."[9]

Put It Into Practice

Building Your Capacity

Just as runners engage in extensive training before a marathon, organizations and their leaders can avoid the negative consequences of operating in a rapidly changing environment by instituting an organizational training regimen that builds individual and organizational capacity for speed. The following practical pointers can guide you in building your capacity, particularly if meeting management in your organization involves multiple individuals, committees, or departments.

1. Assess what types of change your organization (and your meeting management department) is able to handle and where your capacity needs to be increased. Implement strategies to increase your capacity if necessary.
2. Create "express lane" standards for automatically green lighting ideas without having to go through cumbersome review processes. Establish decision-making principles and protocol that can move decisions through your organization more quickly.
3. Create an acceptance for prototyping new types of sessions or conferences where appropriate. Do not ever see yourselves as having the final solution, but strive to create the most appropriate solution for right now.
4. Use technology to automate routine work, freeing up time for more thinking and planning. Whenever possible, leverage technology to let people do for themselves typical tasks that otherwise would require staff intervention.
5. Build relationships among teams and work groups. You have to trust people if you want to give them more latitude for decision-making.
6. When scanning the environment, distinguish between fad and trend. Know when you want to be

an early adopter and when it is more appropriate to let others be the first out of the box.
7. Be prepared for unexpected success. Author Rosabeth Moss Kanter asks, "Would you be able to manage a crowd if they showed up?"
8. Identify the slowest points in your system and concentrate your efforts on revamping those spots. What are the systemic sources that are draining your potential speed and effectiveness?
9. Organize work around functional teams instead of independent silos. Cross-train employees to contribute in a variety of areas. Biking team members take turns riding in the lead position so others can ride behind their draft. Organizations can do the same—allowing those with the training and skills to step into job functions as needed. If you work with volunteer committees, focus their work to leverage their content expertise and contribute your meeting design knowledge and experience.
10. Rethink organizational structure. Consider British management philosopher Charles Handy's concept of the shamrock organization: keep your core functions in-house; use temporary help for administrative work when needed; outsource functions that others can do more efficiently or effectively; and be willing to experiment with new ways of organizing your work. Better that you rethink and revise how meeting management gets done than for other officials to make such changes wholesale for you.
11. Regain clarity around the core purpose and value propositions of your efforts overall, and each meeting or conference individually. What are you uniquely positioned to do? Spreading yourself too thin can cause anxiety as you try to be all things to all people. Know your organization's appropriate balance between quality and quantity of services.

Put It Into Perspective

Design: The Meeting of the Future

It was clear to Chris that this year's annual meeting was going to be a different kind of learning experience than in years past. Though this realization came to him when he received the first marketing postcard for the event, he imagined that strategic conversations behind-the-scenes had been occurring for some time.

An eye-catching direct mail piece invited Chris to visit a special web site for the annual meeting. Upon doing so, he was asked to respond to 10 short multiple-choice questions about current professional issues he was facing and the topics he most needed to learn more about for his current professional challenges.

After completing the survey, he was taken to a customized web page that highlighted components for the upcoming annual meeting that would most meet the needs he had expressed in his survey responses. In addition, it also provided links to content pieces on the web site related to his expressed needs, as well as publications from the organization's bookstore and its other audio/web conferences and in-person seminars that might be of immediate value. Chris used this summary to build his case for attending when requesting funding from his immediate supervisor.

He went back to the web site to register. Besides providing the usual registration information, he was excited to see he could sign up to be placed immediately into online communities of interest, as well as register for an optional coaching/debriefing session with a seasoned professional that would occur on the last day of the meeting. He was sure this would help him synthesize his learning and organize himself to achieve better results upon his return to work.

With his email registration confirmation came additional links to resources he might find of value, as well as an invitation to inform via email up to five of his colleagues that he would be attending and to invite them to register as well.

A few times before he arrived at the conference, Chris was invited via email to participate in an online "highlights" webinar featuring some of the plenary session and concurrent session speakers. This smorgasbord of content offered him some immediate ideas he put into practice, as well as increased his overall enthusiasm for the meeting. He also spent some time online reviewing the individual educational sessions. With so many choices, he found it difficult to select which ones might best meet his needs, but another online tool provided him with a bit of guidance.

When struggling to determine if a session would be right for him, he selected a link that offered a few assessment questions related to his knowledge of the content being addressed in the session. Based on his responses, he was informed as to how his knowledge matched the session's content level and whether it might be a good fit for him.

A seasoned attendee from past meetings, Chris arrived at the convention center to pick up his materials with none of the apprehension he felt his first year when the size and scope of the meeting had overwhelmed him. Much to his surprise, gone were the long cordoned-off lines and check-in stations that in the past had resembled airport check-in. Replacing them were concierge style desks, providing a much more welcoming atmosphere. Mixed among the check-in areas were the award displays and featured offerings from the bookstore giving people some immediate learning opportunities. And since lines were inevitable at peak check-in times, session presenters and some of the "big names" from the profession were working as volunteers, greeting and conversing with participants as they waited to be checked in.

He was greeted by one of a vast volunteer corps that had been recruited to get attendees registered and connected to each other and the meeting, as well as to help build a sense of community from the moment the attendees arrived. After his greeter helped him get his materials, he visited a new type of ribbon station. Instead of selecting ribbons for the committees he served on, he was able to select ribbons for the topical areas where he could be a resource for others attending the conference. This was definitely going to facilitate his networking.

Finally, the greeter invited Chris to the adjacent Internet café and coffeehouse where he could log on and check his email, continue his interaction with the online communities of interest, and respond to some provocative questions posed by the major session presenters. Besides these online opportunities, he could grab a latte and have a one-on-one consultation with a seasoned professional volunteering her time as a coach and mentor.

The meeting enhancements continued to unfold throughout his annual meeting experience. Session rooms were more conducive to interaction and engagement. Speakers allowed more time for exploration of their content and personal reflection and application of the learning. Longer breaks allowed for more networking and informal learning with peers. Participants regularly "hung out" at the Internet café, as it was the place to network and chat about the sessions they had been attending. Everywhere he went, Chris could see the attention to detail that made this year's annual meeting so valuable.

This vision of the future originally appeared in *Convene*, May 2004, as a part of the feature article entitled, "A Curriculum for Change: Making Learning the Metric that Matters Most."[10] Reprinted with permission.

SUMMARY

Meetings are about connections: connecting people to each other, connecting learners to teachers and questions to answers, connecting individuals to the community and the profession or discipline, and connecting problems to solutions. Meeting managers can help ensure that more valuable and relevant connections occur by approaching their work with the mindset of a designer.

Achieving this elevated level of success will require a range of responses: from totally reinventing an entire conference to fine-tuning the individual components of a learning experience and how they flow from one to another. By examining how every element of a meeting or conference can be better designed to promote and support learning and community, savvy meeting managers raise the standard for compelling learning experiences.

It is imperative to put the work of professional meeting management into a larger context: meetings generally are a means to an end, not an end in and of themselves. Whether it is organized for a corporation, association, or government enterprise, a meeting or conference is a container for value. Regardless of a meeting's size or scope or who is responsible for its management, it is meant to make something positive occur for the participants whose interest and attention it targets. Increasingly, meeting logistics and operations that are well-organized and efficiently executed are becoming a minimum expectation, not a value-added attribute. In other words, meeting managers will not accrue goodwill simply by designing a well-run meeting, but they will face criticism and concern for any miscues that participants assume simply should not occur.

Carrying the management and leadership component of the professional meeting manager to the next level, in most instances, translates into the creation of a positive learning experience and ultimately a learning environment that is conducive to achieving the goals and objectives of an event. These become the value-added proposition.

Further, this chapter should have stimulated your thinking about the design and delivery of compelling learning experiences. It is meant to make you think, to reframe or reconsider elements of your work, to cause you to ask different questions, and to consider a broader definition of what a successful meeting or conference entails. It highlights practical concepts, but requires you to connect the ideas and concepts to your own efforts and to make your own determination about the implications they hold for the learning experiences you design and the meetings you manage as you read through the remainder of the book.

REFERENCES

1. Underhill, P. (1999). *Why we buy: The science of shopping.* New York: Simon & Schuster.
2. Lewin, K. (1951). *Field theory in social science: Selected theoretical papers.* D. Cartwright (Ed.). New York: Harper & Row.
3. Bennis, W. & Nanus, B. (1985). *Leaders: The strategies for taking charge.* New York: Harper & Row, p. 92.
4. Pink, D.H. (2005). *A whole new mind: Moving from the information age to the conceptual age.* New York: Riverhead Hardcover.
5. Bennis, op cit.
6. Bennis, op cit, p. 21.
7. Jensen, B. (2000). *Simplicity.* New York: Perseus Publishing.
8. Pink, op cit.
9. Ibid.
10. Cufaude, J. (May, 2004). A curriculum for change: Making learning the metric that matters most. *Convene,* p. 26.

Fast Facts

Useful Reminders About Compelling Learning Experiences

1. People learn best when they feel safe and comfortable, and learning requires a combination of both challenge and support.
2. Program design must embrace the fact that individuals have different learning styles and sometimes learn differently in different circumstances.
3. Realizing the potential for learning and community cannot occur when meeting management and program design are considered separate, almost mutually exclusive functions.

KEY TERMS

Design	Left-brain attributes	Right-brain attributes
Leadership	Management	Webinar

COMPELLING QUESTIONS FOR CONSIDERATION

1. In order to more intentionally focus on learning in every meeting and conference, how might you revise your planning process and/or the way in which your department is organized to plan and design meetings?

2. What support would you need to offer your more presentation-oriented faculty and presenters if you ask them to move toward more interactive and facilitated session formats?

3. How might your future facility and technical needs change based on the more compelling learning experiences this chapter envisions for the future?

4. In terms of designing more compelling learning experiences, what knowledge and resources (both from staff and volunteers) does your organization already possess? What capacity would you need to build and what are your options for doing so?

5. How can you engage program committee members in having meaningful conversations that rethink the types of learning experiences that are offered? What type of reading or information would be valuable for them to complete prior to any such discussions?

6. For which of your events would participants most value pre- and post-program learning opportunities and/or additional content? In what forms might you make that available?

7. When you have been most successful at being a facilitator of learning versus a deliverer of content, what made that possible? How can you create more of those conditions in the future?

8. What is your overall mix of learning facilitation as opposed to content delivery, and how can the learning facilitation be enhanced?

9. What do you know about your members and stakeholders, in terms of their learning needs, learning styles and preferences, and preferred session formats? What data would help your meeting be a better facilitator of learning and how might you begin collecting those data?

10. How can your conferences be modified to introduce more variety (in terms of both session lengths and formats) that might better engage the diversity present among your participants?

11. How might you use your meeting schedules and environments to support more active learning formats during sessions and better facilitate informal learning and interaction?

12. What tangible signs would tell a newcomer to your organization that it is serious about learning? What learning opportunities does it currently offer that might suggest the opposite?

13. What tangible metrics should you use to evaluate the learning that you are trying to promote and the nature of the learning experiences that you are trying to create? How would your evaluation forms and feedback mechanisms need to be revised?

What Is a Professionally Managed Meeting?

This section provides in-depth treatment of all topics related to meeting design and planning. Call it the bread and butter or meat and potatoes of managing meetings. Each chapter explores a component critical to the success of a meeting or conference and offers content to help guide your efforts, including best practices, case studies, and checklists or other planning tools.

CHAPTER 2

STARTING WITH THE END IN MIND: CREATING OBJECTIVES FOR MEETINGS AND EVENTS

Monica Myhill, CMP
PRESIDENT
MEETING RETURNS

Jack J. Phillips, PhD
CHAIRMAN
ROI INSTITUTE

LEARNER OUTCOMES

When the reader has completed reading this chapter, he/she should be able to . . .

1 List the reasons to establish meeting objectives before planning and designing a meeting or event.

2 Describe the necessary data to be collected prior to the creation of meeting objectives.

3 Create measurable meeting objectives for meetings and events.

Dwell in possibilities.

Emily Dickinson

OVERVIEW

In a world that increasingly seeks accountability and return on investment (ROI), the importance of defining objectives for meetings and events cannot be overemphasized. An objective is defined as an outcome or an aim. Meeting objectives are statements that communicate the desired or intended outcomes of a meeting or event for the various meeting stakeholders.

As a meeting manager, you may be asked to plan and organize several different kinds of meetings during your career. The types of meetings you might plan could include educational conferences, sales training meetings, incentive events, marketing events, and trade shows. Some may be as simple as a one-time task force meeting for 20 people, or as complex as an association's annual conference for 3,000 attendees. Since the objectives will differ for each type of meeting, meeting managers must create appropriate, attainable, and measurable objectives. These objectives will be important to your success, the success of the meeting, as well as the success of your organization.

Before meeting objectives can be established, the stakeholders of a meeting or event must be identified and their needs, desires, and challenges established through a needs assessment process. Once these data have been gathered, six levels of measurement can serve as a framework when creating basic statistical type objectives to the ultimate ROI level objective. This chapter will present the foundation for developing objectives, identifying the data to be collected, and measuring the outcomes for meetings and events.

REASONS AND BENEFITS FOR MEETING AND EVENT OBJECTIVES

The reasons and benefits to establish meeting objectives prior to the creation of a meeting are numerous for all stakeholder groups:

For the meeting host or organizer, they tie the meeting or event with the overall strategic objectives of host organization. This is essential for associations because meetings and events are a critical revenue source. Meeting objectives also provide direction to staff, planning committees, and consultants who will create and implement the meeting.

For meeting managers, meeting objectives offer direction and guidance onsite selection, program design, key marketing messages, necessary participant experiences, and other logistical components of the meeting. In addition, these meeting objectives provide the basis for measuring and evaluating the success of the meeting.

Meeting suppliers and vendors can serve as partners and strategic resources for the meeting manager when meeting objectives are shared.

When shared with the meeting attendee, meeting objectives serve as key marketing messages and a contract between the meeting host and the attendee. Meeting objectives tell the attendee both what to expect from the meeting and what is expected from him/her during and following the meeting. An attendee's desire to participate in the meeting and his/her satisfaction level can be enhanced and increased when the meeting objectives are identified and shared.

Meeting objectives are essential to speakers, facilitators, and others responsible for the creation of meeting content, messages, and attendee activities.

DETERMINE MEETING STAKEHOLDERS

Before the meeting objectives can be established, the stakeholders of a meeting or event must first be identified. The Convention Industry Council's Accepted

Practices Exchange (APEX) defines stakeholders as "all individuals who are invested in a project or event such as the sponsors, attendees, vendors, media, and others."[2] According to Daggett, another way to think of a stakeholder is someone "who will directly benefit from or has information critical to the achievement of the meeting's goals."[3]

CONDUCT A NEEDS ASSESSMENT

Nestande notes that "each stakeholder may have their own objectives and it is important that the meeting manager is aware of these."[4] Since objectives are the basis for the marketing, content selection, design, and evaluation of a meeting, meeting managers should take the time to collect key information, through a needs assessment, in order to develop clear, measurable, and compelling objectives. According to Silvers, a needs assessment "helps you determine expectations so that you can define the scope and specifications that result in an event that satisfies the customer's needs and desires."[5] A needs assessment for a future meeting or event would collect and analyze meeting history (if applicable), meeting host information, and stakeholder data.

Meeting history includes:

- Data found within the APEX Post-Event Report[6] (general information and financial details about the meeting itself, facilities utilized, attendees, sleeping rooms, transportation, food/beverage, audiovisual requirements, trade show, etc.)
- Attendance figures and traffic flows for the meeting, breakouts, trade show, and other meeting elements
- Attendee, sponsor, and exhibitor demographics, profiles, and preferences
- Actual expenses and revenues from previous meeting
- Meeting content, messages, and program design
- Evaluation data from individual speakers, sessions, overall meeting, trade show, special events, etc.

Meeting host information features:

- Vision, mission statement, core values, and strategic goals of organization hosting meeting or event
- Internal and external challenges faced by the host organization

Stakeholder data consists of:

- Reasons or objectives for attending or participating (or in some cases, their reasons for not attending or participating)

Fast Facts

The Accepted Practices Exchange (APEX) initiative is tasked with bringing together meeting industry stakeholders to develop and implement accepted practices in order to create and enhance efficiencies throughout the meetings, conventions, and exhibitions industry.

Put It Into Perspective

Stakeholders for an association meeting may include the association itself, association staff, meeting attendees, association members, exhibitors, sponsors, attendees' employers, the city in which the meeting is being held, meeting suppliers/vendors, and industry press.

Stakeholders for a corporate user group conference may include the meeting host corporation, attendees who are current customers, attendees who are potential customers, senior leadership within the corporation, shareholders of the corporation, meeting suppliers/vendors, the city in which the meeting is being held, and industry press.

For example:

- Are your meeting attendees required to attend by their employer? People who are required to attend a meeting may or may not be enthusiastic about their attendance. Often, employers cover all meeting and travel costs for employees whom they require to attend a meeting or event.
- Are they attending to receive credit for Continuing Education Units? Many professions, including medicine, teaching, accounting, and insurance, maintain licensing or certification requirements which require Continuing Education Units.
- Do your attendees want to expand their professional knowledge, renew acquaintances, or make new professional contacts? Some professions and industries are more social and outgoing than others.
- Do your attendees want to learn specific knowledge or skills at your meeting? Some participants may have very specific topic interests that they would like to learn more about during the meeting. Yet, keep in mind that these interests do not necessarily equate to the educational or professional needs of your attendees.

• Benefits they expect or could attain from the meeting

For example:

- Meeting attendees will have different expectations based on their reasons for attending the meeting. Attendees who have been sent to a meeting by their employers for industry-specific training may have different expectations than attendees who have chosen to attend because of personal need or interest.
- Who would they like to meet or connect with during your meeting or event? Many meeting participants attend to expand their network of contacts with other professionals or suppliers.

• Information they possess that will be critical to the design, planning, or success of the meeting

For example:

- What time of the year is best for the majority of your attendees to attend a meeting? Some industries are very busy at certain times of the year and slow at others. Picking a slow time for your industry may result in more people being able to attend your meeting.

• Concerns they have about the meeting, the meeting host, and its success

For example:

- Past meetings or events of a similar purpose or nature will color an attendee's perception or expectations of an upcoming meeting. Bad experiences or less than positive return on investment for the attendee may cause them not to return. Yet, a positive experience may help to attract attendees.

• Challenges they are currently facing in the workplace, their industry, their culture, their community, their country, or their personal lives

For example:

- Information on current challenges can help identify the needs or performance problems of your attendees. According to Louis Phillips, meeting managers "must generate interest in the problem by making their potential audience aware of the problem or issue, explaining how people are affected, and explaining the potential benefits of the planned course in resolving the problem."[7]

High-profile and costly meetings may require a thorough needs assessment, while a needs assessment every 2 to 3 years for other meetings could be sufficient. According to Ramsborg, the 10 steps to follow for conducting a needs assessment are:[8]

- *Step #1*—Make decision to complete a needs assessment
- *Step #2*—Develop focus and specific objectives of the needs assessment
- *Step #3*—Identify meeting stakeholders and specific individuals to be involved
- *Step #4*—Determine the time frame, budget, and staffing required to conduct the needs assessment
- *Step #5*—Select data collection methods (see Chapter 45)
- *Step #6*—Collect data
- *Step #7*—Analyze data
- *Step #8*—Prioritize findings
- *Step #9*—Report the results
- *Step #10*—Utilize the results to create meeting objectives, attendee outcomes, and the program design

CREATING MEETING OBJECTIVES

Once armed with your needs assessment results, analyze this data set to create compelling meeting objectives for each of your key stakeholder groups. Phillips created six levels of measurement, as part of an ROI methodology (see Chapter 46), which can be a useful framework when creating meeting objectives. Each and every meeting may not have objectives created for each level of evaluation. Only 5–10% of an organization's meetings should have level 5: ROI objectives; yet, all meetings should have level 0: Statistics, Scope, and Volume objectives established. Only those meetings which support the organization's strategic objectives and/or incur significant cost/time for the staff and/or attendees should even be taken to level 4: Business Impact or level 5: ROI (see Figure 2.1).

Level 0 – Statistics, Scope, and Volume

Objectives at this level address meeting statistics as well as the scope and volume of meeting attendance, press coverage, budgetary measures, and so on.

Good Level 0 Objectives:

- Identify statistics that are important to the meeting organizer and/or key stakeholders
- Name statistics or key indicators that are measurable and easily collected following a meeting
- Are clearly worded, attainable, and specific to the meeting

Examples of Level 0 Objectives:

- Attain 500 paid attendees at a rate of $795 Canadian per attendee.
- Generate $200,000 U.S. net profit from the annual conference.
- Sell 200 trade show booths at a rate of 2,000 euros each by November 1.
- Have 20 potential clients attend the new product roll-out event.
- Obtain 5 lead meeting sponsors who generate $500,000 in revenues.

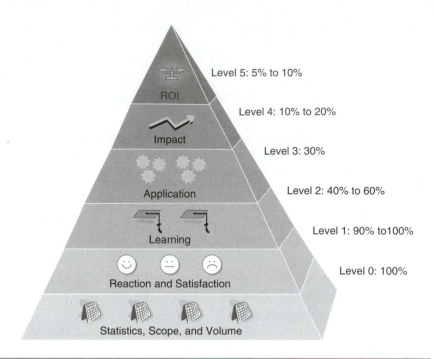

FIGURE 2.1

Recommended Percentage of Meeting Objectives at Each Level
The diagram illustrates the recommended breakdown of measurable objectives at each level. For example, only 5–10% of an organization's meetings should even have objectives at Level 5, while all or a 100% of an organization's meetings should have stated objectives at Level 0.

Level 1 – Reaction, Satisfaction, and Planned Action

These objectives address the desired reaction and satisfaction levels of stakeholders to meeting elements, components, content, speakers, and so on. They also identify the planned actions of the meeting attendees following the meeting or event.

Good Level 1 Objectives:

- Identify issues that are measurable and important to the meeting organizer and/or key stakeholders.
- Are attitude-based, clearly worded, and specific.
- Represent a satisfaction index from key stakeholders.

Examples of Level 1 Objectives:

- Eighty percent of attendees would recommend the conference to others.
- Attendees will rate hotel experience and food/beverage an average of 4.3 out of 5.0 (see Put It Into Practice below).
- Participants will rate the relevance of the meeting to their job success an average of 4.5 out of 5.0 (see Put It Into Practice below).
- Participants will rate the meeting as a good investment for the company with an average of 4.3 out of 5.0 (see Put It Into Practice below).
- Ninety percent of attendees will indicate an intention to implement action plan within 3 months of the meeting.
- Eighty percent of attendees will indicate an intention to implement new sales strategies within 2 months after the meeting.

Level 2 – Learning

These objectives address what the attendees will learn or acquire at the meeting in the form of knowledge, skills, attitudes, opinions, and professional contacts.

Good Level 2 Objectives:

- Begin with an action verb and avoid using verbs that are vague or unmeasurable, such as know, understand, appreciate, comprehend, learn, enjoy, or believe.
- Describe behaviors that are observable, measurable, realistic, and attainable.
- Are outcome-based, clearly worded, and specific.
- Specify what the attendee must do (not know or understand) as a result of the meeting or individual session within the meeting.
- Have three components:
  - *Performance*—identify what the meeting attendee will be able to do at the end of the meeting or event
  - *Condition*—indicate the circumstances under which the attendee will perform the task or behavior
  - *Criteria*—specify the degree or level of proficiency that is necessary to perform the task or behavior

Examples of Level 2 Objectives:

- Successfully demonstrate negotiation techniques during workshop role play.
- Score 75 out of 100 or better on new sales strategy quiz given at the end of the sales meeting.
- Identify two major sponsors of the event and their core business on post-meeting questionnaire.

Within Level 2 objectives, there can be more specific learner outcomes for breakout sessions or concurrent sessions. Learner outcomes describe the skill or behavior that the attendee should be able to demonstrate or the knowledge that he or she should be able to apply or implement at the meeting or workshop's conclusion. For more information on how to provide the learning environment for achieving successful learner outcomes, see Chapter 18.

Put It Into Practice

This numerical average is attained by assigning each possible multiple choice answer a numerical value, adding up all the numerical values of the responses to an individual question, and then dividing this sum by the total number of responses received for that question. For example, a question on a session evaluation asks the attendee to rate the presenter's delivery skills. The possible responses are "excellent" (valued at 5 points), "good" (valued at 4 points), "fair" (valued at 3 points), "not good" (valued at 2 points), and "poor" (valued at 1 point). If 20 persons respond "excellent," 20 persons respond "good," and 20 persons respond "fair," the average score for this question will be 4.0 out of 5.0.

Excellent – value of 5 points × 20 responses = 100
Good – value of 4 points × 20 responses =   80
Fair – value of 3 points × 20 responses =   60
Not good – value of 2 points × 0 responses =   0
Poor – value of 1 point × 0 responses = + 0
240

240 ÷ 60 responses = 4.0 average score

For more information on measuring the success of meeting objectives, see Chapter 45.

Level 3 – Application

These objectives address what the attendees will do with the knowledge, skills, attitudes, opinions, and professional contacts acquired (at the meeting) back in their workplaces or lives.

Good Level 3 Objectives:

- Identify behaviors that are observable and measurable.
- Are outcome-based, clearly worded, and specific.
- Specify what the meeting participant will change or do as a result of the meeting.
- May have three components:
  - *Performance*—will identify what the meeting attendee has changed or accomplished at a specific follow-up time after the meeting or event
  - *Condition*—indicate the circumstances under which the attendee performed the task or behavior
  - *Criteria*—specify the degree or level of proficiency under which the task or job was performed

Examples of Level 3 Objectives:

- Use new customer interaction skills in 90% of situations where they are needed within 3 months of the meeting.
- Ten percent of attendees will submit a request for proposal (RFP) to lead sponsor within 3 months of the conference.
- Achieve 75% of action plan (that was developed at the meeting) within 3 months of the meeting.

Level 4 – Business Impacts

These objectives address what personal, professional or business impact the meeting will have on the attendee, meeting host, exhibitor, sponsor, speaker, and so on.

Good Level 4 Objectives:

- Contain measures that are linked to the skills and knowledge taught as well as professional contacts acquired or strengthened at the meeting.
- Describe measures that are easily collected.
- Are results-based, clearly worded, and specific.
- Specify a business measure that the attendee has accomplished in their job, their own business, or their personal life. Examples of business measures are time savings, greater productivity, reduced costs, increased customer satisfaction, increased sales, and reduced risk.

Examples of Level 4 Objectives:

- Increase sales from existing customers by 5% within 9 months of the meeting.
- Decrease the amount of time required to complete projects by 5% within 6 months of the meeting.
- Save 1 or more hours a week on routine administrative tasks within 3 months of the meeting.
- Attain 20 new association members within 9 months of the meeting.

Put It Into Practice

Association Background

The International Association for Meeting Planners and Suppliers (IAMPS) is the world's largest association dedicated to meeting and event planning. IAMPS' 70,000 members come from more than 100 countries and thousands of organizations—multinational corporations, medium-size and small businesses, government, academia, consulting firms, and industry suppliers.

Annual Meeting

IAMPS' most prominent meeting is the annual International Expo and Conference (IEC), which will be held in Amsterdam next year. This annual conference typically attracts 10,000 delegates, who are members or prospective members, and is regarded as the most important professional development event for meeting and event professionals in the world. Literally hundreds of sessions, workshops, keynotes, panel discussions, and networking events, as well as a multiple-day trade show, are offered during this event.

Stakeholders

The stakeholders for this annual meeting include IAMPS' staff, board of directors, members, prospective members, attendee employers, the city of Amsterdam, the meeting industry within The Netherlands, trade show exhibitors, meeting sponsors, meeting suppliers/vendors, and meeting industry press.

Needs Assessment

Beginning a year and a half prior to this annual conference, several focus groups were conducted with key stakeholder groups and then an online questionnaire was distributed to IAMPS' membership and past exhibitors in order to gather needs assessment data. In addition, the Director of Meetings and Events gathered past meeting information as well as environment scan data.

Below are highlights of key findings:

- For over 75% of the attendees, registration fees and travel costs are covered by the individual's employer. Yet, recently, attendees and their employers have expressed concern over high par-

ticipation costs in this conference, particularly when many other professional development programs are available.

- Meeting managers have expressed a desire to learn more about legal contract issues, emerging technology, and global travel trends.
- Roughly 25% of the attendees register as independent meeting managers or consultants and bear their cost of attending. This segment of attendees is beginning to weigh the value of participating in this meeting and desires more networking opportunities to connect with other independents and potential customers.
- Representing an important income segment of the conference, trade show exhibitors showcase an impressive amount of new products, services, and meeting sites. Recently, exhibitors are also expressing concern about the value of the meeting. Many other meeting industry conferences and trade shows are held each year and they must decide which event is worth the money. Consequently, fewer purchasing decision makers are coming to the conference and the exhibitors have expressed great concern about this.

Meeting Objectives

To better serve meeting attendees and exhibitors, IAMPS decided to create *Level 0: Statistics through Level 5: ROI* meeting objectives for both of these stakeholder groups. These meeting objectives were created in order to design a better conference experience, market the conference appropriately, increase the ROI for attendees and exhibitors, and ultimately measure the success of the meeting.

Senior leadership at IAMPS created meeting objectives from the perspective of IAMPS, attendees, and exhibitors. Due to increased pressure from their board of directors and membership, IAMPS decided that it would conduct an ROI impact study on this conference from the attendee and exhibitor perspectives. For more information on the ROI process, see Chapter 46.

A sampling of objectives at each level for IAMPS' upcoming conference follows; see Figure 2.2.

(continued)

Level	Objective	Perspective
0 **Statistics, Scope, and Volume Objectives**	• Register 1,000 attendees by February 1st at the early bird rate of $550 per attendee. • Sell 500 trade show booths at a rate of 2,000 euros each by November 1st.	IAMPS
	• Greet and converse with 50 or more existing customers during the trade show.	Exhibitors
1 **Reaction, Satisfaction, & Planned Action Objectives**	• Attendees will rate the relevance of the conference to their job success an average of 4.5 out of 5.0. • Attendees will rate the variety, quantity, knowledge level and professionalism of trade show exhibitors an average of 4.0 out of 5.0. • Fifty percent of attendees will indicate an intention to submit an RFP to one or more trade show exhibitors within 3 months.	Attendees
	• Exhibitors will rate the overall conference, trade show registration process, IAMPS staff, traffic flow, and quality of trade show attendees an average of 4.0 or better on a 5.0 scale. • Seventy-five percent of exhibitors will indicate an intention to follow up with 100 or more trade show visitors within 3 months of the conference.	Exhibitors
2 **Learning Objectives**	• During the conference, attendees will acquire a business card or contact information from 10 or more new professional contacts made at the conference. • During the trade show, trade show visitors will provide their contact information to 5 or more exhibitors in order for the exhibitor to follow up with them. • Seventy-five percent of attendees will indicate that they "strongly agree" or "agree" with the statement "I learned new knowledge and/or skills from this conference" on a post-conference questionnaire.	Attendees
	• During the trade show, exhibitors will acquire 50 or more new qualified sales leads.	Exhibitors
3 **Application Objectives**	• Fifty percent of attendees will indicate that they used the knowledge, skills, and/or professional contacts acquired at the conference back on their job either immediately or within 3 months of the conference. • Twenty-five percent of attendees will submit an RFP to one or more trade show exhibitors within 3 months of the conference.	Attendees
	• Within 3 months of the conference, exhibitors will follow up with 25 or more new qualified sales leads attained at the conference. • Within 3 months of the conference, exhibitors will respond to 5 or more RFPs obtained from new qualified sales leads attained at the conference.	Exhibitors
4 **Business Impact Objectives**	• Within 6 months of the conference, 50% of attendees will indicate that the knowledge, skills, and professional contacts made at the conference and applied in their jobs positively impacted 2 or more business measures.	Attendees
	• Within 6 months of the conference, exhibitors will sign 3 or more contracts with new qualified sales leads attained at the conference.	Exhibitors
5 **ROI Objectives**	• Attendees will achieve a 5% return on investment within 12 months of the conference.	Attendees
	• Exhibitors will achieve a 15% return on investment within 12 months of the conference.	Exhibitors

FIGURE 2.2
Sample Objectives for IAMPS Upcoming Conference

Level 5 – ROI

These objectives address what the return on investment will be for the meeting host, attendees, exhibitors, sponsors, and so on. The ROI is calculated using the meeting benefits and costs and can be expressed as the benefit/cost ratio (BCR) or an ROI percentage.

The benefit/cost ratio is the meeting benefits divided by cost. In formula form it is:

$$\text{Benefit/Cost Ratio (BCR)} = \frac{\text{Meeting Benefits} - \text{Meeting Costs}}{\text{Meeting Costs}}$$

The return on investment uses the net benefits divided by meeting costs. The net benefits are the meeting benefits minus the costs. In formula form, the ROI becomes:

$$\text{ROI (\%)} = \frac{\text{Meeting Benefits} - \text{Meeting Costs}}{\text{Meeting Costs}} \times 100$$

This is the same basic formula used in evaluating other investments where the ROI is traditionally reported as earnings divided by investment.

Examples of Level 5 Objectives:

- Achieve a 25% return on investment within 12 months of the meeting.
- Attain a 2:1 BCR on the meeting within 12 months (meaning for each dollar spent on the meeting or event, $2 were returned as benefits).

Not every meeting will need to have objectives at all six levels. Only 5% to 10% of meetings and events should be taken to an ROI level. Meetings appropriate for *Level 4: Business Impact* and *Level 5: ROI* objectives would be those linked to the operational goals and/or strategic objectives of the organization and incur significant costs and staff/participant time. For more information on meetings or events that should be taken to a ROI level, see Chapter 46.

Depending upon the ultimate meeting objective level, create objectives for all preceding levels. A chain of impact should be visible within the objectives as the various levels are addressed.

For example when *Level 4: Business Impacts* objectives are desired, create objectives for Levels 0 through 3 as well to ensure these higher-level objectives can be achieved. If objectives are not created for each level, the meeting manager will have difficulty trying to conclude that the results achieved were actually caused by the meeting or event. Just because attendees were happy with the meeting, does not necessarily mean that attendees have learned or acquired any new skills, knowledge, or professional contacts. Likewise, if attendees learned the desired content or skills at a meeting, this does not mean that the attendee will necessarily implement the content or skills in the workplace.

SUMMARY

In this chapter, the rationale for creating goals and objectives for meetings and events was presented using the Phillips model. Objectives are essential to a successful meeting or event. These meeting objectives provide direction and guidance to staff, planning committees, speakers, suppliers, and other consultants who will create, market, implement, and evaluate the meeting or event.

Prior to the development of meeting objectives, a needs assessment is conducted to collect and analyze past meeting history information and statistics (if applicable); meeting host information; and stakeholder needs, interests, challenges, and preferences.

A six-level measurement framework can be used to create meeting objectives for key stakeholders. The most basic objectives indicate the scope, volume, and statistics of meeting attendance and budgetary measures. The highest level objectives address the ROI for meeting stakeholders.

REFERENCES

1. Russell, M. (July, 2005). Quantifying the value of face-to-face meetings. *Convene*, p. 27-39.

2. Convention Industry Council. (2005). APEX industry glossary. Retrieved February 4, 2006, from http://www.conventionindustry.org/apex/apex.htm.

3. Daggett, J. (July, 2002). BottomLine: Who are the 'players'? *Convene*, p. 13.

4. Nestande, K. F. (1999). Setting meeting objectives. In T. Carey (Ed.), *Professional meeting management: A European handbook*, p. 37–45. Brussels: Meeting Professionals International.

5. Silvers, J. R. (2004). *Professional event coordination.* Hoboken, NJ: John Wiley & Sons, Inc.

6. Convention Industry Council. (2005). The APEX post-event report template. Retrieved December 15, 2005, from http://www.conventionindustry.org/apex/acceptedpractices/posteventreport.doc.

7. Phillips, L. (1994). *The continuing education guide: The CEU and other professional development criteria.* Dubuque, IA: Kendall/Hunt Publishing Company.

8. Ramsborg, G. C. (2002). Process for conducting a needs assessment. *e-Topics newsletter,* December 2002.

KEY TERMS

APEX	Incentive	Questionnaire
Attendee	Incentive event	Request for proposal
Benefit/Cost Ratio (BCR)	Keynote	(RFP)
Board of directors	Logistics	Return on investment
Concurrent sessions	Marketing	(ROI)
Conference	Meeting	Sales leads
Consultant	Meeting manager	Site selection
Content	Meeting profile	Speaker
Continuing education	Needs assessment	Sponsor
Continuing Education	Networking event	Stakeholders
Unit (CEU)	Objective	Statistics
Corporate meeting	Organizer	Supplier
Delegate	Panel discussion	Time agenda
Demographics	Participant	Trade show
Evaluation	Planner	Traffic flow
Event	Post-event report	Vendor
Exhibitor	Profile of attendees	Visitor
Facilitator	Program design	Working program
Focus group	Program development	Workshop

COMPELLING QUESTIONS FOR CONSIDERATION

1. What is the most valuable needs assessment data to collect in advance of creating meeting objectives?

2. Why should meeting managers create meeting objectives based on the six different levels of evaluation?

3. What levels of objectives would you create for an upcoming meeting or event?

CHAPTER 3

EFFECTIVELY MANAGING YOUR MEETING'S BUDGET AND FINANCIAL SUCCESS

Vicky A. Betzig, CMP
PRESIDENT/OWNER
MEETINGS INDUSTRY CONSULTING

LEARNER OUTCOMES

When the reader has completed reading this chapter, he/she should be able to . . .

1 Create a realistic functional income and expense budget for the meeting.

2 Increase income and/or reduce expenses in order to meet financial objectives.

3 Produce specific financial reports that show the financial status of the meeting.

4 Analyze financial reports and make decisions based on findings.

5 Manage funds prior to the meeting and on-site, and evaluate the financial performance of the meeting.

6 Ascertain the financial objectives and desired return on investment (ROI) for the meeting.

> The trouble with a budget is that it's hard to fill up one hole without digging another.
>
> *Dan Bennett*

OVERVIEW

Realistically, budgeting for meetings and events, and the ongoing management of budgets are key skills that CEOs expect of senior-level meeting managers. Additionally, ROI, which takes many different formats when related to meetings, still requires the demonstration of achieving financial objectives as a major indicator of the success of a meeting. Therefore, being able to develop a meeting budget and knowing how to monitor the budget and make decisions based on the financial status of the meeting at any point in time is a responsibility that meeting managers must take seriously. As most meeting managers are not accountants, these tasks could be daunting. This chapter will outline, in simplified terms, the steps required to develop a meeting budget based on the meeting's financial objectives and to manage the actual income and expenses to insure that the objective is attained.

FINANCIAL PLANNING

Establishing the Meeting's Financial Objectives

The first step in successful financial management (as in many other aspects of meeting management) is to determine the financial objectives of the meeting. Generally, there can only be one of three financial objectives: to make a profit, to break-even, or to sustain a loss. Specifically, the financial objective should indicate if the meeting is to break-even, the amount of profit to be made or the loss to be incurred, either as a dollar amount or as a percentage. While it may sound strange, many meetings are budgeted, technically, to lose money. Any meeting that has no income (registration fees, exhibitors, sponsorship) to cover expenses is budgeted at a loss. Typical meetings that are budgeted at a loss include board meetings, committee meetings, training meetings, product launches, and many other types of meetings and events. Typcially, these situations are not viewed as attempting to lose money by the organization holding the meeting, but rather as an investment or subsidy of the meeting that is acceptable because of the benefit of the meeting content to attendees. Having a specific amount of acceptable "investment" in the meeting is important when this is the case.

Specific financial objectives should be developed that are measurable in order to demonstrate the financial ROI to the meeting's sponsoring organization. Asking questions of upper management or those responsible for the meeting to determine specific and measurable financial objectives based on what is an acceptable ROI is a crucial first step in the budgeting process and financial management of any meeting.

Developing the Meeting Budget

Your organization's financial philosophy or other policies and practices may dictate certain aspects of the budget. However, for corporate, association, incentive, government, not-for-profit, or any other type of meeting, developing a budget is the process of identifying and anticipating the expenses and income related to the meeting.

For recurring meetings, the financial history of the meeting must be reviewed. What attendees, exhibitors or sponsors have paid and what expenses have been realistic in the past will direct budgeted income and expenses to some degree. Keep in mind price increases because of the date and location of the meeting. Differences in programming, attendance, and other aspects of the meeting will also dictate increases or decreases in income and expenses. For first-time meetings (zero-based budgeting), research other meetings of similar size and scope and identify all possible expenses to determine a realistic budget. Knowing the demographics of the participants will also impact budgeting. For example, the financial status of attendees and the amount they are willing to pay (if registration fees are charged) for the benefits they receive as a result of the program may impact what can be charged for registration.

Several key issues need to be addressed when developing an overall budget. The budget should include both budgeted and actual figures from previous meetings (using figures from one to three previous meetings is recommended), so that you may easily see how the current meeting compares to past meetings. Additionally, each income and expense line item should be calculated as a percentage of the overall or total budget (for current and previous budgets). This will enable you to easily identify whether certain areas are over or under budget at any time, and will allow for better comparison than would be possible by looking at actual dollars, especially in the case of new locations or programming.

To determine each income and expense line item as a percentage, simply take the amount of the income or expense line item and divide it by the total income or the total expenses. For example, if registration income is $250,000 and the total meeting income is $500,000, then registration income would be 50% of total income ($250,000 divided by $500,000 = 0.5 or 50%). If food and beverage expenses total $300,000, with total expenses of $500,000, the percentage of the total expenses allotted to food and beverage would be 60% ($300,000 divided by $500,000 = 0.6 or 60%).

Avoid the inclination to consider increases in attendance or other revenue areas as trends. If attendance/income increased the previous year or two, this does not always indicate a trend that will continue in the current year. Those increases may be attributable to other factors, such as program content, speakers, new information that was announced, location, and so on.

Generally, budgets should be as realistic as possible. Inflating income above attainable levels may result in problems of not achieving income estimates. Likewise, estimating expenses at lower levels than are realistic may also cause discrepancies in the budget if expenses come in higher. While you may attempt to budget a meeting conservatively (estimating income low and expenses high) in order to provide for a balanced budget in the event that unknown or outside factors negatively affect the meeting, an accurate budget based on all known revenues and expenses that includes all contingencies is the best practice.

Functional Expense Budget

The first step in creating a budget is to determine the expenses of the meeting. A functional budget for expenses allows all expenses to be categorized under the proper functional area of the meeting. This makes for easy monitoring of costs. Figure 3.1 outlines a sample of functional areas, and the expenses that should be considered as line items within each area. These line items are flexible, and Figure 3.1 is not necessarily an exhaustive list of all expense line items. However, this will provide a basis from which to develop your own expense budget.

The key to developing the expense budget is thoroughness—make sure that all possible expenses are listed. Items that are easily overlooked include contingency fees, attrition or cancellation charges, staff salaries, percentages of overhead administrative charges, bank/credit card fees, board and committee planning meetings, site visits, program evaluation costs, complimentary registrations, insurance premiums, legal fees, gratuities, additional service or labor charges, parking fees, on-site first aid services, web site design and maintenance, and other incidental or miscellaneous expenses. Making sure that all expenses are listed in the expense budget will ensure that unexpected costs are kept to a minimum. Expense estimates should be as accurate as possible. This is difficult,

	2006 BUDGET			2006 ACTUAL		
	QTY	AMT	TOTAL	QTY	AMT	TOTAL
EXPENSES						
Administration						
Salary			$35,000.00			
Benefits and Taxes			$4,500.00			
Insurance			$1,500.00			
Staff Travel/Hotal/Expenses			$5,500.00			
Credit Card Fees			$7,000.00			
Legal Fees			$650.00			
Attrition Fees			$10,000.00			
Cancellation Fees			$10,000.00			
Subtotal Administration			$74,150.00			
Program						
Program Committee Expenses	4	$2,000	$8,000.00			
Speaker Fees/Honoraria	20	$400	$8,000.00			
Speaker Expenses	60	$300	$18,000.00			
CME/CEU Expenses			$1,000.00			
Online Abstract Processing System			$1,500.00			
Audiovisual			$45,000.00			
Printing and Copying						
On-site Program/Abstract Book	800	$10	$8,000.00			
Handout Copying			$1,500.00			
Subtotal Program Expenses			$91,000.00			
Facilities						
Meeting Space Rental			$4,500.00			
Service Charges			$2,000.00			
Subtotal Facilities			$6,500.00			
Food & Beverage						
Opening Reception	750	$150	$112,500.00			
A.M. Breaks	3	$3,600	$10,800.00			
P.M. Breaks	3	$4,225	$12,675.00			
Exhibit Hall Reception	750	$38	$28,500.00			
Luncheons	700	$48	$33,600.00			
Closing Banquet	700	$140	$98,000.00			
Misc			$1,400.00			
Subtotal Food & Beverage			$297,475.00			
Marketing (Attendee & Exhibitor)						
Advertising			$5,000.00			
Label Purchase/Rental			$2,000.00			
Design & Layout			$1,500.00			
Printing			$14,000.00			
Postage & Delivery			$6,000.00			
Attendance at Related Shows			$1,500.00			
Meeting Wesite Design/Maintenance			$1,200.00			
Subtotal Marketing			$31,200.00			
Exhibits						
Exhibit Contractor			$6,000.00			
Poster Boards	55	$65	$3,575.00			
Security			$3,200.00			
Facility Rental			$7,500.00			
Lead Retrieval			$1,000.00			
Cleaning			$1,500.00			
Subtotal Exhibits			$22,775.00			
Registration Expenses						
Online Registration System	750	$18	$13,500.00			
Materials & Supplies	750	$14	$10,500.00			
Computers/Equipment			$3,500.00			
Registration Personnel			$5,500.00			
Subtotal Registration Expenses			$33,000.00			
Support Expenses						
Signage	85	$35	$2,975.00			
Shipping			$2,000.00			
Miscellaneous Support			$3,000.00			
Subtotal Support Expenses			$7,975.00			
Miscellaneous Expenses			$3,000.00			
TOTAL EXPENSES			$567,075.00			

FIGURE 3.1
Sample Functional Expense Budget

especially if you are budgeting for a meeting that is more than a year out or for zero-based budgeting. In order to be accurate, obtain reasonable estimates from all suppliers for each function and line item. If the exact cost cannot be guaranteed when you are preparing the budget, use the current cost and obtain a guaranteed maximum percentage increase for the time of the meeting. Add the highest percentage to the current price to budget the expense for the meeting. For example, if continental breakfast is currently $12 per person and the hotel cannot quote firm food and beverage pricing until 6 months prior to the meeting, establish that food and beverage prices are guaranteed not to increase by more than 10% by the time of the meeting. Then use the figure of $13.20 per person ($12 plus 10%) for continental breakfast when budgeting expenses. When budgeting food and beverage costs, remember to include tax and gratuity/service charges, and determine whether the gratuity/service charge is taxable. Depending upon the location, these figures can add as much as 30% to the final costs. All expense line items should be estimated based on contracted/guaranteed prices, or prices calculated with the maximum percentage increase guaranteed/contracted by the provider. If percentage increases are quoted as annual (assuming the meeting is several years in the future), be sure to add the maximum percentage increase for each year (compounded) between the time you are preparing the budget and the time of the meeting.

When obtaining contracted/guaranteed pricing or guaranteed maximum percentage increases for expense line items, estimate the expense based on current pricing and add an appropriate percentage per year for "cost of living" or inflation increases. This can be accomplished by researching the Consumer Price Index (on which cost-of-living adjustments are based) or annual inflation rates through government entities (such as the U.S. Department of Labor or similar government offices in other countries). Meetings industry publications and research also give figures for anticipated price increases in hotel rates and other applicable expenses. Be sure to research the specific destination of the meeting as cost of living adjustments, consumer price indices, and other data tends to vary by location.

You can also use historical data to predict future costs. By comparing the past 2 years' expenses for a particular line item, you can determine the percentage increase and use this as a basis for annual increases in the future. Remember to add this amount for each year (compounded) between when the budget is prepared and when the meeting will take place (for example for a $200 room rate with an 8% annual increase for a meeting to take place in 3 years, use a figure of $252—the 8% must be added each year to the previous year's rate, so year one = $216, add 8%, and year two = $233.28, add 8% and year three = $251.94).

Keep a budget handbook to record how expense line items were computed. This handbook should show all calculations and exactly how expenses were determined. Be extremely detailed and comprehensive in the budget handbook, including all figures used and backup calculations. This document is extremely useful in budgeting for future years.

Expenses should be categorized as either fixed expenses (fixed costs) or variable expenses (variable costs). Fixed expenses do not change and are not dependent on attendance, but remain as a constant. Variable expenses are per-person expenses that change depending on the number of attendees, exhibitors or other participant types. Determining whether an expense is fixed or variable may be difficult. For example, meeting room rental would probably increase if the meeting were for 500 people versus 50 people. However, meeting room rental is a fixed expense. The best way to determine if an expense is variable is to determine whether it is a per-person type of expenditure, such as food and beverage costs. A good general rule is if the cost increases by adding just one person, it is a variable expense. You may also have indirect expenses (indirect costs) and these refer to organizational expenses not directly related to the meeting. Examples include salaries, administrative overhead, or equipment repair and maintenance.

Functional Income Budget

The process of developing the income or revenue budget is much the same as the process of developing the expense budget. A functional budget for income, like its expense counterpart, allows for a comprehensive listing of all income categorized by revenue or income function. Figure 3.2 outlines examples of income functional areas, and the revenues to be considered as line items within each area.

Like the expense budget, making sure all income generating areas are thorough and inclusive is important. Some income areas that are easily overlooked include ground transportation rebates, commissions from facilities, sales of proceedings (audiotapes and videotapes or other products), list sales or rentals, investment or interest income, royalties, administrative fees kept when registrations are canceled, or general grants that are applicable to the meeting.

Many income line items can be projected based on history. The amount of sponsorship and grant revenue, advertising income, material/ product sales, event ticket sales, and interest and investment income can all be based on meeting history (taking any program changes, competitive or economic issues, or other outside factors—as well as realistic projections of sales—into consideration). For zero-based budgeting, extensive research must be conducted to determine levels of participation and pricing guidelines that will be realistic based on the market. Additional research into the demographics of potential attendees and/or exhibitors and what fees they are willing to pay, as well as what competitors are charging, should be conducted.

Other income areas must be calculated, such as registration, commissions or rebates, and exhibit sales. Commissions and rebates can be calculated based on contractual specifications. Determining registration fees and exhibit booth pricing should be based on history, pricing policies of the organization, and/or what the "market" will bear, including researching what competitors charge for similar programs. For example, if registration or exhibit booth rental fees increased by 5% the previous year or if the competition is at lower prices, raising these fees for the current budget may not be reasonable. Therefore, if these fees must stay static, last year's prices should be used in calculating the corresponding income line items.

As the pricing is set, keep a budget handbook that shows accurate, detailed records of the calculations used to determine income for each line item. For example, what expected attendance number was used to determine total registration fee income? How many exhibitors was the total exhibitor income line based on? Be sure to base figures on comparable data from past meetings, but remember to take into account differences in location, economic circumstances, programming changes, and other factors that could reflect either positively or negatively on participation. Remember to keep income projections conservative.

Achieving the Financial Objective of the Meeting

Once all income and expense budgeting is completed, you will be able to review the overall budget to determine if the financial objectives of the meeting are being met. If the financial objective is to break-even, then total income should exactly equal total expenses. If this is not the case, you will need to determine whether income can be raised or expenses lowered to achieve the break-even objective.

	2006 BUDGET			2006 ACTUAL		
	QTY	AMT	TOTAL	QTY	AMT	TOTAL
INCOME						
Registration Income						
Member - Early	300	$495	$148,500			
Member - Late	35	$595	$20,825			
Nonmember - Early	150	$595	$89,250			
Nonmember - Late	40	$695	$27,800			
Students - Early	75	$225	$16,875			
Students - Late	6	$325	$1,950			
Speakers	65	$0	$0			
Emeritus/Honorary	4	$50	$200			
Guest - Early	10	$175	$1,750			
Guest - Late	3	$275	$825			
Exhibitor	45	$0	$0			
Press	10	$0	$0			
Miscellaneous Registration	12	$0	$0			
Gross Registration Revenue	755		$307,975			
Credits/Cancellations	-5		-$2,225			
Net Registration Revenue	750		$305,750			
Exhibits Income						
Commercial	53	$1,200	$63,600			
Non-profit	15	$800	$12,000			
Comps	2	$0	$0			
Nonprofit Literature Displays	3	$500	$1,500			
Subtotal Exhibits	73		$77,100			
Sponsorships & Grants						
Sponsored Sessions	2	$10,000	$20,000			
Sponsored Breaks	2	$5,000	$10,000			
Sponsored Lunches	1	$25,000	$25,000			
Sponsored Receptions	1	$50,000	$50,000			
Unrestricted Educational Grants	1	$10,000	$1,000			
Tote Bags	1	$8,000	$8,000			
Miscellaneous		$2,225	$2,225			
Subtotal Sponsorship			$116,225			
Miscellaneous Income						
CME & CEU Income			$24,000			
Exhibitor Reception Tickets	60	$175	$10,500			
Advertising			$21,000			
List Orders	40	$275	$11,000			
Interest & Investment			$500			
Miscellaneous			$1,000			
Subtotal Miscellaneous			$68,000			
TOTAL INCOME			$567,075			

FIGURE 3.2
Sample Functional Income Budget

To increase registration or exhibit income to get to a break-even budget, you must conduct a break-even analysis to show at what prices or what participation levels all expenses will be covered. Calculating break-even income can demonstrate what the price (registration fee, for example) must be at a given level/number of attendees in order for the total income to equal the total expenses. If prices cannot be raised, then this analysis can show how many attendees are required at the current price in order to break-even. The same can be done for exhibit income or other line items.

The first step in the break-even analysis is to subtract the total amount of income (if any) that has been determined for the "set" revenue line items (those line items that cannot be increased—that is, commissions) from the total expense amount. The resulting figure is the total expenses that need to be covered by the revenue areas for which pricing or attendance/exhibitor participation has been determined to be flexible (registration fee for example). To determine pricing (registration fee required to cover remaining expense total), take this figure and divide it by the number of estimated attendees. This will give you the registration fee that must be charged in order to cover all expenses.

An example of this, using the income outlined in Figure 3.2, may be that the functional areas of Exhibits Income, Sponsorships and Grants, and Miscellaneous Income have been determined to be static or unable to be changed (increasing these income areas has been determined to be unrealistic given specific market conditions for the meeting). Therefore, the total income of $261,325 from these three functional areas ($77,100 + $116,225 + $68,000 = $261,325) cannot be changed. We then must subtract this total of $261,325 from the total income for the meeting ($567,075) to determine how much income must be derived from the remaining income function area (Registration Income). In this example, $305,750 of total income must be generated from registration ($567,075 minus $261,325 = $305,750). Therefore, in order to break even (given that all income except registration is unable to be changed), with the anticipated attendance of 750 people (as in Figure 3.2), you would need to charge a registration fee of $407.67 per person if only one registration fee is charged, unlike the breakdown of different registration categories/fees outlined in Figure 3.2 ($305,750 divided by 750 registrants = $407.67).

If registration fees (using the example above) can not be increased, the same break-even analysis can be used to determine the increase in attendance required in order for the total income to equal the total expenses, thus achieving a break-even financial objective. Subtracting unchangeable income amounts from total expenses to get the resulting amount of expenses that need to be covered by registration fees and dividing that number by the registration fee (price) will give you the number of paying attendees required to break-even. Using the same example as above, if the remaining income of $305,750 must be generated from registration and the registration fee of $495 per person (using only one registration fee to simplify this example) should not be changed due to previous registration fee increases, attendee demographics that show registrants would be unable/unwilling to pay a higher fee to attend, or other reasons, then 618 people must attend at the $495 registration fee ($305,750 divided by $495 = 617.68).

These same calculations can be performed to determine exhibit booth rental fees or number of exhibit booths that will need to be sold in order for the budget to break-even.

If the meeting's financial objective was not to break-even, but to make a profit, additional calculations must be performed. If the profit required is a set dollar amount (for example, the financial objective of the meeting is to net a profit of $20,000), for purposes of determining the budget, the profit amount ($20,000) can be added as an expense line item and then the meeting can be budgeted to break-even (with the $20,000 included in the total expenses, if the budget breaks-even, the profit will be realized). Keep in mind that the $20,000 will not be considered an actual expense and should not be listed as such in the final budget—it is just included in the expenses for purposes of determining the appropriate income required to break-even, which would then cover the $20,000 profit as well. If the profit required is a percentage (for example, the meeting must realize a 10% profit), then the meeting should be budgeted to break-even and either the break-even pricing (registration fees and/or exhibit fees, if flexible) or the break-even anticipated attendance or exhibit booth sales must be increased by 10% to realize the required profit.

Using our continuing example from Figures 3.1 and 3.2, if $20,000 has been added to the expenses to cover the required profit, then the total expenses (in Figure 3.1) and the total income for the break-even budget (Figure 3.2) would increase $20,000 to $587,075. Therefore, the remaining flexible income (Registration Income) would increase to $325,075 and the registration fee for the anticipated attendance of 750 people would increase to $433.43 per person (using the same calculations outlined in the above examples), or if the registration fee of $495 cannot be changed, attendance would need to reach 657 people in order for the budget to break-even and the $20,000 profit to be made (as it is already in the total expenses). Using our continuing example to budget a 10% profit, the calculations in the above examples for the budget to break-even (a registration fee of $407.67 or attendance of 618 people) must be increased by 10%. So, a registration fee of $448.44 ($407.67 multiplied by 1.10) must be charged or 680 attendees (618 multiplied by 1.10) need to register at the set fee of $495 in order for the 10% profit to result.

When developing a break-even budget, understanding the contribution margin is important. Contribution margin refers to the portion of the price (registration fee, for example) that is used to cover non-variable costs (fixed costs and indirect costs). For example, if the registration fee is $495 per person, and variable costs (food and beverage, for example) are $345 per person, then $150 from each registrant's registration fee will be used to pay for the total fixed and indirect costs of the meeting ($495 minus $345 = $150). If the fixed and indirect costs total $150,000, then 1,000 attendees will be required in order for the budget to break-even ($150,000 divided by $150 per person = 1,000).

Several methods exist for increasing non-registration or exhibitor income in order to meet the financial objectives, as well. Additional sponsorships or attractive sponsorship packaging, including or increasing advertising in promotional or meeting materials and/or web sites, and innovative marketing to new target audiences for attendees and exhibitors are ways of increasing income without having to raise prices or attendance/booth sales.

If income cannot be generated to cover expenses (and profit, if applicable), then you must look at expenses for line items that can be reduced. Cost-cutting techniques are available in many functional areas, and should be considered only if income cannot be increased. Determining in which areas expenses can be reduced should be based on minimizing any negative impact on the quality of the meeting or the perception and experience of the attendees. For example, while food and beverage can be one of the budget's largest line-item expenses, cutting costs in this area has a direct impact on attendees. Attempt to decrease other line items first.

FINANCIAL MANAGEMENT

Financial Statements and Reports

Realize that budgets are not static. Costs change and income varies from what was planned. Knowing about variances as early as possible, and the decisions you make to counteract these changes, can be the difference between financial success and failure. Consider the scenario in which attendance is lower than anticipated because of the debut of three new competing meetings in the same month. If you are continuously reviewing the budget and the financial situation based on actual registration figures, you can take action to develop new revenue streams or attendee markets not impacted by the competing meetings to combat the decrease in registration income, and still achieve your financial objectives. If you wait until the meeting is finished and then realize that the bottom-line did not meet original expectations, explaining to your stakeholders why the meeting did not succeed financially will be very difficult.

Continuously updating and reviewing the budget for the meeting is the best way to ascertain, at any given time, how the meeting is doing financially. In order to function as a financial management tool on which decisions about the meeting are based, the budget must be kept current (actual figures must be input on a regular basis), include previous years' budget and actual figures, and include the percentage of the budget that each line item represents. If these areas are all included and updated continuously, the meeting budget itself is the most useful financial management tool.

Additionally, various financial statements and reports can be used to continuously review the actual financial status of your meeting and make decisions/take action accordingly. The most useful of these include the income statement and the spreadsheet control report.

An income statement (Figure 3.3) is a statement of revenues and expenses (also known as a profit and loss statement) which summarizes transactions accumulated over a period of time (a month, a quarter, a year). The bottom-line of this statement shows the meeting's profit or loss for the time frame covered in the statement. This statement can be produced so that it shows the status of income and expenses using the same functional categories as the budgets (work with your accounting department to structure the appropriate function and line items). A clear picture of the actual amounts for each line item is provided for the period for which the statement has been generated. By keeping cumulative totals of

---

Income Statement

May 1, 200X-May 31, 200X

Income

Registration	$ 92,500
Exhibits	$ 17,500
Sponsorship	$ 10,000
Miscellaneous	$ 22,000
Total Income	**$142,000**

Expenses

Administration	$ 8,000
Program	$ 0
Facilities	$ 0
Food & Beverage	$148,750
Marketing	$ 100
Exhibits	$ 0
Registration	$ 5,250
Support	$ 0
Miscellaneous	$ 800
Total Expense	**$162,900**
Income Over Expense	**($ 20,900)**

FIGURE 3.3

Sample Income Statement

line items from the monthl   le statement, comparisons can be made to budgeted figures.   ounting department on a monthly basis can easily generate a   nse statement.

A spreadsheet control   ) is a document that can be created upon completion of the   s. It shows anticipated income and expenses by month. In order to develop this important tool, you must estimate what percentage of each line item will realistically be actualized each month. For example, if your meeting is in early October, registration fee income may begin coming in when marketing begins (for example, early March). In March, April, and May, history may show (or estimates may indicate) that only 5% of attendees will register in each of those months. In June and July, maybe 15% will register each month. In August, perhaps 20% will register. In September, the remaining advance registrations (30%) will come in. In October, on-site registrations will be actualized (5% of total). Therefore, you can break down registration fee income by month, which entails breaking down revenues on a monthly basis as well. If total registration fee income is $100,000, then based on the above example, $5,000 will be realized each month in March, April, and May; $15,000 in each of June and July, $20,000 in August and $30,000 in September. On-site registration fee income of $5,000 would be put into October.

Likewise, the same calculations can be done to spread expenses out over the appropriate months in which they will be paid. Using the same example, most marketing expenses would be paid in February/March, whereas much of the facility costs would be paid in October or November. Most contracts will indicate payment dates for deposits, periodic scheduled payments, and final balances that will help you to determine when expenses will be paid.

Once you have completed the spreadsheet control report, this will show the income expected and the expenses to be paid for each month. Enabling you to easily see if a problem is imminent. If you expected to have a total of 15% (or $15,000) of income received by the end of May (based on the example above) and the income statements show a cumulative revenue of only $5,000 in that period, your budgeted attendance may be in jeopardy. This report also shows any unanticipated expenses or expenses that may be higher than budgeted. Realizing that anticipated income is down or expenses are high for a particular month allows you to research the cause of the discrepancy and take action to make adjustments as necessary to correct a potential problem.

Accounting Methods and Financial Controls

Two types of accounting methods are possible: accrual accounting and cash-based accounting.

Cash-based accounting refers to an accounting method that enters income and expenses into the books at the time when payment is received or expenses paid. A checking account is a simple example of cash-based accounting. The principal advantage of cash-based accounting is its simplicity and the ease with which it can be understood.

An accrual accounting system is a method that enters income and expenses into the books at the time of contract or when they are committed, instead of when they are actually received or paid. This system takes into account receivables and payables and paints a more accurate picture of the financial status of the meeting at any given time, although it is more difficult to understand and interpret. The accrual accounting system is the one most commonly used for meetings.

When analyzing the meeting's financial performance at any point in time, you need to know which system is being used by your accounting or finance department, as the content of reports (income statements) generated will have different meanings, depending on which accounting method is utilized by your

Meeting held in July	January	February	March	April	May	June	July	August	September	October	November	December	TOTAL
INCOME													
Registration	$0.00	$0.00	$30,575.00	$30,575.00	$91,725.00	$122,300.00	$30,575.00	$0.00	$0.00	$0.00	$0.00	$0.00	$305,750.00
	0%	0%	10%	10%	30%	40%	10%	0%	0%	0%	0%	0%	100%
Exhibits	$3,855.00	$7,710.00	$7,710.00	$19,275.00	$19,275.00	$7,710.00	$0.00	$0.00	$0.00	$3,855.00	$3,855.00	$3,855.00	$77,100.00
	5%	10%	10%	25%	25%	10%	0%	0%	0%	5%	5%	5%	100%
Sponsorship	$11,622.50	$17,433.75	$17,433.75	$17,433.75	$11,622.50	$5,811.25	$0.00	$0.00	$0.00	$0.00	$23,245.00	$11,622.50	$116,225.00
	10%	15%	15%	15%	10%	5%	0%	0%	0%	0%	20%	10%	100%
Miscellaneous	$0.00	$10,500.00	$3,550.00	$3,550.00	$21,400.00	$14,450.00	$3,550.00	$11,000.00	$0.00	$0.00	$0.00	$0.00	$68,000.00
TOTAL	**$15,477.65**	**$35,644.00**	**$59,269.10**	**$70,834.25**	**$144,023.15**	**$150,271.80**	**$34,125.10**	**$11,000.00**	**$0.00**	**$3,855.05**	**$27,100.25**	**$15,477.65**	**$567,078.00**
EXPENSES													
Administration	$5,137.50	$5,137.50	$5,837.50	$5,837.50	$7,237.50	$7,937.50	$5,837.50	$10,637.50	$5,137.50	$5,137.50	$5,137.50	$5,137.50	$74,150.00
Program	$2,000.00	$24,000.00	$0.00	$2,000.00	$0.00	$8,000.00	$11,500.00	$41,500.00	$0.00	$2,000.00	$0.00	$0.00	$91,000.00
Facilities	$0.00	$2,250.00	$0.00	$0.00	$0.00	$0.00	$2,000.00	$2,250.00	$0.00	$0.00	$0.00	$0.00	$6,500.00
Food & Beverage	$0.00	$0.00	$0.00	$0.00	$148,737.50	$0.00	$0.00	$148,737.50	$0.00	$0.00	$0.00	$0.00	$297,475.00
Marketing	$2,100.00	$16,100.00	$100.00	$3,600.00	$100.00	$1,100.00	$600.00	$4,100.00	$1,100.00	$1,100.00	$100.00	$1,100.00	$31,200.00
Exhibits	$0.00	$7,250.00	$0.00	$0.00	$0.00	$1,600.00	$500.00	$13,425.00	$500.00	$0.00	$0.00	$0.00	$22,775.00
Registration	$6,750.00	$0.00	$0.00	$0.00	$5,250.00	$5,250.00	$3,500.00	$5,500.00	$0.00	$0.00	$0.00	$6,750.00	$33,000.00
Support	$0.00	$0.00	$0.00	$0.00	$0.00	$3,475.00	$3,000.00	$1,500.00	$0.00	$0.00	$0.00	$0.00	$7,975.00
Miscellaneous	$0.00	$0.00	$0.00	$0.00	$0.00	$0.00	$1,500.00	$1,500.00	$0.00	$0.00	$0.00	$0.00	$3,000.00
TOTAL	**$15,987.50**	**$54,737.50**	**$5,937.50**	**$11,437.50**	**$161,325.00**	**$27,362.50**	**$28,437.50**	**$229,150.00**	**$6,237.50**	**$8,237.50**	**$5,237.50**	**$12,987.50**	**$567,075.00**

FIGURE 3.4
Sample Spreadsheet Control Report

organization. The method used will also impact the spreadsheet control report, as income and expenses must be allocated to the months in which they will be contracted or committed, and not when they are actually received or paid.

If your organization is using cash-based accounting, financial reports including income statements will reflect actual income received and expenses paid as of the date of the report. This information can then be transferred into the "actual" column of the budget and into the spreadsheet control report. If using an accrual system, income may have been received and expenses paid, but these totals will not show up at the same time on reports as they would if a cash-based system is being used. Income would show up on reports when earned (typically when the meeting takes place) and expenses would be included on reports when you become liable to pay them (typically when contracted services are delivered to you). When cash is received or paid out is not important in accrual-based accounting. Accrual-based accounting systems attempt to match income and expense items together in the income statement, and are reflected on the income statement during the period when the event occurs. This will make a difference in figures transferred to the actual column of the budget and the spreadsheet control report and could make it more difficult to determine if income and expenses are on track. The biggest concern is in comparing the current actual figures to past years' figures in the same time frame (e.g. month)—if the accounting system used changes between years, you will be unable to compare the current budget and actual income and expenses to previous years' totals accurately, as the income and expenses on the reports would be accounted for at different times of the year based on the accounting system used.

For example, if your meeting is scheduled for early October and marketing materials were distributed and registration opens in late July, a cash-based system may show registration income on reports in August, September, and October, whereas an accrual system will show all income in October (registrations received during months prior to the meeting will be "deferred" until October). Likewise, using a cash-based system, deposits and prepayments will show as expenses prior to October, while other expenses will not show until after the meeting when the bills are paid. Using an accrual system, expenses will be reflected in October only (deposits will be recorded as "pre-payments" rather than expenses, and invoices received after the meeting will be "accrued" back into the October income statement). Accruals and pre-payments are recorded on your organization's balance sheet, and your organization's accounting or finance department will handle re-booking these items from the balance sheet to the income statement automatically for you. If your organization uses the accrual accounting system, ask your accounting or finance department to provide information to you on the total amount of deferred revenues as well as deposits and pre-payments recorded. This will assist you in tracking income and expenses, as these items will become income and expense during the period when the meeting takes place. Understand whether your organization uses cash-based or accrual-based accounting, as this can certainly affect how actual income and expenses are tracked and how they appear in reports that you are analyzing to determine the financial status of the meeting in any given month.

A chart of accounts is a numbering system used to identify each line item of the budget by a specific account number, allowing deposits and expenditures to be posted to the correct accounts. This system is used primarily by associations to track appropriate income and expenses. Most computerized systems have a chart of accounts already in place. It is important to maintain drastically different assigned numbers for income accounts versus expense accounts, as some may have similar function areas (exhibitor income and exhibitor expense for example). Most systems begin income accounts with a certain number and expense accounts with a different number to differentiate the accounts. The chart of accounts will help to insure that reports generated by the accounting department show actual figures debited or credited to the correct accounts.

Another financial analysis tool that can be used to track the financial progress of your meetings is a variance analysis report. This is a spreadsheet summary of accounts receivable and payable, showing the meeting's cash flow and an analysis of specific expense items. A variance report can usually be generated by the accounting office, as well as a summary of accounts receivable and payable. Analysis of specific expense items (researching why the variance is happening and what adjustments can be taken to correct or offset the difference) should be undertaken whenever the variance between budgeted costs and actual costs are cause for concern.

All of these reports and statements assist in maintaining detailed financial records and provide the information required to continuously review the actual income and expenses of the meeting as compared to the budget. Identifying variances early allows for the required research and action to be taken in advance of the meeting to correct any budget problems so that the meeting's financial objectives will be realized.

Decision Making Based on Financial Statements

All types of financial statements should be reviewed on a continuous basis, at least monthly, to determine the financial "health" of the meeting in order to make decisions to combat any variances from the budget. For example, if a large portion of registration fee income was expected 3 months prior to the meeting and did not materialize, then you need to determine if it is because marketing materials were distributed later than usual, or if it is an indication that overall meeting attendance will be lower than expected. This will allow you to make decisions to offset the changes, such as increasing marketing efforts to increase attendance, identifying additional revenue streams to offset the lower registration fee income, or reducing expenses based on the reduced estimated income.

Continually reviewing how the budget compares to actual results allows you to identify early in the process any changes that may affect vendors (resulting in large fees) and to communicate the changes to the appropriate vendors as early as possible. For example, if registration fee income is down and your research shows that, in fact, final attendance will be lower than anticipated/budgeted, you may be able to limit attrition charges by releasing rooms early. Conversely, if registration income is higher than anticipated/budgeted, and your research shows that final attendance will remain higher, it allows you to contract for more hotel rooms while they are still available.

Changes to the Budget

A formal process should be in place for making changes to the original budget. While compiling ongoing actual revenue and expenses, and updating the "Actual" column of the original budget is a recommended practice, changes will be needed to budgeted amounts. The budget should not be changed without a formal request and approval system. Only authorized persons should have the ability to make changes to the original budget. Documenting any changes, and the reasons for them, is an important process in budget management.

Management of Funds: In Advance of the Meeting and On-Site

Depending on the amount of income you anticipate, and when that income is expected, you may need to set up special bank or investment accounts well in advance of the meeting. If large amounts of income will be received months in advance of the meeting, investment (interest) income could be realized by investing the funds in short-term, interest-paying accounts. Otherwise, setting up a separate bank account for the meeting's income may be recommended. This allows all income directly related to the meeting to be deposited into one account. Doing this is especially important when using online registration. Today the technology available allows attendees and exhibitors to register and pay for items online with credit cards. Depositing these funds into a separate bank account allows easier tracking of income and fees (such as credit card fees). This is also helpful if international attendees will register and pay with bank transfers.

Instituting tax-exempt status (if applicable) well in advance with all vendors is important. Most facilities and other vendors require credit applications and tax-exempt verification when contracting for services. Some organizations are tax-exempt only in certain locations. If your organization has tax-exempt status, you should research whether or not your organization enjoys this status in the meeting's destination, and submit the appropriate verification. Saving taxes on facility and other vendor charges, if applicable, can result in a substantial decrease in expenses.

A determination should also be made regarding the amount of revenue you anticipated collecting on-site at the meeting. If a large amount of income is expected, a bank account at the meeting location may be warranted. Deposits can be made locally each day and then transferred to the main account in the organization's headquarters city at the end of the meeting. This way, funds can begin to draw interest immediately upon deposit. If on-site revenue is not expected to be great, consider depositing all cash receipts with the host facility as an advance payment against master account charges. This provides an effective security measure by avoiding transporting cash, and it may result in a cash-in-advance discount from the facility. Make sure that all registration staff who handle funds on site are bonded. Additionally, clear and well-defined policies regarding cash handling are prudent. Place tight controls on the receipt and disbursement of funds on site and keep the number of personnel handling funds to a minimum.

Master account review is a key element of financial management. Review charges daily, as reconciling and making corrections the day charges are posted is easier than waiting until the meeting is completed. Part of the post-con meeting should include an overall master account review. Again, making changes while you are still on property and everything is fresh in your and the facility representative's minds is much easier than trying to institute changes when you receive the invoice 30 days after the meeting has ended.

When contracting for the meeting, you may want to include language that states that the master account will not be paid until all post-event reports are provided by the facility. The required reports should be requested in the contracting stage. The other aspect of the master account that you may want to address during the contracting process is that all undisputed charges will be paid within 30 days of receipt of the final invoice, while the balance (disputed charges) will be paid within 30 days of successful reconciliation of disputed charges. The bill for a large convention may take 30 days to reconcile, and you do not want to pay interest on the invoice before it can be paid. Additionally, some facilities are slow in providing backup materials and answers to questions, which slows the reconciliation process through no fault of your organization. In these cases, your organization should not have to pay interest charges if the facility is slow in getting the appropriate documentation to you. Many of these problems can be avoided, however, by reconciling the master account on site, both on a daily basis and at the post-con meeting.

Other suppliers should be encouraged to produce invoices by the end of the meeting as well. Again, review all charges either daily or prior to the end of the meeting to make sure they are both accurate and in agreement with contractual arrangements. Completing this task on site will alleviate any misunderstandings later. Negotiating disputed charges may be acceptable on site, but may be difficult or impossible after the fact.

International Financial Management

Budgeting for international meetings follows much the same process as budgeting for domestic programs. However, complications caused by currency and tax issues must be taken into consideration.

If currency exchange rates are anticipated to fluctuate greatly between when the meeting is budgeted and pricing set, and when the meeting will take place, you may want to research "buying forward" at fixed exchange rates, which can lower the risk of fluctuation, at least in the short term. You may also want to set up a bank account in the country where the meeting will be held to deposit income and avoid exchange rate fluctuations that could negatively impact the budget.

Another decision that must be made is in which currency you will accept registration and other income. Requiring funds in one currency may eliminate the need to deal with conversions and currency exchange rates, but may not be convenient for attendees coming from multiple countries and currencies. This practice may also come with hidden costs (for example local suppliers may increase their prices to cover currency exchange). Requiring funds in the currency of the country in which the meeting will be held may make registration fees to attendees in some countries higher, depending on exchange rates.

Exchange rate fluctuations and which currency in which to accept income or pay expenses has been simplified greatly in European countries with the introduction of the "euro" (European Currency Units/ECU—the currency unit of the European Community). Now that many European countries all use the same currency (the euro), conducting business with these countries and avoiding the risks of using multiple currencies and their fluctuations are easier. The use of the Euro also enables attendees to more easily convert currency and use the same currency throughout various countries.

Two tax issues must be addressed when planning international meetings. The first is whether or not attendees and/or the sponsoring organization will be liable to pay income or other taxes in their home country due to the fact that the meeting is being held internationally. While this doesn't necessarily impact the meeting budget, it has ramifications for attendees, which may discourage participation. The second issue is the liability for attendees and the sponsoring organization to pay local taxes in the country where the meeting is being held. Local sales taxes and value-added tax (VAT) (in Europe) are examples. These taxes can be as high as 20%, and the impact on the budget can be substantial. Researching the complexities of different tax rates, rules of what must be paid when and what taxes can be reclaimed after the event is crucial.

Utilizing Technology in Financial Management

Many technology tools can increase the effectiveness of your financial management strategies, and these technologies are ever-changing. Knowing what technology is available, how to use it, and which products match your needs can greatly streamline the budgeting and financial management process.

Software

While numerous types of budgeting software are available, as well as components to most full-service association management or financial management software

Put It Into Perspective

Budget philosophies, as well as innovative and creative ways to increase income (if applicable) or reduce expenses without negatively impacting the quality of the meeting or the attendees' perceptions of value, may vary based on the type of organization that is holding the meeting.

Type of Organization	Budget Philosophy	Increasing Income	Cost Cutting
Association	Most associations are "non-profit" organizations, which simply means that profits can not be excessive and must be used to operate or grow the association. Some "non-profit" organizations are charitable organizations that must distribute all excess income over expenses. All U.S. associations are tax-exempt from U.S. federal income tax and may be exempt from sales tax in some states.	• Add or increase level of advertising in on-site program and on web site; • Consider marketing to related groups, competing organizations and/or students; • Creatively package sponsorship opportunities.	• Create guidelines for staff and speaker/faculty travel and expenses; • Use member speakers at no fee where possible; • Review BEOs and A/V orders to insure no hidden costs; • Print program materials at a discount printer in the destination of the meeting; • Use volunteers, host committee, students from area schools in place of CVB or temp company staff for registration staffing.
Corporation	Meetings typically do not have "income" and companies are under pressure to limit expenditures in all areas, including meetings, so the "loss" or subsidy budgeted must be kept within reasonable limits.	• Income is typically not applicable.	• Consider shortening the meeting by a day; • Hold meetings in smaller cities and/or during "shoulder" or "off-peak" times in order to better negotiate rates and other items at the facility; • Control travel costs by dictating airline and ground transportation preferred vendors; • Negotiate multi-meeting contracts with vendors to receive reduced pricing; • Use creative, fun activities during receptions enabling the reduction of high-end food offerings and reduced quantities of food required.
Government Entity	The overall philosophy is to break even. Registration fees must be kept within reasonable ranges and expenses must be tightly controlled. Attendees must stay within per diem guidelines.	• Increasing registration fees is rarely an option and sponsorships are typically not allowed; • Increasing attendance by including other departments or entities may be an option; • Some vendor exhibits may be allowed, although strict guidelines must be followed.	• Shorten the meeting by a day; • Hold meetings in "nontraditional" venues such as university campuses; • Work with catering or chef to create menus priced within government limits by reducing portion size (meat) or "ganging" menus with another, larger group; • Negotiate food outlet pricing to allow purchases within individual meal per diems; • Use students in place of additional staff for registration and other duties.

Put It Into Practice

The International Association of Widget Manufacturers' (IAWM) annual conference is being planned for 1,000 attendees (no exhibits) and the budget is under development. The financial objective of the program is to break even.

Total expenses are $567,000, broken down as follows:

Administration	$45,000
Program	$129,000
Facility	$35,000
Food and Beverage	$300,000
(1,000 attendees expected, so $300 multiplied by 1,000)	
Marketing	$15,000
Registration	$22,000
Support	$18,000
Miscellaneous	$3,000
TOTAL	$567,000

Total income for last year's conference was $470,000, broken down as follows:

Registration	$375,000
(1,000 attendees, so $375 multiplied by 1,000)	
Sponsorship	$ 80,000
Miscellaneous	$ 15,000
TOTAL	$470,000

Based on the information presented above, the budget can break even only if either the registration fee is increased to $472 per person or, if the registration fee cannot be increased, the number of registrants increases to 1,259 (assuming sponsorship and miscellaneous income are static). The calculations to support these increases are outlined below.

Total expenses equal $567,000. Subtract static income from the total expenses ($567,000 minus $95,000 equals $472,000). The $472,000 of remaining expenses must be covered from registration income. If 1,000 attendees are expected, each would have to pay $472 in order for total income to equal total expenses, thus resulting in a break-even budget ($472,000 divided by 1,000 = $472).

If the $472,000 of remaining expenses to be covered by registration income must be done at the registration fee of $375, then the attendance must increase to 1,259 ($472,000 divided by $375 = 1,259).

applications, many of them are not tailored specifically to budgeting and managing finances for meetings and events. Due diligence is required in order to determine whether these products can be tailored to your specific budgeting needs. If your organization already has such software, see that it works for your meeting budget. However, applications as simple as Microsoft Excel can also be used for budgeting and financial management. Formatting Excel spreadsheets to perform the calculations to determine per-person expenses (variable costs), income and expense percentages, pricing, and overall totals is fairly common. Excel can also be used to format specific reports and financial management tools, such as the spreadsheet control report, variance analysis, and cash flow. If you are looking to partially automate budgeting and financial management, but not necessarily to purchase products to do so, take a look at what tools your system already provides and learn how they can be used to maximum benefit.

Online Tools

While many vendors today offer online registration, housing, travel, and marketing applications, budgeting and financial management components are not as readily available. However, some online tools can streamline the budgeting and financial management process, including online attrition calculators, cost estimators, expense tracking, and budget calculations (see Appendices for a list of the online tools available at the time of printing). Researching available online tools is worth your time as they may provide solutions that will make budgeting and financial management more efficient and less time-consuming in the future.

When considering any technology tool, review what components the tool includes and how it can be tailored to meet your specific needs as well as work with existing technology. Compatibility with databases in order to integrate functions such as marketing and registration is a key feature of any technology.

EVALUATING FINANCIAL PERFORMANCE

Post-Event Financial Analysis

While performing continual financial analysis is important in order to identify potential problems, make changes/corrections, and better inform facilities and vendors of the status of the meeting well in advance of the program, another important step in the financial management process takes place after the meeting has ended. Reviewing actual income and expenses as compared to the budget once the meeting is over and income and expenses have been reconciled allows for an analysis of any variances and the reasons for them. Undertaking this step will allow improved understanding as to why actual financial performance differed from what was anticipated. This understanding may drive new policies for everything from site selection and contract negotiation to speaker guidelines and future pricing. At the conclusion of the meeting, the emphasis should be placed on analyzing the overall financial records to confirm or change financial philosophies based on actual performance.

Return on Investment (ROI)

While the financial ROI (the "bottom-line" of the meeting) and whether or not the meeting's financial objectives were achieved are key indicators of a meeting's success, additional ways exist for demonstrating a positive ROI for your organization.

Utilizing resources to their maximum potential should include a determination of human and technological skill and financial resources. Being able to analyze what resources are available and utilizing all of them to their greatest potential is an invaluable skill for a meeting manager. The bottom-line can be influenced dramatically by this important analysis.

Consider the viability and profitability of outsourcing certain components of the meeting. In many cases, outsourcing may not only be financially advantageous, it may also allow for key resources to remain focused on your organization's core competencies. For example, if your educational program staff is limited, you may consider outsourcing meeting management so that the staff can focus on educational content and/or marketing. Site selection, booth and sponsorship sales, exhibition management, complete meeting management, marketing, housing, and registration services are all areas where outsourcing may be fiscally prudent. Analyzing these options is another means toward providing a positive ROI for your meeting.

SUMMARY

The overall financial objectives of the meeting and the budgetary philosophy of the organization affect all other planning decisions. Specific, measurable budget objectives should be set to allow for realistic budgeting and the financial management required to successfully achieve the financial objectives and demonstrate positive ROI. The budget will determine many components of the meeting and should be communicated to key suppliers to allow everyone to work within a common frame of reference.

Continuous review of the budget and financial reports and tools enables you to analyze the meeting's financial health and make decisions to overcome any potential problems. It allows the control of revenue and expenditures and the identification of opportunities for increasing revenue and/or reducing expenses (if required) far enough in advance to positively impact the meeting's bottom-line. Properly managing finances prior to, during, and after the meeting is a key role for meeting managers and a crucial skill that demonstrates the value of the planner to his/her organization.

KEY TERMS

Accrual accounting
Balance sheet
Break-even analysis
Budget handbook
Cash-based accounting
Chart of accounts
Contribution margin
Fixed expense (fixed cost)

Income statement
Indirect expenses (indirect costs)
Master account
Pre-con meeting
Post-con meeting
Post event report
Return on investment (ROI)

Spreadsheet control report
Value added tax (VAT)
Variable expenses (variable costs)
Variance analysis report
Zero-based budgeting

COMPELLING QUESTIONS FOR CONSIDERATION

1. What are some commonly overlooked income and expense line items and under which functional areas should they be listed in the meeting budget?

2. In Figure 3.1 (Sample Functional Expense Budget), discuss which line items are fixed costs, which are variable costs, and which are indirect costs.

3. What is a break-even budget? Discuss options for increasing income or reducing expenses to get the budget to break-even.

4. What is the difference between cash-based and accrual accounting?

5. What is a spreadsheet control report and how can it be created and used?

6. Discuss the issues relevant to the financial management of international meetings.

7. Identify and discuss cash handling strategies and other tools to manage finances on-site.

CHAPTER 4

SPONSORSHIPS AND STRATEGIC PARTNERSHIPS: A NEW APPROACH

Sherrif Karamat

CHIEF PARTNER RELATIONS OFFICER

PROFESSIONAL CONVENTION MANAGEMENT ASSOCIATION

LEARNER OUTCOMES

When the reader has completed reading this chapter, he/she should be able to . . .

1 Describe the difference between strategic partnerships and event sponsorships.

2 Apply the lessons learned in asset identification and valuation to similar situations in practice.

3 Design strategic partnership packages to achieve the objectives of the organization as well as the sponsor.

4 Explain the benefits of activation and why sponsors should be budgeting for activation.

5 Organize benefits by level for an event or a year-round partnership.

> The Walt Disney organization has been in the world of alliances since Disneyland opened in 1955; Walt himself saw the value of aligning with companies as a way to create experiences for which he needed financial support and as a way to provide opportunities for exposure to those organizations.
>
> *George Aguel, Senior Vice President*
> *Walt Disney Parks and Resorts*

OVERVIEW

Association and corporate meetings are increasingly looking for partners when executing meetings and events for their organizations. Two appropriate strategies for meeting managers to explore are sponsorships and strategic partners. Spending on sponsorships by North American companies grew by 8.7 percent in 2004 representing $11.14 billion in total spending. This growth is expected to continue and the increase in spending is being fueled by both additional spending of current sponsoring organizations and through significant increases in new spending by organizations that are sponsoring events for the first time.[1]

The *Oxford English Dictionary* defines sponsorships as the act of a person or organization that promotes or supports another organization or activity such as a sporting event. An alternative definition comes from the event marketing consulting firm of IEG, Inc.: When a company pays a cash and/or in-kind fee to a property in return for access to the exploitable commercial potential with that property.

In order to define sponsorships for the purposes of meeting management, and to ensure that there is proper understanding of why sponsorships and strategic partnerships differ, we must first define advertising and donations in the context of sponsorships and strategic partnerships.

Advertising is any paid form of non-personal communication about an organization, product, service, or idea by an identified sponsor.[2]

A donation is a cash or in-kind contribution to an organization or foundation with or without taxable benefits but with no expectation of commercial return.

The fundamental difference between a sponsor and a strategic partner is that a strategic partner benefits from the relationship on a year-round basis, whereas a sponsor may only be involved for a single item on a one-time basis. The goals of the strategic partner and the partnering organization must be closely aligned. The relationship is symbiotic; as the organization benefits through the partnership, the benefits and value delivered to the partner grow simultaneously as well.

This chapter will give the reader a basic understanding of sponsorships and strategic partnerships, including the concepts of assets, asset valuation, packaging, pricing, activation, and fulfillment. While the discussion cannot be completely comprehensive (after all, entire textbooks have been written on the subjects of sponsorships and strategic partnerships), the reader should gain a good understanding of how organizations can leverage their strategic partnerships and sponsorships to increase their revenues and at the same time deliver value to their sponsors (see Figure 4.1).

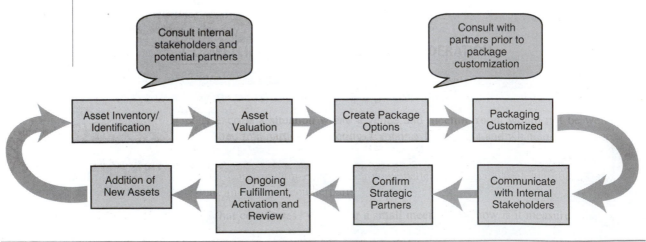

FIGURE 4.1
Strategic Partnership Development Model

BEFORE APPROACHING A POTENTIAL PARTNER OR SPONSOR

In order to realize the full potential of revenues from sponsorships and strategic partnerships, organizations have to take a holistic view of their assets before they approach potential partners. Sponsorships are no longer just a by-product of the association's meeting management department. Most sponsors are looking for a long-term relationship where they can derive increased value over the entire length of that relationship. Potential sponsors want to be sold only once, that is to say that an organization should not have multiple people approaching sponsors on different products at various times during the course of a year.

Prior to even approaching a potential sponsor or strategic partner, any organization must have a complete understanding of:

- Assets and asset valuation
- Packaging
- Pricing
- Activation
- Fulfillment

ASSETS AND ASSET VALUATION

An asset is a product, service, or idea that has value. Assets can be either tangible (such as a product) or intangible (such as a brand). An organization should first embark on a complete inventory of all of its assets. This task is tedious, and it requires the commitment of the entire organization. A template can simplify the process (see Table 4.1).

Clearly each organization will have its own categories for classification of assets. Some organizations may have multiple meetings or conferences per year that vary in size, and may also cater to very different audiences. Organizations may have trade shows, web blogs, and numerous printed products that are all valuable assets. In the intangible category, organizations should consider their brand, logos, trademarks, and rights. For example, Coca Cola and Microsoft are highly recognizable and desirable brands that can offer extremely valuable brand association for potential sponsors.

Additionally, recognizing an organization may have assets that it does not want sponsored is important. For example an association might not want certain educational sessions to be sponsored because sponsorship might be seen as a commercialization of the content, which might ultimately reduce the value of the session to potential attendees.

TABLE 4.1
Asset Inventory

Category	Description	Quantity	Frequency	Current Price
Annual Meeting	Luncheon for 1,000 people	Two	Yearly	$25,000 per lunch
	General Session Speaker	Three	Yearly	$50,000 per speaker
Print Media	Periodicals	30,000	Monthly	$2,500/pg. black & white
Digital Media	Web site banners – home page	10	Rotation – all year	$10,000 per banner
	E-Newsletter	One	Weekly	$5,000 per issue
Intangibles	Logo	One	Continuous	Negotiable

Membership-based organizations may have many assets that are not easily identifiable. The membership itself can represent a huge potential asset for an association. For example, an organization of meeting managers is a natural target for hotels, convention centers, airlines, and audiovisual companies. However, the same organization may be equally attractive to a luggage company, credit card companies, or a high-end shoe manufacturer. While knowing the demographic profile of an organization's membership is vital, much more valuable is the information gathered beyond demographics and insight into the lifestyle choices of the membership. This will open a whole new potential for sponsorships that would not have been visible by merely gathering demographic information. Finally, to ensure that all of the organization's assets are identified and inventoried, you must ensure that all of the employees of the organization are involved in identifying potential assets.

At the same time that the organization is conducting an internal inventory of its assets, it should also be conducting interviews with existing or potential sponsors to find out what assets sponsors perceive as valuable. This process can lead to the realization that the organization has assets that are valuable, but were not previously considered to be assets. Furthermore, the organization will get useful information on how to package their assets and greater insight into what assets are valuable, how sponsors would like to be sold to, and the type of relationship sponsors are seeking.

The value of an asset has little to do with the cost of an asset and more to do with the rights and benefits that it conveys to a potential sponsor. For example, the sponsorship of a luncheon to an audience of medical doctors and pharmacists may be extremely important to a pharmaceutical company if they are introducing a new drug or treatment for a disease. The luncheon may cost only $5,000 to stage, but the value in product sales to the pharmaceutical company may be in the billions of dollars. Thus, the organization is able to value the luncheon at a much higher rate.

Information gathering is critical in order to value any asset appropriately. The first place to start when pricing an asset is to look at what the organization has historically received for that specific asset. Obviously, this will not be applicable to new assets and should just be a starting point as most organization's assets may be valued incorrectly.

The second step is to assess what similar organizations are charging for similar assets. This is not an easy task, because information may not be readily available and—most importantly—similar assets from different organizations do not necessarily convey the same rights and benefits. Some associations tend to list their sponsorship opportunities on their web sites, so this may be an area to consider when conducting the research. A common strategy is that an organization will decide to test the market by introducing the sponsorship at a very high price point in order to see what potential sponsors are willing to pay. However, this approach is not recommended, because the price of the sponsorship should be directly determined by the value and benefits the sponsorship conveys. The key when setting the price for an asset is to realize that the price of the asset is not related to the cost of the asset but rather to the potential value the asset represents to a sponsor. An alternative approach to asset valuation is to hire an independent third-party company that specializes in asset valuation. These companies have various valuation methodologies and techniques that allow them to appropriately value an organization's assets. Third-party companies can be expensive, so weigh the cost of seeking such advice against the increase in return.

PACKAGING

Organizations can no longer expect sponsors to write them blank checks with little or no return on their investment. Sponsors are demanding greater returns, and organizations that can package items that deliver greater value to the sponsors will achieve success. The greater the value for potential sponsors, the more attractive the package, and the result is that the organization can demand higher prices. The number of assets that an organization has identified will determine the number of potential partners, based on the bundling of the assets. Packaging should be done on levels such as Platinum, Gold, and Silver, or Premier Partner, Major Partner, or Event Partners. Some factors to consider in packaging for strategic partners include:

- How many strategic partners can the organization accept and still deliver value?
- What assets should be included in an agreement?
- Length of the agreement
- Termination clause

As stated above, the number of assets an organization has identified in the inventory phase will largely determine the number of strategic partners the organization can pursue. Settle for a smaller number of strategic partners and deliver greater value. The result will be a satisfied partner and one that is prepared to pay a higher price for the package.

Sponsorship packages for strategic partners should be individually tailored to the sponsor. This does not mean the sponsor will be allowed to influence what the organization is offering. Instead, it allows the organization to package those assets that are of interest to a specific sponsor, thereby making the package more valuable and desirable to the potential sponsor. For example, a potential strategic partner may be an employment agency or headhunter and thus they may be interested in programs that target graduating students or, in the case of an association, new members. This information would be very useful for the organization when tailoring the package. As an inclusive, year-round package, the organization could include the following: new member orientation, student programs, e-newsletters that target new members and students, receptions and meal functions that offer marketing and networking opportunities that specifically attract new members and students. All of these items are assets that an employment agency or headhunter might consider valuable.

Agreements that are signed for multiple years can provide an association with a guaranteed source of revenues. It makes the budgeting process for revenues easier as the organization can, at a minimum, budget to receive the revenues in the signed agreement. Longer-term agreements also act as a "barrier to entry" from competitors that are pursuing the same sponsors. When funds dedicated to sponsorships are limited, organizations with multi-year agreements will be less threatened by competitors. Conversely, the downside of a long-term agreement is that the organization may decide they want to discontinue the assets offered in the agreement or that the strategic partner is not the best fit for the organization. Potential partners should be properly qualified as an appropriate strategic fit for the organization. That is to say, at no time should an organization get involved with a partner simply because they can and are willing to pay the package price. If partners are not properly assessed, the potential exists that neither the organization nor the partner will be pleased with the relationship and this may end up causing more harm for future relationships.

Termination clauses can be very important for both parties. A termination clause can be written into an agreement whereby both parties agree to specific situations that may cause the agreement to be terminated. A termination clause can be an option if either party is not adhering to their obligations as stated in the agreement. It can also be an opportunity for the organization to exit from the agreement if a decision has been made to discontinue the assets. Strategic partners will not use the termination clause simply to avoid payment; most strategic partners will consider ending an agreement only as a last resort because the organization has not fulfilled its obligations as outlined in the agreement. To avoid this situation, a review mechanism should be included in the package that would alert the organization to potential problems with any aspect of the agreement. In any agreement, under promise and over deliver; the reverse scenario would most likely result in a dissatisfied partner.

Event-specific sponsors should also be offered by levels such as platinum, gold, silver, and so on, but communication should be clear to those partners who are considered strategic to the organization versus those who are event-specific sponsors, as to the value they are receiving as a strategic partner or an event-specific sponsor. Table 4.2 is an example of an event-specific benefits package by level.

The benefits package in Table 4.2 does not identify what event is being sponsored. Instead, it states the benefits that will be conveyed based on the various levels for platinum, gold, silver, and so forth. This packaging strategy allows the sponsor the flexibility to select the most suitable program. For example, a sponsor might decide to sponsor the opening general session, a luncheon, or the Internet café at the organization's annual conference. In this scenario, if the sponsorship of the opening general session were $100,000 then the sponsor would fall under the platinum category and receive the benefits associated with this category. In addition to the standardized benefits, the organization has the flexibility to provide some extra benefits that are unique to the item that is being sponsored. For example, with the sponsorship of a general session, the sponsor may be allowed speaking time to address the entire conference, show a short video, or hand out a promotional item. The sponsorship of the luncheon could be especially themed with the sponsor in mind, or the default screen on the monitors at the Internet café could show a message from the sponsor. The ideas are numerous; the important point is to work in partnership with sponsors to assist them in achieving their objective without compromising content for commerciality.

PRICING

As previously stated, the price of an asset package should not be based on the cost of the assets it includes, but rather on the value the package represents to potential sponsors. Some of the things to consider before establishing a price are:

- What is included in the package?
- If these items were sold separately, what would they cost?
- What is the competition charging for a similar package?
- Could the potential sponsor target the same market or hold the same event on their own? If so, what would it cost them?

Other factors to consider when pricing a strategic partnership package or an event sponsorship include: How many potential sponsors are available, and how many partners is the organization seeking? What factors other than price are important to buyers? For example, are the benefits conveyed in the package ones that a sponsor would be willing to pay a higher price for? If the strategic partnership is mainly to gain access to the membership of the organization, can the sponsor gain access to these members through another channel or another organization or is this a unique opportunity?

The bottom-line is that price should be based on a combination of factors, such as the value conveyed in the package, the level of competition in the marketplace, the demand that exists for the package, and the uniqueness of the package. If value, demand, and uniqueness are rated high and the competition for sponsors is low, then clearly the package will be more valuable and sponsors will be willing to pay a higher price.

TABLE 4.2
Sponsorship Benefits Grid

BENEFITS	PLATINUM $100,000 plus	GOLD $75 – 99,999	SILVER $50 – 74,999	BRONZE $25 – 49,999	PEWTER up to $24,999
Rotating banner on annual conference home page of the organization's web site	•				
Rotating banner on annual conference program-at-a-glance page of the web site		•			
Logo and description on the "industry links" web page	•	•			
Literature distribution at designated area at the annual conference	•	•	•		
One-time use of pre- and post-annual conference registration list	Two-time use of preliminary registration	•	•		
Acknowledgement during one of the general sessions	Verbal & visual (logo)	Visual (logo)	Scrolling listing	Scrolling listing	Scrolling listing
Recognition in the annual conference preliminary program—circulation approximately 25,000	50-word description + logo	25-word description + logo	Logo	Listing	Listing
Recognition in the annual conference final program—distributed to all annual conference attendees	50-word description + logo	25-word description + logo	Logo	Listing	Listing
Recognition in the annual conference show dailies	Logo	Logo	Logo	Listing	Listing
Recognition in October and December issues of the organization's magazine—circulation approximately 50,000	Logo	Logo	Logo	Listing	Listing
Recognition in the organization's magazine immediately following the annual conference—circulation approximately 50,000	50-word description + logo	25-word description + logo	Logo	Listing	Listing
Recognition on the annual conference sponsor web page, including a link to the sponsor's web site	50-word description + logo	25-word description + logo	Logo	Listing	Listing
Signage recognizing the sponsor at the annual conference	Logo	Logo	Logo	Listing	Listing
Invitation to the president's VIP reception	4	3	2	2	2
Invitation to the chair's reception	4	3	2	1	1
Complimentary annual conference registration	4	3	2	1	0

Sponsors do not necessarily have to pay in cash. Sponsors can bring the organization products or "in-kind" services that reduce the organization's costs, which, in the end, would bring results that are similar to those seen from cash payments. However, if you are entering into an agreement where the sponsorship is in-kind, ensure that the products or services you will receive are relevant to your organization and that the sponsorship really does reduce your costs. If this is not the case, the organization is providing value to a sponsor in exchange for something that does not further the organization's own goals and they will have wasted a sponsorship opportunity. An example of a sponsorship that reduces costs would be an organization that usually budgets $50,000 for shuttle buses for their convention. If they found a sponsor was willing to provide the shuttle buses at no cost, in exchange for marketing exposure and access to the delegates attending the convention, then they have saved $50,000 in budgeted convention expenses.

ACTIVATION

Sponsors who pay a sponsorship fee for a package and then do nothing else, will not get the expected results, and they will end up disappointed when expectations are not met. Successful sponsorships are true partnerships, and sponsors who are not committed to take the necessary steps to achieve their desired results will not be pleased with the outcome and are unlikely to renew their agreement. Thus, the organization must take a proactive role with the sponsor to ensure that they activate their sponsorship to gain the results they expect.

Organizations seeking sponsorships need to explain at the outset of negotiations to potential sponsors that sponsorships require a pre-plan, a concurrent plan, and a post-plan in order to ensure proper results. There is no alternative to proper planning: A pre-plan requires creating buzz about the sponsorship, which may require press releases, a promotional article, and so on. During the event, the sponsor should consider how to maximize exposure. This may include, but is not limited to, showing a promotional video, creating special themed events, and providing product samples to the audience. Following the event, the sponsor should have a detailed plan for following up on all prospects and potential leads. The sponsor should also establish criteria to compare results to their expectations for the sponsorship.

Activation requires the sponsor to budget appropriately to reap the benefits of the sponsorship. The sponsor should consider budgeting as much as 2:1 to properly activate their sponsorship and maximize their results. Thus, if a sponsorship costs $50,000 it is not inconceivable that the sponsor will spend an additional $100,000 to effectively activate the sponsorship.

FULFILLMENT

Fulfillment refers to what the organization does to ensure that it over delivers relative to what has been contracted in the sponsorship agreement. At the beginning of this chapter, reference was made to an organization-wide commitment to inventory the organization's assets; the same is required for fulfillment. While the sponsorship team may sell the sponsorships, the entire organization must ensure that the sponsor is fully engaged and that they have received what has been promised in the contract.

Communication between the sponsor and the organization is key to ensuring proper delivery. In order to achieve good communication, a central point of contact should be established for the sponsor and the organization. This person should be responsible for communicating with the entire staff as to what is expected to ensure proper delivery. A complete fulfillment grid should be established with timelines, work back schedules, assignment of responsibilities, and follow-up.

As tasks are completed, they should be denoted as such and communicated to the sponsor. At no time should the organization depend on the sponsor to automatically fulfill their obligations; the organization should take a proactive approach to ensure that the sponsor is meeting their agreed upon obligations. Most sponsors will appreciate the commitment from the organization toward the sponsors' success. For strategic partnerships, quarterly meetings with the sponsors are recommended to ensure that the sponsor is pleased with the fulfillment of contractual obligations. This will prevent surprises at the end of the year and will result in satisfied sponsors willing to renew their agreement.

At the completion of the agreement, the organization should provide the strategic partner with a full recap of how the terms of the agreement were delivered. The organization should highlight any areas that they over delivered and include any supplementary coverage the partner may have received because of the sponsorship. This should be followed by a wrap-up meeting and discussion of any areas that both sides can improve upon to deliver even greater value to each other.

Summary

Sponsorships and strategic partnerships can be an important source of revenue for an organization if the relationships are managed effectively and the appropriate value is delivered to the sponsor.

Pursue sponsorships that are strategically relevant to the organization; this will help the organization accomplish its objectives. The first step in the process is to identify all sponsorable assets. This process requires the involvement of the entire organization, as well as consultation with potential sponsors.

Asset packaging should not be done in isolation; packages should be tailored to ensure that the value conveyed is relevant to the sponsor and will allow them to achieve their objectives. This requires proper consultation with potential sponsors so that their objectives and needs are clearly understood by the requesting organization. When selecting strategic partners, proper preliminary research should be done to ensure that the objectives of the partner align with those of the organization. If there is alignment of goals, the sale will be easier and will significantly enhance the chance that both parties will be satisfied with the results.

A good strategy for organizations just starting out soliciting sponsorships is to focus on a smaller number of partners and over deliver in value. This will ensure satisfied partners and give room for price increases; never over promise and under deliver.

Sponsorships do not always require the exchange of cash. Sponsorships can be paid in products or in-kind services that reduce the organization's costs. While the cost of an item may be a contributing factor to the pricing of the sponsorship package, prices should focus on the value of the benefits, the demand that exists for the package, competition from other organizations for the same sponsorship dollars, and the uniqueness of the package.

The sponsor's responsibility does not end with the paying of a fee. Sponsors should know they will need to effectively activate their sponsorship, and that this will require additional financial investments on their part—which is usually more than the cost of the sponsorship itself. At the same time, the organization needs to be proactive in their approach to support the sponsor. Organizations soliciting sponsorships should ensure the delivery of any contractual obligations and effectively communicate with the sponsor throughout the agreement. These precautions will negate any unforeseen surprises at the conclusion of the agreement and increase the chances that the sponsor will renew their sponsorship.

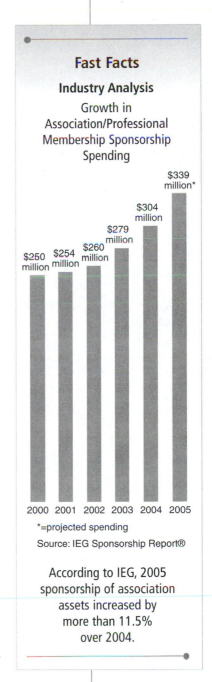

Fast Facts

Industry Analysis

Growth in Association/Professional Membership Sponsorship Spending

$250 million · $254 million · $260 million · $279 million · $304 million · $339 million*

2000 2001 2002 2003 2004 2005

*=projected spending

Source: IEG Sponsorship Report®

According to IEG, 2005 sponsorship of association assets increased by more than 11.5% over 2004.

Strategic partnership involves multi-year agreements whereby organizations partner with each other for mutual benefit. Strategic partnerships are limited based on an organization's assets and ability to deliver value to potential partners. The partnership consists of numerous events/activities and marketing opportunities that are year-round and can be customized based on the partner's objectives and the organization's assets. On the other hand, event sponsorship is "a la carte," and is sold on a one-time basis with most of the value and benefits to the sponsor being delivered during the specific event.

Asset identification is the first step in the process of engaging potential partners. To start this process, involve as many members in the organization as possible—especially those who are closest to the assets. Organizations frequently have assets they are unaware of and that is why it is important to involve existing or potential partners in this process, as they will help identify potential assets. A good place to start when valuing an asset is the current price of the asset. This initial pricing should be followed by thorough research on what potential customers are charging for similar assets, coupled with the intangible benefits that are unique to your organization.

Once assets are identified and their proper value is established, meet with potential partners before embarking on the customization of packages. No two sponsors have the same needs and sponsors will prefer that you tailor a package that will allow them to achieve their strategic objectives.

If you allow a sponsor to pay you a sum of money for a sponsorship package and the sponsor assumes their responsibility is over, then the sponsor will be disappointed and the organization will more than likely lose a valuable partner. Activation is an important process to ensure that the sponsor receives the full benefit of their investment. Activation should include the following phases: pre-planning, during, and post-planning. Sponsors should ensure that the potential audience is aware of their involvement with the organization and a solid plan should be in place for execution during the event and post-event follow-up. The sponsor must budget for the entire process in order to maximize their initial investment.

The benefit an asset conveys can be a simple method for dividing assets by level of sponsorship or partnership. The highest level would convey the most benefits for a potential partner and would command the highest price. On an event-specific sponsorship, you can classify your assets based on the value they represent. For strategic partners, the levels should be based on how the assets are bundled. Assets for strategic partners can be of various values that, when bundled together, represent a specific level.

References

1. IEG, Inc. (2006). IEG, Inc Sponsorship report: Sponsorship spending in North America. Retrieved March 15, 2006 from http://www.sponsorship.com/learn/northamericaspending.asp.

2. Belch, G.E. & Belch, M.A. (2001). *Advertising and promotion: An integrated marketing communications perspective*. (5th ed.). New York: McGraw-Hill Irwin.

Key Terms

Activate	Fulfillment	Sponsor
Advertising	In-kind	Sponsorship
Assets	Intangibles	Strategic partner
Asset valuation	Packaging	Strategic partnership
Donation	Pricing	

COMPELLING QUESTIONS FOR CONSIDERATION

1. What is the difference between a sponsor and a strategic partner?

2. What factors, other than cost, are important in pricing sponsorships?

3. Why should some sponsorship opportunities be declined regardless of revenues?

4. When valuing an asset, what are some factors that should be considered?

5. How do sponsorships and strategic partnerships help an organization achieve its goals?

6. Why is activation important?

7. Discuss potential ethical issues related to sponsorships. How would you establish sponsorship guidelines to avoid this trap?

CHAPTER 5

MARKETING AND PROMOTION: STRATEGY AND COLLABORATION FOR SUCCESS

Ellen J. Toups, CMP
PRESIDENT
OUTSOURCES

LEARNER OUTCOMES

When the reader has completed reading this chapter, he/she should be able to . . .

1 Create an integrated marketing strategy that includes direct mail, press relations, advertising, and the Internet.

2 Prepare a work plan and timeline for implementation of the marketing plan.

3 Analyze the basic features and functions of meeting and convention web sites and how such sites are developed and maintained.

4 Identify avenues of market research to enhance messaging and awareness to new populations of interest.

5 Incorporate integrated marketing strategies into sponsorship and fundraising efforts.

6 Define the term benchmarking and how to use this tool.

7 Establish benchmarks for measuring the success of your marketing efforts.

> Strategy and timing are the Himalayas of marketing. Everything else is the Catskills.
>
> *Al Ries*
> 22 Immutable Laws of Marketing

OVERVIEW

Developing and implementing an integrated marketing strategy will optimize the quality and quantity of participants for your meeting. The American Marketing Association defines marketing as "an organizational function and a set of processes for creating, communicating and delivering value to customers and for managing customer relationships in ways that benefit the organization and its stakeholders."[1] Simply put, your marketing campaign will describe your meeting/event and the marvelous benefits that each attendee will receive by paying the registration fees and attending. The Four Ps of any marketing campaign are product—your education or event; price—registration fees and in the attendees' minds includes travel and hotel; place—where they can find the information; and the promotion—the communication of the benefits of attending.

Additionally, an integrated marketing plan also refers to the interdependence of the various marketing activities. This chapter outlines the activities involved in marketing meetings and events and describes how each piece of the overall marketing strategy should be integrated.

Promotion is the communications tool of the marketing strategy. This aspect of marketing aligns with the benefits or the meeting objectives. These can be as simple as generating program awareness within the target markets to reach specific attendance goals and should identify the benefits for the market(s) that are targeted. Promotional strategies encompass direct mail, advertising, exhibiting at related trade shows, promotional materials, electronic marketing (e-marketing), and meeting and convention web sites. Publicity refers to promotion in appropriate media and encompasses all aspects of press relations.

Association and other not-for-profit organizations use marketing campaigns to promote their events because their audiences normally has a choice of whether or not to attend—or in today's market—which meeting to attend. However, an integrated marketing strategy can and should be used with a variety of corporate, government, and other programs as well. Corporate or government meeting attendees required to participate can learn and enjoy their experience with a marketing campaign that increases excitement and enthusiasm. Studies show that negativity costs corporations in the billions of dollars thereby easily justifying a marketing campaign to assist in disseminating information and promote the events within the program to achieve greater participation levels and a more positive outcome. Marketing helps with the battle when competing for discretionary dollars spent on education.

In this environment, a well-developed and executed marketing plan is invaluable. This chapter will explain the importance of understanding what you are marketing—the essential benefits to your attendees, what vehicles should be utilized in the marketing and promotion, the many parts and strategies of promoting meetings and finally, how to measure your results on the way.

MARKETING STRATEGY

The first step in marketing your meeting is to understand exactly what you are going to market. If you are marketing a meeting of networking for users groups or social activities, your tactics and methods will be much different than marketing a meeting of educational sessions that will make a difference in the every day working life of attendees. Therefore, the key message points will be the first item developed to incorporate in to an overall marketing strategy to reach your target audience.

Identification

Target audiences are the groups to which you are directing your marketing efforts. Identification refers to not only determining who the meeting's audiences should be, but also identifying the key objectives of each audience that attending your meeting will answer. However, at this stage you must identify which products or services within your meeting will best meet their objectives. The more information you can collect about their methods of communication and their lifestyles will assist in preparing not only the marketing messages but identifying the appropriate delivery. While this step can be time consuming and very detailed, the results of your research sets the foundation for the entire strategy. It is important to commit the required resources and time to this step.

Market research is an exploration into the marketplace, target audiences, and/or competition.

This research might take the form of questionnaires, electronic surveys, focus groups (which can take place in person or via tele-, video- or web-conferencing), informal polling, or other methods of gaining information from each of the target audience groups. The research should not only define the demographics of each target audience but also the major generational groupings within the professional segments of attendance. Before you prepare your messages and determine the integration of your marketing check the characteristics of each of the generations and professional segments. There are many generational predispositions that will greatly influence the effectiveness of your messaging. For example, the Baby Boomers are getting older looking for a radical roots message and Gen X'ers want proof and a guarantee message.

Since you have multiple audiences for each meeting—attendees, exhibitors, sponsors, key departments or management groups, volunteer leaders, related groups, and so on, there are many opportunities to locate new attendees that will greatly would benefit from attending. While you survey and analyze what each of these segments would gain by their attendance participation you can also have your strengthened the message delivery strengthened by asking the right questions! The information that identifies the priorities of your targeted audiences may uncover other professional segments that would be potential attendees and/or exhibitors.

Important questions include: Are there any other subgroups within larger organizations that have not previously attended that perhaps have their own meetings? What about vendors of related products or services that your attendees may be interested in learning about and/or purchasing? These untapped niche markets can fuel your event's growth.

The marketing message can now be tailored and delivery to address how your meeting can achieve those objectives.

Consideration must be given to ensure that the essence of the message and purpose of the meeting does meet the objectives of the different subgroups or niche markets that have been uncovered. Marketing and branding experts, Al Ries, and his daughter, Laura, maintain that the loss of focus is the single most detrimental element to any marketing campaign.[2]

Segmentation

Target audiences can be identified and segmented by the criteria and results of your surveys and information gathering. Understanding the different motivations of the groups of attendees will help to determine what the meeting/conference should "look" like and will determine the avenue of promotion that will get the most attention and results. Engineers do not communicate in the same ways that sales people do. Likewise, Baby Boomers and Gen X'ers want different information before deciding how to spend their time and money.

There are as many opinions as there are meetings/conferences as to how to type or analyze your attendees. For example, MPI identifies 5 types of association attendees,[3] whereas, Friedmann, author of *Meeting and Event Planning for*

Fast Facts

Tip: If you are meeting in a college or university town there are many college professors who will give students credit to participate in your conference as part of a course. The actual day-to-day working experience allows the students to apply practical experience to theory. They can poll your members at key points during the conference to get information. And don't forget to ask the students their opinion of your message.

Dummies, describes 12 types.[4] Others believe that segmentation can drill down to two distinct types. First, the attendee who comes to every meeting is interested in the educational program, but also comes to network and support the organization, and second, the attendee who comes for valuable career-building education. This last group, are the attendees that can slip away if attention and detail is not paid to their needs and opinions and, if your marketing messages are not true.

Education is not inexpensive. Writing learner outcomes and or benefits with each segment of the marketing can assist in the attendance decision. Whether an organization pays for an employee to attend or attendees pay their own way, participants must also be able to rationalize their attendance in terms of personal return on investment (ROI).

Interaction

In the age of "information overload," the daily glut of messages people receive through mail, fax, e-mail, Internet, and other media makes it harder for them to notice and retain information. Individuals are no longer engaged by static marketing, the marketing piece must contain an eye-catching and thought-provoking message for the reader to become engaged or interested in its content. Although normally the more interactive a marketing piece is, the more it will be noticed and acted upon, make certain that the piece is well done and answers the basic questions of why an attendee should be interested.

Interesting ways to make your marketing communications more interactive include asking readers to do something in response to receiving a postcard in the mail; allowing them to post ideas or suggestions through a web site; asking for a response to an e-mail message; or engaging them in a creative video or audio message in a web-based invitation. Engage your audience in the message, and they will be more likely to retain it and act positively.

Although most marketing today involves the Internet and email, having a printed document to identify and maintain physical contact will prove helpful. In past years, the direct mail mantra was at least four pieces or "touches" before any results are derived or the logo and organization is easily recognized. This same mantra can be fairly inexpensively done with email postcards. Recently, during their Marketing Makeover Presentation, Ken Esthus of Marketing General presented Direct Marketing Association research and information that in today's environment it takes 10 touches or impressions to be remembered and readily identified.[5]

Integration

Although the content of the messages you develop must be customized for each of the target audiences, the overall theme and identity of the meeting should remain the same. Make sure that your marketing message is consistent and that your meeting has a brand identity that remains constant.

Incorporating a theme and logo specific to the meeting and making sure that all communications promote this theme and logo is one way of ensuring integration. A tag line that describes the overall goal or mission of the meeting is another way to integrate the various pieces in a marketing campaign. When you make this decision, then the financial ramifications of the additional items. Small things make a big difference—consistency all the way to email tag lines should be the same—same color, same font, etc.

Differentiation

The cornerstone of your marketing strategy is what makes your event different from the competition and what the brand of the organization represents. The

---

Fast Facts

To create or maintain a conference identity:

- Logo strictly for conference
- Consistent tagline identifying the event
- Special letterhead with conference logo

essence of a clearly focused message can overcome many competitive messages that are often being scattered messaging to your market. Knowing your competitors' messages and where it is coming from is as important as understanding your own marketing. Competition may take several unconventional forms. Other events with similar audiences are obvious competitors, but there are may others that should be considered. Web-based conferences, vendor programming, self-study or certification programs, online training, organizations' individual company's in-house programs, university courses or industry association, and offerings from other industry associations all compete for attendees' time and dollars. Each marketing message should differentiate your meeting from the competition and expound on the benefit of attending, while clearly reinforcing your brand message.

Finally, your event must deliver on the promise of the marketing message. With the educational offerings at conferences and meetings becoming a larger part of the value of a membership, the marketing promise must be well protected. Many associations are beginning to offer a "money-back" guarantee if the conference does not live up to the advertising and/or descriptors. Maintaining the proper focus of the different parts of the marketing campaign is one of its most important functions.

Promising exhibitors attendance levels or buying power of the attendees that does not materialize will, in a short time span, significantly hurt participation in your event. Misrepresenting program content, keynote speakers, or other aspects of the meeting will end up detracting from the overall program and will damage the reputation of your organization making sponsorship development and other growth much harder to accomplish. Make sure that all marketing messages are truthful and not misleading in any way. Although conferences and events may be viewed as a separate function within the organization it is a representation of the product of the association or corporation and is often the most imprinted experience for members.

Partnering with other organizations that have many of the same characteristics and offering their members a discount can also bring attendees to your convention that other wise might not have attended. Many conferences also offer multiple attendee discounts to enable more than one attendee per company or association.

MARKETING PLAN AND BUDGET

The marketing plan is the written detailed plan of action that integrates all activities for achieving the marketing goals for your event. Once you have solidified your strategy, you will be ready to draft the marketing plan. This process involves identifying the specific tactics and types of marketing vehicles. One of the most important parts of the marketing plan is the work plan and timeline. This portion includes every strategic activity matched with the tactic, deadline for starting and finishing as well as the staff responsible for the action. In order to measure its effectiveness and identify when to rethink the strategic activities there should be measurable goals or benchmarks tied to the marketing efforts. These smaller steps will then feed into the overall goals for the meeting, conference, or exhibit itself.

Keeping accurate records of the marketing plans and results show up earlier but this does not necessarily mean they will be "bigger." Understanding the trends and patterns of registration makes records from past events invaluable. If actual registration numbers and/or booth sales records were not kept from previous events monitoring actual income streams will give an indication of the success of the marketing.

Your marketing plan should also direct the focus of the campaign and keep it on target to the original mission.

Fast Facts

Tip: Don't have previous records? Do your request for proposals (RFPs) before your budget is complete to see where the costs are and how they can be varied and controlled. Managing the creative media, printing and mailing, email blast creation, web site updating, and maintenance are all business opportunities that companies are required to bid on every day.

Fast Facts

Marketing tools
covered here:

- Direct mail
- Publicity and press relations
- Meeting and convention websites
- E-marketing
- Advertising

Integrated Marketing Tools

Many different tools make up an integrated marketing campaign. Understanding the demographics of your audience will help direct some of the marketing tools you will utilize. Alternate media such as audio, Braille, and large print are necessary. Having your information translated into different languages may be necessary.

No single media can successfully market your program since most audiences are incredibly diverse. Key issues to keep in mind when developing these tools include:

- Customizing many materials that bureaus and larger hotels have on hand to save print dollars
- Materials to different market segments must have the same message and look
- Every message and/or touch to the individuals should reinforce the brand identity of the meeting and organization

Throughout your marketing planning and orchestration, the presentation of accurate and complete information concerning both the content and the benefits are a must. The message should be clear and easily updated as the plan progresses.

Setting the Budget

Once you have outlined the marketing strategy and tactics you will use to achieve your marketing objectives, it is time to determine the budget. While this may seem backward if you are accustomed to developing a budget prior to selecting specific tools, budgeting in this fashion will help you to prioritize the tools to use based on cost and potential ROI. A decrease in meeting attendance combined with stricter attrition policies at facilities can combine to severely injure an organization financially. Marketing to increase attendance and/or to get better quality attendees to the meeting can be a financial lifesaver. Therefore, you must look at the overall ROI when budgeting for your marketing campaign.

The stronger the educational content, the more convenient the dates, and the more attractive the location, the less marketing you will need to undertake to attract attendance. When developing an overall marketing budget, review the following:

- Budget for marketing and promotion of previous meetings
- Estimates of costs for each marketing tool you intend to use
- Amount spent by other organizations on marketing meetings of similar size
- Budgets of meetings and timing of other similar conferences that compete directly with your event

Fast Facts

Tip: To determine your marketing budget consider

- Strength of educational program
- Convenience of dates
- Longevity of the meeting/conference/exhibit
- Desirability of location
- Overall cost of attending
- Size and profile of target audience

Researching other meetings or conventions across any and all industry lines and averaging their marketing expenditures can create a baseline for your marketing budget. Additionally, attempt to determine the amount spent by meetings that compete directly with yours for attendees, exhibitors, sponsors, and so on. These factors will help you to determine how much you need to spend to get attention in the marketplace.

As in budgeting for any meeting expenditures, line items should be created for each tool you intend to use as part of your overall marketing strategy. Estimates for each item should be ascertained from prior records or by soliciting bids from vendors. Remember to include items such as creative development and design services, agency fees, ad placements, and complimentary registrations for media personnel.

TABLE 5.1
Annual Meeting Promotion Timeline

When	What
52 weeks (or one year) in advance of the meeting	The best time to announce the date and location of an annual meeting is during the current meeting. Show the dates, location, theme, logo, tagline, and other teaser copy on material distributed at the current meeting (including registration bags, promotional items, signage, graphics at the start of sessions, etc.). Also, devote a page in the current meeting's on-site program to the promotion of next year's meeting.
40 weeks (10 months) in advance of the meeting	Order direct mail lists for all audiences. Also, start a monthly postcard campaign ("save the date," program highlights, etc.).
24 weeks (6 months) in advance of the meeting	Send the first/preliminary brochures to various target audiences via email.
16 weeks (4 months) in advance of the meeting	Mail the second/complete brochures to all target audiences, measure response cards. Send e-cards with the brochure on the website, monitor number of downloads of the brochure.
8 weeks (2 months) in advance of the meeting	Mail the complete brochure a second time. Also, begin sending event and other invitations. Send one last reminder postcard to those who have not yet registered directing them to the web site for registration and/or the electronic registration site.
6-8 weeks (1.5–2 months) in advance of the meeting	Begin sending weekly promotional flyers via fax or email to highlight sessions or other components of the meeting. Send personalized letters to key members of target audiences encouraging their participation and assistance in promoting the meeting to their organization.

Timing

The timeline for marketing material production and distribution is influenced by the timing of the meeting, competition for the audience, the lead time you have to market the meeting, the audiences' preferred timelines, and the cutoff dates for receipt of housing reservations and registrations. Other considerations include the budget year for the exhibitors, sponsors, and the organization with consideration given to the targeted exhibitors and sponsors geographic distribution of prospective attendees (regional, national, or international).

Table 5.1 is an example of a timeline for an association's annual meeting promotion. These guidelines are somewhat flexible according to the objectives and financial concerns of the meeting sponsor.

DIRECT MAIL

While in the past many meeting managers have focused the majority of their marketing resources on direct mail, e-marketing and new media channels have changed that focus. Moreover, the way in which these pieces are sent has diversified. Direct mail to the audience can be accomplished via traditional mail, broadcast fax, and broadcast email. Again, depending on your audiences' preferences, the most effective campaign includes all of these methods. Since spam email has become such a horrendous problem and spam filters have become more and more aggressive, printed brochures and invitations have returned to a higher priority level in the marketing efforts.

Fast Facts

Current definition of Direct Mail now includes postcards, brochures, exhibitor prospectus, event invitations, promotional flyers, and personalized letters

Types of Mailings

A number of different direct mail pieces can be used, in any combination, to promote your meeting to the target audiences. Every mailing should include these essential details:

- Organization name and logo clearly identified and according to style
- Key contact and location information
- Theme and tag line
- Dates and location; and phone, fax, email, and web site address to contact for more information
- Two quotes from past participants extolling how marvelous the meeting or conference was and the great benefits they will bring to their day-to-day jobs

When producing any type of direct mail piece, especially brochures and the exhibitor prospectus, special attention must be paid to the design and content. The fancier the print and the more color makes documents difficult to read via fax. Although it may sound "old fashioned," do check with your post office to ensure that marketing documents can be easily processed at the postage rates that meet your budget.

Design

A direct mail piece should be designed to grab attention, describe the benefit of attending and convey all the critical content in a clear, concise way, and have a great call to action. Since everyone will not utilize the first call to action, make sure the website address is prominent and easy to read. This is the time to promote the benefit of attending not the features of your conference or meeting.

- Use headlines and teaser copy to capture attention and highlight key information.
- Promote the benefits of attending (versus listing features of the meeting).
- Ensure copy is dynamic, written in the active voice with short sentences and specific details.
- Provide instructions for action, i.e., register today, call now for more details.
- Use art, photographs, and color to add visual interest.
- Include photo captions that highlight the benefits, rather than just stating what is in the picture.
- Four-color pieces attract the most attention but are also the most expensive to print. Using creativity and two colors can be just as effective and much more reasonably priced.

Trends in color and design change as often as fashion therefore if possible, the use of a good graphic designer can save time and money in the long run. This professional should also be attuned to what printers need to adhere to budgets and familiar with printer requirements to make mailing documents as economical as possible and adhere to your budget. The graphic designer should guide you in new type fonts, for style and size as well as the paper and color choices.

Content

The content of the piece provides the details that encourage participation. The copy must convince readers of the value of the meeting and elicit a response. It speaks to the key objectives of the target audience segment.

Brochure content should include the following details:

- Title, theme and sponsoring organization name
- Date, times and location, registration fees, cancellation policy
- Program information with objectives
- Housing, transportation and travel information
- Who or what level executive should attend and, if applicable, CEU's
- Name or list keynote speaker or the prominent names
- Who to contact for more information
- Special events during the conference
- Child care and/or guest/spouse program

Copyediting and Proofing

Draft copy must be edited for accuracy and correct grammar, punctuation, and spelling before going to the printer. Having multiple people review the copy provides objective viewpoints, especially if they have no involvement in planning the meeting. Then they can read the content as potential attendees might.

Develop a style sheet to promote consistency across all marketing pieces. This guide should be in alphabetical order and include such items as special spellings, words to be hyphenated and/or abbreviated, and any word usage that is specific to your organization and its audiences. The copyeditor may add to this list during editing.

Printing

The cost of printing marketing materials (including letterhead, direct mail pieces, registration forms, and event tickets) is a major budget item, so it is wise to learn as much as possible about the terminology and techniques involved.

Frequent communication with designers and the printer is essential. Determine your printing needs in advance so you can schedule production and batch print jobs to achieve economies of scale. Ask your printer for estimates and for advice and cost-saving suggestions on all print pieces.

Solicit at least three bids for the printing job. To obtain accurate price quotes, prepare a set of specifications for each printed piece. It is easier to convey accurate specifications when an example accompanies the bid request, which gives the printer a visual representation of the completed piece. State the desired contract terms and set a realistic deadline for the submission of bids. Supply the following information in the bid request:

- Quantity or number of each piece to print
- Final trim size of each piece
- Number of pages in each piece
- Cover, specifying if it will be a self-cover or a separate cover
- Composition, including typefaces and sizes, page size, and format in which the art will be provided (on diskette, CD-ROM, camera-ready, etc.)
- Paper stock, specifying the type, weight, and color for each piece.
- Ink color, including number of
- Furnished inserts, noting quantity, type, size, weight, and die-cut status
- Finishing, or the type of binding to be used—perfect bound (glued), spiral bound, or saddle-stitched (stapled)
- Delivery instructions, with destination and type of packaging
- Production schedule, including when art will be submitted, date proofs will be submitted print date, and shipping date
- What quantities you will accept for over-runs/under-runs

Fast Facts

Bids should include:

- Quantity of printed pieces
- Final trim size
- Number of pages
- Type of cover
- Paper
- Ink colors
- Inserts
- Finishing
- Where to ship!

In the bid, the printer should provide:

- A detailed price list for composition, paper, printing, and binding
- An outline of major contract terms (price escalations, rebates or printing errors, and over-run/under-run policy)
- A working-day production schedule

The printer can be negotiated with as with any other vendor. Great concern and follow-up should be given to references on quality and timeliness. Saving great dollars on printing does no good if the materials are not on time and mailed.

There is no way to keep all the costs updated in this manual so be sure to consult with your in house mail department or the post office about any discounts for presorted mail.

PUBLICITY AND PRESS RELATIONS

Publicity is the marketing tool that encompasses the public relations arm of marketing and therefore includes the communications items and editorial comments in third-party publications or broadcasts (including trade journals, general news media, trade association and other media web sites, etc.). Publicity generated through interviews and public relations, because of its objective and respected third-party nature, can be one of the best ways to promote your meeting. Messages tend to have greater validity when coming from a source outside of the organization. For example, if a neutral trade publication states that your educational program is the best opportunity to gain specific knowledge within your target market, it is more believable than a brochure that you develop with the same message.

To gain publicity, the meeting must be marketed to the appropriate media or press. Identify newsworthy angles on your program, such as a vendor announcing a new product, a cutting-edge educational session, a new technology demonstrated at the meeting, or a celebrity keynote speaker. If at a loss for this type of story, look within the organization for a newsworthy action that can evolve into an article about either a speaker or a subject within the meeting/event.

When writing a press release, remember it has to have a news story within it in order to be captured and utilized in the newspapers. If you do not have newsworthy information in the press release it will be a waste of your time. Creating news may be easier than it sounds.

Ways to create news include:

1. Create contests and announce winners in a press release, or profile local scholarship winners.
2. Announce the story and background of the group and why it is in existence, i.e., to meet the needs of its membership and industry.
3. Announce a high-profile keynote speaker and invite speakers along with an invitation of the press to a private reception with the keynote.

You need to get the press releases to the appropriate people within the media to gain the publicity you seek. In many cases a public relations agency is well worth the money to ensure that your message is distributed through the most appropriate media to reach your target audiences. There are several wire services available to assist for nominal costs, but remember this will be a massive distribution and if you have a finely honed and developed press list you may be well served to utilize your own press list. If you do determine that you need assistance, there are many online organizations that have great lists of press sorted by interests. Some examples of good services are www.bacons.com, www.xpresspress.com, and www.prweb.com.

Fast Facts

Tip: No real stories? Make one happen (notice I did not say make one up). Turn the mirror on your organization and find a success story from the past conference. Or ask one of the experts in the industry to write an article, then highlight it in your story to make it interesting to the local press.

Although still a little bit reticent about attachments, most press will request that the story come through their email. But if they do not, send it utilizing the method that it is requested or it will not make it past the mailroom.

When planning a press conference, prepare your organization's spokesperson to make a statement or be interviewed. Speakers should be informative, to the point, and not too technical. Again, a public relations agency can be invaluable in designing press conferences that create the right kind of publicity targeted to your various audiences.

The timing of press releases and press conferences is a key factor in determining whether the meeting will receive favorable and timely publicity (see Table 5.2). Be sure to find out the production schedule for the publication beforehand, as the media must receive content well in advance of publication closing dates. Sunday publications (newspapers) have greater circulation and have more space for publicity articles.

Press relations refer to the organization's ongoing interaction with the media before, during, and after the meeting. Media representatives should be invited to attend the event with free registration and access to all components of the program. Invite media contacts through personalized invitations and follow up with a phone call. Offering key press members access to keynote speakers or award

TABLE 5.2
Annual Meeting Publicity Timeline

When	What
40 weeks (10 months) in advance of the meeting	Distribute the first press release with general information about the meeting and create the meeting's brand identity. Launch web site/page with information on the conference.
26 weeks (6.5 months) in advance of the meeting	Distribute the second press release with more detailed information about sessions, speakers, and events. Submit articles to industry publications by keynote speakers, have article in association publications by the keynote and/or other well- known workshop speakers. Update web site with the most current information to keep people abreast of latest news and activities, early bird or pre-registration versus regular rates/on-site rates, etc.
20 weeks (5 months) in advance of the meeting	Participate in e-zine activity by writing or giving an announcement about your meeting and the line up of speakers. Speakers may wish to participate by writing articles of interest. Distribute the third press release with newsworthy aspects of the meeting.
12 weeks (3 months) in advance of the meeting	Create a cover story that can be distributed to various publications. Submit another set of different articles to industry publications by keynote speakers, have article in association publications by the keynote and/or other well-known workshop speakers.
10 weeks (2.5 months) in advance of the meeting	Send personal invitations to media representatives to attend the meeting at no charge. Follow up with phone calls to personally discuss the key ideas that will be covered at the conference.
6 weeks (1.5 months) in advance of the meeting	Send a fourth press release that includes feature stories as well as complete details about the meeting.
3 weeks in advance	Send personal reminders to press, arrange for press conference or interview with interested parties.
1 week in advance of the meeting	Follow up media invitations with personal phone calls.

winners can enhance their ability to be published and your ability to get good press. When press is involved, key association staff members should be notified.

A press room should be set up on site to provide work areas with phone lines, fax machines, copiers, and Internet connections, as well as refreshments. This area can also be used for interviews and press conferences, so it should be large enough to accommodate an area for speaking. Media kits that contain newsworthy information on various sessions, speakers, products, or services should be available in advance and in the press room.

Blogs are the newest interactive chat room on the Internet and beginning a blog for comments during the planning stages of a meeting and maintaining the blogs during the meeting create exposure and reach to a market that just might also come to your meeting.

ADVERTISING

Advertising is designed to inform, persuade, remind, add value, and otherwise attract attendees from target markets to your event. Advertising is not used a lot in the promotion of meetings because of its high costs. It can be in print (magazines, newspapers, trade journals), broadcast (network TV, cable, radio), electronic (web site banner ads, blogs, and sponsored email messages), or outdoors (billboards, bus boards, building banners).

Unless your show or conference is a public show, it is doubtful that advertising alone will help your attendance. Additional emphasis should be placed on the other promotional vehicles in order to give the prospective attendee three to four "touches" to maintain a familiarity with your meeting/conference logo. Utilizing the talent in an ad agency can be very cost effective in the particular area as most agencies receive a commission for placements.

MEETING AND CONVENTION WEB SITES

Today's meeting managers have at their disposal the greatest marketing tool ever created—the Internet. Effective use of the Internet can reduce costs while expanding the reach and frequency of the meeting message, something close to nirvana for marketing experts. A meeting web site may well be the most interactive marketing tool you deploy.

Integrating the meeting web site with all other marketing materials is important. The meeting's brand identity should be integrated with the site, including prominent placement of the logo, theme, and tag line. Consider offering exhibitors or sponsors exposure on your web site as a value-added component of exhibiting, or as an additional revenue stream for the meeting. You could place a banner ad, a scrolling column, or a link to the sponsor or exhibitors' web sites.

Basic Site Features

Meeting and convention web sites can be as simple or as complex as budget, imagination, and technology allow, but there are some basic components that should always be considered. It is said that "content is king" on the Internet, and meeting sites are no exception. There must be compelling reasons for potential participants to visit the site and to revisit often.

The most basic and crucial portion of the web site content for most meetings is the program and agenda. These should be prominent on the site and can include hypertext links to speaker information; search engines to pull topics by date, times, or key words; attendee surveys; and even video and graphics presentations from past meetings. Some organizations build communities of interest through their sites with chat rooms, discussion forums, links to speaker and staff email, and attendee lists.

With a trained web designer, newsletters and/or electronic brochures for each segment or track of the meeting/conference can be designed. The site should also direct visitors to action by enticing them to register online. When planning for online registration, it is imperative to provide a secure, encrypted environment for the security and privacy of your registrants. Because a few people are still uncomfortable with purchasing online, having more traditional options such as fax, mail, and telephone transactions is helpful. When the registration procedure is complete, the system should send a separate confirmation email and/or generate printable confirmation page. Generally, the consensus is that fewer clicks required to maneuver around the site and the conference information is always better.

Your event web site should mirror your conference with all the pieces and parts. If you are going to supply weather and local info, add a tab. If you are going to have exhibits make all the portions of the Exhibit, Sponsorship and links for promotions easily definable usable. Don't overlook a virtual Trade Show—these are great for providing added value!

Your meeting web site should be updated frequently and the links tested often! While not everyone answers the call to action the first time, be diligent in ensuring all the links work and information is absolutely as current as possible.

If your meeting has an international component, a separate page with a link highlighting all the new travel regulations and permits needed to travel freely in the United States is also helpful. Provide links from your web site to embassies, airlines, and necessary government agencies. Don't forget the emergency services!

Development and Maintenance

Just as we begin the planning of any event with a look at the desired outcomes, every web site should start with a look at the goals and objectives for the site. What are the strategic reasons for creating a web presence for the meeting? Is it purely a branding initiative? Should it drive an increase in attendance? Will it automate the communication between your office, exhibitors, and the venue? Will it provide for online registration, travel, and/or housing? To construct a truly valuable site, begin with a blueprint of what it should achieve. Some meeting managers may find it easier to develop a web site map, where the site is presented in an outline form with each page listed under the subsection where it belongs.

Work closely with your web developer to ensure the site reinforces the meeting brand identity, conveys a message consistent with other marketing materials, and performs advanced functions as expected. Also work with the developer to be sure that, once created, your web site can be found easily and often. Of course, listing the web address on all marketing materials will help drive prospects to your site for more information.

The information provided here is a very brief overview of web site development and maintenance. With the rapid development of web technology new features and functions will become available in the future. Reading industry publications that specialize in technology applications for meeting management is the best way to stay current.[9] Remember that your web site is your 24/7 marketing representative to anyone in the world and as such is a department in itself combining technology, marketing, and meeting management. Make certain that it represents your meeting and your organization well.

E-MARKETING

Email is the number one function of the Internet worldwide, with trillions of messages sent every year. Although the goal quite often is to use email and faxes to drive visitors to a web site, the fact is that these tools can be a vital component of the marketing campaign.

The key to a successful marketing strategy is reaching the right people with the right message. Carefully building your lists and interacting appropriately with recipients can increase response rates exponentially. Driving the communication through email and fax technologies can also mean success financially, as these tools are much less expensive (or even free) compared to traditional printed materials. Seek out those list vendors who have gone to the trouble and expense of developing detailed data. Increasingly, many email lists today increasingly offer demographic and psychographic sorting that is commonly used in off-line media. These sources may cost more, but targeting in email distribution has proven to produce results that often significantly exceed those of traditional media.

For example, double-digit response rates are not the exception but the rule for many when using high quality email lists today. To battle the anonymity conundrum, seek out the quality providers.

In a corporate environment, meeting invitations can be quite different for senior management and the sales team, for instance. In associations, different messages can go to members, prospective members, speakers, staff, vendors, exhibitors, and sponsors. By segmenting the database, it becomes a simple process to reach the right group with the appropriate message. Consider creating an email signature line highlighting your expertise. Be sure to continually update it from time to time with the dates of upcoming speaking engagements, a list of awards, client testimonials—whatever enhances, and other activities that will enhance your credibility.

Keep in mind it is not just your clients, colleagues, and prospects who will see these email messages. They may be forwarded to others. Your circle of influence is always expanding.

All email messages to persons you do not know or who are not expecting messages from you should include information on how to opt-out of the electronic mailing list. Spam is not only illegal in many countries, including the United States, but can also turn potential customers off completely.

Once you have built your lists, segmented the target audiences, and received permission, you still have to determine the best way to reach and interact with each target group. Many registration Application Service Providers can automate this process quite effectively and provide detailed reports on the e-marketing campaign.[13]

Reporting is a critical factor in determining success, but it is often underused or overlooked. You can test different messages, even subject lines, on target groups and, based on the resulting reports, develop a stronger and more effective message to the rest of the segment. This reporting also has the advantage of being in real time. You can see at a glance who has responded, how they have responded, and (perhaps of equal importance) who has read your email and not responded. These responses can be quickly and efficiently followed up.[14]

Another great e-marketing tool is the online questionnaire or survey. These can be linked from an email message and are an engaging way to solicit information. Most people like to share their opinions, and by providing input into the design of your meetings they may be more apt to attend. Online surveying can be a part of pre-conference planning, customer profile building, meeting evaluation, and post-conference follow up. All are methods to build brand awareness of your organization and its meetings. Reports from these surveys provide not only aggregate responses from all participants, but individual opinions, concerns, and questions that add useful information to their personal profiles. In today's market there are many that are available inexpensively, including Survey Monkey, Zoomerang, and E-Survey.

Having access to personal information places the meeting manager in a position of high responsibility. Your constituents must be reminded and assured that their information is private and will only be used to improve your service to them. Today's technology can be the key to efficient and effective use of personal information to greatly enhance the marketing strategy of your organization and your meetings, without compromising the relationships you nurture with your constituents.

BLOGS

A blog is basically a journal that is available on the web. The activity of updating a blog is "blogging" and someone who keeps a blog is a "blogger." Blogs are typically updated daily using software that allows people with little or no technical background to update and maintain the blog. A blog provides a collaborative space, political soapbox, breaking-news outlet, and a collection of links.

Your blog is whatever you want it to be. There are millions of them, in all shapes and sizes, and there are no real rules. In simple terms, a blog is a web site, where you write stuff on an ongoing basis. New stuff shows up at the top so your visitors can read what is new. Then they comment on it or link to it or email you. Since Blogger.com was launched, almost 5 years ago, blogs have reshaped the web, impacted politics, shaken up journalism, and enabled millions of people to have a voice and connect with others. And we're pretty sure the whole deal is just getting started. The blogging experience is about putting your thoughts on the web and hearing back from and connecting with other like-minded folks. Blogger comments let readers of your site from all over the world give feedback on what you share on your blog. You can choose whether or not you want to allow comments on a post-by-post basis (and you can delete anything you do not like). Group blogs can be excellent communication tools for small teams, families, or other groups. Give your group its own space on the web for sharing news, links, and ideas. Blogger profiles let you find people and blogs that share your interests. And your profile lets people find you (but only if you want to be found). Your Blogger profile lists your blogs, your recent posts, and more. People can click on your interests or location or they can go on to other people's profiles and check out their blogs.

SPONSORSHIP

As part of the overall marketing strategy, or as a separate entity, you may want to add or increase revenues from sponsorships or other fundraising efforts. These functions are treated very similarly to marketing the overall meeting. The key steps of identifying demand, determining the demographics of your audience, analyzing the competition, and creating integrated marketing tools all apply to sponsorship marketing and fundraising.[15]

The first step is to identify the demand for sponsorship or fundraising. What will the policies of the association/corporation allow in the sponsorship. What types of things might be sponsored? What benefits will be achieved from the sponsorship for the sponsor, the host organization and the attendee? How will adding these features improve the meeting and help to achieve the objectives or enhance the meeting experience for your attendees?

A committee rather than just one-staff person should develop the sponsorships and the policies that guide them. This will ensure that there are no impressions of a conflict of interest ensuring that the association is not put in a compromising position. For example, many boards and CEOs do not accept sponsors who contribute to program content. The main competition for these dollars is the money existing exhibitors and attendees will spend on your program, so unless benefits are clearly defined, these additions to your meeting could jeopardize other meeting revenues.

Sponsorship marketing and fundraising tend to be more relationship-based than any other part of event marketing. The most effective way to promote these components is through personal invitations, and personal telephone calls from key staff members. Get your organization's management involved in recruiting sponsors and major donors to fundraising efforts. Personal visits may be required for larger supporters.

Maintaining a relationship with sponsors is crucial. Call past sponsors before sponsorship marketing materials are distributed to offer first right of refusal or the option to repeat their sponsorship. Also give previous sponsors the opportunity to choose another sponsorship opportunity or upgrade their sponsorship.

Sponsorship marketing and fundraising should be patterned along the same steps as marketing any other aspect of your meeting. Letters confirming the sponsorship benefits and obligations as well as the obligation of the association is imperative. This important step is necessary to avoid potential conflicts and misunderstandings between both parties.

Just remember sponsorship is a partnership. Sponsorship is no longer merely a philanthropic venture. Do you want to keep your sponsors year after year? Start by saying "thank you" from every level of your organization to every level in the sponsor's organization. And ask them what they would like to see in a sponsorship for future years. It may surprise you that the sponsors' marketing committees have some great promotional ideas (see Chapter 4).

COST-SAVING IDEAS

By thinking creatively and using available technology, you can easily devise ways to save money on the marketing campaign. The following tips will help you implement a stellar marketing strategy while staying within budget parameters:

- When conducting market research—utilize email!
- Electronic survey companies are great values and do much of the statistical collaboration.
- Try teleconferencing or web conferencing for focus groups.
- Using a variety of mailing lists may increase the response rate and so be more cost-effective than saving by using only one or two lists.
- Trading exhibiting rights with other associations that have a cross section of membership.
- Instead of mailing information to participants, consider sending it via email or broadcast fax.
- Direct traffic to your web site via postcard emails and then have readily available downloads.
- Consider liberal use of electronic advertising, because the costs are much less than traditional advertising opportunities.
- Feature benefits instead of expensive graphics on the covers or marketing pieces. Listing how the meeting will cover attendees' specific long-term objectives may generate more interest.

- Promote other upcoming meetings with every marketing piece by listing future programs on the last page or the back of direct mail pieces.
- Creating a theme, logo, and tag line up front allows consistent branding and saves costs and a cohesive and identifiable theme.
- Proofread everything thoroughly to avoid costly reprints or corrections.
- Adhere to timelines to prevent rush printing, increased postage, or delivery charges.
- Order adequate quantities of pieces during the main run. Reprinting smaller quantities if you run out is cost-prohibitive.

WORKING WITH AGENCIES

In the areas of publicity, press relations, and advertising, working with professional agencies can mean the difference between an effective marketing campaign and wasted marketing dollars. This also holds true in working with marketing specialists to develop your direct mail and e-marketing campaigns, as well as web designers to make sure that your meeting web site is the best that it can be. Although agency services cost money, the increased effectiveness of your marketing can more than offset the charges.

Many agencies specialize in marketing; however, it is important to work with partners who also understand the meeting and convention industry. Inform agency partners of your objectives for the meeting itself, as well as for the marketing campaign. You should also ensure they understand your budget parameters and can work within them.

Communication is the key in working with agencies, as in the relationship with any supplier. Frequent outcome measurement to the communication to make sure everyone understands the desired outcomes and providing input into the marketing process is the meeting manager's responsibility. You must retain control and make sure that those marketing efforts are directed at the appropriate target audiences to achieve results for your meeting.

MEASURING YOUR SUCCESS

The integrated marketing plan has been implemented, the research, found lists, dynamite graphics, and in all accomplished according to plan, but was it enough? How do you know if you have done what should or could be done? The latest business buzzword is benchmarking.

Benchmarking is a comparison-driven evaluation exercise. In the book *Benchmarking for Best Practices—Winning Through Innovative Adaptation*, Bogan and English define contemporary best-practice benchmarking as "the process of seeking out and studying the best internal and external practices that produce superior performance."[17] Benchmarking in large corporations involves surveys, site visits, structured interviews, and other complex research activities. The good news is you can borrow benchmarking basics to help determine if you are getting the biggest bang for your marketing buck.

You'll be amazed how the benchmarks you establish will guide your marketing decisions in the years ahead. Here are some benchmarking steps and suggestions:

STEP 1

To ascertain the best value for your marketing dollars you can calculate the real benefit-cost ratio of your online meeting marketing efforts against your own direct mail and other traditional marketing vehicles. Too often web-based marketing

Fast Facts

Tip: As part of registration always ask attendees what information source most influenced their decision to attend.
Then calculate the revenue produced by each marketing vehicle employed.

masquerades as "free" when compared with multiple runs of four-color printing and mass mailing. In fact, labor and other costs related to posting content online are significant.

STEP 2

Do some research with the objective of selecting 5 to 10 organizations with meetings roughly similar to your own. To ensure apples-to-apples comparisons, base your selections on:

- Organization type—trade or professional association, corporation, or other non-profit
- Organization size—measured in membership/annual budget if you are a non-profit or annual revenue if you are a corporation
- Meeting type—convention, annual conference, educational seminar, or sales meeting
- Number of attendees and exhibitors
- Registration and exhibit booth pricing

STEP 3

Track the meeting marketing of your selected organizations over the next year. Establish criteria to evaluate their approaches compared with your own. Some criteria may be descriptive while others quantitative. A few sample categories:

1. **Investment in web-based marketing**
   - How much do organizations similar to yours incorporate the web into their marketing mix?
     - ○ Post basic meeting announcements and registration information on web site.
     - ○ Post extensive meeting information and provide online meeting registration and tools to facilitate booth sales.
     - ○ Post extensive meeting information and rely on a comprehensive "attendee relationship management" system to automate almost all transactions, provide session self-scheduling, and refine attendee communications.
   - Estimated online meeting marketing budget as a percentage of gross meeting revenue.
2. **Attendee-centric communication:**
   - Frequency with which web site meeting information is updated or in other ways refreshed.
   - Availability of detailed meeting information for potential attendees who want more depth before committing.
   - Ease and speed with which potential attendees' questions are answered.

BENCHMARKING BENEFITS

Benchmarking is not an exercise in "keeping up with the Jones'." In some cases, the comparative data that you collect and analyze may even suggest that you are *overinvested* in aspects of your online marketing. In all cases, benchmarking will help you work with your colleagues to innovate and market wisely in order to stay ahead of the curve while avoiding gimmicks that provide little return on investment. Best of all, you will have comparative data to improve your planning and make your meeting a great success![18]

BUILDING ATTENDANCE

As our industry matures, the responsibility for the growth of our meetings and events is on many different departments. However, the department that plans and operates the meetings and events will normally be responsible for the success of the meeting or event therefore, is also somewhat responsible for increasing attendance at the meetings and conferences. Here are some ideas and hints how to make that happen:

1. Use blogs or listservs to create a sense of community year-round on a topic or subset of your association. This listserv and/or blog would discuss anything and everything on those terms and would contribute to the educational content of the conference or meeting. In doing so, this provides a sense of endorsement and/or agreement that the education is good and these interested members will attend.

2. If there is an exhibit, allow product theater setups so that each exhibitor is able to demonstrate their product with invitations to their clientele.

3. Offer special pricing options because many associations have several qualified employees who would like to attend. Offering sizable discounts for more than two or three from the same organization may alleviate some of the pricing resistance.

4. Put your money and your mouth on the same path. Offer a money-back guarantee to anyone who feels they did not receive value for their dollars. In speaking with several associations with this type of guarantee, only one could remember having to refund money.

5. Have experts speak and attend social functions to mix and mingle with your attendees. Make certain your speakers are leaders in their fields.

6. Offer early bird discounts and anyone repeating two conferences in a row gets a discount by signing up for next year.

7. Offer a drawing at the final general session.

8. Understand the demographics of your organization and where their travel limits are so that your meetings are held in locations they wish to travel to.

9. Create a CD or brochure with snippets of the presentations to entice new attendees but also creates a longer "shelf" life for your conference.

10. Utilize your publications and when signing speakers, ask that they write articles previewing their sessions to peak interest in the subject.

11. Make certain there is followup and then respond to the followup or surveys so that the members know you are listening.

12. Conduct a needs assessment to ensure that their interests, needs, and expectations are met (for more information on conducting a needs assessment (see Chapter 2).

13. Use special technology, pre-meeting tools, or during meeting techniques to facilitate networking between attendees and/or matching up attendees with people they want to meet. Recently "speed networking" was tried and this worked great as an icebreaker.

14. Cite results of past meeting evaluations in the marketing of next year's meeting.

15. Feature sessions that address the up-to-the-minute challenges of the attendees and keep one or two sessions open to cover late-breaking experimental topics or learning procedures.

SUMMARY

A true integrated marketing plan optimizes each communication with the potential participants for your meeting. An integrated marketing strategy defines how to identify and segment your target market, how to engage the audience in an interactive way, how to integrate the varied components of the marketing program, and how to differentiate your event from the competition and deliver the benefits described in the marketing promise. The marketing plan is your plan of action and identifies the tactics for reaching each target audience, as well as the budget and timeline for promoting your event. Marketing is everyone's responsibility. Making certain that your brand maintains its integrity while promoting one of the most important benefits of membership or career advancement is not the responsibility of one person or position.

Without losing the essence of the association/meeting brand and message, create customized materials to each audience segment, engage the audience through interactivity, reinforce the brand identity through integration of materials, and always present accurate and complete information.

Promoting your conference/meeting is much like fundraising. It is a job for everyone! There are many different personalities, so give responsibility to the meeting department to ensure consistency in all mentions and promotions of the meeting or event. Developing a committee can ensure that messages to the varying segments of the group are appropriate and accurately identify ethical concerns.

Today, technology offers incredible e-marketing opportunities. Using this technology in conjunction with traditional marketing tools creates an overall strategy that delivers information appropriate to each market segment.

Marketing is not a static endeavor nor does it involve only one department. If the marketing plan is an integrated strategy, the accomplishment and orchestration of each piece of the plan is a opportunity for collaboration with many different departments. Allowing each marketing step and/or application to have a measurement or a "benchmark" will allow best practices to be established over the promotional period. It may take more than 1 year but best practices and measurement is possible. Although there are many suggestions of what makes a fabulous meeting or a best practice, knowing your market, understanding what your attendees want, and giving them the best value for their expenditure—of time or money —is the true best practice.

REFERENCES

1. Staff (September 15, 2004). AMA adopts new definition of marketing. Marketing News Retrieved March 28, 2006 from http://www.marketingpower.com/content21257.php

2. Reis, A. & Reis, L. (2006). Reis and Reis Focus Consulting. Retrieved March 28, 2006 from http://www.ries.com/Consulting/index.cfm?Page=Overview-Consulting.

3. Welch, S. J. (2000). What lures association attendees? *Successful meetings.*

4. Friedman, S. (2003). *Meeting and event planning for dummies.* Hoboken, NJ: Wiley.

5. Esthus, K. (2006, January 10). Marketing makeover. Presented at the 2006 Professional Convention Management Association 50TH Annual Convention, Philadelphia, PA.

6. Reis, A. & Reis, L. (2002). The 22 *immutable laws of branding: How to build a product or service into a world-class brand.* New York, NY: HarperCollins Publishing.

7. Shimp, T.A. (1993). *Promotion management & marketing communications*. Fort Worth, TX: Harcourt Brace Jovanovich College Publishers.

8. There are hundreds of search engines and different rules for submission at each. Visit www.searchenginewatch.com for helpful hints on submitting your site, and consider using one of the many services that systematically submit your web site to key search engines.

9. Electronic newsletters covering technology solutions for the meeting and convention industry include: *EventWeb Newsletter* (www.eventweb.com), *FLASHfire News* (www.flashpointtech.com), and *TechTalk Newsletter* (www.corbinball.com).

10. Godin, S. (1999). *Permission marketing: Turning strangers into friends and friends into customers*. New York: Simon & Schuster.

11. Ibid.

12. Ibid.

13. Chatfield-Taylor, C. (July/August, 2001). ASP and you shall receive. *EXPO*.

14. Chang, J. (2001). The electronic pitch: How to use e-marketing to build attendance. *Meeting news*, *Successful meetings*, and *Business travel news*.

15. Sunseri, A. & Wickham, K. (March, 2004). Meeting management: Managing your sponsorships. *Convene*, p. 22.

16. Skildum-Reid, K. (2005). *It's not all fun & games*. NSW, Australia: Power Sponsorship.

17. Bogan, C., & English, M. (1994). *Benchmarking for best practices: Winning through innovative adaptation*. New York, NY: McGraw-Hill.

18. Wattanmaker, S., & Toups, E. (June, 2005). Quantifying your return on web site marketing efforts and staying ahead of the curve, *Convene*, p. 72–74.

KEY TERMS

Advertising	Hypertext	Printer error
Author alterations	Integrated marketing	Promotion
Benchmarking	Mailing house	Proofing
Blog	Mailing list	Public relations
Brand identity	Marketing	Publicity
Camera-ready	Market research	Saddle-stitched
CD-ROM	Market segment	Style sheet
Copy	Media kit	Tag line
Copyediting	Opt-in	Target audience
Customer relationship	Opt-out	Teaser
management (CRM)	Perfect bound	Teaser copy
Desktop publishing	Permission marketing	Trade-out
Direct mail	Press conference	URL
Diskette	Press relations	Viral marketing
Dummy	Press release	Web page
Font	Press room	Web site

COMPELLING QUESTIONS FOR CONSIDERATION

1. What signs or indications will help access that your marketing campaign is working?

2. What would be a good focus group for changing or enhancing your meeting—how many different types of attendees will you be able to include? What would help you ascertain the different "population" types to add to this group?

3. Identify three benchmarks that you can apply to your meeting marketing/promotional plan that will help you define your next steps.

4. Identify the benefits that three different segments of attendees will bring back to their professional lives. Write a benefit statement for each that you would include in your marketing brochure and/or website.

5. What are the pros and cons of keeping time slots open in your education for "new" key issues?

CONTRIBUTOR

Generous contribution of Steve Wattanmaker, CEO SimulConference Solutions, Inc., is gratefully acknowledged.

CHAPTER 6

A Strategic Perspective for Meetings Management

Richard (Rick) A. Binford, CMP
Vice President, Field Sales
Conferon Global Services, Inc.

Learner Outcomes

When the reader has completed reading this chapter, he/she should be able to . . .

1 Recognize the impact of strategic sourcing strategies on the changing role of meeting managers.

2 Explain the opportunities for best practices collaboration between procurement professionals and event managers.

3 Identify the major elements of an enterprise Strategic Meetings Management Program (SMMP).

4 Apply the major elements of effective Meeting and Event Policy design and consideration.

5 Implement the concepts of SMMP design to develop an initial best-practices flow for organizations.

> The global business environment is evolving significantly due to a renewed emphasis on accountability, cost consciousness, privacy acts, consolidation, and more….The new reality? You must become fluent in the language of business, adapt to how business is evolving, and articulate the value of meetings to all levels of stakeholders. You must understand the concept of strategic meetings management and learn the benefits of proactively partnering with procurement professionals and others to drive your organization's bottom line.
>
> *Meeting Professionals International*
> *Global Corporate Circle of Excellence*
> *Position Paper: "The Power of Partnership: Capitalizing on the Collaborative Efforts of Strategic Meeting Professionals and Procurement Departments"*
> *January 2005*

OVERVIEW

As the profession of meeting and event management continues to mature, the role of meeting and event managers also continues to evolve. As recognition of the profession began to build during the 1960s through 1980s, initial industry focus was placed upon the various skill sets and functional project management methodologies associated with meeting management—ranging from food and beverage services, to transportation, to vendor negotiations, to registration and housing, and so on. As industry best practices gained recognition and wider acceptance throughout the 1990s, however, meeting managers have experienced a fundamental shift in the expectations placed upon them. In addition to being highly competent in the methodologies associated with event project design, management, and execution, today's meeting managers are being challenged to expand their role from event project management alone to complete event process management across their organizations.

The primary focus for senior leadership within corporations and non-profits, and the audiences to whom they are accountable, is improving total organizational performance. In the corporate world, that often translates into maximizing profits via strategic sourcing and procurement practices. In the association sector, it may manifest itself most directly in membership growth, industry advocacy, or reach, depending on the specific organizational mandate and mission. Regardless of the ultimate measure of success, performance optimization is inherently linked to implementation of process excellence across all possible operational areas and functions—including meeting and event management.

Recognizing the impact of strategic sourcing strategies is critical for meeting managers today as they redefine their roles and value propositions within their organizations.

Increasingly opportunities emerge for true best practice collaboration between meeting managers and procurement professionals in many organizations. By establishing a clearly defined Strategic Meeting Management Program (SMMP), the programs, supporting policies, and procedures can flow to guide the event management process across the entire enterprise; maximizing cost-savings opportunities, minimizing risk, and improving the total return on investment associated with events of all types.

This chapter will identify the benefits and elements of implementing a strategic focus in the management of meetings. Additionally, a design for the development of a strategic policy to guide the execution of meetings will be presented.

THE RISE OF STRATEGIC MEETINGS MANAGEMENT

In the arena of meetings and events, success is driven by implementation of an organization-wide end-to-end process that ensures the best possible outcomes at the lowest possible cost. Events must be more than simply planned and executed flawlessly; the entire lifecycle—starting with why the event should be held in the first place and ending with how the event's results need to drive future decision-making—need to be managed effectively and efficiently with an emphasis on continuous improvement.

This changing view of meetings and events as an integral part of organizational strategy is moving event managers to establish Strategic Meetings Management Programs (SMMP).[1] SMMP advances the earlier concept of "meetings consolidation," which described the centralization of various meeting management functions within organizations. Essentially, this common initial strategy sought to consolidate best practices within skilled work teams as a means to drive anticipated cost savings.

In today's application environment, the term Strategic Meetings Management Program is best described as a strategy to maximize the efficiency and total effectiveness of meetings and events across the entire enterprise.

THE BENEFITS OF HAVING A STRATEGIC MEETINGS MANAGEMENT PROGRAM (SMMP)

SMMP design and implementation offers meeting managers and their organizations several important areas of performance improvement, including:

- Process efficiencies
- Risk management
- Cost reduction
- Return on investment

Process Efficiencies

Without end-to-end SMMP in place, true consolidation seldom occurs. A complete discovery process will routinely uncover multiple areas of overlapping activity and duplication of effort across the enterprise. When multiple work teams involved in similar work have the benefit of a fully integrated network of expertise and resources, great opportunities exist to improve total event activity performance. SMMP streamlines processes and leverages the operational centers of excellence of event management, including contract negotiation, program design, vendor sourcing, logistical planning, on-site event management, budget reconciliation, impact measurement, etc.

Risk Management

Event management requires a wide range of contractual agreements. All such agreements create some type of liability on behalf of the sponsoring organization, either directly in terms of financial obligations, or indirectly in terms of liability associated with the terms of the purchase agreement. Individuals within organizations have varied levels of contractual analysis and negotiation expertise and authority, a fact that can expose the organization to sub-optimal risk levels.

Implementation of a standardized, disciplined process to manage the contractual obligations associated with meetings and events can help to eliminate unnecessary risk exposure (see Chapters 40 and 44). An enterprise-wide contracting process integrated into SMMP should include a number of standardized elements, such as:

- Centralized contract execution (signature) rights
- Predefined contract execution authority levels (determined by expenditure or risk level, or a combination thereof)
- Contractual language, including templates, addenda, riders, etc.
- Contract review and audit
- Document administration and retention

Cost Reduction

Cost reduction is achieved on two different levels: direct cost savings and cost avoidance. Cost savings are realized via two different avenues: productivity gains, which are realized through process efficiencies; and improved sourcing and negotiation expertise, which (when combined with consolidated spend leverage) help reduce the actual costs for purchased goods and services. Cost avoidance, by contrast, results from improved risk management controls over the potential costs associated with contract performance obligations and mitigation, cancellation fees, and other excess contractual liabilities.

Return on Investment

The ability to successfully reduce the costs associated with executing meetings and events is certainly one indicator of a successful SMMP program. The ultimate measure, however, of an end-to-end enterprise strategy is the ability to assess the strategic business impact of dollars invested as a component of total organizational strategy. The design and implementation of a well-structured and disciplined SMMP affords meeting and event managers consistent access to the data critical to assess true return on investment analysis for both direct and indirect costs. The ability to align the total event cost with the total business impact enables informed business decisions when making such investments in the future (see Chapter 46).

THE ELEMENTS OF A STRATEGIC MEETINGS MANAGEMENT PROGRAM

The National Business Travel Association (NBTA) has identified a number of SMMP process components that are considered to be "best practice."[1] Additionally, a truly end-to-end process must also consider the addition of a return on investment analysis element. Thus, in total, a complete SMMP best practices process flow should include the following:

- Event approval
- Meeting registration
- Sourcing and contract negotiations
- Event management
- Payment and reconciliation
- Supporting technology platform
- Data consolidation and reporting
- Return on investment assessment

In reviewing this process flow, the specific sequence of process steps and the specific scope of each must be tailored to the unique needs of each organization. In developing and implementing an SMMP strategy, organizations may choose to start at a different point in the process, resulting in different measures of success.

Within a typical SMMP structure, all roles, responsibilities, and standards for both internal and external resources that may be involved are fully defined. The following section offers a brief overview of each of the program elements and key considerations that any SMMP designer should consider in developing their own process flow.

Event Approval

In an effort to reduce unnecessary resource commitments on behalf of the organization, approval is a critical control mechanism. Defining and integrating the event approval process at the proper levels is integral to the front end of the work flow process. Approval may occur either prior to or in conjunction with the meeting registration described below.

Meeting Registration

The primary objective of this step is to define the goals and objectives of each event early enough to ensure that all decisions support the SMMP process and that all related data and information can be tracked and accumulated. At a minimum, the type of information required includes documentation of the following event details:

- Event type and purpose
- Sponsoring business unit and specific event owner
- Event dates (tentative or preferred)
- Profile of event attendees
- Event budget

Most often, registration of the event includes assignment of a unique event identification code that enables data consolidation and inclusion in a master event calendar.

Sourcing and Contract Negotiations

Once an event is approved and registered, the sourcing of suppliers needed to support the delivery of the event can begin. While many models may be utilized for sourcing of vendors, NBTA's "best-in-class" practices centralize this function within a group or individual specifically skilled in this area and well-positioned to leverage total event and/or travel-related spending. While sourcing of vendors is an integral part of any event management process, the skill set and expertise associated with sourcing are distinct from those of logistical planning and coordination.

The sourcing process typically occurs in three phases:

- Vendor review and selection
- Negotiation
- Contracting and risk management

In the first phase of vendor review and selection, standards must be defined to determine which vendors will be considered and how they will be evaluated. A well-managed sourcing process affords opportunities to leverage benefits for the buyer in two ways:

1. Insuring appropriate competition between qualified vendors to drive best value pricing
2. Leveraging additional vendor value through business opportunity consolidation

Thus the sourcing strategy should define standards relative to request for proposal management, preferred vendors, etc.

In the second sourcing phase of negotiations, both the business terms (service requirements, pricing, concessions, etc.) and the legal terms and conditions of the purchase are defined. Whether that responsibility resides with a single individual or is centralized, roles in the SMMP process flow must be clearly defined.

During the third phase of the sourcing process, the final contractual agreements are defined in writing, with the buyer agreeing to final levels of calculated risk. This phase also ensures legally prudent contract execution and document management standards and processes.

Event Management

Actual management of both the event's content and its logistics is an ongoing process throughout the life of the project. In an SMMP supported environment, all roles and responsibilities for management of internal and external resources are clearly defined, as are any compliance requirements relative to specific policies or procedures.

Payment and Reconciliation

Throughout the event development process, suppliers will need to be paid and related expenses reconciled and consolidated. The SMMP defines all approved methods for purchases of related goods and services as well as the processes and accountabilities for invoice review, expense classification, and so on. Best-in-class programs typically limit the approved methods of payment as a means to consolidate data most efficiently and consistently with desired reporting standards.

Supporting Technology Platform

For most successful SMMP efforts, technology serves as an enabling "backbone" of the entire strategy. Technology is critical to overall success, and provides the primary means to help standardize and streamline processes and manage compliance, as well as to accumulate data to support total program analysis. Numerous technology platform options are available in the marketplace; many are easily self-configurable and customizable to the specific user and SMMP process flow requirements.

Data Consolidation and Reporting

Post-program data analysis is an essential step in comparing results against objectives and fine-tuning budgeting and operational methodologies toward continuous process improvement, as well as accumulating total SMMP strategy impact. Many best-in-class reporting strategies include identifying and reporting a set of standardized metrics across events as a means of benchmarking and tracking aggregate project management performance and trends. Such standardized metrics may include easily comparable measures, such as:

- Average daily total cost per attendee
- Percent variance to budget
- Total cost savings
- Percent of total program budget savings

Return on Investment Assessment

Effective return on investment (ROI) assessment is the ultimate objective of any end-to-end SMMP effort. Providing a model and process from which to reasonably measure the true business impact of event investment is the key to effectively deploying events as part of a total business strategy. Effective ROI measurement involves much more than simply tracking cost savings resulting from SMMP implementation and laying them alongside the cost of supporting the program. Effective ROI measurement tracks both direct and indirect costs of the SMMP effort and aligns them with near-term and long-term financial business impacts based on behavioral changes of event attendees.

This type of ROI assessment is unique to each event and requires a thorough commitment up front in the event development process to clearly articulate specific targeted objectives. The ROI Institute has identified six different levels of measurement that ultimately lead to true event ROI[2] (see Chapter 46). These levels are:

1. Reaction, satisfaction, planned action
2. Learning
3. Application and implementation
4. Business impact
5. Financial return on investment
6. Intangible measures

MEETING AND EVENT POLICY DEVELOPMENT

Once an SMMP process flow has been established, it must be defined through development of an enterprise-wide meetings and events policy. This policy is the "glue" that effectively binds the entire SMMP together from start to finish. Designed essentially as a "user's guide," it defines the rules by which individuals and groups support the SMMP process design through specific policies and procedures, utilizing both internal and approved external (outsourced) resources as applicable.

NBTA has identified eight major elements of a complete meetings and events policy initiative.[3] Development of this policy document must remain an ongoing and dynamic process, serving as an incremental reinforcement and management tool that develops alongside the SMMP implementation process.

1. *Meeting Definition*—This element essentially defines the scope of activities by the enterprise that will be subject to the policy and will ultimately be under the domain of the SMMP effort. Various types of criteria may be utilized to define what qualifies as a meeting or event and may include items such as:

   • Size (number of attendees)
   • Spending (budget type or amount)
   • Type (purpose)
   • Site requirements (on-site, off-site, with or without sleeping rooms, etc.)
   • Travel requirements
   • Planning services required

2. *Approval Process*—This element defines both what approvals are required and the process by which they should be secured in order to be consistent with the SMMP guidelines.

3. *Meeting Registration*—This element details the process by which new meetings and events become "registered" and consolidated into the enterprise event calendar.

4. *Contracting*—This element defines all of the standards relative to sourcing strategies defined in the SMMP.

5. *Logistical Management*—This element addresses specifically who has what responsibility for pre-planning and execution of events as governed by the policy and what types of external resources may or may not be employed and by what means.

6. *Payment Process*—This element clearly defines implementation guidelines for all of the administrative elements associated with the SMMP acquisition strategy.

7. *SMMP Process Tools*—This element typically details what types of standardized tools have been established to support the SMMP implementation. Such tools and resources may include: enabling technology for meeting registration, procurement, expense and attendee management, standardized documents and formats, and other resources available to program stakeholders and users.

8. *Applicable Corporate Policies*—To enhance the adoption rate of the SMMP strategy, the meetings and events policy should be aligned with other related organizational policies, including policies regarding travel, gifts, use of the company name and logo, and so on.

PROCUREMENT AND STRATEGIC MEETINGS MANAGEMENT PROGRAMS

Recently, a dialogue has begun with regard to the role of "procurement" in the meetings industry and its impact on the role of the meeting manager and SMMP

Fast Facts

According to Meeting Professionals International in their annual FutureWatch study, as of January 2005[4]:

- 57% of meeting manager respondents reported either complete or planned implementation of organization wide purchasing policies for meeting and event related goods and services.
- The percentage of organizations reporting full implementation of standardized strategic meetings management policies increased in 3 out of 4 different categories between 2005 and 2004, and those not considering standardization of any kind decreased.

efforts. Especially within the corporate sector, knowing who is, or actually should be, leading any SMMP design effort may be confusing. To best answer this question, one must clearly understand the playing field.

First of all, "procurement," by definition, is not a person or group of persons, nor is it an issue or movement. Procurement, as it relates to most organizations today, simply refers to the process of obtaining the necessary goods and services to conduct the business of that organization. Historically, within most organizations, this function was referred to simply as "purchasing."

Typically the actual process of procurement involves several different facets—some of which we have already discussed as considerations of most SMMP efforts—such as vendor review, negotiating, contracting, and so on. Aside from the widespread development of new e-commerce technology tools that have become available, little has actually changed in the fundamental steps in the procurement process in recent years. What has already changed for many corporate entities, and is fast taking hold within the association sector, however, is a new strategy that is driving this procurement process.

Strategic sourcing involves taking a slightly broader view of the process of procuring goods and services. Contemporary strategic sourcing management focuses not just on prices paid for goods and services, but more broadly on the total lifecycle cost of all the goods and services consumed by the enterprise. This total lifecycle cost is fully inclusive of all the elements of the process, from the labor required to design, execute, and manage the purchasing process, to the costs of maintaining and managing effective relationships with qualified vendors.

To help illustrate this concept of "total lifecycle costs," consider an example. If a meeting manager enters into an agreement with a hotel to contract for use of 250 hotel room nights at a negotiated rate of $200 per room night, the total lifecycle cost of this purchase is not simply $50,000 (250 room nights × $200), but actually comprises many elements, some of which may include:

1. Purchase Price	$50,000
2. Additional Fees (taxes, etc. @ 12%)	$6,000
3. Procurement Costs (vendor research, evaluation, negotiations @ 24 person-hours × $75/hour fully loaded costs)	$1,800
4. Administration Costs (payment processing, invoice reconciliation, etc. @ 12 person-hours × $60/hour fully loaded costs)	$720
Total	$58,520

This strategic sourcing philosophy of evaluating total lifecycle costs focuses on driving maximum value for buyers through cost reductions at every possible opportunity, including process efficiency gains, and prudently managed vendor profit margins. Through effective supply chain management efforts and development of preferred vendor relationships, strategic sourcing strategies also offer sellers advantages to increase their revenues through vendor consolidation.

While "Procurement," or "Purchasing," departments have existed within various organizations for decades, only recently have they gained higher levels of influence and integration across organizations. No longer are these groups viewed simply as tactical support functions. Today's procurement professionals are now viewed as key strategists being charged with implementing consistent strategic sourcing strategies across the enterprise as a means to guide and shape processes and procedures to reduce costs, improve labor efficiencies, leverage best value pricing from vendors, and manage related payment systems. Why is this happening? Because strategic sourcing has become a proven strategy over

Put It Into Perspective

One key component of consideration in the design and implementation of any SMMP effort for all organizations is how to best define supporting policies to align them effectively with any applicable regulatory constraints. SMMP policies and procedures must be aligned to fully support compliance requirements as applicable. In the corporate sector, legislation such as the Sarbanes-Oxley corporate governance law or the Office of Inspector General (OIG) Guidance, in the United States, or Safe Harbor, in the European Union, may need to be considered. In the association sector, profession and/or industry specific regulations such as Continuing Medical Education (CME), PhRMA Code, AdvaMed Code of Ethics, etc. must be considered.

the past 10 years to help reduce costs and ultimately improve total organizational financial performance.[5]

SMMP design and implementation is very closely aligned with strategic sourcing strategies. Taking a SMMP approach within an organization offers the potential to create synergy between the meeting manager and the procurement department and senior leadership, all focused on improving aggregate organizational performance.

While widely based commodity buying practices that are typical across the broader travel industry contrast significantly with the often-complex service-purchasing that is critical to event managers, opportunities abound to apply common principles and strategies to optimize results in all areas. This collaboration opportunity between procurement and event managers is a critical element to the success of any SMMP strategy. Consequently, today's event managers and their supply base must not only be familiar with fulfilling logistical requirements, but also be competent in successfully integrating strategic sourcing methodology into their total business approach.

SUMMARY

This chapter has presented the impact of strategic sourcing strategies on the changing roles of meeting managers. Senior management across all organizations is increasingly focused on total organizational performance. Meeting and event managers must shift their orientation from project management to process management.

The major elements of an enterprise Strategic Meetings Management Program (SMMP) that is identified as the best in class traditionally include eight major components. These are event approval, registration and planning, sourcing and contract negotiation, payment and reconciliation, a supporting technology platform, data consolidation and reporting, and assessing the return on investment.

An effective meeting and event policy provides complete rules of engagement for all stakeholders in the SMMP effort. A well established meeting and event policy typically addresses a number of key elements, including:

- Meeting and event definition
- Approval process
- Meeting registration process
- Sourcing and contracting
- Logistical management
- Payment and reconciliation
- SMMP process tools
- Related organizational policies

Each SMMP process flow must be customized to the operational and cultural needs of each organization. Applying the concepts of SMMP design to develop a SMMP must flow for the individual organization. SMMP process development is in direct alignment with contemporary management emphasis on strategic sourcing initiatives and provides a great opportunity for cross-functional collaboration.

REFERENCES

1. National Business Travel Association. (2004). Framework for success: Building a strategic meetings management program. White paper retrieved March 1, 2006 from www.nbta.org.

2. Phillips, J. (2004). *Phillips ROI methodology*. Birmingham, AL: ROI Institute, Inc.

3. National Business Travel Association. (2005). Building a meetings policy in support of your strategic meetings management program. White paper retrieved March 1, 2006 from www.nbta.org.

4. Meeting Professionals International and American Express. (2005). *FutureWatch 2005*. An official supplement to *The Meeting Professional*. Retrieved February 12, 2006 from www.mpiweb.org.

5. Meeting Professionals International. (January 2005). Position paper: The power of partnership: Capitalizing on the collaborative efforts of strategic meeting professionals and procurement departments. Retrieved February 2, 2006 from www.gccoe.mpiweb.org.

KEY TERMS

Meetings and events policy

National Business Travel Association

Procurement

Project management

Strategic meeting management program (SMMP)

Strategic sourcing

COMPELLING QUESTIONS FOR CONSIDERATION

1. What is the current meeting and event management environment within your organization? Is your current methodology project- or process-centric?

2. What is the total current cost of your meeting and event related activity, including both direct and indirect, as well as internal and external costs?

3. What is the potential opportunity in terms of both cost reductions and efficiency gains from implementation of a well-managed Strategic Meetings Management Program?

4. Who are the key stakeholders in the meetings and events associated with your organization and how can you most effectively engage and communicate with them? How will an enterprise SMMP effort impact those efforts? How do you involve them in the process?

5. What are the key considerations and obstacles for design and implementation of an effective SMMP within my organization? How is your organization both like and unlike other organizations that have already undergone this process?

6. As a meeting manager, what additional skills and competencies do you need to acquire to play a leading role in effective SMMP design and implementation?

CHAPTER 7

INDEPENDENT MEETING PLANNER: ENTERING A BRAVE NEW WORLD

MaryAnne P. Bobrow, CAE, CMP
PRINCIPAL
BOBROW & ASSOCIATES

LEARNER OUTCOMES

When the reader has completed reading this chapter, he/she should be able to . . .

1 Judge the importance of having sufficient self-discipline necessary to work in an unsupervised and undisciplined environment.

2 Identify the characteristics of the self-employed planner.

3 Recognize that self-employed planners are responsible for all facets of running their businesses.

4 Describe the competencies required to successfully operate one's own business.

> Always be smarter than the people who hire you.
>
> *Lena Horne*

OVERVIEW

Industry associations agree on two things. One, that the category commonly called "independent planners" is the fastest growing segment of the meetings industry today, representing about 13% of all meeting managers[1] and, two, this category is populated predominantly by females. Statistics vary among the industry associations as to the exact number of self-employed planners, but that variance is caused in part by the criteria organizations use to identify and classify "independent planners." Further, independent planners probably are undercounted. Some independent planners do not belong to any industry associations and, therefore, would not be counted in this statistical data set.

This chapter explores the self-employed planner role, with particular focus on the planner's need to operate his/her own business in addition to functioning in the role of planner. For the purposes of this chapter, the word planner is used instead of meeting manager because it more accurately describes the role of the self-employed business owner as defined in the APEX glossary.[2]

THE SELF-EMPLOYED PLANNER

According to independent research companies, over three million service and professional jobs will be outsourced overseas by the year 2015.[3] The U.S. Department of Labor, Bureau of Labor Statistics[4] predicts that between the years 2004 and 2014, more than 21% of the civilian work force will reach 55 years of age or older, with more than 75% of the entire work force in the service industries. While these data are not specific to the meetings industry, the concept of outsourcing is relevant.

Outsourcing in the meetings industry ebbs and surges depending on economic climates. The demographics affecting all areas of employment also affect the meetings industry and include economic factors, the aging of the work force, an increasing number of women in the work force, and a lack of experienced or skilled workers to fill the roles currently held by baby boomers reaching retirement age. Just as the number of women in the meetings industry has increased, so has a trend emerged where more women are electing to either work within their organizational structures to have their roles viewed as being of strategic importance, or they are striking out on their own to achieve a greater level of satisfaction in their careers.

ONE SIZE DOES NOT FIT ALL

The self-employed planner comes in many shapes and sizes. Terms commonly used to describe this role include:

- Independent planner
- Contract planner
- Third party
- Independent contractor
- Intermediary, and others

While they all share one commonality—they own their own businesses—the types of services they offer differ, as do their locales and types of business formations. In 2005, Toh, DeKay, and Yates reported in the Cornell Hotel & Restaurant Administration Quarterly that the four services most frequently offered by self-employed planners are:

- On-site management (46%)
- Contract negotiation (28%)

- Full-service meeting management (36%)
- Site inspection and selection (30%)[5]

Who fits into this fastest growing segment of the industry? Home-based independents, those with offices (and perhaps staff of their own), independent contractors working for larger and global companies, and many others may fall under this umbrella, as no single definition exists—and perhaps should not exist. Each is simply a planner who is self-employed.

Each has asked himself/herself the question: "Do I really want to do this and do I have the resolve to make it successful?" And, the answer is affirmative.

STARTING ONE'S OWN BUSINESS

Being a self-employed planner means owning and operating a business. Not all meeting managers are suited for this role. All planners, including self-employed planners, need to have the same core competencies of the meeting manager. As discussed throughout this book, the core competencies will not be fully developed in this chapter. Financial considerations are discussed later in this chapter. In addition to these pre-requisites, the planner must decide a variety of issues, including:

- *Home office or more structured setting*? Many self-employed planners elect to maintain a home-based business. Their business is such that if they need to meet with clients, this is done outside of the office environment. Others prefer the structure of a formal business office or the nature of the business necessitates a more formal setting.

- *Self-discipline*—The decision to "go it alone" requires a great deal of self-discipline, particularly for the home-based person who has difficulty "shutting that office door" at the end of the day. Home-based business owners are challenged to get their families to understand that when the workday begins, their families should treat them as if they had left the house entirely. The home-based planner also may struggle with focusing on work-related issues while being surrounded by happenings around the home.

- *Development of a business plan*—A business plan that includes a marketing plan is essential for the self-employed planner. Does the plan have to be formal and structured? The answer is—*it all depends*. If the planner is seeking outside financial help in the way of small business loans or other financial assistance, then the planner must have a formal business plan. If the planner is not seeking outside financial help, then a plan in outline form that sets out the planner's goals, services, fees, and marketing strategies (at the very least) should be written.

At a minimum, a business plan should include:

- *Description of the business*—What services will the business offer?
- *Ownership of the business*—What is the legal structure of the business? A woman or minority business owner may have advantages. Certain states within the United States offer special incentives to women and minority-owned businesses.
- *Clients*—Has the planner developed a niche? Will the business focus on corporations (large or small) as clients? Will those clients be in a particular sector, e.g., pharmaceutical company meetings? Defining "client" base will enhance the planner's ability to define business and the services offered.
- *Competitors*—Self-employed planners must find ways to differentiate themselves from the competition. By researching competitors' strengths and weaknesses, planners are better able to distinguish their businesses from those of the competition.

- *Marketing*—Determining how to market the new business is critical to the success of the business. Will marketing be by word of mouth (slow, but effective)? Will brochures or other advertisements work for this type of business? What other strategies will help the business succeed?
- *Importance of Networking*—In a published article on independent meeting planners, Toh et al., found that 25% of corporate planners, 33% of association planners, and 50% of independent planners belong to professional associations, such as PCMA.[6] Self-employed planners participate actively in professional associations, community organizations, and other service-related groups for a variety of reasons. Certainly, professional associations offer value through the professional development opportunities they offer. Another reason is the value of networking at annual, regional, or local meetings. Volunteering for these organizations is beneficial, as well. For the independent, the visibility of attending events, and particularly the visibility that comes with volunteer leadership, helps to solidify the credibility of the planner and the perception of that planner's success.
- *At regular intervals*—More frequently in the beginning and at least once a year, the planner should revisit the business plan to determine whether the purposes set out in the plan are being achieved. Do adjustments need to be made? Have new services taken the business in a direction that was not originally anticipated? Does the plan need to be reworked? This review ensures the planner focuses on a forward-moving plan to realize success.
- *Finding a niché*—An independent cannot be all things to all people. Planners' credibility will have greater strength if planners develop their own niché of services and market that as their expertise. In bidding on projects against competitors, this expertise might be the element of the planner's proposal that "lands" the business.

CORE COMPETENCIES OF THE SELF-EMPLOYED PLANNER

Clients assume the self-employed planner has expertise as a meeting manager. What else does the planner need to operate a successful business? The answer to this question may be the deciding factor in whether the planner's business succeeds or fails.

Administration

Running a business means dealing with all of the administrative work that probably was done for the planner by someone else (if the planner was previously employed in a corporate or association environment). Efficiency in maintaining a streamlined office is essential. Questions independent planners should ask themselves about their business administration include:

- Is time set aside for keeping the office neat and tidy (e.g., for filing and other clerical tasks)?
- Is sufficient and regularly scheduled time set aside to process accounts payable and accounts receivable? Bills do not pay themselves and clients do not typically send payments without first receiving an invoice. This is one of the most essential tasks that a small business owner can perform. If the planner does not have the desire or the ability to manage the day-to-day financial operations, then consideration should be given to outsourcing this function to a financial professional (i.e., a bookkeeper or a certified public accountant).

- Does the business have technology resources in place to both operate the business and safeguard the data of the business and the clients? Does the planner have a disaster recovery plan? Recall that in the tragedy of September 11, some businesses had disaster recovery plans with "mirrored" databases residing at off-site locations. The businesses that had such plans in place lost no client information. The businesses that did not have such a plan lost not only the lives of their key employees, but their data as well.

- If the planner's business has a web site, does the planner regularly maintain it and keep it fresh? If the planner has outsourced this function, is there a "maintenance and update" line item in the planner's budget? A web site that never changes is seldom visited.

Communication

Communication with clients is essential. Does the planner reserve time to ensure regular contact with clients? Is the planner responsive to client requests via email, phone, or fax? In times when the planner does not have a current project with the client, does the planner communicate to ensure that the client will think of the planner when a new project is developed? This type of communication is essential to the independent's business.

Another aspect of communication is the importance of staying current. The planner must keep track of trends, not only in the meetings industry, but in the clients' industries as well. Issues such as return on investment (see Chapter 46) and the planner's ability to provide *strategic* solutions are essential. The planner who is able to impart to the client knowledge of trends, challenges, and opportunities in the client's industry is far more likely to gain business from the client. An example of this might be that a current trend in planning conferences is a shift away from the single, national conferences to multiple regional conferences. The planner who follows this trend and provides the client with a report on the trend and its impact on the client may well move from planning one national conference for this client to a variety of regional conferences.

Working with Suppliers

Suppliers can be excellent resources for self-employed planners or they can become the planner's worst nightmare. The planner should act with honesty and integrity in dealing with suppliers. The business the planner brings should be good for the planner, the planner's client, and the supplier. The planner's reputation here is everything. If the planner brings a piece of business to the supplier and does not engage in one-sided negotiations, the next time the planner brings business to the supplier, negotiations will become easier and easier because the supplier will trust in the planner's integrity. Win-win situations are good for everyone.

Preparing the Response to a Request for Proposal (RFP) for New Business

Essential to securing new business is the planner's ability to respond (sometimes quickly) to an RFP. The planner should develop key talking points that address any anticipated requests that will arise in a proposal. Key talking points include:

- The planner's experience and background
- The planner's expertise in providing services. Include specifics; i.e., if the request is to "develop conference brochures and programs" the planner should discuss prior materials previously produced, whether the technology used to create the materials allowed them to forego the services of a graphic designer (and thus reduced the costs to the client), and the effect

---

Fast Facts

Core Competencies
Self-Employed Planner

- Administration
- Communication
- Working with suppliers
- Preparing RFPs

these materials had on attendance at the conference. (Materials alone cannot be credited for any attendance increases, but an increase is worth mentioning in any RFP response.)

- The planner's abilities to complete the project on a timely and accurate basis
- The tools the planner will use to complete the project
- Whether the planner will use any third parties to assist in completing the project

An effectively written response to an RFP helps simplify the contract between the planner and the client, since the contract can simply state that the scope of services is contained in Attachment A, with Attachment A being the response to the request for proposal. Why should the planner use an attachment to describe the scope of services? Simply put, placing all of the actual services in a descriptive attachment facilitates contract consensus by making the contract more uniform.

THE PLANNER'S SUPPORT MECHANISMS

The independent may possess expertise in planning meetings, but he or she probably is not an expert in the law, accounting, technology, or a variety of other areas involved in owning one's own business. The planner who starts a new business after working in the corporate or association world is a lot like the child who ventures out for the first time on a bicycle without training wheels. The self-employed planner no longer has in-house counsel, a financial expert, an insurance expert, or an information technology (IT) person to handle issues that arise in those areas. Sometimes, the first instinct of the planner is "I cannot afford to hire a (lawyer, CPA, and so on.)." Actually, the planner cannot afford *not* to do so. The planner who desires to be viewed by clients, potential clients, and others as the *consummate professional* needs to ensure that all of the business' I's are dotted and T's are crossed.

Many planners shy away from procuring insurance for their business. This is sheer folly and endangers not only the planner's business, but also the planner's personal wealth. At the very least, the planner should have both general liability and errors and omissions insurance. In fact, many client contracts will require proof of insurance before the contract is executed.

What happens when the planner's technology fails? Is the planner going to spend hours trying to determine what is wrong? Alternatively, is the planner's time better spent focusing on the meetings business? Having a technology expert to rely on when technology issues arise will ensure that the planner can focus on the core of his or her business.

THE CONTRACT

Contracts are an important element of any meeting professional's scope of services. This is even more relevant for the self-employed planner because the planner not only is involved in contracts *on behalf of* the client but also is involved in contracts *with* the client.

The overall topic of contracts is covered in Chapters 41 and 42. However, certain elements are common to any contracts between a self-employed planner and the client. Many articles have been written on this subject in meetings industry publications; however, at the very least, elements to include are:

- Identification of the contracting parties and their authority to enter into and/or modify the agreement. Included here should be a recitation of who among them has the authority to make what decisions.

- A scope of responsibilities for both the planner and the client. Provide a detailed description of the services in an attachment to the contract, rather than including the services in the contract itself. (See the discussion on preparing an RFP, above.)
- A specific statement as to how and when the planner is to be paid for fees and reimbursable expenses.
- Mutual indemnification and other insurance and liability-related clauses.
- Termination and cancellation clauses, including specifics on payments for work performed to date, cancellation charges, and when and how notice of termination takes place.

Other important legal considerations may be relevant, depending on the contract and type of services provided. Clients will probably consult their attorneys regarding any contract(s) they enter into. The planner should similarly protect the planner's interests. The reality is that it costs far less to consult an attorney *before* a contract is entered into than it does once conflict regarding the terms of the contract arise. Consulting an attorney before a contract has been signed is less costly than dealing with conflict regarding contract terms. The planner has the expertise to know the parameters of the services planners provide, including any timelines for completion, the scope of services (what the planner is or is not responsible for), and other meeting-related elements. If the planner details the services and brings those to the planner's attorney, the time spent by the lawyer in drafting a contract (and reviewing any subsequent revisions) should be minimal in time and costs.

LEGAL STRUCTURE

One of the many decisions the self-employed planner faces is how to structure the business: sole proprietorship, limited liability company, partnership, or corporation. If the decision is to operate either as a limited liability company or a corporation, the planner must also decide which state yields the most advantages, particularly tax advantages. As discussed elsewhere in this chapter, the planner should seek professional advice in certain areas, and the legal structure of the business entity is one of those areas. In addition to deciding how to structure the business, the planner must decide on a name.

In the United States, fictitious (doing business as) names may necessitate the filing of additional documentation, depending on the location of the business. The planner may also have to secure a business license, permits, have a logo designed, trademark the business name and the logo, and otherwise comply with local, regional, state, and federal laws. Laws vary by state and the planner's research on how to construct his or her business should begin, prior to consultation with legal counsel, with the U.S. Small Business Administration.[7] Prospective business owners can find assistance in starting a business, managing a business, financing a business, and other topics that are useful to the independent for operating in the U.S. and other countries through governmental and commercial web sites.

PRICING, START-UP COSTS, AND OTHER CONSIDERATIONS

One of the biggest challenges for the new business owner is how to price services offered by the new business. Books intended to aid the independent consultant are available, such as *Value Based Fees: How to Charge–And Get–What You're Worth*;[8] although these publications are not specifically aimed at the meetings industry, they are excellent resources for independent planners. Seeking advice from other independent professionals is beneficial. Resist the urge to post pricing questions to industry list servers, as this may invoke antitrust (price-fixing) issues. Ultimately, the independent must decide what and how to charge clients based upon what the market will bear.

Ideally, the decision to "go it alone" is one made at least a year in advance of any business launch, thus allowing the new business owner the opportunity to accumulate at least a year's worth of reserve cash for living and business expenses until revenue streams from the new business become a reality. This allows the new business owner to focus on networking, marketing, and other strategies to acquire new clients for the new business. Unfortunately, the luxury of reserving cash is not available to all, and particularly not to individuals who are downsized or otherwise separated from their prior employment without sufficient severance pay to build a year's worth of reserves.

In the Beginning

What rates to charge clients, be they hourly, weekly, monthly, by the project, or some other agreed-upon method of compensation, are not pulled out of thin air. The first step in determining what rate to charge is for the planner to determine his or her cash flow, based upon the business' financial situation and how much cash is needed to sustain the owner and the owner's family on an annual basis. Start by breaking expenses down into personal and business categories.

Personal expenses include, but are not limited to:

- Rent or mortgage payments
- Food and clothing
- Personal care (including such things as hairdresser appointments, pedicures, and so on)
- Insurance (home, auto, medical, and so on)
- Leisure (discretionary spending)
- Services
- Taxes (property tax, income tax)
- Savings
- Gifts and contributions
- Other obligations
- Contingency (a reserve amount for emergency situations)

Business expenses include:

- Automobile (monthly payments, gas, scheduled maintenance, insurance, and service)
- Insurance (general liability, errors and omissions, and worker's compensation—if applicable)
- Marketing expenses
- Professional fees (legal consultations, CPA or other financial expert)
- Office rent (unless it is a home-based business)
- Office supplies
- Rental/leasing charges (including office equipment)
- Taxes
- Travel
- Dues
- Professional development
- Licenses (local, regional, state)
- Retirement

- Bank charges
- Parking
- Postage and delivery
- Telecommunications (telephone, fax line, broadband services)
- Publications and other professional/learning tools

The planner then determines how much money will be needed for each expense category and places the amounts into a spreadsheet, with columns for each month of the year. For instance, if the planner knows that auto insurance must be paid in January and July, the projected amount of the auto insurance expense will be entered in those two months only. If specific months cannot be projected, then the planner takes the total expense, divides it by twelve, and enters an equal amount into each month's expense line item. The same process is followed for projecting revenue. These items then form the basis for a pro forma budget for the new business. When calculating tax liability, payments to federal, state, and perhaps even local governments must be ascertained. In the United States, taxes on the federal level, including income, FICA, Medicare, and social security taxes, are all the responsibility of the self-employed person. Similar considerations must be made by those who are forming new businesses in other countries.

Once the pro forma budget is in place, the planner must then decide how many hours will be devoted to the business. While a year typically consists of 365 days, the planner needs to deduct hours not only for weekends, holidays, and time with family and friends but also for time spent administering and managing the business and marketing or acquiring new business. Once these time frames are decided, a realistic figure for the number of billable hours emerges.

Regardless of whether the planner bills on an hourly, weekly, monthly, project-based, or other basis, the next step is the determination of a satisfactory hourly rate. All fees are based on this calculation.

A planner may have different rates for different services. Certainly, in the initial phase of building one's business, the new independent may discount fees in order to *get* the business. Regardless of how the independent chooses to structure the fee base, factors that affect the hourly rate must be considered. Those factors include:

- *What the market will bear*—One cannot expect to charge $200 per hour in a geographic region where competitors top out at $125 or $150 an hour. Be realistic! Research local salary ranges and other regional considerations.

- *Professional experience*—While the independent may wish to offer a bundle of services, the planner may actually have greater expertise in a specific service. Here, the independent may charge higher fees in the area where greater expertise exists.

- *Type of services offered*—Sometimes, the service itself demands a higher fee/hourly rate because of the complexity of the service offered. The planner should not be reluctant to require a higher fee for more complex services. After all, that is one of the expectations when a company outsources—receiving a high standard of service in return for a fee.

- *Degrees, certifications, and education*—College and graduate degrees in the hospitality industry are becoming more common and add to the self-employed planner's credibility, as do industry certifications and, to a more limited degree, meeting planning certificates. According to Toh et al., research on independent meeting planners, while "only 12% of corporate and association planners have professional designations (such as certification in meeting management and the Certified Meeting Professional (CMP) designation), 27% of independents have professional designations."[9]

Once an hourly billing rate is established, the rate is then applied to the specific piece of business the planner is seeking to secure. If the projected fee total appears to be excessive, the planner may either take a flat discount on the proposed fee, or rework the hourly fees, understanding the impact this will have on the planner's annual financial goal.

Commissions and Other Potential Conflicts

Sometimes, certain planner services are offered on a commission basis, rather than on a flat or hourly fee basis. For example, a planner may provide services to a client but may also accept a commission from the hotel, based on sleeping rooms booked. Views vary on the ethics of third-party commissions. Some planners simply refuse to accept commissions. Others, particularly those who focus on-site selection as a core element of their business, consider the commission critical to their being able to provide the services to the client. In fact, some clients, with limited ability to pay hourly or other fees, may request that the planner consider commissions as part of their overall project fees. With full disclosure of arrangements among the parties, including commissions, the behavior is ethical.

Other potential areas of conflict include the acceptance of meeting points from hotels and whether commissions are calculated inclusive of attrition charges. Blind commissions are yet another area of concern. While the debate on the ethics will continue for years to come, the ethical planner will always engage in full disclosure (see Chapter 39).

SUMMARY

Independent planners serve the interests of their clients as well as themselves if they adhere to professional standards and ethical behavior. Home-based business owners are challenged to get their families to understand that when the workday begins, their families should treat them as if they had left the house entirely.

Successfully operating as an independent planner requires confidence and discipline. Usually the choice to strike out as an independent planner results from a feeling that the current employer does not value the meeting manager as a strategic partner. As an independent business person, the independent planner must have good business skills, such as writing a business plan, budgeting, and communication.

The independent planner must have the same competencies as other meeting managers, along with a large dose of self-confidence. At stake here is the planner's reputation, the likelihood of receiving referrals and, most importantly, the ability to acquire and maintain working relationships with peers, including other independents, clients, and suppliers. Appreciation of these relationships will help to ensure the planner's survival as an independent and the profitability of the planner's business.

REFERENCES

1. Toh, R.S., DeKay, F., & Yates, B. (2005). Independent meeting planners: Roles, compensation and potential conflicts. *Cornell hotel & restaurant administration quarterly, 46(4),* p. 431–443.

2. Convention Industry Council (2006). APEX Glossary. Retrieved March 28, 2006 from http://www.glossary.conventionindustry.org/noresults.asp.

3. Friedman, T. (2005). *The world is flat.* New York: Farrar, Straus and Giroux.

4. Toosi, M. (2005). Labor force projections to 2014: Retiring boomers. *Monthly labor review 128(11)*. Retrieved March 1, 2006 from: http://stats.bls.gov/opub/mlr/2005/11/art3exc.htm.

5. Toh et al., op. cit.

6. Ibid.

7. United States Small Business Administration–http://www.sba.gov/.

8. *Weiss, A. (2002). Value based fees: How to charge–and get–what you're worth.* San Francisco, CA: Jossey-Bass/Pfeiffer.

9. Toh et al., op. cit.

KEY TERMS

Blind commission
Business plan
Budget
Cash flow
Contract planner
Independent contractor/
  planner

Intermediary
License
Networking
Outsourcing
Planner

Return on investment
  (ROI)
Third party
Win-win situation

COMPELLING QUESTIONS FOR CONSIDERATION

1. List the various skills an independent planner might excel in and promote to potential clients.

2. What kind of credentials should an independent planner offer in your area to be competitive?

3. What kind of suppliers might work with an independent planner and offer a commission to that planner as part of his/her compensation package?

4. Investigate the services provided by a destination management company and differentiate between that and an independent planner's typical services.

5. What benefits does a corporate or association meetings planner enjoy in comparison to independent planners? What are the advantages to being independent?

CHAPTER 8

SMALL MEETINGS MANAGEMENT: SMALL DOES NOT MEAN UNCOMPLICATED

MaryAnne P. Bobrow, CAE, CMP

PRINCIPAL

BOBROW & ASSOCIATES

LEARNER OUTCOMES

When the reader has completed reading this chapter, he/she should be able to . . .

1 Identify three types of small meetings and compare and contrast them with large meetings.

2 Discuss the value of the small meeting.

3 Demonstrate an improved ability to negotiate contracts for smaller meetings.

> The secret of getting ahead is getting started. The secret of getting started is breaking down your complex, overwhelming tasks into small manageable tasks, and then starting on the first one.
>
> *Mark Twain*

OVERVIEW

What is a small meeting? As yet, there is no consistent, industry-wide definition of this term. However, as it is usually employed in industry articles and publications, a small meeting is a meeting with 100 or fewer participants. That is the definition that will be used in this chapter. A small meeting may last for a single day, with or without room nights, or it may be a multi-day meeting with room nights, food and beverage functions, and audiovisual (A/V). This chapter explores the types of meetings that fall under this classification, the challenges of managing a smaller meeting, and the value of these meetings to the entities that produce them and the participants involved.

DIFFERENTIATING BETWEEN SMALL AND LARGE MEETINGS

A small meeting is classified by the number of participants, not by its perceived importance or the size of its budget. A meeting of a corporation's or an association's board of directors, a corporation's sales or incentive meeting, and an association's board retreat are just a few examples of small meetings. While the large, annual meeting may include thousands of attendees and exhibitors, it is at the smaller meeting that important decisions are made and a majority of the group's business is conducted. Smaller seminars and workshops are more likely to be conducive to adult learning styles and learner outcomes. Small meetings may equate to smaller numbers of meeting rooms, sleeping rooms, and quantity of food and beverages or audiovisual services. However, size does not mean that its management is uncomplicated.

Small meetings typically have a much shorter time line than their larger counterparts. In some organizations, responsibility for meeting management may be assigned to someone other than a meeting manager, such as an administrative assistant or a volunteer board member of an association. When this occurs, staff from the chosen venue is relied upon heavily in planning and executing meeting logistics and may often provide on-the-job training for the administrative assistant or volunteer meeting manager.

In managing large meetings, a variety of social events are typically incorporated into the agenda so that attendees are afforded choices for leisure time and after hours' activities. Smaller meetings, however, tend to be more focused and structured, which allow participants little free time, and they tend to offer little in the way of optional events.

TYPES OF SMALL MEETINGS

Small meetings have the flexibility to use a variety of formats, including conclaves, retreats, workshops, symposia, strategic planning sessions, and so on. These run the gamut from informal to very formal gatherings, and everything in between. The individual meeting goals and objectives, agenda, invited participants, and budget will, and should, help drive the selection of facility and meeting format. Some of the types of meetings classified as *small* include:

- Board meetings and other business meetings
- Board retreats (including visioning/strategic planning sessions or board training/orientation meetings)
- Sales meetings
- Incentive meetings
- Regional meetings
- Small association annual meetings
- Staff meetings (large corporations or associations)

Unlike larger meetings that have many components and participants, smaller meetings generally have no more than one or two people in leadership roles. For the board or business meeting, this is customarily a volunteer leader (for associations) or a manager or executive (for corporations) who chairs the meeting. In the case of board retreats, this type of meeting is typically led by an outside facilitator who is experienced in both facilitation and visioning/strategic planning or board orientation/training. Other meetings are chaired by people in leadership roles, such as a sales manager for sales meetings or a management-level employee for staff meetings.

SMALL MEETINGS DEVELOPMENT

Increasing workloads and other time constraints make it imperative that meeting objectives be clearly defined and communicated to participants well in advance of the meeting. Breaking down the elements common to most meetings and then mastering those elements is essential to producing effective meetings. These elements include developing an agenda and identifying the meeting participants.

Developing the Agenda

Agenda development is essential to running a successful and efficient meeting. In order to create an effective meeting agenda, involve key meeting participants and ask them and yourself two questions:

1. What are the overall desired outcomes of the meeting?
2. What activities need to occur to reach those outcomes?

Identifying Meeting Participants

Who should attend a meeting depends entirely on what is to be accomplished at the meeting. Look at the meeting objectives and then determine three things:

1. Whose participation is desired?
2. Whose participation is needed in order for a decision to be made?
3. Whose consensus is needed in order to move forward after the decisions are made?[1]

Communicate with each of these participants, advising them of the purpose of the meeting and why their attendance is important to the success of the meeting. Follow up the call or other form of communication with a written meeting notice that includes:

- The purpose of the meeting
- Where and when it will be held
- The proposed agenda
- A list of participants
- Whom to contact for questions

CONDUCTING THE SMALL MEETING

If you are involved with conducting the meeting on-site, keep in mind the following essential elements of a successful small meeting:

- Opening the meeting
- Establishing ground rules for the meeting
- Time management
- Establishing the discussion management process

- Evaluation of the meeting process
- Closing the meeting[2]

Opening the Meeting

Always start meetings on time. This shows respect for those who arrived on time and reminds latecomers that the scheduling is serious. Begin by welcoming attendees and thanking them for their time. Review the agenda at the beginning of the meeting and give the participants the opportunity to understand all of the proposed major topics. Make any modifications to the agenda based on participant feedback and then accept the modified agenda. Assign one participant to take notes that will be translated into the meeting minutes. Provide a draft of the minutes to participants shortly after the meeting. It is important that, once the preliminaries of the meeting are established, everyone's role in the meeting is clarified.

Establishing Ground Rules for the Meeting

The basic ingredients for a successful meeting include creating ground rules for the meeting. There are four significant rules that must be followed by all meeting participants:

1. Be an active participant.
2. Focus on the discussion and/or issue at hand.
3. Stay involved in order to maintain momentum.
4. Agree to support the outcomes of the meeting, even those that you did not vote for.[3]

If there are participants who are new to the process, be sure to review each ground rule thoroughly, ensuring not only that the ground rules are posted at all times but that the participants completely understand the need for consensus.

Time Management

Time is valuable to meeting participants. In order to keep the process moving, maintain momentum. Time typically runs out before all of the agenda items have been addressed. Involve participants by asking them to help you keep track of time. If it appears that the planned time for the meeting will be exceeded, ask the group for their ideas for resolving the problem.

Evaluating the Meeting Process

Never wait until the end of the meeting to solicit feedback from participants. Instead, conduct "satisfaction checks" at intervals throughout the meeting.[4] That way, participant feedback can be addressed immediately. Then, at the end of the meeting, reserve five or ten minutes for a more formal evaluation. Have each member rank the meeting using a scale of 1 to 5, with five being the highest ranking. Ask each member to explain his or her ranking. Note any constructive criticisms made during this process and act on them to improve future meetings.

When it is not feasible to conduct the meeting evaluation in person at the close of the meeting, an evaluation form should be created that asks, in the fewest possible questions, the participants' opinions regarding the meeting. Be sure to include questions regarding:

- Speakers
- Food and beverages
- Audiovisual services

- Registration process
- Meeting format and logistics, including room set-up

Online survey tools are a good way to develop the evaluation form and streamline the participants' responses. While brevity is important in order to maximize responses to the request, be sure to include one or two open-ended questions about the participant's overall impression of the meeting and suggestions for improving service at future meetings. If response rates on previous evaluations have been low, consider using some type of prize drawing or incentive to increase the response rate.

Closing the Meeting

Always end the meeting on time and attempt to end it on a positive note. At the meeting's conclusion:

- Review action items, assignments, and due dates.
- Set the time for the next meeting, if any.
- Clarify each person's commitment to attend any follow up events.
- Keep the momentum moving by committing to produce the minutes within seven days.

Small Meeting Site Selection

Matching the venue to the type of meeting is critical to its success. A meeting room with four walls and no windows is not the best choice for meetings where participants are expected to "envision," brainstorm, or otherwise be creative. Certainly, large hotels, convention centers, and other facilities have adequate space to house small meetings, but they may not be the best choice, depending on the type of meeting. Smaller or boutique hotels, unique venues, conference centers that offer complete meeting packages, and airport properties may make more sense for meetings that are upscale, participatory by nature, or require convenience due to time constraints.

In selecting a site for a small meeting, the meeting manager should seek answers to the following questions:

1. Are there other major conventions in town?
2. If so, is it feasible for the meeting manager to piggyback his or her meeting on the larger meeting (assuming that there is some commonality)?

If the answers to these questions make co-locating the small meeting look promising, proceed with making arrangements. On the other hand, if the other meetings in the city do not coincide with the meeting's objectives, another site should be considered (see Chapter 17).

Typically, small meetings are planned with shorter lead time than larger meetings. One of the main reasons for this short time frame is the difficulty in securing meeting space with longer lead times. Hotels are reluctant to book a small piece of business a year or more out in the hopes of securing a larger event. Meeting managers who require a longer lead time should focus the site selection search on smaller properties for which the small meeting will be a "big piece of business."

Meeting managers should consider other alternatives as well. For example, a downtown hotel may offer better rates on weekends and holidays, while a resort property might be ideal during its low season.

Try to match the meeting and its participants to a facility that best suits the needs of the participants and the purpose of the meeting. If meeting participants are flying in from various locations, an airport hotel may be the best choice. If they are driving, a conference hotel near a major highway may be desirable. If the meeting takes the form of a focused, interactive workshop, a facility that lends itself and its location to this type of meeting might be the better choice. If participants are expected to attend a larger meeting, attempt to schedule your meeting just before the start of the other meeting. Although the facility housing the larger event may not be able to accommodate the smaller meeting, check availability at nearby properties.

Depending upon the specifications for the small meeting, a variety of facilities may meet the criteria for the meeting, including conference hotels, suite hotels, conference or convention centers, resorts, universities, restaurants, museums, or other unique venues (see Chapter 11).

Conference Centers

While most of the discussion thus far has focused on hotel facilities, small meetings may find both value and benefit in using a conference center accredited by the International Association of Conference Centers. These venues specialize in small meetings, and offer complete meeting packages that include meeting rooms, standard audiovisual, sleeping rooms, meals, and refreshment breaks. These centers are excellent choices for a variety of small meetings. But they are particularly good options for those meetings that require participants to do a great deal of creative thinking (see Chapter 15).

Alternative or Unique Venues

For some meetings, alternative or unique venues not only offer interesting options but also may serve to increase overall meeting attendance. Unique venues come in all shapes and sizes and include museums, corporate centers, historic properties, and, yes, even aircraft carriers. Transportation to these special venues is much less complicated than it would be with a large group. Catering for small groups off-site may also be less challenging, as many venues have on-site capabilities or recommended caterers. There are many web sites that offer search engines for unique venues, such as http://www.uniquevenues.com.

Restaurants and Private Dining Rooms

Whether it is for the main portion of the small meeting or for an after-hours team-building event, small groups can often be accommodated in private dining areas in many restaurants. Costs can be controlled by ordering from the standard menu or by selecting a menu that is being used by another in-house group. It may be possible to partner with the local convention and visitor's bureau as they can help to identify facilities that may meet your needs and have some flexibility.

SMALL MEETING SITE NEGOTIATIONS

Whether you choose to use one of the smaller meeting facilities or a larger property, the following suggestions are useful in maximizing your negotiating position once you find the right location.

History

Be prepared to provide the facility with a history of the meeting and its attendees. Include:

- The number of years the meeting has been held
- The number of meeting rooms used in past years

- The number of sleeping room nights used in past years
- The average food and beverage consumption expressed in terms of dollars
- Locations where the meeting was held in the past

Attendees

How well do you know your attendees? Understanding the profile of the attendees helps you communicate the value of the meeting to the facility. Answers to the following questions will assist you in offering a composite profile of the meeting's attendees:

- Are the participants decision-makers, and are they likely to bring other business to the facility?
- Are they members of an association community that might consider use of the facility for a future, major conference?
- Are there high-ranking dignitaries or VIPs attending the meeting?
- Are press conferences planned at the facility?

Providing this type of information to the facility managers acquaints them with the potential for additional business and not only helps in negotiations but may also result in better room rates for the meeting's attendees.

Date Flexibility

If there is no specific need to hold the small meeting on specific dates, date flexibility can work to the meeting manager's advantage. The ability to shift arrival and departure patterns of guests for the meeting to the hotel's slowest days can be advantageous as well. The ability to hold the meeting either during the hotel's low season or shoulder season can almost guarantee lower rates. While, typically, the rule of thumb is that the larger the group, the better the rate, if the meeting manager demonstrates that the meeting's date flexibility will fill a gap in the hotel's schedule, lower rates can be negotiated.[5]

Networking and Relationships

There is nothing more valuable to a meeting manager than his or her reputation. Those who build strong relationships with industry suppliers, including hotel sales representatives, will reap the reward of an enhanced ability to negotiate meetings with short lead times.

SMALL MEETING CONTRACTING

There are some contracting issues that are unique to the small meeting. The meeting contract for a small meeting should specify the meeting room assignments and contain a requirement that the meeting manager will be contacted if the hotel would like to change the room assignment. Obviously, if a meeting's sleeping room reservations fall significantly below expected levels, the meeting manager will want to work with the hotel to adjust the meeting room assignments. However, the hotel should not relocate the meeting without the meeting manager's advance knowledge and consent. If a move is agreed upon, the meeting manager may find some room for negotiation on some items, such as free coffee, a cocktail party, or a credit to the master account. Consider including a clause in the contract that speaks to relocating both the meeting space and the room block.

These clauses serve to make the site responsible for honoring confirmed room reservations. It is the meeting manager's responsibility to have a "walk clause" included in the contract. The clause may contain any or all of the following, depending upon your group:

- Transportation to and from lodging within close proximity with rooms of equal or greater value
- Facility to cover the cost of the hotel room until the attendee can return to the original hotel
- Transportation to and from all meeting locations
- Facility to pay for a limited number of long distance calls to family and office each day

Beware of clauses in some meeting contracts or letters of agreement that indicate that the hotel will provide certain services based on average food and beverage revenue. Ensure that no contract details are left open to interpretation. Always ensure that specific numbers and dollar amounts are stated concerning any service provided for the meeting. Read the information carefully and do not hesitate to add items or clauses to the proposed contract or letter of agreement. Reasonable requests or additions are rarely refused (see Chapter 39 and Chapter 40).

MEETING FORMATS

Meeting room configurations should depend upon the goals and objectives, size, and format of the meeting. While presentational or instructional meetings may be arranged in the conventional classroom or theater style, alternative setups may be preferred. Interactive meetings likewise may fare better in a less conventional or traditional meeting format. As population demographics and generations change, so do the needs of participants. Meetings are focused on learner outcomes and learning styles and, consequently, are using alternative meeting formats. Use of open space sessions is becoming more widely accepted, and this set-up is commonly used for smaller meetings.[6]

Provide a detailed event specifications guide (ESG) to the facility as soon as is feasible. Although Chapter 34 covers this topic in detail, it is useful to reiterate some basic information for the small meeting manager. Every ESG should, at a minimum, include:

- Key personnel and other parties with signature authority and their contact information
- Billing instructions
- Participant profiles
- Service requirements (e.g., room temperature, times)
- Any additional information the facility personnel need to know in order to execute the meeting

The main portion of the ESG contains the detailed room set-ups and schedule, audiovisual needs, and food and beverage requirements for the preparation of the facility banquet event orders (BEOs). Use a simple but detailed format (see the template in Chapter 34), understanding that the facility will transfer the information into its own system and subsequently print it in their format. When this occurs, be sure to confirm that the information on the facility's paperwork matches the information that you originally submitted for the meeting. Double-check all of the paperwork you receive from a facility or vendor, as the meeting manager is ultimately responsible for reviewing and approving these documents.

Following the meeting, a post-convention meeting with selected facility staff will allow you to identify both the positive and the negative experiences of the meeting. The dialogue should go both ways, with you giving feedback to the facility, as well as hearing what you could have done sooner or better to help the facility prepare for your meeting.

Put It Into Perspective

The XYZ Association held a retreat for its board of directors. An experienced facilitator is brought in to lead the retreat. At the meeting's conclusion, desired outcomes are forthcoming. Fast forward one year. The Association's chief staff executive is trying, without success, to move the plan forward to achieve the desired outcomes. Constructive suggestions from staff are rejected by the board out of hand. The level of frustration among the stakeholders is high. What went wrong? No one took the pulse of the board members to assure that they (as meeting participants) agreed to support the meeting outcomes and, thus, there was no buy-in and no progress in achieving the desired goals.

FINANCIAL CONSIDERATIONS AND THE VALUE OF THE SMALL MEETING

Many organizations require return on investment (ROI) or return on objectives (ROO) for meetings. An in-depth discussion of ROI is given in Chapter 46. In the context of the small meeting, it is important to remember that when participants (including suppliers) invest financially in a meeting, they will require a return on their investment. If there is no financial consideration, the measurement is of objectives achieved, as opposed to monetary investment returned. However, whatever the meeting's objective, the outcome must be measurable.

In recent years, some organizations have reduced the number of meetings they hold, while others have altered their reporting structures to reassign the meeting manager position to the organization's procurement department. Today's meeting manager, whether in a corporate or an association environment, must assume a more strategic role within the organization and must be able to articulate the value of each meeting. To accomplish this goal, concisely written financial objectives for each meeting must be created to demonstrate such value. These objectives must be SMART, which stands for specific, measurable, achievable, realistic, and timely (see Chapter 2).

The per-person cost for smaller meetings is usually higher than it is for larger conferences, while the lead time for planning will be significantly less. The costs associated with meeting space rental, food and beverage, and audiovisual services will also be proportionately higher per capita for smaller meetings. With smaller meetings, there may be additional costs involved, such as offering participants a buffet luncheon or requesting bar service for the smaller meeting. Be sure to itemize all these additional fees when preparing the meeting budget.

For very small meetings (fewer than 10 people) renting a hotel suite and ordering room service may provide a better solution from a cost standpoint. Convention centers may also have small rooms available for short-term rental.

One way to increase the meeting's ROI is to keep costs accountable and as low as possible. To avoid prepayment of estimated charges, request direct billing or establish a master account. It is important to specify what charges are acceptable, which are not, and who is allowed to sign or authorize charges prior to the meeting and on-site. In some cases, the authorized on-site person may not be the meeting manager. A statement in the contract indicating what is necessary from the facility prior to authorization of payment is appropriate. Once the final itemized billing and other requested information is received, conduct a detailed review of all charges and discuss any questions with the facility immediately. To keep the group's credit history strong, be sure to pay all undisputed charges within the normal billing cycle established.

SUMMARY

Smaller meetings are just as important as larger meetings but with fewer people. All of the skills and knowledge that are employed in managing a large meeting should also be applied in managing a small meeting. However, the budgetary constraints and shorter planning cycle frequently associated with small meetings can present additional challenges to the meeting manager.

Understanding the goals and objectives of the meeting and the desired outcomes for the attendees, building strong relationships with facility managers and suppliers, and being flexible on meeting dates are essential to producing a meeting that is well positioned, well planned, well executed, and considered to be successful by the meeting stakeholders and participants.

REFERENCES

1. Avery, C.M. (August, 2002). Anatomy of a small meeting. Retreived March 31, 2006 from http://meetingsnet.com/religiousconferencemanager/meetings_anatomy_small_meeting/index.html.

2. Ibid.

3. Ibid.

4. Pelletier, S. (December, 2000). Balancing act. Retrieved March 28, 2006 from http://meetingsnet.com/associationmeetings/meetings_balancing_act_8/index.html.

5. Pelletier, S. (December 2000). Scoring a good deal. Retrieved March 15, 2006 from http://meetingsnet.com/associationmeetings/meetings_scoring_good_deal_22/index.html.

6. Doyle, M. (August, 2002). Great expectations for small meetings. *Corporate and incentive travel, 20*(8), p. 3.

KEY TERMS

Agenda	Low season	Shoulder season
Banquet event order (BEO)	Master account	Small meeting
	Open-ended questions	SMART objectives
Complete meeting package	Open space session	Specifications guide
	Post-convention meeting	Time lines
Direct bill	Return on investment (ROI)	
Facilitator		

COMPELLING QUESTIONS FOR CONSIDERATION

1. Why is it so important to not only carefully select the meeting participants for a small meeting but also to get their buy-in to the desired outcomes?

2. Describe a situation where a venue and meeting room would not be well-suited to a particular meeting. Explain why it is not and what could be done to improve it.

3. Why are small meetings able to take better advantage of date flexibility than are their larger counterparts?

4. What constitutes "value" for a small meeting and how is it measured?

CHAPTER 9

COMMITTEES, VOLUNTEERS, AND STAFF: WORKING TOGETHER TO MAKE MEETINGS SUCCESSFUL

Kelly Peacy, CAE
VICE PRESIDENT
STRATEGIC AND ORGANIZATIONAL INITIATIVES
PROFESSIONAL CONVENTION MANAGEMENT ASSOCIATION

LEARNER OUTCOMES

When the reader has completed reading this chapter, he/she should be able to . . .

1 Develop a volunteer program for meeting management and support functions.

2 Utilize a program committee in planning and implementation.

3 Identify the key components of a volunteer policy manual.

4 Determine when it is appropriate to outsource projects and responsibilities.

5 Identify appropriate ways to educate and develop volunteers and staff.

> People come to [work at associations] not realizing that working with volunteers is 80 percent of the job, and 20 percent of it is what you learned in college.[1]
>
> *Thomas McKee*

OVERVIEW

Most meeting managers enhance their teams with volunteers to ensure that all event details and customer service needs are attended to. Volunteers are passionate about the organization, its mission, meeting, or all of the above. They want to be of service and want to feel as if they are making a difference. At the same time, today's busy lifestyle equates to less time that volunteers can provide, and effectively managing the time they do provide to meetings can make all the difference between an inefficient meeting and a successful one that runs like a well-oiled machine.

Traditional volunteer roles in meeting management range from program committee chair to registration assistant to evaluation coordinator, but as today's meetings and conventions evolve, the role of volunteers will also expand into other areas. Couple this fact with a volunteer's limited time availability, and several factors should be considered when creating and managing a volunteer program:

- *Types of volunteers*—Organizations need volunteers with specific competencies; therefore, organizations should blend traditional volunteers with distinctly skilled volunteers.
- *Time*—People have less free time, and the time they do have may not fit the traditional 9-to-5 schedule. More volunteers want short-term commitments with flexible schedules.
- *Motivation*—Organizations need to provide compelling, interesting, and focused work for volunteers. Individuals need a clear sense of organizational purpose, mission, and goals to be certain their commitments are well-focused.
- *Changes in the population*—These changes demand an increased sensitivity to diversity.
- *How people work*—The trends in alternative work schedules, telecommuting, and working in home offices impact how to find, manage, and reward volunteers.
- *Technology*—From recruiting volunteers via the Internet to using web-based collaboration and project management tools, technology is changing how organizations communicate and conduct business with volunteers.

In today's climate, volunteers expect to be included in meaningful work that is clearly focused on the organization's mission. Organizations should make every attempt to include volunteers in program work; however, volunteer assistance should enhance, not replace, paid staff work. Volunteers give staff more time in their work schedule to add a strategic dimension to their current job responsibilities. In an era when organizations are focusing on operational efficiency, volunteers can play a vital role in achieving strategic goals.

This chapter will address how to establish and build a strong volunteer base in support of operating successful events and meetings. Strategies for the development of educational and support environments for effective volunteers will also be presented.

ESTABLISHING THE VOLUNTEER PROGRAM

Establishing and managing a volunteer program is well worth the investment of organizational resources. Volunteers provide organizations with:

- Delivery of services at reduced costs
- Access to additional expertise
- Better contact with the community
- Better assistance to attendees and customers

However, managing volunteers also has its challenges, such as:

- Lack of control and reliability of volunteers
- Time demands for volunteer supervision
- Potential negative impact on paid jobs
- Difficulties in recruiting enough qualified volunteers

Defining the Volunteer Program and Establishing the Recruitment Plan

To ensure that the potential volunteer's first impression of the organization is positive, staff must be trained and a volunteer management system must be in place *before* any recruitment effort is made. Staff should be well-versed in the major functions of the meeting as well as in the various roles of the volunteers, including what the volunteers' specific responsibilities are and how they may or may not differ from those of staff.

When developing a volunteer program for meetings, the following should be taken into consideration:

- Objectives for the volunteer program. Why will the organization recruit volunteers and what will constitute a successful volunteer program? Ensure that top management has shown support for volunteer placements and initiatives.
- A volunteer needs analysis, given the parameters of the meeting or event. What types of volunteer positions will be needed? Again, be sure to enhance current staffing instead of replace paid staff work. What is the best use of paid staff's time? Where can volunteers be used in order to give staff more time in their work schedules? How long will the volunteers' assignments be?
- A budget for the volunteer program. Keep in mind any reimbursable expenses incurred by volunteers, volunteer communications and materials, staff time needed to supervise volunteers, and volunteer recognition.
- A volunteer policy manual. More about this later.
- The necessary skills for the defined volunteer positions—clerical, technical, creative, or managerial? From these skill set requirements, write specific job descriptions for each of the volunteer positions.
- Screening and selection of volunteers. Communicate this process in all recruitment efforts.
- Volunteer recognition—how will volunteers know that the organization appreciates their efforts?
- Volunteer evaluation and minimum standards of performance.

From a volunteer management perspective, it is also important to have the following in place before recruiting:

- Staff is prepared to assist in interviewing, screening, orienting, training, and supervising volunteers
- Volunteer materials have been developed and produced
- There is a place for volunteers to work
- Policies, procedures, and record-keeping systems are in place
- Legal and liability issues pertaining to volunteer involvement have been resolved
- All staff knows how to handle and direct calls from potential volunteers

At this point, create a recruitment communication that clearly defines the organization's mission and event goals, volunteer opportunities, and expectations including position titles, descriptions, and performance expectations. It is important to also include time commitment, financial commitment (if any) and evaluation and recognition programs. Finally, it is important that an organization's constituents are taken into consideration when determining the best way to target the volunteer pool—is it via email, letter, phone call, word of mouth, or a sign-up sheet at an earlier event?

Developing the Volunteer Selection Process

Unless the organization will accept anyone who responds to a call for volunteers, it is likely that some type of screening is being done. However, many organizations need a more structured approach to ensure consistency in the selection process. Once it has been determined who will be selected into the final pool of volunteers, screening and interviewing potential volunteers is similar to an employee recruitment process and should be handled with the same professionalism. Standard interview questions should be appropriate for the position, recruiters should be properly prepared, the scope of work and expectations for performance should be carefully explained, and candidates should have an opportunity to talk about their motivation and qualifications. Evaluating candidates using predetermined criteria will ensure each receives fair consideration.

Selecting a diverse group of volunteers will help to ensure that all of perspectives of the organization's constituents are represented. However, diversity can also create barriers to effective communication. When communicating desired outcomes to volunteers, it is important to take into consideration the various languages, customs and generational differences that may be present. The success of organizations that engage volunteers depends in large part on how different value systems can be incorporated into ongoing programs.[1]

A diverse volunteer group can assist in ensuring that various aspects of the meeting or event are addressed and can help meeting managers plan for various aspects of culture and custom.

Volunteer Policies

One of the first steps in implementing a volunteer management program is to create a volunteer policy manual. The purpose of volunteer policies is to provide guidance and direction to staff and volunteers as they work together in the organization. These policies often match the human resource policies of an organization. Policies should include:

- Material that describes the mission, vision, and goals of the organization and the role played by volunteers
- Descriptions and qualifications for each volunteer position (this should include work to be done in that position, measurable indicators of whether the work was accomplished, and appropriate timelines for accomplishment of the work)
- Volunteers should be included in and have access to memos, materials, and meetings relevant to their work assignments (primary responsibility for ensuring that the volunteer receives such information rests with the direct supervisor of the volunteer or chair of the committee)
- A reimbursement-of-expenses policy to identify specific reimbursement items as well as approval processes
- Evaluation process

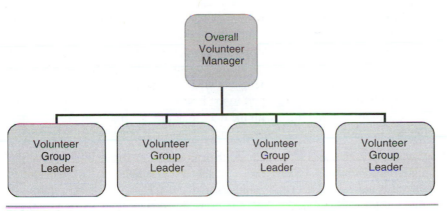

FIGURE 9.1

Volunteer Lines of Communication Reporting to the Meeting Manager

Risk and Liability

Organizations carry insurance to cover their employees in the case of damages, but has the organization considered the implications of damage as a result of a volunteer's action?

Volunteers for nonprofit entities have a line of defense against the threat of personal liability since Congress passed the Volunteer Protection Act of 1997. The act is intended to encourage volunteerism and facilitate volunteer recruiting by reducing the legal liability risks to volunteers. The law provides that volunteers will not be personally liable for their acts or omissions if they are acting within the scope of their responsibility for the organization and the harm is "not caused by willful or criminal misconduct, gross negligence, reckless misconduct, or a conscious, flagrant indifference to the rights or safety of the individual harmed."[2]

The Volunteer Protection Act does not mean that volunteers will be immune from lawsuits nor does it mean that a nonprofit organization will be not be sued for the actions of its volunteers. What is most important is that the organization has insurance that covers both staff and volunteers.

WORKING WITH COMMITTEES

Typical Committee and Task Force Structures

Committees have varied roles and go by various names within an organization, but a majority of the time they are composed of volunteers. They may include standing committees, subcommittees, ad hoc committees, project teams, task forces, panels, advisory groups, and so on. Committee names should accurately reflect their role and scope (see Figure 9.1). Committees typically involved in meeting-related functions include:

- *Standing*—Committee with ongoing responsibility for furthering the organization's interests, programs, and projects. These committees are frequently mentioned in the bylaws of the organization such as nominating, program, and finance. They usually have a chair and may include a board member who acts as a liaison between the committee and the board of directors. They assist the board in its work by examining issues in depth and bringing policy recommendations for board consideration.
- *Ad hoc*—Formed at the time it is needed for a specific reason (also called a task force). After it finishes its task, it disbands. There is a trend toward

Fast Facts

Meeting-Related
Committees

- Standing
- Ad hoc
- Advisory
- Steering
- Executive

using ad hoc committees rather than standing committees so that organizations can better meet the time constraints of their volunteers.

- *Advisory*—Group of people appointed by the board, whose advice is sought on a particular subject. Its members are people with expertise in that area.
- *Steering*—Group with expertise in an area to help guide a specific initiative. It may or may not report to the board of directors.
- *Executive*—Committee with the duty to administer rules and manage the affairs of the organization or meeting.

Many organizations have changed their governance structure to reduce the number of committees. Instead, project teams are assembled based on the areas of interest and expertise of the members and staff. The teams tackle narrowly defined tasks that are often of short duration. This concept can be used in meeting management to put to optimum use the pool of volunteers who can offer a significant amount of time but only for a short duration. For example, program committee responsibilities may be segmented into project teams such as guest programs, fundraising, special events such as a newcomer's orientation, session review, and speaker selection. These components allow volunteers who cannot commit to an entire year of work to take on one project within the committee's focus.

Committee members should be selected on the basis of their dependability, accessibility, and knowledge of the subject matter. The better informed volunteers are about performance expectations, background information, and timelines, the more productive the committee will be.

Program Committees

Program committees are most often charged with responsibility for planning the conference program content. The scope of the committee's responsibilities can vary from one organization to the next depending on staff size and the commitment of the volunteers. Some organizations empower their program committees to negotiate and sign contracts with meeting facilities. This can bring significant risk to an organization; before taking this approach, it is important to understand the implications of a volunteer signing a contract on behalf of an organization. It is also not uncommon for smaller organizations to include the responsibilities of exhibit and sponsorship sales under the program committee.

The program committee typically has the following responsibilities:

- Suggest innovative approaches to enhancing the educational value for attendees.
- Ensure that the content of the conference is in accordance with the strategic goals of the organization.
- Select papers for presentation (if there is a call for papers).
- Identify potential keynote speakers.
- Identify and develop program components according to conference theme.
- Define session topics.
- Review session titles, descriptions, and content, often done by way of web-based abstract management systems.
- Assign appropriate audience level to sessions.
- Recommend potential speakers for sessions.
- Review session objectives.
- Identify session moderators and, in some cases, moderate sessions.
- Work with staff, as needed, to confirm speaker attendance.
- Handle on-site duties as needed—session introducers or monitors, for example.

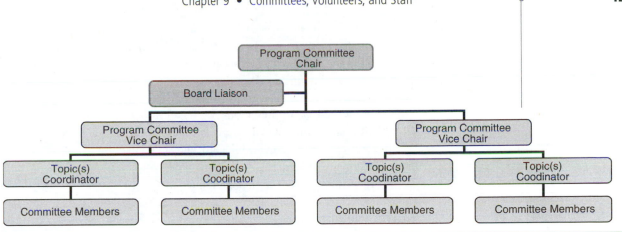

FIGURE 9.2
Program Committee Structure Reporting to a Board of Directors

The program committee chair plays a key role in providing leadership and strategic direction for a conference and can be structured in a number of ways—see Figure 9.2 for an example of a program committee structure.[3] Select a program chair who is familiar with the organization's conference and has previously served on the program committee. Because the chair may also help recruit volunteers, the individual should have an established network of contacts within the organization's constituency. The chair may be responsible for:

- Recruiting and managing volunteer subcommittee chairs for the content areas of the conference
- Contributing to development of conference policies and procedures and managing committee compliance
- Facilitating timely communication with committee members to provide direction and solve problems
- Representing the conference to other organizations, the media, and the public at large
- Chairing all meetings of the program committee
- Attending all conference committee meetings and other meetings as appropriate

Committee Communication

When a committee is formed, members should receive the background materials and resource information they will need to fulfill their duties and make informed decisions. This can be done by compiling a committee notebook or by using a web-based team management tool that allows the group to store and organize electronic files. For example, a program committee notebook may include:

- List of committee members with contact data
- Committee goals and objectives
- Meeting goals and objectives
- History of program structure
- Previous years' promotion pieces
- Evaluation summary and analysis
- Policies regarding remuneration and fees
- Summary report from previous year's program committee chair
- Convention site information
- Estimated attendance and attendance history report

- Meeting budget, or specific information from the budget that is applicable to the committee, such as speaker expenses
- Planning timeline and deadlines
- Restrictions such as meeting room capacities, labor regulations, and audiovisual (A/V) limitations
- Information on ancillary aspects of the meeting, such as satellite programs, guest programs, childcare, and social events
- Information pertaining to continuing education units
- Agenda topics for the first committee meeting

Staff Liaisons

The role of the staff in working with committees is to provide background information and act as a resource for the committee. Staff members may also provide administrative support, such as assisting the chair in the preparation of agendas and other resource material, distributing meeting minutes, and maintaining files and other background material concerning committee activities. During transition periods, staff serves as a vital link in the continuity of the committee's work and provides historical perspective in committee deliberations.

Staff liaisons should have proper training in dealing with committees and volunteers and should be well-versed in the organization's mission, bylaws, and the committee's goals.

LEADERSHIP AND MANAGING VOLUNTEERS

Leading Volunteer Teams

Effective volunteer programs and committees require strong and inspired leadership. Failure to understand the importance of effective volunteer leadership undervalues the contribution volunteers make to the organization. Whether it is paid staff or another volunteer, the challenge of an effective leader is to cultivate the attitudes necessary for success:

- A clear understanding and a strong commitment to the meeting or event's goals and objectives and a desire to see it succeed
- Fairness and the willingness to listen to and involve all volunteers
- Recognition of individual volunteers' potential capabilities rather than formal credentials
- Openness to tapping a variety of volunteers (diversity)

Managing volunteers is like managing employees, in that volunteers need clearly defined jobs, orientation and training, supervision, and recognition for a job well done.[5] Unlike employees, however, the rewards for volunteers are less tangible, and it takes diplomacy and tact to retain and motivate good volunteers.

Volunteer Positions

In thinking about how volunteers might be involved with the meeting, consider the capabilities and limitations of the current staff. Are there types of work that the staff is unable to do? Perhaps they are not skilled in a particular type of work, or they are too skilled for the work and would be better utilized if they could concentrate their efforts in another area. Are there areas in which there is too much work for staff to do alone, and volunteer assistants could extend staff resources? Or are there areas where volunteers would allow the meeting manager to begin work that might not otherwise be accomplished?

Also consider using volunteers in positions of direct assistance to meeting participants, such as very important person (VIP) or speaker escorts. The following jobs are frequently given to volunteers for meetings:

- *Registration assistant*—During registration, volunteers can meet and greet, answer questions, and assist with crowd control.
- *Room monitor*—Educational conferences typically need volunteers to monitor each of the meeting rooms to ensure that the speaker's needs are met and that the attendees have materials needed.
- *Room monitor coordinator*—The coordinator is an experienced volunteer who is familiar with the program and can work closely with staff in developing volunteer schedules and training. This position oversees the meeting room monitors.
- *Hospitality coordinator*—Groups use hospitality suites for many reasons ranging from a check-in location for volunteers to a room where VIPs and speakers assemble. Coordinators meet and greet and provide information about the host city or about the meeting.
- *Meeting evaluations coordinator*—Volunteers can assist with the distribution and collection of all meeting evaluations, including individual session evaluations as well as overall program evaluation.
- *Local committee*—A local or "host" committee is typically comprised of volunteers from the surrounding area who can coordinate and be the information resource for local events, dining, and goings-on. They may also be responsible for planning social events, promoting the meeting through local media channels, and obtaining area sponsors and exhibits.

No matter how big or how small the job performed by a volunteer, the volunteers should enhance staff competency rather than challenge it. Educate staff about the skills volunteers have; recruit skilled volunteers for specific jobs—don't just recruit "warm bodies"; value volunteers enough to treat them like "customers."

Training Volunteers

Volunteer job descriptions should delineate responsibilities, time frames, qualifications, benefits, decision-making authority, accountability, and evaluation criteria. A written job description should be part of the orientation packet volunteers receive upon joining the organization. An orientation and training session should be scheduled to provide new volunteers with the information, tools, and resources that they need to be effective. A good orientation program includes a description and history of the organization, an overview of the conference.

The training session should be developed and implemented for all volunteers based on the individual job descriptions. For ease of training, volunteers with similar responsibilities, work locations or assignments can often attend the same training session. Training can be done on-site or prior to the event depending on the responsibility, but before work begins, volunteers need to know how they are expected to perform their duties.

In volunteer training sessions, be sure to cover:

- A brief education on the attendee, the schedule of events and what to expect
- Process and procedures of the job
- Volunteer supervisors and who to go to with questions and the best way to handle problems
- The event's emergency plan and procedures
- Volunteer shifts—start and end times

Evaluation and Recognition

Volunteers need feedback on their performance, and the organization will need to assess the effectiveness of its volunteer training and supervision. A well-rounded evaluation process includes assessment by each of the stakeholders, including staff, volunteers, and meeting participants. Additionally, there should be a method for volunteers to evaluate their experience as it relates to their goals for volunteering with the organization.

Volunteer recognition is the means for staff and the organization to demonstrate appreciation for the time and commitment of the volunteer. How volunteers are recognized can vary widely, from a one-to-one thank you to a volunteer recognition special event. Recognition should be designed to motivate volunteers. It can take a variety of forms, for example:

- Give regular feedback
- Match volunteers with jobs appropriate to their skills and expertise
- Treat volunteers as part of the overall organization team
- Find ways to show them and others that their accomplishments have been noticed
- Listen and act on their ideas and suggestions
- Organize a special event to recognize volunteers

Recognition and appreciation of volunteers is something that should not be overlooked. What motivates volunteers differs from one person to the next, but all like to feel included, involved, and *appreciated*. Simple handwritten thank you notes, a personal phone call or an inexpensive token gift help to express appreciation. Volunteers can be *recognized*, however, in a number of ways including on-site signage, special volunteer apparel or ribbons, listings in on-site publications or newsletters if available, or through various leadership speaking opportunities at the event.

STAFF TEAMS AND STAFF SUPERVISION OF VOLUNTEERS

Staff Teams

One way an organization can manage its staff prior to and during a meeting or event is to divide it into teams with each one accountable for the delivery and execution of certain program functions. For example, the information technology (IT) staff of an organization would be the staff team responsible for all computer networking and equipment at the meeting. The membership team may be responsible for on-site member service at the registration desk and other membership related tasks. Each team may have a team leader who is responsible for ensuring that staff is fulfilling their assignments, and the number and size of each team will depend on the organization and the complexity event. Some staff teams

Put It Into Practice

Your meeting or convention may have more breakout sessions than you have staff to monitor them. This is where volunteer assistance can be invaluable. The Professional Convention Management Association (PCMA) uses volunteer room monitors—up to 20 at a time—to pass out handouts and collect evaluations, monitor any A/V challenges, as well report any other issues that could arise in a session. The overall goal is to deliver an exceptional learning environment to the attendee, and volunteers help ensure that happens.

may also expand to include volunteers. Staff and volunteer teams allow smaller groups of people to focus intensively on one particular area of a meeting or event. When all areas of an event are covered by a staff or volunteer team, there is not only clear accountability, but the opportunity for the group to focus on the work that it does best.

Staff Supervision of Volunteers

Volunteers may be used in all programs and activities of an organization and serve at all levels of skill and decision-making. However, volunteers should not displace paid employees from their positions. Productive use of volunteers requires staff involvement in identifying productive and creative volunteer roles, recruiting suitable volunteers, and tracking and evaluating the contribution of the volunteers to the organization.

Depending on the staff size and their involvement in the organization's meetings, there may be times when volunteers also supervise other volunteers. This should only be done if a supervising volunteer is under the direct supervision of a paid staff member.

Staff supervising volunteers should be responsible for regular communication with the volunteers. Technology has made this easy through tools ranging from email group messaging to web-based team collaboration tools. Use the organization's web site to make resource information available to volunteers. Have open discussions and shared files capability so that volunteers can communicate easily with each other. Post training, orientation material, newsletters, and volunteer schedules online, or send a periodic email newsletter to volunteers updating them on the progress of meeting preparations.

TEMPORARY PERSONNEL

Typical Uses of Temporary Personnel

To reduce staff travel costs, organizations may hire local personnel to handle a number of on-site responsibilities. Local residents can be a valuable resource for assisting attendees with restaurant recommendations and local directions. Temporary personnel may be hired through the local convention and visitors bureau, temporary personnel agencies, and destination management companies to handle a variety of responsibilities.

Some questions to consider when using temporary personnel:

- If temporary personnel will be using computers on-site, will they have the basic computer skills necessary to perform the job?
- Are temporary personnel familiar with the conference program and the types attendees expected?
- Are temporary personnel bonded? This is critical for temporary personnel working with money.

Identify the specific responsibilities within each area for which local personnel will be hired. Determine what skills are required, and write a job description for each post that needs to be filled. Develop a schedule of required dates and hours for each post, and add time for orientation. Arrange for a sufficient number of individuals to provide relief during breaks and lunch periods.

Discuss job descriptions and the overall schedule with the agency providing the personnel. Take into consideration the following as well.

- Determine the hourly rate for each post and the minimum number of hours for which an employee must be paid.

Fast Facts

Tasks for Temporary Personnel

- Registration personnel, typists, and cashiers
- Ticket sales
- Information and message center clerks
- Badge checkers and meeting room monitors
- Receptionists
- Exhibitor product demonstrators
- Poll-takers and evaluation form distributors
- Computer-trained personnel

- Ask about overtime rates and rates for the weekend, early morning, and late evening.
- What expenses should be expected? Some agencies ask that parking fees be reimbursed, and others add a dinner allowance for evening work.
- Inquire about the extent of supervision that is provided by the company, and find out how a responsible individual may be contacted over the weekend and before and after regular business hours in case of a problem.
- Because it is sometimes difficult to anticipate on-site needs accurately, ask how long it will take to obtain an additional person, and how much notice must be given if an individual will not be needed.
- Also, confirm insurance coverage by the agency for each temporary employee.

Send copies of job descriptions and the daily schedule to the selected agency in sufficient quantity and in time for advance distribution to hired personnel. Include with the instructions the name of the individual to whom each employee is to report, the exact location, and a telephone number to use in case of last-minute changes.

Schedule orientation and training time for temporary personnel well in advance of the time their duties are to begin. Conference attendees should not notice a difference in service because the temporary personnel are providing service; adequate training is paramount.

Evaluating Temporary Personnel

It is important to evaluate the performance and on-site management of temporary personnel so that the organization can make improvements at subsequent events. Create an evaluation form for the personnel agency and the temporary personnel to evaluate their experience working with the group. Require the personnel agency to provide a post-conference report detailing the number of temps used, how many hours they worked, and in what areas (registration, room monitoring, etc.). Ask the personnel agency to make suggestions regarding where additional support may have been needed and areas where temp hours could have been reduced. The report should also detail the temporary support hours added once the group is on-site.

Outsourcing

Outsourcing is the tool that allows organizations to focus on their core competencies. As organizations outsource activities that are non-core, it frees management time and resources to focus on essential activities. With the benefit of additional staff time and resources, the core competencies are reinforced and enhanced, keeping the organization focused on where it adds the most value to its stakeholders.

The pressures of downsizing has led management to review whether all activities that have traditionally been done in-house should stay there, and whether hiring additional staff is the right step whenever a new program is undertaken. For example, is it cost-effective for an organization to have a full-time meeting manager to handle one large convention or trade show a year plus a few relatively routine board and committee meetings? Or could it outsource management of the convention, while other staff can handle the smaller meetings? If meetings are a core service to the organization's customers, then outsourcing their management may not be an option.

Put It Into Perspective

An association planner may have a somewhat easier time recruiting volunteers for a meeting or event as there is generally a membership base pool to draw from—people who are already engaged and have invested in the organization at some level. Another plus is that volunteers from the association generally have an advantage in that they already understand the attendee and event. Often, the easiest way to recruit volunteers at an association meeting is to just ask them.

While corporate and government planners may have a more difficult time recruiting volunteers from within their own organizations, colleges and universities with meetings management programs can be great resources for volunteers. Students are usually very eager to develop "hands on" and "behind the scenes" experience in meetings management.

Whatever function is chosen to be outsourced, it is important to negotiate an agreement that clearly defines services, agreed cost, and a level of performance. The following components should be included in the agreement:

- *Service specification*—Spell out specific and measurable terms for the services required, how they will be delivered, and the duration of the agreement.
- *Service levels*—Specify performance expectations for each of the services that will be provided.
- *Roles and responsibilities*—Identify the obligations of the outsourcer and the boundaries of responsibilities.
- *Prices, payment, and duration*—State the pricing and payment policy for services delivered, including the basis of charging for any additional requirements such as travel, parking, and meals.
- *Agreement administration*—Define how the agreement will be managed and administered, including when payments are due and what types of reports are required from the outsourcer.

If the organization chooses to outsource meeting management or related support services, there should be a system in place for monitoring the activities of the outsource provider and ensuring the duties are performed to meet the organization's expectations.

SUMMARY

A volunteer program for successful meetings consists of the identification of available volunteer positions and the goals for each, as well as a budget, training procedures, policies and identified ways to motivate and recognize volunteers. Volunteer policy manuals provide guidance to staff and volunteers as they work together. Key components of a volunteer policy manual include material that describes the mission, vision and goals for the meeting, descriptions and qualifications for each volunteer position, lines of communication, standard operating procedures for volunteers, reimbursement policies, and evaluation procedures. If the organization charges a program committee with the task of planning and implementing the program content, appoint a qualified chair who can provide the leadership and strategic vision necessary to make the event a success. The chair must be intimately familiar with the organization, connected to the professional community it serves, and able to manage the diverse group of professionals who volunteer to serve on the committee.

Outsourcing projects and responsibilities may allow an organization's staff to focus on core activities. For example, is it cost-effective for an organization to have a full-time meeting manager to handle one large convention or trade show a year plus a few relatively routine board and committee meetings? Or could it outsource management of the convention, while other staff can handle the smaller meetings? If meetings are a core service to the organization's customers, then outsourcing their management may not be an option.

The training session should be developed and implemented for all volunteers based on the individual job descriptions. For ease of training, volunteers with similar responsibilities, work locations or assignments can often attend the same training session. Training can be done on-site or prior to the event depending on the responsibility, but before work begins, volunteers need to know how they are expected to perform their duties. Volunteers can bring the organization closer to their constituency and can help to the meeting manager become more successful.

REFERENCES

1. Rodriguez, S. (1997). Diversity and volunteerism: Deriving advantage from differences. *Journal of volunteer administration*, 15(3), p. 23–29.

2. *Volunteer Protection Act of 1997*, Public Law 105–19, 105th Cong. 1st Sess., Section 4, Limitation on Liability for Volunteers, (a)(3).

3. Lynch, R., & McCurley, S. (1998). *Essential volunteer management* (2nd ed). Downers Grove, IL: Heritage Arts Press.

KEY TERMS

Ad hoc committee	Program committee	Volunteer policies manual
Advisory board	Standing committee	Volunteer protection act
Committee notebook	Steering committee	Volunteer training session
Diversity	Temporary meeting	Volunteer recognition
Executive committee	personnel	

COMPELLING QUESTIONS FOR CONSIDERATION

1. How can volunteers help ensure a successful meeting?

2. What trends are changing the way organizations recruit and engage volunteers?

3. Discuss the qualifications and responsibilities of a program committee chair.

4. What types of attitudes do successful volunteer leaders strive to cultivate?

5. What are some of the considerations in developing an effective volunteer management program?

6. Discuss ways organizations can use technology to communicate with volunteers.

7. If you outsource a component of your meeting, will your job be in jeopardy? Why or why not?

CHAPTER 10

TECHNOLOGY TOOLBOX FOR MEETING MANAGERS

James Spellos, CMP
PRESIDENT
MEETING U.

LEARNER OUTCOMES

When the reader has completed reading this chapter, he/she should be able to . . .

1 Identify technology tools that can be implemented to support the goals of the meetings.

2 Assess the application of new technologies' impact on an organization's meetings.

3 Integrate new technologies into a meeting that provides value-added potential.

4 Describe how to select a technology vendor for their work integration.

5 Identify critical new technologies and terminology that will impact future work applications.

> Any sufficiently advanced technology
> is indistinguishable from magic.
>
> *Arthur C. Clarke*

OVERVIEW

It is frequently stated that 80% of the technology that we are going to use 5 years from now has yet to be invented. This statement is justification for many meeting managers to not even bother learning about current technologies. The inference is that they will be out of date before they use them.

However, meeting managers like any business professionals, do not have the luxury of ignoring the technological advances occurring on a daily basis. Their bosses want them to find ways to reduce planning time and save money (which properly used technology can do). Meeting attendees want organizations to provide the services which they have come to expect back at their office or at other meetings. And the hotels are looking to the meeting managers (and, naturally, their attendees) to define which technologies are critical to embrace and implement.

The extent of available technologies is enormous. From desktop to web-based, from virtual gatherings to enhancing face-to-face meetings, the meeting manager's approach to technology needs to resemble their knowledge base on the myriad of tasks they manage. The meeting manager needs to understand the information well enough to know whether it will enhance the needs of their organization and their attendees.

Only one fact about technology is stable—it is constantly changing.

DESKTOP APPLICATIONS

Much to the chagrin of many industry software developers, the Microsoft Office suite is still the product used by most to manage their event. From the intuitiveness of Excel, to the sophistication and customization of Access, managing lists, creating résumés and banquet event order (BEOs), printing name badges and tent cards, and almost any task they need can be accomplished by this software suite. Yet still, these products are not always the best ones to manage certain aspects of an event.

APEX and The OfficeReady Professional

The OfficeReady Professional templates work with Microsoft Office products. These templates were created by the Convention Industry Council, through the Accepted Practices and Exchange (APEX) initiative.[1] Beginning in 2001, APEX started working on seven key areas as to how we do business and exchange information. The seven key areas defined by APEX include:

- Terminology
- History/Post-Event Reports
- Résumés and Word Orders
- Requests for Proposals (RFPs)
- Meeting and Site Profiles
- Housing and Registration
- Contracts

The technology component of this initiative is being driven by the APEX Technology Advisory Council (TAC) and has prepared the OfficeReady Professional templates. These templates interface with Word, Excel, and Power Point to attempt to create standards in the processing and distribution of hospitality industry documents. The resulting toolkit should save significant time.

Greatly assisting the APEX technology process is the development and more widespread usage of eXtensible Markup Language (XML). This facilitates the

Put It Into Practice

For many years, meeting managers have used their computer desktop tools to assist them with standard industry tasks such as registration and housing block management. As computer software became more functional in the 1990s, specialty applications were designed to not only improve how these tasks were handled, but to also help automate tasks such as the conference résumé and the site selection process. With more robust options available, today's meeting manager has a great number of technology options to help with their pre-planning and industry communications, but also to use technology to enrich the attendees experience on-site.

technology communication process by using a web-based language that can be easily user-specified (as well as industry specified). Unlike HTML (Hypertext Markup Language), XML elements are sufficiently flexible to allow users to more easily interface with data on the web, such as how an online registration database can interface with the company's own database.

Office Suite

For many planning professionals, the Microsoft Office suite is the most utilized desktop software. Combining database, spreadsheet, and word processing, the software is the choice for many professionals to do all of their tasks, from registration and housing lists, to conference budgets, to name badges and name tents. The solution is inexpensive (as it does not require an additional investment), and is more user friendly (since there is a great deal of familiarity with the products already).

A host of companies provide streamlined databases to aid the meeting manager in managing registration and housing. If this task requires an online registration component, the meeting manager needs to be certain that the product they select can seamlessly interface with a database product, such as Access or Excel in the Office suite. Otherwise, the meeting manager may be forced to re-enter information, as well as remove any system duplications, tasks that require extra time as well as creating a higher possibility of error.

ASP SOLUTIONS & WEB-BASED APPLICATIONS

An Application Service Provider (ASP) is a web-based service provider. In the technology world, the first larger scale ASP was Microsoft's Hotmail. By definition, an ASP allows the user to have full functionality of a service (such as email), without having to install any software. For many years now, rumors continue to surface that Microsoft one day plans on providing their Office suite solely as an ASP. Without a large majority of businesses and individuals having high speed bandwidth, that option has not yet become a reality.

Web-based applications are the preferred technology platform for marketing and promotion; registration, housing and travel management (frequently referred to as Attendee Management); and market surveys. The ability to access and process data through a standard web browser, in real time, is a fundamental benefit that web-based applications have over stand-alone software. Well-defined and integrated applications can greatly reduce cost and workflow.

The labor savings from web-based meeting management, online registration, and integrated marketing can have a tremendous effect on a meeting's profitability, especially meetings and conferences of a larger scale.

Adopting a web-based solution requires careful assessment of your computing needs as well as an understanding of your attendees' computing habits and comfort level. Issues of privacy of information and security are tantamount to address and implement to ensure a successful web-based process. Some of the questions to ask include:[2]

- Do the prospective attendees have Internet access? Are they receptive to entering their data online when registering for an event, including payment and credit card information?
- What happens if a system crashes during meeting registration?
- How will a web-based solution integrate with your existing system?
- What additional costs are involved to customize or integrate the system? This should include customized reporting functionality.
- What happens to your data if the vendor goes out of business?
- Who owns the data?

Enterprise-Wide Solutions

One of the challenges in large organizations is that there are many decentralized users of meeting management tools. With an enterprise-wide solution, all users can be connected via the company's Intranet, share the same data, and have access to commonly used applications.

Enterprise-wide solutions make value chain management possible. They are either web-based or client-server based solutions, depending on the product. Through value chain management, companies, their vendors, and downstream users can share the data they need to do their part of a process. In the meetings industry, this phenomenon is evident in applications that enable meeting managers, attendees, exhibitors, service contractors, and facility managers to access the event data they need to participate in or service an event.

The benefit of an enterprise-wide solution is that it enables an organization to track and analyze the cumulative dollars spent on meeting services across the organization. Armed with this data, the organization has tremendous buying power, which they can leverage in negotiations with vendors.

Enterprise-wide solutions are not only for attendee management processes. Critical planning functionality, such as understanding how many sleeping rooms a company has booked within its organization, are areas where, for the right organization, an enterprise-wide solution can provide significant savings. This holds true, as well, for other scalable purchases such as audiovisual and ground transportation.

Enterprise-wide solutions also lower the cost of technology support and management, since all users run the same solution throughout the organization. This optimizes the investment in training and support costs.

Selecting a Vendor

The following items should be considered when selecting a vendor for a software application or web-based service:

- Do they support the industry? Are they members of primary organizations?
- Number of employees?
- Years in business?
- What are the training options? Is it with their system or your converted system? Cost of training?
- Number of active users?
- Can they provide at least three references who match your meeting profile?

- How do they handle system upgrades? Are they included in the purchase price? How do they affect any customization?
- What is the technical support policy and how is support charged? Hours of availability?
- Is the application developed in-house or do they use outside services?
- Do they use or license any third-party vendors? If so, how are you protected?

If you are considering an ASP, ask the following additional questions:

- How do they handle security data?
- Do they monitor downtime from remote regions of the country?
- How is your data and access to the system protected from theft, viruses, fire and other disasters?
- How often and where is your data backed up?
- How are financial and personal data protected?
- Where are credit card, employee ID, and social security numbers stored, and with what level of encryption?
- Do they have an errors and omissions insurance policy with adequate coverage?
- Can the application work with your legacy system, if needed? (Make certain this is clearly addressed by those with technical knowledge of both systems.)

In addition to these questions, carefully check the service contract. Review pricing, exit strategies, and protections in case of downtime during your peak registration period.

ONLINE MEETINGS

Another web-based tool is to hold part or all of a meeting online. Using services that are widely available (and relatively inexpensive), meeting managers can save time and money by having some of their meetings virtually held (also see the note later about online exhibit tools).

However, there are drawbacks to online meetings. First, it does not, and possibly will never, replace the need for people to physically meet face-to-face. For meetings where networking is a critical component of the success of the event, online meetings rarely meet that goal.

Online meetings also work best in meetings of shorter duration (a few hours maximum). An excellent example of a successful type of online meeting would be a committee meeting, where attendees need to meet (and would have difficulty making the time to meet face-to-face) to discuss specific agenda items.

An understanding of the demographics of your group is also in order to hold successful online meetings. Younger generations, more accustomed to working on the computer, feel more comfortable holding a meeting online than folks who did not grow up with computers. While this is a general assumption, it is important to understand your group well enough to identify if online meetings can be a successful component of their meeting strategy.

WEB SITES AS MARKETING TOOLS

The most useful application of the web site within our industry is the marketing brochure approach. In the *2005 State of the Industry Report*, only 68.6% of all meeting managers used the web in the past 12 months to promote meetings and events.[3] While still not 100% used, the web site is the most cost-effective way to market your meeting and communicate with attendees. The various web-based communication options and tools will be discussed later in this chapter.

All of the information on a meeting web site should be geared toward building interest and excitement about the event and enticing prospects to participate, while providing a clear, easy to navigate interface. Meeting web sites should include, at the very least, the following components:

- The 5 Ws about the meeting
  - Who are the attendees
  - What is the meeting objective
  - Where is the meeting location
  - When is the meeting taking place
  - Why should this meeting occur
- Frequently updated content about the meeting and organization
- Highly visible registration button or hyperlink
- Links to sites of interest and use for visiting attendees (link to meeting destination CVB is always a great link to include)
- Straightforward, simple navigation around the site
- Methods of providing communication between attendee and meeting management

Attendance Promotion

The greatest trap in producing a meeting web site is to initially establish content, and then not update it at all. Unlike the traditional printed brochure, the web is a dynamic marketing tool. Groups who do not frequently update their content provide a reason for individuals not to return to the web site, which can lead to reduced numbers of attendees at the conference.

Many industry solution providers now also provide the meeting manager with the templates to create their own web site, if the option is not viable from within the organization. These templates can be branded with the company's look and feel, so that without any programming knowledge, a meeting manager can establish a professional-looking web site in a short amount of time.

E-marketing campaigns can have tremendous impact, linking critical news from the email blast to information on the meeting web site. However, meeting marketers need to be sensitive to the volume of junk email that most people receive. Providing useful content is the most important tool the e-marketer has to ensure that their e-blast is not relegated to the spam or junk email folder.

Online Registration

For most groups, especially those meetings where the attendee must attend (as opposed to having a choice to attend), an online registration component is critical. The amount it is used is clearly dictated by the demographics of your potential attendee. Like almost every other task in this industry, understanding your group is critical in this regard.

Many meeting managers use third-party online registration/attendee management ASPs to handle that portion of the event. Some larger organizations build their own online registration functions, which better integrate into their own system.

Processing registrations online can have tremendous advantages and create possible cost savings for an organization. Accuracy of information can and should be an immediate benefit. When interfaced successfully with an organization's central database, the organization reduces the data redundancies and typos often encountered in traditional practices.

Costs for implementing online registration vary widely, depending on whether the organization develops an in-house solution or purchases a web-based solution from an ASP. Web-based solutions frequently include online registration as one of several modules, and there is often an initial licensing fee that provides access to design templates and support. In addition to the licensing fee, there may be charges for customization, as well as a fee per transaction for each registrant. It is important to clarify what defines a transaction. For example, does a registration transaction fee allow multiple changes to a person's record, or is a charge assessed each time the record is modified?

Before implementing an online registration solution, be sure to understand the registration patterns of your attendees. When reviewing past data, look for the total number of registrations, total number of record changes, total number of deletions, and total number of those paying by credit card. In addition, gather any labor costs charged back to the registration process and calculate a per-attendee labor cost. Armed with this type of history, you can project an estimated cost for handling registrations. There are other cost savings as well as potential expenses to implementing an online solution, so be certain to identify the major costs and savings when calculating cost comparisons.

The meeting manager should be aware that web-based online registration data frequently needs to be integrated into a desktop database system. The meeting manager needs to be certain that the data from the online, ASP service can seamlessly be mapped and integrated into their own database. If the data does not go into the proper fields, then the amount of time and cost for handling this process can increase astronomically. Unfortunately, these issues frequently become best understood only after the first meeting is managed utilizing both systems.

Using an online registration system entails certain risks, including the possibility of stolen information or identity theft crimes. Data can be compromised where personal information is stored if proper security measures are not followed. As a safeguard, clearly identify the ramifications should a security breach occur. Security protocols should become a part of the contract for services between the organization and the application vendor.

Exhibit Sales

Applications exist for virtually all elements of trade show management, including exhibitor and vendor management, floor plan design, booth sales, electronic brochure distribution (including but not limited to exhibitor prospectus and exhibitor service kits), on-site communications, lead retrieval systems, and reporting and analysis. Virtual trade shows, creating expanded sales and purchasing opportunities for your vendors, can extend the event to become year-round.

Implementing an online component to a trade show can increase show revenue and promote and extend the life of the trade show. An online booth provides year-round visibility to sponsors and exhibitors, as well as assisting in the promotion of the physical show. The use of streaming media can allow vendors to conduct online product demos, present live testimonials or simulcast directly to their audience.

Beyond generating exhibit sales, there are many sponsorship opportunities available when conducting a virtual show. Revenue can be generated from banner advertising, booth packages offering varied degrees of physical and virtual exposure, and marketing affinity programs that promote services or serve as an extended distribution channel for e-newsletters.

Technology can help integrate information provided at registration with the needs and wants of the exhibiting companies. Lead retrieval has become a two-way process. Traditional lead retrieval systems allow the exhibitor to scan and capture information from the attendee's badge. This can be done using bar codes, magnetic stripes, and Radio Frequency Identification tags (RFID). Additionally, lead retrieval systems have morphed into a reverse lead retrieval process, where the attendee, using a hand-held scanning device given to them at registration, can scan information at the exhibitor's booth, then download the information at designated stations with the appropriate call to action.

PORTALS AND ONLINE SEARCHING

Meeting industry portals are web sites designed to be the source for your information needs. It is worth the time to register for these resources.[5] A portal can help with site selection, submission of requests for proposals (RFPs), job searches, researching best practices, and staying up-to-date on industry news.

Using industry wide site selection search engines (which include search options from convention and visitors bureaus (CVB) and national sales office web sites) can save enormous amounts of time when looking for a meeting venue. You can filter searches using criteria such as destination, climate, proximity to attractions, distance to airports, number of sleeping rooms and size of meeting space, among other options. When you select a facility from the list, you are presented with a fact sheet containing information the facility has posted, which can include rate information, room capacities, floor plans, and photos or other multimedia presentations. Once completed, RFPs can be sent to a single property, multiple properties within a city or around the world, national sales offices and/or CVBs. Response time is typically 48 hours or less.

Additionally, industry portals can also help check hot dates and rates, as well as various services within the selected city. A number of portals provide educational content, and some provide a chat or listserv functionality for industry professionals to gather or provide information for others.

Standard Specification Formats

Submitting an online RFP requires you to supply the core information about your meeting and organization. Additionally, the APEX initiative is also addressing the need for standardization in the preparation of RFPs. However the RFP is prepared, the specifications should include:

- Required decision date
- Preferred and possible alternative meeting dates
- Room block requirements with arrival and departure dates, and number and type of sleeping rooms
- Event schedule, identifying the size, times, and setup requirements
- Basic catering needs
- Meeting history, where available

Facilities typically rate RFPs using yield management (a revenue management process), which enables them to estimate the meeting's ability to generate revenue for the facility. If the meeting makes good business sense, then the sales office can review date patterns and room availability. Sales offices will factor in the history of the meeting along with the potential revenues from catering and other areas, as well as the total space required and the amount of setup time. Generally, they will determine the maximum revenue to be generated from the meeting, so it is essential that your RFP reflect the value of your meeting to the facility.

Online and Reverse Auctions

Online auctions, also called open bidding, allow the meeting specifications to be bid upon by facilities. The meeting manager submits the meeting criteria to the site, where the provider will identify pre-qualified facilities, CVBs, or other providers based on the specs, and then schedule a bidding time online or in real time. During the bidding process, you can negotiate a number of previously determined variables with the qualified facilities. The end result is that a decision on a meeting venue can be made in a short amount of time.

In a reverse online auction, a facility can post available dates and potential buyers of the space bid on the business. To participate in a reverse auction, you need to be well informed about prevailing rates, the facility, and the destination to be certain that your meeting specifications can be met.

COMMUNICATION TOOLS

Recently, a technology publication blared on its front cover the question, "Is Email Dead?" The cover created some controversy, and generated a great deal of discussion in chat rooms. However, the premise may not be so far fetched. Consider the following: One spam watchdog group, Mail-Filters.com, indicated that the percentage of spam email has increased to as much as 93% in January 2005.[6] In a generation, email has gone from being the great hope of business communications to the standard bearer to nearly becoming a time-consuming burden.

What happened? Once email accounts proliferated among business professionals and consumers, marketers realized that email was the cheapest and easiest way to sell their products. While email is still a communications tool used widely, a large number of other communication tools have become available to the meeting manager to facilitate the way they and their attendees communicate.

Email

Email is the lifeblood of most corporate communications. However, with the large amount of spam, as well as the proliferation of viruses and other email-driven maladies, the meeting manager needs to reconsider how they "use or do not use" email in their meeting communications.

Just a few years ago, it was thought that the best way to communicate and market your meeting was to send frequent email announcements, updates and information. However, it is becoming clear that recipients do not like receiving the constant bombardment of information. In fact, email programs provide the user the ability to establish blacklists that can block anyone they wish. While this is used often to help prevent viruses from reaching your computer, it also allows the recipient to stop the flow of large amounts of marketing information from a given source.

To best utilize email as a marketing tool (and one of its main advantages is the very low cost of sending large numbers of emails), the sender must make sure that the information they send is pertinent to the recipient. Providing content (as is the case with many successful e-letters) in a non-selling environment is a great method to ensure that communication from the sender is not blacklisted. Even great content can be compromised if the sender uses email as a daily communication tool with their audience. Judicious use of email is the meeting manager's best strategy.

Providing email access at an event is a very popular service, becoming part of the event's message center. These email kiosks are known to be "sticky" services, keeping people in the area of the event, as opposed to having them go to their guest rooms or back to their offices to keep up with their email messages. Naturally, there are costs involved in setting up such an infrastructure at an event, including but not limited to the rental of computers, establishment of high speed connectivity, networking of terminals, as well as management of the service on-site.

Antivirus Issues

A few words about email viruses are critical in any discussion about email. Everybody needs an active antivirus program. However, in a corporate environment, this decision should be made by the information technology (IT) professionals. The meeting manager independently installing their preferred antivirus program runs a significant risk of crashing their computer, as it is well known that antivirus programs do not interface well with one another. However, the independent meeting manager, or those folks who do not work off a corporate technology infrastructure, must be sure to have an antivirus program running, with automatic updates turned on to ensure the latest definitions are downloaded to their computer.

Viruses tend to come in as attachments to emails. Even if a sophisticated antivirus strategy is in place, it is critical that the meeting manager is aware of email that looks suspicious. It is not sufficient to just look at the "to" line of an email to determine the safety of an email message. "Spoofing" is a technique where people are able to masquerade as someone else, even using a friends or colleagues email address in the "to" line.

Here are a few points to consider when trying to prevent a computer from virus infection:

- Ensure a complete antivirus strategy is implemented on your computer (speak with IT professionals in corporate environments).
- Be aware of suspicious email content; if it looks odd, it should not be opened.
- Do not open an attachment from anyone you don't know.
- Even if you know the receiver, be aware about opening attachments unless you are expecting it.
- Many file extensions are blocked by corporate anti-virus firewalls; file extensions such as .exe, .mdb, and .zip are frequently quarantined.

Instant Messaging/Chat Rooms

Instant Messaging (IM) provides real time messaging capabilities from and to one's computer or mobile device. While many folks believe that IM is more for social than business communications, a large number of Fortune 500 companies have embraced IM as a critical business communications tool.

From the meeting managers' perspective, IM has its greatest impact as a communication method within online meetings and chat rooms. These virtual meetings, both using one-to-one and one-to-many communications, frequently use an IM interface to enable discussion to occur within the online meeting.

While the main instant messaging providers are not inherently compatible, IM cross-platform compatibility tools exist, facilitating communications between the various IM products. Enterprise-wide versions of IM are also developing to provide IM functionality with higher levels of protection and security available to the network infrastructure.

Blogs

A blog (web log) is an online diary. Writing a blog (also known as blogging) is becoming a critical information distribution tool, allowing everyone to create their own web-based presence. Most blogging services are free to use, and can be set up in a matter of minutes.

Meeting managers can create and update blogs to distribute updated information about their event, or to create a "buzz" for the upcoming function. Since blogs are intended to stimulate dialogue, a meeting blog can be a critical marketing tool for the meeting manager to utilize.

Attendees can also create useful meeting-based blogs. One example of this is the attendee who blogs while sitting in on the meeting's general or concurrent sessions. These blogs enable a dialogue to occur with the staff not in attendance, generating more questions and information about the content distributed at the event. For this level of blogging to take place on a significant scale, the meeting manager will likely need to setup and utilize a wireless network in the meeting space of the hotel.

Really Simple Syndication (RSS)

RSS is a way to share or aggregate information from various sources onto a web site or a blog. Using XML formatting, RSS is a content aggregator, culling topical content from a large number of sources. The Google News site (http://news.google.com) is an excellent example of an RSS feed. Meeting professionals can and should consider using RSS as a means to continually update web content. If updated content is the main driver for people returning to a web site which they have visited, then RSS is a critical tool to support that objective.

Voice Over Internet Protocol (VOIP)

VOIP allows people to use their high-speed Internet connection to make and receive phone calls. By definition, an internet protocol (IP) address is the unique address used to identify each device on a network or on the web. While an IP address technically is a combination of four numbers, most people access an IP address by entering "www," followed by the name of the web site. (One side note about IP addresses is that when the meeting manager is providing connectivity at an event, he/she may need to pay for each individual IP address that gives access to the internet to the user).

Since most businesses, and many individuals use broadband services (T1, cable modem, and DSL) for their internet connectivity, and since broadband-based connection is at a much higher speed, VoIP is developing into a standard for making and receiving phone calls by using that connectivity.

With both free and premium services available, companies are beginning to move to VoIP systems to reduce telecommunication costs. Planners should investigate VoIP services as a way to handle their on-site telephone/telecommunication needs.

Radio Frequency Identification (RFID) Tags

As discussed in the exhibit sales section above, regarding lead retrieval, RFIDs are devices that share information between a receiver (such as a handheld device) and a small transponder (which can be contained as part of a name tag). RFIDs are not only finding use in lead retrieval systems, but many meeting managers are using them to help track continuing education units (CEU) by being able to track attendance at their various sessions.

Put It Into Perspective

Technology affects all kinds of meeting managers, including association and corporate meeting managers, large city-wide conference meeting managers and special event meeting managers, incentive meeting managers, and religious conference meeting managers. It does not matter what type of meeting manager you are, technology can impact your job. What does matter, within any meeting type, is a thorough understanding of the needs of your group, as well as a palette of technology options. By being able to combine those two aspects, the meeting manager can make intelligent decisions about the use of technology, rather than just using the first technology that appeals to them. The technology is nothing more than a tool that can enhance the value and experience of a meeting.

ROOM DESIGN

Since the days of DOS-run computers, the hospitality industry has offered software which assist the meeting manager and to better communicate with their partners by providing computer-aided design (CAD) programs for meeting room design. Using these tools (within a simple drag-and-drop interface), the user can quickly and accurately draw to scale their meeting room, complete with room setup, audiovisual aids, and other room requirements. These tools support and enhance the communication process between meeting manager and supplier, by providing visual support of the written meeting specifications.

Audience Response Systems (ARS)

Audience response systems allow presenters to elicit instant feedback from your audience. They can be implemented online, as electronic surveys or polls, or on-site during a presentation. In meeting rooms, typically, these are radio frequency devices (as are RFIDs). These devices do not need a clear line of sight to properly function, making them easier to use. Additionally, radio frequency devices have a greater transmission range than other types of transmissions, such as infrared.

These systems typically come with predefined polling questions, but also allow for modification and editing as you go. This technology allows the meeting organizer and speaker to gain instant information (demographic or otherwise) about attendees, and can be used to highly customize content and direction of educational sessions.

HANDHELD DEVICES AND WIRELESS CONNECTIVITY

The immediate future of technology can be summed in two words: wireless and portable. Smaller devices are proliferating, with freedom from hard wired connectivity at the forefront of many travelers' needs. However, wireless connectivity is not a panacea. It can be costly, and the consistency of the signal is not as strong as it needs to be in some locations.

Wireless Issues

Within the context of the hospitality industry, a debate has emerged about the cost of wireless connectivity in hotels. Some properties have decided to provide the wireless (or wired) connectivity at no cost, to entice travelers and meeting managers to book their space. Other properties have designated it as a cost center, anticipating revenue from meeting manager and hotel guests using the technology.

Another issue pertaining to wireless technology is in its stability. Depending on the type of wireless network deployed, as well as the location and frequency of wireless access points, some wireless connections can drop the signal periodically. This can cause frustration in the users from their inability to read their email while on the road, to preventing the use of web sites in presentations by conference speakers. For many meeting managers, an on-site connectivity strategy of using wireless, while having hard wired backup is the only way to ensure seamless event connectivity.

Mobile Technologies

A few years ago, many technology pundits predicted that the personal digital assistant (PDA) would be the next super tool, replacing computers as the single device for connectivity. And, with the convergence of data and voice, many PDA/smart phone devices (such as the Blackberry and the Treo Communicator) have become a single communication tool for the business professional. With the ever shrinking laptop size, it seems that PDAs and Smart Phones, many using Bluetooth technology (which provides wireless exchange of information between devices, such as a smart phone and a headset) have found their niche, but may not become the super tool.

PDAs and handheld devices are being used more frequently to help distribute meeting information to attendees. A number of companies provide meeting managers the ability to take the meeting program and beam or synchronize it to the PDA of the attendee, allowing for a more mobile program, which would interface with their own contact management system, helping customize the event schedule of the attendee. One such example of program mobility is having the conference newspaper designed for the PDA, then synchronized every day to the user's device.

These devices are also being integrated into name badge/networking devices at conferences. By asking questions of attendees at the point of registration, the portable device can not only become a badge, but it can communicate with other badges to find commonality between attendees. In some cases, these devices can help locate attendees through wireless communications with the other devices.

As with the use of all technologies, one of the biggest caveats is to understand the technological savvy of their attendees. Providing high tech solutions for a group uncomfortable with those products does not necessarily advance the goal of the meeting.

SUMMARY

The only constant about technology is that it is continually changing. For many meeting managers, this constant change is of great concern, as they feel that they cannot get a handle on a technology to be able to understand and utilize it before it becomes dated.

However, meeting managers need to approach the use of technology from a different mindset. Most critical to the process is the understanding of the group. Knowledge of how comfortable their members and attendees are with technology, coupled with a clear understanding of the objectives of their meeting, will provide a clearer path as to which technologies could best support their meetings. It does not make any sense to provide really cool handheld devices to a group that is intimidated by technology.

Cost is also a large factor in technology implementation. However, the meeting manager needs to look beyond the cost and better understand the ROI that the technology could provide. For many meetings, costs of technology services can be offset entirely by selling sponsorships for the service. A great example of this is in the establishment of the email kiosk, which at many conferences is a successfully sponsored service.

Once these factors have been addressed, the meeting manager needs to keep a basic understanding of technologies available. By attending industry events, reading the trade publications (including the online versions) and networking with other meeting managers, the meeting manager can learn what is "hot" and how it is being used successfully in the industry. The meeting manager who stays abreast and implements the technologies most useful for his/her own groups will continue to grow and ensure that meetings meet and exceed the needs of the attendees and their organization.

REFERENCES

1. APEX. Convention Industry Council. Retrieved April 1, 2006, from http://www.conventionindustry.org

2. Ball, C. (2006). Application service providers (ASPs)—88 key questions to ask before you buy. Retrieved April 4, 2006 from http://www.corbinball.com/articles/art-ASP.htm.

3. 2005 State of the Industry Report, *Successful meetings*. Retrieved March 31, 2006 from http://www.mimegasite.com/mimegasite/research/state_of_industry.jsp.

4. Hardin, T. (2005). The scope of planners' Web usage. *Successful meetings*. Vol. 54, No. 1, p. 59–61.

5. Popular industry portals include the Meetings Industry Mall (www.mim.com), mpoint (www.mpoint.com), Corbin Ball (www.corbinball.com), Conworld (http://www.conworld.net), Trade Show News Network (www.tsnn.com), and the Meetings Industry Megasite (http://www.mimegasite.com).

6. McGann, R. (2005). The deadly duo: Spam and viruses. January 2005. Retrieved March 15, 2006 from http://ww.clickz.com/stats/sectors/email/article.php/3483541.

KEY TERMS

APEX	Enterprise-wide	Request for proposal
Application service	Extensible markup	(RFP)
provider (ASP)	language (XML)	Résumé
Audience response	IP address	Reverse lead retrieval
system	Lead retrieval	Reverse online auction
Banquet event order	Legacy system	Simulcast
(BEO)	Listserv	Smart phone
Blacklist	Online registration	Spoofing
Blog (Web log)	Personal digital assistant	Streaming media
Bluetooth	(PDA)	Virtual trade show
Computer aided design	Portals	Voice over internet
(CAD)	Radio frequency ID tags	protocol (VoIP)
E-letters	(RFID)	Web browser
E-list	Really simple syndication	Wireless access points
Email	(RSS)	Yield management
E-marketing	Registration transaction	(Revenue management)
E-newsletters		

COMPELLING QUESTIONS FOR CONSIDERATION

1. Which of the technologies discussed in this chapter have the potential to have the greatest impact on your responsibilities as a meeting manager? Select three and discuss how they affect your job.

2. Define APEX. How are the APEX OfficeReady Professional templates intended to assist the meeting manager in doing their job more efficiently?

3. Discuss the pros and cons of using email as a meeting marketing tool?

4. What components are essential to a successful meeting web site?

5. Identify and discuss at least three new communication tools? How would you be able to use them to manage your next meeting?

CHAPTER 11

SITE SELECTION

Kevin C. Lewis

VICE PRESIDENT OF CONVENTION SALES

GREATER MINNEAPOLIS CONVENTION
& VISTORS ASSOCIATION

LEARNER OUTCOMES

When the reader has completed reading this chapter, he/she should be able to . . .

1 Identify the eight basic steps in the site selection process.

2 Recognize the value of knowing meeting objectives, history, physical requirements, and attendee expectations before the site inspection.

3 Compare different types of meeting facilities.

4 Recognize the types of items that should be included in a site inspection checklist.

> Perfection is a road, not a destination.
> Every time I live, I get an education.
>
> *Burk Hudson*

OVERVIEW

Selection of a meeting site, whether for an event 3 months away or an annual convention 10 years away, is a critical factor in the success or failure of the meeting. The site selection process is straightforward with an outline of the steps the meeting manager must follow, yet it is also complex, because each meeting and each site has important differences. The distinctions require excellent perception skills and close attention to details. Needs of the event must first be identified and matched to the sites that can appropriately accommodate them. The setting must provide a comfortable and pleasing environment as well as be logistically suitable for the meeting.

THE SITE SELECTION PROCESS

The site selection process involves eight basic steps:

1. Identify the meeting objectives.
2. Gather historical data.
3. Determine the physical requirements of the meeting.
4. Consider attendee interests and expectations.
5. Select a destination and the type of facility.
6. Prepare meeting specifications and a request for proposal (RFP).
7. Review and evaluate sites.
8. Select the site.

IDENTIFY MEETING OBJECTIVES

The major purpose of a meeting may be to deliver education, to discuss business, to attend a trade show, or to provide a social setting for personal enjoyment or professional growth. Few events, however, serve a single purpose. An association's annual meeting often combines educational sessions and business meetings with leisure-time activities. A corporate meeting may consist of training or motivational seminars, and feature leisure activities such as a golf tournament. The purpose and expected outcome of the meeting must be clearly understood before the RFP is prepared. Before considering potential sites, a meeting manager must do a needs assessment of the meeting and the attendees. Ask the important question: What is to be accomplished as a result of this meeting? Often, the purpose(s) of an event must be identified first by a group or groups of employees, volunteers, or potential attendees. Your organization's culture may determine this process. If not, you must assume this responsibility before proceeding further.

The meeting's objectives will indicate the appropriate setting. An airport facility might be the better choice for a brief business meeting with an agenda of intense discussions about specific short-term goals. If informal discussion and reflection will facilitate the meeting's objectives, a resort may be more appropriate.

GATHER HISTORICAL DATA

Historical data on the meeting is very valuable. Gather all past records of the meeting regarding attendance, room block pick-up, financial performance, and service use. Hotels and facilities typically require 3 years of history. When you prepare your RFP, provide as much historical detail about the event as possible. Sleeping room usage (block and pick-up), daily meeting space allocations, food and beverage requirements (numbers served), and exhibit space needs are just a few of the items that should be documented within the RFP. The master schedule or group résumé from a previous event can provide a facility with a comprehensive overview of the meeting.

If the event is being conducted for the first time, gather historical data from previous similar meetings conducted by the group. Current demographic data for the group, such as location of the majority of attendees, purchasing habits, educational needs assessment, and related commentary, can provide a profile of the potential audience and, thus, establish the need for an event. This supporting data is important for facilities that are considering a new piece of business that is uncertain or unproven.

DETERMINE PHYSICAL REQUIREMENTS

The meeting format will dictate many of the physical requirements for the event. In addition to determining guest room and other requirements based on historical data, use the program plan and schedule to help determine the number of rooms needed for general sessions, simultaneous or concurrent sessions, food and beverage events, registration, exhibits, offices, and storage (see Chapter 19). As space needs are identified, determine the length of time each meeting room, office, storage, and service area is needed on a daily basis. Be sure to take into consideration the amount of time required before the event begins for facility personnel and equipment suppliers to set up, and the time needed after the event for move-out of equipment and supplies. Determine if space for a specific service area is needed continually, or whether the area can serve a dual or changing purpose.

Whether from previous data or current projections, the following information is needed to develop a meeting profile.

Preferred Dates

- Is the meeting limited to a specific set of dates or time period?
- Does the meeting have date/pattern flexibility?
- Is there a need to avoid certain religious, ethnic, state, or federal holidays? If the meeting is in another country, are there local holidays that must be considered?
- Must scheduling conflicts with allied or kindred groups be avoided?
- Will seasonal hotel or facility rates or local labor laws affect the decision?
- Are any construction or remodeling projects scheduled near the meeting dates?

Attendance

- What is the anticipated attendance for the meeting?
- What has been the attendance at the past 5 years' previous meetings of this type? Three years is adequate. 5 years will provide information on outside influences that could have a negative impact on a meeting.
- What internal/external factors could impact future attendance?

Sleeping Rooms

- What will be the total number of sleeping rooms needed each night, from the earliest arrival through the last departure?
- How many rooms are needed for staff members, speakers, exhibitors, and others who may not have been included in the attendance estimate?

- If using previous data, must the arrival and departure pattern be adjusted for the proposed location because of flight schedules?
- What is the percentage of single versus double room occupancy?
- What are the requirements for one- and two-bedroom suites?
- Are large suites needed for entertaining? How many and what size? Who will use the suites—members, VIPs, exhibitors? On what dates?
- What is the average percentage of people who cancel reservations?
- What is the average percentage of people who fail to claim reservations (no-shows)?
- What has been the average room rate for this meeting? The highest? The lowest?
- Are room rates important to the group? Are discounted rooms needed for students, retired members, speakers, and/or staff? If so, how many?
- Are rates to be commissioned back to group or third party?
- Are rebates and/or housing fees to be added to and/or included in the room rate?

Meeting Space

- How many meeting rooms will be required on a daily basis? How many are needed simultaneously on a daily basis?
- Should any meeting rooms be held on a 24-hour basis (may be required for rooms with extensive audiovisual (A/V) set-ups)?
- In addition to the formal program, will meeting rooms be needed for committee and business meetings and ancillary group functions?
- What is the estimated attendance for each meeting/food and beverage event/session?
- Are rooms to be set up theater, classroom, conference, or banquet-style?
- How will the A/V plan impact requirements for meeting rooms? Does the room need to have high ceilings and no columns for clear sight lines?
- Will meeting rooms separated by air walls be sufficiently quiet, or do you require the sound insulation of permanent walls?
- Does the program require high-speed wireless Internet access or other advanced technology for presentations?
- Is space needed in or near the meeting room(s) for refreshment breaks?
- Determine the facility's flexibility concerning the tentative agenda (increases or decreases in meeting space).
- Does the schedule require meeting rooms in close proximity to each other, to exhibits, and to public areas where traffic flows?
- Where are restrooms in close proximity to meeting/event/exhibit space? What is the ratio of restrooms to your projected attendance?

Food and Beverage Events

- How many food and beverage events will be held, and when? What types—casual, formal, or themed?
- What kinds of food and beverage events will be held, i.e., breakfast, lunch, dinner, refreshment breaks?
- What is the estimated attendance at each event? What has been the attendance at previous functions?
- Are you planning any indoor or outdoor events? Do you need back-up space (space not already being used for your other meeting requirements is preferred) in case of inclement weather?

Exhibits

- Are there exhibits in conjunction with the meeting? If so, what is the gross and/or net square footage required?
- Will exhibits and aisle signage require high ceilings and/or column-free space?
- How much time is needed for move-in and move-out of displays?
- Is close proximity of loading docks and freight elevators important?
- Are your exhibits suitable for the facility, i.e., hotel versus convention center? For example, if your exhibitors require utilities (water, electricity, gas) a hotel is less likely to have those utilities set in the floor. An exception would be if the hotel has an exhibition hall.
- Do you require a carpeted exhibit hall? If yes, a hotel would most likely be able to provide you with carpeted space. Most convention centers do not have carpeted exhibit facilities (except in their ballrooms). Your general services contractor can provide any carpeting needs of the exhibit space and charges are passed on to the organization.
- If using a convention center, is the center attached to or within walking distance of your headquarters or primary hotel?
- Are the facility's (hotel and/or convention center) workers part of a union? More than one union?

Registration

- How large an area is needed for registration purposes? Is the designated registration area in a high-traffic area, or away from general public? Can the area be secured after registration closes?
- Are adequate utilities available including wireless high-speed Internet, electrical outlets, and ample lighting?
- Is space needed for additional services, such as restaurant reservations, tours, local information, or video and/or audio tape sales?

Ancillary Space Needs

- Are all dates and times determined?
- Is storage space needed?
- How many rooms are required for headquarter offices and press offices? What size must each be?
- Does the A/V supplier need an equipment room?
- Will a speaker preparation room be needed?
- Are special lounge areas desired for exhibitors or international attendees?
- Are hospitality suites needed?
- Are additional rooms required for spouse/guest or children's programs?

Other Logistical Considerations

- Are there special needs for some participants, such as people with disabilities? (See Chapter 43)
- Are there any potential language barriers, either with facility staff or meeting attendees? If so, does the hotel have fluent translators on staff?
- Will tours of local related-interest facilities be required (universities, hospitals, or manufacturers)? Does the facility have space for loading/unloading buses?

- Are there allied or ancillary groups that may wish to convene immediately before, after, or during the meeting? Do they book direct with the facility, or do they book through the organization and does your organization need to hold additional space?
- Does your meeting warrant the presence of convention and visitors bureau (CVB) representatives during the event (visitor information desk/restaurant reservation desk)?
- Does your primary facility contact have an immediate means of communication with facility staff throughout the facility?

Site Inspection Requirements

- How many site visits are required prior to and after confirming an event?
- How frequently are site visits conducted?
- Who conducts the site visits? Are staff and suppliers included? Any volunteer groups or individuals?
- What is expected of the destination and facilities in accommodating site visits?
- How long do the site visits last (how many days)?
- Who pays for the specific components of the visit — airfare, hotel accommodations, ground transportation?
- Site visits/inspections should be set up as far in advance as possible to ensure all parties/facilities are available.

External Factors

- What is the meeting's future growth potential?
- How will this impact economic development in the selected site?
- What other external factors may have an impact on the meeting (union regulations and contracts, supplier availability, hotel construction/renovation, industry economics)?

CONSIDER ATTENDEE INTERESTS AND EXPECTATIONS

Fulfilling attendees' expectations plays an important part in site selection.

- What surroundings will please attendees?
- Does your group prefer large, glittery lobbies, or small European-style facilities?
- Will the facility food and beverage outlets fulfill attendees' needs or are gourmet restaurants expected?
- Must lounges or show rooms be available, or is a quiet setting preferred?
- Will sporting events play a role in leisure-time activities?

A profile of attendees can be developed by evaluating the following:

- What is the average age of the meeting participants and how does their age affect expectations for the meeting site?
- What percentage of the group is male versus female?
- Will attendees want to bring family members?
- Are spouse/guest or children's programs desired?
- How important are local attractions and cultural opportunities to attendees?
- Are recreational activities such as golf, tennis, or skiing important to attendees? Is a golf tournament included as part of the meeting?

- Are spa services and fitness facilities desired?
- Is the availability of nearby shopping and restaurants expected?
- Will international attendees require special services?

The local environment has become an integral part of the marketing effort for a meeting in selling perceptions of the site to attendees. Potential attendees' interest in visiting an area can contribute to a significant increase in attendance and revenue. In fact, some meeting managers evaluate localities to determine which can accommodate their groups and then present their board or executives (occasionally attendees) with a list of possible sites to help rank desirable destinations.

SELECT DESTINATION AND FACILITY TYPE

Although there are endless worldwide possibilities, the meeting's objectives and physical requirements will usually indicate the general area and type of facility where the meeting should be located. Political and economic factors may play a part in narrowing the choices, or organizational policy may dictate the general location.

Some organizations require a bid or invitation from a local member, or sponsoring group, before considering a destination and facility type for a future meeting. If this is the case, convey accurate projected meeting requirements so local representatives can research and recommend facilities that can realistically accommodate the meeting. Provide clear instructions to local representatives as to the limit of their involvement in facility or site selection. Convey this information to the facility and/or CVB as well, so they know whom they are to be working with and who has the authority to make decisions on behalf of the organization.

Many groups establish a rotational pattern for future sites, moving from one region to another, holding a meeting in the same area every 3 or 4 years. Using familiar facilities has many benefits. If a rotational pattern is too rigid, however, you will be unable to review new facilities as they are constructed. A major consideration is the number of prospective attendees in the geographic area and whether they will be likely to continue to support the meeting.

Consider travel convenience and cost for the maximum number of potential attendees. You probably will not hold a meeting on the East Coast when five out of every six attendees are from the West Coast—unless special circumstances require an East Coast site.

Determine potential attendees' usual means of travel: airplane, private car, bus, or train. Investigate major airline availability, the number of daily flights, and whether connecting flights are necessary to reach the destination. The CVB can provide you with this statistical information. If most attendees will arrive by car, review expressway accessibility, parking facilities, and the availability of valet parking.

Once the general area is identified, determine the type of facility that will best match the meeting's objectives and physical requirements. Advantages and disadvantages exist for each type of meeting site.

Metropolitan Area

Downtown locations usually offer a high concentration of quality metropolitan hotels, many with extensive meeting and banquet space. Businesses providing services and equipment to the meeting are located nearby. Museums, theaters, and art galleries provide cultural opportunities for attendees. Taxicabs, buses, light rail, and other mass transit options are readily available. Additionally, diverse restaurants, shopping, and strolling the streets provide attendees with a flavor of the city.

The activity that makes a metropolitan area attractive for some meetings may be too distracting for others. Traffic may be a problem. Taxicabs can be difficult to find, and airport buses may run infrequently. Parking is usually limited downtown and may be expensive. Depending on the specific location and general activity in the downtown area after business hours, safety during the evening hours may be a concern.

Suburban Area

Many suburban areas are new and fashionable. They include chic boutiques, luxury hotels, and trendy restaurants. There is usually less traffic than the city, and free parking is readily available. Sports and recreational facilities are generally nearby. However, large suburban hotels are rare, limiting the space available for exhibits and other facets of the meeting. Also, suburban hotels are very similar in appearance to metropolitan hotels, but they may not offer the unique flavor of a downtown facility.

Airport Area

Airport hotels offer excellent space for brief committee meetings or one-day sessions. Complimentary shuttle bus service is often available to and from the airport. Many of these facilities are new and have full-service meeting capabilities. Since many attendees can fly in and out in just 1 day, airport-area meetings offer an excellent opportunity to save both time and money for your attendees. Unfortunately, nearby restaurant options may be limited, and the potential for airport noise may be a factor. For longer meetings, attendees may feel confined in this environment; however, most hotels now offer exercise facilities to satisfy longer stays.

Resort

The resort facility provides a relaxed environment in which attendees feel removed from day-to-day pressures. Some resorts are posh and offer every amenity; others are more rustic. Distances from airports become a major consideration because of cost, time, and transportation factors. Suppliers of equipment and services critical to the success of the meeting must be available within the facility or nearby.

Off-season rates and group meal plans can offer a considerable savings to attendees and/or the meeting sponsor. Resorts usually offer a full American Plan (all meals provided) or a Modified American Plan (two meals provided, breakfast and one other meal).

A resort location should not be selected for a meeting with a full program that completely absorbs attendees' time. Attendees at such a meeting would likely express some concern as to why the site had been chosen if they have little time to enjoy its benefits.

Conference Centers

The distinction between a conference center and a hotel is often blurred. In general, however, a conference center can be defined as a facility that is especially constructed for and devoted to meetings. There is typically a higher ratio of meeting space to sleeping rooms; in fact, some conference centers do not have sleeping rooms within their facilities. A conference center provides dedicated space for you to use as needed, usually on a 24-hour basis. A meeting that runs past its allotted time or an impromptu evening session would be unlikely to cause problems. It is also less likely that a noisy social function will be booked next door in a conference center than in a hotel facility.

Facilities often include state-of-the-art A/V equipment and a full-time technical staff. All services required for the meeting — furniture, equipment, registration personnel — can be provided by the facility. Most conference centers offer a wide variety of recreational facilities in secluded, park-like surroundings. Another popular advantage of booking meetings at conference centers is that many offer complete meeting package (CMP) pricing. These centers price their meetings by the person either with or without lodging. Included in the package are continuous breaks, A/V, meeting amenities, and meals.

However, one weakness of some conference centers may be in the area of guest services. Many conference centers offer high-quality accommodations and amenities, while others provide only sparse guest quarters, or none at all (see Chapter 15).

Convention Centers

Most convention centers are designed for a multi-group, multipurpose use. They can accommodate very large meetings and exhibitions—events that do not fit into a hotel or conference center setting. A wide choice of meeting rooms in varying capacities, and one or more exhibit halls specially constructed to support the technical needs of a major exhibition will be part of the facility.

Guest rooms are not part of the facility's design. In some locations, convention centers are adjacent or connected to a hotel and may be used in conjunction with the hotel's facilities. In most cases, however, the distance from the majority of sleeping rooms and the cost and availability of shuttle bus service become primary considerations.

The wide variety of food and beverage outlets found in a hotel is not available in a convention center, although most centers do contract with caterers to provide food service from concessions or for group functions. Guest services are more limited in convention centers, but many centers are adding services such as business centers, food and beverage outlets, gift shops, and concierge services (see Chapter 14).

PREPARE SPECIFICATIONS AND RFP

An RFP is the written meeting specifications document prepared for facilities to assist them in evaluating the appropriateness of their property for the group. The RFP presents the meeting objectives, historical data, physical requirements, and attendee interests and expectations and identifies the general area and type of facility desired.

Preparing the RFP requires careful thought and articulation of the group's needs. The professionally prepared document facilitates consistent communication to all suppliers. All site requirements are outlined, including:

- Key information about the group or organization holding the event
- Purpose of the event
- Information about the meeting attendees
- Preferred dates and optional dates (if available)
- Number and type of guest rooms required each day
- Number, size, and usage of meeting rooms, along with estimated times they are needed
- Range of acceptable rates
- Number and types of food and beverage events, including dates and estimated attendance
- Food and beverage expenditures per event (exclusive of service charges and taxes)

- Exhibits and any other special events or activities
- Any related information, such as complimentary requirements
- History of the meeting to include: guest room pick-up, food and beverage expenditures
- When the proposal must be received by, who will review the proposal, and when a decision will be made regarding site selection

The RFP should present the meeting requirements in an agenda format by day, time, and hour so that it can be reviewed easily and compared to space availability in the facility.

REVIEW AND EVALUATE SITES

Most meeting destinations have a local CVB charged with assisting meeting managers in obtaining information about the potential site as well as sending out RFPs to hotels/facilities as directed by the meeting manager (see Chapter 12). Available resource materials include facility descriptions with names and addresses of key contacts, city maps, details on visitor attractions, and transportation information. Most CVBs also provide assistance with arrangements for the initial review of the site. CVBs can save the meeting manager quite a bit of time before, during, and after the site selection process.

In addition to the CVB, many other sources of information are available about potential sites, such as trade publications, web sites for the meetings industry, facility and destination web sites, destination management companies, and regional offices of hotel chains. Using any of these sources will provide ample options for consideration. By reviewing the wealth of information available online, you may be able to narrow your choices fairly quickly. Many web sites—such as meeting industry, CVB, and national hotel chain web sites—allow RFPs to be submitted online by filling out a form or attaching a document. For example, the Destination Marketing Association International (www.destinationmarketing.org), formerly the International Association of Convention & Visitor Bureaus, allows you to distribute RFPs to multiple sites simultaneously. The advantage of this process is communicating identical information to each site and receiving quick replies from sales managers, usually within 24 to 48 hours. The CVB sales managers will in turn submit your information to the hotels/facilities that can accommodate your meeting.

Initial contact with the facility representative is for the exchange of basic information. Based on your RFP, the facility will determine if it can satisfy the physical requirements, then submit an offer or proposal with detailed information about the property. Carefully review each proposal to determine which facility best meets your meeting requirements and attendee expectations.

Assessing Space Adequacy

The facility will provide information outlining available public space and the capacities of the meeting rooms when set in various configurations. The numbers used in figuring room capacity vary widely from facility to facility, and the meeting demands of organizations vary greatly.[1] Each event will use a facility differently, so be aware of the square footage required for special activities associated with your meeting.

As you evaluate the available space, keep in mind the purpose and requirements of each session, along with any unique or high-priority factors that affect the overall meeting. If audiovisuals are important to the success of the meeting, space must be allotted for projection platforms, screens, and head tables (see

Chapter 23). A large coffee break area in the rear of the room will also leave less space for seating.

A primary consideration in determining if appropriate space is available for planned meal functions is whether the facility's banquet tables seat 8 or 10 people. As a rule of thumb, allow 13.5 square feet per person to comfortably accommodate 8 people per 60-inch table or 10 people per 72-inch table.[2] Room capacity will vary depending on whether there are pillars in the room or special facility requirements for food service. Providing a dance floor, head table, or A/V presentation will also affect room usage and capacity.

For stand-up receptions, estimate that 9 to 10 square feet are required per person. A larger allowance provides for a more comfortable event. Space will be needed for bars and bartenders away from entrance areas and exits. Depending on the facility and the type of reception planned, it may also be necessary to allow space for a cashier. Plan sufficient space for food service areas if extensive hors d'oeuvres will be served. Keep buffet lines and food service areas away from entrances/exits allowing space for people to queue.

Site Inspection

Although it may not be possible or economically feasible to personally visit all facilities under consideration, a site inspection is invaluable for judging the suitability and current condition of a property—as well as the professionalism and attitude of facility employees.

Site inspections do not have to be costly. Most hotels are more than eager to provide a complimentary room night for the meeting manager to conduct a site inspection. This is a standard practice that should never be abused. Only use it for properties that are *seriously* being considered for the meeting. Most organizations also budget a certain number of site inspection airline tickets per year. Some destinations provide airline tickets for site inspections pertaining to conventions considered to be citywide when using two or more hotels and/or the use of a convention center or event complex.

Some associations conduct site inspections with committees of volunteers who assist in determining locations, especially for larger meetings and conferences. Again, careful planning and thoughtful use of resources and time are mandatory in order to convey the most professional image possible.

Site Inspection Checklist

Whether you visit one destination or several, using a site inspection checklist helps ensure that you do not overlook important features and services during your visit. At a minimum, your checklist should include the following:

The Destination
Accessibility
❏ Ease and cost
❏ Proximity to airport
❏ Accessible to people with disabilities
❏ Adequate taxi/limousine service (cost)
❏ Sufficient parking space (cost)
❏ Availability and cost of shuttle service
❏ Adequate airport assistance
❏ Adequate number of flights into destination
❏ Seasonality of destination (peak season versus off-season)

Environment

❏ Availability of local attractions

❏ Shopping

❏ Recreation

❏ Restaurants

❏ Business services

❏ Weather conditions

❏ Appearance

❏ Safety of destination

❏ Impact of local ordinances on your organization (e.g., smoking laws, gaming laws, liquor service)

❏ Economic health of community

❏ Reputation of area/facility for hosting meetings

❏ Support and services available from local convention bureau

❏ Availability of experienced suppliers, such as A/V firms, exhibit service contractors, temporary help, and security

Hotel Accommodations

Accessibility

❏ Registration desk easy to find; sufficient space and personnel in relation to guest rooms; ability to handle peak check-in/check-out times for major groups; efficient front desk personnel

❏ Modern elevators and escalators in sufficient number to serve guests when the facility is full

❏ Accessible, fully staffed message and information desk; rapid response to telephone calls; quick delivery of messages

❏ Availability of guest services; e.g., business center, drug stores, banks, emergency services, gift shop, concierge, safety deposit boxes, and so on

❏ Availability of beverage and ice machines on each floor

❏ Service elevator accessibility

❏ Rooms equipped for people with disabilities

❏ Availability of executive floor offering special guest services

Environment

❏ Efficient, friendly doormen and bellmen

❏ Attractive, clean lobby

❏ Comfortable clean rooms: furniture in good condition, modern bathroom fixtures, adequate lighting, adequate closet space and hangers, iron/ironing board, coffee maker, refrigerator and/or mini bar, work desk with Internet and telephone

❏ Smoke detectors in all public areas, audio and visual fire alarms, sprinkling system in all public areas and guest rooms, and fire exit information clearly posted

❏ Adequate lighting and cleanliness of hallways

❏ Size of standard room versus deluxe room

❏ Number and types of suites and availability of suite floor plans

❏ Reservations procedures and policies

❏ Room category classifications (floor number, nonsmoking, ocean view, and so on) and number available in each category

❏ Number of rooms available for early arrivals and late departures (luggage storage for early arrivals)

❏ Current convention rate and rack rate for individual guests (not part of the group)

❏ Date hotel will provide firm rates (confirm 1 year out or more if possible)

❏ Best rate guarantee policy including Internet reservation providers

❏ Guarantee and deposit requirements

❏ Check-in and check-out hours

❏ Cut-off date for the room block

❏ Check-cashing policies and types of credit cards accepted

❏ Refund policy for cancellations

❏ Number of nonsmoking floors (standard and concierge)

❏ Dates of any planned renovations

❏ Any change in hotel ownership being discussed

❏ Availability of a health club, hours, and cost

❏ Telephone access charges (long distance, local, and calling card)

❏ High-speed wireless Internet accessibility in guest rooms (Is there a fee?)

❏ Card or key system for guest rooms

❏ Adequate parking space (free or for a fee?)

❏ Hotel emergency plan (meeting manager should review)

❏ Hotel emergency exits clearly marked

❏ Comparison of king-bed versus double-bed room categories

❏ Additional room fees, if applicable (resort fees, room occupancy taxes, and so on)

❏ Charges for early departures

❏ Room service and hours of operation

❏ Ability of hotel to accept Internet reservations either through hotel's web site and/or CVBs

❏ Competing meeting currently booked into the facility

❏ Willingness to work with third-party planner, destination management company, and so on

❏ Hotel's union status (is all or part of the hotel unionized?)

❏ Hotel handling fee for incoming organization's shipments (excludes exhibit drayage)

Meeting Space

Accessibility

❏ Accessibility for people with disabilities

❏ Proximity of space for refreshment breaks

❏ Restrooms in proximity to meeting space

Environment

❏ General suitability of meeting rooms for designated uses (current floor plans)

❏ Number of meeting rooms adequate for requirements

❏ Size of rooms (prepare scale diagrams; incorporate all equipment, staging, and decorations; and calculate the desired square footage per person for required setup)

❏ Ability to accommodate required setup: theater, classroom, conference, or banquet style

❏ Capacity of each room compared to expected attendance at session

❏ High ceilings (10 feet is considered minimum) and no columns or obstructions for A/V presentations

❏ Adequacy of lighting: adjustable controls, brightness

❏ High-speed wireless Internet accessibility (is there a fee?)

❏ Meeting rooms available for committee and business meetings or ancillary group functions

❏ Pre-meeting and post-meeting space available for affiliated ancillary groups

❏ In-house sound and A/V company available

❏ Electronic signage outside each meeting room (or will manual signs be required?)

Food and Beverage Service

Public Outlets

❏ Availability of food and beverage outlets, types, and hours of operation

❏ Appearance and cleanliness

❏ Cleanliness of food preparation areas

❏ Adequate staffing at peak times

❏ Attitude of personnel

❏ Prompt and efficient service

❏ Variety of menus

❏ Cost range

❏ Reservations policy

❏ Feasibility of setting up additional food outlets for continental breakfast and quick luncheon service, if necessary

❏ Feasibility of using public food outlets for group functions during non-peak hours

Group Functions

❏ Quality and service

❏ Diversity of menus

❏ Costs: tax and gratuities; projected price increases by the time of the meeting; extra labor charges for small-group functions (set menu pricing 1 year out)

❏ Liquor laws (restricted times)

❏ Cash bar policies: bartender cost and minimum hours, cashier charges, drink prices

❏ Current banquet menus

❏ Guarantee policies: when a guarantee is required, number set and prepared for beyond guarantee

❏ Special services: tailored menus, theme parties, unique refreshment breaks, food substitutions available, table decorations, dance floor

❏ Size and inventory of banquet rounds (60-inch rounds, 72-inch rounds, and standard seating capacity 8 or 10 people)

❏ Room service: diversity of menu, prompt and efficient telephone manner, prompt delivery, quality, hours of operation

Exhibit Space

❑ Number of loading docks and proximity to exhibit area
❑ Truck marshalling area
❑ Availability and location of freight receiving area
❑ Location of utilities (type, location, and number)
❑ Maximum floor load
❑ Security of area (officers required?)
❑ Location of fire exits
❑ Proximity to food service areas, restrooms, and telephones
❑ Availability of sufficient time for move-in and move-out
❑ Reputation of facility regarding union relations
❑ Decorations to enhance facility appearance
❑ Availability of supplemental lighting
❑ High-speed wireless Internet accessibility
❑ Proximity of exhibit hall to other portions of the meeting
❑ First aid station
❑ Availability of office space for exposition manager, service contractors, and suppliers
❑ Crate storage areas and policies
❑ Fire marshal regulations
❑ Air conditioning, heating, and lighting restrictions during set-up and take-down
❑ Floor plans of convention center including ceiling heights
❑ Exclusive services, i.e., security, food and beverage, hall cleaning
❑ Aisle signage, banners, hanging weight restrictions, and so on

Offices and Other Services

❑ Is designated group registration area out of general public/high traffic area?
❑ Sufficient space for furniture and equipment necessary to perform the business at hand
❑ Good lighting
❑ Easy for attendees to locate
❑ Adequate electrical outlets
❑ Availability of house telephones or telephone jacks
❑ Ability to secure space after hours
❑ Flexibility regarding tentative agenda versus meeting space locked in by a signed contract
❑ Accessibility for people with disabilities

Equipment

❑ Inventory sufficient to meet set-up requirements for simultaneous functions
❑ Tables: number and condition of each type (6-foot long, 8-foot long, 30-inch wide, 18-inch wide, 60-inch round, 72-inch round, half rounds, and high-top cocktail tables)
❑ Chairs: types and sizes
❑ Riser sections, stages

Fast Facts

Site Selection

1. Identify the meeting objectives.
2. Gather historical data.
3. Determine the physical requirements of the meeting.
4. Consider attendee interests and expectations.
5. Select destination and type of facility.
6. Prepare meeting specifications and a request for proposal (RFP).
7. Review and evaluate sites.
8. Select the site.

SELECT SITE

The final selection process can include a number of steps internally for the organization depending on the reporting needs and approval required. Often, a board of directors or other governing body must be consulted or provide final input on the decision. You may need to provide data to verify the various steps and processes employed in determining the final recommendation. A spreadsheet outlining your choices and findings can help provide a clear picture to all those concerned.

Once you are satisfied that the facility is appropriate for the meeting and that all requirements can be accommodated, the facility will offer a letter of agreement that outlines the space requested and held. Negotiations on usage and cost follow in subsequent communication between the meeting manager and the facility (see Chapter 39).

VIRTUAL SITE SELECTION

It is important to address that through continual advances in technology, virtual site selections are growing in popularity. Online features such as 360-degree virtual reality tours, photo galleries, floor diagrams and specifications, live web cams, 3-D exhibit diagrams, meeting space configuration builders, and more offer the convenience of being introduced to a site from the comfort of the office.

Although virtual site tours cannot replace the value of a live, on-site inspection, they are very useful tools that can provide a solid introduction to hotels, convention facilities, and offsite venues. This is similar to how you can be introduced to and begin a dialogue with a colleague over email, without really getting a sense for knowing that colleague until you meet in person.

As technology continues to progress at a rapid pace, new and exciting online and virtual tools will become available to aid meeting managers in the future.

SUMMARY

Meeting managers are responsible for accurately projecting organizational requirements and evaluating the site's ability to meet these requirements. The site selection process should follow eight basic steps.

You should have a firm grasp of the meeting's objectives, physical requirements, and attendee expectations before visiting a potential site for inspection. Each of these factors plays a key role in site selection. How well these needs are matched with the facility will be the determining factor in the meeting's success.

A wide variety of facilities from which to choose are available when deciding where to hold a meeting. Consider the logistics of meeting in a metropolitan area, suburban area, airport area, resort, conference center, or convention center. Each has unique advantages and disadvantages. The suitability of each will depend on the needs of the meeting being planned.

Numerous important details need attention during the site inspection. The checklist included in this chapter provides a good starting point. It can be revised and customized as needs mandate.

REFERENCES

1. The Professional Convention Management Association (PCMA) offers a space verification program that enables facilities to have their room capacities verified and posted on the PCMA web site (www.pcma.org). Meeting managers can download the floor plans of all PCMA space-verified properties.

2. Harris, B. (2000). Function room set-up. *The convention industry council manual*. (7th ed.) McLean, VA: Convention Industry Council.

KEY TERMS

Airport hotel	Letter of agreement	Proposal
American plan	Meeting profile	Request for proposal
Bid	Meeting specifications	(RFP)
Conference center	Metropolitan hotel	Resort
Convention center	Modified American plan	Site inspection
Facility	Offer	Site selection
Hospitality suite	Profile of attendees	Suburban hotel

COMPELLING QUESTIONS FOR CONSIDERATION

1. Briefly describe the importance of each step in the site selection process.

2. In what way do meeting objectives impact the site selection process?

3. Which meeting facility would be most suitable for a small, intense corporate meeting that will last only one weekend?

4. Which meeting facility would be most suitable for a large annual convention to which most attendees will bring family members?

5. Which items on the site inspection checklist do you think are most important in the decision-making process? Why?

CHAPTER 12

CONVENTION AND VISITORS BUREAUS: PARTNERING WITH MEETING MANAGERS FOR SUCCESS

Paul Vallee

EXECUTIVE VICE PRESIDENT

TOURISM VANCOUVER—THE GREATER
VANCOUVER CONVENTION AND VISITORS BUREAU

LEARNER OUTCOMES

When the reader has completed reading this chapter, he/she should be able to . . .

1 Describe the role and mission of a convention and visitors bureau (CVB).

2 Explain the value of the Destination Marketing Association International (DMAI) and other associations that represent CVBs.

3 Identify how a CVB can work to assist the many diverse needs of a meeting manager.

4 Evaluate the variety of services that may be available through a CVB for your organization.

5 Discuss recent initiatives to accredit and certify service standards with CVBs.

> The conference was a great success!
> From the beginning site visit through the
> follow-up after the conference, the
> Bureau did an outstanding job of making
> the convention easier to maneuver...
> [They] made our job easy.
>
> *Cindy Winter, CMP*
> *Conference Director/Section Liaison*
> *The National Council on Family Relations*

OVERVIEW

Meeting managers often need a significant amount of local expertise and assistance during the meeting management process. Convention and visitors bureaus (CVBs) can provide the services that will help a meeting be successful by saving the meeting manager time and effort.

A CVB is generally a not-for-profit umbrella organization that represents a destination in the solicitation and servicing of all types of travel and tourism-related business. CVBs serve as the destination's official contact point for meeting managers, tour operators, and individual visitors. Understanding the role and mission of the CVB, knowing how to work effectively with them, and being aware of the value-added services that are available, will help the meeting manager maximize attendance and increase their return on investment.

ROLE AND MISSION OF THE CVB

CVBs are represented at the local, state/provincial, and national level throughout the world. In recent years, CVBs have also been referred to as destination marketing organizations (DMOs). The primary responsibility of a CVB is to deliver economic benefit to its constituents through attracting and hosting overnight nonresidents to their jurisdiction. Even in the most far-reaching places on the globe, CVBs have been put in place to generate foreign spending and retain domestic spending that might be drawn elsewhere.

CVBs are usually the entity that brings together the interests of the private sector (hotels, restaurants, attractions, local transportation, convention suppliers, and so on) and the quasi-public and public sector (convention centers, airports, city and state/provincial governments), in building and servicing convention and visitor traffic to the area. CVBs act to transform general destination information to local knowledge, provide convention management consulting, and promote the destination to relevant markets. Although marketing remains the primary focus, many CVBs now delve into such matters as infrastructure enhancements and investments, public policy matters, crisis management, and labor issues.

CVB Business Flow

As CVBs' mandates have grown, so has the way in which they build their strategic planning. Although the bread and butter for CVBs remain sales, marketing, and servicing, they also develop and implement plans for other interrelated, core business considerations (see Figure 12.1). CVBs endeavor to have influence through the various phases of the business flow that lead to a customer purchasing and, ultimately, experiencing their destination (see Figure 12.2).[1]

The core purpose of a CVB is to generate visitor demand to its area. The success of the CVB and the destination is usually determined through such measures as number of overnight visitors, hotel room nights, visitor spending, and economic impact. The CVB commonly achieves its goals by working to:

- Solicit, qualify, and confirm groups to hold meetings, conventions, and trade shows in the area it represents
- Assist meeting groups that have confirmed through attendance building and convention servicing
- Manage the destination brand through awareness building and customer relationship management
- Market to leisure travel trade and individual travelers through targeted promotional and sales activities

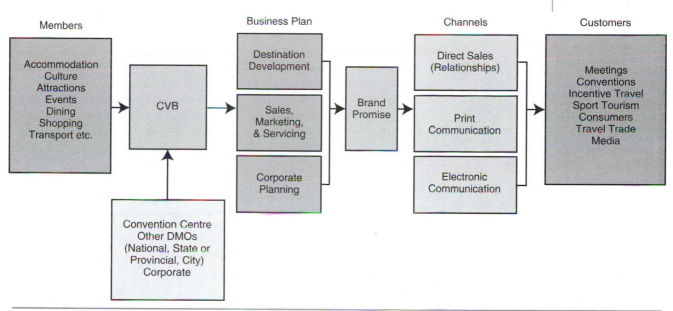

FIGURE 12.1
Typical CVB Business Flow

- Facilitate relationships between meeting manager and travel trade buyers and sellers, with sellers generally composed of local businesses offering products and services
- Service visitors, including convention delegates, in the destination to encourage them to stay longer and see more of the area

In some cases, a CVB only conducts the convention side of the business. In other words, it does not get involved in leisure marketing or visitor servicing. In these instances, those responsibilities are often handled by a regional, state/provincial or national body. Note that a CVB does not actually organize meetings and conventions. It does, however, assist meeting managers by providing unbiased, one-stop shopping of the products, services, and facilities that the destination has to offer.

CVB Structure

CVBs are organized, governed, and funded in a number of different ways. The CVB may be an independent organization, a department or branch of a chamber of commerce or an economic development agency, or a department within city government. In some jurisdictions outside North America, the CVB responsibilities rest with a state/provincial or national agency. For example, the Hungarian Convention Bureau and the Korea Convention Bureau are national organizations that act as CVBs.

Often in the United States and Canada, the CVBs primary funding is provided by dedicated transient occupancy tax or hotel room tax, which is not as common in other areas of the world. Other sources of funding include government budget allocations, membership fees and dues, corporate sponsorships, or a combination of these and other methods of funding.

FIGURE 12.2
Vancouver, British Columbia

In most cases, bureaus are membership-based organizations with a portion of funding coming from the private sector in the form of membership dues. CVB members generally include businesses that are active in the tourism industry, such as convention centers, lodging facilities, restaurants, attractions, retail outlets, destination management companies, caterers, ground operators, and convention service contractors. Bureaus also have less obvious benefactors from the visitors industry, such as accounting firms, law firms, banks, and others who elect to join the bureau to demonstrate their support for what the industry means to their community.

Many CVBs are legally registered as not-for-profit agencies and require a duly elected board of directors and by-laws to govern the affairs of the association. The board reports to the members of the association on fiscal, marketing, and membership performance measures.

Outside of the United States, many CVBs operate with a corporate label that includes "tourism."[2] The tourism label is meant to cover a broad spectrum of responsibility; unlike in the United States, where tourism tends to be used to describe activities related to leisure travel, elsewhere tourism can define all types of activities, both leisure and business.

CVBs endeavor to be fair and impartial as they represent a broad base of stakeholders in the community, such as members if they are an association. CVBs will provide sufficient information on local products and services so that intelligent decisions about using a particular business can be made.

Marketing convention destinations is closely linked to the area's convention facilities. The CVB has knowledge of the facilities' booking policies and, in some instances, manages the schedule and maintains a master calendar for the convention facility. In other instances, the bureau has booking authority enabling it to commit facilities to a meeting group. In more isolated instances, the bureau is not only the marketing arm for the convention facility, but also has operational control. Recently, some cities have merged the operations of the convention center and the CVB; however, for the most part, these organizations remain separate, albeit with some overlapping responsibilities.

CVB Relationships

The operating methods of any given bureau depend on a number of factors, including the geographic area they represent, their organization mandate, and the resources available to them. Some CVBs allocate a significant amount, if not all, of their human and capital resources to attracting convention business, while others diversify their investment. The size and deployment of the CVB sales staff depends largely on the individual city. Bureaus focus their sales efforts by region, account type or category, and account size as well as by event function, such as conventions, meetings, and trade shows.

CVBs actively solicit meeting and convention business from associations and corporations regardless of size. The CVB is eager to attract business to its location whether that means a sale of 10 guest rooms at one property or 10,000 guest rooms at properties on a citywide-event basis. Most bureaus have specialists assigned based on market segments who are experts in their particular field. These specialists become the meeting manager's point of contact with the bureau.

Developing relationships with meeting manager customers is at the core of a successful CVB. Building and maintaining these relationships comes through a variety of distribution channels, including face-to-face and remote communication. More traditional forms of communicating, such as trade show participation, advertising, and promotional materials, continue to play an important role in disseminating information and building the destination brand.

CVBs also extensively leverage technology to more effectively sell and market their destination. Database management, email marketing, and integrated web strategies are heavily utilized by the industry.

CVB web sites serve as the official destination presence on the Internet. These web sites strive to provide extensive information about the services of the CVB as well as meaningful information about the destination, convention facilities, conference centers, hotel properties, convention services, and area attractions. Many sites include the capability of submitting a request for proposal (RFP) online. This online process has several advantages:

- An RFP is submitted to the CVB at no cost.
- Facility and city information is current and accurate.
- Citywide meeting requirements can be submitted more easily than going through individual hotel properties.
- Utilizing web portals, managed by such organizations as DMAI, can send RFPs to CVBs around the world in a matter of minutes.

ASSOCIATIONS REPRESENTING CVBs

Destination Marketing Association International

The Destination Marketing Association International (DMAI) (formerly the International Association of Convention & Visitor Bureaus) was founded in 1914 to promote sound professional practices in the solicitation and servicing of meetings, conventions, and leisure markets. Located in Washington D.C., DMAI's mission is to enhance the professionalism, effectiveness, and image of destination management organizations worldwide. Today, this organization boasts more than 600 member bureaus actively involved in generating visiting group and independent business.

Membership in DMAI is a strong indication of a CVB's professionalism. DMAI is recognized worldwide as an authority on destination marketing and provides its members with opportunities for professional dialogue and exchange of information. Its intent is to continually improve the scope and caliber of its service to the meetings industry. To that end, DMAI is moving forward with the development of an accreditation program for CVBs (see Put It Into Practice).

DMAI also operates a certification program for individuals who work within CVBs. The Certified Destination Management Executive (CDME) is an advanced educational program at the executive level. DMAI also offers the Professional Destination Management (PDM) program to certify CVB employees in the basics in management and marketing.

DMAI offers web site portals that contain information from its CVB members.[3] For meeting managers, DMAI's web site enables you to search for destinations, select a city, and submit an online RFP/bid proposal form that is emailed directly to the selected cities. Moreover, the web site can link you to the official web sites of tourism organizations of worldwide travel destinations. Each destination provides information about accommodations, attractions, dining, events, entertainment, shopping, sports/recreation, and transportation. The site provides access to over 1,250 CVBs around the world, including non-DMAI member destinations.

DMAI also operates the Meetings Industry Network (MINT), which profiles over 27,000 meetings from 14,000 organizations around the globe (e.g., associations, corporations, military reunions, sporting events, and government agencies). MINT is the collaboration among 150 CVBs, which share detailed demographic and historical information about meetings held in their cities enabling the participating bureaus to source and qualify convention leads for their destinations.

Since its inception, DMAI has taken a position of leadership in the convention industry and maintains a close relationship with various other organizations concerned with conventions and leisure travel. The association actively presents its position on various issues relevant to the industry and provides an educational platform for its membership. Ultimately, their efforts identify qualified CVB organizations and individuals to work with the meetings industry.

Other Associations

Headquartered in Amsterdam, the International Congress & Convention Association (ICCA) represents a global network of 750 suppliers to the international meetings industry, with members in almost 80 countries. Membership categories include CVBs, destination management companies (DMCs), professional congress organizers (PCOs), airlines, hotels, and convention centers. Close to 200 members of ICCA are CVBs. ICCA is focused on the international meeting and congress market. Through professional development, conferences, and a shared database of international meetings, its members look to develop a competitive edge by enhancing expertise in this area. This supplier network assists meeting managers in such areas as destination knowledge, venue selection, technical advice, assistance with delegate transportation, and full convention planning.[4]

Additionally, various other organizations have international membership on more of a regional basis. For example, the Pacific Asia Travel Association (PATA) is a membership organization that provides information, advocacy, and support for the development of Pacific Asia's travel and tourism industry. PATA has some 100 government, state, and city tourism bodies, and thousands of travel professionals belonging to more than 70 PATA chapters worldwide.

Put It Into Perspective

From association to corporate to independent planner, CVBs work with a broad range of clients. CVBs provide support to groups of all sizes, whether it is a large city-wide event or a small board meeting. In addition, they assist meeting managers who are on a short-term time frame, as well as on much longer time frame.

Recognizing that the needs and expectations of meeting managers can be fairly diverse, CVBs commonly tailor their sales and servicing by type of account (e.g., association, corporate, independent). Generally, a CVB's level of involvement with associations is more extensive given that association meeting managers require a great deal of coordination and information beyond hotel rates and dates. Associations have larger groups with multiple properties and hotel brands required in a single destination. Also, given that associations go on rotation and typically have a formal bid process, they need to start with the broad destination information first before looking at confirming hotel selections.

On the corporate meetings side, CVBs work closely with these meeting managers who tend to book shorter-term business and require quicker decisions. These meeting managers usually operate in a fast pace environment and the successful CVB will be able to respond with timely information and contacts in the community. Corporate meeting managers can benefit enormously from the local knowledge a CVB provides, ensuring they are current and up-to-date with developments in the community. Many times a meeting manager will have a hotel determined prior to dealing with a CVB; in these cases, the CVB works to make certain that the meeting itself is a success.

Finally, CVBs will work in a similar fashion with independent planners as well. If the independent is representing a large or citywide type group with a longer-term planning horizon, the CVB will act to build a successful bid by pulling together the various facets in the local community that are required.

Regardless of the type of meeting manager, CVBs that are organized, client-focused, and professional will nurture the relationship to ensure the meeting manager receives all the services he or she needs. From providing basic destination information to organizing complex bids and servicing requirements, CVBs in cities and towns around the world are in business to deliver results for the meeting manager client.

Another example is the European Federation of Conference Towns (EFCT), which represents 90 destinations in 30 European countries. EFCT aims to provide information to meeting industry professionals who organize events in Europe and provides specialized training for the meeting industry players.

Additionally, other regional and national associations that represent convention destinations are found throughout the world. For example, the Confederación de Entidades Organizadoras de Congresos y Afines de América Latina (COCAL) looks after Latin American convention interests. The Australia Association of Convention and Visitors Bureaux (AACVB), and the Canadian Association of Convention and Visitors Bureaux (CACVB) have a national focus.

WORKING WITH MEETING MANAGERS

Successful CVBs are focused on satisfying the overarching needs of meeting managers, such as:

- Minimizing risk and optimizing success of meetings
- Being a trusted partner for the meeting manager
- Providing timely and accurate information
- Delivering creative and innovative service offerings
- Ensuring ease of doing business
- Making certain the meeting manager has no surprises

The Sales Cycle

CVBs will work with meeting managers during various phases of the sales cycle. Beginning with research and qualification, where the CVB determines what meetings are potential matches for their destination through to the post-event phase, CVBs need to understand what is important to the meeting manager customer at different points (see Figure 12.3).[5]

Site Reviews and the Leads Process

Determining if a site or location can accommodate requirements for a meeting is critical. The CVB is a central information source for advice on site selection, transportation, and available local services, all with no cost or obligation to the meeting manager. CVB representatives have the knowledge and information to provide up-to-date data about the area, as well as planned future developments.

Regardless of the meeting size, the CVB can serve as the first stop in the site review process. When a meeting manager contacts a CVB, a sales manager will be assigned to assist in securing the necessary information and facts needed to produce a successful meeting. The sales manager can gather information about preferred dates for the event and find out what facilities are available, if there are adequate sleeping rooms and meeting rooms, and whether convention facilities are available for the entire time period, including time for exhibitors to move in and out. CVBs have a lead process, wherein the sales manager circulates meeting specifications to facilities and lodging entities that can accommodate the requirements.

Often a first step in the process of a meeting manager determining which destinations to seriously consider involves the meeting manager completing an RFP/bid proposal form (Figure 12.4). As discussed above, RFPs are commonly done online through the DMAI web site or an individual bureau web site. Once the RFP is distributed to the sales manager at the selected destination(s), the CVB takes the information, qualifies whether the meeting is a fit for the community, and in turn distributes it to their local industry (referred to as a lead).

CVB Phase	Important Customer Needs
Research and qualification	• Suppliers are as unobtrusive as possible
Building awareness with targeted clients	• Information about options • Communication in the form customers want
Solicitation	• Accurate, timely, and detailed information about the destination • Familiar reps who understand the customer's needs and have expert local knowledge about the product • Communication in the form customers want • Trust
Bid	• Confidence that their needs can be satisfied by the CVB and destination and meeting facilities • Innovative suppliers who are solution-oriented • Local contacts
Negotiation and contracting	• Fair price and terms • Trust • Confidence in the suppliers
Event promotion and exhibitor and delegate attendance building	• Promotional materials • Advanced technical expertise • Supplier commitment to customer success • Minimize risk, optimize success
Planning and managing the event	• Ease of doing business • Access to knowledgeable local services and suppliers • Seamless destination and facility interface • Local contacts • Accurate and timely documentation
Post-event and re-booking	• Accurate, informative financial and other documentation • Timely wrap-up • Participant feedback

FIGURE 12.3
The CVB Sales Cycle

The sales manager sends the lead to all accommodation properties capable of handling the meeting. However, the meeting manager may limit the lead distribution by establishing certain parameters, such as specifying a location downtown or near the airport. In such cases, the lead would be forwarded only to properties that meet the requirements identified. If a meeting manager is familiar with the city's properties, he/she may express interest in certain facilities by name. Then, only those facilities receive the lead.

The CVB sales manager will request that the receiving property send all relevant information directly to the meeting manager; or the CVB sales manager may collect the information, compile it into a package, and send it to the meeting manager. Most jurisdictions prohibit CVBs from discussing pricing policies with hotels under consideration. All pricing discussions must take place between the meeting manager and the prospective property. A CVB salesperson may relate to a property that a meeting manager is looking for a specific range of room rates but cannot negotiate on the meeting manager's behalf.

The CVB sales manager will communicate with the meeting manager and the facilities to ensure that all information is disseminated, received, and understood. Any additional questions will be answered, and the meeting manager will

Destination Marketing
Association International

MINT RFP System

Contact Information

Prefix:	First Name:	Last Name:
Suffix:	Title:	Professional Designation:
Phone:	Fax:	Email:

Organization Information

Organization Name:

Address	Address:
City:	State/Province:	Postal Code:
Country:	Web Site:

Organization Type:

Meeting Name & Dates

Meeting Name:

Preferred Start Date:	Preferred End Date:	Meeting Held:
Alternate Start Date:	Alternate End Date:	
Response Date to RFP:	Decision Maker:	

Arrival/Departure Information

| Preferred Arrival Day: | Preferred Departure Day: | Alternate Arrival Day: | Alternate Departure Day: |

Guest Room Information

| # of Days Required: | Room Rate Range: |
| Peak Rooms Block: | Total Rooms Block: | % Single Rooms: | % Double Rooms: | # of Suites: |

Meeting Management Company

Management Company Name:

| Contact Name: | Phone: | Email: |

Meeting Profile Information

| Meeting Type: | Meeting Scope: | Total Attendees: |
| Largest Meeting Setup: | Largest Meeting Attendees: | Concurrent Breakout Rooms: |

Please indicate the continent(s) in which this meeting can be held.
Asia/Pacific Rim   Caribbean Europe   Central America   South America   North America

Please indicate whether this meeting uses official Airline/Hotel/Car Rental.
Airline   Hotel   Car Rental

Preferred Location/Facilities Information

| Preferred Location 1 ▼ | Preferred Location 2 ▼ | Preferred Location 3 ▼ |

Exhibit Information

# of 8'x10' Booths:	# of 10'x10' Booths:	# of Tabletops:	# of Other:	Other:
Gross Exhibit Area (Square Feet):	Net Exhibit Area (Square Feet):	
# of Move In Days:	# of Move Out Days:	# of Show Days:	Show Start Day:

Food & Beverage Information

| # of F&B Functions: | Largest Meal Period: | Largest F&B Attendance: | # of Off-Site F&B Functions: |

FIGURE 12.4
Online Request for Proposal (RFP)

? Did You Know?

According to DMAI, the roots of present-day CVBs in North America stretch back to 1895 when a group of businessmen in Detroit put a full-time salesman on the road to invite conventions to their city. Formed in that year, the Detroit Convention and Businessmen's League (now the Detroit Metro Convention & Visitors Bureau) is one of the oldest CVBs in the world.

be encouraged to visit the city to personally review the properties under consideration. The CVB can be of significant assistance by arranging site inspections. The CVB sales manager will develop a complete itinerary and schedule appointments with salespeople at each property. If other facilities must be reviewed during the visit, the bureau will contact the necessary parties and include them on the itinerary. In most cases, the sales manager will accompany the meeting manager on the site reviews and respond to any questions that may arise.

The CVB can also make its customer aware of any local laws and regulations that may impact the meeting. Important issues to consider often revolve around unions, taxes, alcohol serving regulations, customs requirements, and any other peculiarities during the information-gathering process. Meeting managers should be sure to discuss the condition of the local economy and local economic trends that could have an impact on their meeting. The CVB sales manager will provide the necessary information for the meeting managers to make informed decisions.

The CVB's Convention Services Manager

Once a decision is made to meet in a city, the CVB will assign a convention services manager (CSM) to the meeting group. The CSM is responsible for helping plan and conduct a successful meeting by working as an extension of the meeting manager staff in the host city (see Chapter 35).

The duties of a CSM at a convention bureau differ from those of a CSM at a hotel or convention center because they are usually carried out before the group checks into the city. The CVB's CSM has the ability to work throughout the community, rather than within just one facility, and is familiar with the full range of services and suppliers available.

CVB Services

A CVB's job is to ensure the meeting manager gets the services he/she needs. The services a CVB provides itself vary from city to city, but some are fairly standard throughout the convention industry. The BestCities Global Alliance (see Put It Into Practice) has established the following set of service standards that are practiced by its CVB members (see Figure 12.5).[p] These standards have relevance for bureaus throughout the world:

- Destination expertise
- Bid development
- Convention planning
- Attendance building
- On-site event support
- Post-event support

Put It Into Practice

Two significant efforts are underway at the moment to enhance the level of service standards delivered by CVBs. One is being led by the BestCities Global Alliance, the world's first and only alliance of CVBs, which is comprised of the CVBs from Cape Town, Copenhagen, Dubai, Edinburgh, Melbourne, San Juan, Singapore, and Vancouver. The other effort has been initiated by the Destination Marketing Association International (DMAI).

BestCities is undertaking a certification process of their quality management system that covers the evaluation and enhancement of 35 client service standards specifically focused on the meetings market. This system will be certified by Lloyds, an external certification body. The purpose of the process is to provide international meeting managers with a commitment by the eight partner CVBs to continuous improvement in servicing clients and providing the marketplace with an assurance of quality and reliability.

DMAI is in the process of developing an accreditation program to identify CVBs that have met predetermined standards and criteria to achieve this recognition. A general accreditation program will be offered and higher levels of recognition are proposed for CVBs that demonstrate consistent performance exceeding minimum accreditation standards. Accredited bureaus will be expected to pursue a philosophy of continued improvement in their operations.

The DMAI program will be broader than BestCities in that it will be available to all interested CVBs and will touch on various aspects of the organization including but not limited to the meetings area. DMAI itself will be the accrediting body. The BestCities program will be specific to the partners of the alliance, focused on the meetings area and the credentialing will be done through a third-party credentialing body.

FIGURE 12.5
The BestCities Global Alliance Brochure

Destination Expertise

CVBs provide a valuable information resource for their respective destinations. Each has access to a comprehensive range of local products and services to assist with event enquiries. Services usually include:

1. *Dedicated Meeting Manager Web Site*
   - CVBs typically have a web site link that allows meeting managers to research suitable venues and services with the ability to make contact electronically with CVB staff and/or listed members.
2. *Dedicated Meeting Manager Guide*
   - CVBs provide a printed destination planner guide available at no cost to meeting managers.
3. *Request for Proposals that Serve as a Brief for Site Selection*
   - CVBs will prepare proposals for clients, based on the requirements expressed by the client.
   - CVBs will research and propose suitable venues to client.
   - CVBs respond in a timely manner to client with venue/service options based on the time frame given by the client.
   - CVBs will set up and accompany site inspections of viable venue options where appropriate.
   - Upon request, CVBs arrange meetings for clients with suitable service suppliers.
4. *Expertise on Local Products and Services*
   - Sales and service managers provide firsthand knowledge of the venues they recommend.
5. *Access to Local Industry and Government Contacts*
   - Upon request, each CVB should be able to acquire letters of invitation/welcome from local and governmental contacts in a timely manner.
6. *Itinerary Planning and Suggestions*
   - CVBs can provide both suggestions and contacts to assist in the planning of any conference-related activity.

Bid Development

CVBs are specialists in putting together a convention bid. They provide meeting managers with bids that reflect a detailed level of local knowledge and expertise to assist the decision-making process.

1. *Detailed Event Research*—Pre-event research undertaken by the CVB to determine the historical pattern of the event, which includes:
   - Delegate numbers
   - Venue profile
   - Accommodation requirements and pricing
   - Event organizer
   - Identification of a local ambassador where appropriate
   - Previous budgets (if possible)
   - Social program details (hospitality programs, meeting specifications)
     - Hospitality programs
     - Meeting specifications
2. *Customized Bid Strategies*—Working with the meeting manager, CVBs will develop a bid strategy for each event, which includes:
   - Determining when and where bid will take place

- Determining if bid is to be submitted to national association first
- Quantities of bid documents required
- Whether CVB will be required to be present at bid
- Where appropriate, assisting in developing the strengths, weaknesses, opportunities, and threats (SWOT) analysis of the destination

3. *Customized Bid Document*—For groups where a customized bid document is required, provide the following details:
   - Features and attributes of the destination
   - Letters of support
   - Destination, venue, access, accommodation (including room blocks and rates)
   - Social program
   - Pre- and post-convention details
   - Budget consultation, guidance, and assistance

4. *Bid Presentation Support (if applicable)*
   - Airfare support for local hosts
   - Preparation of presentation
   - Promotional material on destination
   - May include support for a reception, or provision of entertainment for a reception

5. *Provision of Audiovisual Aids*
   - Video/CD/DVD
   - PowerPoint presentation
   - Images, graphics

6. *Venue and Accommodation Selection and Proposals*
   - CVBs will give an overview of relevant venues and hotels that match the specific client's requirements.
   - CVB inquires into the general availability of venues and hotels.
   - CVB assists with collection of data needed to fit a meeting's needs, arranges site inspections, distributes hotel leads, and collects proposals.

7. *Secure Provisional Room and Venue Allocations*
   - CVBs approach hotels for a tentative allocation of rooms for the conference.
   - Hotels will hold allocations until after the decision on destination selection. CVB will advise hotels on the outcome of the decision.
   - If the destination is successful with securing the meeting, hotels hold allocation until the housing service is determined.

8. *Site Inspection Support*
   - CVBs provide site inspection support for the association on a case-by-case basis. This may include transport around the city, accommodation, meals, and so on. Where possible, this is hosted by members of the CVB.

9. *Local Government and Industry Liaison*
   - CVB holds details of various local government and industry contacts.

10. *Post-Bid Questionnaire*
    - A post-evaluation questionnaire of the client's satisfaction with the CVB's services in the bid phase

Convention Planning

CVBs provide local assistance during the initial planning stages of a convention after the destination has been selected to host the meeting.

1. Housing Service

- For citywide meetings, CVBs often provide a housing service. This service is usually performed only for groups using three or more properties. Service may include housing, pre-registration, and booking airline and ground transportation. Fees may be involved.
- If a CVB does not provide this service, it may recommend to the meeting manager an outsourced third-party provider.
- Upon completion of meeting, the CVB can provide a housing report, which details information and data relevant to the completed meeting.

2. Planning Visits of Local Venues, Accommodation, and Infrastructure

- CVBs will facilitate a planning visit that may include provision of ground transportation and accommodation and setting up meetings with the relevant suppliers and local government in the city.

3. Appointment of a PCO or DMC

- CVBs provide information on the usage of a Professional Congress Organizer (PCO) or Destination Management Company (DMC), if required.

4. Development of Social Program and Pre/Post-Tour Programs

- CVBs provide suggestions for social programs or refers to a PCO or DMC depending on the situation.

5. The Selection of Other Products and Services Relevant to the Event

- CVBs will refer clients to relevant industry members that can provide the product or service.
- CVB will provide a list of suppliers that offer a range of services from registration to A/V assistance to off-site venues.

Attendance Building

CVBs will help to make each event successful and maximize delegate attendance through a variety of promotional techniques. These programs are designed to present the city in an attractive, compelling way and to ensure the meeting attendees are familiar with the destination prior to their arrival.

1. Access to Promotional Collateral

- The majority of CVBs provide information through a web site, as well as supply publications, maps (electronic and printed), and other brochures with details about the local area. These materials usually include such information as what to see and do, where to shop and dine, and points of interest.

2. Publicity Assistance

- CVBs provide background information including stock photography, slides, and video presentations.
- Some bureaus offer email capabilities and web site development to the meeting, including links to the CVB's site and digital marketing promotion.
- Standard press releases and other stock story material can be provided for incorporation in pre-convention publicity, convention magazines, and other periodicals of the meeting group.
- CVBs will provide media lists with contact information of local media for distributing press releases about the event.

3. Assistance with Attendance Building

- CVBs will work with the client in developing a delegate recruitment strategy.

- On a case-by-case basis, CVBs will help boost attendance by promoting the destination at the meeting prior to when the meeting is held in the city. It may include setting up a display booth, distribution of brochures, and showing destination videos.
- CVBs may also send a representative to address decision makers within the sponsoring organization, such as the board of directors.
- CVBs will work with airlines to provide meeting managers with offers to their delegates in the way of special fares.

On-Site Event Servicing

CVBs may provide a number of value-added services on-site to ensure the meeting manager continues to receive full attention.

1. *Visitor Guides for Delegates*
   - Provision of visitors guides and other collateral, e.g., materials, maps, events calendar.
2. *Visitor Information Booths*
   - For some events, the CVBs will staff a booth/counter at the event for information and reservation on restaurants, entertainment, and shopping.
3. *Registration and Event Support*
   - Some CVBs provide staff for tasks associated with the on-site registration process.
   - Individuals to serve as room monitors, ticket collectors, and credential/badge checkers are also provided by some CVBs.

Post-Event Support

CVBs can provide some value-added services after the event has been completed to assist the meeting manager in evaluation and follow-up.

1. *Post-Event Research and Debrief—Organizer Level*
   - To gain valuable feedback on how effectively the city facilitated the conference, CVBs may conduct one-on-one interviews or conduct surveys with the organizers. The feedback will be communicated to the appropriate sources in the destination. A post-event report will provide details and activities of the event.
   - If housing has been provided, information will be provided from all hotels on actual pick-up, cancellations, and no-show percentages. The information is also reported by the CVB to DMAI to be entered into the MINT system. With these historical statistics and current requirements at hand, the next bureau will be prepared to plan and serve the meeting.
   - CVBs can work with the meeting manager to determine the overall impact of the event, based on estimates of delegate spending and economic spending.
2. *Follow-up Communications*
   - If desirable, some CVBs are able to provide e-marketing tools to meeting managers to communicate directly with attendees after the event.
   - CVBs may assist the meeting manager in establishing a relationship with the CVB in a future city where the group is meeting.

Additional Services

CVBs can provide a list of other available services that may be needed during the meeting or convention. As most CVBs are membership organizations, such suppliers have been qualified and evaluated prior to being recommended by the bureau. In addition to the services already discussed, below are just some of the additional service providers a bureau may help identify:

- audiovisual companies
- caterers
- coach lines, limousines and taxis
- charters
- convention and exhibition service contractors
- currency exchange
- customs brokers/packaging and forwarding services
- decorating services
- display companies
- entertainment companies
- florists
- furniture rentals
- golf courses and spas
- insurance brokers
- office supplies

- photography
- printing companies
- promotional items/specialty gifts
- prop rentals and sales
- registration companies
- restaurants
- sightseeing companies
- special event and sports planners
- team building companies
- temporary help
- telecommunication services
- translation services
- unique venues
- vehicle rentals

SUMMARY

This chapter described the role and mission of a convention and visitors bureau (CVB). CVBs exist to deliver economic benefit to their respective communities through attracting and hosting nonresident visitors. They are primarily not-for-profit organizations that facilitate relationships between buyers (e.g., meeting managers) and sellers (e.g., hotels, convention facilities). Since the CVB represents all components of the hospitality and tourism industry within a given area, it is the ideal coordinating agency between these businesses and those who wish to use their services. Bureaus often serve as intermediaries, catalysts, and liaisons working for the destination, visitors, and meeting managers.

The value of the Destination Marketing Association International (DMAI) is that it is the only international association composed solely of CVBs. The organization strives to enhance the professionalism, effectiveness, and image of destination CVBs worldwide. Other associations, such as ICCA and PATA, also represent CVBs on the world stage.

CVBs work to satisfy the needs of meeting managers by minimizing risk, being a trusted partner, providing timely information, delivering creative solutions, ensuring business is done as easily as possible, and eliminating surprises. A successful CVB will work with the meeting manager throughout the sales cycle process.

The job of a CVB is to ensure the meeting manager receives attention to detail and commitment to service. Services can be fairly extensive in the areas of destination expertise, bid development, convention planning, attendance building, on-site event support, and post-event support.

Recently, the CVB industry has embarked on an effort to further elevate its service standards. The BestCities Global Alliance and DMAI are both putting into place systems to entrench services through credentialing and accreditation. The goal is to make sure that meeting managers receive an assurance of quality and reliability when they deal with CVBs.

REFERENCES

1. Tourism Vancouver (January, 2005). Business plan: Exceeding expectations.

2. Harrill, R. (Ed) (2005). *Fundamentals of destination management and marketing (IACVB)*. Lansing, MI: Educational Institute- American Hotel and Lodging Association.

3. DMAI (2006). Retrieved February 16, 2006 from http://www.destinationamarketing.org.

4. ICCA (2006). Retrieved February 25, 2006 from http://www.iccaworld.com.

5. Tourism Vancouver (2003). Draft joint marketing strategy. Vancouver, Canada.

6. BestCities Global Alliance (2004). Strategic Plan 2005-2008. Retrieved February 8, 2006 from http://www.tourismvancouver.com/meetings/vcec_expansion/vcec_newsreleases.php?id=69.

KEY TERMS

Bid	Housing	Post-event report
Booking policies	Housing report	Professional Congress
Citywide event	Lead	Organizer (PCO)
Convention and Visitors	Not-for-profit	Request for proposal
Bureau (CVB)	No-show	Site inspection
Destination Management	Occupancy tax	Site selection
Company (DMC)	Pick-up	Transient

COMPELLING QUESTIONS FOR CONSIDERATION

1. What is the prime responsibility of a CVB?

2. What are the main benefits of working with a CVB?

3. What purpose does the lead process serve during site selection?

4. What are the advantages of submitting online RFPs?

5. What are the six main areas of service that can be provided by a CVB?

6. Why is credentialing and accreditation of CVBs important?

CHAPTER 13

From Bits to Webcasts: The Technology Relevancy Factor

David Angeletti, CASE
Chief Marketing Officer
Conference Archives, Inc.

Learner Outcomes

When the reader has completed reading this chapter, he/she should be able to . . .

1 Select the most efficient and effective technology services on-site to meet the goals and objectives of the meeting.

2 Define your meeting's requirements for Internet connectivity.

3 Name the technologies available for meetings and conventions today, and what developments to prepare for in the near future.

4 Distinguish meetings for which audio, video or web conferencing would be a suitable solution.

5 Explain the terminology and technical considerations involved in producing a multi-point meeting.

6 Perform the basic functions that can be employed with web-based conferencing tools.

> The whole of science is nothing more than a refinement of everyday thinking.
>
> *Albert Einstein (1879–1955)*

OVERVIEW

Much of what Albert Einstein is known to have introduced to the world had to do with relativity. Much of what technology has to offer meeting planners, too, is relative. This chapter, in part, will illustrate how the information presented in the preceding chapter can be implemented relative to working in high-tech facilities, and/or multi-point meetings. There will also be an introduction to many of the technologies inherent to these facilities and types of meetings.

Not too long ago on-site technology for meetings and conventions revolved around electrical, audiovisual (A/V), and telecommunication services. Facility site inspections noted locations of microphone inputs, telephone jacks, and power plugs. Today, on-site technology is more relative to the needs of the group booking the site(s).

Meeting managers are incorporating the Internet and new tools such as streaming media, cyber cafés, wireless networks, and radio frequency identification (RFID) into their requirements. Exhibitors are demanding sophisticated lead retrieval systems, high-end A/V presentations, and high-speed connections to the Internet from their booths. Attendees expect speedy access to their office systems on the road and unfettered service and communications on-site. Meeting facilities from hotels to convention centers have geared up to meet a new level of requirements.

Many venues today highlight their high-tech capabilities on nearly equal footing with the amount and quality of their physical space and level of service. Advertisements for venues sell their miles of fiber optic cable network infrastructure and high-speed Internet access alongside, and sometimes above, their more traditional services. Online facility directories that allow planners to search for properties based on space and other requirements now include criteria for such services as high-speed Internet and videoconferencing.

Entirely new in-house service groups have emerged to assist meeting managers with bookings and managing their meetings on-site; especially in venues where the complexity of technology offerings is magnified by the physical size of the facilities. Many of these groups are quite capable of assisting the planner in choosing the right technology for the needs expressed, and represent larger, nationally-based firms.

Facilities are also looking for ways to better serve the customer and beat the competition. Their web sites are no longer simply Internet-enabled versions of the facility's printed color brochures. Some now provide online interactive floor plans, panoramic or three-dimensional photos, videos, reservation services, forms and contracts, and exhibitor packets. Advanced technology has become a marketing tool. Availability of these types of marketing tools should be viewed as a hint as to the level of understanding the staffs of those respective facilities possess.

The expansion of high-tech tools is not a domestic phenomenon. Facilities around the world have woven technology into their offerings to become attractive and competitive venues for organizations reaching out to global audiences. Like their U.S. counterparts, they provide complex on-site networks; reception and transmission of data, audio, and video over satellites; large numbers of high-speed Internet connections; and secure links to corporate computer networks on an international scale.

The term multi-point meeting refers to a real-time gathering of people in two or more distant locations for the exchange of ideas and information through the use of technology or a mix of technologies. Whether the technologies employed are telecommunication, satellite transmission, and/or the Internet, the gathering is still a meeting. And as a meeting, it includes many of the same elements of a traditional, face-to-face gathering—goals and objectives, a program or planned agenda, teaching tools and/or visual aids, possibly even registration procedures, exhibits, and special events.

It is important to remember that the main focus is the meeting itself—not the technology. Finding the right technology to meet the goals of the meeting is the planner's goal. Multi-point meeting technology is confusing to those who do not make it a point to at least understand the basic terminology. The options can be manifold, and the appropriate choice for a given meeting is, of course, relative; and depends upon factors such as availability of equipment and technical assistance, production costs, compatibility of computer platforms, and user comfort level with the technology.

This chapter focuses on three types of multi-point meetings—audioconferences, videoconferences, and web conferences—and provides information about the rationale for choosing each option. While it is not meant to offer all the technical information required to implement each option, it will provide a basic understanding of the technology involved so that discussions with a trusted technology partner can be more productive.

FACILITY INFRASTRUCTURE

Most meetings that cannot be held in an organization's own facilities because of size, nature of the group, or purpose of the event are conducted in hotels, conference centers, or convention centers. The growth of these facilities has been on a rapid pace in the past decade, both in number of venues and square footage devoted to meeting and exhibition space. In North America alone, more than 2.1 million square feet of new exhibit space was added in one year, from August 2000 through July 2001, according to *Tradeshow Week*'s *Major Exhibit Hall Directory*. Another 16.8 million square feet is under construction or on the drawing boards to be available for meetings by 2010.[1]

New properties are being built and existing properties are undergoing renovation and expansion to accommodate a steady growth in the size and number of meetings worldwide. However, there remain thousands of others that have not built in advances in technology due in part to the expense of retrofitting older buildings. Meeting managers should not ignore these venues if they meet all of the goals of the event, and should also recognize that the technology exists, now, to bring in a portable/temporary network, depending on how that network will be used. However, if features such as high-speed Internet connections and wiring for sophisticated on-site networks are required, the cost to supply these features in an outdated facility can substantially increase expenses.

When selecting a site for a meeting or convention, consider the goals and objectives of the overall event and how well the facility is equipped to meet these goals. This is true for technology just as it is for the size and quality of meeting space, staging considerations, or food selection. If one of the goals of the meeting is to allow participants to stay in close communication with the home office, site selection criteria may include Internet access in guest rooms, kiosks for e-mail connections in the exhibit hall, and cell phone transmission systems on property.

In addition to the needs of your meeting participants, consider how you and your staff will stay "connected" while on-site. You may use a wireless digital telephone, laptop computer with email and Internet access, a handheld personal digital assistant (PDA), two-way radio, and pager. A wide area network (WAN) may need to be established to link registration and offices internally and to an off-site office. A property-wide wireless communications system may need to be established to keep you, your staff, and facility personnel in close contact. These virtual local area networks (VLANs) enable you to create privately networked

---

Fast Facts

Types of Multi-point Meetings

- Audioconferences
- Videoconferences
- Web conferences

Put It Into Practice

Portable Networks

The American Heart Association (AHA) implements a VLAN structure to facilitate moving large volumes of data and files within the meeting venues they occupy for their annual Scientific Sessions meeting. Offering nearly 3,000 presentations from thousands of presenters, and hosting over 25,000 attendees, Scientific Sessions is a living example of why VLANs exist. AHA needs to manage tens of thousands of registration records, move presentation files throughout a centralized network to ensure the right files are available in the appropriate session rooms, and report on various logistics throughout this citywide meeting. The VLAN remains secure, and available only to AHA-designated personnel while on-site. Once the meeting concludes, the network is disconnected.

zones that can be controlled within the facility, and not necessarily be linked to the public Internet.

Setting up many meetings and conventions today can be complex. When discussing the more sophisticated needs of your event, it is beneficial to speak to each property's chief engineer early in the decision stage. Make them aware of the various technology solutions planned for implementation, regardless of whether those plans will be actualized. This allows the facility to be better prepared to help reach the goals set for the meeting.

Wired Networks

As facilities first began wiring their structures for the needs of computer networking, the standard at the time was category cable, specifically Category 3 (Cat 3) copper cabling. This network infrastructure allowed signals to pass through it at a speed of 10 mbps (10 megabits of data per second). This speed was sufficient for the computing needs then, but technology quickly outpaced the performance offered by this type of cabling.

Further development in copper cabling has produced much greater efficiencies in data transfer, introducing Category 5 (Cat 5) lines capable of transmission speeds of 100 mbps. Category 6 (Cat 6), still relatively new in convention and meeting facilities, is a super-fast network running at speeds of approximately four *billion* bits (or four gigabits) per second.

Thanks to the advent of fiber optics—which transmit voice (telephone), data, and video signals over glass fiber cables at essentially the speed of light—facility networking infrastructures can provide the bandwidth required for hundreds or thousands of simultaneous users and multiple data sources.

The state-of-the-art in facility infrastructure now includes a fiber optic backbone with Cat 6 or Cat 5 cabling expanding the network out to the distribution points. This is an important baseline to keep in mind when negotiating for space at a center where networking will be a crucial element for the event.

An Internet connection is brought into the building via one or more DS3 (also know as T-3) lines, providing access at 45 Mbps each from the facility's Internet service provider, 30 times faster than the more common T-1 lines. Capabilities also include slower lines, such as ISDN and DSL, for more economical solutions not requiring the full capabilities of the network.

If Internet access will be used only for communication kiosks (email stations), or for passive Web connections (allowing people to use web-based email or other communication tools, and not mission-critical tasks) T-1 or DSL type connections are likely to be just fine, depending on the number of workstations that will be on the network. The facility engineer can help you to determine which of these connections are most suitable. If you have a large exhibit hall, and/or a number of services (included educational session needs) that will, for example, require access to the Internet for demonstrations, it is best to move up to the more substantial connection.

One interesting point to note is that, especially in older facilities, these connections are sometimes brought into the building by a provider (e.g., Verizon, BellSouth) on a temporary basis only. This means that a sufficient amount of time should be allotted for the facility to have the service installed, and can typically take anywhere from 30 to 90 days to order and have installed in time.

Wireless Networks

Many properties have added wireless networks to their existing systems, and this is a key trend to watch. With wireless technology, the facility manager can simply activate an area rather than going to the location and wiring it, resulting in tremendous savings in staff time and a convenience for the end user. Setup in the property using overlapping cells for best coverage, a wireless network gives users full Internet or network access on their desktop computer, laptop, or PDA from anywhere in the facility with a special wireless receiver card. While there are several benefits, it should also be noted that wireless networks are suspected to be one of the most prevalent access points for unauthorized access to a network, thereby posing a security issue.

There are a few wireless protocols or standards in use today, and it is important to understand what the property supports if a wireless network is to be used for an event. Two standards are used for transmission ranges of 100 feet or more, IEEE 802.llb (also known as wireless fidelity or Wi-Fi) and HomeRF. These wireless systems are already installed in hotels, from public space to guest rooms, throughout convention facilities, in airports, and even the corner coffee shop. As wireless technologies continue to be developed, it is smart to continually monitor what is available in the facilities you intend to book.

Bluetooth, a third wireless protocol, has a shorter transmission range of about 30 feet. Bluetooth is intended to eliminate the need for many of the inconvenient cables connecting computers, printers, telephones, PDAs, and other devices. Bluetooth provides more of a personal network because of its shorter range but has numerous applications in the meeting environment. It is being incorporated in hotels, from curbside check-in to wireless printing in the guest room. In meeting space, Bluetooth-enabled devices can send questions to a presenter or be used for instant audience response. Bluetooth in the exhibit hall can be used to alert attendees to their proximity to a particular booth, or to exchange pertinent information between buyer and seller without the clumsiness of some traditional information retrieval systems. Bluetooth technology is still in its infancy, but offers a great deal of promise for interactivity in a conference environment.

Applications for Meetings

A sophisticated network provides an entirely new set of capabilities for the event attendee, exhibitors, and the meeting manager. Increased bandwidth and the convergence of technology means that any access point can handle any machine that might benefit from network access, including telephones, computers, credit card systems, badge and card readers, videoconferencing, lead retrieval systems, display signage, security cameras, and fire systems.

With a coded name badge or card with a person's general information, a swipe of the card eliminates tickets, confirms entrance into sessions, works with

Fast Facts

Wireless Options
- WiFi
- Home RF
- Bluetooth

exhibitors' lead retrieval systems, and can even be used as money to buy a latté or a newspaper, use the Internet, or buy a soda from a vending machine. The technology exists to make smart cards do everything from serve as the key to your hotel guest room to transmit a request for proposal (RFP) to an exhibitor at the booth.

Registration desks and each meeting room can be linked to staff offices. Exhibitors can show their web site as part of their display, or even webcast their demonstration from the exhibit hall floor to customers and prospects who could not physically attend. In the same manner, worldwide audiences can "attend" keynote and other presentations live, or at their convenience, by downloading archived webcasts from the event web site.

The real convenience for facility managers and meeting managers alike is that by having properties fully wired and networked, "plug-and-play" connectivity to networks and the Internet is easily achieved. Gone are the days of having engineers run cables to every computer and configuring every system. A technology layout today should include floor outlets with data, voice, video, and power access on at least a 30-foot grid in exhibit halls, on every fixed wall in meeting rooms, and on all fixed walls in public areas for best overall access. Whatever the requirement, the end user plugs into the access point, goes through a simple configuration procedure, and begins to work.

Do not overlook the networking needs of your vendors either. While most are adept at including their networking requirements during the proposal process, it is still wise to inquire about them before signing a contract, and then learning on-site that something was missed.

TELECOMMUNICATIONS

Telecommunications services required by meetings have expanded from analog phone lines to include mobile phones, pagers, wireless PDAs, and other gadgets. Take that connectivity away, and you may be faced with irate customers. Unfortunately for many facilities, the location or the building construction materials may create a block between users and their telecommunications services, especially digital/cellular telephones. Some properties rent or otherwise provide cellular phones using an outside vendor with a nearby receiving antenna. This enables clear communication, but also forces the user to adopt a new telephone number.

Another way facilities bring cell service into the site and provide clear signals is to have small cellular transmission sites known as repeaters installed. These receive signals within the building and transmit directly to a larger main tower of the cellular service provider. The clarity of these channels has to be balanced with the expense of setting up the service, however. Repeaters can cost more than $25,000 and each cellular provider needs a separate system.

The communication needs of the meeting staff have also increased over time and are being met by modern facilities. There are still requirements for basic analog systems, providing access to local telephone services and dial-up Internet connections. Two-way radios continue to provide communication between far-flung staff members and facility personnel. Wireless telephone systems are being included in many properties to allow instant access throughout the venue, combining the best of standard telephone service and radio.

Rather than deal with the din of two-way radios, sometimes with dozens of conversations on the same channel, small wireless handsets allow the meeting and facility staff to keep in close communication. The devices can be preconfigured to speed-dial key staff and include the ability to call local or long-distance telephone services.

INTERNET SERVICES

Many considerations revolve around Internet access for meetings. Questions to consider, and to discuss with the Internet service provider (ISP) for the facility, include:

- What are the overall meeting goals, and how can Internet technology meet those goals?
- What are the needs of speakers, attendees, exhibitors, meeting staff, and the press?
- How many devices will be hooked up to the Internet?
- How will the devices be used?
- Does each device need its own IP (Internet protocol) address?
- What is the maximum amount of data that will be transmitted?
- Will there be massive data streams such as videoconferencing or webcasts?

Once the technology structure and Internet needs of the meeting are defined, facility staff can appropriately configure their systems. Many venues have DS3 lines available, but this is not yet standard. Others have T-1 lines, DSL, cable, ISDN, all of the above, or none at all. Even for moderate Internet use during a conference, broadband access is desirable, meaning at least a DSL or cable connection to the Internet. If the selected property does not have the capacity to support your technology needs, those services can be obtained, but it can be costly.

If the facility already has permanent Internet access through an ISP, or is itself a service provider, budgeting for access and networking should be straightforward. In-house service providers are not common but do exist. For proper negotiation of services and rates, knowing who is providing the service can help avoid confusion.

Also knowing exact requirements can save literally thousands of dollars. Costs for connectivity vary wildly and are plummeting. Prices for individual Internet connections range from under $100 to over $500 but associated services may or may not be included. If you have a large number of connections, it can be advantageous to purchase blocks of IP addresses. A Class C Internet address includes approximately 250 addresses, which can be used for a period of time. Expect to pay $2,500 or more (with individual setups contracted separately). Compared to an average $300 per connection standard price, those same 250 connections would cost $75,000. The difference can purchase plenty of technical support for those individual needs. Again, be sure to inquire about the amount of time it could take to have the service made available to you. In some cases wait time can be as long as 90 days.

SUPPORT SERVICES

Developing a good working relationship with the technical staff of your chosen facility means the difference between glowing reviews and disappointment. Even if you have or hire your own engineering team, the property staff are probably the only ones who know where all the switches are and can manage the network efficiently. During your site inspection, ask about in-house support services. If you have complex networking requirements, have your networking specialist or consultant talk directly to the facility staff about their capabilities.

LANs, WANs, and VPNs

If you are going to be operating one or more local area networks (LANs), for instance a staff office, press room, cyber café, and hands-on computer laboratory,

---

Fast Facts

Internet Connection Transmission Speeds

Keep these parameters for data transmission speeds in mind when deciding how much bandwidth you need:

- ISDN   128 kilobits per second (kbps)
- T-1   1.5 mbps
- Cable   1.5-2 mbps
- DSL   1.5-9 mbps
- DS3 (T-3)   45 mbps

you must know your configuration down to the last computer, printer, and other network peripheral. Diagram the systems and share the diagrams with the network administrator as early as possible.

If the systems will be connected to outside networks in a WAN, further consideration needs to be given to how that link will be made. It may be advantageous to bring network administrators from the host organization and property together to discuss details.

Knowing that networks will be connected via the Internet poses additional considerations, such as privacy and security. A firewall may need to be added to the network to restrict access to or from certain systems via the Internet or block them out entirely.

A virtual private network (VPN) may also be configured, creating a secure way to transmit information between the on-site system and a corporate network and enabling users to stay connected to their offices.

Multimedia Services

In addition to networking and Internet services, a host of hi-tech multimedia functions are coming to hotels and conference and convention centers. Discuss the facility's capabilities and consider the implications for making your programming accessible to a broader audience than ever before.

Videoconferencing is becoming increasingly popular as an adjunct to larger conferences or to make more efficient use of time and resources. Some facilities have conference rooms equipped with specialized tables that have built-in microphones, speakers, power and network inputs at each seat. Cameras are mounted in the walls, with multiple monitors and video projection systems strategically located. Transmissions are sent and received over permanent satellite uplink and downlink stations, or over secure broadband connections. Professional-looking videoconferencing can be as simple as walking into a room and flipping a few switches.

In many locations, on-site production facilities can rival commercial television studios. Trained crews use broadcast-quality equipment and transmission systems for all types of point-to-point multimedia communication. Want to create a closed-circuit television network to keep attendees up-to-date with convention news? Need to do a live webcast of the keynote presenter, or a demonstration from the show floor? In more and more venues, excellent broadcast production services are available in house.

Put It Into Practice

Multimedia Services

The American Society for Microbiology has all of its sessions recorded during their Annual Sessions conference each year. The resulting recordings, as well as Adobe Acrobat (PDF) versions of the authorized presentations are then released on the Web as an added value to attendees. A parallel site for media organizations is also created allowing medical journals of all sorts to access the science presented each day of the conference.

These services are pre-arranged and carefully constructed to offer the best use of the technology inherent to the facility, or that is erected within the facility (e.g., VPNs). Where available, the recording company interfaces with the contracted A/V company to ensure clean audio feeds, and records the sessions in a digital format. The resulting files are produced in a manner that matches them up with the related presentation file in PDF format, and presented to the media on the web . . . directly from the conference.

Technology nerve centers can also control the environment, and manage electronic signage throughout the facility and on outside marquees. Conference proceedings can be fed to hotel guest rooms, or over the Internet to anyone who could not make the event. Need to produce audio recordings of sessions? Chances are they can be digitally recorded at a central location, rather than running cable and setting up recorders in every room. Sophisticated systems may provide simplified translation services, or a central distribution point for presentations to each session room. Your recording vendor sits in an optimal position to rate the feasibility of recording from a patch bay of this sort. The quality of the audio feed varies greatly among facilities, and this is something that requires professional insight.

Wired facilities include central processing points for conference proceedings. Whatever is recorded in any format, can be gathered, edited, and prepared for distribution on CD, DVD, audio tape, printed and bound, downloaded to a PDA, or posted to a web site.

The captured media (audio, video, visuals) can then be produced into a variety of integrated archives that can include searchability, synchronized elements (audio to visuals), and even continuing education opportunities, though these level of services are most often available only through third-party suppliers.

THE VIRTUAL WORLD OF HI-TECH FACILITIES

Before you ever set foot in a facility, technology can greatly assist in the planning process. Meeting venues have blossomed on the web, with full-featured sites that offer a wealth of information and services. Today's savvy planner can take a virtual tour that includes panoramic photographs, three-dimensional modeling of meeting space in a variety of setups viewed from various angles, and downloadable floor plans that can be manipulated to show preferred setup designs and returned to the venue for their files. While this level of sophistication is reserved for only the most visionary of facilities, it can be expected that more and more facilities will begin to implement technologies of this manner in the coming years.

Major hotel chains are already posting available dates and value opportunities on their web sites, and you can check availability and book meetings online with some properties, especially for smaller meetings. Online housing forms allow attendees to reserve rooms and receive instant confirmations. You can manage you room blocks, check attendance, and report results online.

Online RFPs, service agreements, and exhibitor packages are common. Food-and-beverage selections, A/V equipment inventories, and other meeting necessities will soon be selected on the web and entered into an online event order. In many convention centers and hotels, exhibitors can order electrical, Internet connections, computer equipment, telecommunications, and a host of other services from their office, or wherever they happen to have an Internet connection and web browser.

Because the better web sites today are backed up by powerful databases, service-oriented facilities can turn their web visits into valuable management information. RFP and meeting histories can be stored online for the customer's convenience in a secure and private database. Customer profiles can be constantly updated. As more information about the planners, exhibitors, and their meetings is acquired, intelligent systems can report out on trends and requirements, helping the sales and operations teams provide personalized service with much greater ease than traditional paper-based systems.

It is these types of meeting logistics and attributes that are being addressed by APEX. APEX promises a standard means for providing and exchanging attributes and logistical information between meeting planners and suppliers.

The more entrenched these practices become, the more easily it will become for planners to compare facilities and other suppliers to each other, thereby making the decision process more informed, and balanced.

AUDIOCONFERENCING

When voice contact between meeting participants will suffice, an audioconference is the least complicated option for a multi-point meeting. Audioconferencing has become integral to the way business is done today, and conference calls are being handled in a variety of ways. Typically, participants join the conference by dialing a special telephone number at a prearranged time. When participants are connected to the conference, they have two-way audio capabilities—that is, they can speak to and hear the other participants.

In some instances, the Internet can also be used as a streaming audio resource where participants log onto a web site that carries the conferencing program live—bypassing some international long distance barriers. Participants need a microphone and speaker on their computers, and a compatible web browser.

In any case, the integration of the human voice in a collaborative discussion, while using only the sense of hearing, is still one of the most effective business tools and provides a valuable, readily available option for holding meetings with participants around the world. As is the case with most services of this nature, recordings of the actual conference can be made available in many formats for delivery to other audiences at a later date.

It should also be noted that hundreds of audioconference providers are in business, each typically reselling the same services from a tier one provider, e.g., Sprint. They differentiate themselves typically by price and additional services (operator assisted options, reporting options), but ultimately the base service is all coming from just a few true providers. Let price and service options be your guide to choosing your provider.

Videoconferencing

While videoconferences have existed for quite some time, the various methods and applications have continued to evolve. The technology takes two basic routes—satellite or cable (fiber optic or copper). Regardless of which transmission method you use, the essential questions are the same:

- Where does the video originate?
- Where does it need to go?
- How many sites need access?
- Do you need one-way or two-way communication?

Video may be transmitted between one point and another point (point-to-point), or between many points (multi-point). Point-to-point satellite transmission is relatively simple to understand, in that an origination site is captured on video, encoded digitally, and transmitted via satellite from an uplink site to a downlink site, where it is decoded and displayed. This may take the form of one-way communication, where one site sends and the other receives live video data; or two-way communication, where both sites are sending and receiving. A multi-point satellite videoconference involves three or more locations with uplink/downlink capabilities. Satellite videoconferencing can be costly for small meetings and is typically reserved for larger gatherings.

More common on a day-to-day basis are videoconferences that use some type of cable—either fiber optic communication cable or hard cable such as that available from the local phone provider. ISDN service is typically used for many business applications.

While satellite videoconferencing uses standard video, cable-based video-conferencing uses compressed video. This means that the signal is processed and transmitted through a video modem called a CODEC, which compresses the signal on the transmission end and decompresses it on the receiving end. In some applications, this compressed video travels through high-speed digital data lines, such as T-1, DSL, or T-3 lines. The speed of transmission and the quality of the video are directly related as you go from a single ISDN line at 128 kilobits per second (kbps), to 3 ISDN lines at 384 Kbps, to DSL at 1.5 megabits per second (mbps), to T-1 at 1.5 mbps, to T-3 at 45 mbps. Naturally, the faster the speed, the more costly the service.

What type of criteria should exist to consider a videoconference to meet the needs of your organization? There are several factors that lend themselves towards using videoconferencing as a solution; when more than one geographic location where audience members will be participating *and* the content being presented can only be conveyed in a video format, and is critical to the success of the meeting; or when visual confirmation of the attending audience is required to validate participation.

There are several important factors to consider in planning a videoconference, including technical considerations, physical setup, and how you will conduct the program.

Put It Into Practice

Technical Considerations for Videoconferencing

- Is the videoconference to be point-to-point or multi-point between three or more locations?
- Will the videoconference be held at your site or at a rented videoconferencing facility?
- If multi-point videoconferencing, is the facility equipped with a multi-point bridge?
- How many participants will be at each location?
- Will each participant have good visibility and camera and microphone coverage?
- If using a cable-based system, what connection speed is available at the facility?
- What other equipment will be needed for the (video, computer, etc.)?

Physical Setup

- Determine the type of equipment used at the remote sites.
- Identify and confirm the ISDN numbers for the remote sites.
- Test the system with a call in advance to ensure compatibility between local/remote sites and systems.
- Test all video equipment at least 30 minutes before the meeting.
- Be sure cameras are adjusted for best visibility.
- Adjust all lighting in the rooms to ensure best visibility for the camera image.

Pre-Conference Planning

- Determine the time of the videoconference. Consider time-zone differences for international participants.
- Prepare an agenda, allowing enough time for audience interaction.
- Distribute the agenda, along with the date, time, and a list of participants with locations.
- If materials are to be distributed, do so before the conference begins to save time during the conference.
- Provide instructions for the participants to follow in the event of technical difficulties.
- Plan on using a facilitator, particularly for multi-point conferences.
- Ask participants to arrive 15 to 20 minutes early to ensure an on-time start.

Attendee Apparel Guidelines

- Avoid wearing plaids and prints; they may be emphasized on screen.
- Pastel colors are preferable; white causes a glare.
- If you must wear a white shirt, add a dark jacket.
- Avoid wearing red; it may "bleed."

Day of Program

- Introduce all the participants at each location.
- Review and follow the published agenda to maximize time and cost efficiencies.

(continued)

Put It Into Practice, continued

- Ask all participants to address each other by name to avoid confusion during the conference.
- Use short segments of information for better audience retention and smoother question-and-answer sessions.
- Use color graphics where helpful in communicating key points.
- Reduce background noise by putting participants in listen-only mode when they are not speaking.
- When international connections are used, allow for slight delays in response time to avoid overlap and interruption in responses.

Videoconferencing Etiquette

- Be yourself, speak naturally, and identify yourself as necessary.
- Look into the camera to establish eye contact with remote participants.
- Pause occasionally so others may make comments.
- Let the other sites know when you are going to display a graphic so they do not transmit an image at the same time.

- Minimize extraneous noise. For example, avoid coughing into the microphone, shuffling papers, and engaging in side conversations.
- Pay attention to which camera is in use. If a document camera is being used to show a graphic, be sure to switch back to the main camera when the discussion moves on to another topic.

Ending the Videoconference

- Conclude your meeting on time if at all possible.
- Reserve time at the end for wrap-up and good-byes.
- If your meeting will run longer than planned, contact your videoconferencing coordinator to determine if the meeting can be extended.

Post-Conference Follow-Up

- Record the conference and offer audio or videotapes.
- Have minutes taken through the conference and follow up with printed conference proceedings.

Web Conferencing

The fastest-growing type of multi-point meetings is being held over the Internet. Much like other conferencing techniques, the web conference takes on a variety of configurations from point-to-point to multi-point to collaborative applications. Web-based multi-point meetings allow two or more people to communicate and collaborate as a group over the Internet or corporate Intranet in real time. This involves both desktop and audio communication either over the computer network or through standard phone lines. In some instances, web cameras may be integrated into the system to enhance the meeting with the addition of live streaming video.

Web conferencing applications vary widely, from systems that integrate voice, video, and data over web-based, carrier-class communications services; to streaming services that use fiber optic and copper cable to send video signals to multiple distribution sites, which then distribute a high-quality signal via satellite. Dozens of service providers have emerged to provide the technical know-how and hosted applications needed to implement web-based meetings. Your information technology department or a qualified consultant can assist with selecting and implementing an appropriate service.

Web conferencing offers several benefits over alternative multi-point conference formats, including:

- Attendees can participate without leaving their offices, using an Internet connection, computer, and phone, thus saving both time and travel expense (conversely, they can participate even when they're on the road).
- A web conference can augment a face-to-face conference, broadening the reach of an event to include many who may not be able to travel or who would not normally be able to participate in an event. The same attribute

allows for additional revenue to be generated by allowing for web conference participants to attend your live event virtually, though they never would have been on-site regardless of price or schedule.

- Using the Internet rather than satellite uplink/downlink services is less costly for the sponsoring organization; and typically does not exhibit as much latency with regard to delivery of the content (sound is delivered more immediately, and with less delay than with satellite signals).
- Hosted web conferencing applications are frequently priced on a volume basis, so the more meetings you hold via the Web, the less the per-meeting cost.

System Capabilities

Most web conferencing tools revolve around the ability to show presentation slides, such as a Microsoft Power Point presentation. Additionally, web conferencing systems provide several secondary functions that enable the conference facilitator to more actively engage conference participants: application sharing, chat, white boarding, file transfer, polling, and web browser sharing. Regardless of the platform you choose to provide your web conferences, realize that participants may be required to install proprietary software on their PCs in order to participate. This can provide a major impact if your participants are not aware of this requirement, and must first get approval or assistance to install the software.

- *Presentation mode*—Intended for presentations, briefings, and distance-learning applications, presentation mode allows the presenter to show slides to remote participants. There is typically a short pause between the time a presenter changes the slides, and the web audience sees the change, however, the pause is negligible at best. Most platforms also do not enable the use of animations in these presentations, since the slides are actually translated into images for easy sharing on the web.
- *Application sharing*—Allows users to share an application that is running on one computer with other online participants in the conference. Those participants can then review the data or information live and see actions as the person sharing the application works on a document (editing content, presenting information, etc.). The person sharing a document can choose to collaborate with other conference participants and even let others take turns editing a document. Only the person sharing the program in which the edits are taking place needs to have the shared application installed on his/her computer.
- *Chat*—Users enter text messages to discuss topics with other participants. A chat log can be used to record meeting notes and list action items during the meeting. Additionally, participants can use text-based discussion to communicate privately with other participants in the conference without interrupting the audio communication between the bigger groups of participants. It is wise to review the chat log before publishing it as part of a post-event archive to ensure there are no issues with regard to liability.
- *Whiteboarding*—Provides a multi-page, multi-user drawing application that allows users to sketch diagrams, designs, or charts and to display other graphic information to participants in a conference. A user can import a digital image into the whiteboard and use the whiteboard as a focus for discussing the image, annotating it with questions and comments. In addition, a remote pointer or highlighting tool can be used to point out specific content or sections of shared pages.
- *File transfer protocol (FTP)*—Allows conference participants to send files to one or all of the other participants. The file transfer occurs in the

Fast Facts

Tip: The practice of contracting with a specific provider is not widely used since price-matching is very typical. Again, let service offerings be your guide when choosing.

Fast Facts

Tip: Application sharing is considered by some IT professionals as a high security risk, so be sure that participants are aware that application sharing will be used during a specific event.

background as participants continue to meet, share information or work on graphic files. Some systems allow participants to share a hard copy document with all participants by faxing it into a meeting. It should be noted here that file transfers represent a security risk and may be blocked by some organizations. This is an aspect of your meeting that you'll want to pre-announce for your participants.

- *Web browser sharing*—With this feature, any participant can navigate the web and synchronize the browsers of other participants to display the navigated sites. Co-browsing is fully interactive, and control can be passed to any participant, thus enabling users to complete web forms together and annotate the web pages.

- *Audience polling*—Allows presenters to solicit immediate feedback from attendees. The presenter composes questions with multiple-choice answers and displays the questions to participants as an aside to the ongoing discussion. Participants select an answer and submit their response. The poll is automatically tabulated, and results can be displayed to participants in graphic format, such as a pie or bar chart. Results can also be logged and be included as part of a post-event archive.

- *Web conferencing archives*—Some providers allow for the recording of all interactions in a meeting for later reference, training or demonstration purposes. These archives can be made available on the web for participants to access later as an added value, or can be accessed on a purchase-based basis to create a new revenue stream for the organization. This function can also be performed by your archiving vendor of choice.

- *Security*—Many systems work independent of existing firewall technology and can offer unlisted meetings, password-protected entry into meetings, and data encryption to protect sensitive data.

More services and software features are being added each day as organizations find new and varied applications for web-based meeting technology. The key is to stay abreast of the trends as they develop and make logical choices based on your needs. As with any technology, the only features that are important are the ones that help achieve your meeting goals. Acquiring features that no one will use or that become more of a distraction for your participants can be counterproductive. Examine available features and select only those that fit your needs and budget. This will keep your meetings effective and your budget under control.

Although most systems enable platform-independent meeting participation on Windows, Mac OS, and UNIX, testing the functionality in advance is the only way of ensuring acceptable performance.

Interactivity

A web-based meeting environment offers numerous advantages; however, there are disadvantages that must also be weighed. While the technology makes it practical for people from all over the world to meet online, it can be difficult to keep participants focused and involved in the meeting. In most instances, each participant sits at his/her own workstation and can attempt to multi-task to more pressing matters or become distracted when a topic is not particularly interesting.

To ensure that an online meeting is productive for all participants, plan interactivity into the program. Actively engage participants and solicit their response using voice, visual, and text contact. Vary the format between presentation, discussion, and collaboration, and allow for questions and answers during the presentation. Ask for feedback on the effectiveness of the format, and adjust the program as needed.

Collaborative Meetings

Real-time collaboration is rapidly becoming a critical tool for groups of all sizes, providing new opportunities to meet, collaborate, and work on documents across geographic boundaries. These virtual meetings can reduce travel costs, improve productivity, and support problem solving anytime and from anywhere.

The average business professional can make three to six trips each month to attend meetings. At the same time, organizations are constantly under pressure to keep travel costs down. Web-based meetings provide an alternative to the traditional business meeting. The relatively low cost also allows for more frequent collaborative meetings and greater speed in communicating between participants.

SUMMARY

Technology infrastructure can be a key to success, but according to property managers it is rarely a profit center. Adding technology infrastructure, upgrades, and services adds value, and increased value draws and keeps customers; but it is expensive, and the shelf life is short. It is increasingly important for meeting managers to stay abreast of these developments and how they can impact their events.[2]

During the site selection and inspection process, include a technology checklist for the features and capabilities that can help your event fulfill its goals.[3,4] Assess the infrastructure for wired and wireless networking capabilities, data transmission speeds, and plug-and-play connectivity. Inquire about telecommunications services and how the facility accommodates mobile phone usage throughout the building. Find out whether Internet services are provided in-house or by an outside ISP, and determine the costs associated with meeting your bandwidth requirements for programming and participants. Determine how in-house support services can add value to your meeting through videoconferencing, webcasting, and production and distribution of multimedia conference proceedings. Finally, familiarize yourself with the venue's web site features and functionality and consider how online booking, event orders, housing, and other services could improve service to your participants and impact your bottom-line.

In other words, make sure the options available from the facility meet the needs and goals of your meeting, not only from an infrastructure point of view, but from the perspective your group represents with respect to Internet accessibility. Use the referenced checklists to ensure that the technology solutions you require (or think you require) are either available or can be arranged for from each of the venues you are considering.

In reality, we are in a transition period for technology in meeting and convention facilities. A few use their technical prowess to provide better service, gain business and grow market share, but others lag. Technology is changing the way everyone is doing business and driving many of the decisions made by both meeting managers and facilities. However, technology is simply a tool. In the rush to be high-tech, it is easy to overlook your goals and, therefore, miss the mark for your event.

Advanced technology in facilities is becoming the standard instead of the exception, and meeting managers are beginning to understand how the technology can help them meet or exceed the goals and objectives set for their events. It is no longer simply locating the light controls and microphone inputs. Today's meeting managers are bringing technology into meetings and conventions with the help of the facilities that support them, and they are raising the bar for meetings with every new application.

Any meeting conducted using technology sacrifices some of the human dynamics that are achieved in face-to-face meetings. People express themselves in more than words or speech. Nonverbal aspects are not easily translated in a

Fast Facts

Web Conferencing

NACHA—The Electronic Payments Association partners with a conferencing provider and archiving provider to ensure all of its audioconference series presentations are documented in full. The user interacts with a phone and PC, thereby hearing what is said, and seeing what the speakers are presenting in a simultaneous fashion. At the same time, the archiving vendor records the audio portion of the program, and receives the presentation file from NACHA. The resulting files are synchronized and presented back to the conference participants online as an added value, and sold to those who were unable to participate.

technology-based meeting. For this reason, meeting managers need to balance the use of technology with the more traditional gatherings of people. Audioconferencing, videoconferencing, and web conferencing should be considered as a complement to, not a substitute for, traditional meetings. Take the time to become familiar with the key terms of this chapter and the implications they represent for your meeting and group.

Whatever the goals of the meeting—education, motivation, or collaboration—multi-point meeting technology can be used to reduce or eliminate travel costs for some participants. It can extend the reach of the event beyond the traditional audience to segments who might not otherwise be able to participate, such as international members. The technology also facilitates meetings where working groups must reach consensus, make decisions, and produce deliverables. These are just a few of the scenarios for which multi-point meetings have application.

In selecting the meeting format, consult with a knowledgeable service provider about the costs, equipment, and potential technical difficulties that could impact the success of the meeting. Find out how many participants the format can effectively handle; how transmission speeds will affect quality of audio, video and data transmitted during the meeting; what features are available to enhance interactivity among participants; what conditions could interrupt service; and whether the provider will have technical support available during the meeting. If participants will want to share materials before, during, and/or after the meeting, ask how these materials can be distributed. Also find out whether audio and video recordings and text transcripts of the meeting can be produced and distributed, and at what cost. For example, some services have pay-per-view fees for on-demand webcasts of prerecorded web conferences.

Register for a number of meetings industry web conferences and other online offerings to gain greater familiarity with the technology, and how to use the various options available. Your ability to market these opportunities to your members will be a direct result of how well you understand and use the same technology.

As the technology evolves, multi-point meetings will improve the way organizations communicate. Integrated audio, video, and data communication will become more commonplace. People will be able to communicate their ideas using the most effective means possible—whether preproduced graphics, live video images, document mark-up, interactive polling, or new technology that has yet to be introduced. Regardless of how people meet, the experience and skills of the informed meeting professional will be key to making their meetings successful.

REFERENCES

1. NA (2001). *Major exhibit hall directory.* Los Angeles: Tradeshow Week.

2. Siwik, E. (2006). Break through the maze: Managers guide to meeting technology. Hague, NY: Flashpoint Technologies, LLC.

3. Ball, C. (2001). Meeting planners technology checklist. Retrieved March 22, 2006 from http://www.corbinball.com/tipstools/index.cfm?fuseaction=cor_ArticleView&artID=370&sectionCode=tipstools.

4. Rasco, J. W. (2001). The tech check: Site inspections for today's wired meetings. Retrieved March 15, 2006 from http://www.corbinball.com/articles_site/index.cfm?fuseaction=cor_ArticleView&artid=482&sectionCode=art_site.

KEY TERMS

Application sharing	Firewall	Point-to-point
Audience polling	Gigabit	Repeater
Audioconference	Homerf	Smart card
Backbone	IEEE 802.11b	Streaming
Bandwidth	Internet service provider	T-1 line
Bit	(ISP)	T-3 line
Bluetooth	ISDN	Uplink
Broadband	Kbps	Videoconference
Category cable	Kilobit	Virtual private network
Chat	Local area network	(VPN)
Codec	(LAN)	Webcast
Cyber café	Mbps	Web conference
Digital subscriber line	Megabit	Whiteboarding
(DSL)	Multi-point bridge	Wide area network (wan)
DS3	Multi-point meeting	Wireless fidelity (Wi-Fi)
Fiber optic	Personal digital assistant	Wireless network
File transfer protocol	(PDA)	
(FTP)		

COMPELLING QUESTIONS FOR CONSIDERATION

1. For what types of meetings could a facility's infrastructure be a deciding factor in site selection?

2. List three applications for a wireless network on-site and explain how these applications could add value to your meeting.

3. What telecommunications services might you use during a 4-day convention with exhibits?

4. How should you determine what type of Internet service you need for your meeting?

5. Identify five ways to make conference proceedings available after a meeting using multimedia support services.

6. What features of a facility web site would be most helpful during the site selection process? During the pre-meeting planning?

7. Discuss what types of meetings could be held most productively via an audioconference.

8. What are the potential benefits and limitations of a multi-point videoconference?

9. What factors influence the quality of a videoconference transmission?

10. Which web conferencing features would you use to make a multi-point meeting more interactive?

11. How would you use the Internet to facilitate a working group whose participants are located in distant offices?

CHAPTER 14

CONVENTION CENTERS: UNRAVELING THE MYSTERY

Michael T. McQuade
DIRECTOR, SALES & MARKETING
WASHINGTON STATE CONVENTION
& TRADE CENTER

Julie Burford
ASSISTANT GENERAL MANAGER
SMG/THE MOSCONE CENTER

LEARNER OUTCOMES

When the reader has completed reading this chapter, he/she should be able to . . .

1 Identify the purpose and functional differences between a convention center and other convention or meeting venues.

2 Recognize the philosophy behind the development and management of convention centers.

3 Describe the relationship between the Convention and Visitors Bureaus (CVB) and the convention center.

4 Name the reasons for the booking, pricing and contracting procedures associated with the use of convention centers.

5 Explain the breadth and quality of meeting services that meeting managers can expect from a convention center.

6 Discuss the nuances and practical implications of a convention center's relationship with the labor organizations that support the convention industry.

7 Distinguish the role of the exclusive and preferred providers in a convention center.

We shape our buildings;
thereafter they shape us.

Winston Churchill

Overview

Convention centers have become ubiquitous elements of the urban landscape throughout the United States and much of the world during the last two decades. They have been developed by cities, counties, states, and in some instances by private developers or through public/private partnerships. Regardless of ownership, all convention centers are a reflection of their community's goals and the intentions that led to their development. These goals, whether they are those of urban renewal, economic development, accommodation of community events and activities, or tourism development, are typically reflected in the center's booking policies and operating practices. They may be operated by government entities or, increasingly in recent years, by private management companies. Understanding this essential background offers a useful perspective, whether you are a student of meeting management curricula, a meeting manager just beginning to use convention centers, or an experienced meeting manager continuing to learn about this highly dynamic subject.

The last decade has witnessed more dramatic change in how convention centers work than in any similar period. These forces of change are driven by rapid innovation, technology, economics, globalization, politics, and geography. Much of this change is rooted in the inexorable demand for both education and qualified markets. As a result, more communities have developed centers or expanded existing ones, contributing to an unprecedented increase in the supply of space. More centers have invested in new and more sophisticated building design and infrastructure in order to compete effectively. While convention centers of earlier decades were largely concrete boxes offering flexible, although impersonal, meeting and exhibition spaces, today's centers tend toward sophisticated urban design, advanced technology for telecommunications and audiovisual presentation, upscale food and beverage operations, extensive in-house services, and an emphasis on enhanced service levels.

Organizations of all kinds continue to seek the most cost-effective yet responsive ways to meet the needs of their members, employees, customers, and markets. As their events grow in size, reach, and sophistication, they seek the larger spaces and service capabilities of convention centers in an increasingly global environment. As such, convention centers tend to accommodate the largest events in terms of attendance and occupied square footage, and the ways in which their services are organized and delivered are necessarily very different from those of hotels and conference centers.

This chapter will explore the reasons behind those differences and offer insights and approaches that are intended to help meeting managers effectively navigate the planning and execution of convention center events.

Formulas for Success

The first step to successful management of convention center events is to define the critical relationships between the convention center and its customers. Who are the key players, and how do they relate to each other throughout the planning and execution of an event?

- *The Customer*—Whether the event is an annual meeting, a trade show, a corporate meeting, a product launch, or an educational conference, the customer is the association, company, or partnership whose goal is a successful event. The meeting manager's role is to partner with service providers and the convention center staff in setting objectives, clarifying expectations, and providing all of the necessary information to plan and execute each element of the event. While the meeting manager may be responsible for other smaller events throughout the year that are held in hotels or conference centers, their largest events are held in convention centers and are typically among their organization's most critical activities for the year.

- *The Convention Center Team*—Unlike a hotel where the focus is on selling and servicing sleeping rooms, a convention center's focus is solely on the logistics and operation of events. The management team represents the services and operating elements to support each event from sales and contracting to event management, from technical services to operations and housekeeping, from food and beverage services to building engineering and security. Centers will differ in the range of in-house services they offer, but all centers share the common goal of successful service delivery to the customer.

  Convention centers are most commonly owned by public agencies, but they can be operated under a variety of management structures. While many continue to be operated by public agencies, operation by private management companies or public/private operating corporations is becoming more common.

- *Service Providers, Contractors, and Vendors*—Today's conventions, conferences, and trade shows are complex events that require an ever-expanding range of services to support the event's objectives. They include the following:

  1. *General services contractors* are selected by the organization's meeting manager to execute everything from design to drayage. They execute the meeting manager's direction for dressing the facility's spaces in color and theme, provide furnishings beyond those offered by the center, deliver electrical and plumbing services to exhibition and registration spaces, manage the movement of freight and décor into the facility, and take responsibility for overall logistics of materials used throughout the event.

  2. *Exhibitor-appointed contractors* are selected by individual exhibiting companies to install and dismantle their booths once the freight has been delivered to the venue. They are often involved in initial design and construction of the exhibit structures as well, and they typically maintain ongoing relationships with the exhibitor irrespective of venue.

  3. *Production companies and audiovisual contractors* are selected by the meeting manager to produce general sessions, keynotes, special event elements, and for the delivery of sound and video presentations. They are often offered as non-exclusive in-house services by the center or can be outside providers, often with multiple-year relationships with the organization.

  4. *Registration companies* are selected by the meeting manager to provide computerized registration (and often lead retrieval) services to the event. They provide the computer equipment, programming, and supervisory staff to oversee the installation in the area designated for attendee and exhibitor registration.

  5. *Plant and floral contractors* are usually chosen by the meeting manager to enhance the look of the event with plant and floral displays in the lobbies, exhibit halls, and public concourses of the center.

  6. *The caterer* is responsible for meeting all of the meeting organization's food and beverage needs throughout the event. This is typically an

Fast Facts

Convention Centers Ownership

In the US:
Private companies = 40%
Government agency = 60%

In Canada:
Private companies = 34%
Government agency = 66%

Source: Tradeshow Week's 2006 Major Exhibit Hall Directory

exclusive service provided by the convention center. Its exclusivity derives from the substantial investment in facilities and equipment and the need for consistency and continuity in product and service levels to all of the center's customers.

7. *Security contractors* are selected by the meeting manager to provide security staff surveillance for event spaces. The convention center itself typically provides perimeter security for the building, but security for the equipment and materials delivered for the event, as well as crowd control in the meeting and exhibition spaces, is the responsibility of the security contractor. If the event is the target of protests or demonstrations (as is more frequently the case today), many centers have considerable expertise in helping to manage such actions and can take the lead in suggesting strategic plans. However, the meeting organization needs to provide adequate event security to respond to challenges and protect their attendees from interference.

8. *Telecommunications and Internet service providers* play an increasingly active role in supporting today's conventions and exhibitions given the growing emphasis on connectivity in both meetings and exhibitions. They are typically provided either as in-house services (often exclusive) or through a third-party provider. The exclusivity tends to derive from the extensive level of investment in both infrastructure and expertise made by the provider.

9. *Transportation companies* play a role in multi-property and citywide events by furnishing the shuttle services that move attendees from hotels to the convention center and often to other off-site venues throughout the event.

10. *Electrical contractors* are responsible for delivering electrical services to exhibition and registration spaces. These contractors may also provide temporary electrical power distribution to the customer's production and audiovisual contractors. Some of the companies providing the electrical services are divisions of the companies that provide decorator services. Whether the center has an exclusive contract or not, the facility and decorator have an understanding that the service order forms for the center's contractors are included in the service kits prepared by the decorator. In the process, any other contractors who need electrical services usually know or learn of the exclusives in a center and make arrangements directly with the electrical contractor.

11. *Emergency medical contractors* have an increasingly critical role in centers as the first responders to unanticipated medical emergencies. Due to the size of and nature of the facility, as well as the varied types of events, some convention centers have exclusive providers for this service, which may include up to a fully staffed and equipped First Aid room and direct relationships with local hospitals and emergency rooms.

COMMUNICATION: THE CRITICAL FACTOR

While other, more specialized, service providers unique to certain types of events may be available, the service providers listed above are the typical entities that support the majority of convention center events. Because there are so many providers, each with a specific task or role, the most critical element in combining their efforts into a unified and successful outcome is communication.

Since successful events are the result of good planning, communication is the logically essential vehicle for turning plans into results. The best communication occurs in the context of an effective partnership. Since convention centers operate today in an intensively competitive environment, they are increasingly invested in creating partnerships between their customers, themselves, and all of the service providers who play a role. The most successful centers recognize that the shortest route to repeat business and a positive market image is a reputation for delivering successful events through focused partnerships.

Communication starts early and never really ends. It begins with the initial site visit or sales call, and it identifies the essential facts of dates and space. It involves the convention and visitors' bureau and/or convention center sales staff in the selected city and continues through the process of confirmation and contracting, often many years in advance of the actual event date. Factors affecting this process include the meeting organization's site selection criteria and the booking policies of the center as a reflection of the community's objectives.

Once the event is booked and contracted, the center expands the partnership with the meeting organization. It begins with sales but moves quickly into the actual planning process, and the meeting organization's key partner in that process is their event team. While terminology varies among venues, the team consists of the event manager or convention services manager (CSM) who is the chief point of contact for delivering all of the center's services; the catering manager who will handle all of the details of menu planning, tastings, and the myriad details of food and beverage service throughout the event; and the technical services managers who coordinate the provision of telecommunications and Internet services, as well as managing house sound and rigging systems.

The next step for successful management of convention center events, after identifying the players and defining the roles and relationships, is to look more closely at some specific guidelines that are intended to assure a trouble-free planning process for meeting organization and venue alike. While they may appear fairly obvious or rudimentary to the experienced meeting manager, they are often overlooked or misunderstood.

- *Block space in the center as far in advance as possible.* Centers often confirm space holds 10 years or more in advance, subject to the convention center's booking policies.
- *View the booking process as a firm business commitment.* Once the space reservation is confirmed, the convention center will hold that time and space out of their working inventory. Be certain that you have booked adequate time to move in and out of the center. This means leaving time not only for your exhibitors' move-in but for your service contractors as well.
- *Review the date/space hold from time to time to make sure needs have not changed and that the booking remains appropriate and practical.* If changes occur update the hold through the convention and visitors bureau or convention center sales staff, whichever is appropriate. As the date of the event approaches, you will find less flexibility to accommodate changes.
- *Respond promptly to the center's contracting process.* Most centers contract between 12 and 24 months of the event date. Some centers will contract even further out, including as early as a group makes their decision on a city. Until there is a signed and executed contract and a deposit has been paid, there is no firm deal.
- *Schedule site visits well in advance.* Busy convention centers have activities in progress most of the time. This means that key staff members often have to juggle demands from events in progress with requests for tours and planning meetings for future events. There may be events in the convention center that do not permit tours in their contracted space once their event is in progress.

- *Submit floor plans well in advance for convention center and fire department approvals.* The center has to evaluate many event requirements in the context of operational and safety guidelines, contractual conditions, fire department codes, and the requirements of other events using the facility. Most importantly, if exhibits are involved in the event, do not sell booth space until the floor plan has been approved. Selling from an unapproved floor plan can result in the embarrassment of having to alter booth locations after booth orders have been taken.

- *Provide detailed event requirements for the use of each space and room for each time period of the day as far in advance as possible.* Most centers require these data anywhere between two weeks to a month in advance. This information should include the specifics of room set-ups, timetables for use, and operating hours for exhibit halls and registration areas. It should also include a copy of your exhibitor service kit and the published event program. Timely receipt of this critical information allows the center to anticipate labor requirements and schedule crews so that the event's need's can be handled smoothly—especially in the case of tight turnovers. Keep in mind that, unlike hotels where staffing is maintained around the clock, convention centers staff directly around event requirements and plan staffing needs around the event's production schedule and event specification guide.

- *Let your convention center team know immediately when there is a problem.* This could be anything from information concerning possible demonstrations or protests, to changes in program elements, to unusual security conditions.

- *Let the convention center management know how well the team met your expectations and your event's needs.* Convention center staff members are usually groups of experienced professionals who take pride in their work. Let them know where they excelled, as well as where they could use some improvement. They will appreciate the feedback.

MISCONCEPTIONS

There are some common misconceptions about convention centers that deserve to be debunked:

Misconception: Conventions centers are public buildings run by bureaucrats.

Fact: Today, convention centers are more likely to be operated as if they were private enterprises. They have professionally trained management and staff members who are expected to bring accountability and business ethics to the operation.

Misconception: Convention centers are only interested in large citywide conventions for national and international associations.

Fact: Many convention centers host local and regional meetings, conferences, trade shows, consumer shows and community events ranging in size from single-day, one room events to multi-day events drawing over 100,000 attendees. It depends on the community's vision and goals for the center. The center's booking policies define the priorities that are applied to the booking process. In some cities where economic impact is the defining criterion, local events that make little or no use of hotel rooms can only hold events on a short-term basis, with long-term priority given to room-night-intensive events with a proven record of economic impact to the community.

Misconception:	Convention center rental is always negotiable.
Fact:	Convention centers are under increasing pressure from cities and counties to produce sufficient revenue to cover their operating costs. While the mission of most centers is to generate economic impact and hotel taxes through visitor expenditures, the days when convention centers could operate at a deficit and be considered loss leaders are gone. Negotiation of the rent is possible, but limited to certain criteria, such as, events scheduled over holidays or during the low season; in consideration of alternate revenue sources (e. g. hotel/motel room tax, but more importantly, from other direct operating revenues such as catering revenues).
Misconception:	Convention centers are unreasonably inflexible in contracting.
Fact:	Convention centers, more often than not, make concerted efforts to accommodate requests for reasonable changes in language or mitigation of some contractor requirements. However, the center's governing authority often fixes a center's contract clauses, particularly those dealing with insurance requirements and terms of indemnification. Those centers may not be in a position to make changes.

FACILITY DESIGN

Other than the obvious differences in scale, the most fundamental difference between a center and a hotel is that the convention center is a purpose-built facility, in most cases constructed, owned, and operated by the state or local government to generate economic impact for the community. While most publicly owned convention centers are publicly managed many are privately managed. Other convention centers are privately owned and operated, although this is a small percentage of the total.

Even though differences are common in how hotels and convention centers are owned and operated, these differences should not be viewed as a hurdle for any group considering a convention center for the first time.

As previously mentioned, a convention hotel's focus is on selling and servicing its sleeping rooms, filling its restaurants, and servicing the in-house events. A convention center's focus is solely on the success of the event and not on ancillary activities. One could say that all a convention center does is meetings and conventions.

The growth in the convention/meeting industry over the last few decades continues to create a demand not only for more space but also for better quality facilities and services.

As the highly visible demonstration of a community's vision, desires, and pride, the convention centers of today are architectural statements—inside and out. The result: the "concrete boxes" of decades ago are few and far between. Most convention centers today are soaring glass and steel sculptures enclosing open, airy, and naturally lit lobbies and registration areas. Centers also contain and display considerable collections of art for the benefit of out-of-town attendees and local citizens. Many centers are the recipient of architectural and community design awards for improving the look and feel of the community they occupy. Furthermore, in this day of being green, more and more convention centers are designed with energy saving measures as well as the infrastructure to reduce the environmental and ecological impact of the facility and the conventions they support.

Convention centers know it is not enough to be pretty on the outside. The interior spaces of the center must be practical, offer high quality interior finishes with a pleasing and functional physical environment, and provide great flexibility to support the various groups that will use the center. It is in this area that today's centers are best suited for larger conventions, as they offer all of the above. Depending on the size of the group, more and more centers are sized to offer the opportunity for groups to essentially "own" the building much like they would in a large convention hotel. Some centers are designed to provide the feel of an intimate conference center, while supporting large citywide conventions.

At the same time that mega-convention hotels such as those operated by Gaylord Hotels or found in Las Vegas, continue to come online, offering customers additional destination options, convention centers still offer the largest variety of space options for the customer. From more flexible exhibit hall combinations—with high ceilings for exhibits or general sessions—to small and large meeting rooms with numerous combination capabilities, to large ballrooms suitable for elaborate general sessions and AV productions, to elegant formal dining, to sloped floor auditoria for small intimate congresses with special technical support, to large open airy prefunction spaces to support the most complex and extensive registration requirements and activities to the most unique special event spaces, the choices for the customer are extensive.

Since convention centers are typically larger than convention hotels they are more likely to have more than one group in the facility at any one time. A customer should discuss with the convention center representative, well in advance, the guidelines about putting signage on the outside of the center, in public areas, or in common space shared with other groups in the center. Some convention centers have restrictions on signage on the outside of the building or in public spaces, but most convention centers are willing to work to meet customer's needs in advance. While some centers may have an outdoor marquee, meeting managers should not assume that another center without an outdoor marquee will allow signs on the outside of the building. Meeting managers with this assumption may find that they have to develop an alternative, and expensive, plan.

When convention centers upgrade, refurbish, or expand, names of existing rooms are sometimes changed. If the facility being used is undergoing expansion, meeting managers clarify if rooms or area names are changing so that signage and final program information agree.[1]

BOOKING AND NEGOTIATING

Meeting managers should understand the role of the CVB in the marketing, selling, and booking of the convention center (see Chapter 12). In some cities, the role is limited to simply making the customer aware of the center and then to put the planner and convention center in touch with each other. In other cities, the role may be as involved as managing all the marketing and sales as well as the details related to date and space, pricing proposals, and commitments. In the latter case, the center simply issues the contract to the group based on the agreed upon proposal.

Do the CVB and convention center share the same goals and intentions? In some cities, where the CVB and center are managed by the same organization, this unity of focus is more obvious (e.g., Hawaii, Las Vegas, Providence/Warwick). In most cities, however, the CVB and center are two totally separate organizations and operations, and report to separate governing bodies, yet they share the same goals and vision. In some of these cases, the center may have a marketing agreement where the CVB is the sales and marketing contractor for the convention center. In some cities the CVB and center have separate sales and marketing teams that work together. In privately owned and managed convention centers, the center has its own sales and marketing team that may work independently of the local CVB.

A convention center's booking policy is generally tied to its community's goals and intentions. Related to nearly all convention center booking policies is a peak hotel room night pick-up.[2] The premise for this requirement is for the CVB and convention center to secure groups with the largest hotel room pick-up further in advance than groups with smaller pick-ups. This is simply a matter of economic impact, which is why most centers were conceived, funded, and built. For those convention centers whose booking policy is tied to room pick-up, there is usually a room tax (also known as an occupancy tax), which is applied to hotel rooms used by convention attendees to pay the debt service on the convention center's construction/expansion costs, operating costs, or marketing costs. It is for these primary reasons that booking policies vary slightly from one convention center to the next. Customers should ask the CVB for the specifics of their convention center's booking policy, as it relates to the booking date window in which the meeting manager can obtain a confirmed date.

By comparison, convention hotels have no such booking policy and make their own decisions about when they can and will commit dates to any group, regardless of the number of hotel rooms. In essence, a convention hotel has a great deal more latitude in date and space booking commitments than does a convention center. This freedom may be the same with privately owned and managed convention centers. Booking policies are an important nuance to understand for groups that are considering a convention center for their meeting.

Before a group has made a final decision on a convention center for their meeting, the meeting manager should cover important items with the convention center rather than simply discussing them with the CVB.

Most convention centers have standardized license/lease agreements (contracts), rules and regulations, and general operating guidelines. When considering a convention center, groups should ask for copies of these documents to assist them in site selection. Most convention centers will provide these documents when asked. Too often groups wait until after deciding on a city and finalizing the contract process with hotels before asking for the convention center's contract, rules and regulations, and operating guidelines. By this time, the group may have lost negotiating leverage, since they have already committed to the city. Chapter 41 will address contracts, legal terminology, and negotiation in greater detail.

The meeting manager should be sure to understand the terms and conditions of any agreements, including asking the convention center about unclear details and reviewing agreements with legal counsel. While the old adage says: "All things are negotiable," negotiation is a two-way street. If the center is asked to give on some items, the meeting manager should be prepared to give on some items as well (see Chapter 40).

While Chapters 41 and 42 address contracts, legal terminology, and negotiation in greater detail, most centers do understand that each group has different issues to address—some resulting from past experiences and some resulting from the nature of the customer's organization. Convention centers do understand that a corporate customer will have different contract issues than will an association customer or a government customer.

Some conventions can fill an entire convention hotel, which provides them protection from having other events (competitive or otherwise) on-site at the same time. When considering a convention center, understand that the larger the center is, the more likely that center can and will have multiple events taking place at the same time. Meeting managers should request the names of other groups that will be in the center over their dates, as well as on either side of their dates. Convention centers, as a courtesy, may offer a right-of-first-refusal at the time of the contract and contact the meeting manager in advance of booking another event in the remaining available space. Customers should ask if this is an option.

FACILITY LABOR AND SERVICE CONTRACTOR RELATIONSHIPS

Like any great undertaking, and a convention is just that, all the parties involved with supporting the convention need to work together as a team. The convention center, its exclusive or preferred service providers, the customer's contracted service providers, the exhibitor appointed contractors, etc., are all members of the customer's team. Without these members, the event cannot be successfully completed. Therefore, the better these members work together, the more successful the event will be, and the more successful each member will be.

Convention centers, just like most large convention hotels or general service contractors, operate using various types of union labor for everything from food service employees to the staff that set-up and clean meeting rooms to exhibitor services to badge checkers and door monitors. Some convention centers have labor agreements with individual unions, and a few centers have what are called joint-craft agreements. The latter covers all unions operating in the convention center under one labor agreement. Under either arrangement, convention centers are obligated by the conditions of the labor agreement (as are convention hotels and general service contractors). Some of the labor unions, which a customer is likely to encounter in a convention center, are:

- District Council of Carpenters
- International Brotherhood of Electrical Workers
- International Alliance of Stage and Theatrical Workers
- International Brotherhood of Teamsters
- Painters
- Sign and Display Workers
- Unite HERE
- International Union of Operating Engineers
- Service Employees International Union

Which labor union a meeting manager may encounter in a center depends on the history and strength of the unions in that city. For example, the predominant union that provides labor for trade show set-up (whether in a convention center or a convention hotel) in San Francisco is the Teamsters. In Seattle, the predominant union that provides labor for trade show set-up is the Carpenters, and in Portland, Oregon, the predominant union that provides this same work is the Sign and Display Workers.

Most convention centers have exclusive contracts that are tied in to or related to their labor agreement (food and beverage services, room set-ups, conversions, and housekeeping). In some centers, other functions such as badge checkers, ticket takers, door monitors, and crowd control are considered union jurisdictions. Even in centers where such functions are jurisdictions covered under the labor agreement, meeting managers may still have a great deal of latitude in the hiring of other contractors for such services as registration, or to hire their own security for inside the trade show, general session, and registration areas.

In short, the union jurisdictions in a convention center are not that much different from what would be expected in a convention hotel or through service contractors. Meeting managers should have an understanding of the union jurisdictions in the center as part of their decision making process, as well as during their planning process.

WE ARE FROM THE GOVERNMENT AND WE ARE HERE TO HELP YOU

As scary as that may sound, it is actually true.

Local government agencies such as the fire marshal, police, and city, county, or state business-licensing can all impact a convention program. Therefore, meeting managers should make them a member of the team early on and avoid the problems that can befall a convention later on.

Since convention centers are typically the largest meetings facility in town, they are typically targeted for stronger enforcement of local laws and regulations (life safety issues with the fire marshal, taxes and permits with city and state agencies, and traffic management issues with the police or other city agencies). Meeting managers should ask about these and any other situations they may have experienced in other cities, and, normally, the convention center can easily identify these early on in the sales and booking process. The sooner this process starts, the easier it is.

More often than not, the local fire marshal gets the worst rap. A meeting manager might believe different cities and convention centers operate under different fire codes and one city seems to have more lenient rules than another. The reality is that two very similar national fire standards exist for cities to follow. One is known as the International Fire Code.[3] The other is known as the Uniform Fire Code.[4] The differences are slight, and relate mostly to construction issues and generally have little impact on temporary events such as a convention or a trade show. However, what is different is how each city's fire marshal applies their limited resources to enforcement of the "fire code."

As disasters occur around the country and the world, additional attention is being given to new areas of concern. One city's fire marshal might have a stronger feeling about aisle widths in a trade show than does another city's fire marshal. Or in one city, they are more concerned about two-story booths than another city is. Remember to never allow the AV contractor or decorator to block a fire exit without providing adequate and acceptable alternatives. In short, here is where the customer's team working together can be most helpful. The general service contractors and AV contractors should know from firsthand experience what each city's fire marshal is sensitive to. Everyone's best interest is served if the group's contractors bring this information to the table when they are pre-planning with the customer, rather than ignoring that known sensitivity and making the fire marshal or the convention center the "bad guy." To avoid potential problems with the fire marshal, many centers now require that all floor plans be reviewed and approved by the center before selling booth space or before finalizing a general session production stage.

Some highly important specific areas that meeting managers should be aware of include:

- *Life safety*—With the high concentration of attendees at convention centers, the fire marshal is very concerned with issues related to safety. As a result, they are more stringent in the enforcement of such guidelines as:
  - Clear access to fire exits, fire hose cabinets, fire extinguishers, and pull stations
  - Exit pathways from large sessions and activities
  - Informational displays and registration equipment in lobbies (a convention center lobby is typically considered an exit pathway, not a function space)
  - The types and concentrations of exhibits in the exhibit hall
  - Potential obstructions created by audiovisual requirements (drapery or cabling across entrance or exit doorways, pyrotechnics, mobile microphone and camera cables, etc.)
- *Taxes and permits*—Some cities, counties, and states have become more aggressive in enforcing existing tax and permits ordinances as they apply to trade shows. Other cities are trying to modify those ordinances to reflect the distinct nature of the trade show versus a local business.
- *Traffic management*—Again, due to the large concentration of attendees, traffic, and truck deliveries at convention centers, some cities are concerned about the impact on city streets from foot traffic in and out of the center, shuttle buses, and attendee and contractor vehicles (i.e., drayage, audiovisuals, and deliveries) during a convention and may impose additional requirements on the sponsoring organization.

RISK MANAGEMENT AND EMERGENCY PREPAREDNESS

Managing risk and planning for the various emergencies that can occur in today's environment is a mutual responsibility. Every organization that plans and executes events has their own well-defined approach and practices for ensuring the safety of their attendees and the orderly completion of their program. The convention center, regardless of ownership or management structure, has the obligation to prepare a viable plan for managing any type of emergency. The center's goals are to support the risk management of their customers in ensuring safety and protecting the event's integrity.[5]

As with everything else that contributes to a successful event, planning and communication are once again the key factors. Every convention center has developed an emergency preparedness plan. Such a plan outlines how the center's staff and management function under each kind of emergency situation, such as fire, bomb threat, hurricane, flood, terrorist attack, or earthquake, among others.

Here is a suggested approach for combining forces and cooperatively planning for emergencies during your event:

- At the beginning of your planning process, ask for a copy of the center's emergency preparedness plan. Once you have read their plan and understand how they would execute their role, develop your own plan according to your individual priorities and policies.
- Share your plan with your convention center team.
- If you would like their assistance in developing your plan, enlist the help of the center's fire marshal or safety manager, as well as your event manager. Centers often keep copies of particularly well-prepared plans they receive and should be happy to provide them to you as models.

- Be sure that your plan and the accompanying communication with your convention center team include such often overlooked items as:
  - identifying specific responsibility for making the decision to evacuate
  - designating a location outside to which your own staff would relocate (see Chapter 44)

FACILITY SERVICES, TECHNOLOGY, AND FACILITY CONTRACTORS

The increasing demands of meeting programs for a consistent, reliable, and available technical infrastructure for such services as wireless cyber cafes for attendees, streaming video for live surgical feeds into the convention, and live Webcasting have required that centers become more technologically focused and expand their infrastructure and level of technical capabilities.[6] Installing and maintaining this infrastructure is a considerable financial cost to the facility. The complex nature of the variety of the larger events that take place in a convention center put centers on the leading edge of having most, if not all, of this technical infrastructure in place already. Like any investment there has to be an appropriate return on that investment. This is the same as a convention hotel's exclusive contractors. Meeting managers would rarely think of asking a convention hotel to allow them to use, at no charge, meeting rooms or on-site services just because they are there or to bring in a company that is different from the hotel's exclusive provider.

Convention centers have established exclusive contracts with specific service providers to remain competitive, and to provide a consistent, reliable, and high level of service at a competitive price. Exclusive contracts also provide the center with an additional revenue source that, while small compared to other revenue sources, helps defray the cost of operation and keep the center's rental prices low. Since the convention center's reputation is on the line, exclusive contracts allow the center to ensure that companies who are experts in their trade manage certain services in the center in a professional manner. This arrangement is no different than contracting with one of the many different third-party meeting management or multi-management firms to handle day-to-day association operations, or to negotiate hotel contracts, or to manage details of the annual meeting or trade show. These exclusive contracts are awarded to companies run by professionals who are experts at what they do, leaving meeting managers with the overall responsibility, authority, and time to deal with issues and responsibilities that are better kept in-house.

Just as each convention center has different goals and objectives, each center has different reasons for establishing which exclusive contracts they have. The most common exclusives are for catering, electrical services, and telecommunications/connectivity. Some centers have contracts for other services, ranging from drayage and decorating to security and audiovisuals. Convention centers may also have preferred contractors or a recommended list of contractors. Just as a convention hotel may have different exclusive contractors, each center has a different approach to exclusive, preferred, or recommended contractors. Therefore, meeting managers should ask, just as they would in considering a hotel, about these service providers and discuss early in the process whether the center has any flexibility in allowing exceptions to their exclusives. This does not suggest that a center will risk putting itself in default on its contract with that exclusive; however, if discussions are begun early enough, a mutual understanding might be achieved.

CATERING

In concert with the changes in program content that require higher levels of professional and technical support from a center's staff, the expectations have grown for food and beverage product quality, presentation, and service delivery. No longer can a center expect to be successful just by having dates and space. Sponsoring organizations are voting with their feet, and convention centers fully understand that more options are available to them now than ever before. The days of rubber chicken and canned peas or mystery meat with a brown sauce are fast becoming a thing of the past.

Food and beverage is a major budget line item for a convention and therefore a potential major revenue source for the facility. Meeting managers would never think of asking a convention hotel to allow them to bring in their own outside food service caterer. They know the hotel has a major investment in the equipment and catering facilities and in their food service reputation. Therefore, they should not think of asking for this at a convention center. Convention centers have exclusive food and beverage service for the same reason that a convention hotel does.

However, because each center is different, the conditions of the contract for the food service in the center may be different from other centers. Most convention centers contract national firms to operate and manage the catering operations, while others have contracts with local firms, and still others operate their own food service. In some centers, the catering contractor has full control of all catering related matters, which might limit the customer in their catering options.

Other centers have management contracts whereby the catering contractor manages the operation similar to how a third-party meeting manager manages the details of a customer's event. In this scenario the contractor is able to bring their professional experience and resources to the table and the center has available to them a similar level of national resources as a nationally flagged convention hotel. Specifically, if the size or scope of an event requires additional equipment, staffing, or culinary expertise the center can draw on additional support for the existing on-site staff. This is no different from what happens in convention hotels. What many may not know is that centers use the same professional cadre of wait staff, banquet captains, and bartenders that work in convention hotels.

Also not exclusive to convention hotels are the culinary teams that manage the day-to-day details of the largest kitchen operations in any city. Whether you are working with the executive chef and chef de cuisine, or the sous chef and dedicated pastry kitchens, convention center kitchens and their culinary capabilities are no longer just a meeting manager's pipe dream. Customized menus to meet budget, cultural, or dietary restrictions, program or award themes, or corporate logos are more the menu of the day than ever before. Some centers have developed seasonal fresh menus to showcase the locale's strengths in fresh fruits and vegetables, beef, seafood, and alternative options, not to mention the "fruit of the grape." Chef's tables, once the domain of only four- or five-star hotels, are a standard operating procedure in most convention centers. How better to demonstrate to a customer what the center can do? The chef's table offers the customer an opportunity to sample the menu prior to the event and make whatever adjustments are required. This also allows the chef to learn more about the customer needs. If scheduled and planned accordingly, meeting managers can observe meals being served in the center for another group on the day of the tasting.

SUMMARY

Today's marketplace is characterized by increasing competition as more and more cities build and expand convention centers. This competition can only benefit the customer, as centers will be able to distinguish themselves from their competitors only through the level of service they offer.

Convention centers, while existing solely as function space for conventions and trade shows, are a reflection of their communities. As a result, the policies and procedures for each center vary, even if the center is one of the many managed by a private management firm.

Because of the public ownership of most convention centers, many rules and regulations and contractual terms are not negotiable.[7] These include life safety issues, tax and permit requirements, and liability.

Often convention centers work closely with their CVB. In some cases, the role of the CVB is in the marketing, selling, and booking of the convention center. However, in other cities, the role may be limited to simply making the customer aware of the center and then to put the planner and convention center in touch with each other. Meeting managers must understand the structure between the center and its CVB.[8]

While convention center ownership and policies may differ from those of convention hotels, they are not entirely different in operation. Centers operate under labor agreements similar to the labor agreements in a convention hotel or with a general service contractor.

Convention centers may hold exclusive contracts for a variety of services, just as in a convention hotel. These exclusive contracts reflect substantial investments on the part of the center to ensure the highest quality and most consistent delivery of services.

Food and beverage quality in convention centers has improved greatly over the past several years. Today's convention centers offer pricing, creativity, and flexibility that rival even the most renowned hotels. Centers have invested significant resources—financial and personal—to ensure the highest quality, broadest variety, and most competitive pricing for their customers.

Convention center managers are constantly thinking about new ways to make their customer's jobs easier. They are convinced that when customers and convention centers talk to each other and share ideas, customer service will be a reality for all.

REFERENCES

1. Wallace, C. (May, 2000). Questions to Ask a Center Undergoing Expansion. *Convene*, p. 30.

2. Dunn, J. (October, 2000). Growing Up and Out? Centers Offer an Alternative. *Convene*, p. 27.

3. International Fire Code. Retrieved March 3, 2006 from http://www.iccsafe.org.

4. The Uniform Fire Code. Retrieved March 3, 2006 from http://www.ufca.net.

5. Russell, M. (April, 2003). Planning Convention Center Security. *Convene*, p. 46.

6. Fox, D. (March, 1999). Questions to Ask Convention Centers. *Convene*, p. 69.

7. Golding, M. (October, 2003). Comparing Apples and Oranges. *Convene*, p. 23.

8. Rushing, A. (October, 2005). Uncovering 'hidden costs' at Convention Centers. *Convene*, p. 24.

KEY TERMS

Ancillary activities	Debt service	Low season
Booking policy	Exclusive contracts	Multi-management firms
Chef's table	Exhibitor appointed	Peak hotel room night
Convention center	contractors	pick-up
Convention and Visitors	Hotel/motel room tax	Right-of-first-refusal
Bureau (CVB)	(room tax or bed tax)	Third-party meeting
Direct operating revenues	Joint-craft-agreement	managers

COMPELLING QUESTIONS FOR CONSIDERATION

1. Why do convention centers often have special non-negotiable legal requirements?

2. What are some problems a customer could encounter with a convention center if he/she plans to use the same tested and true caterer that handles all the organization's meetings?

3. When might a customer exercise his/her right-of-first-refusal regarding convention center bookings?

4. Is it fair for local authorities to target convention centers for strict enforcement of laws and regulations? Why or why not?

5. Discuss the advantages and disadvantages of convention center facilities and services as compared to hotel facilities and services.

CHAPTER 15

THE CONFERENCE CENTER DIFFERENCE

Tom Bolman, CAE
EXECUTIVE VICE PRESIDENT
INTERNATIONAL ASSOCIATION OF CONFERENCE CENTERS

LEARNER OUTCOMES

When the reader has completed reading this chapter, he/she should be able to . . .

1 Classify the conference center concept as a specific segment within the hospitality industry.

2 Clarify the differences between conference centers and other meeting facility venues.

3 Describe sub-sets within the conference center industry.

4 Determine the types of meetings that work best at conference centers.

> I am a strong advocate for conference centers. You not only get a proven commodity—a facility that provides the optimum learning environment in which you can present your meeting— you also get great value.
>
> *Joan Eisenstodt*
> *Chief Strategist*
> *Eisenstodt Associates, LLC*

OVERVIEW

Pressures continue to mount on corporations and other organizations to maximize the productivity of their meetings. The expectation level of meeting managers, those who sponsor meetings, and those who attend them has risen dramatically over the past two decades. Time—in business, in universities, in organizations of all sizes and descriptions—is too precious a commodity to waste or put at risk.

In the quest to maximize the return on an organization's meeting investment, dedicated conference center facilities represent a powerful, dependable resource.

While the term conference center is generic, the type of facility described in this chapter is one that specializes in smaller meetings and that strives to provide the most productive environment for adult learning. The trade organization for the conference center industry is the International Association of Conference Centers (IACC) and this organization provides information to support operators of conference centers as well as education for meeting managers of the services provided by these facilities. This chapter will provide an exploration of the unique niche of services that conference centers offer and the contrast of these facilities to larger hotels, resorts, and convention centers options.

THE CONFERENCE CENTER'S UNIQUE ROLE

Conference centers occupy a unique niche in the hospitality industry. They exist for one purpose: to provide an optimal environment that will support and facilitate meetings—particularly smaller-group meetings, averaging from 25–75 people.

The basic difference between conference centers and convention hotels and resorts is the focus. Conference centers specialize in accommodating conference groups; their physical plant, staff, and amenities are combined and customized to provide the best possible environment and services for productive meetings.

Of necessity, hotels and resorts must cater equally to a variety of market segments: transient guests traveling for business or pleasure (or both); conventions, trade shows and other large-scale events; social and civic segments from banquet groups to wedding receptions; individuals patronizing on-site restaurants and bars; and, of course, conference business in the form of small and medium-size meetings.

Given this broad spectrum of clientele, conventional hospitality facilities cannot focus their systems or services on any one segment. They must design facilities for multiple functionalities, just as they must train staff to handle a constantly changing mix of diverse tasks.

Because of their specialized focus, conference centers offer physical, operational, and philosophical differences in virtually every aspect of their operations. Some are subtle; others are quite apparent to even the casual observer. However, five major areas of difference exist: meeting facility design, meeting furnishings and equipment, personnel, food and beverage services, and packaging.

Put It Into Perspective

A host of corporate and association meetings are ideal for conference centers: training, strategic planning, budget and audit meetings, board of directors meetings, departmental and committee meetings, sales and marketing meetings, team-building retreats, and new product introductions. In fact, any smaller meeting in which the audience is a known quantity will thrive in the productive environment of a bona fide conference center.

Facility Design

From the ground up, a conference center focuses on group meetings. Its physical plant is organized to keep different group functions apart and private, minimize distractions, and emphasize both convenience and productivity for conferees. Conference rooms are positioned for convenient access to support services; such as refreshment areas, restrooms, on-site business center, and the offices of conference services staff. At the same time, conference meeting and breakout rooms are separated from—and distinct from—banquet and dining rooms as well as other high-traffic areas to eliminate, as much as possible, any outside distractions.

Meeting room interiors are dedicated, single-purpose spaces designed specifically for conference activities, not multi-function space that also must accommodate receptions, banquets, and other social functions. Everything, from lighting and acoustics to wall surfaces and overall color schemes, is designed to enhance meeting productivity.

Often, the interaction of participants outside of a meeting is as valuable and productive as what occurs inside the meeting, so conference centers have built-in public spaces that encourage discussions and networking (see Figure 15.1). In addition to meeting rooms, conference centers provide many informal gathering places such as secluded lounges, seating alcoves, patios and courtyards, as well as workrooms and offices for visiting meeting managers (see Figure 15.2).

FIGURE 15.1
Conference center meeting rooms are designed specifically for comfort and productivity.

Furnishings and Equipment

The multi-purpose nature of hotel and resort space for group functions dictate that meeting furnishings and equipment be designed for easy movement to maximize the efficiency and functionality of the space.

By contrast, conference centers' dedicated approach places the emphasis on the comfort of the user, as well as supporting productivity. Ergonomic, executive-style chairs are designed specifically to keep conferees comfortable and alert for long periods of time. They are padded and have arm rests; they swivel, tilt, and have casters. Conference tables are typically heavy and not easily moved. Their stability and smooth, wide writing surfaces provide noticeable comfort and utility, offering ample room for laptop computers, briefing notebooks, and other workshop or meeting materials.

Conference centers tend to have a much broader and deeper in-house inventory of conference technology (A/V), which allows better control of equipment quality and faster response to on-site requests. Additionally, conference centers employ full-time professional media technicians to operate and maintain A/V equipment and to advise presenters on its use for their programs.

Personnel

The same basic skills and knowledge are required of both hotel/resort and conference center personnel. While similar principles apply, the focus and orientation are different.

The attitude, appearance, and general hospitality approach of service staff are basic components of a conference center's operating profile. The concept of an aggressive hospitality program, in which each service individual takes a highly proactive approach to anticipating and accommodating customer needs, is particularly important in the conference center, where customers expect a flawless meeting environment.

FIGURE 15.2
Customers of conference centers anticipate a flawless meeting environment and proactive service.

Conference services personnel must be prepared to provide substantial service and assistance to meeting managers. In contrast to hotels and resorts, where a meeting manager must deal with each functional area of the property individually, conference center clients deal with a dedicated conference manager. This one person will generally have full responsibility for the success of the client's program, and has the authority and stature within the conference center to combine the services of all departments and personnel on the client's behalf.

Conference services personnel are able to assist the group's meeting manager in every aspect of the meeting: designing the program, coordinating the details, providing gracious service during the group's time on-site, and conducting the post-conference evaluation.

Another specialized service offered by conference centers is a conference concierge, typically provided in the form of a separate desk staffed by individuals with administrative skills who provide a variety of business services for conference groups and individual conferees.

Food and Beverage Services

The conference center dining room provides buffet service for breakfast and lunch, and either a la carte or buffet service for dinner. This enables conferees to dine in groups at their convenience while at the same time allowing each conferee to make individual menu selections. While allowing great freedom of menu choice, the conference dining concept enables groups to complete breakfast or lunch within one hour. The concept also allows the meeting manager to organize a program without making any decisions regarding individual banquet meals, pre-selecting menus, or stipulating specific dining times.

The approach to conference center refreshment breaks is another departure from the traditional hotel or resort. Conference centers have dedicated refreshment areas—often referred to as "kiosks"—that are contiguous to conference rooms, and these areas are continuously refreshed while conferences are in session, allowing conferees to break at will, in groups or individually, with the assurance that refreshments are always available to them (see Figure 15.3).

Put It Into Perspective

Corporate business tends to be the primary market segment for most conference centers, with less business generated from other sectors such as associations, government or military groups, and academic functions. This is significant because corporations generally mandate attendance at their meetings, while other groups tend to have "invited" attendance. For conference centers, required attendance translates into more reliable business.

Because conference centers focus on the small meetings market, they are not able to replace lost business as easily as facilities that serve a variety of markets. Conference centers, therefore, tend to have stricter attrition and cancellation clauses in their contracts and they work better for organizations—whether corporate or association—that are able to give accurate estimates of their meeting attendance.

Packaging

Conference centers offer and promote (sometimes exclusively) a per person/per day package plan, often called a Complete Meeting Package (CMP). The CMP wraps together all the essential components of a meeting, including guest rooms and three meals a day, continuous refreshment service, conference space, conference services, conference technology (A/V) and service charges covering gratuities for food and beverage. Conference centers also normally provide Day Meeting Packages that include conference space, conference technology, lunch, and continuous refreshment service.

A conference center's all-inclusive packaging and pricing approach provides strong benefits to the customer: it eliminates a myriad of decisions and details that meeting managers would otherwise have to shoulder; it streamlines both advance planning and billing reconciliation; and it eliminates surprises, especially in the area of budgeting.

Conference centers do not generally "unbundle" the package and sell the facility on an a la carte or European Plan (EP) basis—but they often customize packages to meet the needs of a particular group.

FIGURE 15.3
Conference centers provide continuous refreshment service outside of meeting rooms.

CONFERENCE CENTER STANDARDS

The International Association of Conference Centers (IACC), the industry's trade association, has 31 brand standards that are incorporated into IACC's universal criteria.[1] These standards govern the priority of business, conference room design, conference and business services, food and beverage, technology, and guest rooms at all member conference centers. Before conference centers can become a member of IACC they must meet all of the brands standards identified by the association. Routinely, evaluations are made of IACC members to insure that these quality standards are being maintained.

TYPES OF CONFERENCE CENTERS

The IACC divides conference centers into six basic types:

1. *Residential*—Full-service facilities that serve the entire spectrum of market segments, from entry-level training to meetings restricted to captains of industry. They tend to be located in suburban locations surrounding major metropolitan areas.
2. *University*—Facilities located on college campuses that are also available to outside groups. They are built to "executive" rather than "student" standards and are often able to bring additional resources of the university (e.g., faculty and advanced technology) to the table.
3. *Corporate*—These are owned by corporations that use them for internal training while usually leasing under-utilized space to groups outside of the corporation.
4. *Resort*—Full-service facilities that also have on-site recreational amenities that may include golf, swimming, tennis, spa services, and comprehensive fitness centers.
5. *Non-Residential*—Facilities that have all the amenities of a full-service conference center with the exception of guest rooms. They tend to be connected to, or in close proximity to, hotels.

Did You Know?[2]

- 75% of guests at conference centers are likely to stay as part of a package plan.
- Business organizations, followed by academic institutions, generate the greatest demand for conference centers.
- The greatest percentage of meetings at conference centers are training or continuing education sessions.

- Conference attendees comprise 63% of occupied rooms at conference centers. The remaining occupancy is fairly evenly split among commercial, leisure, and other transient guests.

6. *Ancillary*—Readily identifiable conference centers that are part of a larger hospitality complex—a floor or wing of a hotel or a conference center on the grounds of a resort.

SUMMARY

Conference centers exist for one purpose of providing an optimal learning environment for smaller-group meetings. They compete with other meeting venues by offering complete meeting packages that include everything that is needed for a successful meeting.

Five major areas of difference exist between conference centers and hotels and resorts. These include facility design, furnishings and equipment, personnel, food and beverage services, and packaging. Each of these areas found in conference centers are designed to maximize privacy and productivity of the groups using the facility.

Conference centers can be classified into six types: residential, university, corporate, resort, non-residential, and ancillary. These different types of conference centers offer amenities unique to their target market, which distinguishes them from other meeting venues.

Typically conference centers are attractive for groups where the meetings have reliable attendance. Groups often prefer conference centers when they require a facility that will cater specifically to their meeting needs, without making them compete with other facility guests who are at the venue for non-meeting activities.

REFERENCES

1. International Association of Conference Centers (IACC) (2006). Illustrated Universal Criteria. Retrieved March 10, 2006 from http://www.iacconline.org.

2. PKF Consulting (2005). Conference center industry trends: A statistical and financial profile. San Francisco: PKF Consulting.

KEY TERMS

Ancillary conference centers	Corporate conference centers	Residential conference centers
Complete meeting package	Day meeting package	Resort conference centers
Concierge	European plan	Universal criteria
Conference center	Hospitality program	University conference centers
	Non-Residential conference centers	

COMPELLING QUESTIONS FOR CONSIDERATION

1. What is a conference center?

2. How do conference centers differ from conventional hotels and resorts?

3. What are some of the industry standards for conference centers?

4. What are some different types of conference centers?

5. What kind of meetings work best at conference centers?

CHAPTER 16

INTERNATIONAL MEETINGS, CONVENTIONS, AND EXHIBITIONS

Leigh Wintz, CAE
EXECUTIVE DIRECTOR
SOROPTIMIST INTERNATIONAL OF THE AMERICAS

LEARNER OUTCOMES

When the reader has completed reading this chapter, he/she should be able to . . .

1 Describe two types of international meetings.

2 Adapt the meeting management process to accommodate an international audience.

3 Identify key differences in managing a meeting outside of the United States of America.

4 Discuss the different resources available to help make international events successful.

> Integrate with the local culture—
> don't fight it.
>
> *Ulla Buchner-Howard, CMP*
> *President UBH International*
> *Faculty, Preston Robert Tisch Center for*
> *Hospitality, Tourism and Sports*
> *Management, New York University*

OVERVIEW

An international meeting is defined as an event that draws an international audience from three or more countries. International meetings that are hosted in one's own country are termed inbound meetings. International events convened in a foreign country are termed outbound meetings. Business practices in the meetings community vary from country to country, as do the expectations of participants. Because there are greater challenges in doing business outside one's own country, this chapter will focus primarily on outbound meetings and exhibitions.

Successful international events in any country are the result of good design and thorough planning and execution. They require an understanding of the meeting objectives, as well as an open mind as to how those objectives can best be met in the host country. In addition to expertise in managing and organizing meetings and exhibitions, meeting managers also need intuition, common sense, diplomacy, and respect for the culture of both the host country and the international participants.

Potential challenges with communications make it advisable to begin planning for international meetings further in advance than for domestic meetings. A sound timetable allows for unexpected events, such as mail or transportation strikes and delays in communications due to language differences. Allow additional time for working with more than one counterpart (e.g., travel agent, professional congress organizer, destination management company) and arranging for professional language interpretation.

WHY HOLD AN INTERNATIONAL EVENT?

Increased globalization has caused many U.S.-based organizations to host meetings outside the United States in order to accommodate a growing base of international members. An invitation to meet may be issued by a local chapter, foreign government, or an affiliated national organization. Some organizations elect to meet internationally because they are global in nature, for social reasons, for recreation, or for cultural exchange.

In the current business environment, if U.S.-based manufacturers are looking to expand or increase their market share, the opportunities available internationally can provide expanded growth and increased sales. Increasingly, organizations are multinational through mergers, acquisitions, strategic partnerships, and collaborations. Pursuing international business opens up new, potentially lucrative markets.

Meeting managers, whether corporate or association-based, can play a major role by identifying destinations that will allow their organizations to accomplish strategic goals and objectives.

SITE SELECTION AND INSPECTION

The decision about where to hold a meeting is dependent on many factors. For some organizations, the choice of site may be linked to support from members in the area, or perhaps the ability to visit state-of-the-art manufacturing complexes. Factors such as convenience, cost, safety/security, and the desirability of the destination frequently come into play. The attractiveness of the location, for example, may be an important factor if you anticipate that attendees will link holiday travel to the meeting trip.

Most major international cities offer exhibition facilities; however, their sizes and standards vary greatly. Select a facility that contributes to the meeting's objectives, offers value to participants, and accommodates the needs of exhibiting companies. International site selection is similar to domestic site selection. In addition to the site selection factors outlined in Chapter 11, a review of international destinations and facilities must allow for the uniqueness of the site. Give special attention to the following elements:

- Customs regulations and visa limitations
- Political and economic climate
- Availability of assistance from local members and tourism officials
- Availability of required support services and personnel
- Import restrictions and duties
- Currency exchange restrictions and controls
- Availability of medical facilities
- Transportation access

A large amount of preliminary information can be gathered online; however, a quick inquiry from a stranger via an email to gather additional data may be less well received than one that comes with an introduction from a trusted third party or mutual acquaintance. As a general rule, Europeans, Asians, and Latin Americans prefer personal relationships in the conduct of business than do North Americans.

Given the wide range of facilities available and the language differences that exist even among English-speaking countries, a site visit may be essential before committing to a given location. Allow twice as much time for the site visit as you would allow for a site visit to a U.S. city. If you have organized events before in the site under consideration, the time can be reduced because you will already have established the personal relationships that will help the meeting go smoothly. Arrange the site visit at approximately the same time of year as the organization expects to meet, so you can fully appreciate local customs, climate, and typical weather conditions.

BOOKINGS

Local Partnership

For all but the smallest meetings, most experienced international meeting managers hire the services of a professional congress organizer (PCO) when hosting meetings outside of North America. A PCO can make almost all the arrangements for your program, including airline bookings, housing arrangements, facility bookings, transportation needs, social programs, and special events. They typically can secure a favorable rate due to the volume they do locally and at the same time provide a single point of contact for planning. The PCO is a partner in the meeting and the specific services are arranged via a contract that can provide for a full range of services or just those services necessary to supplement the expertise of staff or local volunteers.

Some countries require the involvement of a domestic company to organize a meeting or exhibition. You may be required to use a company that is at least 50 percent locally owned in making arrangements and contracting for domestic services. If such a partnership arrangement is required, allow the locally owned company to guide you in various decisions related to schedules, protocol, and customs.

Even without a specific requirement, consider hiring a local management company to assist in organizing the meeting and exhibition. A local firm can be helpful in identifying compatible organizations and/or government agencies that might be willing to host and contribute to the event. Whether local advice is secured voluntarily or by government requirement, it can have an impact on the overall budget and should be decided at an early date.

Fast Facts

Most Widely Spoken Languages in the World

Language	Approx. number of speakers
1. Chinese (Mandarin)	1,075,000,000
2. English	514,000,000
3. Hindustani	496,000,000
4. Spanish	425,000,000
5. Russian	275,000,000
6. Arabic	256,000,000
7. Bengali	215,000,000
8. Portuguese	194,000,000
9. Malay-Indonesian	176,000,000
10. French	129,000,000

Source: Ethnologue, 13th Edition, and other sources.

Transportation

If attendees are likely to travel as a large group, a travel agent is essential. If attendees are more likely to travel individually, an agency may be less interested in offering group rates. Some companies may require employees to use a specific travel agent, further reducing group potential. The key is to understand the composition of the group and anticipating their travel preferences. Be flexible when designing a group program and recognize that individual travelers can be accommodated without having to purchase airline tickets through a certain agent or leave from a specific gateway city.

Group transportation bookings for international flights do not always yield the lowest available airfare. Frequently, you can negotiate specific tariffs as well as special cabin services for your group by dealing with a single carrier. The national airline of the destination country frequently offers additional incentives for group movements. Consider all alternatives—including the use of a travel agency—before determining the best value in air transportation. Name an official airline, even if the organization is also naming an official travel agency.

Accommodations

Many international destinations do not have hotel accommodations for the thousands of people who sometimes attend an event, and housing services are not readily available in most cities. Delegates typically book both their hotel and registration from the same form, so if you handle registration for your organization, but leave the hotel reservations up to the delegate, you will need to use either a PCO or a travel agent to handle the housing portion of your program. One or more nights' deposit will be required upon receipt of the reservation request; and in some cases, full payment will be required prior to arrival, depending on the city or facility.

In some cities, the largest hotel in the city may have fewer than 500 rooms, while its convention center is one of the largest in the world. Many exhibitors and attendees will secure accommodations outside the city limits and travel to the exhibition by train, other public transportation, or by private vehicle. If you want your participants to stay as close as possible to the event, make reservations as early as possible.

Most non-U.S. hotels are accustomed to dealing with travel agents rather than with meeting managers. Typical contracts will include commissionable rates, but will not include meeting or exhibit space. The meeting manager must be involved in these negotiations and have a clear understanding of the booking of space, and any costs associated with using that space for meetings and exhibitions, at the time the guest room commitment is made. Depending upon the country and season, guest room rates may be fairly inflexible; however, if the room block is linked to the use of function space, room to negotiate on the cost of the function space is usually available.

International participants attending a U.S.-based meeting may be used to having a travel agent make all their arrangements to attend (registration, hotel, and air). They may be unaware of the need to stay at one of the official hotels. U.S.-based hotels should be made aware of the names of those travel agencies to insure that rooms secured by those agents come from within the contracted room block.

Have a good understanding of food-and-beverage requirements for any meeting so these can be negotiated in the booking contract. Basic knowledge of meal plan options is essential. Be sure to ask what meals, taxes, and services may be included in any quoted rate. Outside of North America, room rates often include breakfast. Four categories of rates are possible:

- *European Plan (EP)*—The rate quoted includes the cost of the sleeping room only. Usually, tax and service charges are additional.
- *Modified American Plan (MAP)*—This rate includes the sleeping room plus breakfast and dinner. Meals may be provided in several ways:
  - group meals in a function room with a set menu and time for breakfast and dinner
  - individual menu selections in one of the regular food outlets
  - individual meals with a separate menu for people on this plan. The menu may not offer the same variety of selections as the normal restaurant menu.
- *Full American Plan (FAP)*—This package is the same as a MAP except that lunch is also included.
- *Voucher Plan*—Some meal plans allow a set, daily dollar credit per person that may be used in any outlet within the facility. Charges over the stipulated amount are billed to the guest's account.

Meeting Space

Unlike hotels in the United States, fees for meeting space in hotels in other countries are not often tied to a room block. The quoted rental rate for a meeting room may not be negotiable, depending on local business practice. Attrition clauses are just beginning to appear in a few contracts in Europe. In addition to the rental fee for the meeting room, the facility may charge a daily delegate rate. It may include full use of available audiovisual equipment as well as one or two coffee breaks, and even lunch. Be sure to ask what is included and what the standard room set will be. Some of the creative room sets that are common in North America may not work in a meeting room that is designed for one set.

SERVICES AND EQUIPMENT

Services and equipment are similar to what is available in the United States, but may be called different things and may be charged differently. Be sure to outline specific needs when doing your site research. For example, exhibition service contractors as we know them in the United States are not common outside of North America. Many times, the meeting manager will have to coordinate each service component, including booth installation (stand building), electrical service, telephones, and shipping, as well as compile the exhibition service kit for exhibitors. Again, a local service provider such as a PCO can assist with this type of service.

Regarding equipment, always remember to check the electrical requirements of the country in which you will be hosting your meeting, including telephone modems and adapters. Current electrical packages for laptops are able to convert the electricity from 110V to 220V and only require an adapter, not an electrical converter. Clarification of these needs prior to sending information to delegates and speakers alike will prevent problems when the meeting occurs.

BUDGETING

Booking facilities and arranging for services begin the budgeting process. Contracting usually is accomplished during the second planning trip or through correspondence after the first trip. Use meeting and exhibition checklists as source guides in anticipating expenses. Once all usual expenses have been identified, however, a significant number of additional factors should be considered in the international arena. Some expenses can be identified in advance, but for those that cannot, a 10–20 percent contingency expense category is essential.

The budget process for an international event differs from one for domestic events in the following ways:

- Prices quoted do not necessarily include the full range of facilities and services that they do in the United States.
- Each requirement needs to be disclosed and questioned in regard to associated costs.
- The cost of foreign exchange must be factored into the budget.
- The risk/reward relationship inherent in currency exchange should be examined, and the organization must determine how it wants to manage the risk.
- Meeting managers need to understand the base currency to calculate prices in contract agreements, determine when payments will be made, and specify in what currency.

Payment options will be part of the negotiating process. Consider the obligations inherent in all contracts, and then negotiate payment schedules that coincide with the meeting's income timetable. Deposits and advance payment schedules for international facilities are usually significantly greater than for U.S. facilities. Be sensitive to these timetables and negotiate adjustments so the payment pattern properly tracks the income pattern. Again, review what hotel deposits may be required and discuss how they can be managed.

Government Fees

One fee that is not found in the U.S. and must be added to the list of budgeted expenses is the fees that the host government may assess the meeting organization. These fees may be for identified services, such as exit visas or receiving fees; or they may be expressed as a service charge and related to total revenues generated or total number of participants. For example, a host government may hold a reception for attendees and then recover the cost by assessing the organization a service charge for the event. Ask each supplier and government contact what charges are associated with these services.

Taxes

Another significant budget item may be taxes. This is an area that is particularly complex, and it may be wise to engage an accounting firm to handle taxes for the meeting. Most major accounting firms have an overseas office or a corresponding firm in the country where the meeting is being held. Negotiating a consulting agreement with the local office could pay for itself many times over.

Tax liability within a host country should be determined prior to any commitment to meet there. Some taxes can be reduced or waived entirely if negotiated in advance. Many countries have reciprocal agreements that waive certain taxes, such as value added tax (VAT). This is particularly true within the European Union. Host city convention and visitors bureaus (CVBs) can be especially helpful in identifying how to plan for local taxes. Assess attendees and exhibitors for taxes at the time they are invoiced and to identify the amounts as such.

The VAT varies in each country, from as low as 6 percent to as much as 25 percent in Europe. The VAT increases as the expenses of your event increase. This is the cost of doing business internationally and must be budgeted appropriately. In addition, find out in advance how the VAT refund program works and if you qualify. Applying for a refund may be an arduous task and you need the expertise of someone with firsthand experience. Be prepared, because it can be a frustrating, time-consuming aspect of managing an international event. Once you have applied for a refund, allow from three to 18 months before you receive your money, but the amount can be significant. A VAT refund can make the difference between the event making a profit or taking a loss. However, due to the uncertainty of when or if a refund may be received, do not include the refund in your budget in case the refund cannot be applied within the current year's financials.

In addition to VAT, budget for duties that may be applied to inbound materials under customs regulations.

Currency Exchange Problems

During the site selection process, establish the base currency. In general, money must be received in the same currency and at the same exchange rate as it is spent. Countries with hard currency typically negotiate only in their currency, because the currency can be traded outside its borders. Your organization assumes the foreign exchange currency risk associated with exchange rates fluctuating over time. In many developing and controlled-economy countries, the local currency (soft currency) has no value outside that country's borders. In these countries, most negotiations are undertaken in U.S. dollars. This practice puts most of the currency exchange risk on the supplier, provided the organization collects its revenue in U.S. dollars. Confirm how payments can be made when dealing with soft currency, because you may be unable to use wire transfers as forms of payment. Both alternatives have inherent risks. Understand those risks and determine how to manage them.

Official, exclusive exhibition contractors can also have a significant impact on the budget. In addition to standard selection criteria, you must establish a common vocabulary for describing equipment, services, and prices. Currency exchange can be a major factor in total cost. To compound the problem, if a contractor from a third country is selected, the contractor will likely quote prices and require payment in the third country's currency. In addition to budgeting the cost of converting the local currency, you will need to budget the cost of converting U.S. dollars into the currency of the third country.

Managing Foreign Exchange Risk

Two basic ways to manage foreign exchange currency risk are open to you. One is to negotiate fixed-rate exchange contracts, then insist that all income be priced at an exchange rate that is equal to or greater than the fixed rate. This option still has some risks. The second, and safest, technique is to buy foreign currency on the futures market at the rate prevailing when the contracts are negotiated. Factor in the time value of money when assessing risk of currency exchange fluctuations; then determine the relative advantage of insuring against a loss by buying futures. Buying forward should not be seen as an opportunity to make money, but only to ensure the exchange rate for budgeting purposes. If the amount of money involved is relatively insignificant, or if the value of the dollar is considered to be low at the time of negotiations, your organization may elect to take the risk with the hope of some reward. Be sure to inquire about insurance coverage on the amount you are considering buying forward, as you may find limits depending on the amount you wish to purchase. For example, there may be insurance coverage of only up to $100,000 by the company you are securing to buy forward. If you need to purchase more than their insurance covers, it may not be worth the risk.

To minimize the impact of currency fluctuations on your budget, you may be able to open a bank account in the city/country that is hosting your event, although some restrictions will apply. This can be extremely beneficial if you plan to hold an international event on an annual basis. As you receive revenue generated by exhibit sales and registration, you can make scheduled payments and forward the funds to an international bank that will convert the U.S. dollars into the appropriate currency. In addition, you can write checks in the appropriate foreign currency from this bank to pay for on-site expenses. This will eliminate the exchange rates, which can be quite costly as the number of transactions goes up. This has been made more attractive by the introduction of the euro.

Currency Restrictions

Currency restrictions vary considerably among different countries, so become familiar with currency requirements, restrictions, and limitations imposed by the host country. Failure to observe proper limits and procedures can result in money being confiscated or impounded in the host country indefinitely. If they have an international department, your organization's bank can be a big help. An experienced travel agency or PCO can be a valuable resource in matters related to currency exchange and currency restrictions.

EXHIBIT SPACE SALES

Prior to undertaking an international exhibition, extensive market research must be conducted to ensure sufficient demand. Typically, profit margins on international events are narrower than on domestic events, and many industries have a much smaller base of potential exhibitors from which to draw. Early decisions must be made on the eligibility of companies to participate. Exhibitions can be national events, available only to home-country-based manufacturers, or international events, with eligibility open to companies from other countries as well.

After you have completed your market research and have identified the event that best fits your objectives, you will need to develop specific exhibition criteria that may include the following for a first-year event:

- Exhibit floor space
- Frequency of show
- Main product groups
- Total number of exhibitors
- Total number of attendees

Based on these criteria, you can identify exhibitors who would be willing to make a commitment to participate in this program.

Establishing a source of potential exhibiting companies will affect sales promotion costs, such as multi-language brochures and overseas postage. A list of buyers in attendance and the applicable product groups that are represented will provide you with the appropriate direction.

National financial support of an exhibition is a common practice outside the United States. In many cases, exhibit space sales success can best be achieved by contracting with a local firm experienced in the sale and organization of exhibitions. Proper representation of the exhibition to the host country's department of trade may result in a government subsidy that measurably stimulates exhibit space sales. Information on producing international exhibitions—including a list of potential agents and suggested contract forms—can be secured from UFI, the Global Association of the Exhibition Industry (www.ufinet.org).

Pavilion Programs

Hosting a U.S. pavilion at an existing international event can be a cost-effective way to give participating companies an opportunity to benefit from other companies that have already made a commitment to the global marketplace. Existing trade events have already established a base of buyers that would be interested in

U.S. products. Organizing a group of U.S. companies in a pavilion in one location gives international buyers the opportunity for one-stop shopping for all of their needs.

A pavilion program also reduces the cost incurred per company. Because most international exhibitions use a hardwall set-up, exhibitors can share equally in the expenses incurred to provide a lounge, food and beverages for their guests, and business center capabilities (phone, fax, and Internet access) so their members can communicate with their home office. Fees for exhibit space are also lower. For example, for one fee, a standard booth and available equipment could include:

- 3-by-3 meter booth (stand)
- Display panels
- Wall-to-wall carpet
- Fascia with company name
- Storage room with shelving and counter space
- Pavilion director

The pavilion program could also include:

- Assistance with hotel reservations
- Freight coordination/customs clearance
- Interpreters
- Exhibitor services (security, cleaning, electricity)
- Promotional support
- Association/staff support

Another cost-saving advantage to participating in a pavilion program is that you can make special arrangements for freight forwarding. You may be able to provide your exhibitors with consolidation points in the United States to coordinate the shipment of products. For instance, you can offer a consolidation point in Los Angeles or San Francisco for West Coast participants, Chicago to accommodate the Midwest, and New York to accommodate the East Coast. These three consolidation points would then be combined and shipped to their destination.

To save money for your exhibitors, your organization should submit one commercial invoice listing all companies under the organization's name. Many freight forwarders charge by the cubic meter/kilos, whichever is greater. You could pro-rate the cost so the exhibitors are not paying for additional charges.

ATTENDANCE PROMOTION

Attendance promotion for an international event is complicated by language and cultural barriers, local government restrictions on mailing list usage, and the unpredictable nature of overseas mail service. In general, you will apply many of the same promotional techniques as you would for a domestic event, but allow more time and budget dollars for translation and mailing. Because costs can quickly escalate, be selective in choosing your promotional strategies, which may include the Internet, direct mail, print advertising, and local promotion.

International attendance promotion has been greatly enhanced by worldwide Internet access. A web site and email marketing are especially useful strategies for educational, scientific, and technical groups whose members are likely to be frequent users of the Internet. Using the Internet to promote your event is not only cost-effective but also avoids problems with mail delays (see Chapter 5).

Whether in print or online, promotional information for the meeting may be translated into a foreign language to capture the right tone for the intended audience.

This may require rewriting as well as direct translation. To ensure correct translation, ask someone who is originally from the country where the translated language is spoken to read the translation for the correct message. Also provide the original English version for comparison purposes. Note that translation of print materials will greatly increase the size of the brochure, depending on the number and types of languages. Also, be sure that providing materials in more than one language does not convey the idea that the meeting itself will be translated (if it will not). If marketing materials are translated, the official language(s) of the program should be stated.

To allow for the sometimes unpredictable nature of mail service, begin the promotional process at least a year in advance. If the budget permits, plan at least two mailings. Preliminary announcements can be distributed 16–18 or more months before the meeting, followed in a few months by a second mailing that describes the program in more detail. The latter containing pre-registration forms can be directed primarily to those who responded to the first mailing. This method is best when the original promotion list is quite broad. Mailing the more detailed program only to those who have indicated an interest will save printing and postage costs. Be sure to also check holiday periods so that marketing materials do not arrive during these extended periods. For example, Europe has extended holiday periods during June, July, and August. Any materials received during that time will sit on desks or in mailrooms for up to six weeks while delegates are out of their offices.

When promoting your event with direct mail pieces, keep in mind that some companies can provide this service internationally, so you can cut down on postage and shipping costs and, more importantly, reduce the time needed for the direct mail piece to arrive at its destination.

Use of trade journal advertising and other forms of print media may be more effective than direct mail. Publications in the host country can reach thousands of potential attendees, and trade journals have a circulation directly related to your industry. Using their circulation lists for direct mail pieces is also beneficial. Ask appropriate professional journals or trade magazines and newsletters in all participating countries to publish announcements of the meeting and, when possible, include pre-registration forms. Travel agents and airlines may also be able to assist in promoting the meeting.

Support from a local organization that can provide a mailing list and advice about other visitor promotion activities is valuable. Local sponsorship that opens such doors usually must be negotiated prior to confirming the exhibition. Sponsorship agreements should be well defined, with a clear understanding of the level of support to be provided and the quality and quantity of potential visitors who can be reached through the sponsoring organization. The sponsorship agreement should also identify what payments, if any, will be made to the sponsoring organization by the exhibition organizer.

Controlled-economy countries usually identify and organize their own visitors to an exhibition. The only cost to the organizer may be the expense of printing admission tickets. Visitors to an exhibition in controlled-economy countries usually do not pay an entrance fee.

Unlike most U.S. events, an international exhibition may be of great interest to the local public. If attendance at the exhibition is a major concern of the organizer, consider scheduling advertisements in the local press both before and during the event. Advertising can generate additional editorial coverage and more interest in the event. In addition to paid advertising, standard public relations activities can help promote the event as well. Distributing press kits, targeting news releases, and developing on-site press contacts are just a few examples. Many practices that work well in the United States work equally well overseas.

Put It Into Practice

Before selecting an international destination, savvy meeting managers do their homework by consulting a variety of online and print resources to learn about the customs, climate, food, and business practices of the country. Investigate hotels, meeting facilities, and social event possibilities online and through U.S.-based representatives. If the site still looks promising, contact colleagues who have held events in that country. If the site is suitable for your organization and meets the event's objectives, plan a visit to build relationships with potential local suppliers. Use your organization's network to contact local people to make introductions and help pave the way for a productive information gathering site visit.

Remember to:

- Learn some simple phrases in the native language
- Carry plenty of business cards
- Keep spoken language simple
- Know some of the customs and culture of the country, including how to dress, how to handle introductions, and seating
- Use safe conversation topics
- Understand how to negotiate
- Appreciate the place of women in international business

COMMUNICATION

Language differences appear to be the most intimidating barrier to international meetings and exhibitions. Actually, this problem can be overcome by hiring professionals who provide interpretation for oral communication and translate written communication without losing the meaning in the process. Rarely does one individual possess talents in both translation and interpretation. They require different skills and talents.

An interpreter must be able to think and speak in the host-country language, as well as understand the meeting's objectives. Ideally, the interpreter should be familiar with meetings and exhibitions, as well as the industry the organization represents. An interpreter acts as a bridge between you and your suppliers in the host country. If you are unsure about the interpreter's ability, describe what you wish to convey and then ask him/her to tell you what you said before it is spoken to the other person.

Consecutive interpretation, which requires the speaker to stop after 3 or 4 sentences to allow the interpreter to speak, can easily double the length of time for a meeting. Simultaneous interpretation allows a person to speak at normal pace with only a short lag time for interpretation; however, special equipment is necessary with individual receivers in order for anyone to understand the one language in which they are listening. If you are expecting an interpreter to translate both from English to another language and also from that language back into English, be sure you make that known and hire someone with the correct credentials and rating.

Written communication in advance of the event allows the receiver time to translate the message clearly and accurately. It can also help call attention to unfamiliar words and jargon that may be unique to the home country. A question about the meaning of a word from the translator is a signal to avoid using that word in oral communication. Ultimately, most negotiations and planning details must be discussed orally in order to communicate effectively. Translation of preliminary correspondence is excellent training in preparing for oral communication.

Perhaps the greatest danger in oral communication is the false sense of security that develops when carrying on a conversation under the assumption that all parties understand. Language nuances are common in the English-speaking

Fast Facts

- Learn how to say "please," "thank you," "hello," "goodbye," and "pleased to meet you" in the host country's language.
- Smile; it is the one safe universal gesture.
- Make two photocopies of your passport. Keep one in your suitcase and leave one copy at home. Doing so will speed replacement of a lost or stolen passport.
- Did you know that different sources list 189–194 independent countries of the world?
- Most of the world uses A4 paper—not 8 1/2" x 11" paper as in the United States and Canada.
- Except in the United States, dates are written dd/mm/yy; for example May 10, 2006 would be written 10/05/06.

world; you should not be surprised that significant differences outside the English-speaking world exist. To minimize confusion, avoid using jargon, idioms, imprecise words, and different words to convey the same thought.

Exhibiting companies must also cope with language differences. Ideally, companies will staff their booths/stands with employees who know the products and services and also speak the local language. Rarely, however, do companies have sufficient staff with language capability and product knowledge, plus the personality and sales skills necessary to effectively staff an exhibit. In many countries, exhibiting companies should hire two people to assist with communication: one with technical knowledge of the products and services displayed, who can be the explainer; and one with multi-lingual language skills, who can be the interpreter. This method can also be applied to other services within your meetings, such as registration.

Hiring an interpreter is not inexpensive, and if your event is in Europe, you may need an interpreter who speaks three or more languages. If you promote the exhibition as a pavilion program, you can hire three or four interpreters and the exhibitors can share the expenses to minimize costs.

Finally, be prepared for negotiations to take longer for international events. This is particularly true when variances from standard practice are requested. Patience and diplomacy are essential. Since services are to be provided in the host country, all agreements and commitments must be understood in the host-country language. It is recommended that contracts should be written and signed by all parties in both languages.

Simultaneous Interpretation

When conducting a meeting in a country whose principal language is not English, a decision must be made regarding the official language of the meeting and whether simultaneous interpretation services will be required. Some groups avoid the need for simultaneous interpretation by designating an official language of the organization and conducting all worldwide meetings in that language, regardless of the location. If one of the meeting's objectives is to communicate with indigenous participants or if participants are coming from several countries, simultaneous interpretation may become a meeting requirement regardless of the organization's stated position.

State-of-the-art simultaneous interpretation equipment is available in most countries. Government agencies, CVBs, audiovisual companies, and local broadcasting companies are usually good sources for renting the equipment if it is not available from the meeting facility. If a meeting is being organized as a result of an invitation from a host government, simultaneous interpretation and interpreters may be provided at no cost. If, on the other hand, the organization has to pay for renting equipment and hiring interpreters, the decision to use simultaneous interpretation equipment will have a significant impact on the meeting budget and on administrative costs. Sometimes this cost can be passed on to the delegates by charging a per-person cost per language with a signup minimum.

For simultaneous interpretation, at least two interpreters are required for each language being spoken. Typically, the stress under which interpreters work necessitates frequent breaks (typically 20 minutes on, 20 minutes off); thus two or three interpreters for each language are recommended. Since the effectiveness of communication will depend on the quality of the interpretation, organizers should seek well-qualified people. Ask interpreters to provide references from organizations similar to yours to confirm their abilities in interpretation for your industry. For formal remarks, each speaker could be required to produce a written text. The presentation text should be received far enough in advance to provide time for translation. This will permit interpreters to read the material rather than interpret what they are hearing. If all presenters submit a written script well ahead of time and do not deviate from it appreciably, you may be able to reduce the number of interpreters. Sessions that rely on questions and answers or discussions among panelists ultimately will have to rely on phrase-by-phrase interpretation.

The interpretation problem is further complicated by technical requirements. Meetings dealing with specific subjects such as engineering, medicine, or manufacturing may need interpreters familiar with technical language. Adding technical requirements to language proficiency further complicates the task of employing good interpreters. You may need to decide whether to sacrifice language skills or technical familiarity when selecting interpreters. Many global organizations maintain a cadre of interpreters for the most common languages in their organization and pay travel expenses regardless of where the meeting is located with the idea that more effective communication is worth the extra cost. Maintaining a glossary of organization-specific terms may be a useful strategy to ameliorate this challenge.

CUSTOMS REGULATIONS

Moving goods in and out of a country requires specialized knowledge. Customs regulations are unique to each country, and customs inspectors have authority to delay or impound questionable shipments. The time-sensitive nature of meetings and exhibitions usually cannot accommodate such delays. Thoroughly investigate host-country requirements to identify restricted materials and applicable duties or tariffs, and pass this information on to attendees and exhibitors.

All materials being shipped into a host country must be specifically documented. Generalizations such as "meeting paraphernalia" are not acceptable. International freight forwarders and/or customs brokers are the best source of information regarding customs regulations. They can also provide forms and assist in completing them. (When the process has been accomplished once, you can make a template to simplify the process for the next event.) An international freight forwarder can also provide an estimate of the time that must be allowed for materials to clear customs once they have arrived in the host country. Purchasing or renting necessary materials and equipment in the host country can help minimize problems or additional costs in clearing customs. If you secure a freight forwarder/customs broker from the United States, be sure to ask who their partner is in the country and/or facility in which your meeting will be held. This will ensure a clear connection when executing the return shipment.

Customs regulations can affect the cost of shipping freight and can be a little intimidating for exhibitors who are not familiar with the paperwork or the advance planning that may need to occur. The implications of these regulations need to be made clear and understandable to exhibitors. Being able to refer them to a trusted customs broker to help deal with concerns may positively influence a decision to exhibit for the first time in a foreign country.

Meeting attendees must also be advised of any customs regulations that might affect their personal travel. Embassies, CVBs, and travel agents all are good resources for gleaning information that has particular application to the visitor. Many countries have customs regulations that restrict the amount of currency that can be brought in, as well as restrictions on certain books, films, records, tapes, or other items that may be considered detrimental to the country's politics, economy, culture, or ethics. Plants, foodstuffs, pornographic literature, and, in some countries, alcoholic beverages are the items most frequently confiscated from international travelers. Advise attendees of restrictions on imports and exports to avoid embarrassment, expense, and possible violation of local laws.

Most countries have adopted specific regulations related to exhibitions. In general, goods imported for display at an exhibition are exempt from duty, provided they are shipped out of the country within a reasonable time. The event sponsor may be liable for payment of duty on equipment that is not shipped out of the country if the exhibiting company fails to pay. For this reason, appoint an official freight forwarder who will be responsible for tracking essential paper-work that deals with the movement of goods into and out of the host country. The freight forwarder can also function as a liaison with customs on items purchased at the exhibition. Failure to properly manage customs regulations can have a significant impact on the profitability of an exhibition.

IMMIGRATION

U.S. passports are generally accepted throughout the world. Passports must be current, and all meeting participants should be advised to renew their passports in advance if the expiration date is within six months of the date of travel for the meeting. Visas, on the other hand, are far more complicated. Frequently, a visa service is engaged to expedite the visa process. While the cost for the service may seem high, it can be worthwhile when time is a factor. Frequently, visa applications must be hand-carried from one embassy or consulate to another. In some cases, the host government agency with which the organization is dealing must initiate the visa approval process.

When meetings involve delegates from several countries, special attention must be paid to the immigration requirements of the host country. Many countries impose immigration restrictions even for the purpose of attending meetings. Information on immigration restrictions for all the anticipated delegates should be determined during the site selection process. Members may request visa letters from the hosting organization. To ensure that your organization is not issuing letters to those who would like to enter the country but may have no intention of attending your meeting, a non-refundable fee, applied to registration, may be charged. In your letter, be specific about what expenses of the delegate you are or are not paying. In some countries, to issue an invitation means that you will host the attendee.

The U.S. Department of State (www.state.gov) provides current travel warnings, consular information, and other information for U.S. citizens abroad.

IMMUNIZATIONS

Many travelers have a relaxed view toward immunizations and other health precautions. Vaccinations are not easily accessible in all countries; therefore, the international traveler should take precautionary measures. Many inoculations, such as tetanus, are good for long periods of time. It is wise to get current inoculations before leaving home, since they may not be available in the host country.

The Centers for Disease Control and Prevention (www.cdc.gov) provides information for international travelers regarding disease outbreaks and immunization needs in specific countries. Diseases such as yellow fever, malaria, and cholera can erupt on short notice and cause a health warning to be issued. Travelers coming from areas under a health warning must be able to produce current immunization records. Local health departments and travel agencies are also good resources for current health warnings in effect around the world. Individual travelers need to consult a travel immunization health clinic well in advance of travel to assure that necessary immunizations are obtained. In some cases, visas will not be issued without documentation of immunization against certain endemic diseases. Hepatitis A vaccination (a series of three injections) is recommended for any international meeting manager who did not receive this immunization which is now routine in the United States.

LOCAL CUSTOMS

Host-country customs pose the most common challenges for meeting managers and meeting participants alike. Americans generally have an informal business style compared to many countries. To successfully adapt your meeting to local customs, learn as much as possible about the host country. Ample information about a country's history, culture, traditions, and people is available in libraries and on the Internet. A few hours of research and study can pay handsome dividends during business and social discussions.

Cultural differences around the world are significant, and the successful international event will demonstrate the utmost respect for local customs, whether or not participants understand or agree with them. Religious, racial, and sexual discrimination still exist in many parts of the world. Avoid discussion of these subjects in business and social situations. Provide attendees with guidelines concerning appropriate customs in the country they are visiting.

Scheduling

Be aware of local customs that might directly affect the event schedule. For example, in the Middle East, the weekend is observed on Thursday and Friday. This can have a significant impact on event scheduling. Religious, national, or local holidays can also wreak havoc with an event schedule, so investigate details of the local calendar before setting dates. For various social and political reasons, the workday can vary from one country to another. In countries with tropical climates, a midday siesta is common. Take care to ensure services will be available and uninterrupted during your programming. Find out usual meal times in the host country. For example, many countries routinely break for tea or a substantial snack in the late afternoon and then eat dinner later in the evening.

Although the group may be accustomed to early-morning sessions in the United States, traffic patterns and customs may call for a later start, particularly if participants will be using public transportation to and from the meeting facility. Exhibit hours can extend well into the evening in some countries, so prepare exhibitors for traffic patterns that differ from those at a U.S. exhibition.

Food Functions

Banquets can frequently become major problems overseas. Listen to the caterer in matters relating to menu selection, timing of service, and gratuities. Attempts to require caterers to serve menu items they are not accustomed to preparing can produce disastrous results. Basic arrangements, such as guarantees and oversets, need to be understood clearly. Caterers usually prepare menus only for the guaranteed number with no excess capacity, and guarantees may be required much earlier than you would normally expect.

Menus for international participants must provide alternative selections. Reasons for requiring alternatives include religious, medical, and personal-choice issues. Failure to recognize and be prepared for these situations can result in serious problems for guests and embarrassment to the host.

Protocol

Protocols associated with such matters as greetings, formal ceremonies, meal functions, and flag displays should be respected by all event participants. Properly brief the leadership of the sponsoring organization, and advise attendees and exhibitors of protocols that may affect their conduct in the host country. Failure to follow proper protocol—even out of ignorance—can result in embarrassment, formal protest, or a break in friendly relations with the host country.

For example, protocol violations relating to the display of flags are common. Flag protocol differs for each country. Unless expert advice is available, avoid the issue altogether. A variety of brightly colored fabrics flying from poles can provide the same decorative effect and is politically safer than displaying national flags.

Event participants should adapt to customs of the host country. Many practices and social customs have been developed over hundreds, even thousands, of years. If an organization is unwilling to respect and comply with local customs, the event would be better held in another country.

Controlled Economies

Controlled-economy countries can present unique challenges. By their very definition, these countries exert control over their citizens, and they expect organizations sponsoring events to supervise their delegates in a similar manner. Have a complete itinerary for the entire time the group will be in the country. Set aside blocks of time for meetings with government officials if they are requested, and urge participants to be flexible if they are called to a meeting on short notice. Remember that your organization is there at the invitation of the host country. All participants should assume an invited-guest mentality.

INTERNATIONAL MEETINGS IN THE UNITED STATES

Many organizations within the United States are affiliated with an international body. A formal invitation to meet in the United States is extended to the international committee and, if accepted, the U.S. group becomes the meeting's host and may assume primary financial responsibility.

When hosting an international group, plan the program to include the perspectives of all of the countries that are participating. Participants naturally expect to see their representatives among the speakers on the program. The individual or committee selecting speakers should attempt to satisfy national sensitivities and identify the best authorities on a variety of program topics from a number of geographic regions.

Registration materials also require special attention. Specify in registration materials that fees must be paid in U.S. dollars and drawn on a U.S. bank. A copy of the foreign bank transfer draft should accompany the registration form. Regardless of instructions provided, be prepared to deal with registrations that arrive without payment and bank drafts received with no indication of the originating party. Another problem may be encountered by the custom in some countries of using the family name as the first name. Word the registration form to ask for "family" or passport name rather than "last" name. Cross-file registration information under both names to ensure registration personnel can easily locate the material.

As for an international event held outside the United States, on-site translation of written communications and interpreting of oral communications may be necessary to accommodate non-English-speaking participants. Make multi-lingual resources available through a visitors desk, lounge, and/or special reception for international visitors.

INTERNATIONAL MEETING MANAGEMENT RESOURCES

The best resources for managing international events are colleagues who have conducted events in the cities and countries you are considering. In addition to your professional network, a host of organizations, government agencies, and companies can be helpful in managing international events.

The U.S. Department of Commerce offers its services to managers of domestic meetings and trade shows and can be helpful in building traffic at these events. In addition, many embassies around the world provide specific services for U.S. organizations that are interested in expanding and promoting their products and services to international markets. Many U.S. embassies have a marketing department that can provide meeting space for appointments with local representatives, as well as assistance in coordinating trade missions. These trade missions may include small table-top exhibits, depending on the size of their facility. (See appendix for list of resources.)

U.S. Commercial Service

The U.S. Commercial Service, located in more than 150 overseas offices in 85 countries, can help you find potential overseas agents, distributors, sales representatives, and business partners. One of the services they offer is the Gold Key Matching Service, which includes:

- Customized market and industry briefings with trade specialists
- Timely and relevant market research
- Appointments with prospective trade partners and key industry sectors
- Post-meeting debriefing with trade specialists and assistance in developing appropriate follow-up strategies
- Help with travel, accommodations, interpreter services, and clerical support

The U.S. Commercial Service office also offers a matchmaker program to help small- and medium-size U.S. companies establish key business relationships in major markets abroad. Matchmaker trade delegations are industry-specific and target two to four countries with strong sales potential for U.S. goods and services. The matchmaker program provides the following services:

- Three to six appointments
- Market briefing by local trade specialists
- Welcome kit
- Office space for the day of the scheduled appointments
- Domestic use of fax, telephone, and Internet
- Hotel arrangements
- Interpretation and transportation services
- If requested, a Commercial Service staff person will accompany you to your appointments

SUMMARY

An international meeting is defined as an event that draws an international audience from three or more countries. International meetings that are hosted in one's own country are termed inbound meetings. International events convened in a foreign country are termed outbound meetings.

Adapt the meeting management process to accommodate an international audience. In addition to expertise in managing and organizing meetings and exhibitions, meeting managers also need intuition, common sense, diplomacy, and respect for the cultures of both the host country and the international participants.

Differences exist in booking, budgeting, marketing, equipment and services, negotiating contracts, culture, and customs that need to be considered when managing a meeting outside of the United States of America.

A wealth of resources are available to help make international events successful: books, articles, web sites, convention and visitors bureaus, country-based offices of tourism, and meeting managers who have managed events in that country or hosted international attendees.

KEY TERMS

Attrition	Full American Plan (FAP)	Outbound meetings
Base currency	Hard currency	Pavilion
Consular information	Hardwall	Passports
Customs	Health warning	Professional Congress
Customs brokers	Inbound meetings	Organizer (PCO)
Duties	International freight	Protocol
European Union	forwarders	Receiving fees
European Plan	International meeting	Tariffs
Exhibition service	Interpretation	Translate
contractors	Local sponsorship	Value Added Tax (VAT)
Exchange rate	Modified American Plan	Visa
Exit visas	(MAP)	Voucher Plan
Foreign exchange	Official language	
currency risk		

COMPELLING QUESTIONS FOR CONSIDERATION

1. Why might an organization choose to hold a meeting overseas?

2. Why does the site selection process for an overseas meeting generally require more time than that for a meeting held in the United States?

3. In what ways might the budget for a meeting held overseas be different from that of a similar meeting held in the United States?

4. Why should you spend time learning about the country where your event will be held?

5. What information should be provided to attendees before they leave to attend a meeting held in a country other than their own?

6. Why use a PCO?

7. How will the meeting need to be marketed differently to an international audience?

CHAPTER 17

CO-LOCATING TRADE SHOWS

Mike Muldoon
PRESIDENT
CONVENTION MANAGEMENT GROUP, INC.

LEARNER OUTCOMES

When the reader has completed reading this chapter, he/she should be able to . . .

1 Describe how co-location allows meeting managers to provide a more dynamic platform.

2 Summarize how co-location of events gives organizations the opportunity to offer a wider range of educational programming and a broader scope of products and services.

3 Explain why co-location helps sponsoring organizations gain exposure to more potential members.

4 Debate the pros and cons of sharing the costs of systems, infrastructure, and professional services in a co-located event.

> Good ideas are not adopted automatically.
> They must be driven into practice
> with courageous patience.
>
> *Admiral Hyman Rickover*

OVERVIEW

Associations sponsor trade shows, expos, conventions, fairs, and other exhibitions to provide a platform for association issues. An association trade show can improve professionalism in the industry; promote products and services that improve productivity, safety, and profitability; and, provide industry networking opportunities. In short, what can be achieved at one trade show may save weeks or months to accomplish the same if employees stayed home. And, it may be less expensive. According to the Center for Exhibit Industry Research, it costs 62% less to close a lead generated from a trade show than one that originated in the field.[1]

Given the increase competition for attendees and exhibitors along with a shrinking pool of attendees, many associations are looking at holding their meeting in association with other industry groups. This is referred to as co-location. However, for co-located trade shows to be successful—and benefit all parties—there has to be good alignment between the two shows. The attendees at Show A must have a legitimate interest in the exhibitors of Show B and vice versa. Otherwise, attendance crossover will be minimal, and the intended benefit of creating more synergism and activity on each show floor will not be realized.[2]

This chapter focuses on the advantages of co-location from an association's point of view. Key issues associated with co-locating managers will be discussed that should provide insights into the development of a strategic plan for associations that wish to explore this option.

ASSOCIATION GOALS FOR SPONSORED CONVENTIONS AND EXPOSITIONS

An association's annual meeting and trade show should be a marketing vehicle to integrate the association's goals into one forum. Common goals of trade shows or expositions typically include:

- To provide a platform for association issues
- To improve the professionalism of the industry it serves
- To promote products and services that improve productivity, safety, profitability, and so on
- To provide networking opportunities
- To reinforce the association's position as an industry advocate and resource
- To interact with the current membership
- To attract potential new members
- To operate within the financial guidelines of the budget

In theory, trade shows are the lifeblood of most associations, providing up to one third of the association's income. When new ideas and strategies are implemented yearly, a trade show can thrive. However, even the healthiest of trade shows needs to be monitored. The average attrition—at even the dynamic of trade shows—can run to more than 30%. Many associations tend to rely heavily on the success of their trade show to help support the financial success of the association. The business of an association is the business of its trade show.[3]

TRADE SHOW OBSTACLES THAT ASSOCIATIONS FACE

The days of "build the exhibit and they will come" are long gone. Competition and a more complex marketplace fueled, in part, by the Internet, have made it imperative to be sensitive to the needs and demands of both exhibitors and attendees at every trade show. Bigger, faster-growing events in other industries have priority for preferred dates, facilities, hotels, and cities. The cost of keeping up with systems, processes, procedures, and infrastructure and expertise has its boundaries, and often is not justified for a "single" event.

The distraction of consolidation among members has resulted in a shrinking audience, dwindling registration numbers, and a reduction in revenue from dues.

Increasingly, the challenge of providing general business sessions to a broad horizontal membership and, at the same time, presenting specific technical programming to vertical segments of the industry has proven to be a difficult task for associations to overcome. Additionally, there is the tendency of expanding into related services and activities which may already be served by other organizations.

WHY CO-LOCATE?

More than 10 years ago, the American Society of Association Executives (ASAE) suggested that associations should do the one or more of the following:

1. Look for co-location possibilities with other shows
2. Consider co-sponsoring with other associations
3. Seek alliances and partnerships
4. Provide exhibitors with more sophisticated and targeted buying information on show attendees[4]

Since ASAE's proclamation, the consistent trend is that companies from all industries have been reducing the number of trade shows in which they are exhibiting. The larger exhibitors are pressuring show management to increase the size and traffic density of their shows to ensure their participation. Co-located shows offer exhibitors a stronger, more comprehensive event where they can get a greater return on their investment (ROI).

To accomplish all of the above, meeting managers must plan carefully and establish goals. Clear objectives must be established. For example, a clear set of objectives for the creation of an effective exhibition are to:

- Facilitate interaction within the current membership
- Attract potential new members
- Reinforce the association's position as an industry resource
- Operate within financial guidelines

Using the objectives stated above, meeting managers could apply these objectives to their trade shows and improve them by making sure they are specific, measurable, achievable, realistic and timetable for achievement is stated. It is important to note that the association's objective must be congruent with the partner in the co-location opportunity.

Co-located shows can take one of many forms:

- Two (or more) shows agree to co-locate in one venue over the same dates but plan to keep their identities, brands, ownership, and finances completely separate.
- One show locates as a pavilion within another (usually larger) show. This can also include clearly defined educational tracks added to an existing program.
- Two (or more) shows merge completely—including ownership, finances, and a new identity or brand.
- A stand-alone conference locates within a larger event, such as a trade show.

THE ADVANTAGES OF CO-LOCATING

If two organizations have a high level of compatibility, it would seem likely that combining their events would increase value for both of the organizations and attendees while increasing attendance. While this can certainly be true for many co-located shows, this strategy does not automatically improve a show. Co-located shows must have a logical reason to exist. More specifically, the attendees must benefit from being able to visit both shows at one time. The best co-location is one where there is 100% compatibility for the attendee and 0% for the exhibitor—so as to avoid creating a competitive exhibitor base.

Co-locating two trade shows certainly creates a more dynamic platform for attendees and exhibitors alike. It creates a broader scope of products and services and can offer a wider range of educational programming.

The benefits of co-locating are bountiful. Simply being able to use the following sales pitch to both attendees and exhibitors can have a substantial effect: "Come to this mega-event, and you will use your time and dollars more effectively."

A traditional, stand-alone trade show is a forum for an association to interact with their current membership. A co-location not only reaffirms the associations' strong identity with its members, but it also provides exposure to more potential members.

Merging a 150-booth show with an existing 500-booth show is much more cost-effective than running the 150-booth show as a stand-alone event. The 650-booth show is likely to be considerably more profitable than the two individual shows.

Additionally, co-located shows can produce better sites and/or dates. Joining forces with a show that already has a prime location and dates increases the marketability of the show that does not yet have an ideal setting. It can also benefit the show that made the original reservation: a convention center will always treat a 1,000-booth show better than two 500-booth events. Moreover, a meeting-heavy show can take advantage of another that may have surplus meeting rooms.

Co-locating shows allows rapid entry into a market, particularly from an international perspective. It also permits expansion of the exhibitor base for other shows. Finally, co-locating is a good way to "box out" the competition. An organization can co-locate directly with a competitor or with a competitor's competitor, using the old adage, "the enemy of my enemy is my friend."

SUCCESSFUL CO-LOCATING

Done well, co-location is good for both parties because it creates a stronger, more comprehensive event that will be larger on the radar screen of the key exhibitors, who then take larger booths. The dominant show of an industry attracts more attention—meaning more attendees, more press coverage, more financial analysts, more international visitors, and thus a larger exhibit. This makes for a much more rewarding and profitable event. However, co-located events require diplomacy, coordination, and careful management in order to meet the goals of all of the parties involved.

An initial step to a successful co-location is to examine how well a potential partner's goals and culture align with the association. The following are some questions to test the compatibility of different shows and organizations:

- Who are the principal members of the organizations?
- What is the major focus of each meeting?
- Are operations, promotions, and administrative decisions driven by the board, staff, or a committee?
- How are priorities ranked and success defined by both parties? Improving education? Expanding exhibits? Achieving greater visibility?

Put It Into Practice

The American Meat Institute holds the largest expo for the meat and poultry industry in North America—the AMI Meat, Poultry & Seafood Exposition. From 1990 to 1995, machinery, equipment, and supplies exhibits grew from 150,000 net sq.ft. to 208,000 net sq.ft., representing a 28% increase. In the same period, attendance rose from 9,000 to 14,000, in which reduced domestic attendance was offset by mid-level managers, non-members, and international attendees. AMI was committed to a strong technical and business program and targeted facility, distribution, refrigeration, and greater international attendance for future growth. At the same time, the International Dairy Foods Association (IDFA) was the largest expo for the dairy industry in North America. From 1990 to 1994 machinery, equipment, and supply exhibits grew from 100,000 net sq.ft to 170,000 net sq.ft., representing a 42% increase. In addition, attendance rose from 7,000 to 14,500. They also offset shrinking domestic attendance with mid-level managers, non-members, and international attendees.

In 1997 AMI and IDFA agreed to co-locate under the name World Wide Food Expo. They also partnered with the International Association of Food Industry Suppliers (IAFIS, formerly DFISA), and the National Food Processors Association (NFPA).

The agreement between these groups included separate exhibit sales and services, coordinated exhibit space rates, and the understanding that there would be no poaching of potential exhibitors. Specialized pavilions were created on the trade show floor, which added an additional 200,000+ sq. ft. The specialized pavilions included areas focused on facilities/distribution/refrigeration, product development/ingredients, logistics, canning/packing, and food formulating.

The groups also shared international attendance promotion, including creating marketing collateral in eight languages. The domestic attendance promotion was handled separately and the individual organizations' member promotions were personalized. There was a coordinated direct mail campaign as well as coordinated trade press ads and public relations. There were advertisements in a total of 41 industry publications (16 meat, 10 dairy, 15 food).

The agreement meant shared housing and registration services, security and shuttles, a general services contractor, an international business center and translation services, and a facility and schedule.

The educational program included a total of 60 educational sessions, which included 20 sessions on the dairy industry, 20 sessions that related to the meat industry, and 20 shared sessions on food processing. To augment the educational sessions, there were three general sessions. One was meat specific, one was dairy specific, and there was a joint or shared general session featuring Walter Cronkite. Food and beverages expenses were separate and entertainment expenses were shared.

The bottom-line was that all of the sponsors were able to maintain their own identities with their respective members. Attendance for WWFE grew 23% and international participation increased by 25% (a total of 5,100 international attendees, representing 127 countries). The show simultaneously provided broad horizontal and specific technical and vertical programming. The sponsors enjoyed improved systems, processes, and infrastructure, all within their budgets. They also secured preferred future dates, facilities, and hotels. Cost efficiencies funded improved promotion, services, and programming. The Worldwide Food Expo exceeded all financial goals, both cash flow and net.

In addition to ensuring that both parties' needs and working style are in alignment, there are several other steps that meeting managers can take to create lasting partnerships. Whatever the form that the partnership and co-located event take, here are 10 tips that will help make them successful:

1. Be aware of all of the events that occur in your market niche (e.g., other exhibitions or conventions, conferences, or private events). View all of them as potential co-locations. Then test their alignment with the organization and show, based upon the compatibility test above.
2. Take a positive approach to the other event—how will they benefit from co-locating with the organization? Assure them that they will not be lost within the larger event.

Put It Into Perspective

Share the risk and the reward. In a time of decreased budgets, groups are looking to partnerships to help diversify their offerings and increase their chances of financial success.

This is especially crucial when show revenues contribute inordinately to association operations—an average of 12 cents of every association revenue dollar comes from trade shows, according to the *2005 Association CEO Survey*, conducted by the PCMA Education Foundation.[5]

The trend to co-locate has been further accelerated by the following developments:

- A downturn in the economy, which has decreased participation in shows by both attendees and exhibitors.
- In general, exhibitors are cutting down on the number of shows that they are doing. The larger exhibitors are pressuring show management to increase the size and clout of their shows.
- There are just too many shows out there, each attracting a diminishing response.

3. Be sure the agreement is a win-win for both parties—each organization must walk away with one or more tangible benefits, such as free access to the other's attendees.

4. Divide up the major tasks among the partners, as appropriate. For example, one group might do the attendance promotion while the other handles operations. Do not share responsibility for a single task or the task will not get done effectively.

5. Do not allow poaching. The lower-priced show may not approach exhibitors in the higher-priced show and say, "Come into our show and save money." Actually, the best solution is for both shows to charge the same exhibit rate.

6. Strongly encourage crossover attendance—make it free, make it easy, massively publicize it, and offer an incentive (such as a free seminar pass or a T-shirt). Note there must be a common registration or lead inquiry system for both shows, since exhibitors will demand this.

7. Agree on common days for the exhibit—but not necessarily the same hours. Generally, attendees will not come back the next day to attend a co-located event.

8. Keep the financial agreement as simple as possible, and charge only direct expenses to the common budget. Salaries and overhead expenses should come out of each party's profit split.

9. Make it work as a partnership. Ensure that the deal is driven from the organization's top management and that each party considers the other an equal, no matter what the size differential.

10. Decide in advance how to dissolve the partnership. Include a non-compete clause in the agreement so that the partner who wants out is prohibited from re-entering the market for an agreed-upon period of time.

ECONOMIC CONSIDERATIONS

Economic effects are essential to the decision to co-locate a trade show. This section outlines some economic considerations that associations should address in writing before deciding whether to co-locate their trade shows. This written agreement on the finances of the partnership is sometimes referred to as a memorandum of understanding (MOU).

In general, there should be no exchange of money, except for sharing the costs of registration and security. These costs should be shared equitably—based on the size of each show's exhibit square footage or registered attendance. However, there may be a situation where one show benefits more than the other. In that case, the benefiting partner should pay a fee. The other general consideration that applies to any kind of co-location partnership is the length of the contract. Are future contracts confirmed for the long term? Are they renegotiable, and are they open to new partners?

When one show is located in a pavilion inside of another show, several financial considerations should be decided in advance. If the floor space is rented from the main sponsor's show, what is the discount off of the posted rate that is charged to the pavilion sponsor? In most cases, the same rate should be quoted to exhibitors inside and outside the pavilion. Note that the sponsor makes its money off the differential between the posted and the discounted rate. If there is to be sharing of revenue, what percentage is to go to the main sponsor and what percentage goes to the pavilion sponsor? In the case of a revenue split, the following guidelines help to determine what the split should be:

- Which group will pay to promote exhibit-only attendance?
- What on-site operations costs will be borne by each association?
- What support will the prime sponsor provide in exhibit sales (e.g., will the overall show prospectus include information on the pavilion)?
- Who is responsible for collecting from the pavilion exhibitors?

Thus, for example, if the main sponsor is responsible for all promotion and operations, the split might be 60% (main sponsor) / 40% (pavilion sponsor).

When the two exhibitions are completely integrated, the following financial considerations should be agreed upon in advance and included in the MOU:

- What is the common rate that will be charged for exhibit space? Usually it is the higher of the two shows.
- What portion of revenue does each organizer keep for those exhibitors unique to each show?
- How will revenue from common exhibitors be shared? Also, who sells to key accounts?
- What does each do to promote the common event as well as their own event?
- Who pays for operational costs and other expenses?

SUMMARY

Before deciding to co-locate meetings, meeting managers should analyze the alignment across the shows to determine the potential for success of the co-location decision. A significant number of co-located events do not create more value for attendees or significant ROI for exhibitors. Often one show benefits at the expense of the other.

However, co-location strategies can be an important means of growth for many associations' events and trade shows; therefore, careful consideration should be given to the decision. Co-location is most successful when there is high audience and exhibitor alignment that results in positive synergies across the floors of both shows. Before co-locating, the meeting management of both associations should agree upon the details of the show's finances and promotion, and divide other responsibilities equitably. The partnership should extend to how best to brand the co-located events and how to lay out the exhibit floor in a way that benefits both associations.

REFERENCES

1. Hough, M. (2003). *The profitable tradeshow.* http://www.profitabletradeshow. com.

2. Cox, S. (July, 2003). Is your trade show ready for the future? *Convene*, p. 44.

3. Littlejohn, M. (July, 2005). The association trade show business. *Convene*, p. 28.

4. American Society of Association Executives. (1993). *Report.* Washington, DC: author.

5. PCMA Education Foundation. (2005). *Association CEO survey.* Chicago: Author.

KEY TERMS

Alignment	Exhibition	Pavilion
Attendance	Expositions	Return on investment
Attrition	Fairs	(ROI)
Co-location	Horizontal show	Trade show
Consolidation	Marketplace	Traffic density
Convention center	Memorandum of	Venue
Conventions	Understanding (MOU)	Vertical show
Educational tracks		

COMPELLING QUESTIONS FOR CONSIDERATION

1. What are the advantages of co-locating?

2. What are the obstacles to co-locating?

3. How is the right co-location partner found?

4. What should be included in the MOU (memorandum of understanding) or financial agreement between the co-location partners?

5. What are appropriate goals as a co-locator?

CHAPTER 18

STRATEGIES TO EMBRACE THE ADULT LEARNER

Sandra K. Strick, PhD

ASSOCIATE PROFESSOR
SCHOOL OF HOTEL, RESTAURANT,
AND TOURISM MANAGEMENT
UNIVERSITY OF SOUTH CAROLINA

LEARNER OUTCOMES

When the reader has completed reading this chapter, he/she should be able to . . .

1 Discuss the characteristics of adult learners.

2 Adapt learning content to the generational issues of adult learners.

3 Apply adult learning principles in the development of educational programming.

4 Define visual, audio, and kinesthetic learners

5 Describe the application of learning styles to optimize learner outcomes.

6 Identify elements of the learning environment that affect how adults apply what they have learned.

> The illiterate . . . (is) not the individual who cannot read and write, but one who cannot learn, unlearn, and relearn.
>
> *Alvin Toffler*

OVERVIEW

Education is a key component of most meetings. According to the American Society for Association Executives, 95% of associations offer education programs for their members, making it the single most common association function. Moreover, continuing education and the resulting continuing education units (CEU) are often the main objective of professional and association meetings.[1]

Adult education provided by meetings is integral to the concept of lifelong learning. Business, industry, and professional organizations as well as the academic community have eagerly embraced a commitment to lifelong learning. Meetings influenced by the concept of lifelong learning encourage learners to acquire new skills, knowledge, and perspectives. By definition, the lifelong learner never graduates.

A meeting manager's effectiveness and value will increase significantly with the ability to develop the educational component of a meeting in a way that ensures successful learning. In order to do this, the meeting manager must understand the adult learner, factors influencing adult learning, and the importance of lifelong learning. This chapter will provide you with the skills and resources to be better prepared to meet this challenge.

WHAT IS LIFELONG LEARNING?

Lifelong learning is the commitment to and the process of learning throughout one's life. It is the collective set of activities that includes both formal and informal delivery modes, such as college or university credentialing programs, basic job skills training, apprenticeships, English as a Second Language (ESL), work-related courses, and courses of personal interest.[2]

Lifelong learning is an ongoing process by which an individual actively seeks to understand and contribute to change in the workplace and in society. It pervades every aspect of adult life. K. Patricia Cross and others have observed that "There is no such thing as a separate 'permanent' part of education that is not lifelong . . . Lifelong education is not a system, but the principle on which the overall organization of a system is founded and which accordingly underlies the development of each of its component parts."[3]

As R.H. Dave writes in his book *Foundations of Lifelong Learning*, "Lifelong education seeks to view education in its totality. It covers formal, nonformal, and informal patterns of education and attempts to integrate and articulate all structures and stages. . . . It is also characterized by flexibility in time, place, content, and techniques of learning, and hence calls for self-directed learning, sharing of one's enlightenment with others, and adopting varied learning styles and strategies."[4]

WHO ARE ADULT LEARNERS?

By definition, an adult learner is any person 16 years or older who is not enrolled as a full-time student. According to the National Center for Educational Statistics, 42% of the relevant population participated in adult education in 2001. This amounts to some 92 million people taking a variety of courses. However, the majority of the courses attended were either work-related (30%) or courses of personal interest (21%).[5]

Adult learners are experienced, tough-minded consumers who lead busy lives. They are given to voicing their frustrations and concerns with the learning environment and to viewing the learning process differently than the traditional student.[6]

Adult learners have been described as self-directed people who are responsible for their own lives and who should be acknowledged as such. They are internally motivated and usually enter the learning environment with pre-established goals that feed their need to achieve the ends they have set for themselves or that have been set for them.[7]

Unlike younger learners, adult learners bring a variety of life experiences with them to the learning environment. They are sophisticated consumers who will make their needs known and work hard to have them met. These adult learners can choose whether they want to participate in the learning process. Although they may be physically present, they must make a conscious decision as to whether their participation fulfills their personal goals and addresses their needs.[8]

The demographic profile of the adult learner has changed very little in the last three decades. Participants are usually middle class and educational attainment is the principal motivation. In 1992, Cross estimated that one of every three adults was involved in some type of organized learning activity.[9]

The learning experiences in which adults engage can be as informal as the casual pursuit of a subject of interest, or as formal as pursuing an academic degree. Adult learners also participate in continuing education programs to keep their skills current or to acquire new ones that enable them to keep up with changes in their jobs.

CHARACTERISTICS OF ADULT LEARNERS

Adult learners are self-directed, have a wealth of life experiences on which to draw, and are oriented to problem solving.[10] As a result, their physical, mental, and emotional characteristics have important implications for learning.

Self-Direction

Lifelong learners accept and assume responsibility for their own lives. Because of the high value they place on autonomy and responsibility, they respond positively when their maturity is acknowledged and respected. Adults want to be actively involved in the learning process and are usually less responsive in a passive learning environment. The focus of learning must be on what they perceive as important.

Adult learners are motivated by the desire to maintain or improve their economic position or professional status and to gain opportunities for self-actualization or a sense of accomplishment. Such learners have a need for socialization with peers during learning. They are self-directed and are drawn to interactive learning situations with a high level of practicality.

The use of computer-aided instruction, simulators, and distance learning are all examples of self-directed learning that meet the adult learner's need for interaction and provide a powerful incentive to learn.[11]

Multiple Life Experiences

Adult learners hold fixed ideas, habits, attitudes, opinions, and beliefs that the facilitator must be aware of in order to tailor information to the specific needs of the group. If the facilitator ignores the experience and expectations that learners bring to the educational situation, the desired learning will not occur. While most developmental education takes place within a traditional classroom atmosphere, providing alternative methods and opportunities can enhance adult learning. Relating new knowledge and skills to what learners already know increases retention.

Group activities, such as roundtable discussions, in which learners exchange ideas and information, add a new dimension to learning. Listening and socializing are both essential because the collective knowledge and experience of the individuals in a learning situation can be a valuable resource. A skilled instructor capitalizes on the contributions of participants in the learning environment by acting as a facilitator so learners can learn from one another.[12]

Problem-Solving Orientation

Adult learning peaks when the content helps the learner solve a problem. Unmet needs and unsolved problems motivate adult learners, who will use the information when it is practical and immediately applicable. The learner's belief that an activity can help solve a problem provides a powerful motivation for taking part in the learning experience. The response from learners will be greater when there is relevance and value to the material being presented. Likewise, the dropout rate will be highest when the content is considered to lack applicability.

The focus of educational planning should center on problems that face the learners rather than on content. Because problems are multifaceted and often impinge on each other, addressing them will further demonstrate the applicability of the content. A good facilitator is more people-oriented than subject-oriented and will be more focused on the learners than on the subject. Your challenge as the meeting manager is to help plan an educational program that achieves this goal. Here are some principles to keep in mind as you plan the educational program for your meetings:

- Adults need to be involved in the planning and evaluation of their instruction.
- Experience (including mistakes) provides the basis for learning activities.
- Instructional formats should take into account the wide range of backgrounds among learners. Learning materials and activities should allow for different levels of experiences of the audience.
- When using learning materials involving the use of or application of technology, the instructor must be mindful of the varying degrees of comfort and familiarity of the audience with the technology.
- Since adults are self-directed, instruction should allow learners to discover things for themselves, providing guidance and help when mistakes are made.
- Instruction should be task-oriented instead of requiring rote forms of learning such as memorization.
- Adults are more interested in learning about subjects that have immediate relevance to their jobs or personal lives.
- Adult learning is problem-centered rather than content-oriented.
- Adult learning programs should attempt to cater to the age limitations of participants.
- Adult learners should be challenged to move to increasingly advanced stages of personal development.
- Adult learners should have as much choice as possible in the access and organization of learning programs.[13]

APPLICATION OF ADULT LEARNING PRINCIPLES

Leading adult theorist Malcolm Shephard Knowles emphasized that self-motivation is the best stimulus for learning, with a "need to know" also being a critical component of adult learning success. Knowles' theory of andragogy is an attempt to develop a theory specifically for adult learning success. In his theory, Knowles suggests that the design of learning should include experiential learning and problem solving. In practical terms, andragogy means that instruction for adults needs to focus more on the process rather than the content. Case studies, role-playing, simulations, and self-evaluation are useful techniques. With these teaching strategies, instructors become facilitators rather than lecturers and graders.[14]

In his book *The Modern Practice of Adult Education*, Knowles developed underlying principles that synthesized the way adults look at the learning environment.[15] He argued that learners must exhibit these principles for the learning to be successful. These principles are a need to learn, a need for ownership of the learning, and the importance of the relevance of the content. These principles provide the foundation for the adult learning process, as well as a framework for designing and developing successful educational activities.

The Need to Learn

Adults must feel a need to learn, and their individuality must be recognized and respected. An atmosphere of mutual respect, friendliness, and support creates a climate conducive to adult learning. In non-threatening learning situations, adults are more likely to gain insight into their needs and discover what they can learn.

Adult learners do not appreciate being herded from place to place, being passive listeners, or being told they must do something. Therefore, learning activities that emphasize responsibility rather than obedience produce the best results. Activities that require group problem solving may help to satisfy this need.

The key to learning is a felt need, which represents the disparity between desired and actual levels of knowledge. The learner must be able to identify the relevance of the material being learned to the fulfillment of the need.[16]

The Need for Ownership

The adult learner's focus on self-direction must be the principal consideration in designing and developing learning activities. Having made the decision to attend a workshop or seminar, the attendee must have already consciously determined that what will be presented will be helpful in meeting their learning needs.[17]

The Importance of Relevance

The ability to draw on life experiences in putting material together for a presentation is crucial to capturing the interest of potential participants. The provision of real-life examples and material that is directly applicable to the learner's situation helps maximize the success of the educational experience.[18] Failure to demonstrate relevance of the content to the learner will result in unsatisfactory results of learner outcomes.

Putting Knowles' andragogy theory into practice, the following is an example of applying these principles to the design of personal computer training:

1. Instruction should explain why specific things are being taught and how they can be applied to the learner's situation (commands, functions, operations).
2. Instruction should take into account the wide range of backgrounds of learners. Learning materials and activities should allow for different levels/types of previous experience with computers.
3. Instruction should be task-oriented. Instead of memorization, learning activities should be in the context of common tasks to be performed.

4. Instruction should provide for learners to be self-directed, allowing learners to discover things for themselves while providing guidance and help with mistakes.[19]

FORMATTING THE LEARNING EXPERIENCE

Educational content can be formatted and organized through proven methods known as organizational patterns. These patterns categorize learning from the perspective of the format that the learning experience will take and the learner's own educational objectives. Since the characteristics of the adult learner have been well documented, organizational patterns that support the learning of adults are especially applicable to the meetings industry. Organizational patterns appropriate for adult learners include:

Individualized Learning

Individualized learning is well suited to specific learning activities. The learning can occur independently or through person-to-person interaction with the instructor/facilitator, who explains, clarifies, and encourages or supports the learner. Typically, this approach is informal and fosters freedom in learning; however, it can assume a more formal arrangement, depending on the goals identified by the instructor/facilitator or the learner. Examples of individualized learning are networking at a refreshment break, individualized follow-up to a group discussion, self-guided programmed instruction, and self-study.

Small Group Learning

Adults learn better when they are actively involved in the process. Small group learning situations, such as workshops, promote interaction among participants and allow learners to be actively involved in the learning process. Learners like to have input into the educational activity and are willing to play a direct role in it, such as teaching other learners. The challenge lies in preparing a learning activity that is creative and varied. This approach offers a great opportunity to develop activities that can be individualized and adapted to larger groups. The greatest challenge in small group activities is that the leader must be an attentive listener because learner participation is the primary focus. An example of small group learning would be a workshop with limited registration. The small group experience can be enhanced by using round tables for optimal interaction. For more information regarding room sets for educational sessions (see Chapter 23).

Large-Group Learning

Large-group sessions are very efficient for conveying information or content. The environment is formal, structured and can be disconcerting sometimes, not only to the learner, but also to the leader. This environment could be a large workshop in a large room with chairs in a classroom setup (see Chapter 23). The challenge for the leader is to use a variety of techniques and strategies to maintain learner interest and involvement. An element of showmanship in the presentation is critical in order to fully engage the learner in the process.

Mass Learning

The kind of learning that can occur in this format is more like mass communication than education. This approach offers the learner the greatest anonymity; however, it requires the expertise of educators, as well as the participation of writers, producers, communication specialists, and others. An example would be a large general session at a convention.

PERSPECTIVES OF THE LEARNER

The need and desire for learning can take two perspectives—developmental and transformative. These are closely aligned with the age of the adult and his/her life stage.

Developmental Perspective

Developmental perspective of learning occurs during the first half of life, when education is directed at building a personal life, a career, and a future. The focus is on the acquisition of new competencies and skills. Developmental learning begins at birth and continues through the fourth decade of life.

During the first half of their lives, adults pursue learning to enable them to feel at home in the world. Their focus is on increasing their proficiency in their jobs and personal lives. As a result, most formative adult learning is competency based, with a goal of mastery in specific fields of study, professional practice, and performance.

Although some of this learning occurs in the classroom, much of it takes place in experiential settings and involves experts, mentors, and colleagues. Attendance at learning activities sponsored by employers and professional organizations and participation in a variety of continuing educational opportunities helps prepare these individuals and integrate them into working cultures.

Transformative Perspective

During the second half of life, learning becomes directed at attaining a new consciousness and self-understanding, with a focus on fulfilling the human experience through imagination and self-expression. Such learning is viewed as the transformative perspective of learning.

At this stage adult learners develop new ways of looking at the world. They search for alternative ways of living their lives and shaping their culture. They are seeking new ways of touching the world and leaving their mark on it. In this perspective, learning is more all-encompassing and eclectic than learning in the developmental stage. As the adult's commitment to learning intensifies, energy is channeled into development and renewal.

When developing an educational program, focus on the priorities and learning perspectives of the target audience, taking into account the range of ages of the group and their association with the organization. However, when the audience includes individuals from several age groups, the challenge is to design a program that will reach all participants. The interests of the participants should dictate the scope of learning activities and the opportunities for participation.

GENERATIONAL INFLUENCE ON LEARNING

Most organizations bring multiple generations together at board meetings, staff functions, and annual conferences. Behaviors and attitudes can vary greatly from one generation to the next, and managing those differences effectively is critical to a meeting's success. Understanding the predisposition of each generation will help meeting managers to better understand the audience and enable them to adapt content and format appropriately.

For the first time in history, there are five living generations of Americans and each bring vastly different experiences to our meetings:

- GI Generation (born 1901–1926)
- Silents (born 1927–1945)
- Boomers (born 1946–1964)

Fast Facts

- GI Generation (born 1901–1926)
- Silents (born 1927–1945)
- Boomers (born 1946–1964)
- Gen X (born 1965–1981)
- Millennials (born 1982–present)

- Gen X (born 1965–1981)
- Millennials (born 1982–present)

Four of the five (all but the GIs who are mostly retired) are not only active in, but also critical to, the American workplace and marketplace. Each generation experienced significantly different formative years (birth to roughly age 20), so each generation molded different core values. Those values exert tremendous influence over their attitudes, decisions, and preferences.

Silents (Born 1927–1945)

Silents have decades of business wisdom and experience and can be invaluable to today's workplace. Many Silents will not retire at the traditional age. They are excellent mentors to younger employees. They came of age with workplace values such as courtesy, inclusiveness, loyalty to the company, discipline, strong work ethic, respect for the company's history, and respect for authority.

Since they came of age before the computer, Silents prefer to be taught by human beings, not a CD or DVD tutorial. For them, a lecture format is preferred; however, they do need to be engaged in an interactive discussion. Technological enhancements to the session are fine as long as Silents are comfortable with those enhancements and they do not substantially diminish the human touch.

Be sensitive to their age:

- Provide comfortable seating
- Allow stand-up-and-stretch or restroom breaks
- Determine if the audio can be heard clearly. Eliminate ambient noise that might compete with speaker such as close doors, do not speak when dishes are being cleared, etc.
- Use 14-point or 16-point font on handouts
- Avoid starting too early

Silents are good listeners and have made their mark in the workplace as helpers and facilitators.

When Silents attend a meeting, they want a training session that is courteous, free of vulgarity and off-color remarks, respectful of their experience and wisdom, physically comfortable, analytical and inclusive, and not overly combative or argumentative. Silents are also looking for training sessions that develop skills to enhance their employable and marketable value within their company.

Boomers (Born 1946–1964)

Since we are the products of our formative years boomers tend to be idealistic, aggressive, confident, and career-minded. Boomers are big thinkers. They work late and on weekends. This is the workaholic generation. Boomers are less politically correct and less company-loyal than Silents. They are bigger risk takers and very entrepreneurial.

This group came of age during a comparatively safe time in America, so they never met a stranger. Boomers are people who have a need to network. They favor the development of relationships with everyone, especially their coworkers. Boomers are technologically savvy. However, like Silents, they prefer interpersonal learning formats instead of impersonal computer training. They like to learn and work in teams. When placed in teams, Boomers are willing and likely to take control, be assertive, and fight aggressively for what they believe.

When Boomers attend a meeting, they expect a learning experience that is time-efficient and not bogged down by meaningless corporate drivel, and is factual, accurate, and thorough. Boomers want to know the "why" behind everything. They are visionary and bold, always exploring new horizons. Boomers tend to be extremely ethical. They want a learning experience with plenty of social interaction. Boomers are looking for ways to enhance their ability to build financial security for retirement.

Gen X (Born 1965–1981)

Generation X (X'ers) is the least nurtured and least supervised of our five living generations. They are the most independent, self-reliant, and misunderstood. This group went through their formative years just as the divorce rate skyrocketed, the women's movement produced a generation of latchkey kids, and a generation of parents experimented with a new parenting philosophy: "the rules are negotiable."

Also during their formative years, X'ers saw one major institution after another fail to deliver on its promise; government (Agnew resigns in scandal, Nixon resigns in scandal, America "quits" a war in Vietnam, Challenger ends in disaster, and news erupts on the Iran-Contra scandal); big business (layoffs of their mothers and fathers; despite Mom's and Dad's loyal, diligent hard work for the company; corporate corruption); and most importantly, the failure of the institution of marriage. They also grew up more isolated from older people than any generation of kids before, as X'ers were the first generation of children to have radio stations and TV channels solely targeted to their interests. The number of radio stations multiplied dramatically in the 1970s, whereas television did the same with cable networks in the 1980s, each targeting a smaller niche in the market. The comfort with isolation and these solitary experiences were continued with the widespread availability of the personal computer (not yet connected to the Internet). Moreover, X'ers have molded core values with a huge distrust of government, big business, and older people.

In an educational environment, X'ers are more comfortable learning and working independently than in teams. They are the first generation to mature with personal technology and take great pride in that fact. Learning by way of the computer is quite comfortable for them, especially when it is interactive. X'ers tend to be problem-solvers.

This is the MTV generation. It is a visual generation. The use of images—both moving and still—is usually important. However, do not assume that everything has to be in short snippets, bulleted points, and small bites.

When teaching X'ers, quantify the educational session. Consider giving the X'ers a written certificate to verify that they have received special formal training, because X'ers fully expect to be job-hopping throughout their careers. One-company-for-life is something X'ers do not expect in America in their lifetimes. X'ers want to build a skill-set they can carry with them to each new job.

When X'ers attend the meeting they want to get down to business and stay focused. They expect efficiency of time and word. They expect sessions that are fact-based, and that will enhance and quantify their skill-set. They seek teaching that is formatted for individuals rather than for teams, e.g., present a problem and then let them find the solutions. Most importantly, X'ers want their educational experience to be relevant to their careers and their lives.

Millennials (Born 1982–Present)

In the '80s, as the Millennials were entering the world, American parents decided they needed to make a significant change to the way they had parented. GenX is America's least nurtured, least adult-supervised generation, and the Millennials are the most nurtured and most adult-supervised of the generations. Consequently, Millennials have grown up extremely close to their parents, teachers, and coaches.

Put It Into Practice

Chuck Underwood often presents training seminars on one of two topics: "Generational Marketing/Advertising/Media Strategy" and "Generational Workplace Diversity and Human Resource Strategy." Because his audiences are always multigenerational, Underwood accommodates the unique learning preferences of the Silents, Boomers, Xers, and Millennials in several ways, including:

1. He makes a rule to "never leave anybody behind," so he prepares a script that explains the ABCs of his topic and, right from the beginning, gets the entire audience—from the youngest to the oldest—to the same starting point; he does not speak esoterically and does not use "insider jargon and buzzwords" without explaining each one.

2. He immediately asks the audience if they can hear him clearly, no matter how small or large the room, he always asks; because of loud music concerts and stereo headphones, we have a hearing diminution in this country that is now reaching down into the 30-something age bracket.

3. He immediately tells the audience where the restrooms are located, since most presentations are off-site for the audience.

4. He jumps right into the content after a sincere but brief "thank you" to start the session and a quick introductory bit of humor with multigenerational appeal. With multigenerational audiences, the wrong humor can instantly get you negatively labeled as "old" or "young" or "unfunny."

5. He never talks about himself and avoids personal opinions. He presents business seminars with well-researched information and makes it a point to tell audiences they are NOT getting his opinion, but rather documented truth.

6. He creates Power Point slides that are not text-intensive and that use oversized type; he often displays newspaper headlines, magazine covers, and archival photographs instead of his printed documents to enhance visual interest; he never uses clip-art.

7. He uses video and sound in Power Point, usually television and radio commercials that are good examples of generational advertising strategy. This gives the audience a break from his voice and renews their energy and interest. He always arrives 30 to 60 minutes before the audience to set up the Power Point equipment and to test the audio to make sure the microphone volume matches the embedded TV commercials' volume.

8. He uses a speaking pace that has a "gearbox"; he speaks more rapidly through uncomplicated passages but slows down when the content is complex or to punctuate a point.

9. He enunciates every word.

10. He moves around the stage, using gestures and facial expressions only when they are appropriate and without exaggeration; younger generations, especially, will put his physical performance under a high-powered microscope.

11. He makes it interactive, announcing at the outset that audience members should raise their hands any time they have a question or comment; when time permits, he asks questions of the audience to engage them in the material.

12. He offers breaks whenever the audience feels they need breaks, not when he needs them.

13. He supplies extra-comfortable chairs which are not crammed tightly together, and set up in classroom style.

14. He (almost always) avoids cuss words, even the milder ones.

15. He always acknowledges an audience member, who raises a hand to comment or ask a question, with "Yes, ma'am?" or "Yes, sir?"; courtesy and respect, even if not always practiced by audience members, are always appreciated.

16. He always concludes with a sincere "thank you" for their time and interest in his topic.

Most Millennials were aware of the tragedies of September 11, 2001, and many were involved in some type of school activity designed to send aid or letters of support to the families of the September 11, 2001 victims. As a result, Millennials are patriotic and have a sense of charity that they will embrace for life.

Millennials feel like a generation, and they think big. In these respects they are different from X'ers and similar to GIs and Boomers. They want to make a positive difference in the world. Teenage social pathology (pregnancy, crime, substance abuse) is declining. Millennials prefer team play and are comfortable with older people. They have a sense of being protected, a strong commitment to corporate ethics, tremendous drive to earn good grades, and a keen inclination to schedule every hour of the day.

Child psychologists fear that Millennials are being pushed too hard to achieve by their parents, although at the same time they are being nurtured too much. They fear that Millennials will become workaholics like the Boomers, but will be soft when they enter the work force, having relied too much on their elders. Many fear that Millennials will not be tough-skinned, independent, and entrepreneurial, as the times now require.

When Millennials attend a meeting, they want a team-oriented experience that is technologically advanced, focusing on the company's big picture. They want an educational session that gives them a solid foundation of the ABCs of life in the workplace. They are extremely ethical and want motivation to make a big contribution to the company and to their country. Planners should keep in mind that the potential for maximum creativity often lays at the points of intersection, or commonality among these generations.

ADULT LEARNING STYLES

Learning styles are ways that people's brains learn and store information. The style of the educational program should be based on the educational needs of the attendees and tailored to their learning styles. Meeting managers need to recognize that each attendee prefers a particular style of learning and that using one method of presenting material will not necessarily be beneficial to everyone. The three basic learning styles are *visual, auditory, and kinesthetic*. We are all born with a tendency toward one style or another.[20]

Visual Learners make up approximately 40% of the population. These individuals like to see things written down. They learn best through software slides (such as Power Point), diagrams, and illustrations.

Auditory Learners make up approximately 30% of the population. They remember best by talking out loud and verbal repetition. They prefer class discussions, and opportunities to discuss new concepts.

Kinesthetic Learners make up the final 30% of the population. These learners need time to practice. They enjoy hands-on activities and learn best by imitation and practice. They prefer to "touch" the material being covered (see Figure 18.1).[21]

> To identify your personal learning style preference, ask yourself:
>
> **When you spell, do you:**
>
> *Visual* - try to see the word
>
> *Auditory* - sound out the word or use phonetic approach
>
> *Kinesthetic* - write the word down and see if it feels right[22]

Through a careful needs analysis (see Chapter 2), you can learn more about attendees' learning style preferences, and their content needs.[23] Synthesizing this information carefully will help meeting managers design a program that will match the needs of the individuals in the group.[24]

Besides an individual's innate preference for one learning style or another, there are several other issues that affect learning.

Technology Issues

Technology has become a major force in today's educational offerings, and its influence will continue to grow. Although technology should be fully utilized by

Fast Facts

Visual

- Needs to see it—to know it
- Written instructions
- Handouts
- Background noise distracting
- Reacts to colors
- Remembers faces and not names

Auditory

- Remembers—once it is heard
- Listens and learns
- Verbal repetition
- Talks through a concept
- Enjoys class discussions
- Difficulty with written instructions

Kinesthetic

- Physical involvement
- Project orientated
- Hands-on activities
- Imitation and practice
- Well coordinated
- Athletic ability

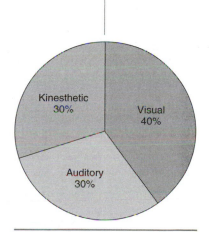

FIGURE 18.1
Learning Styles

curriculum designers and instructors, it is important to remember that this form of learning also represents a learning-style preference. Some audiences embrace new technology, while others are more reluctant and prefer face-to-face learning formats. Not surprisingly, younger learners tend to embrace the Internet as an effective learning medium more readily than do older learners.[25]

Self-Directed Versus Group Activities

Adults tend to prefer self-directed learning projects over group learning experiences led by a professional. The adult learner also often prefers more than one medium for the program.[26] Consequently, combining learning methods can be effective. For example, face-to-face sessions with electronic bulletin board connections afterward are often a good teaching approach.

Synchronous Versus Asynchronous

Not all learning needs to take place at the same time and place. Your educational program can combine synchronous and asynchronous learning. Synchronous learning is when all learners are learning the same thing at the same time. It is characterized by time scheduled for a learning experience and typically offers live interaction. A face-to-face conference, a teleconference, or a Web conference are all examples of synchronous learning. Conversely, asynchronous learning is designed to allow learners to "patch in" to the learning at a time that is suitable and convenient for them. Although there is a defined beginning and ending, asynchronous learning allows the learner much more discretion in choosing a time and place for the experience.

VARIABLES THAT AFFECT ADULT LEARNING

The lifelong learner faces a full array of learning experiences. The effect of those experiences is determined not only by content, but by many factors found in the learning environment. Some of these factors are unique to the learner, but might be accommodated by the meeting planner, if the meeting planner recognizes them. Meeting planners typically coordinate variables in the learning environment, such as technology, service, and personnel. All of these factors have some bearing on the success of an adult learning experience: physiological, psychological, social/cultural, industry, nutritional, technological, physical, service, personnel, and evaluation (see Figure 18.2).

Physiological Factors

As you plan your program, take into account the fact that the aging process affects memory span and reaction time—our memory span becomes shorter and reaction time slows as we age. C. L. Finkel suggests that adult learners have "lost the discipline required for 'classroom' learning. We must help them become learners again."[27] To help adults learn, the learning environment must be as comfortable and as distraction-free as possible.

Psychological Factors

Psychological pressures might adversely affect learning. Whereas learners may hear what is being presented, they may mentally "check out" from time to time as they process what they have heard and apply it to a life experience. Consequently, the facilitator must keep in touch with the audience and allow time for processing. In such instances, real-world examples become an important presentation technique.

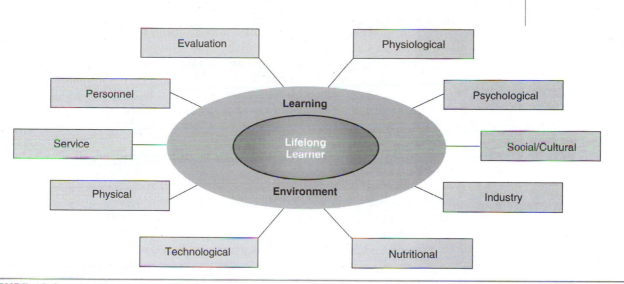

FIGURE 18.2
Factors in the Learning Experience
Designed by Glen C. Ramsborg, PhD. Copyright 2003. Used with permission.

Adults have different reasons for learning, such as a desire to improve their economic position or professional status, and a preference for self-actualization opportunities. Some adults have a need for socialization with their peers, especially if they perceive that this need is not satisfied in their work environment. For example, individuals who must cope with a difficult work environment may take solace in learning their peers face similar challenges.

Emotional associations forged by words, attitudes, situations, concepts, people, and examples can impede or assist the learning process. Learning styles also affect the learning experience. These psychological factors should be considered when organizing the learning environment.

Social/Cultural Factors

Meeting attendees have expectations of the learning experience. Some of these expectations are based on perceived social expectations, like the desire to balance family, work, and personal needs. Some expectations may be based on cultural influences, such as ethical decision-making or what should be consumed during a specific meal. Meeting planners and facilitators will deliver more successful learning experiences if they understand and accommodate the social and cultural expectations of their audience. This will be particularly challenging when meeting attendees originate from a variety of social settings and cultures.

Learners derive some satisfaction from feeling accepted by other members of their social group, as well as being treated as an equal by the facilitator and the host organization. The concept of "we" serves the social/cultural needs of learners and may result in a higher level of satisfaction at the conclusion of the learning experience. As J.W. Johnson wrote, "No one has yet perfected a way to duplicate the energy generated by a group of people in the same room where individuals stand up and share their ideas with the entire audience."[28]

Industry Factors

Related to social and cultural factors, the industry providing a context for the learning event will have an influence on the adult learner. Some industries require hands-on learning (fire-fighting, for instance), while others suggest a typical classroom-style environment (continuing education for teachers). The industry context may require cutting-edge "bells and whistles" (electronic gaming), while others require a setting that approximates the work environment as much as possible. Effective learning environments and facilitation strategies may be dictated by the industry for which the learning event has been developed. Meeting planners are often reminded to meet not only the expectations of meeting attendees, but also the expectations of the attendees' employers.

Nutritional Factors

High performance in a learning environment depends on proper nutrition. Although foods carry multiple emotional and cultural connotations, meals and refreshments must be selected with an emphasis on providing energy and fuel for the brain. Nutritionists advise that proteins and complex carbohydrates promote alertness. Fats and sugars promote sluggishness. Attention must also be paid to proper hydration and dietary restrictions of meeting attendees. Comfort goes beyond the attendee's chair or the temperature of the meeting space—a hungry attendee is not comfortable.

Technological Factors

Fritz Steele notes an organization that creates "an information-rich environment with or without bells and whistles is the key factor in a successful meeting.... What's important is to make information visually and audibly available so everyone can access it as needed."[29] The effect technology will have on the educational process and the learner is difficult to predict. The temptation to think that technology will replace face-to-face meetings should not overshadow the human need to be together. Learning is a part of socialization, socialization is a part of learning, and both are an integral component of human nature.

With technology selections in mind, the meeting manager must also consider the physical arrangement of the environment, so that the technologies offered can be utilized by all attendees.

Physical Factors

The physical arrangement of an educational setting will affect the learning and interaction that occur. Physical factors include architectural design, spatial arrangement of furnishings, proxemics (the distance between communicators), environmental quality, and the patterns of learner-facilitator and learner-learner interactions.[30] These factors are highly interdependent; none is more important than one of the others.[31]

For example, temperature, humidity, air circulation, odor, background noise, lighting, and cleanliness (all elements of environmental quality) have significant effects on learners and may contribute to or subtract from the learning experience.

Psychologist William Ryan shared these concepts with his workshop audiences:

- No "ideal" room arrangement is effective for everyone.
- Congruence should be evident between the goals of the teacher, the teaching method, and the physical structure.
- The arrangement of the classroom should coincide with the technique or method used in the learning environment.[32]

Control of the physical environment is an important part of the meeting planner's responsibilities. Sommer refers to the meeting room as a "network of interconnected and varied micro-environments," observing that "the physical and social systems of the classroom are inextricably entwined. Change one, and you inevitably change the other." The meeting room is seen not as "something fixed and determined by an abstract external authority, but as a group interaction space under the joint jurisdiction of the class."[33] Levels and quality of interaction will be determined by the configuration of furnishings in the meeting space.

Service Factors

Although numerous physical factors influence the learning experience, less tangible factors are also important considerations. The hospitality a learner receives will influence how that learner perceives the experience. Thorough preparation, attention to the details, quality in service during the learning event, and even the presence of amenities will impact the learning experience positively.

Personnel Factors

Successful implementation of all the variables that affect adult learning is dependent upon having appropriate personnel, including planning and operations staff, service staff, the host organization, presenters, and all team members who contribute to the learning experience. Each member of this team has the potential to improve or damage the effect; therefore, all must be aware of the responsibility placed on them and their importance to the success of the learning event.

Evaluation Factors

Adult learners seek education on the basis of need, problem-solving goals, and many of the factors explained above. The variables that provide an effective learning environment will lead directly to the learner's perception of quality, usefulness, and applicability of the content. These factors are amazingly interdependent. Even the process of evaluation will influence the learner's perception. The evaluation process may improve or detract from the perception, but will, at the least, solidify that impression. Therefore, mechanisms for monitoring progress and measuring value should be incorporated in a variety of ways and at various times throughout the learning experience. These evaluation mechanisms should encourage thoughtful responses, while being a positive activity for the learner.

SUMMARY

Meetings can be ideal venues for the kind of lifelong learning that typify professional and personal development. Understanding the importance of lifelong learning and the characteristics, learning patterns, learning styles, and motivations of adult learners will help meeting managers plan successful educational components for their meetings.

Adult learners generally are self-directed, bring multiple life experiences to the learning process, and are oriented toward problem solving. Key principles of adult learning are: adults must feel the need to learn, they must achieve some ownership of their learning, the learning must be relevant to their lives, and they must be active participants in the learning process.

The characteristics of adult learners are related to a series of predictable stages in an individual's life cycle. Developmental learning is that which takes place in the first half of life and focuses on building a personal life, a career, and a future. Transformative learning occurs during the second half of life and focuses on attaining new self-understanding. Generational predispositions, as well as the innate learning styles (such as visual, auditory, or kinesthetic) of the participants affect learning outcomes and should be considered for success.

Many factors affect the learning experience—physiological, psychological, social/cultural, industry, nutritional, technological, physical, service, personnel, and evaluation. Providing an effective and efficient learning environment requires paying attention to all of these factors.

REFERENCES

1. U.S. Department of Education, National Center for Education Statistics National Household Surveys of 2001. (2004). *Participation in adult education and life-long learning 2000-01.* Washington DC: US Department of Education.

2. Faure, E., Herrara, F., Kaddourn, H. R., Lopes, H., Petrovskyh, A.. V., Rahnerma, M. and Ward, F. C. 72). *Learning to be: The word of education today and tomorrow.* Paris: UNESCO.

3. Cross, K. P. (1981). *Adults as learners.* San Francisco: Jossey-Bass Publishers.

4. Dave, R. H., ed. (1976). *Foundations of lifelong education.* Oxford: Pergamon Press.

5. U.S. Department of Education, National Center for Education Statistics. (2003). *The condition of education.* Washington DC: US Department of Education.

6. Leed, K., & Leed, J. (1987). *Building for adult learning.* Cincinnati, OH: LDA Publishing, Lead Design Associates.

7. Slotnik, et al. (1993). *Adult learning on campus.* London: Falmer Press.

8. Ibid.

9. Kim, K., and Creighton, S. (2000). *Participation in adult education in the United States: 1998–99* (NCES 2000-027). U.S. Department of Education. Washington, DC: National Center for Education Statistics.

10. Ramsborg, G. C. (1993). *Objective to outcomes: Your contract with the learner.* Birmingham, AL: Professional Convention Management Association.

11. Ibid.

12. Ibid.

13. MacLaurin, D. (2001). The yearn to learn: How learning styles differ across generations. *Convene,* 50–52.

14. Cannon D., & Gustafson, A. A. (2006). *Training and development for the hospitality industry.* Lansing, MI: Education Institute of the American Hotel and Lodging Association.

15. Knowles, M. S. (1980). *The modern practice of adult education: From pedagogy to andragogy.* San Francisco: Jossey-Bass Publishers.

16. Ramsborg, *Objectives to outcomes.* op. cit.

17. Ibid.

18. Ibid.

19. Knowles, *The modern practice of adult education: From pedagogy to andragogy.*

20. Channer, C. (2001). A matter of style. *MPI,* 9.

21. Ibid.

22. Ibid.

23. MacLaurin, *The yearn to learn.* op. cit.

24. Cufaude, J. (2001). Association learning: When learning matters most. *FORUM, 1,* 6–7.

25. Ibid.

26. Zemke, R., & Zemke, S. (2001). Thirty things we know for sure about adult learning. *Convene,* p. 6–8.

27. Finkel, C. L. (1980). The total immersion meeting environment. *Training and development journal, 34*(9), 32–39.

28. Johnson, J. W. (1994). Technology has yet to find a way to duplicate the energy of meetings. *Convene*, p. 37–38.

29. Steele, F. I. (1973). *Physical settings and organizational development*. Reading, MA: Addison-Wesley Publishing Co.

30. Ryan, W. P. (1974). Workshops about the physical structure of the classroom: An interesting way to work with teachers. *Journal of school psychology 12*(3), 242–246.

31. Sommer, R. (1969). *Personal space*. Englewood Cliffs, NJ: Prentice-Hall.

32. Ryan, op. cit., p. 242–246.

33. Sommer, op. cit., p. 175.

KEY TERMS

Adult learner
Andragogy
Arranged environment
Asynchronous learning
Auditory learners
Developmental learning
Distance learning
Emotional factors
Individualized learning
  patterns
Interactive learning

Kinesthetic learners
Large-group learning
  patterns
Learning environment
Lifelong learning
Mass learning patterns
Multiple life experiences
Physical factors
Physiological factors
Problem-solving
  orientation

Psychological factors
Self-direction
Small group learning
  patterns
Social-cultural factors
Synchronous learning
Technological factors
Transformative learning
Visual learners

COMPELLING QUESTIONS FOR CONSIDERATION

1. Why is it important for meeting managers to understand the principles of lifelong learning?

2. Why will adults learn better when they have had a role in determining the session topic?

3. What issues should be considered when designing a program related to participants' learning styles?

4. Describe some of the variables that affect learning.

5. What factors should be considered when designing the learning environment?

CONTRIBUTOR

The generous contributions of Chuck Underwood, Founder/President of the Generational Imperative, are gratefully acknowledged.

CHAPTER 19

PROGRAM DESIGN AND DEVELOPMENT

Wanda Johnson, CMP
SENIOR DIRECTOR, MEETINGS & EDUCATION
THE ENDOCRINE SOCIETY

LEARNER OUTCOMES

When the reader has completed reading this chapter, he/she should be able to . . .

1 State the elements used in program design.

2 Create a program planning timeline.

3 Explain when to use the different education and presentation formats.

4 Identify the role and responsibilities of a planning committee.

> Design is a plan for arranging elements in such a way as best to accomplish a particular purpose.
>
> *Charles Eames*

OVERVIEW

Once the purpose of the meeting has been identified and the educational goals and objectives have been established, planning can begin to match the best educational format to achieve the desired outcome. Organizations are increasingly demanding an appropriate return on investment (ROI) from meetings and conventions that they host. These events are often showcase events and a source of revenue for the organization. Meeting managers must understand the strategic value of meetings and conventions for their organizations and how the quality of the program content and way the content is delivered generate both attendance and revenue.

Increasingly meeting managers are responsible for the quality of the educational content at their meetings. Based on the educational goals and objectives, a meeting manager's duties may include identifying appropriate program delivery formats, developing a planning timeline, developing the program schedule, selecting and working with a program-planning committee, and assisting with speaker selection.

Additionally, as technological advances such as videoconferencing and the Internet make communication and education more accessible and efficient, meeting managers must understand and promote the value of face-to-face interactions to their constituents and recognize how to use technology to expand the reach of their meetings.

Constructive and well-organized program-planning sessions are vital to the successful development of educational programs and the selection of subject material and speakers. An effective meeting manager assumes a leadership role with the organization's staff, the program-planning group, and with outside suppliers, maximizing each individual's contributions in order to plan a program that offers attendees a productive and educational meeting experience. This chapter will explore the elements to consider in designing and developing the programming for meetings and events. Strategies for extending the program reach before and after the meeting will also be presented.

PROGRAM DESIGN

Program design provides structure of event program elements to achieve specific goals and objectives. The basic elements of program design are the outline, program content, program format, and the environment where the program will be presented. Figure 19.1 shows how the program design is built once the objectives have been identified. The program design requires research and the development of a timeline working with a program or planning committee who will be responsible for identifying the final program/agenda or content. The keys to success are to carefully select the members of the program committee, work with the volunteers to meet goals and adhere to the timeline, provide guidance and direction, and create clear agendas for planning sessions.

In some organizations such as medical societies, the program design may be influenced by accreditation requirements that govern program design and planning documentation. Understand the exact requirements for accreditation documentation and adjust the program design process to comply with these requirements.

Research

Once the meeting objectives have been established, additional research is necessary to profile the target audience and their preferences, and the instructional method best suited for the group. Is the broad emphasis on education, networking, or recognition for the organization or participants? What are the expectations

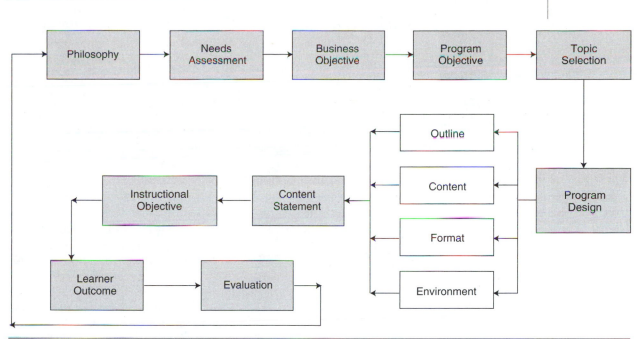

FIGURE 19.1

Program Design and Development Flow Chart

Designed by Glen C. Ramsborg, PhD. © 2002. Used with permission.

of the attendees? Collecting demographic information about meeting attendees is a prerequisite to selecting a meeting location or environment, determining the appropriate meeting length, estimating the potential audience size, and designing program content. Consider the age, gender, education level, experience, and economic status of attendees.

Historical statistics and evaluation summaries from past meetings are valuable research sources. Questions that can be answered by historical information are: Were a large percentage of past attendees from the same region in which the convention site was located, or were they geographically dispersed? What are the common characteristics among attendees? Do family members and/or guests typically accompany attendees? and Are recreational activities important to the group?

If one goal of the program is to attract new audiences, in-depth market research may be required to gain an understanding of the competitive environment and opportunities for growth or expansion. Answering questions such as these and gathering as much information about attendees and past meetings as possible is the first step in designing a successful meeting program.

Meeting History

The meeting history is the record of an event over time. Convention centers and/or hotels used for past meetings can provide information on room pick-up, and check-in and check-out patterns, as well as usage patterns for room service, hotel restaurants, recreational facilities, and concierge and business services. Meeting managers are responsible for collecting this information and verifying its accuracy following each meeting and should outline specific requirements for this information in the contract for the facility. This information can be valuable in planning the program and schedule for the next meeting. The APEX Toolkit offers a template to assist the meeting manager in keeping this information current and readily available.

Attendee Preferences

Evaluation summaries from past meetings can be very helpful when determining attendee preferences in several areas, such as preferred destinations, type of accommodations, meeting format, and the importance of networking opportunities. Information such as likes and dislikes from previous meetings and which activities are worth repeating or eliminating, can also assist in making informed decisions.

The destination itself can be a vital element in the success of a meeting, helping to boost attendance and revenue. Many attendees use a convention as a starting point for a personal vacation. Because of the expense of hotels and airfares, attendees may combine a business trip with a vacation since this often enables attendees to travel to a location that might otherwise be too expensive to visit. If attendees are using the meeting as a prelude to a vacation, their expectations and the need for guest activities will be important factors to consider when planning the program.

Other types of information gleaned from evaluations will also affect programming decisions. Any information that is available about attendees' preferences will provide a clearer understanding of their expectations. For example, do attendees learn best in interactive workshops where they can express their views, or do they prefer to learn from experts in a lecture format? Do they want scheduled meal functions or the opportunity to explore area restaurants? Do they expect a program during meal functions or do they prefer to use that time to network with colleagues?

Special Needs

Identify any special needs of meeting attendees early in the program-planning process. For example, attendees from other countries may require special arrangements such as translation services to fully understand the presentations. Attendees with disabilities may need special accommodations in order to participate such as amplification devices, sign language interpreters or special seating. Other special needs you must address include dietary requirements, religious observances, and holidays that occur during the meeting dates. It is preferable to schedule meeting dates that do not conflict with religious and cultural holidays. Consideration should also be given to time zone adjustments that may be faced by attendees when building the program schedule.

International Attendees

Attendees from other countries face increased scrutiny when traveling to the United States and need to allow more time for processing visa requests. They may require assistance from meeting organizers to obtain visas to enter the country. At a minimum, meeting managers should provide general information on how to request visas to enter the country with contact information for the U.S. State Department and a list of the current requirements to obtain a visa. Some countries may require an "invitation letter" from the meeting organizer that acknowledges the traveler is registered for the meeting. The invitation letter will also include information on the meeting such as date and location (see Chapter 16).

Timelines

The timeline includes each task to be accomplished and is the core of the program plan. A fully developed, formalized planning timeline is especially helpful when a committee is involved in program planning. The process is most likely to be successful when members of the planning group know what is expected of them from the start.

Timelines may differ based upon the meeting objectives and the type of organization sponsoring the meeting. Timelines can incorporate the planning steps for the meeting content or educational program and all of the logistic steps required for producing the event. Figure 19.2 shows an example of a logistics timeline for a mid-to-large annual meeting. Figure 19.3 provides a timeline for a smaller meeting and incorporates both program planning and logistics. Although the components will likely be the same for any meeting, the times for completion of tasks may vary widely depending on the organization's structure and the size of the meeting. The timeline will also need to be adjusted for international meetings, which require more time to facilitate the various activities. The timeline should includes deadlines required for planning the entire meeting—from site selection through post-meeting evaluation and can be compressed or expanded as needed for an individual event.

PROGRAM OUTLINE, CONTENT, AND SCHEDULE

The program outline organizes the meeting into the various activities. The outline combines the appropriate number of educational hours with social and recreational activities. The outline should include time for registration, the opening ceremony or general session, exhibition hours, meal and social functions, breaks, and a formal closing session, if appropriate for the meeting type. If customary to do so, select a meeting title and/or theme before developing program content. Figure 19.4 is a generic program outline for a multiple-day meeting.

The program content is the educational component of an event. Using the objectives of the meeting and considering the information gathered from the research, content is identified that will fulfill the objectives and meet the needs of the target audience with varying levels of skill and experience, and different learning styles. Program content is the specific sessions or activities that are scheduled using the program outline. The program content will dictate the number of general sessions and simultaneous or concurrent sessions that are required to achieve the meeting objectives. As the content is being developed, it is important to consider if there are any required sessions that must be included for certification or recertification purposes.

The program schedule provides the table of time and location for all functions related to an event. This information should be included in the Event Specifications Guide (ESG) for an event. Figure 19.5 is a generic program schedule for a multiple day meeting.

Breaks

A break is a short interval between sessions at which time coffee, tea and/or other refreshments are served. Scheduled breaks not only help attendees stay refreshed and alert, but also serve as additional networking opportunities. Many factors affect the program schedule, including the logistical constraints of the meeting site and the timing of key sessions. Consider the time attendees will take to get from one location to another, as well as the locations of rest rooms. As a general rule, provide at least a 10-minute break for every 50 minutes of instruction. If refreshments are provided during breaks, they should be conveniently located with ample access that does not impede traffic flow.

Proximity of Housing

If everyone is to be housed in one facility, such as for a meeting at a hotel or conference center, events may be scheduled to begin earlier in the morning and extend later into the evening; however, if attendees are to be housed at locations separate from the meeting facility, allowance must be made for travel and transit time.

	Advance Planning Timeline	
Date Due	**Date Completed**	**Task**
6 years		Solicit site proposals
		Establish convention and visitor bureau contacts
5 yrs 6 mos		Schedule site inspection trips to review and evaluate facilities
		Board and/or site selection committee approves site selection
5 years		Finalize convention dates and site
		Approve and sign convention center space hold
		Negotiate headquarters hotel room rates
		Identify preliminary housing blocks at overflow hotels
2 yrs 6 mos		Site inspection trip • Inspect convention facility • Review hotel public space and rooms • Finalize overflow hotels • Initiate supplier contacts and negotiations
		Finalize facility/hotel arrangements
		Update files - schedule periodic review of files
		Review room block from meeting histories and adjust accordingly
18 months		Site inspection trip: • Review city activities, information, maps, etc. • Inspect hotel public areas • Review information about convention bureau forms/procedures, temporary help, equipment rental, media contacts, events, support literature, VIP contacts, hospital lists and contract for local labor unions (setup and A/V)
		Preliminary research for: • Shuttle buses • Tour/special event company • Message desk/phone equipment • Decorating company (drayage/equipment) • Entertainment • Auto rental • Airline (prime carrier), post-tour • Local host committee: guest program, local VIPs, dining guide • Local printer • Duplicating company contact • Banking arrangements • Audiovisual (A/V) supplier • Security firm • Photographer • Emergency services • Child care
		Develop budget
		Appoint planning committee
		Set planning committee meeting date/location
		Review room block from meeting histories and adjust accordingly
		Finalize marketing plan
		Draft exhibitor prospectus

FIGURE 19.2
Sample Advance Planning Timeline for a Large Annual Meeting

Date Due	Date Completed	Task
12 months		Assemble planning committee materials to include: • Schedule of events • Agenda • Synopses of program/course evaluations • Resource materials/contacts • Worksheets/instructions • Philosophy/background information/theme • Educational program direction/curriculum • Deadlines/time frames • Develop committees/staff performance criteria • Summaries of any research conducted
		Site inspection
		Finalize budget
		Obtain event insurance
		Sports arrangements contacted
		Hotel contract finalized & signed by both parties; obtain: • Hotel rack brochures & photos • Suite diagrams • Menus
		Contact DMCs for spouse and special events
		Tentative schedule of events outlined
		Airline contract finalized
		Car rental contract finalized
		Print and mail exhibitor prospectus
		Event stationery printed
11 months		Convene program planning committee • Approve and distribute program committee minutes • Develop program topics/formats
		Select & obtain information from suppliers
		Develop and mail "save-the-date" or initial promotion
10 months		Finalize selection of topics/speakers using planning matrix
		Set up session/speaker files (names, contact info. and biographies)
		Begin booth contract processing
		Draft exhibit services manual
		Obtain order forms from suppliers
		Draft invitation letters to speakers
		Finalize marketing plan with deadlines & distribute internally
9 months		Send confirmation letters to all speakers
		Begin developing preliminary brochure & event web page
		Hotel reservation form to hotel for review & approval
		Prepare meeting registration form
		Prepare sports registration form

FIGURE 19.3
Sample Planning Timeline, continued

Date Due	Date Completed	Task
7 months		DMC contract signed for spouse programs and special events
		Establish registration policies and fees
		News release & launch of event web site
		Request visitors guide and local information from CVB
		Sporting events confirmed
		Mail exhibitor services manual
		Distribute press release to related organizations
		Complete social program
		Finalize banquet and hospitality arrangements
		Preliminary brochure mailing
		Finalize registration confirmation letter & information package
		Registration & housing open for meeting
6 months		Site Inspection • Meeting with convention center and/or hotel CSM and catering departments • Tour special event venues
		Information received from Convention & Visitors Bureau
		Name badge holders & card stock ordered
		Begin preparation of final brochure
		Order mailing lists and labels
		Review price quotes against budget for adjustments in plans
		Update crisis management plan
5 months		Send reminders to speakers concerning dates/contracts, A/V requirements, audio and videotaping release form
		Meeting room assignments finalized
		Begin preparation of course materials
		Print & mail final brochure
		Finalize and print on-site registration form
3 months		Prepare initial A/V summary
		Photography arrangements confirmed
		Send reminders to speakers concerning A/V, setup requirements and session handouts
		Promotion in trade magazines
		Conduct final site visit and meeting with facilities & contractors
2 months		Review room block and pick-up with hotel(s)
		Tickets prepared and printed
		Orders placed for: • Awards • Ribbons • Plaques • Trophies • Certificates • Sports items

FIGURE 19.3
Sample Planning Timeline, continued

Date Due	Date Completed	Task
		Speaker information due: • A/V requirements • Hotel reservations • Handouts • Biographies
		Process speaker/staff room reservations
		Mail awards banquet invitations and tickets
		Mail special invitations
		Order carrier and schedule for shipping materials to convention site
		Draft Event Specifications Guide (ESG) • Hotel schedule and instructions • Convention center instructions • Decorator instructions • Order A/V equipment • Order signs • Order registration/temporary personnel • Order flowers • Finalize shuttle bus schedule(s)
7 weeks		Memo to staff attending meeting for housing and travel
6 weeks		Finalize all instructions to facilities & suppliers
		Program materials to printer
		Review hotel block and pick-up
		Airline & car reservations made for staff
4 weeks		VIP room list to hotel, including staff, volunteers, speakers
		Review hotel block and pick-up
		Promotion in newsletters and trade magazines
		Send final instructions and Event Specifications Guide (ESG) to facilities & suppliers
		Packing list developed
		Begin development of lectern guide – scripts
		Items determined for hospitality center or information desk, including membership information, products, local tourist information
		Housing cut-off date
		Decide all on-site staff needs and make a chart of staff responsibilities
		Review final program page proofs
3 weeks		Review room pick-up with hotel
		Evaluation forms prepared and printed or copied
		Begin preparing registration packets, including: • Evaluation forms • Name badges/holders • Tickets • Registration envelopes/labels
		Receive/review suppliers' versions of final instructions

FIGURE 19.3
Sample Planning Timeline, continued

Date Due	Date Completed	Task
		All staff briefing on meeting site & logistics
		Packing for shipment: • Registration packets/materials/extra forms • Credit card materials • Pre-printed receipts • On-site registration forms • Trophies • Binders • Podium signs • Signs • Plaques/awards • Office supplies • Cash boxes • Extra tickets • Badge stock • Badge holders • Hospitality center items • Registration lists • First Aid Kit • Crisis Management Plan
2 weeks		Golf handicaps to pro shop and golf chair
		Tennis assignments to tennis chair
		Attendee list prepared/copied
		Lectern guide/scripts finalized
		Program book received from printer
		Name badges prepared
		Receive from hotel and review BEO's
		Review room pick-up with hotel
		Finalize staff assignments and schedules
		Carrier picks up convention materials for transportation to site
1 week		Travel to meeting destination
		Transport last-minute materials
4 days		Conduct final walk through meeting facility to confirm details
		Set up staff meeting office
3 days		Hold pre-con meeting with facility staff
		Start exhibit/registration setup

FIGURE 19.3
Sample Planning Timeline, continued

Date Due	Date Completed	Task
2 days		Conduct staff tours
EVENT		Conduct/manage the meeting • Educational programs & sessions • Exhibit • Guest programs • Social functions • Business meetings • Announce date and location of next meeting • On-site evaluation
		Invoice review/gratuities paid
1 day after		Hold post-con meeting with facilities – convention center & hotel(s)
1 wk after		Send thank-you letters to: • Convention center • Hotel • DMC • Speakers • Suppliers • Program committee
2 wks after		Post event news release/report of convention in trade magazines
4 wks after		Pay BMI/ASCAP/SESAC
		Reconcile all invoices: • Convention Center • Hotel • DMC • Decorator • A/V • Shuttle
		Attendee evaluations summarized
		Compile post-convention report
		Send post-meeting statistics to exhibitors
2 mo after		Reconcile income/expenses with finance department

FIGURE 19.3
Sample Planning Timeline, continued

General Program Outline

Day 1
| | | |
Morning: Office and press room setup begins
                Registration setup begins
                Exhibition setup begins

Afternoon: Meeting room setup begins

Day 2
Morning: Governance and/or committee meetings
                Registration opens
                Office and press room open
                Exhibition and meeting room setup continue

Afternoon: Pre-meeting workshops

Evening: Opening reception

Days 3-5
Morning: General session
                Exhibition opens
                Registration, office, press room open

Afternoon: Concurrent sessions
                Annual business meeting (Day 4 only)

Evening: Annual reception and banquet (Day 4 only)

Day 6
Morning: Exhibition move-out begins
                Closing general session

Afternoon: Move-out of registration area, office, press room

FIGURE 19.4
General Program Outline

EDUCATIONAL FORMATS

The methods of instruction that are most adaptable to the meeting environment are expository, participatory, and evaluative.[1]

In expository learning, the instructor presents to the learners and the learners remain passive and watch or listen. This is generally the format for large plenary sessions.

Participatory learning occurs when the participants share knowledge and experience and work together to learn. The role of the instructor is to join the group as a member and to share experiences. The more participants are induced to share ideas with each other, the greater the level of participant interest and commitment.[2]

The evaluation learning method tests whether participants learned what was expected, and if they can use the information effectively. Verbal questions, tests and exercises, and self-assessment are used to test a participant's knowledge of the subject matter.

Program Schedule for Multiple-Day Meeting

Saturday – Monday (exhibit hall open)

8:00 - 9:15	Plenary Session
9:15 - 9:30	Break
9:30 - 11:00	Concurrent Symposia
11:00 - 12:00	Poster Session
12:00 - 1:00	Lunchtime Workshops & Break
1:00 - 2:30	Oral Presentations
2:30 - 3:00	Networking Break
3:30 - 5:00	Concurrent Symposia
5:30 - 6:30	Plenary

FIGURE 19.5
Sample Program Schedule for Multiple-Day Meeting

Adults learn best through involvement and experience. Meetings that consist primarily of expository learning sessions led by individuals and panels may have difficulty holding participants' attention. The best educational programs combine all three methods of instruction. One effective program design is to begin with an expository approach, move on to participatory learning, and end the session with evaluative learning. Provide attendees with as many choices as possible. If a plenary session with a keynote speaker is planned for the morning, offer a choice of afternoon sessions designed for participatory and evaluative learning.

The following formats can enhance educational delivery:

- *Break-out session*—Small group sessions, panels, workshops, or presentations, offered concurrently within the event, formed to focus on specific subjects. The event is apart from the general session, but within the event format, formed to focus on specific subjects. These sessions can be arranged by basic, intermediate, or advanced, or divided by interest areas or industry segment.
- *Case study*—An intensive analysis of an individual unit or situation.
- *Colloquium*—An informal meeting for the purpose of discussion, usually of an academic or research nature and in order to ascertain areas of mutual interest through exchange of ideas; conducted when convenient, but with little regularity.
- *Concurrent sessions*—Multiple sessions scheduled at the same time; programs on different themes or subjects offered simultaneously.
- *Controversy panel*—To stimulate interest and debate, arrange for two or more views on a controversial issue to be presented. A moderator (person who presides over panel discussions and forums) is sometimes used to challenge the panelists and sharpen the focus of the discussion.
- *Demonstration*—The act of showing how to do something. For certain topics, products, and services, a hands-on demonstration is the most interesting and useful presentation format. This is especially true for technical products and services, such as information technology or medical equipment and procedures.
- *General session*—A meeting open to all those in attendance at an event.
- *Lecture*—An informative and instructional speech.

- *Keynote*—Opening remarks or presentation at a meeting that sets the tone or theme of the event and motivates attendees.
- *Keynote address*—A session that opens or highlights the show, meeting or event.
- *Q&A*—A question-and-answer period after a speaker or presentation at a meeting.
- *Opening address*—A formal speech given at the commencement of a meeting to welcome participants; usually given by an eminent person (see Keynote).
- *Oral presentation*—A contribution made verbally.
- *Panel discussion (presenter/discussant format)*—A panel of three or four experts in certain subject areas are identified, with each giving a brief presentation. After each lecture, the other panelists become discussants of the material just offered. At the conclusion of the presentations, the audience is given an opportunity to ask questions of the entire panel.
- *Poster sessions*—1) Display of reports and papers, usually scientific, accompanied by authors or researchers. 2) A session dedicated to the discussion of the posters shown inside the meeting area. When this discussion is not held in a special session, it can take place directly between the person presenting the poster and interested delegate(s). This format is often used at medical meetings or other meetings where research is presented. In a moderated poster session, a subject matter expert leads a small group in reviewing several posters on a specific topic. The moderator guides the discussion and provides input on the science during the review.
- *Plenary session*—A general assembly for all participants (also known as general sessions).
- *Roundtable*—A group of experts who meet on an equal basis to review and discuss specialized, professional matters, either in closed session or, more frequently, before an audience.
- *Simulation encounter*—An interactive instructional technique in which an individual simulates certain behavior that can then be examined, studied, and discussed by the attendees.
- *Structured question*—A 1-hour presentation with previously prepared 8 or 10 questions to be distributed in advance of the session to selected attendees. Following each major presentation, attendees ask questions from the list.
- *Symposium*—A meeting of a number of experts in a particular field, at which papers are presented and discussed by specialists on particular subjects with a view to making recommendations concerning the problems under discussion.
- *Workshop*—1) Meeting of several persons for intensive discussion. The workshop concept has been developed to compensate for diverging views in a particular discipline or on a particular subject. 2) Informal and public session of free discussion organized to take place between formal plenary sessions or commissions of a congress or of a conference, either on a subject chosen by the participants themselves or else on a special problem suggested by the organizers. 3) Training session in which participants, often through exercises, develop skills and knowledge in a given field.

WORKING WITH A PROGRAM COMMITTEE

A committee is a group of people appointed for a specific purpose. A program committee is appointed to develop the educational content for a meeting. Program committee members should be recognized authorities in their fields and are selected on the basis of their dependability and accessibility. The ideal committee chair is one who is well organized and has enough confidence in the planning process to delegate responsibilities and keep the committee on track.

A meeting manager should provide committee members with a tentative schedule of committee meetings, a copy of the reimbursement policy for travel expenses, and the planning timeline. The more background information committee members receive in advance of each meeting, the more productive the planning sessions.

A list of guidelines for program committee members might include the following:

- Adhere closely to the program-planning timeline and deadlines.
- Report to the committee chair and staff liaison immediately if a deadline cannot be met.
- When contacting speakers, follow the guidelines set forth by the committee with respect to content and format expectations, fees, manuscripts, and handouts.
- Report immediately to the staff liaison and chairperson if committee assignments are inappropriate or cannot be completed in the time frame allotted.

Resource Workbook

A resource workbook is usually a loose-leaf binder in which additions and deletions are made as the program develops. The workbook is a comprehensive source of information that will be helpful to the program committee when planning the program. It should be sent to the committee members before the first planning meeting.

The resource workbook should include the following:

- A list of committee members and their contact information
- The committee charge and/or performance criteria
- The meeting goals and objectives and/or a brief description of the program
- The program and promotion pieces from the previous year
- An evaluation summary of the previous program
- Minutes of previous program-planning meetings
- Policies regarding speaker remuneration and fees
- A list of contacts and resources
- Meeting dates
- Information about the meeting site and a map
- Estimated attendance
- Meeting budget
- Planning timeline and deadlines
- Session format descriptions
- Audiovisual (A/V) guidelines and restrictions
- Information on other aspects of the meeting program (exhibits, guest programs, food and beverage functions)

Committee Agenda

An agenda is a list, outline, or plan of items to be done or considered at an event or during a specific time block. This may include a time schedule. The agenda for planning meetings will reflect the stage in the timeline at which the meeting takes place. A typical agenda for a program committee's first meeting follows:

1. Introduction of committee members and staff
2. Meeting philosophy, objectives, and theme
3. Committee charge
4. Overview of meeting site and physical arrangements
5. Organizational policies
   a. Reimbursement of committee members' expenses
   b. Complimentary registration for committee members and speakers
   c. Remuneration to speakers (honoraria and travel expenses)
6. Review of evaluation summary, previous program, and attendance
7. Review program formats
8. Program schedule
9. Speaker suggestions
10. Committee assignments
11. Timeline and reporting forms
12. Date of next meeting

Topic and Speaker Selection

Distribute topic and speaker worksheets to committee members in advance of the planning session. Ideally, the worksheets will include the presentation format at the top (e.g., workshop, luncheon, round table), with columns in which the committee member can list suggested topics and speakers with contact information for each. For later use, the worksheet can also include columns to indicate whether the speaker accepted or declined, and the name of the committee member responsible for the session.

Another method is to divide the program planning process into topic or format areas for assignment to individual committee members who will be responsible for the development of one or more areas. Assignments are made on the basis of the professional interests of each committee member.

Using a planning matrix (grid) during committee meetings can be a useful way to develop the program content. A planning matrix is a grid used to plan meeting formats and finalize subject areas, topics and assignments. Key elements, such as topics and session titles, are identified at the top of each column, and the rows are used to represent specifics for each, such as subtopics or time segments.

Research reports are a mainstay of many technical and medical meetings, and the programming for these reports often requires extensive committee involvement. The usual procedure is to initiate a call for abstracts, which are sent to members and other interested individuals. Abstracts are: 1) written summaries of speeches or papers, generally between 200–500 words; 2) laser presentations, graphic designs, or patterns that are not representational of concrete objects; or 3) a brief statement of content.

The call for abstracts or announcement includes information about the meeting, a form on which to submit a summary or abstract of the research, guidelines regarding who may submit abstracts, and the deadline by which they must be received. Many organizations have instituted electronic processes for submission and review of abstracts. The program committee, or a subcommittee, has the responsibility to review the abstract submissions for possible inclusion in the program following selection criteria developed by the organization.

Minutes

Keeping minutes of all planning sessions helps keep the process focused and on track, and provides documentation of the committee's progress. Minutes are the formal written record of a meeting. However, an exhaustive account of all discussion is not necessary. Goal-oriented minutes are more useful in ensuring action. Include only the most important points of the discussion, and an itemized listing of action items with the name of the individual responsible for completing each task and the date by which it is to be accomplished.

EXTENDING PROGRAM REACH

Technology can extend the impact of a meeting far beyond the walls of a hotel or convention center. Information from live presentations can be recorded for rebroadcast in other formats such as CD-ROM or web casts. Programs can also be distributed using videoconferencing. For example, videoconferencing enables interested individuals or groups from across the country or around the world to participate in a live session. Educational programs created in alternative formats can be maintained for a specific duration on the organization's website. Procedures should be developed to periodically review and retire programs as the content becomes dated. Consideration must also be given to any accreditation rules that may apply for education delivered in these formats. Determine both the interest level and the preferred method of delivery for this type of education before initiating new technology that allows distance learning programming for the organization.

Online learning is a type of education where students work on their own at home or from an office, and communicate with faculty and other students via email, electronic forums, chat, web conferencing, and other forms of online communication. Meeting and event websites can facilitate distance learning by offering online educational programs.

Distance learning can be completed without using these electronic devices, i.e., print-based resources. Distance learning can incorporate other forms of electronic communication such as audioconferencing and videoconferencing. These can be cost-effective ways of making a meeting more accessible.

Pre-meeting and post-meeting educational offerings may enhance the experience as well. In fact, a face-to-face meeting may not always be required. In some cases, an organization may serve the needs of its members more efficiently through distance learning or other methods of presenting educational sessions via technology. In any case, the basic principles of program planning and organization still apply.

SUMMARY

Meeting managers are becoming increasingly responsible for the quality of the educational content at their meetings. An effective meeting manager assumes a leadership role with the organization's staff, the program-planning group, and with outside suppliers, maximizing each individual's contributions to create an educational program that fulfills the meeting objectives.

The basic components of a program plan include affinity group research, a timeline, a program committee, and the final program/agenda. The keys to success are to carefully select the members of the program committee, work with the volunteers to meet goals and adhere to the timeline, provide guidance and direction, and create clear agendas for planning sessions.

The timeline for program planning includes each task to be accomplished and is the core of the program planning process. Well-organized program-planning sessions are vital to the successful development of educational programs and the selection of subject material and speakers. The agenda for planning meetings should reflect the stage in the timeline at which the planning meeting takes place.

Fast Facts

- Learners must be actively involved in the learning process. Adults learn best by doing. Expository learning (e.g., "talking heads") is becoming less prevalent as the next generation of adult learners enters the workplace.[3]
- Use of technology to expand the reach of meetings has almost doubled since 1997.[4]
- Adults prefer self-directed and self-designed learning projects 7:1 over group-learning experiences led by a professional.[5]

The methods of instruction that are most adaptable to the meeting environment are expository, participatory, and evaluative techniques. They can be used in a variety of formats, including presenter/discussant, structured questions, workshop, roundtable, hands-on participation, simulation encounter, controversy panel, and poster session.

A committee of people will need to be appointed to carry out the role of recommending the content of the program. These committee members should be recognized as authorities in their fields. The ideal chair of this committee will be well organized and have good delegation skills. The more background information committee members receive in advance of each meeting, the more productive the planning sessions will be. Prepare a comprehensive resource workbook and send it to committee members before the first planning meeting.

REFERENCES

1. Rogers, A. (1987). Education for development. ERIC Document Reproduction Service No. ED 290 838.

2. Munson, L. S. (1989). *How to conduct training seminars*. New York: McGraw Hill.

3. Shure, P. (March, 2004). 13th Annual Meeting Marketing Survey. *Convene*, p. 28–40.

4. Siwek, E. J. (April, 2002). Meeting technology: A better way for program content. *Convene*, p. 60.

5. Draves, W. (October, 1997). Why meeting managers must become adult educators. *Convene*, p. 58–63.

KEY TERMS

Abstract	Expository learning	Presenter-discussant format
Affinity group	Hands-on participation	Program committee
Agenda	Keynote	Program design
Break	Keynote address	Resource workbook
Break-out session	Keynote speaker	Roundtable
Case study	Meeting history	Schedule
Colloquium	Minutes	Simulation encounter
Concurrent session	Moderator	Structured questions
Content	Panel discussion	Symposium
Controversy panel	Participatory learning	Timeline
Demographics	Planning matrix	Workshop
Demonstration	Plenary session	
Evaluative learning method	Poster session	

COMPELLING QUESTIONS FOR CONSIDERATION

1. Why should you research the educational needs of your prospective meeting attendees?

2. What should be included in a program-planning timeline?

3. What role does the meeting manager play in developing the educational content for a meeting?

4. Describe three methods of instruction and several educational delivery formats.

CHAPTER 20

WRITING EFFECTIVE LEARNER OUTCOMES

Brian Miller, EdD
ASSISTANT PROFESSOR
HOTEL, RESTAURANT, AND INSTITUTIONAL MANAGEMENT PROGRAM
UNIVERSITY OF DELAWARE

Glen C. Ramsborg, PhD
SENIOR DIRECTOR, EDUCATION
PROFESSIONAL CONVENTION MANAGEMENT ASSOCIATION

LEARNER OUTCOMES

When the reader has completed reading this chapter, he/she should be able to . . .

1 Differentiate among the three domains of learning.

2 Apply the concept of learning domains in writing learner outcomes.

3 Select verbs that clearly and succinctly state the intention of the outcomes of the proposed learning activity.

4 Evaluate learner outcomes in relation to the content presented.

5 Compare learner outcomes with program objectives.

6 Incorporate the integral parts of learner outcome statements in planning a program.

> What we see depends mainly on what we look for.
>
> *Sir John Lubbock*

OVERVIEW

Most organizations view providing educational content as a key component of their mission. Therefore a common element of most meeting managers' job descriptions is the organization of educational content for their organization's meetings and conferences. Even though most meeting managers are not experts in the field or industry that their organization supports, nevertheless, it is important that they understand how to develop specific educational outcomes that are appropriate to their audience. This is an essential element of a successful meeting.

Organizations are charged with meeting the needs of many stakeholders. In order to focus on meeting their affinity groups' needs, most develop objectives that guide them in carrying out their daily activities. Objectives written for educational content are commonly referred to as learner outcomes, learning outcomes, learner objectives, instructional objectives, learning goals, and other terms. In this chapter the term learner outcomes is used to encompass all of these commonly used terms.

Learner outcomes are statements that identify what learners should be able to know or do at the end of a defined learning activity. They should be specific and are likely expressed as knowledge, a skill, or an attitude. Given the significance that education plays in most meetings it is imperative that meeting managers ensure that learner outcomes are developed for the educational sessions of their meetings.

Well-written learner outcomes include the following characteristics:

- Focus on changing the learner's behavior
- Serve as a guideline for the development of content, instruction, and evaluation
- Identify specifically what should result from the experience
- Convey to the learner what is to be accomplished

Based on three domains of learning, knowledge (cognitive), attitudes (affective), and skills (psychomotor), well-written learner outcomes provide meeting attendees a guide to evaluate and predict the outcomes they will receive by participating in the learning experience.

While the meeting manager may not be the individual involved in curriculum development or the writing of the learner outcomes, it is incumbent upon meeting managers to understand and use learner outcomes in the development and marketing of program content to demonstrate educational value to their attendees. However, too often learner outcomes are vague, include multiple constructs, and cannot be measured effectively.

This chapter will provide meeting managers with information to ensure that the educational content that is developed, supported, and distributed has clear, well-written, and measurable learner outcomes. The concept of forming a contract with the attendees will also be discussed.

DOMAINS OF LEARNING

Learning is change. It modifies behavior or performance. While the process of learning may not be directly observable, the external manifestations of the experience in the learning environment are directly related to changes in the learner.

An awareness of the domains of learning is the foundation of planning educational programs. The essence of fulfilling the needs of the adult learner is executed within a planned sequence using the framework to be explored in this chapter and then applying the concept as written statements that reflect what the learner is going to know how to do at the end of the experience.

Bloom,[1] Krathwohl,[2] Simpson,[3] Harrow,[4] Anderson and Karthwahl,[5] and others have identified three areas of behavior, which are generally referred to as the domains of learning. The three domains—cognitive, affective, and psychomotor—can be further subdivided into a series of categories arranged in hierarchical order from simple to complex that enable all possible learner outcomes to be classified in a taxonomy.

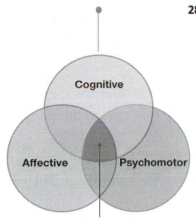

An Historical Perspective

The idea for organizing learner outcomes into taxonomies resulted from an informal meeting in 1948 of college examiners who were trying to devise a theoretical framework to facilitate communication in the discipline. Kinney[6] and Travers[7] were among the early educators who advocated the use of written objectives for educational events. The domains of learning were developed in an effort to bring focus and order to learner outcomes.

They decided that a taxonomy, or classification system, of educational objectives would provide the basis for building curricula and tests, as well as a starting point for educational research. The original taxonomy included two of the three domains of learning—cognitive and affective. The psychomotor domain was subsequently defined, delineated, and added to the other two.

How Does the Taxonomy Work?

The taxonomy is a simple classification system that uses specific terms to determine which characteristics are fundamental to other characteristics. As the complexity increases within a domain, the ability of the lower levels is subsumed within the higher ones.

In terms of learning, the existence of a hierarchy acknowledges that some higher-level behaviors cannot be attained until lower-level behaviors have been achieved. If the levels in the taxonomy are thought of as a mountain incline, a climber cannot reach the summit unless he or she starts at the base. For example, knowledge and comprehension must be present before information can be applied. When writing outcomes in order to analyze the results of a learning situation, the learner must understand the content before he or she can be expected to accomplish the outcomes of the learning activity.

The taxonomy of educational objectives[8-9] is a valuable resource for identifying and defining learner outcomes. Gronlund states that "the taxonomy provides a classification of educational objectives that is analogous to the classification scheme used for plants and animals."[10] Such a taxonomy consists of outcomes that are useful in instruction, learning, and measurement.

Depending on the type of learning that is taking place, it may be desirable to use several levels of learning. For example, within the cognitive domain, knowledge, comprehension, and application might come into play and would be appropriate for the given instruction. In the following section, each of these domains is briefly defined and a discussion of the levels within each domain is given.

DEFINITION OF DOMAINS

Cognitive Domain

The cognitive domain attends to what the learner knows or understands. It encompasses recall or recognition of information and the development of intellectual skills that provide the learner with the ability to conduct rational tasks. It is the knowledge-acquisition phase of learning and emphasizes intellectual outcomes, such as comprehension and analysis skills. It includes six cognitive levels, ranging from knowledge to evaluation.

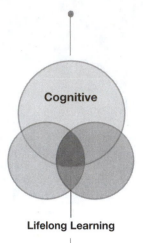

Cognitive

Lifelong Learning

The cognitive domain will include learner outcomes that emphasize intellectual ability, such as knowledge, understanding, and thinking skills. They begin with knowledge and proceed through increasingly complex levels of cognition.

Knowledge: Knowledge is the ability to recall or recognize content in a form that is virtually identical to the way it was originally presented. Knowledge is defined as recalling past experiences or previously learned material in order to apply them to a situation. It represents the lowest level of learner outcomes and depends on an individual's ability to use words and symbols to manipulate elements of past experience.

Comprehension: Comprehension involves the learner's ability to manipulate knowledge elements meaningfully. It includes the ability to change the content presented from one form to another, to explain or summarize a body of content, and to go beyond that content to determine its probable implications, consequences, or effects, given the conditions described. These learner outcomes go a step beyond the simple recollection of information to encompass translation, interpretation, and extrapolation.

Application: Application refers to the ability to use material in new and concrete situations, including the use of content learned in one situation to either solve a problem or to facilitate learning in a new situation. These learner outcomes are based on applying the knowledge and comprehension of previously learned material. The demonstrated use of problem-solving, communication, and self-actualization is primary at this level.

Analysis: Analysis involves the ability to identify relevant knowledge components that foster an understanding of the whole. Analysis of both the elements and the relationships is required; for example, breaking down the components of presented content into their constituent parts. The analysis of relationships requires the learner to see the connection between one part of an aggregate of content and the other parts. These learner outcomes occur on an intellectual level that requires an understanding of both the content and the structure of the material so the relevant elements and their relationships to one another can be identified.

Synthesis: Synthesis entails the ability to take parts of previously acquired knowledge elements and produce a unique response. It requires the ability to arrange and combine content in such a way as to produce a new structure, pattern, or idea. The learner must be able to communicate effectively at this level. These learner outcomes put major emphasis on the production of an appropriate product with unique characteristics. Communication, or the solution to a problem, is evident in the manner in which the analyzed elements are manipulated into a feasible course of action.

Evaluation: Evaluation refers to the ability to appraise or judge the value or appropriateness of a proposed or applied behavior and to make both quantitative and qualitative judgments about the way in which particular elements or aggregates of content meet external or internal criteria. The learner must make a judgment about the value or worth of something in relation to some purpose. Learner outcomes at this level are the highest in the cognitive hierarchy and contain all the elements of previous categories, as well as a conscious value judgment based on clearly defined criteria.

When developing educational content the instructional developer should consider the appropriateness of the content to their intended audience. Using the cognitive domain taxonomy facilitates this effort to ensure that the educational content matches the abilities of the learner.[11]

Cognitive Domain

Examples of Learner Outcomes and Action Verbs

Knowledge

- Recite an attrition policy.
- Quote room rates from memory to a meeting manager.
- List the safety regulations for a convention center.

Action verbs: cite, define, describe, draw, identify, label, list, match, name, outline, recall, recognize, record, repeat, reproduce, select, state, and underline.

Comprehension

- Rewrite the meeting learner outcomes.
- Explain the steps for completing a marketing plan.
- Translate a meeting's revenue equation into a computer spreadsheet.

Action verbs: compute, comprehend, convert, defend, describe, discuss, distinguish, estimate, explain, express, extend, generalize, give examples, identify, infer, interpret, locate, paraphrase, predict, report, restate, review, rewrite, summarize, tell, and translate.

Application

- Use a manual to calculate an employee's vacation time.
- Apply statistical tests to evaluate attendee evaluations of a meeting.
- Interpret the elements of a hotel's attrition clause.

Action verbs: apply, calculate, change, compute, construct, demonstrate, discover, dramatize, employ, examine, illustrate, interpret, manipulate, modify, operate, practice, predict, prepare, produce, relate, schedule, show, sketch, solve, and use.

Analysis

- Troubleshoot a piece of equipment by using logical deduction. Recognize logical fallacies in reasoning.
- Gather information from a department and select the required tasks for training.

Action verbs: analyze, appraise, break down, calculate, categorize, compare, contrast, debate, diagram, deconstruct, differentiate, discriminate, distinguish, examine, identify, illustrate, infer, inventory, outline, question, relate, select, separate, and test.

Synthesis

- Write an organization meeting department's operational manual.
- Design the flow chart for the meeting management process.
- Integrate educational programming to meet the meeting's objectives.

Action verbs: arrange, assemble, categorize, collect, combine, compile, compose, create, devise, design, explain, formulate, generate, integrate, manage, modify, organize, plan, prescribe, propose, rearrange, reconstruct, relate, reorganize, revise, rewrite, summarize, tell, and write.

Evaluation

- Select the general services contractor for a meeting.
- Hire the most qualified candidate.
- Explain and justify a new budget.

Action verbs: appraise, assess, choose, compare, conclude, contrast, criticize, critique, defend, describe, discriminate, estimate, evaluate, explain, interpret, justify, measure, rank, rate, rule, relate, revise, score, select, summarize, and support.

Affective Domain

The affective (attitude) domain is concerned with how the learner feels, that is, their interests, attitudes, feelings, and values, as well as how they internalize values and beliefs. It is organized according to the degree of internalization involved. The emphasis is on feelings and emotions, or the degree to which the attitude or value has become a part of the individual. This taxonomy includes five levels, ranging from receptivity to character.

If the objective of an activity is for the learner to show increased interest or motivation in a topic or activity, or to change some attitude or value, then that out-

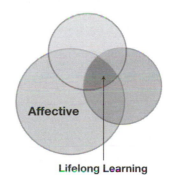

come falls within the affective domain. Each of the outcomes in the affective domain is characterized by a value or attitude based on a performance or behavior. Affective outcomes are difficult to write and measure because it takes more time to change someone's attitude or values and such change is not easily identifiable.

The affective domain is concerned with attitudes and feelings and involves a process of internalizing values and beliefs. It includes learner outcomes that emphasize feelings and emotions, such as interests, attitudes, appreciation, and methods of adjustment. The affective domain focuses on awareness, attention, and values. It filters the stimuli received by the sensory nerves so the mind can separate the important from the unimportant.

The amount of learning that occurs in the affective domain is abstract and difficult, if not impossible, to measure. Over time, it changes values and attitudes. These changes are subtle and become part of the learner after he or she has practiced the knowledge, awareness, values, and aspirations and integrated them into his or her normal daily experiences.

Therefore, a learner must be directly involved in a learning situation. It is not enough to tell an individual something he or she needs to know, nor assume that he or she hears what is being said. The information must be analyzed in the learner's center of consciousness. Allowing for interaction and immediate feedback thereby strengthens the learning process. The maintenance of affective domain outcomes in the planning of educational activities is important to ensure that the learning activities continue to address whatever attitude is to be changed.

Receptivity: Receptivity refers to the learner's willingness to pay attention to a particular stimulus or educational activity. Learner outcomes at this level range from a simple awareness that an educational activity is available to a receptivity to learn.

Response: Response involves the active participation of the learner, who is responding to a stimulus, such as an advertisement for an educational activity. It is some type of reaction to the stimulus. These learner outcomes emphasize that the individual shows an interest in a subject or participates in an educational event.

Valuation: Valuation concerns the value or worth an individual places on a particular object, phenomenon, or behavior. It is a voluntary display of an attitude or an interest. It can range from simple acceptance (a desire to improve group skills) to a more complex level of commitment or conviction (assumes responsibility for the effective functioning of the group). It is based on the internalization of a set of specified values. Learner outcomes in this area are concerned with behavior that is consistent and stable enough to make the value clearly identifiable.

Organization: Organization involves the bringing together of different values, resolving conflicts among them, and beginning the development of an internally consistent system. Emphasis is placed on comparing, relating, and synthesizing values. These learner outcomes recognize the responsibility of each individual for improving human relationships or the organization of a value system. An organized individual understands and accepts his or her own strengths and limitations.

Character: Character can develop only when a value system has controlled an individual's behavior for a sufficiently long time so that the learner has adopted a characteristic lifestyle. The learner's behavior or response to a situation would then be pervasive, consistent, and predictable. While learner outcomes at this level cover a broad range of activities, the major emphasis is on the fact that the behavior is typical or characteristic of the learner.

Fast Facts

Affective Domain

- Attitudes
- Values
- Beliefs
- Priorities
- Feelings

Affective Domain

Examples of Learner Outcomes and Action Verbs

Receptivity

- Listen to others with respect.
- Describe the importance of having a diverse staff.
- Follow the organization's ethics policy.

Action verbs: accept, ask, attend, choose, describe, develop, erect, follow, give, hold, identify, locate, name, point to, realize, receive, recognize, reply, select, sit, and use.

Response

- Participate in organization meetings.
- Give a presentation.

Action verbs: answer, assist, aid, behave, complete, comply, conform, cooperate, discuss, examine, greet, help, label, obey, observe, perform, practice, present, read, recite, report, respond, select, tell, and write.

Valuation

- Demonstrate belief in the democratic process in their office.
- Demonstrate sensitivity toward individual and cultural differences.
- Inform management on matters that the participant feels strongly about.

Action verbs: accept, balance, believe, complete, defend, demonstrate, devote, differentiate, explain, follow, form, influence, initiate, invite, join, justify, prefer, propose, pursue, read, report, seek, select, share, study, value, and work.

Organization

- Explain the role of systematic planning in solving problems.
- Apply professional ethical standards.
- Prioritize time effectively to meet the needs of the organization, family, and self.

Action verbs: adhere, alter, arrange, codify, combine, compare, complete, defend, discriminate, display, explain, favor, formulate, generalize, identify, integrate, judge, modify, order, organize, prepare, relate, synthesize, systematize, and weigh.

Character

- Use an objective approach in problem solving.
- Display a professional commitment to ethical practice on a daily basis.
- Revise judgments and change behavior in light of new evidence.

Action verbs: act, discriminate, display, influence, listen, modify, perform, practice, propose, qualify, question, revise, serve, solve, and verify.

Psychomotor Domain

The psychomotor (skills) domain focuses on how a learner uses manual skills, with an emphasis on the performance of motor skills. It can be seen as a progression in the degree of coordination required to complete a specific task and encompasses seven psychomotor levels, ranging from perception to originality.

The psychomotor domain is the "doing" phase of learned behaviors or motor skills. It is an integral part of performance because the cognitive and affective domains are interrelated with performance and are, in fact, prerequisites. The learner must have the knowledge and the desire in order to actually perform the required or specified task, and be able to integrate previously acquired knowledge and attitudes in order to accomplish more complex tasks.

Each level of this domain contains skills that are performed daily. However some skills may require higher levels of cognition for successful performance of the skill. For example, the effort required to plan a meeting on paper is simple enough, involving a sketch of the room layout that includes the outer walls, doors, and various obstacles. Such a sketch basically entails copying the specifications from the facility brochure—a simple and straightforward task. However,

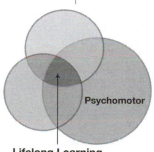

Psychomotor

Lifelong Learning

placement of the riser for the speaker, the screen for the visuals, and the chairs for the learners require that the learners have a higher level of cognition to draw upon. Application of knowledge to consider the sight lines and audio requirements is required by the learner to successfully demonstrate the psychomotor skill.

The types of learning activities required to provide a physical environment conducive to learning psychomotor skills may necessitate a different kind of physical layout than is needed for the other two domains. For instance, if a learner outcome is to display negotiating skills, interaction and group dynamics will be required and will not be conducive in a room that is permanently set up theater style. Therefore, when educational content will focus on psychomotor skills outcomes, meeting managers should carefully consider the physical space of the learning environment.

> ### Fast Facts
>
> Psychomotor Domain
> - Developing skills
> - Performance
> - Changing behavior patterns
> - Complex tasks

Perception: Perception involves the use of the senses to obtain cues that guide a motor activity. This category ranges from sensory stimulation (awareness of a stimulus) to cue selection (selecting task-relevant cues) to translation (relating cue perception to action).

Set: Set refers to the readiness to take a particular type of action. It includes mental set, physical set, and emotional set. The perception of cues is an important prerequisite for this level.

Guided Response: Guided response occurs during the early stages of learning a complex skill. It includes imitation, repetition of an act that has been demonstrated by a facilitator, and trial and error—a multifaceted approach to identifying the appropriate response. The adequacy of performance is judged by an instructor or by applying a suitable set of criteria.

Mechanical: Mechanical relates to performance when the learned responses have become habitual and the movements can be performed with some confidence and proficiency. Learner outcomes at this level are concerned with the performance of skills of various types, but the movement patterns are less complex than at the next higher level.

Proficiency: Proficiency focuses on the skillful performance of motor acts that involve intricate movement patterns. Proficiency is demonstrated by a quick, smooth, accurate performance that requires a minimum of energy. It includes the resolution of uncertainty; that is, the learner performs automatically and without hesitation. The learner's movements are executed easily and with good muscle control. Learner outcomes at this level include highly coordinated motor activities.

Adaptation: Adaptation concerns skills that are so well developed that the individual can modify his or her movement patterns to fit special requirements or deal with a problem situation.

Originality: Originality refers to the creation of new movement patterns to fit a particular situation or problem. Learner outcomes at this level emphasize creativity based upon highly developed skills.

MOVING FROM OBJECTIVES TO OUTCOMES

Since educational sessions are only one function of an organization's meetings and conferences, it is important that meeting managers gain an understanding of the theoretical principles behind learner outcomes and learn how to apply them in the development of their educational programming, while ensuring that they are congruent with the meeting's overall objectives. The development of learner outcomes lets the potential attendees know what they can expect to learn from the educational program at the meeting or convention.

Psychomotor Domain

Examples of Learner Outcomes and Action Verbs

Perception

- Detect non-verbal communication cues.
- Select the menu after tasting the food to meet the preferences of attendees.
- Detect when the temperature of the meeting room needs to be adjusted after complaints from attendees.

Action verbs: choose, describe, detect, differentiate, distinguish, hear, identify, isolate, relate, select, smell, taste, and touch.

Set

- Adjust sales pitch based upon the sequence of steps in the sales process.
- Recognize one's abilities and limitations.
- Prepare a meeting room for social interaction.

Action verbs: adjust, approach, begin, display, explain, locate, move, place, position, prepare, proceed, react, show, state, and volunteer.

Guided Response

- Perform a mathematical equation to forecast.
- Follow instructions to create a floor plan diagram.
- Respond to the instructor's hand-signals of instructor while learning to operate a forklift.

Action verbs: copy, determine, discover, duplicate, imitate, inject, trace, follow, react, repeat, reproduce, and respond

Mechanical

- Use Excel for creating a line-item budget.
- Repair a bicycle tire.
- Drive a car.

Action verbs: adjust, assemble, build, calibrate, construct, dismantle, display, fasten, fix, grind, heat, illustrate, indicate, manipulate, measure, mend, mix, organize, set up, and sketch.

Proficiency

- Maneuver a car into a tight parallel parking spot.
- Operate a computer quickly and accurately.
- Display competence while playing the piano.

Action verbs: assemble, build, calibrate, construct, coordinate, dismantle, display, fasten, fix, grind, heat, manipulate, maintain, measure, mend, mix, organize, operate, and sketch.

Adaptation

- Respond effectively to unexpected experiences.
- Modify instruction to meet the needs of the learners.
- Perform a task with a machine that it was not originally intended to do (machine is not damaged and there is no danger in performing the new task).

Action verbs: adapt, alter, build, change, develop, rearrange, reorganize, revise, supply, and vary.

Origination

- Construct a new theory.
- Develop a comprehensive training program.
- Create a new gymnastics routine.

Action verbs: arrange, build, combine, compose, construct, create, design, initiate, make, originate, and produce.

Pipe[12] has proffered two critical reasons why outcomes should be used in planning educational activities: "Before you can tell whether you're getting the results you want, you need to know how you will judge success when you see it," and "If you know your 'destination,' you can make better decisions about how to get there."

It is important to make product decisions before process decisions when developing educational programming for meetings. That way, meaningful change can occur for attendees. The greatest danger in making process decisions before product decisions is the user continues to do things "the way we have always done them." Ideally, the educational programming for meetings is developed to provide a variety of learning opportunities (product), outcomes of what the learner will know at the conclusion of the learning activities (product) are identified, and then the process of instruction is determined.

BUILDING AN EDUCATIONAL EXPERIENCE

Learner outcomes are the end products of instruction or a learning activity and describe the behavior that the attendee should be able to demonstrate or the knowledge he or she should be able to apply at the program's conclusion. Writing objectives and stating them as learner outcomes are components of the overall development and design process involved in building an educational program.

Once the goals of the meeting have been established, they will be used as inputs to develop the educational program which supports these goals, and then be followed by writing learner outcomes. Objectives are outcomes or aims. They are statements that communicate instructional intentions to both the facilitator and the learner. They are the end products of instruction or a learning activity and describe the behavior that the attendee should be able to demonstrate, or the knowledge he or she should be able to apply, at the program's conclusion.

In other words, learner outcomes are directions, instructions, or statements of what the sponsor of a learning activity hopes to achieve. Learner outcomes are formalized statements of what is to be anticipated as a result of the teaching process. They assist the facilitator in selecting content, resource material, and appropriate instructional methods. Outcomes give the learner a means of self-evaluation after the learning process. Well-written outcomes also provide mechanisms for measuring and evaluating learning to help minimize the frustration and dissatisfaction expressed by both facilitators and attendees alike.

When writing learner outcomes it is important that the wording of the outcome is clear, a single action, and is measurable. To achieve this, learner outcomes should be written in behavioral terms. A behavioral outcome is a precise statement that sets forth specified behavior(s), a standard of performance, conditions of the performance, and an indicated evaluation. It describes the exact behavior expected upon completion of a learning experience. Changes in behavior provide abundantly clear evidence that something has been learned. The behavioral change is manifested as something done by the learner.[13-14]

Intended Learner Outcomes

While the concept of learning outcomes may sound new, the term has been in use for a long time. The word *intended* is equally important, implying that there is control and direction to the educational process. An educational offering may result in a number of outcomes, and some of them may be quite accidental, whether good or bad. In adult learning, acceptable unintended outcomes often end up being more significant to the learner than the intended ones. There is nothing wrong with this, as long as the facilitator has also delivered the stated learner outcomes. When discussing learner outcomes, the word "intended" may not appear, but it is always implied.

The word *learning* is also used advisedly, because it serves to emphasize that the major purpose of the activity is to change the program participant. Educational activities, meetings, and other programming are for the learner, not the teacher or facilitator. Learners are the reason for the activity in the first place.

Finally, the word *outcome* puts the emphasis on what the learner can gain or achieve from the educational offering to which he or she has been exposed. For the sake of understanding, acceptability and brevity, the word "intended" has been removed. It has become more acceptable to use the phrase "learner outcome."

Defining Learner Outcomes

Learner outcomes are the end products of instruction or a learning activity. While they are sometimes called behavioral, performance, or instructional objectives, learner outcomes more precisely describe the behavior that the program's participants should be able to demonstrate at its conclusion as evidence that they have learned something.

The primary product to emerge from the planning phase is a set of learner outcomes, or behavioral objectives. The term outcome is already used in business and medicine and is surfacing in the meetings industry. It is a statement of what a program participant can expect to learn as a result of attending the educational activity. An outcome may be a statement of principles, skills, values, or feelings. While a set of learner outcomes can be altered, reconsidered, and refined, the primary focus must remain on the desired outcome in the learner.

WRITING LEARNER OUTCOMES

Writing clear, succinct learner outcomes takes practice. Writing a meaningful learner outcome takes time and effort. Refining, rewriting, and reorganizing what is to be communicated to the learner are very demanding tasks. Whether it is for the first time or part of the ongoing process of writing, success in making such information "come alive" takes effort and thought.

After the learner outcomes have been written, colleagues should be asked to read them to ensure that what the participant is going to learn is clear. As with any skill, the more writing practice you gain, the better and easier the process will become. There are a few important principles to keep in mind when writing learner outcomes. The next section explains these principles and brings them together with educational activities used as examples to give meeting managers a clear understanding of how the theory can be applied in the real world.

Format

In the 1970s, the U.S. Office of Education supported the Instructional Development Institute, which promoted the ABCD mnemonic as an approach to writing learner outcomes. Based on the institute's work, four basic components of an outcome are described below. Writing an outcome is similar to writing a sentence. A well-stated outcome starts by identifying the intended audience of learners. Then, the behavior or capability is specified along with the conditions under which it would be observed. Finally the degree to which the new knowledge, attitude, or skill must be mastered—the standard by which the behavior or capability can be evaluated—is set forth.

Regardless of the format of the outcomes developed, the single most important consideration is evaluating the written outcomes in terms of their ability to communicate the intent of the learning activity to the end user, the audience (e.g., attendees, employees, or students). The real test of the effectiveness of learning would be to query attendees three, six, or even nine months later to see whether there had been a change in their behavior as a result of the learning that occurred. This goal is a real challenge for every meeting manager. Even if only a very small number of previous attendees are contacted, it could provide some very useful feedback.

The final evaluation of any outcome is determined by the learning's usefulness to all involved: the meeting manager, the facilitator, and the learner. Certain steps are involved in writing objectives and outcomes so that an identifiable change in performance can be ascertained after the learner has participated in the instruction.

The most important characteristic of a useful outcome is that it describes the kind of performance that will be accepted as evidence that the learner has mastered the outcome. It is a carefully thought-out description of what the competent person does (or is supposed to do) when he or she performs a task. It is possible to derive

Put It Into Practice

Audience: Who is to do something?

The focus of lifelong learning is on what the learner will be able to do, not what the facilitator will be doing in the learning situation. An actively involved participant is most likely to learn in an environment that is conducive to interaction, be it mentally processing an idea or practicing a skill.

Because the focus of the outcome is on what the learner will be able to do and not what the facilitator will do, the written outcome begins with the stem of the outcome and addresses whose behavior is going to be changed. For example, "engineers attending this workshop," or "newly hired convention services managers" or "the attendees" will be sufficient when the written outcome is directed at the individuals attending the educational event.

Behavior: What is to be done?

The core of the outcome is the action verb, which describes the new behavior or capability that participants will possess after instruction. Clear communication is the primary reason for writing learner outcomes. By selecting an action verb, the writer of the outcome can more clearly communicate the intent of the learning activity. The behavior stated in the outcome should reflect real world situations and specify how the learner should use the information. Vague, difficult-to-understand beginnings should be avoided. They only cloud the intent of the anticipated learning experience.[14]

Condition: What is to be learned?

There may be limitations to determining whether an individual has achieved an outcome in a formal classroom setting. However, in a meeting format, the criterion becomes the content of what the learner can learn as a result of participating in the educational activity.

Degree: How is it to be done?

The degree of accuracy or proficiency used to determine mastery of the outcome is less often applied to adult learning situations because, generally, there is no opportunity to test the knowledge acquired, either by paper and pencil or by return demonstration. This aspect of the outcome format is generally employed in the classroom or by a testing agency, as in the Certified Meeting Professional (CMP) Examination or other certification programs. Quantitative or qualitative criteria should be incorporated into the outcome when they are appropriate or feasible (see Chapter 46).

outcomes for instruction that are closely tied to the reason for instruction (see Chapter 46).

Analyzing the outcome is important to determine whether there is a significant difference between what someone is already able to do and what is desirable for him or her to be able to do. It is important to determine whether a difference does exist and whether instruction or some other course of action is needed to eliminate that difference.

PRINCIPLES OF WRITING OUTCOMES

The following principles provide guidance in writing learner outcomes, as well as good and not so good examples of the different types of objectives and outcomes. While there usually is no single correct or incorrect way to make such statements, refining them helps the writer focus more clearly on the intent of the educational activity being planned. The following are 10 principles that meeting managers should keep in mind when developing or evaluating learner outcomes for their meetings. As each principle is presented, both an inappropriately stated outcome(s) will be provided followed by a more appropriately stated outcome(s).

Principle #1: The statement must be specific

The objective or outcome statement must be clear, concise, and specifically relate to one of the program's goal statements. It must include only one type of behavior the learner is expected to demonstrate with respect to one category of content. For example:

At the end of the session, the learner will be able to:

1. Develop and implement appropriate learner outcomes for his/her educational programs.
2. Write learner outcomes for specific content areas of the educational activity.

The first example incorporates two different performances, "develop" and "implement," while the second example is specific to behavior or performance. This allows for easier evaluation of the learning that occurs.

Principle #2: The statement must be measurable

The statement must be worded in such a manner that the behavioral change resulting from it is measurable after the educational program has occurred. This may not happen immediately after the learning has taken place; it may occur after attendees have gone back to their work environments, where they have put the new knowledge, attitude, or skill to a specific application.

At the end of the session, the learner will be able to:

1. Understand the principles of green meetings.
2. List four practices that make a meeting or event more environmentally responsible.

In the first instance, there is no way to measure an individual's understanding. "Understanding" is a vague word that defies evaluation. Granted, there will be evidence of understanding through discussion or other behaviors, but the second example clearly states what the individual must be able to do at the end of the educational activity: list the six principles.

Principle #3: The statement must be attainable

Within the given period of instruction, there is only so much that can be learned. Consideration of the entire educational experience should be the guide in developing statements of what can be achieved by the learner within the time allotted for learning.

At the end of the session, the learner will be able to:

1. Evaluate the global effects of green meetings.
2. Implement three green meeting practices at the next annual meeting.

It is unrealistic to expect that the learner will be able to evaluate a process that is explained in an introductory learning situation in a short amount of time. At the evaluation level, it is assumed that the individual has used the process enough to develop some expertise. This would not be possible after an introductory learning activity. However, the second statement reflects a more reasonable expectation of attainment following an introduction to the concept.

Principle #4: The statement must be relevant

Outcomes must be relevant to the material presented. An outcome that is not directly relevant will not be learned, especially if it is presented outside the context of the primary reason for attending the learning activity.

At the end of the session, the learner will be able to:

1. Discuss the basic concept of green meetings as applied to the meetings industry.

Principle #5: The statement must be timely

Attainability is closely aligned with timeliness. In constructing the program format and instructor objectives, care must be taken to allow a reasonable amount of time for the facilitator to meet the objectives. The attempt to carry out an overly complex program and/or allow only a minimal amount of time to implement it will result in frustration for the facilitator and, ultimately, create an impediment to learning. Likewise, the expectation that learners can digest a large amount of information in a short time fragments attention, decreases retention, and frustrates the learners.

At the end of the session, the learner will be able to:

1. Evaluate the impact of green meetings with regard to employee acceptability.
2. Explain three ways to reduce waste through recycling exhibit hall trash.

The first example involves a high-level learner outcome that could be attainable only after significant study and experience with using the concept in the organization. The duration of an initial workshop would not be long enough to cover the material in sufficient depth to permit the learner to meet the stated outcomes. By contrast, the second outcome is both timely and attainable in terms of learning the small segment of material presented.

S	Specific
M	Measurable
A	Attainable
R	Relevant
T	Timely

The first five principles presented—specific, measurable, attainable, relevant, and timely—can be summed up by the acronym SMART. The origin of the acronym is unknown, but it has been widely used in the management-by-objectives area. It is easy to remember and should be kept uppermost in the writer's mind when writing any goals, objectives and, in this case, learner outcomes. The following principles add depth to the understanding of the concept and serve as an additional guide when writing and refining learner outcomes.

Principle #6: The statement describes the end (product), not the means (process)

A learner outcome should be described in terms of the observable behavior the learner will be able to demonstrate as a result of the learning experience. The educational intent should be clear and succinct.

The following statements are examples of what the facilitator will do; each representing a teaching strategy, or instructor objective.

1. Talk about procedures for evacuating a ballroom.
2. Break through the self-limiting myths that drive so much of organizational life.
3. Teach the specifics of what is and is not negotiable.
4. Gain an awareness of green meeting objectives.
5. Diagram a classroom-style meeting room set-up.

The preceding examples are not measurable learner outcomes; they are instructional objectives, or what the instructor intends to present. By contrast, the corresponding statements that follow are worded in terms of the results of the instruction, or learner outcomes that are measurable.

1. Diagram the paths to evacuate 1,500 people from a ballroom using fire exits.
2. List six self-limiting myths that apply to organizational culture.
3. Differentiate the negotiable and non-negotiable points of a hotel contract.
4. Discuss the impact of reducing linen changes in guest rooms.
5. Diagram the layout of audiovisual equipment for a classroom set-up.

Principle #7: Write a separate statement for each outcome

Each outcome must be expressed in a separate statement that includes only one type of behavior the learner must demonstrate with respect to one category of content. As a general rule, the more statements written the better the chance for clarity. Include only one type of behavior the learner will be expected to demonstrate with respect to one category of content. Inclusion of more than one verb or action

---

Fast Facts

Focus on the Learner

What will the learner do to demonstrate achievement? Remember, an outcome is *not* a description of what the facilitator does or teaches.

in the statement will make it difficult for the learner to understand, and impossible for the meeting manager to evaluate the intended learner outcome. For example:

At the end of the session the learner should be able to:

1. Plan and conduct stimulating follow-up discussions and activities.
2. Compare and contrast various items that are appropriate for a formal food and beverage event.
3. Design and develop a learning activity for a sales meeting.

The preceding statements all contain two action verbs, each of which requires a separate skill from the learner. The following examples are six outcomes made from the three above. Note the degree of specificity that is achieved by wording them so that they reflect only one behavior each. Then consider the degree to which an evaluation of the skills of the learner following the attendance at the learning activity can take place.

At the end of the session the learner should be able to:

1. Plan a stimulating discussion on the topic of international meetings.
2. Select a facilitator who is capable of conducting a discussion group on the interpretation of scientific proceedings at the annual meeting.

Note that the learner, a meeting manager in this instance, will be able to put together a program that provides an opportunity for the attendees to have a stimulating discussion of the topic. Secondly, they will possess the skills necessary to select an instructor/facilitator to conduct the discussion group.

At the end of the session the learner should be able to:

1. Compare a list of foods to be served at a formal reception with those appropriate for an informal event.
2. Select food and beverage for an event, using specifications related to a reception.

In this instance, the requirement of the learner is to focus on specific foods and beverages for different types of events. Note that this particular learning activity was designed for individuals who are employed in a meeting department or a hotel catering operation.

At the end of the session the learner should be able to:

1. Synthesize the sales goals for the projected fiscal year as they relate to the current sales force.
2. Evaluate selling strategies from the perspective of timeliness to market segments prior to implementation.

The preceding two outcomes reflect the expected results of a sales meeting designed for upper management sales personnel. In this instance, additional business-oriented outcomes or objectives may be imposed on the individual when the learner hat comes off and the sales hat goes on. While the individuals may accomplish the outcomes, the manifestation of a change in behavior from the learning experience may require that a report or additional activities be employed to demonstrate learning and compliance with management directives (see Chapter 46).

Principle #8: Write a statement that reflects different levels of skill attainment

The phrasing of the outcome statement reflects the extent to which the learner is expected to have mastered the content or the attitude to be assumed.

At the end of the session the learner should be able to:

1. Name the three domains of learning.
2. Define "learner outcome."
3. Identify the fire exits on a ballroom layout.

Fast Facts

Verbs to Use

- List
- Define
- Accept
- Report
- Demonstrate
- Balance
- Support

Fast Facts

Verbs to Avoid[15]

- Know
- Understand
- Appreciate
- Comprehend
- Learn
- Enjoy
- Believe

Fast Facts

See Action Verbs[SM],
a handy resource
associated with this text
for selecting verbs within
each of the domains.

Each of the preceding outcomes is an example of level one in the hierarchy of learning. Now compare the following examples that require a higher level of knowledge and skill in fulfilling the expectations of the learner.

At the end of the session, the learner should be able to:

1. Write one learner outcome in each of the three domains of learning.
2. Evaluate the congruence of the learner outcome with the planned content.
3. Diagram the egress of people from the ballroom using all fire exits.

These are examples of learner outcomes intended for the advanced learner. They use higher-level action verbs and assume a significant amount of prior knowledge. The focus of this learning activity is informational, and the educational experience.

Principle #9: Start each statement with a concrete action verb

The use of action verbs makes a statement a more powerful communication tool. The learner outcome must specify a response on the part of the learner. Since that response must be observable, the verb must connote action. Therefore, the verbs listed in the box to the left should be avoided because they are not concrete action verbs and are open to many interpretations.

It is better to use concrete verbs that infer a specific action than it is to use ones that are not easily defined and are more difficult to evaluate retrospectively. Verbs to use, in Fast Facts, are specific and measurable.

Principle #10: Attitudes themselves cannot be measured; they can only be inferred from behavior

Some feel that affective domain objectives and learner outcomes are difficult to write, and others feel that they should not even be included. The challenge for the meeting manager and facilitator is to look for behaviors that demonstrate that there has been a change in the behavior of the learner. The instructional strategy for an orientation session of new employees may be expressed as follows:

At the end of the session, the learner should be able to:

1. Present the standards regarding how the company uniform is to be worn.

This statement sets forth an instructional strategy. It states what the facilitator will do during the orientation program. Consider the following outcome, which falls in the affective domain and would be difficult to evaluate other than through the employee's conformance to standards regarding how the company uniform is to be worn. The outcome that follows demonstrates a behavioral change.

At the end of the session, the learner should be able to:

2. Conform to dress code standards for wearing the company uniforms.

In this instance, the employee has accepted or changed their behavior as a result of the learning activity. The evaluation of such a learning activity would be that the employee is wearing the uniform in a manner that demonstrates acceptance and willingness to make changes.

A Contract with the Learner

The concept of a contract spells out the nature of the relationships among the instructor, the learner, and the meeting manager. One of the advantages of basing an educational program on a contract is that it requires greater precision, especially when increased competence is the primary focus. In such instances, the contractual relationship provides a basis for the attendee to reconcile his or her initiative and commitment with the expectations of others, such as employers and supervisors.

Influencing the Learner's Decision to Attend

Just as the meeting manager has gone to considerable effort to produce the educational activity and make the meeting happen, so the attendee goes through a similar process in deciding whether to attend. From the learner's perspective, Smith[16] has postulated several questions that the learner will ask himself or herself regarding attendance at an educational activity (see Fast Facts box at right).

Smith goes on to suggest that questions such as those that follow are legitimate concerns the learner should ponder before, and most certainly after, the educational experience:

- How will I know when I have achieved my goal?
- How can I measure the extent to which my goals and purposes have been achieved?

A contractual relationship is established when the educational program communicates the desired goals, objectives, and learner outcomes to the facilitator. Likewise, the meeting manager also lets the learner know about the educational activity that is being planned, including learner outcomes. The facilitator also should confer with the meeting manager to ensure that the planned content matches the stated goals, objectives, and outcomes.

Share Learner Outcomes with the Facilitator

Clearly stated learner outcomes are necessary to help convey the instructional intent to the facilitator so that he or she can decide what learning experiences to provide. Simply asking a facilitator to conduct a learning experience is not sufficient, especially when a specific agenda has been developed for a particular target audience. An overly casual approach can condemn an educational offering to failure. It fosters very loose control and almost no assurance that the attendees will realize what they set out to achieve.

At the other end of the informal-formal continuum is the written contract with the speaker or facilitator. Many meeting managers who use this approach find themselves with a contract that defines logistics like time, place, fees, and expenses. There usually is very little, if any, mention of the content to be delivered. Even when there is a content statement and some written objectives to guide the facilitator, they are seldom substantive.

By clearly defining the intent of instruction through the use of learner outcomes, the meeting manager provides valuable information to the facilitator, because such outcomes define the instructional strategies or methods to be used to achieve the learner outcomes.

Let the Prospective Attendee Know the Outcomes

Learner outcomes should be used as a tool to communicate with the potential attendee. They tell the attendee what he or she can expect to learn as a result of participating in the educational activity. The learner outcomes of the educational programming should be published in all promotional materials. This is especially important when a meeting has many options from which to choose. As a result of publishing the intended outcomes, the attendee will be able to make a more informed selection and is less likely to be disappointed.

The Role of a Learning Contract

In a learning contract, as described by Knowles,[17] the learner devises a document that states his or her expectations regarding the learning objectives, resources, strategies, proof of accomplishment, criteria, and ways of validating achievement.

In effect, the learner has made a "deal" with the instructor that certain things will take place. The more that is achieved, the higher the rating the attendee is likely to give the facilitator on the evaluation of the learning experience.

However, most adult learning situations, especially meetings, are not conducted in a controlled academic setting like the example suggests. Attendees at such meetings are not going to be able to develop a formal learning contract with the meeting manager and the facilitator. Or are they? In reality, their expectations are the same as if a formal contract existed. Time, money, and effort are all being expended. In some instances, an employer or some other sponsor is paying the fees, but often the meeting is an out-of-pocket expense for the learner.

The contractual relationship that exists between the meeting manager, the facilitator, and the learner becomes more meaningful when considered in these terms. This is the key process that separates a good educational experience from a bad one, and a worthwhile expenditure of time and money from a waste of time and money. It is critical that the educational experience achieves certain goals and objectives and that the learner realizes these benefits as a return on his or her investment. Then, at a minimum, a learner can say, "I learned this by attending." The service that was advertised has been delivered. A contract also demonstrates the accountability of the meeting manager and the facilitator to the learner. It is a yardstick that can be used to ensure that the facilitator delivers what was promised.[18]

Marketing the Educational Program Effectively

When reading attendee evaluations following an educational event, a meeting manager may sometimes wonder if all the attendees were in the same room, listening to the same presentation. While comments run the gamut from highly positive to completely negative, the most disconcerting are those that read: "This was not what I expected to learn. It was not what was advertised." The following excerpt from one facilitator's experience illustrates this phenomenon.

"I recently addressed a group of meeting professionals on the topic of speaker selection. My premise was that there is a whole design process that precedes the selection of speakers. I continued to present the process as I saw it. As the interaction among the program participants continued, there was obvious negativism in some comments. One participant flatly said that this was not what she wanted to learn. There was a definite disparity between her expectations and the actual content of the learning situation."

The disparity from this example could have been averted or minimized if the preliminary promotional materials had stated that participants would have an opportunity to learn particular segments of information by attending the session. If this has been done, then it is the responsibility of the learner to decide if he or she wants to learn what is advertised. At the same time, the instructor/facilitator should make every effort to deliver the material the adult learner came to receive so expectations can be fulfilled.

When outcomes for a learning situation are published in promotional materials, they become the expectations of the learner, who ultimately will decide whether he or she actually learned what was advertised in the advance promotion. Repeated and consistent fulfillment of this contract generates the best possible form of advertising—word of mouth. Once this has been achieved, the expectation level will rise, as will learner satisfaction. A previous satisfactory experience becomes the yardstick the learner uses to decide whether to attend another learning experience and evaluate its quality.

Using Outcomes as Benchmarks

Learner outcomes not only become the primary focus of evaluation, but also potent selling points in the marketing program. Promotion of successful learner outcomes in advertising will let learners know what they can expect to learn. It will whet their interest in the educational offering and, it is hoped, tip the scales in favor of attendance. Learner outcomes are themselves the agreement the meeting manager has made with the facilitator to ensure that the information advertised is presented to the attendees in the learning environment. They are an assurance of at least a minimum level of learning based on the published learner outcomes.

While there are those who may feel that writing outcomes is too cumbersome, time consuming, or not part of their job, clearly developed and written outcomes that are communicated to both facilitators and learners become the benchmark for the evaluations made at the conclusion of the learning event, as well as the basis for marketing future programs. If what was advertised was in fact delivered, the contractual agreement with the learner has been fulfilled. It is then the responsibility of the learner to incorporate the knowledge, attitudes, and/or skills he or she learned into his or her work environment or personal life.

What If the Learning Contract Is Not Fulfilled?

The meeting manager's entry into a contractual relationship with the facilitator and the learner does have its ramifications, especially if the learner's degree of satisfaction with the experience is not fulfilled. In the interest of avoiding such a shortfall, here are some thought-evoking questions to be directed at the organization when developing the educational program:

1. What level of sophistication is the speaker to address?
2. Is it more important for the speaker to be a content expert or a polished presenter?
3. Will the professional speaker deliver a canned speech and fail to personalize it to his or her audience?
4. Has sufficient information been provided to the speaker to enable him or her to prepare and deliver what has been advertised?
5. Has a needs assessment been completed so that the target audience's wants and needs are known?

These and other aspects are extremely important areas to address. The satisfaction of learners with a speaker becomes an influential factor in future speaker selection decisions. Competition among speakers is keen, and those who are successful will continue to flourish, while those who are mediocre will either drop out or be unable to get bookings.

SUMMARY

The result of decades of research and discussion among educational theorists, the classification system presented in this chapter has relevance for meeting managers as they develop programs, educational events, and learning activities for adult learners. When it is used as a guide, it can enhance the quality of the program design and the development of programming. Such a system can help meeting managers to focus on being conduits for learning. Effective use of the system adds strength and direction to the programs that are being planned and managed.

Learner outcomes should be written in the future tense as a continual reminder that the outcome will be realized only after the learning has taken place. Use of the phrase "will be able to" forces the writer to structure the outcome in terms of performance after the educational event.

Reviewing the attributes and guidelines of writing objectives and learner outcomes before developing the statements will assist meeting managers in focusing on the intent of the proposed educational programming. After learner outcomes have been developed a few times, writing them will soon become second nature and they will flow more easily.

When writing outcomes, it is always helpful to have another individual or group ask pointed questions about the intent and the scope of the outcome statement. A quality control element will emerge, and the words will become clearer, not only to the meeting manager but also to the ultimate customer, the learner.

An outcome-based educational format enables the potential attendee to be aware of the program's objectives or learner outcomes in advance. The attendee will know what to expect from the speakers from having received a list of outcomes to be covered in their presentations. At the conclusion of each learning activity, he or she will be asked to evaluate the presentation on the basis of how well the speaker met the learner outcomes.

Learner outcomes focus on what the attendee is going to learn. They form a "contract" between the learner and the program planner and let the potential attendee know what he or she is going to receive from the program before a decision is made to attend. Each outcome must be stated in terms of what the attendee should be able to do at the end of the presentation or learning activity.

The concept of a learner contract is superficially simple and straightforward. The key to a successful program is the degree to which the learner's expectations of the learning situation are fulfilled. The use of outcome statements as a beginning and end for the specific learning relationship can set a meeting manager apart from his or her competitors.

REFERENCES

A portion of this chapter was extrapolated from: Ramsborg, G. C. (1995). *Objectives to outcomes: Your contract with the learner* (2nd ed.). Birmingham, Alabama: Professional Convention Management Association.

1. Bloom, B. S. (1956). *Taxonomy of educational objectives, handbook I: The cognitive domain*. New York: David McKay Co Inc.

2. Krathwohl, D. R., Bloom, B. S., & Bertram, B. M. (1973). *Taxonomy of educational objectives, the classification of educational goals. Handbook II: Affective domain*. New York: David McKay Co., Inc.

3. Simpson, E. J. (1969). The classification of educational objectives, psychomotor domain. *Illinois teacher of home economics*, 9 (10), 110–114.

4. Harrow, A. J. (1972). *A taxonomy of the psychomotor domain*. New York: David McKay.

5. Anderson, L. W., & Krathwohl, D. R. (Eds.). (2001). *A taxonomy for learning, teaching, and assessing: A revision of Bloom's taxonomy of educational objectives*. New York: Longman.

6. Kinney, L. B. (1948). Operational plan in the classroom. *School and Society,* 68, 145–148.

7. Travers, R. M. W. (1950). *How to make achievement tests*. New York: Odyssey Press.

8. Bloom, B. S. (1956). *Taxonomy of educational objectives, handbook I: The cognitive domain*. New York: David McKay Co Inc.

9. Krathwohl, D. R., et al. (1964). Taxonomy of educational objectives, handbook II: Affective domain. New York: David McKay.

10. Gronlund, N. E. (1985). *Stating objectives for classroom instruction* (3rd. ed). New York: Macmillan Publishing Co., Inc.

11. Bolin, A., Khramtsova, I., & Saarnio, D. (2005). Using student journals to stimulate authentic *learning*: Balancing Bloom's cognitive and affective domains. *Teaching of psychology, 32* (3), 154-159.

12. Pipe, P. (1975). *Objectives—tools for change.* Belmont, CA: David S. Lake Publishers.

13. Passig, D. (2003). A taxonomy of future higher thinking skills. *Informatica,* 2(1), 11-35.

14. Kizlick, B. (2005). Definitions of behavioral verbs for learning objectives. Retrieved April 21, 2006 from http://www.adprima.com/verbs.html.

15. Kruse, K. (2004). How to write great learning objectives. Retrieved April 29, 2006 from http://www.e-learningguru.com/articles/art3_4.htm.

16. Smith, R. M. (1982). *Learning how to learn: Applied theory for adults.* Chicago: Follett Publishing Company.

17. Knowles, M. S. (1986). *Using learner contracts.* San Francisco: Jossey-Bass Publishers.

18. Kealey, D., Protheroe, D., MacDonald, D. & Vulpe, T. (2003). Instituting a competency-based training design and evaluation. *Performance improvement,* 42 (5), 8-35.

KEY TERMS

Affective domain	Evaluation	Outcomes
Analysis	Cognitive domain	Psychomotor domain
Application	Knowledge	Stakeholders
Comprehension	Learner outcomes	Synthesis
Domains of learning		

COMPELLING QUESTIONS FOR CONSIDERATION

1. Explain the use of the domains of learning for the meeting manager, even though he/she may not be responsible or involved in developing the educational content.

2. What role do learner outcomes have in providing a strong educational program?

3. Explain the process of writing a learner outcome using the ABC mnemonic.

4. Write three learner outcomes that focus on three different levels of learning, and that use the SMART principle.

5. What steps can be taken to ensure the content advertised is actually delivered?

6. Discuss the meeting manager's role in implementing the educational program, e.g., explore matching content with room set-ups. How would you go about ensuring the learning environment is conducive to the learning that is supposed to take place?

CHAPTER 21

HIRING SPEAKERS AND WORKING WITH SPEAKER BUREAUS

Brian D. Palmer
PRESIDENT
NATIONAL SPEAKERS BUREAU

Donald C. Jenkins, CASE
ACCOUNT EXECUTIVE
NATIONAL SPEAKERS BUREAU

LEARNER OUTCOMES

When the reader has completed reading this chapter, he/she should be able to . . .

1 Recognize the importance a speaker has on the success of a meeting.

2 Identify details that must be included in a speaker's contract or offer letter.

3 Discuss ways to affirm, confirm, and reaffirm all arrangements made with speakers.

4 List steps that help prepare a speaker for a meeting.

> Annual meetings for associations have struggled to maintain audiences in recent years. Having the promise of something memorable taking place is one of the ways to promote these meetings.
>
> *Rand A. Baldwin, CAE*
> *President*
> *Aluminum Extruders Council*

INTRODUCTION

The importance a speaker plays in the success of your meeting cannot be overstated. A report conducted by the MPI Foundation titled *Making Meetings Work: An Analysis of Corporate Meetings*[1] showed that well-prepared speakers ranked number one among attendees on a list of key meeting success factors. Similarly, another report conducted by the MPI Foundation, this one based on association annual meetings and titled *Who Attends Association Annual Meetings...and Why?*[2], revealed that quality of speakers ranked second with association members when deciding whether to attend annual meetings.

This chapter presupposes that you have clearly defined the purpose of the meeting, developed goals, written objectives, chosen a site, and set a schedule. Once these elements are in place, selecting the right speakers will be an important key to the success of your meeting.

FINDING A SPEAKER

When it comes time to develop your program content, there are several variables and methods to consider in conducting your search and identifying the right speaker. For larger meetings where multiple speakers are presenting, a meeting manager may choose to start the search by sending out a speaker Request for Proposal (RFP) or issue a Call for Papers. A speakers bureau may be another option and can help your selection process by narrowing the search and screening potential speakers. Additionally, your informal network can also be an effective resource. Consider maintaining an ongoing physical or electronic file to collect information on speakers you have encountered and found to be effective.

If your meeting requires a large number of speakers, you may need to use a Document Management System. A document management system (DMS) refers to a system by which a paper is received, edited, reviewed, scheduled, and assigned a room for presentation at a convention or meeting. A DMS can be internal, database-driven, or web-based. Some applications on the market allow for some customization specific to an organization's needs.

TYPES OF SPEAKERS

Plan to use different presenters to achieve varying objectives of the program. A motivational speaker may be an excellent choice for a keynote presentation, however, such an individual often will not be able to provide the detailed content necessary for directed learning and problem solving. Consider each presentation in terms of the goals and objectives of the session. Consider also the type and timing of the session. A general session keynote often calls for a different type of speaker than a breakout or training session. Time of day also will play a part in your speaker selection. Will the session occur before or after lunch? Will food or alcohol be served? Is the session late in the day or the last session after several days of intense training? In cases like these a less content-heavy, more entertaining speaker might be most appropriate. While one type of presentation might call for a high-energy, dynamic professional speaker, another might need to allow for PowerPoint® projection and note-taking.

Professional Speakers

A professional speaker is a speaker who is paid a fee for performances and makes a living by presenting information to various organizations. A professional speaker is typically a polished, effective orator, who is capable of making a presentation in a style that satisfies the audience's need for information, advice, or entertainment. A professional speaker may be a subject expert and/or an expert speaker. The challenge is to make sure that each professional speaker you choose is both.

To lay the foundation for an excellent event, here are some steps to consider before retaining a speaker.

- Verify references. Ask permission to call a speaker's most recent clients; then ask those clients for additional references. If you are calling people based on reference letters, make sure the letters are no more than 6 months old.

- Arrange to see the speaker deliver a live presentation. If possible, the presentation should be for an audience somewhat similar to yours.

- If seeing a live program is not possible, view a video of a live presentation. If possible, the video should be of an entire program. Short preview videos typically show only presentation highlights.

- Schedule a conference call with the speaker. Most professional speakers are willing to discuss the event with you to help determine whether they are a fit. Clearly define and discuss your group, your objectives for the meeting and the session, your expectations of the speaker, the speaker's availability, and any financial requirements. Most professional speakers will be direct and tell you if they feel their presentation is not right for your meeting. High-profile speakers may not be willing to participate in a conference call either prior to or after being confirmed for your meeting. When dealing with high profile presenters, you might be better served working with an agent or speakers bureau.

Do not assume that a professional speaker can present on any subject desired for your meeting. If you request a topic other than the speaker's usual material, before signing a contract ask for outlines and, if possible, written text to be sure the topic will be covered appropriately.

Volunteer Speakers

Volunteer speakers are typically not professional speakers. They could be members of a professional organization, or somehow linked to it, and are asked to speak as content experts. As with professional speakers, get written confirmation of any agreements with volunteer speakers. The same information included in the contract or letter of agreement for professional speakers should be spelled out for volunteers. This ensures that both you and the speaker are operating under the same assumptions regarding the presentation expectations and expenses.

Avoid the tendency of exempting volunteer speakers from established deadlines or requirements you have set for your program. Handle the arrangements and assignments for volunteer speakers and hold them to the same standards that you would someone you are paying. Better events will result.

Speaker Bureaus

An alternative to searching for speakers directly is to work with a speaker bureau. A speaker bureau serves as a professional broker or agent for many speakers. The bureau can facilitate finding appropriate speakers for your meeting and can often provide videos of speakers for your review. The bureau can also professionally handle details and contracts for speaker engagements. Most bureaus have developed large databases and personal knowledge of specifics regarding hundreds to thousands of speakers, and because bureaus are generally paid a commission by the speakers and do not charge those planning the meeting a fee, they may serve as a great, no-cost resource.

Put It Into Perspective

How much lead time should you have to hire speakers? As those that speak are individuals and approach the marketplace in a unique way, it is difficult to draw any hard and fast conclusions. The points below are intended to serve as guidelines:

- Associations book most speakers between 4 and 7 months prior their event. The range for corporations is 2 to 4 months prior.
- The honorarium a speaker requests is often a function of demand. The higher the fee, the greater the demand, so consider planning earlier for such people. Invite these people 6 to 12 months in advance.
- A corollary to the above scenario is the group of desirable potential speakers who prefer not to plan too far ahead. These speakers tend to have acute responsibilities that are constantly evolving. If someone on their staff suggests an invitation is premature, ask for a specific, appropriate date.
- The pool of potential speakers is large. High quality alternatives are generally available at a moment's notice.

When working with a speaker bureau, the following are some factors to consider:

- How long has the bureau been in business?
- Is the bureau reputable? Are references available for both the bureau and the speakers?
- Can you contact speakers directly before making a decision?
- How are payments made? If payments are made up-front, then the money should be placed in a special account until after the presentation, in case there is a problem such as a cancellation.
- Is it a full-service bureau that will handle all arrangements and payments, or will you have to deal directly with speakers after the contract is signed and the deposit is paid?
- Is the bureau's contract clear? Be sure you understand the cancellation clauses. Look for other areas of the contract that you might need to modify.
- Ask the speaker bureau how they may differ from other bureaus.
- Does this speaker bureau broker speakers, or is it a lecture agency that promotes specific speakers?

CONTRACTING/BOOKING A SPEAKER

Offer Letter (Affirm)

When you have verified references and decided to hire a speaker, prepare an offer letter. This is the negotiation phase of the agreement. You may prefer to have a speaker bureau assist with the details and specifics of the offer. The offer letter should cover all the details of the arrangement, including details regarding presentation/performance, compensation and expenses, termination, intellectual property and risk management.

Do not confuse an offer letter with an agreement or contract. Though an offer letter, if it is written as such, may be considered binding once agreed to and signed by all parties, it is not uncommon for an offer to go back and forth unsigned once or twice before all parties have agreed to the terms. Once the terms of the offer have been agreed upon and the offer letter has been signed by both the meeting manager and the speaker, an agreement or contract is written.

Speaker Compensation and Benefits

Most professional speakers choose not to negotiate or make exceptions to their fee schedule. However, there may be circumstances that allow for a reduced fee. Some professional speakers offer a local fee if the meeting is within driving distance from their home or may offer a discount for charities and non-profits. If you wish to negotiate a fee reduction, think about what your organization can offer the speaker in return. Occasionally simply allowing the speaker to sell products is enough incentive for a lower fee, provided the audience is large enough. Ad space or a series of articles by the speaker may also be offered in the organization's publication. Other options include complimentary conference registration, extra nights at the meeting hotel, travel for the speaker's guest, a free booth at the trade show, or guaranteed dates for future programs. Fee reductions are often given for booking multiple programs throughout the year.

For volunteer speakers, some organizations do not offer any reduction in registration fees or room rate, nor do they provide any reimbursement for travel. Other organizations provide some form of consideration for volunteer speakers. Whatever your organization decides to do, be sure the terms are stated in the contract or letter of agreement. As you would with professional speakers, indicate who will handle airline and hotel reservations, as well as other details, for volunteers.

Speakers who are government officials are subject to a variety of rules which often govern whether they may charge a fee and, if so, how much. Many request a donation to a favorite charity in lieu of payment. Contracts with government speakers often include clauses that allow last-minute cancellation because of their official duties. Speakers from the news media may also require such cancellation clauses so that they are free to cover breaking news events. These clauses often allow a speaker to cancel as little as 24 hours before the event.

Speaker Contract (Confirm)

The speaker agreement or contract contains all the stipulations agreed to in the offer letter. It must be countersigned and it must indicate that it memorializes the offer letter. The speaker contract is the business side of speaker selection. All changes to the contract must be agreed to by all parties and should be in writing (see Put It Into Practice).

Final Details (Reaffirm)

As the meeting date approaches, communicate again with your speakers to ensure everyone is on the same page. A good way to do this is with a cover letter attached to a final details form. The cover letter is a good place to again express your group's anticipation of the presenter's presentation and remind the speaker of any key points that are to be discussed in or omitted from the presentation. A final details document or reminder is a clear, concise document that contains confirmation of all the information the speaker will need on site.

Remember that changes to the original agreement must be agreed to by all parties. The final details should not contain any surprises, although you might highlight changes agreed to along the way.

Thank-You Letter

Event organizers customarily acknowledge or thank those that speak at their meetings with a letter. This should be done approximately 7 days following the conclusion of your event and should accurately reflect your impression of the presentation. As speakers often use these letters to market themselves, the accuracy can guard your credibility and that of your organization. Be prepared to be asked for such a letter. If you are not comfortable sending one for any reason, you are welcome to decline. These letters are not required. Such letters can also serve as a reminder to send expense invoices or tie up any loose ends related to the meeting.

To show the organization's appreciation, you may choose to provide speakers with commemorative photos or videos of the event, or other tokens of appreciation. Speakers also appreciate receiving copies of any evaluations conducted of their presentations. Be sure to copy the speaker bureau, if applicable, on thank you letters and evaluations.

SPEAKER PREPARATION AND MANAGEMENT

Since a key factor in the success of a meeting is well-prepared speakers, you should help the speaker be as prepared as possible.

Conference Calls

The process of preparing speakers begins at the first conference call prior to contracting the speaker. As previously mentioned, the meeting manager should define the group in great detail, discuss the objectives of the meeting, and clearly explain how the speaker will contribute. Have another conference call with the speaker approximately two to four weeks out from your event to refresh his/her memory of your group, your expectations, and provide any additional details that will help the presenter gain a better understanding of the audience and to customize their talk. If the speaker has a pre-program questionnaire, complete and return the questionnaire to the speaker, or their designated representative, prior to the conference call. This will lead to a more productive call by answering basic questions and allow more time for discussion about the meeting and what is expected of the speaker. Also, be sure all speakers have been provided the same conference brochures and notices sent to attendees. This will help speakers get a better feel for the audience and who else is presenting at the conference. Inform speakers of how many attendees have registered for their presentation so they will be properly prepared for the number in attendance. Topics to discuss with the presenter on the conference call might include:

- Why he/she was selected to speak at this meeting
- Audience demographics
- Education level and personality of the audience
- Current industry trends or hot button issues
- Topics, issues, or language best avoided
- Key terms, industry terminology, or keywords that will help a speaker customize their presentation
- Programming elements which will proceed or follow the speaker
- Confirm how the presenter prefers their name to appear on the conference badge or materials
- How they would like to be introduced. Most speakers will have a prepared introduction.
- Information on the sponsor, if applicable

Most professional speakers are well accustomed to conference calls and very proficient in asking the questions that allow them to best craft their speech. In addition to conversations with those responsible for planning the meeting, the speaker may request to interview a handful of attendees or association members to gain a greater understanding of the typical audience member.

Fast Facts

The number one area of speaker criticism is the degree to which a speaker personalized his/her presentation or made it relevant to the group and event. Interestingly, the number one topic of speaker praise has to do with the same thing. Studies have clearly shown that well-prepared speakers are one of the key determinants of attendee satisfaction. The lesson: Establish a process that emphasizes and helps make certain those you engage can and will thoughtfully account for your group and event in their presentation.

Put It Into Practice

Checklist of Considerations for Speaker and Entertainer Contracts

When creating/reviewing a speaker or entertainer contract, planners should ensure the following items have been considered and properly addressed in the contract.

Presentation/Performance

- Does the contract include the name and description of the presentation/performance to be given?
- Is the date, arrival time, starting time, duration, and location properly stated in the contract?
- Are any other obligations on the speaker/performer clearly defined in the contract, e.g., mandatory dress rehearsal, attendance at a post-program reception?
- Are due dates for handouts and other materials clearly defined in the contract?
- Does the contract address the environment and equipment for the program, e.g., an appropriately lighted, well-heated or cooled, location, with an adequate audio-visual system, maintained and operated as required by law?
- Does the contract state that Speaker/Performer shall make a conscientious effort to communicate and cooperate with the Sponsor's contact person regarding customizing the presentation/performance to the Sponsor's goals?
- Does the contract state that the material presented by Speaker shall be timely and shall be presented to the best of Speaker's ability? Often these types of provisions also state that a Speaker may refer to notes during the presentation, but shall not read any substantial portion of the presentation from a prepared text.
- Does the contract require the Sponsor to provide the Speaker with written evaluations concerning Speaker's presentation?

Compensation and Expenses

- Does the contract clearly definite the fee to be paid to the speaker/entertainer including any deposit or prepayments? Some contracts state the final payment is due upon completion of the presentation/performance.
- Does the contract specify how the Speaker/Performer's expenses are to be handled, i.e., who makes the travel, hotel and ground transportation arrangements, whether there are any limitations on class of air travel, what the reimbursement policy is relative to receipts and expense reports?

- Is there a provision stating that the Speaker/Performer is acting as an independent contractor and is solely responsible for any and all federal, state and local taxes and fees imposed in connection with Speaker/Performer's services, and the procurement of and payment for any and all necessary licenses and insurance?

Termination

- Does the contract include a provision regarding termination? The contract might state that neither party may terminate the agreement or it might state that either party may terminate the agreement with a certain amount of notice.
- Does the contract address the issue of whether the Speaker/Performer, their bureau or agency will, upon termination of the Agreement by Speaker/Performer, assist the Sponsor in securing an alternate speaker? Some contracts also require the Speaker/Performer or their bureau or agency to pay the costs of notifying attendees of the new speaker/performer.
- Does the contract address a termination due to an Act of God or other force beyond the parties' control? Generally this type of provision allows the parties to terminate the contract without liability and requires that any deposits be refunded to the Sponsor.

Intellectual Property

- Does the contract state that the Sponsor can use the Speaker/Performer's name, picture, and title for purposes of promoting the program/performance?
- Does the Sponsor have the right to audiotape, videotape or photograph the presentation/performance? If so, are their limitations on the use/distribution of the reproduction? Is the author granting ownership in the work (assignment) or granting permission to use/distribute the work (license)?
- Does the contract address the Speaker/Performer's use of the Sponsor's name and logo? Generally this type of permission grants the Speaker/Performer the option to use the Sponsor's name and logo so long as their use is limited to promotion of the program/performance.

Risk Management

- Does the contract indicate that because the Speaker/Performer is an independent contractor, the Sponsor shall not be liable for any acts, omissions, statements or commitments of Speaker/Performer, nor shall either of them be liable for any injury or loss suf-

(continued)

Put It Into Practice, continued

fered by Speaker/Performer or those claiming through Speaker/Performer?

- Does the contract include the Speaker/Performer's representation and warranty that none of the material contained in the presentation/performance to be made by Speaker/Performer will violate or infringe upon the proprietary or statutory rights of any person or entity, or constitute an invasion of anyone's right to privacy, and that Speaker/Performer shall not libel, slander or defame anyone in making the presentation/performance? These types of provision typically also state that in the event Speaker/Performer is alleged to have engaged in any conduct which, if true, would constitute a breach of such warranty, Speaker/Performer shall defend, indemnify and hold the Sponsor, its officers, directors, employees and agents, and each of them, harmless from any and all claims or causes of action, including court costs and attorneys' fees, resulting from such conduct.

Miscellaneous

- Does the contract prohibit the Speaker/Performer from assigning his/her rights and duties under the contract without the Sponsor's prior written consent?
- Does the contract state that it may be amended only in writing and signed by both the Sponsor and Speaker/Performer?
- Does the contract include a provision which states that a waiver by either party of any term or condition of the contract or any breach of the contract shall not constitute a waiver of any other term or condition or subsequent breach of any term or condition of the contract?
- Does the contract include a provision which states that the contract constitutes the entire understanding of the parties and supersedes and replaces all agreements, oral or written, between Sponsor and Speaker/Performer relating to the presentation/performance?

©Copyright 2005. Howe & Hutton, Ltd. used with permission.

AUDIOVISUAL REQUESTS

The quality of a presentation is directly related to the quality of the A/V equipment and materials utilized by the speaker. Improve speaker performance by providing guidelines on the selection and preparation of A/V materials. Coordinating speaker requests for equipment and materials may be facilitated by utilizing a standard speaker A/V request form for audiovisual equipment.

Selecting Audiovisual Formats

Each type of media has advantages and disadvantages. Consult with the speaker and your A/V technician regarding the best A/V setup to accomplish your goals. Consider the type of presentation, the presenter, the size and setup of the room, and the cost of the equipment. While an exciting audiovisual display is impressive, consider the cost to effectiveness ratio. While the audiovisual component is crucial to the effectiveness of the presentation, for some speakers it may have little to no effect on the quality of the talk.

Audiovisual Materials Preparation

Established standards for the preparation of visual materials have been developed, tested, and proven over a number of years by professional societies and manufacturers of projection equipment and video. Those that affect the quality of the projected image are based on these key principles of good projection:

- Size and spacing of visual elements
- Contrast in the projected images
- Brightness of the projected image
- Size of the projected image

By providing guidelines in the preparation of A/V materials, you can help improve the speaker's quality and effectiveness. Inform the speaker of the size and setup of the meeting room, anticipated attendance, and any unusual features of the projection facilities as early as possible.

Some generally accepted guidelines regarding visual materials, such as overheads, slides, and Power Point presentations:

- Only one thought or concept per screen.
- Follow the six-by-six rule; no more than six words per line, no more than six lines per screen.
- Graphs work better than tables when projected.
- Use uppercase and lowercase letters in the text of visual materials.

Speaker Requirements

The outcome of an efficient speaker communication system involves not only accurate provision of equipment, but also cost-effective management.

- Make early contact with speakers
- Provide a timeline of specific deadlines and milestones for your event
- Develop a good A/V request form
- Follow up on the return of forms
- Send copies of the forms, or an order summary, to the A/V contractor
- Confirm speakers' requests

The A/V request form is the foundation for providing the correct equipment and should be separate from other speaker forms such as registration and housing. Be sure to include the option of indicating, "No A/V equipment required," since a lack of response does not necessarily mean that equipment is not needed. Make sure that you include only the equipment your group is willing to provide.

Sending an A/V confirmation to each speaker is critical. Along with a reiteration of the equipment needed, use this communication tool to remind speakers of the availability of the speaker preparation room, as well as an update on any schedule or program changes.

Handouts

Handout materials are an excellent complement to any presentation. Handouts may contain a summary of main points, conclusions, references, case studies or examples, graphs or tables, or any additional information that will support or reinforce the presentation.

For larger conventions and meetings, meeting managers may require speakers to be responsible for the duplication, delivery, and any costs related to the production of handout materials for their presentations. If this is the case, inform speakers of the anticipated size of their audiences, so they can prepare accordingly. In many cases, however, the organization is responsible for the duplication, delivery, and cost of handout production, as well as the development of the materials. If speakers plan to provide handouts, be sure to get digital copies in advance for reproduction. As an incentive for speakers to provide their handouts in a timely manner, indicate that presenters will have to make their own reproduction arrangements after the deadline.

When preparing handout materials, consider how they will be used during the meeting. Handouts that will be used as a workbook during the conference may require a different format than handouts intended as a post-conference reference manual. When setting deadlines for handouts, consider editing and proofreading requirements, the complexity of production, and printing time.

Fast Facts

The most frequent criticism of speakers by attendees of PCMA's 50th Annual Meeting was the lack of handout materials provided by the speakers.

Speakers increasingly allow their handouts to be accessed via the conference website following the conference, or in a CD provided for attendees during registration or sent to attendees after the meeting. If you are planning to make the materials available to attendees in one of these or a similar format, obtain written permission from the speaker.

Copyright Waiver/Conflict of Interest

If your organization plans to make audio or video recordings of presentations, either by professional or volunteer speakers, you must obtain signed copyright waivers from each participant—even if your organization is not planning on selling the tapes. If sessions are to be taped, it is important to clearly communicate this to all presenters well in advance of the meeting. Some presenters prefer not to be taped and any miscommunication in this area could cause a cancellation. If you plan to sell the tapes, speakers may wish to negotiate for a percentage of the profits. Arrange all such details in advance. Often in return for the right to tape the presentation, the speaker will request a copy of the video (generally in a beta or digital format) and may use this footage for their preview videos.

If a speaker's remarks will be edited for publication in a newsletter or magazine, the speaker must grant specific written authorization for such publication and should guarantee that materials used in the presentation are his or her own original work. In addition, ensure that permissions have also been received for any portion of the speaker's material restricted by a copyright held by another person. Before implementing a copyright waiver form, have a copyright attorney review a draft of the form.

You may also wish to protect the audience from speakers who may use the podium to offer opinions, value judgments, or endorsements of specific products or services described in the presentation. A conflict-of-interest statement asks the speaker to identify any conflicts of interest that may be relevant to the presentation.

Put It Into Practice

Who Owns It?

Consistently, the issue of intellectual property is an ongoing concern for the meeting professional. Well-drafted and carefully crafted contracts outlining who owns what will go a long way in alleviating that burden, not to mention clarify who is responsible for somebody who goes astray and unlawfully infringes someone else's property rights. Make sure you do own the right to record or reproduce the program materials and use it in any media you might want to employ, such as print, electronic or otherwise. Following is some language to consider including in that contract.

Warranty and hold harmless. *The Speaker represents and warrants that none of the material contained in the Presentation will violate or infringe upon the proprietary or statutory rights of any person or entity; or constitute an invasion of anyone's right to privacy; and that the Speaker shall not libel, slander or defame anyone in making the Presentation.*

In the event of a breach of this warrant, the Speaker shall defend, indemnify and hold the Client, all of its officers, directors, employees and agents, and each of them, harmless from any and all claims or causes of action, including court costs and attorneys' fees, resulting from such breach. The Client shall select legal counsel acceptable to this.

By signing such a statement, the presenter agrees that any materials he or she uses are not otherwise copyrighted, nor do they infringe upon someone else's intellectual property rights unless they have been given specific written authorization to use the material.

Additionally, the contract should specifically state that *the speaker or author will not defame or otherwise castigate someone else. Such actions could lead to liability, since the sponsor could reasonably be considered a "publisher" of the defamation.*

Copyright 2005. Howe & Hutton, Ltd. Used with Permission.

Speaker Host

If the staffing of your event allows, consider assigning a host to each speaker. For a high profile speaker, you may want to arrange for the host to meet with the speaker at the airport. If this is not possible, leave a message with the speaker's registration packet as to who the host is and where the host may be reached. Many speakers, even volunteers (unless they are members of the organization), are not comfortable in a room full of people they do not know. Have someone whose responsibility it is to introduce the speaker to the organization and to give some insight into the group. Speakers may be more comfortable with an audience when they have met some attendees socially before the program.

The host should also be able to handle last-minute needs of the speaker, such as extra copies of handouts, changes in room setup, and audiovisual (A/V) equipment testing. After the program, the host can ensure that the speaker has transportation and is properly thanked.

If the event will involve special staging, be sure that both professional and volunteer speakers have seen the set and have the opportunity to rehearse before the program. Introduce speakers to the technician who will be working the room so they know who to see about equipment problems. Even if the host will be present for the entire presentation, the speaker and the A/V technician should meet prior to the session.

You or the host should also discuss lighting with each speaker. Bright lights on stage make the speaker look good to the audience, but they inhibit a speaker's ability to see and, in some cases, relate to the audience. A speaker's on-stage request to adjust house lights can be distracting to the audience and embarrassing when there is a delay.

If you do not have the staff to assign a host to each speaker, try to arrange a time to meet the speaker prior to his/her presentation to discuss any last minute needs. Show the speaker the room, the set-up, and explain the flow of the program to include how the speaker will be introduced. An alternative to the use of a host is to assign room monitors to each room to handle the speakers needs prior to, during, and following the presentation.

Speaker Preparation Room

Depending on the number of speakers and the size of the event, a meeting manager may want to provide speakers with the courtesy of a speakers' lounge (also known as a speakers' ready room) in which they can relax before their presentations. The room should be quiet and comfortable. The speaker preparation area can be a separate room, a section of the meeting management office, a section of the A/V equipment room, or a room primarily designed as a speaker lounge with an area draped off (for privacy) for speaker preparation. A room dedicated only to speaker preparation works best for meetings with a large number of speakers. If the budget permits, have an A/V specialist available in the speaker preparation room at all times.

Summary

A contract or letter of agreement is a necessity for professional speakers and advisable for volunteer speakers as well. The contract should include the details of all arrangements made between the speaker and the organization.

A speaker bureau can facilitate finding appropriate speakers for your meeting, assist with drafting professional agreements, and take care of the details surrounding your speaker. Speaker bureaus are paid a commission by the speaker, not those planning the event.

The basic rules for communicating with speakers are affirm, confirm, reaffirm, and thank. Speakers should also be provided with the same publicity and materials that attendees receive. Schedule a conference call with the speakers to ensure they have the information needed to prepare the best possible presentation for your audience. If you plan to record a presentation or publish a speaker's remarks, the speaker must first grant specific written authorization.

The quality of a presentation may be related to the quality of A/V equipment and materials utilized by the speaker. You can help improve speaker performance by providing guidelines on the selection and preparation of A/V materials and coordinating requests for equipment and materials.

REFERENCES

1. Webb, W. (1998). Making meetings work: An analysis of corporate meetings in the U.S. Dallas: MPI Foundation. Retrieved March 6, 2006 from http://www.mpi-web.org/CMS/MPIweb/MPILandingPages/PublicationResearchLanding.aspx.

2. Trombino, J. (2000). Who attends association annual meetings? Dallas: MPI Foundation. Retrieved March 6, 2006 from http://www.mpiweb.org/CMS/MPIweb/MPILandingPages/PublicationResearchLanding.aspx.

KEY TERMS

Agreements	Final details	Speaker A/V request form
Cancellation clause	Host	Speaker bureau
Conference call	Keynote	Speakers' lounge
Conflict-of-interest statement	Offer letter	Speakers' ready room
Copyright waiver	Presenter	Volunteer speaker
	Professional speaker	

COMPELLING QUESTIONS FOR CONSIDERATION

1. What factors should be considered prior to deciding on the type of presenter to have at your meeting?

2. What steps can be taken to ensure the speaker is appropriate for your meeting?

3. What items should be discussed during a conference call with the speaker prior to the event? What purpose does this serve?

4. Should a contract or letter-of-agreement be prepared for volunteer speakers, as well as professional speakers? Why or why not?

5. If the organization is only planning to videotape the presentation of a volunteer speaker for the sole use of organization employees, is written permission from the speaker necessary? Why or why not?

CONTRIBUTOR

Kristin Crane
Manager, Education
Professional Convention Management Association

CHAPTER 22

MULTICULTURAL ASPECTS OF MEETINGS

Sue Tinnish
PRINCIPAL
S.E.A.L. INC.

LEARNER OUTCOMES

When the reader has completed reading this chapter, he/she should be able to . . .

1 Explain the characteristics of culture.

2 Identify the concepts and issues related to cross-cultural communications.

3 Analyze how culturally diverse audiences impact meetings.

4 Recognize the communication differences in dealing with international attendees and business partners.

5 Assess cross-cultural communication challenges and roadblocks.

6 Implement strategies to avoid miscommunication due to cultural differences in meetings.

> No culture can live if it attempts to be exclusive.
>
> *Mahatma Gandhi*

OVERVIEW

Multicultural awareness is a reality of our global economy. Today's world is a global world with historical barriers (time, distance, and communication) minimized through technology, travel, and international commerce.

Meeting managers must understand the dimensions and impact of multicultural communication in a variety of situations, including:

- Managing events where international attendees will come to the United States for a meeting or conference
- Managing a meeting or conference in an international destination
- Managing events in the United States that will attract local and multicultural attendees

This chapter focuses on improving the communication within a variety of meeting settings to enhance productivity, increase participants' comfort, and maximize the human capital assembled.

The terms diversity and multicultural are being used more frequently in today's society and are often used as synonyms. For the purposes of this book, this chapter will focus on cultural differences that impact communication. The study of culture and cross-cultural communication is complex and subtle. Cultural identities stem from race, ethnicity, gender, class, religion, country of origin, and geographic region. Therefore, this chapter will focus on culture as defined by country of origin, recognizing that other characteristics—including race or lifestyle—can also define culture.

The ideas presented in the following pages about culture and cultural communication are intended to provide guidelines and promote understanding. Awareness of multiculturism is not intended to perpetuate stereotypes nor cast people in specific roles. The challenge to you, the reader, is to extract the germ of truth without over-generalizing.

The multicultural exploration presented in this chapter will provide an overview of the current demographics found in the United States. Additionally, the role of culture in communication, aspects of cultural differences (e.g., attitudes toward time or respect for authority), and cultural frameworks will be addressed. Finally, this information will be applied to meetings, and strategies for success will be identified.

THE CHANGING FACE OF U.S. DEMOGRAPHICS

Most meeting managers realize that cultural factors will impact international meetings and U.S.-based conferences that attract international attendees. However, cultural elements are less obvious when the meeting is held in the United States and involves only people who live and work in the United States. Yet, even in this familiar situation, a degree of cultural awareness is important. The United States is a culturally diverse country, and it is becoming increasingly so. According to the 2000 Census, the United States includes 31 ethnic groups of at least one million members each, and numerous others represented in smaller numbers.

The majority of Americans consider themselves to be "white." In the most recent census, Americans who classified themselves as white had ancestors who came from such countries as Germany, Ireland, England, Italy, Scandinavia, Poland, Russia, and other Slavic countries. This majority, totaling 69.1 percent in 2000, decreases each year, and is expected to become a mere plurality within 50 years.

Hispanics are the largest minority group in the United States, comprising 12.5 percent of the population. Hispanics are a very diverse ethnic group, coming from

South America, Mexico and Central America, Africa, Europe, and even Asia (Filipinos of Spanish descent). People of Mexican descent made up 7.3 percent of the population in the 2000 census, and this proportion is expected to increase significantly in the coming decades. African Americans (blacks) constitute 12.3 percent of the U.S. population. Asian Americans, including Native Hawaiians and Pacific Islanders, are the third most significant minority (accounting for 3.7 percent of the population in 2000). The largest Asian American subgroups are immigrants or descendants of immigrants from the Philippines, China, India, Vietnam, South Korea, and Japan. Indigenous peoples in the United States, such as American Indians and Inuit, constitute 0.9 percent of the population.

In the near future, minorities will represent almost half the U.S. population; this change is predicted to occur within 50 years. The Hispanic and Asian share of the total population will double to 25 percent and 8 percent, respectively. The black population is expected to grow by 71 percent, which would increase its share of the population from about 13 percent to 15 percent.[1]

DEFINITION OF CULTURE

Culture is not easily defined; scholars, philosophers, and even politicians lack consensus as to what exactly the concept should include. Culture is seemingly invisible and inherent in all that we do, say, believe, and act. Craig Storti in his book, *Figuring Foreigners Out: A Practical Guide,* defines culture as:

> The shared assumptions, values and beliefs of a group of people, which result in characteristic behaviors.[2]

This definition captures two essential points. Culture includes an invisible dimension (assumptions, values, and beliefs) and a visible dimension (behavior). Assumptions, values, and beliefs (the invisible) impact behavior (the visible) in a cause and effect relationship (see Figure 22.1).

People learn their cultures. Culture, as a set of learned values, beliefs, and behaviors, acts as a model or guide. Culture helps shape behavior and consciousness within a society from generation to generation. As a model, culture helps guide:

- Systems of meaning and primary language
- Ways of organizing groups and society, from kinship groups to states and multinational corporations
- Distinctive techniques, processes, or ways of thinking

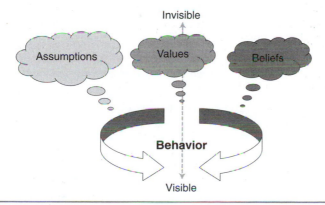

FIGURE 22.1
Definition of Culture

Culture's invisible nature (assumptions, values, and beliefs) affects our behavior. Behavior is neither arbitrary nor spontaneous. Behavior is the direct result of what people assume, value, or believe. What seems completely natural and right to the members of one culture may send a totally inappropriate message to a person from another culture.

A simple example of business dining etiquette will point out how differences in our beliefs impact behavior and create misunderstandings based on culture:

> A group of businessmen assemble after a meeting. The group includes a Japanese man and several Americans. This is their first business meeting and they do not know each other.
>
> The group goes to a small restaurant and orders a pitcher of beer. As is the custom in Japan, the Japanese man fills the glass of everyone at the table but himself. He leaves his own glass empty, because in Japan, it is very poor manners to serve yourself. The American businessmen at the table look at the Japanese man in surprise. One asks him if he wanted a drink. The Japanese man smiles and nods, assuming that now someone else will fill his glass for him. The men wait for him to fill his own glass. When he does not, they dismiss it and begin to talk. Throughout the night, the Americans or the Japanese man continue to fill the Americans' glasses. The Americans assume that the Japanese man does not drink beer and leave his glass empty.[3]

A caveat about culture: People think of culture as defining their values and identity. Racial definitions may not define cultural differences. For example, the term "Hispanic" used in the U.S. Census to define race does not take into account cultural differences between Cuban-Americans and Mexican-Americans.

ANALYZING CULTURE

Researchers, sociologists, and others advocate different ideas for analyzing culture and communication. Terence Brake, Danielle Medina Walker, and Thomas Walker, authors of *Doing Business Internationally: The Guide to Cross Cultural Success,* identify ten frameworks for understanding multicultural communication for meetings and business.

Environment

Different cultures view their environments in different ways. Using the three concepts of control, harmony, and constraint, cultures can adopt these various orientations:

- *Control*—Humans can mold their environment, including other people, to fit their needs.
- *Harmony*—People are an integral part of nature; their actions and thoughts should facilitate harmonious relations with the world and with others.
- *Constraint*—In a constrained culture, people do not claim direct control over an environment.

Time

Cultures treat time very differently. Various cultures may take a single or a multi-focus use of time. Additionally, various cultures view time as either fixed or fluid. Finally, a culture may possess a past, present, or future orientation. Using these terms, cultures assume various orientations:

Fast Facts

1. Environment
2. Time
3. Communication style
4. Space
5. Competitiveness
6. Individualism
7. Action
8. Power
9. Thinking
10. Order[4]

- *Single focus*—In this culture, people place a high value on doing one task at a time and meeting set deadlines.
- *Multi-focus*—People place greater emphasis on doing simultaneous tasks with a high commitment to relationship building rather than just completing tasks or meeting arbitrary deadlines.

- *Fixed*—In this orientation, people see time as a valuable quantity not to be wasted.
- *Fluid*—Time is defined in looser terms; delays are expected, deadlines and other commitments are not written in stone.

- *Past*—These cultures place a high value on the maintenance of historical sensibilities.
- *Present*—The aim is for quick results and the emphasis is on the here and now.
- *Future*—These cultures demonstrate a willingness to trade short-term gains for long-term results.

Communication Style

From culture to culture, people communicate very differently. When analyzing communication styles, cultures may exist along either high context/low context, direct/indirect, expressive/instrumental, or formal/informal communication styles. Using these terms, cultures can take various orientations:

- *High Context*—In high context cultures, people conduct business based upon contextual information about an individual. Business is personal and trust is critical to the relationship.
- *Low Context*—In low context cultures, the communication is task centered. Business is impersonal; trust and compatibility are not primary considerations. Meaning is communicated directly and explicitly.

- *Direct*—Direct cultures meet conflict head on.
- *Indirect*—Indirect cultures use a mix of conflict avoidance and third parties to handle conflict. These cultures possess a strong desire to save face, protect honor, and avoid shame.

- *Expressive*—Expressive cultures are not shy when it comes about displaying emotions.
- *Instrumental*—In these cultures the communication is problem centered, pragmatic, impersonal, and goal oriented. What is said is placed above how something is said. The stress is on the accuracy of the communication rather than on its appropriateness or style.

- *Formal*—Formal cultures place a high value on following business protocol and social customs.
- *Informal*—Informal cultures stress informality.

Space

Anthropologist Edward T. Hall coined the term proxemics to address how different cultures use space. People require different space needs in different settings. In *The Hidden Dimension,* Hall defined four types of distance:

- Intimate
- Personal
- Social
- Public[5]

People operate in various comfort zones of space, depending upon the setting. If one person violates a second person's comfort zone for that situation (social, public, personal), then both people will feel uncomfortable—and they may not understand why.

Proxemics helps explain why people from different cultures may feel that others are infringing upon their space or creating too much distance. For example, in North America, the normal social distance is 4 feet to 12 feet for business communication and meetings. Public distance ranges from 12 to 25 feet. In some cultural groups in South America and the Caribbean, the normal conversation distance is 14 to 15 inches. For certain cultures in the Middle East, that distance is as small as 9 to 10 inches.

A simple matter of how far away a person stands from another one can create unintended consequences. In Saudi Arabia if you stand 20 inches from a Saudi Arabian, which is normal by North American standards, it would communicate reserve, unfriendliness, and a sense of superiority (see Figure 22.2).

Competitiveness

Cultures vary in the relative value they place on competition and cooperation.

- *Competitive*—Competitive cultures place a high value on ambition, decisiveness, initiative, performance, speed, and size.
- *Cooperative*—Cooperative cultures stress quality of life, sympathy, nurturing, and relationships. They utilize consensus decision-making.

Individualism

Cultures vary in the value they place on individual accomplishments versus collective accomplishments. Also, cultures vary in how they value generalizations, rules, and standard procedures. These differences manifest themselves in differing orientations:

- *Individualistic*—Individualistic cultures place a high value on independence; social bonds between people are relatively loose and flexible.
- *Collective*—These cultures subordinate individual interests to group interest. Collective groups protect their members in exchange for loyalty and obedience.

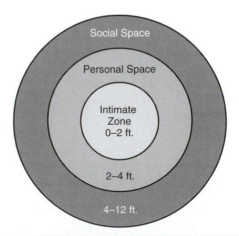

FIGURE 22.2
Proxemics in North American Culture

- *Universalistic*—Universalistic cultures stress consistent application of rules and procedures.
- *Particularistic*—In particularistic cultures, generalization is of limited value; uniqueness is celebrated. Special circumstances and unique relationships are recognized.

Action

Cultures vary in the relative value they place on doing and being:

- *Doing*—Doing cultures emphasize achieving external measurable accomplishments, achieving goals, and improving standards of living.
- *Being*—Being cultures stress affiliations, character, and personal qualities. These cultures place a premium on nurturing, caring, and relationships.

Power

Cultures vary in the way that they organize power; power in cultures tends to be either more hierarchical or more equitable:

- *Hierarchical*—In hierarchical cultures, power and authority are centralized and organizational structures are tightly controlled.
- *Equality*—In equality cultures, inequality is considered an unsatisfactory condition.

Structure

Cultures vary in the relative value they place on order and flexibility:

- *Order*—Order cultures seek to reduce ambiguity and uncertainty. Conflict and change are perceived as threatening.
- *Flexibility*—Flexible cultures tolerate unknown situations, people, and ideas. These cultures exhibit a greater willingness to take risks.

Thinking

Cultures process thoughts very differently. The predominant thinking styles in a particular culture can be thought of as being either deductive or inductive, and either linear or systemic. Using the concepts that these terms represent, cultures can take various orientations:

- *Deductive*—Deductive thinking emphasizes abstract thinking, and develops ideas, moral values, theories, and the principles from the abstraction process. The influence of past and future is greater in this type of thinking.
- *Inductive*—Inductive thinking derives principles and theories from the analysis of data. It is oriented more toward the present.
- *Linear*—Linear thinking cultures dissect information into small chunks. Linear thinkers link cause and effects, and emphasize detail, precision, and pragmatic results.
- *Systemic*—In systemic cultures, the thought process seeks an integrated or holistic approach—integrating viewpoints and focusing on relationships between parts and the whole.

CULTURE, LANGUAGE, AND COMMUNICATION

Language is the primary way in which humans communicate meaning. Yet, communication truly occurs only when a receiver gets a message from a sender.

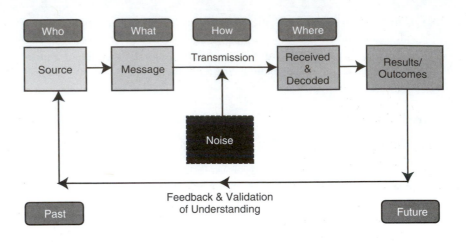

FIGURE 22.3
Communication Takes Two People

Communication requires more than one person. (See Figure 22.3 for a model of how communication actually works in practice.)

Embedded in communication, in addition to the spoken words, are tone, volume, inflection, and other nonverbal cues. In the seminal work of Koneya and Barbour the total impact of a message occurs through:

- 7 percent verbal (words) communication,
- 38 percent vocal (volume, pitch, rhythm, and so on) communication, and
- 55 percent body movements (mostly facial expressions).[6]

All senses—hearing, smell, sight, spatial perception, taste, touch, and awareness of time—are channels for nonverbal cues. Nonverbal communication is as important, if not more important, than the actual words that are used.

Examples of nonverbal communication include:

- Body language
- Gestures
- Facial expressions
- Tones of voice
- Eye contact
- Spatial arrangements
- Patterns of touch

The example of how differently Saudi Arabians and North Americans perceive space, used before, directly illustrates how nonverbal actions impact communication.

CULTURAL FRAMEWORKS

Individuals within a culture may behave differently than their cultural expectations might predict. These differences from their dominant culture are based upon the person's own experiences, family, history, and other elements that help frame an individual's personality. Hence, we cannot rely on cultural analysis to stereotype an individual.

Additionally, cultural differences exist on a continuum. Edward Hall created a popular classification defining cultural differences.[5] He classifies cultures as either low context or high context. The United States, Swiss German, German, and Scandinavian cultures are considered low context cultures. High context cultures include Asian, Latin American, African, and Middle Eastern countries.[7]

In low context cultures, people are less aware of nonverbal cues, the environment, and situations. Low context cultures rely less on developed networks. These cultures require detailed background information. People operating in low context cultures tend to segment and compartmentalize information. They control information on a "need to know" basis. Solving problems in this type of society consists of stating all of the known factual details and then evaluating their significance one by one. When drawing conclusions regarding the problem at hand, facts play the chief role (rather than intuitive speculation). Another important aspect of low context communities is their freedom to openly question and challenge authority. This type of freedom reinforces the idea that individuals exhibit behaviors of personal power and individualism. People are encouraged to verbalize their desires for answers and change if necessary. "Individualism" is the one word that characterizes low context. Low context countries are primarily found in North America and much of Western Europe.

High context cultures use a greater amount of shared knowledge. As a result, different assumptions are made as to the amount of information a verbal or written message carries. Information may be implicit and may be transmitted as ambiguous and fragmentary clues. Emotions and behaviors are more openly expressed and more highly valued than pure reason or words. The context of a situation, such as a speaker's tone of voice, gestures, postures, and sometimes even the person's historical family status, holds greater significance than the information itself.

These cultures prefer group harmony to individual achievements. Emphasis is placed upon group and interpersonal relationships over individual desires. Developing trust between individuals plays the most crucial cultural function within any high context society. "Collective" is the one word that defines high context cultures. Asia, Africa, South America, and much of the Middle East are classified as high context cultures.

Hall's work also presented a second concept, polychronic versus monochronic time orientation. This concept deals with the ways in which cultures structure their time. The monochronic time concept follows the notion of "one thing at a time," while the polychronic concept focuses on multiple tasks being handled at the same time, and time is subordinate to interpersonal relations.

Monochronic ties to low context cultures and polychronic ties to high context cultures. Table 22.2 identifies characteristics of monochronic and polychronic cultures. Reisner captured the importance for meeting planners to incorporate multicultural awareness into their planning process.[8] (In *MeetingNews*, June 1993. Figure 22.4 and Tables 22.1 and 22.2 summarize that article.)

CULTURE'S IMPACT ON MEETINGS

Meetings are places for people to learn, socialize, network, recognize their peers (and be recognized), and gain access to new information. A meeting is successful only if successful communication occurs.

While multicultural communication is challenging between two people, the stakes are even higher with a group, such as in a meeting. The speaker may be communicating to people from multiple cultures with differing perspectives, values, experience, and beliefs.

Thus, multicultural issues have major implications for communication within meetings. The full details and subtlety of multicultural communication extends beyond the scope of this chapter. Chapter 16 "International Meetings, Conventions, and Exhibitions" in this text will help meeting managers plan the logistics

---

Fast Facts

Elements in the Communication Model

- Source—the sender or initiator of the communication.

- Message—the words and non-verbal aspects

- Noise—anything that can interfere with the communication of the message. Includes distractions or a disconnect between the words and body language.

- Receiver—the person who receives and interprets the message. The impact of the communication is visible through the results or outcome which serves as a feedback loop back to the sender.

Fast Facts

Real life example: In low context cultures, award ceremonies and celebrations of individuals are normal. Competitions, like sales incentive programs or competitive teams, are introduced throughout the culture.

TABLE 22.1
Characteristics of Low and High Context Cultures[7]

Low Context Cultures	High Context Cultures
Logical and linear	Relational and intuitive
Personal control over the environment	Love and harmony with nature
Present and future oriented	Past oriented
Reliance on the verbal over the nonverbal message	Reliance on nonverbal codes over verbal messages
Competitive	Cooperative
Change over tradition	Tradition valued over change

Adapted from Reisner, R. "How Different Cultures Learn." *MeetingNews* June 1993. Used with permission.

TABLE 22.2
Characteristics of Monochronic and Polychronic Cultures[8]

Monochronic	Polychronic
Low Context Cultures	**High Context Cultures**
Need information	Are high context and already hold information
Adhere religiously to plans	Committed to people and human relationships
Emphasize promptness	Change plans often and easily
Do one thing at a time	Do many things at once
Concentrate on the job	Highly distractible and subject to interruptions
Take time commitments seriously	Consider time commitments an objective worth achieving, if possible

Adapted from Reisner, R. "How Different Cultures Learn." *MeetingNews* June 1993. Used with permission.

of an international event. The elements covered in this chapter offer an overview of the elements that are necessary to effectively communicate across cultures.

Before proceeding to specifics, consider seven general guidelines to help insure successful multicultural communication:

1. Do your homework. You can prepare by reading some of the numerous books and web sites with country-specific cultural information.
2. Learn from generalizations about other cultures, but do not use those generalizations to stereotype, "write off," or oversimplify situations or people. Cultural norms may not apply to the behavior of any particular individual.
3. Do not assume any culture (or situation) has only one correct way to communicate. Question your assumptions about the "right way" to communicate. Focus on verbal and nonverbal communication.

Fast Facts

Real life example: In high context cultures, flowery language, humility, and elaborate apologies are expected and normal.

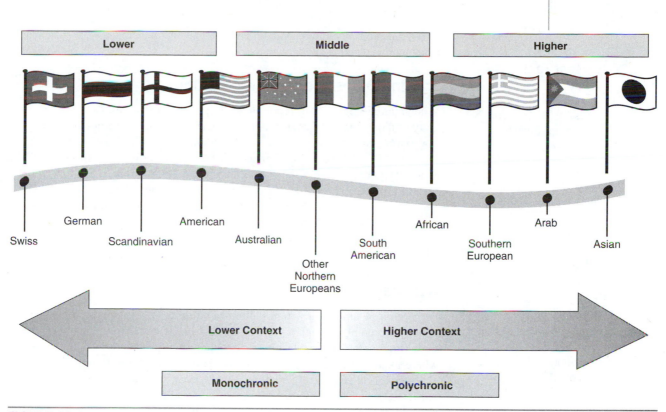

FIGURE 22.4
Cultures of the World Arranged along the High/Low Context and Monochronic/Polychronic Continuum
© 1993. *MeetingNews.* Used with permission.

4. Do not assume that breakdowns in communication occur because other people are wrong. Search for ways to create successful communication, rather than searching for breakdowns.
5. Listen actively and empathetically.
6. Stop, suspend judgment, and try to look at the situation as an outsider. You may need to operate from the edge of your comfort zone.
7. Communicate in good faith, with openness and honesty. A positive attitude will help bridge many gaps (or gaffes).

STRATEGIES FOR SUCCESS

This section discusses twelve strategies for success. Paying attention to these areas will make the difference between a meeting that facilitates communication across cultures and one that fails.

Audience

Speakers, meeting managers, and other suppliers can find it easier to be respectful of the audience's cultural orientation when they understand the cultural and communication characteristics of the participants.

Selection of Dates

Consider the impact of holidays and religious days in scheduling meetings. The traditional work week will vary around the globe. In the Middle East, Thursdays and

Fridays are considered weekend days (except in Israel, where the weekend extends from sundown on Friday through Saturday).

Printing Dates and Time Information

When numbers, not words, represent dates, people may be confused by the ambiguity of a date order. When the numbers representing the day, month, or year are low, participants may find it impossible to tell which order is being used.

The United States and Canada follow a convention of printing dates in Month/Day/Year order. Most European and South American countries use the Day/Month/Year order. Canada (French), China, Hong Kong (Chinese), Hungary, Japan, Korea, Latvia, South Africa (English), Sweden, and Taiwan use the Year/Month/Day convention.

Consider using military (24-hour) time to indicate the start and end times on your agenda.

Agenda

Perception of time varies from culture to culture. This suggests being flexible about proceeding through a meeting agenda under circumstances when people view time more fluidly. Meetings can wander off the stated agenda in cultures where ideas are not considered individually or sequentially.

Networking can be of paramount importance. In much of Europe and North America, business is contractual in nature. Personal relationships are seen as unhealthy as they can cloud objectivity and lead to complications. In South America and much of Asia, business is personal. People form partnerships with those they know, trust, and feel comfortable with. Investing in relationship building is necessary before moving to the business at hand.

Meeting Expectations

North American meetings incorporate a larger number of presentations and business issues into a day. In other cultures, meetings dedicate time to developing relationships with colleagues.

Western societies are conscious of time. Time is money and punctuality is crucial. This is also the case in countries such as Japan or China where being late is an insult. However, in South America, southern Europe and the Middle East, being on time for a meeting or keeping meetings to a timetable does not carry the same sense of urgency.

Communication Styles

Many elements go into a person's communication style. Communication occurs through language combined with nonverbal cues. Some of these nonverbal clues include:

- Eye contact
- Gestures
- Personal space and touch

Eye Contact

In the United States, the United Kingdom, and much of northern Europe, strong, direct eye contact conveys confidence and sincerity. In South America, steady eye contact indicates trustworthiness. However, in some cultures, such as the Japanese, prolonged eye contact is considered rude and is generally avoided.

Gestures

Perfectly accepted gestures in the United States, such as a "V" for victory or the "OK" sign formed with the thumb and forefinger, convey significantly different meaning in other cultures (see Figure 22.5).

Avoid specific gestures unless you know that the audience understands their meaning and will not misinterpret them.

Personal Space and Touch

In Europe and North America, business people maintain a certain amount of distance between themselves when interacting. Touching takes place only between friends. In South America or the Middle East, business people are tactile and like to get up close. In Japan or China, people commonly leave a gap of four feet when conversing. Touching only takes place between close friends and family members.

FIGURE 22.5
Inappropriate Gestures. The common "V" for victory sign in the U.S. is inappropriate in other cultures.

Humor

Humor is a double-edged sword. On the side of caution: Humor is often culturally specific. Humor is often dependent on cultural context and/or language to be funny. In many cultures, business is taken very seriously, and people closely observe protocol and professionalism. Many cultures will not appreciate the use of humor and jokes in a business context.

However, when humor is shared across cultural lines, it can function as a bonding experience, an energy source, and a great communication tool.

Group Activities/Feedback

In some cultures, reverence for experience, age, and job level may restrict people's ability to speak out, challenge authority, or participate on equal terms in decisions. Large group discussions may not elicit honest and open feedback. Therefore, build in brainstorming sessions, small group discussions among employees of the same level, or anonymity to solicit ideas.

Consider the groups' time orientation when setting up group activities. Also, how the group views power and their degree of competitiveness or cooperation affects how they will deal with any group activity.

Negotiations

Several factors complicate international negotiations. The first is that the parties must deal with the laws, policies, and political authorities of more than one nation. These laws and policies may be inconsistent, or even directly opposed. Secondly, a second currency complicates any legal agreement (see Chapter 16). Finally, governments often play a much larger role in foreign business than Americans are accustomed to.

Legal issues aside, reaching an agreement requires skills in cross-cultural negotiations. Considering cross-cultural issues in a negotiation can help favorably impact the desired outcome. When considering cultural issues, you can:

- Tailor your approach to the negotiations using insight about cultural differences
- Endear yourself more to the other negotiation team by acknowledging and respecting their approach, values, and beliefs

When negotiating, evaluate two elements in the negotiation:

- Use of information
- Negotiation style

Use of Information

Western business culture places emphasis on clearly presented and rationally argued business proposals using statistics and facts. Other business cultures rely on similar information but with differences. For example, South Americans—who are more visual and oral communicators—may prefer information presented through speech or using maps, graphs, and charts.

Negotiation Style

The way in which we approach negotiation differs across cultures. For example, in the Middle East, rather than approaching topics sequentially, negotiators may discuss issues simultaneously. South Americans can become quite vocal and animated. The Japanese negotiate in teams and reach decisions through consensual agreement. In China, negotiators are highly skilled at gaining concessions. In Germany, decisions can take a long time due to the need to analyze information and statistics in great depth. In the United Kingdom, negotiators employ pressure tactics and deadlines to close deals.

Protocol Issues

Protocol comes from the Greek word meaning "the first glue," or that which holds civilization together. Protocol is "the generally accepted code of etiquette and precedence within a particular group or entity."[10] International protocol includes:

- Introductions and greetings
- Seating
- Displaying national and organizational flags
- Business card savvy
- Gift-giving ideas and practices

Introductions and Greetings

Most international business people greet one another with a handshake. In some countries, this is not appropriate between genders. Some cultures view a weak handshake as sign of weakness, whereas others would perceive a firm handshake as aggressive.

Introductions and the proper use of names are an important part of cross-cultural communication. In general, North Americans are very informal compared to other cultures. Research and understand the degree of formality, the use of titles, and the structure of names (order of first name, surname) prior to any meetings.

Seating

Whether seating issues will arise depends upon the formality of the culture and the formality of the event. If the event is informal, the primary goal is to seat people with common interests together. For formal events, you should consider the protocol of seating. For business seating, guests are seated in order of rank. Evaluate the formality of the event and the site of the event to determine how important the seating protocol is.

Displaying National and Organizational Flags

Flag etiquette is also very important. Flags of nations may change from time to time. Obtain the proper national flag for display. Acquire information about the proper display of national flags from any protocol officer from the local government office. Usually the host national flag takes precedence and is placed in the center when surrounded with an odd number of flags. With an even number of flags, place the host flag to the right.

Exchanging Business Cards

In North America or Europe, a business card has little meaning other than a convenient form of capturing essential professional details. In other parts of the world, the business card has very different meanings. Research or closely observe business card etiquette, especially in countries like China, Japan, and India. In general, a business card represents the person whose name appears on it and should be treated with the same respect as you would the person. Present business cards with respect and seriousness; study the business card handed to you, and do not casually place it in your pocket. Nor should you flip it over and use the back for writing notes. Research country-specific details for business card protocol prior to meeting in that country or receiving conferees from that country.

Gift Giving Ideas and Practices

Gift giving customs vary greatly from country to country. Gifts are a social gesture that may be expected in some countries, and could be considered a bribe in others. Understanding the gift guidelines for the country will help make your meeting a success.

Countries in which a gift is expected:

- Europe—Czech Republic, Poland, Russia, Ukraine
- Latin American—Bolivia, Columbia, Costa Rica
- Pacific Rim—China, Hong Kong, Indonesia, Japan, Korea, Taiwan, Malaysia, Philippines, and Thailand

Countries in which a gift is not expected on the first visit, but would be expected on a subsequent visit:

- Europe—Portugal, Spain
- Latin American—Brazil, Chile, Guatemala, Nicaragua, Panama, Peru, Venezuela
- Pacific Rim—Malaysia, Singapore
- Scandinavia—Finland, Norway

Countries in which a gift is not expected, or gifts are less frequently exchanged:

- Africa
- Australia
- Europe—England, France, Hungary, Italy
- Latin America—Uruguay
- Scandinavia—Denmark
- Middle East—Pakistan, Saudi Arabia
- United States

Cultures with detailed rituals for gift giving are the Japanese and the Chinese. And Nomadic cultures in the Middle East have a tradition of hospitality to travelers, while Latin cultures consider all relationships, including business relationships, as personal. So people from these cultural backgrounds will exchange gifts as a normal part of building relationships and doing business.

Research the specific country for gift giving guidelines and practices. When giving gifts consider:

- Who is receiving the gift? Is it a person or a group? What is the status of the receiver(s)?
- What is the protocol associated with gift giving and receiving?
- Should gifts be reciprocated?

In general, you should:

- Always be cognizant of religious laws. For instance, pork is prohibited in the Jewish and Muslim religions, so do not select a gift made from pigskin. In India, don't offer a gift made from cowhide. Another prohibition for the Muslim faith is alcohol, including products like perfume that use alcohol as an ingredient. Also forbidden in Muslim cultures are products or foods from scavengers, which includes birds and shellfish.
- Avoid gifts (or gift wrapping) that invoke superstitions or are symbolic. Sharp objects, such as knives, letters or scissors, often imply the severing of relationships. In some cultures, a particular color or type of flower is associated with romance or funerals; avoid these colors and flowers in business situations. Certain numbers are symbolic in various cultures. For example, in China, red is a lucky color, pink and yellow represent happiness, and the number 8 is the luckiest number. The colors black, white, and blue, and the number 4 or four of anything, are negatively associated with death or funerals.
- Gifts should be quality items. They need not be expensive or ostentatious but should be something that is difficult for the recipient to obtain. Avoid

Put It Into Perspective

Avoiding a Cultural Clash

Your association has invited a group of Korean students to attend your annual conference. The idea is to allow them to attend the conference and either present their research or participate in a debate on leading research issues. The association is contemplating sponsoring a contest for the winners of the presentation or debate. Your management also wants them to actively participate in the welcoming reception. You are the meeting manager organizing the logistics and content of the conference.

From your research you know that Koreans identify as one ethnic group speaking one language. This creates a strong national identity. They follow the teachings of Confucius which describes the position of the individual in Korean society. Confucianism stresses duty, loyalty, honor, filial piety, respect for age and seniority, and sincerity. The concept of *kibun* is very important in Korean life. *Kibun* does not translate literally into English; the closest terms are pride, face, mood, feelings, or state of mind. If you hurt someone's *kibun*, you hurt their pride, and cause them to lose dignity and face. Korean interpersonal relationships operate on the principle of harmony. Maintaining a peaceful, comfortable atmosphere at all times is important, even if it means telling a "white lie" or responding "yes" even when that is not the true answer. *Nunchi* is the ability to determine another person's *kibun* by watching body language and listening to the tone of voice as well as what is said. Knowing how to judge the state of someone else's *kibun*, how to avoid hurting it, and how to keep your own *kibun* at the same time is very important.

At the same time, Koreans are extremely direct communicators. They are not averse to asking questions if they do not understand what was said or need additional clarification. In social situations, Koreans wait to be introduced. Many South Koreans shake hands with expatriates after the bow, thereby blending both cultural styles. The person of lower status bows to the person of higher status, yet the most senior person initiates the handshake.

How will you use this information to construct the meeting to include the Korean students?

> ### ? Did You Know?
>
> North Americans wave their hands up and down to signify "goodbye"; Japanese make the same gesture to indicate "come here."
>
> In the Chinese culture, receiving a clock as a gift is considered bad luck.
>
> Latin Americans typically place great emphasis on authority. People wait for instruction and seek approval from authority figures.
>
> When doing business in the Middle East, handshakes are always used and can last a long time. Islamic etiquette recommends that one waits for the other to withdraw their hand first before doing the same. Men may also escort other men by leading them by the hand.
>
> Negotiations with Russians often involve flared tempers. During negotiations and meetings, temper tantrums and walkouts often occur.
>
> Body language is significant in Argentina. Argentineans maintain long periods of eye contact. Placing the hands on hips when speaking usually means the person is angry. If someone taps their middle finger against the thumb this means "hurry up."
>
> In India, people maintain diverse dietary restrictions influenced by religion. Hindus do not eat beef and many are vegetarians. Muslims do not eat pork or drink alcohol. Sikhs do not eat beef.
>
> Silence often indicates disapproval in Chinese culture, where openly negative responses are considered rude.

items that are locally produced. In Belgium, France, Greece, Italy, Portugal, and Spain, don't give an item with your company logo. Avoid highly personal items like clothing.

Food and Beverage

Mealtimes distinguish cultures—not just the food itself, but the purpose of mealtimes which varies from nourishing the body to nourishing relationships. For example, food in Europe is a conduit to social relations, never nourishment for its own sake. In contrast, in North America, meetings may include lunch during a presentation. This would not happen in most European countries.

Food choices should also be based upon cultural appropriateness. For example, pork should not be served at a meeting with Muslim or Israeli participants, and vegetarian choices should always be available to participants from India.

Marketing and Promotion

Language is key to effective cross-cultural advertising. The advertising world is littered with blunders from launching products or services. Examine themes, graphics, symbols, numbers, and color for cultural suitability before approving any marketing plan.

SUMMARY

This chapter introduced the concept of culture. Culture includes the accepted assumptions, values, and beliefs (not visible) and behavior (visible) of people. While culture should not be used to stereotype people, understanding culture can help us understand how people communicate, how they organize their society, and their ways of thinking. Using the work of Hall, you can use the concepts of low and high context cultures and monochronic and polychronic frameworks to evaluate your meeting audience.

As culture is composed of beliefs, assumptions, values, and behavior, multicultural differences play a central role in effective communication. Communication is a combination of verbal and nonverbal cues. Nonverbal cues are a significant portion of communication (80–90 percent).

Good communication is typified by sending and receiving the same (or similar) message. Meetings are all about communication—whether the communication occurs from one speaker to a group, one on one, or in a small grouping.

Uncertainty is a barrier to good communication. Communication with strangers involves relatively greater degrees of uncertainty, due to the difficulty involved in predicting a stranger's responses. We cannot predict the stranger's attitudes, feelings, and beliefs. We are also uncertain of how to explain the stranger's behavior. Both sides may feel anxiety or be tense.

Gaining more information about the other person reduces uncertainty and increases the accuracy of our communication. This is the central reason that everyone participating in meetings should tune into multicultural differences.

Ten dimensions aid our understanding of how cultural beliefs, assumptions, and values vary. Multicultural differences arise because of varying perspectives. These ten multicultural dimensions affect logistics and meeting strategy for both domestic and international meetings.

The global economy has changed the essence of a "U.S.-based corporation." Corporate meetings for a U.S. company may involve people from around the globe, while foreign companies increasingly employ significant numbers of North Americans. At the same time, U.S. society is extremely diverse and will continue to be even more so. Travel abroad is no longer necessary to become involved in a meeting or conference with a diverse audience. All these developments necessitate that meeting managers understand and plan for cultural differences in their audiences.

Steps that exhibit good meeting management in a cross-cultural setting are ones that allow for:

- Assessment of cross-cultural communication challenges and roadblocks
- Implementation of strategies to avoid miscommunication due to cultural differences

This assessment and implementation affects pre-planning, logistics, and program content. Negotiation strategies, currency differences, and legal differences are just three manifestations of multicultural differences in the pre-planning stage. From logistics such as food and beverage service and date selection, to re-examining the programmatic elements (receptions, teambuilding, networking), meeting managers hold the opportunity to facilitate the communication at meetings, conventions, conferences, and expositions. In doing so, these meeting managers will enhance productivity, increase their participants' comfort, and maximize the human capital assembled at the meeting. That, in turn, delivers real value for the organization hosting the meeting.

REFERENCES

1. Census Scope.Org (2006). CensusScope. Retrieved March 21, 2006 from http://www.censusscope.org/us/chart_race.html.

2. Storti, C. (1998) *Figuring foreigners out: A practical guide.* Yarmouth, ME: Intercultural Press.

3. Axtell, R.E. (1993). *Do's and taboos around the world* (3rd ed.). Indianapolis, IN: Wiley Publishing.

4. Brake, T., Walker, D., & Walker, T. (1994). *Doing business internationally: The guide to cross cultural success.* New York, NY: Irwin Professional Publishing.

5. Hall, E.T. (1976*). Beyond culture.* Garden City, NY: Anchor Press/Doubleday.

6. Koneya, M., & Barbour, A. (1976). *Louder than words: Nonverbal communication*. Columbus, OH: Merrill.

7. Hall, E. T. & Hall, M. R. (1990). *Understanding cultural differences*. Yarmouth, Me., Intercultural Press.

8. Reisner, R. (June 1993). How different cultures learn. *MeetingNews*.

9. Hall, E.T., & Reed, M. (1987*). Hidden differences*, Garden City, NY: Anchor Press/Doubleday.

10. Searchnetworking.com. Retrieved March 21, 2006 from http://searchnetworking.techtarget.com/sDefinition/0, sid7_gci212839,00.html.

KEY TERMS

Cross-cultural communication	Low context culture	Polychronic framework
Culture	Monochronic framework	Protocol
Diversity	Multicultural	Proxemics
High context culture	Nonverbal communication	

COMPELLING QUESTIONS FOR CONSIDERATION

1. What "standard" practices exist within U.S.-style meetings that may intimidate, confuse, or create anxiety for participants from other cultures?

2. How can you effectively convey multicultural information to speakers, suppliers, or others without further reinforcing stereotypes?

3. What predictions can you make about the attendees at your meetings, conferences, and expositions? How will they change over the next five years and what things might you need to adjust in your meeting management to accommodate those changes?

4. What nonverbal behaviors have you witnessed in the meetings you manage? What do those nonverbal clues tell you about the communication within the meeting (these may be cultural or not)? How can you use those clues in your future meeting management efforts?

5. Analyze a meeting audience using each of the ten factors discussed in the chapter. Does this analysis suggest any changes for that meeting?

6. Identify the positive impacts a low context culture will have on a meeting. Identify at least three ways that low context cultures can negatively impact a meeting or conference.

7. Identify the positive impacts a high context culture will have on a meeting. Identify at least three ways that high context cultures can negatively impact a meeting or conference.

CHAPTER 23

THE ENVIRONMENT FOR MEETINGS AND EVENTS

Jeffrey Beck, PhD
Assistant Professor
The School of Hospitality Business
Michigan State University

LEARNER OUTCOMES

When the reader has completed reading this chapter, he/she should be able to . . .

1 Discuss factors to consider when designing the environment for a meeting or event.

2 Identify the factors that affect an attendee's psychological and physical comfort level.

3 Describe how the choice of meeting room can affect the achievement of the goals and objectives of the event.

4 Identify basic meeting equipment requirements.

5 Identify the planning, space, and equipment elements necessary to support the logistics of the meeting or event.

> There are two ways of being creative.
> One can sing and dance. Or one can
> create an environment in which
> singers and dancers flourish.
>
> *Warren G. Bennis*

OVERVIEW

The elements of space use and function room set-up design have evolved over the past five years to include the notion of an experience. Many meeting managers are seeing the link between a meeting or event, for whatever the purpose, and the art of theater. According to Pine and Gilmore in *The Experience Economy*, meetings and events should be designed to provide a theme, send positive cues for learning and meaning, eliminate cues that do not support the goal of the meeting or event, and incorporate all five senses.[1] This requires taking into consideration the objectives of the meeting or event, designing the function space set-up creatively, planning for the physical and psychological comfort of the participants, and using space efficiently.

An on-site inspection of a proposed meeting facility should take place before the planning process is concluded (see Chapter 11). It is critical that the meeting or event's objectives are clearly understood at the time of the site inspection to ensure the facility can accommodate the needs of the meeting manager. A critical step in completing advance arrangements is the selection of the proper space, equipment, and set-up for all events. Depending on the size, duration, and complexity of a meeting or event, subsequent planning sessions may be needed to monitor facility maintenance and to finalize details of function room selection and set-up.

It is the meeting manager's responsibility to create a positive environment through efficient and effective space use and set-up design. Set-up design should be customized to the unique needs of the current event. The movement of attendees throughout the day, the lighting needed in the room, the use of technology, and the level of experience of the speaker(s) or entertainment all affect set-up design.

If a speaker or entertainment is part of the meeting, the meeting manager must define their needs, including furniture requirements (e.g. stool, lectern), the degree of interaction with the audience, and technological requirements. Other key factors of function room selection and set-up include group dynamics, degree of participant involvement, visibility issues, ability to hear the presentation, and choice of formal or informal meeting style.

Once the meeting manager has established the group's needs and formulated a clear direction, the facility staff becomes involved as consultants in determining the correct rooms for the set-ups desired. The meeting manager should be aware of local fire and safety codes and take care to incorporate these restrictions in the planning process. This chapter will address the many issues that must be considered regarding the environment of meetings and events to ensure success.

MEETING AND EVENT DESIGN FACTORS

Meeting managers work closely with facility staff to use meeting space correctly and effectively, and should consult an audiovisual (A/V) contractor if meetings or events will require projection, special effect lighting and/or data transmission. The selection and assignment of meeting rooms are based on the meeting objectives, the type of event, capacity required, and physical factors, such as:

- General location in relation to other facilities, including traffic flow
- Configuration of room, including dimensions, ceiling height, door placement, and maximum room capacity
- Dropped ceilings, obstructions, or chandelier placements
- Restroom accessibility, including facilities for people with disabilities
- Room acoustics
- Lighting system and location of switches (fixed and remote)

- Ventilation, heating, and air conditioning
- Location of kitchen in relation to meeting room if food and beverages will be served
- Quality and placement of portable walls
- Sound system
- Control panels for recording output or tie line to central record location
- Noise leakage from hallways, service corridors, and portable airwalls
- Appearance and decor, including cleanliness
- Security

FUNCTION TYPES

The Accepted Practices Exchange (APEX) approved by the Convention Industry Council (CIC) lists a variety of uses for space as part of the event specifications guide (ESG) template. The types of functions include:

- *Break out*—Small function rooms set up for a group within an event as opposed to a plenary or general session.
- *Coat check*—A room or space used for checking coats or other personal items when a coat rack is insufficient.
- *Green room/hospitality room for VIPs*—Room, stocked with refreshments, for artists, featured speakers, and entourage to meet guests and media representatives.
- *Exhibits*—Individual display area constructed to showcase products, services, or convey a message.
- *General session*—A meeting open to all those in attendance at an event.
- *Meeting*—An event where the primary activity of the attendees is to either attend educational sessions, participate in meetings/discussions, socialize, or attend other organized events.
- *Office*—Similar to a hospitality suite, but geared more exclusively toward typical office communications services.
- *Photo room*—A room or space used for a photographer typically following award ceremonies.
- *Poster session*—Display of reports and papers, usually scientific, accompanied by authors or researchers.
- *Registration*—Designated area where event registration takes place.
- *Speaker room/ready room*—Area set aside for speakers to meet, relax, test A/V, or prepare prior to or between speeches.
- *Storage*—Space at a show set aside for storage of crates or materials.
- *Workshop*—Training session in which participants, often through exercises, develop skills and knowledge in a given field.[2]

The complexity of the meeting or event will dictate the space required and for what function. Whatever the space is to be used for, it must support the purpose of the meeting or event.

ATTENDEE COMFORT

The biggest single physical factor that impacts comfort level in an educational session is the room used as the classroom. In *How to Size Up and Set Up a Meeting Room*, Jeannie Drew wrote, "A meeting room can enhance or inhibit productivity, encourage or discourage communication, promote or stifle creativity, and make participants feel relaxed or tense."[3]

There are several factors to consider when choosing the best room for meetings or events:

- Is the room size adequate for the number of potential attendees? If a room is too small, some people may become claustrophobic or unable to concentrate. If a room is too large, people have a tendency to spread out, and any sense of group cohesion is lost.

- Is there adequate ventilation? Poor air quality and circulation tend to make people drowsy.

- Does the room have independent, adjustable temperature controls that can be moderated depending on the number of people in the room and the ambient temperature? Room temperature should be 70°F to 74°F. As a general rule, it is better for participants to be too cool than too warm.

- Is lighting too harsh or too dim? Fluorescent lights are hard on the eyes. Studies have shown that this type of lighting reduces energy levels and the ability to concentrate. Meetings in rooms with fluorescent lighting should be limited to less than two hours.

- Is there natural light and/or windows? Natural light provides a softer, brighter light. Windows provide a welcome momentary diversion that helps recharge mental batteries during long sessions.

- Do acoustics vary from section to section within the room? The room should be thoroughly checked and seating arrangements positioned in the best areas. Carpets and drapes help absorb noise and diminish echoes.

- Is there ambient noise from heating/cooling systems that could distract attendees?

- Does noise from adjoining rooms or corridors bleed into the room? Air walls or moveable walls should be soundproof, and there should be a buffer zone between service and traffic corridors and the meeting room. Meeting managers should listen for outside noise from construction, automobile traffic, airplanes or trains.

- Are access and egress points at the back of the room to allow people to come and go with minimal distraction to the rest of the group?

- Do low ceilings or columns crowd the space? Ceilings under nine feet can be oppressive, as well as hinder A/V presentation. Columns impede sight lines and the ability to set a room to maximum advantage.

Other elements to consider when choosing a suitable meeting room include the sound system, electrical outlets, and built in presentation equipment such as pull-down projection screens. A final consideration is for special needs—for those who have disabilities and for special services such as simultaneous translation (see Chapter 43).

If a learner is not psychologically comfortable within the learning environment, then learning may not take place. Look at the learning environment from the learner's perspective and consider the psychological factors that affect the learner's comfort level. Psychological comfort means the environment is seen as being "safe," a place where the learner is able to take mental risks.

To determine how to create a psychologically safe learning environment, look at the program and learner outcomes. Program objectives will help determine the operational parameters—what meeting rooms are available, for example. Learner outcomes indicate what people will learn as a result of the session. This information helps determine content delivery, room set-up, etc.

Work with speakers and/or facilitators to create a comfortable environment for meeting participants. Ask the speaker to arrive early and greet attendees as they come into the room. Have the speaker circulate an agenda of what is going to take place during the session, especially if it is a longer one. Encourage the speaker to use small groups so that people who are timid about speaking in public will be able to express an opinion in a less threatening forum.

Consider learning styles when planning the function room set-ups (see Chapter 18). Most adults have a preferred way of taking in and processing information. If the speaker tends to use a lecture format, many adults will tune out. Encourage the speaker to use a variety of teaching strategies throughout the session to reach as many learners as possible.

CREATE A LEARNING EXPERIENCE

Learning is a multi-sensory experience. Adults learn more when engaged in the learning process on several different levels. Music, color, movement, and interaction are all factors that work together to create the optimal learning experience for meeting attendees.[4] Pine and Gilmore, in their seminal work, *The Experience Economy*, advocate a model that contains four realms of an experience, which dovetails nicely with the aim of meetings and events.[5] These realms of an experience can vary from active to passive participation on the part of the attendee. The degree of connection to the event, from being aware of, to physically placed in the environment of the event dictates the amount of interaction. The implication, as Gilmore puts it, is that meeting managers must use theatrical concepts as a means for planning more effective meetings and events.

Beyond A/V presentations and handouts, sessions can be enriched by other visual and audio stimuli. Meeting room peripherals, such as wall displays, mobiles, or floor displays, add variety and interest to a setting. Choose from content-related displays to enhance learning, or decorative displays to beautify the meeting site. Visual displays and décor should be used to link the purpose of the event with the experience the meeting manager wishes the attendee to encounter. Some examples include using artwork from local artists to enhance otherwise uninteresting meeting rooms or using visual "cues" for attendees as they move from place to place, such as old the style rhyming highway signs. As Lena Malouf in *Behind the Scenes at Special Events* suggests, the type of event and its purpose will influence theme, décor, and the extent of creativity required.[6]

Using Sound

Although the effects of music on adult learning capacity are difficult to measure, most people acknowledge and experience on a daily basis the psychological impact of music. Whether venting frustration to rock-and-roll while exercising, unwinding from a tense day at work by listening to the radio on the drive home, or simply relaxing to classical music or jazz, people use music to influence their moods. A song, rhythm, or melody can also evoke a particular time and bring back memories. Sounds can have a similar effect as the meeting manager links the theme of a meeting or event and sense of hearing. Julia Silver in *Professional Event Coordination* recommends the use of sound sculpting, or composed sounds, to provide a mood appropriate for a meeting or event.[7]

In the meeting or learning environment, music has a similar effect. It can be used to reduce frustration caused by stressful or intensive encounters or to raise spirits and energize people as they enter the room during an early morning session. Music played before sessions also welcomes people into the room and breaks the initial silence. The music should be played in the background so as not to interfere with conversation. Although not everyone will consciously notice the music being played, it will have a subtle effect on the group. If the conference meets over a number of days and attendees become accustomed to music before a session and at breaks, they will comment if the music is not playing when they enter the room.

Music affects digestion, circulation, respiration, and the immune system. Emotionally, music releases endorphins that relieve mental fatigue, calm tension, focus thinking, and stimulate creativity and self-esteem. When using music to enhance the learning environment, the most important concept to keep in mind is that the music should match the educational objectives of the session. Research has demonstrated that classical music is a means by which learning can be enhanced. Inappropriate music can distract the learner from the tasks at hand. Additionally, keep in mind the demographics of the meeting attendees. Current events can help suggest the type of music; the author has used soundtracks from current movies and popular composers. Care must be taken to insure that copyright laws are followed. The LIND Institute, San Francisco, has developed a catalog of music appropriate for any number of meeting environments and objectives.[8]

Using Activity

Current research shows that exercise increases the potential for learning. Ensuring that attendees have time for exercise during a conference will increase the mental receptivity of the adult learner. This can be accomplished by allowing sufficient time for a workout between the afternoon session and dinner, by organizing a group aerobics class, or by making exercise or jogging trail information part of the registration packet so that attendees can plan ahead and bring their workout clothes. For attendees without an active exercise schedule, plan brief walks or walking tours during the day. Exercise will reduce tension, stimulate learning, and make attendees more alert and open to new ideas.

It is important to schedule recesses throughout the day, particularly if attendees are receiving large amounts of information in long sessions. Have session leaders lead the group in simple stretching exercises, particularly in the afternoon when many people return from lunch feeling sluggish. If the meeting involves attendees working in teams, exercise breaks can be used as an opportunity to build team spirit. Even walking briskly around the parking lot can energize attendees and revitalize them for the rest of the session. The time spent in 5- to 10-minute exercise sessions will pay off immediately, producing less irritable and more alert attendees.

ACCESSIBILITY

The Americans with Disabilities Act (ADA) (see Chapter 43) has afforded all attendees with disabilities equal access to each meeting room and also to the seating within it. This means, among other things, that meeting managers must accommodate the special needs of each attendee with a disability.

The most common concern deals with wheelchairs. Wheelchair access to all types of room sets require more space than standard seating would require. This does not mean that the entire room needs to be redesigned to make this accommodation.

As part of the registration form, attendees should be requested to identify their special needs and have a staff member contact these attendees individually to make arrangements to meet these special needs. An ADA booth in the registration area can help accommodate special needs that may include access to the meeting room, seating in the meeting room, arrangements for guide dogs, access to a "signer," arrangements for a hearing amplification device, and access to a stage or platform. A staff member should be available at a designated ADA booth to distribute motorized chairs/scooters and hearing amplification devices.

Tips for Wheelchair Accessibility

- For classroom- or theater-style programs, aisle seats and the back row must be wheelchair accessible.

- A wheelchair-accessible aisle should be at least 6 feet wide to provide passage of two wheelchairs.
- When setting up the room, remove two chairs for every wheelchair.
- Tape a laminated sign on the floor designating space reserved for wheelchairs/scooters.
- For classroom seating, allow 6 feet between tables in the row(s) designated for wheelchair attendees.
- Provide at least 3 to 3.5 feet of table space per wheelchair at the table.
- For seating at banquet rounds, remember that a wheelchair occupies approximately 1.5 times as much space as standard seating.
- Provide at least 3-foot wide aisle access to banquet tables where attendees in wheelchairs have chosen to sit. Tables should be 6 feet apart (edge to edge) on the route to the requested seating.

Accommodations for the Deaf or Hearing Impaired

A special seating area may be required for attendees who are hearing impaired and require a signing translator. The seating area must be close to the stage area where the signer will be communicating. The seating must also provide easy viewing of slides and other presentation material. This seating can be identified with a designated sign.

If the lights are lowered for A/V presentations, some arrangements must be made to enable these attendees to see the interpreter's face and hands when they are signing. Some hearing-impaired attendees may request a hearing amplification device. A/V contractors typically offer rentals and installation of such a device.

REGISTRATION AND OFFICE AREAS

Space requirements for registration and office areas should be communicated at the time of booking. The location and size of the registration area should receive special consideration. Where possible, the registration area should be located in a highly visible and accessible location with the back of the registration booth facing unusable space, such as a wall, alongside a set of stairs or an escalator railing. Close proximity to the meeting rooms and other meeting services is ideal. If counters are needed for registration, an outside decorating contractor is usually needed to install them. The meeting manager should also consider adequate space for auxiliary functions such as audiotape sales and or product sales, and concierge or other ancillary services to be offered.

The meeting manager must take into account the types of queuing (wait lines) for registration to use at different times of the meeting or event. For example, during slower times for registration, having a straight-line queue may be appropriate, whereas during peak registration times, a serpentine queue may be necessary (see Figure 23.1). The type of queuing system used will also be a function of the space available in the registration area.

The use of office space will vary by the complexity of the meeting or event. While some organizations need only a storage area, others need a place where they can actually work at conference-related duties. To take care of on-site organizational business, one or more rooms may be needed. Larger meetings may require extensive space for headquarter offices, an exhibit management office, a speaker and/or very important person (VIP) lounge, and space for membership services and guest programs. Storage areas may be required for A/V equipment and for the organization's meeting supplies. Additional space may be required for hotel housing desks, guest programs and/or group tour registration

Registration Desk							
A to C	D to F	G to J	K to M	N to Q	R to T	U to W	X to Z

FIGURE 23.1
Serpentine Queue

and information, transportation arrangements, and general information kiosks. The meeting manager must work with facility staff to ascertain proper locations.

The meeting manager can determine the office equipment that is available from the facility, what may be acquired from outside vendors, and what may be brought from the meeting manager's offices. Facilities customarily provide some office and service space at no charge, but those arrangements must be clear at the time of booking the meeting or event. The meeting manager should evaluate suggested locations for registration, office or service area with space and equipment requirements in mind. Can the area accommodate the desired set-up and also provide adequate space for those working in and visiting the area? Lighting should be adequate for paperwork, and heating and/or air conditioning levels must be comfortable. Electrical services for computers fax machines, and adding machines may be required. Also consider the best location for telephone and data lines.

Be alert to the need for securing cash, equipment, and supplies. Many facilities will allow the meeting manager to re-key guest and function rooms where valuables are kept. Some can also provide a safe for securing cash. As part of the preconference meeting and tour, the meeting manager should verify that the facility's security cameras are operational. It may be appropriate to hire an outside security company to guard the entrance to offices or other areas requiring the appearance of additional security.

If anything beyond a few 6-foot tables and chairs will be required in the office area, draw a floor plan of the office to scale and include the necessary desks, counters, chairs, and tables. A room-diagramming program is a useful tool for this process. Most floor plan diagramming software applications programs are also capable of laying out office set-ups. A floor plan will also serve as an instructional layout for facility set-up personnel and outside suppliers. The decorator will know where to drape off a specific area, the company delivering desks will know exactly where they are to be placed, and the telephone company will know where phones and longer cords will be needed.

THE SCHEDULING PROCESS

All facilities maintain a calendar of bookings and the rooms reserved for each booking (see Figure 23.2). Space or booking diaries are usually handled via com-

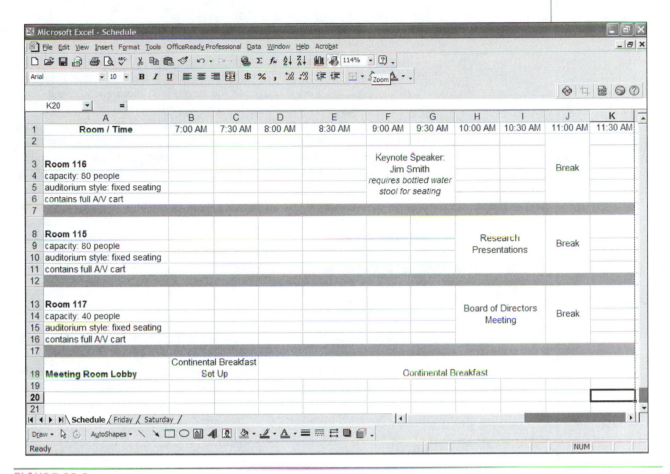

FIGURE 23.2
Example of Booking Diary

puter, with a few manual calendars still in use. Proper allocation of space and time is critical to the meeting management process. Like the facility representative with whom they are working, meeting managers should also use a space diary. This chart of room assignments will avoid scheduling conflicts and point out potential problems with traffic flow and timing, even if only two or three meeting rooms are required. A simple space diary can be designed using spreadsheet software by listing the rooms and capacities down one side and the meeting time periods across the top. The format can be expanded to include A/V requirements, recording requirements, session titles, and set-up notes.

During the scheduling process, meeting managers must determine if there are, or will be any potential conflicts with other groups that are using the facility. Rooms can be reserved on an hourly or on a 24-hour hold. Holding rooms on a 24-hour basis can be more expensive. When reserving rooms on an hourly basis, allow enough time for set-up and turnover. To avoid conflicts with other groups, hold the room for an hour before and after the scheduled event. Costs can be reduced if the A/V equipment can be set once and not moved from room to room. Charges associated with electronically recording a meeting are usually based on a per-room, per-day rate. Scheduling of sessions requiring recording in the same block of rooms throughout the day can reduce this expense.

The Professional Convention Management Association (PCMA) and Meeting Matrix International have engaged in a program to certify meeting room sizes so that calculations and function room set-ups will be accurate. This program is of value to the meeting manager by providing the structural details of each meeting room.

Using room-diagramming software such as Delphi Diagrams for Meeting Managers, Meeting Matrix, and Room Viewer can help the meeting manager use space more efficiently, make changes to the set-up plan more quickly, and communicate final designs to facility staff in electronic and/or print format. Newer programs, like Vivien from Cast Software, allow the meeting manager to construct a 3-D rendering of the meeting or event environment. Products such as these can help meeting managers with complex themes, decorations, and set-ups to communicate their visions to facility housemen, other staff, and outside contractors. Many hotel companies use room-diagramming software and, in fact, offer free copies of the software to their clients as an added service. All details gathered during the planning process are used in the preparation of final set-up instructions that should be sent to the facility four or more weeks prior to the event. Written instructions are necessary to ensure that meeting rooms and service areas are prepared correctly, on time, and that all arrangements are handled as planned.

FACILITY EQUIPMENT

Before discussing the various means by which space can be set up and arranged, an overview of the various equipment used for meeting and event set-ups is appropriate. As the meeting manager is considering set-ups, the planner must also determine whether the venue has the equipment necessary. An inventory of available equipment aids in the decision to change a set-up, rent additional equipment, or modify a set-up.

Tables

The use of 72-inch round tables (rounds) is standard within the meetings industry, although some facilities also maintain a supply of 60- and 66-inch. Rounds provide ample workspace and the best setting for small-group interaction.

Cabaret tables vary in size from 15 to 30 inches. The height of the table can vary from 36 to 50 inches. Also called cocktail rounds, these tables are used for cocktail parties, receptions (also called walk and talks), and in seating for entertainment venues.

Most hotels have 6-foot and 8-foot rectangular tables in standard widths of both 18 and 30 inches. Tables that are 18 inches wide are typically called classroom tables. In conference centers, 24-inch wide tables are common. There are 10 different table lengths ranging from 3.5 feet to 8 feet long.

Serpentines, also known as half moons, are used for displays, food buffets, and as part of the hollow square set-up.

Chairs

Standard chairs are 20 inches front to back at base. Seat widths vary from 17.5 inches to 18.5 inches. Most chairs for meetings and events are not as wide as the average person.

For the learning environment, C.L. Finkel in *The Total Immersion Learning Environment*, recommends a chair that is 1) adjustable in three directions, 2) has wheels or casters, 3) swivels, 4) arms that are flat versus round, 5) a firm seat covered in fabric, 6) a reclining back covered in vinyl, 7) nonreflective metal parts, 8) a width appropriate to the table it is paired with.[9]

Tablet chairs, also called writing chairs, can be used when space is at a premium. Unfortunately, these chairs can be uncomfortable, too small for some attendees, and the writing surface can be too small.

Podiums, Lecterns, and Head Tables

After the tables and chairs, the podium, lectern, and/or head table is the next important equipment component of the function room set-up. Lecterns can be either a table top style or free-standing floor model. A panel discussion can require both a lectern and a head table. A talk show set-up includes a desk and comfortable armchairs. Ideally, the floor-standing lectern is combined with the head table, allowing adequate space for people seated at the table. Risers are frequently used to elevate the head table and lectern, making it easier for speakers to view the attendees and vice versa.

Miscellaneous Equipment and Supplies

Meeting managers should also consider items that add to the comfort of the attendee, such as:

- Water service for speakers and head table participants
- Water service for tables
- Water service tables at the back of the room
- Paper and pens or pencils at each seat
- Hard candies on tables

Meeting Room Set-ups

The most commonly used set-up styles are roundtable, schoolroom, meeting (or conference), and theater. Set-ups can include tables and chairs, chairs only, or tables only. Special set-ups, such as perimeter seating, or an autograph table can be used in conjunction with the set-ups presented below. Use the following general guidelines when choosing rooms for meeting room set-ups.[10]

Roundtable Set-up

Two variables have a bearing on attendee comfort when they are seated at roundtables: The number of chairs at each table should be kept to a minimum, and the distance between the tables (generally measured center to center) should be as great as space permits. Sound bleed from nearby tables and poor full-room interaction can be expected. Some attendees may have trouble hearing conversation across a large round table, particularly if background noise level in the room is excessive

A meeting room can be set up with a series of round tables, with a discussion leader stationed at each table. The 72-inch round table comfortably seats 10 people, up to a maximum of 12 people. The 60-inch table comfortably seats 8 people, up to a maximum of 10 people (see Figure 23.3). A note of caution: Setting for the maximum allows each person only 18 inches of table space, which is too little for comfort.

If used as part of a presentation session that requires a quick set from or to a meal, the round tables can be set with chairs around one side (4 people at a 60-inch round) facing the podium or head table and lectern. This is known as a crescent round set-up. This allows participants to move their materials aside as the meal (typically a buffet) is served.

Shorter cabaret tables can be set with two to four chairs depending on the table size as part of a cocktail reception. Taller tables can be used to facilitate networking during a reception, or

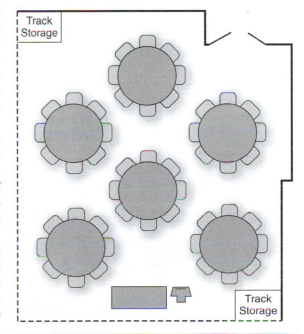

FIGURE 23.3
Roundtable Set-up Seating Eight People per 60-inch Table

TABLE 23.1
Schoolroom (Classroom) Guidelines

Schoolroom (Classroom)	
Description	Long tables with standard seating are placed in rows facing the speaker or focal point in the room. The surface is ideal for note taking and enables water pitchers/glasses to be close to attendees.
Best Uses	Ideal for attendees who must take notes or refer to handouts and/or material in binders. Also helpful if computer equipment or other tools/props are needed. This is the most comfortable set for long sessions. The speaker/entertainer does most of the talking. Not ideal for stimulating conversation among attendees.
Best Design	Tables abut forming rows facing the speaker. Ideally, rows that extend beyond the stage should be tilted toward the speaker (herringbone pattern), thus providing a better angle to the screen or speaker.
Set-up Hints	The distance from the back of one table to the front of the table in the row behind should be at least 3.5 feet to avoid attendees having to scoot in sideways to get to their seats.
	Try to avoid long rows. Rows should be 24 feet or less and have aisles on both sides. If the entrance doors are on the side of the room, be sure to have cross-aisles to help attendees get into the room.
	Allow at least 2 feet of table space per person (three people per 6-foot table, four people per 8-foot table). For meetings where a lot of materials, binders, or computers are used, allow 2.5 feet to 3 feet of table space per person (two people per 6-foot table, three people per 8-foot table).

as part of a "working lunch." When cabaret tables are set with a stage to create a nightclub atmosphere the set-up is referred to as a cabaret set-up.

These tables are also perfect for adding décor to the function room as part of the event.

Schoolroom/Classroom Set-up

The schoolroom or classroom set-up is most often used for lecture-formatted meetings (see Table 23.1). While both terms are used interchangeably in the APEX glossary, the term schoolroom set-up will be used here. In this style, attendees are seated at tables facing the speaker so the presenter can see all the participants. However, minimal interaction is possible between participants, and participants only see each other's backs. In the schoolroom setting, allow 17 to 22 square feet per person.

Most facilities have a supply of 6-foot and/or 8-foot by 18-inch tables used for this purpose. The standard in most facilities is three people seated per 6-foot table and four people per 8-foot table. For comfort during daylong education sessions, some meeting managers prefer two chairs per 6-foot table and three chairs per 8-foot table, especially when attendees will be using laptop computers or resource manuals (see Figure 23.4).

Conference or Meeting Set-up

The set-ups described below vary according to meeting objectives and group needs. For maximum effectiveness, these seating styles should be limited to groups of no more than 25 to 30 people. To prevent crowding, allow a minimum of 2.5 feet per person (3 feet is preferable) and avoid table legs in the placement of chairs. Also avoid seating two people in the adjoining corners of the table. Microphones may be needed to ensure that all participants can clearly hear the proceedings.

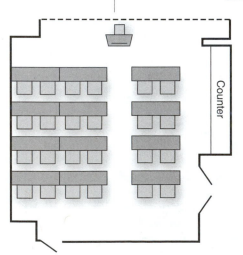

FIGURE 23.4
Schoolroom (Classroom) Set-up

TABLE 23.2
Boardroom Set-up Guidelines

	Boardroom Style
Description	The boardroom style set-up refers to a table where attendees may be seated on all four sides. For smaller groups (16 people or fewer), 6-foot or 8-foot by 30-inch tables are combined to make a solid rectangular table. Some facilities have rooms with a permanent table and suitable chairs, in which case the room is known as a boardroom set-up. For larger groups, the table becomes a hollow square or hollow rectangle.
Best Uses	This style is designed to encourage dialogue between participants. Often used for a board of directors, committees or small discussion groups.
Equipment	Many facilities have permanent conference tables. The permanent boardroom table should be at least 5 feet wide, and the width should increase as the number of attendees grows. For hollow squares, use 30-inch wide tables or double up 18-inch wide tables to create a 36-inch width.
Best Design	The longer each side is, the harder it will be to see others who may be speaking. For groups of 25 people or more, consider an octagonal set-up to provide better communication and sight lines for participants.
Set-up Hints	No chair should ever be within 1 foot of a shared corner on a conference table or hollow square/rectangle. For hollow squares/rectangles, skirt the sides and inside of each table section. For these sets, no corners will have two attendees, so seats can go within 1 foot of the corner.
	These set-ups require approximately 30 square feet per person at the table. Allow at least 2 feet of table space per person. For meetings where a lot of materials, binders or computers are used, allow 2.5 feet to 3 feet of table space per person (two people per 6-foot table, three people per 8-foot table).
	Place the speaker or facilitator at the side opposite the entrance door whenever possible. On the entrance door wall, place extra seating for those who may be observing or presenting to the board or committee. This way they can enter and leave the room with the least amount of disturbance.

Specify the type of table arrangement desired:

- *U-shape set-up*—A horseshoe-shaped arrangement of tables, usually used for interactive and board-style meetings. Indicate if seating is to be placed inside as well as outside the U (see Table 23.3 and Figure 23.5).
- *T-shape set-up*—Self-explanatory. If only chair people or presenters are to be seated at the top of the T, specify the number of chairs to be placed in that location (see Figure 23.6). This style can be used for small banquets, possibly with a guest speaker who does not have a visual presentation.
- *Boardroom set-up*—This is preferred by industry over the term 'conference style,' however, both refer to the same set-up. Two or more tables are put together to provide extra room for notebooks and other meeting materials or to create a solid table. This style is typically used for committee and board meetings (see Table 23.2 and Figure 23.7).
- *Hollow square set-up*—Self-explanatory. Chairs are placed on the outside only (see Figure 23.8). This style is sometimes confused with the boardroom style (above).
- *Rounded hollow square set-up*—Same as Hollow Square, but with serpentines or half moon tables at corners of the square (see Figure 23.9). A word of caution: When hollow-square or rounded hollow-square styles are used for meetings, 20% to 23% of the participants will not be able to see each other while seated.
- *Geometric shapes set-up*—These may include diamond, octagon, or oval designs. These designs are preferred for larger groups of 20 or more.

TABLE 23.3
U-shape Set-up Guidelines

U-Shape	
Description	U-shaped configurations consist of rectangular tables placed to form a "U." Seating is generally around the outside of the "U;" however, it is possible to seat attendees on both inside legs.
Best Uses	Used for board of directors, committees, and breakouts when audiovisuals are involved. Occasionally used for banquets with seating at all sides.
Equipment	Use tables that are 6 feet or 8 feet long and 30 inches wide. Table widths of less than 30 inches are not recommended.
Best Design	The length of the configuration depends on expected attendance and on the facility's inventory. Allow a minimum of 2 feet of table space per person; 2.5 feet to 3 feet if materials, binders or computers are used. You may need more space if larger chairs are used. For "outside-only" set-ups, avoid U-shapes of 25 people or more. The sides become so long that attendees' participation is stifled.
Set-up Hints	Allow 2 feet for each standard hotel chair. If board room-type chairs are used, provide the actual chair width plus 6 inches per person. Don't place any attendee within 1 foot of a shared corner. For outside seating only, skirt the inside. Do not skirt the inside if interior seating is used.

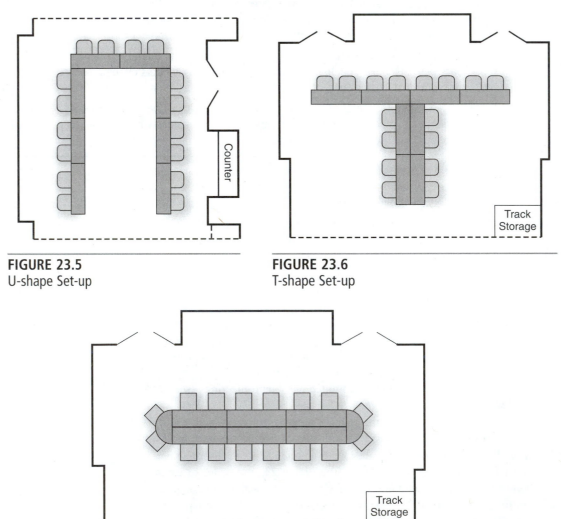

FIGURE 23.5
U-shape Set-up

FIGURE 23.6
T-shape Set-up

FIGURE 23.7
Traditional Boardroom Set-up

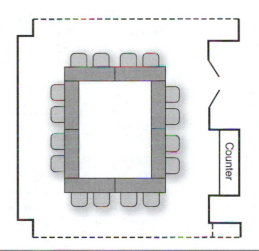

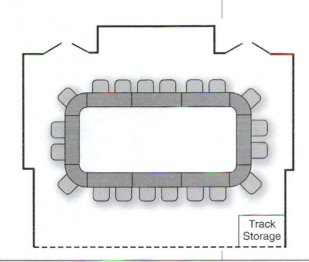

FIGURE 23.8
Hollow Square Set-up

FIGURE 23.9
Rounded Hollow Square Set-up

TABLE 23.4
Theater (Auditorium) Set-up Guidelines

Theater (Auditorium)	
Description	Chairs are lined up in rows facing the speaker or focal point in the room. Padded, stacking chairs are usually used. There is no writing surface or area for handout materials.
Best Uses	When attendees take on the characteristic of an audience (i.e., listening to a speaker or entertainer, viewing a movie or slide presentation), this is the most efficient room set-up. Not recommended for note taking or food events. This style is used to maximize attendance in meeting rooms to allow the audience to be as close to the speaker as possible.
Best Design	This is the most flexible set-up from a design perspective. Theater should be set up in rows facing the speaker. The rows may be semi-circular, circular, straight or herringbone (i.e., angled toward the speaker). If space is not a problem, offset each row so that the attendee is not looking over the person in front but rather between people, and avoid a center aisle unless it is necessary for the program.
Set-up Hints	For a capacity audience, the space between adjacent chairs should be at least 2 inches (preferably 4 inches to 6 inches for comfort). However, if chairs interlock, there will be no option on spacing. The space between rows of chairs should be at least 24 inches from the back of one row to the front of the next row. Each row should be no more than 30 feet long. The first row of chairs should be no closer than 6 feet from the edge of the platform, or 2 times the vertical dimension of the screen, whichever is farther. *CAUTION: Many hotels place chairs so that they are touching or near-touching side to side. Avoid this whenever possible. Because standard chairs are narrower than most people's bodies, attendees will be spilling on to the next chair. This actually reduces capacity in a room, as not all chairs will be used.*

Theater (Auditorium) Set-up

Theater or auditorium set-ups are good for large groups where reading and writing are not required (see Table 23.4). Platforms for presenters may be necessary for very large groups. Allow 10 to 11 square feet per person for groups of more than 300 people, 11 to 12 square feet per person for groups of 60 to 300 people, and 12 to 13 square feet per person for groups of fewer than 60 people.

There are many variations of the theater-style set-up, but the focal point is always the speaker and the A/V support area. Chairs are set in straight rows facing the speaker. They can also be placed in a semi-circle or chevron set-up (also called or herringbone set-up). A modification of the chevron arrangement for use with larger audiences has a straight center section and two side sections that are slightly slanted to face the speaker, providing better visibility for the attendees who are seated on outer edges (see Figure 23.10). A theater-style arrangement can also be set up with additional side aisles framing sections of chairs, and cross aisles can be added (see Figure 23.11).

In any case, set up the front edge of the first row of chairs at least 6 feet away from the edge of the speaker's table or platform. Length of rows should be limited to 14 chairs, so that participants will not cross over more than six attendees from aisle to seat. For a capacity audience, the space between rows of chairs should be at least 24 inches from the back of one row to the front of the next row.

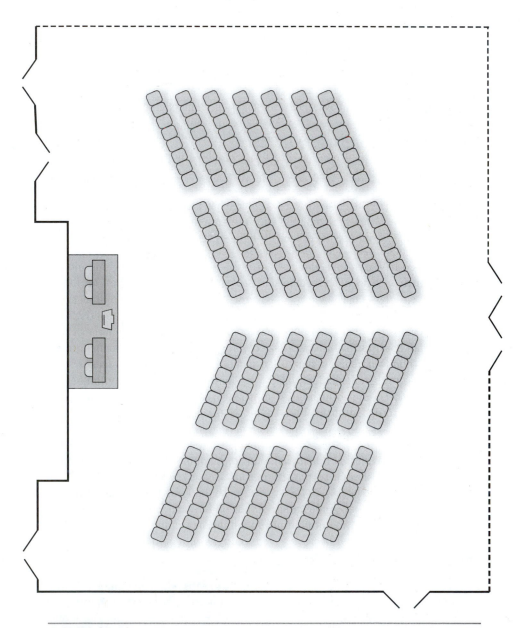

FIGURE 23.10
Theater-Style Set-up in Modified-Chevron

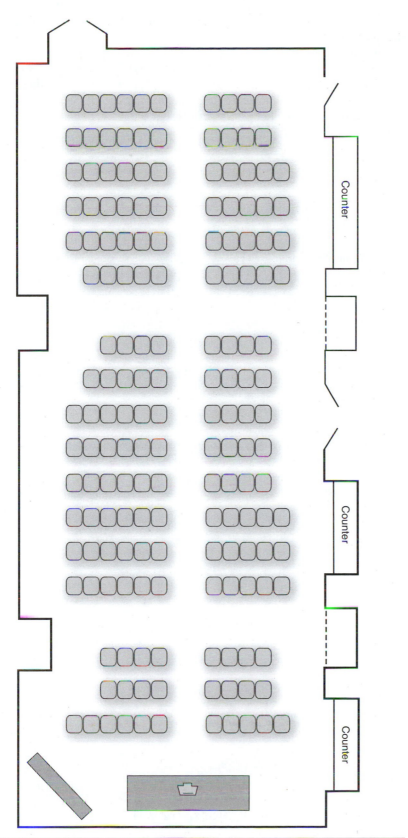

FIGURE 23.11
Theater-Style Set-up with Wall and Cross Aisles

Avoid a center aisle unless it is necessary for part of the program. Otherwise, the speaker looks directly into empty space.

Required capacity and fire codes can dictate the space between chairs, the distance between rows, and the number, width, and location of aisles. Some local fire codes dictate that meeting facilities use chairs that lock together in a theater-style set-up. Fire codes can also require the placement of aisles across a room's front and rear and along both sides. Extra room should be planned near exits for proper traffic flow.

TABLE 23.5

Set-up Uses, Advantages, and Disadvantages

Set-up Uses	Advantages	Disadvantages
Theater (Auditorium)		
Sessions with a staged performance or elaborate audiovisuals. Large groups (more than 200 people).	Maximum number of people can be seated. Any kind of space can be adapted to this set-up.	No writing surface for participants. Limited (if any) interaction between speaker and participants. Often sight lines are obscured when seating is on a flat (as opposed to an inclined) floor. Set-up tends to discourage attendee participation on most levels.
Schoolroom (Classroom)		
Large groups or long sessions where workspace is required. Session with a speaker. Training sessions for groups of 40 to 50 people.	Good sight lines to front of room. Ample work space if you allow for 2.5 to 3 feet per person is allowed. Allows for some small-group interaction when participants at every other table turn to face those in back of them.	Uses a lot of space. People in back of room may have impaired sight lines and trouble hearing people near the front of the room. May limit participation by people at the back of the room. Often presents a psychological barrier between presenter and attendee.
U-shape		
Group problem solving, information sharing, and decision-making. Ideal for groups of 6 to 12 people.	Allows presenter to get close to participants. Allows for good group interaction. Good sight lines and workspace. Good access and egress without disturbing others. Openness often encourages participation. Promotes good eye contact within group and with presenter. No sense of preferential seating, so there is a sense of equality among participants.	Uses a lot of space. For optimal learning, group size is limited to 20 to 24 people.
T-shape		
Small groups where defined leadership is desired/necessary. Labor and other negotiation-based sessions.	Allows for interaction between facing rows in stem of T. Provides good sight lines for participants when audiovisuals are placed at bottom of T. Defines leadership/authority figure(s).	Poor group interaction across top of T.

TABLE 23.5

Set-up Uses, Advantages, and Disadvantages, continued

Set-up Uses	Advantages	Disadvantages
Hollow Square		
Small groups where there is a facilitator guiding discussion. Decision-making, problem-solving sessions. Groups of up to 30 people.	Good sight lines and eye contact between participants. Ample workspace. No sense of preferential seating, so there is a sense of equality among participants. Efficient use of space in a room.	Not good for session requiring audiovisuals.
Roundtable Style		
Informal sessions such as creativity/brainstorming sessions. In-depth, small-group discussions.	Good eye contact around the table. Good workspace depending on diameter of table and number of people per table. No preferential seating so there is a sense of equality among participants.	In a room set with several round tables, some people may have their backs to the speaker. Not good for a session requiring audiovisuals. May limit interaction with speaker. May be loud because of simultaneous discussions at tables.
V-shape		
Technical training sessions where facilitator can be inside V. Training, demonstrations, simulations. Groups of up to 25 people.	Good eye contact and sight lines for all participants. Allows for good interaction with facilitator. Allows a student in technical/computer training to see both their monitors and the facilitator.	Not good for session requiring audiovisuals. Limits group interaction.
Learning Circle (Circle of Chairs)		
Intimate sessions that require risk taking or sharing of personal experiences. Groups of up to 20 people.	Sense of equality among participants. Sense of connectedness (unity) in-group. Promotes feeling of safety for participants. Any kind of space can be adapted to this set-up.	No writing surface for participants. Limited to smaller groups. Not good for session requiring audiovisuals.

LIGHTING, TEMPERATURE, AND NOISE

Lighting, temperature, and noise levels in the meeting space impact attendee learning and comfort. Meeting rooms should be adequately lit and well ventilated. Temperatures should be maintained at 70°F to 74°F. Generally, it is better for participants to be too cool than too warm.

Noise from heating/cooling systems, adjacent rooms and corridors, nearby construction, and automobile traffic, airplanes, or trains can seriously detract from a meeting. Evaluate the noise level in the meeting space, and consider how that noise will affect the event. For example, a conference-style set-up with 30 people may require microphones to enable all participants to hear the proceedings.

Consider the type of lighting and control system when selecting the meeting space where participants are viewing audiovisuals and/or reading and writing. Some lighting systems are zoned to enable sections of a room to be dimmed for

A/V presentations, while allowing the audience area to remain adequately lit. Remote controls may be placed for the speaker's use or for the use of an assisting technician. The room monitor should be instructed in the operation of lighting.

The main lighting systems in meeting rooms will most likely be incandescent, fluorescent, or halogen. Each has its advantages/disadvantages:

- *Incandescent*—Regular light bulbs with tungsten wire filaments of varying wattage, capable of dimming if needed; provides good lighting for meetings.
- *Fluorescent*—High-intensity discharge electric arcs combined with phosphors; produces bright light throughout the room; incapable of dimming, produces high glare, and can cause eyestrain.
- *Halogen*—Quartz or quartz iodine lighting, with a small size relative to the light generated; capable of dimming if needed.
- *Ambient lighting*—Collected from windows and skylights; lighting is dependent on the time of day and weather conditions.

Artificial lighting produces consistent lighting throughout the course of a meeting. Ambient lighting may be suitable for banquet events but can produce serious glare that may impede the effectiveness of audiovisuals. The ideal meeting room lighting system is user friendly, with low glare, enough light for the chosen task, and flexible enough to allow multi-task functions to be performed simultaneously (i.e., lights turned low over the projection screen, brighter over the speaker/presenter, and bright enough over attendees so that they may take notes or do other tasks).

The use of various lighting techniques can help to achieve the goals of the meeting or event. The meeting manager can work with the facility or an outside contractor to achieve the desired affect. The use of other techniques adds aesthetic quality to the meeting or event, while serving a specific purpose. For example:

- *Accent lighting*—Directional lighting used to highlight an area or object, and to draw the attendee's attention to that field of view.
- *Back lighting*—Used to illuminate transparent and translucent materials, or to give depth to a speaker or image when videotaping.
- *Ellipsoidal spotlights*—An adjustable spotlight used to focus a pool of light on a lectern, sign, or area.
- *Wash lighting*—Lighting, which may be colored, that softly illuminates an area, for accent purposes.

Recalling the metaphor of the theatre cited by James Gilmore earlier in the chapter, the meeting manager would be wise to study theatrical techniques from various forms of entertainment to achieve the desired purpose.

SUMMARY

Selecting the appropriate room set-up design and equipment will result in effective and efficient use of the meeting room space. The best design is one in which meeting space and set-up support the meeting's purpose, provide a comfortable environment, promote the communication process, and minimize any environmental distractions.

The physical components of a learning environment include the meeting room, tables, chairs, temperature, individual space, and so on. The psychological components of the meeting or learning environment include the attitudes and expectations of the attendee, the degree in which the attendee participates and interacts with the environment and the attitude of the speaker or presenter. All of these components must work together to create an effective environment that supports the learning objectives for an educational session and/or the objectives of the meeting or event.

There is a wide variety of meeting room set-ups to chose from. The meeting's program objectives and individual session learning objectives will determine which is appropriate for a given situation. When selecting the style of room set-up, the meeting manager must take into account the purpose and size of the meeting, lighting and audiovisual requirements, plans of the speaker or entertainment, fire codes, and special needs of the attendees. There are many set-up styles to choose from, ranging from theater to roundtables, and each has an ideal purpose. The style must suit the purpose of the meeting or event.

Planning for equipment needs in advance will help in negotiating and planning with facility representatives. It also enables the meeting manager to determine early on whether the facility can meet all of the group's needs or whether an outside supplier must be contracted. Establishing and constantly updating a detailed inventory list of equipment needed is a good idea.

It is also important to plan in advance for logistical space needs, such as registration, tour desks, information kiosks, housing registration desks, storage, and office space. Having adequate space and staff necessary to support the goals and objectives of the meeting and/or event can determine whether a favorable impression is given to the attendees. Taking advantage of the capabilities of room diagramming software and space diaries can make the process more accurate and streamlined.

The unique aspect of meetings and events are the possibility of interaction between the speaker and attendees, and among peers in an organization or common field. Creating an environment for success, whether it be educational sessions, meetings for discussion, social gatherings, or other organized activities is essential.

REFERENCES

1. Baraban, R. (January, 2000). Every meeting is a stage. *Corporate meetings and incentives.* Retrieved March 15, 2006 from http://meetingsnet.com/corporate-meetingsincentives/meetings_new_perspectives_every/index.html.

2. APEX event specifications guide template (2004). McLean, VA: Convention Industry Council.

3. Drew, J. (June, 1994). How to size up and set up a meeting room. *Meeting news.*

4. Andersen, O., Marsh, M., & Harvey, A. (1999). *Learn with the classics: How to use music for learning, teaching and studying.* San Francisco: The LIND Institute.

5. Pine, B. J. II, & Gilmore, J.H. (1999). *The experience economy.* Boston, MA: Harvard Business School Press.

6. Malouf, L. (1999). *Behind the scenes at special events.* New York: John Wiley & Sons.

7. Silvers, J. R. (2004). *Professional event coordination.* Hoboken, NJ: John Wiley & Sons.

8. Andersen et al., op. cit.

9. Finkel, C. L. (1987). *The total immersion learning environment.* New York: Conference Center Development Corp.

10. Harris, B. (2000). Function room set up. *The convention industry council manual. (7th ed.)* McLean, VA: Convention Industry Council.

KEY TERMS

Accent lighting	Head table	Serpentine queue
Accessibility	Herringbone set-up	Set-up
Air wall	Hollow square set-up	Set-up drawings
Ambient light	Horseshoe	Set-up personnel
Auditorium set-up	Housemen	Set-up plan
Autograph table	Incandescent	Set-up time
Back light	Learning environment	Speakers' ready room
Boardroom	Lectern	Speakers' room/lounge
Boardroom set-up	Panel discussion	Tablet chairs
Cabaret set-up	Perimeter seating	Talk show set-up
Cabaret table	Podium	Theater semicircular
Ceiling height	Ready room	set-up
Chevron set-up	Registration area	Theater set-up
Classroom table	Risers	T-shape set-up
Crescent round set-up	Room capacity	Traffic flow
Dais	Round	Turnover
Ellipsoidal spotlight	Rounded hollow square	U-shape set-up
Fluorescent	set-up	V-shape set-up
Function space	Roundtable	Walk and talk
Green room	Schoolroom set-up	Wash light
Guest program	Serpentine	

COMPELLING QUESTIONS FOR CONSIDERATION

1. What factors should be considered when selecting meeting room set-up styles that will enhance the learning environment for participants?

2. For what types of meeting sessions would you use a theater-style set-up?

3. For what types of meeting sessions would you use a roundtable set-up?

4. Discuss how you would accommodate a speaker who uses a wheelchair in a general session, and an attendee who uses a wheelchair in a schoolroom-style setting.

5. What are the benefits of knowing in advance what meeting equipment you will need? How can you develop such an inventory?

CHAPTER 24

TAMING THE REGISTRATION BEAST

Kenneth G. Carlisle, CMP
VICE PRESIDENT
OUTSOURCES

LEARNER OUTCOMES

When the reader has completed reading this chapter, he/she should be able to . . .

1 Identify the advantages of advance registration for both the meeting manager and the attendee.

2 Explain the uses for information about attendees that is gathered during the registration process.

3 Discuss details involved in the set-up and procedural management of online registration.

4 Discuss the physical set-up and procedural management of on-site registration.

5 Assemble a complete registration packet.

As the line you left starts moving.

Eddie Lewis

OVERVIEW

Registration is the transitional phase between the marketing of a meeting and the meeting itself. It is the first interactive experience a potential attendee has with the meeting. A poor registration system will frustrate attendees and potential attendees, limiting their ability to register properly and completely. Improper and incomplete registrations can also result in additional staffing expenses as well as reduction in revenue. A carefully planned registration process that is quick, thorough, and easy to navigate will be appreciated by attendees, welcomed by the meeting manager, and reflect positively in the meeting's financial bottom-line.

Technology has revolutionized the way we work. The blending of computers, software, and the Internet has transformed how we process meeting registrations as well. Each year more registrations are conducted online than were the year before. While the rules of processing registrations are the same today as they were in the past, the means by which the process is completed and the meeting manager's necessary knowledge base have changed. Today, meeting managers who are responsible for meeting registration also need to have a basic understanding of the relevant computer hardware and software, how databases work, and the role of the Internet in meeting registration.

ADVANCE REGISTRATION

The first step in designing an effective registration process is to offer attendees the opportunity to register in advance. Regardless of the size of the meeting, this will dramatically simplify on-site traffic problems, improve attendance, and generate cash flow during the months preceding the event. Moreover, advance registration provides an early indication of marketing strengths and weaknesses.

Careful planning and skilled organization are required to prevent advance registration from creating more problems than it solves. A misplaced check or incorrect paperwork can result in a frustrated, angry registrant.

Today, computerization of advance registration is vitally essential for any sized meeting. A computer, database software, and access to the Internet are key tools in today's registration processes. Special attention needs to be paid to database development. Whether using an in-house or a third-party database, ensure that adequate time and expertise are allocated to its design to ensure that all of the necessary information is being captured, as well as that the information captured can be formatted into the reports that are need. A registration database that is flawed in data or design can result in frustration when the reports that are needed cannot be produced.

In addition to the opportunity to register for the meeting, advance registration is a great opportunity to market products, services, or additional events to attendees. Attendees may be encouraged to purchase tickets for additional events, such as social functions and tours; services, such as babysitting; or products, such as CDs of meeting program content. Some organizations plan special in-depth conferences and workshops requiring separate, additional fees. Usually, the more programs that are included in the advance registration package, the more attractive the meeting will be to prospective attendees.

Other than a discount on fees and tickets, which may or may not be offered, the primary incentives to register early are the avoidance of standing in line for on-site registration and the guarantee of reserved tickets for events that might become sold out. Advance registrants should be assured of getting all necessary materials by mail or email before leaving home for the meeting or of having a packet of material, including a badge, waiting for convenient pick up at the on-site registration area.

Advance Registration Announcement

Whether it is sent by mail, email, or fax, or posted on the organization's web site, the advance registration announcement should contain complete information about registration procedures.

Never assume that including pertinent information on the registration form is sufficient. Once the application has been completed and returned, the attendee often will have no reference to important details. A good practice is to provide important details on the organization or meeting web site and in the promotional brochure text as well.

General information regarding advance registration procedures, including the refund policy, should be highlighted in the promotional materials. Generally speaking, there should be some leeway for refunds. If the promotion states that there will be no refunds for cancellations after a specific date, the date should be extended internally, by a week to 10 days. Using a postmark deadline assists registrants and staff alike by removing the question: "Did my registration get there on time?" This allows for delays in mail, and so on. Refunds should be made within seven to 10 days of the receipt of the cancellation notice. However, for cancellations made within 30 days of the event, refunds need not be made until after the event. Some organizations reduce the refund by a nominal amount of $10 to $50 to cover the administrative costs of processing and refunding a registration. While these "administrative fee" charges may help cover the administrative costs or registration processing, they may also keep people from registering until the last moment—resulting in a deluge of registrations just before closeout of advance registration. It is important that organizations think through this issue thoroughly.

Many organizations include all meeting activities in the registration fee. This method simplifies registration and accounting since one fee covers everything. Other organizations keep registration fees as low as possible so as not to discourage budget-conscious people from attending. Activities and special events cost extra and are paid for as optional fees added to the registration total. Organizations need to decide which method is most suitable for the program design and attendees' needs, then implement procedures that allow for the collection of payment and accurate tracking all types of registrations—attendee, exhibitor, speaker, and VIP.

Pre-Registration Methods

Most organizations offer a variety of pre-registration methods. Attendees should be able to register by mail, phone, fax, or via the Internet. The method of registration often correlates with the method of payment: the majority of forms that are mailed include a check (for some organizations a purchase order) as the payment method. The majority of forms that are faxed have a credit card as the payment method. Most online registration systems require a credit card as the payment method. There is no clear advantage of one payment method over another. Credit card and check payments risk being rejected for insufficient funds. Checks may take a little more time to clear through the bank but are not open to the risk of charge back fees. Both forms of payment have associated processing costs, such as staff time, bank fees, or credit card fees (the percentage taken on the sale processed).

Some organizations allow attendees to register by phone. This trend seems to be declining for a variety of reasons. Taking phone registrations is both prone to errors and time consuming, particularly if the program includes multiple tracks, limited seating, special events, and other options. It is difficult to properly staff for phone-in registrations, since it is often unpredictable when peak periods will fall during the day. Other registration methods allow the organization to manage the data entry staff's workload. In peak periods it may appropriate to add several hours to a work shift or split the workload over several shifts while maintaining

Fast Facts

Contents of Registration Announcement

- How to register
- Who may register
- Credentials, if required
- Fee for each category of registrant
- Materials and amenities included in the fee
- Deadline date for receipt of advance registration
- Policy about checks, purchase orders, foreign funds, wire transfers, and credit cards
- Cancellation and refund policies
- Date that badge and final program will be mailed, if not distributed on site
- Information for attendees with special needs
- On-site fees that will apply, if different from advance fees
- On-site registration location and hours

timely issuance of confirmations. There are also a few less obvious disadvantages to phone-in registration, such as:

- There is no audit trail (no paper forms with a signature as proof of purchase).
- It leaves the organization open to "he-said/she-said" situations on-site.
- Should the database crash or become corrupted, there will be no method of recreating the registration files.

The methods of pre-registration offered will depend on the history and level of comfort the organization and their attendees have with each method.

Timely Confirmations

Confirmations should be expedited, with a follow-up confirmation notice emailed, faxed, or mailed within 48 hours. The faster the confirmation is sent, the fewer telephone calls the organization will have to field. Today's online registration systems can provide confirmations instantaneously once the online registration process has been completed.

The confirmation, at a minimum, should clearly indicate meeting dates and the fact that it is a confirmation. It should provide a clear summary of registration fees paid, registration ID number for future reference, balance due, and activities or courses selected. If possible, list all of the information that was entered into the registration system and request the attendee to review and advise of any errors. This will help minimize any on-site corrections. For the attendee's convenience it may be useful to include other information, such as on-site registration location and schedule, and shuttle bus information. More advanced registration systems offer a confirmation letter that is customized to each registration category or activity selected (e.g., a speaker could be invited to the speaker ready room, international attendees could be reminded to take advantage of the international attendees' reception, and so on).

It is also useful to recap the organization's refund policies. The confirmation should include the phone and fax numbers of the registration desk and instructions for how attendees can make changes to their registration record. If the confirmation serves as a confirmation of both registration and the attendee's hotel reservation, the hotel's address should be included and, if possible, the reservation confirmation number.

REGISTRATION FORMS

Form development presents an interesting challenge. The form must be designed for efficient handling and accurate entry into the reporting system database, and at the same time be understandable and easy to use, particularly in calculating applicable fees. The registration form can either be a part of a brochure or a separate sheet or card with one or multiple copies. Use what best fits the meeting's specific needs.

First, determine what is required for statistical and financial reporting (name, title, contact information, registration category and fee, and so on). Then consider additional questions concerning the demographic profile of attendees. Attendee data are a valuable by-product of the registration process. Information about the buying power of attendees, and the services and products they use, is generally significant to exhibitors, vendors, and the facility. This information is also valuable for the meeting manager in marketing the event to potential exhibitors and sponsors. Information gleaned from one meeting is essential for promoting future meetings, and demographic information can provide guidance for planning and improving the next meeting.

Design the form to be clean in appearance and easy to read, keeping the copy simple and concise:

- Do not use a variety of typefaces, and reserve bold face and *italic type* for important directives.
- Avoid the use of long blocks of copy set in CAPITAL LETTERS.
- As a general rule, do not ask attendees to fill in blanks; have them choose between alternatives.
- Procedures and instructions for attendees should be included on the same page as the form to be completed. If this is not possible, the procedures and instructions should be on the page facing or immediately preceding the actual form (for printed materials).
- Identify on the form the required information that is specific to the meeting. Required information should be designated with an asterisk (*) and a notation should be made on the form that "*These fields are required in order for this form to be processed."[1]
- Avoid using a glossy finish that is difficult to write or type on and colors (such as blue) or shading (like grays) that do not photocopy or fax well.

If pre-registration will be offered via fax, design the form with that in mind. Keep artwork and large black areas to a minimum, since they slow down fax transmissions. Do not use any shading on the form; it will appear as a solid gray area when faxed. If the form extends to more than one page, provide a place for the registrant's name and phone number on *each* page in case some pages are not received or are separated from the others.

Ensure that the payment section of the form is easy to complete. Some organizations require attendees to sign the registration form to acknowledge the organization's cancellation and refund policy. Other organizations require a signature with credit card payment, not only to authorize the credit card payment, but also to authorize the organization to charge the correct amount of fees if the attendee has miscalculated the total fee.

Figure 24.1 illustrates the APEX Event Registration Form. This form is the industry accepted structure for forms by which attendees can register to attend events of all types. The form can be produced on paper or electronically, and may be designed by event organizers to reflect the "look and feel" of the event or the host organization. All design should be clear, concise, and, if printed, include enough room to handwrite information. (Downloadable electronic copies of this form are available from the Convention Industry Council's web site: www.conventionindustry.org.)

Online Forms

The Internet has greatly eased the function of pre-registration, and most organizations continue to see an increase in the number of registrants who register via the web.

Processing registration over the Internet poses some unique challenges and provides unique benefits. Most of the unique challenges to online registration are the up-front technical issues that occur when setting up the system. Once it is set up, the benefits of online registration include reduced staffing for data entry and greater emphasis on quality control of data.

If the organization offers pre-registration, it is important that registrations from all sources, including the Internet, can be entered in a single database. Many association management software providers currently include web modules that facilitate this process. Specialized registration firms can also integrate data collected from online forms into their statistical and financial reporting systems. The Internet has also facilitated the ability to connect to a registration database from a remote location. Today's registration software offers various levels of access to registration data, coupled with a variety of web-based reporting tools and search capabilities.

APEX EVENT REGISTRATION FORM TEMPLATE

[HEADER]

[At a minimum, the following information should be included in this area:
    Event Name
    Event Dates in <<MonthName StartDate-EndDate, Year>> Format
    Name of Primary Event Facility
    Event City, State/Province, Country
    Deadline for Submitting the Event Registration Form & Receiving Event-Specific Rates

Additional form header content may include:
    Event Logo
    Event Organizer Logo
    Other pertinent information determined by the event organizer]

ATTENDEE INFORMATION

*These fields are required in order for this form to be processed.

Prefix *(Mr., Ms., Dr., etc.)*: _____   Given Name/First Name: _____   MiddleName/Initial: _____

Family Name *(as appears on passport)*: _____   Suffix(s) *(Jr., MD, CPA, etc.)*: _____

Preferred Name *(for badge)*: _____

Employer/Organization: _____   Job Title: _____

Preferred Mailing Address:
    Address1:_____   Address2:_____
    City: _____   State/Province: _____   Zip/Postal Code: _____   Country: _____

Employer/Organization Mailing Address: ☐ Same As Preferred Mailing Address
    If different from preferred address, complete the following:
    Address1:_____   Address2:_____
    City: _____   State/Province: _____   Zip/Postal Code: _____   Country: _____

Preferred Phone: _____ *(Include appropriate country, city, and area codes)*
Mobile Phone: _____ *(Include appropriate country, city, and area codes)*
Fax: _____ *(Include appropriate country, city, and area codes)*

Email: _____

Preferred Method for Receiving Acknowledgement of Registration: ☐ Email   ☐ Fax   ☐ Mail

Would you like to be contacted by event sponsors and exhibitors prior to the event? ☐ Yes By Email ☐ Yes By Fax
☐ Yes By Mail ☐ No

Attendee Type *[List all attendee categories the Event Organizer desires to track, for example, Member, Speaker, Exhibitor, Guest]*:
    ☐ [Attendee Type 1]
    ☐ [Attendee Type 2]
    ☐ *Additional Attendee Types As Necessary*

Do you have any special physical ♿, dietary *(for example, vegetarian, kosher)*, or other needs: ☐ Yes ☐ No
    If yes, please describe: _____

[Event-Specific Attendee Information - Use this section to add additional questions that are specific to this event. For example: Are you a first-time attendee for the XYZ Conference? ☐ Yes ☐ No and, If No, How many times have you attended? _____]

FIGURE 24.1
APEX Event Registration Form Template. Used with permission.

ON-SITE EMERGENCY INFORMATION

Where you are staying during the event? _____ *(for example, name of hotel, with a family member, at home)*

In Case of Emergency:
    Name of Person to Contact: _____
    Phone: _____ *(Include appropriate country, city, and area codes)*
    Relationship to You: _____

REGISTRATION FEES

All fees are in *[note type of currency]. [Note if any functions are limited by space or other requirements]*

	Before [Date]	After [Date]	Additional Date Categories As Necessary
[AttendeeType1]			
[FeeType1]	☐ <<$Amount>>	☐ <<$Amount>>	
[FeeType2]	☐ <<$Amount>>	☐ <<$Amount>>	
Additional Fee Types As Necessary			
[AttendeeType2]			
[FeeType1]	☐ <<$Amount>>	☐ <<$Amount>>	
[FeeType2]	☐ <<$Amount>>	☐ <<$Amount>>	
Additional Fee Types As Necessary			

Additional Attendee Types as Necessary

Note any discounts that are available

Total Cost—Payment Due $_____ $_____

[An event's Fee Types could be Full Registration, One-Day Registration, Special Session/Event #1, etc.]

PAYMENT INFORMATION
Please—only one form of payment per registration!

[Include any special event-specific instructions (for example, Any registration form received without a valid deposit will not be processed). Indicate all methods of payment that are applicable to the event including, but not limited to:]

☐ Check ☐ Money Order

    If paying by check or money order, make it payable to <<Payee>> and mail with this form to: <<Payee>>, <<MailingAddress>>, <<City>>, <<State/Province>>, <<Postal/Zip Code>>, <<Country>>.

☐ <<CardTypeAccepted1>>   ☐ <<CardTypeAccepted2>>   ☐ <<CardTypeAccepted3>>   ☐ *Additional card types as necessary*

    Credit Card Number: _____
    Expiration Date: _____ *NOTE: All credit cards must be valid through the dates of the event.*
    Card's Security Code: _____
    Cardholder's Name: _____
    Cardholder's Signature: _____
    Today's Date: _____
    Billing Address *(If Different from Preferred Mailing Address)*:
        Address1: _____ Address2: _____
        City: _____ State/Province: _____ Zip/Postal Code: _____ Country: _____

  Additional Forms of Payment As Necessary (such as wire transfers or purchase orders)

ACKNOWLEDGEMENTS
[Reiterate all policies outlined in the Registration Procedures regarding acknowledgements.]

SEND COMPLETED REGISTRATION FORMS TO:
[Reiterate all methods by which reservations can be made outlined in the Registration Procedures.]

FIGURE 24.1
APEX Event Registration Form Template, continued

If registration will be available via the Internet, ensure that the paper form and web forms match—both in terms of content (registration fees and activities or courses offered) and in terms of the refund policy in force. Published forms with discrepancies among various versions can generate a lot of phone calls and frustration for registrants and staff.

Many organizations have developed extensive web sites for their annual meeting or convention. However, web sites and online registration processing are not the same thing. A web site is an Internet location where attendees can retrieve information about a particular event's registration, hotels, programming, and so on. Web sites can act as a portal to direct attendees to an online registration form. This form (or forms) is the façade that the attendee sees and interacts with. Behind this façade is the online registration system that processes the information.

Whether it is created in-house or provided by a third party, the components of an online registration system should include:

- Internet access, preferably high speed
- Web-based software used for the creation of the online registration form and the creation of customized back end reporting (this software may be purchased and installed in-house, or it may be provided by a third-party service that charges a fee for access and use)
- A database in which all of the information captured via the online registration form is stored. Usually the database is part of the software package or, if in-house, it may be part of the association management software
- An online payment service, which usually is provided by a third-party provider that processes online credit card transactions
- A merchant account number, which allows credit card payments to be deposited into the organization's bank account

DATA SECURITY AND PRIVACY

With computer viruses and hacker attacks going around the world in an instant, database security and attendee privacy protection must be top considerations when setting up registration procedures. Ideally, data are hosted and maintained in-house by information technology professionals, or by a professional firm that has the technical resources to maintain system integrity and security. The following points should be addressed when evaluating database security, whether the database is maintained in-house or by a third-party provider:

- How robust and secure is the server that hosts the data?
- What human resources are available to monitor the system?
- What back-up procedures are in place and what contingency plans exist to recover data in the event of a system failure?
- What kind of virus protection system is in place?
- What procedures are in place to ensure that data are not accessed or misused by unauthorized parties?

With software and hardware technology changing at an ever-increasing pace, it is wise to consult a specialist to find the best technology to ensure proper database security.

Privacy Protection

When data are collected from registrants, they are entrusting the organization with information that they may prefer not to share with others. Policy guidelines drafted by organizations such as TRUSTe (www.truste.org) and the Responsible

Electronic Communication Alliance (RECA, www.ResponsibleEmail.org) set forth procedures to protect customer privacy.

The privacy policy should be easily accessible at any point where attendee information is collected, such as online registration forms and email surveys. It is recommended that attendees are given choices about what information they reveal and how the organization will use that information. For example, an online registration form with extensive profiling should indicate which questions are optional. Attendees should also be able to indicate their preference for receiving additional information about the event, or products and services related to the event.[3]

ON-SITE REGISTRATION

Ideally, most meeting managers would like to receive all of the registration forms in advance. However, this just does not happen. On average, 70% of attendees pre-register. The remaining 30% of attendees expect to register at the meeting easily and without delay. (The number of advance registrations is dependent upon the organizations' past history, and as few as 40% could register in advance.)

It is very difficult to process on-site registration without some waiting. The cost to handle on-site registration without any delay is prohibitive to most organizations. Because on-site registrants probably had the opportunity to pre-register, some inconvenience is acceptable and is part of the motivation to register in advance for the next meeting. However, the meeting manager should try to keep the registration process as streamlined as possible. The feasibility of this goal, of course, will vary depending on the various registration categories on the form, the amount of courses/seminars offered, as well as ticket exchanges and the number of attendees in line.

Today's on-site registration has gone high-tech. It is not unusual to see on-site registration systems that consist of several computers and printers networked to one another and to the pre-registration database, along with Internet access. A registration staff member with a computer should be able to process 10 to 15 attendees per hour, depending on the amount of information to be entered and the tasks that need to be completed at the registration desk (credit card processing, membership verification, course selection/modification, and so on).

Provide written instructions, in advance, for all registration staff members, and conduct an orientation session before registration. It is important that registration staff members understand all procedures for receiving fees, issuing badges and tickets, and cash accounting and checkout. Registration staff should be provided with answers to standard attendee questions and explanation of the organization's policies regarding refunds, lost badges, press passes, guests, and children.

Place supply tables for program books and other handouts behind registration counters. Rope off the registration counter to prevent registrants from entering the work area. Make sure lighting is adequate and there are sufficient electrical outlets. Provide plenty of wastebaskets, ice water, and drinking cups for the registration staff and keep each station supplied with appropriate materials (cards, badges, badge holders, final programs, and receipts).

A knowledgeable staff member should be in charge and supervising the on-site registration area at all times. If this is not possible, registration staff members should know how to get assistance quickly. If space allows, have a small office behind the registration area for staff breaks, refreshments, and tabulating money at the end of each day.

Registration Traffic Flow

The physical layout of the registration area is a major factor in its success. Determine how the on-site registration area will be laid out and segmented between registration options. Will there be just two sections; on-site registration and pre-registration? Or will additional sections be needed for exhibitors, ticket purchases, or badge corrections? If more than just a few tables or counters are required, draft a rough (to scale) floor plan to determine the location of each station and supporting furniture, staffing, and equipment. Ask the facility representative or supplier for specific dimensions of the registration counters and/or tables that will be used. If using counters, ask for the type that comes with lighted signs and advise the supplier of the sign copy or message to be inserted in each header. Have extra generic header signs (e.g., "REGISTRATION") made to use when stations are merged after peak hours. Provide separate, clearly marked areas for such needs as information, ticket exchange, lost and found, and so on.

Most meeting managers ask registrants to present completed forms to registration attendants. This has proven to be the fastest method for accurately capturing registration. In many cases, setting up on-site registration forms in an NCR format (carbonless multiple copies) can expedite the registration process by automatically providing copies of the registration form for everyone who needs a copy. If the registration form will be set up as a NCR format, think through how many copies will be needed and for what purpose, and ensure that each form is printed accordingly (e.g., "Registration Copy," "For Accounting," or "Attendee's Copy").

Some organizations prefer using an interview technique, where the attendant asks the registrant questions to gather data. Others allow attendees to register themselves at self-registration stations or kiosks—computer workstations that are networked to the registration desk. Whether this type of set-up works for the organization will depend upon the volume and complexity of the registration process.

When a large number of people require extensive processing, the most common procedure is to bring them into a reception area first. This area should be well stocked with program literature and equipped with stand-up writing surfaces. Be sure to include counters that are accessible to people in wheelchairs. Place a supply of registration forms and tethered pens on writing tables and affix signs above head level instructing attendees "How to Register." Use large lettering for the instructions, which should be brief, clear, and numbered. Assign someone to monitor the sign-up tables to ensure they are supplied and neat.

After completing the necessary form, the registrant moves to the appropriate registration counter. If there are several categories of registration (member, nonmember, student, and so on), base the number of stations for each category on the most recent registration experience. If statistics are not available, be prepared to be flexible; open and close stations based on need and keep tallies for the next meeting of how many individuals registered in each category each half-day. The area that will serve the heaviest volume should be given the most depth in the layout, allowing space for lines to stretch out. Establish separate registration counters for speakers, exhibitors, and others who are not standard attendees.

If proof of eligibility to register is required, consider a separate credentials station at the head of the line, prior to reaching the registration counter. An employee having the knowledge and authority to evaluate registrants' credentials and make exceptions and rejections should be assigned this function.

If there is one common fee, registrants can be moved into a serpentine queue (line) that feeds to stations for fee payment and badge typing. The serpentine is more than just a way to organize a crowd. It recognizes the fact that, for most people, a certain amount of waiting is tolerable if there is movement and a sense that progress is being made. Even though a serpentine may contain many people, the line will move forward almost constantly if it is feeding four or five stations, keeping everyone as happy as possible under the circumstances (see Figure 24.2).

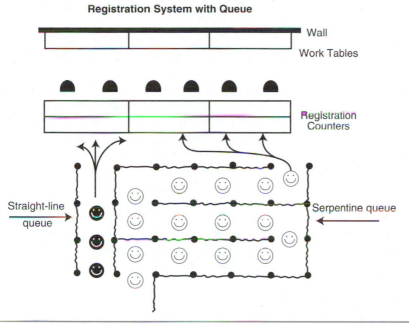

FIGURE 24.2
Layout with a Straight Queue and a Serpentine Queue

Consider placing "traffic managers" at strategic points in the registration queue to verify registration forms before registrants reach the counter. If the program requires registrants to purchase tickets for individual sessions or courses, make sure that a listing of courses that are sold out or closed is clearly displayed. This will prevent delays caused by attendees who stand at the registration counter pondering what replacement course to select.

After traffic has slowed, some stations can be merged and personnel reduced. Do not, however, change the registration location and do not remove too many counters. This may give the appearance that the meeting is over.

Payment Collection

Unless there is a single registration fee for everything, separate data fields should be created in the on-site registration database to account for the various registration and event fees. The confirmation form should double as a receipt, verifying how each dollar spent was utilized relative to registration, event, and so on. Arrangements for depositing money at the end of the day should be made in advance. If considerable sums are collected on-site, consider hiring a specialized firm to pick up and transport money. Coordinate on-site financial management with the organization's finance department to ensure continuity and consistency.

Things can get hectic during on-site registration for large meetings. Control over the process can easily be lost if proper control systems are not in place. This often will occur with the volume of forms to process in a short period of time, inadequately trained temporary staff, registration software with limited abilities to track payments and transactions, or a combination of all of the above. Whether the decision is to hire a professional registration firm, or use in-house staff for the registration, detailed reports on funds collected and transactions processed at the end of each day must be developed and available. The more advanced registration service providers will be able to provide a detailed paper trail of transactions, as well as detailed reporting of various types of funds collected. Whether the organization handles registration or hires a registration service provider, assign one person to be in charge of on-site finances.

REGISTRATION PACKETS

Registration packets may be mailed in advance (15 to 21 days before the meeting) or picked up on-site. The packets should include all necessary documentation, plus name badges and event tickets. If packets are mailed in advance, bulky items may be picked up on-site. Name badge holders are generally picked up on-site and should be placed in a convenient area. Mailing packets in advance enables attendees to forego visiting the registration area and generally cuts down on traffic there. Mailing badges, however, may increase the number of badges that will have to be re-made because the registrant either left the badge at home or never received it.

Many registration systems offer the ability to track actual attendance. An attendee's presence is recorded at the time a badge holder is picked up. This will allow for building historical data of pre-registration figures and actual attendance. Often, these data correlate well with the housing pick-up.

Name Badges and Holders

The two main types of badges are adhesive and plastic holder. The stick-on variety is rarely used for large meetings that extend over several days, since the adhesive fails after a period of use. The plastic case or sleeve badge is available with hook pins, safety pins, revolving clips, a neck cord, or in a pocket-insert version. The most versatile is the combination safety pin/moveable clip-style holder, because it permits the badge to be clasped onto a pocket or rotated 90 degrees to hang from a collar. Some meeting managers avoid the use of coarse pin-on badges, which can damage clothing, and some order several different types to give registrants a choice.

Inserts for plastic badges must be sized to fit the sleeve snugly (not too tight and not too loose). To avoid mistakes, order the badge holders before inserts are printed. Most badge holders and inserts are a standard size. Be certain to order well in advance to avoid problems. Badges can be printed professionally, printed from a computer, typed, or handwritten. They can also include a picture of the attendee (usually for security), be coded by color or number to indicate various categories of attendees, or have barcodes that allow exhibitors or others with the appropriate readers to retrieve profile information on the attendee. Choose a style that meets the organization's needs and budget and projects the desired tone of the meeting.

Most computerized registration programs produce a badge as a by-product of the registration process. Before approving such a program, be sure the resulting badge can be accommodated in commonly available badge holders.

If some categories of registrants are given privileges that other categories do not enjoy, such as access to the exhibit hall or voting rights, color-code the inserts, but avoid dark background shades in the area where the name will be printed. Consider printing a legend explaining the various color codes on the back of the insert and in the final program book. Some meeting managers use self-adhesive ribbons that may be color-coded and/or embossed with identifying information (i.e., past-president, new member, and so on). These can be attached to the plastic badge holder.

Function Tickets

For ease in accounting, pre-number function tickets consecutively and verify numbering before issuing tickets to the registration personnel selling the tickets. If more than one ticketed event is offered, use different colors. Print the time and location of the event on the tickets; attendees do not always carry programs to meals and social events and will have no other reference. Establish ticket prices in whole dollars to save time in making change at the function or registration sales desk.

Receipts

Most registrants, particularly those who register on-site, will require a receipt for tax purposes or reimbursement from their employers. Computerized registration systems will have this feature included. More advanced systems detail the types of fees paid (e.g., registration fees, social events, membership dues, and so on). The registration attendant can initial the receipt, and/or the signature of the appropriate official can be preprinted on the form.

WORKING WITH REGISTRATION CONTRACTORS

If the organization elects to hire a registration contractor, a variety of firms offer a wide range of services. Types of contractors include:

- *Full-service registration contractor*—It is possible to outsource the entire registration process. A full-service contractor will process pre-registration, handle inquiries, process payments, provide financial reports, and provide on-site registration equipment and training of temporary staff.
- *Application service provider (ASP)*—ASPs offer web-based registration applications with online registration forms and database management tools. ASPs allow the organization to set up, customize, and manage the registration on virtually any web browser that is connected to the Internet.

Which approach the organization should take depends upon the requirements of the meeting. ASPs are perceived as more valuable among smaller organizations where registration and marketing responsibilities are more integrated. As a general rule, ASPs offer lower cost and some additional functionality compared to traditional registration vendors, but at a comparable decrease in flexibility and service. Overall, the simpler the event, the more attractive an ASP will be.

In evaluating the available registration services, begin by matching the specific event needs with the capabilities of the service provider.[5] As a general rule, it is best to investigate traditional registration vendors if the program is complex and likely to change in the future. If managing multiple events with less complex registration needs, an ASP may be worth consideration.

Full-Service Contractors

Full-service registration contractors often work with the latest technologies. There are a handful of national registration firms that serve a variety of markets. If the organization elects to hire a professional on-site registration firm, it must be sure that expectations are realistic and the following are considered during the selection process:

- What is required from the registration firm—producing name badges or managing the complete registration process?
- If the organization processes advance registrations and wants a professional firm to handle on-site registration, how will pre-registration data be exported to the firm's database? How should the data be formatted?
- What additional costs are associated with importing and managing the financial data in advance or on-site? Such import procedures tend to be rather complex so be sure to involve the organization's technical and financial staff in this process.

- If the contractor will manage pre-registration and on-site registration, is the same registration system used during both processes? What type of reports will the contractor provide and how often will they be available? Is there direct access via the web to the meeting information on the contractor's database?
- If the vendor is managing concurrent meetings, does it have sufficient resources to give the meeting appropriate attention?

The complexity of the meeting and data requirements will determine the registration firm that is best suited to the organization's meeting. For example, providing registration for a large trade show differs greatly from registration for a smaller but much more complex medical meeting. Each meeting offers its own challenges, and the potential registration contractor must receive the needs of the group expressed clearly. The organization should request a proposal and provide a profile of the event, procedures, and expectations.

When evaluating the proposals and pricing the meeting manager should consider the sophistication of the software and hardware used and the customer service that is being offered to the organization and their attendees. Contacting the contractor's clients who have held meetings that are similar in profile will be very informative. It is important to verify the internal procedures the registration firm has in place. If possible, a tour of their office is appropriate to gain an understanding of the firm's capability to handle the complexity and volume of the meeting. Ask if the organization will deal with the same contact person both during pre-registration and on-site. Staff of the vendor having knowledge of the meeting's pre-registration process is key during on-site registration. Verification of the person's projected workload during the meeting's pre-registration period is important to ensure that he or she will be available during critical dates, such as the early-bird registration cut-off date.

Once a firm is selected, the meeting planner should be open to their suggestions; they bring a wealth of expertise and experience to the table. The registration firm should be an extension of the sponsoring organization. They are a partner and should be expected to uphold the organization's customer service standards and registration policies. There should be clear explanation of the registration policies and procedures to both the contractor and staff. A professional registration firm can and will enforce them. Make sure one or several staff members of the organization are available during registration hours to handle questions and exceptions.

If choosing to combine registration with housing, keep in mind that only a few firms truly have expertise in both. Typically, firms specialize in one task and offer the other as a necessity. Ensure that if hiring a housing firm, there is no compromising of the quality of registration or vice versa. One way to test this is to ask if they are willing to accept just the housing portion or just the registration portion for the organization. Avoid housing firms that subcontract on-site registration. Speak with the firm's references or visit one of their clients' events.

Application Service Providers

Web-based applications are rapidly evolving. What was available six months ago is dramatically changed today; and what will be available for future meetings may be a generation ahead of today's capabilities. When evaluating ASPs, consider not only their current capabilities but also where the provider has been and where it is going. Follow these guidelines, recommended by *EventWeb Newsletter*.[6]

- Review the product literature to ensure that the application has the features and functionality that is needed.

- Find out about the company: How many employees? How many full-time programmers? What is their experience and expertise? When is technical support available? What about customer service?
- How many customers use the application? How many online registrations have been processed? How has the application been enhanced and upgraded over time?
- Talk to current customers. Ask specific questions about what works and does not work, and how the vendor responds to problems.
- Test the application using both a high-speed Internet connection and a dial-up connection, during different times of the day. Notice if the servers are slow or if they encountered any technical problems.
- Ask the company if they have independent tests and monitoring conducted by third parties. Some companies hire outside security firms to try to hack into their own servers. ASPs may have the results of such tests that they can share. In addition, some companies hire third-party monitoring services that ensure that a web site is up and running and can be accessed from anywhere in the world.

In addition to processing online registrations, most ASPs offer email marketing tools to help promote attendance and reduce costs by driving more registrations online. Using these web-based applications, additional services can include:

- Import a contact database
- Customize invitations from templates
- Blast messages by email, fax, and print mail
- Segment lists by target audience
- Personalize messages for each segment
- Track click-throughs
- Send follow-ups to those who have not registered[7]

Although ASPs offer powerful tools to attract and register attendees, be sure the company has the technical and customer support in place to support the size and complexity of the event. Above all, confirm that database security measures are in place to protect attendees' data and privacy. The ASP should have procedures for ensuring system integrity, data mirroring in remote locations, regular system backup, robust firewall maintenance, and virus protection capabilities.[8]

SUMMARY

The goals of any registration process, whether in advance or on-site, are accuracy and efficiency. Both must be achieved within certain time and budget constraints. The responsibility of the meeting manager is to develop a precise method of dealing with paper and people that saves time, minimizes attendee frustration, and provides needed and accurate data.

Hours saved in the advance registration process will provide additional time to apply the finishing touches that are so important to logistical arrangements. Advance registration can simplify traffic flow during on-site registration, improve meeting attendance, provide more accurate guarantees, and generate cash flow during the months preceding the event.

Attendee data collected during the registration process can be valuable in many other ways. Such data can provide exhibitors with information about attendees' buying power and spending habits; it can help build negotiation leverage for the next meeting; and it can help to analyze the current meeting and make plans to improve the next meeting.

The keys to a smooth on-site registration process are careful planning; use of technology; detailed preparation; good traffic control; and an efficient, well-informed staff.

REFERENCES

1. Convention Industry Council. (2005). *APEX housing and registration accepted practices*. Retrieved March 31, 2006 from http://www.conventionindustry. org/apex/acceptedpractices/housingregistration.htm.

2. Chatfield-Taylor, C. (September, 2001). Privacy, please. *Meeting planners' guide to using the web*. A supplement to *Meeting News, Successful Meetings,* and *Business Travel News,* p. 23.

3. Ibid.

4. Wolfson, S.M. (1986). *The meeting planners' guide to logistics and arrangements*. Washington, DC: Institute for Meeting and Conference Management.

5. For a checklist of features and functions to consider, see Fox, D. (February, 2001). Registration checklist. *EventWeb newsletter*. Retrieved January 29, 2006 from http://www.eventweb.com/022001.html#one.

6. Fox, D. (January, 2001). Evaluating Internet technologies. *EventWeb newsletter*. Retrieved February 15, 2006 from http://www.eventweb.com/011901.html#1.

7. Chatfield-Taylor, C. (July/August, 2001). ASP and you shall receive. *EXPO*.

8. Ball, C. Online registration: The 3rd generation. Corbin Ball Associates Web site. Retrieved January 11, 2006, from http://www.corbinball.com/articles/art onlinereg.htm.

KEY TERMS

Advance registration	Full service registration	Registrant
Application service	contractor	Registration
provider (ASP)	Function ticket	Registration data
Attendee data	Interview technique	Registration form
Badge	Online registration	Registration packet
Confirmation	On-site registration	Serpentine queue
Demographic profile	Refund policy	

COMPELLING QUESTIONS FOR CONSIDERATION

1. Discuss the advantages and disadvantages of offering advance registration for a meeting.

2. Develop a list of attendee information items that can be gathered on a registration form. How can each piece of information be used for the current meeting? For future meetings?

3. What do you need to do to set up an online registration system? Use the attendee information items you developed in question two. What issues would you need to address when setting up your database to accept the information and provide you with the appropriate reports?

4. Diagram the set-up for a registration area. What factors did you consider in designing the layout?

5. Prepare a detailed list of items that should be included in a registration packet and explain why you included each item.

6. Discuss the relative advantages and disadvantages of a full-service registration contractor and a registration application service provider.

CHAPTER 25

HOUSING AND ROOM BLOCK MANAGEMENT

Susan Bracken

PRESIDENT

J. SPARGO & ASSOCIATES, INC.

Peter Shure

DIRECTOR, STRATEGIC MARKETING

CONFERON GLOBAL SERVICES, INC.

LEARNER OUTCOMES

When the reader has completed reading this chapter, he/she should be able to . . .

1 State why housing has become a critical factor in planning and executing a meeting.

2 Employ the housing method that is most appropriate for your group.

3 Develop a room block management strategy to yield high participation rates.

4 List all pertinent information required to process all types of reservations.

5 Evaluate the overall housing process of your organization.

> Our block had been deteriorating for some time. We decided we had to do something.
>
> *Carol Tobin*
> *AIHA's Director of Education and Meetings*

OVERVIEW

The housing process has changed dramatically in recent years, but one thing remains constant: Meeting participants want and need comfortable and convenient accommodations, arranged with minimal effort and to their exacting requirements. Your role is to ensure this happens.

This seemingly simple function has become one of the riskiest aspects of meeting management. A housing shortage by early 2000 created a seller's market, and hotels are increasingly using attrition clauses to guarantee group fulfillment of contracted room blocks. Litigation can result when these contract clauses are contested. You must manage that risk by understanding the dynamics of your group, arranging for appropriate accommodations with the hotel(s), and actively monitoring and adjusting your room blocks throughout the entire housing process. Retaining a detailed group history, including your group's housing requirements, is essential.

Technology has dramatically changed the reservation process. Today, real-time online processing allows for instant reservations and credit card processing, immediate acknowledgment back to the attendee, and accurate reports for both the hotel and the meeting manager. As the number of reservations made through the Internet has increased, so has the opportunity for attendees to find alternate housing outside the contracted block. Rather than go through the designated web site for housing reservations, attendees may choose to search for the best rates through discount travel agents. This chapter will present the process commonly used to coordinate attendee housing requirements, guidelines for selecting housing providers, and strategies to manage your organization's room block.

HOUSING RESERVATION PROCESS METHODS

Five different options are available to facilitate housing for your group. The advantages, disadvantages, and general process for each option are listed below to help you determine the best solution for your organization.

1. **Meeting attendees contact any hotel directly to make their own reservations.**

   Application: This method works well for extremely small meetings usually requiring one hotel.

   Advantages:

   - No financial liability for the organization
   - Minimal staff time required
   - No hotel cut-off

   Disadvantages:

   - Organization does not earn complimentary room nights
   - Organization does not receive discounted room rates
   - Room availability not guaranteed for attendees, which may impact overall meeting attendance
   - Higher rates may deter attendance

   Process:

   - Provide attendees with a list of hotels in the area along with phone numbers, addresses, and web sites

2. **The organization negotiates a contract with the hotel, and attendees respond directly to the hotel via a reservation request (form, telephone, or hotel's web site).**

Application: This method works well for small meetings usually requiring one hotel.

Advantages:

- Discounted room rates for attendees
- Discounted staff rates offered (usually 50% off group rate)
- Complimentary room nights earned
- Guaranteed room availability

Disadvantages:

- Financial liability for rooms contracted (attrition)
- Limited control of inventory

Process:

- Negotiate hotel contract(s) (see Chapters 40 and 41)
- Contact the hotel to determine the best reservation method (form, telephone, or hotel's web site)
- Inform attendees on how to make reservations
- Monitor and analyze room block pick up with hotel

3. **The organization manages housing through its own in-house meetings department.**

Application: This method works well for mid to large size meetings requiring one or more hotels.

Advantages:

- Total control over the housing process
- Meeting participants appreciate the personalized service
- Protection for very important person (VIPs) and committee members by ensuring they are housed in specific hotels
- Discounted room rates for attendees
- Discounted staff rates offered (usually 50% off group rate)
- Complimentary room nights earned
- Guaranteed room availability

Disadvantages:

- Requires additional full-time staff
- Can impede planner's ability to manage other aspects of the meeting properly

Process:

- Select the meeting site
- Negotiate hotel contracts
- Determine the software you will use to process reservations:
  - Off-the-shelf software program
  - Custom software
  - Application service provider

- Prepare housing form for attendees. Whether in print or online, the reservation request form should include the following information:
  - Name and date(s) of the meeting
  - Name, address, telephone, fax number, and email address of individual requesting reservation
  - Names of other individuals who will share the accommodations
  - First, second, and third choice for hotel property requested
  - Room type and rate preferred
  - Arrival date and time
  - Departure date
  - Credit card number, expiration date, and signature for advance deposit per the terms in the hotel contract
  - Special accommodations request (e.g., wheelchair-accessible room with roll-in shower)
  - Deadline for submitting reservation request to confirm group rate
- Protect rooms for special groups by creating sub-blocks at each hotel. If, for example, you have 1,000 rooms at the headquarters hotel, your block may include the following: BOD (20); other VIPs (50); press (5); exhibitors (200); persons with disabilities (5); staff (20); speakers (10); and general attendees (690).
  - Establish and communicate an earlier deadline for these subgroups so you may put rooms back into general inventory if they will not be utilized
  - Inform attendees within the special blocks of cut-off deadline
- Generate housing list for hotel. The list should include the following information:
  - Name and date(s) of the meeting
  - Name and address of the organization
  - Contact information for the meeting manager
  - Name, address, telephone, fax number, and email address of individual requesting reservation and name of additional individuals sharing the room
  - Room type
  - Arrival and departure date
  - Special needs (wheelchair-accessible room with roll-in shower, smoking or non-smoking, king bed, etc.)
  - Billing instructions including room, tax, and/or incidentals charges
  - Reservation guarantee information or advanced deposits paid
  - Once the housing list is turned in to the hotel, the hotel will process the reservations, and you may instruct the hotel to send confirmations to the attendees.
  - Request hotel rooming list and cross reference against your list for accuracy.

4. **Utilize the housing bureau services of the convention and visitors bureau (CVB) of your host city.**

   Application: This method works well for any size meeting, but depends on the host city CVB's capabilities.

   Advantages:

   - In-depth knowledge of hotels and local area
   - Established relationship with hotel representatives
   - Web-based solutions

- Customized acknowledgements/confirmations sent electronically to attendees

Disadvantages:

- CVBs differ from city to city and not all will offer the same array of services
- Financial liability for rooms contracted
- Limited control
- Staff time required to provide instructions and guidance to CVB
- Staff time required to handle VIP arrangements

Process:

- Negotiate hotel contracts
- Contact the CVB to determine if their services meet your needs.

5. **Hire a housing vendor to manage your housing process.**

Application: This method works well for mid-size to large city-wide conferences where multiple hotels are needed to accommodate the group.

Advantages:

- Employs latest technologies to facilitate housing process
- Real-time, online reporting for client and hotel partners
- Consistent service from year to year
- Knowledge of hotels
- Established rapport with local hotel representatives as well as national sales representatives
- May be able to handle vast array of services including site inspections, site visits, and contract negotiation
- Greater buying power resulting in lower room rates and/or increased concessions for your organization

Put It Into Practice

How Hotels Can Help

Partnering with the hotel to maximize pickup can help. Hotels can do the following to add value to the attendee's experience:

- Offer an early bird room rate—a discounted room rate until a certain date or until a certain number of rooms are sold, whichever comes first.
- Give vouchers or discounts at the hotel's restaurants and other amenities to those who stay within the block. These can include complimentary drinks, restaurant coupons, free use of the health club, or parking, Internet, and phone access.
- Offer double or triple hotel points for staying within the block.

- Offer express check-in and check-out services for those staying in the block.
- For citywide meetings where transportation to and from the center is offered to those who book within the block, hotels can have room keys imprinted with the organization's name. A member of the bell staff could check for room keys at the bus stop. The bureau could provide the same service at the convention center.
- Waive the resort fee, which pays for amenities like Internet, access to the workout room, and complimentary bottles of water.
- If hotel is oversold, honor the integrity of the group's housing service by not relocating, or "walking," the reservations made through group housing.

- Housing vendors may offer other conference planning services such as registration, conference logistics, and exhibit sales and management
- Optimize room blocks
- Maintenance of historical housing data
- Customized confirmations/acknowledgements sent electronically to attendees
- Offer solutions to increase block performance

Disadvantages:

- Possible fees

Process:

- Send out a request for proposal (RFP) for a housing vendor (See Choosing a Housing Provider below for general guidelines that are appropriate for selecting either a housing provider or vendor)
- Consider asking the housing vendor to assist with site selections and contract negotiations
- Execute a mutually agreeable contract between your organization and housing vendor
- Adhere to the terms of the contract

CHOOSING A HOUSING PROVIDER[1]

A written request for proposal (RFP) is the best and most effective vehicle for selecting a housing provider. In many cases, the housing provider will be a hotel; however, today, non-traditional venues are becoming popular for holding meetings such as conference centers, college campuses, and cruise ships. The RFP provides the prospective housing provider with the comprehensive and accurate group historical data necessary to properly forecast the group's needs, prepare the appropriate proposal for consideration, and ultimately plan the most efficient approach to reserving and managing the room block.

In preparing to send out the RFP, identify at least three possible housing providers that have managed groups of a similar size to yours. Review the hotel contract(s) to determine whether there are terms and conditions that would preclude or limit the use of a housing vendor. Also consider whether the hotel's policies and conditions allow housing provider fees to be included in the group room rate and study the agreement to identify any housing policies and responsibilities that may have an impact on the services you will require of the housing provider.

Use the sample RFP form (see Figure 25.1) to write a housing provider RFP. Specify your group's history and include any attendee information that may affect housing needs. Ask the provider to include information on the company's history; staffing levels that will be available; methods that will be used to manage subblocks; cut-off date procedures; and technological capabilities, including the systems and timelines to be used to generate and reconcile reports. Ask the provider the following questions:

General

- How will reservations be processed (via phone, fax, mail, the Internet, or a combination)?
- During what hours will reservations be accepted and processed?
- How will lost reservations and incomplete forms be handled?
- Will confirmations be made by the housing vendor only or also by the hotel(s)?

- If housing vendor is used:
  - What assistance can be expected if blocks are sold out?
  - Will you assist in securing additional rooms?
  - When are reservations turned over to the hotel(s)?
  - How will you handle reservation requests that are received after the cut-off date?
- Will you accept hospitality or meeting room requests?
- How will suites be sold and confirmed?
- How are room blocks and sub-blocks managed?
- What are your capabilities for providing specific group services (such as housing sub-blocks for exhibitors and international attendees)?
- What management procedures will be used for sub-blocks (such as assignments, deposits, cut-off dates, cancellation fees, and the maximum number)?

Data Transfer

- When and how will reservations be transmitted to the hotel(s)?

Confirmation/Acknowledgment Process

- What is the timeframe for acknowledgments/confirmations?
- How will acknowledgments/confirmations be made (via fax, mail, or the Internet)?
- Will both acknowledgments and confirmations be sent? If so, by whom?
- Provide sample of actual confirmation form, identifying a space in which the sponsoring organization can provide a message, such as advertisements or instructions.

Deposits and Refunds

- What are the options for handling deposits?
- How are deposits transferred to the hotel(s)?

Changes and Cancellations

- How will changes be handled?
- How will replacements for cancellations be processed?

International Attendees

- What are your capabilities for assisting international attendees?
- How will information be provided to international attendees?

Travel Arrangements

- Will supplier/vendor coordinate with a shuttle company? If so, explain.
- Do you have the capability to book airline tickets, rental cars, tours, or other services? If so, please describe.
- What benefits from booking airline tickets, cars, tours, or other services for attendees will be passed on to the sponsoring organization?
- What travel expenses will you be responsible for?
- What travel expenses will be passed on to the sponsoring organization?

Request for Proposal Form

The following information should be supplied by the association, management company, or sponsor:

Convention Information and History

Sponsor and sponsor profile:

_____

_____

_____

Name of event:

_____

Date(s):

_____

Convention housing profile:

_____

_____

_____

Attendee profile:

_____

_____

_____

Previous locations:

_____

_____

_____

Future locations:

_____

_____

_____

Sponsoring Organization Information

Contact person:

_____

Title:

_____

Address:

_____

Telephone and fax numbers:

_____

Email address:

_____

Web site address:

_____

Convention Specifications

City:

_____

Hotels in block:

_____

Housing inventory:

_____

Suite inventory and assignment:

_____

FIGURE 25.1
Sample Request for Proposal Form

Special room blocks:

Number of attendees:

Number of exhibitors:

Exhibitor regulations (blocks and sub-blocks, including special needs):

Percentage of reservations made via telephone, mail, fax, e-mail, and the Internet:

Projected date that housing registration will open:

Timeline for advance promotion and/or attendance building:

How attendees will register for the meeting:

Contracts and Site Inspections
Your requirements for assistance with contract preparation, tracking, and/or site inspections:

On-Site Management Support
On-site assistance that the sponsoring organization will expect:

Expectations for handling walks and relocations:

Expected parameters for handling complaints:

Requirements for reviewing daily no shows and report findings:

Requirements for managing post-cutoff inventory:

Criteria for selection:

Deadline for responding to the RFP:

Contract award process (including the award date, contingent upon final contract negotiation):

FIGURE 25.1
Sample Request for Proposal Form, continued

Put It Into Practice

Insurance Accounting and Systems Association (IASA)

THE CHALLENGE

In 2002, IASA faced a $200,000 attrition damage fee after realizing that 54% of all exhibitors (512 out of 995 total) booked Rooms Outside the Contracted Block (ROCH). An additional 12% of attendees did the same.

THE SOLUTION

The association chose to motivate their exhibitors and attendees to stay inside the convention-contracted hotels by doing the following:

1. Educated the exhibitors and attendees on the previous year's $200,000 attrition liability far in advance and well before the next show's materials were scheduled for distribution. The new policy was explained in a letter sent to the group, and pre-show materials reinforced the registration changes and incentives. The centerpiece of the incentives was based around the registration fee. The base registration fee was raised by $100 and only those staying in the group hotel received a $100 discount.

2. Created a separate package of incentives for exhibitors. Incentives included:

   • Up to three complimentary exhibitor badges per 10' x 10' booth, up to a maximum of 12. Badges entitled exhibitors access to the opening reception, one breakfast and one luncheon; access to IASA's general session; and admission to seven technical sessions.

• Each exhibiting company also received two priority points for each hotel reservation made at an IASA contracted hotel and through the IASA housing bureau. (IASA uses a point system for space selection for future shows.)

Exhibitors outside of the IASA housing bureau did not receive a complimentary allotment of badges. Each badge cost them $100 and no special access tickets were attached to those badges for meals or sessions.

THE RESULT

In the first year the program was introduced, 88% of exhibitors booked rooms within the block, nearly double the previous year's percentage. In addition, the number of attendees staying in the block increased to 92%.

IASA's Successful ROCH (rooms outside the contracted hotel) Plan

Exhibitor Attendance

Year	Site	IASA Hotels	ROCH	% of rooms outside the contracted block
2001	San Antonio	595	392	40%
2002	San Francisco	433	512	54%
2003*	Denver	694	93	12%

* First year of the incentives

Reports

• What are your reporting capabilities (including alpha lists, pick-up reports, and post-show reports)? Please describe each report.
• What is your method of transmission and frequency of hotel reports?

Fees and Costs

• What is your fee and commission schedule?
• Will the fee be based on each room night, each reservation, or a percentage of the room rate?
• Will you process rebates for the sponsor (such as a shuttle bus rebate)?
• What cancellation or change fees may be incurred?

Contract Negotiations

- Do you have errors and omissions insurance?
- What is your number of contracts per year?
- Do you maintain relationships with national sales representatives?

Request, from a vendor, at least three references from similar-sized groups that held meetings in the current convention site during the last 18 months. The RFP should make your expectations for the housing provider clear. Identify the criteria to be used for selection, establish the provider's timeline for responding to the request, and specify when the contract will be rewarded.

ROOM BLOCK MANAGEMENT

At the end of the day, the goal of both event organizers and host properties is to maximize the number of heads in contracted beds. Room block management is a process that begins with the RFP and does not conclude until a thorough post-event audit of actual room night pickup has been conducted. This section addresses room block forecasting, tracking of pickup, incentives for booking within the block, room block audits, and measures that should be taken to protect the block.

Determining the Number of Rooms

On the front end, a number of variables help determine the number of rooms that should be blocked. Among them are future destinations, dates, program format, anticipated shoulder night usage, and the geographic distribution of prospective attendees.

Meeting Destination

A resort or city known for family attractions may increase the number of attendees who bring their families to the meeting with them. Meeting in such a destination may also increase the number of those who stay for extra nights before or after the meeting.

Meeting Dates

Consider how specific meeting dates might affect arrival and departure patterns. For example, if your meeting is during spring break or over a holiday weekend, some attendees may choose to bring their families and stay longer.

Program Format

The most important predictor of room-night needs is the format of your meeting. Changing your program format can change the entire pattern of attendance and the number of rooms needed. Keep in mind that meeting space and guest rooms go hand in hand; on the days that you need more meeting space, you will most likely need more guest rooms, except on departure days. Use your workshop schedule to determine how many guest rooms might be needed: Start with the number of sessions offered on a given day and estimate how many people will attend each session.

Shoulder Nights

When determining how many rooms to block, pay attention to more than the peak nights of your event. Take time considering your shoulder nights as well as the nights before and after the meeting. These nights will fluctuate more from year to year, so you must watch them closely. For instance, if you notice that you aren't filling enough nights on the front end of the meeting, you may not be able to fill your rooms on peak nights. If your shoulder nights are not booked properly, it can dramatically impact your ability to pick up your peak night commitment.

Geographical Area

The area of the country where you hold your meeting can greatly influence whether attendees will need extra room nights before or after the meeting. The timing of the first and last events also has a huge impact on room blocks for those dates. Whenever an early arrival or extra late night is needed, do not assume that 100% of attendees impacted will actually stay the extra night.

Once registration opens, the room block situation changes every day. Regular pace reports should be used to track pickup patterns. For example, if a group has a history of heavy booking 4 weeks in advance, a hotel should not be concerned if only 50% of a block has filled 8 weeks out. Pace reports are also essential in monitoring the bell curve, an invaluable tool in determining how many rooms to block. Maintain communication with your hotel sales representative to alert him/her of the progress between registration and the rooms booked.

Using the Bell Curve

The bell curve formula tracks the number of rooms blocked per night, expressed as a percentage of the peak night block.

Your meeting's bell curve can be one of your most effective tools for determining how many rooms to block. The bell-curve formula looks at the room block per night, expressed as a percentage of the peak night. Most effective when portrayed graphically, the bell curve shows arrival numbers for each day of the meeting, building up over the first few days and cascading downward following peak nights. You can figure the percentage of peak for each night by dividing the number of rooms used by the number of rooms on peak night.

Figure 25.2 shows an example of the bell curve for a typical meeting with 1,650 rooms required on the peak nights.

Use your history to determine the meeting's average bell curve, which can help you anticipate how many rooms to block on any given night of your meeting. When booking citywide events, or events that will use multiple hotels, you can also use the bell curve to compute the number of rooms needed at each hotel on each night.

For example, if Hotel A can commit 500 of your needed 1,650 rooms on peak night, you would multiply 500 by the percentage required each night. That

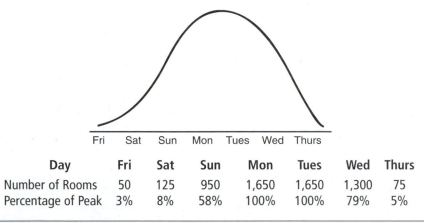

Day	Fri	Sat	Sun	Mon	Tues	Wed	Thurs
Number of Rooms	50	125	950	1,650	1,650	1,300	75
Percentage of Peak	3%	8%	58%	100%	100%	79%	5%

FIGURE 25.2
Bell Curve for 1,650 Committable Rooms

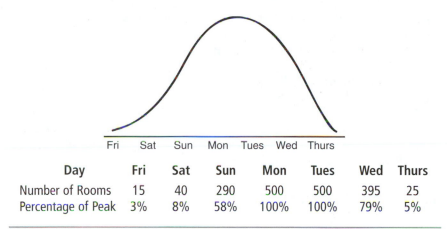

Day	Fri	Sat	Sun	Mon	Tues	Wed	Thurs
Number of Rooms	15	40	290	500	500	395	25
Percentage of Peak	3%	8%	58%	100%	100%	79%	5%

FIGURE 25.3
Bell Curve for 500 Committable Rooms

calculation will determine how many rooms you need that hotel to provide each night throughout the meeting's duration.

Figure 25.3 shows how it worked for Hotel A which has 500 committable rooms.

Maximizing Pickup Within Your Block

What's at Stake?

While attrition—the failure of an event organizer to meet contracted performance thresholds—makes headlines, a number of other reasons make maximizing and accurately reporting room pickups critical.

- *Attrition Fees*—Perhaps the most feared consequence of low pickup is attrition, which can result in catastrophic damages for your association. In the aftermath of September 11, 2001, six-figure attrition fees were not uncommon.

- *Leverage*—The value of your business is largely dependent on the number of guest rooms your meeting brings to a hotel or destination. If attendees book outside a contracted hotel, your organization will lose negotiation leverage in future years. Plus, your group's reputation could be damaged if you fail to fill your block.

- *Lost Concessions*—Many of the concessions routinely negotiated in a contract, including comp room ratios, upgrades, free Internet access, and even complimentary coffee breaks between sessions, depend on a group's ability to meet their pickup goals. Excessive slippage may limit a hotel's willingness to grant future concessions.

Educate your attendees about the importance of staying within the block by communicating what's in it for them. Consider creating and marketing a list of reasons to stay inside the contracted hotel block and include this list directly in your meeting brochure or web site.

Creating Incentives

Only about one-fifth of all meeting attendees are aware that their groups could suffer attrition fees if they choose to stay in hotels outside the block, according to a poll taken by the Convention Industry Council's Project Attrition. A third of attendees said they would help their groups if inducements were given, which supports the survey's finding that cost is the main concern for attendees when making housing decisions.

Survey respondents said that money-saving incentives would encourage them to use the group's hotels, but these incentives need to be substantial enough to make a real difference in attendees' wallets. A $25 discount on registration is not enough to make an attendee want to stay in the block, but an incentive worth $100 to $150 will eliminate the desire to book elsewhere. Another important thing to remember about incentives is that they should be presented as encouragement for staying in the block—not as a penalty for booking elsewhere. Incentives always work better than penalties.

INCENTING THE ATTENDEE

Here are some of the most popular and successful attendee incentives:

- Raise the registration fee by $100 or more and then offer registration discounts of that same amount only to those who stay within the block. Not only will it keep attendees inside your block, it will protect the revenue you receive from registrations.
- Allow attendees staying within the block to earn points toward products and services provided by your organization.
- Offer drawings for amenities, suite upgrades at the host hotel, round-trip airport transfers, or free registration at next year's conference, open only to those staying inside the block. (These are not as effective when used without a registration incentive.)
- Offer special incentives, such as free merchandise credits, a reduced fee pass for local attractions, or attendance at a special networking reception only for those staying in the block.

INCENTING THE EXHIBITOR

There's no doubt that it's a much harder task to get exhibitors to stay in the block. What works is to create an incentive that is worth more to the exhibitor than the money saved by staying outside the group's hotels.

For exhibitors who stay in the group block, these incentives work:

- Complimentary exhibitor badges, which provide access to events like technical sessions, opening receptions, luncheons, breakfasts, and the general session
- Higher priority status in exhibit space drawings at future meetings
- The chance to earn points toward more advertising or sponsorship exposures
- Requiring exhibitors using 10 or more rooms to sign a hotel contract for all rooms
- Some meeting managers even refuse freight to exhibitors who are not staying within the contracted block, while others require each exhibitor to purchase two rooms for each 100 net square feet of space rented

CONDUCTING ROOM AUDITS

Ask a meeting manager who has been faced with attrition fees for advice and he/she will give you two words: room audit. Room audits are the most effective way to find rooms outside the block (ROB), and they can help you establish history and avoid attrition fees.

Put It Into Perspective

10 Reasons to Book within the Block

Repeated studies have shown that "cost" is the primary reason attendees choose to stay outside the block. But there are numerous advantages that result from booking within the block.

Ed Harris, the president of ITS, which developed many of the best practices in room block management, detailed the benefits in an article that appears on CIC's web site, www.conventionindustry.org.

Among them:

1. One-stop shopping
2. Convenient customer service
3. No full prepayment required
4. Easy-to-change reservations
5. Reservations backed by meeting sponsor
6. Convenient shuttle bus service
7. On-site service desk
8. Full frequent traveler benefits
9. Increased networking opportunities
10. Support of sponsoring organization's financial commitments

Why Audit?

For one reason or another, meeting attendees might book at the contracted hotel, but through a different channel, such as through membership in the AARP, AAA, or U.S. military. Other sources of miscoding can include a corporate rate plan, corporate travel policy, or hotel loyalty plan. Still, if people attend your meeting and stay in your contracted hotel, your association should get credit for those rooms. Sometimes hoteliers can be reluctant to help you find these rooms.

Remember: Identifying rooms outside the block or outside the contracted hotels is especially important for future bookings because the bigger your actual room block pickup this year, the more bargaining power you will have for next year's conference.

Getting Started

Whether your association has faced attrition fees or not, performing pre-audits keeps the registration and housing process on track. For example, if your conference is six months out, and you've only picked up 150 rooms in an 800-room block, you probably do not want to wait until you are on-site to perform the first room audit. Look for red flags like very light pickup or pickup that does not match the previous year's pace. The sooner you find room books outside of your room block (ROB), the sooner you can get credit for your rooms. The sooner you find ROCH (rooms outside the contracted hotels), the more time you will have to either convince those attendees to rebook inside the block or reduce your block.

How Audits Work

Because of privacy issues, some hotels are unwilling to release a list of guests to a third party, fearing that the third party might contact guests or sell their names and contact information. When hotels have this concern, they might offer to conduct the room audit itself. However, you will generally uncover more rooms if you are present during the audit.

In order to reap the full benefits of a room audit, set the expectation in the contract that you will conduct an audit and determine how concessions and other entitlements will be handled for the additional rooms. As long as your pickup rate matches what you expected, the best time to conduct a room audit is the day after each of the conference's peak nights. If your conference is a citywide with small

Put It Into Practice

Ten Reasons that Address Attendees' Priorities

1. **Networking.** Make the most of your conference by spending more quality time with other attendees or exhibitors.
2. **Convenience.** Ride the elevator to and from the sessions and events.
3. **Support your association.** Help it earn free or discounted meeting space, more concessions, and decrease its liability for unused rooms to keep your registration fees lower and more competitive.
4. **Cost savings.** Save money on rental cars, parking, and taxi fares.
5. **Conference shuttle.** Enjoy the convenience of complimentary shuttle service to and from the convention center.
6. **Customer service.** Take advantage of superior reservation procedures. Rooms booked through Internet channels are often difficult to cancel or change and often require prepayment. Plus, the non-chain Internet channels do not offer frequent stay points.
7. **Low-rate guarantee.** Shop for competitive rates by viewing conference hotels on their chain-branded web sites. Many chains now offer a lowest-rate guarantee on their branded site.
8. **Prize drawing.** Earn a chance to enter a drawing for a free registration or complimentary guest room.
9. **Lower registration fees.** Take advantage of any registration discounts for using the conference hotel.
10. **Hotel incentives.** Look for additional incentives from your hotel. These incentives might include additional hotel points, free high-speed Internet, free health club, or other inducements to stay in the conference hotel.

group blocks in several hotels, you may want to start the room audit process even earlier.

PROTECTING YOUR BLOCK

You will undoubtedly have to work hard and smart to motivate your attendees and exhibitors to stay in the block. What happens, though, when events beyond your control conspire to erode your block? Online price shopping, hotel reward programs, and "housing pirates" make block protection an ongoing challenge—but one that can be overcome with astute planning and preparation.

Online Travel Sites

Five years ago, few people knew how to search the Internet for lower hotel rates. Today, everyone is accustomed to checking hotel rates online and usually on more than one site. Sites like Travelocity, Expedia, Hotels.com, and even hotel web sites themselves sometimes offer lower rates than the ones for which you contracted. What many attendees do not know is that taking advantage of lower rates cannot guarantee them a room at an overbooked hotel. Often, the attendee will need to forego loyalty points, may need to prepay, and could be on the hook if the reservation needs to be canceled or changed. Further, the rooms often for sale at these lower rates may be located next to an ice machine or elevator, not the place to be the night before an intensive educational session.

Exhibitor Sub-blocks

Exhibitors often book large blocks and are more likely to do it on their own, rather than through your housing service. In many cases where associations have faced attrition fees, the lack of pickup in exhibitor sub-blocks was the primary culprit.

Housing Pirates

A meeting manager's worst nightmare, housing pirates are unauthorized, unaffiliated housing providers that offer rooms at reduced rates to your attendees, often under the guise of an affiliation with your show. They often target exhibitors and obtain membership lists before a show's official housing block opens. If successful, their efforts to siphon rooms from a block can result in tens of thousands of dollars in attrition penalties.

STAYING VIGILANT

Protecting a housing block requires event organizers to be part sociologist, part researcher, and even part cop. Success demands the scrupulous monitoring of many of the foundation steps in the room block management process.

THE GOLDEN RULE

The best way to protect your block is to make sure your housing blocks accurately offer a cross-section of the desired price points of your attendees and exhibitors. To do this, you must have a thorough understanding of your attendees' wants and needs. Remember the golden rule: If the lowest rate in your hotel mix is too high for any segment of your audience, they will book elsewhere.

Often, the convention and visitors bureau in the city where your meeting will be held can help you identify potential problems. Because meeting sites are booked so far in advance, it is possible that a new hotel (and a different price point) might be available after you book. The CVB or your housing partner can be very helpful in letting you know if you have left a hotel out of the mix.

The size of the destination and number of rooms available will affect contracted pickup. If your peak night pickup will be 1,000 rooms, booking a city with 40,000 rooms may give your attendees more options than you would like. Booking outside of contracted hotels is far more likely when the city has many other hotel options available to attendees. If your group is large enough to cause compression—when you consume the majority of the rooms available in a destination—then attendees are more likely to end up in your block because fewer alternatives are available.

During the contract phase, make sure you include a clause that prohibits—with a few exceptions—the hotel from offering a lower rate to the general public than the group rate. If there's no protection in your contract, chances are good that your attendees will book outside the block at the lower rate. In the event that attendees book at a lower rate, but in the same hotel, your contract should include a clause that credits those rooms—even though not part of your block—toward your overall pickup.

To preempt the dreaded call from a disgruntled attendee who informs you that he or she has found a better rate elsewhere—and to make sure the hotel honors the no-lower-rate guarantee in your contract—you will need to do some price monitoring of your own. Call the hotel to find out the lowest rate they are offering and check the hotel's web site, as well as a couple of the sites for major online travel companies. Travelaxe.com can show you side-by-side prices that you would find individually at each of these sites.

BATTLING THE BANDITS

Because most housing "pirates" operate from the platform of legal businesses, planners can do little to shut down these organizations, no matter how detrimental they are to your block. Pirates are only successful because they offer lower rates—

or at least promise lower rates—than the groups they attack; they cannot win against groups that have strong registration incentives.

Here are some measures that can be implemented to curb even the peskiest pirates:

Provide Strong Registration Incentives

Attendees will have no reason to search the Internet or respond to pirates if they know that, by doing so, they will lose the registration discount. The higher fee

Put It Into Practice

International Dairy-Deli-Bakery Association (IDDBA)

THE CHALLENGE

Housing pirates targeted the 2003 annual IDDBA convention. A Las Vegas event company solicited exhibitors, offering them reduced rates at more than 60 hotels in Las Vegas, including some within IDDBA's room block. "We received many complaints because the salespeople were extremely aggressive and persistent," Christison says.

THE SOLUTION

The association took a proactive approach to battling the housing pirates. Not only did Christison call the company that was sending faxes to her exhibitors and ask them to stop, she also alerted members—through faxes, e-mails, articles in the IDDBA newsletter, and posts on the association web site—to the problems that pirates can cause both to individual exhibitors and the entire association. The association motivated its exhibitors and attendees to avoid booking with pirates by doing the following:

- Providing the name of the official IDDBA housing bureau.
- Warning them against the common practices of housing pirates with the following language:
  - Many of these agencies do not have contracts for a block of rooms with the hotels.
  - They will contact a housing wholesaler to see if anything is available that can be resold to you.
  - Even legitimate wholesalers cannot knowingly book convention attendees in the convention room block. Only IDDBA's housing agent can book our block of rooms. If the hotel determines a convention attendee has been solicited or contacted by a legitimate wholesaler, those rooms may be canceled or increased in rate to match or exceed the group rate. A rate quote from a room broker is not a guaranteed rate.

  - Rooms must be fully prepaid up front. (A one-night deposit isn't enough; they want it all and for every room you book, when you book.)
  - Reservation confirmations and numbers are generally not available until three to seven days before the first day of arrival. Even then, there is no guarantee a room will be available when you arrive.
  - Generally, they cannot get a large block of rooms; only one or two at a time.
  - It's difficult to do name changes on rooms with unofficial wholesalers/room brokers.
- Incenting them to use IDDBA's housing bureau with the following language:
  - The IDDBA has negotiated reduced rates with the hotels in our block.
  - The IDDBA gets a credit for the rooms booked. We are able to use this credit for speaker rooms and staff rooms. (This is one of the reasons we have not had to raise registration fees since 1988.)
  - The IDDBA provides and pays for busing from official hotels to the convention center. You would have to arrange your own transportation from other hotels.
  - Our hotel contracts include clauses that protect you. They also include clauses that require the IDDBA to pay for hotel rooms that we book on your behalf but are not filled. Unfilled rooms could cost the IDDBA hundreds of thousands of dollars. In short, it's good business to stay in the association hotels.

THE RESULT

Because the IDDBA acted as soon as they found out wholesalers were soliciting exhibitors, they were able to prevent the pirates from booking many rooms for exhibitors and attendees. As a result, the IDDBA avoided costly attrition fees that could have caused them to increase registration fees for future meetings.

they pay to go outside the block would negate any savings that pirates could offer.

Communicate the Issue

Tell attendees and exhibitors to be suspicious if they receive an unsolicited phone call, fax, or email that offers lower hotel rates than the group rate. Coach them to "play dumb" and obtain as much identifying information as possible. Communicating the name of the official housing bureau associated with your association can help them identify the unfamiliar pirates. Also, communicate the potential threat to your members and instruct them on the benefits and importance of staying within the block.

Protect Your Lists

Do not publish the lists of attendees and exhibitors on the Web or share them outside of your exhibitor or sponsorship organizations. If you do post a list of attendees on your association's web site (a common practice to show the value of attendance to exhibitors), make sure its password-protected. Also, seed your list with some false names at addresses of employees, so that you can learn firsthand if pirates have obtained your list.

Know Your Exhibitors

If a suspicious firm asks to exhibit, make sure it is legitimate. Some pirates buy a small booth, wait until they get an attendee list, then cancel the booth and start attacking the list.

Work with Contracted Hotels

When you are working out the hotel contract, include a clause that guarantees the group will have the lowest rate over the meeting dates. This guarantee should apply to all rates except opaque channels—like Priceline or Hotwire—where the customer cannot choose the hotel or brand. Also make sure that your hotel contracts contain terms that allow for all rooms to be credited towards the group pickup, no matter what the rate or how the reservation was made. Find out if your hotel has an agreement with its wholesalers preventing them from selling to meeting attendees. If not, as the meeting date approaches, ask your contracted hotel if they are aware of any inventory outside their distribution channel. Make sure the hotel knows to alert you of any blocks being requested that appear to be in conjunction with (ICW) your event.

Consult Legal Counsel

As soon as you find out housing pirates have targeted your association, call your attorney, who can apply legal pressure. If pirates use the logo or the trademarked name of the association in its marketing pitch—which is in violation of intellectual property law—or if pirates state that their solicitation was approved or sanctioned by the association, you could legitimately shut them down. Normally a good cease-and-desist letter will do. Legal counsel can also check to make sure your anti-pirate communications with attendees and exhibitors cannot get you into trouble.

DECISION-MAKING PROCESS

You must decide which method suits your meeting and your organization's ability to manage the housing process. All but the first option presented above require your organization to negotiate group rates and book room blocks with one or more hotel properties. When an organization contracts with a hotel or conference center for guest rooms, it asks the property to commit a certain number of rooms in a given pattern for the individuals who will be attending. That room block, once contracted for, is considered sold for that one-time opportunity. Unless provisions in the contract specifically state how and when the block can be adjusted, the organization is bound to use and pay for the guest rooms in the negotiated block. Understand the impact your particular housing process might have on the site selection and negotiation process. Decide how you will handle housing during site selection and negotiations. Lead-time to manage the housing process is determined by meeting size, special requirements, property or housing vendor limitations, and technology.

When you evaluate your options for outsourcing the housing function, understand the process the CVB, contractor, or hotel will use, how they price their services, and how payments are made. Cost is determined by the services requested and is based on either a fee per transaction or a percentage of the room rate. Hotels generally build the cost of housing services into the guest room rates. Housing vendors may take a commission from the hotel for rooms booked there. The decision to use a CVB or housing vendor should be made before the hotel contract is fully executed. The contract should spell out how the service charges will be billed, who is responsible for payment, and what disclosure, if any, is required either in the contract or to the attendee.

Comprehensive and accurate data are required by the CVB or housing vendors to properly forecast your housing needs and efficiently use the guest rooms reserved for your attendees. The CVB and housing vendors have the ability to monitor and report on hotel inventory in real time. That results in more accurate room block management and less chance of attrition charges to the organization.

If you have a medium to large size meeting, offer your attendees the option to book rooms online. Online housing has introduced real-time inventory management, resulting in better room block management, less attrition, and more accurate histories for future negotiations.[2] Whether provided by the organization, CVB, or housing vendors, web-based reservation processes offer a number of benefits for all parties. Attendees get better access to information about available properties and instant confirmation of their choice, so they are less likely to make changes later. For the meeting manager, real-time reporting allows for more informed decisions and better management of the housing block, thereby reducing the risk of penalties. Hotels also like the technology because it eliminates the re-keying of reservation data and provides real-time inventory control.

In addition to full-service housing providers, application service providers (ASPs) can offer integrated invitation/registration, housing, and travel processes to the planner and the attendee. These have proven most valuable to the corporate event sector where the billing is centralized for the services. Association planners are beginning to find value in this approach as well. The one-stop shopping approach is convenient to many. ASP services and pricing should be evaluated and competitively bid along with other housing service providers.

GENERAL INFORMATION OF THE HOUSING PROCESS

Guest Rooms

Most hotels have a variety of guest rooms. The experienced meeting manager will be able to anticipate and reserve the right mix of rooms to accommodate all attendees. Standard definitions of room types should be printed on reservation requests or included in online reservation forms:

- *Single*—room for one person with one bed of single, queen, or king size
- *Double*—room for two people with one bed of double, queen, or king size
- *Double/Double*—room for two people with two beds of single or double size
- *Triple*—three people occupying a double/double room
- *Quad*—four people occupying a double/double room
- *Parlor Suite*—hotel living room, usually with a hide-a-bed sofa, connected to an adjoining sleeping room
- *P+1*—parlor suite with one connecting room identified as single, double, or double/double
- *P+2*—parlor suite with two connecting rooms identified as singles, doubles, or double/doubles

Typically hotels also have designated smoking floors and accessible rooms for people with disabilities.

Housing Reports

If you select a CVB or housing vendor to manage your housing, you should insist on real time up-to-date housing reports. The most common housing reports are: 1) summary of reservations confirmed by each hotel, 2) room pickup by day for each hotel, 3) rooming lists for designated sub-blocks including VIPs, exhibitors, and master account. The CVB and housing vendors should be able to print these reports in alternative formats, which needs to be made clear to all parties before the housing process begins.

After the meeting, the CVB or housing vendor should provide a final pickup report, showing the number of rooms actually used. This report includes the total number of rooms originally blocked at each hotel on each night (arrival/departure pattern), and how many of these rooms were sold on each night. This final report may be submitted to the Destination Marketing Association International (formally, IACVB) and becomes part of the MINT database available to its members. These reports should be filed and become part of your meeting history and used as an important tool in negotiating contracts for future meetings.

PCMA WHITE PAPERS ON HOUSING

The Professional Convention Management Association (PCMA) Housing Committee published its first white paper report on housing in 1992, identifying specific problems and recommending solutions for improving the process.[3] Despite advances in technology, including the introduction of online housing in 1996, the housing process continued to be a challenge for the meetings industry. In response, the PCMA Housing Committee published "Best Practices" for housing management in 1998.[4]

The committee recommended the following steps for managing the housing process:

- Establish agreement with hotels and the housing provider relating to policies, timelines, block adjustments, reports, mutual expectations, and responsibilities for the housing process.
- Confirm the format for communicating reservations, changes, substitutes, and cancellations.
- Establish a date to open housing and verify the published cutoff date with all parties. Also establish the format, content, and regularity of reports.

- Finalize the housing form with the approval of all parties (meeting manager, hotels, and housing provider) and include the reservation method (whether it is to be done via telephone, fax, mail, and/or email).
- Define sub-block management policies, exceptions, preferences, special needs, room types, and allocation before the housing process begins. Maintain open communication among all housing partners.
- Devote ongoing attention to arrival/departure dates, sub-blocks, and special needs; alert the housing provider to irregularities on a timely basis.
- Communicate regularly with hotels to review group pick-up, provide reports on time, pay special attention to shoulder dates, assist in locating overflow rooms, and work with contracted hotels after cutoff to accommodate late requests for rooms and/or date changes.
- Determine the method and type of disclosure of rebates, subsidies, and/or commissions.
- Provide the meeting manager with a pick-up report (in the format agreed to) for rooms, suites, and sub-blocks within 30 days of the close of the conference.

In addition to these general guidelines, the white paper covered:

- Determining group housing needs
- The process required for choosing a housing provider
- Requesting a proposal from the housing provider
- Parameters for hotel contracts
- Guidelines for managing the housing process, including procedures, reservation forms, sub-blocks, block management, history, and disclosure
- Post-convention reporting
- A glossary of hotel terms

PCMA continued to monitor housing trends with its annual Housing Trends Study, co-sponsored with the American Society of Association Executives.[5] By 1999, only 18% of respondents indicated maximizing room blocks as a significant problem when asked to identify the most significant problems in the housing process.

As housing solutions and related technology evolve, it is essential meeting managers stay informed about best practices, new procedures, and advances in technology that can make this function efficient and cost-effective. Consult your professional association publications and online resources to stay up-to-date.

SUMMARY

Emerging technologies and world events have led to a dynamic environment for the meetings and events industry. This has resulted in a very competitive market, which requires meeting managers to pay close attention to the housing needs of their groups. Attendees have more choices in selecting where to stay when attending a meeting than ever before. Additionally, they are better informed as to the quality and the price of lodging options in any city. Therefore, an important role of today's meeting manager is to develop strategies to keep attendees booking within the room block to ensure lower room rates, and improved attendee services, as well as meet the provisions of the contract with the housing provider. Failure to meet the negotiated room block numbers often leads to additional expenses for the sponsoring organization.

Room block management is not an exact science, but the spectrum of attrition damages has turned it into an art. Variables such as destination, dates, program design, and past history help determine future blocks. Bell curve tracking is an especially useful tool for tracking pickup. Event organizers must educate attendees about the importance of booking within the contracted block. Money-saving offers, such as registration discounts, have proven to be the best incentives. Offering a wide range of rates is an essential method of protecting blocks from so-called "housing pirates." The entire room block management process should be measured by a detailed post-show audit; be vigilant in identifying rooms outside the block.

Five ways are available to handle the housing process. The method you choose depends on staff resources, the size and complexity of the meeting, services required, and the cost. Decide what method you will use before negotiating with housing provider(s). Whether you outsource the housing function or not, send out a request for proposal to at least three qualified providers or vendors who have managed housing for meetings similar in size to yours.

To make the housing process easier, standard forms and technologies are commonly used, such as toll-free telephone numbers, hotel web sites, a single-property reservation form, a multiple-property reservation form, a housing list, or full online housing through a housing vendor. Regardless of the method used, the essential core information includes: name of the organization; meeting name, location, and dates; guest room types, rates, and how they will be paid for; deadline for requesting a reservation; the need for special accommodations; guarantees or advance deposits; how payments will be accepted; and change or cancellation penalties. Additional information will depend on the specific nature of the meeting.

CVBs and housing vendors can provide many services to a meeting manager, such as acknowledgment and confirmation of reservations and final housing reports. Online housing enables real-time monitoring of the room block usage and hotel inventory, provided you receive timely and up-to-date reports. Define what reports you need and when you want to receive them at the beginning of the housing process, and require a post-conference final report that can become part of your meeting history.

For all meetings, small and large, the housing process is a cooperative effort. Changes in the housing process have created some misunderstandings, confusion, and frustration. The PCMA Housing Committee has proposed best practices to improve the housing process. By implementing these best practices and working in partnership with hotels, CVBs and/or housing vendors, you can better manage the risk and ensure the housing process for your meeting is successful and meets the needs of your attendees.

REFERENCES

1. Excerpted and reprinted with permission from PCMA Housing Committee. (1998). Best practices in the citywide housing game. *Convene*. Retrieved March 1, 2006, from http://www.pcma.org/publications

2. Chatfield-Taylor, C. (2001). Hype and hyperbole. *EXPO*.

3. PCMA Housing Committee. (1992). White paper report: City-wide housing. *Convene*, April 1992. Retrieved February 28, 2006, from http://www.pcma.org/publications.

4. PCMA Housing Committee. (1998). Best practices in the citywide housing game.

5. CIC Research, Inc., American Society of Association Executives, and PCMA. (1999). 1999 ASAE/PCMA Housing Trends Study (Chicago: PCMA, 1999). Retrieved March 1, 2006, from http://www.pcma.org/publications.

KEY TERMS

Application service
  provider (ASP)
Acknowledgments
Advance deposit
Arrival/departure pattern
Attrition
Attrition clauses
Bell curved formula
Book
Committable rooms
Complimentary rooms
Confirmations
Convention and Visitors
  Bureau (CVB)

Double/double
Double room
Group history
Guaranteed
Housing
Housing list
Housing provider
Housing vendor
Incidentals
MINT
Online reservation
Parlor suite
P+1
P+2

Pick-up report
Peak room night
Quad
Request for proposal
  (RFP)
Room block
Room block management
Rooms outside the
  contracted hotel
  (ROCH)
Single room
Sub-blocks
Triple

DISCUSSION QUESTIONS

1. Discuss when a housing list should be used and when a housing vendor may be preferable.

2. What information should you provide on a housing reservation request for a small meeting?

3. What information should you provide on a housing list?

4. How can you work with a housing vendor to reduce the risk of attrition?

5. What are the advantages of using an online housing provider? What are the risks?

6. Identify three ways to reduce attendee cancellations and no-shows.

CHAPTER 26

FOOD AND BEVERAGE ARRANGEMENTS

Patti J. Shock, CPCE
PROFESSOR AND DEPARTMENT CHAIR
DEPARTMENT OF TOURISM AND CONVENTION ADMINISTRATION
UNIVERSITY OF NEVADA, LAS VEGAS

LEARNER OUTCOMES

When the reader has completed reading this chapter, he/she should be able to . . .

1 Recognize the role food and beverage plays in a meeting.

2 Discuss several types of meal functions and some of the service options for each.

3 Evaluate cost-saving options for food-and-beverage events.

Champagne and orange juice is a great drink. The orange improves the champagne. The champagne definitely improves the orange.

Philip, Duke of Edinburgh

OVERVIEW

Almost all meetings include some type of food and beverage service. It may be as basic as dry snacks and nonalcoholic beverages for a refreshment break, or as elaborate as an elegant six-course sit-down dinner for an awards banquet. Food and beverage, and the manner in which they are served, can help make the meeting more memorable and more productive.

Food and beverage functions should support the objectives of the meeting.[1] If a corporation plans a 3-day training meeting, they will want attendees to be alert and comfortable. This requires balanced, nutritious, and appealing menus. An association holding a gala awards dinner is likely to have somewhat different objectives. For the gala, the food must be impressive and spectacular, with a celebratory atmosphere.

The catering manager of the facility facilitates the planning of what foods and beverages to serve, how they will be served, what seating arrangements will work best, and what décor should be used. To ensure success, provide the catering manager with a clear vision of the objectives for the event, as well as a history of the group's food and beverage preferences from historical information documented at previous meetings. In addition to the date, time and location, consider the following items:

- Why is the event being held? Is it for business, networking or social purposes?
- Will the event have a theme?
- What are the demographics of the attendees? Will there be any VIPs?
- Will the event be formal or casual?
- What type of service is preferred (buffet, table service)?
- Will entertainment or presentations take place during the event?
- Will other scheduled activities precede or follow the event (a meeting, a reception, a dance)?
- What is the event budget?[2]

This chapter will explore the world of food and beverage for meetings and will identify key strategies that will help ensure that these offerings support the group's meeting objectives.

MENU PLANNING

The choice of the main course is important and serves as the starting point for selecting the rest of the meal. If the choices on the standard menu do not seem appropriate for the meal function, ask for a customized menu. If there is uncertainty as to whether particular dishes will appeal to the meeting's attendees, asking to taste menu items in advance is appropriate. For large or very important person (VIP) meetings where a committee decides on menu choices, ask for a Chef's Table, which is an opportunity to sample a variety of offerings.

When selecting food and beverage offerings consideration of the geographic location should also be made. Every region has its own specialties and most guests will want to sample the special foods and flavors of the area they are visiting. For example, salmon is a specialty of the U.S. Pacific Northwest and barbecue is a specialty of the southeast United States.

Guests will come from all demographic groups, so menu planning must take this into consideration when choosing food items. Average age, sex, ethnic backgrounds, socioeconomic levels, diet restrictions, where the guests come from, employment and fraternal affiliations, and political leanings can indicate the types of menu items that might be most acceptable to the group. Psychographics, guests' life styles and the way in which they perceive themselves, are also useful indicators. Age is often an excellent indicator. For example, senior citizens usually do not want exotic foods or heavy, spicy foods. In this case, avoid excessive use of garlic, hot spices, and onions. Often it is wise to avoid other distress-causing foods, such as monosodium glutamate (MSG), cabbage-family vegetables, beans, and legumes.

Only serve food that is eaten with the hands, such as barbecued ribs, at very informal affairs, and when it is known that the dress will be casual—and provide plenty of napkins.

The time of year is also a factor. Some seasonal foods are available year-round, but at higher prices and often lower quality. People tend to eat more during cold weather and prefer hot meals.

It is important to provide alternatives for attendees who are on special diets or have other special food requirements. Some meeting managers print menus in the meeting program, so attendees will know in advance what is being served and can make other arrangements if necessary.

Consider the following when planning menus:

Seasonal food	Food is at its peak flavor when it is locally grown and served in-season.
Ethnic foods	American tastes have grown beyond the ethnic foods of the past—Italian, Chinese and Mexican—to include the foods of many Asian countries, the Middle East, and South America.
High quality, fresh and safe ingredients	When people are away from home, they want only the best. The loss of flavor during preservation has made fresh food highly prized. Frozen, canned, and dried foods are not appreciated. Organic food consumption is increasing rapidly and many people prefer foods free from pollution and pesticides.
New and unusual ingredients	With improved transportation, new foods items are available that were once unknown to most Americans. A great web site for exploring exotic fruits and vegetables is: http://www.friedas.com/

Nutrition

Nutrition is a consideration for all meetings, but especially for groups that will be at a hotel or conference center for several days during a convention. Since virtually all meals during their stay will be consumed on the premises, special attention must be paid to nutritional requirements when planning menus. Many attendees will appreciate it if alternatives are provided, including some low-fat, low-calorie, or high-protein meal options as well as a variety of low carbohydrate foods.

Whenever possible, serve sauces and dressings on the side so that guests can control their own portion sizes. Use fresh ingredients instead of processed foods that contain preservatives and other additives. Today's consumers want fresh choices. They also are becoming more adept at recognizing pre-prepared, processed foods.

While the trend is toward healthier, more nutritious foods, many meeting attendees see eating out as an opportunity to change their routines and splurge a little. The key to satisfying attendees' nutritional needs, as well as their expectations for a special dining experience, is to serve a variety of foods in appealing combinations and appropriate portions. Most foods, even those that are high in fat and salt, can be part of a well-balanced meal if the portions are controlled. The catering manager can work with the meeting planner to develop menus that are creative, nutritious, and satisfying.

Allergies and Food Restrictions

Many attendees cannot eat certain foods due to allergies, health considerations or religious or cultural beliefs. Some attendees may be vegetarians. Some common food allergies include peanuts, shrimp, wheat and strawberries. Others cannot tolerate MSG. Health considerations include not eating salt or fat for those with heart ailments, diabetics that cannot eat sugar, and those with hypoglycemia that must eat something every few hours.

Some guests consume special diets for religious or life-style reasons. For example, devout Moslems and Jews will not eat pork or shellfish. Orthodox Jews require kosher-prepared foods. Accommodating some ethnic/religious requirements may create added expenses due to outside specialized personnel (e.g., a Rabbi to supervise kosher preparations), acquiring special food items, and so on.

There are three types of vegetarians. Type one does not eat red meat, but will eat chicken and fish. Type two, referred to as lacto-ovovegetarians, will not eat anything that must be killed, but will eat by-products such as milk and cheese. Type three is known as vegans and will not consume anything from any animal source, including butter, honey and marshmallow. When in doubt, if someone identifies as a vegetarian, to be safe, assume they are vegans.

Politics of Food

Politics can play an important role in menu planning. Some groups will not consume certain types of foods. The catering department and the meeting manager must often see to it that politically correct foods are available. Serving veal to animal-rights organizations can anger guests because these groups believe that veal is raised and processed under inhumane conditions. Politically active groups may insist that the facility purchase and serve politically correct products. For example, the meeting manager may be prohibited from purchasing beef raised on recently deforested tropical rain forest land or be asked not to purchase tuna from countries that use drift nets that trap and kill dolphins and other sea life indiscriminately. Additionally, when planning food and beverage events the meeting manager should inquire about the client's "green" concerns, as it may prohibit the packaging finished of food products in disposable containers, and will require the need to use reusable containers.

Other Considerations

It is risky to offer items such as fish or lamb to a large group as these items are not universally appreciated. If the meeting manager would like to be a bit adventurous, a split entrée, known as "dualing menus," may be appropriate, which would still provide something "safe" for the meat and potatoes diner. An example would be surf and turf, perhaps a small filet mignon with three grilled jumbo shrimp.

When people are hungry, they are more likely to become irritable. Well-balanced meals with adequate portion sizes leave attendees calm, satisfied, and ready to learn. Refreshment breaks also help to stave off hunger, elevate the mood, and thereby enhance learning.

Caterers notice that many guests are reluctant to give up their dessert course. Ironically, when people are "good," they like to reward themselves with a rich dessert. Even while people are becoming more health-conscious, fancy desserts are expected at a catered meal. The typical guest feels cheated if the meal ends without a dessert, or if the dessert offered is viewed as mediocre.

The dessert creates the last impression of the meal and should attempt to be spectacular or unusual. A small portion of a rich dessert is sufficient if the presentation is very artistic. For instance, ordinary desserts can be very impressive if served on a colorful coulis (a fruit puree) on an oversized plate, and/or prepared at tableside.[3]

Meal Functions

Breakfast

With some groups as many as 50% of attendees skip breakfast. They may wish to sleep later or prefer to exercise. It is important to know the history of the group, so that the catering manager can plan accordingly and not waste food and money. There a several choices for breakfast meals.

- *Continental breakfast*—A continental breakfast is fast and encourages prompt attendance at morning meetings. It is often set up in the pre-function space just outside the meeting room or in the back of the meeting room. A basic continental breakfast includes coffee, tea, juice, and some type of bread or pastry, such as bagels, muffins, Danish, or croissants. A deluxe continental breakfast can also include several types of juices and an assortment of breads, yogurt, fruit, and cereal. It is typically a self-service buffet, although wait staff may serve beverages. There should be one attendant and a separate buffet table for every 100 attendees. The breakpoint for setting up a second buffet is 120 attendees. Continental breakfasts usually run from 30 minutes to an hour. Many guests arrive within the last 15 minutes, so be sure the tables will be replenished for this wave of attendees.
- *Full breakfast buffet*—A full breakfast buffet features two or three types of meat, two or three styles of eggs, one potato dish, three to six types of bread or pastry, cereals (cold and hot, with nonfat and whole milk), fresh fruit, yogurt, juices, coffee, and tea. A full breakfast buffet usually should run about 1 hour.
- *English breakfast*—An English breakfast includes the same foods as a full breakfast buffet, and also features action stations at which foods such as waffles, omelets, or crepes are made to order. It also should last about 1 hour.
- *Full, served breakfast*—There are occasions that call for a seated, served breakfast (e.g., an opening breakfast to kick off the meeting, an awards presentation, or a special speaker). This format, of course, will require more time for service.

Refreshment Breaks

Most meetings include a mid-morning and a mid-afternoon break. Thirty minutes is the minimum amount of time that should be scheduled for a refreshment break. Attendees need time to visit the restroom and make phone calls, in addition to having refreshments. Breaks are for networking as much as for refreshment, so be sure to allocate enough time.

The meeting budget will dictate what can be served. Many breaks include beverages only. Coffee, tea, bottled waters, and soft drinks are the mainstays. Many attendees prefer cold drinks, even in the morning. Depending upon the budget, muffins or fruit breads are a pleasant addition in the morning, especially since many attendees will not have made it to breakfast. Additions for the afternoon break may include yogurt, fruit, cookies, or soft pretzels.

Costs for breaks may be quoted per person or on a consumption basis. Paying for coffee by the gallon and pastry by the dozen is usually more cost effective than paying a per-person price. The sugar and creamer should not be placed in front of the coffee urns, since it takes twice as long to add cream and sugar as it does to pour coffee, this setup will create a real bottleneck. At least one attendant should be scheduled for every 100 attendees. Request that setup be completed at least 15 minutes prior to the scheduled break time, as a session may end early.

If the meeting room is large enough, the break may be set up at the back of the room. However, noise during setup could be distracting for session participants. The break can also be set up in the pre-function space just outside the meeting room, if the space is secure and the area is large enough to accommodate the group. If space is available, an even better option may be to set up the break in an adjoining room.

When a break has to sit out continuously, it is best to use whole fruit and wrapped cheese and crackers, rather than cutting it up where the air can dry it out or it could attract insects.

It is essential to determine the quantity of food and beverage to order at breaks. To verify and apply the information, check with the facility to confirm the size of the coffee cups as some may use 8-ounce or 10-ounce mugs. Whatever is the case, remember there are 128 ounces in a gallon. Divide 128 ounces by the appropriate mug size and the results will give the number of cups use by the facility per gallon. For example, 128 divided by 8 equals 16. Then divide the 300 cups by 16 for a total of 18.75 gallon or round it up to 19 (see Put It Into Practice).

Luncheons

Luncheons, like breakfasts, are intended to provide attendees with the convenience of remaining on the property and ensure their being on time for afternoon sessions. Prompt service is important in order keep the afternoon's programming on schedule.

A typical seated lunch takes 1 hour and 15 minutes to serve, so a 90-minute time period should be scheduled. If this is not feasible, have part of the meal preset in order to cut down on service time (e.g., salad and/or dessert already on the table).

Luncheon buffets can include deli setups for working lunches in boardrooms to hot buffets with a variety of options.

Put It Into Practice

How Much Should You Order?

For a Morning Break

Drinks	All Male	All Female	50/50
Regular Coffee	Attendance x 60%	x 50%	x 55%
Decaf Coffee	Attendance x 20%	x 25%	x 25%
Tea	Attendance x 10%	x 15%	x 10%
Soda	Attendance x 25%	x 25%	x 25%

For an Afternoon Break

Drinks	All Male	All Female	50/50
Regular Coffee	Attendance x 35%	x 30%	x 35%
Decaf Coffee	Attendance x 20%	x 20%	x 20%
Tea	Attendance x 10%	x 15%	x 10%
Soda	Attendance x 70%	x 70%	x 70%

How to use these charts: Locate the percentage associated with the makeup of your group and multiply that percentage by your overall attendance. Then divide the resulting number by 20 (6-ounce cups per gallon) to determine the number of gallons needed. Round each partial gallon up to the next highest half-gallon. For example, for a morning break at a conference that has an audience of 500 predominantly male attendees, the formula should be calculated as follows:

Regular Coffee = 500 x 60% = 300 cups / 20 = 15 gallons

Decaf Coffee = 500 x 20% = 100 cups = 5 gallons

Tea = 500 x 10% = 50 cups = 2.5 gallons

Soda = 500 x 25% = 125 sodas

Box lunches can be ordered for service on the exposition floor, to eat outside in a park area, to eat on buses en route to another destination, or to consume at an off-site event.

Receptions

Receptions are often referred to by caterers as "walk and talks." Most meetings have an opening reception, often followed by a dinner. Such receptions allow people to gather and be seated at the same time instead of straggling into the banquet room.

If possible, serve food before alcoholic beverages are offered to keep guests from drinking on an empty stomach. Serve starchy and high-protein foods, which stay in the stomach longer and delay the absorption of alcohol into the bloodstream. Avoid salty, greasy, spicy, or sweet foods that create a thirst that guests will quench with additional drinks.

The types of hors d'oeuvres to serve at a reception will depend on the available budget. When the budget is small, dry snacks, raw vegetables with dip, and/or cubed cheese with crackers may be appropriate. When there is more money to spend, hot and cold hors d'oeuvres set on attractively decorated buffet tables placed around the room will increase the movement of guests and encourage socializing.

Using plates can add as much as one third of the cost of food. Finger food, where attendees do not need utensils, is often preferable to fork food. When food does not require utensils to eat and often, not even plates, it is called finger food. Utensils require more landing space (tables, etc.). People can't hold a drink in one hand and eat from a plate with a fork with the other. Additionally, people will eat less when they do not have plates to load up.[4]

Butler service is where servers are passing trays of food is one way to control consumption at a reception. Trays can be sent out on a timed schedule rather than having large quantities of food openly available on a buffet table. This decreases consumption, yet gives the appearance of abundance and added style. This is a good option with shrimp, which is very expensive. Increase the elegance of the service by having servers wear white gloves. Boxes of disposable white gloves are readily available. It is preferable to only have one item per tray. It slows service when people have to ask what each item is before they choose.

When the reception is scheduled immediately after a meeting, food consumption will be less than if the reception is held later. When given the opportunity to go to their rooms to rest and change clothes, attendees are more relaxed at a reception and will enjoy the food and drink more. When a dinner follows the reception, less food, but more drinks will be consumed, because many guests will carry drinks from the bar to their table. Pre-poured wine and mineral water on trays to be passed are a good idea for a short reception.

Distractions, such as music, entertainment, or dancing, cut down on the consumption of food or drink; however, the music should never overpower comfortable conversation. Discuss decorating options with the caterer, who can arrange for flowers, ice carvings, or special lighting.

Seating should be minimal at receptions. Do not encourage guests to sit and eat. Seating for 20% to 25% of the attendees is optimal. There should be one attendant for every 50 guests.

Some general guidelines:

- Guests will generally eat an average of seven hors d'oeuvres during the first hour.
- Guests will usually eat more during the first hour of a reception.
- The demographics of the group are a factor. A group that is predominately male will usually consume more than a group that is predominately female. Older attendees will usually eat less than their younger counterparts.

Type of Reception	Type of Eaters	# Hors d'Oeuvres per person
2 hours or less (dinner following)	light	3-4 pieces
	moderate	5-7 pieces
	heavy	8+ pieces
2 hours or less (no dinner)	light	6-8 pieces
	moderate	10-12 pieces
	heavy	12+ pieces
2-3 hours (no dinner)	light	8-10 pieces
	moderate	10-12 pieces
	heavy	16+ pieces

Consumption also depends on how many square feet are available for guests to move around in (the tighter, the less consumption).

Space Requirements for Receptions

Minimum (tight)	5 1/2 to 6 square feet per person
Comfortably crowded	7 1/2 square feet per person
Ample room	10+ square feet per person

Seated, Served Dinners

Dinner guests are usually not on a tight schedule, and typically dinner service will take about 2 hours. If entertainment, dancing, awards, or other activities are included, the time may be increased to as much as 4 hours or more.

Since dinner is usually a more formal event, this is a great opportunity to include a spectacular menu item, such as an upscale dessert. Ask the chef for suggestions.

Seated Buffet Dinners

Several buffet or action stations around the room are preferable to one long buffet.[5] If there is a program during the evening, separate buffets with the same foods allow attendees to locate a station close to their dining table and avoid long lines and bottlenecks. If there is not a program, each station can feature a different theme, allowing attendees to wander to each station throughout the evening trying different dishes. Buffet tables more than 16 feet long should be two tables wide. Consider allowing service from both sides of the table to keep the lines moving more quickly.

Theme Parties

A theme party can be as simple as a mariachi band playing while Mexican food is served. Often the theme will reflect the local region, such as a "Gone with the Wind" theme in Atlanta, a clambake in Boston, or a beach or surfing theme in Southern California. A theme can be developed around almost anything. Ask the catering manager what themes have been successful in the past. Ask to see videos or photos of the event and consider these elements:

- *Moving décor*—Staff can wear costumes. They could be the servers or actors (hired from a local college).
- *Lights*—Tiny Italian lights look magical in ficus trees. Pin spots can be directed on turning glass balls that reflect light around the room, used to

highlight props, directed at the centerpieces on each table, or aimed at the stage. Strobe lights, black lights, and rotating beacons can also be used.

- *Special effects*—Confetti cannons (some with Mylar confetti), streamer cannons, bubble machines, fog machines, balloon art, and laser presentations can all add an exciting touch to a theme party.
- *Props*—Most major cities have one or more décor companies that rent a great variety of props. Some props are basic, such as columns and trellises. Visit a prop house to get an idea of what is available and what the costs are.

Hospitality Suites

Hospitality suites may be hosted by the meeting's sponsoring organization or by other organizations catering to the entire group or to a particular subgroup of attendees. Often, suite sponsors host evening hospitality functions; but, increasingly, breakfast or luncheon events are hosted as well. Hospitality suites are often auxiliary business to a hotel or facility, referred to as in conjunction with (ICW) business. While ICW business does not necessarily come from the meeting sponsor, it should be part of the meeting history used in negotiations because it increases the value of the meeting to the hotel. Meeting sponsors often develop guidelines on the times that events can be scheduled. These guidelines should be clearly published so that the host and attendees are aware of these restrictions.

Hospitality suites are usually held in a suite on a sleeping room floor, perhaps one of the hotel's top floors with a spectacular view. These types of functions are typically sold by the catering department, but serviced by room service. At times, hospitality suites are held in public function rooms, which, while less cozy, are easier for guests to locate, generally accommodate more people, and have ample room for live entertainment and dancing. When hospitality suites are held on public meeting room floors, catering sells and services the event.

Some hospitality suites feature a full bar, while others offer only offer beer and wine. The amount and type of food depends upon the budget, the event sponsor, and what other activities are planned for the event.

Underground hospitality suites, where a group brings its own liquor and raids the ice machine on the floor, should be discouraged. When a meeting promotes or encourages underground hospitality suites, there is an increased liability risk.

SERVICE

Service quality is just as important as food quality; they go hand in hand. Poor service can spoil even the most well-prepared meal. Service at a sit-down function is timed and more efficient, especially if there is a speaker or a planned presentation. A sit-down affair may be somewhat lower in price than a buffet, since every dish is pre-portioned. French or Russian service is elegant, but be prepared for a longer service time and a higher cost.

A buffet requires a bit more time, as guests have to select their food and take their seats before any program or entertainment can begin. Since the kitchen staff has to prepare more food, not knowing which items will be more popular, as well as not being able to control portion size, buffets tend to be more expensive.

The director of catering must stay within his or her payroll budget, but it is important to have good service. Instead of cutting labor to the bone, and possibly inconveniencing the meeting's attendees, it is better to pay a modest labor surcharge so that the meal can be prepared and served professionally. If the time allotted for the meal is tight and if paying a labor surcharge is the best option, this should be planned for it in advance; it should not be a last-minute consideration.

Types of Service

- *American service*—The food is portioned and plated in the kitchen, then served by attendants. Side dishes are used for bread and butter and salad. Food is served from the left, beverages from the right, and all items are removed from the right. This is the most common, functional, economical, controllable, and efficient type of service. Less movement and space are required for this service.

- *Buffet*—The food is arranged on tables. Guests serve themselves and take food to a dining table to eat. Servers may provide beverages. A variation would be plated buffet service, for which a selection of pre-plated foods are set on a buffet table and guests choose from among them.

- *Butler service*—Butler service is usually used at receptions; servers offer a variety of both hot and cold hors d'oeuvres on platters or trays to guests. Sometimes called "tray service. " (see Russian banquet service)

- *Cafeteria service*—This is similar to buffet service, except that attendants serve food to guests and the food is carried to their tables on trays.

- *English service*—This service is similar to Russian service as a tray of food is brought to the table and presented to the host. The host then either cuts the food or has it done by the server away from the table. Accompaniments (like vegetables) are placed in bowls on the table for guests to serve themselves and pass to other guests—family style.

- *French cart service*—A pattern of service (usually for smaller events) involves the use of serving pieces (usually silver); heating and garnishing of food table-side by a captain; and the serving of food on a heated plate, which is then served to the guest by a server. Plated entrees are usually served from the right, bread and butter and salad from the left and beverages from the right. All are removed from the right.

- *French Banquet Service*—For French service "banquet style" platters of food are prepared in the kitchen. Each food item is then served from the guest's left by the server from platters onto individual plates. Any course can be "Frenched" by having the dressing put on the salad or the sauce added to a dessert after it is in front of the guest. French service is impressive, but requires an experienced captain and servers to implement, as well as more time and ample space between tables.

- *Preset*—Some food is already on the table when guests arrive. Water, butter, bread, salad, and cold appetizers are the most commonly preset foods. However, at informal luncheons, the dessert or even a cold entrée may be preset as well.

- *Russian banquet service*—The food is fully prepared in the kitchen. All courses are served either from silver platters or an Escoffier dish. Tureens are used for soup and special bowls for salad. The server places the proper plate in front of the guest. After the plates are placed, the server returns with a tray of food and, moving counter-clockwise around the table, allows guests to help themselves from a platter presented from their left. Also called "butler service."

- *Russian restaurant service*—The food is cooked at table-side. Servers put the food on platters and present platters to guests seated at dining tables. Guests serve themselves. Russian service requires sufficient space between tables for servers to move about freely.

Service styles at a single function can be mixed. The evening could begin with a reception at which hors d'oeuvres are served butler style. For dinner, the appetizer may be preset, the soup served French style, the salad American style, the entrée Russian style, and dessert on a buffet.

Standard Service Ratios

It is important to ask how many tables will be assigned to each server and clarify the timing of all aspects of the event. Provide all of the details of the food and beverage event to the venue in writing (including the scheduled times for performances or speeches, equipment setup, and so on.).

When the food and beverage function will be having introductions, speakers, or presentations it may warrant a request that servers be out of the room or stationed at the back during these activities. Ensure that at least one room captain will remain in the room after the meal has been served, since assistance may be needed during the course of the program. Servers should know the ingredients and preparation method of everything on the menu in order to answer questions from guests.

Discuss with the catering manager the level of service that can be expected. Dinner service levels can range from one server per eight guests to one server per 40 guests. Most hotels plan one server per 32 guests. It is appropriate to request one server per 20 guests at a standard dinner and one per 16 if wine is served or an upscale type of service (French or Russian) is planned. The number of servers is always negotiable, but the group may be assessed an additional labor charge.

For optimum service levels:

Rounds of 10	1 server for every 2 tables
Rounds of 8	1 server for every 5 tables
Bussers	1 for every 3 servers

With poured wine or French service:

Round of 10	2 servers for every 3 tables
Round of 8	1 server for every 2 tables
Buffets	1 server for every 40 guests
	1 runner per 100–125 guests

French or Russian:

Rounds of 8 or 10	1 server per table

Supervision

For a dinner buffet, the setup and location are very important. Ask the facility how many buffets will be provided per 100 attendees. Buffet tables should not be placed too close to the entrance of the room. Sufficient space is required for adequate service lines to accommodate the variety of food and the number of people to be served. For more efficient service, have a separate dessert table away from the main buffet tables or provide dessert service with coffee later in the meal. There should be one room captain, and one section captain for every 250 guests (25 rounds of 10).

Set Over Guarantee

The set over guarantee is the percentage of guests that the caterer will prepare for beyond the guarantee, in case additional and unexpected guests show up. The calculation is negotiable.

Average overset is 5%

However, it is important to look at the numbers, not just the percentages.

100 guests = 10% overset
100-1000 guests = 5% overset
Over 1000 guests = 3% overset

Cocktail Servers

Cocktail servers can only serve from 48 to 64 drinks per hour. They can carry from 12 to 16 drinks per trip—counting the time to take the order, the time to wait for the drinks at the service bar, and the time it takes to find the guest and deliver the drink—it takes at least 15 minutes per trip to the bar. Hence, cocktail servers are usually only used at small or VIP functions.

SEATING ARRANGEMENTS

Casual Seating

The most casual method of seating diners is to let them select their own seats. This allows them to socialize with whomever they choose. This type of seating is typical with buffet service. If networking is the objective for the meal, suggest that particular groups or subgroups of people sit together at tables designated by different color tablecloths or different centerpieces or balloons for each subgroup so that they can readily find each other.

Formal Seating

The most formal method is assigned seating. An official of the sponsoring organization determines where individuals will sit and place cards are used at the tables. Have charts or lists made and staff available to help guests find their seats. Escort cards indicate to which table the guest has been assigned, place cards indicate the place at the table where the guest is to sit. Many groups are exploring the use of RFID technology to assist in this service (see Chapter 13).

A seating method often used for large and/or formal banquets is a *ticket exchange*. This allows guests to turn in a ticket by a pre-determined time to self-select seating with whoever they wish to sit with. This can be accomplished easily with web-based or software-based registrations. This allows the meeting manager to cut the guarantee for their final banquet, which is often the most expensive meal function.

Open Seating

Open seating is an alternative for meetings that do not have a history, or if there are too many variables to determine an accurate guarantee. As an example: If the hotel accepts a guarantee for 500 people and agrees to set 5% over guarantee, there would be 525 places set. Perhaps it is believed that 10 to 20 additional people may show up for the meal, but the group is not willing to take a chance on the guarantee. Open seating provides one or more extra tables that are not completely set as they are only covered with tablecloths. Should the group go over the guarantee, the partially set tables would then be set for service. The paid count would increase by the additional individuals who showed up. However, the meeting manager may have to accept that these additional guests may not be served the same entrée as the rest of the group. It is customary for hotels to set places for a certain percentage over guarantee—usually 3% to 5%, but again, the number is negotiable.

DETERMINING COSTS

The caterer has certain built-in costs for food. Other costs include labor for purchasing, setup, preparation, service, cleanup, and overhead (utilities, etc.). The flexibility for negotiating prices is narrow. Ask for menu items based upon a set budget and discuss cost-saving possibilities.[6]

For smaller meetings, such as a board meeting with a luncheon, the hotel may charge a service fee for a guarantee of fewer than 25 meals. Check the fee. For example, if only 20 meals are ordered, it may be less expensive to guarantee and pay for 25 than to pay the service fee.

If prices for food-and-beverage events cannot be negotiated prior to the time that the meeting manager must set the meeting registration fee, it may be possible to negotiate a written guarantee stating that the organization will not be charged more than the current price plus the estimated increase percentage, or the actual price if that is less than the early estimate.

Remember that the costs outlined above do not include décor or other peripherals to will make the meals memorable. There is usually more room for negotiation on props, linens, and décor that the hotel already owns than there is on decorations that must be rented from a decorating company.

GUARANTEES

One of the greatest challenges is to provide the catering department with accurate meal guarantees—the final number of guests expected. Weather, popular speakers, unusual locations, or particularly interesting areas may cause fluctuations from year to year that skew traditional meeting patterns. It is the combination of historical data and current conditions that are used to arrive at final guarantees.

Most hotels require a guarantee 48 hours before the event in order to allow adequate time to order and prepare food and schedule required personnel. They may require the guarantee 72 hours in advance if the time frame is over a weekend or a holiday, or if they are in a remote location without a frequent delivery system. Because of on-site registration and last-minute ticket sales, usually the standard minimum guarantee 48 hours in advance requirement can be negotiated so that the guarantee can be increased, but not decreased, within 24 hours in advance. As already mentioned, hotels usually plan to set places for 3% to 5% over the guarantee.

To ensure the promised quality of service, guarantees should be as accurate as possible. The average no-show factor is 3%, which may vary by the group and the destination. Do not forget to include the number of head table guests and staff members in the guarantee. A guarantee that is too low can ruin an event if a large number of attendees must wait an extra 30 minutes to be served.

Ideally, a large event should have tickets. The tickets should be numbered and/or have attendees' names on them and computer software makes this possible. At a seated dinner, empty seats can be counted and subtracted from the total set to get an accurate head count, but at a reception, only tickets can give an accurate attendance figure.

Another way to gauge potential attendance is to have the convention service manager check with the front desk to see how many checkouts are scheduled for the last day. Most checkouts will not remain for the evening banquet.

COST-SAVING IDEAS

The chef at the venue can come up with suggestions that will fit any budget. Chefs usually enjoy meeting with the client and appreciate the opportunity to be creative.

Consider the following cost-saving strategies:

- *Ganging menus*—Ask what other groups in the hotel are being served during the same mealtime. If the same menu can be served to another group in the hotel, a better price might be negotiated because of the economies of scale.

- *Provide small servings of high-end items*—Lobster medallions on a salad provide elegance at a lower cost than lobster for the entrée.
- *Limit portion size*—Enjoyment of a meal does not depend on quantity. The visual appeal and taste of food is just as important as the amount. An 8-ounce steak can be served instead of a 10-ounce steak.
- *Pass the food*—Guests usually consume less food when it is passed on trays or platters, and they appreciate being able to control their own portion size.

The catering manager and the chef can help add special touches that make an event even more spectacular. Consider the following:

- *Napkin folds and linens*— Ask what unusual or elegant options the catering staff can provide. There are many linen rental companies—and the meeting manager does not have to use what the hotel has in stock.
- *China and silver*—Most facilities have several patterns available, try something different. Even if the meal does not require a full place setting, it will create a more formal, elegant atmosphere.
- *Music*—Music can enhance the atmosphere of the event at a relatively low cost.
- *Lighting*—Lighting can have an impressive effect on an elegant evening. Small votive candles, or dimming the lights in the banquet room add to the effect.

GRATUITIES

The difference between a tip, gratuity, or service charge is that a tip is voluntary and given at the time of service, a gratuity is voluntary and added to a bill and a service charge is mandatory and an automatic amount that is added to a bill to defray labor costs. Tips may be given in addition to a gratuity or service charge for special or outstanding service. Gratuities added to the bill will go entirely to the staff. Service charges added to the check will range from 18%–22% of the total. Hotels will retain a portion of service charges. Ask the hotel what portion will go to the staff.

Facilities vary in regard to how they reach the bottom line. Ask the catering manager whether the gratuity is taxable or if the gratuity is figured on the base price plus tax.

BEVERAGES

Careful selection of both alcoholic and nonalcoholic beverages can add to the success of a reception or a meal. Placing sample bottles of what brands are being served on the top of the bar allows guests to make up their minds what to order while they are waiting in line, which speeds up the service.

Alcohol

The choice of whether to serve alcohol with a meal will depend upon the event budget and the impression the host wishes to convey. In general, beverages should not exceed 20 percent of the budget for a catered meal.

If people prefer a low-alcoholic wine, for example at lunch before going back to work, they should try German Rieslings. They are tasty, refreshing and very low in alcohol, often only about 8%. Alsatian Rieslings have a little higher content. California Rieslings are higher in alcohol.

Wine is the most popular alcoholic beverage to be served with dinner. Many caterers use a standard formula of about one half bottle of wine per person for a seated affair. Consumption will average about three glasses of wine per person during a 2-hour reception. Whenever possible, try to obtain the history of the group for an accurate estimate.

The nature of the event should also be considered, including the average age of the guests (younger people tend to drink more wine and beer, an older group will drink more hard liquor). Also consider the location and the season. At an outdoor party, more white wine will probably be consumed as a thirst quencher. More red wine is consumed in winter.

For every 10 bottles of white or sparkling wine ordered for a reception, only two bottles of red are needed. Of course, at a dinner with red meat as the entrée, the opposite would be true. There are people who do not drink red wine, even when the entrée is red meat, so always have some white wine available.

When making spirits or hard liquor available, be sure to request that bartenders use jiggers with pour spouts to control portions. For liability reasons, do not allow doubles to be served.

The great variety of beers now available includes light beers, nonalcoholic beers, and specialty beers. Beer has become increasingly more popular and guests appreciate having choices.

Number of Drinks per Bottle

		1 ounce	1 1/4 ounce	1 1/2 ounce
Liter	33.8 ounces	33	27	22
750 milliliters	25.4 ounces	25	20	16

Neutral Beverages

It is important to provide neutral (nonalcoholic) choices for those who do not drink alcohol. Neutral beverages include effervescent or still waters, sodas (including diet and caffeine-free), coffee and decaffeinated, herbal and decaffeinated teas, nonalcoholic beers and wines, iced tea, fruit punches, and fruit juices.

Themed Beverages

The catering manager may be able to suggest beverages that go well with the theme of the event. For example, serve fruit smoothies for an exercise event, tropical drinks for a luau, or root-beer floats for a sock hop. A dinner featuring regional fare might include beer from a local microbrewery. Add to the theme with appropriate glassware or stirrers.

Matching Food and Wine

Generally speaking, delicate, less-flavorful foods should be served with white wines. Red meats, pastas with meat and tomato sauce, and other strong-flavored foods should be served with red wines.

BEVERAGE PURCHASING OPTIONS

Cash or No-Host Bar

A cash bar is an option when drinks are not paid for by a host. Guests pay the bartender directly or present a ticket for each drink. Tickets may be the same price for all drinks, or there may be different colored tickets and different prices for wine, beer, spirits, and soft drinks.

Most facilities place a minimum on the number of drinks sold per bartender. If the minimum dollar amount is not reached, the organization must pay for each bartender's time for a minimum number of hours. These minimums are generally negotiable.

The per-drink price may or may not include a gratuity and may be only for house brands rather than premium or name brands. Be sure to ask what will be served and what the price includes. Snacks or hors d'oeuvres may be added and charged to the organization on a per-person or quantity basis.

Beverage consumption with a cash bar is usually much lower than when a host is paying the bill. When the party is scheduled at the usual cocktail hour following a meeting, approximately half of the meeting participants will stay for the event. Consumption typically averages 1.5 drinks per person for a 1-hour cash-bar function.

Open or Hosted Bar

When a sponsor is hosting the reception as an open bar, expect much higher consumption and costs than for a cash bar. When cocktails and hors d'oeuvres are hosted at the usual cocktail hour, 80 percent of the group may be expected to attend. Average consumption is 2 to 2.5 drinks per person for a 1-hour open bar, 3 to 3.5 drinks for 1.5 hours.

Methods of paying for an open bar include:

- *By the person*—The organization pays a flat amount for the duration of the party, or per person, per hour, whether the guest chooses a cocktail, a soft drink, or no drink. The per-person price may cover only beverages or may include snacks and hors d'oeuvres. The number of attendees for which the sponsor is charged may be based on a guaranteed number and/or the number of tickers collected at the door.

- *By the drink*—A per-drink charge is tallied and a single check presented to the function host. Prices are negotiated in advance.

- *By the bottle*—The hosting organization pays only for those bottles opened (whether or not any beverage has been poured from the bottle). The meeting manager controls the inventory of the number of bottles present before the party and the number remaining at the close of the function. Partial bottles (sometimes referred to as stubs) become the property of the organization at the end of the event.

- *Limited consumption bar*—The host organization establishes the maximum dollar amount they are willing to spend. This works best on a per-drink basis when a cash register is used or there is a time limit for the open bar. When the cash register reaches the set amount or the bar has been opened for the pre-designated time period, the bar closes or is converted to a cash basis.

Package Plans

While most facilities offer several methods of paying for liquor, not all hotels offer all options. Purchasing by the person, per hour is easiest for the meeting manager, as costs are known up-front based on the guarantee and is the most profitable for the facility.

Cocktail Reception Package Plan

The cocktail hour is a package designed to ease the budgeting plans for groups of 50 or more attendees. Under this arrangement the group will be provided a full-service cocktail reception with portable bars, experienced bartenders, and full setups.

Once the package is chosen the venue will charge per person, based on guaranteed attendance or actual attendance, whichever is higher. The complete bar setup includes call or premium brand liquors, California wines, domestic beers, and soft drinks. Bar service includes vermouth, mixers, juices, and garnishes.

Hours	One	Two	Three
Premium Brands	$20	$22	$24
Call Brands	$15	$18	$21

Generally, prices for alcoholic beverages are subject to gratuity and sales taxes. It is common that for cash bars and package plans the facility will have a sliding bartender charge such as $75 for the first hour, $50 for the second hour, and $25 for each additional hour. One bartender should be provided for every 100 guests if they are arriving at intervals. If guests are all arriving in one group, one bartender for every 50 guests is more appropriate.

Put It Into Practice

Catering Checklist

The following checklist is a starting point to help when planning a food and beverage event. Instructions to the catering manager as well as any other vendors providing service to the event should be very specific.

Food and Beverage

- What is the estimated attendance?
- What is the budget for the event?
- What are the objectives for the event?
- Is there a program to be presented?
- What food and beverages will be served?
- How many places are required at the head table?
- How will the meal be served (to the head table and to the other tables)?
- Are there any guests with special dietary restrictions? If so, what are they?
- Will any part of the meal be preset?
- How are taxes and gratuities or service charges calculated?

Décor/Setup

- Is there a theme for the event?
- What table linens, china, and silver will be used?
- How many seats will be at each table?
- What type of centerpieces and decorations are needed for each table, the head table, and buffet tables?
- Are programs or menus to be preset on tables or chairs, or distributed at the door?

- Are banners, flags, or signs needed, and where will they be placed?
- How much time is needed for setup?
- When will the room be accessible?
- Are platforms and stages to be skirted and/or carpeted?

Audiovisual (A/V)

- Will the head table be on a platform?
- Is a floor or table lectern needed? If so, where should it be placed?
- Is a microphone needed? If so, what type and where?
- Will there be an A/V presentation? If so, what type?
- Is there any music or special lighting planned? Will it be throughout the event or only during a portion of it?
- Will there be entertainment for which an additional stage or platform is needed? If so, what size and height?
- Is a rehearsal planned? If so, when?

Other

- If tickets are to be used, will staff collect them? Where will they be collected, at the door or at the tables?
- Is a coat-check room needed?
- At what time will the doors be opened?
- What is the timing for all aspects of the event (pre-program music, entertainment, meal service, formal program and presentations, dancing, etc.)?

LIQUOR LIABILITY SAFEGUARDS

The sponsoring organization as the social host (the organization providing alcohol to their guests) could be held liable if any of their guests becomes intoxicated and causes injury to themselves or others, or damage to property, or if liquor is served to someone younger than the legal drinking age.

While dram shop laws vary from state to state and even within states, there are at least four types of liquor sales that are illegal in the United States:

1. *Sales to minors*—Liquor may not be served to anyone under 21 years of age.
2. *Sales to intoxicated people*—Liquor cannot be served to anyone who appears to be intoxicated.
3. *Hours of operation*—Most areas restrict the hours during which alcohol may be served. Beyond those hours, sale of liquor is illegal.
4. *Proper liquor license*—A hotel's on-premises liquor license would not be valid for an off-premises event. A temporary license would be needed.

SUMMARY

Almost all meetings include some sort of food and beverage function. The food and beverages, and the manner in which they are served, can help make the meeting more memorable and more productive.

The meeting manager will be working closely with the catering manager, who will help them plan what food and beverages will be served, the type of service, seating arrangements, and the décor. Meeting managers should provide the catering manager with the objectives for the event, as well as a history of the group's food and beverage preferences, and other details, including date, time, location, budget, entertainment, and presentations.

The key to satisfying attendees' nutritional needs, as well as their expectations for a special dining experience, is to serve a variety of foods in appealing combinations and appropriate portions. Most foods can be part of a well-balanced meal if the portions are controlled. The catering manager can work with the meeting manager to develop menus that are creative, nutritious, and satisfying.

Service quality is just as important as food quality—they go hand in hand. Service at a sit-down function is timed and efficient, especially if there is a program planned. A sit-down affair may be somewhat lower in price than a buffet, since every dish is portioned. French or Russian service, at which courses are served individually and sequentially, is elegant, but take longer to serve and cost more than other styles of service, such as American or preset service. A buffet also requires a bit more time, as guests have to select their food and take their seats before any program or entertainment can begin.

Most meetings include a mid-morning and a mid-afternoon break. Thirty minutes is the minimum amount of time that should be scheduled for a refreshment break. Whether beverages only or beverages and snacks are served will depend upon the meeting budget.

Hospitality suites may be hosted by the meeting's sponsoring organization or by other organizations catering to the entire group or to a particular subgroup of attendees. The amount and type of beverages and food served depends upon the budget and what other activities are planned for the event.

The choice of whether to serve alcohol with a meal will depend upon the event budget and the impression the host wishes to convey. In general, beverages should not exceed 20% of the entire food-and-beverage budget for a catered meal. Most hotels and other venues offer a variety of beverage purchasing options.

The sponsoring organization as the social host (the organization providing alcohol to their guests) could be held liable if any of their guests becomes intoxicated and causes injury to themselves or others, or damage to property, or if liquor is served to someone younger than the legal drinking age. Take appropriate precautions to prevent guests from becoming intoxicated.

Although food and beverage events may have significant variable expenses, there are ways to control costs without sacrificing quality, and there are always special touches that can be added at little cost. Utilize the creativity of the chef and the advice of the catering manager to plan functions that meet both the objectives of the meeting and its budget.

REFERENCES

1. Conferon. Retrieved March 28, 2006 from http://www.conferon.com/.

2. Meeting planner's guide to food and beverage. Retrieved April 6, 2006 from http://www.pcma.org/templates/food_bev/.

3. Sturken, C. A. (October, 1999). Kitchen aid. *Meetings & conventions.* Retrieved April 7, 2006 from http://www.meetings-conventions.com/convertedarticle.aspx?articleid=2419.

4. Shock, P. J., & Stefanelli, J. (2001). *On-premise catering.* Hoboken, NJ: Wiley.

5. Teitler, A. D. (May, 2000). Building a better buffet. *Meetings & conventions.* Retrieved April 7, 2006 from http://www.meetings-conventions.com/converted article.aspx?articleid=929.

6. Edelstein, L. J. (May, 1998). Fifteen ways to cut F & B costs. *Meetings & conventions.* Retrieved April 7, 2006 from http://www.meetingsconventions.com/convertedarticle.aspx?articleid=1111.

KEY TERMS

American service	French service	Open bar
Auxiliary business	Finger food	Open seating
Banquet	Full breakfast	Place cards
Buffet	Ganging menus	Plated buffet
Butler service	Gratuity	Preplated
Cafeteria service	Guarantees	Preset
Cart-style service	Head count	Russian service
Cash bar	Hors d'oeuvres	Service charge
Chef's table	Hospitality suite	Ticket exchange
Continental breakfast	Host	Tip
Dram shop laws	In conjunction with (icw)	Underground hospitality
Dualing menus	Lacto-ovovegetarians	suite
English breakfast	Limited consumption bar	Vegans
Escoffier dish		

COMPELLING QUESTIONS FOR CONSIDERATION

1. What are some of the factors that affect menu planning?

2. Describe several types of service and the type of functions for which each would be appropriate.

3. Discuss ways a meeting manager can make the meal guarantees as accurate as possible.

4. Discuss dram shop law and some of the precautions to be taken to prevent guests from becoming intoxicated.

5. For a predominately female group, how many gallons of coffee, decaf and tea would a meeting professional have to order for the morning break when the facility is using 8-ounce cups?

CHAPTER 27

EXHIBITIONS: IT'S SHOW BUSINESS AFTER ALL

David A. Weil

SENIOR DIRECTOR, CONVENTION AND TRADESHOW SERVICES

SMITHBUCKLIN CORPORATION

LEARNER OUTCOMES

When the reader has completed reading this chapter, he/she should be able to . . .

1 Discuss the factors to be considered when choosing a facility for an exhibition.

2 Determine how much exhibit space is required for an exhibition.

3 Develop an exhibition budget.

4 Identify the elements that should be included in an exhibitor prospectus.

5 Describe the four basic booth configurations.

6 Identify the elements to be included in an exhibitor service kit.

> With the advent of the Internet and the decline in personal sales calls, exhibitions have become the last bastion of face-to-face marketing.
>
> *Doug Ducate*
> *President and CEO*
> *Center for Exhibition Industry Research*

OVERVIEW

Adding an exhibition (trade show) to a meeting or educational conference creates a viable marketplace for buyers to meet sellers. A well-planned exhibition can provide a substantial source of revenue for the organization, a valuable learning opportunity for its members, and a marketing opportunity for exhibitors.

This chapter focuses on providing information on the overall planning, selling, marketing, and site selection for an exhibition. Launching a new exhibition requires research to critically evaluate many factors, including the necessary market for the exhibition, for both potential exhibiting companies and attendees, current and future economic conditions, staffing, financing, and other resources.

WHY PLAN AN EXHIBITION?

In addition to the financial benefits for the sponsoring organization, an exhibition (also referred to as an exposition) that is held in conjunction with a meeting or educational conference can help stimulate or enhance attendee participation in the overall event. Exhibits can be an extension of the program, offering attendees the opportunity to see exhibitors' products and services, and enabling them to make purchasing decisions in the context of a comparative marketplace.

Exhibitions provide a cost-effective marketing opportunity for exhibit companies, compared to the costs of reaching the same number of customers through direct sales, according to research available from the Center for Exhibition Industry Research (CEIR). CEIR has more than 200 research reports available in its database (www.ceir.org), which can provide valuable information for use in planning an exhibition.

The International Association for Exhibition Management (www.iaem.org) and the Society of Independent Show Organizers (www.siso.org) also provide information on the value and role of exhibitions, as well as extensive information on exhibition management. Practical tips and how-to information for exhibiting companies are also available from associations such as the Trade Show Exhibitors Association (www.tsea.org).

CHOOSING A FACILITY

Many different types of facilities can hold exhibitions, but the ideal venue should have adequate space to house both the meeting and the exhibits under one roof. Most major convention centers have such facilities, as do many larger convention hotels. Other types of facilities to consider, depending upon the needs of the organization and exhibiting companies, include trade centers, market centers, colleges and universities, and even tents and other outdoor facilities (see Chapter 11).

Exhibit Space

Convention centers and convention hotels publish the gross square footage available in each of their exhibit halls (or ballrooms). If the organization previously held its exhibition in another location, determining whether a hall is the right size for the needs is relatively easy.

As a general rule, double the estimated net square footage needed for booths (to account for aisle space) to determine the gross square footage needed for exhibits. If, for example, the exhibition had 400 standard (10-foot-by-10-foot) booths and occupied 40,000 net square feet last year, it is anticipated to have a 5 percent growth in exhibit space this year with aisles the same width, and the registration area uses 5,000 gross square feet, then the organization will need 42,000 net square feet of exhibit space plus 5,000 gross square feet for registration. In the example, the exhibition will require 89,000 gross square feet of space (42,000 net sq. ft. x 2 + 5,000 gross sq. ft. = 89,000 gross sq ft.).

Other factors to consider when determining space needs include:

- the number and size of nonstandard booths (e.g., island booths, peninsula booths)
- the amount of space needed for the organization's displays, special feature exhibits, lounge areas, and concessions
- whether the registration area and show management office will be located inside the exhibit hall

Also, it is advisable sometimes to provide Internet cafés, food and beverage service areas, or other specialized space on the show floor.

Determining space needs for a new event is more difficult. Surveying potential exhibitors, discussing marketing and production plans with exhibitors, and reviewing other events in the specific industry can all help the meeting manager reach a reasonable estimate of the space needed.

Floor Plan

For most exhibitions, a general services contractor (GSC) will diagram the exhibit space and any other areas that may be needed on the exhibit floor. The GSC can save the meeting manager time and money by creating the most cost-effective floor plan that meets the needs of exhibitors and attendees, as well as by being familiar with the facilities and with local fire rules and regulations.

Many architectural features of the facility can affect an exhibition floor plan, including columns, rigging points, escalators, stairwells, and elevators; ceiling heights and other obstructions such as lighting fixtures and heating and air conditioning ducts; and floor loads (weight limits), floor coverings, and utility ports.

Basic utility requirements for an exhibition are lighting and electricity. Some exhibitors might also require compressed air, hot and cold water, steam, drains, or gas. Most utility ports are usually spaced evenly throughout exhibit halls, but in some facilities, irregular outlets and hanging wires or pipes requiring ceiling or aisle access might prove inconvenient or cost-prohibitive. Even local fire regulations can affect the allowable width of the exhibition's aisles.

Freight

Most convention centers have a designated number of loading docks and freight elevators to expedite moving freight. However, exhibitors' equipment, skids, and crates can come in a wide range of sizes, so it is important to advise them of the dimensions and capacities of freight elevators and doors, as well as floor-load limits within the exhibit hall.

It is not uncommon to find even convention hotels with only one loading dock and ramp for both exhibition freight and hotel suppliers. Some hotels carpet the ballroom or exhibit hall and prohibit forklifts on the carpeting. These factors can slow material handling for the exhibition, so schedule exhibit hall or meeting room access, and move-in and move-out times accordingly.

EVALUATING A FACILITY CONTRACT

Hall rental fees vary from facility to facility, as do the methods used for determining those fees. Here are some of the questions to consider when evaluating a hall rental contract (see Chapter 40):

- Is the square footage rental rate for the entire term of the lease or per day?

- Are move-in and move-out times covered in the basic rental rates or is there an additional charge?
- Are the number of move-in and move-out days limited in the basic rate? (Dock access, marshaling yards, and the general facility layout all factor into negotiating the starting and ending hours.)
- Is there a guaranteed minimum or buy-out (cancellation) rate? If so, is it clearly defined in the agreement?
- Under what circumstances will show management be compensated if the facility moves the event to another hall?
- What does the rental rate include (e.g., meeting rooms, equipment, and so on)?
- Will there be extended-use charges for failure to vacate the leased areas at the end of the period designated in the rental agreement?
- Is a security deposit required?
- What is the payment schedule?

FACILITY RULES AND REGULATIONS

The most important rules and regulations governing exhibition facility use are fire regulations, union labor rules, and rules regarding the use of exclusive, in-house services. There will likely be other policies as well, so it is important to

---

Put It Into Practice

A Facility Checklist

Prepare for the Selection Process
- ❏ Event Goals and Objectives
- ❏ Requirements and History
- ❏ Event Specifications
- ❏ Site Inspection Checklist
- ❏ Facility Questionnaire

Research Potential Venues
- ❏ Convention Centers
- ❏ Conference Centers (executive, resort, corporate, educational, non-residential, ancillary)
- ❏ Hotels (full-service, mid-level, limited-service, resort)
- ❏ Non-Traditional Venues (museums, galleries, restaurants, cruise ships, and so on)

Schedule Site Inspection(s)
- ❏ Before Contract Negotiations
- ❏ 1 to 2 Years Before Event Dates
- ❏ Before and After Property Renovation
- ❏ At Same Time of Year as Event Dates

Conduct Site Inspection(s)
- ❏ Make Appointments with Sales Manager and/or CVB Representative
- ❏ Bring Notepad, Cassette or Video Recorder, Camera, Facility Brochures and Floor Plans
- ❏ Meet with Sales Manager, Operations Staff, Bureau Representative, Service Vendors, National Sales Representatives
- ❏ Ask Each Contact/Vendor About Checklist Points Pertaining to Their Areas
- ❏ Record Responses to Questions and Note Concerns to Discuss in Negotiations

If Delegating Site Inspection Duties, Then...
- ❏ Choose Staff Members or Volunteers who Live in or Can Travel to Destination
- ❏ Provide Written Event Specifications
- ❏ Define Purpose of Site Inspection
- ❏ Delimit Responsibilities and Expected Outcome
- ❏ Provide Guidelines for Reporting Recommendations

APEX Facility Checklist Template, Copyright 2004 by Convention Industry Council. http://www.conventionindustry.org

review a copy of all of the facilities' rules and regulations and determine their financial impact before signing a contract.

Fire Regulations

It is common for facilities to require having the fire marshal approve the floor plan prior to its being published, in case changes are required. A fire inspector will usually tour the exhibition during set up and give final permission for the show to open. Sometimes an additional inspection takes place during the exhibition to ensure that all fire regulations continue to be met.

In addition to submitting floor plans for the exhibit space and meeting rooms, the meeting manager must also submit plans for any other areas that are being used (e.g., registration area, book store, membership booth, information counters, and so on).

Many facilities now require both facility approval and fire marshal approval for each floor plan. In some cases, the facility or the fire marshal's office may charge for this review service. Often the GSC will assist in preparing and sending exhibit floor plans to the fire marshal.

Union Rules

Exhibitors have a responsibility to follow the union labor rules that apply in the host city. The GSC and the appropriate locals of each union sign most labor contracts. Labor rates are negotiated between the GSC and the unions on a city-by-city basis. Facilities may also sign union agreements for work performed within the facility. Labor contracts require that only members of a particular union (e.g., carpenters, riggers, electricians, decorators, millwrights, plumbers, stagehands, and teamsters) perform specific types of labor. The GSC will provide the meeting manager with a copy of the labor rules and rates as they apply to the exhibition, and the meeting manager can publish them in the exhibitor service kit.

If exhibitors adhere to the labor rules, few, if any, problems should arise. A business agent or union steward for each of the unions involved will inspect the site to ensure that exhibitors are following regulations and that union personnel are performing correctly. Depending upon the size of the organization's staff, the meeting manager can either appoint a staff member to act as floor manager or hire a professional. Any floor manager represents the best interests of the organization on the exhibit floor and helps handle any work-rule disputes that may arise.

Even when the exhibition is held in a "right to work state," where laws prohibit employers from making union membership a condition of employment, the use of union labor may still be necessary to perform certain tasks. For example, labor rules might allow an exhibitor to set up a display as long as tools are not used and the job is completed within 30 minutes. Otherwise, the exhibitor must employ union labor.

Moving in during straight-time hours, and avoiding holidays, weekends, and overtime can save money on labor, but getting the job done within these time frames is not always possible. Communication of these budgetary implications to exhibitors should always occur.

Exclusive and In-House Contracts

Some facilities reserve the right to provide many of the services required by exhibitors and show management through in-house departments or exclusive contractors. Services provided on this basis might include electrical or other utilities, telecommunications, cleaning, catering, AV, floral, or registration. The facility may also offer to provide services, but not necessarily insist upon being the official provider.

Outside Contractors

Numerous outside contractors are needed to put on a trade show, including the general services contractor (GSC) and contractors for audiovisual, computer rental, security, floral, custom furniture, cleaning, and bus shuttles. Most convention centers and hotels have certain exclusive contractors that all shows must use.

The general services contractor is the most important outside contractor, for its employees have the most direct contact with the group's exhibitor base and it supplies the essential equipment (e.g., tables, chairs, carpets, signs) and labor (e.g., freight movement, forklifts, carpenters). Therefore, the meeting manager

---

Put It Into Practice

Basic Expenses in the Exhibition Budget

Management expenses

- Salary and commissions for show management, sales personnel, other staff
- Allocated office expenses (e.g., rent, utilities, and so on)
- Telephone, fax, photocopies
- Liability and cancellation insurance
- Fees for an outside exhibition management company (optional)

Marketing and sales expenses

- Design and graphics for the exhibit prospectus
- Design, graphics, and printing for stationery
- Printing and postage for the exhibit prospectus
- Prospect and database development, including purchase of mailing lists
- Printing and postage for follow-up mailings
- Fees for mass faxes or marketing via email
- Development, distribution, and analysis of the evaluation instrument (survey to determine exhibitor satisfaction)

Exhibitor services expenses

- Printing, binders, and tabs for exhibitor service kits (Note: The GSC may provide the exhibitor service kits.)
- Graphics and printing of guest passes for exhibitor distribution
- Design, graphics, and printing for the exhibit directory
- Exhibitor communication (newsletters, email updates, general information)

Exhibition production expenses

- Hall rental
- Carpeting for the aisles, concessions, registration area, and lounges
- Furniture for the show office, lounges, and registration
- Booth set up (labor, pipe and drape, signage)
- Registration counters, headers and fill-in counters, labor, and graphics
- Directional signs (graphics and labor)
- Registration services (badges, badge holders, data entry, programming and reporting, online usage fees, computer equipment or self-registration terminals)
- Registration personnel (including travel expenses)
- Temporary personnel (show office and so on)
- Security services, including guards and badge checkers
- Media relations
- Catering for breaks and receptions
- Construction, graphics, and labor for special displays
- Staff for first-aid station
- Exhibit hall cleaning and trash removal
- Electrical and other utilities
- Shipping and drayage (material handling) of freight for show management and registration
- Vendor travel and expenses
- Staff travel and expenses
- Telephone line connection and usage charges
- Office equipment rental (computers, telephones, fax machines, photocopiers)
- Shuttle bus service
- Printing registration forms and special event tickets
- Sponsorship expenses (signs, banners, and so on)
- Union labor (movement of boxes, show management requirements)

should devote adequate attention to selecting this company. Send an request for proposals to several GSCs, both national and local to the site city.

BUDGETING

Estimating Expenses

Before setting the booth space rate, the meeting manager must determine how much it will cost to stage the exhibition. Substantial expenses can be incurred for managing the event, marketing exhibit space, providing exhibitor services, and producing the exhibition. The GSC can help estimate many of the production costs. If the exhibition is a stand-alone event (not part of a convention or meeting), the organization will also incur the expenses for attendance promotion.

Estimating Revenue

Once the meeting manager has estimated the expenses involved in producing the exhibition, the next step is to anticipate how much exhibit space will be sold and determine how much revenue is expected to be generated from booth sales. These figures must be determined before establishing the cost of booth space.

Exhibit Space Rates

Divide the total anticipated expenses by the anticipated number of booths or net square feet to form the basis for pricing exhibit space. Compare these rates with other events in the same industry to ensure they are similar to other shows. The projected net square feet times the price per square foot will be the estimated exhibit space sales revenue for the exhibition.

Be sure to factor in how many exhibitors might receive any special pricing that is granted to members of the organization, how much space will be sold at premium rates (e.g., corner locations or islands), and any other special considerations.

Registration Fees

Registration fees charged to attendees and exhibitors are another potential source of revenue.

Some shows allow exhibitors an unlimited number of badges, while others set limits based on the amount of paid exhibit space and charge for additional badges.

Some exhibitions charge no registration fees for attendees, while others allow pre-registered attendees to attend at no charge and charge a nominal fee for on-site registration.

Put It Into Practice

What can be done if exhibitors are complaining about the high cost of exhibiting and their poor return on investment?

Help control Exhibitor Costs:

- Offer a package deal appropriate for the show, such as free furniture or drayage costs

- Encourage exhibitors to order furniture and labor early to save money and time
- Review exhibitor rates very closely (e.g., look closely at overtime costs and surcharges)

Sponsorships and Other Income

Sponsorships can help an exhibiting company gain additional exposure and access to attendees. Determine what metrics exhibitors will use to gauge sponsorship success and then build and customize the sponsorship around those metrics. These include:

- Brand name awareness—seeing their name everywhere
- Business leads—driving traffic to their booth
- Media coverage—getting reporters to cover their product launch

The organization can provide a variety of sponsorship opportunities related to the exhibition and meeting, such as refreshment breaks, receptions, special events, signs, banner advertising, or tote bags for attendees.

After the event is completed, ensure that sponsors have an opportunity to provide feedback to the meeting manager through a survey, which should include questions on customer service, delivery of benefits, and the value of the program based on their objectives.

Merchandise sales are another revenue-generating activity. Items bearing the show or organization logo, such as pens, coffee mugs, and T-shirts are popular. Industry-related books, CD-ROMS, or software are another potential revenue source. However, always be aware of local city or facility regulations and taxes for trade show sales.

The organization can sell advertising in the show directory or show dailies. The directory is a listing, with booth numbers, of all of the exhibitors in an event and a map showing booth locations. A show daily is a newspaper that is published each day during the run of the show. It includes articles about the exhibits and events and often advertising as well.

EXHIBIT MARKETING AND SALES

The first step in developing an exhibit sales strategy is to understand the unique rationale for the show and the specific need the show fills that no other event does. This will allow the meeting manager to identify the differentiation in the marketing message to current and potential exhibitors.

The marketing message must also address the goals and objectives of potential exhibitors, in order to attract them to the event instead of other marketing opportunities. The exhibit marketing material should demonstrate how the event can help exhibitors increase awareness of company products, impart product knowledge, provide one-on-one time with prospects, strengthen relationships with current customers, obtain new customers, and generate leads. The exhibitor prospect database is the backbone of any exhibit sales effort; therefore, managing additions, changes, and deletions to the database, and how qualified prospects will be handled throughout the year leading up to the event is vital.

Sales staff should be able to develop relationships with prospects, exhibitors, and sponsors. The exhibit sales staff should become an expert on industry issues, trends, and areas of potential new growth.

THE EXHIBITOR PROSPECTUS

The exhibitor prospectus is the most important marketing piece that will be produced for the event. The prospectus should include the following:

- A cover letter from an industry leader inviting the exhibitor to the show
- The show's unique rationale
- The show's important statistics and successes

- The features of the show and benefits for exhibitors
- A listing of attendee categories and demographics (location, buying power)
- A listing of the products and services that will be displayed at the show
- General information (hours, days, booth furnishings)
- Exhibiting companies that will participate
- Brief highlights of education content
- Exhibitor and attendee testimonials
- Photos of the show (crowded aisles)
- The exhibitor contract with rules and regulations (include the return address)
- Pricing, payment schedule, and deposits
- The exhibit floor plan

EXHIBIT SPACE CONTRACTS

The design of the space application should be uncluttered, but it must allow enough room for an exhibitor to provide all of the information required for the space assignment process. Many shows provide online forms, as well as printed ones.

Distribution of the exhibit prospectus is an invitation to apply for exhibit space. Acceptance as an exhibitor is not guaranteed until the show management signs the contract, acknowledging the company's eligibility and space assignment.

A basic contract should include the following:

General Information

- The show name, producer, location, and dates, including move-in and move-out schedules
- The address for mailing the application and deposit
- Acceptable forms of payment

Exhibitor/Space Selection Information

- Space for the company name, contact, address, phone, fax, email address, and exhibitor's signature
- Space to list several booth location choices, dimension and height requirements, products to be exhibited, and the names of any competing firms the exhibitor prefers not be located nearby

Payment and Cancellation Policies

- State the deposit payment schedule (50% is common) and exactly what the booth fee includes (e.g., pipe and drape, sign, electricity, and so on).
- Outline the cancellation policy and emphasize that cancellations must be in writing. State whether the deposit or any payments are refundable, or which portion is refundable depending upon the date of cancellation or whether the organization is able to resell the space to another exhibitor. (Refund and cancellation policies vary widely.)

Other Terms and Conditions, Rules, and Regulations

- Include the standards for design, construction, hanging signs, decoration, and safety of exhibits, including restrictions on sound, lighting, balloons, videos, or other attention-getting devices such as contests.

- List regulations for the conduct of exhibits, such as rules for distributing literature outside the booth, demonstrations, direct sales, animals, and so on.
- List the general rules on eligibility and acceptance of exhibitors, and the subletting of space policy.
- List display rules and regulations.
- Include the standards for fire safety, electrical connections, and so on.
- Include a clause that reserves show management the right to reassign space if it is deemed necessary for the overall good of the exhibition.

Liability and Insurance

- Include a liability clause that states who will assume liability in the event of damage to the facility, loss or damage to the exhibitor's property, or the injury or death of an attendee or third party. Usually the sponsoring organization limits its liability to any personal injury or property damage resulting from its own negligent use of the premises. Show management usually requires that the exhibitor indemnify or "hold harmless" the organization, the facility, their agents, and employees for any claims arising from or in connection with the exhibitor's occupancy and/or use of the exhibit hall. The contract should also indicate the liability in the case of an "act of God."
- Specify who is responsible for music licensing, fees, and permits for copyrighted material.
- Specify which party must obtain property, liability, and business interruption insurance on the exhibitor. In most cases, it is the exhibitor.

THE FLOOR PLAN

The floor plan becomes a major tool for selling exhibit space. The GSC can prepare a floor plan drawn to scale on a template of the facility's space. It should be updated as the selling and planning process progresses. In addition to sending an exhibit prospectus, many exhibitions also offer their floor plans for review online. Electronic versions of floor plans can be updated quickly and easily.

The meeting manager may combine some of the standard booths to form larger exhibit spaces, including peninsula booths and perimeter booths (see Figure 27.1).

Standard Booth (Linear Booth)

The standard booth (also called a linear booth or inline booth) is a basic back wall booth designed to stand back-to-back with an opposite row of booths. One or two sides of the booth face an aisle. The usual depth from aisle to back wall is 10 feet (3.05 meters), although hotel showrooms sometimes scale down this dimension to 8 feet (2.44 meters). While the standard width is 10 feet, a booth can occupy two or more adjacent 10-by-10-foot (3.05-by-3.05-meter) spaces. The back wall height for standard booths is 8 feet 3 inches (2.51 meters). This uniformity ensures that no booth will interfere with or detract from a smaller adjacent (or back-to-back) booth.

To provide each exhibitor with an unobstructed sight line from aisles, standard booths are restricted in the dimensions of their side walls. These side wall "wings" can be 8 feet (2.44 meters) high only in that part of the exhibitor's space that is 5 feet (1.52 meters) from the aisle line. The remaining 5-foot (1.52-meter) side rails to the aisles are restricted to a 4-foot (1.22-meter) height. Similarly, exhibit furniture or fixtures more than 4 feet (1.22 meters) high must be located behind this 5-foot (1.52-meter) sight line. This guideline applies only within 10 linear feet (3.05 meters) of an adjacent booth on either side; beyond this margin,

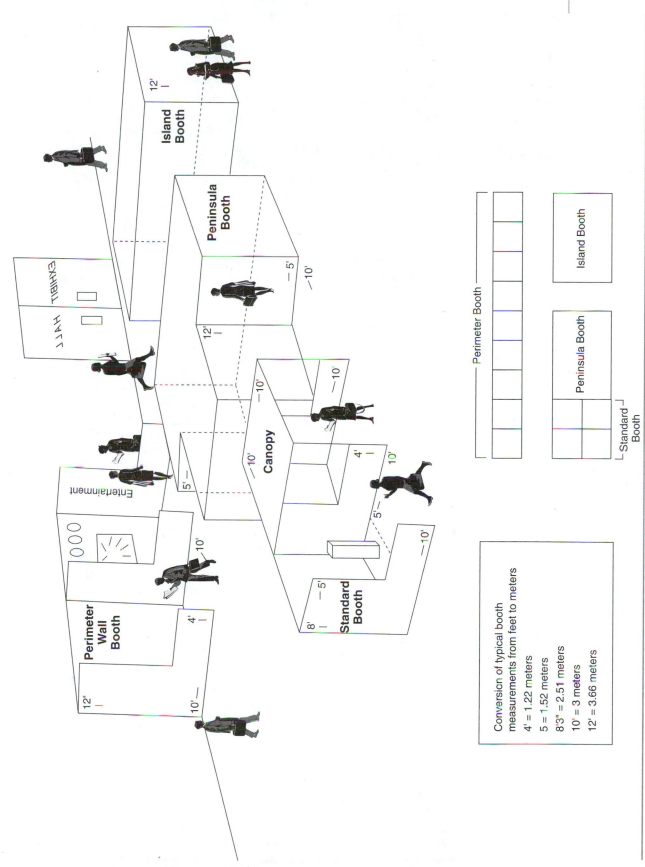

FIGURE 27.1
The Four Basic Booth Types
Adapted from *The Convention Industry Council Manual*, 7th edition, p. 211. Used with permission.

Put It Into Perspective

Many factors that are out of the meeting manager's control can affect the results and bottom-line of the event. The following external factors can hurt or help the event:

• The industry is booming and new innovative products are being launched. New companies are contacting the organization about the show.

• Major exhibitors within the industry are merging, which is causing a serious reduction in the overall demand for booth space.

• The show's attendance is affected by the popularity of the selected destination, which can affect overall attendance and show traffic.

• Venue and supplier pricing can change from city to city, really affecting the exhibitor's bottom line.

larger booths may be built to maximum height all the way out to the aisle. Vertical supports for the front corners of canopies must not exceed 3 feet (0.91 meters) so they do not create excessive obstructions for adjacent booths.

Perimeter Booth

The perimeter booth (also called a perimeter wall booth) is similar to the standard booth in all respects except in the height of the back wall and adjacent wings, which may be up to 12 feet (3.66 meters) high. Since these booths are designed for set-up against a wall, their added height will not detract from neighboring booths. The 5-foot (1.52-meter) sight-line restrictions still apply for wing extensions (side rails) to the aisles and for exhibit fixtures. Many exhibitors take advantage of the extra height permitted for a perimeter wall booth by designing their booths to work for heights of either 8 or 12 feet (2.44 or 3.66 meters) in order to be able to use the same booth in venues where perimeter space might not be available.

Peninsula Booth

Surrounded on three sides by aisles, the peninsula booth usually consists of four or more booth units 10 feet by 10 feet (3.05 by 3.05 meters) each. The standard height for a peninsula booth is 16 feet (4.88 meters). On the sides and corners bordered by aisles, peninsula booths may be built up to 16 feet (4.88 meters) all the way out to the aisles. Where peninsula booths have adjacent neighbors, all previously described sight-line restrictions apply.

Note in Figure 27.1 that the near wall of the peninsula booth borders two standard booths, and exceeds their height. In this case, the bordering wall of the peninsula booth must be finished (laminated, painted, and so on) and may not carry identification signs or other copy that would detract from the adjoining exhibits.

Island Booth

Bordered on all four sides by aisles, the island booth has no adjacent neighbors and none of the sight-line restrictions imposed on other booth types. The only restriction is height (16 feet or 4.88 meters). The rationale for imposing height restrictions on island (and peninsula) booths is to avoid a height contest among exhibitors, who understandably look for any attention-getting edge in the visually competitive environment of the exhibition floor. All display structures more than 12 feet (3.66 meters) high should have drawings available for review onsite. The drawings should be stamped or signed by a structural engineer and by the firm that built the exhibit.

EXHIBIT SPACE ASSIGNMENT

There are several methods for assigning exhibit space. Keep in mind that once the meeting manager has chosen a method, it may be difficult to change it in subsequent years. Exhibitors seek consistency in policy design and implementation. Consider several options before deciding which is best for the exhibition. Include the space assignment policy in the exhibit prospectus.

The following factors should be considered when assigning exhibit space (to be equitable, as well as to limit exposure to potential antitrust liability):

- An exhibitor's past performance (e.g., number of years in the show)
- The amount of space requested
- Date application and deposit are received
- Space preferences and the locations of competitors
- The products or services to be exhibited
- Eligibility to exhibit
- Whether a company is a sponsor
- Member or nonmember status

The following sections discuss some of the most common methods for assigning exhibit space.

First Come, First Served

In the first come, first served method for assigning exhibit space, applications are processed in the order of receipt or postmark, when accompanied by the required deposit. When several applications arrive on the same day, show management can assign priority for multiple-booth requests prior to single-booth requests, or assign members before nonmembers, or use some other criterion. The drawback to this space assignment policy is that there is no incentive or benefit for exhibitors who return year after year.

Priority Point System

Using a priority point system, the show management awards every exhibitor points for each year of participation in the show and/or for the amount of space requested. There may be a deadline for exhibitors to submit their applications in order to exercise their priority points in the first round of exhibit space assignments. Exhibitors are ranked by points and assigned space accordingly. In the case of a tie, the date the application and deposit are received or the size of the space requested may be considered. After the deadline, the show management assigns space on a first come, first served basis.

Unless the meeting manager awards exhibitor points for the size of the contracted space, there are few drawbacks to this system. Some shows award points for advertising and/or sponsorships. If points awarded are strictly based on the number of years an exhibitor participates in the show, both small and large companies have the opportunity to receive prime locations. If points awarded are for how much space is taken, it will be more difficult for a smaller company to receive a prime location. Another consideration is to decide upon a policy for handling ownership of priority points in the case of a merger or acquisition.

Advance Sale

The show management may make space assignments for the next show during the current show. This often guarantees exhibitors the same space or their preference for a better space. Some shows offer exhibitors a discount if space for the next year is confirmed before the current show ends. Some shows mail the contracts to exhibitors before the show and accept applications at the current show or by a mail deadline.

There are a few drawbacks to this method. Company representatives at the show may lack the authority to make a commitment for the next show or to choose an exhibit location. Exhibitors who are unable to attend the current show and new exhibitors have no opportunity to choose locations unless the show management accepts mail-in applications.

EXHIBITOR SERVICES

Exhibitor Service Kit

About 90 days prior to the exhibition, an exhibitor service kit should be sent to each exhibitor. The kit includes all the information and order forms an exhibitor needs in order to participate in the exhibition. In many cases the kit is provided by the GSC, and it may be made available online, as well as in notebook form. Online ordering offers many advantages, including round-the-clock access and reduction of printing and mailing costs.

The exhibitor service kit usually contains the following information and forms:

- A table of contents and index
- A list of official service contractors
- A checklist of forms by deadline date
- The days, dates, and hours for move-in and move-out
- General information on show colors, booth carpet, and furnishings supplied (if applicable)
- Target dates for heavy freight shows, or shows with tight move-in/move-out schedules
- Display rules and regulations
- Facility rules and regulations
- Labor union rules
- Fire and safety regulations
- Rates and order forms for exhibitor-appointed contractors
- Pricing and order forms for furniture, carpeting, and signs
- Pricing and order forms for labor and equipment
- Pricing and order forms for utilities
- Shipping and drayage information
- Pricing and an order form for booth cleaning
- Pricing and order forms for AV services, photography, floral vendors, greeters, and demonstrators
- Pricing and order forms for phones, computers, and pagers
- Contractors' payment policies, liabilities, labor, and material-handling authorization
- Booth security
- Exhibitor insurance
- Marshaling yard location and directions
- Booth catering pricing and order forms
- Lead retrieval pricing and order forms for tracking sales leads

The service kit may also contain information and order forms for promotional opportunities available to exhibitors. For some exhibitions, a separate promotion-planning guide may be produced. The promotional opportunities offered may include the following:

- Pre-registration lists, labels, and disks for use in preparing pre-show and post-show direct mailings, broadcast faxes, and email blasts
- Customized exhibitor invitations (guest passes)
- Sponsorship opportunities
- Media information sheets
- Show logo sheets
- Participation in exhibition-sponsored traffic-generation programs
- Show program guides
- Web site advertising

Exhibitor Education

Many exhibitions offer an exhibitor-training workshop prior to the opening of the show. In this case, the show management retains an expert to provide tips and practical advice on how to manage a booth effectively. This training may be offered on a complimentary basis or for a nominal charge. Sometimes exhibitor-training workshops, or exhibitor training webcasts, are held several months in advance of the exhibition.

Another way to communicate with the exhibitors and to provide educational material is through a monthly, bimonthly, or quarterly exhibitor newsletter, which may be distributed by mail, fax, or email. This communication tool can be used to provide exhibitors with timely information on exhibiting, pre-show promotion, shipping, budgeting, and other exhibit planning tips. The newsletter can also report deadline reminders and schedule changes.

Exhibitor Advisory Committee

By establishing an exhibitor advisory committee, a means for communicating the needs and suggestions of exhibitors to the show management is created. Such a committee should include representatives from both large and small exhibiting companies and represent various market segments of the exhibitor base. In addition to meeting before the show, exhibitor advisory committees often meet during the second or third day of the exhibition to provide show management with feedback and suggestions. This feedback is important when it comes to formulating strategies for growing the show, expanding the attendee base, marketing, and evaluation (see Chapter 45).

PRODUCING THE EXHIBITION

Depending upon the size of the exhibition and the staff, the meeting planner may choose to appoint a staff member as floor manager to oversee the details of the exhibition and assist exhibitors, or hire a professional to do so (in other words, outsource).

Operations

The show management plans the exhibition, and is supported by various contractors to implement the plan. Exhibitors order the services outlined in the exhibitor kit and the GSC ensures the orderly and efficient installation, dismantling, and removal of exhibits. For guidelines on selecting a GSC and a list of services the GSC provides for show management, as well as information on selecting other service providers (decorators, floral, security, furniture rental, equipment rental, telecommunications, photography, and so on) (see Chapter 37).

The following is a list of services the GSC provides for exhibitors:

- Receiving and storing advance exhibitor shipments at the warehouse
- Assigning and overseeing labor for booth set up and dismantle
- Booth packages (pipe and drape, furniture, booth carpeting)
- Drayage (material handling), including unloading incoming trucks, reloading freight onto trailers to be taken to the show floor, removal and storage of empty crates and skids, returning empties at the close of the show, and reloading the freight
- Checking utility hookups
- Hanging signs and banners
- Delivering rental furniture and equipment
- Clearing trash
- Booth cleaning
- Laying aisle carpet

Exhibitor-Appointed Contractors

There are many different contractors that an exhibitor may employ. For example, some exhibitors employ the services of an installation and dismantling (I&D) company for their exhibits. In such a case, the exhibitor must inform the show management and the official GSC in writing of the contractor's name and the work to be performed.

The exhibitor-appointed contractor should do the following:

- Provide a certificate of insurance on a specified date to the show manager with specified limits for comprehensive general liability with respect to injuries to more than one person in any one occurrence and a specified amount with respect to property damage.
- Provide Workers Compensation Insurance, including employee liability coverage.
- Agree to abide by all show rules and regulations.
- Provide the show management with all of the required information and documentation no later than 30 to 60 days prior to the show.
- Wear identification badges or wrist bands at all times while on-site.

When exhibitor-appointed contractors are used, there are costs involved for the show management, including staff time for processing certificates of insurance, preparation and production of admission credentials, extra cleaning, and liability. Some show management companies charge exhibitor-appointed contractors an "outside contractors" fee.

Summary

An exhibition is a valuable addition to a meeting, providing a cost-effective marketing opportunity for exhibiting companies and a source of revenue for the organization, while also providing product solutions for attendees.

There are a variety of factors to consider when choosing an exhibition facility and determining the amount of space that is needed for an exhibition, including the square footage needed for exhibit space and aisles, the number and size of nonstandard booths, and the space required for concession and lounge areas.

Hall rental fees and the methods for determining them vary from facility to facility. The number of show days, the time required for move-in and move-out, guaranteed minimums, the services required from the facility, and a range of other factors affect costs.

Establishing a budget includes first understanding management, marketing, and exhibitor and exhibition production expenses. Exhibit space revenue can be established once it is determined how much exhibit space the organization will be able to sell and total show expenses are forecasted.

The exhibitor prospectus will help define the unique aspects of the show within the organization's industry and how they can help accomplish exhibitor objectives and goals.

The four basic booth types are the standard booth, perimeter booth, peninsula booth, and island booth.

The exhibitor service kit includes all the information and order forms that an exhibitor needs in order to participate in the exhibition. In most cases, the kit is provided and distributed by the general services contractor (GSC) and is available both in notebook form and online.

REFERENCES

1. Reprinted with permission from: Convention Industry Council. (2000). *Convention industry council manual*. (7th Ed.). McLean, VA: Convention Industry Council.

KEY TERMS

Booth	Floor load	Move-out
Booth package	Floor manager	Peninsula booth
Demographics	Floor plan	Perimeter booth
Drayage	General services	(perimeter wall booth)
Exhibitor advisory	contractor (GSC)	Priority point system
committee	Inline booth	Sales leads
Exhibition	Installation and dismantle	Show office
Exhibit hall	(I&D)	Show dailies
Exhibitor-appointed	Island booth	Show directory
contractor	Linear booth	Sponsorship
Exhibitor service kit	Loading dock	Standard booth
Exhibit prospectus	Move-in	Webcast
Exposition		

COMPELLING QUESTIONS FOR CONSIDERATION

1. What factors should be considered when determining how much space an exhibition will require?

2. What questions should be asked when negotiating a hall rental contract?

3. How do union work rules affect exhibitor costs?

4. Describe the four basic booth configurations.

5. List some of the types of information and forms provided in the exhibitor service kit.

6. What objectives do exhibitors want to achieve at a trade show?

7. List the responsibilities of the show organizer, the GSC, and the floor manager.

CHAPTER 28

SIGNAGE AND WAYFINDING FOR MEETING MANAGERS

Carol J. Sconzert

PRINCIPAL

OSMOSIS CREATIVE, LLC

LEARNER OUTCOMES

When the reader has completed reading this chapter, he/she should be able to . . .

1 Differentiate the three functions of signage and demonstrate how to apply them appropriately in composing sign orders and in determining placement.

2 Distinguish audience variables and create signage that supports meeting attendees' successful navigation of an event.

3 Discuss the term "wayfinding" as it applies to the event industry and its application to the formulation of strategic signage plans.

4 Describe the basics of print production and how it affects the graphics ordering process.

> Good signage is good customer service.
>
> *Carol J. Sconzert*

OVERVIEW

Signage is more than just text on a panel. In trade shows and conferences where large groups of people are assembled, effective signage is critical to the success of your meetings and the satisfaction of attendees. When they are done correctly, signs serve to inform, protect, and direct people efficiently throughout facilities. Incorrect use of signage can result in confusion, frustration, and risks to personal safety. Meeting managers are charged with the responsibility of guiding the movements of a large number of people who are in unfamiliar territory and conducting business under time constraints. By understanding how your attendees' needs change over time, your signage can help or hinder their success, as well as their overall perception of your event.

WHEN AND WHERE TO USE SIGNS

All event signs fulfill one or more of the following functions: identify, inform, or direct. Yet, as simple as this sounds, these seemingly elementary functions can be problematic when they are done incorrectly. When planning the signage for an event, you should be cognizant of the specific objective of each sign and how it functions for your audience.

Identification Signs

Identification signs include the name of the event and the names of places and features within the event, such as "Ballroom," "Speakers' Lounge," "Sales Office," and so on. They are used to establish an endpoint of a destination or to define the ownership of activities as belonging to the event at hand.

A significant number of identification signs are used to identify an event's key sponsors. Sponsorship of an event or activity is also often identified as a byline on general signage, or is featured on an overall panel or banner with a thank you message. In either case, the message conveyed to the reader is that sponsors have contributed to bringing this content to fruition. Sometimes an event organizer will want to re-name permanent facility signs to brand the event, such as changing the Grand Ballroom to "XYZ (Sponsor's Name) Ballroom." However, you should resist the suggestion to completely re-name building areas to honor sponsors or designate content, despite coaxing from the sponsorship committee. Use of the building as a vanity plate serves the needs of only one customer, and may actually hinder navigation by attendees. Your guests will use a broad array of tools to find their way around your event, including maps and data from outside your meeting. Re-naming the rooms or areas within the building will hinder their efforts to reach you, especially when facility or security staff members have never heard of the room that the attendees are trying to find. More dramatically, obscuring facility signage with differing names can become a safety issue if emergency teams need to quickly respond to someone in need. Good signage is good customer service.

Informational Signs

Informational signs provide background data and/or instructions for the reader. A sign displaying "Exhibit Hours" is informational, as are signs with instructions for filling out registration forms. Sometimes informational signs have heavy content, involving the reader for a long period of time, such as when attendees need to look up a session title and room number on a "Schedule-@-A-Glance" display. Shorter informational signs are important to convey changes in the event that happened after the final program was printed, and are used to remind guests of facility regulations such as smoking areas, and rules concerning age limits for admittance to your event.

Directional Signs

Directional signs assist attendees in moving safely and efficiently throughout a facility as they visit exhibit halls, keynote presentations, plenary sessions, and so on. Not all directional signs require copy—international symbols, a proprietary color, event mascots, and logos often can provide enough information to direct traffic. Directional signs often contain arrows to indicate a path to follow; the best practice is to order signs with a space for loose arrows to be attached on-site with Velcro™-type material. This ability to adjust the arrows allows maximum flexibility in placing the signs once you arrive at the event.

You will also find that sometimes the same content of your message will need to be displayed in different types of signs. For example, announcing the location of a wireless hot spot could be on a directional sign. Arrival at that location would be confirmed when the attendee reads the identification sign, and he/she would then look for the informational sign which instructs him/her about how to log on to the service.

Often, more than one function can and will be combined on a sign. You should be aware of the priority of what is presented. Event logos are an important clue to the reader that the content within will be relevant to him or her (especially in non-exclusive facility rental); however, the layout of the sign should give precedence to the message that is most important at the time that the viewer is reading it.

Tips on Writing Sign Copy

Writing sign copy need not be a stressful exercise. Do not feel that you must be formal in your communication simply because your words will be printed on a sign. Stilted phrases such as "shall and shall not" are unnecessarily distracting to the reader, and risk creating a psychological barrier between you and your audience if the words are perceived as overly authoritarian or as "legalese." The most effective sign copy is simple in phrasing and terminology. Today's event attendees are accustomed to a less formal "conversational voice" in all areas of business—reading the signs at your event should be a seamless activity that quickly conveys information and allows them to act on it efficiently. Consider these tips when writing your sign orders:

- Consistent terminology—Follow the communication style of activities such as pre-show mailers, web sites, and preliminary programs. Keep copies of these and be consistent in the terminology used for the event. Names such as "Email Center," "Communications Central," "Cyber Center," and "Attendee Lounge" may all in fact be referring to the same area; however, check to ensure that only one title is used consistently from program materials to website to signage.

- Concise editing—Be succinct.
- Avoid confusing terms—Some words add a qualifying or conditional element to a message which causes confusion. Avoid such phrasing as: *"Proceed to Point A **Unless** Your Badge is Coded for Point B or D."* This message lacks specific information about how the badges are coded, and omits any information about a "Point C."
- Public events—Plan for more directional signs in public "open" events, to help manage the broader range of capabilities and experience in these types of crowds. Copywriting should be simple and layouts large with high contrast between type and backgrounds. Signage can be a significant aid in crowd safety for the public audience.
- Use of symbols—Symbols and icons are a great way to convey information quickly to a broad audience. Icons may appear in proximity to a message or may be used in place of words. Plan to use a symbol key every time icons are used in a stand-alone fashion. Be aware that overuse of icons can be counterproductive, especially custom icons that are not found outside your event.

Sometimes the inclination to combine content on a sign is driven more strongly by budget concerns than by the logical relationship of the information. Be aware that if there is no obvious relationship among the various content items presented together on a sign, your reader's mind will try to make a relationship. For example, an informational sign for the keynote session contains information about the shuttle bus schedule. Although these two items are not related, you risk confusing the audience into making a connection with negative results.

SIGNAGE PLANS/WAYFINDING FOR MEETING MANAGERS

The proper placement of signage is critical to its function. As you consider the message that you wish to convey in a sign, you must also consider the ability of the attendee to receive that message. What are your attendees doing at the moment they encounter each sign? What is in their hands, and where is their attention? Are they moving or static?

A common mistake in event signage is to place too much copy on structures or signs located at critical points of traffic patterns, such as posting an exhibitor list on the entrance tower for the exhibit hall. Placement of detailed information in this location requires the reader to stop walking in order to read the directory—blocking ingress and egress to the room and thus, creating a hazardous situation. A similar example of inappropriate placement of content is found when signage placed close to escalators and stairwells is overloaded with text, such as an archway unit or overhanging banner loaded with heavy directional copy. It is neither safe nor effective to request someone's attention on a sign when they are about to step onto another level of flooring, especially if it is moving. Misdirecting someone's attention to a sign when that person is about to step onto another floor level, especially a moving floor, is neither safe nor effective. In a situation where an overhead sign is near a stairwell or escalator, consider an abbreviated version of the information you wish to convey, such as "Level Three Sessions," and then augment that with another sign placed a safe distance away containing the session schedule. The proper placement of detailed signage, such as directories and schedules, is in a highly visible, well-lighted location with enough room around it for several people to read it at once and enough floor space to accommodate several readers at the same time.

When planning graphics in a structure, such as registration counters or entrance units, resist the temptation to "fill up" every available surface of your structures with copy—the overload of information will be counterproductive. Once again, consider the movements and attention of your intended reader as a stage manager would plan the movements of the actors: first movement is to Line A, next movement to Counter B, on to materials pick-up at Station C, turning toward walkway D, and so on. Then convey your sign copy in appropriate chunks, addressing what they need to know at that particular moment, and guide them on to the next information, matched to their needs and their location in your event. In this manner, you are creating a flow and positively impacting the pace of the crowd's movement.

Signage plans are a factor in the larger discussion of the term wayfinding, which addresses the evolving responses to the human need to "find our way." The term was first used by American architect David Lynch[1] to describe the layout of streets, numbering systems, and the use of visual cues in urban design, which allow people to form their personal mental maps of orientation. Today, the term encompasses all forms of stimuli that feed the human senses with information and reference points to guide us. For example, in the meetings industry, when someone comes upon clusters of comfortable chairs, he/she understands that this is a lounge area. Logos appearing on the screen or the dimming of lights communicate without words that a session has come to its end. You may choose to include references to these alternative information modes in advanced signage plans.

Put It Into Practice

PCMA Annual Meeting Wayfinding Plan

Strategic Signage Plans are a set of documents that plot the location and copy of your directional signs throughout the venue. Executing the process of developing a coordinated set of documents ensures that you do not miss any crucial directional information for your attendees' movements. The process should also reveal opportunities to advance important marketing messages to your audience. This concept is illustrated here through the mini-example of the directional sign plan for PCMA's Annual Meeting in Philadelphia (see Figures 28.1 and 28.2A and B).

While signage plans can be done in many ways, some common methods are useful and adaptable to the specific needs of the facility or organization. The first document needed is a facility floor plan of the entire property, obtained from either the venue itself or the General Service Contractor (GSC). In this case, we utilized a website tool provided by Freeman Decorating, called PlanTour®. On this website, a nationwide roster of facilities is displayed with floor plans that are marked to indicate the most common sign locations. Data sheets can be downloaded with specifications for sizes and recommended materials, along with a photo of the sign location in the building. The latter is very handy to add to a signage plan and to attach to signs as they are being distributed for installation.

Often a summary list of signage options will be included in your contract, identifying quantities and types of signs negotiated for your event, and sometimes a price list based on a square foot rate for additional signs. This list is the second necessary document. In the partial example shown here, the master contract allowed for the following directional signs:

- Eight double-sided panels in bases, 3.28' x 8'
- Six double-sided foam panel signs to overlay existing building signs
- Three 4' x 10' vertical banners, double-sided

Lastly, the plan included a simple spreadsheet to track between the first two documents and the wording of the actual copy to be written on the sign. The spreadsheet employed a numbering system that incorporated information about which floor the sign was to be placed on and a letter to indicate what type of sign material would be used. All signs on the lower level of the Pennsylvania Convention Center were numbered in the 100-series, prefaced by the letter M (meter board), B (banner), or O (overlay sign). The spreadsheet lists the sign number with the letter "a" or "b" to identify the two faces of the sign, with the floor plan following along with the "a" and "b" shown in the corresponding position.

The strategy behind the placement of the directional signs was simple: The planning began at the farthest point that an attendee would be from the "hub" area of activities created in the registration area, called the "PCMA Plaza." The meeting managers then penciled in a series of locations—spread out fairly evenly along the path of travel—for more potential signs. At that point, what type of signs they would be (freestanding meter panels, overlays, or banners) was not clear. The summary of signage list indicated that three banners would be located on upper level, since there were hang points identified for that purpose. Because banners are larger and more visible from farther away (since they are overhead), they reduce the number of ground signs that are necessary to convey information. Therefore, the next decision was to use more of the free-standing meter boards on the lower level.

Once you have penciled in a framework for the locations of signs, if you shift your mindset to thinking about the activities of the attendees in those areas, you will find that your sign copy nearly writes itself. For example, now that almost all convention and conference facilities nationwide are non-smoking venues, frequently you should identify the closest routes to street access on second-level signs. At the farthest points from the hub, PCMA's attendees were in session rooms for 75 to 90 minutes at a stretch, with short breaks in the concourses. Many were staying in the same vicinity to prepare for their next session. Others traveled to the second-level session rooms, and some headed to the PCMA Plaza for refreshments or to visit the Communications Central hub for email access. Attendees who need to move relatively long distances must quickly learn "where I need to be and how I get there," and the communication should be repeated consistently along their path of travel so that they do not miss it. For this reason, the signage plan for the PCMA meeting placed directional copy on the signs overlaying the facility signage—the facility signs were high on the wall of the concourse or spanning directly over the escalators, so they were easy to see and read over the heads of a crowd. Layout was simple, arrows were bold, and the copy was kept to essential directional information, such as "PCMA Plaza," without a long list of features, distracting irrelevant information, or busy logos.

(continued on page 445)

PCMA Wayfinding Plan

	A	B	C	E	F	G	H	I	J	K
	Date	Name	Location	Copy/Description	Qty	Print Count	S/S D/S	Horizontal (inches)	Vertical (inches)	Graphic Sq. Ft.
3		M-101a	rm 113	Chapter Events (Prelim program pg 20)	1	1	D/S	38	96	25.33
4		M-101b	rm 113	**The PCMA Plaza—Your Official Meeting Place for PCMA 2006!** Communications Central, daily continental breakfasts and refreshment breaks, Free Wireless, Philadelphia Pavilion, Toronto Pavilion // **PCMA Annex—** KnowledgeOnDemand, Relaxation Therapy, PCMA Sponsors Lounge, Student Resources	1		D/S	38	96	25.33
5		M-102a	rm 111	Evening Events: (Copy from pg 11 Prelim Program)	1		D/S	38	96	25.33
6		M-102b	rm 111	Gen'l Session recap	1		D/S	38	96	25.33
7		M-103a	rm 109	> Meeting Rooms 109-113, Lecture Hall 114	1		S/S	38	96	25.33
8		M-103b	rm 109	[none]	1	1		38	96	25.33
9		M-104a	12th St ent.	You Are Here locator	1	2	D/S	38	96	25.33
10		M-104b	12th St ent.	You Are Here locator	1		D/S	38	96	25.33
11		M-105a	rm 105	Evening Events: (Copy from pg 11 Prelim Program)	1		D/S	38	96	25.33
12		M-105b	rm 105	Gen'l Session recap	1		D/S	38	96	25.33
13		M-106a	rm 103	Chapter Events (Prelim program pg 20)	1		D/S	38	96	25.33
14		M-106b	rm 103	**The PCMA Plaza—Your Official Meeting Place for PCMA 2006!** Communications Central, daily continental breakfasts and refreshment breaks, Free Wireless, Philadelphia Pavilion, Toronto Pavilion // **PCMA Annex—** KnowledgeOnDemand, Relaxation Therapy, PCMA Sponsors Lounge, Student Resources	1		D/S	38	96	25.33
15		O-101a	Freem PT09	Meeting Rooms 101-107 >> Meeting Rooms 108-114	1		D/S	34	89	21.01
16		O-101b	Freem PT10	Upper Level PCMA Plaza, PCMA Annex, General Sessions,Hall C Luncheons, Meeting Rooms 201-204	1		D/S	34	89	21.01
17		O-102a	Freem PT56		1		D/S	38	89	23.49
18		O-102b	Freem PT57	Upper Level PCMA Plaza, PCMA Annex, General Sessions,Hall C Luncheons, Meeting Rooms 201-204	1		D/S	38	89	23.49
19		O103a	Freem PT47	Upper Level PCMA Plaza, PCMA Annex, General Sessions,Hall C Luncheons, Meeting Rooms 201-204	1		D/S	38	89	23.49
20		O-103b	Freem PT48	This Level for Meeting Rooms 101-113 and Lecture hall 114 // Shuttle Buses and Taxis at 12th & Arch Streets	1		D/S	38	89	23.49
21		B-201a	Freem PT17	Hall C Luncheons (arrow angled down)	1		D/S	48	120	40.00
22		B-201b	Freem PT17	Hall C Luncheons (arrow angled down)	1		D/S	48	120	40.00
23		M-201a	Freem PT17	What's Up With The Pears?	1	1	S/S	38	96	25.33
24		M-201b	Freem PT17	[none]	1					0.00
25		O-201a	Freem PT26	Lower Level Meeting Rooms 101-114 Street Level Access, Shuttle Buses & Taxis	1		D/S	34		0.00
27		O-201b	Freem PT27	PCMA Plaza, PCMA Annex, Grand Ballroom General Sessions, Meeting Rooms 201-204, < Hall C Luncheons	1		D/S	34		0.00
28		B-202a	Freem PT25	Thank You Host City and Platinum Sponsors	1		D/S	48	120	40.00
29		B-202b	Freem PT25	Thank You Host City and Platinum Sponsors	1		D/S	48	120	40.00
30		M-202a	Freem PT25	You Are Here locator	1	2	D/S	38	96	25.33
31		M-202b	Freem PT25	You Are Here locator	1		D/S	38	96	25.33
32		O-202a	Freem PT 53	Street Level Access, Shuttle Buses and Taxis	1		S/S	24	153	25.50
33		O-202b	Freem PT 53	<<Hall C Lunches PCMA Plaza, Meeting Rooms>>	1		S/S	24	153	25.50
34		O-203a	Freem PT51	< PCMA Plaza, Meeting Rooms Hall C Lunches	1		S/S	24	153	25.50
35		O-203b	Freem PT51	Street Level Access, Shuttle Buses and Taxis	1		S/S	24	153	25.50
36										
37										777.97

FIGURE 28.1
Sample Wayfinding Plan

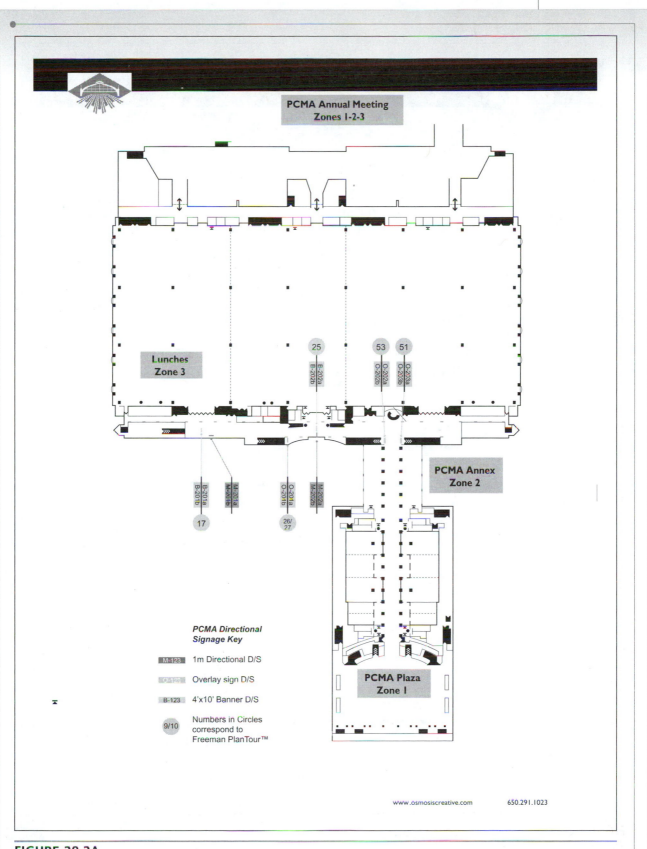

FIGURE 28.2A
Directional Sign Plan

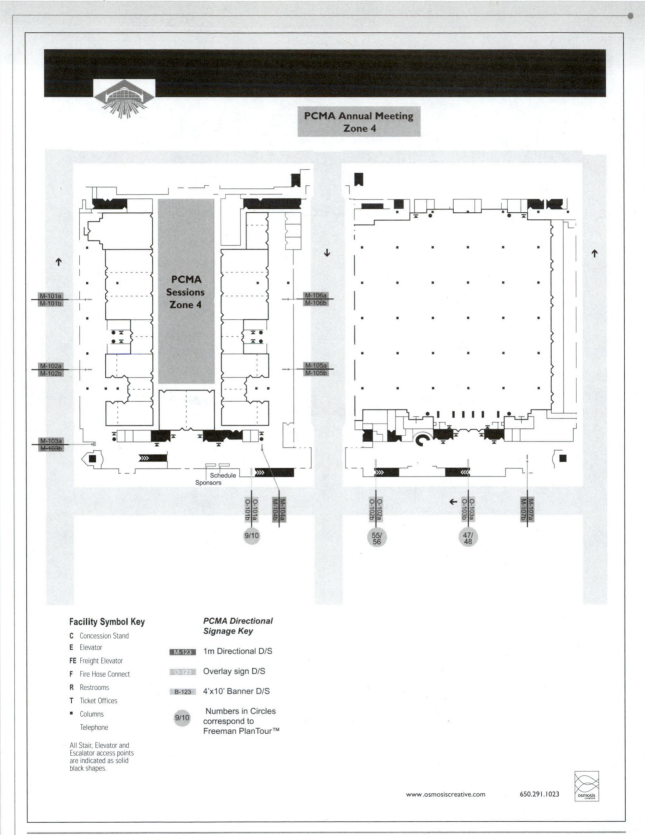

PCMA Annual Meeting Zone 4

PCMA Sessions Zone 4

M-101a / M-101b
M-102a / M-102b
M-103a / M-103b

M-106a / M-106b
M-105a / M-105b

Schedule Sponsors

O-101a / O-101b   M-104a / M-104b   9/10

O-102a / O-102b   55/56

O-103a / O-103b   47/48

M-107a / M-107b

Facility Symbol Key

C   Concession Stand
E   Elevator
FE Freight Elevator
F   Fire Hose Connect
R   Restrooms
T   Ticket Offices
■   Columns
    Telephone

All Stair, Elevator and
Escalator access points
are indicated as solid
black shapes.

***PCMA Directional
Signage Key***

M-123   1m Directional D/S

O-123   Overlay sign D/S

B-123   4'x10' Banner D/S

9/10   Numbers in Circles
       correspond to
       Freeman PlanTour™

www.osmosiscreative.com   650.291.1023

FIGURE 28.2B
Directional Sign Plan

Put It Into Practice—continued

In contrast, attendees who stayed in the immediate session area could use that time to learn about special features of the event schedule, such as general session speakers, activities in the next few days, or off-site events. Panels with informational copy such as this also function as conversation points among attendees who may coordinate plans with each other, thus supporting them in their networking goals for the event. Some panels listed activities and indicated that further details could be found in the PCMA final program; in these instances the signs provided indirect support to the advertisers in the program by driving attention to that resource.

Once the signage plan was fleshed out, the meeting managers discovered an opportunity to use a 4'x10' banner in the upper concourse for recognition of the Host City Partners and the Platinum Sponsors, which was an added value for them that extended beyond the sponsorship agreements.

Taken together, the marked floor plan and the spreadsheet of copy for each sign face can be shared and reviewed by several people before any expensive fabrication begins. Once copy was approved, the sign vendor works directly off the spreadsheet, literally copying and pasting the text into their sign layout software, adding the backgrounds, and formatting it according to the design style guide. During the event's move-in period, the labor foreman can use the signage floor plan to install the panels and plan for special equipment needs, such as high-lift equipment to hang banners. With all of the information contained in two documents, everyone is better prepared to support one another as the event production moves from one phase to the next. A strategic signage plan is a powerful tool on many levels.

In the case of the PCMA Annual Meeting, the event spread across three buildings and three different levels of the Pennsylvania Convention Center. To assist attendees in quickly orienting themselves to the building and the activities, the signage plan specified custom "You Are Here" panels for the event. The panels displayed the relationships among the buildings, the levels, and the activity areas, and indicated all modes of transfer available: stairs, elevators, and escalators. Supporting copy provided a quick recap of which event features were located on each level.

CROWD DYNAMICS

Attention to signage can be an important tool in managing crowd dynamics,[2] a related area of growing importance to meeting managers. Dr. Keith Still is the founder and chief science officer of Crowd Dynamics Ltd., an international consultancy that advises on emergency and disaster preparedness for municipal planning, stadium design, and other environments where large groups of people congregate. He defines crowd dynamics as the study of how people move and interact with others and their surroundings. Crowd dynamics takes into account factors such as,

- *Crowd Movement*—How much space do people occupy? How does the crowd affect how people walk?
- *Human Characteristics*—How do people behave and respond to information or the conditions around them?
- *Spatial Analysis*—How does the layout of a venue influence movement?
- *Queuing (lines of people)*—Why do queues build up? What are the consequences for safety?

Communication is a critical aspect of crowd management—correct messages, clear sight lines to exits, and properly located signage for identification, information, and directions can positively impact a crowd's dynamics to reduce safety risks and enhance an experience.

INDIVIDUAL AUDIENCE MEMBERS

Once the safe and efficient movement of crowds is addressed, you will want to consider ways in which signage can support your attendee in achieving his/her

Put It Into Perspective

Historically, sign orders were funneled through the meeting manager as one of the logistical tasks for execution. Overall event graphics packages consisted of orders submitted by the Program Committee for the sessions they created, and the meeting manager added orders for directional and informational signs.

This workflow has changed dramatically in recent years due to several significant factors. In addition to the technological advances which allow for an expanded scope and scale of sign production, the internal positioning of trade shows has shifted to reflect the strategic goals and events within corporations and organizations. As a result, senior level executives and other depart-

ments such as marketing have become more integrated into the planning process for events, introducing more layers of input and review.

Newer initiatives and features of sponsorship programs generate even more layers of content handling for detail checking, reviews, and approvals. The net result is that the sign ordering process for most organizations now requires more dedicated resources.

Consider the risks to your event goals before handing the sign order process to an intern-level worker without proper training, and re-evaluate the budget allotted to the graphics management portion of your operations.

individual objectives during the time spent at your event. A good starting point is to examine the demographic of your group with these questions in mind:

- How many of your visitors are veterans of your show, and how many are new attendees? What will the new visitors need to understand about the format of your event and how can they best learn the information? Consciously prioritize information for them.
- Does your show have a large international base? Consider using international symbols on your signs. If multi-lingual signs are not possible for your budget, consider at a minimum, the customer-service effect of using multiple languages on your "welcome" and "thank you" signs.
- What is the average age and gender split among your guests? Since visual impairments are more prevalent among specific ages and genders, you might decide to adjust the font size and styles of your signage accordingly.

GRAPHICS MANAGEMENT AND WORKING WITH GRAPHICS VENDORS

Few areas of event management reflect the evolution of technology in recent years more dramatically than event signage and graphics. The increases in the size, complexity, speed of production, and sheer volume of signage for events in recent years has helped to transform the look of even the most simple conference topic into a customized experience. Yet all of the bells and whistles that new graphics technology can bring to a show can also wreak havoc on a meeting manager's budget in short order if approached without clarity and a plan. The intensification of graphics in trade shows and meetings demands that meeting managers achieve similar growth in their knowledge of graphics techniques, terminology, and options.

In fact, the pace of change in graphics production techniques makes presenting a definitive recap of this portion of the industry impossible. Many signs for meetings are produced digitally on some variety of inkjet technology. Logos, text, and colors are merely computer bytes of data that are processed with printers and inks to make an image. These images may be printed directly onto substrates (the physical base material of which a sign is made, such as a banner, cardstock, or foam panels) or may be printed on paper and then laminated onto a panel. Multiple options are available in the equipment and processes to fabricate graphics. Your designer or graphics vendor will review options and make recommendations based on the sign's intended use (e.g., the lifespan of the sign, indoor/outdoor protection) and budget.

The procedure for ordering overall event graphics differs greatly from ordering graphics for an individual exhibit or display. Signage for an event involves a much larger volume of signs that include related and overlapping content. This interconnectedness means that even the smallest changes in content may ripple through many different signs in production, incurring expensive revisions.

Four distinct phases should be considered in managing graphics orders. Ideally, each phase of the process is completed, as much as possible, before moving to the next phase, and all participants are committed to agreed-upon due dates. In the sequential nature of sign production, missed deadlines in the beginning phases create expensive bottlenecks or, worse, no sign at all when the event opens.

The first phase is the internal process of identifying other entities within your organization who will be involved with sign orders, and setting up schedules for the delivery of their orders. Many organizations have developed internal forms for this purpose to facilitate the task and to help prompt the person placing the order for pertinent information, such as dates and times for installation of the sign. This phase also involves setting up a system to manage the volume effectively—most often a spreadsheet (with its flexibility and ease of modification) is the tool of choice. Using a spreadsheet in conjunction with the venue floor plan is also the simplest way to approach copywriting for directional signs.

The second phase of graphics management is the communication of your orders to the graphics vendor. The same spreadsheet (or a similar one) can be used for this purpose, or you may choose from an array of specialized products. Some vendors utilize web-based interfaces for uploading orders and/or reviewing layouts; other options include using Adobe PDF files for their ability to include comments and their tracking features. Web-based interfaces are particularly useful because they allow multiple parties to access layouts and add comments from any web browser; this eliminates tedious or confusing rounds of email forwarding and tracking, and relieves traffic on mail servers. Whichever tool is used, this second phase will involve your copy orders being transferred to actual sign layouts on the approved design backgrounds. Most vendors prefer to work from your digital sign order so that they can copy and paste your text directly from your file into their layout software, and then make formatting adjustments for the actual dimensions and specifications of the order. This process ensures the highest level of accuracy for unusual or technical spelling and grammar; therefore, carefully proof your work before submitting it for production. The layout portion of sign production is at least half of the labor involved in making your signs. Changes to the copy after layout—even if the sign has not yet been printed—represent a significant expense to the graphics vendor. Usually, each sign layout is sent back to the meeting manager for approval before it is actually printed for final review and approval—this is referred to as the proof cycle. You will be expected to read the sign for accuracy of spelling and consistency of presentation, such as using the same format for display of all dates and times ("9:00 a.m." versus "9 AM" or "9am," and so on). Spelling changes should be minimal, since provided copy was checked before submission. Be aware that radical changes to actual text which require a new layout may be construed as a new order, and may be charged at a different rate depending on the terms of your contract.

Once you have approved the layouts, you enter phase three of the process, and your signs will go into a queue for printing and fabrication. Both the layout and the fabrication tasks are done by the vendor in a production mode. That is,

Fast Facts

- 8%–12% of adult males are color blind; most people with color blindness are challenged by red/green colors in the same tonal value range, while 1%–2% suffer a deficiency in perceiving blue/yellow difference.[3] The best practice to eliminate difficulties for color blind readers is to avoid the proximate use of red and green in the same tonal range—if they are used near each other, one of the hues should be represented in a darker shade to help the reader discern the transition points.

- According to Prevent Blindness America (1998–2000),[4] cataracts are a leading cause of blindness among adults in the United States, accounting for one out of every seven cases of blindness in people age 45 and older. Cataracts affect 20.5 million (one in six) Americans age 40 and older. According to studies of Americans age 40 and older, a higher proportion of females have cataracts (20%) as compared to males (14%). Increasing the contrast between a sign's type and its background will improve readability for cataract patients.

Put It Into Perspective

Industry Sector Factors

Events for some industries, such as the scientific and financial sectors, may make more use of charts and graphs on informational signs. Technical vocabulary requires particular care in proofreading your copy. You can export the "custom dictionary" feature in Microsoft Word to provide your graphics vendor with correct spellings to load into their layout software before they begin working on your project.

orders are batched together and processed en masse. Maintaining consistency of formats, colors, and finishes is easier when signs are made together than it is during the more tedious process of making signs one at a time. Changes to orders at this stage are more costly, since an order must be pulled from queue and handled individually. Phase three is complete when the finished signs are tagged for placement and readied for shipment to your venue.

Phase four of graphics management is performed in different ways. Essentially, it is the final installation of your signs at your event venue. Some meeting managers prefer to schedule a final round of review of the signs on-site, before they are installed. This may not be necessary if all of the orders were proofed carefully in advance of production and all of the orders contain complete instruction for placement. If you choose to request an on-site review, be sure to inform the vendor in advance so that labor schedules can be adjusted to allow a window for that purpose. On-site reviews may be performed by someone on the show management staff, a contractor hired for graphics management, or a graphics account executive from your vendor contractor.

A WORD ABOUT ALTERNATIVE EVENT MESSAGING

Advances in technology also bring alternatives to traditional signage. Digital signs are flat screen displays for your messages, sometimes used in key gathering spots for special announcements or reminders, or even used to replace session listing signs in meeting room areas. The initial cost is higher (because of rental of units, programming costs, and electrical orders) but many meeting managers find savings in reduced charges for late-order changes and the labor that is required to switch placards out daily. A reduction in environmental impact is also a motivating factor for the move to digital signs.

An alternative messaging mode is personal audio equipment. The Acoustiguide®[5] company has developed audio tour technology that is used in many museums worldwide. Their recording devices and headsets are provided for personal use, to guide a visitor through a space with a narrative. The narrative can also function as a crowd management tool because the participant's movements are prompted by instructions. Use of a system such as this one may be best suited to an event's display area, and as a creative alternative in self-guided tours for programs for spouses or for off-site activities.

SUMMARY

Effective signage is conceived with a clear objective to communicate to the reader either the identification of an area or feature, some critical information or instruction, or directional information to assist in navigation. More than one functional message can be successfully combined on a sign as long as the intent and priority are considered.

Proper sign management also takes into consideration the ability of the reader to successfully receive the information. Individual factors such as vision issues, attendee experience, and industry demographics factor into decisions about copywriting, layout, and use of icons, symbols, charts, and graphs.

You can fulfill your responsibility to guide attendees efficiently and safely throughout your venue with a variety of tools and techniques. The integration of your marketing materials, web communications, signage, floor plan, and décor into a strategic sign plan will frame robust and cohesive communication. This holistic view—wayfinding—is the sum of all the parts of your users' movements at your event. As such, your skill in managing their movements can define their perception as "easy and effortless" or "frustrating and distracting."

Managing overall event signage requires an additional layer of management tasks and procedures to track copy changes, proof cycles, and placement instructions, and a host of other criteria unique to your event. Tools ranging from spreadsheet software to web-based interfaces allow all parties access to the information they need for their roles. Clear and frequent communication with the design and production teams is essential to ensure the accuracy of your signs and décor properties of the facility.

REFERENCES

1. Lynch, D. (1960). *The image of the city.* The MIT Press.

2. Symonds North America Inc. (2004). Retrieved November 28, 2005, from http://www.symondsna.com/crowd-dynamics.htm.

3. Hoffman, P. (1999). Usability interface, accommodating color blindness. *Usability interface.* (Vol 6, No. 2). Retrieved December 12, 2005 from http://www.stcsig.org/usability/newsletter/9910-color-blindness.html.

4. Causes of vision impairment (1978). Estimates reported from National Society to Prevent Blindness, 1980. Retrieved December 12, 2005 from http://www.visionconnection.org/Content/Research/EpidemiologyandStatistics/Statistics/CausesofVisionImpairment/default.htm?cookie%5Ftest=1#cat.

5. Acoustiguide®5 company (2006). http://www.acoustiguide.com/index.html.

KEY TERMS

Crowd dynamics	Laminate	Strategic signage plan
Digital signs	Layout	Substrate
Directional sign	Proof cycle	Symbol key
Identification sign	Signage	Wayfinding
Information/instructional sign		

COMPELLING QUESTIONS FOR CONSIDERATION

1. Develop comparison strategies for a public event versus a closed industry event for the tasks of copywriting and placement, with an explanation of your reasoning and assumptions.

2. Construct a sample spreadsheet for managing an overall event signage program. Consider all parties who will use this tool and what items they will need to see in order to best perform their roles. If you include formulas, explain how the resulting calculations will be used by you or others.

3. Select a floor plan from a facility website and create a set of documents that comprise a strategic sign plan. Using content from an existing show or your own creation, explain how your placement of signs and the content will assist your attendees' navigation of the event and support your event's goals.

4. Develop both a checklist and a timeline for your event graphics procedures. Consider all parties involved in the ordering process, placement process, and production and installation. Consider the factors that will threaten each party's ability to meet their deadlines, and describe how you will mitigate their impact.

5. Prepare a list of signs for your event and obtain price quotes for the production (only) from at least three sources. Include as many sign types as possible (banner, foamcore, cardstock, and so on) and describe what criteria you will use to evaluate each bid and any risks to be considered.

CHAPTER 29

AUDIOVISUALS: PRINCIPLES THAT IMPROVE MEETING COMMUNICATION

Greg Van Dyke

SENIOR VICE PRESIDENT, MARKETING
PRESENTATION SERVICES/AUDIOVISUAL HEADQUARTERS

LEARNER OUTCOMES

When the reader has completed reading this chapter, he/she should be able to . . .

1 Discuss how audiovisual services (A/V) can facilitate improved meeting communication.

2 Identify barriers that impede the audience from listening.

3 Deploy A/V into programs that have the audience engaged from the moment they arrive.

4 Recall the various types of A/V equipment available for use.

5 Recognize appropriate applications for A/V equipment.

6 Implement a meeting process that is more efficient for meeting managers, presenters, and attendees.

> Leadership is about change. It's about taking people from where they are now to where they need to be. The best way to get people to venture into unknown terrain is to make it desirable by taking them there in their imaginations.
>
> *Noel M Tichy*

Fast Facts

There is 1 minute until showtime. Let's go.

Fast Facts

• According to the International Communications Industries Association, the audiovisual industry represented $18.9 billion in revenue in 2004.
• A study by psychologist Albert Mehrabian found that just 7% of what the listener understood was verbal content. 93% of the information came from how the presentation looked and felt. 38% of the information received was from how the presentation sounded and 55% came from visual cues.

ICIA press release, June 10, 2004, reference study done by Acclaro Growth Partners

Mehrabian, A. (1981). *Silent messages: Implicit communication of emotions and attitudes.* 2nd edition. Belmont, CA: Wadsworth.

OVERVIEW

Why do organizations hold meetings? There are so many things to consider including travel, accommodations, food, beverage, insurance, and more that it is easy to forget the reason attendees are there. At the most basic level, the point of a meeting is to communicate a message, most of it via the presenters. A/V services are the conduit between the presenters and the audience.

A/V has become more sophisticated, and the expectations of the audience have also increased. The result? The audience takes less than a minute to decide whether a presentation is worth listening to. If they are not engaged quickly, the audience's attention can wander. And all the money and time invested in travel, catering, and planning sink without a trace: not a good return on investment. So let us examine this 1-minute concept more closely.

First why are visual presentations so important? According to educational psychologist Richard E. Mayer in his book, *Multimedia Learning*, research has found that people learn better from graphics and text than from text alone. One study found that when graphics were added to the text elements of a multimedia presentation, the ability to remember the information increased by 23% and the ability to apply the information increased by 89%.[1] These kinds of results should get the meeting manager focused on how to deliver the right audiovisual experience for his/her audience.

When the audience arrives at an event, they walk through the door wondering: "What's this going to be like?" Their subconscious mind compares the look and feel of the room to every other event they have attended. They draw a fast conclusion. By creating the right environment up front, the audience is put in the right frame of mind to listen to the message. However, the presenters still have only that minute to prove themselves and most of them are somewhat nervous. A speaker who has rehearsed feels more comfortable on stage. They get used to the stage lights, the microphones, and how to control the presentation systems. Instead of a hesitant, microphone-tapping, paper-shuffling start, they get right down to it. The audience picks up on these cues. And if the lighting is right and the sound is right, it creates the cycle of positive feedback that is so essential for getting the message across. Now an effective meeting is ready to go.

The goal of this chapter is to acquaint the meeting manager with the issues to consider regarding the application of A/V, rather than making him/her an expert in A/V systems. The A/V supplier that the meeting manager selects will be a critical partner helping to produce a successful event. A/V suppliers come in a broad range of capabilities, skills, specialties, and expertise. It is important to understand if they are providing equipment, technical service, creative support, and production as part of the quoted services. Before selecting an A/V partner, the meeting manager should seek references from others and view samples of their past work.

Finally, it is important to realize that A/V and technical meeting support services continue to rapidly evolve. New technology continues to provide more efficient, flexible, and innovative ways to help presenters deliver the message to their audience. This chapter will refer to some technologies that may well be obsolete by the time it is read. The key understanding to take away is not the technology, but an understanding of how the meeting manager and A/V supplier can use the available technology to help deliver their message with more impact.

This chapter is presented by discussing the key areas of implementing A/V including audio, visual display, lighting, and specialty systems. Finally, strategies for running the show in an efficient and cost-effective manner are described.

AUDIO EQUIPMENT

Sound plays a critical role in the meeting environment. It starts with the obvious; *the audience needs to hear the presentation.* It really goes beyond that. Sound has a deep subliminal effect on people's thoughts and moods. If you are presenting rational information, the main requirement of sound is simply that everyone in the room can hear clearly. When you are presenting an emotional message, sound enhances the message and affects how the audience feels. Similarly, when showing a video on the big screen, it is easy to get excited about the picture quality. However, the quality of the sound that delivers that emotional impact is equally important.

Also consider the role of walk-in music. Walk-in music sets the tone when people arrive. It is a strong emotional communicator. It creates energy and anticipation. When it is time to start the show, fade the sound down and the audience automatically stops talking and turns to face the stage. Similarly for major events, use "play on stings"—short bursts of energetic music—as presenters move to the podium. It can make an amazing difference in the energy of the audience.

Microphones

An important decision to make when planning a meeting is to determine the number and types of microphones necessary for the meeting. The A/V technician can play the best role in advising what type of microphone the meeting should have. Here are some of the things to be aware of when it comes to making the decision:

- Microphones can be unidirectional or omni-directional. Unidirectional microphones are far less prone to feedback, but have to be in very close proximity to the source of the sound. Omni-directional microphones pick up sound from a greater distance away. Each type can be good or bad depending upon the application or even the speaker's tendencies. Consult the A/V tech as to which is the right solution for the purpose.

- Microphones can be wired in a fixed location such as on a lectern. A lectern microphone should be attached to a flexible metal gooseneck so that its position can be changed to accommodate the height of various speakers. Ideally the microphone should be positioned 6 to 10 inches directly in front and below the level of the speaker's mouth.

- Wireless microphones allow presenters to move freely around the stage and they are extremely reliable. A lavaliere microphone is one that can be clipped on clothing or hung around the neck. An entertainer or extremely dynamic speaker will likely benefit from a handheld microphone or a wireless microphone that fits on an earpiece around the head. But there are tradeoffs—lavaliere microphones are great for speaking. However, the hand-held or head-worn microphones can deliver better fidelity.

- A key part of a professional presentation is smooth changeovers as presenters come on and off stage. Consider the number of lavaliere microphones necessary to allow each presenter to be wired up before they arrive on stage. This allows the incoming presenter to focus on their speech rather than on technology.[2]

- For a panel discussion, the moderator and each participant on the panel should have a microphone. Panel microphones should be placed on table stands. The microphones can be voice-activated so only one presenter is amplified at any given time.

- Questions from the audience are best handled by installing stationary microphones on floor stands throughout the aisles. Someone at a floor microphone is easy to spot, and floor microphones facilitate smooth transition to the next question. Alternatively, technicians can pass a handheld microphone throughout the audience.
- As more open microphones are added, the potential for trouble is heightened. This is where the mixer (mixing board or sound board) comes into play, as well as audio technicians to monitor and run the mixer. Unfortunately there is no set rule for when to add a mixer and a technician. It all depends upon the application. The A/V technician should be able to explain why and when the investment is appropriate.

Speaker Systems

There is a wide range of choice available for loudspeaker and sound systems. Many facilities will have their own installed in house audio systems. Sound quality is usually adequate for the spoken word (rational presentations) but is often inadequate for music reproduction, theatrical style reproduction, or living up to the quality of multimedia presentations. Does the audience need to "feel" the music for an emotional presentation?

To determine the acceptability of a built-in sound system, listen to it in use and check it again the day before the meeting. If the room is part of a multi-room complex, check to see that sound feeds only into the individual room(s) being used. Ask about the sound proof capabilities of moveable walls and what events are scheduled in neighboring rooms.

If there are concerns about the built-in sound capabilities of the facility, the A/V partner should offer a range of solutions including the following.

Portable sound systems start with a single microphone and a powered speaker. This sort of mono system offers good audio reproduction and maximum flexibility for smaller groups of people. It is quick and simple to move around. It can also play CDs for background music with some systems have the option of running under battery power.

The next level of speaker systems is stereo sound systems. These systems include passive left and right speakers for stereo sound. When delegates are listening to presentations for extended periods, any level of distortion will affect their ability to pay attention and absorb information. A good stereo sound system will enhance intelligibility by reproducing speeches with maximum clarity, delivering clean powerful sound in medium-sized rooms. It suits almost any event audio application, including music, video soundtracks, and computer audio.

There are a myriad of speaker system options as the meeting becomes more complex. The meeting manager may need distributed systems with a bi-amp or tri-amp main cluster in the front of the room and speakers distributed throughout the room. Professional sound-processing and equalization racks allow the sound to be crafted to suit the room's individual acoustics, which prevents feedback even with presenters who walk around the room.

For the ultimate in sound quality consider line array systems. Line array speakers use advanced new audio technology, with multiple speakers hung in vertical rows. This allows accurate sound to all members of the audience: not too loud, not too soft. It also reduces audio "reflections" from floor and ceiling, and helps create ultimate clarity and intelligibility.

Recording Equipment

If the organization will be making an audio recording of the meeting, placing extra microphones next to the main public address microphone or taking a feed from the facility's public sound system will be important. If multiple micro-phones are to be used, it is usually much easier to tie into the output of the house system. Most facilities are accustomed to providing this service.

If the recording is for transcription and distribution in printed form, record directly onto cassettes using two recorders. The second one can start recording before the first one is finished, preventing the loss of material that normally results from changing tapes in the middle of a speech.

If individual cassettes will be needed of each speaker's presentation, inform the person recording the event ahead of time, in order to avoid having to edit the material later. A higher quality recording can be made using a digital recorder and can be edited to eliminate pauses or other interruptions.

Technological advances in digital recording devices have made them virtu-ally as easy to set up and use as traditional cassette recorders. They typically allow longer recording times and produce better quality recordings that can be reproduced over and over with no loss of quality. Digital recording also provides the flexibility for distribution over the web.[3]

Unless audience microphones are used, the moderator should repeat audi-ence questions or comments so they are included in the recording.

Visual Equipment

Visual support provides a broad range of options for meeting managers to con-sider. Let us consider some of the basic categories.

Presentation Software

With its dominant share of the presentation software market, Microsoft Office PowerPoint™ is the tool that most speakers use to prepare their presentation mate-rials. Although PowerPoint is easy to use, there is a growing chorus of critics and researchers who say that reading bullet points from a slide actually disrupts learn-ing. At the same time PowerPoint can be used in a manner that is aligned to the extensive body of research by Dr. Mayer and other researchers. One such guide would be Cliff Atkinson's book, *Beyond Bullet Points* (Microsoft Press, 2005).[4] Being familiar with these resources can help meeting managers work with presen-ters to get the maximum impact from their visual communication.

Heritage Systems

Two main items play a role here, the overhead projector and the slide projector.

- *Overhead Projector*—The simplest of all A/V equipment. It uses a mirror system to project a transparency of up to 10 by 10 inches on a flat projec-tion screen. The overhead is versatile despite its simplicity, allowing a speaker to develop an impromptu visual idea during presentations. If a presenter will be writing on the transparencies during the presentation, make sure there is an ample supply of acetate sheets and special marking pens.
- *Slide Projector*—The 35mm slide projector is often referred to as a carousel projector. It uses a 2 by 2-inch slide in the United States. This piece of equipment has largely been replaced by LCD projectors, which allow transmission directly from a digital source. At some meetings, some presenters with older material may require the projector.

Video Projection

Most meetings today require the projection of images. The source is frequently a computer displaying a PowerPoint presentation or a DVD player displaying video. Today's projectors can interface with almost any type of computer including all PC and Mac platforms as well as many high-end engineering and architectural design workstations.[5] Mac platforms often require a simple adapter be attached; therefore, meeting managers should make sure this is checked in advance.

- LCD projectors are the most common type of projector in the market. There are a lot of considerations that go into looking at which projector is right for the meeting including size of the room, size of the screen, ambient light, projector placement, and type of information being displayed. The more detail that can be discussed with the A/V supplier about these sorts of inputs, the easier they can recommend the appropriate projector solution for the event.
- DLP projectors utilize a unique technology developed by Texas Instruments. This technology allows for the brightest possible image and has the capability of extremely high light output. It is more expensive than comparable LCD projection, but tends to be higher quality as well.

Here is a quick review of some of the considerations:

1. *Lumen*—This refers to the brightness thrown out by the projector. A general rule of thumb is the higher the number the better the picture. Small projectors can display large images such as PowerPoint slides adequately in a boardroom. When presenting detailed spreadsheets, say in Excel for budget meetings, or when projecting onto a larger screen in a ballroom, the presenter may run into some problems. A good way to review this with the A/V supplier is to review the options they have for a boardroom meeting, a quarter to half ballroom meeting, and for a full ballroom presentation. They are likely to recommend a different projector with a different lumen count for each application.
2. *SVGA vs. XGA*—It is tempting to launch a technical dissertation regarding resolution, pixel count, and aspect ratios. But here is the key information about this description of projectors:
   - *XGA*—This is the current standard for professional presentations today. This technology ensures seamless translation of all forms of computer resolution and video
   - *SVGA*—This is an adequate form of projection, particularly for video instead of computer data
3. *Rear Projection vs. Front Projection*—This refers to where the projector is placed, behind the screen for rear projection and in front of the screen for front projection. Rear projection offers a brighter picture and avoids any need to place the projector with the audience. It does require more space (the space required behind the screen in the front of the audience) and more labor to drape off the area around the screen. This space can be minimized by the use of a short throw lens, which requires less distance between the projector and the screen. Front projection avoids the space and labor issue, but there is a sacrifice in terms of image brightness when room design requires the use of a front projection projector.

Display Devices

A wave of technical innovation is opening options to communicate with audiences with display devices instead of projection devices. Traditionally the only available display device has been the CRT monitor. This is effective for communicating to small audiences, but the prevalence of the LCD projector has reduced its role in meetings. However the emergence of flat panel and high definition technology has rejuvenated the role and relevancy of display devices. Older CRT devices use a 4:3

aspect ratio (think of a portrait photo or TV screen) while newer devices use a 16:9 aspect ratio (think of a landscape photo or a wide-screen movie). A 4:3 device displays images with 4 units in width to 3 units in height; a 16:9 device displays images with 16 units in width to 9 units in height. Popular devices include:

- *Plasma Displays*—As consumers increasingly adopt plasma televisions at home, they will look for the plasma display in the meeting environment. Plasma displays can interface with the full range of data devices to display TV, video, computer images, or graphic displays. The plasma is capable of displaying high definition images if content is provided in a high definition format. The flat design also provides a sleeker, high tech image for audiences. Plasma screens are ideal for displaying video images from sources like cameras, DVD players, and other videotape sources. Plasma displays provide excellent gray scales for superior color reproduction. The plasma screen also provides a better viewing angle for audiences seeing the screen at wide angles. Prevalent sizes include 42, 50, and 61 inches.

- *LCD Displays*—This is another form of flat panel display that also allows for high definition images. The A/V partner can advise which of the two technologies is better for the application. LCD images tend to be brighter than plasma and are excellent in displaying images in areas of high ambient light. LCD displays do an excellent job of recreating digital images exactly, which makes them great for displaying computer-generated images. LCD displays start very small in size, but the 16:9 aspect ratio starts at 26 inches and goes to 47 inches. Much larger sizes are starting to be produced. LCD displays tend to be more flexible in their size.

Projection Screens

Selecting an appropriate surface on which to project an image is equally as important as selecting the projection equipment. The first decision is the size of the screen, which is based on capacity, dimensions, and ceiling height of the meeting room (see Table 29.1). Another way to impact size is to use multiple screens on either side of a stage.

The most portable screen is the tripod. It is a pull-up surface with three legs and a support rod. Tripod screens range from 4 feet to 8 feet. There are two types of larger screens. The cradle screen is available in sizes of up to 12 feet. It is a wall screen turned upside down, and the surface is pulled up and out of the container and supported by a rod on the back. It must be set on a table or a riser. The fast-fold screen is available in sizes ranging from 5 to 30 feet. It is made of a folding aluminum frame that accommodates interchangeable snap-on front or rear projection fabrics. Fast-fold screens come with legs that can be adjusted to various heights or the screen can be hung from a ceiling or support truss.

Here are some general A/V rules for screen size and placement:

- Divide the distance from the screen to the last row of the audience by eight, and use the resulting number as the height of the screen. For example, if the distance between the screen and the last row is 120 feet, 120 divided by 8 equals 15. Therefore the screen should be 15 feet high. Sometimes it is impossible or impractical to use the ideal screen size because of ceiling height or other physical restrictions.

- In terms of the projector distance to the screen, assume that the projector should be placed approximately 1.5 times the width of the screen. So if the screen is 8 feet high, the projector should be 12 feet away.

- The 2-by-8 principle states that no one should be seated closer to the screen than 2 times the height of the screen, nor further from the screen than 8 times the height of the screen.

TABLE 29.1
Projection Screen Specifications

Screen Height	Screen Width	Screen Format	Image Height	Image Width	First Row (2x Image Height)	Last Row (8x Image Height)
6' 0"	8' 0"	4 x 3	6' 0"	8' 0"	12' 0"	48' 0"
		16 x 9	4' 6"	8' 0"	9' 0"	36' 0"
		Square	6' 0"	6' 0"	12' 0"	48' 0"
7' 6"	10' 0"	4 x 3	7' 6"	10' 0"	15' 0"	60' 0"
		16 x 9	5' 8"	10' 0"	11' 3"	45' 0"
		Square	7' 6"	7' 6"	15' 0"	60' 0"
9' 0"	12' 0"	4 x 3	9' 0"	12' 0"	18' 0"	72' 0"
		16 x 9	6' 9"	12' 0"	13' 6"	54' 0"
		Square	9' 0"	9' 0"	18' 0"	72' 0"
10' 6"	14' 0"	4 x 3	10' 6"	14' 0"	21' 0"	84' 0"
		16 x 9	7' 11"	14' 0"	15' 9"	63' 0"
		Square	10' 6"	10' 6"	21' 0"	84' 0"
12' 0"	16' 0"	4 x 3	12' 0"	16' 0"	24' 0"	96' 0"
		16 x 9	9' 0"	16' 0"	18' 0"	72' 0"
		Square	12' 0"	12' 0"	24' 0"	96' 0"
15' 0"	20' 0"	4 x 3	15' 0"	20' 0"	30' 0"	120' 0"
		16 x 9	11' 3"	20' 0"	22' 6"	90' 0"
		Square	15' 0"	15' 0"	30' 0"	120' 0"

• Finally the bottom of the screen should be at least 5 feet off the ground. Why? It allows the audience to see the image over the person in front of them.

Video Equipment

There are three broad quality groups for video equipment: broadcast, commercial, and consumer. Commercial quality is the most prevalent form in the meetings industry. By consumer quality, we are referring to VHS or SVHS tapes that play in a standard VCR. This does not provide adequate quality to be projected on a big screen. If the image is to be of high quality, use a format like Betacam or DVC Pro. However, one cannot take a poor quality VHS tape, transfer it to Betacam, and expect a better result. The original source material must be of sufficient quality to start with. The key consideration as a meeting manager is to understand what video formats presenters will be using well in advance of the meeting.

Video cameras are often used in the meeting environment to enable the audience to see the presenter's image more clearly on a large screen. This is usually done in large ballroom style venues and is referred to as image magnification or I-mag. Cameras can also be used to show close up detail of documents, medical procedures, or other on-stage activities that would otherwise be difficult for the audience to see. Finally consider having two cameras. That allows the camera operator to get each shot fully set before it goes up on the big screen. Seamless switching allows the operator to go back and forth between each camera.

Finally, it is important to remember that video playback and recording equipment has different standards throughout the world. The standard used in the United States is NTSC. The PAL standard is found in Europe, Africa, Australia, and Southeast Asia. SECAM is used in Russia, France, and the Middle East. PAL and SECAM equipment are available in the United States, but will require advance planning to arrange.

Lighting

Good lighting is critical to the success of any session. Poor lighting can cause presenters to have problems with A/V as well as divert attendee attention away from the program and the speaker. Theatrical lighting is not just for the opening special event. Lighting has become an integral part of meeting rooms, exhibit floors, and walkways, allowing low cost enhancements to the look and feel of an event. The basic instruments of meeting lighting include:

- *Par Can*—This is a lighting instrument that acts like a floodlight providing an even light over a specific area. These are simple wash lights.
- *Fresnels*—This lens produces a soft edged beam of light. It is a theatrical fixture with adjustable lens. It is a type of semi-focusable light used for stage washes.
- *Lekos*—Type of adjustable spotlight used to light lecterns, signs, and areas that need a tightly focused pool of light.
- *Gel*—Interchangeable colored filters for lights.
- *Gobo*—A pre-cut, etched pattern fabricated from metal or glass that fits in the focal plane of a lighting instrument to form projected light into a shape (logo, graphic, or even scenery). Templates can form light images on ceilings and walls. The pattern or template can be used in a projection type spotlight, to project decorative patterns on the walls.
- *Wash*—Broad unfocused light for covering a wide area evenly. The opposite of a spot.
- *Spotlight*—Strong focused light thrown upon a particular person or object, such as on a stage.
- *Barndoor*—Movable hinged flap used on stage lights to control light spill.
- *Intelligent Lighting*—Lighting instruments that can be computer controlled to move light around the room, and project color and patterns on screens, scenery, walls, or floor.
- *LED*—Light Emitting Diode. A solid-state diode rectifier whose atomic properties cause it to emit light when electric current is passed through it. Current LED technology allows the emission of light from infrared through green frequencies, and visible light LEDs are available in colors from deep red to green. Allows color changing capability.

For the speaker to look his/her best, using three lights per podium will provide the best results. That is two in front and one behind. Using two in front prevents shadows; the third behind provides depth and provides a three dimensional image of the presenter.

Lights can be a great way to add life to even a simple set. Add wash to a simple fabric to add life through different colors. If the budget does not allow for a set, a cool look can be achieved with the use of internally lit truss uprights. Put different color lights at each end, and an instant budget-friendly set is created.

Add more excitement by adding some color textures with intelligent lights. Intelligent lights give the meeting manager everything needed to control the mood of the audience. Imagine that the meeting manager wants the audience to feel calm and relaxed. Cool colors—blues and greens—have an instant soothing effect on people. Now we add some soothing music, and we are in business. When you are expecting a tough audience for some reason, it is a good way to keep them as calm as possible.

Now imagine that the meeting manager wanted to get the audience excited and energized. We just change the colors over to hot reds, yellows, and oranges, and kick in some punchier music. Lights can instantly control the mood.

It also helps with multi-day events, where lighting can change the whole feel of the show overnight without set changes.

Finally do not underestimate the power of a gobo. All association executives and corporate sponsors love seeing their logos up in lights. It is a great way to add branding and exposure at minimal cost throughout the meeting location.

Specialty Systems

Some events can be greatly enhanced by taking advantage of the technological innovation that is available to meeting managers today. The following applications typically require advanced technical support from the A/V partners.

Multi-Image Display Technology

Sophisticated audiences are expecting ever more sophisticated presentations to capture their attention and motivate them. At one point, multi-image display technology required multiple screens and multiple projectors choreographed together. Today state of the art technology allows multiple images to be placed on a single screen with extremely high-resolution display for wide-screen formats.[6] With this new class of technology from companies such as Barco/Folsom Research or Vista Systems, the meeting can use portions of a given signal, overlap images, and blend images to provide a seamless presentation that merges input from one or more devices. Audiences see a clearer high-resolution image that can incorporate branding, advertising, polling results, and other images all on the same display real estate. Screen size is limited only by budget. Applications vary from incorporating live video, with graphics detailing the visual, and an I-mag of the speaker presenting. As this can be constantly varied, the meeting manager can change the look and feel of the room day-to-day or speaker to speaker.

When looking into this technology:

- Research A/V vendors who have successfully deployed multi-source technology and networks
- Make a detailed site visit to ensure successful room set-up. The A/V vendor should accompany the meeting manager on this site visit
- Create a detailed storyboard including the presenters, the types of display, and a ranking of image importance. The most important information should always be in the same real estate
- Allow extra time to preview all visual content

Virtual Speaker Systems

The use of web technology can greatly facilitate the exchange, coordination, and collaboration between the organization, the A/V vendor, and the speakers. The A/V partner can create an Internet site for the meeting. This site will include a 24/7 guide to presentation templates, fonts, colors, and A/V requirements.[7] Speakers can upload their presentations on the site in advance of the meeting. The A/V company can review the slides in advance and coordinate edits with the speakers well in advance of arriving on site. As speakers arrive on site, their presentations have already been uploaded on the local area network and are ready for their final review. Speakers can visit the on-site speaker ready room for a final review. A central server and network will ensure that the right presentation is ready for the speaker in each of the breakout rooms when they arrive. Most national A/V companies offer some form of this service.

High Definition

High Definition (HD) is generally defined as any format other than NTSC video. The improved resolution, clarity, and crispness of the image have made broadcasting in a HD format an attractive option for associations and meeting managers to consider. While HD comes in a variety of formats, the two most common are 720p (1280 x 720) and 1080i (1920 x 1080). These numbers refer to the pixel count (width vs. height). HD provides the best quality images possible today. The further benefit of HD is that once the content is in digital format, an incredibly high degree of flexibility in editing and re-purposing content is gained.[8]

Here are some considerations to approaching an HD deployment:

- Meet with the A/V vendor and clearly identify the requirements early.
- Map out where and how the group would like to incorporate HD into the venue's floor plan. Many venues' existing cabling systems may not be rated for HD.
- Balance high definition against scenic treatments and backgrounds. HD will show details that are not readily visible today, so this application may require the meeting manager to consider upgrading lighting, scenic backgrounds, and make up for presenters.
- The site visit is a must. HD can change the room set-up. Viewing distances stay the same based on screen height but projection distances will increase because of the wider aspect ratios.

Planning the Show

Most meeting managers strive to have their show work smoothly and be stress free. It can be done. Here are some critical elements to consider:

Site Inspections

For any serious event, meeting managers need a site inspection with a technical expert. Do it as early as possible. More time means more scope to arrange the event to suit the budget. Check:

- *Room capacities*—Yes, there is enough room for the meeting's expected numbers, but will the stage and the dance floor fit? Audiences feel uncomfortable sitting too close to the stage.
  - For a quick estimate of the maximum room capacity for an A/V application, divide the square footage of the room by 10 feet per person for theater style set-up or 17 feet per person for a classroom style set-up.
- *Ceiling heights and hang points*—If the event needs anything more than basic lighting, lights will need to be hung (and possibly the sound). This means careful checking of ceiling heights and "hang points."
- *Access times*—Find out how long it will take to set up and rehearse the event. If there is a function already booked immediately before the event, this may not allow enough time to adequately set up. If time is tight, be sure to review this with the technical team in advance. They can specify the load in and set-up.
- *Internet access*—There is more on this in a later section. Just remember that time moves at a different speed for a presenter on stage. If there is a need for the Internet in the presentation, make sure to have broadband access and know what kind of speed should be expected.

- *Get a run sheet*—Help the crew stay in control with a run sheet. Big shows use complex run sheets with every cue broken up into video, audio, lighting, and staging. For complex sessions/events the meeting manager will need a producer to create one of these, but for the average event a simpler run sheet is fine. Just list everything that is going to happen during the event with the approximate times. List all the presenters, where they will be speaking from, and what presentation material they will use. This will alert the crew as to segments with specific needs like panel discussions, Q&A, or awards.
- *Plan for back up*—Computers crash. Have the A/V company run two computers in tandem, slide for slide. If one fails, they switch to the other one and nobody is the wiser. The same rule applies for content like CDs, tapes, and other materials.
- *Crew Rules*—When booking any major event, be sure to consider local crew rules. Check in advance, as the budget figure the organization is projecting might not be accurate. A/V managers and project managers will be happy to advise on what rules apply and will help manage crew labor to deliver the best possible result.

The Internet

High-speed Internet access (HSIA or broadband) has quickly moved from luxury status to an integral requirement for most meetings. High-speed Internet access is possible due to digital technologies that compress vast amounts of voice, video, and data information. The deployed technologies move this information far more efficiently than traditional dial up connections.

Here are some of the ways HSIA can play an integral part of the meeting:

- Email kiosk stations
- Online registration management
- Member services
- Meeting services (from weather to news to airline reservations)
- Remote broadcast
- Trade show deployment
- Integrated into individual presentations

Considering how vast the potential reach of HSIA is to the meeting, meeting managers need to understand the Internet capabilities of the host facility and ensure they are sufficient to meet the needs. The term HSIA is used very casually and can vary from a phone line running at 56K to a T1 line.[9]

So the first critical question to ask is "Is the Internet mission critical, or nice to have?" If it is critical, the meeting manager will need to consider how they can make sure the facility has sufficient bandwidth and build in some level of protection to ensure a successful meeting. Considerations include:

- What is the Internet being used for (e.g., live presentations, streaming presentation content from a corporate server, checking email)? Is each one equally important?
- If the meeting will need email access for attendees, how many users may be connecting at one time and how mission critical is the ability for everyone to connect?
- What connection speeds are included in the agreement?
- Does the supplier guarantee bandwidth? (If someone next door is streaming video and the meetings are sharing the general hotel connection, how does the meeting manager protect his/her meeting's needs from other events?)
- How can the meeting secure incremental or a guaranteed bandwidth? How long does it take and at what cost? Will this provide redundancy?

- Test all meeting space and function spaces for the desired connectivity in advance.
- What are the available options for wireless as well as wired connections?
- Understand the hotel's cost structure and what drives it. For instance what are the charges for public vs. private IP addresses?
- Who is the technical support for the meeting and are they on site or in another state? Many facilities have escalation procedures for Internet issues. The meeting manager will need to understand who is responsible for supporting the group on site at the facility. Many times the Internet provider is different than the A/V provider.

The key component to remember is to determine if the Internet is critical to the success of the meeting. If so, will the organization work through the supplier to secure the service needed or just use what is available?

A/V Costs

Efficient management of an A/V budget includes close control over program costs, speaker requests, equipment, labor, and the performance of contractors and meeting facility personnel. The speaker A/V request form should be an accurate reflection of the types of equipment that are available. The form should clearly identify the types of equipment that will not be made available. Avoid asking the speaker to indicate special requests unless the organization is financially capable of providing anything that may be requested.

Equipment costs will vary depending upon the location of the meeting and the specific type of A/V supplier being used. Whether the facility has union labor may affect the budget. If equipment must be totally removed at night because the facility has sold the room to another group for the evening, reset charges will be incurred. Review all electrical requirements for audiovisuals to determine what will be provided by the facility and at what charge, and what must be arranged through an electrical contractor.

Typically the facility electrician handles routine tasks, provides extension cords where needed, and completes special electrical arrangements. Special electrical arrangements are likely to encounter additional costs. Dimmers and remote control light switches are not standard in most facilities but can be supplied by the facility engineering staff or the A/V supplier. Again, these costs must be considered as part of the budget.

Technological advances continue to expand the range of possibilities for using audiovisual services to make a dramatic impact on the meeting's communication. These new technologies frequently cost more. But the meeting manager should equally expect more, specifically a greater ability to effectively deliver the communication goals of the meeting. New technology costs can also provide greater efficiency as they are rolled out. Discuss the impact of the new equipment to provide savings in labor, pre-, and post-production work, reduced scenic hard set requirements, and a greater ability to use digital and graphic elements after the show.

Finally, the best advice is to plan ahead. The earlier that the meeting manager can share A/V expectations and requirements, the more time is allowed for a creative solution that maximizes the communication impact while respecting the event's budget.

SUMMARY

A/V equipment can be as simple as a single microphone and a flip chart or as complex as a multi-image display in a theater-style presentation. The key is that the meeting manager understands how the A/V strategies can help them to more effectively deliver the message to the audience. It all depends upon the goals of the organization and the size of the meeting that is being held.

This chapter reviewed the various types of A/V equipment available for use. Basic considerations include providing sufficient audio support so speakers are heard clearly by their audience; visual support so presenters and their content are seen clearly by their audience; and advance planning so that both the audio and the visual elements maximize the communication within the specific constraints of the meeting facility. Meeting managers responsible for arranging A/V services should return to this chapter and use it as a resource to ensure that the appropriate application of A/V technology is utilized and to be able to ask better questions of the A/V partner for their specific recommendations.

Technology continues to facilitate the meeting experience. Virtual speaker systems utilize the Internet and local networking to provide a more professional and efficient meeting experience for attendees and the presenters. Meeting managers must articulate the experience they want their audience to have, and a creative and skilled A/V company can deliver several options that can meet their budgets.

Finally, planning is the key to a successful meeting's A/V setup. Critical environmental issues such as ceiling height, walls and floors, obstructions, windows, lighting, air conditioning, electrical requirements, and even the meeting next door can have a major impact on the design of the meeting. These considerations can even impact the decision on the meeting room itself. The earlier the meeting manager establishes their communication goals and budget with the A/V team, the more time both will have to deliver a creative, powerful, and meaningful A/V presentation.

REFERENCES

1. Mayer, R. E. (2001). *Multimedia learning*. Cambridge University Press, p. 74–76.

2. Siwek, E. J. (December, 2005). Innovative meetings: Making your presenters look great. *Convene*, p. 35.

3. Siwek, E. J. (May, 2005). Innovative meetings: Taking advantage of digital technology, *Convene*, p. 23.

4. Atkinson, C. (2005). *Beyond bullet points*. Redmond, WA: Microsoft Press.

5. Siwek, E. J. (July, 2004). Display technologies: A new wave of technical innovation. *Convene*, p. 27.

6. Siwek, E. J. (October, 2004). Multi-sourced displays, *Convene*, p. 31.

7. Siwek, E. J. (December, 2004). Virtual speaker ready rooms, *Convene*, p. 31.

8. Siwek, E. J. (February, 2005). High definition production. *Convene*, p. 27.

9. Siwek, E. J. (July 2005). High-speed Internet access. *Convene*, p. 23.

KEY TERMS

Audiovisual	Lavaliere microphone	Overhead projector
Barndoor	LCD projector	Par can
Broadband (or HSIA)	Lekos	Plasma display
CRT monitor	Lectern microphone	Rear projection
Fast-fold screen	LED	Run sheet
Fresnel	Loudspeaker	Slide projector
Front projection	Lumen	Spotlight
Gel	Mixer	Tripod screen
Gobo	Multi-image display	Unidirectional
Hang points	technology	microphone
High definition (HD)	NTSC video	Virtual speaker systems
I-mag	Omni-directional	Wash
Intelligent lighting	microphone	

COMPELLING QUESTIONS FOR CONSIDERATION

1. How long do you have to make an effective impact upon your meeting attendees?

2. What is the most prevalent method for displaying information at meetings today?

3. What are key considerations for audio equipment in your meeting?

4. Name two key ways lighting can impact meeting communication.

5. Name one of the primary considerations for planning high speed Internet access for your meeting.

6. What does the 2-by-8 principle mean?

7. Are audiovisual guidelines for applications fast and finite, or general advice from which a meeting manager and his/her A/V supplier should work?

CHAPTER 30

ENVIRONMENTALLY AND SOCIALLY RESPONSIBLE MEETINGS AND EVENTS

Amy Spatrisano, CMP
PRINCIPAL
MEETING STRATEGIES WORLDWIDE

Nancy J. Wilson, CMP
PRINCIPAL
MEETING STRATEGIES WORLDWIDE

LEARNER OUTCOMES

When the reader has completed reading this chapter, he/she should be able to . . .

1 Define a green meeting.

2 Explain how producing green meetings positively affect the environment.

3 Apply green meeting practices to make a meeting or event environmentally responsible.

4 Implement environmentally responsible practices into future meetings.

> The earth and the human community
> are bound in a single journey.
>
> *Thomas Berry*

OVERVIEW

The hospitality industry has a tremendous sphere of influence because meetings touch so many other industries. Think about how many industries we rely on to produce meetings.

- *Energy*—natural gas, electricity, and oil used to produce meetings/hold events
- *Transportation*—airplanes, airports, cabs, buses, trains, rental cars
- *Food*—farms, dairy, cattle, poultry, fisheries
- *Local community*—employment, financial, retail
- *Accommodations*—hotels, cleaning products, soft goods market

The rates of consumption at meetings can be staggering. For instance, during a typical 5-day conference, 2,500 attendees will use 62,500 plates, 87,500 napkins, 75,000 cups or glasses, and 90,000 cans or bottles.[1]

Large corporations are already beginning to understand and take on new green initiatives as part of their long-range planning. General Electric's Chair and CEO, Jeffrey Immelt, was quoted in May 2005 as saying "It is no longer a zero-sum game—things that are good for the environment are also good for business. General Electric is embarking on this initiative not because it is trendy or moral, but because it will accelerate economic growth."[2]

GE is a great illustration because it is not necessarily considered an environmentally minded organization and Immelt admits he is no environmentalist. Organizations like Nike, Starbucks, Interface Carpets, VNU Expo, Shepard Exposition Services, and many more now have sustainability departments, green teams, or some other unit devoted to reducing their environmental impact. If you think greening is a perspective that only environmentalists and fringe groups have, think again.

So, what does this have to do with meetings? Everything! Green meetings and events hold a hope for the future by reducing their impact on the environment and improving financial outcomes for our organizations. By adopting just one environmentally responsible practice meeting managers can reduce consumption of the earth's resources and their organization's expenses—a win-win situation for everyone. This chapter will explore how meeting managers can shape their organization's meeting to be more sensitive to the environment and play a positive role in the communities in which meetings are held.

WHAT ARE GREEN MEETINGS?

When most people think of being "green" or environmentally sensitive, recycling is usually the first thing that comes to mind. A green meeting or event goes beyond recycling.

"Greening" a meeting or event encompasses all aspects of the strategic planning process. By making choices at every level of meeting management, from site selection to serving condiments like ketchup, mustard, and sugar from bulk containers, the environmental impact of the event can be significantly reduced. Green meetings also incorporate social aspects including charitable contribution and humanitarian efforts. There are many ways that meetings can have a positive impact in the community where it is held. Well-planned volunteer activities can incorporate fun and instill a sense of common purpose and goodwill within a group while supporting a worthy cause. For the purposes of this chapter, both environmentally and socially responsible meetings are included in the term green meetings.

While many organizations are working to make their meetings more eco-efficient, misconceptions about environmental practices are holding back many

Fast Facts

Definition of Green Meeting

A green meeting incorporates environmental considerations throughout all stages of the meeting in order to minimize the negative impact on the environment.[3]

others. Meeting managers working to green their meetings may encounter one or all of the "myths of green meetings":

- *Myth 1: Environmentally responsible meetings are too expensive.*

  Many green strategies actually reduce rather than increase expenses. The simple act of asking a hotel to change sheets and towels by request rather than on a daily basis reduces the environmental impact, saves the hotel money and empowers the attendee—all at no cost to the host organization.

- *Myth 2: If conservation cannot be 100 percent, why bother?*

  In fact, every effort toward sustainability has an impact. According to Green Suites International, if one hotel adopts the bath and linen program mentioned above, 200 barrels of oil are saved per year—enough to run a family car for 180,000 miles.

- *Myth 3: Eco-efficiency requires too much effort.*

  Most green practices are a matter of setting environmentally oriented policies and letting hotels and vendors know it is an important selection criterion. Green practices become a part of the normal meeting management cycle, from site inspections and contract negotiations to promotion and logistical management.

- *Myth 4: Only "environmental types" are making efforts to go green.*

  Not true. For example, Fortune 500 hotel chains are participating in environmental benchmark programs through The Prince of Wales International Business Leaders Forum. Sustainability is keeping company with mega-retailers like The Home Depot, which is committed to selling wood that is only from sustainable forests.

- *Myth 5: Individuals are powerless to change their workplaces and communities.*

  The burgeoning green marketplace is filled with success stories of individuals who came up with environmental solutions and helped meet the growing need for earth-friendly products and services. Empowerment is a primary goal of eco-efficient conference management, giving attendees the opportunity to reduce their own environmental impact and adopt responsible behaviors. These individual changes continue beyond a single event.

THE BENEFITS

Whether someone is a meeting manager or a supplier, producing green meetings can be rewarding by providing economic and environmental savings and increasing the organization's competitive advantage. However, green meetings must make business sense in order to be sustained.

Economic Savings

For a meeting manager, green meeting practices offer a variety of cost-saving opportunities without compromising quality. For example, selecting properties within walking distance to events can eliminate thousands of dollars in shuttle services. The added benefit is attendees get a chance to get some fresh air, a little exercise, and see a little more of the surrounding area. There are many other cost-saving green practices meeting managers might want to consider. For example, eliminating individual bottled water service will not only save money but also is environmentally friendly. Instead, provide a refillable container—a great sponsorship opportunity—with large containers of water. This practice can save hundreds or thousands of dollars depending on the size of the group. Another practice is to eliminate or significantly reduce speaker handouts. Make them available on a CD or online during or after the event. This saves time and money. These two ideas represent a sampling of possible economic savings from green meetings. The intention is to get meeting managers thinking about potential opportunities to reduce stress on the environment without reducing service to their attendees.

Suppliers, especially hoteliers, have a multitude of green economic-saving opportunities available to them. For hotels adopting environmentally responsible practices, energy efficiency, water conversation, and waste management offer the most cost savings. Green Seal is a great resource for information about the savings associated with such practices for hotels. To help organizations estimate savings potential, Green Seal, which also offers green hotel certification, has developed averages for a 296-room hotel:

- *Water savings*—Replacing 3.5 gallon-per-flush (gpf) toilets with 1.6 gpf toilets will result in 307,914 gallons of water saved per year or a cost savings of $1,163 annually.
- *Energy savings*—Replacing lobby lights with compact fluorescent bulbs saves $711 annually plus the cost of maintenance staff time and a drop in heat generated in the lobby.[4]

However, one does not need to be a hotelier to realize economic savings by incorporating green meeting practices. Caterers, food service providers, and general service contractors have ample opportunities as well. For example, condiments served in bulk containers instead of individual containers can offer up to 50% savings. By providing online exhibitor kits, general services contractors save money in production time, mailing, and staff time by not having to produce hard copy versions.

These are a very small sample of the economic savings realized from implementing green meeting practices. Suppliers should examine how and what they provide to their clients and customers and look for ways to go green. Consider alternatives that provide the same or greater level of service while minimizing the negative affects on the environment.

Environmental Savings

While some green meeting practices produce actual, measurable financial savings, others are more subtle. For example, by requesting that water glasses at a served meal not be pre-filled, a facility can save hundreds of gallons of drinking water on an event serving 2200 attendees. Also, using china service instead of disposables with the same size group can eliminate over 1800 pounds of plastic products being sent to a landfill. If food composting is available for the same size group over a 3-day period, as much as 6.5 tons of food waste could be diverted from a landfill. [5]

All of this is to illustrate the environmental impact meeting managers have in the decisions they make about products and services used at their events. Recognizing and relaying information about the economic and environmental savings realized at meetings can be a powerful message that can influence behavior and attitudes about how meetings are implemented.

Competitive Advantage

Producing green meetings can have a dual competitive advantage. The meeting manager can increase their value to their organization by providing an elevated level of expertise. Recording the economic and environmental savings as a result of green meeting practices quantifies their ability as an innovative and successful meeting manager.

Organizations can gain a competitive advantage for implementing an innovative, environmentally responsible meeting. Demonstrating a commitment to minimize the meeting's ecological footprint gets people excited. Evaluations after green conferences for non-environmental groups have shown a marked increase in satisfaction levels and many comments thanked organizers for taking environmental responsible steps. [6]

GETTING STARTED

Set Goals and Objectives

As with any conference or meeting, setting goals and objectives is essential to producing a successful event. During this process, make sure green meeting practices are incorporated. If the sponsoring organization is greening the meeting for the first time, they will need to establish the commitment of the organization to "go green." Once the organization's level of support is received, meeting managers can determine what green strategies or practices to put into place.

Meeting managers should begin by understanding how greening their meetings will fit into their company or client's mission and values. Chances are some environmental commitment, however subtle, may already exist. For example, Intel's mission states "We strive to conserve natural resources and reduce the environmental burden of waste generation and emissions to the air, water, and land." Alternatively, 3M expresses "It is 3M policy to provide a safe and healthful workplace for all, and to minimize the impact of our production processes and products on the environment."

Here are some fundamental questions to consider when setting goals and objectives for green meetings:

- *Why does the organization want to incorporate green practices?*
  This question may seem self explanatory, but ask it anyway. The answers received may be different than expected and will shape the approach taken.

- *How much is the organization willing to contribute?*
  It is extremely helpful for meeting managers to know if their organization is willing to spend more resources if some of the green practices recommended cost more than traditional practices. Although it may be difficult to provide actual costs, knowing approximately what the organization is willing to spend will save a lot of time and effort and focus the meeting manager on appropriate practices.

- *Is this a one-time effort or part of the organization's core practices?*
  This question clarifies the company's long-term commitment and purpose for adopting greening practices. The meeting manager can build on any level of commitment.

- *What aspects of the conference are most important to green?*
  The answer to this question will provide direction and focus on where to spend time and resources. Showing success in an area that is considered important, for whatever reason, may lead to greater support in the future.

These questions are just a beginning. Be open to exploring other questions as the dialogue continues with the organization.

Once there is a commitment to green the meetings by the sponsoring organization, work to build on this by developing a green strategy. It is easier to get financial and management support if a greening plan is developed, as it can show how to implement environmental practices that will be deployed. Sometimes the best way to enroll and engage the organization is to start with one or two new practices with the intention of building on their success.

Fast Facts

Steps to Realize
Green Meetings

1. Set goals and objectives
2. Develop guidelines
3. Communicate objectives
4. Negotiate green practices
5. Measure results

Develop Guidelines

The second step is to develop minimum guidelines to incorporate in all meetings. Criteria should be created for all of the vendors used, such as convention centers, hotels, caterers, transportation services, and even convention and visitors bureaus. The Convention Industry Council's *Green Meetings Report* offers helpful guidelines in eight areas of meeting management to get started.[3] It is important that clear guidelines are included in the request for proposal (RFP) stage of planning. This will make negotiating and implementing the practices much easier.

Communicate Objectives

Meeting managers will need to communicate expectations for the meeting very clearly, especially if greening practices are new. Communicate with the organization first. Let them know what policies or new practices are being put into place to green the event, why they are important, and the plan to implement them.

Be sure to say the same thing to all of the parties involved. The better they understand, the more motivated they will be to implement these requests. After all, everyone wants the meeting to be successful.

Inform attendees. Attendees will get engaged in what is being done if the what, why, and how is communicated to them. Let them know why the organization is doing things differently, and why it is important to make a change. Attendees do not usually respond well to surprises, but they frequently are open to new practices and ideas, if they are explained well.

Market greening practices. Informing the media about greening efforts could offer a press-worthy angle to the meeting.

Negotiate Green Practices

The fourth step is negotiating green practices. Many of the organization's greening practices may be new to their suppliers. Know what practices the organization is willing to compromise on and which ones they are not willing to relinquish. Also, be aware of which practices are easily implemented and are cost saving or cost neutral. For example, there may be resistance or refusal to donate food from the food and beverage provider because of a perceived liability issue. The fact is that the national Good Samaritan Law was written to support the donation of food in good faith. The law protects organizations that donate food to charity from liability related to the donation. If food donation is against a vendor's policy, the meeting manager may decide that vendor is not a good fit.

Most green practices are actually cost saving or cost neutral for suppliers. The crucial component to remember is, whatever is negotiated, ensure it is included in the contracts.

Measure Results

The final step is measuring the results. Do not skip this step. Tracking both the environmental and economic results provides the ability to quantify the results. For example, track the pounds of waste recycled or how much money was saved by eliminating conference bags. Ask attendees for feedback. Did the attendees notice and like any of the changes? Do they have suggestions for next time?

Then, publish what was measured. People love data. Tell attendees, use the information on the sponsoring organization's web site or as marketing for next time, share it with the team or organization, and tell their suppliers. Sharing the measured results is a great way to enroll and engage people to want more greening action taken by the sponsoring organization. This multilevel approach moves the notion of "greening" a meeting from a fringe behavior perspective to a mainstream practice.

Fast Facts

Good Samaritan Law supports donation of food in good faith.

Put It Into Perspective

PCMA's Network for the Needy was developed to unite meeting professional, city officials, and members of the hospitality community in helping the needy nationwide through donation of surplus convention goods. The Network for the Needy initiative has developed local contacts in many destination cities that will help arrange for surplus food and products to be distributed to local area shelters or food banks. More about Network for the Needy can be found on the PCMA website at www.pcma.org.

RESOURCES

There is no need to re-invent the wheel when adopting green meeting practices. Many resources are now available that provide sources for products and services, information about best practices, and opportunities to network with other industry professionals. A comprehensive list of resources is included in the appendix of this book.

START NOW

The key to getting started is to just start. Start anywhere in the process. Think of green meeting practices not as another thing to add to a "ToDo" list. Rather, incorporate the practices in the meeting management processes that are already being employed. For example, on the site inspection list for a hotel add such questions as: Do they have a towel and sheet reuse program? Do they have environmentally responsible practices? Do they use earth-friendly cleaning products?

Even if the meeting manager is able to implement only one environmentally-responsible practice, they will have made a difference.

The remainder of this chapter provides green meeting practices in the meeting management categories that are outlined in the Convention Industry Council's green meeting report.

DESTINATION SELECTION

Does the location of the meeting really make a difference? Absolutely it does. Choosing a destination that is conducive to the event's purpose, is held in an environmentally responsible destination, and takes into account the location of attendees is the first step in producing an earth-friendly meeting. The following are some green meeting practices for destinations:

- *Understand the event's purpose and the attendees' geographic locations*—The first step in managing a green event is choosing a destination that meets the organization's purpose for the meeting. Is it a board retreat, a fundraiser, an incentive trip, or an industry conference? Does the meeting manager know the demographics of the attendees? If so, then determine a site that requires minimal travel for all participants.
- *Obtain a list of environmentally-responsible organizations*—The meeting manager should ask the convention and visitors bureau (CVB) or a destination management company (DMC) for a list of venues, properties, and suppliers that have environmental practices in place. A list of green organizations may not be readily available. However, the request is an excellent opportunity to drive the demand for green meetings and will provide an indication about how environmentally responsible the location is.

Fast Facts

In 2004, the Convention Industry Council (CIC) produced the *Green Meeting Report* that set minimum and recommended guidelines for green meetings and events. This well-respected organization of over 30 meeting and event management, hospitality, and tourism associations is defining green meetings by offering specific guidelines and practices that provide meeting managers and suppliers a template for a green meeting. This report can be downloaded for use from www.conventionindustry.org.

- *Include environmental criteria in the RFP and contracts*—When sending out the RFP for events, meeting managers should include the environmental criteria. Specify the importance of environmental criteria in the site-selection process. For example, ask if recycling is available and implemented in the venues that are being considered. Details of specific environmental criteria are discussed in each of the remaining categories. Cities that understand the importance of eco-friendly meetings and have prepared a list of green vendors will be more effective partners as the meeting manager moves into other aspects of managing the meeting. It is important that green practices are included in contract language with all vendors.
- *Evaluate all aspects of the city and venue*—Weigh all the factors related to the city. Is the city's mass transit system adequate? Is it linked to the airport? Does the city publish walking maps? Are hotels and restaurants within walking distance of the venue or on public transportation?

While it is unrealistic to believe that all destination decisions will be made on environmental considerations alone, these factors can be important when choosing between comparable cities. The more a city and venue understand and embrace environmentally responsible practices, the easier it will be to green the event. If the meeting manager chooses a city or venue based on environmental considerations, communicate this fact with them. It is important for cities and venues to know they either gained or lost business because of their commitment to the environment.

ACCOMMODATION AND VENUE SELECTION

The location of the attendees' sleeping accommodations is often the same location where the meeting or event will take place. Therefore, those categories have been combined in this section. Meeting venues and accommodation locations can provide the greatest opportunity to minimize the event's negative environmental impact by implementing green meeting practices.

Green practices benefit venues not only by helping them present an environmentally responsible image to guests, but also by helping them realize significant economic savings. Remember to incorporate the following green meeting practices into all meeting pre-planning tasks such as RFPs, site inspections, and contract negotiations.

Determine Environmental Guidelines for the Sleeping Rooms

The following are some basic environmentally responsible practices to include in the meeting's minimum guidelines:

- *Linen and towel reuse program*—Guests are encouraged to decide whether their sheets and towels are changed daily during their stay or less frequently. By following the hotel's system, guests make their own choice. Ask about the training program for housekeeping staff.
- *In-room energy savings program*—Hotel employees are instructed to shut the blinds, minimize heating/air conditioning, and turn off all lights while rooms are unoccupied.
- *Amenities*—The hotel has guestroom dispensers for soap, shampoo, and lotion or they donate unused portions of amenities to charity. Request that soaps not be changed daily.
- *In-room and property recycling programs*—Offer guests recycling in their room, including paper, metal, glass, and plastic products. If in-room recycling is not available, the housekeeping or operations staff should sort these items after the room is cleaned. Determine if the hotel has a program to donate or reuse old linens, fixtures, and furniture.

- *Paperless registration and communication*—Ask if the hotel has paperless check in/out and billing procedures. Also request to be emailed (rather than mailed) all banquet event orders (BEOs), contracts, and master accounts. Finally, ask if in-room television service can be used to communicate to attendees.

General Venue Practices

The following are green practices for all venue types. Specific practices for food and beverage are discussed below.

- *Environmental management program or certification*—Has the property been certified by a third-party organization or have they established an environmental management program and training for all staff? The property should purchase environmentally friendly cleaning supplies and energy-efficient equipment.
- *Recycling program*—Does the venue routinely implement a recycling program for cardboard, paper, metal, glass, and plastics? If not, is it available to them and will they ensure one is implemented for the event?

Send an RFP with the Minimum Guidelines

Once the meeting manager has chosen the minimum green guidelines they should include them in their RFP and ask properties to respond to the guidelines. If the sponsoring organization has not developed their own guidelines, they should ask if they have an environmental certification program or use the Ceres Best Practices survey, found at http://www.ceres.org/pub/docs/Ceres_GHI_BPS_survey.pdf.

Include Environmental Commitment as a Factor in Rating Properties

Weigh each hotel or venue's environmental policies and procedures along with other determining factors. Ask hotels that do not already have policies in place if it is possible to establish them for the meeting and ask if they will continue them after the requesting group checks out.

Conduct a Site Inspection to Determine if Practices and Policies Are in Place

Experience has taught many meeting managers to conduct a back-of-the-house tour as part of the green site inspection. It is important to actually see where the recycling is sorted and where it is stored before pick-up. Take a look at the kitchen to see the amount of individual packaging that is used, as well as the venue's recycling or composting efforts, and where they store food for donation to local food banks.

Request a Commitment to Comply with Environmental Guidelines in the Contract

It is vital to include a clause in the contract outlining the environmental components that will be in place during the conference and event and the consequences for not complying.

Ensure Practices Are Occurring and the Measurable Data Is Being Tracked

Once on-site for the meeting, tour the back-of-the-house again to see how green practices will be implemented. Be sure to ask for measured data, such as how much cardboard, paper, plastic, and aluminum is collected from the event. If the group is not the only one in-house, actual numbers may be difficult to obtain; in that case, ask for estimates. Ensure the organic and local food that is ordered is purchased and used, and that all environmental guidelines established are followed.

Specify Environmental Programs in the Contract

Include a clause in the contract outlining the environmental programs to be in place during the event; be clear about the impact of non-compliance.

Choosing an environmentally responsible venue is one of the most important decisions a meeting manager will make. Guests often cite their experience with the venue on evaluations; they consider it a reflection of the meeting manager's efforts to green the event. The venue's commitment to green practices provides attendees and their guests with tangible evidence of the environmental awareness of the sponsoring organization.

TRANSPORTATION

Participants, meeting supplies, food, exhibit booths, and audiovisual equipment all travel to an event regardless of the meeting manager's efforts to choose a green destination. Because of the inherent value of face-to-face communication, minimizing transportation and working with companies to provide the most environmentally responsible transportation will never completely eliminate emissions or waste.

However, measures can be taken to minimize the negative impact of transportation in the following areas: attendees, transportation vendors, ground transportation, shipping freight, and carbon offsets.

Attendees

Attendees will be making many of their own decisions regarding transportation when coming to the event. Educate them and provide resources so their decisions can be as environmentally responsible as possible. The following are some examples of green transportation options:

- Alert attendees to environmentally preferable transportation, such as mass transit and carpooling. Commuter trains and other mass transit systems are preferable to car travel.
- Provide information about local public transit or arrange for shuttles to transport attendees to and from the airport and the hotel or meeting venue.
- If it is available in the city, provide car-sharing for attendees who need a car for only short periods of time. Car-sharing is an excellent option for conference and event staff members who need vehicles only sporadically. Having a few bicycles to share is also popular.
- Provide public transit passes and maps in attendees' welcome packets.
- Provide incentives to cycle or walk to events. And allow time between events for an enjoyable walk.
- If business attire is not important, encourage dressing down so attendees feel comfortable walking or biking to events.
- Provide carbon-offset opportunities for attendees.

Transportation Vendors

Inform potential transportation companies of the sponsoring organization's environmental commitment and initiatives and ask about their environmental practices. Include a clause in the contract with the transportation provider that confirms their commitment to comply with the environmental requests.

Ground Transportation

The following are questions to ask when choosing a ground transportation company:

- Do they perform environmentally responsible maintenance and recycle used oil, batteries, antifreeze, and tires?
- Do they train drivers to minimize idling and use of air conditioners, especially when no passengers are in the vehicle?
- Do they offer fuel-efficient or alternative fuel vehicles? Or, are they willing to use bio-diesel fuel in their existing vehicles?

Shipping Freight

When choosing a freight carrier for supplies, keep in mind the environmental costs and ask the carrier about them, including reducing and recycling packaging. Use the questions in the air or ground transportation sections of this chapter to choose a carrier.

Carbon Offsets

To offset inevitable emissions from an event, carbon offsets are often offered on behalf of the event and participants. A carbon offset is a way of counteracting the carbon emitted when the use of fossil fuel causes greenhouse gas emissions. Offsets commonly involve investing in projects such as renewable energy, tree planting, and energy efficient projects. Meeting managers attempting to green their meeting will likely hear quite a bit about carbon-offset programs and they will need a basic understanding of the complicated world of carbon offsets.

- *Carbon Offset Programs*—Various programs are available to calculate the emissions caused by the energy use associated with events. Resources include the Climate Trust's carbon counter (http://www.carboncounter.org), which is used for calculating the carbon emissions involved in travel, and the Leonardo Academy's Cleaner and Greener Event Certification program to offset most aspects of a conference.
- *Funding a Carbon Offset Program*—There are few scenarios for funding carbon-offset programs that meeting managers currently employ. One option is to use this program as a sponsorship opportunity and publicize that the sponsoring company has offset the entire event's greenhouse gas emissions. This strategy gains powerful recognition for both the sponsor and for the event. A second scenario is to ask attendees to offset their own travel by contributing a specific amount as part of their registration fee (this can range from $6 to $25). Make their contribution optional, then those who participate will be taking an active role in contributing to improving the environment. Or include the offset as part of the conference budget and let attendees know that the organization is doing this on their behalf.

Although travel may never be completely sustainable, it is a necessity. Currently, there is no experience that replaces the face-to-face interaction of humans at meetings and events. There are many choices meeting managers can make with transportation to minimize its effects. So this is an area in managing a green event where it is wise to listen to Buddha's last words, "Do your best."

FOOD AND BEVERAGE

As individuals, meeting managers make personal choices every day. Paper or plastic? Window or aisle? Debit or credit? As meeting managers, they make choices too, but for a their organization and attendees. Beef or chicken? China or disposable? Local or organic? Plated or buffet?

The choices meeting managers make about food and beverages are critical to the well being of their guests, budget, and planet. Meeting managers have the responsibility for making these food choices for the large number of people attending their meetings and events. These choices have become increasingly complicated as guests have come to expect food that fits their daily way of life, whether that is low-carbohydrate, organic, or one of the many other options. Not only do meeting managers make choices about the food and beverages served, but also about how it is served. The following list of ideas will help make those decisions easier:

- *Choose food in season*—From economic, health, and environmental standpoints, choosing food in season in the local area has great benefits. Buying locally grown products helps support the local communities and offers fresher, seasonal, and regional choices without the transportation impact. It is also a great way to celebrate the local flavor of the region. From a green perspective local and organic products are certainly the best if they are available.

- *Choose seafood from sustainable fisheries*—Increased consumer demand for seafood is depleting fish stocks around the world and harming the health of the oceans. Today, nearly 75 percent of the world's fisheries are fully fished or over-fished.[7] Two guides are available to take the guesswork out of menu selection: The Monterey Bay Aquarium publishes Seafood Watch, a guide for consumers. They provide a free pocket guide that can be downloaded and carried (www.montereybayaquarium.org). Blue Ocean Institute publishes the Mini-Guide to Ocean Friendly Seafood. It is available for free at www.blueoceaninstitute.org.

- *Choose food based on the history of the attendees' preferences and attrition*—The meeting manager should know the group's preferences (e.g., whether a hearty salad is plenty for them, or a full warm meal is necessary) and can order accordingly. In addition, guarantee meals based on their history. Are they early risers and all show up for breakfast or do they arrive just before the general session—rushing in at the last minute and grabbing a cup of coffee? Do they skip the conference lunch to have smaller business meetings at local restaurants? If there is no history for the group, ask attendees to sign up for meals in advance. This will save both money and food.

- *Choose china service*—Disposable cups, plates, and flatware not only add to the landfills, they do not have the same "first-class" service experience. The Environmental Defense Council reports, "Using 1,000 disposable plastic teaspoons consumes over 10 times more energy and natural resources than manufacturing one stainless steel teaspoon and washing it 1,000 times."[8] Using cloth instead of paper napkins also adds to the experience.

- *Choose not to serve individual water bottles*—Serving water from large pitchers or containers saves a tremendous amount of money ($5 to $10 per guest per day depending upon the venue). For one conference, that was $25,000 in savings over the course of the conference.[9] Additionally, it also saved all those plastic bottles from getting into the waste stream.

According to the Oregon Food Bank, one in five people in Oregon and southwestern Washington eat donated food at least once a year. Thirty-eight percent of these people are children. Most likely, the statistics are similar in most communities. Donating leftover food from conferences and events is an important component of social responsibility. There are some urban myths surrounding food donation and legal liability. Meeting managers should know about the Good Samaritan Food Donation Act:

Federal legislation provides limited liability to food donors, absent gross negligence or intentional misconduct. The Emerson Good Samaritan Food Donation Act converts Title IV of the National and Community service Act of 1990, known as the Model Good Samaritan Food Donation Act, into permanent law within the Child Nutrition Act of 1966. Specifically, the Act states that donors (persons, gleaners, and nonprofits) shall not be subject to civil or criminal liability arising from the nature, age, packaging, or condition of apparently wholesome food or apparently fit grocery products received as donations. Check with the state attorney general's office to ascertain whether the federal statute takes precedence over any applicable state Good Samaritan law.[10]

The law was signed by President Clinton on October 1, 1996. It is designated as House Rule 2428, 42 United States Code 12672, Section 402. Check with local food banks for a complete text of the law and any interpretation which has been given to it by legal counsel. Donated food must meet applicable health department regulations.[11]

At the time of this printing, no case involving food donation liability has been brought before a U.S. court. However, a surprising number of catering departments are not aware of this and have no established relationship with local food banks. Write a clause into the contract requiring the hotel or caterer to donate leftover food and request they start an ongoing program. This is a wonderful legacy to leave behind.

A good deal of the food and beverage waste is in both the packaging and the serving. The following are tips for reducing this waste:

Purchasing and Packaging

- Request minimal packaging on all food products.
- Purchase environmentally responsible cleaning products.

Serving

- Eliminate or minimize use of forest-based and petroleum-based products, such as paper plates and plastic eating utensils.
- Do not allow polystyrene products to be used.
- Use cloth instead of paper napkins. If cloth is not available, use recyclable napkins with a high post-consumer content.
- Use china and glassware when possible.
- Use biodegradable, disposable serviceware when possible.
- Serve condiments, spreads, and jams in bowls (or appropriate containers) rather than in individually wrapped packages.
- Serve water and juice in pitchers, and soft drinks in returnable containers.
- Consider using reusable beverage containers. Consider offering a conference mug and stock corporate meeting spaces with glassware.
- Do not preset drinking water; serve it upon request at banquets.
- Eliminate the use of boxes for lunches. Use reusable containers, fabric lunch bags, or picnic baskets.
- Minimize the use of tablecloths, especially for layering.
- Table decorations can include live, potted flowers or plants, a bowl of fruit, or a special dessert on a pedestal.
- Provide signage that tells attendees whether food is locally grown, organic, or seasonal.

Reduce, Reuse, and Recycle

- The venue and caterer should recycle paper, glass, plastics, cans, aluminum, corrugated boxes, and kitchen grease.
- Provide recycling bins for paper, bottles, and cans. Assure the bins are actually used for recycling. If the facility does not have recycling capability, contract with an independent hauler to provide and remove recycling bins.
- Food and food-contaminated paper waste should be composted.

EXHIBITION PRODUCTION

Exhibitions and trade shows are often the component of a conference or event that has the most significant impact on the environment. Exhibitions use large amounts of energy, require considerable transportation, and generate a tremendous amount of waste—all of which affect air quality. For example, a 3-day conference with 496 exhibit booths and 8100 attendees can consume over 617,000 kilowatt hours of electricity, over 28,000 thermals of natural gas, and over 376,000 gallons of fuel. Additionally, it is estimated that for a meeting of this size over 8 million tons of carbon is emitted into the air.[12] This example represents only one exhibition held in the United States. Imagine how many are produced daily worldwide.

Other environmental factors to consider are water usage and the products and services purchased to produce the show. Food and beverage service and restroom usage are among the larger contributions to water usage during an exhibition. Meeting managers should consider facilities and caterers that have water conservation practices in place. The U.S. Environmental Protection Agency estimates the average conference participant uses 846 gallons of water.[13]

Decisions about products and services can have a considerable environmental impact. Some examples of such decisions follow:

- name badges printed on recycled paper
- recycle name badge holders
- conference bags made of recycled materials
- programs printed on 100% post-consumer recycled paper with soy-based ink

Exhibitions offer a tremendous opportunity to minimize their negative environmental impact by the choices made by the organizers, facility, general services contractor, and exhibitors. Collaboration among those players is crucial to creating an environmentally responsible exhibition or trade show.

It is important to remember that the venue where the exhibition is being held also plays a crucial role in the ability to implement environmental practices. For example, if the venue does not have a recycling program in place, minimizing the impact of waste will be virtually impossible.

The following recommendations help ensure that the exhibit hall floor reflects environmentally responsible practices.

Facility

- Recycle bins on the show floor
- Collection bins for less common materials (batteries, vinyl table coverings)
- Information for exhibitors outlining what material is collected
- An area to donate leftover signage, giveaways, and flowers to schools or civic organizations
- Organization names to contact for the donated items
- Lighting and electrical conservation practices using half-lights and no HVAC during move-in and move-out

General Services Contractor

- Use recycled, recyclable, and/or environmentally responsibly cleaned trade show materials (drapes, carpets)
- Use recyclable or biodegradable shipping and packing materials, such as paper and corrugated boxes instead of polystyrene and plastic wrap
- Coordinate with the organization to collect donated items
- Provide carbon-offset programs for shipping and freight

Meeting Manager

- Accurate expected attendance numbers so exhibitors can bring the corresponding number of materials for distributing, thereby cutting down on waste
- Electronic scan cards for attendee profiles
- A clause in the agreement with the facility and/or general services contractor to:
  - Provide recycling services for cardboard, pallets, paper, cans, plastic, glass, and other recyclable materials that are generated; and provide trained clean-up crews who will keep recyclable and reusable items out of the garbage
  - Request specific environmental practices
  - Make available measured results of recycling materials, waste, and any water or energy conversation data
- A clause in the exhibitor agreement to comply with the following:
  - Minimize the use of collateral materials and, for any necessary materials, request they are produced on post-consumer paper stock, using vegetable-based inks.
  - Minimize their packaging and participate in recycling packaging when appropriate.
  - Use recycled or consumable products as giveaways when possible and do not use gift items made from endangered or threatened species. In addition, attempt to use locally grown/made products.

Exhibitors

- Use soy-based ink and post-consumer recycled paper to produce materials
- Use recycled or consumable products as giveaways
- Do not have gift items made from endangered or threatened species
- Avoid bringing large quantities of collateral materials—send them upon request instead
- Trade show booths to be made from sustainable or reusable materials and/or designed as environmentally consciously as possible
- Minimize packaging materials and/or use recyclable or biodegradable shipping and packing materials
- Purchase supplies that have minimal packaging
- Assist the move in/out process with recycling of cardboard, freight boxes, and plastic wrap

COMMUNICATION AND MARKETING

Communication and marketing are not just about the paper, ink, and electronic methods used, they are about spreading the word and building understanding. They are about sharing with the media, employees, attendees, stakeholders, and

Fast Facts

Spread the Word

Share what efforts that are being done with everyone.

the world the difference the meeting manager is making by planning the event in an environmentally and socially responsible way.

Share what efforts that are being done with everyone. This point is often overlooked; but it is vital to the continued success of a green program. Tell the sponsoring organization's board, the membership, meeting attendees, the press, peers, and clients. Communicate all environmentally responsible efforts in all promotional materials, including press releases, conference programs, and web sites.

Publishing the green practices of meetings in a case study with quantifiable results is an excellent marketing piece for the conference and sponsoring organization. Post it on the conference web site for all to review. Meeting managers should share data with professional associates. They will be interested in what efforts were done, how it was done, and the outcomes. Networking with other meeting managers who employ green meeting practices is important as well.

Meeting managers should submit a press release or write an article for their organizational newsletter, industry trade publication, or local media. Include statistics and quotes from attendees on how their participation in a green meeting affected the quality of their experience.

Apply for an award. There are award programs for green management in the environmental and social arenas as well as from meeting management organizations. These awards showcase the exciting, new innovations in green meeting practices.

The following are communication and marketing ideas that engage and involve attendees:

- Appoint recycling advisors to assist attendees.
- Give attendees a prize when caught doing something right.
- Provide walking and public transportation maps so attendees can visit the city without renting a car.
- Suggest attendees take full advantage of the hotel's commitment to reuse linens, turn off lights, and participate in their recycling programs. Also suggest they pass on the daily paper unless they intend to read and recycle it.
- Encourage attendees not order room service or take out.
- Ask attendees to bring their favorite water bottle or coffee cup from home.
- Provide a list of suggestions for attendees to continue the effort back home. Make the list available on the conference web site or through confirmation or follow-up emails.
- Include questions in the formal evaluation about the event's environmental stewardship and attendees' suggestions on how to build on the success.

The event's communication materials should also demonstrate the organization's commitment to environmental responsibility. For the more formal communication involved with a conference, the following green practices are recommended:

- Reduce paper usage by using the web and email lists to promote events. Publish the registration brochure online.
- If a flyer needs to be mailed, use post-consumer content, chlorine-free paper printed on both sides with vegetable-based inks.
- Send media and sponsorship packets electronically.
- Conduct all conference correspondence via email.
- Encourage online registration and send confirmation emails to attendees.
- Use name badges made of recycled material; collect and reuse them after the conference.

- Consider not providing a conference bag. If one is provided, make sure attendees have an option not to take one and let them know it will be donated on their behalf. Also, ensure the bag is made from eco-friendly materials.
- Limit sponsor handouts for the bags or print all sponsor information in a newsletter format that is produced in an eco-friendly way.
- Consider making the final program available for PDAs (personal data assistants) instead of on paper.
- Ask hotels for electronic check in/check out services. All correspondence with hotels should be electronic, including BEOs.

OFFICE PROCEDURES FOR CONFERENCES AND EVENTS

Recycling at home is probably being done already, but what about the office and conference? The command base for green meeting management should exemplify the principles of environmental responsibility.

The following practices apply to an on-site office at a conference or event. While these recommendations are not comprehensive, nor do they consider all aspects of a work space, they can be applied directly to any work environment.

General Practices

Whether in the office at work or at an event, energy-efficient equipment provides both cost and environmental savings:

- Purchase/rent Energy Star™ products.
- When purchasing/renting laser printers, choose a model that reduces energy consumption when idle.
- Consider using a laptop computer. On average laptops use only 10 percent or less of the energy consumed by desktop computers.
- Buy recharged toner cartridges.
- Choose copy machines that can duplex all documents. Also look for a machine that can also handle multiple functions such as a fax and printer.
- Encourage employees to turn off equipment and lighting and turn down thermostats when leaving for extended periods of time.

Communications

- Email communications whenever possible.
- When emailing is not possible, make double-sided copies using paper with at least 30 percent post-consumer recycled content.
- Ask attendees to sign up for hand-outs or proceedings.
- Make sure email and mailing lists are kept up-to-date.
- Use signage that can be reused whenever possible. Directional signage can be used with different clients and organizations. Signage from the same organization can be used again if the year and destination do not appear.
- Use the hotel's in-room television station to publish information.
- Ask for recycled paper flipcharts.

Recycling

- Make sure to use the facility's recycling systems to recover cardboard, paper, glass, cans, glass, batteries, and toner cartridges.
- Donate all leftover supplies (including conference bags) to a local school or day care.

SUMMARY

The outcomes of this chapter for the learner were for the reader to be able to define what a green meeting is, to explain why green meetings are important, to apply green practices to make a meeting or event more environmentally responsible, and to be able to implement those practices. Remember, green meeting management is not an extra step to take, or even more work. The green practices outlined in this chapter can and should be incorporated into current practices of finding a venue, choosing a hotel, ordering food and beverages, and communicating with the organization's stakeholders. The ability to utilize these practices will put the meeting manager at the cutting-edge of meeting management and increases their value to their organization.

Green meetings and events can save organizations money while reducing their impact on the environment. It does not need to be done all at once. Start anywhere in the process, but just start.

REFERENCES

1. Meeting Strategies Worldwide. (2000). Conference data. Unpublished raw data.

2. Little, Amanda. (2005, May 10). It was just my ecomagination, *Grist magazine*, Retrieved April 18, 2006 from http://www.grist.org/news/muck/2005/05/10/little-ge/index.html

3. The Green Meetings Task Force, Convention Industry Council. (2004, April 6; Updated 2004, June 15). *Green meetings report*. Retrieved April 18, 2006 from http://www.conventionindustry.org/projects/green_meetings_report.pdf

4. Green Seal, Inc. (2002, April 19). *Virginia case studies report: Environmental pollution prevention opportunity assessments for the hospitality industry*, Retrieved April 18, 2006 from http://www.deq.state.va.us/p2/lodging/pdf/report.pdf

5. Meeting Strategies Worldwide. (2002). Greenbuild International Conference and Expo data. Unpublished raw data.

6. Meeting Strategies Worldwide. (2002). Conference data. Unpublished raw data, p. 8.

7. Monterey Bay Aquarium. Seafood watch guide, frequently asked questions. Retrieved April 18, 2006 from http://www.mbayaq.org/cr/SeafoodWatch/web/sfw_faq.aspx

8. Environmental Defense Fund. (1998, June). An ounce of prevention: Think before you buy, *EDF Letter, XXIX: 3,7*.

9. Meeting Strategies Worldwide. International conference and expo 2004 data collected.

10. APPENDIX C: Text of Emerson Good Samaritan Food Donation Act, PUBLIC LAW 104-210. (1990). Retrieved April 18, 2006 from http://www.usda.gov/news/pubs/gleaning/appc.htm

11. Chef's collaborative. Retrieved February 15, 2006 from http://www.chefnet.com/cc2000.

12. Meeting Strategies Worldwide. (2004). Greenbuild International Conference and Expo data. Unpublished raw data.

13. United States Environmental Protection Agency (2000). *A method for quantifying environmental indicators of select leisure activities in the United States.* EPA-231-T-00-01.

KEY TERMS

APEX	Fair trade	Processed chlorine free
Biodegradable	Fossil fuel	(PCF)
Carbon offset	Greenhouse effect	Recycled paper
Climate neutral	Kilowatt hour	Recycling
Compost	LEED	Shade grown coffee
Ecological footprint	Organic foods	Trawling
Ecology	PDA	Volatile organic
Ecosystem	Pesticide	compounds (VOC)
Ecotourism	Post-consumer material	
Energy star equipment	Post-consumer waste	

COMPELLING QUESTIONS FOR CONSIDERATION

1. How can the choices a meeting manager makes impact the community in which the event is being conducted?

2. How can you involve meeting attendees in the effort to have environmentally responsible meetings?

3. What are some options in choosing food and beverages to make meal functions less harmful to the environment and benefit the community?

4. What should you look for when choosing an environmentally responsible meeting venue?

5. Name three ways to save money as well as the environment through green meeting practices.

6. What can exhibitors do to minimize their impact on the environment?

7. What do you see as the competitive advantage of green meeting management for your organization?

CHAPTER 31

GUEST PROGRAMS, HOSPITALITY, AND RECREATION

Andrew Schorr
GENERAL MANAGER
IN THE LOOP CHICAGO, INC.

LEARNER OUTCOMES

When the reader has completed reading this chapter, he/she should be able to . . .

1 Discuss the importance of providing hospitality and recreation events in conjunction with a meeting.

2 Describe the services a destination management company can provide.

3 Develop plans for a hospitality suite.

4 Compare the advantages of various child care options at meetings.

> That's the secret of entertaining. You make your guests feel welcome and at home. If you do that honestly, the rest takes care of itself.
>
> *Barbara Hall*

OVERVIEW

One of the extra touches that can enhance a meeting is providing attendees and their guests with opportunities for social interaction and recreation. If such hospitality events and optional activities are well planned and marketed, they can also boost meeting attendance, add value to the meeting experience, and enhance the image of the organization. This chapter will focus on how to develop hospitality and recreational activities in conjunction with meetings and conventions. Strategies for developing a budget to pay for these programs will also be discussed.

GUEST PROGRAMS

Attendees' spouses are not the only ones to be considered when planning guest hospitality programs. It is increasingly common for children to accompany their parents to meetings, and for unmarried professionals to bring traveling companions and significant others. As a result, meeting managers must design guest, hospitality, and recreation programs to appeal to a wide range of interests.

Whether a meeting manager is planning guest programs sponsored by the organization or events for which guests must purchase tickets, the first step in the planning process is research. Gather demographic information on attendees and guests (age, work experience, educational background, interests, and so on.). A meeting manager must maintain a list of previous events with notes on which ones were successful, which were not, and why. More importantly, meeting managers must keep a history of these events, including the number of guests who preregistered and the number who actually attended. If a conference has an international contingency, it is important to track those specific numbers as well and include offerings that will appeal to that audience. Tracking the price points and scheduled times of each guest program is important as these are factors that can affect attendance. It is also a good idea to ask for feedback from both those who attended each event and those who did not to find out what factors influenced their decision. As appropriate, meeting managers should consider putting together a comment card to secure immediate feedback following the participant's tour or activity experience. Managers should set a participation goal for their guest program and determine the best avenues to reach their audience.

Destination Management Companies

A local destination management company (DMC) can arrange and manage almost any activity for a meeting, saving both money and staff time. Most DMCs offer a range of services, including special events, tours, transportation, guides, theme parties, entertainment, airport greeting, VIP gifts, staffing hospitality rooms, and providing registration and housing services.

Meeting managers can find a DMC through the local convention and visitor bureau (CVB), the Association of Destination Management Executives, or through recommendations from other meeting planners or your hotel convention services manager. Meeting managers should select a DMC as far in advance of the meeting as possible in order to ensure the maximum amount of time for planning events that are well suited to the needs and interests of the attendees and guests. Meeting managers must clearly define the organization's needs, the selection process and the scope of those services required from DMCs and then decide on the number of DMCs they would like to interview for their program. Managers must also establish a list of DMC profile characteristics that will best suit the culture of their organization.

Provide the DMC with attendance projections, as well as demographic information, and ask about the following:

- Tour and program suggestions, both creative and classic to the destination
- Current price of proposed tours and anticipated increases, if any; request price ranges to best understand what is appropriate for the destination
- Deadline for supplying final count for each tour
- Date by which each tour or program can be canceled without penalty
- Number and experience of company staff
- Qualifications of tour guides and group escorts, what are the DMC's resources for securing and training staff
- Type, condition, and capacity of buses, as well as minimum and maximum hours
- Process for developing tours and activities
- Qualifications and process for selecting vendor partners
- Opportunities to experience a tour or meet one of the organization's guides
- Written format and descriptions, photos, and videos to be used for promotion
- Signage
- Insurance
- Method of collecting fees or payments
- Online guest program registration and marketing capabilities
- Marketing tools for tour and activity promotion

Ticketed Tours and Events

The most common guest activities are sightseeing tours, educational programs, and demonstrations.

Consider repeating the traditional programs that have proven popular with your group, but also offer new and creative options. Many guests are interested in participating in activities that might not otherwise be available to them. Always consider program possibilities that are unique to the destination — tours of historic areas, local companies, museums, and galleries. It is equally important to include classic tours that the destination is known for. A guest program with a combination of creative and classic offerings tends to be the most successful. Local colleges, universities, theaters, musical groups, and other organizations can also be excellent sources for speakers and entertainment. Another idea is to plan a service project with a local charity, one with a mission that is consistent with the mission of your organization. With strong communication between the organization and the DMC you can make selections that have strong value, timing, and content, which are essential to any guest program.

A successful guest program offers unique options that attendees would not necessarily find on their own. Provide as many options as possible (at different price points), including half-day and full-day tours with and without lunch, in-house seminars, and demonstrations. But do not create an overly demanding schedule or provide too many choices that might cause options to compete with

Put It Into Practice

Be sure to create recreational events that are appropriate for both genders and all fitness levels. Morning walks, aerobics, and yoga are all excellent options.

There are more and more hotels that have spa facilities for those looking for facials, massages, body scrubs, wraps, and hair and nail treatments.

each other, as this will affect attendance and could force program cancellations if there are minimum attendance requirements.

Additionally, provide information on local attractions and shopping for those who wish to explore the destination on their own. Be aware of any special exhibits or events that may be occurring during the program that might be of interest to participants. Extra touches that are appreciated include signs, name badges, and small gifts (such as a book or photo) as mementos of the event.

Budget

Whether the guest programs and hospitality are subsidized by the organization, sponsored, or paid for entirely by participants, develop a budget that includes cost controls and provides an accurate overview of program income and expenses. Meeting managers must make sure that if they are adding fees to prices the DMC has quoted that they are not inflating the price of the offerings to the point that it makes the option too expensive or unappealing.

Among the budget items to be included are:

- Income from registration fees, ticket sales, sponsorships, donations, as appropriate
- Tour costs (guides, DMC registration fees, admission fees, transportation, food and beverage, taxes, gratuities)
- Costs associated with on-site tour desk ticket distribution and sales
- Speaker fees, honoraria, transportation, per diem
- Hospitality room (supplies, equipment, furniture, food and beverage, flowers, signs)
- Badges and holders, tickets
- Amenities and gifts (e.g., bags, souvenirs)
- Promotional expenses
- Expenses for in-house programs (audiovisual, microphones, other equipment, and supplies)

When meeting managers use a DMC, they must be sure that the budget reflects the method of paying their fees. Some charge on a per-person basis, while others charge a percentage of the total cost. These costs can be built into the ticket prices for individuals, if desired, or absorbed by the organization.

Promotion and Publicity

Provide detailed information on all guest programs in the meeting information sent to attendees. If online registration is available, meeting managers should include all guest programs and special events. This will provide instant updates on the number of reservations made for each event or tour. Meeting managers must ensure that access to their online guest program is easy to get to and has good visibility. The DMC may have marketing suggestions on ways to best promote the options and drive participation.

Put It Into Perspective

Corporations use golf outings as rewards as well as networking activities. They may bring in golf pros to give clinics and/or play with the guests.

Associations very often use golf tournaments as fundraisers. Sponsorships are sold to create a revenue stream in addition to the golf registration fee.

If there is to be a special program for a select group of individuals (e.g., the guests of the board of trustees), meeting managers should send them information about the day's events, including date, time, location, a description of the event, and possibly suggestions on appropriate attire.

Prepare registration packets for guests that include a name badge, meeting program, required tickets, a map of the area, and information on restaurants, attractions, and shopping.

The Hospitality Suite/Room

Audience responses often confirm that attendees are more alert, attentive, and receptive when opportunities for social interaction and recreation are available during the meeting. Guests also enjoy having a place to relax, mingle, and obtain information. The hospitality suite (or hospitality room) is usually viewed as a social gathering place where attendees may meet up with their guests during the day, or for guests to meet and socialize with other guests. If the size and type of meeting warrants this service, be certain to designate space and develop a budget to support it properly.

The hospitality suite should be comfortable and aesthetically pleasing. Sometimes it is possible to secure a room near the pool, cabana, or tennis courts, or a strategically located suite near other meeting activities. There are several ways to make the room comfortable and enticing. First, provide comfortable furniture, either from the facility or through the show decorator. Decorate tables with colorful linens and floral arrangements. Second, provide plenty of refreshments. Coffee, tea, soft drinks, and water are mainstays. Depending upon the budget, add juices, muffins, and rolls or croissants in the morning; cookies and fruit in the afternoon; and hors d'oeuvres and bar service later in the day. Make sure the catering department schedules several cleanups and refreshes food and beverages regularly. Third, stock the room with information about the city. The room should be staffed with a host, especially if alcohol is available. An added plus is to hire staff through your DMC to provide local information on sites, attractions, restaurants, and so on. Select staff that will best suit audience in the hospitality suite.

There are clear differences between how associations and corporations use, and/or fund hospitality suites. For example at an association convention with an exhibition component, exhibiting companies may use suites as an event marketing or sponsorship recognition opportunity. Some associations have a hospitality suite for long-time members. Associations may all use them as a gathering area for their tour and activity program. Typically they are located within the headquarter hotel of the convention. Corporate groups, such as incentives or as part of sales meeting use the more traditional hospitality suite for social and networking opportunities.

CULTURAL EVENTS

Many meeting attendees appreciate a schedule that allows them time to explore the destination. You can provide options for cultural or sporting events, or arrange to add a performance to the social program.

The easiest way to provide entertainment options is to work with the hotel concierge or DMC to compile a referral list of cultural and sporting events, as well as special exhibits at museums and galleries, thus allowing attendees and their guests to make their own reservations. The information provided should include descriptions of the events, dates, times, locations, ticket prices, payment options, addresses and phone numbers of facilities, and transportation. Some hotels will send a member of the concierge staff to your hospitality room to assist attendees and guests.

If you decide to reserve a block of tickets or buy the house for an event, consider the following suggestions:

- Consider using the DMC to handle cultural events as part of the guest program offerings.
- Decide whether the organization wishes to accept ticket orders to maintain control of the tickets, or whether orders will be received and processed by the theater/facility directly.
- Decide on the specific number of tickets to be held and the date the remaining tickets revert to theater/facility management for sale to the general public.
- Decide whether tickets will be mailed directly to attendees, or whether they should pick them up with their registration materials.

There is some risk associated with reserving a block of tickets, as the organization may be required to guarantee the number of tickets that will be sold.

SPORTS ACTIVITIES AND TOURNAMENTS

Many people have become more health conscious and welcome opportunities to exercise. Provide attendees with information on exercise and recreation options and facilities within or near the hotel or convention center.

Sporting events can be excellent opportunities for networking and team building. When planning sporting events, keep in mind that the goal is for everyone to have a good time. Maintain a balance between competition and enjoyment, so that both the best players and less skilled participants can enjoy themselves. Some organizations successfully offer concurrent events for less athletic attendees.

The key to producing a successful sporting event is the advice and assistance of professionals and volunteers who are active in the sport. There are many consultants, including DMCs and team-building professionals, available. However, the best advice and guidance often comes from within the organization. Select a member of the sponsoring organization to serve as chair of the event, someone who participates regularly in the sport and can assist with both organizing and marketing.

If looking for ways to conduct a sports tournament, but have a limited budget, consider bringing in sponsors. Whether sponsoring the entire tournament or an individual segment, a sporting event offers an excellent marketing opportunity for the right vendor, while helping to offset the costs and providing a great event for attendees.

Golf Tournaments

Once the course for a golf tournament is selected, contact the golf pro or director of golf at the course. This individual can provide valuable advice regarding which format works best on the course, help make logistical arrangements, and coordinate the tournament. Provide the pro with a history of other tournaments the organization has held, the estimated number of participants, and their skill levels (handicaps). (Note: Handicapping is a system used in amateur events and tournaments that allows golfers of varying abilities to compete on the same level.)

Advance registration of golfers is necessary for the receipt of fees (if the tournament is not hosted) and to obtain information such as the golfer's handicap, shirt size (if giveaways are ordered), and any other special requests. This is also a good time to relay information, such as playing hours, deadline for turning in score cards, transportation arrangements, and any local ground rules or special instructions.

One type of tournament recommended by the U.S. Golf Association is the shotgun scramble. Teams of four are formed based on handicaps, with good, intermediate, and inexperienced players mixed together. The "shotgun" refers to the fact that everyone will start at the same time from a different hole with the goal of completing play at approximately the same time. In the scramble format, every player tees off, but the team plays its second shot from where the best first drive landed (the other three shots are not counted). Play continues in this manner through putting. The most ideal aspect of this type of tournament is that it ensures speedy play and makes all players comfortable, regardless of their skill level. An added bonus is the team building that occurs.

A scramble is not the only option available for your organization or corporate golf tournament. In a best-ball tournament, each golfer in a foursome plays his or her own ball from tee to cup, but only the best score on each hole is counted. There are many variations of this type of tournament; such as having a two or three best-ball event, meaning you count two or three of the best scores of the foursome on each hole. These tournaments are usually geared toward the better golfers, since all holes will be finished by each foursome member.

Other tournament formats to consider are an individual stroke tournament (lowest score for 18 holes, with adjustments for handicaps), or team match-play (each golfer is paired with an opponent and whoever wins the most holes, regardless of overall score, wins the match). These two types of tournaments are best for very skilled and competitive golfers, and may not be appropriate for a tournament with golfers of varying skill levels.

There are many other options for organizing a tournament. The golf pro or director of golf can provide more suggestions, including providing a golf clinic before the tournament if your budget permits.

Additional considerations when planning a golf tournament include providing shirts, making food and beverage arrangements (such as a beverage cart), and photo opportunities.

Prizes may be awarded for both low-gross and low-net scores. A closest-to-the-hole prize on a par three and a longest-drive prize on a par five are also appropriate awards. Keep in mind the inevitable tie-breaking play for duplicate prizes. Also, when ability levels vary, it may be a good idea to provide prizes based upon participation rather than skill.

Tennis

As with planning a golf tournament, the best advice on planning a tennis event may be found within the sponsoring organization membership. Well in advance of the meeting, select a member to serve as chair of the tournament. The chair can work either with a DMC or directly with the hotel or sports facility. Since all participants cannot be on the courts at the same time, advance planning is required to schedule a smooth-running tournament. Obtain a commitment from the tennis pro or courts manager regarding the number of courts that can be made available. A written letter followed by an acknowledgment verifying the arrangements is essential. Advise the tennis pro or courts manager how much time can be devoted to the event and discuss an appropriate schedule.

Instead of a tournament, another option is to schedule specific court times for attendees to reserve or to provide an instruction session with the tennis pro.

Other Sports Activities

If the meeting is located at a facility on or near water, several sports and recreation opportunities may be available, depending upon the time of year. Many hotels and resorts have departments that make arrangements for guests to

---

Fast Facts

- There are 12.8 million adult golfers in the United States.
- Twenty percent of adult golfers are women.

participate in water sports, including water skiing, fishing, boating, scuba diving, and snorkeling.

DMCs can arrange group activities, including scavenger hunts, fun runs, team-oriented sporting events, field days, and other team-building activities.

When planning outdoor events, be prepared with alternate plans in case of inclement weather, and be aware of how cancellations or delays due to weather affect contract performance and deposits.

CHILD CARE PROGRAMS

According to the Travel Industry Association of America, 15.3 million business trips in 2003 included children, more than half (53%) were taken by parents who are Baby Bommers (35-54).[1] The factors that influence the statistics vary from an increase in two-career couples and single parents to parents wishing to combine business trips with vacation or simply desiring to spend more time with their children. Whatever the reasons, the growing number of attendees bringing children to meetings means that meeting planners are increasingly being asked to provide child care programs.

The first step in planning for a child care program is determining the need. First consider the destination city or resort location. Some cities are viewed as more child-friendly than others. What are the attendee demographics? For example, Generation X parents are statistically more likely to travel with their children, and professional parents appreciate the educational value of travel in general, and some destinations in particular.

Here are some questions to be considered:

- Would offering a child care program be a way of recognizing the needs and diversity of the organization's members?
- Is offering a child care program in line with the organization's core mission?
- Have attendees taken or attempted to take their children onto the show floor?
- Have exhibitors or the exhibit manager complained about having children on the show floor?
- Have children shown up at inappropriate places, such as the president's gala?
- Have attendees complained about the distraction of having children in educational sessions?
- Have children been seen in the hallways of the meeting facility?
- Would there be more meeting attendees if a child care program were available?

If the answer to any of these questions is "yes," it may be time to offer a children's program that recognizes the needs of your attendees.

When selecting a child care program, it is important to understand that one size does not fit all. For some groups, the best solution to child care concerns is to offer parents a referral list of babysitting services. For other groups, because of the meeting location (e.g., a resort), it is best to use the hotel child care service. But for many groups, the best choice is for the meeting planner to work with a child care company to create a customized program to accommodate the various age groups and interests of the children, as well as the meeting hours. Such companies can provide off-site field trips, and age-appropriate activities and entertainment.

While referral systems, hotel services, and companies specializing in child care and children's programs are all valid options for meeting planners, there is one option that is never a good idea. It is not advisable for the organization sponsoring the meeting set up a child care program on its own because of the liability, risk, and financial burden involved.

Referral System

The most cost-effective plan is to provide a referral child care list of bonded and licensed child care agencies. Two good sources for this information are the CVB and the hotel concierge.

Before publishing agencies' names and numbers, check their references and ask the following questions:

- Is the agency insured and bonded?
- Do they have experience working with conventions?
- Are bilingual care providers available?
- What are the operating hours?
- How close are they to the convention center or hotel?
- What are the ages and maximum number of children they will accept?
- Do they provide transportation?
- Are they equipped to serve children with disabilities?
- What are the daily and hourly rates?

Once a list of qualified agencies is provided, it is up to the parents to make arrangements directly with the agency. It is very important that the sponsoring organization publish a liability disclaimer releasing the organization from responsibility for any arrangements.

Hotel Services

Many hotel chains have recognized the needs of today's business travelers by expanding their services to include day camps and play areas. The advantages of such programs are that they are generally high quality, the meeting planner's only role is to publish the contact information, and parents make all of the arrangements. The disadvantages are that the hours often do not coincide with meeting hours, the age range is usually limited to children 3 years old and older, and they are open to all hotel guests, not just meeting attendees. So in order to address the security concerns of parents, you may want to provide an exclusive program for meeting attendees.

Child Care and Children's Programming Services

A convention child care program is designed to care for the children of convention attendees during a meeting, reception, special event, or exhibition. Several companies specialize in providing child care on-site, tailored to the needs of meeting attendees, their children, and the meeting schedule. The child care program will be located at the convention center or headquarters hotel.

These companies are, in essence, destination management companies for children, and are staffed with qualified and trained caregivers. The services they provide include complete care and programs for children of all ages, coordination of children's events, customized tours and companion programs, age-appropriate parties, teen hospitality suites, and registration. They also work with planners on promotional materials.

The following checklist can be used when selecting a child care/children's programming company:

- How long has the company been in business?
- Does the company have experience in the convention and meeting market?

- Is a complete list of client references available?
- What is the average number of years of experience of caregivers?
- Are background checks performed on staff members?
- What kind of training does the staff receive?
- Are they trained and equipped to handle children with disabilities?
- Are they trained in pediatric first aid and CPR (cardiopulmonary resuscitation)?
- Does the company have written policies on safety and security?
- Are they licensed and bonded?
- What level of insurance do they provide?
- Can your organization be added as additionally insured?

Risk Management

In order to manage risk and limit liability, it is fundamental that all parents registering their children for care sign a disclaimer releasing your organization from any potential liability. The waiver should also grant authorization for any necessary emergency medical treatment. The release must state the name of the person or persons who have the authority to take custody of the child. As part of the program, security measures such as numbered wristbands, photo identification, and verified signatures should be provided.

Safety and Security

Child care licensing agencies recommend a minimum of 35 square feet per child; however, in convention child care programs, the standard is 50 square feet per child. The program should be held in rooms with both smoke detectors and sprinkler systems. It is advisable that the room is away from heavily trafficked areas. The room should be child-proofed, and it may be prudent to inquire whether the provider offers a beeper service in order to contact parents in an emergency.

Name tags should be used for all children. And a plan for check-in and check-out must be developed to prevent children from leaving with someone other than the authorized person.

SUMMARY

Since many meeting attendees are accompanied by family members, companions, and guests, arranging guest programs and child care options has become an important part of meeting planning. When guest, hospitality, and child care programs are well planned, received and marketed, they can help boost meeting attendance and enhance the sponsoring organization's image.

Destination management companies (DMCs) can provide valuable assistance with optional meeting activities. Most DMCs offer a full range of services, including special events, tours, transportation, guides, theme parties, entertainment, airport greeting, VIP gifts, and staffing hospitality rooms. They should be used as the local destination experts.

The most common guest activities are sightseeing tours, educational programs, and demonstrations.

Programs that are unique to the destination are especially popular, such as tours of historic areas, local companies, museums, and galleries. It is a good idea to provide as many options as possible, including half-day and full-day tours, in-house seminars, and demonstrations.

A hospitality room or suite can also enhance the meeting experience for attendees and guests by providing a place to relax, mingle, and obtain information about the city. The room should be attractive, comfortable, and well stocked with refreshments.

Sports and recreation activities are excellent opportunities for networking and team building. The key to success is to maintain a balance between competition and enjoyment, so that both the best players and less skilled participants can enjoy themselves. Professionals and volunteers who are active in the sport can provide valuable assistance in planning sports tournaments, and there are also many consultants available, including DMCs and team-building professionals.

There are a number of options to consider when planning child care programs, including referral systems, hotel services, and companies that specialize in providing child care and children's programming services for meetings and conventions.

REFERENCES

1. Travel Industry Association (2005). Domestic travel fast facts – travel trends from "A to Z". Retrieved March 31, 2006 from http://www.tia.org/pressmedia/domestic_a_to_z.html.

KEY TERMS

Concierge	Hospitality program	Networking
Demographic	Hospitality suite	Referral child care
Destination management company (DMC)	Liability disclaimer	Sightseeing tours

COMPELLING QUESTIONS FOR CONSIDERATION

1. How does a meeting benefit from the inclusion of hospitality and recreational activities?

2. What questions should be considered when choosing a destination management company?

3. What are the steps involved in planning a golf tournament?

4. What options are available for child care programs and what are the advantages of each?

CHAPTER 32

PLANNING SPECIAL EVENTS

Max Suzenaar
CEO
MINDING YOUR BUSINESS, INC.

LEARNER OUTCOMES

When the reader has completed reading this chapter, he/she should be able to . . .

1 State five different types of special events.

2 Specify when and how to incorporate special events into a meeting or convention.

3 Summarize the process for designing, planning, and producing a special event.

4 Identify the challenges involved in producing special events off-site.

5 Explain the services offered by a special events company or destination management company.

> Our show is a very busy show, and I needed someone to come up with a theme for the dinners and run with it and the only way to do this and have peace of mind was to sit down with the planner and explain exactly how I wanted people to feel when they walked away from the event.[1]
>
> *Terri Bartlett*
> *Vice President of Communications*
> *Toy Industry of America*

OVERVIEW

All meetings, conventions, and conferences are events in the broadest sense of the term. A special event is a unique group activity produced to celebrate a special occasion, recognize the achievement of goals or successes, or network with fellow members or peers. This chapter presents the reasons for incorporating special events into a meeting, describes the different types of special events that might be appropriate, and explains how to produce them within the context of a larger meeting or convention.

WHY PLAN SPECIAL EVENTS?

Special events enhance the meeting or convention experience by making it especially memorable. They can provide an opportunity to relax during a period of intense training or study, increase attendance, reinforce educational messages, and celebrate corporate culture.

Special events can be designed to meet specific marketing or sales goals when they are used for product roll-outs or sales incentive programs, or for client entertainment, providing a relaxed environment for networking and relationship-building. Employee parties, team-building events, and award presentations can build morale and increase corporate teamwork and production. Special events are effective because people are drawn to gatherings that celebrate actions, occasions, and achievements.

TYPES OF SPECIAL EVENTS

Once considered simply "parties," special events have become much more strategic and targeted. In the most general sense, "parties" are social in nature and tend to focus on non-work-related gatherings or occasions. Changes in the economy and in business philosophy have modified how organizations evaluate—and substantiate—the dollars they spend. As a result, special events have evolved to incorporate goals and objectives—honoring attendees, providing networking opportunities for members, celebrating successes, and "wowing" clients.

Today's special events are also much more customized to meet the needs and preferences of their audiences. Whether they are members, clients, or employees, understanding the target audience is a key variable in the initial planning an event. For example, an association target audience may comprise several different segments—members, board of directors, sponsors, and exhibitors. A corporate event may encompass very different groups, such as sales people, customers, or executive committee members. Simple demographics, which are basic statistics about the guests attending a special event, will define the target audience. Age range, percentage of male/female attendees, and geographic information can be helpful in designing an event to meet the event's objectives. Additional profile information can also be valuable in the planning stages of an event. If the meeting takes place annually, the planning process should take into consideration the history and locations of previous special events and feedback on them. Drill down a step further and ask questions about the dynamics of the attendees. Are the attendees fun loving? Do they like to dance? Are they conservative? Do they expect to be "wowed" every year? Are they a "meat and potatoes" crowd? Answers to these seemingly simple questions can greatly impact the management and success of a special event.

There are several different types of special events. Those described below are designed to give the reader an overview of the various types of special events that are typically incorporated into a meeting or a conference. However, there are many other types of special events, such as client appreciation events and employee outings that are not necessarily associated with a meeting. These types of events share many of the same characteristics and considerations as those listed below and the same basic management principles apply.

Receptions

Receptions are the most flexible type of event. They can be designed to achieve any number of objectives and, as a result, are used during many meetings. From creating a welcoming and dynamic conference "kick-off" to a bonding closing event, receptions provide an exceptional opportunity to network with peers and build loyalty with attendees.

A common challenge is to make the reception stand out in peoples' memories. Themed parties are a popular and easy solution. An opening night welcome reception featuring local themes enhances the destination. A cowboy theme in Fort Worth, a Caribbean theme in South Beach, or a Blues theme in Chicago will meet attendees' expectations and give them a taste of the local culture and history. Exceptional food, décor, and entertainment can make this an enduring memory for attendees and guests.

Luncheons

Luncheons tend to be the most sedate special events. However, luncheons are unique in that they fulfill a need for attendees (lunch) while creating a forum for education, presentation, and even solicitation. And because they are typically only one to two hours long, attendance is met with strong success. Keynote speakers, annual updates, and recognition programs are common during a seated luncheon. Networking luncheons are typical on the trade show floor to generate interaction among the attendees and exposure to exhibitors.

Because of the business nature of luncheons, the décor can be simple; yet, it still should be "finished." This can be accomplished in a subtle manner with centerpieces, which can enhance the theme with flowers or other creative decorations. Carefully selected linens can create a comfortable and attractive environment for the exchange of ideas, with or without a speaker. Occasionally, luncheons can surprise attendees with unexpected flair or engaging activities, such as incorporating musical or comedy entertainment. Take care to ensure that such entertainment advances the objectives of the meeting and does not become a distraction.

Dinners

Dinners can run the gamut from sedate to exceptionally entertaining events. Awards presentations can be especially difficult to stage in interesting ways. Look for creative ways to recognize people and avoid the usual parade of presenters and recipients across the stage. Staggering the awards presentations throughout the evening and adding some short entertainment in between can be an effective way to hold attendees' interest. Script the program to keep both introductions and acceptance speeches short. Tactfully convey the length of time (one to three minutes) that both the presenters and award winners have in which to speak. Provide some exciting activities as guests enter the venue. Be creative—singers, musicians, stilt walkers, jugglers, or other entertainers greeting the guests at the entrance can set the stage for an exciting evening. Take the event theme to the next level and incorporate it into the menu. Dessert is an opportunity to provide a great climax to an outstanding dinner. Set off fireworks and drop a curtain to reveal a pyrotechnic dessert buffet, or have flaming desserts created at the table.

Galas

A dinner becomes a gala when it is planned as a particularly lavish and festive occasion. Galas frequently require formal dress and are commonly used to close a meeting or conference, or are held mid-meeting and combined with awards presentations. A gala can serve the function of community building through celebration and recognition, as well as promoting the following year's program.

More formal dinners or galas usually entail assigned seating. Table numbers should be written on the seating card. Diagrams of the seating chart and layout of the room should be given to banquet staff, sponsoring organization staff, and/or volunteers to direct guests to their tables. An innovative approach to orient guests to the seating arrangements is the use of radio frequency identification (RFID) technology (see Chapter 13).

Fundraisers

Fundraising events are often held as galas and may include silent and/or live auctions or raffles. Be sure to allow time in the program and space in the venue for a silent auction, and make sure that the items are secured (guarded) at all times. These events will have higher ticket prices. It is important (by law) to let the guests know the amount of the ticket price that can be used as a charitable tax deduction. Include this information on the original invitation and on-site program.

MANAGING SPECIAL EVENTS

Because of the many facets and details involved in managing a meeting or conference, logistics tend to drive the process. However, special events are an opportunity for the meeting manager to have a little more freedom. Although managing a special event requires the same attention to detail and flawless execution of logistics, it also requires a creative approach. Every special event presents an opportunity to design a one-of-a-kind experience. It should engage guests and create a lasting memory. Although each event has its own unique features, there are four fundamental steps that are universal in managing any special event:

1. Understand the needs of the group
2. Select a venue
3. Design a "big picture" concept or theme
4. Plan and produce the event

Understanding the Needs

As was mentioned previously, it is important to understand what the objectives of the special event are and the target audience. A simple question to ask when initially planning the event is how success will be defined. This question will help define priorities regarding the qualities and features of the event: What is success for your event? A simple congratulation from the executive director? High marks on post-event surveys? Increased attendance? Rebooking of sponsorship? It could be a number of variables, so it is important to look ahead to ensure that the path to get there is planned properly.

It is also key to have a clear understanding of the budget. Obviously, designing an extravagant event with a limited budget does not make sense. Additional parameters that are important to consider are specific needs or expectations. For example, a CEO may require an opportunity to address his or her guests. Hence, a stage, podium, and microphone with sound system may be required—which will impact the floor plan. From a design standpoint, the speech will impact the flow and the tone of the event. It is important to be aware of each variable and its impact during the early stages of planning the event.

Select a Venue

Identifying the right venue for the experience, flow, and budget is essential. Hotels and convention centers typically negotiate food and beverage minimums as part of their overall contract. Hence, during a meeting many special events will take place within those facilities. Designing an event can be challenging or limiting in these facilities because they are designed to support meetings or trade shows, not special events. Although somewhat of a blank palette, they can seem cavernous, sterile, or uninviting. Transitioning the space may require extensive lighting, décor, and entertainment. Conversely, hotels of more traditional styling may have ornate décor, heavy draperies, and period styling. This holds special challenges when trying to convert the space to a 70s Discothèque or Hawaiian Luau.

Off-site venues can offer wonderful alternatives for hosting special events. There are several benefits and considerations when assessing whether to use an off-site venue for a special event, which are discussed in the section on off-site events later in the chapter.

Design a "Big Picture" Concept or Theme

It is always best to create a central concept or theme for a special event during the early planning stages. This will help spawn innovative ideas with suppliers and create continuity throughout the event. Listed below are a few key considerations for planning and designing an event with a central theme.

Create the Environment

Creating the environment can be one of the most enjoyable tasks in staging a special event. Whether creating upscale ambience for a gala, or a casual theme event for a welcoming reception, the appropriate environment will support the goals and objectives of the event.

Use the venue floor plan as a foundation to design the event. This will allow for balancing both the logistics and flow of the event with the guest's experience. Start "big picture" and plot out where the stage and dance floor will be, key décor elements, and interactive activities. The meeting manager should think of themselves as an attendee and "walk" through the floor plan. What is being seen, heard, and experienced? Be creative and do not be afraid to make mistakes. The meeting manager can make as many changes as they like at this stage of the planning and find that it will quickly evolve into a "big picture" overview of the event. From this point, drill down with more features and details.

Lighting can help create the desired ambience and transition a space in the most effective manner. By using uplighting to highlight props, plants, or room features, and spots or downlighting to highlight food, floral decorations, ice sculptures, or centerpiece displays, can create visual drama that builds excitement. Gobos are gelled spotlights that can be used to project a company logo or theme message onto the wall and provide a more interesting and sophisticated look than traditional banners.

It is most cost-effective to use local resources and existing décor and props. However, custom-designed meeting décor and props can be a very effective way to promote a company or an objective. If working with a limited budget, do not try to spread it too thinly. Instead of covering all of the walls with décor, concentrate available resources on key areas for maximum effect. Coordinate an entrance, stage décor, and something nice on the tables. Centerpieces can carry the entire room if there are sufficient tables, but they should not interfere with the

Fast Facts

An easy litmus test is to establish financial estimates for the 10 basic elements of any special event:

- Venue rental fee
- Food
- Beverages
- Tax
- Gratuity
- Floral
- Linens
- Rentals
- Lighting
- Entertainment

While it is not comprehensive, this simple budget will help determine the overall budget—or how to best allocate monies from an overall budget that is already in place.

other elements of the event. While guests may not be able to talk across a 60-inch or 72-inch round table, it is still inappropriate to use centerpieces that block the view. Depending upon the theme, using a nontraditional table setup, such as square tables or, for smaller groups, one continuous table set banquet style or in a U-shape may enhance the ambience of the event.

Plan and Produce the Event

As the design of the event evolves, the logistics become more prominent and integral to the management process. The success of any design requires a solid and detailed plan for its execution. The following key variables are necessary in planning and executing a successful special event.

Food and Beverage Needs

Food and beverage selections are critical, both in terms of menu selection and style of service. Consider using food stations that are more interactive, featuring chefs preparing entrees in the room, or using "live" props. For example, stage people as part of the display and have them interact with the attendees.

A gala awards presentation requires that the guests are seated, so buffet stations would interfere with the objectives of the event. A theme dessert buffet after the program, however, could add interest to the event and give the guests an opportunity to stretch their legs while networking.

Working directly with the catering manager, meeting managers can develop creative menus and presentations. If the event is large enough and a plated meal will be served, request a tasting to ensure the appropriate food quality and presentation before making a final decision regarding the menu. Acclaimed restaurant chef Will Greenwood asks meeting managers to communicate their group's likes and dislikes, yet be willing to be more adventurous.[2] For the "meat and potatoes" crowd, he suggests considering simple meals that can be memorable, such as juicy roast chicken, truffle mashed potatoes, and haricot vert. Greenwood also suggests asking the chef to serve the food as he would in a restaurant (i.e., stacked and layered rather than placed clockwise around the plate). For example, a grilled veal chop can be placed on garlic mashed potatoes and a bed of braised spinach.[1]

A wine tasting featuring local or regional wines could prove to be a unique and well-received special event for the right group. Ask the chef and sommelier for suggestions for creative pairings of food and wine.

If funds are limited, ask the catering manager to design several sample menus (to include all courses, tax, and gratuity) within the event budget. Also consider issuing a limited number of drink tickets (two) and have a cash bar for the remainder of the beverages.

For more suggestions regarding food and beverages for functions, see Chapter 26.

Providing Entertainment

Entertainment can be a major enhancement to an event. Top-name entertainers can be used to attract attendees, add prestige, and provide an unforgettable experience. Good local bands and entertainers can create atmosphere, get people dancing, and generally add fun to an evening. However, inappropriate or exceptionally loud entertainment can detract from the experience.

The three key factors that influence the choice of entertainment are the budget, the preferences of attendees, and the objective of the event. A good special event manager, destination management company (DMC), or entertainment agency can help locate appropriate acts and maximize the entertainment dollar. Provide them with the demographics of the group, as well as the goals of the meeting and the objective of the particular special event. Be sure to let them know whether certain types of music or humor might be inappropriate for the group. Also, provide the agent with any announcements that the sponsoring organization would like the entertainer(s) to make. Provide the bandleader or booking agent with a copy of the script and/or banquet program. Regularly check with the band leader to let him or her know if the event is on schedule or running late. Each set usually includes a short break (about 10 minutes) every hour. The contract will clearly state that any music performed after the original set will be paid at time and a half. If the budget is flexible, this may not be a problem. If it is tight, there will be a need to keep track of timing and let the band know that they will not be playing overtime.

Before signing any contracts for entertainment, pay close attention to the contract rider. This is an attachment to the contract that describes certain specific requirements, such as travel, accommodations, stage size, lighting, sound, and much more. When signing the entertainment contract this commits the organization to the terms of the rider. The cost of providing the rider requirements is in addition to the contract price. Sometimes this information is included in the body of the contract at no additional cost. Two small areas that the client may seriously want to consider including (even if they are not in the contract) are to provide box lunches and sodas/coffee for the band and to validate or "comp" their parking. This is especially important if the event is at a downtown venue (with expensive parking). Also, find out where freight elevators are located so that the musicians can load their equipment in and out of the hotel/venue. Feeding the band and validating parking can make all the difference to entertainers—it is the little extra touch that is not expensive.

Security

Security is a real-world issue now, so it is important to plan for security and a contingency plan for an emergency (not just rain). Have a couple of staff members or, if necessary, security guards (depending on who is attending the event), stationed at the door to discreetly monitor guests. Many will not wear a badge to an evening gala, but registration staff could also check guests off as they arrive. Even if the doors to a banquet room are closed during the evening, make sure that they are not locked in case people need to leave quickly. Make all guests aware of emergency exits at the beginning of the program.

Accessibility and Special Needs

It is important to determine accessibility for on- or off-site events. Include a question about special needs on the registration form or invitation and follow-up directly with those guests prior to the event. This consideration should also include dietary restrictions.

Engaging Participants

Engaging the audience in opportunities to interact can be an important element in the success of a special event. Interaction can be stimulated through a formal, structured program put together with the assistance of a team-building facilitator, or through employing incidental entertainers who interact with the guests, such as magicians, jugglers, or sketch artists. Depending on the group, a dance can be a wonderful way to engage participants in the spirit of the event.

Invitations

The tone for a special event is set as soon as attendees receive their invitations. For printed invitations, the range of paper choices includes numerous colors and textures. A nontraditional invitation can also help build excitement for the event,

Put It Into Practice

A Checklist for Planning Off-Site Events

- Must transportation be provided for guests? If so, will motor coaches, limousines, minibuses, or something more unique, such as a trolley or double-decker bus?
- If transportation is to be provided, where will the vehicles discharge passengers and where will they park until the conclusion of the event?
- What equipment must be brought in? Does the facility have tables, chairs, platforms, linens and tableware, coat racks, refrigeration, a water source, and sufficient electrical outlets?
- Is the facility accessible to people with disabilities?
- Are there enough restrooms? Where are they located? What is their condition? Plan one toilet per every 100 guests.
- Is the facility heated or air-conditioned?

- Depending upon the weather, will a coat-check area be necessary? If so, are there facilities for this or will they need to be created?
- If it is an outdoor venue, what is the contingency plan in case of inclement weather?
- Is liquor service permitted? Is a permit required?
- What type(s) and quantities of wine, beer, and/or spirits will the caterer be supplying?
- Is there a kitchen? If not, is there an area large enough for the caterer to work?
- Are there times, sound levels, or other local restrictions in place?
- Are permits and licenses required? If so, who is responsible for obtaining them?
- Will the sponsoring organization's insurance cover events at the venue?

such as a "message in a bottle" for an event with an island theme, or even a "talking" invitation that features a recorded message that plays upon opening. Whether the invitation is traditional or not, it must include these key event information:

- Time
- Place
- Address
- Appropriate attire
- RSVP instructions
- An agenda, if appropriate

OFF-SITE EVENTS

Off-site events take special planning and may cost more. However, they provide attendees with an opportunity to experience a unique venue. This is especially important if they have been in a meeting all day. Events can be held at parks, public gardens, pool areas, golf courses, courtyards, historic homes, museums, or any number of other attractive venues.

Many meeting destinations have unique venues that are ideal for a special off-site event. They provide significant value in that each has several features that make them special. Hence, a majority of décor and entertainment elements need to be built into the plan. A museum, for example, offers galleries of art, artifacts, and private viewings of traveling exhibits. Adding simple touches—hors d'oeuvres served on artist palettes, a "create your own dessert art" station, interactive painting stations—can make the theme "pop" and keep attendees engaged.

Some off-site venues are prepared to host events. However, the more unusual venues, will incur additional costs, with the final cost soaring to three to four times as much as for an on-site event. Equipment and furniture may need to be brought in, including tables, chairs, china, silver, and linens. In addition to catering services, there may be a need to hire sound and lighting contractors.

Power can also be a major factor, especially if 220-volt power is required for some of the equipment or for the entertainment. Another consideration may be the need to provide portable lavatories. Mobile trailers with standard restroom facilities are available and are much nicer than the types of portable units used at construction sites.

Outdoor events are the most time-consuming and complicated, and can also be the most expensive. Risk management issues need to be carefully considered and require back-up locations and contingency plans, especially in the event of bad weather. Keep in mind that tents leak and may collapse in high winds. Lack of drainage can also pose problems when using a tent. Inform attendees of how to dress for an outdoor event—what type of shoes to wear and whether to bring a jacket or sweater.

Entertainment can pose special challenges at an off-site event. The contract rider may include conditions that will be difficult or impossible to fulfill at the site; these issues should be addressed before signing. Contracts with major entertainers require payment in full even if the event is canceled due to weather. Make sure entertainers also have directions to the venue, maps, parking information, and so on. Most contracts with entertainers do require a 50% nonrefundable deposit at the time of signing and the balance either 10 days prior to or at the time of the event. The contracts are usually "play or pay." Contractual clauses protect the entertainers, to some degree, from losing revenue if the client cancels.

Catering options at some sites may be limited to a list of approved or exclusive suppliers. In any case, it is best to use a caterer who has worked at the site before.

Transportation and parking are also key considerations. If shuttle transportation is not provided, note where the nearest parking is and provide directions/maps for guests.

Despite the challenges, off-site events usually prove to be truly special events.

SPECIAL EVENTS COMPANY AND DMCs

The design and management of a special event can be done either in-house or by hiring a special events company or DMC. Hiring a special events company or DMC requires the same care used in selecting a meeting site or hiring other meeting suppliers. Trusted meeting managers and professional associations are good sources for recommendations. Local convention bureaus and hotels can also be great referral sources. The International Special Events Society administers the Certified Special Events Professional program. Professionals who have earned that designation have passed a rigorous exam testing their competency, as well as meeting other requirements.

Utilizing these organizations that concentrate on special events can provide many benefits. For example, The Endocrine Society has used a DMC for its last 10 citywide annual meetings, according to Johnnie White, CMP, director of meetings and CME services. White has had DMC's coordinate special events from 100 to 2,000 people. "I probably could not find or have access to a number of venues we have used over the years without the DMC," White said. "DMC's can open doors, where a planner can't ... private homes and mansions, private clubs, private golf resorts," said Karen Gordon, DMCP, president of Activity Planners Inc. in Las Vegas. "If there are certain things that need to be negotiated, venues or vendors would more likely negotiate with the DMC which is a known entity than a one-shot contact they'll never see again," said Linda Simon, DMCP, executive vice president of The Best of Boston Ltd. "You're more likely to have a negotiating relationship with a customer who's back regularly."[3] The combination of knowledge and relationships can create an enviably smooth meeting experience.

The decision to hire a special event manager should be based on several factors. Is there time to plan the event, particularly if this is part of a larger meeting for which the meeting manager is responsible? How sophisticated is the special event and are there in-house creative and technical resources to design, contract, and implement it? Because special event managers have different styles, pricing structures, and specialties, finding the right match for an event may require some research. Be sure to ask for descriptions and photos from events they have managed for similar groups and be sure to check references.

The special event manager can provide creative ideas, negotiate outside vendor costs, develop and manage the event budget, and handle all of the details and logistics involved in producing the event. In addition to planning and design, this will include creating a script for the event and overseeing all aspects of production—from décor and props to entertainment, sound, and lighting.

SUMMARY

Special events are a significant addition to the meeting experience. The objectives of the meeting can be promoted through the components of the event, including environment, food and beverages, entertainment, and activities that engage attendees. By strategically using special events, meeting managers can "wow" their attendees at luncheons, dinners, galas, and fundraisers.

Producing receptions, luncheons, dinners, or galas as special events is a detailed and complicated process that requires hiring professionals, such as a caterer, entertainers, sound specialists, and lighting companies. When the event is complex, the prudent decision may be to hire a special events company or DMC, such as for off-site events, which have special challenges. Communication between knowledgeable professionals is the key to producing successful special events.

To make an event truly special for attendees consider holding the event off-site from the primary meeting location. In every city there are a plethora of venues that are well suited for a remarkable backdrop to any special event. However, coordinating an off-premise event has many challenges, such as transportation, catering, equipment, and adequate insurance. With careful planning, off-site events can be very successful.

Finally, when considering the application of special events as a part of the programming for a meeting, meeting managers do not need to go through this alone. There are many vendors who specialize in these events that are available to outsource the management. Hiring an outside special events company or DMC frees the meeting manager from arranging all of the details and considerations required to hold a special event. These professionals typically will handle all of the arrangements that are necessary to ensure a successful event.

REFERENCES

1. Ritzer-Ross, J. (September, 2003). An extra pair of hands. *Convene*, p. 24.

2. Torrence, S. (September, 2000). Bring the white tablecloth experience to your special events. *Convene*, p. 29.

3. Phillips, G. (March, 2005). Creating an extension of yourself: Working with DMCs. *Convene*, p. 44.

KEY TERMS

Accessibility	Meeting décor	Sommelier
Catering manager	Off-site event	Special event
DMC	Props	Special event manager
Entertainment	Reception	Target audience
Fundraising event	Rider	Team building
Gala	Risk management	Theme party
Gobo		

COMPELLING QUESTIONS FOR CONSIDERATION

1. In what ways do special events benefit a meeting?

2. What are the potential problems or challenges in incorporating special events into a meeting?

3. In what ways can an entertainer's contract rider affect event costs?

4. What event elements require special attention when producing an off-site event?

CHAPTER 33

TRANSPORTATION STRATEGIES AND SOLUTIONS

Steve Weathers
PRESIDENT
SEAT PLANNERS
INCORPORATED

Kathleen Eddy
MANAGER, ASSOCIATION,
INCENTIVE, TRADE SALES
DELTA AIR LINES

LEARNER OUTCOMES

When the reader has completed reading this chapter, he/she should be able to . . .

1 Discuss the advantages of contracting with an official airline.

2 Describe the benefits of online travel arrangements and online, integrated meeting-management programs.

3 Develop preliminary plans for shuttle service between multiple hotels and event sites.

4 Determine the advantages of contracting with a professional travel management company to handle pre-meeting and post-meeting tours.

> No one traveling on a business trip would be missed if he failed to arrive.
>
> *Thorstein Veblen*

OVERVIEW

In the initial review of prospective meeting sites, the availability, convenience, and cost of transportation to the area are factors in the selection process. Once the site is selected, it is the meeting manager's responsibility to identify travel options that are convenient and cost-effective for attendees.

The ease of transportation to the meeting events can affect attendee attitudes toward the entire convention or meeting. Make sure transportation plans ease access to the meeting; allow ample time for attendees to arrive at the site; are communicated clearly, accurately, and well in advance; and are as economical as possible.[1] This chapter presents strategies for managing transportation needs before, during, and after an event.

AIR TRANSPORTATION

The sponsoring organization may elect to manage travel costs on the behalf of attendees or leave transportation arrangements for the attendees to make. Many options are available, including contracting with an official or preferred airline (or airlines) that provides a discount, in most cases, on published airfares to meeting attendees. In most situations, a meeting manager will select two air carriers to partner with for their meeting, thus offering attendees a choice. In today's environment more and more travelers prefer to purchase their tickets online. It is beneficial for the association/organization to work with an airline representative to provide a link from the meeting web site to the airline partner's web site to realize the maximum benefit to the attendee and association/organization. A direct link to the airline's web site offers members a simple way to make their travel plans and allows attendees to manage their own travel. Another option to consider would be to utilize a web-based transportation management application.[2]

A key component in selecting a carrier to be an official or preferred airline is the frequency of flights scheduled into the meeting city. Most airline carriers have account managers who will discuss mutual benefits and facilitate a meeting contract. Once the contract is signed, a travel management company can be used to help with administrative details such as promotion, reservations, ticketing, and tracking; however purchasing tickets from the airline's web site is usually more cost effective for the attendee and association/organization.

The primary benefit associated with designating an official or preferred carrier is the discount available to meeting attendees. In most cases the discounts offered are standard percentages off published fares. Depending on the airline, the meeting location and passenger volume may factor into the discounts offered. Additionally, zone fare programs, offering guaranteed unpublished fares from predetermined sections of the United States and Canada to the meeting destination, are available. Zone fares provide discounts which eliminate restrictions such as the Saturday night stay requirement. This is most beneficial to attendees when the meeting is scheduled for mid-week travel. With most discount programs, the attendee will earn mileage credits on the airline's frequent flyer program. As noted, programs vary; therefore, it is beneficial to consider more than one airline. The most cost-effective approach is to request packages from two to three potential airline partners.

Additional benefits of designating an official or preferred carrier can sometimes, but not always, include site inspection tickets, productivity tickets, and marketing assistance. Site inspection tickets can be either complimentary or offered at a reduced rate that may be fully refundable after a meeting or convention has fulfilled its contracted number of flight reservations. Productivity tickets are awarded after the meeting and are based on the number of attendees who actually flew on the airline (e.g., one complimentary round-trip ticket for every 40 passengers, which is a negotiable component, that were ticketed against the meeting contract number). The details of site inspection and productivity tickets vary depending on the air carrier.

Once an official or preferred carrier is selected, review meeting schedules with current flight times in mind. For example, if the meeting is on the West Coast, the last flights to the East Coast, other than the red-eye overnight service, depart early in the afternoon. If possible, consider travel benefits and limitations before completing the program schedule. Would concluding the event earlier in the day allow attendees from the Midwest and the East to arrive home the same evening? Would extending the program over a Saturday night permit more people to qualify for an additional fare reduction?

It is also very important to consider the lead time necessary to promote an official airline program. Negotiate the contract far enough in advance so there is time to disseminate information and include the airline in promotional materials for the meeting. Motivating attendees to travel on the designated carrier will increase the number of complimentary tickets earned by the organization. As mentioned above, promoting the airline partners online is cost effective for all concerned.

In summary, in today's economic environment, the following guidelines should be heavily weighted when contracting with an airline:

- Partner with no more than two airlines to maximize the benefits offered to the association/organization and its members.
- Provide a link on the association/organization's web site to the airline's web site to make immediate reservations for air transportation. This allows self-managed travel and cost savings; additional benefits may be available to the association/organization and member.
- Assess the options and select an official/preferred carrier based on scheduled flight frequency to the meeting city. This offers flexibility and choice to all travelers.
- Contact the airline's account manager to discuss available programs. Benefits may include discounts, frequent flyer program bonus miles, and earned travel certificates based on total flights booked (programs vary depending on the airline).
- Contact the airline far in advance to allow time to publish benefits via mailings, e-blasts, and online.

Online Travel Arrangements

Online bookings are increasing[3] and the Internet is constantly improving as a travel solution. Because of the number of web services available, some meeting managers elect not to name an official carrier, and instead encourage attendees to purchase individual airline tickets using airline web sites or consumer discount online travel sites. Note that online travel agencies such as Expedia, Travelocity, and Orbitz charge fees for their services, while most airlines do not charge service fees for tickets that are bought directly on their web sites.

Online web sites provide ease of booking and discount pricing (negotiated discounts from the airline not included). However, those web sites do not provide tracking and reporting mechanisms or other benefits to the organization and attendees as an official airline would. This component of a negotiated contract with an airline is very important to most associations/organizations. Alternatives to track attendee travel are: 1) appoint a designated travel agency to book attendee reservations, or 2) utilize a meeting technology solution or Web-based travel tool (for example, a transportation-management application offers meeting managers integrated services such as online registration, housing, and transportation solutions, giving attendees access to zone fares and other event-specific negotiated airfares).[5]

Remote Locations

A meeting site, such as a conference center or resort, may have been chosen for team-building exercises, recreation, or seclusion, rather than for ease of transportation. Local air, rail, or bus service may be minimal or nonexistent. Investigate alternatives: chartered planes into nearby small commercial or private air fields, shuttle buses from the nearest airport or railroad station, limousines, or rental cars. Review all options with frequency, comfort, cost, and travel time in mind.

Arrangements for larger groups may be made with a local ground operator that can provide shuttle service from the nearest transportation hub on a predetermined schedule. Attendees can indicate arrival locations and times on a return card or registration form. Attendees should also be given a 24-hour telephone number to accommodate emergencies and last-minute changes.

SHUTTLE BUSSING

Shuttling bussing is a shared ride system for transporting people between their hotels and the convention center (or other venue). Because the ride is shared, the individual passenger sacrifices the personal advantages of privacy, route, and schedule that they would enjoy using a personal vehicle, taxi, or hired car. Decisions about whether to provide shuttles are made more on a basis of what is best for the group rather than for the individual. The goal of a successful shuttle program is reliability—that the guest can expect the transportation to run as promised.

As a meeting's attendance increases, it outgrows the ability to meet in a single venue where the elevator is the primary mode of transportation. The meeting now relies on a large venue linked to multiple hotels by a shuttle bus system acting as a horizontal elevator.

The size of citywide conventions can overwhelm the local infrastructure's ability to provide for parking or enough taxis to move everyone in a timely fashion. Consequently, a shuttle bus system for the meeting is needed to provide the necessary lift or seating capacity to get attendees to and from the convention center efficiently.

The development of modern convention facilities that can accommodate thousands of people that paralleled the rise of citywide meetings spawned firms that design and operate shuttle bus systems for citywide meetings. They are known as transportation management companies. These types of contractors are in addition to the same services provided by either destination management companies (DMC) or in-house staff who set up and operate the shuttles internally.

If the organization chooses to operate their own shuttle system and hire buses directly, use a DMC or engage a transportation management company, and familiarize yourself with some of the fundamentals of shuttle bussing. This knowledge will save money and increase the value of the service to the attendees.

The fundamentals of a shuttle program include the following:

- Management
- Vehicles and drivers
- Passengers, route, and bus stops
- Schedule and signage
- Budget with funding

There is much to consider regarding each of these fundamentals.

Shuttle Bus Management

Citywide shuttle programs are complex and require preplanning, careful execution, and post-meeting analysis. Most commonly, meeting managers engage either a transportation management company or a DMC to handle the shuttle service. These companies have the skills and experience to do the job, and more importantly, have the trained staff to coordinate and dispatch from the sidewalks. Choosing a company early enough to help establish a budget gives the meeting time to secure adequate funding or make adjustments to the program or room blocks to keep costs under control.

The duties of the management company include designing the shuttle service, setting an accurate budget, securing and arranging the various elements, executing the program with supervision and coordinators, and providing a post-meeting report.

Selecting the shuttle service manager requires a request for proposal (RFP) containing the following:

- *Client information*—the organization's purpose and the purpose of the meeting; the main contact and alternate; due date and decision date; meeting history with ridership numbers; average number of guests needing special transportation services; anticipated registration numbers for attendees, spouses, exhibitors, and day visitors; demographics about attendees

- *Housing information*—full name, address, and phone number of each hotel; name of housing bureau or coordinator; bell-shaped curve of the housing block (or the daily percentage of the block compared to the peak night); average guests per room; which hotels are to be served and which are considered to be within walking distance; hotels with special distinctions such as headquarters, board of directors, staff, speakers, VIPs, and so on

- *Schedule information*—Days and dates of the shuttle; daily start and end times; daily peak and off peak times; acceptable wait times between buses at peak and at off peak

- *Program and location of activities with estimated attendance*—Exhibit hours; registration hours; general sessions; breakouts with combined attendance; receptions; banquets; functions such as concerts, dances, corporate sponsored symposia, and so on

To find qualified bidders, research the local CVB's (convention and visitors bureau) members, approved companies of the venue, and ask the housing bureau and other meeting managers. Consider local DMCs or ground operators, as well as nationally operating transportation management companies.

Some shuttle management companies and DMCs are national in the scope of their services. They offer multiple-year contracts in order to provide continuity to the meeting from year to year. This is especially valuable to the meeting manager in setting future budgets.

There are three times when the meeting manager should examine a particular shuttle program:

1. Before selecting the city or venue, as cost can vary widely
2. When developing the budget for the meeting
3. Six to nine months prior to the meeting to get the most accurate cost estimate

Fuel, insurance, labor, and traffic change all the time; so an accurate cost is difficult to know more than six months before an event. Fuel cost fluctuations may cause the need for adding a fuel escalator clause to the contract based on the prevailing cost of fuel at the time of the execution of the shuttle program. The

U.S. Department of Energy maintains a weekly retail average fuel cost by region on the Internet.

Have a plan for what to do with items lost on the shuttle buses. Decide if items are to be returned to the bus company, shuttle management, convention center, or meeting office.

Shuttle Vehicles and Drivers

Shuttle programs usually utilize 47 to 53 passenger, 40 to 45 foot long chartered motorcoaches from local or regional companies. Occasionally it may be prudent to utilize school buses or transit buses, but these are rarely used. The drivers are employees of the bus company whose driving duties vary from day to day so that many different drivers may work over the several days of the meeting. This requires drivers to be thoroughly briefed before each shift. Gratuities are an important part of driver's wages and should be budgeted. There is no universally agreed-upon formula, but an amount between two and five percent of the charter bus cost is customary (plus more if luggage is handled).

The drivers communicate using cell phones and sometimes radios. Make certain that the drivers have a policy concerning safe use of communications equipment while driving, such as not allowing personal calls, limiting the length of calls, and requiring the use of hands-free devices. The on-site staff needs to be able to communicate with the drivers, meeting manager, venue, hotels, and guests as each situation dictates. Attendees use cell phones to check on the schedule, lost and found, and report shortcomings.

Motorcoaches are charged according to either hourly or mileage charges, whichever is greater (although hourly usually applies for conventions). A minimum charge of three, four, or five hours plus the cost of additional hours is the rule. On occasion deadhead (the distance between the bus yard and the charter) is charged. Buses are regulated by the state, and sometimes the city, in which they operate. A few jurisdictions charge tax. Normal statutory insurance minimums are $5,000,000 liability. The meeting should be included as "additionally insured" on the bus company's policy.

Shuttle Bus Passengers, Routes, and Stops

The number and location of the passengers needing transportation influence the cost and success of a shuttle service more than any other factor. There is a correlation between cost and the travel time to and from the hotels. Closer-in hotels use fewer buses because the buses can make several trips to carry people, compared to farther-out hotels that may get only one or two trips per hour per bus. Bus routes with round trip travel times of 20 to 25 minutes are the most efficient and cost effective. Longer routes cost more money because they require more buses. Carrying capacity is the key; as is demonstrated by Table 33.1.

TABLE 33.1

Hourly Capacities Based on a Single 47 Passenger Bus

20 minute Round Trip	30 minute Round Trip	40 minute Round Trip	50 minute Round Trip	60 minute Round Trip
3 trips	2 trips	1.5 trips	1.2 trips	1 trip
141 passengers	94 passengers	70.5 passengers	56.4 passengers	47 passengers

Note: a round trip is the time it takes the bus to leave the convention center, discharge, and board passengers at all the stops on the route and return.

As Table 33.1 shows, a 60-minute round trip route requires three times as many buses as the 20-minute round trip route. Consequently, the equipment cost is three times higher for the same number of passengers. For instance, if a route is anticipated to have 400 passengers ride in a one hour period, it would take three buses if the route is 20 minutes round trip and nine if the route is 60 minutes round trip.

Integrating housing selection with the ability to shuttle efficiently is important for more than just the meeting budget. The meeting manager, housing bureau, and shuttle contractor should work together when adding hotels. How attendees feel about the length and circuitousness of their ride influences their feelings about the shuttle and meeting overall.

Overloading can occur on bus routes when attendees who have booked around-the-block utilize the shuttle service. The design of the bus routes is forecasted using the pick-up report from the housing bureau; so having inaccurate numbers can leave the system unprepared to cope with the unintended riders. The meeting manager needs to decide if these attendees are to be accommodated (because they registered for the meeting) or denied service (because they booked outside the block). If the meeting manager limits ridership to those within the block, a simple solution is to provide a specially printed sticker for the attendee badge that is distributed by the hotel's front desk at check-in for those on the housing list. The stickers can also be handed out at the housing desk at registration. To save on the cost of the labor needed for checking the stickers, usually a route coordinator at the convention center only checks for stickers when people attempt to board. Then those who are denied a ride have a chance to go back to registration to get a sticker and a potentially negative event can be avoided. Bus drivers can also check for stickers; but they tend not to be effective screeners and it sets drivers up for conflict. The policy regarding the stickers needs to be clearly stated on the published bus schedule and in all collateral materials.

Dealing with farther-out hotels can be a conundrum. The attendees may feel they are too far away from the meeting and isolated from the total event. A way to counteract this perception is to provide sufficient bus service to keep the waits between buses down.

Bus stops need to be located where there is shelter and adequate room for the vehicles. The meeting manager needs to have the bus zones at the convention center reserved for the meeting's exclusive use. Each route needs to have access for free movement and will require a zone of between 65 and 110 linear feet or a diagonal sawtooth at least 12 feet wide with room for safe backing. It is better to have bus stops that do not require buses to back up in order to depart. The loading platform (sidewalk) at the convention center needs to be adequate for the number of attendees.

Passengers with impaired mobility must be accommodated. Preplanning helps to make certain that the right equipment is available when it is needed. There should be a question regarding special transportation needs on the registration form. Anyone requesting special transportation should be contacted in advance to verify how they can be best served. Sometimes all that is needed is an accessible parking space or a room in the headquarters hotel. In any case, the meeting manager needs to secure wheelchair lift-equipped buses or vans appropriate for the size of the meeting. Keep track of each year's use and provide that information to the next year's operator. Personal mobility devices, which are battery-powered scooters, are available for rent in major cities. Many attendees who rent them do not consider themselves "special needs" and consequently do not identify themselves on the registration form. Be sure to provide a phone number on the published schedule telling attendees with impaired mobility how to arrange transportation.

Shuttle Schedules and Signage

The classic shuttle service is set up in two shifts: peak service and off peak service. Peak service is during those times when the greatest numbers of people are expected to ride, and off peak is the fill-in service between the peaks. Most peaks are three to four hours in length. How many minutes apart the buses operate is called frequency (or headway). Ideal frequency at peak times is 10 minutes or less. Off peak frequency is dependent on the level of service the meeting wants to provide its attendees, the budget, and the size of the block on the route. There is no clear policy regarding off peak service, but experience has shown that guests perceive frequencies of 20 to 25 minutes as reasonable, and frequencies of 30 minutes or more contribute to a feeling of isolation or impatience.

There are many ways to deal with mid-day shuttle service: from no service at all, to doing the bare minimum of one bus per route, to having departures every hour, every 20 to 25 minutes, or every 10 to 15 minutes. This decision is based on how well the meeting manager wants to treat attendees and the budget for the meeting. Always remember that shuttling is in two directions. In the middle of the day for every attendee who leaves the meeting there is another attendee at a hotel who needs a ride to the convention center. People need the bus service in the middle of the day for many reasons: an exhibitor break or shift change, a problem back at the attendee's office, forgotten belongings, a fax to be picked up, a meeting with a colleague, and so on. Attendees have free will and may resent not being able to exercise it.

The length of the event day affects the cost of the shuttle. Buses and staff are billed by the time they are used, so a shorter day will cost less than a longer one. The buses should begin service from one-half to one hour before the program begins, depending on the size of the activity. If a major program is anticipated to attract large numbers is to begin that day, then a one-hour lead time helps ensure that all arrive in time; a half hour works if the day begins with a build up such as registration first, then posters, then the general session.

The most expensive shuttling cost is when everyone must be carried at the same time, as each bus was not be able to make multiple trips. Avoid having everything at the convention center begin at once (e.g., registration, exhibits, posters, and breakouts). Conversely, programs that end suddenly require more buses to accommodate everyone who shows up at the bus stop at the same time. Concerts usually end this way.

Communicating the timetable of the shuttle is important. Putting the schedule in the meeting's program book is good; but that makes it necessary to have the bus schedule set by publication time. The program book should carry a preliminary schedule with the basic daily start and end times. A more current printed schedule published just before the convention begins can be distributed on the shuttle buses, at on-site registration, and in the hotel lobbies. Posters (generally 22" x 28") can be provided for each of the hotel lobbies as well as at the convention center.

Each bus stop at the convention center needs to be clearly marked with a sign that identifies the route and hotels served. The route signs need to be able to withstand the elements; especially the wind. Every bus needs to have identifying signs in the front and side windows that list the route and hotels served. Caution must be used in the size and placement of the signs so that the bus driver's vision is not obscured.

Local Tours

It may be advantageous to use the shuttle bus supplier for sightseeing tours, too. If a DMC is being used for sightseeing tours, the company could manage shuttle service as well. Using a DMC can maximize equipment usage more cost-effectively because of the DMC's awareness of tour participation. It also reduces the likelihood that tour buses inadvertently load passengers at shuttle stops, wreaking havoc with schedules for both activities. In some locations, more than one company must be utilized to achieve shuttle service; the DMC can coordinate this. Depending on the minimum time requirement, extra buses needed at peak times may be used for guest tours after high-volume traffic has eased.

Regardless of which company is used, information about local tours should be provided in a separate proposal, which should include the same information as the shuttle bus proposal, as well as the following:

- Tour descriptions and prices
- What is included in the tour price (admission, guides, meals)
- A contingency plan in case a tour is undersubscribed
- Whether minivans are available for smaller groups
- The cutoff date for cancellations in order to avoid paying a penalty
- The lead time required in order to provide an additional bus or van
- The organization's responsibilities (promotion, sales, and ticket pricing)

Shuttle Service Budget and Funding

There are many ways a meeting can cover the cost of a shuttle program. The five most common ways are:

1. Hotel room rebate
2. Sponsorship
3. Locale and/or venue subsidy
4. As a part of the registration fees
5. Charging fares

Usually it takes a combination of funding sources to pay for the shuttle program.

A hotel room rebate is a disclosed amount of money added on to each guest's room charge. The amount is agreed upon in advance as part of the housing contract and is often only enough to cover part of the shuttle expense. Some hotels will require that the hotel be on a bus route as a part of the fee. Oftentimes the rebate is paid by all hotels, including the walking hotels, to create a large enough pool of money to cover the expense.

Sponsorships involve fees paid by exhibiting companies in return for advertising opportunities. These can take many forms, including the following:

- Attribution on collateral materials like the printed schedule and lobby signage
- Headrest covers with printed artwork
- Small signage inside the buses
- Exterior wraps of varying sizes
- A video and/or audio message played within the bus

The meeting charges for the rights to the space or opportunity, while the sponsor provides the ad or promotion collateral. Because some charter bus companies charge for placing sponsorship advertising on their buses, make certain that the shuttle contractor is aware of the possibility of this happening before reserving the buses. Some buses do not accept exterior advertising.

Some cities and venues offer shuttle subsidies as an inducement to attract the meeting. Sometimes the subsidy covers the difference between the cost of shuttle service in a competing city and the cost in the hosting city.

Including the shuttle expense as part of the registration fee is the most common source of shuttle funding.

Charging a fare is a possibility, but it is fraught with challenges. It is difficult to determine in advance how many people will purchase bus passes in order to reserve the correct number of buses. Selling the passes requires handling money and accounting for it. Checking the passes requires more labor than normally needed so the cost is even higher. Charter bus drivers have little experience in checking bus passes which can lead to problems.

PRE-MEETING AND POST-MEETING TOURS

Pre-meeting and post-meeting tours are an increasingly popular option utilized to attract more attendees to a meeting. However, managing tours outside the meeting area requires different skills and priorities. Keep in mind that the organization is not just providing transportation, but a total experience for the duration of the trip. Participants are the responsibility of the organization from start to finish.

Along with negotiating the airline contract, professional travel management companies also have the resources to plan tours. These agencies can help determine if there is sufficient interest to make it feasible to charter an airplane, or if tour airfare can be built into the round-trip price of traveling to the meeting. In most cases, there is not additional cost to the traveler or the organization for using a travel consultant. Where there is a charge, it is worth paying in order to avoid a job that can be time consuming, if not downright risky, for the inexperienced meeting manager. It is important to understand the liability aspects of conducting pre-meeting and post-meeting programs. Consult legal counsel prior to embarking on this component of any event.

A professional travel company can often negotiate the lowest, most comprehensive arrangements. There can also be last-minute problems that occur without notice. A travel company's resources and contacts can be valuable in an emergency. Also, the travel agent is knowledgeable regarding the reputation of local DMCs and can provide information about hotels included in the tour. This can eliminate the need for the meeting manager to make a site visit to review facilities or sample programs.

Once everyone has assembled at the airport or rail station, every effort should be made to give the group the feeling that special arrangements have been made on their behalf. Personalized badges and lists of participants with names and affiliations will help the group bond. Ask the airline or station official if there is a lounge or private area where the group can gather prior to departure to get to know one another. The meeting manager may also request that the group be seated together in a special section of the plane or train. Ask passengers in advance about seating preferences and special meal requirements.

Upon arrival at the destination, the transportation supplier helps claim, identify, and load luggage for the next stage of the journey. Travelers should be provided with current hotel information, as well as a day-by-day itinerary.

SUMMARY

It is the meeting manager's responsibility to identify travel options that are convenient and cost-effective for attendees. Contracting an official airline enables attendees to take advantage of lower group rates for air transportation. It can also benefit the organization by providing complimentary or reduced-price site inspection tickets, productivity tickets, freight discounts, and other benefits. In today's high-technology business environment, meeting managers should become familiar with transportation-management applications and tools that offer integrated services such as online transportation planning and reservations.

Ground transportation is also an important responsibility. Choices may include local rail and bus systems, airport service buses, hotel service vehicles, taxis, private limousines, and shuttle buses. When arranging for shuttle service between meeting locations, determine how expenses will be met, coordinate routes and times with the meeting program, and choose a service provider carefully. Also be sure to publish all transportation options for attendees.

A professional travel management company can greatly enhance pre-meeting and post-meeting tours. They can determine the level of interest among attendees, negotiate lower rates, and handle other tour details. Their contacts and knowledge of the destination can help make the tour successful.

REFERENCES

1. Torrence, S. (March, 1997). Shuttling your attendees in style . . . and within budget. *Convene*, p. 31.

2. Block, S. (2000). Letter to the editor. *Meetings and conventions*.

3. Sacks, J. (2000). *The Conferon guide to meeting management*. Chicago, IL: Professional Convention Management Association.

KEY TERMS

Chartered
Citywide meeting
Complimentary
Dispatcher
Itinerary
Last-seat availability
Lead time

Lift
Meet and greet
Official airline
Pre-meeting and post-
 meeting tours
Productivity tickets

Schedules
Shuttle buses
Site inspection tickets
Yield management
Zone fare

COMPELLING QUESTIONS FOR CONSIDERATION

1. Compare the advantages and disadvantages of contracting with an official airline versus promoting discount online travel sites. What effect do these sites have on achieving low-priced group rates through the official carrier?

2. Discuss some key elements that should be included in a proposal submitted by a shuttle service provider.

3. What are the advantages of having a professional travel management company organize pre-meeting or post-meeting tours?

4. Why is it important to publicize all transportation options for attendees?

CHAPTER 34

IT'S SHOWTIME: FINAL INSTRUCTIONS TO THE FACILITY AND YOUR SUPPLIER TEAM

Gail E. Mutnik, MPA

DIRECTOR OF MEETINGS

AMERICAN ASSOCIATION FOR CLINICAL CHEMISTRY (AACC)

LEARNER OUTCOMES

When the reader has completed reading this chapter, he/she should be able to . . .

1 Explain the importance of detailed, written on-site instructions.

2 Identify information that should appear in the staging guide.

3 List the different types of signage required on-site.

4 Develop an event specifications guide and function sheets to create a comprehensive meeting document.

5 Describe the key contents of final instructions to facilities and suppliers, and the approximate timing of these instructions.

> Reading maketh a full man, conference a ready man, and writing an exact man.
>
> *Francis Bacon*

OVERVIEW

After putting considerable effort into developing an event, you will need to orchestrate the plan of action. The meeting manager is the focal point of intelligence, determining how, where, and when all things must come together. Regardless of the teamwork developed in planning the event, if information is not communicated in an effective and timely way to the on-site support team, the hard work of planning the event could be lost in transition.

This chapter is about communicating internally within the meeting management team and externally with the multitude of suppliers and contractors, including your convention services manager, who will help you produce a memorable, smooth-running event.

The vernacular used by meeting managers and suppliers to describe the tools of their trade can differ. For example, the APEX Glossary of Terms refers to and defines an event specifications guide (ESG) (also known as the meeting résumé or staging guide) as a "comprehensive document that outlines the complete requirements and instructions for an event."[1] It further defines this document as "typically authored by the event planner [meeting manager] and shared with all appropriate vendors as a vehicle to communicate the expectations of services for a project." The lack of standardized terminology can be confusing, especially to the novice meeting manager. Regardless of the terms you use, make sure the person who receives your instructions knows exactly what each item will encompass, what is expected of all parties, and when their services are required.

The creation of the ESG should not be done last minute; rather, it should be created as part of the overall planning process for the management of a meeting. It is a useful tool to track and organize all of the individual bits of information that are required to successfully manage a meeting or event.

FACILITY INSTRUCTIONS

The comprehensive information provided by the meeting manager, in the ESG, must be concise and clear, describing how the meeting will proceed. It includes activities (by day, time, room, set-up, and requirements), complimentary room assignments, signature authority, and many other details that will be outlined here. In essence, the ESG encompasses the full operational guidelines of the meeting, and it is shared with all of the key individuals. This guide is the heart of the meeting—the diary of every minute detail—as authorized by the meeting manager.

The ESG comprises a number of comprehensive function sheets. Each function sheet provides your explicit instructions pertaining to a single, scheduled event, session, or activity within the scope of your meeting. The final function sheets should be sent to the convention services manager (or event coordinator) at least five to six weeks prior to the meeting. This is the minimum time needed for the facility to review, question, and communicate the requirements to their departments, then send a copy back to you for final approval. The facility may also respond with a banquet event order (BEO), which is a form used to provide details to its own staff reflecting your requirements for room set-up, food and beverage, and so on. The BEO is then distributed to the appropriate functional departments within the facility.

ESG CONTENTS

The following is a comprehensive listing of what should be placed in an ESG. However, some events may require more than one staging guide for each facility that is involved in managing an event. Staging guide information should be tailored for the facility where the meeting will take place. For example: For a meeting that is confined to a single hotel, you may wish to include all the elements that are listed below. For a citywide meeting, you may wish to have several staging guides: one for the main or headquarter hotels, one for the overflow hotels, and one for the convention center or the location where individual events will take place. Be sure to give each facility all the information they need to be able to successfully manage your event. APEX has approved an Event Specifications Guide template that you may find useful.

The following components might be included in your ESG:

- *General overview*—Group name, day(s) and date(s), contract details pertaining to the meeting, and information about the organization (including attendee profile, philosophy, and objectives)

- *Event profile*—event name, start and end dates of event, pre- and post-event dates and locations

- *Meeting requirements by day, time, and place*—Include floor plans of the meeting room design, audio visual (A/V) requirements, function name and number (if code numbers are used), name of room and floor number, time room should be set-up, times when the function begins and ends, expected attendance, number of speakers, head table set-up, staging, special requirements (computer set-up, meals, accommodations for persons with disabilities), signage, menu selections and times, scheduled breaks for refreshing rooms, and the person in charge

- *List of key personnel* (contractors/suppliers, meeting staff, VIPs, and hotel staff)—Include contact names for all contractors, staff, and those in authority and how they can be reached immediately (office telephone, pager, cell phone, and/or hotel room extension); also name VIPs who should receive special attention

- *Meeting policies*—Include all policy statements of the organization as they relate to the meeting (e.g., policies regarding advertising, exhibit regulations, staff expenses, use of cameras, and taping)

- *Staff responsibilities*—Each staff member should be listed with specific on-site responsibilities and a schedule of times and days of involvement.

Figure 34.1 is an example of what might be included in a specifications guide.

FUNCTION SHEETS

As a way of managing meetings and events, some meeting managers prefer to use a series of function sheets, which are formatted templates used as a check-off system to manage the details of each event. Appropriate requirements are selected from a list of possibilities on a pre-designed form. One form is completed for each function or room set-up and is placed in a binder in chronological order. Figure 34.2 is an example of a function sheet form.

The advantages of this system are the convenience of adding or deleting information; it also reduces the likelihood of omitting important details. This works well in a small to medium-sized meeting. Although the binder can be cumbersome for a large meeting, you must give your facility this level of detailed information in order to set up your function(s) correctly. Binders may be organized in a number of ways, depending on how they will be used. For hotels, many meeting managers organize their information by placing their function sheets for each day behind a tab, starting with the earliest starting session and ending with

---

Fast Facts

Components of Event Specifications Guide

- General overview
- Event profile
- Meeting requirements by day, time, and place
- List of key personnel
- Meeting policies
- Staff responsibilities

MASTER COPY

Staging Guide of:

Name of Sponsoring organization and event

Contact: Name of individual in charge of meeting (meeting manager)
Name and address of company
Telephone numbers, fax, email address

With

Name of the event hotel or facility
(In the case of a citywide meeting, list all facilities involved.)

Contact: Name of convention services manager
Name and address of hotel/facility
Telephone numbers, fax, email address

Date Created:

Inclusive Dates: Indicate day, date, and year when group begins arriving; list each day group is in-house through departure.

Anticipated Attendance: Provide an expected number of people based on previous history or, if this is a first-time event, work with the facility to determine a realistic forecast. Segment the list by type of attendee, if possible.

Room Block: Designate arrival patterns; anticipate that some attendees will arrive early and some will stay extra days. Suggest check-in, check-out patterns.

Rate: List the negotiated guest room rate(s) and meeting space charges (if applicable). Indicate meeting space rental charge and the cost for each meeting room or, if space is provided on a complimentary basis, note the terms.

Reservations: Include the methods used to make reservations. Provide a rooming list of staff, VIPs, and speakers in alphabetical order. Note each person's address, phone number, arrival and departure dates, type of room, and special room requirements (and hotel, if a citywide meeting). Clearly explain how charges will be paid. For VIPs, speakers, and staff, indicate if the master account will pick up all charges, room and tax only, or any variation of costs determined. Indicate guest relocation instructions (if any) and guest room deliveries to be expected. Specify the details of a guest room attrition policy if this is an integral part of the facility contract.

Complimentary Rooms: Provide the negotiated complimentary room allotment; also specify who will receive the complimentary rooms.

Master Account: Indicate those items for which the organization will be responsible and the charges to be billed to the master account, with any other charges authorized by the meeting manager (indicate name). The invoice, with accompanying back-up receipts, should be directed to: name of individual (usually the meeting manager) at the headquarters office indicated. Also include billing instructions and remember to reiterate the negotiated items/services that may be over and above what is standard in your contract. This may include rebates or commissions to be paid to third-party vendors.

Authorized Signatures: Indicate individuals who have signature authority to make changes and approve invoices/charges. The fewer individuals who are involved, the more effective the financial control will be. Ideally, just one person, the meeting manager, has authorization to sign contracts. However, this is not practical with most organizations. The executive director and conference chair may also have signature authority.

Special Attention: List the names of individuals who are to be provided VIP status. The hotel/facility may extend special check-in and amenity packages to VIPs. Determine with the hotel the number of individuals to include on this list (e.g., VIPs, president, president-elect, executive director, conference chair, and key speakers).

FIGURE 34.1
Example of an Event Specifications Guide

Meeting Office: Indicate the name of the meeting office room, when move-in will begin, office hours, and room set-up and equipment requirements (copy machine, fax machine, computer connections, and so on).

Registration: Identify the room or area where attendee registration will take place, as well as the hours of operation.

Exhibits: Name the room, area, or separate facility in which there will be exhibits (if applicable) and the hours of operation.

Transportation: Indicate airport transfers for VIPs and staff as provided by the facility and shuttle services with time for off-site events.

Contracted Services: List outside vendors and contractors for services such as audio taping, ground operations, drayage, and so on. Indicate the company that will be providing A/V services and computer equipment, and what the facility will provide.

Engineering: If power and/or extension cords for computers or exhibit hall set-ups will be required, be sure to include this information, providing details of when, where, and who receives what.

Restaurants: Advise the hotel/facility of times during the program when the group will be using the restaurants.

Room Service: Provide times during the program when the attendees will utilize room service most heavily.

Telephone: List the extension numbers for the registration desk, meeting office, speakers' room, and so on, and describe the long-distance calls' policy.

Security: If security services are to be provided, indicate the name of the security company, the number of uniformed guards, their schedules, their locations, and to whom they report.

Bell Service: Advise the facility of any special needs related to staffing of the bell desk (i.e., heavy arrival or departure times).

Coat Check: Indicate if a coat check is required, where it will be located, the cost (or charge arrangements), and the hours of operation.

Housekeeping: List suites and rooms that need special or frequent attention.

Receiving: Describe anticipated shipment of boxes, the number and size expected, delivery date(s), and established storage area.

FIGURE 34.1
Example of an Event Specifications Guide, Continued

the latest starting session. This can be used, then, as a daily event guide by reviewing each day's section. For convention centers and other suppliers, the binder may be organized by tabs for each room. Within each tab, the function sheets are organized by day and by the earliest starting session to the latest starting session in that room on that day. This helps facilities and suppliers set a room each day with the most equipment for that day, whether or not all the equipment is used for each function in that room, so that set-up time, changes, and per day charges are kept to a minimum.

The function sheets are a very helpful way to get an overall picture of what is required for your event. Use them as a tool to help organize your communications as well as to organize your meeting.

Catering Instructions

All food and beverage requirements for an event should be included in the function sheet. From this sheet, the facility will send you their banquet event order (BEO). Figure 34.3 is an example of a catering function sheet that serves as a checklist or reminder of all of the details to be noted when a session includes food and beverages.

Function Sheet

Date _____   Event # _____

Facility _____   Room _____

Event _____   Time (from) _____(to) _____

Attendance _____   Room Set-up Completed _____

Posting? Yes _____ No _____ Post as: _____

Room Setup
- ❏ Theater
- ❏ Conference
- ❏ Classroom
- ❏ Crescent rounds of _____
- ❏ Hollow square
- ❏ Banquet
- ❏ Reception
- ❏ Breakfast
- ❏ Lunch
- ❏ Dinner
- ❏ Special _____

Visual Aids
- ❏ A/V stage—draped (size) _____
- ❏ Projection table (size) _____
- ❏ LCD projector
- ❏ Computer
- ❏ 35mm slide projector
- ❏ Overhead projector
- ❏ 16mm projector
- ❏ Video player (VHS/Beta)
- ❏ Movie screen (size)_____
- ❏ Lighted pointer
- ❏ Conference phone

Platform Requirements
- ❏ Stage size _____
- ❏ Stage carpeted & skirted
- ❏ Head table—skirted (size) _____
- ❏ Head table—# of chairs _____
- ❏ Lighted standing lectern
- ❏ Lighted table lectern
- ❏ Lighted podium
- ❏ Ice water station
- ❏ Pitchers of ice water on tables
- ❏ Flipchart & markers
- ❏ AC outlet (number)_____
- ❏ Lectern mic (#) _____
- ❏ Podium mic (#)_____
- ❏ Table mic (#) _____
- ❏ Floor mic (#)_____
- ❏ Mic mixer (#) _____
- ❏ Sound engineer
- ❏ Light engineer
- ❏ Other _____
- ❏ Sound controls to AV platform
- ❏ Light controls to AV platform

Audio Requirements
Diagrams/special instructions _____

Other Equipment	Location	Signage (list)
Easels_____	_____	1. _____
Tackboard_____	_____	2. _____
Whiteboard _____	_____	3. _____
House phone _____	_____	
Coat rack _____	_____	
Extra tables _____	_____	
Extra chairs _____	_____	

Person in charge of meeting _____
Copy to
- ❏ Hotel _____
- ❏ Suppliers
- ❏ Diagram (attach)

FIGURE 34.2
Example of a Function Sheet

Catering Function Sheet

Function Sheet #: _____   Hotel BEO #: _____

Name of Event: _____

Posting? Yes _____ No _____ Post as: _____

Day/Date: _____   Facility & Room: _____

Time of Event: _____   Time Ready By: _____

Estimated Attendance: _____   Guarantee: _____

Type of Function:
- ❏ Breakfast
- ❏ Lunch
- ❏ Dinner
- ❏ Reception
- ❏ Refreshments

Setup Format:
- ❏ Buffet
- ❏ Sit-down
- ❏ Head table for _____
- ❏ Lighted table lectern
- ❏ Lighted standing lectern
- ❏ Banquet rounds
- ❏ Conference tables
- ❏ Cocktail tables and chairs
- ❏ Roll-in cart
- ❏ Easel
- ❏ Whiteboard
- ❏ Flipcharts/markers
- ❏ Mic(s): _____
- ❏ Ashtrays
- ❏ Waiter during service
- ❏ Waiter throughout event

❏ Floor plan attached
❏ Service to be provided for meeting already in progress and previously set-up
❏ Other _____

Time of food service: _____   Time of beverage service: _____
Waiter to collect tickets: Yes _____ No _____ If yes, at table _____ at door _____

Menu: _____

_____

_____

_____

_____

Cost: _____

Bar requirements: ❏ Hosted   ❏ Cash

Start time: _____   End time: _____
Open bar at: _____   Close bar at: _____
❏ Premium brands   Snacks/hors d'oeuvres
❏ House brands   _____
❏ Beer/wine only   _____

Signage (list)
1. _____
2. _____
3. _____

Bartender: Yes _____ # _____ No _____

Additional information: _____

_____

_____

_____

Staff Responsible: _____
Charges to be posted to Master Account. Authorized Signature: _____

FIGURE 34.3
Example of a Catering Function Sheet

Housekeeping Instructions

Housekeeping services include proper cleaning of the meeting rooms and public areas each day, as well as freshening rooms between sessions. Allow as much time as possible between meetings to replenish water at the head table. Provide instructions on the proper disposal of handouts and other materials left after each session at the close of the day. If materials should not be removed, inform the services coordinator.

At the hotel, the housekeeping instructions should also include any special requirements that you have for your VIPs, such as cleaning their rooms or suites twice a day at specified times or after a reception in a suite.

FACILITY SPECIFICATION FORMATS

Standardization of the facility specification format is becoming more common. A number of facilities already provide a standardized format tailored to their own facility's needs. Some facilities now post their event order forms on their web sites, where meeting managers can complete the forms online, then access and revise their orders through a secure interface.

Whether you choose to work with the facility's format or create your own is a matter of preference. Once the hotel receives your instructions, they will translate them into their own format. Although this duplicates the effort, it provides a valuable double-check at the on-site pre-conference briefing (see Chapter 36). At that time, you will read your function sheet as the convention services manager outlines what will happen at the meeting. The important thing is to be aware that your instructions have been transferred to the facility's standard format, and to confirm that both you and the facility personnel are working from the same instructions.

GENERAL GUIDELINES

The instructions that the convention services manager prepares for the facility staff should reflect the information provided by the meeting manager. Be logical and concise when writing instructions. Take time to walk through the requirements and double-check that every detail is included:

- Review the agreement letter or contract and correspondence.
- Confirm the chairperson and speaker requirements.
- Provide general instructions and summarize agreements in the specifications guide.
- Use stage directions (stage right or left) and compass references (north wall) to indicate the placement of platforms and other equipment.
- Provide pictures or diagrams of floor plans.
- Number all floor plans and attachments, referencing by number in the text of the function sheets.
- Proofread the function sheets and send them to the facility at least five to six weeks before the meeting.
- Ask to review a copy of the facility's version of the function sheet in sufficient time before the event, and make corrections and additions immediately by telephone and followed up in writing.
- Schedule a pre-convention meeting (pre-con) with facility representatives to review the function sheet.
- As the meeting progresses, note all on-site changes and additions as a reference for comparing the final statement of charges and for use in developing instructions for the next meeting.

APEX OfficeReady for Meeting & Event Planning

Easy-to-Use Templates Written for Microsoft® OfficeSuite

Jointly developed by the Convention Industry Council and KMT Software, Inc. © 2006

- When making changes on-site, clearly indicate the date in order to track when changes were made.
- Supply all major service contractors with a copy of the schedule of events and set-ups.
- Have all major contractors and suppliers attend the pre-con.

SUPPLIER INSTRUCTIONS

Large meetings typically require several major contractors, such as a general services contractor (decorator), A/V supplier, security service, transportation, and so on. All contractors should receive the same set of instructions as the facility does. Knowing one anothers' instructions may help generate questions and suggestions that will be helpful, and everyone will be operating from the same document.

AUDIOVISUALS

Your A/V supplier is an important member of the meeting management team (see Chapter 29). Include the A/V contact in the planning stages wherever possible and appropriate. Provide information on the whole program—not just what A/V equipment is needed and where.

Arrange the technical aspects of meeting room design when the set-ups are being developed. They are a lot easier to change in the early planning stages than on-site. Also provide information on food and beverage set-ups, evening functions, set-up times, staging requirements, time allotments between each function, requirements for a speakers' room, and whether a technician will be needed on-site or on call.

Provide the contractor with a copy of the function sheets and a printed program five to six weeks in advance, and include this person in the pre-con with the meeting facility.

SIGNAGE

To move attendees through the facility with the least amount of confusion, provide clear, concise directional signs throughout the areas in use by your meeting. Walk through the facility to determine where signs are needed (see Chapter 28).

SHIPPING INSTRUCTIONS

An important aspect of meeting management involves forwarding supporting materials to the event location. Shipping documents, publications, equipment, and meeting-related materials from the organization's headquarters or other locations to the site of the event involves numerous steps to ensure the timely arrival of these important items.

Several weeks before the event, information regarding shipments should be forwarded to the people within the organization who will need to ship materials. If the meeting is small, only one or two people may be shipping materials to the site. If the meeting is large, however, many people within the organization, as well as outside the organization, may be responsible for forwarding vital documents and equipment. Information sent to those responsible for shipping items should include details such as: what can be shipped, the maximum sizes of boxes or crates that can be utilized, and the date(s) that materials can be received. For a smaller meeting with only a few boxes or items to be sent, the materials probably can be sent directly to the facility in care of the person who needs them or in care of the convention services manager. All boxes should be sent only a few days before the event and clearly marked with the following:

- the name of the person who is receiving the package
- the group name
- the address of the facility
- the recipient's arrival date

For a large meeting, this method would not work effectively, particularly if a convention center is involved. In that case, prior to the meeting, a shipping instruction document should be prepared and distributed to staff and vendors. Include information such as shipping deadlines, labeling instructions, and addresses for delivery and return shipment. Keeping everyone informed will make the shipping process efficient and cost-effective. People who ship items should keep a list of the number of boxes they have shipped, as well as the contents of each box. As materials are packed, make a list of the contents of each box, then number each one (e.g., 1 of 130, 2 of 130, 3 of 130, and so on), and record the total number of boxes, each box number, its general contents, the name of the person to whom it should be delivered, and the location to which it should be delivered. This saves time when boxes are being delivered on-site and makes accountability easier.

Generally, you may have four or five locations to which boxes will be delivered, particularly within a large facility, such as registration, headquarters office, speakers' lounge, and so on. You may wish to color-code each box with stickers that relate to the specific area of delivery (i.e., red = registration, blue = headquarters office, and so on), so that separating the boxes on-site will go more smoothly. Indicate your color coding system to the convention services manager.

Depending on the arrangements made, a large shipment may be forwarded via your general services contractor acting as the shipping agent. If this is the case, the shipment will go to a warehouse or staging location prior to being dropped at the meeting site. Using this method may require the materials to be sent no less than 10 days prior to the event (depending on location) and no more than one month prior to the event. This is usually the most economical method of transporting large quantities of materials to a meeting site, since the service contractor has access to its own trucks or can contract with ground carriers to obtain a considered rate based on frequent usage. Convey to staff and vendors using this shipment method that their materials and boxes will not be accessible until the contractor delivers the entire shipment to the facility. Be sure to work with your specific contractor regarding shipments to and from the meeting site, and keep a copy of the bill of lading (receipt of goods shipped) for your records.

Last-minute or priority shipments usually occur after the larger shipment has departed. In this case, use a reputable air express carrier for smaller or lighter shipments or a two-day carrier for heavier or bulkier items. These can generally be shipped directly to the facility or hotel. Items that are valuable, irreplaceable, or so important that the conduct of the meeting would be impaired by their loss should be hand-carried to the site.

STAFF INSTRUCTIONS

Meet with your staff prior to the meeting to go over all program details. Develop a duty roster that outlines hourly schedules for each staff and volunteer member and includes the event or job location, exact times, and functional responsibilities. Compiling a personal schedule for each staff member is time-consuming but extremely worthwhile. The more information your staff and volunteers have to work with, the smoother the meeting will go.

Once on-site, meet with your staff and walk through all their responsibilities as determined prior to the meeting. Tour the facility to introduce yourselves to convention services personnel and to familiarize your staff with the location of meeting rooms, restrooms, telephones, in-house restaurants, and shops.

SUMMARY

The irony of a well-run meeting is that from the attendees' perspective, everything happens just as it should. Their guest rooms are ready when they check in; their meeting rooms are comfortable and provide an environment for learning and networking; they find their way easily from room to room; and the educational content and social functions are memorable.

Meeting managers know all the work that goes on behind the scenes, but a meeting is a success when attendees walk away with fond memories and a sense of accomplishment. The secret of this success, after the detailed planning outlined in previous chapters, is communicating every minute detail to all of the staff and suppliers that are concerned in a timely, efficient manner.

Make sure that all communication between you and the facility is done (or followed up) in writing. This not only helps everyone remember and perform their jobs better, but also provides documentation that can be valuable if details of the meeting management are questioned. The specifications guide is a written document that formally summarizes important information about the meeting. Function sheets or event orders typically address the requirements of a single event. Whether you use one of these formats or the format of the host facility, the purpose is to accurately convey important information to all key personnel in a concise and organized manner.

Another crucial element of a well-organized event is signage. Directional and informational signs will help attendees get to meeting events on time with minimal hassle.

Finally, help the meeting staff members to do the best job they can by providing them with complete information about the meeting and a clear understanding of their responsibilities. The operations manual should be complete and accessible to all key staff. Providing the right kind of information before the meeting will make your job significantly easier during the meeting.

KEY TERMS

Banquet event order (BEO)	Facility specifications	Meeting résumé
Bill of lading	format	Pre-conference meeting
Directional signs	Function sheet	(pre-con)
Event specifications guide	Housekeeping	Signage
(ESG)	Meeting bible	Staging guide

COMPELLING QUESTIONS FOR CONSIDERATION

1. Why should a meeting manager provide (or follow-up on) all meeting details in writing?

2. Compare the examples of function sheets and the event specifications guide included in this chapter. What are the strengths and weaknesses of each? Which do you prefer?

3. If the meeting manager's function sheet is different from the convention services manager's format, what should be done?

4. What are some purposes of signage for a meeting? Is it possible to have too many signs?

5. Who should receive the event specifications guide? Is this something for everyone and should all relevant parties get the same document? Why?

CHAPTER 35

CONVENTION SERVICES MANAGER

Association for Convention Operations
Management (ACOM)
EDITORIAL COMMITTEE

LEARNER OUTCOMES

When the reader has completed reading this chapter, he/she should be able to . . .

1 Discuss the role of the convention services manager (CSM) in meeting management.

2 Differentiate between the roles of CSMs in convention and visitors bureaus, hotels, and convention facilities.

3 Recognize the different responsibilities involved in sales and services.

4 Explain the convention services manager's "3 R's" for successful meeting management.

5 Develop timelines for effective management of citywide and non-citywide meetings.

> Quality in a service is not what the
> supplier puts in rather it is what the
> customer gets out and is willing to pay
> for. Customers pay only for what is of
> use to them and gives them value.
> Nothing else constitutes quality.
>
> *Peter Drucker*

OVERVIEW

The convention services manager (CSM) assists the meeting manager with coordination of meeting details and services before, during, and after a meeting. The CSM is the lead contact between the customer and the city, hotels, convention facility, and local suppliers (see Figure 35.1). CSMs are employed by convention and visitors bureaus (CVBs), hotels, and convention facilities and can have titles that vary by facility. Some of the different titles a meeting manager might encounter include:

- Director of convention services
- Conference services coordinator
- Event coordinator
- Event services manager
- Operations manager

Ideally, the CSM help customers obtain resources for promotional and publicity material, identify personnel for registration and other related purposes, and provide for their contractual needs. In essence, the CSM becomes the client's on-site liaison. The CSM evaluates and offers goods and services that increase the event's efficiency and provide cost savings. Done properly, this action can help the client increase attendance, gain access to the goods and services that they and their exhibitors or vendors need, and make the community aware of the organization's presence and mission.[1] This chapter begins with a brief history of the CSM followed by an explanation of the roles and responsibilities of CSMs in convention and visitors bureaus, hotels, and convention centers while providing guidance as to how meeting managers can best benefit from their services. The information in this chapter is useful for both convention services managers who want to improve their knowledge and skills as well as for meeting managers who work with CSMs while performing their job.

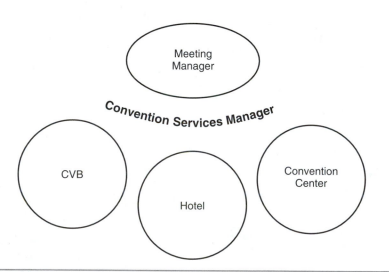

FIGURE 35.1
The Role of the Convention Services Manager

HISTORY OF THE CONVENTION SERVICES MANAGER

The idea of the CSM was conceived in the mid-1950s, at the Stevens Hotel in Chicago (now the Chicago Hilton and Towers), to expedite the movement of client orders between hotel departments. Jim Collins, a Stevens Hotel employee, now retired and a member of the Convention Industry Council (CIC) Hall of Leaders, promoted the concept of communication between the convention services group and other hotel departments. The concept was formalized and the position increased in responsibility in response to client need through the 1980s.

The Association for Convention Operations Management (ACOM) was founded and incorporated as not-for-profit organization by William H. Just, CAE, CMP in 1988 as the first and only professional association for Convention Services Managers (CSMs). The association provides educational programs, networking, and leadership opportunities for CSMs. Convention services managers are employed at hotels, convention centers, and convention/visitor bureaus and work with association, government, and corporate meeting managers to produce conventions, meetings, trade shows, and public events.

THE CONVENTION AND VISITORS BUREAU CONVENTION SERVICES MANAGER

The duties of a convention and visitors bureau (CVB) CSM differ from those of a CSM for a hotel or a convention center. The most obvious difference is timing. The CVB convention services manager generally provides most of his or her services before the meeting begins.[2]

CSMs are an integral part of the CVB sales process and often participate in site inspections before the host city is selected. During the site inspection, the meeting manager provides an overview of the group's needs and establishes a relationship with the services provider. Once the meeting manager signs a contract with the meeting destination, the CVB assigns a CSM to the group. The CSM is responsible for helping to plan and conduct a successful meeting by serving as an extension of the meeting manager's staff.

The CSM provides continual assistance during the meeting's initial planning process, on-site during the actual meeting, and after the meeting is over. The CVB/CSM's broad-based knowledge allows them to work throughout the community providing clients with access to a full range of destination services and suppliers. The CVB/CSM can educate the meeting manager on local policies and procedures, products, services, and venues. An experienced CSM can help save organizations money by minimizing costs. The CSM knows about discounts and amenities available to attendees, unique locations for special events, and local speakers and themes that work well in the area. The CSM can also establish contacts for the meeting manager among the many available suppliers, and can be an excellent source of ideas for building audience attendance and developing programs for spouses.

For citywide events that are utilizing multiple hotels and conference facilities, contacting the CVB/CSM with updates or changes will save the meeting manager time and work. As the primary point of contact in this citywide scenario, the CSM will communicate with all of the involved partners.

The CVB/CSM is not limited to working with meeting managers who are using hotels or convention facilities. Their expertise can also be helpful when contracting with venues such as fairgrounds, sports facilities, college campuses, and auditoriums. Additionally, CVB/CSMs often assist meeting managers with housing, registration, referrals, pre- and post-convention meetings, tours, spouse programs, and pickup reports.

Whom Does the Convention and Visitors Bureau CSM Serve?

The CVB/CSM does not serve a single master. Instead, CVB/CSMs must meet the needs of three separate customers:

1. *External client*—the meeting manager
2. *Internal client*—bureau partners
3. *Employer*—city or CVB corporation

The CSM must walk a fine line in balancing the needs and expectations of all three customers, especially when there is a conflict. For example, a meeting manager who finds fault with a hotel or convention center and blames the facility for the failure of a conference may draw the CVB into the situation by demanding that the CSM act as advocate for the meeting manager to resolve the conflict. If the CVB is a partnership bureau, it has to answer to the hotels and conference center as dues-paying members. The CSM has a responsibility to help mediate the situation if it appears to jeopardize future business for the city, while preserving his or her relationship with the meeting manager (external client) and the hotel (internal client).

The CSM must have excellent communication skills as the liaison between city-owned venues, which could include offsite facilities and convention centers, supplier partners such as shuttle companies, hotels, caterers, or tour operators, and the end user, the convention delegate. By being proactively involved in preparation for the arrival of an event and effectively communicating with everyone involved, the CSM can keep the process flowing successfully.

The CVB/CSM should, ideally, have a relationship of trust with the supplier partners, especially the CSMs at the hotels and convention center. Each must rely on the other to fulfill the client's expectations and written instructions fully. Yet, in the event of a misstep, the CSMs must also rely on their abilities to address any failure immediately and appropriately, so the meeting manager is satisfied and the convention delegate is not aware of any disruption of service.

The nature of the meetings world means that the CVB/CSM will work with meeting managers of varying abilities and experience. Managers who are employed by professional associations and are active participants in professional organizations such as Professional Convention Management Association or Meeting Professionals International will have opportunities for continuing education that prepare them for their positions. Often, however, groups that are loosely organized or managed by volunteers, such as military reunion groups, hobby groups, and religious and fraternal organizations, have less—or sometimes no—experience at managing meetings.

With many meetings departments downsized and an increased number of meeting managers who are volunteers, CSMs today are becoming more integrally involved in every step of the meeting management process. CVB/CSMs work under three basic rules for successful meeting management, commonly referred to as the "3 R's": resources, relationships, and reliability.

Resources

CSMs supply resources to their clients. They are familiar with their destination suppliers and can efficiently handle client requests for external services. They have an established resource network of suppliers in their respective communities that can be accessed for a myriad of services, including transportation, off-site venues, entertainment, and speakers. That local network is expanded nationally for CSMs who are members of the ACOM, an association that is dedicated to the advancement of the convention services practitioners and best meeting practices.

In recent years, clients' requests for non-traditional services have increased. CSMs are seeing more demand for items such as special city permits, sponsorship assistance, and creative ideas for promoting meeting attendance and avoiding audience attrition. Because CSMs are familiar with city services and requirements, they can help meeting managers comply with most such requests, using their resource network to obtain city permits and services.

Finally, meeting managers who rely largely on volunteers to help with conference logistics often depend on CSMs to serve as an extension of their staff.

Relationships

The CSM establishes a relationship with the client during the site selection process. CSMs understand the importance and long-term value of a good working relationship with meeting managers, and work hard to earn their trust and respect. The meeting manager comes to rely on the CSM to meet or exceed their expectations and complete assignments on time.

Reliability

Most CSMs manage numerous conventions, trade shows and other events each year. CSMs are masters at managing multiple meetings, and strive to provide the same level of service and attention to each client before, during, and after their event.

From the moment of the meeting manager's initial contact with the CVB's sales manager, the CVB staff must manage each step in the booking and the servicing process. While the sales manager will ask the meeting manager about hotel and site selection, it will fall to the CSM after receiving the confirmed booking to help the client through the process of program development, supplier resources, and successful implementation of a convention plan. The CSM will do this by keeping a file of resource materials, a bibliography of meeting-management related books and articles, a list of helpful web sites with meeting manager toolkits that can be downloaded and printed, and referrals to third-party meeting managers if they are requested or needed. The "3R's presented above are also important skills for CSMs at hotels and convention centers as well.

The Non-Citywide Convention Services Model

Successful implementation of the 3 R's of convention services management requires good communication between the meeting manager and the CSM. The following suggested scenario for a non-citywide meeting is a representation of the process from the perspective of the CSM. Following this timeline will help even highly experienced meeting managers to get the most value out of their relationship with a CSM (see Table 35.1).

This proactive timeline keeps an inexperienced or volunteer meeting manager on track and focused on the information that the host city and facility need to make the meeting successful. The professional meeting manager may have a separate task timeline that works well consistently, and the CSM will adapt to this timeline as required.

The Citywide Convention Services Model

The services that a CVB/CSM provides to a non-citywide meeting and a citywide convention share many similarities, but they do differ in the quantity of material, staff time, and resources supplied. Planning for a citywide convention should begin five years in advance, and a CVB/CSM will be working on the convention to some extent from the time of booking until the convention takes place.

Fast Facts

Convention Services
Manager 3 R's

- Resources
- Relationships
- Reliability

TABLE 35.1
A Suggested Scenario for a Non-Citywide Meeting

Timing	CVB/CSM Responsibilities
15 months out	Sales manager sends out leads to appropriate size facilities, or to specific properties requested by the meeting manager.
13 months out	Site tour and hotel selection. CSM accompanies the meeting manager on-site to determine the needs of the group. Arrange for attendance-building brochures and/or a display booth to be shipped to the current convention site. CSM arranges for a special web page or a link to the CVB web page to help with promotion.
9 months out	CSM sends out requests for proposals for support services as needed, such as group tour operator, off-site banquet facility, entertainment, coach transportation, airport ground transportation, special coupons for the group, photographer, decorator, and keynote speaker. Responses are gathered and given to the meeting manager for review and selection.
6 months out	CSM confirms with the meeting manager the selection of suppliers, logistics, and program needs. If a welcome letter from a city or state dignitary is needed for the event program, the CSM makes the arrangements.
Monthly	CSM calls monthly to check on the progress of registration and any adjustments being made to the hotel blocks. CSM also stays in touch with the hotel convention services department to make sure that all the needs of the client are being communicated. If registration assistance is hired through the CVB, CSM gets details of staffing needs and handles the request. If volunteers are needed, this is also handled by the CSM. Welcome program, amenities for VIPs, airport signage, spouse orientation, welcome address by CVB representative, and a pre-convention meeting (pre-con) with the hotel staff are all on the CSM's task list for completion prior to the start of the event.
During the meeting	CSM checks on meeting manager's arrival schedule, airport pickup, meeting and VIP pickup. CSM ensures that there are welcome/thank you gifts for the meeting manager and VIPs, supplies pre-meeting attendance figures, and checks in daily with the meeting manager on-site or by telephone. CVB provides a visitor information table/booth, perhaps staffed by a volunteer information specialist. CSM is on call via cell phone 24/7 for the duration of the convention through the departure of the meeting manager.
Post-Convention	CSM sends a thank you letter to the meeting manager with a survey, either via email, online, or mail, to review the meeting and the level of satisfaction with the city and the facilities used. The client is asked to return to the city with future conventions. Completed surveys are shared with the facilities managers. Sales manager contacts the meeting manager to review their experience in the city and to inquire about future opportunities to bid on conventions.

Transition from Convention Sales to Convention Services

The process of managing a citywide meeting begins with the transition from the CVB's convention sales department to its convention services department. This transition has six phases:

1. Account distribution
2. Account history
3. Financial requirements/commitments
4. Servicing procedures
5. Welcome program
6. Post convention servicing

Account distribution is the first step in the transition from the sales department to the service department. The factors that are considered in determining which CSM will receive the assignment should include:

- The CSM's knowledge of the client
- The CSM's history of collaboration with the sales manager
- The CSM's current volume of clients
- Any other factors that are particular to the CVB

The CSM will then receive an account history from the sales manager. A complete account history should include the following:

- The dates of the event
- The client's space needs
- Any hotel blocks that have already been reserved
- Past cities' history with the client
- Any third-party involvement
- Housing information
- An overview of financial commitments that have been made, and any other financial information that the CSM might need to know

Most CVBs will have turnover procedures in place that include worksheets and other documentation.

The sales manager will make the CSM aware of any financial requirements and/or commitments that have been made during the sales process. These may include:

- The year(s) of monetary disbursement
- The use of monies that have been committed (e.g., for space, transportation, special events)
- The source of financial commitments
- Any rebates or promotional assessments (including the percentage to be collected and the source to bill and collect)
- Housing fees (including the source of service, amount of fees, billing arrangements, and whether the fees are included in the promotional assessment or rebate)
- Any financial commitments in the sales/service document (e.g., procedure for notifying the in-house department that is monitoring the commitment, source for questions on financial requirements)
- A report on the collection and disbursement of funds (e.g., documentation to substantiate disbursement or billings)

Put It Into Practice

Convention Services Initial Checklist

Initiate and maintain contact with the client. Building a relationship means serving their needs in a way that is smart and consistent.

1. Confirm the contact(s). Include name(s), title(s), address, telephone number, fax number, and email address.
2. Confirm the hotel room block.
3. Who is handling the housing needs (the CVB, the client, a third party, or attendees themselves)?
4. Is there a rebate of the promotional assessment? Are there any other financial considerations or obligations promised by the CVB?
5. Are the clients using the convention center, hotel or conference center? If so, what are the details of the space that has been blocked? Has the event coordinator at the facility been assigned?
6. Has the contract been signed at the meeting facility?
7. Have the hotel contracts been negotiated and signed? Is the room block flow accurate?
8. Has the client representative been to the host city prior to this visit?
9. Is there a local organizing committee? What duties/responsibilities does it have? Has the CSM met the chair?
10. Will the attendees use a shuttle service? Who will pay for it?
11. Will the client need off-premise facilities for special events?
12. Will the client need a Destination Management Company?
13. If there is a third-party involved, what are their responsibilities? (i.e., contract negotiations, housing, meeting set-up, shuttle arrangements, off-premise operations, overall management, or something else.)
14. Does the client need registration services?
15. Has the client seen the city, including the convention center? Are they in need of other meeting facilities? Are they aware of the labor costs and other related expenses at the meeting facility?
16. Has the client met with the food service provider at the convention center?
17. Has the client met with the security firm at the convention center, hotel, or conference center?
18. Is the client expecting attendees with special needs?
19. Does the client need translation services?
20. Does the client need tour services, including itineraries and equipment?
21. Does the client need a decorator, audiovisual services, or a production house?
22. Does the convention center understand the client's move-in, set-up, and move-out arrangements?
23. Has the client met with hotel officials to talk about use of their properties?
24. Do the clients need special equipment or décor items?
25. Does the client need an event specialist to handle their special event(s)?
26. Does the convention center have an accurate list of the client's executives, board of VIP's, and so on?
27. Are there other considerations, information, or requirements that the CVB needs to obtain for this client?
28. Did the CVB send a thank you note at the time of the booking? (Remember also to send a thank you and a post-event survey at the conclusion of the event.)
29. Call the client and offer assistance in providing the following:
    - Hotel accommodations
    - Itinerary development
    - Making appropriate contacts at facilities being used
    - Arranging for outside contractors (if required)
    - Providing transportation (if applicable) from the airport
    - Arranging at least one dinner/lunch with the client
    - Tying into an entertainment feature (if applicable)
      - Major or minor league sports
      - Cultural events or museums and so on
    - Arranging for amenities
    - Sending itineraries to all parties concerned
    - Arranging for transportation to the airport (if applicable)
    - Sending follow-up letters detailing the results of the visit and outlining next steps or needs
30. Follow through on all of the items detailed in the "Prescription for Success—Convention Services Manager" template (see Figure 35.2).

**Convention Services Manager
Prescription for Success Checklist**

Group: _____   Sales Manager: _____

Date: _____   CSM: _____

Convention Center
Event Coordinator: _____

Convention Center
Sales Manager: _____

Activity	Completed Task	Status Alert	Follow-Up
24 Months Out/Or Upon Turnover			
18 Months Out			
13 Months Out			
12 Months Out			
11 Months Out			
9 Months Out			
6 Months Out			
90 Days Out			
30 Days Out			
14 Days Out			
Client Arrival Date Through Convention Date			
Post-Convention Activity			

FIGURE 35.2
Checklist Template for Managing a Citywide Convention
Use with the Citywide Convention Task List (Table 35.2)

TABLE 35.2
Citywide Convention Task List
Use with Checklist Template (Figure 35.2)

Citywide Convention Task List	
Event Name: _____	Event Dates: _____
Contact Name: _____	Phone: _____
Email: _____	Fax: _____

Timing	CVB/CSM Responsibilities
24 Months Out Or Upon Turnover	CSM sends a letter to the meeting manager. Reviews and confirms fees and promotional assessments with the sales manager. Obtains pertinent information from sales (history, financial information, rebate information).
18 Months Out	CSM helps client with facility contracts (including space needs/issues, rules/regulations, and labor concerns/issues), hotel block/contracts, and off-site venue needs (including program needs and transportation implications). Together, the CSM and the meeting manager conduct site visits. Meeting manager gives CSM marketing registration plans/timeline. CSM sends membership directory/other promotional items.
13 Months Out	CSM reviews history. CSM sends good luck letter/amenity to group's current convention site. Convention center or other meeting facility contract is signed, and event coordinator is assigned. CSM gets update on the housing process. Together, CSM and meeting manager start pre-promotion planning (including purpose, plans, and contacts to be made requiring information for convention center or other meeting facility and hotels). CSM creates web site links for promotion. CSM and meeting manager discuss welcome program.
12 Months Out/ The Pre-Promotion	CSM assists with: • Staffing the city promotions booth • Exhibit contacts on the trade show floor • Convention center contacts • Hotel/CVB contracts • Preparing reports on the activity
11 Months Out	CSM: • Obtains housing pickup reports (Meeting Industry Network (MINT) and hotels) • Confirms convention center or other meeting facilities contracts • Arranges future site visit(s) • Helps with local organizing committee (LOC) needs, if required • Confirms the opening date for housing • Reviews notes/reports from the client's most recent convention

TABLE 35.2
Citywide Convention Task List, continued

Timing	CVB/CSM Responsibilities
9 Months Out	CSM looks for block changes CSM assists with the program and catering contracts Meeting manager may want to do a site visit CSM helps with convention center planning, including security, catering concerns, etc. CSM and meeting manager begin public/media relations
6 Months Out	Obtains updates on housing, hotels, and off-site events. CSM updates meeting manager on the convention center (including decorators, events, catering, labor issues, and outside contractors). Checks on transportation/shuttle contracts. Meeting manager supplies program information for the convention profile. Checks hotel pickup and reviews numbers. Reviews one-stop shop forms. Meeting manager and CSM check web site for program details.
90 Days Out	Reviews expanded housing report, and confirms cut-off date. Reviews convention center issues (including labor, decorators, and information booth). Updates material for convention profile and gets background information to CVB's media reps. CSM and meeting manager review off-site event issues.
30 Days Out	Housing cut-off date. CSM and meeting manager begin preparing convention profile for distribution. Reviews convention center, catering, and decorator issues, any contract concerns, and any unforeseen issues.
14 Days Out	• Confirms arrival dates of key clients • Distributes convention profile • Determines date of any "welcome program" material to be distributed • Distributes current housing list(s) to client if CVB is handling housing • Finalizes welcome reception • Orders amenities for selected (VIP) clients • Determines date for convention center pre-convention meeting • Establishes a date for post-convention analysis before the client leaves city • Finalizes information/restaurant booth dates, personnel, and locations
Client Arrival Date Through Convention Date	Ensures in-room amenities delivered (prior to arrival). Arranges pick up of clients from the airport (including lunch or dinner). Provides pre-convention meal opportunities, on-site assistance, and host-city welcome reception. CSM is available 24/7 via cell phone throughout the convention.
Post Convention	Meets with meeting manager, followed up by a post-convention survey. Reviews comments from the client, and sends the client a thank you letter. Sends meeting manager the final housing pickup.

While each CSM will have their own servicing procedures, a general outline of their responsibilities in preparing for a citywide convention is provided in the Convention Services Initial Checklist.

The CVB/CSM may provide a welcome program. Not every event will qualify for an "all-out" welcome program from the city. In general, citywide conventions usually justify a CVB-organized welcome program. Other groups that might require a welcome program include ones that are attempting to generate awareness of their mission in the city itself, or ones that have a local organizing committee that is important to the city. The welcome program should take place on the event's peak nights, as determined by the CVB. Communicating the city's welcome to the convention's participants can take the form of some or all of the following:

- Hotel and concierge signage
- Front line personnel identification via buttons
- Electronic signage
- Other exterior/interior signage as warranted
- Supplemental "guides" for distribution as needed or warranted (e.g., a special event in the city)

The final element in the transition from the sales service department to the convention management department is post-convention servicing. Post-convention servicing usually involves:

- Thank you letters from sales and service managers
- Post-convention surveys
- Billing activity, if any, related to housing services and/or financial collections and payments to vendors
- Follow-up (e.g., finalize any uncompleted tasks or client requests)

Sales and Service Collaboration

Every department in the CVB must work together to manage an event that is the size of a citywide convention. Once the contract has been finalized, the sales manager who made the sale should review the account in person with the CSM who has been assigned to the convention. At that meeting, the sales manager should communicate any special instructions (e.g., requirements, concessions, special billings or invoicing). In addition, the following should be placed in a source database, for ease of validation:

- Client information
- Financial commitments
- Commitment letter

Record Keeping

Good record keeping can save meeting managers a great deal of effort and conflict. For a citywide meeting, a CSM will keep hard copies of the following information:

- Booking notice/information (also in the CVB database)
- Housing information (database print outs)
- Account notes/memos (includes itineraries and so on)
- Sales information (notes and instructions from the sales manager)
- Letters and hard copies of important emails from the client

THE HOTEL CONVENTION SERVICES MANAGER

In contrast to the CVB/CSM, the hotel CSM coordinates the services that are required to support a meeting held in a hotel. A hotel CSM is well-versed in the operation of each hotel department, and assists meeting managers with all the details involved in their meetings. A meeting manager can request that the hotel CSM join the hotel sales manager during the initial site visit. The hotel CSM is a valuable source of information throughout the booking process and can offer alternatives to both parties based upon experiences with similar events.[3]

Based upon the size and business type, a hotel may operate as either a uniserve property, where the CSM handles all of the logistics (including catering), or a duoserve property, where the logistics are handled by the CSM with a separate catering manager assigned to handle the food and beverage service. During the booking process, the meeting manager may request either the uniserve or duoserve method. In either case, the CSM is the primary contact and is ultimately responsible for the delivery of a successful event.

Once the booking agreement is finalized, the hotel CSM is assigned to handle a group's meeting management needs, from initial planning to post-meeting reporting, including arrangements for the pre-conference and post-conference meetings. The hotel CSM is responsible for administering the hotel contract, representing each party's needs, and ensuring that both the hotel and the organization meet their obligations. The CSM will determine the appropriate actions and follow-through to meet the terms of the agreement. Any request for a change in the agreement by either party is handled by the CSM. The CSM has an open line of communication with the hotel manager and all hotel personnel during the entire process.

The hotel CSM will use a timeline to proactively anticipate the group's needs (see Figure 35.3). Review the booking agreement with the hotel CSM 11 months prior to an annual event (or as soon as possible) and revise both the guest room block and function space as needed (based upon the group's most recent event history). This is the time to reserve a guest room sub-block for VIPs, staff, and speakers. The CSM will provide a list of ancillary activities with confirmed prices for review, as well as catering menus with confirmed prices.

If the event includes an exhibit area, the hotel CSM will work with the meeting manager and any designated outside contractors to ensure that proper floor plans and fire code approvals are obtained. The move-in schedule, exhibit hours, and move-out schedule should be reviewed and included in the exhibitor prospectus along with a list of all hotel services and exhibit regulations (see Chapter 27). The hotel CSM should also review and follow the sponsoring organization's policies and procedures governing event participants.

The hotel CSM should obtain a draft of the meeting program to review and ensure that they are placed on the event's mailing list. The CSM will attend the hotel's weekly financial forecast and operations meetings to update all departments on changes in the group's status and to keep current with anything that may affect the group. The hotel CSM will advise the meeting manager of any situation that might affect the event, and will seek direction before changing any element in the agreement.

Efficient communication between the CSM and the meeting manager in the months and weeks leading up to the event will maximize productivity. These parties should take advantage of current technology—including voice mail, email, fax, and conference calls—and prearranged telephone appointment times to ask questions and provide any new updated information. During site visits, the CSM will introduce the meeting manager to key department heads. These early introductions foster good working relationships throughout the meeting management process.

Convention Services Event Checklist—Hotel

Event Name: _____   Event Dates: _____

Contact Name: _____   Phone: _____

Email: _____   Fax: _____

Timing	CVB/CSM Responsibilities
Upon Receipt of Turnover	Complete an overall review of the sales manager's turnover sheet, booking ticket, and sales contract. In doing so, look for following items. Place appropriate paperwork in the event file if needed. • Reservation method & cut off date • "Preferred Meeting Manager" points included in contract • Confirm that contract date & method match booking ticket • Paperwork processed once payment received • Commissions/rebates due at conclusion • Addendums/rate confirmations sent by sales manager • Contract suites • Food & beverage minimums • Comp room/suite clause • Special contracted menu pricing • Pre-planning agreement, if any Review meeting space noted in contract versus what is being held in the system. If there is a "Hold All Space" (HAS) included in the contract, note deadline for client's program being due. Complete Room/Suite Protection form—include exact room names, dates, and rates for each room. Forward to reservations. Send introduction letter to client. Include the following information: Reservations method, cut-off dates, HAS deadlines, credit application or credit card authorization form, current banquet menus, and A/V brochure.
Six Months Prior to Group Arrival	Receive accurate program from client and confirm it reflects what is in the system. Discuss specifics with client, such as: • A/V, meeting set-up and food and beverage fit in the assigned rooms? Confirm set-up & teardown times; obtain names of drayage company, decorators, outside A/V company, and so on. • Input accurate food and beverage cover counts and revenue for forecasting. • Obtain "In Conjunction With" (ICW) list from client if applicable. • Re-verify suite requirements and dates with client. • Confirm billing and submit posting master request accompanied by appropriate back up. • Confirm whether or not group is sales tax exempt. If exempt, obtain certificate and send it to accounting.
Three Months Prior to Group Arrival	Confirm receipt of credit application, if not already received Re-check client's program to confirm any changes or additions Re-verify cover counts in system and re-verify food and beverage revenues are forecasted accurately

FIGURE 35.3
Sample CSM Checklist for a Convention Hotel[5]

Timing	CVB/CSM Responsibilities
Three Months Prior to Group Arrival	Monitor reservation procedure and pickup numbers. Keep client informed throughout process. Request VIP information and suite assignments from client. Confirm menu pricing if special pricing is contracted. Contact group's decorator/drayage companies to confirm arrangements.
Two Months Prior to Group Arrival	Receive client's final program with specifications, including menu selections, room set-ups, AV requirements, and so on. Begin to generate Banquet Event Orders (BEO's). Continue to re-verify cover counts in the system so that food and beverage revenues are forecast accurately. Review "housing opportunities" with reservation manager.
One Month Prior to Group Arrival	Review room block, pickup, and cut-off date with client. Distribute special request paperwork (electrical, phone, banner). Generate BEO's, if not already completed. Confirm and complete purchase orders for special details you are taking care of for the client such as floral deliveries; transportation arrangements, entertainment, etc.
Ten Days Prior to Group Arrival	Confirm receipt of signed BEO's from client. Distribute BEO's to operating departments. Distribute the Event Specifications Guide—including reminder of pre-conference meeting, if scheduled. Reconfirm any special arrangements you have made for client.
One Week Prior to Group Arrival	Distribute amenity request forms.
Three Days Prior to Group Arrival	Obtain all food and beverage guarantees from client. Update BEO book. Verify VIP flight arrival times/flight numbers, if necessary.
One Day Prior to Group Arrival	Send pre-conference meeting voicemail reminder. Attend daily BEO meeting beginning today through group's departure.
On-Site	Attend daily BEO meeting while group is in-house. "Opportunities" identified and rectified while group is in-house. Act as "hotel liaison" at all times. Schedule post-conference meeting, if client requests.
One Day After Group Departs	Send thank you letter to client.
One to Two Weeks Following Group's Departure	Receive and review bill from hotel group billing coordinator.

FIGURE 35.3
Sample CSM Checklist for a Convention Hotel, continued[5]

The CSM will involve these staff members as often as possible to acquaint them with an organization's needs. An experienced CSM will delegate tasks to hotel departments based upon the event's complexity and the meeting manager's individual working style. The goal is to build a proactive team of hotel staff working together to anticipate the group's needs.

The hotel CSM documents the event in the Event Specifications Guide (ESG), also known as a résumé, which provides hotel staff with a summary of the organization (including its history), organization leadership, meeting manager and key staff, VIP arrangements, attendee profile, and meeting objectives.[4] The ESG highlights the operational details of each department's responsibilities, as previously arranged by the CSM. The ESG will also contain a schedule of the meeting's events with anticipated attendance and is distributed to hotel department heads one to two weeks prior to the event.

Upon arrival on-site for the event, the meeting manager should review the ESG during a pre-conference meeting with the CSM, hotel manager, and department heads. Throughout the event, the hotel CSM will stay in touch with meeting management staff using two-way radios, pagers, and/or cellular phones. The CSM should also schedule a daily 15- to 30-minute face-to-face meeting to review the events for the next 24 hours and to discuss any unresolved issues from the previous 24 hours. The hotel CSM will also arrange to have a daily review of the group's master account to prevent accounting errors.

Often, the CVB/CSM will attend the pre-conference meeting. For citywide conventions, CVB/CSMs schedule the pre-convention meetings and invite representatives from the group's hotels, convention center, and third-party suppliers.

After the event, the hotel CSM will schedule a post-conference meeting with the meeting management staff and invite members of the hotel's executive committee and key department representatives. This event review is an opportunity to critique the hotel's performance and recommend improvements. The CSM will also arrange for a final review of the group's master billing (see Chapter 3). The hotel CSM is available after the event to address any outstanding issues and will work with the sales manager to determine the group's future booking potential. The CSM may be assigned to all the group's future events.

The CVB/CSM usually sends a post-event evaluation form to the meeting manager that addresses the evaluation of the host city, including the meeting managers' satisfaction with the hotels, CVB, and third-party services.

THE CONVENTION CENTER CSM

The role of the CSM in a convention center has unique features and responsibilities unlike those of a CSM in a hotel environment or at a convention and visitors bureau. Multi-tasking, a part of all three disciplines, is expanded for the CSM at a convention center.[6] Sales manager(s) from the center and, in some cases, the CVB are the first to interact with the CSM at the center. Subsequently, a myriad of vendors, labor sources from both inside and outside the facility, catering concerns, billing and other accounting services from multiple departments, together with a host of personnel managers from various departments within the center are all centralized and, to some degree, managed or, at least, directed by a single source in the convention center: the CSM.

This one-stop management system is not necessarily universal. Some centers employ a CSM to initiate action with and engage in-house departments and outside vendors for the client. Once engaged, the convention center CSM's role becomes one of pre-planning and encompasses only duties that occur prior to the event itself. On-site management comes from an individual(s) assigned to interact with a variety of vendors and in-house personnel who are assigned to various duties for the client.

A job description for a CSM at a center, in some cases referred to as an Event Coordinator (EC), might include the following duties:

- Maintain communication with client(s) to assist in management of events in the building (center)
- Coordinate physical set-up requirements and service needs
- Work with the center's sales department to assure that clients' requirements are met
- Create set-up diagrams and drawings as needed (in house)
- Act as liaison to outside service contractors
- Perform other duties that may be assigned by the CSM's manager or the building's executive director

A CSM at a convention center works from a checklist that encompasses many proactive duties as well as information that is to be given to the meeting manager. The checklist includes data the center needs for its own purposes to ready the facility for the customer. Other information relates to policies and procedures the building employs for its users. The basic checklist might include the following:

- General facility information
- Goods and services for which the client will incur an expense
- Security items
- Set-up issues
- Sound and lighting issues
- Ticket office issues
- Policies and procedures in the center

The CSM's interaction in advance of the meeting will normally include a series of site visits. The focus of these site visits is dependent on the attendees during the site visit. The meeting manager needs information (both logistical and budgetary) for use of space and operations within the center. Whereas, vendors supporting the client are in need of information relating to facility, including labor contracts, power access, floor loads, access to the building, loading dock rules and regulations, AV information, and so on. These site visits, less visible to sales sources, may be numerous and require considerable time from the CSM, depending on the size and scope of the trade show or convention.

Another key element that distinguishes the life of an CSM at a center from the life of a hotel is the greater potential for multiple events within the same building. Convention centers are designed to host multiple events at the same time. As a result, the move-in, set-up, and move-out may create real challenges for the CSM. Accordingly, interaction with other CSMs in his or her organization is crucial to ensure that adequate planning is being conducted to support more than one event. It is incumbent upon a good CSM to communicate with in-house representatives working with other clients routinely in order to ensure that the access, scheduling, material, and labor needs meet the capabilities of the center and multiple tenants within it.

The ultimate tool for any CSM will be a comprehensive Event Specifications Guide. Created through the input of the meeting manager and in conjunction with a myriad of in-house departments within the center, this document details every physical need for space, labor, and equipment required by the customer. Merged with pre-convention meetings and daily meetings with the meeting manager, the document is the road map from which decisions are made to confirm, alter, or delete requirements set out in it. It also serves as an adjunct to the billing process conducted by the accounting department.

The meeting manager's post-convention meeting(s) with the CSM may include billing information, concerns, unresolved issues, and information from both sides that will help both parties in the future. The sources for this information may flow from meeting manager to CSM for a period of time after the event, resulting in the meeting manager having a good record of the trade show or convention—one that will assist the customer in the future.

SUMMARY

The convention services manager is the professional at a convention visitors bureau, hotel, or convention center who is responsible for event operations management on all levels. While the specific duties at each venue may differ slightly, the responsibilities of all CSMs remain consistent. The CSM acts as an extension of the meeting manager's staff, fulfills contract commitments and obligations, facilitates referrals and use of resources at a destination, and is the main facility contact for on-site convention operations.

REFERENCES

1. Ramsborg, G.C. (May-June, 1995). Convention services: Proactive or reactive? *Convene,* p. 32.

2. Daggett, J., & Betzig, V. (December, 2004). Core competencies: Step 10: Convention services manager and facilities staff roles. *Convene*, p. 16.

3. Smith, K. (June, 1998). "That was the week that was": A meeting manager and a CSM trade places: A meeting manager walks in the shadow of a CSM. *Convene*, p. 56.

4. Daggett, J., & Betzig, V. (May, 2005). Core competencies: Step 14: Specifications guidebook. *Convene*, p. 16.

5. Convention Services Department, Westin Hotel, Indianapolis.

6. Ibid.

KEY TERMS

Ancillary activity
Association for
   Convention Operations
   Management (ACOM)
Bible
Booking
Citywide event
Conference service
   coordinator

Convention services
   manager (CSM)
Convention and Visitors
   Bureau (CVB)
Duoserve property
Master account
Post-conference meeting
   (post-con meeting)

Pre-conference meeting
   (pre-con meeting)
Résumé
Specifications guide
   (spec guide)
Uniserve property
Venue

CONTRIBUTORS

Robert E. Desautels, CMP
Senior Manager, Convention Services
Indianapolis Convention & Visitors
   Association

Mary A. German, CMP
Director of Convention Services
Arlington Convention & Visitors Bureau

Marilyn J. Healey, CMP
Senior Convention Services Manager
Hyatt Regency Orange County

Denise Suttle, CMP
Assistant Director of Convention
   Services
Albuquerque Convention & Visitors
   Bureau

CHAPTER 36

EFFECTIVE MEETING COMMUNICATIONS AND ON-SITE OPERATIONS

Steve Drew

ASSISTANT EXECUTIVE DIRECTOR
SCIENTIFIC ASSEMBLY & INFORMATICS
RADIOLOGICAL SOCIETY OF
NORTH AMERICA

Janet M. Cooper, CMP

DIRECTOR, CONVENTION OPERATIONS
RADIOLOGICAL SOCIETY OF
NORTH AMERICA

LEARNER OUTCOMES

When the reader has completed reading this chapter, he/she should be able to . . .

1 Recognize the purpose and procedures for pre-conference and post-conference meetings.

2 Recognize the importance of daily logistical meetings and staff briefings.

3 Plan an on-site office as the headquarters for your operations.

4 Set up risk management procedures.

5 Plan equipment requirements for on-site use of telephones, cell phones, pagers, walkie-talkies, PDAs, and Internet on-site.

6 Arrange for an information kiosk.

7 Arrange for a message center.

> It is time for us all to stand and cheer for the doer, the achiever—the one who recognizes the challenges and does something about it.
>
> *Vince Lombardi*

OVERVIEW

Successful on-site operations depend upon a well-defined plan for program management. Excellent program management is contingent upon excellent communication. Communication starts before the meeting, when precise expectations are conveyed to all site facilities in a thorough and timely fashion. Communication during the meeting means daily meetings to review logistical details. Communication after the meeting takes the form of feedback from the organization staff, attendees, exhibitors, and representatives from all participating facilities. Effective communication is the essential ingredient for successful on-site operations and a successful event.

PRE-CONFERENCE MEETINGS

Before departing for your meeting destination, meet with your staff to review pertinent information about the meeting facilities, program, and logistics. The objective is to orient your staff to all the activities surrounding the meeting and make clear your expectations for them on-site. Review the following information:

- Name, address, and phone number of all meeting venues
- Staff arrival/departure dates and times
- Emergency preparedness plan
- Floor plans of meeting space, with details on how the space will be utilized
- Summary of events and room assignments
- On-site job responsibility

Once on-site, require your staff to tour the facility and familiarize themselves with the location of meeting space, emergency exits, and all public areas.

The pre-conference meeting (pre-con) is an essential meeting between you and your team, the site's key decision-makers, and outside contractors. The pre-con meeting's purpose is to reconfirm all written and verbal details of the meeting, discuss the meeting arrangements, and answer any questions pertaining to the program. The pre-con is a time to put names to faces and resolve last-minute questions. It is not meant to substitute for providing ongoing, up-to-date logistical information. Rather, it is a final confirmation of previously articulated specifications. A pre-con meeting should be held no matter how small or large the meeting. It is usually held 24 hours prior to the first event of the meeting. For large meetings or citywide events, hold the pre-con meeting a week in advance to allow for all participants to review the information in detail before the start of the event.

Depending on the complexity of the meeting, the pre-con meeting may be one to two hours in length.

Whether the meeting is held in a hotel or convention center, essential participants for the pre-con meeting include:

- Association or organization staff members, inclusive of the meeting professional and meetings team
- Convention services manager (CSM) and designated convention services personnel
- Sales manager
- Banquets or catering manager, if food and beverages are involved
- Audiovisual (A/V) department representative or your independent A/V contractor, if audiovisuals are involved
- IT department representative, if computer and networking are involved
- Convention and visitors bureau (CVB) representative

- Outside suppliers (general service contractor, security, transportation, DMC, etc.), as appropriate
- Safety/security department representative

If the meeting is held in a hotel, other participants who are usually involved in a portion of the pre-con meeting include

- General manager or representative
- Accounting manager
- Bell staff manager
- Engineering/special utilities representative
- Front desk manager
- Guest services manager
- Housekeeping manager
- Recreation (golf/tennis/health club) coordinator
- Receiving/shipping representative
- Reservations manager
- Restaurant outlets manager
- Telecommunications manager
- Transportation manager

If the meeting is held in a convention center, other participants who are usually involved in at least a portion of the pre-con meeting include

- General manager or representative
- Accounting manager
- Engineering/special utilities representative
- Receiving/shipping representative
- Restaurant outlets manager (if different from the catering company)
- Telecommunications manager
- Transportation manager

The pre-con meeting should establish the mindset and expectation that this entire group of people will operate as one team. Contractors must be included in the pre-con meeting. Not only do they need to hear about and see the big picture, their experience with other groups provides them with an extensive knowledge base, and they can contribute worthy recommendations and suggestions to the discussion.

Pre-Con Meeting Agenda

The pre-con meeting gives you the opportunity to set the tone of the meeting, show appreciation for the work that has been done prior to the meeting, and inspire teamwork among all strategic partners present for the upcoming event. A U-shaped or hollow square room set is most conducive to the purpose of the meeting, because it enables all participants to see one another and facilitates communication.

The convention services manager (CSM) assigned to your group generally helps chair the meeting. The CSM generally welcomes the organization to the facility, asks each person around the table to introduce himself/herself and to give a brief description of his/her respective role in the meeting. The CSM, then turns the meeting over to the meeting manager. Begin by giving a brief profile of your organization and state the purpose and objectives of the meeting. Review key information, such as meeting attendance (domestic and international), housing pick-up, net square footage of exhibition space (if applicable), hours of operation, very important person (VIP) concerns, any major difference between current event and previous one held at the facility, if this is a repeat event, and any "hot topics." Distribute the meeting program (or a condensed version) to all attendees at the pre-con meeting.

Before opening the meeting to questions, the meeting manager, along with the facility security department representative, should review the organization's emergency preparedness plan and distribute pertinent materials (inclusive of contacts and cell phone numbers). Review the overall security/safety operation within the facility, policy regarding medical/emergency calls, first aid/EMS coverage, as well as any political concerns or weather considerations specific to the area.

Following specific questions your team may have for a particular department within the facility or vise versa, thank the support staff for attending and allow them the opportunity to excuse themselves from the balance of the meeting, if they wish. During the remainder of the meeting, the meeting team, CSM, banquets or catering manager(s), audiovisual (A/V) representative, and any appropriate outside suppliers walk through the logistical details of the meeting. The basis of this discussion will be the materials you have sent to the site four to six weeks earlier and the function sheets that the facility has returned to you two weeks prior to your arrival.

Function Sheet Review

The function sheets (created by the meeting manager) or the banquet event orders (BEOs created by the facility) summarize all of the meeting requirements. These documents should list key meeting team member's name, hotel, and cell phone number. Other key personnel in the organization should also be identified with the same information. Advise the CSM who is authorized to sign for the master account. Some facilities give the meeting management team a unique pin to wear during the meeting, identifying them as decision makers.

You and your team should also receive the contact list of all facility department managers, including the cell phone number for the CSM assigned to the group. In the event of a non-medical emergency that occurs at a time other than when the CSM is on property, you must have a way to reach this key person. The CSM is responsible for handling on-site problems and requests. If the CSM has major decision-making ability within the facility, the rest of the managers need never be contacted. However, this list is an essential piece of information for backup procedures.

Most pre-con meetings go over the details of each event in chronological order, beginning with VIP arrivals, board and committee meetings, general sessions and breakouts, late checkouts, and the post-conference meeting (post-con). Review meeting room turnover timing, setups, and changes. At the hotel pre-con meeting, confirm key organization members, board of directors members, speakers, or other VIPs who should receive special treatment, be given room upgrades, or be pre-registered in the hotel. Dates and times of off-site events, and arrival and departure patterns should also be discussed.

If the event is of a longer duration and/or consists of multiple simultaneous sessions, you may not have time to go over all meeting details at the pre-con meeting. In that case, a daily meeting time should be established to cover the next day's events.

DAILY LOGISTICAL MEETINGS

An excellent communication tool for multiple-facility meetings is the daily logistical meeting. This meeting is held at a pre-set time each day, and is attended by key facility and contractor personnel from each participating hotel or facility, in addition to the meeting team. Getting all responsible parties together at one time enables everyone to be informed about the events planned for the next day.

This meeting allows you to advise appropriate personnel about cancellations or additions to the program, changes to food-and-beverage orders, increased needs for A/V equipment, and more. It is also a time to review operations over the past 24-hours and discuss how communication or strategies can be improved in anticipation of the next day's events.

Although these meetings can sometimes be tedious, they frequently produce an additional level of camaraderie for the entire group. While this is an excellent opportunity to manage problems, be sure to compliment staff for the activities that are progressing according to plan.

Be sure to note, in writing, all on-site changes and additions as a reference for analyzing the final statement of charges.

Staff Briefings

Daily briefings of your organization's on-site team provide an opportunity to evaluate the previous day's events. These briefings do not have to be long, particularly if everything is going well. Some meeting managers prefer to have the briefing at the end of the day, first thing in the morning, or mid-day, provided that all staff members are available to attend. A preferable alternative is to hold the meeting in conjunction with the daily logistical meetings to make the best use of everyone's time. The briefing should take place in an area free of distractions.

During the briefing, identify and discuss issues or concerns from the past 24-hours and review the next day's schedule and assignments. Ask for suggestions about how to address sensitive issues. Attitude is important. No matter what has transpired, facing it with a "can-do" attitude is critical to the meeting's success. This is a time to find solutions, not cast blame. This is also a time to congratulate team members for a job well done and to show support for their efforts.

ON-SITE OFFICE OPERATION

Every meeting needs an on-site office as the designated location where you and your staff can confer, access private phones, and store and retrieve meeting materials. Large meetings may have an office suite in the convention center or hotel. In this case, one office should be designated for you and your staff, and one as the organization's on-site headquarters. Ideally, these offices should be clustered together to facilitate communication between members of the meeting team.

Many organizations designate the on-site office as the center of operations for the meeting. This office differs from the meeting manager's office because it is designed to answer questions from attendees, leadership, and staff. The meeting manager's office is the place to interact with the operations staff of the facility, communicate program changes, and carry out directives from the chief executive officer (CEO) or board. These two offices communicate regularly and complement each other in their responsibilities.

The staff person in charge of the on-site office has a key role because, in many instances, this office becomes the central communications center. The office manager should have a listing of where all staff members are located on a daily and hour-by-hour basis. The on-site office manager must have the means for instant communications with all pertinent parties at all times.

Identifying Meetings Staff

The meeting manager is in charge of the entire meeting, and all offices turn to you for help with issues of all types. From locating an attendee who has an emergency phone call, to alerting the program committee that a speaker has cancelled, you will field questions, troubleshoot problems, and direct operations for the duration of the meeting. You will have the best perspective on all that transpires and know how to direct communications to your team.

Many organizations identify the meeting team, and sometimes the entire organization staff, by having them wear specific clothing (e.g., a brightly colored shirt). This allows attendees, volunteers, facility staff, and others to easily identify knowledgeable staff capable of facilitating communication and expediting problem solving.

STAYING IN COMMUNICATION

Staying in communication with key personnel throughout the meeting enables you and your staff to anticipate and resolve problems before they become emergencies. Several communication tools have been proven effective for meetings of all sizes.

Risk Management Procedures

Following the pre-con meeting, and before any show management equipment is brought in to the facility, the meeting manager, CSM, security department representative, and any appropriate contractors should walk through all meeting space being utilized to note any existing property damage and/or debris. This should be documented through a written report (photograph or video taping is recommended) and signed by all parties. During the course of the meeting, if a damage incident is determined, the meeting manager should be notified immediately. All representatives involved should meet and determine responsibility for the damage. An incident report should be completed and signed by all parties.

Telecommunication Services

If the event is a small meeting, such as a board meeting with a single room setup, you may not need any communication devices on-site other than a telephone or cell phone to communicate with the CSM. For mega-meetings with a staff of 20 or more people in several offices, however, you may need to set up a more extensive communication system with multiple incoming lines for voice, fax, and Internet access. Also consider the needs of your attendees. Because most people carry cell phones today, telecommunication is not the logistical issue it used to be. If, for some reason, your group is unique and the majority of attendees do not utilize personal cell phones, be aware of the facility's pay phone infrastructure. Most facilities have reduced the number of available pay phones. In this situation, groups may overtax the facility's phone banks. Be sure to work with the facility to make arrangements for alternate attendee telecommunication services (cell phone rentals, portable/temporary pay phones, etc.). The temporary solution must be convenient to accommodate the needs of your attendees.

Most modern facilities are capable of providing adequate on-site telecommunication services. In some cases, however, you may need to contract with an outside provider to procure telecommunication services for your special requirements. Ordering services in advance allows you to identify phone numbers for respective offices. Promote the phone number of your on-site office and message center to all participants in advance of the meeting. Detailed diagrams of office layouts should identify locations of all furniture and equipment (phones, faxes, computers, etc.). To insure a smooth and accurate installation, diagrams should be distributed to the general contractor/CSM and posted in each office before setup. If your operations rely on the Internet, determine bandwidth requirements and order the service. Most facilities are capable of providing Internet service; if not, contract with a dependable Internet service provider (ISP).

Wireless Communication

Walkie-talkies remain a suitable means for communication with staff and contractors. Be sure that identical frequencies are available on the walkie-talkies used by all parties. Instantaneous communication is a major advantage when responding to a question or emergency. A major drawback is that no one else can talk until you finish your conversation, unless they switch to another channel. In the event that you need to have a lengthy conversation, find a telephone and alert the other party to call you at that number. This will keep the radio frequencies open for operational issues.

Meeting professionals often use cell phones to stay in touch with staff and operations personnel in charge of the event. Combination devices are available and efficient. They not only allow cell phones communication but also provide direct-connect communication similar to walkie-talkies. A major advantage of direct-connect devices is the flexibility available for programming private and group channels.

Cell phones and walkie-talkies are good tools for communication, *as long as they work*. Check each facility for "dead spots" and other areas that have difficulty picking up signals. This is an important service that can be provided by your A/V and telecommunication contractors. Try a test run with your communication products in advance of the meeting to determine dead spots. Take corrective action by installing repeaters or identifying alternate communication devices. Pagers are effective uni-directional communication devices. They can be purchased or rented from an A/V contractor or telephone company. Typically, each pager is assigned a telephone number. When that number is dialed, the caller enters a return call number and/or a message, using voice or the phone's keypad. The pager then either beeps or vibrates to alert the receiver. The range is typically much longer than a walkie-talkie.

Personal digital assistants (PDAs) are an emerging trend at meetings. Computer terminals can be setup to download data to PDAs through a hot sync cradle or infrared beaming station. Attendees and meeting staff alike can use beaming stations for wireless e-mail messaging, meeting and delegate information, and up-to-date event schedules.[2] See Figure 37.1 for examples of wireless communication.

INFORMATION KIOSKS AND MESSAGE CENTERS

Every organization holding a meeting should recognize the need to provide an information kiosk and message center for meeting participants. For small, simple meetings, this may be a cork bulletin board where people can post telephone messages, schedule changes, etc. A logical location might be adjacent to the information kiosk. The information kiosk may be a freestanding unit or it may be part of the registration and/or help desk. You may decide to make available an alphabetical listing of attendees so that registrants can easily check to see if colleagues are in attendance. Offer attendees the opportunity to provide cell phone and email contact information during the registration process; with their permission, include contact information on the attendee list. If additional contact information is not available, leaving a message at this center may be the best way for attendees to contact fellow registrants.

A more advanced system is the electronic message center. Two options are available when choosing a message system: (1) open email functionality via the Internet, or (2) closed email functionality with no Internet access. Many third party contractors provide either or both systems. Some systems include a large display (liquid crystal display or plasma) that scrolls an alphabetical list of message recipients. This system is effective for small groups, but is not efficient for larger groups

FIGURE 36.1
Wireless Communication Options

because of the wait time for a name to appear when scrolling. Ease of access to the system can be accomplished via magnetic strip or bar code name badges.

Consider deploying wireless access points (Wi-Fi zones) in lounge areas so that attendees may access their personal email accounts via their personal notebook computer or PDA. The majority of hotels and convention centers have the infrastructure and personnel to provide Wi-Fi access.

Follow these guidelines to provide the most efficient information kiosk and message center:

- Place the information kiosk and message center in a central area relative to the majority of meeting activities.
- Be sure the space is adequate for the intended layout of equipment, electrical wiring, and Internet access, if desired.
- Provide a thorough orientation for the person(s) staffing the information kiosk.
- Docents providing assistance to message center users should be fully trained in all aspects of the system.
- The information kiosk should include information about restaurants and extracurricular activities; offer electronic access to this information as well, generally available through a web site by the local CVB.
- For a non-electronic message center, provide telephone directories, message paper, and envelopes for private messages.
- Provide signs to identify Wi-Fi zones and include appropriate addressing/access information.

All offices and information kiosks should be equipped with a written summary or policy for managing emergencies. This information should be shared with each member of the organization staff and appropriate facility personnel during the pre-con meeting. The organization will need to determine how emergency calls should be delivered, i.e., by the temporary staff or volunteer in charge

Put It Into Practice

Sample Hotel Pre-Con Meeting Agenda

1. Welcome and introductions
2. Brief profile of organization and meeting overview
3. Contracted room block and actual pick-up
4. Number of guests expected, main arrival and departure dates
5. VIPs and special considerations
6. Procedures for master account
7. Meeting room activity update
8. Food-and-beverage activity update
9. Security/emergency preparedness plan
10. Overview of facility services
11. Function sheet review (with selected individuals)

Sample Daily Staff Meeting Agenda

1. Evaluate the previous day's events and discuss any unresolved issues

2. Review the current day's activities and highlight any cancellations/changes/additions/concerns
3. Discuss following day's activities
4. Review responsibilities and procedures
5. Reemphasize communication lines
6. Congratulate members of the team

Sample Post-Con Meeting Agenda

1. Congratulate members of the team
2. Critique the facilities' performance and recommend improvements
3. Identify outstanding efforts made by the facilities' employees
4. Ask what information you could have provided earlier, or in a better way, to help the facility prepare for the meeting
5. Review the master account

of the message center or by organization staff. Immediate delivery of emergency messages is the highest priority.

POST-CONFERENCE MEETING

At the conclusion of the meeting, a post-conference meeting (post-con) held on-site can be a vital source of feedback on the meeting just held and for reference when planning future meetings. It is essentially your report card for the on-site operations of the meeting. It is also an opportunity for the organization to receive candid feedback on how well it performed in the planning and management of on-site logistics.

The end of the meeting is the time to reflect on what worked well, as well as what did not work. Your meeting team, and key facility and contractor personnel should attend the post-con meeting. Open the discussion with compliments on the service of the facility personnel. Then move on to any problem areas. Despite the fact that your daily logistical meetings identified procedures that were inadequate, some of the issues bear repeating at the post-con. Most CSMs welcome constructive criticism and suggestions for improvement of their operation. All will welcome well-deserved praise for exceptional service.

Meeting professionals do not hesitate to ask the CSM and other facility personnel, "What can we, the organization, do better in the future?" This is a time to learn and receive a candid perspective, recognizing that the CSM has broad-based experience from which your organization can benefit.

You might have a separate meeting with your meeting staff and extend a special thank you to all the people who contributed to a successful event. You might want to share a small token of thanks with your staff members during this time. Remember, attitude is everything and it flows from the top.

SUMMARY

On-site operations is all about timely and thorough communication. Providing comprehensive information to all parties, including those remotely involved in the meeting, helps ensure success. When all parties involved understand the big picture, a smooth-running, crisis-free event will likely result.

Before departing for your meeting, confer with staff to review pertinent information about the facilities, program, and logistics. Once on-site, use the pre-con meeting with CSM, facility staff, and key contractors to confirm all the arrangements, review the function sheet, and answer questions. Go over the details of each event in chronological order, and confirm contact information for all participants, as well as emergency contact information for decision-makers.

Plan daily logistical meetings with key facility and contractor personnel, as well as daily staff briefings, to discuss program changes, problems that occurred, and preparations for the next day's activities. Staying in communication with key personnel throughout the meeting enables you and your staff to anticipate and resolve problems before they become emergencies.

Designate one location (office) to serve as the communications center for the meeting team, and stay in touch with key personnel throughout the meeting using telephones, walkie-talkies, cell phones, pagers, and/or PDAs.

You can facilitate communication among meeting participants with a well-equipped information kiosk and message center, placed in a central area relative to the majority of meeting activities. The message center can be as simple as a bulletin board, or as advanced as an electronic messaging system with Internet access. Consider deploying wireless access points (Wi-Fi zones) for attendees to access their personal email accounts via their PC or PDA. The information kiosk should include information about the meeting, restaurants, and local attractions.

All offices, the information kiosk, and message center should be equipped with a written summary or policy of how to manage emergencies.

At the conclusion of the meeting, solicit feedback from all key personnel during a post-con meeting, and use this feedback to assess the meeting just completed, as well as to improve on-site operating procedures for future meetings. Remember to acknowledge a job well done.

REFERENCES

1. Chatfield-Taylor, C. (April, 2001). More bandwidth for your buck. *EXPO.*

2. Chatfield-Taylor, C. (January, 2002). From paper to portals. *EXPO.*

KEY TERMS

Banquet event order (BEO)	Message center	Post-conference meeting (post-con)
Cell phone	Office suite	Pre-conference meeting (pre-con)
Convention services manager (CSM)	On-site office	Walkie-talkies
Function sheet	Pager	Wi-Fi zone
Information kiosk	Personal digital assistant (PDA)	

COMPELLING QUESTIONS FOR CONSIDERATION

1. Who should be present at the pre-con meeting, and why should they attend?

2. What should you try to accomplish during a daily logistical meeting? Discuss ideas for making this meeting as productive as possible.

3. How does the daily staff briefing differ from the daily logistical meeting, and what procedures should both include?

4. What are the relative advantages and disadvantages of the communication devices typically used by meeting personnel?

5. Develop a policy to handle and deliver emergency calls.

6. Discuss the ideal location for an on-site office, based on the functions of this office.

CHAPTER 37

SUPPLIERS AND CONTRACTED SERVICES

Carol J. Sconzert
PRINCIPAL
OSMOSIS CREATIVE, LLC

LEARNER OUTCOMES

When the reader has completed reading this chapter, he/she should be able to . . .

1 Identify the different types of third-party providers, their roles, and relationships with the meeting manager.

2 State the different types of suppliers required for a successful meeting.

3 Integrate the various supplier and contracted services vendors into a coordinated vendor team.

4 Describe how labor agreements are managed and plan these resources strategically.

> No one can whistle a symphony. It takes an orchestra to play it.
>
> *H.E. Luccock*

OVERVIEW

Suppliers and third-party providers are important members of the event team. Meeting managers contract with industry suppliers to provide everything from function space and event catering to show decoration and ground transportation services. Working in partnership with supplier contacts, meeting managers will find that coordinating all the details of the meeting goes much more smoothly.

Both corporate and association meeting managers have come to rely upon suppliers and third-party providers to function as extensions of their staffs and assuming key decision-making responsibilities. Depending on whether an organization will manage meetings in-house or outsource all or part of this function, these contractors may provide full-scope meeting management services, or special services such as guest program planning, event production, and exhibition management. For many associations, the meeting manager *is* the third-party provider.

Meeting managers can ensure that their meeting team works together as a cohesive unit focused on the meeting's success if they clearly communicate the meeting requirements, understand the relationships between the various players, and know what services to expect from whom. When service capabilities overlap among some vendors, the meeting manager will be expected to make final determinations and assign responsibilities. Understanding the contractual issues of each player will provide guidance in making the most effective decisions. The strength of the communications and the interpersonal relationships they have built in this team will elicit the highest level of customer service from each member. This chapter will focus on an understanding of how meeting managers develop positive working relationships with suppliers to better meet the needs of the meeting or event and the organization.

SUPPLIER SELECTION

The suppliers selected to provide services for the event are an important part of the meeting management team. Although the contractual agreements will delineate the specific services, timelines, and terms of delivery and payment, the working relationships and ongoing communications ultimately determine the quality of the services received. Establishing mutually beneficial and cooperative relationships with supplier contacts will go far to ensure services are delivered as required.

Meeting managers typically evaluate two or three potential suppliers for each service required. Contract evaluation should begin during the request for proposal (RFP) process. The RFP outlines specific requirements for the meeting. The proposals should demonstrate how the supplier will fulfill those requirements, why they are qualified to do so, and all the costs associated with the service.

The selection process can be influenced by many factors, ranging from low bid to superior qualifications. Personalities and a good fit between the contractor's company and the organization may also play a significant part. Once a facility is chosen, the choices for suppliers of certain services may be limited by facility rules and regulations.

All potential suppliers should submit sample contracts with their proposals. This includes hotels and convention centers, as well as drayage, decorating, ground transportation, and other service contractors. The supplier contracts reflect their current operating policies and cover issues such as space and room commitment, attrition, key dates, liability/insurance, assigned responsibility/performance, and finances. All contracts are subject to negotiations and amendment and should be reviewed by legal counsel before execution (see Chapter 42). Some organizations develop standard contracts, especially when multiple hotels are used.

In-House Contractors

Many facilities have in-house contractors for services such as audiovisual (A/V) support, Internet/telecommunications, and security. These contractors are retained by the facility to be on-site and provide services as needed. Although the meeting manager is not required to use their services, there may be surcharges or a fee for bringing in an outside contractor for the same service. Frequently there are distinct advantages to using the in-house contractor. The contractor is familiar with the facility and staff, has likely served similar meetings in the same facility, and may propose cost-saving solutions based on past experiences. When considering using an in-house contractor, RFPs from at least two outside providers is strongly suggested to compare services and pricing.

Exclusive Contractors

An exclusive contractor is designated by facility management to be the only contractor who has the right to provide a given service within that particular convention center or hotel. If there is an exclusive contractor for catering, for example, the meeting manager has no choice but to use that contractor. Rather than be dismayed by this limitation, most meeting managers are confident that the in-house contractor will provide the best available service.

Hotels have a major investment in their food service reputation and in equipment and facilities. Many convention centers have exclusive contracts with food service and other services for the same reason. The convention center must, in order to remain competitive, provide a consistent and high level of service at a competitive price. Exclusive contracts allow the convention center to ensure that professional companies that are experts in their trade manage certain aspects of the facility.

Some convention centers have exclusive contracts for electrical services, and a few have contracts for a variety of services, ranging from drayage and decorating to security and audiovisual; however, these are not in the majority. It is important to ask about all potential service contracts in the convention center and discuss early whether the convention center is willing to be flexible in allowing exceptions to their exclusives. This is not to say that a convention center will default on its contract(s) with its own contractors; however, if discussions are begun early enough, some mutual arrangement may be possible, and that understanding should be reflected in the license agreement. This will also help the meeting manager decide whether to pursue that particular venue for a meeting.

Communication

Remember that contracts are not final until they are fully executed. Do not hesitate to negotiate the terms of any contract. Some suppliers have difficulty in amending the terms of a contract, especially if they are a state or municipal agency. In these cases, contract addendums should be considered.

It is the meeting manager's responsibility to be proactive by ensuring that the organization adheres to the terms of the contract. If questions arise in the interpretation of the contract, the parties should engage in immediate dialogue to ensure that there is no misunderstanding. If circumstances change or new ones arise that cause the parties to amend the contract, this should be discussed, negotiated, and executed as quickly as possible. Talk with each contractor about the preferred method of communication (phone, fax, email, or prescheduled conference call).

General Service Contractor

The general service contractor (GSC) is the company appointed to provide services for meeting's trade show and exhibitors. The GSC is responsible for everything from the show floor to the loading docks, including material handling (drayage), setup, storage, signage and graphics, furniture rental, labor, and, in some cases, utilities and cleaning. The GSC works closely with the trade show manager to coordinate show management requirements and exhibitor requirements throughout the meeting.

The GSC should assign an account executive to provide the meeting manager one main point of contact from preconvention meetings through the actual meeting dates. The meeting manager may also request that the account executive travel with them to at least one site visit. For exhibitors, the GSC should provide a customer service line prior to the meeting, and customer service representatives on-site. The meeting manager should ask if the service representatives provides any extra services, such as calling all exhibitors to remind them of deadlines or providing guidance for first-time exhibitors.

The GSC can prepare an exhibitor floor plan scaled to the trade show's particular needs. They also produce the exhibitor service kit, which includes information from show management, as well as information and order forms from all suppliers. Exhibitor service kits typically are provided in both online and print versions.

When writing an RFP, meeting managers should ask what prices exhibitors will be charged for material handling, labor, furniture rental, and carpeting. These rates should be compared with the average rates charged in the destination city. This information is tracked annually and published by *Tradeshow Week* magazine.

The following is a list of services and equipment the GSC may provide for show management.

- Develop working drafts of floor plans and secure the necessary approvals from the facility and local authorities.
- Design service to provide an overall cohesive look or theme for an event.
- Standard booth setups to include drapery and ID signs. If there are any special booth setups at the meeting, these should be included in the RFP.
- Additional drapery for masking, crowd control, function rooms, and so on. This is usually priced per linear foot.
- Aisle carpet in the exhibit hall to include the cost of daily cleaning. This is priced per linear foot.
- Registration setup to include counters with headers, draped work tables, chairs, and wastebaskets. The trade show manager may want to also include back drape, carpet, special graphics, rope and stanchion, or easels.
- Entrance unit at the main entrance to the exhibit area to include graphics and all labor to install and dismantle.
- Aisle signs in the exhibit hall and labor to install and dismantle.
- Décor and props for general areas, meeting rooms, and exhibit hall.
- Directional and customized signage.
- Material handling (drayage) for all show management materials received in the GSC's warehouse, held in storage for delivery prior to the regular move-in, and reloaded at the close of the show.
- Lounge areas on the show floor, including furniture, carpet, and accessories. This may include an exhibitor lounge or empty booths.
- Hardwall to be used to build offices, partitions, and so on. This is priced per linear foot.

- Furniture, including office furniture and other accessories.
- Labor for show management services.
- On-site service desks.
- Coordination of special props or décor necessary to add interest to an event.

The meeting manager may be able to negotiate significant discounts in many of the above areas, based upon the consideration of the cumulative value of the business and cost efficiencies which can be leveraged within the GSC. Keep in mind that what is negotiated for show management may affect the prices that exhibitors pay. Alternatively, some of the above services may be fulfilled by specialty contractors. If separating some line items, be sure to let the GSC know in advance to avoid set-up costs for those services. As with all contracts, make sure that the GSC chosen has adequate insurance.

TYPES OF THIRD-PARTY PROVIDERS

The dynamic state of the meetings industry in recent years has turned legacy event business models on their heads. As the definitions of meetings, conferences, product launches, special events, trade shows, and so on, have morphed into a different kind of experience for the attendee, the resources to meet these new needs have changed, and may be beyond the logistics or scope of the GSC. In some instances, a more focused specialty vendor may be brought in to address a particular challenge for the event. Specialty vendors may include prop houses, graphic designers, event marketing specialists, sign production companies, sponsorship development firms, entertainment and/or speaker agents, special technology providers—the list grows daily. The meeting manager should consider all of the options when assembling a team based on the value the event will derive, and consider hidden costs when comparing bids. Rest assured that specialty vendors and the GSC will work together to coordinate décor and set-up times, as a successful event is the common goal of all dedicated professionals. As the meeting manager, clear communication and coordination among vendors will be a top priority for the role. Following are some of the types of service providers who may act as third-party providers for the event:

1. *Multi-Management Firms*
   - Offer complete turnkey organizational support, including administrative and meeting management services, as well as more limited services depending on organization's needs and budget.
   - Services are often fee-based to the end-user, but can also be commissionable.
   - Can sign contracts with other providers while acting as agents for the end user.
2. *Meeting Management Companies*
   - Handle site selection, negotiation, front-end planning, and on-site logistics management for an organization.
   - Services can include exhibit management and sales, registration, and marketing.
   - Compensation may come from commissionable room rates or by a flat project fee.
   - Relationship with the event owner may be transaction by transaction, or a longer term contract, or may even be in-house or an outsourced former employee of the end user.
   - Most often, the event owner organization signs contracts.

3. *Housing Companies*
   - Can be, but typically are not, involved in site selection or negotiation.
   - Services are commissionable (typically 5%–10%) or fee/transaction based on housing services.
   - Generally used when housing requires multiple hotels.
   - Services are sometimes contracted by the event owner after the business is confirmed with city and hotels.

4. *Site Search Companies*
   - Supplement an organization's meeting managing function, focusing on uncovering qualified, available sites for future events and meetings.
   - May or may not control negotiation, actual site selection, or contracting, but may have influence over these issues.
   - Services are most often compensated by commissioning hotel room rates.

5. *Incentive Companies*
   - Actively pursues fulfillment of reward-and-recognition-based travel and potentially merchandise programs.
   - Purchasing may be centralized and separate from their account management process.
   - Provide turnkey support for the event and, in some cases, are involved in a consulting role within the end-user organization
   - Most often, they sign contracts acting as agent for the end-user organization.
   - Fee structure can include commissioning hotel room rates, a percentage of gross event cost, or a flat fee.

6. *Event Design companies*[1]
   - Assist in the creation of theme development to effectively communicate with the audience demographics.
   - Develop a graphic "look and feel" for the event based on meeting's marketing messages and objectives
   - Provide a comprehensive style guide of graphic elements, fonts, and approved colors
   - Provide graphic templates and production specifications to all pertinent vendors to ensure consistency of presentation across the event.
   - Copywriting services
   - Marketing materials, advertising campaigns, and program layout and/or production
   - Space planning and guidance on effective use of traffic patterns
   - Development of specialty areas of the event such as commemorative and feature displays
   - Graphic management services for order production
   - Contracts are usually signed directly with the event owner. Some activities (theme development and marketing materials) may begin far in advance of actual production timelines.

7. *Event Production Companies*
   - Provide a turnkey solution to events such as opening ceremonies, large social events, concerts, etc. Event production companies will contract and manage talent, venue, lighting, sound, catering along with all other elements of the event.
   - For events that include an exhibition, the services of a trade-show management company can include assistance in developing the exhibit floor plan, preparation and distribution of exhibitor service kits (furniture, electrical, carpeting, labor), exhibit drayage, exhibit decorating, labor, move-in, setup, floor management, and tear-down.

SECURITY AND SAFETY

Meeting managers and organizations have an obligation to provide a safe and secure atmosphere for all meeting participants. Planning for security should begin during an early site-inspection trip.

Security needs vary for each meeting. Check the security staff in both the meeting and hotel facilities to see if there is a need for additional security personnel. The local police department can also be a good source of information.

Exhibit Security

Exhibitor security needs have increased significantly with the regular usage of audiovisual and technical equipment by many exhibitors on the show floor.

The show manager should present a final floor plan in advance to the convention center or hotel security staff and discuss the characteristics of the show and the type of equipment that will be on the floor. These experts know their facilities and can recommend the amount of staff needed in order to provide adequate security.

Many facilities require security. Obtain a copy of the rules and regulations to determine particular requirements for security and other services, and to find out if the facility has an exclusive contract with a security company requiring the meeting manager to use that company. The facility manager may also be able to provide the names of security companies that regularly work in the facility and know how to provide maximum protection. Companies that cater to the meeting and exhibition industry are often preferable. In giving instructions to the security company, include not only the number of individuals needed and when, but also information on each officer's specific responsibilities. If guards will be checking badges, provide badge samples and recommendations for handling problems.

Qualities to look for in a good security company include the flexibility they have in making personnel changes and additions on-site, and the extent of on-site supervision provided. Superior companies have ongoing training programs for their personnel. The ideal security staff person is polite, personable but firm, tactful, alert, and knowledgeable.

Obtain references and ask other meeting managers about the characteristics of the company's personnel and their dependability and punctuality. If possible, attend a show at which the security company is working in order to observe them and ask questions. Determine the hourly rate for security officers, supervisors, relief officers, and any other costs to be included. Ask what minimum rates will be in effect, as well as details on overtime charges and how they are applied. On-site personnel may use cellular phones, pagers, walkie-talkies, and so on, to stay in constant communication with one another. Require a description or photograph of the uniforms worn by guards and supervisors.

Discuss security with facility personnel who can advise which entrances and exits can or cannot be locked and assist in identifying other areas that need attention. In the case of a large trade show, indicate on a floor plan the specific duty location for each officer and indicate if the officer is to be stationary or is to move between certain points.

Contact all other suppliers who will need to enter the hall (e.g., florist, caterers, computer rental, furniture). Compile a list of the number of employees, and names (if possible), and give the list to security staff. A duplicate list should be kept in the meeting office. It is important to have adequate roving security when the number of suppliers is greater than what stationary officers can handle. For example, cleaning crews often consist of a large number of workers all arriving at one time, and stationary officers at a few doors cannot possibly protect exhibitor booths. Review the security plan in advance with the convention center or hotel security director. The security company should coordinate its efforts directly with the facility's security staff.

With such a wide range of individuals involved in the production of a meeting, especially a trade show, the potential for theft and tampering is high. The most crucial times for security are the move-in and move-out periods, and after the exhibit area is closed each day. Hours especially likely for theft are the time spans between the delivery of equipment and its display, and from the close of the show until merchandise and equipment are packed for shipment. If possible, the booth should not be left unattended during these periods. If the exhibitor's budget permits, hiring booth security is an effective measure.

Encourage all personnel to remove small items of value. The exhibition manager may provide lockable, guarded security rooms, or the facility or contractor may have security cages available for this purpose. Unauthorized removal of items from the exhibit area can be controlled by several methods—merchandise removal passes on which the trade show manager's signature is required, a business card with matching photograph and ID, and/or restricting the removal of any merchandise until the conclusion of the trade show.

Shortly before the event, send a special mailing to exhibitors with exhibitor security tips. Encourage all exhibitors to have their own security plan to protect their booth and product. Video cameras and bar code security measures are recommended.

Monitor the performance of security personnel as frequently as possible, observing the alertness and courtesy with which they fulfill their responsibilities. It is difficult to know if the organization is getting its money's worth in the case of evening security; a surprise night visit to the exhibit hall in the early stages of the meeting is recommended. If possible, a different person should pay a surprise visit at a different hour each evening.

Ask bidders to recommend the amount of security based on the nature of the event and the floor plan. Compare their recommendations with the advice of the facility's security staff and review all requirements outlined by the facility. Use the floor plan as a vehicle for negotiations.

Meeting management or the organization should distribute a map to all staff, exhibitors, and official service providers in advance and on-site, with instructions on what to do in case of fire or other emergencies (e.g., bomb threat, power failure). Key staff should be trained before the event in what to do in case of emergency (see Chapter 44). Instructional safety signs should be posted for exhibitors and attendees if not adequately displayed by the facility.

Badges

Issuing badges to participants is standard operating procedure. Badges may be simple or more complex photo badges encoded with identifying information. For exhibit events, badge scanners are offered for rental to exhibitors to facilitate the retrieval of contact information from interested attendees. Bar codes and magnetic strips are common on badges used for this purpose. Sessions may also require tracking for educational credits, and the same badges scanners can be used. New technology enhancements include embedding of RFID chips (Radio Frequency Identification), which identify the attendee and track their participation in sessions and movements around the event facility. As technology increases the level of detailed information gathered about the attendees, it should be expected that the meeting manager will field more questions concerning privacy issues. As is the case in society at large, decisions on the scope of use of technology will be an ongoing balance of customer service to personal rights.

The level of security for the event will determine what type of badge to use. Meeting managers should always utilize professional security staff in areas where safety and money are involved.

OFFICE FURNITURE AND EQUIPMENT

To conduct extensive organization and committee business on-site, staff members may find a desk more efficient and comfortable than the usual draped tables provided by facilities. A copying machine in the meeting services office or show office is also more convenient than numerous trips to the nearest copy center. A number of companies can provide business furniture and equipment required for meetings, and furniture may also be obtained through the GSC. Once again, the keys to success are advance planning, thorough review of available resources, exactness in preparing orders and instructions, and requiring early confirmation of order receipt.

Office Furniture

In most major cities, there are specialty or custom furniture companies available to handle the needs of the trade show and convention industry. These companies can supply catalogs with pictures and descriptions of the furniture that they have in stock. If furniture requirements are extensive or unique, visit the supplier's warehouse and inspect the merchandise before placing an order. It is important to know the supplier's warehouse location and whether they are capable of handling last-minute, on-site orders or changes. Do not hesitate to inquire about the size of the supplier's inventory and whether they can accommodate requests for large quantities. Before contacting the furniture supplier, determine the amount of furniture needed and the style desired. The contact should work closely with the meeting manager to choose the proper furniture based on availability and the budget.

In determining the specific kinds of furniture required, it is helpful to draw a scaled floor plan of the office or area where the furniture will be needed. Once space availability and general furniture requirements have been reviewed, determine the specifics (e.g., secretarial chair or executive swivel chair; four-drawer, letter-size file cabinets or six-drawer, legal-size file cabinets; desks and cabinets, with or without locks). The order must be clear and precise, but be prepared to be flexible. Include a copy of floor plans showing the placement of each piece of furniture.

If the meeting is held in an area with limited availability of convention and meeting-type resources, allow sufficient time for delivery of business machines and office furniture. Also provide time for a thorough inspection and replacement or repair of faulty equipment and damaged furniture before actual use. Again, ensure that suppliers coordinate with the facility to plan delivery for appropriate times when the loading dock and freight elevators will be available for their use.

If the meeting includes a trade show and a GSC is hired, ask the GSC whether they have their own furniture inventory or use a furniture supplier. If the meeting manager is not using a GSC, the CVB can assist in locating a specialty furniture rental contractor. Most suppliers will extend a show management discount based on the quantity of furniture needed.

Office Equipment

Rental equipment takes a great deal of abuse and is costly to keep in good operating order. Membership in a local convention and visitors bureau generally indicates that an office equipment supplier understands the basic nature of the meeting industry and recognizes the unusual time frames that apply.

The supplier should be willing to provide a full price list that includes delivery and pickup of equipment, a discounted rate for backup equipment, and 24-hour emergency service.

The order must be specific as to the type of machines required. In the case of computers, for example, indicate if they are to be full-size or laptop. Make certain the operating system is appropriate, software is preloaded, and that the computer is capable of running the software. Also specify requests for any peripheral equipment that is required—printers, modems, and so on. When renting printers, determine if paper is included or must be ordered separately.

Renting the correct computer equipment can greatly enhance the meeting. The company selected must be worthy of the sponsoring organization's trust and have all the equipment that is needed, plus backup, as well as technical expertise. If the meeting manager plans many shows that utilize computers, building an ongoing relationship with a company that can help in other cities as well may be beneficial.

Sufficient technical support and replacement equipment readily available to get through any problems that might arise during the rental period is a prime consideration. It is important that the rental company offers unbiased, trained specialists who will recommend the correct technology for the sponsoring organization's needs. If the meeting requires a networked system, the company should have trained technicians who can network their equipment with the organization's existing system. The meeting manager will want to rent computer equipment that is compatible with existing hardware. Brand name equipment is always best, according to the experts, even though it costs more.

Ensure that appropriate electrical outlets are available in the room/area where the equipment is to be installed and that the amount of power is adequate. Before the installer leaves, verify that the appropriate people know how to use the equipment and that the repair service telephone numbers, including weekend and after-hours service, are in hand.

Meeting managers who have seen the lights go out at a major trade show because of a power failure will advise that the most important piece of equipment that can be rented is a backup source of power to save the information and data from being lost.

TELECOMMUNICATIONS

The communications needs for a show can be extensive. Some may need computer labs, Internet connectivity, videoconferencing, and other capabilities. Dealing with several suppliers (e.g., phone company, Internet service provider, computer company, and facility telecommunications staff) can be overwhelming. If available, the best option is to have a single contact at the facility.

Phone Service

Phone service may be needed in many meeting areas, such as registration, the show office, meeting rooms, or by exhibitors on the show floor. The facility may provide these services in-house or they may contract with an outside company to provide these services within the facility.

If there are requests for speaker phones, the meeting manager will need to find out whether there will be more than one person on the outside call. Many times if there is more than one person involved, it is better to have an outside service set up a conference call for a specific time. Ask the service provider or convention services contact what the procedures are for that facility.

If the meeting includes a trade show, the organization will want to offer phone service to exhibitors. The facility or service provider will normally supply the meeting manager with order forms that can be inserted in the exhibitor service kit. This service is not in demand as much anymore since the use of cell phones has become common.

The meeting manager should forward the requirements to the service provider well in advance of the meeting. Along with the requests, it is helpful to provide a floor plan or diagram with the locations for each phone line, the time the phones will need to be available, and when they can be removed. The phone numbers for these lines can usually be made available before the meeting begins, which enables the group to publish the numbers in programs, and other collateral material. As with any service, the meeting manager should make sure they have a contact with a pager or cell phone in case of emergency.

INTERNET SERVICE

Internet access is becoming a critical element in the success of meetings and trade shows. Hotels and convention centers have found it necessary to provide Internet connections. Most hotel sleeping rooms now provide additional phone lines that allow the guest to use a laptop and modem to connect to the Internet. Meeting rooms and exhibit halls are designed for Internet access. It is important to find out ahead of time if the facility has already installed high-speed data connections, so that it will be able to accommodate any last-minute changes to the meeting requirements. If high-speed lines from an outside vendor are needed to be ordered, the meeting manager may not be able to connect a new local area network or add extra computers at the last minute. Also, it is more likely that the meeting's costs and their exhibitors' costs will be lower when working with a convention center that has installed permanent and versatile connectivity options.

It is a continual challenge for hotels, and especially convention centers, to keep up with the rapid pace of technological change. Here is what is being offered at many facilities today:

- Internet service providers (ISPs) may be exclusive, nonexclusive, or preferred at a facility. An exclusive or preferred ISP has the advantage of knowing the facility's infrastructure and having full-time staff available on-site. Using the sponsoring organization's own ISP may be best if there is a complex network and the same requirements from year to year. To assess a meeting's needs and deliver appropriate service, ISPs need to know how many devices will be hooked up, how the devices will be used, and whether each device needs its own IP (Internet Protocol) address. This information determines how much bandwidth and how many connections will be needed.
- The most basic form of Internet access utilizes a meeting facility's regular phone lines. These ISDN lines are traditionally slow. One step up from an ISDN line is the T-1 line. Although access is good, it is relatively slow (1.5 megabits per second). The most reliable and cost-effective Internet access is the T-3 line, which is the best connection for multi-user access.

Cost should not be the only factor when choosing an Internet service provider. The provider needs to have the equipment that is needed for the meeting, the staff and technical support, and someone who can solve problems on-site. As with other contracted vendors, the meeting manager will want worry-free service and support in order to make their meeting a success.

PHOTOGRAPHY

In addition to the usual use of photographs of special events and dignitaries by the media and meeting sponsor, a number of organizations keep a photographic record as an aid in planning setups and decorations for future meetings. Some exhibiting companies use photographs as a reference for installation of their displays at other trade shows, or for annual reports or sales brochures. Photographs can also serve as a reference for special sales appeals and products featured in the past.

It is wise to select an official photographer who specializes in meetings and trade shows. The company should be able to provide service throughout the meeting and ensure fast delivery of proofs and prints. Ideally, the photographer will have access to lab facilities (or use digital photography) to offer the quickest and best customized service. Photographers can have the same quick turnaround as 1-hour photo processing centers if the client has rapid response needs. Additional qualifications include dependability, adequate equipment and personnel, and a high-quality product.

Put It Into Perspective

Working with Third Parties[2]

The Professional Convention Management Association (PCMA) Ad Hoc Committee issued the "PCMA White Paper on Third Party Issues" in February 2001 identifying concerns about relationships among meeting managers, suppliers, and third-party providers and recommending best practices for working with third parties. The committee defined a third party as any service provider that is compensated by acting as an agent for another supplier. This role can encompass facilitating, recommending, and/or contracting services on behalf of an end user. As such, depending upon the business relationship, third-party providers can include, but are not limited to, housing and registration companies, site search and meeting management companies, travel agents, trade show decorators, convention centers, and hotels.

The use of third-party providers has been on the rise, primarily because they fill a business need for organizations that require assistance with everything from membership and accounting to housing and meeting managing. This trend to outsource began in the corporate sector and has since caught on in the association community as well. As more organizations outsource to third-party providers, the traditional delineations between customer and supplier become hazy. The most controversial issues center on the methods of compensation, i.e., rebates and commissions. The committee examined the vendor-supplier business relationships to better understand who pays and who receives the benefit of the vendor service, then identified guidelines by which all parties can interact in an ethical and professional manner.

Recommended Best Practices

The PCMA Ad Hoc Committee recommended these best practices, which focus on disclosure, value for fees paid, and fair and equitable business practices, to engender a better understanding of roles and expectations and a more honest and forthright business environment:

1. Disclosure
   - A meeting facility, i.e., hotel, convention center, conference facility, should have an obligation to disclose any and all rebates, overrides, commissions, fees, or incentives committed to a third-party provider that will be passed on to the organization or attendee.
   - The organization should have the obligation to provide appropriate disclosure to attendees whose expense for attending will be increased due to agreements for rebates, overrides, commissions, fees, or incentives paid to third-party providers or the organization itself, its governing body, paid staff, or elected officers.
   - A third-party vendor, i.e., A/V company, exhibit company, florist, destination management company, housing company, meeting management company, site selection company, or other, should have an obligation to provide appropriate disclosure to the organization contracting the services of any rebates, overrides, commissions, fees, or incentives that will be passed on to the association, company, or attendee. This adds new responsibility to third-party vendors for communicating with the customer about fee structures and pricing.
   - An organization purchasing group services from a hotel should have an obligation to disclose any known costs that will require funding through the hotel, convention bureau, or other vendors during the RFP stage of site selection and negotiation (i.e., housing or transportation cost).
2. Value for Fees Paid
   - All parties acknowledge that there is a need and a value inherent to all vendors either directly or indirectly and that fair market practices, the competitive environment, and price-value perception should be the guideposts for establishing fees and pricing.

Put It Into Perspective—continued

- If a vendor, i.e., hotel, convention bureau, is responsible for all or part of the fees paid for a commodity or service provided to the buyer or attendee, that vendor should be consulted for input on a service provider.
- All parties should agree that the fees charged are fair and equitable based upon the services performed. This protects the attendee or end user from paying supplemental fees or assessments caused by poor planning or mismanagement.

3. Fair and Equitable Business Practices
- All fees, commissions, rebates, and incentives should be disclosed by all parties as part of the RFP (or as soon as known) and subsequent contract, including expected assignment of responsibility for paying the fees.
- A third-party provider, contracting on behalf of an end-user group, should disclose the name of the end-user and all known information about the name, type, and scope of its event before a hotel or destination is obligated to hold tentative space or quote rates.
- A hotel or destination should not contact an end user directly about an event which they have already discussed with a third party that is serving as agent of record for the end user, without discussing that contact first with the third-party agent of record.
- In a competitive bid situation, prior to establishing an agent of record, any tentative arrangements held for the event would belong to the end user until such time as the option expires, space is released by all bidding agencies, or an agent of record is selected by the end user.

- A third-party agent has a responsibility to present all information received from bidding hotels and destinations to the end user for review. While it is appropriate for the third party to make a recommendation to the end user, the agent should not withhold information that would allow a bidding party an unfair advantage in the bidding process.
- The end user should have the ultimate right and responsibility to determine the amount and nature of direct contact and involvement they wish to maintain with hotels and destinations.
- Commission paid by facilities, destinations, or other vendors to create or direct business to their facilities or services is not re-assignable and in such cases should be paid to the original agent of record. If the end user, at some future point, decides to terminate its agreement with the original third-party agent of record, the end user should not be able to reassign any fees, commissions, rebates, or incentives that were promised the original agent of record to the new agent. The vendor has no obligation to compensate the new agent of record in any manner for business already contracted.
- The third-party agent should have the obligation to disclose to the end user any inducements, fees, overrides, or incentives that would influence his or her recommendation of one destination over another.
- A third party should not take incentives or complimentary arrangements meant for the end user and intentionally price them or mark them up for the purpose of increasing profit to the third party.

Ask the prospective photographer to provide work samples, and to quote prices to the sponsoring organization and to exhibitors for color and/or black-and-white prints in specific sizes. Also, get information on any other services the meeting manager may be interested in, such as digital photography or videography. Ask if there is an additional hourly rate for the photographer and charges for film, processing, and contact sheets. Give the photographer information on the volume of sales from exhibitors in the past. This will help determine the photography costs in the agreement. If there is an hourly rate, the meeting manager may be able to negotiate a certain number of complimentary hours that the organization can use.

If coverage is desired for all sessions, provide the photography company with a complete program as soon as it is available in order to determine if one photographer can cover the sessions in the time frame allowed. Also provide a detailed schedule indicating all areas and events to be photographed.

If photography of exhibitor booths is to be offered, the photographer should provide a form to be included in the exhibitor service kit. Exhibit photography requires scheduling and a willingness to accommodate the client at odd hours. For example, the exhibitor may wish to have photos of the empty booth, which are more easily shot in the morning before the doors open. To provide coverage of a large trade show, the photographer may have to proceed aisle by aisle on a daily basis. The meeting manager must be able to contact the photographer or an associate at all times. The schedule may be changed by an exhibitor who wants to have a photograph taken only when all staff are present in the booth.

Schedule photographs of committee meetings in such a way as to avoid disrupting the proceedings. Give the photographer complete information, so that the chairperson and committee members will not have to waste time discussing camera angles or dealing with questions. Ask the photographer to be as unobtrusive as possible when taking lectern pictures during sessions, and be specific about the kinds of photographs needed.

DIGITAL PHOTOGRAPHY

Most professional meeting photography companies are now offering digital photography services to meeting management and exhibitors. With digital photography, the meeting manager has the capability of posting images at a web site almost instantaneously. They can also be presented on a CD-ROM and uploaded onto a web site, or prints can be made from the images. This may be particularly appealing to the organization's public relations staff.

Other digital services include having negatives scanned for storage or manipulation. Also, immersive photography, a 360-degree immersive photo, is an ideal way of promoting the meeting or exhibition via the Web. QuickTime Virtual Reality (QTVR) is an extension of the QuickTime technology developed by Apple Computer, which allows the user to interactively explore and examine photo-realistic, three-dimensional virtual worlds. QuickTime Virtual Reality can be used to add an interactive dimension to web pages, presentations, and other applications.

VIDEOGRAPHY

Many meetings and trade shows hire videographers to record a 10- to 15-minute videotape to promote the show. Meet with the videographer to create a list of events to be recorded. The videographer can also conduct interviews with attendees or exhibitors. Another option is to create a video of the proceedings and activities over the course of the meeting and show it as part of the closing ceremonies or at the final session. The tapes can even be a revenue source if copies are made for sale to attendees. In using vendors to support archiving the meeting through the use of these media, the meeting manager must insure that there is clarity in the vendor's contract as to which party has ownership of the product and the appropriate use by both parties.

LABOR CONSIDERATIONS

The labor situation in the destination city can affect the cost of services to meeting management and, if the meeting has an exhibition, the exhibitors as well. Facilities located in a right to work state may be free of labor union rules and regulations. But many hotels and convention centers operate under various types of union labor agreements. Some unionized convention centers have contracts with individual unions, and a few have joint craft agreements, where all the unions operate under one labor agreement. Under either arrangement, the facilities are obligated by the conditions of the agreement. Before selecting a facility, be sure to understand the labor situation and how this will affect the meeting requirements and budget.

Some convention centers have tougher guidelines and restrictions from being the largest potential labor user. Many convention centers have exclusive contracts tied in or related to their labor agreement (food and beverage services, room set-ups, electrical services, and housekeeping, for example). In some convention centers, functions such as badge checkers, ticket takers, door monitors, and crowd control are considered under the broad spectrum of "security." Even in convention centers where such functions are covered under the labor agreement, the meeting manager may still hire their own security for inside the trade show, general session, and registration areas.

SUMMARY

Suppliers and third-party providers are an integral part of our industry, and they provide a wide variety of specialized services. Clear communication, full disclosure, and accountability are the hallmarks of productive and successful working relationships with suppliers and third-party providers. Beginning with the first site visit and ending with the post-con, the meeting manager and their staff can rely on industry partners for quality service.

The contracted services required for meetings and trade shows are as numerous and varied as the interests and industries represented by sponsoring organizations. When arranging for any contracted service for a meeting, plan as far in advance as possible. Establishing a cooperative relationship with supplier contacts begins during the selection process, with an RFP that delineates specific requirements and proposals that demonstrate superior qualifications and value for fees paid. The selection process can be influenced by factors such as availability of in-house contractors, limitation to use of exclusive contractors, and labor agreements that restrict who can perform certain services. Investigate the quality and reliability of the service provider thoroughly, and obtain references and recommendations from several sources. Obtaining quality service at the best possible price will help the meeting manager enhance the value of the event by staying within their budget and ensuring a safe, secure, and enjoyable experience for all meeting attendees.

A good general service contractor (GSC) is key to the efficient operation of the exhibition. Choose a GSC with a proven record of providing top-quality service to both show management and exhibitors. A good security company offers flexibility in assignments, continual training for personnel, and employs only high-quality security guards.

Third-party providers fill a business need for organizations that require more specialized and often less costly assistance with meeting management functions. The PCMA Ad Hoc Committee on Third Party Issues recommended 16 best practices focusing on disclosure, value for fees paid and fair and equitable business practices. The committee's recommendations may prompt further discussion among organizations and their third-party providers and eventually be incorporated in the Accepted Practices Exchange (APEX) for industry-wide consideration. By discussing these recommendations with colleagues and implementing the practices in their organization, meeting managers can contribute to a more open business environment.

Once the meeting manager has assembled a quality team to produce the event, leadership and communication skills are the most important factors to continued success. Even the most experienced vendors need input to turn the organization's vision and goals into reality. Vendors can offer cutting edge solutions as well as the depth of their experience, but ultimately the meeting manager's decisions are followed. Knowing the underlying issues of contractual scope and labor enable the meeting manager to ask the right questions and make the best determinations for overall success.

REFERENCES

1. Provided by Carol Sconzert, Osmosis Creative LLC, Pacifica CA.

2. Excerpted and printed with permission from PCMA Ad Hoc Committee on Third Party Issues. PCMA white paper on third party issues (Chicago: PCMA, February 2001).

KEY TERMS

Ancillary services
Booking
Commission
Conference services
   coordinator
Contracted services
Convention services
   manager (CSM)
Drayage
Exclusive contractor
Exhibitor service kit
General service
   contractor (GSC)
Hardwall

Inducement
In-house contractor
Internet service provider
Joint craft agreement
Labor union
Master billing account
Material handling
Outsource
Pbx
Post-conference meeting
   (post-con)
Preconference meeting
   (pre-con)

Rebate
Request for proposal
   (RFP)
Résumé
Right to work state
Security
Set-up
Signage
Third-party provider
Uniserve property
Videographer

COMPELLING QUESTIONS FOR CONSIDERATION

1. How should you communicate your requirements to suppliers before, during, and after an event?

2. Discuss the factors that influence the selection process for suppliers of services such as A/V support and catering.

3. Identify three best practices for working with third-party providers that, if implemented, could have the most significant impact on the success of your meeting.

4. Why is it important to plan as far in advance as possible for contracted services?

5. Why is it advisable to obtain more than one reference or recommendation for a supplier?

6. What are some of the criteria that should be used to evaluate a security company?

7. What best practices can you develop to address the management of change orders?

CHAPTER 38

THEY CAME, THEY MET, THEY LEFT— NOW WHAT?

Glory Wade

CONFERENCE COORDINATOR

VANGUARD INTEGRITY PROFESSIONALS, INC.

LEARNER OUTCOMES

When the reader has completed reading this chapter, he/she should be able to . . .

1 Develop concise, detailed plans for returning rented equipment, and retrieving and shipping materials to be used again.

2 Discuss appropriate guidelines for gratuities and tipping.

3 Summarize the importance of keeping detailed financial records and generating accurate post-event reports.

4 Explain the importance of obtaining post-meeting feedback from various groups involved with the meeting.

5 Recognize what to look for when reviewing the bills to be paid.

> The world is round and the place which may seem like the end may also be only the beginning . . .
>
> *Ivy Baker Priest*

OVERVIEW

The close of an event is usually very busy with everyone wanting to wrap it up. Attendees and exhibitors are leaving in a rush. The event sponsor's staff is eager to go home. The facility staff is preparing the space for the next event. Ensuring a smooth wrap-up for the meeting begins during the initial planning stages. Plans and systems need to be in place to ensure that the process of move-out and wrap-up is as efficient as the move-in. Preparing concise, detailed instructions and checklists for both the staff and the facility personnel is important for success. The topics in this chapter are presented in a loosely chronological order and cover items that need to be addressed in the wrap-up process of meetings and events.

RENTAL EQUIPMENT

Meetings frequently require rental equipment, including computers, printers, copiers, telephones, walkie-talkies, and audiovisual (A/V) equipment. Once it has been decided what equipment is needed and for how long, as well as when and where it is to be delivered, complete the planning process by determining when and where the equipment will be picked up and who is responsible for the pick-up, return, and billing. Be sure to include the vendor contact data. It is wise to include this in the event specifications guide (ESG), also known as the résumé. The ESG should also include a diagram of placement in the room. The facility event manager must be aware of the scheduling of all incoming and outgoing shipments, including the sponsoring company's items to be shipped back to the office. This information is then distributed to the appropriate hotel personnel to avoid confusion when the supplier(s) arrive(s).

Just before the meeting ends, call the vendor to reconfirm pick-up times and locations. If the supplier can only pick up during regular business hours, and the event closes in the evening or on a weekend, make arrangements with the facility to store the equipment in a secure place and to put someone in charge of it. Most facilities are willing to provide this service, but arrangements must be made in advance.

Prepare an inventory list to use in collecting rental equipment and check off items as they are moved out. If time does not permit preparation of a checklist, save all receipts to use as verification that items have been returned. If any items did not function properly upon delivery, the supplier should have been called immediately and informed of the problem. A written note should have been made of the call, the day, time, nature of the problem, and name of the person receiving the message. If a replacement was not sent or repairs were not made, there is no obligation for payment. Be sure to hand carry the copy of the inventory list, which should include contact name, phone, and email address.

Equipment left in an empty room after the meeting can be easily stolen. If the supplier was not given a specific pick-up time, the organization will be billed for the missing property. Additionally, if the organization's equipment (pointers, lectern seals, banners, etc.) is to be used in meeting rooms or public areas, label each item with the organization name, then plan for a timely and orderly pick-up at the conclusion of each session or event. In the daily schedule prepared for staff, note the room, the equipment, and the time that it must be retrieved, as well as the staff member responsible.

SIGNS

Review the inventory list of all signs and highlight those that will be returned and placed in storage for use next year. Many signs will not be reusable because they are specific to the current meeting, but money and time will be saved if the generic signs (those without specific dates or meeting themes) are collected at the end of the meeting. There are two options for retrieval:

- If staff is available, assign someone to make a sweep of the facility and gather all reusable signs as soon as it is feasible to do so. In a facility with numerous signs, a list with sign titles and locations will be helpful. It is best if this is the same person who has been responsible for placement and pick-up of signs throughout the event.
- Provide the facility's event coordinator with a list of the signs to be saved, noting their location. It then becomes the coordinator's duty to pass those instructions on to the house crew. A word of caution—reconfirm the orders just before the end of the meeting; instructions do not always get transmitted to the appropriate department.

Once all reusable signs have been collected, check them off on the list and put them aside, clearly noting "Do not throw out, to be shipped back to the office" on a sheet taped over the edge of the top sign. Next year, when inventorying the existing signage, the copy, size, and condition of each sign will be noted in the inventory. If the meeting was in a convention center, the sign order might have included large, overhead (hanging or standing) signs constructed by the general service contractor (GSC). When designing these costly signs, keep multiple-year usage in mind. When the meeting is over, signs can be crated and stored until the next meeting. If the organization has a multiple-year contract with a GSC, the company should be willing to store signs and deliver them to the next meeting.

RETURN SHIPMENTS

It is especially helpful to prepare a shipping instruction document to distribute to staff and vendors. Include details such as shipping deadlines, labeling instructions, and addresses for delivery and return shipment, and contact information. Keeping everyone informed will make the shipping process efficient and cost-effective. There may be a considerable amount of material to be shipped back to the main office. As materials are packed, make a list of the contents of each box, then number each one (e.g., 1 of 24, 2 of 24) and record the total number of boxes, each box number, its general contents, and the name of the person to whom it should be delivered. Keep a copy of the list and give a copy to the facility's event coordinator and/or whoever is responsible for shipping. If the materials need to go through customs, be sure that all required paperwork and parameters are being met.

If the service contractor is also the shipping agent, shipping labels will be provided. If not, labels must be made for all boxes. They should be prepared in advance to expedite wrap-up. Some organizations print their own labels on bright colored stock with the organization's initials and the words "convention materials" printed in bold letters. A simple, inexpensive method for making labels is to print a label on an 8.5-by-11-inch paper in large, uppercase type and make copies on appropriately color-coded stock, e.g., blue for marketing department materials. Do not use markers as they may get wet and become illegible (unless waterproof markers are used). Affix the label with clear strips of tape at least 3 inches wide. As an additional precaution, print large, self-adhesive stickers of the organization's logo to clearly identify the boxes to eliminate confusion during the storage and shipping process. For smaller meetings, most hotels can provide return shipment of materials through their package rooms if given proper information on how they are to be shipped.

Find out in advance if there are size or weight limitations for the type of delivery service chosen. Charges can be applied directly to the organization's master account. A member of the hotel staff can collect packaged materials, sign for them, and arrange for shipment. Those using a GSC can request contract labor to collect the boxes, sign the waybills, and ship them by air or truck as directed. Airfreight is expensive; do not insist on it unless the materials are needed immediately upon return from the meeting. There are two options for air-freight delivery:

- *Door-to-door*—Packages are picked up at the site and delivered to the organization's office.
- *Terminal to terminal*—Packages are taken to the shipper's terminal and must be picked up from the terminal in the destination city.

Decide which option is more feasible considering budget, labor, resources, and time. Hand-carry valuable items to ensure their safe return to the office. Boxes carried onto aircraft may be assessed baggage charges, but if the materials are irreplaceable, the expense is justifiable.

When the materials are delivered back to the office, confirm that all of the items and their contents are received intact. If not, follow up with the shipping agent immediately.

GRATUITIES AND TIPPING

There are no hard-and-fast rules when it comes to gratuities and tipping. In the absence of a prescribed policy, the best thing to do is share information within the industry regarding who should receive tips and gratuities and how much is appropriate. The meeting manager can also ask the salesperson about the usual practice at a particular facility before preparing the budget for the event since this must be included. The facility staff and some other vendors who are closely involved in the event look forward to the gratuities and it is important to provide them if at all possible. If none is given, it is usually assumed that there was no budget for it. If the level of service has not been good, this will be communicated to the appropriate management personnel in the vendor's organization.

The words "tip" and "gratuity" are often used interchangeably, but there is a distinction.

The word "tip," believed to originally mean, "to insure prompt service," is now defined by the Accepted Practices Exchange (APEX) as "a voluntary and selective amount of money given at will for special or excellent service." Tips are usually given as a token of gratitude when services are rendered by bell staff and valets in hotels, limousine drivers, food servers in restaurants, and other service personnel. A tip is a way of saying, "thank you for serving me."

A gratuity is defined by APEX as "a voluntary payment added to a bill to signify good service." Note that a gratuity is commonly added automatically to food and beverage bills for organized functions and is a set percentage of the total bill. By automatically adding gratuities to the bill, facilities may be eliminating a strong incentive to provide good service. The gratuity gets paid, no matter the quality of service received.

Tipping—Who and Why

Most meeting managers have no specific system, but award tips based on the quality of service, duties beyond the normal scope of the job, visibility, courtesy, cooperation, availability, response time, overtime, and overall attitude.

Individuals who hold executive or high-level positions on properties or in facilities are generally not given tips. It is considered inappropriate; instead, letters of thanks and appreciation should be sent to these individuals immediately following the event. The same holds true for contract service provider owners or executives. Observe employee operations during the meeting and determine who met or exceeded expectations, gave extra effort, and/or worked extra hours. Does he or she receive a portion of any mandatory gratuities?

Give meeting staff an opportunity to identify individuals who provided exceptional service in areas for which they were responsible. Ask the facility event coordinator for the names of individuals who are not on the list and should be included. Based on the budgeted allowance for tips and gratuities, draft a list of the recipients, their department, the amounts, and indicate if there will be some reward other than cash. Include a column for "thank you cards" and for "distributed" with sufficient room to enter the applicable date.

General Guidelines—How Much

When creating the budget for the event, the following options should have been considered before determining the one that best suits the organization, except where the method has been laid out by company guidelines:

- Set dollar amount per attendee
- Set dollar amount per sleeping room used
- Percentage (ranging from .025%-1.5%) of the total bill or added to the banquet/catering bill beyond the automatic gratuity
- Set percentage of the total meeting budget (ranging from a small fraction of 1% to a full 2%)

When it is not feasible to tip on a per-attendee or per-sleeping-room basis, the following criteria may be used:

- Number of food and beverage functions
- Number of meeting rooms used
- Complexity of setups and number of room changes
- Duration of meeting
- Demand placed on service people
- Performance
- Organization's meeting budget or total expenses at the facility

Ask the facility event manager how the mandatory gratuity (on food and beverage) is distributed and who is reliant on tips as part of their wages. Take this into account when reviewing the list of recipients that has been compiled.

Tipping at Resorts

If the meeting is to be held at a resort, inquire in advance about tipping policies. Many resorts automatically add a specific dollar amount per day to the room bill to cover tips to the bell staff, housekeeping, and other service attendants.

Meeting attendees, staff, CEO, and his/her spouse should be aware of tipping arrangements prior to arrival to eliminate double tipping. Resort staff should also be aware of tipping arrangements so they will not expect or accept tips from meeting attendees. Prepare a special note card to be placed in each attendee's room explaining the tipping policy. If the organization is going to give a lump sum gratuity at the end of the meeting, print that on the card so that both attendees and facility staff are informed. The card should include the name of the organization, an expression of appreciation, and the gratuity arrangements.

Tipping at Other Facilities

Ensure that the CEO and his/her spouse are aware that gratuities are already included in the charges for all food and beverage delivered to the president's suite.

Each facility may have somewhat different policies for gratuities and tipping. For example, some convention centers do not permit their employees to accept cash; others simply discourage it. Clarify the tipping policy in advance.

Fast Facts

Employees Who Most Frequently Receive Tips

- Head houseman
- Bell captain
- Bellman
- Banquet manager
- Catering manager
- Catering captain
- Bartenders
- Electrical/sound staff
- A/V aides
- Convention services manager
- Individuals who moved boxes
- Reservations/front office personnel
- Telephone operators
- Housekeeping

Others to Consider

- Security
- Limousine drivers
- Night club manager
- Recreational professionals
- Maitre d´
- Wait staff (beyond the gratuity)
- Chefs
- Room service (as a department)
- Doormen
- Stage hands
- Concierge
- Sales department secretaries
- Package room attendants
- Parking lot attendants

Before the meeting, ask the facility sales director for a list of individuals who will be working on the meeting and identify the role each will play. Ascertain who receives a percentage of the automatic gratuity charged for a food and beverage function. This information is sometimes in the fine print on catering contracts; some contracts even specify the exact percentage of the total gratuity distributed to each position. This does not preclude giving an additional tip to the banquet captain and the head of the wait staff when they go out of their way to provide exceptional service.

Distributing Tips and Gratuities—How, When, and Where

There is a difference of opinion among meeting managers as to whether tips should be distributed before or after a meeting. Some believe they will receive better service if the facility staff has already been compensated, while others believe that a tip is a reward for extra service and, therefore, should be given after the service is rendered.

Recognition is not always given in the form of money. Often flowers, candy or items from the conference are given to deserving individuals. A letter to the general manager (or facsimile thereof depending upon the type of vendor) naming those the organization would like to recognize is always greatly appreciated by the individual and their organization.

Some facilities can arrange for employees to be given paid-out slips charged against the organization's master account (also known as billing account). The employee presents the slip to the facility cashier to receive the cash tip. Most meeting managers prefer this method as it avoids the necessity of handling cash.

There will be situations requiring that a lump sum of money be given to a supervisor, who then distributes the designated amounts to others. It is acceptable and appropriate to ask that the supervisor obtain a receipt from each person. This protects those who are to receive the tips, as well as the meeting manager, whose accountant and auditors may require proof that the money was actually distributed.

It is acceptable for meeting managers to prepare individual envelopes with thank you notes for each person who is to receive a tip, along with a list of all recipients. As recipients receive the tips, they sign the list. The original list is then returned to the meeting manager and provides proof that tips were distributed.

It is ideal to distribute gratuities personally before leaving town if at all possible. A handwritten note of thanks usually accompanies the cash or paid-out slip. Make it clear that this is a token of the organization's gratitude for exceptional service. Keep accurate records of the recipients of gratuities and the amount given, and for non-cash awards the cost of the gift.

THANK YOU LETTERS

Facility Staff

Write letters of gratitude and appreciation to everyone involved immediately upon returning from the meeting. Those who did not receive a tip (because of their executive position) appreciate this feedback. Send copies of letters of recommendation and praise to supervisors or the general manager of the hotel or facility. They need to know who is performing well. If the meeting manager is unable to give someone a tip personally, they should include it with the letter. Letters to department managers may include special mention of specific people who did outstanding work and a request that the organization's gratitude be passed on to them.

Provide criticisms or suggestions in a separate letter. Such comments detract from the purpose of a letter of appreciation and are not appropriate.

Speakers

After the meeting manager returns to the office, they should process and print the evaluation results for each of the speakers sessions and send them with the thank you letters (applicable to keynotes and session instructors). This should be in addition to the thank you card that accompanies the speaker gift given to them on-site (if the organization does this).

POST-CONVENTION MEETING

The meeting manager should schedule a wrap-up meeting with the facility department heads. If that is not possible, they should meet with the event coordinator to critique the meeting. This is not a time for placing blame for things that went wrong; it is an opportunity to find out how everyone performed. Asking if facility representatives were provided with enough information, and whether instructions were complete, understandable, and prompt are important. Review the gratuities list and ask if any key non-commission persons who contributed to the success of the event are missing.

This is a partnership. If accurate information is not conveyed, the facility cannot provide adequate service. If areas of facility operation were lacking, cite them. Most properties would prefer to know what departments are not functioning properly. They need repeat business and should welcome constructive criticism. Also asking if there are areas where the staff could improve, or if another organization does something in a more effective way is appropriate. Specific examples and recommendations should be requested.

PAYING THE BILLS

It is important to carefully review every item on every bill that is received to confirm that the group was correctly charged. The individual preparing the bill may not have reviewed the contract and taken concessions into consideration, and they may be unaware of pertinent communications between the staff member and the meeting manager. The meeting manager should watch for double billing, any charges that shouldn't be there, e.g., charged for an extra booth, incorrect dollar figure per meal or per booth. Comparing the charges to the contracts and to any pertinent notes subsequent to the contract should be done.

Facility

If a good job has been done with the budget, attention paid to cost controls on-site, and copies of invoices signed during the meeting kept in order, there should be no surprises when the bills arrive. Most facilities can provide an opportunity at the conclusion of the meeting to review charges posted to the master billing account. It is not always feasible to do this review on-site before the meeting manager leaves but it is well worth the time and effort. Errors can be corrected before the final invoice is sent, and missing charges can be identified. Be sure to confirm that all concessions in the contract were correctly applied, e.g., comp nights. Stress the necessity of backup material for all charges, e.g., copies of signed function checks and sleeping room bills, which should be submitted with the final invoice. If the organization is exempt from state taxes, provide all suppliers and facilities with a copy of the tax-exempt certificate in advance and be certain that taxes have not been added to invoices. It is much less work to correct errors such as these before they are posted to the final statement. Ask key staff members who were responsible for different aspects, e.g., rooming lists, food and beverage to also review the pertinent sections of the bill. They may be aware of important information that the meeting manager is not.

Ask if the final billing is done within the hotel or at a centralized location elsewhere. If the latter, ensure that the bill is made available to review before it is sent for creation of the final statement.

When the final statement is received, the meeting manager should review every charge carefully, confirming that all concessions stipulated in the contract were applied correctly. Was the group charged for quantity put out versus consumed for those items that were on a consumption basis? Noting any questionable or incorrect charges or calculation errors. If a team member was the point person for any aspect of the bill, i.e., rooming list, food and beverage arrangements, ask them to also review the pertinent sections. They may catch something the meeting manager was not aware of. Confirm that the comp room nights were accurately applied or credited to the master account. Check the food and beverage portion of bill to confirm that charges were on a consumption basis where applicable, versus the requested quantities. If unable to actually count the items at the end of each event and the figures don't make sense, ask about it.

For functions and guest room charges which belong to another budget, note the correct department name on the copy of the bill and be sure to bring it to the attention of the accounting department, keeping a log of them in the front of the reconciliation folder. When the meeting manager receives the profit and loss statement (P&L) from the accounting department, they should review and confirm that all appropriate charges were removed from the budget.

In reviewing the guest room charges, note any staff charges for which the employee must reimburse the company. Alert the accounting department to the need to compare that individual's expense report to this bill and to collect the appropriate amount.

Items on the bill that are not in dispute should be paid in a timely manner. Mail a list of disputed items along with the payment for the undisputed portion of the bill. Contact the vendor and go over all questionable items. Then, ask for a final, corrected invoice.

If the group is facing attrition, a comparison must be made between the attendee list and the hotel guest list (see Chapter 42).

Other Vendors

Some of the other vendors whose charges are not included in the facility bill will send an invoice after the event. This could include but not be limited to destination management companies, independent transportation companies, A/V, GSC, and child care. Review with any applicable team members for accuracy and pay as quickly as possible.

Music License Fees

The organization must pay ASCAP and/or BMI if music is played anywhere during an event. The fee varies depending upon if it is performed live or pre-recorded, and the number of attendees at the function. If held outside of the United States, fees will be due to SESAC. Visit their web sites to determine who is owed payment and how much: www.ascap.com, www.bmi.com, and www.sesac.com.

Speaker and Staff Expenses

In order to facilitate the reimbursement of speakers' expenses within established parameters, it is advisable to restate the reimbursement policy that was given to each speaker before the meeting. Attach another copy of the expense reimbursement voucher as well. Immediately following the event, send program participants a thank you letter praising their efforts and reminding them to submit their expense vouchers as soon as possible.

Follow up with the accounting department to confirm that they reviewed the expense reports of staff that had charges on the hotel bill that were not covered by the company and have requested reimbursement where applicable.

Honor reimbursement requests for both speakers and staff within 30 days. Maintain a copy of each in the meeting's files.

REPORTS AND STATISTICS

Accurate statistics, financial and non-financial, are crucial to future planning. Inform staff members about the type of information that will be gathered and why. Develop forms for information gathering and compile reports as quickly as possible after the meeting. To facilitate comparisons, be consistent in the methods used to formulate reports. Good records will provide the tools necessary to accurately reflect fiscal return on investment (ROI), to track growth (or decline) and trends, and to determine future requirements. Ideally, these statistics and reports will be compiled into a final Post-Event Report (PER), which will provide an overview of the entire event for the CEO, staff, board members, and committees. Include comments regarding any circumstances that had a major impact on the event, e.g., lower attendance because of Mother's Day, or a political or economic situation. Independent planners will provide the appropriate statistics to their client for them to compile their PER. If reports or statistics are required from vendors or facilities, the meeting manager can ensure delivery of this information by holding final payment for services until the requested information is received. This stipulation should be articulated in the initial contract when booking the business. The PER should contain all of the applicable data below, and whatever else is specific to the meeting. Visit www.conventionindustry.org to see the sample PER created by APEX.

Registration

Separate registration totals into categories such as members, nonmembers, guests, exhibitors, and press. Include advance ticket sales for social events, tours, children's programs, seminars, and workshops. If weekly totals were made during advance registration, plot them on a graph, along with figures from the previous meeting, and compare the patterns. Base the time spans to be compared on the number of weeks from the brochure mailing date (or from the start of the meeting) to ensure that returns are related on an equal basis.

The registration report should include information on meeting promotions—the target audience, the number of mailings, dates, expenses, etc. When this information is related to registration figures and dates, it should indicate the success of promotion efforts.

Keep daily totals of on-site registration, broken down by the same categories. The daily figures will provide guidance for registration staffing needs for the next meeting. The cumulative daily totals can be combined with advance registration totals for a complete overview of total attendance by category. These figures can then be compared to budget projections, thus providing valuable assistance in budgeting for the next meeting.

Calculate percentages for advance and on-site totals, breaking the figures into categories. Compare the percentage of members to nonmembers, and the percentage of increase or decrease over the previous year. Many organizations also track attendance by demographic categories (function, title, etc.) and geographic data (state, region, international). This is useful in negotiations, as it shows what percentage of attendees are likely to travel by what means and how many hotel rooms will be used.

Do not neglect statistics for educational programs. If there were workshops, courses, or seminars for which additional fees were charged, track the advance and on-site sales for these also. Combined with written evaluations, this data will prove valuable when planning future programs. Provide this information to speakers as well.

Publish registration statistics and growth comparisons in the organization's newsletter, magazine, or other appropriate medium. If the meeting included an exhibition, send a letter or news release to each exhibitor with attendance figures emphasizing growth (if applicable) and exhibit data (number of companies, total booths, percentage increase). Conclude the letter with a note about the next meeting, including the dates, location, and information about when the prospectus will be sent.

Ticket Sales for Social Events

The figures compiled for social functions may be tracked in a slightly different way, as the major concern is how sales related to the guarantee and actual attendance. Compare the actual attendance figure with total sales to arrive at a percentage of no-shows. Some insight will be gained as to how to better determine a guarantee for the same event in the future. Over several years, a pattern will develop. If figures vary greatly, look for other factors affecting attendance, such as time, weather conditions, location, cost, and conflicting or competing events.

Media Attendance and Publicity

If a newsroom is part of the on-site operation, keep records of how many media representatives attended. What publications or types of media did they represent? How much coverage did the organization receive? Such information may be useful in post-meeting publicity, especially to exhibitors, and to track any articles or coverage generated after the meeting is over.

Facility Reports

Collect data from the hotel or conference center and/or housing bureau regarding room pick-up, percentage of singles, doubles and suite usage, and percentage of no-shows, early check-outs, and late check-ins. In addition to rooming statistics, request food and beverage stats including room service and bar usage, and habits of the group. What was the actual number of people served per function versus the guarantee? When were the peak traffic periods? Was room service heavily used and, if so, when? Were there many hospitality suites and private parties held in conjunction with the meeting?

It is wise for the meeting planner to let the facility know up front that they will require this information within a specific amount of time after the conference. Ideally, it is stipulated in the contract. As a rule, they do not provide it automatically. The meeting manager must request it. Be persistent. Using a standard form that is provided to the event coordinator in advance should make it easier to obtain the information. It is a good idea to incorporate data reporting in all facility contracts.

An accurate profile of the group will provide leverage in future negotiations, showing what the meeting is worth to facilities and how much room there is for negotiating.

THE GRAND FINALE

It is vital to confirm that the accounting department removed charges for other departments/divisions from the financials and questioned any discrepancies. The meeting planner's performance and value to the organization is tied to the success of the event. The meeting manager should be sure to maintain a record of where and how much they saved the company for consideration when annual review comes up, filing all of the appropriate paperwork/records for future reference.

Put It Into Practice

Evaluation/Feedback

Attendee/Speaker Feedback

Collate the feedback from attendees' overall evaluations and from those for each of the sessions. Send a thank you letter to every attendee, along with any applicable certificates e.g. completion of a specific track. Each speaker also receives a summary of the feedback for their sessions, accompanied by a thank you letter. When planning the next event, all of the input received will be taken into consideration.

Staff Feedback

Request feedback from all staff who were involved in the meeting/conference—the good and the bad. Their observations and information gleaned or overheard from attendees is valuable. This will assist in future planning and as an added bonus, reinforce the value of each team member.

Supplier Feedback

Contractors or vendors supplying goods and services can be valuable sources of feedback and recommendations for future meetings. Following is a partial list of suppliers and the type of information each can provide:

A/V Firm

- What kind of equipment was most needed?
- What equipment was requested that was not anticipated or offered?
- What was the firm's assessment of the facility's A/V capabilities

Convention Bureau

- Was the number of temporary personnel sufficient?
- What were the peak hours and days of registration?
- Was there an adequate number of visitor and reference guides available?

- What assistance was given with advance and on-site promotion?

General Service Contractor

- Were move-in and move-out times adequate?
- Were directional signs adequate?
- Was the floor layout conducive to good traffic flow?
- What was the extent of special furniture and utility requests from exhibitors?
- What was their assessment of the facility?
  Security/First Aid
- Were there any incidents/breaches?
- How often, where, when and why?
- Who was notified and when? Action taken?
- How could the incident have been prevented?
- Was the insurance company notified (if applicable)?

Tour Operators

- What kinds of tours were most popular?
- Were there too many offerings, or not enough?
- Did attendees prefer having meals included or not?

Transportation (Shuttle Buses, Official Airline)

- How many tickets were purchased from the official airline, and how many complimentary tickets were earned?
- Were buses utilized to capacity?
- What were the peak shuttle bus hours?
- Were signs adequate?
- How frequently was the wheelchair-accessible bus used?
- Were there any unusual requests from those who used the wheelchair-accessible bus?

Request similar information from all other suppliers who supported the meeting.

SUMMARY

This chapter has focused on the tasks that are required to wrap a meeting or event. At this point in the meeting, staff and vendors are eager to shut down and return to their home base. Additional stress is often caused by the venue's efforts to bring in a new show. It is important that the meeting manager maintains a document of pick-up details for all rental equipment and items being shipped back to the home office and assign one person to be responsible. Confirm that all is on track a day or two before they are due, keeping the facility event manager in the loop regarding scheduled pick-ups. Pull and ship re-usable signs back to the organization's office for use next time.

According to the APEX Glossary gratuities and tips are not the same. There are different methods of determining gratuities and tips—how much, who, when, and how. The budget should have included this expense. When deciding how much to give to an individual, bear in mind that event budget and quality of service is key. Also take into account if they already receive a portion of any mandatory gratuities, e.g., on food and beverage.

It is imperative to keep detailed records, financial and non-financial, to accurately determine the meeting's ROI, to track growth (or decline), and to assist in planning future conferences. Compile all of the statistics and reports from vendors and staff incorporating them into the PER. Include any circumstances that had a major impact on the event. Knowing the strengths and weaknesses, the areas that ran smoothly, and those that need improvement are key to successful future planning.

Get feedback from the vendors to determine what could have been done to make the process smoother/better. It is standard practice to have a post-con meeting with the facility department heads or facility event coordinator to recap and to identify elements that went smoothly and areas for improvement. Do not play the blame game. Get feedback from all stakeholders including staff and use the information to make the next meeting or event better.

Finally, carefully review every charge on the bills from all the different vendors for the event. Be sure to involve key staff responsible for any aspect of a bill. Confirm that the bills correctly reflect all related concessions in the contract. Confirm that the accounting department removed from the budget charges that belong to other departments, and correctly processed any other discrepancies.

REFERENCE

1. Rosenberg, G. (February, 2004). Tips on tipping. *Convene*, p. 59.

KEY TERMS

APEX	Master account	Résumé
Backup material	Paid-out slips	Return on investment
Feedback	Post convention meeting	(ROI)
Final statement	Post event report (PER)	Shipping agent
Generic signs	Profit and loss statement	Specification guide
Gratuity	(P&L)	Tip
Inventory list	Reimbursement policy	

COMPELLING QUESTIONS FOR CONSIDERATION

1. What are some of the details involved in returning and shipping equipment and materials?

2. How do you determine who should receive tips and gratuities and how much to give?

3. Why is it important to gather detailed financial and attendance information about the meeting?

4. What is a PER? What information is it composed of and where does the data come from?

5. What types of feedback can the facility staff and suppliers provide?

6. What should you be looking for when you review the final statement from the facility?

7. What should you do when you receive the P&L statement from the accounting department?

CHAPTER 39

ETHICS

Tyra W. Hilliard, JD, CMP

ASSOCIATE PROFESSOR

DEPARTMENT OF TOURISM AND CONVENTION ADMINISTRATION

UNIVERSITY OF NEVADA, LAS VEGAS

LEARNER OUTCOMES

When the reader has completed reading this chapter, he/she should be able to . . .

1 Explain why codes of ethics are important to the meetings industry.

2 Apply ethical principles and tests to meetings industry practices.

3 Analyze the role of ethics in establishing meetings industry best practices.

4 Assess the ethical boundaries of common meetings industry scenarios.

> Ethical axioms are found and tested not very differently from the axioms of science. Truth is what stands the test of experience.
>
> *Albert Einstein*

OVERVIEW

In a world of immediate gratification, intense competition, and fluctuating economies, ethics is sometimes seen as separate and less important than other business elements like strategic planning, return on investment, or risk management. The reality is that ethics plays a vital role in these and other key business elements. Allegations of unethical behavior can ruin a business and can ruin a person professionally. For this reason, ethics is not just a "do-gooder" personal choice, but an important business practice.

Common and consistent ethical principles also help to maintain the meetings industry as a profession. For this reason, it is important that those employed in the meetings industry help develop, support, and enforce industry codes of ethics in their own organizations as well as in meetings industry associations.

Although ethical standards are not law, there has been a renewed effort to legislate minimum levels of corporate behavior due to certain scandals. Such laws are surfacing not only for for-profit companies, but also for nonprofit organizations. Even without such laws compelling these ethics-based business practices, organizations should adopt best practices and codes of ethics and ensure that all employees receive training in ethics.

DEFINING "ETHICS"

Ethics is one of those difficult to define "you know it when you see it" concepts. The dictionary defines ethics as "a system of moral standards or values."[1] Based on a definition like this, people instinctively know that they should behave ethically and avoid unethical behavior. The reality, however, is that ethics are subjective—whose "moral standards" should be followed? Moral standards vary from person to person, not because some people are "bad" and others are "good," but because individual moral standards are developed from various influences encountered throughout our lives. Such influences may include (and this is not an exhaustive list) family, religion, school, work, professional organizations, life experiences, news, politics, and even pop culture. Influences vary not only from person to person but may be quite different for people from different generations or from different parts of the world. Although personal values can never be completely set aside, it is professional ethics that are the subject of this chapter. Professional ethics provide common and consistent principles of ethical behavior for those who are employed in a certain profession—in this case, meeting managers.

PROFESSIONAL ETHICS

The responsibility for ensuring ethical behavior in the workplace is not limited to behaving ethically yourself. Part of supporting professional ethics is bringing behavior that may be of a questionable ethical nature to the attention of owners, managers, clients, partners or other decision-makers. Unethical behavior on the part of a single person in a business can affect the reputation and success of a business. Likewise, the stamp of being "unethical" can rub off from one person onto other people in the business. Whether fair or not, a business with one "bad apple" can spoil the whole bunch.

A recent survey indicated that 31% of workers in the United States had witnessed unethical behavior by coworkers.[2] Only half of those who witnessed ethical misconduct or illegal acts reported it to someone in authority.[3] It is easy to think that the enforcement of ethics is someone else's job. Certainly, revealing such behavior can put the whistleblower in an uncomfortable or awkward position. Being ethical is not always easy. In fact, sometimes doing the right thing is very, very hard. At its most extreme, doing the right thing can sometimes mean turning away a needed client, risking job security, or being disliked by coworkers. Being ethical takes a strong constitution, but if ethical behavior is adopted throughout a business or an industry, it can become the rule and not the exception.

CORPORATE ETHICS

Many meeting managers may feel far removed from corporate accounting scandals that make national and international news. There is an inclination to believe that such scandals occur only in other companies or that if they do happen, they have nothing to do with the meeting manager. Not so! An example of direct involvement by a meeting manager is the Tyco International, Ltd. case. Scattered across the news stories was information about how the event manager for Tyco helped her boss host a $2.2 million birthday party for his wife, allegedly at least partially paid for with company funds.[4] Inappropriate use of company resources for personal gain is not uncommon. Because the meeting manager often has experience with different destinations, travel options, and hotels, there is a natural tendency for people to ask the meeting manager for suggestions about personal travel. This innocent inquiry can go too far when the meeting manager is asked to use business connections and relationships to benefit someone's personal travel.[5]

An example of indirect impact on the meeting manager is any corporate scandal that may hurt the company enough to cause financial impact. It is not a far stretch to imagine that a company that is hurting financially may end up reducing the number or size of meetings and possibly even resort to downsizing or outsourcing the meetings function. The frightening thing about ethical issues is that the allegations do not even have to be true to have a negative impact on the companies, organizations, and people involved. Sometimes the bad press alone is enough to create a negative impact.

ETHICAL ISSUES IN THE MEETINGS INDUSTRY

Although ethical issues arise in many shapes and sizes, a few specific situations are mentioned here to provide a framework for considering ways to deal with other situations. These examples are not intended to be exhaustive—only illustrative.

Convention and Visitors Bureaus

One area of the meetings industry that has faced great scrutiny is convention and visitors bureaus (CVBs). Because many CVBs are funded at least partially through hotel occupancy taxes, activities and spending patterns of CVBs are often subject to great scrutiny by the public and the press. One CVB discovered a misuse of funds by its president after an audit. The president resigned and eventually pleaded guilty to the inappropriate use of thousands of taxpayer dollars.[6] The CVB president was ultimately sentenced to 840 hours of community service and required to make financial restitution.[7] This instance of ethical violations was prosecuted, but many are not. Likewise, some unfounded allegations are made that may have a negative impact on a company or an organization. It is important that people act ethically; but unfounded allegations of unethical behavior should be vehemently defended. Just the hint of impropriety and questionable ethical practices can have a negative impact on a company or organization.

Put It Into Practice

Hotel staff members are sometimes put into awkward positions because of their relationships with meeting managers and others in the meetings industry. Because the convention and meetings industry is a relationship-oriented business, the line between business relationships and personal relationships can become blurry. For example, a hotel sales manager may find himself in an awkward position when a meeting manager calls to say that she is coming to the hotel's city for a vacation and asks if the hotel sales manager can help her out. The hotel sales manager does not want to jeopardize his/her relationship with the meeting manager; but neither does he/she want to be an unwitting party to unethical behavior if such personal courtesies violate the meeting manager's or Hilton's organizational code of conduct or other ethical standards.

To address this issue and facilitate disclosure, Hilton Hotels Corporation has implemented the use of this letter and acknowledgement card.

Dear Business Associate,

Hilton values your business and our relationship, which we have worked hard to develop and nurture. From time to time, we are asked and may provide customers certain courtesies associated with a leisure stay in one of our hotels.

While is our pleasure to extend these courtesies, in this climate of heightened ethical awareness and increased scrutiny of business practices which we read about every day, we believe it is advisable to ask our customers and business associates who enjoy a business courtesy to have their supervisor or superior confirm that their acceptance of this courtesy will not violate their organization's code of conduct or similar ethical policies, and that appropriate disclosures have been made.

To help both of us satisfy this requirement, please have your supervisor or superior sign and return the attached acknowledgement form.

We look forward to our continued relationship and hope you embrace and understand the spirit behind this request.

Acknowledgement Card

Please detach this card and mail or fax to _____. Your supervisor may also complete and return this form by email to _____. Thank you.

On behalf of ___(name of company or association)___, I hereby acknowledge that ___(name of recipient)___ may accept ___(description of courtesy)___ from Hilton Hotels Corporation, and that such acceptance is in compliance with our internal policies.

_____   _____   _____

      Authorized signature*   Title   Date

_____

      Print Name

*If returned by email, your supervisor's return email address will suffice as an authorized signature.

Used by permission of Hilton Hotels Corporation.

Familiarization Trips

One of the most typical ethical "gray areas" involves familiarization trips, or fam trips. Convention and visitors bureaus or hotel companies sometimes invite meeting managers on an all-expense-paid trip to visit and tour the city or hotel properties. While the host of the fam trip should qualify meeting managers—that is, verify that the meeting manager has business to bring to the destination or hotel company in the foreseeable future—a less than truthful application to go on the fam trip or a less than thorough qualification process can result in unqualified meeting managers or travel agents taking a spot on a fam trip that would be better filled by someone else. Because fam trip expenses are paid for with marketing dollars spent by a destination or hotel company, the dollars should be wisely spent. It is, unfortunately, not unheard of for someone to show up on a fam trip who is obviously there to be wined and dined and not to learn about the destination.[8]

Loyalty Program Points and Miles

Another issue that is discussed frequently in the meetings industry is the accumulation of airline miles or hotel points earned on business travel.[9] Should the meeting manager who travels 150 days a year get to keep those points and miles to use for personal travel or should the points go into a business account for company use for business travel? Some organizations expressly specify their policy on this issue in codes of ethics or staff handbooks. When the policy is spelled out in writing, this is an easy call to make. It becomes questionable when the organization has nothing in writing about this situation. In that case, the safest thing to do is to ask for something in writing that settles the issue one way or the other. It is much better for the meeting manager to find out that the company is going to perceive the use of airline miles and hotel points for personal use as inappropriate this way than to be accused of unethical behavior later.

Gifts

It is considered polite, and even necessary, in some cultures to exchange gifts as a part of conducting business. However, the exchanging of gifts can also create an ethical conundrum. One issue with gift-giving is the timing of the gift. For example, a gift given by a hotel to a meeting manager on the day before a decision is to be made about whether to choose that hotel or another property may be construed as a gift intended to influence the decision—also known as a bribe. A gift given by the same hotel to the meeting manager while the meeting manager is on-site for the meeting may be considered standard business practice. If it is given after the meeting is over as a token of appreciation, the gift may be perceived as a gracious and polite gesture. Another issue with gift-giving is whether the gift is intended for the meeting manager personally or is intended for the benefit of the company or organization as a whole. To avoid even the hint of impropriety, some organizations have created ethical guidelines that do not allow their staff to accept any personal gifts or that put a dollar value limit on personal gifts. Sometimes gifts that benefit the organization may be accepted on behalf of the whole organization, but personal gifts, such as fruit baskets, plants, or chocolates, must be refused or put in public areas to be enjoyed by all of the staff. Again, it is to everyone's benefit to ask about the organization's gift policy. If one is not available in writing, write one for review and consideration by management or the board of directors.

Other Issues

As mentioned previously, these scenarios illustrate some of the ethical dilemmas that occur in the meetings industry, but it is certainly not an exhaustive list—it is not even close, unfortunately. There are many other situations that arise daily and in different organizations. The best way to address these issues is for every organization to have a code of ethics and ethical training for staff. Even a written code of ethics will probably not have a comprehensive listing of every conceivable behavior or action that may be construed as unethical. This is why ethical training and refresher courses for staff are important. Training helps employees understand and apply the spirit of ethics to everyday business activities and actions.

THIRD-PARTY ISSUES

As the meetings industry continues to evolve and change, so does the environment in which it does business. It is now common for third-party vendors to help meeting managers with everything from site selection to choosing suppliers and contractors for support services. In 2000, the PCMA Task Force on Third-party Issues was charged with identifying and addressing concerns surrounding the business relationships among third-party providers.

The following was included in its Recommendations for Industry Best Practices:[10]

Disclosure

1. The hotel should have an obligation to disclose any and all third-party rebates, overrides, commissions, fees, or incentives that will be passed on to the association, company, or attendee in the form of increased pricing.
2. The association or company should have the responsibility to provide appropriate disclosure to attendees, either individual or corporate, whose expense for attending will be increased due to agreements for rebates, over-rides, commissions, fees, or incentives paid to third-party vendors or the organization, its governing body, paid executives, or elected officers.
3. The third-party vendor (e.g., A/V company, exhibit company, florist, desti-nation management company, housing company, meeting management com-pany, or site selection company) should have a responsibility to provide the association or company contracting the services with appropriate disclosure of rebates, overrides, commissions, fees, or incentives that will be passed on in the form of increased pricing if the law requires it.
4. The association or company purchasing group services from a hotel should have an obligation to disclose any known costs that will require funding through the hotel, convention bureau or other vendors during the RFP stage of site selection and negotiation (e.g., housing cost).

The third point is important in that it should add new responsibility to third-party vendors to be accountable for communicating with the customer about fee structures and pricing. If a hotel and an A/V company have an arrangement through which the hotel receives a commission on business serviced by that com-pany in the hotel and this cost is added on to the normal rental prices, the A/V company, not the hotel, should have the responsibility of disclosing this infor-mation to the customer. However, if such arrangements are designated by the vendor as a cost of doing business (such as rent to a hotel by a gift shop for retail space), disclosure may not be needed.

Value for Fees Paid

1. All parties acknowledge that there is a need and a value inherent to all ven-dors either direct or indirect and that fair market practices, the competitive environment, and price value perception should be the guideposts for estab-lishing fees and pricing.
2. If the vendor (e.g., hotel or convention bureau) is responsible for all or part of the fees paid for a commodity or service provided to the buyer or attendee, the vendor should also participate, when possible, in contractor selection and definition of the scope of work for that contractor.
3. All parties should agree that the fees charged are fair and equitable based upon the services performed. This protects the attendee from usurious assessments caused by poor planning, mismanagement, or malfeasance.

Fair and Equitable Business Practices

1. All fees, commissions, rebates, and incentives should be disclosed by all parties as part of the RFP and subsequent contract, including expected assignment of responsibility for paying the fees.

2. The third-party agent contracting on behalf of an end user group should disclose the name of the end user and all known information about the name, type, and scope of the event before a hotel or destination is obligated to hold tentative space or quote rates.

3. The hotel or destination should not contact an end user directly about an event that they have already discussed with a third party, serving as agent of record for the end user, without discussing that contact first with the third-party agent of record.

4. In a competitive bid situation, prior to establishing an agent of record, any tentative arrangements or price quotations held for the event would belong to the end user until such time as the option expires, space is released by all bidding agencies, or an agent of record is selected by the end user.

5. The third-party agent has a responsibility to present all information received from bidding hotels and destinations to the end user for review. While it is appropriate for the third party to make a recommendation to the end user, it is unethical to withhold information on hotels or destinations that responded to the RFP and meet the minimum specifications for the event.

6. The end user should have the ultimate right and responsibility to determine the amount and nature of direct contact and involvement to be maintained with hotels and destinations.

7. Commissions paid by hotels or destinations to create or direct new or unique business to their facilities is not reassignable in such cases. If the end user, at some future point, decides to terminate its agreement with the original third-party agent of record, the end user should not be able to reassign to the new agent any fees, commissions, rebates, or incentives that were promised to the original agent of record. The hotel has no obligation to compensate the new agent of record in any manner.

8. The third party should not withhold or alter RFP information to allow any bidding party an unfair advantage in the bidding process.

9. The third-party agent should have a responsibility to disclose to the end user any inducements, fees, overrides or incentives that would influence the recommendation of one destination over another.

10. The third party should not take incentives or complimentary arrangements meant for the end user and intentionally price them or mark them up for the purpose of increasing profit to the third party.

LEGISLATING ETHICS

Ethical precepts are not law; but, as indicated in some of the scenarios above, some ethical violations can be illegal. It is important to note that the reverse is not true—just because something is not illegal does not automatically make it ethical. The law provides a minimum standard of behavior—what you must do, or what you cannot do. Ethics are voluntary and sometimes represent a higher standard of behavior. For example, the law says that a parent must provide food, clothing, and shelter for a child. Ethics would dictate that a child needs more from a parent than basic physical necessities.

Although law and ethics are two different things, they are interrelated. In response to the corporate and accounting scandals of Enron, Tyco, and other public companies in 2001–2002, the Sarbanes-Oxley Act of 2002[11] was enacted as a federal law. Sarbanes-Oxley, abbreviated "SOX," makes corporate accountability mandatory for public corporations. Sarbanes-Oxley requires that publicly-traded companies—those that sell stock—comply with new stringent governance standards which serve to strengthen the role of board members' oversight of financial transactions and auditing procedures.[12] The goal of Sarbanes-Oxley is to hold corporate board members responsible for the actions and financial management of a company. No longer will board members be able to shrug and say "we did not know."

The main provisions of the Sarbanes-Oxley Act address the following issues:[13]

- *Independent audit committee*—Members of the audit committee cannot be part of the management team or compensated consultants for other professional services.
- *Responsibilities of auditors*—The lead partner of the auditing firm must rotate off of the audit every five years, and the audit firm is prohibited from providing bookkeeping, human resource, legal, and other professional services concurrent with auditing services.
- *Executives must certify financial statements*—The chief executive officer and chief financial officer must attest to the appropriateness of company financial statements.
- *Insider loans*—Company loans to directors or executives of the company are generally prohibited.
- *Disclosure*—In an effort to increase the "transparency" of operations of a company, internal control mechanisms, corrections to past financial statements, and material transactions not reflected on the balance sheet must be disclosed.
- *Whistle-blower protection*
  - Whistle-blowers (employees or other "insiders" who report illegal or unethical business practices) are protected and criminal penalties are addressed for retaliation against whistle-blowers.
  - This is one of the two provisions of Sarbanes-Oxley that expressly applies to nonprofits as well as publicly traded companies.
- *Document destruction*
  - The law makes altering, covering up, falsifying, or destroying documents to prevent their use against the company in litigation or other investigations a criminal act.
  - This is one of the two provisions of Sarbanes-Oxley that expressly applies to nonprofits as well as publicly traded companies.

Since the law was enacted, there have been suggestions that associations and nonprofits use the SOX requirements as a voluntary guideline for business practices, but more formal recommendations are also beginning to surface. In 2005, the Panel on the Nonprofit Sector, "a collaboration among leaders of America's charitable organizations," drafted a report to the U.S. Congress and nonprofit community entitled: "Strengthening Transparency, Governance, and Accountability of Charitable Organizations."[14] The report recommends that nonprofit organizations adopt, implement, and publicize policies and procedures related to audit procedures, policies on travel expenses, conflicts of interest, and whistle-blower protection.[15] The report outlines actions that should be taken not only by charitable organizations themselves, but also by Congress and the Internal Revenue Service.

Further, some states have enacted, or are discussing enacting, laws similar to Sarbanes-Oxley but directed specifically at nonprofit organizations. For example, the California Nonprofit Integrity Act of 2004 became effective on January 1, 2005. This law contains many provisions that mirror SOX provisions, but is directed expressly at charities.[16] Reminiscent of Sarbanes-Oxley and the recommendations of the Nonprofit Panel of 2005, the California Nonprofit Integrity Act includes provisions related to governance, including audit provisions and compensation review.[17] Unique to charitable organizations, however, are provisions relating to fundraising activities, including misrepresentations, prohibited fundraising acts, contracts, and record retention.[18] In this environment, associations and other nonprofit organizations should consider voluntarily adopting best practices now.

Joshua Grimes recommends the following best practices for businesses and associations:[19]

- Ban conflicts of interest for officers, directors, and senior employees.
- Implement ethics rules for personnel.
- Conduct annual audits of finances.
- Assemble an audit committee.
- Adopt a policy expressly protecting whistle-blowers and encouraging them to come forward.
- Implement a document retention policy

Learn your organization's code of conduct and consider how it applies to you as a meeting manager. If your organization does not have a code of conduct or statement of ethical principles, consider helping to develop one. Start by evaluating standards outlined by professional organizations or associations to which you belong, as well as those with which your industry is associated. Professional publications and online resources are also valuable references.

INDUSTRY CODES OF ETHICS

Ethics are important in a professional, or business, context. Common ethical standards help to define a profession, whether that profession comprises doctors,

---

Put It Into Perspective[20]

Like some other professions, physicians are required to earn a certain number of continuing education credits (called continuing medical education, or CME, credits) each year. In September 2004, the Accreditation Council for Continuing Medical Education (ACCME) announced its Updated Standards for Commercial Support. One of the major issues addressed in the ACCME's Updated Standards for Commercial Support is conflicts of interest in CME programs.

The speakers and presenters at CME programs are often physicians themselves. These presenters have long been required to disclose whether a presenter had a real or potential conflict of interest due to the presenter's financial relationship with a pharmaceutical or other medically related company. The new ACCME Standards require even more stringent disclosure. The CME provider has to "have disclosure from anybody who is in a position to control CME content." This means that disclosure is required not only by the presenter, but also by volunteers and staff involved in the CME program.

In addition to the ACCME Updated Standards for Commercial Support, managers of medical meetings have a number of other sources of ethical guidance. A few pertinent sources of ethical information include:

PhRMA Code (2002): The Pharmaceutical Research and Manufacturers of America developed a voluntary set of guidelines for medical meetings and the ways that pharmaceutical companies interact with physicians. www.phrma.org

ACCME Updated Standards for Commercial Support (2004): The Accreditation Council for Continuing Medical Education not only provides standards, but also provides a toolkit for meeting managers to address managing conflict of interest. www.accme.org

AdvaMed Code of Ethics (2003): The Advanced Medical Technology Association, an organization that represents medical device manufacturers, has issued this code to address interactions with healthcare professionals. www.advamed.org

Alliance for CME: www.acme-assn.org

accountants, or meeting managers. One reason a code of ethics is so important in the meetings industry is that the perception of a meeting manager's job by those outside the industry is that the meeting manager's job is a glamorous life of travel and being wined and dined. While the travel part may be true, there are few meeting managers who would describe their work as "glamorous!" Having ethical standards helps to ensure that those outside the meetings industry understand that meeting management is not just a job; it is a profession.

Many professions and organizations develop codes of conduct or ethical guidelines, usually consisting of general statements that must be interpreted for specific situations. The code of conduct is the benchmark—compliance is the challenge. To be successful, a code of conduct must be accepted at all levels of the organization and integrated into all business practices.

PCMA Principles and Recommendations

The PCMA upholds the highest level of professional and ethical behavior for the convention and meeting industry. The organization has adopted the following statement of principles for its members to use as a standard of honorable behavior by which they may evaluate their relationships with their organizations, suppliers, clients, and colleagues.

PCMA's Principles of Professional and Ethical Conduct[21]

PCMA represents the highest levels of professional and ethical behavior in the convention and meetings industry. This association has adopted these Principles of Professional and Ethical Conduct and its members use them as standards of honorable behavior by which they may evaluate their relationships with their organizations, suppliers, and colleagues.

As a member of the Professional Convention Management Association, I will:

  I. Approach all meetings in accordance with the highest ethical standards of professionalism and personal conduct.
  II. Negotiate all agreements in good faith respecting the rights of all parties involved.
  III. Respect the policies and regulations of those organizations with which I deal.
  IV. Participate and encourage others to participate in continuing education related to the convention and meetings industry.
  V. Refrain from activities that will cause damage to or discredit to myself, my organization, or the convention and meetings industry.
  VI. Not use my position for personal gain or benefit to the detriment or disadvantage of my organization, and I will advise all parties, including my organization, of any circumstances that may have the appearance of a conflict of interest.

Professional Convention Management Association Educational Foundation. (2002). PCMA Principles of Professional and Ethical Conduct, 144–145.

ETHICAL TESTS

When faced with a decision, several "gut level" ethical tests have been suggested to determine whether an action is ethically questionable:

- Would you tell your mother what you are about to do?
- Would you want this reported on the front page of your hometown newspaper?
- Would your children, partner, or faith leader be proud of you if they knew what you were doing?
- Would the person with whom you are dealing trust and respect you if they knew what you were doing?

If the answers to any of the above questions are "no," then consider giving the decision and situation a harder look and seek input and advice from others.[9]

SUMMARY

The most important and effective ways of exercising ethics are honesty and disclosure. Much of the text of laws, codes of ethics, and best practices boil down to these two things. If an action could possibly be construed as a conflict of interest or an activity for personal gain, be honest and disclose it to management, to the board, to the client, or whoever has the power to put their stamp of approval (or disapproval) on the action. When you are not sure how an action may be construed by a colleague or client, be honest and tell them about it and ask for their feedback. Ethical standards are not black and white, but shades of gray. What is acceptable in one organization may be deemed unacceptable (or even illegal) in another organization. Meeting managers need to be guided by a personal sense of ethics, but governed by professional or organizational ethics. Having a written code of ethics and engaging in ethics training can contribute to a better work environment, a more successful business, and a stronger meetings industry profession.

REFERENCES

1. Neufeldt, V. (1996). *Webster new world college dictionary* (3rd ed.). New York: Simon & Schuster Macmillan.

2. Hudson Employment Index. (2005). One in three workers witness ethical misconduct despite clearly communicated guidelines. Retrieved March 5, 2006, from http://www.hudson-index.com/node.asp?SID=5337.

3. Ibid.

4. Johnson, C. (2003, October 29). Kozlowski jurors shown videotape of lavish party. *The Washington Post*, E01.

5. Doyle, A. (February, 2006). When the line gets blurred. *Convene*, p. 40–44.

6. Bain, B. (2005, November 4). Former president of the Long Island Convention and Visitors Bureau sentenced to 840 hours of community service, $10,000 in restitution for filing bogus expense reports. Retrieved on March 5, 2006, from http://www.hotel-online.com/News/PR2005_4th/Nov05_LongIslandCVB.html.

7. Ibid.

8. Doyle, op. cit., p. 42.

9. Doyle, op. cit.

10. Professional Convention Management Association. (n.d.). Recommendations for industry best practices. Studies and white papers. Retrieved on March 5, 2006, from http://www.pcma.org/resources/resources/whitepapers/thirdparty.asp.

11. Sarbanes-Oxley Act of 2002. 15 U.S.C. § 7201 *et seq*. Retrieved on March 5, 2006, from http://caselaw.lp.findlaw.com/casecode/uscodes/15/chapters/98/sections/section%5F7201%5Fnotes.html.

12. BoardSource and Independent Sector. (2006). The Sarbanes-Oxley Act and implications for nonprofit organizations. Retrieved on March 24, 2006, from www.boardsource.org/clientfiles/Sarbanes-Oxley.pdf.

13. Ibid.

14. Nonprofit Panel. (2005). Strengthening transparency, governance, and accountability of charitable organizations. Retrieved on March 24, 2006, from http://www.nonprofitpanel.org/final/.

15. Ibid.

16. California Nonprofit Integrity Act of 2004. S.B. 1262. Retrieved on March 5, 2006, from http://www.icnl.org/JOURNAL/vol7iss2/ar_silk.htm.

17. Ibid.

18. Ibid.

19. Grimes, J. (October, 2004). Sarbanes-Oxley meets the convention industry: Best practices for businesses and associations. *Convene*, p. 20–24.

20. Littlejohn, M. (April, 2005). CME's bugaboo: Medical meeting planners deal with conflict of interest issue. *Convene*, p. 42–49.

21. Professional Convention Management Association Educational Foundation. (2002). *Professional meeting management* (4th ed.). Chicago: Author.

KEY TERMS

Ethics	Restitution	Values
Familiarization (fam) trip	Sarbanes-Oxley Act of	Whistle-blower
Moral standards	2002	
Professional ethics		

COMPELLING QUESTIONS FOR CONSIDERATION

1. Name three things that have influenced the development of your moral values and ethics. How might these influences differ from someone else's influences (e.g., someone older or younger, someone from a different country, someone with different spiritual beliefs, and so on)?

2. What is the most unethical act you have ever witnessed in the workplace? What did you do? Would you do something different today?

3. How should you make a decision if your personal ethics differ from your organization's code of ethics? What if the organization's code of ethics seems unreasonably strict? What if your personal ethics demand a higher standard of behavior than the organization's code of ethics?

4. What is the relationship between law and ethics? What is the difference between law and ethics?

5. What role do the media play in ethics?

NEGOTIATING STRATEGICALLY: BUILDING RELATIONSHIPS AND STRIVING TO DO BETTER THAN WIN-WIN

Samuel R. Tepper, PhD

MANAGER, ORGANIZATION AND CHANGE STRATEGY

ACCENTURE

LEARNER OUTCOMES

When the reader has completed reading this chapter, he/she should be able to . . .

1 Comprehend a process-oriented approach to negotiations.

2 Comprehend the data preparation necessary for the best negotiation outcomes.

3 Discuss the win-win concept as it applies to negotiations.

4 Use negotiations to build relationships and move from an adversarial to a collaborative environment.

> Let us never negotiate out of fear, but let us never fear to negotiate.
>
> *John F. Kennedy, Inaugural Address, Jan. 20, 1961*

OVERVIEW

Negotiations are the subject of much research, of much discussion, and even much trepidation. In fact, some would say that it is impossible *not* to negotiate since communication itself "is a process wherein humans collectively create and negotiate social reality."[1,2] When we reach a *great* deal, our world is brighter, we have a skip in our step, and nothing could be better. When we come out of a negotiation feeling brutalized, however, it seems that the weight of the world is on our shoulders and nothing could be worse. The problem is that there are a number of core skills that business people need to have and very often, simply haven't had the chance to learn them in a concrete way. While business schools are fantastic at churning out graduates with skills in economics, strategy, and analysis, if they do cover the subjects at all, their focus on negotiations, sales, and procurement are cursory at best. Without these core competencies, most organizations could not function. And what happens to those poor hapless souls that have not even gone to business school?

Another problem that we encounter is the very perception of negotiations themselves. How many books or seminars cover the *art* of negotiating? It seems that there are countless. Is negotiating an art? Are artists born or made? Most tend to think of artists as those with an inner drive to be creative, putting their souls on canvas, in sculpture, in words. If you take an art class, you will be able to learn about colors, about media, about composition, but you will not be taught *what* to create. So at best, most of those who attend art classes learn some inter-

? Did You Know?

Did you know that 95.2% of polled business organizations have a formal sales strategy while 82% have *no* formal negotiation strategy?[1]

The answer is that top-notch negotiators are *made*, they are not born. While some people definitely have a more intuitive sense about communicating with people, are great at networking, putting others at ease, and making deals, it does not mean that those who do not have these skills are lost from the outset. You can be taught to more ably read body language or be more nonverbally sensitive. You can be taught the analytical or scientifically proven skills necessary to create better outcomes than merely following your gut. On the flip side of the coin, we see quite a number of people doing deals by playing hard ball, by threatening, by engaging in coercive behaviors. Does that lead to ultimate success? It's easy to see that these sorts of people take negotiating one deal at a time and do not focus on relationships, on strategic partnerships, or even on their bottom line. So whether you take a tactical approach or a "gut" approach to negotiating, there's obviously room for improvement. And at the end of the day, like in all social sciences, the truth in the art or science question lies somewhere in the middle. Negotiating is *both* an art and a science.

So what is the key to being the best negotiator possible? Preparation, preparation, preparation, and using a process that will increase the likelihood of success. If one can be taught to increase one's abilities to read others' nonverbal behaviors as well, so much the better. There are quite a number of books on the subject, but it's best to get a good process under your belt before worrying about how to physically read the person on the other side of the negotiation table. The best negotiators are not only strategic in their thinking, but they focus on building relationships, on making the most money over time, and on ensuring that their tactics are motivated by their goals. At the end of this chapter, you will know the simple steps you need to prepare for your negotiations, the likely items that will be on the negotiation table, where to get further data you need to negotiate, how to build your relationships via your negotiations, and most importantly, an overall process that will guide you through the sometimes tumultuous difficulties faced whenever you have to make a deal. Please note that the information that follows has been gleaned from a variety of sources, including Bazerman & Neale,[5] Fisher, Ury, & Patton,[6] Harvard Business Essentials,[7] Lum, Tyler-Wood, & Wanis-St. John,[8] and Ury.[9]

esting facts and skills but could not call themselves artists when they leave. Would you?

The point is that negotiating is *not* merely an art! But is it a science? Social scientists have long turned their trained eyes on bargaining and negotiations, explaining not only the foundations of strategic decision making and game theory involved in negotiations[3,4] but also on those skills that, once enacted, actually increase the likelihood of success and the greatest individual and/or joint gains. Does this mean that it's purely a science? Of course not. When we study human behavior, we can only predict responses with a particular probability, not a given certainty. Under various conditions, we can know what a person will *probably* do, not what they'll *definitely* do. Are negotiations inherently uncertain then? Since it's neither purely an art nor purely a science, what are we to do? How can we gain this competency?

THE NEGOTIATION ARENA AND ADVERSARIAL TRAP

When we think of negotiations, what metaphors do we use and what images come to mind? It is time to get down to brass tacks. It's time to roll up our sleeves and pull no punches. We think of an adversarial arena in which two fighters are vying to best each other and come out ahead. We've all heard of the idea of "win-win" but it generally falls to the wayside as we try to ensure that we "win" more than the other side. We simply want to get the best deal possible and in order to do that, we have to come out ahead, right? Aren't negotiations confrontational by their very nature?

This attitude is truly astounding, especially if we are on the seller side using a sales process in which the approach is all about "selling value" and becoming a "strategic partner" or "trusted advisor." When it comes to getting the actual deal done, however, we are told to "sharpen our pencil" or that we "can do better than that." At the end of the day, we are told, in essence, that we are really just vendors.

Yet this is also true on the procurement side. If we are buying, we talk a good game about strategic alliances and can even make reference to sole-sourcing agreements, preferred vendor arrangements, and most-favored supplier status designations, yet at the negotiating table, we really just want the lowest price possible even if partnering might make us a heck of a lot more money in the long run. And is the seller *really* trying to be our partner or just trying to get the most from us? Basically we trust each other up until the point when it comes down to talking turkey. Then it is no holds barred and our guard comes up, our armor comes back on, and it is time to do battle in the arena.

Once we are adversaries, we are serving to create distrust, harming our relationships, and creating legacy issues, or those factors that create expectations of current and future negotiations based upon past negotiations, with which we or our team will have to deal *every* time we negotiate down the road. Yet we know that it is much easier to negotiate with people with whom we get along, so how do we break this cycle? How do we *actually* become strategic partners? How do we show that we are *genuinely* interested in not only getting a "win" for our side but that we know we'll *BOTH* make more money in the short and long run if the other side gets a "win" too? And what does getting a "win" even mean?

Luckily for us, we can think about negotiations differently. There are underlying concepts that are the same across ALL negotiations. No matter which side of the negotiation table you are sitting on, no matter what you're negotiating, whether it is a personal matter like trying to buy a house or get a raise, a business matter, like trying to find a vendor or partner to supply a convention with A/V needs, trying to negotiate with a hotel chain to offer discounted room rates for a conference series, or trying to negotiate with internal staff in order to get them to actively come on board with a new corporate initiative, all negotiations have the same fundamental principles and all negotiations can be used to *build* relationships instead of falling into the adversarial trap. Let's review what these fundamental concepts are and how they can be used to change the rules of the game so that both sides work together.

FUNDAMENTAL NEGOTIATION CONCEPTS

The Negotiation Goal

According to an old Buddhist maxim, if you have no goal, any path will get you there. The problem with this sort of thinking is that in business we are governed by the bottom line. Many negotiate deals that are focused on getting revenues, on beating the other side down and winning this round, on ensuring that they simply walk away with a signature on a contract. But is this acceptable? What is missing here? Can you make a deal happen that pulls in revenue but still loses money? If you beat the other side down and do all you can to win this round, do you think the other side will be happy? Will they do all they can to ensure that you are happy in return? If small service issues crop up, for example, will they bend over backwards to help you or will they get to you when it is convenient for them? What will happen in the next negotiation? Will they try to be as fair as possible or will they remember the last negotiation when you played hardball? If you do all you can to simply get a signature on a contract, what lessons have you taught the other side? Have you taught them that you will ensure that you get a win or will they think that next time around they can push you to the wall in order to get more out of you and have you sharpen your pencil?

Every behavior you enact will be perceived by the other side in a negotiation and if you have no goal, it will be far more likely that you teach them some unintended and perhaps negative lessons. Without a negotiation goal you are far more likely to:

- be reactive versus proactive
- abandon any plans you may have had and cave into the other side's demands
- let your tactics define your strategy
- fail to take into account the other side's plan, strategy, and/or tactics
- allow emotions to control the negotiation
- think short-term versus long-term
- be less creative in finding solutions appropriate for both sides.

Any of these blunders can be very costly. So how can we avoid them? Start by choosing an appropriate goal. A good suggestion would be that for *every* negotiation, your overarching objective should be to build your relationships through your negotiations and move beyond win-win. As mentioned, it is easier to negotiate with people with whom you get along and, you will actually be able to make more money over time. This is true whether you are buying or selling simply because when you focus not only on getting a win yourself but having the other side win as well, you will build a reputation for trustworthiness over time, for fair dealing, and for finding business solutions that focus on overall value. All other objectives in your negotiation should be subordinate to this. If you want to make a particular profit and hold steadfastly to a particular margin, if you want to meet certain revenue goals, if you want to ensure that your boss is happy, all become sub-goals while you ensure that both sides get the best deal possible. Now that we have our goal in place, where do we go from here? How do we concretely build our relationships? What is a win?

STEP 1: ANALYSIS, PLANNING, AND PREPARATION

What's the first thing we do when faced with an upcoming negotiation? Obviously we have to have a plan for our negotiation, but what does a negotiation plan, or the analytical tool that helps to guide the analysis of an upcoming negotiation, look like? What should be in our plan? What data points do we need? There are two fundamental concepts that we will focus on which will guide our analysis. Once you have these firmly under your belt, you will see that negotiations do not have to be as complicated or as combative as they often can be. These are:

- The END™ Analysis
- The RINT™ Analysis

The END™ Analysis

Often in any analysis, it is best to start at the end and work backwards. This notion can be applied here as well. The first thing we have to do when thinking about negotiations is look at the worst-case scenario. Occasionally negotiations simply fall apart and die with both parties walking away to pursue other interests. They walk away from a negotiation because they can do better elsewhere. If that happens because we simply cannot reach agreement with the other side, we are going to be left with another situation. You might be saying to yourself that you won't let that happen, that the deal *can't* fall through because you really *need* for it to go off, that you *have* to meet your numbers, that there are too many political pressures to allow you to fail or any other of a myriad of reasons why the thing just has to be made to work. We all want the deal to work out, but sometimes life just does not happen the way we plan it. So if the negotiation does face a demise, we are going to feel some sort of effect. The other side will feel some sort of effect. What are those effects?

We call this the END™ Analysis or *Effect of the Negotiation Demise*™ Analysis. If we cannot reach agreement, we will be facing something, an *end* to that agreement with the person across the negotiation table and we'll feel some sort of effect due to that end. If we are on the *sales side* of the table, the END™ will be that we will either have to:

- Sell to someone else
- Do nothing and maintain the status quo with regards to our current relationship, whatever that might be

If we have to sell to someone else, what is the market demand for our products and/or services and how many deals will we have to make to equal what we could have gotten here? If we are on the *procurement side* of the table, the END™ will be that we will either have to:

- Buy from someone else
- Do nothing and potentially use the budget for another purpose
- Build or service it ourselves
- Find a realistic substitute

If we have to buy from someone else, what does that look like? Is the seller the incumbent? Are there switching costs? How long will it take to build a new relationship? What is the cycle of our procurement process? How fiscally stable is the other seller? What is their service record? What is our total cost of ownership, return on investment, or total business value if we go with someone else? As you can see there are a myriad number of questions we have to ask and analyze. It is not simply as easy as thinking to ourselves that we can get it potentially better or less expensive elsewhere.

If we do nothing, what does that mean? How will we be able to service our customers? What else would we do with the money we've budgeted? If we build it ourselves, what's involved with that process?

In thinking about any of these issues, from acquiring from another supplier to finding a substitute (if available or even feasible), we have to analyze the END™ further. What are the effects of a negotiation's demise for the long and short term? Long- and short-term effects will have hard and soft costs and gains associated with them. Hard costs and gains are those we can more easily and quantifiably measure numerically such as dollars or time. This is why it is important to focus on the total value of a deal rather than getting hung up on percentages.

Soft costs and gains are those that are a bit "fuzzier" and harder to measure such as relational issues, hassles, or morale. The foremost short-term soft costs are those associated with missing your goals. Any time we miss our business goals, it affects us psychologically and emotionally as well. In the long term, you might also be faced with a possible hit to your organization's stature and standing because of the associated issues of lowered customer satisfaction.

The long-term soft costs for the other side would be possible market repercussions in terms of their organization's reputation. Word gets out in the community and it would not look good if a relatively prominent convention center partnered with anyone other than your organization. There would also be short-term relational hassles they would have to deal with. Their boss would not be happy and the other sales folks would be perturbed with them should the negotiation go south.

In analyzing the ENDs™, we have to remember to think about all of these issues as they apply to BOTH organizations *and* for the specific individuals involved in the deals. If I am selling to you, for example, I am not only worried about my company making a profit but also about my commission that I will be making as well as making my boss happy. If I am buying from you, I not only have to worry about how the products or services I get will affect my projects and immediate needs, but also my customers, my career, and my organization.

And remember an important point: often, the other side's understanding of their own END™ may be skewed. It is for this reason that we must analyze the ENDs™ thoroughly so we know the difference between opinion and reality. Should there be a gap there, we may have to discreetly inform them of the actual situation at hand. This is especially poignant since the other side will view anything you say or any proposal you put on the table through a lens of their estimation of their END™. If the buyer feels as if he or she can really get your products or services cheaper elsewhere, for example, but you, as the seller, know for a fact that it is not true, then that buyer must be shown subtly yet confidently where the truth lies.

The END™ also gives us insight as to how far we can get pushed before it is better to walk away from the negotiating table and how far we can push the other side before it is better for them to walk away. The ENDs™ define the Zone of Possible Agreement (ZOPA), or the area where it is better for the individuals or organizations involved to reach a deal rather than walk away. It defines the boundaries or ends of the negotiation table and the win-win situation (see Figure 40.1).

The END™ also lets us know who has more muscle in the negotiation. Whoever has the *worse* END™ has *less* muscle. Without muscle, you cannot exert as much force. If I am selling services that are in great demand I won't have to work too hard to get another buyer. If I am buying services that are in great demand, however, and there are few adequate sellers in the market, I'll be hard pressed to get these services elsewhere. In this situation, the seller has more mus-

FIGURE 40.1

Defining the Zone of Possible Agreement (ZOPA)

cle because their situation isn't as bad if the negotiation faces a demise. We need to analyze the END™ *objectively*, however, in order to recognize where we truly stand. If we outline how we *wish* the situation were or try to paint a rosy picture for ourselves, we are doing ourselves a disservice since we'll end up skewing the entire analysis. An important note is that if we have more muscle than the other side, we must *tactfully* and *cautiously* inform them of this, *IF* we actually have to flex that muscle, in order to preserve the relationship. If we can reach agreement without having to go there, so much the better.

Remember, when analyzing the ENDs™, look impartially at the long- and short-term effects, and more specifically:

- All hard costs and gains
- All soft costs and gains

Most people usually focus on those things they will get out of the negotiation if it succeeds. They forget that sometimes there are actually things to be gained by *not* reaching agreement. If a customer is consistently hard to deal with, for example, one of the things that one gains by not selling to them is peace of mind. Another key point here is that we have to do this analysis to understand the long- and short-term effects. Of course we want to get a good deal here, but what sorts of legacy issues will this deal create down the road? If we constantly hammer the seller down on price, how will they get back at us in the future? If we give away something for free to the buyer in order to get the deal signed, where will the next negotiation start? Will we be able to get it back the next time around or will this negotiation be the starting point and the buyer will expect us to go down from there? Have we taught the buyer that the item was important to us or unimportant enough to merely give away? Again, we must realize that everything we do will have an effect and be perceived by the other side. We therefore want to ensure that we take more proactive approaches and *own* our behavior.

In sum, the END™ analysis allows us to:

- Understand who has more muscle in the negotiation and when that muscle should be flexed
- Define the ZOPA (Zone of Possible Agreement)
- Define the boundaries or ENDs™ on the Negotiation Table

The RINT™ Analysis

Once we have analyzed the END™ on both sides of the table we must continue our analysis. Most prepare for a negotiation by creating a list of the things they want to get out of the negotiation. They often forget that the other side also has such a list. We must actually take this into account and try to decipher not only what we want but *specifically* what the other side wants as well. In other words, what is on the table? We call this the RINT™ or *Ranked Items on the Negotiation Table*™ Analysis. Not only do we need to know what the items are that we will be negotiating and their ranked importance, but the boundaries for each item (the upper and lower ends that each side will be willing to accept), *how* important they are, and *why* they're important. In other words, we have to act like a newspaper reporter, trying to figure out:

- What is on the table
- What the order of importance of the items on the table are
- How each item on the table is weighted, i.e., how important they are in relation to each other
- Who is involved in the deal, i.e., who the key stakeholders are and how they will be affected by it
- Where the upper and lower boundaries of each item are
- Why they are on the table in the first place

This list is, in essence, the sub-goal sheet for both sides (recall our overarching goal from above). We want items A through J for example, and it is our goal to get them. The other side wants items Q through Z and they believe that it is their goal to fulfill their list. The problem arises, however, that more often than not, there's overlap on the lists and both sides are looking for the same items but with different limits attached to them. Price is often on the list for both sides, for example. Obviously the buyer wants a lower price and the seller wants a higher price. How do we reconcile this? The only way for the seller to achieve this is to get more money from the buyer and the only way for the buyer to get a lower price is to pay less money to the seller! When only talking about price, the seller gets a "win" if the price is above the minimum cost, and the buyer gets a "win" if the price is below the cost of providing the service elsewhere. Even when talking about one issue, we have a win-win situation! But we want to move beyond that. We can do better.

The crux of this issue is that we have to learn to exchange items of differing value. By adding more items into the mix, it becomes easier to be more creative in finding appropriate solutions that are acceptable to both sides. This is why we need to know what's most to least important for both sides as well as the boundaries for each item. If we are selling, we need to know how much we are willing to go down on price for example, but only if we exchange the lowered price for something else, like volume. I'd be willing to come down on price for my services, for example, if I reach a much larger agreement in which the buyer purchases more of my services for a longer period of time. It is a rather simple exchange but creates quite a bit of value for me.

We also need to know how each item is weighted, or how important each item is so that we don't get stuck talking about unimportant issues or so that we can more easily reach agreement by exchanging items of differing value and importance. If the buyer is in a cash flow problem and the seller isn't as concerned about payment terms (let's say payment terms is number three on the buyer's list and number eight on the seller's), the seller could probably get a higher price in exchange for more amenable payment provisions. It is easier for the seller to give this since it is not as high on the list, but of much more value to the buyer. Remember that just because something is third on the list doesn't mean that it is almost as important as the second item. The seller might fall on his or her sword for the first two items but items three through ten might be up for grabs! More often than not, the RINTs™ for both sides will *not* be in the same order. In fact, that makes it easier to negotiate since it is more simple to see where good exchanges might be.

Finally, we have to know *why* each item is on the list. If we understand what is motivating each side to get a certain item, we might be able to provide a more creative way of getting it. If the buyer wants a lower price, for example, we might want to know why. It sounds rather silly, right? Buyers *always* want a lower

Fast Facts

Some examples of CasualDrive™ for the buyer are:

- Cost cutting and revenue generation
- Avoiding repercussions
- Lowering the number of vendors you deal with

For the seller:

- Being more firmly entrenched with the client
- Future possibility of up-selling
- More face time with clients
- Cover costs of employees' salaries
- Increase the value of the relationship

price. But what is the Causal Drive™ that is creating the need for that lower price? By knowing what's causing each party to behave in a certain way, it is easier to see where value is truly being added in the negotiation. It allows both sides to be more creative in their ability to exchange items of different value. This is where relationship-building comes into play as well as the idea of moving *beyond* win-win. We will talk about these issues shortly. Before we move forward, it would be helpful to discuss where we get the data for our analysis.

Data Collection and Items on the Negotiation Table

The steps for collecting the proper information for your analysis are quite simple. First, start by collecting information about the ENDs™. Our own should be relatively simple. The other side's will be a bit more difficult. There are quite a number of sources of information available that will allow us to understand where the other side's organization is headed. These include the company's web site and publicly available information. If the company is publicly traded, you'll be able to find information in its shareholder prospectus, its marketing materials, and its filings with the SEC. You can also find company profiles and information from such places as www.hoovers.com, Yahoo! finance, or a number of research data providers. You can also ask those in the organization who are advocates for you, those in your organization who have dealt with them before, or even your own past experience. While these sources might give you overarching goals and mission statements, to find out about this deal, you'll have to use a bit of logic. If you're on the buyer side, remember that the seller will more than likely have to sell to another organization or do nothing, as above. If you're on the seller side, recall that the buyer will have to either do nothing, buy from another seller, find a substitute, or do it themselves. Decide which is the most appropriate for the situation and analyze the necessary components outlined above.

For the RINT™ Analysis, you'll have to use information from past experience, other deals that you've done like this, or even past deals with the organization or person on the other side of the table. You would first start with your list, and then try to ascertain what items would correspond on the other side's list. In the convention management arena, you might want to develop a meeting profile.

A meeting profile outlines the meeting history, anticipated use of all services, attendee profile, occupancy patterns and other details. To compile the necessary information, consider the following:

For All Facilities

- *Meeting history*—including facts and details about previous meetings, such as receptions, banquets, dinners, audiovisual (A/V) requirements, recreational events (golf, tennis, health club, spa, etc.), and other sponsored functions that generate money for the site. These statistics demonstrate the potential for revenue derived from sources other than room rates, for example.

- *Profile of attendees*—which outlines their number, economic level, and spending habits. Financial statistics from prior years' histories will establish the meeting's value to the site.

- *In-house vendors*—and what services are exclusive or preferred (such as drayage and A/V companies). Investigate any facilities surcharges as this can affect the budget, especially if you do not have any ability to negotiate.

- *Outside vendors*—for equipment, decorations, services, and suppliers not provided by the site. Who are they, how many are needed, and at what costs? This can affect the budget and any cost savings meaningless if there are too many added expenses.

- *Labor union rules*—if they apply, can affect the budget and make a lower rate or fee meaningless in some meeting venues. Be sure to check for any applicable rules.
- *Transportation*—for the geographic distribution and off-site activities of attendees during the event. These include air, auto rental, bus, and limo services.
- *Space pattern*—Guest room nights, meeting room, and exhibit hall requirements that use the entire facility will result in a better rate and negotiated rental fees.
- *Other meetings or functions to be held in conjunction with (ICW)*—your meeting that have the potential to increase the facility's income. If the meeting will spin off or draw additional business before, during, or after the event, this enhances the total meeting value.
- *Anticipated use of outlets*—such as room service, cocktail lounges, ice cream parlors, pool, and cabana snack bars, gift shops, dry cleaners, etc. Food and beverage is an important income item. Document anticipated functions as well as other potential food sales at outlets and cash stations in and about the property.

If in a Hotel

- *Room occupancy pattern*—broken down by the number of single and double rooms and suites. High multiple-room occupancy rates usually help in negotiating better rates. No-shows (those making reservations but do not attend and do not cancel) are also important, since a low no-show percentage may help reduce rates. Room pick-up rate and total room night history enable the hotel to estimate the number of rooms that will be available to fill other reservation requests, which will enhance its potential profit margin.
- *Room gap analysis*—or the difference between the total number of attendees and the number of hotel rooms used on peak night. Many factors can affect the arrival and departure pattern, and these should be analyzed before negotiating the room block. The destination may also affect international attendance and how the meeting draws from the local population. For example, the number of medical schools in an area may impact attendance at a medical meeting.
- *Length and time of stay*—The arrival and departure pattern may provide the hotel with extra days for premeeting and post-meeting and/or weekend stays that would otherwise be difficult to sell. If lower occupancy days can be used for arrivals, rates may be lower. In some areas, the season affects room rates also, and off-season or shoulder season are usually favorable. Using this time can be especially advantageous for first-time events.
- *Expense accounts*—including who pays guests' bills may affect spending for hotel services. Depending upon the type of organization and purpose of the meeting (corporate, association, government, religious, social, academic, or fraternal), the hotel can usually anticipate more revenue when the meeting's sponsor pays the bill.
- *Other services*—such as parking, nearby shopping, local entertainment and attractions, and children's activities. If the hotel charges for additional programs, activities or services that attendees require, these services should be included in the meetings' total value.
- *Exhibitors*—may block rooms on their own or hold hospitality functions that produce income for the hotel. This can increase the total value of the meeting. Such functions should be placed under your control by having exhibitors' reservations and functions monitored.

The First-Time Event

An event or meeting that is being held for the first time presents a complex problem since there is no event history. The only information available is the perceived needs of the event, the topic and anticipated interest, and reports and results of similar meetings. Many suppliers and facilities have experienced financial losses on such events and are cautious in negotiating. Be prepared with information regarding anticipated spending habits, general program plans, and data such as:

- *Space requirements* for events, meetings, and other functions
- *Meeting profile,* including information about attendees, food-and-beverage functions, and other events either as part of or in conjunction with your meeting
- *Projected budget* and profit sources
- *Reports from similar events* on the same or related topics with a comparable audience

Past files of hotel or convention center bills, registration reports, and financial statements may be available from various organizations. Hotel chains usually have records of similar meetings held previously (either at the site or at another property). Convention and visitor bureaus (CVBs) and chambers of commerce can also produce useful data regarding past meetings held in their area. Other meeting managers are usually more than willing to share useful information.

Remember that much of the above information may be incomplete and not first-hand. Research all available sources thoroughly.

Data Sources for Events

A valuable source of information for all events is the Destination Marketing Association International (DMAI) Meeting Information Network (MINT) system. The MINT system is a shared repository of information about association and corporate meetings. It is accessible only by those who subscribe to it through DMAI; however, meeting managers can request MINT reports through CVBs that subscribe to MINT. You can learn more by checking the DMAI web site at www.destinationmarketing.org.

Requesting post-convention reports from the headquarters hotel, any overflow hotels, or other venues used during the meeting is the best way to maintain an accurate meeting history. To ensure that you get the information you need, consider making a provision in the contract that the master account will not be paid until the post-convention report is received.

Regardless of the event being planned, gathering pertinent data about the site and area selected for evaluation is essential. Become familiar with competitive rates for all services that may be required at the selected site. This includes recently advertised hotel rates or promotions. Supplier availability, vendor sources, and costs should also be considered so that the budget does not get out of hand.

There are many sources to investigate for this information. Research rates and dates on the Internet for the suppliers under consideration as well as their competitors. These sources may be of assistance:

- Chambers of commerce and CVBs
- Organization files
- Business publications and trade journals
- Destination web sites
- Trade associations, individual hotels, and hotel chain national sales offices
- Professional/peer information gathered through personal contacts, online networks, and referrals

Also remember that depending upon whether you are negotiating with a hotel, a convention center, with exhibit services, or any other context, each will have different RINTs™ associated with them and must be analyzed appropriately. There may even be hidden costs that must be taken into consideration. Some things to think about follow, but should not be taken to be an all-inclusive list. Please be aware that they are only *some* of the items to consider in various contexts.

SOME ITEMS TO CONSIDER WITH A HOTEL

Hotel room rates are usually the primary item on the meeting manager's list of responsibilities. Be sure to select sites that offer rates within attendees' cost expectations. There are many factors (dates and arrival patterns, room block, budget, food and beverage, business value, season, etc.) that influence room rates. Depending on the circumstances, a resort hotel may offer better rates during a less costly and slower off-season or shoulder season, or a smaller site or city may offer reduced prices at less busy times in order to sell space. Consider the size of the facility and compare it to the size of your meeting. A hotel's booking calendar may have open space that may provide a better bargain if the organization has the flexibility to use those dates. Loyalty to hotel chains, multi-year contracts, and future commitments can influence room rates with some properties.

Most hotels will not confirm a guaranteed room rate more than a year in advance. However, if meetings are planned and scheduled several years in advance, you can negotiate a price for a future date based on the rack rate, group rate subject to a percentage of change formula, or the Consumer Price Index (CPI) rate. The terms of this formula become a part of your contract and are designed to keep rates within an acceptable range and still be fair to the hotel. If the group rate is used as the basis for setting future prices, the contract should also reflect the percentage of discount from the rack rate that will be used to establish the group rate.

Some Items to Consider

It is important for the hotel and the meeting manager to negotiate reasonable hotel rates that reflect the current economic environment, so the hotel has every chance to fill. If the industry or economy does not warrant the contracted room rates at the time of the meeting, you should reevaluate the formulas used to arrive at the maximum rate. You do not want your attendees booking hotel rooms outside the block if they can get a cheaper rate at a comparable hotel.

The room rate will be either a flat room rate for singles and doubles, or cover a range of prices from standard to deluxe. Depending on the amenities, various levels of décor, and views from the windows (golf course, ocean, mountains, etc.), you may be able to negotiate a run of the house for everyone, which offers any available room as reservations are made. This is preferred if the majority of rooms in the hotel are deluxe or better.

Prices will vary from city to city and within a particular area, so obtain several competitive bids in order to get as much information about END™ as possible. This is especially true when the meeting is in a single hotel. However, if the meeting requires a majority of the hotel's function space, but not a comparable number of rooms and/or room nights, the business might not be as desirable to the hotel. Also consider the size of your meeting. Whether it is the main event in the hotel or one among many other meetings will affect room rate and the attractiveness of your business to the hotel.

When discussing meeting and function space, have the complete program schedule in hand and identify specific meeting rooms rather than place a "hold all space" request in the contract. This enables the hotel to rent remaining space to others. Use the space rate structure of other properties as a guide. These may be obtained from the sales department, other meeting managers, or the CVB.

For multi-property meetings, one or more hotels may be designated as headquarters. These should be selected and contracts negotiated many years prior to the meeting date. Lower rates may be difficult to obtain due to almost total use of available space within the hotel and adjacent properties. However, the potential publicity from very important person (VIP) use and official events held exclusively on the property may make competition for headquarters hotel favorable. Request proposals from several potential headquarters hotels, then negotiate the headquarters contract first. Try to offer a variety of hotel room rates within your attendees' price limits.

If hotel management resists your rate requests, emphasize the special features of the meeting, such as large or lavish food-and-beverage functions, recreational activities, and favorable use of the property that will provide additional income in place of total room nights. Be prepared to discuss any issue the hotel salesperson raises, such as recent renovations, new services available, and so on. You must judge whether or not the improvements justify the rate.

Do not set unrealistic goals or hold out for rates that are so low that other features of the meeting will suffer. "Inexpensive" can mean staff cuts, and the resulting loss of service will wipe out the positive effects of the rate bargain. Remember: You get what you pay for.

In addition to room rate, other items can be negotiated based on the meeting's perceived business value. Negotiable items may include:

- Waiver or reduction of meeting room rentals for food-and-beverage functions
- Minimal or no exhibit space rental fees with an adequate sleeping room block
- More favorable complimentary room ratio (usually one complimentary room for every 50 attendee rooms) Room quantity counted on a cumulative basis over all of meeting days, rather than per night, is best
- Complimentary room nights for site inspection and preconvention set-up trips
- Complimentary presidential or executive suite during the meeting for the meeting sponsor and VIPs
- Complimentary room for the meeting manager during the scheduled event
- VIP room upgrades at the group rate
- Speaker and staff rooms discounted during the meeting
- Hospitality suites and receptions (complimentary beverages or wine-and-cheese party)
- Revision of percent of room block on specific dates and protection from slippage charges if registration falls below expectations early enough to inform the hotel
- Room block reservation cutoff closer to the meeting date
- Optional or reduced service charges for bell service and housekeeping
- Pads, pencils, easels, bulletin boards, candy dishes, and white boards in function rooms
- Lecterns and risers, microphones, and other A/V requirements for meeting rooms
- Assurance that adjacent space will not be used for programs that could adversely impact your functions, and right to review and approve a questionable booking

Amenities

A hotel can compensate for higher room rates in many ways. Many amenities and services can be complimentary or offered at reduced group or meeting rates. From the hotel's point of view, a fair room rate, room nights expected, and the anticipated increase in business volume for in-house functions will influence the number of services and complimentary amenities that can be negotiated.

Amenities and services may include:

- Housekeeping services (such as twice-a-day service, turndown, and extra and upgraded toiletries)
- Children's programs and childcare services
- VIP gifts and services (flowers, welcome packages, and airport pick-up)
- House limo or van shuttle service to nearby attractions
- Hospitality cabana at the pool (if available)
- Discounts for golf, tennis, spa, health club, beach chairs, umbrellas, sports equipment, and other on-site services
- Separate group and VIP check-in with extra bell staff available
- Upgrades to concierge, club, or business class floors for VIPs at a group rate
- Concierge lounge keys available to guests who are not assigned to the concierge floor
- Free or reduced parking fee or valet service
- Free self-mail registration and preprinted promotional brochures
- Free local phone calls

Other Services and Suppliers

Many sources of supplies and services can be used during a meeting. Those located in the hotel are in-house and others are outside vendors or sources. Prices for these supplies and services may be subject to negotiation. However, it is equally important to consider the quality of equipment and service required. This is especially critical with A/V service, when equipment must work well, with adequate backup and readily available technicians. For ground transportation, modern and well-maintained buses, limos, and vans are desirable. Be sure to include adequate liability and insurance protection for these services.

The success of the event may depend upon the decision between cost and quality, so carefully investigate vendor sources for all services. These services and suppliers may or may not be contracted directly with the hotel:

- Business center services (printing, fax, computer, hours of operation, etc.)
- A/V services and teleconferencing
- Destination management companies (DMC)
- Agents for music and entertainment, off-site events, local transportation, parties, gifts and decorations, guest or children's programs
- Security
- Registration service (CVB staffing, computer services, supplies and programs, printing, and signs)

If negotiated separately, once again, the perceived business value of the meeting is important to each individual supplier and vendor. If the hotel has exclusive contracts with suppliers that you must use, compare their prices to the competition.

SOME ITEMS TO CONSIDER WITH CONVENTION CENTERS

Convention centers are usually owned by local governments and are subject to established city or state regulatory policies. Convention center rental rates vary widely. Some rates are formulated on a cost per square foot for exhibit space, with meeting rooms provided at no charge, whereas others require additional fees. If no exhibit space is required, rates may depend on the rental of individual rooms or blocks of rooms and the days or portions of days for which they are needed. Rentals also vary with the inclusion of a set-up (chairs, platforms, lecterns, and microphones, etc.). Some centers' costs relate to the rental space alone, with additional charges for all other supplies and services, such as furniture move-in and move-out, cleanup, electricity, air conditioning, and daily room changes.

Just as with hotels, most convention centers will not confirm a guaranteed rental cost more than two years in advance. However, if meetings are planned years in advance, prices for future dates may be based on the current costs subject to a percentage-of-change formula. If you need to secure a meeting location three or more years in advance, request a letter of agreement from the CVB or directly from the center (each city works differently). The letter of agreement should include:

- Exhibit hall and meeting room rental rate subject to percentage of change formula
- Listing of exclusive suppliers
- Equipment lists
- Sample menus
- Center policy guidelines, rules, and regulations
- Special charges and surcharges for security officers, exhibit hall cleaning, etc.
- Copy of the space contract

Be sure to understand the total business value of the meeting. It is in your best interest to have complete knowledge of your meeting history and current requirements. Be sure to request post-convention data from previous venues, including food-and-beverage function costs and number of people served, dollars spent by ICW events, and food cart and restaurant totals.

Although cost reductions are not the rule in most convention centers due to government regulations, there are several items that can be negotiated. These may include:

- Deposit and payment policy
- Number of complimentary move-in and move-out days for exhibit and meeting room set-up. (The industry standard is one free move-in and move-out day for each show day.)
- Full service of utilities (air conditioning and electricity) during move-in and move-out
- Contract clauses pertaining to indemnification, termination, renovation, operating rules and regulations, cancellation, and space resale
- Equipment rental charges for lecterns and risers, microphones, table and stage skirting, and linen changes
- Dollar minimums for food-and-beverage cart locations
- Room change over fees
- Location of signage and type of signage
- Restaurant hours of operation

- Assurance that adjacent space will not be used for programs that could adversely impact your functions
- Right to review and approve a questionable booking

You may also get information from other meeting managers who have used the facility to determine if they have received any special considerations in the past. Investigate what other groups are occupying space in the center before/during/after your proposed meeting dates. Understanding the schedule and logistics of the other shows can determine whether or not your show will fit in to the center or if you will be a preferred client.

Local convention bureaus may be able to assist with information regarding rules and policies as well as flexibility. Be aware that many facilities are union houses and retain exclusive vendors that must be used. Discussions with these suppliers and union stewards before contracting for space are helpful in establishing relations and costs and identifying key contacts to work with in the future.

What Is Not Negotiable

Convention centers have standardized license/lease agreements (contracts), rules and regulations, and general operating guidelines. Ask for copies of these and be sure you understand the terms and conditions. Most items in the rules and regulations are nonnegotiable. As a public facility, convention centers are targeted for strong enforcement of local laws and regulations, such as safety issues with the fire marshal, taxes and permits with city and state agencies, and traffic management issues with the police.

With the high concentration of attendees at a convention center, regulations related to safety are more stringently enforced. These may include guidelines regarding:

- Clear access to fire exits, fire hose cabinets, fire extinguishers, and pull stations
- Exit pathways from large sessions and activities
- Informational displays and registration equipment in lobbies (considered to be exit pathways, *not* function space)
- Types and concentration of exhibits in the exhibit hall
- Potential obstructions created by A/V requirements (drapery or cabling across entrance or exit doorways, pyrotechnics, mobile microphone and camera cables, etc.)

Be sure your meeting requirements can be adequately met without violating such regulations, since you will be unable to eliminate them from your contract.

STEP 2: CONFIRMING YOUR ANALYSIS: RELATIONSHIP-BUILDING THROUGH NEGOTIATIONS

Once the END™ and RINT™ Analyses are accomplished, it becomes much easier to discuss needs with the other side. Just because you have done your analysis does not mean that you are done, however. There are items about which you are unsure. If you have exhausted all of your data sources, where do you get this information? The easiest place is to ask the other side. This sounds rather odd, but we know that BOTH sides get the best deal possible if they are actually exchanging items on their lists that help them achieve their goals. They both win! Schedule a pre-negotiation meeting and set it up as an information-gathering and -sharing session. If you're buying or selling, you need a bit more information in order to ensure that both sides come out ahead and do better than they could do elsewhere. Remember, do not negotiate the end of the contract during this meeting! Simply ask questions about those things you do not know and take notes. Share appropriate information. You do not want to tell the other side about your END™ for example, but you might want to tell them your RINT™ because you'll be discussing it when you hammer out the details of the deal anyway. It will allow them to know how they can best make exchanges as well. Be wary of sharing your boundaries on each item, however, but you will help build your relationship if you tell them the items on your list and their ranked importance. Make sure you do not react to the things they tell you as you might mistakenly reveal information that would be inappropriate to share or the tone of the meeting could shift from information gathering to actually trying to hammer out a deal. Simply take notes and ask more questions.

You'll know if the meeting is successful if you come away with more information about their END™ and RINT™. Make sure you ask WHY each item is important to the other side. You can read between the lines and understand more about their END™. Use the meeting as a chance to not just confirm your analysis, but to fine-tune your data and find out where you missed the boat. Once you have this information you will have the tools in place to get the best deal possible. You can creatively come up with offers that will be *better* than both sides' ENDs™ and exchange items of different worth based on your RINT™ Analysis in order for both sides to win.

Moving Beyond Win-Win

As can be seen, there are quite a number of issues to consider in your analysis. The use of ZOPA will allow you to see that it is possible to add more value to the negotiation table than would be available if we didn't do a thorough RINT™ analysis. Once you get at those issues driving the buyer's desire to get a lower price, you can understand how best to expand the ZOPA in order to increase the deal's total business value.

We have now moved *beyond* win-win because with one item on the table, we also had a win-win situation since any negotiation that ends within the ZOPA is a win for both sides. If, on the other hand, we add and exchange items to the mix that serve to expand the ZOPA, we have done *better* than our initial win-win situation!

We have to remember a key point, however. Not every item on the table helps to expand the ZOPA. We must make exchanges that only add to the negotiation table.

In order to ensure that we are actually expanding the ZOPA based on our RINT™ Analysis, remember the following key points:

- Moving beyond win-win involves exchanging items of different worth and importance
  - Only exchange items that EXPAND the ZOPA
  - Take out those items that SHRINK the ZOPA
- Only give in to the other side on an item if you get something in return.
- Only negotiate items in relation to others in the mix.
- Negotiating at the Causal Drives™ level allows for more innovative solutions.

By exchanging items of differing importance, you can find a number of ways in which you can expand the ZOPA. Once it has been expanded, you will have an easier time in reaching agreement because of the simple fact that there's more money and other items to help find innovative solutions and ensure that the negotiation falls within the appropriate zone. If you try to exchange items in the wrong direction, however, you will be more likely to deadlock and have the negotiation be pushed towards demise. If, for example, both parties have an item that's very low on their lists, there's no reason to get hung up on it. Just because both sides have items on their lists does not mean that all the items must be included in the final deal. Further, some items can actually detract from the value of the deal. If it costs more for a seller to provide an item than a buyer can get it elsewhere, take it off the table since it actually shrinks the ZOPA!

Another key point to remember is that all of the items on the table should be taken as a whole. One side generally tries to split the other side's apart and negotiate the items singly, line by line. The problem with this is that it sets up a number of discrete sub-negotiations, each with the potential of being win-lose rather than win-win. If items on the table are interdependent and systemic, no part of the deal can be changed without it affecting another part. In this way, everything is up for negotiation, but the negotiation becomes far more reasonable when the rules of the game dictate that if you ask me for something, for example, I am going to ask you for something in return. It is only fair, right? As the buyer, you would be willing to pay a higher price for A/V services if you could get a better warranty and customer service response time.

Note that this is not the same thing as compromising. People often approach negotiations with the idea that if you compromise, you'll do better. According to the Thomas-Kilman Conflict Mode Instrument,[10] people adopt varying conflict styles depending upon how they balance the concern they have for their own needs versus the concerns they have for the other side's needs. If we have a medium amount of concern for both parties, we will compromise. In other words, we will both give up something that we want in order for the sake of harmony and to reach an agreement. There's an inherent problem if both sides do not get what they want in a conflict or a negotiation. Neither side will truly be satisfied!

If, on the other hand, we have a HIGH concern for both sides' needs, then we will take a problem-solving, or collaborative approach to resolving conflict or negotiations. If we collaborate and work together to reach the best agreement possible, we can use problem solving techniques to create new and creative solutions where all parties get what they're seeking in the negotiation, and perhaps even more. We might not get them in the original way we thought we would, but that's where expanding the ZOPA becomes so important. We've seen how this works numerically by focusing on Causal Drives™ and getting at the underlying motivating factors for negotiators to seek to fulfill their sub-goals.

Once the pre-negotiation meeting is accomplished and we have confirmed and fine-tuned our analyses, we can truly seek to expand the ZOPA by coming up with offers that will be acceptable to both sides. These offers will be based on our analysis of this particular deal as well as our subsequent pre-negotiation meeting data. They will NOT be based simply on our needs alone. By looking at the RINTs™, we can see which items are of differing worth and can be easily exchanged in order to increase the overall business value from the deal. We can seek those exchanges that increase revenues and profits, while trying to limit exposure to risk, for example. Keep in anything that helps add value and take out those items that do the opposite.

STEP 3: EXCHANGING TO EXPAND AND SHARE THE ZOPA

When your analysis is complete and you're prepared to hammer out the details of the deal, we must have a plan of action for the next meeting with the other side. Expectations will be higher for both sides since we have had a pre-negotiation meeting and found out what the other sides' needs are and have shared some of our needs as well. The side that has more muscle and the side that has better data about the other sides' END™ and RINT™, will often determine who opens first. But what offer should be made and at what point in the ZOPA?

The answer to the latter part of the question is easiest. Under the best possible circumstances, we should open as close to the other side's END™ as possible while allowing them to get a "win" and allowing us to garner as much of the ZOPA as feasible. We call an opening offer an anchor since it is a data point that serves to fix the negotiation and will affect the final deal. Other anchors also exist. They can be anything from one side mentioning budgetary constraints to service requirements to future deals to competitive pricing. We must be constantly vigilant of the anchors that we place in the negotiation and how the other side might respond to them. We can do this tactically and purposefully, such as revealing our RINT™. We can also do this unintentionally, however, by mistakenly mentioning our END™ if we are not coming from a position of strength, for example. We must also be aware of the anchors that the other side uses. If they anchor unreasonably, such as outside of the ZOPA, we should not respond with a counter-anchor, but rather, disregard them and re-focus the discussion around reasonable issues within the ZOPA based on the RINT™s and END™. If we anchor unreasonably, the other side might walk away or think that we are not serious about negotiating in good faith. So ensure that you have the best data possible and take your goal of building your relationships through your negotiations and moving beyond win-win seriously.

The key here is to ensure that when we make an offer, we are setting a strategic anchor on the entire deal to be negotiated, including ALL of our terms, conditions, and RINT™ and meeting the needs of the other side as well in order for both sides to do better than they could elsewhere. Note that this does not mean splitting the difference or compromising, but trying to claim as much of the ZOPA as necessary in order to get a deal done and it truly depends on the specifics of each deal. Again, this is why proper analysis is so important and why if we have more muscle than the other side, in order to flex it properly with a concern for the relationship, we must discreetly show it to the other side so they, too, understand their own END™.

A useful tool to help with the exchange process is the CEA™, or Categorized Equivalent Anchors™. These are two or more anchors that we strategically create based on the RINT™ and END™ analyses, which are roughly equivalent to us but hold differing values to the other side and outline the *entire deal* parameters. This does not mean that all of them will hold the same dollar value to us, but it does mean that we would be satisfied if they chose any one of them. CEAs™ can help us further our RINT™ or END™ analysis and help us stave off pressures to give in on particular issues. If a buyer wants a lower price, for example, it is now easy to point at the price line item on one of the offers and say that it can be changed as long as something else in the matrix changes in order to compensate. Your focus is on doing better than you can elsewhere and this helps to ensure the truth of that sentiment.

Make sure that each offer is categorized, or labeled, based on its intent. One could outline a long-term relationship, for example, and one could cover just the next convention.

Sharing the ZOPA

Once you've come up with one, two, or even three offers that meet the criteria for both sides, you need to actually hammer out the details of the negotiation. Remember to anchor on the CEAs™ you've created and share as much of the zone as appropriate while building your relationship by showing a good faith effort to meet the other sides' needs while also fulfilling your own. Remember that the object here is to collaborate and problem solve. You will make more money over time, have more repeat business, and help to build your relationships through your negotiations.

It is in this step that you might face the possibility of deadlock, or a stalemate in which both sides either threaten to or actually do leave the negotiation table. There are three major reasons why this might happen:

- structural deadlock
- emotional deadlock
- behavioral or environmental deadlock

With a structural deadlock, an offer is on the table that is simply outside the ZOPA (see Figure 40.2).

The offer made by the seller to the buyer is outside of the ZOPA. The buyer can choose to walk away since he or she can do a better deal elsewhere, thereby enacting his or her END™. The danger, in fact, of making an offer that is outside of the ZOPA is that not only do you threaten to stop the negotiations in their tracks from the outset, you create mistrust. If, in this case, the seller were to keep on coming down in price until the offer was back in the ZOPA, the buyer would not know where the bottom end was and keep on pressuring the seller to continue to lower the price. It is therefore incredibly important that you have GOOD DATA about the other side's END™. If you simply throw an offer on the table that is not based on analysis, it will either be outside the ZOPA, it will be near your END™ because that's the number you know, or you might get lucky and have it fall in a reasonable place in the ZOPA. Unfortunately luck is not a repeatable process with any degree of certainty, so it is best to fall back on the process outlined above. In order to resolve the deadlock, exchange items in the RINT™ to bring the offer back into the ZOPA, or walk away since one party or the other can do better with their END™.

In Figure 40.2B, the situation is one in which both parties can do better elsewhere. The seller can get more money from another buyer and the buyer can get it for less money from another seller. In this situation, it is appropriate to stop the negotiation, maintain a good relationship and walk away amicably. Remember to not burn any bridges.

With an emotional deadlock, an offer on the table is within the ZOPA but for some reason the other side simply isn't accepting it. In this case, one must deal with the egos and perceptions of those involved in the negotiation. If you've done your research properly, you know what the other side's END™ is, so it is best to discreetly compare their *actual* END™ to the offer on the table, discuss what their *opinion* of their END™ is, and resolve the differences between the gaps. If it is an issue of ego, ensure that the other side can save face by being able

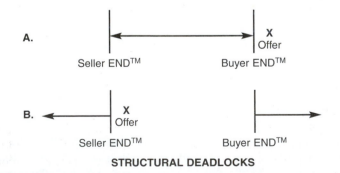

FIGURE 40.2
Example of ZOPA: Structural Deadlocks

to explain their win to their colleagues, and if it is a personality issue, just remember your goal, your strategy, and your plan. Just because someone yells at you, for example, does not mean that the END™ or RINTs™ have changed. Be calm and tactfully make use of your data, showing the other side that the offer is a good one and that, in fact, they will do worse if they have to enact their END™. Reframe the issues involved in a way that the other side will be more likely to understand and accept.

Finally, a behavioral, situational, or environmental deadlock is one in which outside forces impact the parties' ability to actually negotiate. If it is behavioral, it could be that the parties have different rules on the timing or place in which the negotiation is to actually occur. Simply make sure you know the prevailing culture, rules of etiquette, and any other pressures that the other side might be facing. Ensure that it is a good time to reach a deal! The same holds true if there really are environmental issues affecting the ability to negotiate, e.g., acts of God, such as a hurricane, personal issues that the other side is facing, or a schedule that simply does not allow for the time. Obviously, take these into account when creating any schedules, being sensitive to both sides' time and availability.

STEP 4: REACHING AGREEMENT

In your final discussion with the other side, once you've overcome any deadlocks or objections, reach agreement by making some final exchanges where appropriate, and sign the contract. Remember when you reach agreement, ensure that *all* of the items to which you've agreed are *explicitly* stated in the contract. This will save time, energy, money, and hassles later should disagreements arise. Remember your goal, your strategy, and your plan. You do not have to cave in to the other side's demands, for example, just because they ask you to do so. If their needs change, redo your RINT™ Analysis and make another offer. Any tactics they use can be diffused by using this process. And if they're using the same process, so much the better! Your negotiations will be far less combative, far less emotional, and focused more on the issues at hand rather than on beating the other side.

There's no magic here. We can only prove ourselves trustworthy over time. We can only build our relationships one good-faith negotiation at a time. If we prove, over time, that we do what we say we will do and that we are actually concerned with both sides coming out better than they can do elsewhere, we will not only have better relationships with our negotiating partners, but make more money in the long run.

Graphically, then, we can represent the entire process as ACES™. Follow it as outlined above and it will help you move more expeditiously through your negotiations, navigate trouble spots, and reach better deals than you would otherwise have been able to do (see Figure 40.3).

STEP 5: FEEDBACK

Finally, feedback is one of the most important parts of this model. We must remember that since legacy issues, expectations, and quite a number of other variables affect every aspect of the negotiation, each time we come across new data that can potentially help us with any step of the process, we should use that data wisely, informing on every aspect of every step. Just because we have three outlined steps, it does not mean that we can't backtrack should we need to do so in order to get the best result possible. Should we find out new information about the other side's Causal Drives™ after putting our CEA™ on the table, for example, we can take a couple steps backward and re-analyze the situation in order to

The ACES™ Negotiation

Your Goal: Build relationships THROUGH your negotiations and move BEYOND win/win

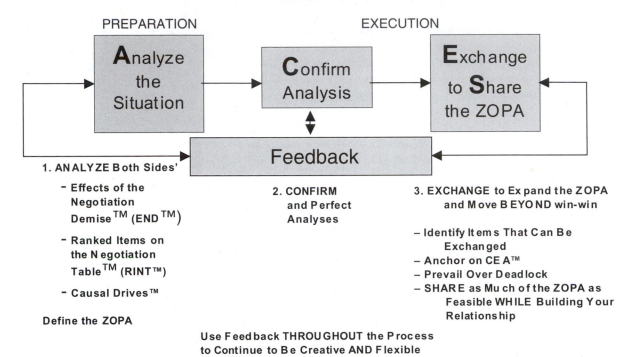

PREPARATION   EXECUTION

1. ANALYZE Both Sides'

- **Effects of the Negotiation Demise™ (END™)**
- **Ranked Items on the Negotiation Table™ (RINT™)**
- **Causal Drives™**

Define the ZOPA

2. CONFIRM and Perfect Analyses

3. EXCHANGE to Expand the ZOPA and Move BEYOND win-win

- **Identify Items That Can Be Exchanged**
- **Anchor on CEA™**
- **Prevail Over Deadlock**
- **SHARE as Much of the ZOPA as Feasible WHILE Building Your Relationship**

Use Feedback THROUGHOUT the Process to Continue to Be Creative AND Flexible

FIGURE 40.3
The ACES™ Negotiation Process. Used with permission.

make a better offer down the line. We must use the process model as a guide to the preparation, data collection, analysis, and discussions with the other side but remember that occasionally we might have to take two steps forward and one step backward in order to truly move beyond win-win.

SUMMARY

As can be seen, negotiations can be complex inasmuch as they have multiple items on the table and analyses involving a number of uncertain data points. Even more frustrating is the fact that negotiations involve people and very often people simply do not act as expected, are subject to their moods and emotions, and occasionally behave irrationally. Given all of these vagaries and seemingly random notions we are lucky to have at our disposal the fundamental underlying concepts common to all negotiation situations as well as a process that allows us to apply them.

Is negotiating an art? As we have seen, partially. We still have to show trust, build rapport, and even discreetly show the other side that our analysis more closely resembles reality than theirs. Luckily we can incorporate our own communication styles and be comfortable with the fact the process works regardless of the other side's intentions.

Is negotiating a science? Also as we have seen, partially. A repeatable step-by-step process allows us to bring specific concepts to bear based on the methodical analysis of data. We start by choosing to have our negotiations build our relationships and move beyond win-win. We then collect information from both sides' *effects of the negotiation demise (END)*[TM] and see that if a negotiation falls apart there are long and short term effects that define the negotiation table and ZOPA or zone of possible agreement. We then analyze the *Ranked Items on the Negotiation Table (RINT)*[TM], acting like a reporter to find out the what and why of those items that are actually being discussed to understand the *Causal Drives*[TM] that motivate the desire to achieve specific outcomes and obtain the items on the table.

Once the preliminary analysis is accomplished, we seek to fill in any gaps in our knowledge by meeting with the other side. In fact, we should start thinking of the person across the table from us as our negotiation partner, as our collaborator, helping us solve the puzzle of how we can put the pieces of the negotiation together to come up with the best solution for both sides. When we confirm our analysis we then exchange items to expand and share the ZOPA, overcoming deadlock, using *Categorized Equivalent Anchors (CEA)*[TM] and feedback throughout the process to help us garner as much of the ZOPA as possible while building our relationship and moving beyond win-win.

Is this process difficult? No. As we can see, there aren't that many moving parts and it is relatively simple to navigate. Is it easy to do? No. Like the musician who gets to Carnegie Hall, it takes practice, practice, practice. The more we use a process, the more it becomes second nature and we can apply it without much thought. We can then spend our time focusing on the issues contained therein and dealing with our negotiation partner with a communication style that makes us feel most comfortable. Remember that the negotiation process is a cooperative effort, blending art and science in order to reach a successful outcome for all parties. Even if the other side tries not to play by the rules of fairness, it does *not* change the fundamental underlying concepts of the negotiation, it does *not* change the ENDs[TM], the RINTs[TM], the Causal Drives[TM], or your ability to present CEAs[TM]. Fall back on the process when troubles arise and you will find that deadlocks and objections will be much more easily overcome and that over time, the negotiations with that partner will have a much more collaborative focus.

In negotiations as in life we teach people who we are based not on our words, but on our actions. If we do what we say time and time again, our reputations for fair-dealing, for ethicality, and for strategic partnership will be virtually assured.

REFERENCES

1. Dietmeyer, B. J., & Tepper, S. R. (2002). *Negotiation: Organizational alignment of strategy and execution process*. White paper. Strategic Account Management Association and Society for Sales.

2. Trenholm, S., & Jensen, R. (2003). *Interpersonal communication, 5th ed*. New York, NY: Oxford University Press.

3. Lewicki, R. J., Saunders, D. M., & Barry, B. (2006). *Negotiation, 5th ed*. New York, NY: McGraw-Hill.

4. Raiffa, H., Richardson, J. & Metcalfe, D. (2003). *Negotiation analysis: The science and art of collaborative decision making*. Cambridge, MA: Belknap Press.

5. Bazerman, M. H., & Neale, M. A. (1992). *Negotiating rationally*. New York, NY: The Free Press.

6. Fisher, R., Ury, W., & Patton, B. (1991). *Getting to Yes: Negotiating agreement without giving in*. New York, NY: Penguin Books.

7. Harvard Business Essentials. (2003). *Negotiation*. Boston, MA: Harvard Business School Publishing.

8. Lum, G., Tyler-Wood, I., & Wanis-St.John, A. (2002). *Expand the pie: How to create more value in any negotiation*. Seattle, WA: Castle Pacific Publishing.

9. Ury, W. (1993). *Getting past no: Negotiating your way from confrontation to cooperation*. New York, NY: Bantam Books.

10. Thomas, K. W. & Kilman, R. H. (1974). The Thomas-Kilman conflict mode instrument. Palo Alto, C.A.: Consulting Psychologists Press.

KEY TERMS

Amenities
Anchor
BATNA
Business center services
Categorized Equivalent Anchors™
Causal Drive™
Collaborate
Complimentary room
Consumer price index (CPI) rate
Deadlock
Exclusive contract
Flat room rate
Group rate
Hard costs or gains
Headquarters hotel
Hold all space

In conjunction with (ICW)
In-house
Legacy issues
Letter of agreement
Meeting history
Meeting profile
Negotiation goal
Negotiation plan
Occupancy rate
Off-season
Outside vendor
Percentage of change formula
Pick-up
Profile of attendees
Projected budget

Rack rate
RINT™ Analysis
Room gap analysis
Room nights
Room occupancy pattern
Room rate
Run of the house
Service charge
Shoulder season
Slippage
Soft costs or gains
Statistics
Total business value
Union house
VIP
Win-win situation
ZOPA

COMPELLING QUESTIONS FOR CONSIDERATION

1. Should you ever compromise what you hope to gain from negotiations? Why or why not?

2. What is an appropriate goal for your negotiations? Why?

3. When planning for a negotiation, what are the key points that must be analyzed? Why? How do these help move beyond win-win?

4. From a hotel's point of view, what historical information about your meeting would help to negotiate more favorable room and function space rates?

5. Do you think amenities should be offered as a cost-of-doing-business service by a site or vendor? Should some amenities always be offered?

6. How do anchors affect the negotiation and what can be done to counteract unreasonable offers?

7. What methods can be used to overcome deadlock?

CHAPTER 41

FACILITY CONTRACTS IN THE MEETINGS INDUSTRY

John S. Foster, Esq., CHME
PARTNER
FOSTER, JENSEN & GULLEY, LLC

LEARNER OUTCOMES

When the reader has completed reading this chapter, he/she should be able to . . .

1 Describe the basic principles applicable to all contracts.

2 Identify the key clauses in a well-written hotel contract.

3 Explain the differences between convention center licenses and hotel contracts.

4 Identify key license terms that require special attention.

> It's easier to stay out of trouble than
> it is to get out of trouble.
>
> *Will Rogers, American humorist*

Chapter Legal Disclaimer

This chapter is designed solely to provide basic information on the subject matter covered. The author and publisher are not engaged in rendering legal advice. If legal advice or other expert assistance is required, it is advised that you seek the specific advice of a legal expert in the meetings and conventions industry.

OVERVIEW

All meetings and events involve contracts between the meeting sponsor and the supplier of the product or service. This chapter covers contract basics and contract terms in hotel contracts and convention center licenses that meeting managers must understand to survive and advance in the meetings industry. The most complex contracts are between meeting sponsors and facilities. Whether the meeting is planned for 100 or 10,000, the operational issues, risks, and liabilities are still present and must be addressed in the contract.

World events have pushed the trend for longer and more complex contracts in order to include all of the terms and conditions necessary to host a successful meeting and protect the legal interests of both parties. Today's hotel contracts include terms that shift more risk to meeting sponsors through performance clauses. Hotel owners and management companies have become stricter in enforcing performance clauses with lawsuits against meeting sponsors.

"Meeting sponsor," "event sponsor," and "group" refer to any person, company, association, or other entity that plans and sponsors a meeting, convention, trade show, exhibition, or special event. "Facility" refers to the hotel, convention center, conference center, or other facility used as a venue for a meeting. "Meeting professional" refers to meeting managers and suppliers.

MUTUAL OBJECTIVES FOR A WELL-WRITTEN CONTRACT

A well-written contract should accomplish both parties' mutual objectives and include the following items:

- All *rates and prices* specified
- Statements of the *intents and expectations* of both parties
- All applicable *deadlines*
- *Allocation of liability* between the parties for injury to persons and damage to or loss of property
- *Specific remedies* for breach or default by either party
- Contract language that is legally clear, precise, and inclusive of all important terms

The final contract should have enough detail and clarity so that an independent third party can read the contract and understand the intent of the parties without asking any of the people involved for explanations. Consider whether the lengthy time to negotiate a contract is worth your time, trouble, and effort.

BASIC PRINCIPLES APPLICABLE TO ALL CONTRACTS

A contract[1] is "an agreement between two or more parties that creates in each party a duty to do or not to do something and a right of performance or a remedy for the breach of the other's duty."

Fast Facts

If you ask the other side for something before a contract exists, it is called negotiating; if you ask the other side for something after a contract is signed, it is called begging.

Did You Know?

- If a party changes a material term in a contract proposal, the original terms are voided.
- Contracts that cannot be performed in one year from the date they are made are unenforceable.
- Other legal standards besides impossibility exist that allow a party to terminate their contract performance obligations.
- If a liquidated damage clause for attrition or cancellation is calculated to be a penalty, the clause is unenforceable.
- Deposits are not required to have an enforceable contract.

Five Requirements for the Formation of a Contract

An agreement must meet the five requirements below in order to be a legally enforceable contract.

1. *An offer with definite terms*—An offer[2] is a promise, proposal, or other expression of willingness to make and carry out a contract under proposed terms with another party who has the ability to accept it upon receipt.

   In the meetings industry, an offer is usually referred to as a proposal.[3] Either the supplier or the meeting sponsor can send a proposal to the other party. Frequently, the meeting sponsor will send a request for proposal (RFP) to generate offers.[4] The offer must be made with the intent to be bound, and not as a mere inquiry. Preliminary negotiations, such as inquiries or requests for proposal, advertisements, and price quotations are not offers. They are considered invitations to receive offers.

   A court will not enforce an agreement if its material terms[5] are vague or not included. If definite rates or prices are to be quoted in the future, the offer should have a definite formula or method for setting rates and prices.

2. *Mutual acceptance of the same terms*—Acceptance of the exact terms of the offer is required for a contract to exist. This is called the mirror-image rule.[6] If a proposal is made, it is accepted if the party receiving the offer (offeree) signs the offer as submitted. If the offeree revises or adds any terms, the original offer is voided and the offeree returns a counter-offer. If the party making the original offer (offeror) accepts the revisions with their signature, a contract is formed. If the offeror makes additional revisions, the process continues until the two parties establish mutually agreeable terms.

   An offer or counter-offer can be withdrawn at any time until the other side accepts it. The mailbox rule[7] states that acceptance is effective when it is sent by any commercially reasonable means, regardless of whether it reaches the offeror. The mailbox rule includes faxes, emails, overnight letters, and so on. The offeror may negate the mailbox rule by stating in the offer that acceptance is effective only when received by the offeror.

3. *Consideration*[8] is the motive or price that induces a party to enter into a contract. Consideration can be bargained-for promises that each party makes to the other. In the meetings industry, consideration is the facility's promise to deliver a specific room block and/or function space on specific date(s), and the meeting sponsor's promise to use the block and/or space on those dates under the terms negotiated.

4. *In writing when required*—Certain types of contracts are required to be in writing to be enforceable under the Statute of Frauds.[9] Under the statute, two

Fast Facts

Five Requirements for a Legal Contract

1. An offer with definite terms
2. Mutual acceptance of the same terms
3. Consideration
4. In writing when required
5. Legally competent parties

types of contracts in the meetings industry must be in writing: a) contracts that cannot be performed within *one year* from the date that they are made, and b) contracts for the sale of goods (i.e., catered food and beverage items) over $500 (in some states the amount is $1,000).[10] Oral contracts are enforceable unless the Statute of Frauds applies.

5. *Legally competent parties*—To be enforceable, a contract must be signed by persons with legal competence (also referred to as "capacity").[11] Generally, legal competence includes:

   • *Legal age*—minors cannot enter into contracts. In most states, a minor is anyone under the age of 18 years.

   • *Mental competence*—people who are not of sound mind, including people with mental disabilities and people who are incapacitated by drugs or alcohol, cannot enter into contracts.

   • *Legal authority*—a person who signs a contract on behalf of another person or entity must have authority to do so from that person or entity.

Defenses to Performing a Contract

Generally, when a contractual promise is made, the party making the promise must perform its obligations or pay damages. Exceptions may exist. The most common defenses to performing a contract include the following:

• *Contingencies*[12]—A contingency is an act or event that qualifies a duty to render a promised performance. A contingency can be a required act incumbent on a party or an act or occurrence outside either party's control. A party may include certain contingencies that must occur before they are obligated to perform the contract.

• *Impossibility of Performance*[13]—If the performance of a contract has been made impossible by events outside the control of the parties that occurred after the contract was made, the performance obligations of the parties may be discharged. Impossibility must be judged objectively.

• *Impracticability of Performance*[14]—Termination of obligations under a contract may be granted when performance has been rendered excessively difficult or harmful by an unforeseen act or occurrence outside of the control of either party. The Restatement of Contracts 2nd, §261 defines impracticability as follows: "When, after a contract is made, a party's performance is made impracticable without his/her fault by the occurrence of an event, the non-occurrence of which was a basic assumption on which the contract was made, his/her duty to render that performance is discharged, unless the language or the circumstances indicate the contrary."

• *Frustration of Purpose*[15]—In frustration cases, the party seeking discharge is not claiming that he/she "cannot" perform in the sense of inability to perform. He/she is claiming that said performance would be nonsensical, because what he/she will get in return does not have the value he/she expected at the time he or she entered into the contract. The main factors courts use to decide whether to apply the frustration doctrine are:

   • The object of one of the parties in entering into the contract must be frustrated by a *supervening event*

   • The attainment of this object was a basic *assumption common to both parties*

   • The principal purpose of the contract must be *totally (or nearly totally) frustrated*

   • The party seeking to use the defense *must not have contributed* to the frustrating event or non-occurrence

Remedies for Breach of Contract

The general rules regarding damages[16] for breach or under-performance of a contract are well established (see below). Contract law provides a remedy for breach of contract called damages, defined as a sum of money awarded as compensation to put the injured party in the same financial position as if the contract had been performed. The general rules for breach of contract follow:[17]

- Breach by one party entitles the other party to damages (*not penalties*).
- Generally, damages are defined as lost profits, not 100% of lost revenue.
- "Lost profit" is defined as gross revenue minus variable expenses.
- Damages are collectible if they are foreseeable, certain, specific, and contemplated by both parties.
- When parties agree to specific damages in advance, this is called liquidated damages and may be expressed as a *flat fee, sliding scale*, or *formula*. (In order for liquidated damages to be enforceable, the actual damages must be difficult or impossible to calculate, and the liquidated damage amount must be a close approximation of actual damages.)
- The injured party has a duty to mitigate its damages unless the parties agree to reasonable liquidated damages.
- Penalties exist if the injured party would benefit more financially by enforcing the liquidated damage clause than if the contract was performed. *Penalties are not enforceable in contract law.* If a liquidated damage clause is held to be unenforceable, the injured party is still entitled to their actual damages.

Types of Contract Damages

Two basic types of contract damages are referred to in meetings industry contracts: actual damages[18] and liquidated damages.[19]

Actual damages (also called compensatory damages or general damages) are the compensation for losses that can readily be proven to have occurred and for which the injured party has the right to be compensated. Actual damages can be ascertained only after the time for performance of the contract has passed. When a contract is breached (or under-performed), the injured party has an affirmative legal duty to take reasonable steps to reduce the damages, injury, or costs that were reasonably foreseeable. This affirmative duty must be met and proved before the injured party can legally enforce the contract. This is called the duty to mitigate damages.[20]

A liquidated damage clause is enforceable *only* if it meets strict criteria for reasonableness. Liquidated damage clauses are frequently held to be unenforceable in court if the amount stipulated is out of proportion to the actual damages and amounts to a penalty clause.[21] Generally, reasonableness must be judged as of the time of contracting rather than at the time of the breach.

When preparing a liquidated damage clause, parties must agree on what revenue to include in the fixed amount or formula. In a hotel contract, the choices are revenue from guest rooms, catering food and beverages, and ancillary activities[22] (usually referred to as ancillary revenue). Revenue from ancillary activities is the most controversial because it is unquantifiable in advance and totally at the discretion of individual guests.

A liquidated damage clause in a hotel contract must provide for the possibility that the unused guest rooms and/or canceled food and beverage function(s) may be resold to other individuals or groups with credit given to the first meeting sponsor to reduce its potential damages. If a liquidated damage clause is actually a penalty clause, and held unenforceable in court, the injured party is still entitled to its actual damages.

Fast Facts

Types of Contract Damage

- Actual damages[18]
- Liquidated damages[19]

How to Sign a Contract Correctly[23]

A contract can be signed in only one of two capacities: as a principal,[24] or as an agent.[25] If you sign the contract as a principal, you are the person primarily liable for performance. If you sign as an agent on behalf of another person or entity (the principal), the contract you sign is legally enforceable against the person or entity you represent, as long as the other person or entity gave you the authority to be their agent. An authorized agent can be an employee or an independent contractor.

Two types of legal authority exist: "actual" and "apparent." Actual authority[26] is the authority actually granted by a principal to an agent. It can be given orally or in writing by contract or job description. Apparent authority[27] occurs when a principal represents or makes it appear (purposely or through negligence) to third parties that a person or entity has specific authority when such authority has not been granted in reality. If a third party relies on this representation or appearance, the principal is responsible for actions taken or promises made by the agent on the principal's behalf.

A person signing a contract should indicate in which capacity he/she is signing. If a person's legal status is not indicated, the law will assume that the person is the principal and hold him/her responsible for the terms of the contract. A person signing as an authorized agent should always name the organization he/she is representing (i.e., the principal) and should state his/her job title. If a third party meeting manager is signing, he/she should use the words "as its agent" or "authorized agent for" with the name of the principal.

How to Review a Contract Proposal

Many meeting managers are good negotiators, but they lack the training and skill to prepare, review, or revise contracts. Contracting skills include, among other things, ensuring that

- All terms agreed to are in writing
- All terms important to your side are strategically written to cover the important points
- No written terms give your side more risk than it is willing to accept
- Understanding how legal concepts affect every term in the contract
- Understanding what legal concepts control issues not covered in the contract

Here is a three-step approach to reviewing a contract proposal.[28]

- Identify clauses that are vague, inappropriate, one-sided, or over-burdensome and need to be deleted or revised to be more acceptable.
- Identify terms that are missing and need to be added to protect your side and clarify the intent of the parties.
- Determine the best way to incorporate the revisions, additions, and deletions. The options are revising the contract proposal, preparing an addendum with new or revised terms, or preparing a new contract with all revisions and new terms included.

Preparing a Well-Written Contract

Proper Way to Revise a Contract or Proposal

To advance the negotiation process and avoid a dispute over what terms are in the final contract, negotiating parties must understand the proper way to revise or amend a proposal or existing contract. Suggestions follow for revising contract proposals electronically and revising hard copies of contract proposals.

Whichever method is used, all parties should initial the bottom of each page of all revised documents, and sign and date the agreement and addendum.

Revising or Amending Electronic Copies

The party who prepares the initial proposal should provide an electronic version to the other party via email.

The party who desires to revise the initial proposal has the choice of making all of the revisions and additions on the initial proposal, making all of the revisions or additions in an addendum, or a combination of the two.

The revising party should track electronic changes so that deletions are shown with a colored line through the deleted text and additions are underlined with a different color.

If additional terms are added in an addendum, the addendum should be cross-referenced on the last page of the revised proposal or contract and on the first page of the addendum. Terms in the initial proposal or contract that contradict the terms in the addendum should be crossed out and a reference to the addendum should be added in the margin.

Create a new document that merges all of the changes. Send both parties a merged and a redlined copy (for the reader to follow the changes) and the addendum.

Revising or Amending Hard Copies to be Faxed or Mailed

Strike through terms in the initial document and write new terms in the margin. Both parties must initial and date all changes (handwritten or other) on the proposal.

If additional terms are added in an addendum, the addendum should be cross-referenced on the last page of the revised proposal and on the first page of the addendum. Terms in the initial proposal that contradict the terms in the addendum should be crossed out and a reference to the addendum should be added to the margin.

Put It Into Perspective

Meeting managers need to understand the basics of contract law and how the various terms and conditions relate to their circumstances as an association meeting manager, a corporate meeting manager, a government meeting manager, or an independent meeting manager.

Meeting managers for associations generally plan meetings and sign contracts several years prior to the actual event. Contracts for associations must be much more strategic when forecasting room blocks and preparing for every contingency that could affect the meeting.

Corporate meeting managers plan meetings on a short-term basis. Negotiating and signing contracts one to six months prior to the event is typical. Because of the constantly changing corporate environment, corporations tend to cancel on shorter notice than their association counterparts—thereby necessitating strategically written cancellation clauses.

Government meeting managers for both state and federal agencies have their own set of challenges. Government agencies are usually required to book meetings within a calendar or fiscal year and are subject to government travel regulations, per diems, and last-minute budget cuts. Some government agencies can sign contracts, others can sign only purchase orders. When contracting for government business, the parties need to incorporate the various government regulations that are non-negotiable.

Independent meeting managers can serve as independent contractors and agents for associations, corporations, or government agencies. Contracts negotiated by independent managers need to specify the legal status of the managers, how they are compensated, and their authority in managing the meeting.

On the facility side, contracts terms with resort hotels will differ from contracts with downtown, suburban, and casino hotels. Contracts with conference centers may or may not involve terms for guest rooms.

If the crossed out terms and addendum become lengthy and difficult to follow, the parties should consider preparing a new original with all of the revisions agreed to by the parties.

Understand the Proper Way to Create an Electronic Contract

An electronic contract[29] is a contract created wholly or in part through communications over computer networks. An electronic contract can be created entirely by the exchange of emails where an offer and an acceptance are evident or they can be made by a combination of electronic communications, paper documents, faxes, and oral discussions. For those who want to engage in online contracting, two major issues arise: 1) The person with whom you are communicating may not be who he or she claims to be, and 2) a confidential document may be intercepted by unauthorized parties. In order for a wholly electronic contract to be legally sufficient, it must meet the requirements of authenticity, integrity, non-repudiation, writing and signature, and security. Legal and technical experts developed digital signatures[30] to meet these requirements. A digital signature is an electronic substitute for a manual signature (a digital signature is *not* a replication of a manual or typed signature scanned into your computer, such as "signed, Jane Smith"). It is generated by a computer software program. A digital signature serves an important information security purpose that a manual signature cannot. Digital signatures allow the recipient to determine if the digitally signed communication was changed or not after it was digitally signed.

Specify Terms for Deposits (Group and Individual)

Generally, group deposits are applicable only if the "buyer" has bad credit or the vendor must put down a deposit with subcontractors for materials. Deposits can be a term of performance in a contract, but are not required to have a valid contract. If deposits are required from the group or from individuals, the contract should specify the following to avoid potential disputes:

- the amount of deposit (*never pay 100% up front*)
- the date(s) when deposits are due
- whether the party holding the deposit(s) is required to segregate the funds, and/or pay interest for the time the deposits are being held
- when title to the deposits passes from one party to the other
- under what circumstances the deposits are refundable

Specify a "Remedy" for Every "Right"

Contracts are basically a recitation of "rights" and "obligations" that each party has to the other under certain circumstances. For every "right" contained in a contract, there should be a corresponding clause specifying the remedy to each side if their rights are not honored or obligations are not performed as promised by the other side.

UNDERSTANDING HOTEL CONTRACT CLAUSES AND LEGAL TERMS

The following are typical (the list is not all-inclusive) contract clauses that are used in the hotel industry.

Guest Room Block

This clause ensures that the hotel holds the appropriate number of guest rooms in its inventory (called the room block[31]) on each night of the meeting for the exclusive use of the meeting sponsor's attendees at a negotiated rate. Typically, the room block is broken down into guest room type, such as singles, doubles, or suites. Ensure that the room block is adequate to cover anticipated needs, but not so large as to trigger attrition damages if the group's attendees do not reserve and use all of the guest rooms. Consider whether all participants will stay the entire time of the event, how many local attendees will not need guest rooms, and whether attendees may stay at other hotels.

Room Rates

This clause establishes the definite room rates that will be offered to attendees, or a formula for how rates will be set in the future. Guaranteed room rates should be provided if the contract is signed within one or two years of the event. If the contract is signed too early to obtain a definite rate, a date on which guaranteed rates will be provided should be stated. This date is typically one year prior to the meeting. The clause should include a formula for how the future rates will be established. The formula can be based on the lesser of

- A percent discount off published rates,
- The current year rates plus a percentage cap, or
- The change in the Consumer Price Index

Include terms that all rooms occupied by the group's attendees will count toward any performance clauses based on room pick-up, regardless of the rate paid.

Reservations and Individual Guest Deposits

This clause specifies how reservations will be made by attendees (e.g., individual reservations, housing bureau or third-party housing company, rooming list, reservation cards) and individual deposit requirements. An individual guest deposit is usually required to guarantee a guest room reservation for one night. This clause should clearly state when a guest deposit is due, by what date the guest will receive a refund if the reservation is canceled, and that revenue from forfeited deposits will be applied as a credit to reduce any attrition damages.

Early Departure Fees[32]

Some hotels charge an early departure fee to guests who check-out earlier than the original departure date indicated in the reservation. The contract should state the amount of the fee and that the guest will be given the opportunity to change their departure date at check-in. It should provide that all early departure fees collected by the hotel will be applied as a credit to reduce any guest room attrition damages.

Dishonored Reservations

A dishonored reservation clause is also called a relocation (walk) clause.[33] The purpose of this clause is to establish the hotel's duty to honor all reservations guaranteed by attendees and specify what concessions the hotel will make to the attendee if this duty is not met. Meeting sponsors should negotiate to include a formula for liquidated damages due to the organization as well. Damages to the organization could be a fixed amount per room night or a percentage of the room rate.

Overbooked Hotel Prior to Cut-Off Date[34]

An overbooking clause protects the group from the hotel selling into its room block before the cut-off date. The clause requires the hotel to pay liquidated damages to the group when attendees cannot make reservations at the hotel before the cut-off date and the room block is not filled. This is distinguished from the dishonored reservations clause covering situations where guaranteed reservations are not honored. This clause should state that the group will be credited with the number of room nights not accepted for purposes of calculating attrition, meeting room rental, or any other calculation dependent on the number of room nights used.

Cut-Off Date

This clause establishes the last date the hotel will hold out of inventory the meeting sponsor's guest room block for exclusive sale to the group's attendees. Any guest rooms that remain in the meeting sponsor's block after the cut-off date that are not reserved or guaranteed by the meeting sponsor or its attendees are released to the hotel for sale to attendees or the general public on a first-come, first-served basis.

State whether the hotel will honor reservations from the group's attendees after the cut-off date at the negotiated group rate. If the contract contains a guest room attrition clause, consider negotiating language saying that the hotel will accept late reservations after the cut-off date at the negotiated group rate on a space available basis. Space available basis should be defined as up to the last room available in the hotel.

Guest Room Attrition

Attrition[35] (also called underperformance) is the difference between the actual number of guest rooms picked up (or food and beverage covers or revenue) and the number of guest rooms or minimum amount of revenue guaranteed by the meeting sponsor in the contract. Before an attrition provision is contemplated, the parties must agree on whether the meeting sponsor is guaranteeing any portion of the room block or is merely giving the hotel the right to receive reservations from attendees who want to stay there. If no guarantee is given, then no attrition damages should be included in the contract. In this instance, a statement that the meeting sponsor is not responsible for unsold rooms is sufficient.

If the meeting sponsor is guaranteeing guest rooms or revenue, the contract should include an attrition clause. The attrition clause is usually stated as liquidated damages and establishes a percentage of allowable attrition and a method of calculating damages if the actual amount of attrition exceeds the allowable amount.

No standard wording exists for attrition clauses. Suggestions for what an attrition clause should contain include the following:

- A statement that attrition damages are based on either a room night guarantee or revenue guarantee. Room night guarantees are preferable to meeting sponsors and are easier to track. Revenue guarantees are preferable to hotels. With revenue guarantees, the meeting sponsor accepts the full risk when an attendee goes around the room block and gets a less expensive rate from the hotel.
- Review date(s) for adjusting the group's room block with or without liability based on history.
- The percentage of attrition the group is allowed before damages apply. The percentage generally ranges from 10% to 30%.
- A requirement that the hotel will attempt to resell the unused rooms and credit the resulting room nights or revenue to the meeting sponsor to reduce its potential attrition damages.

- The formula for determining attrition damages, if any. The formula should include the following:
  - the group's average rate excluding suites
  - calculation of attrition on a per night basis then added to reach a cumulative amount
  - credit for resold rooms
  - definition of "sold rooms" to include rooms billed to individuals or other groups for attrition, cancellation, or no-shows over the same or overlapping dates
  - a statement that ancillary revenue is or is not included in damages
  - a statement that off-market rooms will be deducted from the hotel's total inventory before the number of unsold rooms are calculated
  - a statement that sales tax will not be applied to attrition damages unless required by state and/or local law
  - a percentage by which to multiply revenue subtotals to represent estimated lost profit to the hotel. The industry average profit margin for guest rooms is 70% to 80%
- Other credits that will be applied to potential attrition damages. These might include offsets for:
  - comp rooms that are earned but not used
  - unpaid rebates and commissions
  - early departure fees
  - non-refundable deposits
  - room nights from early arrivals and stay-overs
  - room nights from the hotel's overbooking prior to the cut-off date
  - room nights from dishonored reservations

Third-Party Agent and Commissions

The purpose of this clause is to identify the third-party agent by name and address and state the amount of commission payable (*10% is the industry standard*). The authority of the third-party agent should be stated in this clause. Some hotels require a statement that the meeting sponsor will disclose the hotel's payment of commissions to its attendees.

Concessions

This clause specifies what concessions the group will receive for bringing its business to the facility over and above the standard contract clauses. Typical concessions include complimentary rooms (usually stated in a ratio, i.e., 1:50, 1:40), room upgrades, concierge privileges, VIP amenities, preferred location for guest rooms, discount staff rates, late check-outs, and so on.

Hotels may tie concessions to guest room pick-up expressed as a percentage of the guest room block or as a specific number of guest rooms. If any of the concessions are tied to guest room pick-up, clearly state how concessions will be affected in case of a shortfall. The meeting sponsor should have the right to either pay for the guest rooms needed (lost profit) to get the full concessions or reduce the concessions on a pro rata basis. State that any guest rooms paid for under the attrition clause will count toward the group's pick-up when calculating concessions.

Pre and Post Pick-Up Reports

The pick-up reports clause requires the hotel to provide pick-up reports to the meeting sponsor and should be included in every hotel contract. Pre-meeting pick-up reports should be furnished two to three months prior to the meeting and should indicate how many rooms the hotel is blocking per night for the group, how many rooms have been reserved, and how many rooms are available to be sold. Post-meeting pick-up reports should be sent with the group's final invoice indicating the total number of rooms and suites occupied per night, total room revenue, catering revenue, A/V revenue, and revenue from recreational activities, if applicable.

Master Account Procedures/Method of Payment

This clause specifies what charges individuals are responsible for and what charges the meeting sponsor will pay, what supporting documents the hotel is required to submit to substantiate the charges posted to the master account, due dates for the hotel's submission of the final bill, the time allowed for the group to identify disputed items, and a procedure for handling disputed items on the bill. Usually, individuals pay their own deposits, guest room rates, and incidentals. The meeting sponsor is responsible for staff, guest, and VIP rooms, tax, catering functions, and for all other items or services requested and authorized by the group.

State whether the group is requesting credit and direct-billing privileges; if so, include which procedures and deadlines apply. If the group's credit is accepted, requirements for group deposits should not apply. If the group's credit is rejected, the due dates for deposits and whether the hotel is required to hold deposits in escrow and pay interest should be stated.

Food and Beverage Requirements/Food and Beverage Attrition

This clause establishes the obligations of the group with regard to food and beverage functions. Obligations are usually stated as a guaranteed minimum amount of revenue. If the meeting sponsor is allowed a certain percentage of attrition, that must be included. This clause should state what the hotel is owed if the group does not meet its guaranteed minimum revenue amount. Based on contract law, the hotel is owed its lost profit on the incremental difference between the guaranteed minimum revenue and what was actually spent multiplied by a percent to represent estimated lost profit to the hotel. The parties should agree in advance what percentage will represent estimated lost profit and state it in the contract.

Note that hotels require all groups to guarantee the number of people who will attend each catered function. This allows the hotel to purchase the exact amount of food necessary to service the function. Guarantees are usually required from 48 to 72 hours before each catered function. After a meeting sponsor gives the hotel a guaranteed number of people for a function, the meeting sponsor must pay 100% of the revenue represented by the guarantee, or for the amount of people actually served, whichever is greater.

The contract should state that if a catered food and beverage function is canceled (or attendance is reduced to the point the hotel moves the function to a smaller meeting room) and the hotel is able to book another group into the original space, the first meeting sponsor will receive credit for the resold revenue.

Meeting and Function Space Requirements

This clause specifies what public space will be reserved for the exclusive use of the group for general sessions, breakout rooms, receptions, and exhibits. If the meeting sponsor can give only a preliminary program to the hotel at the time of the contract, the date when the final program will be submitted to the hotel should be stated.

Fast Facts

The industry average profit margin for catered food and beverages is 20% to 40%.

The contract should state if the facility is required to get the group's consent before the group can be reassigned to alternate meeting space. In the alternative, state that the facility may reassign the group to alternate space as long as the alternate space meets certain square footage requirements.

Meeting and Function Room Rental

This clause specifies whether the group will pay meeting room rental and the amount. Generally, meeting and function space is provided at no charge to the group if the group picks up a certain number or percentage of guest rooms. Pick-up requirements are negotiable and can range from 80% to 90%. Some hotels allocate complimentary meeting space in the same ratio as the number of rooms the group is using in the hotel. For example, if the group is using 30% of the rooms in the hotel, the group is entitled to 30% of the meeting and function space at no charge. If the group's meeting and function space requirements exceed this ratio, the group pays the meeting room rental based on a sliding scale tied to the number of guest rooms used.

If a sliding scale for meeting room rental is based on guest room pick-up, the contract should state that guest rooms paid for under the guest room attrition clause will count toward the group's pick-up for purposes of calculating rental.

Condition of Facility

The Condition of Premises clause requires the facility to be in the same or better condition over the meeting dates as it was when the contract was signed. Generally, this clause is used only if the meeting is 12 months or more from the contract date. The criteria to be used in determining the condition of the facility may include "star" or "diamond" rating by a specified rating service, reference to photos used in the hotel's marketing material, or comparison to other comparable hotels. This clause should state a deadline date when the meeting sponsor will notify the hotel of its reasonable concerns and a remedy if the hotel cannot or will not correct the deficiencies.

Renovation and Construction/Noise Control

This clause acknowledges the hotel's obligation to disclose any current or future plans for construction and renovation. This clause usually requires the facility to control other groups so they do not cause undue noise or other disturbances that would materially affect the group's attendees. Include remedies for the group if future renovation or construction materially affects the group's activities.

Warranties, Representations, and Duties of the Parties

This clause states certain warranties, representations, and duties made by each party upon which the other party may rely in performing the terms of the contract (e.g., the hotel warrants and represents that it maintains policies and procedures concerning safety issues and will provide adequate security in all of the public areas it controls. The group will comply with all anti-terrorism laws and will cooperate with the hotel and governmental authorities to ensure compliance).

Indemnification/Responsibility for Property Damage[36]

The purpose of an indemnification clause is for one party to agree to pay damages or compensate the other party for legal claims asserted against that party under certain circumstances. Indemnification (hold harmless) clauses pertain to claims made by third parties (e.g., attendees, contractors, and so on). In contracts between meeting sponsors and private facilities (e.g., hotels and conference centers), the best practice is for the parties to agree to mutual indemnification. Mutual indemnification clauses provide that both parties agree to defend and/or compensate the other party for asserted claims against, or liability damages incurred by, the other party due to the acts or omissions of the first party.

Insurance

This clause requires both parties to carry specific insurance coverage over the meeting dates that protects against losses incurred from the meeting's activities. Consider including a mutual waiver of subrogation[37] for property damage or a statement that neither party's liability to the other for property damage will exceed the amount of property insurance contractually required. Typical insurance coverages required include the following items:[38]

- Commercial General Liability (CGL) insurance (meeting sponsor),
- Commercial Liquor Liability Insurance (facility),
- Basic Property Insurance (both parties), and
- Workers Compensation (meeting sponsor).

Americans with Disabilities Act (ADA) Compliance

This clause allocates what requirements the meeting sponsor and the facility will be responsible for under the Americans with Disabilities Act (ADA), a federal statute[39] that prohibits discrimination in employment, public services, and public accommodations. The ADA requires a public accommodation to

- Remove physical barriers (if readily achievable) to make facilities accessible
- Reasonably modify its policies, practices, or procedures to avoid discrimination
- Provide auxiliary aids and services that are necessary to provide equal access to the goods, services, facilities, privileges, or accommodations that it offers unless an undue burden or a fundamental alteration would result

Both the user and the provider of a public accommodation can be held jointly and severally liable for noncompliance with the law. The industry practice is for meeting sponsors and hotels to specify in the contract that the facility is responsible for meeting the requirements that affect the physical structure, including the public areas and guest rooms, and the meeting sponsor is responsible for adherence inside the rented space, including the furnishing of auxiliary aids.

Termination and Excuse of Performance[40]

A performance clause is sometimes referred to as force majeure or act of God and allows either party to terminate their obligations and excuse their performance *without liability* if that party's performance is made illegal, impossible, or commercially impracticable by acts or occurrences outside that party's control.

Terminating a contract is not the same as canceling a contract. If a contract is "terminated," neither party has any continuing obligation to the other. If a contract is "canceled" it means one party has breached or defaulted on their performance and potentially owes the other party damages. Circumstances triggering a right of termination should be clearly specified. Consider adding "specific threat of terrorism" and "reasonable fear of personal safety" and references to the Homeland Security Advisory System.

Variables to consider for inclusion are

- a certain percentage of attendees that must be affected by a *force majeure* act or occurrence before the meeting sponsor may terminate the contract in full,
- a change in the hotel chain affiliation or management company,
- the sale or transfer of 51% or more in the ownership of the hotel,
- the unavailability of a sufficient number of suitable overflow hotel rooms over the meeting dates, or
- the inability or unwillingness of the contracted convention center to provide its facilities over the contracted dates.

Cancellation by the Group

If the meeting sponsor cancels the meeting, or moves it to another facility for reasons other than a *force majeure* event, it has breached the contract and potentially owes the hotel damages. A cancellation clause is usually stated as liquidated damages. Its purpose is to specify a fixed fee or a formula for determining the amount the meeting sponsor will pay to the hotel. The following are suggested guidelines on what a well-written cancellation clause should accomplish:

- Define "cancellation" to differentiate it from "attrition" and "termination."
- Establish potential damages for cancellation due to the hotel if cancellation by the group occurs.
- Specify a sliding scale or fixed amount applicable for determining the cancellation damages owed to the hotel based on when the cancellation occurs. The sliding scale or fixed amount can be based on room nights or anticipated lost revenue. If it is based on revenue, clearly specify what revenue sources are included in the fixed fee or sliding scale, i.e., guest rooms and/or catering food and beverage (ancillary revenue may be included if the parties agree).
- If the fixed fee or formula is based on a percentage of "anticipated lost revenue," define how that term is calculated. The formula should be based on the group's estimated average rate (excluding suites rates) and should include an offset for any commissions, rebates, and housing fees not paid. The formula should include an offset for a percentage of allowable attrition and credit for rooms resold by the hotel.
- Every fixed fee or formula should provide a calculation to reduce anticipated revenue to estimated lost profit in the agreed upon revenue sources.
- Establish when payment of the cancellation fee is due and payable. Set the due date after the anticipated meeting dates to determine if any business has been recouped by the hotel.

Cancellation by the Hotel

Hotels sometimes breach the agreement with the meeting sponsor by canceling the contract. Cancellations by hotels occur most frequently in a growing economy when the hotel has the opportunity to book another group at a higher rate.

The cancellation by the hotel clause is to protect the group if the hotel cancels by providing for payment of damages to the group. The following are suggested guidelines on what this clause should accomplish:

- Define "cancellation" by hotel to differentiate it from "termination," and "excuse of performance."

- Include a statement that the meeting sponsor is due damages if cancellation by the hotel occurs.
- Explain how damages will be calculated to compensate the group as liquidated damages. The typical options are to: 1) specific amount, 2) sliding scale of revenue based on when the cancellation occurs, or 3) actual out-of-pocket expenses and lost revenue from moving the meeting date and/or location.
- Include a statement establishing when the cancellation payment is due. Payment can be due the time of the cancellation, or after the actual amounts are incurred.
- Include an agreement by the hotel to return deposits within a specific time frame.

Audit[41]

The audit clause should acknowledge the meeting sponsor's right to independently verify the accuracy of the hotel's occupancy and pick-up figures when calculating any guest room attrition or cancellation damages. This clause will specify how the audit will be conducted and the parties' compliance with privacy laws.

Dispute Resolution[42]

This clause specifies in advance how any disputes will be resolved. The commonly used methods for resolving contract disputes are mediation, arbitration, and litigation. This clause is also used to specify which state's (or country's) laws will govern the interpretation of the contract, and the city and state where the mediation, arbitration hearings, or the litigation will take place. It can also provide that the substantially prevailing party will be awarded costs and expenses, including attorney's fees, or that this issue will be at the discretion of the arbitrator or judge.

CONVENTION CENTER LICENSES ANALYZED[43]

Convention Center Licenses Distinguished from Hotel Contracts

Most convention centers are owned by state or local government municipalities and there is only one per city. Because they are government-owned, negotiating with convention centers is substantially different from negotiating with hotels or other vendors. Another reason is that the contracts are essentially real estate license agreements prepared by real estate attorneys, not service agreements. A license agreement[44] is a permission granted by an owner of land to another person or entity to occupy the land for a specific purpose and for a specific period of time. Whether the document issued by the convention center is called a "license," "lease," or "permit," it is still a contract and most of the legal rules applicable to contracts apply. "License" or "license agreement" will be used throughout this section to mean the contract between a convention center (also referred to as a "facility") and an event sponsor.

Most license agreements are prepared by the convention center to protect the facility and specify the event sponsor's performance obligations and liabilities. Event sponsors should focus on negotiating terms that protect them and clarify the performance obligations and liabilities of the facility.

Terms That Require Special Attention

Letters of Intent

The purpose of the Letter of Intent (also called a Letter of Agreement) is to hold the space at the convention center prior to signing the license agreement, usually 12–18 months before the event. The danger of signing a letter of intent is that it can become a contract that binds the parties even though it does not include all of the terms the parties want and need. If a letter of intent is necessary to hold space at the convention center before the license agreement and other vendor contracts are signed, the letter of intent should contain a contingency clause to protect the event sponsor. The contingency clause should state that the event sponsor is not obligated to use the convention center unless the event sponsor can negotiate 1) mutually agreeable rates and terms in the actual license agreement, and 2) mutually agreeable rates and terms with a sufficient number of hotels to accommodate all of the anticipated attendees.

Indemnification Clause and Insurance

Like its counterpart in a hotel contract, the purpose of this clause is for one party to agree to pay damages or compensate the other party for legal claims asserted against that party under certain circumstances. Mutual indemnification clauses are preferred; however, municipally owed facilities will not always agree to them. In some states, municipally owned facilities are prevented by local law from agreeing to mutual indemnification clauses that require them to pay costs up front. Most municipalities will agree to include wording requiring the municipality to be liable for the acts or omissions of its employees, agents, and contractors and to reimburse the event sponsor for any defense costs it incurs defending itself against claims asserted by third parties (e.g., attendees) resulting from the acts or omissions of the facility.

Event sponsors should insist on an indemnification (hold harmless) clause that states that the event sponsor is not required to indemnify the convention center when the convention center is "solely" or "grossly" negligent. Insurance requirements for the event sponsor are usually included in this clause.

Condition of Facility

Many licenses offered by convention centers require the event sponsor to accept the convention "as is" over the event dates. Like its counterpart in hotel contracts, this clause requires the convention center to be in the same or better condition over the meeting dates as it was when the license agreement was signed. This clause is used only if the meeting is 12 months or more from the contract date.

Condition and Inspection of Returned Premises

The standard license requires the event sponsor to return the premises at the end of the license period in the same condition that they were in when the event sponsor took possession, normal wear and tear and acts of God excluded. Additional terms may be added to jointly inspect the facility prior to and after the event, and to specify that the event sponsor will not be required to pay for repair costs that exceed the amount of property insurance required in the license.

Compliance with Future Operating Rules and Regulations

The standard license incorporates the facility's operating rules and regulations by reference and requires the event sponsor to agree to be bound by all future changes. Event sponsors should obtain a copy of the operating rules and regulations for review before the license is signed. Consider adding that the facility's right to make changes will not apply to the event sponsor if the changes would result in a substantially negative impact on the event sponsor's event (e.g., operationally or financially).

Exclusive Services Added After Execution of the License

This clause addresses the rights of event sponsors when exclusive services are added after the license is signed. The event sponsor should negotiate for guarantees that the convention center's exclusive service providers will match or beat competitive quotes from non-exclusive service providers.

Other Events in the Facility

The typical license gives the facility the right to book other groups into the facility over the event sponsor's event. The license should state that incompatible groups will not be booked over the same or overlapping dates. An event sponsor should always ask what other groups are already booked in the facility before it signs the license. An incompatible group is defined as any other group or individual who may have a conflict of interest with the event sponsor or who is in the same industry and seeks to attract the same attendees. If possible, the event sponsor should provide specific names of organizations or individuals it specifically does not want in the facility at the same time. Event sponsors should consider negotiating a right of first refusal[45] on all available function space before another group is booked by the facility.

Notice of Default and Opportunity to Cure

A "Notice of Default and Opportunity to Cure" clause should be included in every license agreement. The purpose of this clause is to require the facility to give written notice to the event sponsor if it is in default of the license and the opportunity to cure the default within a specific time frame before the facility is allowed to terminate the license agreement and hold the event sponsor liable.

Cancellation

Cancellation by the Event Sponsor

Typical licenses provide a liquidated damage clause specifying what the event sponsor will owe. The typical liquidated damage clause requires 1) payment for total cancellation, and 2) payment for partial cancellation of space.

Payment for total cancellation is usually stated in a sliding scale. Typically, the sliding scale will require forfeiture of the first deposit if cancellation occurs more than five years prior to the event, payment of 50% of the license fee if cancellation occurs between two and five years, and payment of 100% of the license fee if cancellation occurs less than two years prior to the event. These percentages and time frames are negotiable, and depending upon the group, the location of the facility, and the event dates. Payment for partial cancellation of space is usually calculated on a pro rata basis.

This clause should require the facility to use its best efforts to re-license any canceled space to other groups and apply the revenue toward the cancellation damages owed by the event sponsor. This clause should establish when the cancellation payment is due. *Payment can be due at the time of cancellation, or after the contracted event dates in order to apply credit for any resold space.*

Cancellation by the Facility

The typical license *does not* include a clause for compensating the event sponsor for cancellation by the facility. Some facilities address this issue in the license agreement by stating that, in the event of total cancellation by the facility, the facility's only obligation is to return any deposits already paid by the event sponsor.

The parties should discuss additional terms to include in this clause to protect the event sponsor. Damages due to the event sponsor would include a return of all deposits plus reimbursement for the cost and expense of postponing or relocating the event to another facility. Damages may include lost revenue from exhibitors and sponsors who cancel due to the event's postponement or relocation.

Use of Force by Facility

Most licenses proposed by the facility contain a clause that facility personnel have the right to use force to eject disorderly people from the premises and a requirement that the meeting sponsor indemnify (hold harmless) and defend facility management from such action. Event sponsors should revise this provision so it does not apply to claims of excessive use of force by facility personnel.

Use of the Facility's Equipment

The typical license states the facility will provide chairs and tables to the event sponsor up to the facility's inventory. Since the facility's inventory, and the requirements of other groups in the facility, are unknown to each event sponsor, the license should be revised to specify the facility will provide all chairs and tables in each meeting room up to their maximum capacity.

Force Majeure

The typical license states the obligations of parties can be terminated without liability only when providing the facility to the event sponsor is impossible. This is very one-sided and incomplete. See the discussion of "Termination and Excuse of Performance" for hotel contracts.

SUMMARY

One of the most important responsibilities of a meeting manager is to negotiate and sign hotel contracts and convention center licenses with their counterparts in those facilities. Meeting managers must understand basic contract law and critical terms and conditions in facility contracts that protect both sides.

Meeting managers cannot possibly be experts in every aspect of contracting for a meeting, but they are responsible for knowing the experts. If contracts and legalities are not your strong point, you are advised to use your in-house legal resources for advice, or obtain the services of an outside legal counsel that is an expert in hotel contracts and convention center licenses.

Meeting managers must be able to complete the following tasks:

- Describe the basic principles applicable to all contracts.
- Identify the key clauses in a well-written hotel contract.
- Explain how convention center licenses differ from hotel contracts and key license terms that require special attention.

REFERENCES

1. Calamari, J.D., & Perillo, J.M. (2004). *Contracts.* (4th edition, 2004). St. Paul, MN: West Publishing (Black Letter Law Series). See also: (2004). *Black's law dictionary.* (8th edition), St. Paul, MN: West Publishing.

2. Ibid.

3. Ibid.

4. Ibid.

5. Calamari & Perillo.

6. Ibid.

7. Ibid. See also: *Black's law dictionary.*

8. See Convention Industry Council. APEX Glossary. http://glossary.convention industry.org/. See also: Calamari & Perillo.

9. Calamari & Perillo. See also *Black's law dictionary.*

10. Uniform Commercial Code (UCC) §2-201

11. Calamari & Perillo. See also *Black's law dictionary.* (8th edition).

12. Uniform Commercial Code (UCC) §2-201

13. Foster, J.S. (2006). *Meeting & facility contracts.* (4th edition). See also APEX Glossary and *Black's law dictionary.*

14. Ibid.

15. Ibid.

16. Convention Industry Council. APEX Contracts Panel Report. In: APEX Glossary. http://glossary.conventionindustry.org/. See also Foster.

17. Foster.

18. APEX Contracts Panel Report. See also Foster.

19. Ibid.

20. Ibid.

21. Ibid.

22. Ibid.

23. Ibid.

24. Ibid. See also *Black's law dictionary.*

25. Ibid. See also APEX Glossary.

26. Ibid. See also *Black's law dictionary.*

27. Ibid.

28. Foster.

29. *Black's law dictionary.*

30. See ABA Digital Signatures Guidelines Tutorial at www.abanet.org/scitech/ec/isc/dsg-tutorial.html.

31. Ibid. See also APEX Glossary.

32. APEX Contracts Panel Report.

33. Ibid.

34. Ibid.

35. Foster.

36. Ibid.

37. Ibid.

38. Ibid.

39. Ibid. See also Insurance Information Institute. Glossary of Insurance Terms. http://www.iii.org/media/glossary.

40. See 42 USCA §§ 12101-12213

41. Foster. See also APEX Contracts Panel Report and APEX Glossary.

42. Ibid.

43. Ibid.

44. Foster.

45. See APEX Glossary and *Black's law dictionary.*

46. See APEX Glossary.

KEY TERMS

Act of God
Acceptance
Actual authority
Actual damages
Agent
Americans with
   Disabilities Act (ADA)
Ancillary activities
Apparent authority
Attrition
Block
Breach
Cancellation clause
Capacity
Concessions
Condition of premises
Consideration
Contingency
Contract
Counter-offer
Damages
Digital signature
Duty to mitigate damages

Early departure fee
Electronic contract
Food and beverage
Force majeure
Frustration of purpose
Function space
Impossibility of
   performance
Impracticality of
   performance
Incompatible groups
Indemnification (hold
   harmless)
Legal competence
Letter of intent
License agreement
Liquidated damages
Mailbox rule
Material terms/Material
   breach
Mirror-Image rule
Mitigate/mitigation
Mutual assent

Offer
Offeror
Offeree
Overbooking
Penalty clause
Performance
Performance clause
Pre and post pick-up
   reports
Principal
Proposal
Remedies
Request for proposal
   (RFP)
Right of first refusal
Room block
Signatures
Statute of Frauds
Termination and excuse
   of performance
Waiver of subrogation
Walking

COMPELLING QUESTIONS FOR CONSIDERATION

1. What are the five requirements for the formation of a contract?

2. If the United States is attacked again, or a severe weather catastrophe occurs, affecting a contracting party's ability to plan or host a meeting, what are the legal defenses available to terminate that party's contractual obligations?

3. What are the requirements for a liquidated damage clause to be enforceable?

4. Why is an audit clause in a hotel contract important to a meeting sponsor?

5. How do convention center licenses differ from hotel contracts?

6. What is the difference between "penalties" and "damages" in a contract or license?

7. What are the advantages of a digital versus a manual signature?

CHAPTER 42

DEVELOPING SUPPLIER CONTRACTS

Mary Catherine Sexton
EXECUTIVE VICE PRESIDENT
CHIEF LEGAL COUNSEL
GES EXPOSITION SERVICES

Julia W. Smith, CEM
VICE PRESIDENT, SALES
GES EXPOSITION SERVICES

LEARNER OUTCOMES

When the reader has completed reading this chapter, he/she should be able to . . .

1 Develop a comprehensive request for proposal (RFP).

2 Review and compare proposals from suppliers and vendors.

3 Identify elements that will impact the success of your working relationships.

4 Select suppliers that share your organization's vision and provide the quality of services and/or products required at the agreed-upon pricing structure.

5 Negotiate an agreement that is win-win for your organization and your selected supplier partner.

> I'm only as good as the supplier teams around me—and they are only as good as the information I provide to them.
>
> *Pat Phillips*

OVERVIEW

Negotiating contracts are an important part of every meeting manager's job. The days of striking deals with a handshake are long past—meeting managers must protect themselves, the organization, and the interests of all of the parties involved in the production of an event by spelling out the agreements concisely and thoroughly.

The potential for terrorism, pandemics, natural disasters, or legal claims and disputes has created an environment that calls for careful documentation. If the risks presented by the vendor's service is understood, the meeting manager can better tailor the agreement to address those risks in a manner that reflects the parties' understanding.

In this chapter, information regarding how to customize vendor agreements to address the unique needs of an organization's meeting(s) to protect the sponsoring organization and meeting attendees will be presented. All agreements have essential elements such as a description of services, insurance, indemnification, payment, and pricing.

While the meeting manager works with the organization's attorneys to develop or review and approve the terms and conditions portion of any contract, the responsibility lies in the details that outline the scope of services or products to be supplied, in what manner, and at what cost. The clearer meeting managers are in setting expectations for a supplier, the more likely that the supplier will be able to provide services that meet expectations at the prices quoted.

All suppliers have standard contractual language, and if the meeting manager signs a proposal produced by a vendor, the organization's legal team should review the terms and conditions to protect the organization's interests. As the meeting manager, the obligation is to ensure that the language outlining the scope of services or products to be provided, and the affiliated pricing structures, is complete and clearly defined.

IDENTIFYING POTENTIAL VENDORS

There are many sources for identifying suppliers for your meetings. Most facility staffs maintain a list of recommended suppliers, and may maintain a list of companies that are restricted from working at the property if there were issues with prior performance. The facility can also provide a list of in-house or exclusive providers, such as the catering company, that must be used when working in the hotel or convention center.

Convention bureaus provide lists of members that provide services and products to the meetings industry; the lists may be available in a printed guide or online.

The network that meeting managers work with are excellent resources for recommending suppliers based on recent experience, and other trusted contractors have contacts for use in the selection process.

While a current contractor could be doing an excellent job, the meeting manager has a fiduciary responsibility to the organization to get competitive bids periodically, and ensure that the pricing and services provided by current suppliers are competitive. Whether seeking a supplier for a new service, looking for a change, or negotiating an extension to a current agreement, the basic tenets of developing an effective, legally binding document hold true.

THE REQUEST FOR PROPOSAL (RFP)

The surest way to get a contract that meets the meeting manager's needs is to ask for it by means of a carefully constructed request for proposal (RFP). The RFP acts as a road map for the respondents, outlining the specifics of the event and the needs pertaining to that supplier group.

A well-constructed RFP generates proposals that are easy to compare and contrast. The responses not only provide all of the information needed to make an informed decision, but also give a good indication of how well the supplier takes direction.

The content of an RFP will vary, depending upon the type of supplier (general service contractor, audiovisual (A/V) company, security firm, florist, and so on), but all RFPs should include the following:

- Official name of the event
- Sponsor(s) of the event
- Meeting/show management (if different from the sponsor)
- Location of the event, including specific space being used
- Dates of the event, including available move-in and move-out times
- Future dates and locations, if available
- Event history
- Profile and number of attendees
- Profile and number of exhibitors
- Scope of work (a detailed list of the services to be provided)
- Applicable completion times for all tasks (so the vendor can calculate labor costs effectively)
- Contact information and guidelines for posing questions prior to the proposal submission
- Proposal due date
- Delivery method (via mail or other form of delivery, email, or in person)
- Presentation schedule, if applicable
- Names, titles, and roles of decision makers
- Date of decision
- Implementation plan

Using a generic RFP results in a generic proposal that may not provide sufficient information to judge a supplier's capability to meet the organization's needs. No one knows more about the meeting and the organization's expectations than the meeting manager and the organization's staff. The more that is provided in terms of detail in the RFP, the better quality responses provided by suppliers. Also resulting are fewer time-consuming questions to the meeting manager and staff from the bidding contractors.

Each of the sections that follow includes tips for items that should be a part of an RFP sent to that vendor group—the first step in setting clear expectations for the delivery of services.

General Services Contractor (GSC)

The general services contractor (or GSC; also known as an official services contractor or decorator) is defined by the Exhibition Services and Contractors Association (ESCA) as "an organization that provides show management and exhibitors with a wide range of services, sometimes including, but not limited to, installation and dismantle (I & D), creating and hanging signage and banners, laying carpet, material handling, and providing booth furniture."[1]

The scope of services that a GSC provides includes both exclusive services, and non-exclusive, or discretionary services.

Exclusive services are services that show management and exhibitors must order through the selected general services contractor. The services may be exclusive to the GSC due to the types of skills and/or equipment required to provide them, or because of the logistics or liabilities associated with working within a facility. For instance, if any number of contractors were permitted to operate mechanized equipment such as forklifts or scissor lifts, it would be difficult to ensure the safety of individuals on the show floor, and to protect the facility from damage.

Contractors are also asked to guarantee pricing for the products and services they are providing to an event. In order to do so, as well as to assume the costs for the materials and labor to provide the services, contractors must be able to count on revenue streams from designated lines of business. A single contractor must control the dock areas, freight staging areas, freight elevators, storage of "empties" (crates and other containers), and other major logistical aspects of the event set-up and tear-down to ensure that the exhibition and other events open on time and in an orderly fashion. A list of the services that may be exclusive to the GSC:

- Material handling (sometimes referred to as drayage)
- Forklift labor
- Rigging/sign-hanging labor
- Furnishings rental
- Electrical and plumbing in selected facilities (in some facilities, facility staff or an in-house contractor provide these services)
- Carpet rental
- Cleaning (unless it is an exclusive service of the facility)
- Modular booth components rental

Discretionary services may be provided by the GSC, or by an exhibitor appointed contractor (or EAC). An EAC has to provide proof of sufficient liability insurance and any applicable permits, and must follow facility, local, and state regulations. If a union claims jurisdiction for the type of work provided by the EAC, the EAC must employ qualified union personnel. To ensure that only qualified personnel are operating on your event floor, set a deadline (a minimum of 30 days prior to move-in) by which time exhibitors must provide proof of insurance and the individual names of the EAC employees for credentialing. The meeting manager need to have a process for check-in of the EAC personnel to protect the sponsoring organization against unauthorized personnel doing work, or uninsured parties from working on the floor.

EAC personnel should not be permitted to solicit new business on the event floor, in competition with your selected general services contractor, as that would be a breach of the organization's obligations to the GSC.

Discretionary services can include the following:

- Custom booth fabrication
- Production of signs and graphics
- Labor for installation and dismantling of booths
- Prop and specialty item rental
- Transportation of exhibit materials (also known as shipping or logistics)
- Custom/plush carpet rental
- Specialty furnishings rental
- Custom lighting packages

These are a sampling of the services and products that can be obtained through the general services contractor, but also can be rented or purchased through an outside contractor pending event and facility rules and regulations. The contract defines which services are exclusive and which services are discretionary. These will change based upon the facility, and will affect the overall pricing of services.

The GSC may request being designated by the sponsoring organization as the recommended contractor for certain discretionary services, such as shipping, to help drive revenue. If the GSC captures a greater percentage of the discretionary revenue available on the event, the company can offer cost savings or new services to the organization or their exhibitors on future events, or cover rising costs of materials and labor without significant pricing increases. The key is to determine how to get the best prices, while creating efficiencies that improve customer service.

The RFP for the general services contractor should request details on the bidder's capabilities to provide any of the following applicable products and services, as well as the affiliated pricing, any minimums that apply, and deadlines for submitting requirements:

- Aisle carpet (and available colors)
- Exhibitor draped booths (and available colors)
- Aisle signs (and available styles)
- Registration counters and other items, such as fill-in counters, for the registration area
- Exhibitor furnishing or booth packages, if applicable
- Labor
- Material handling services (receipt of exhibitor materials at the GSC's warehouse or at the event site; delivery to the exhibitors' booths; storage of empty containers during the event, and return at the close of the event; load-out of the exhibitor materials onto selected transportation carriers at the close of the event)
- Signs, banners, and other graphic elements
- Floor plans (including information on the AutoCAD or other design systems used for updates, and how they might work with any system used by the organization)
- Design capabilities, to integrate your marketing message into décor elements
- Customer service capabilities, both in advance, on-site, and post-show. Does the company have a call center? Is it centralized, regionalized, or local? How are orders processed? What are the staffing levels and hours? What is the average wait time for a call to be answered, and the abandonment rate (the number of callers who hang up before talking to a service representative)? What are the methods by which orders can be placed (i.e., via phone, fax, mail, online)? How is the exhibitor service center staffed at the event site? Are there additional customer service representatives on the floor to take orders and problem solve at the exhibitors' booths?
- Exhibitor service center—how is it staffed? How much space is required? Will the contractor provide service counters for other contractors within the space?
- Exhibitor service manual—the meeting manager should ask for a sample to review the forms and view the marketing slicks showing the furnishings, carpet, and other rental items. Can the service manual be made available via pdf file, CD-Rom, or online through a web-based system? What are the production deadlines? Will the contractor assemble the manuals and include your information?
- Feature area designs—if an association booth, a cyber café, a new products area, or other focus on the event floor is needed, what does the GSC recommend to fulfill your needs?
- Cleaning services—are they subcontracted, or provided by the GSC?

- Specialty (upgraded) furnishings and carpet, and do they come from a third party?
- Staging capabilities, if needed
- Storing and warehousing of materials
- Rental furnishings and carpet
- Modular rental components and standard configurations
- Lighting packages and electrical and other utilities (if not exclusive to the facility)
- Special event requirements
- Custom drapery
- Ability to recommend and coordinate with specialty contractors (such as florists, photographers, and so on)
- Show management discounts offered for areas such as standard furnishings, signs, labor, and material handling
- Local labor rules and regulations

The meeting manager may also request:

- Company history and financial health
- References for events that are similar in size, scope, and required services, and for those held in the facilities in your meeting rotation
- Capabilities within the local operation (warehouse size and location, production capabilities, inventory, staffing)
- An positional organizational chart
- An implementation plan
- A list of any services that will be subcontracted, and to whom

The information listed above is more pertinent if the meeting manager is considering a change to a new contractor.

A GSC's typical terms and conditions section will cover the following:

- The term of the agreement (effective date and end date)
- A list of both exclusive and non-exclusive services
- The payment policy, terms, deposit amounts, and due dates
- Confidentiality/proprietary information terms
- An excusable delay or non-performance clause
- Insurance coverage (minimum coverage to be carried by each party for workers' compensation, commercial liability, and automobile liability insurance) for the GSC, for event management, and for any third parties (EAC or subcontractors) hired and present on the event floor
- Indemnification/hold harmless language
- Protection relating to changes in the dates, location, or scope of the event
- Dispute resolution procedures (such as negotiation, mediation, arbitration, and so on)
- Limited liability (addresses what the contractor can be held liable for as a breach of the agreement)
- Successors and assigns language (to address the sale, merger, or acquisition of the event)
- Governing law (defines which state's laws will govern the agreement)
- Cancellation (any recourse should the event be postponed or cancelled)
- Other potential inclusions that address policies relating to exhibitor appointed contractors, notices, modifications, and the binding nature of the agreement

Unless the meeting manager has a legal background, engaging an attorney's assistance is advisable to ensure that the contractor's "standard" language is in the best interest of both parties. However, the more experience with suppliers, the better understanding the meeting manager will have of the terms, and which suppliers truly protect the organization's best interests.

Audiovisual Company

One of the most visible vendor selections for the meeting manager is the audiovisual (A/V) company. The right contractor can enhance their meeting with high impact visuals, sound systems, presentations, and other equipment; a contractor without sufficient capabilities could cause a high profile service failure. Asking the right questions in the RFP will help the meeting manager identify the best contractor for a simple board meeting or a complex annual meeting and exposition. Questions to be posed in the RFP for audiovisual services include:

- Who owns the equipment—the A/V contractor or subcontractors?
- Who is providing the skilled labor (for operating sound boards, technical equipment, or theatrical lighting)? If it is primarily local or union labor, how much supervision will be provided by your contractor?
- If union labor claims jurisdiction for any of the work, how do they interact with the facility and other contractors (such as the GSC and electrical contractors) when working on stage sets and other joint projects? What union locals are used, and what is the contract status with the local? Can they provide the full complement of labor required over the event dates? Who establishes the labor call?
- How often is the equipment updated and serviced?
- What is the staffing schedule on-site?
- What kind of storage space will be needed, and will security be needed (or re-coring of door locks)?
- Can the company respond to on-site orders or changes?
- Does the staff possess the technical capabilities to consult on major projects (such as a general session), provide floor plans, and offer solutions?
- What is the pricing structure for equipment? Are there price breaks for weekly rentals? When are labor charges incurred for equipment set-ups? What discounts are available to the event producer?
- What computer hardware, software, and networking capabilities are available?
- What are the labor rates? Are there minimums? What are the breakdowns for straight-time, over-time and double-time? When are supervisors required?
- What is the company's experience in the facility and relationship with the in-house staff?
- Can the A/V contractor unload and distribute their own equipment, or must they work through the GSC (another budget line item)?
- When and how will the equipment be delivered (and picked up)? Make sure that dock space and time are available. If the event is in a hotel, scheduling freight elevator time may be necessary. If the A/V contractor is delivering equipment, are they aware of facility rules and regulations for use of wheeled carts in lobbies, on tile or marble floors, or across carpet?
- Can the company provide other services, such as session recording and CD or DVD sales?

- How are exhibitors serviced? Is there a revenue share based on exhibitor orders? Are commissions paid to the facility? How will they market to exhibitors? How will they protect your exhibitor list?
- Who is responsible for damage to equipment or theft?
- Are there charges for travel and/or housing?
- Are there cancellation or change charges? If so, what are the cut-off dates for making changes without incurring penalties?
- What are the payment terms?

To get the information that is needed to make an educated choice, the meeting manager should provide a detailed day-by-day event schedule with equipment needs, installation, turnover, re-set, and removal schedules. The manager may need to refer to the prior year's actual usage, as the next event details may not be solidified at the time of the bid process. The selected audiovisual company can provide an updated estimate when final requirements are provided.

If the meeting has unique requirements, the meeting manager should be sure to provide this information during the proposal development phase, to verify that the provider can meet their needs. For instance, a medical event with physicians presenting papers may require a high level of individual customer service to interact with the speakers.

The meeting manager should check with the facility, convention bureau contacts, general services contractors, and other meeting managers before making your final selection. As with any supplier, the A/V company's ability to provide a consistent level of service may vary by city or facility, and local users can provide valuable feedback.

Registration Company

Chapter 24 addresses the intricacies of registration in more detail. Registration needs are so unique to each meeting and event that the RFP should be highly customized with detailed information about attendees and their needs and habits. Some of the information that the meeting manager might ask for in soliciting bids from registration specialists includes:

- Current client list and contacts
- Company history
- Organizational chart, both support and on-site
- Is there a call center? How is it staffed? What hours?
- What computer hardware and software systems are used?
- What services are handled in-house, versus outsourcing?
- What sort of software/programming customization of registration screens is available?
- What are the financial processing systems?
- If you are changing to a new contractor, what sort of hourly costs are there for set up of the new system?
- Can the system be used in multiple locations (including remote/satellite registration areas) on-site?
- How flexible is the system?
- Detail customer service programs and VIP treatment
- Web site capabilities
- Attendee and exhibitor confirmation
- Types of badges and badge holders available to interface with the system and costs (ask for samples)
- On-site equipment needs

- Attendee verification capabilities
- What types of reports are available? (Pre-show, daily on-site, and post-show.) Ask for samples.
- Sample registration forms
- Self-registration capabilities
- All cost schedules for travel, telephone/fax, postage, bank charges, transportation of equipment, staff, stationery, printing, programming, email transmissions, and reports. Ask about minimums, sliding scales, and discounts.
- Revenue tracking and financial reports
- Key contacts and contact information, including emergency numbers
- Guarantees against service failures
- Confidentiality terms to protect your ownership of the data gathered during the registration process
- Benefits of a multi-year agreement

Before signing an agreement with a new registration firm, the meeting manager should visit a show being serviced by the company, and observe the activities in the registration areas. If possible, the manager should meet at the company's headquarters to view their activities and set up. Telephone the call center, and see how long it takes for the call to be answered, and how proficiently and pleasantly it is handled.

Security Company

Heightened security concerns have given new weight to the selection of a security team. Before soliciting bids for security firms, the meeting manager should confirm the requirements set by the facility where the event will be held. Hotels and convention centers may require employing facility staff for at least some of the services (such as fire watch), or that any security firm brought onto the property be on a recommended or approved list.

If the event is large, complex, or has special security needs, there may be value in employing a security consultant who can negotiate and supervise on the organization's behalf and perform day-to-day responsibilities. A consultant can get to know the members, attendees, and exhibitors and their special needs, and adapt them to each facility if the event travels.

A security RFP should request the following information:

- Recent references for similar events and within the selected facility
- Emergency response procedures
- Certification process for guards (background checks, training to industry standards, drug testing, and so on)
- Knowledge of all applicable rules and regulations
- Resources such as security cameras
- Access to qualified armed guards or off-duty police if needed
- Pricing and minimums
- Types of personnel, definitions of their roles and qualifications (e.g., badge checkers, rovers, door guards, VIP escorts, supervisors)
- List of on-site managers providing guard staff supervision
- Guard positions and a proposed guard schedule, based upon a meeting schedule provided by the organization
- Insurance coverage
- Procedures for dealing with valuables
- Procedures for dealing with theft and other incidents; the company's relationship with the local police force

- Limits of liability for theft and damages; warranties
- Procedures for performing baggage checks
- Any legal actions pending
- Their role in, and understanding of, the communications and jurisdictions during protests, bomb threats, health emergencies, natural disasters, and other unexpected events
- Badge checking procedures
- How much space they need for office/staff sign-in/dispatch
- How is cash transported to banks (e.g., off-duty police, armored car)?
- Communication methods
- Uniforms/attire of staff

The ability of the security team to represent the organization's interests during an event, as well as to respond promptly to unplanned events, mitigates some of the risks and challenges associated with producing any meeting, large or small.

Security should act as the organization's eyes and ears during the meeting. This requires more than a "badge check" function to note issues like high value items moving in and out of the facility.

Shuttle Bus

Getting attendees to and from the meeting and special event venues can be a challenge if the event requires the use of multiple hotels. If engaging a shuttle or transportation company to move your attendees, the meeting manager should review the company's credentials and history of providing safe, efficient, on-time people movement.

Areas to be addressed in the RFP include:

- Experience moving groups of a similar size, with recent references
- Relationships with the owners of the buses (or do they own their own vehicles?)
- How are the bus routes established?
- How is the timing of the routes determined during both peak and off-peak hours?
- What sort of liability insurance is carried by the company?
- What is the firm's accident record?
- How does the company interact with city traffic control?
- Are there construction plans that could impact the traffic flow?
- What kind of staffing will be provided, and how are the supervisors qualified?
- Driving records of the operators
- Interaction with the Department of Transportation (DOT), if applicable
- Security and emergency response plans
- What form of communication do the supervisors, ground crew, and drivers use (i.e., cellular phones, two-way radios, Nextels, or pagers)
- How will the attendees be identified (badge, wrist band, and so on)?
- Can sponsorships be shown on the buses (such as on seat covers, magnetic signs, or LED screens with on-board advertising)? How much does each option cost?
- Can show publications/dailies be distributed on board?
- Can beverages or food be consumed on board the vehicles?
- Who prepares, prints, and provides bus route signage and fliers with schedules?

- Are individual contracts available (e.g., for exhibitors or sponsors who may want to transport attendees to private functions)?
- Number of riders to be serviced by the agreement
- Date that schedules will be finalized
- Are smaller vehicles, such as limousines and limo buses, available for VIP transportation?
- Pricing programs and any current add-ons (such as gasoline surcharges).

Recent reference checks are particularly important prior to finalizing contracts with a transportation provider. Some larger organizations find value in employing a transportation consultant who knows the organization's event(s) and travels from meeting to meeting to oversee the local transportation provider.

Photographer

Important moments at the event could be lost forever if the contracted photographer misses the shot. Selecting the right photography firm, and scheduling the staff accordingly, will ensure that the sponsoring organization will have photos to use in future marketing materials, on the web site, and for VIP recognition.

Contracts with your photography firm of choice should include:

- Staffing coverage
- Photo ownership rights
- Pricing programs (i.e., hourly rates, daily rates, costs for housing and/or travel for staff)
- Formats to be provided (e.g., hard copy, CD-Rom, originals, or prints)
- Ability to respond to on-site orders and changes

To receive a contract that meets your needs, provide:

- A daily "shot schedule"
- Specific areas of interest
- A schedule of celebrity appearances
- Event marketing goals
- Guidelines for interaction with the media
- A revenue recap from prior shows
- Expectations for marketing to exhibitors

Meeting managers should always check references when considering hiring a company that the organization has never used.

Floral Contractor

Often, the floral contractor is selected on recommendation of the GSC's local office (for inclusion in the exhibitor service manual), with little due diligence on the meeting manager's part. However, if the organization has official needs, it is worth the time to document requirements and obligations.

Keep in mind that the potential plant and floral revenue on the event floor declines as exhibitors tighten their budget belts. So the meeting manager should be realistic in the expectation of discounts and complimentary items.

Questions to ask in your RFP include:

- The formula for complimentary items (comps) versus paid plants/arrangements
- Staffing at the event site
- Means of contact (pre- , during, and post-show)
- How does the contractor plan to market the show?

- What quality guarantees are there?
- Does the contractor require storage space?

Information to provide to the floral company:

- The event's demographics
- Theme or décor colors
- Requirements for specific areas
- Delivery and pick-up schedules
- Types of plants or cut flower arrangements preferred
- Types of containers requested
- Length of the event (and any care needed after delivery, such as watering)

Other Suppliers

As meetings, events, conventions, and exhibitions respond to the need to enhance an attendee's experience, and add value to the sponsors' or exhibitors' investment, an expanded pool of vendors are becoming involved in the industry.

Computer rental companies, marketing firms, advertising agencies, talent/model firms, temporary labor agencies, operators of temporary business centers, specialty food vendors, and shipping companies are just a few of the businesses involved in the temporary marketing and education environments created by meeting managers.

The meeting manager should start selection process by soliciting referrals from peers and trusted professionals who are part of the meeting department's team. Convention center, hotel, and bureau personnel are excellent sources, and most convention bureaus publish directories of local suppliers. Remember that other event managers will need to observe confidentiality clauses which prohibit sharing specific details about their agreements, but information about overall experiences, service levels, or problems can be shared.

General services contractors with local offices will make recommendations of ancillary services suppliers, and will include order forms for some of the services in the exhibitor service manuals or kits supplied to exhibitors, helping to drive orders to the organization's recommended providers.

In every case, select vendors that carry appropriate levels of insurance to ensure that the organization is protected in the event that the vendors cause harm to attendees, facility space, or exhibitors.

MULTI-EVENT AGREEMENTS

There can be a variety of benefits to entering into multi-year or multi-event agreements, including financial incentives or added services. Staying with one vendor over the course of time can also provide continuity of service, as well as saving the meeting manager the time and energy of reviewing and negotiating new agreements.

If opting to enter into a multi-event agreement, the meeting manager must be sure that price increases are outlined, and that there are remedies for performance issues. The terms and conditions section should address change of ownership of either organization during the course of the agreement, and survivability of the agreement post-sale.

Remember to request facility specifics that could impact how the supplier services the organization from event to event. For instance, a general services contractor may be able to provide electrical services in one convention center, while the facility has an in-house provider in the next. There could be opportunities to negotiate better pricing based upon the multi-year commitment; a contractor may also offer a sliding scale pricing structure based upon potential growth over several years.

TIPS FOR CONTRACT NEGOTIATION

The goal in negotiating contracts with suppliers should be an agreement that benefits both parties. A fair negotiation process and contract can set the tone for many years of collaboration and mutual benefit. Some tips for negotiating win-win contracts follow:

- If the contractor offers discounts, request the price sheets from which the deductions will be made. Make an informed choice, as nothing is really free—it is just an offset for other sources of revenue. Is there a need to guarantee a minimum to receive a discount?

- Do not expect elaborate presentations that can cost thousands of dollars. Challenge the bidders to develop value-added solutions for exhibitors or attendees instead. Know the event's exhibitors' major issues, and encourage respondents to address these concerns.

- Most contractors have a standard contract format that addresses the areas of risk pertaining to their particular business. In contracts, one size does not fit all, so start with the contractor's standard terms. That will help the contractor to understand risk in providing the pricing offered in their RFP response. Have attorneys review the terms and conditions; establish business decisions that are within your ability to alter. Try to avoid the "battle of the forms," by using the supplier's terms as the base.

- If any of the work will be performed by union employees, request the status of all union contracts and their expiration dates. The meeting could be negatively impacted by work slow-downs, pickets, even strikes or worker shortages if a contract is up for a disputed renewal around the time of the event. Request a plan for servicing the show if an agreement is not reached in a timely fashion.

- Once a contract is executed, remember to document any changes and additional quotes in writing. Not only will this ensure that there is no misunderstanding by either party, the practice will help fulfill Sarbanes-Oxley Act compliance requirements also. Addenda or letters of agreement are the most legally binding methods for supplementing a contract's scope of work, and both parties should sign any change to ensure a clear understanding.

- More vendors are requiring performance clauses in the form of minimum amounts of guaranteed revenue to lock in pricing. Review these clauses carefully, and be sure that the organization's history and current trends are on track to exceed any minimums before signing on the dotted line. Be upfront about the level of commitment the group is comfortable making when discussing guarantees. The meeting manager should not promise more than what can be delivered to get better pricing. This will create unrealistic expectations, and could result in surcharges for revenue short falls, as well as impact the manager's relationship with the affected supplier.

- Be careful with commission-based services, as the commissions add costs to the ultimate user, the exhibitor.

- Negotiations should take place during the proposal process; items not covered in the agreement should be quoted in writing with pricing during the ordering phase. The meeting manager should not expect to negotiate during the invoice phase post-show, when the work is already completed.

- Understanding the overall value of the business to each supplier group prior to entering negotiations, will provide meeting managers realistic expectations for the overall package. The event may be an excellent piece of business to a registration company, but be a barely break-even proposition to a florist, for example. The meeting manager should attempt to build a reputation as a fair and informed negotiator.

Summary

Every supplier contract should contain the same basic components:

- a description of services
- insurance
- indemnification
- payment
- pricing

The detail in the scope of services is dictated by the type of service provider and the event's unique needs. It is important to be as specific as possible (outlining an agreement that could be executed by any meeting manager), and negotiate a contract that is truly win-win for the organization and for the supplier.

References

1. NA (2006). Exhibit industry glossary of terms. The Exhibition Services and Contractors Association. Retrieved April 12, 2006 from http://www.esca.org/resources.htm.

Key Terms

Abandonment rate	Exclusive services	Letter of agreement
Addenda/addendum	Excusable delay	Limited liability
Attendee	Exhibitor	Multi-event and multi-year agreements
Attendee verification	Exhibitor appointed contractors (EACs)	
Audiovisual (A/V)		General services contractor (GSC)
Business decisions	Exhibitor service center	
Cancellation	Exhibitor service manuals	Pandemics
Decorator	Governing law	Proprietary information
Demographics	Hold harmless	Recommended contractor
Discretionary services	Indemnification	Request for proposal (RFP)
Dispute resolution	In-house providers	
Drayage	Installation and dismantle (I & D)	Sarbanes-Oxley Act
Empties		Scope of work
Exhibition Services and Contractors Association (ESCA)	Insurance coverage	Successors and assigns
	Jurisdiction	Terms and conditions

Compelling Questions for Consideration

1. Why is it important to use an RFP to generate a proposal?

2. What are exclusive services?

3. What are in-house or preferred services? Explain both.

4. Why is it important to understand local labor jurisdictions?

5. When should you contact references?

6. What are the key components of a supplier contract?

CHAPTER 43

THE AMERICANS WITH DISABILITIES ACT

Jonathan T. Howe, Esq.
PRESIDENT AND SENIOR PARTNER
HOWE & HUTTON, LTD.

Barbara F. Dunn, Esq.
PARTNER
HOWE & HUTTON, LTD.

LEARNER OUTCOMES

When the reader has completed reading this chapter, he/she should be able to . . .

1 Define the purpose of the Americans with Disabilities Act.

2 Explain the types of disabilities covered by the ADA.

3 Provide general guidelines for accommodating people with disabilities at a meeting.

4 Identify sources of information and assistance regarding ADA compliance.

> Now we must begin to dismantle the architectural barriers we have created and the attitudinal barriers we have allowed.
>
> *Former President George H.W. Bush*
> *Signing Ceremony for the Americans*
> *with Disabilities Act, 1990*

OVERVIEW

The Americans with Disabilities Act (ADA) of 1990[1] is a civil rights statute that promises equal access to opportunities in education, employment, and society for people with disabilities. The intent of the ADA is to prevent discrimination against the millions of Americans with disabilities.

The "general rule" states, "No individual shall be discriminated against on the basis of disability in the full and equal enjoyment of the goods, services, facilities, privileges, advantages, or accommodations of any place of public accommodation by any person who owns, leases (or leases to), or operates a place of public accommodation."

Title III of the ADA provides definitions of public accommodations and guidelines about what must be done to make them accessible. Generally, the facility has the responsibility to make the facility accessible. The sponsoring organization, organizer, and/or producer has the responsibility to make the program accessible. Meeting participants with disabilities should be able to attend the meeting in the same way as attendees who are not disabled. In order to be in compliance with the ADA, the meeting manager must be proactive in determining the arrangements necessary to accommodate people with disabilities.

From a meeting manager's standpoint, the ADA simply mandates the full participation of a great number of potential attendees who may have been underrepresented in the past.

SPECIFICS OF THE LAW

The ADA consists of five titles, or major sections: Title I governs employment of persons with disabilities; Title II covers activities of state and local governments, and it governs public transportation services; Title III directs places of public accommodations; Title IV addresses telephone and television access; and Title V.

The title most directly applicable to meetings and meeting managers is Title III, Public Accommodations. According to Title III, an entity is a public accommodation if it is "a private entity that owns, leases (or leases to), or operates a place of public accommodation. It is the public accommodation (that is, the private entity that owns, operates, leases, or leases to), rather than the place of public accommodation, that is subject to the nondiscrimination requirements."

Both the facility at which the meeting is being held and the organization sponsoring the meeting are public accommodations under this definition. Thus, they are jointly responsible for providing reasonable accommodations to allow people with disabilities to participate. This includes both barrier-free meeting space and the provision of auxiliary aids and services necessary for individuals with disabilities to have equal access. Auxiliary aids and services are "… any measures to ensure communication accessibility for persons with impaired vision, speech, or hearing." Examples include visual alert systems in hotel rooms, sign language interpreters, and Braille materials for the meeting.

The joint responsibility of the organization sponsoring the meeting and the meeting facility is a clear, legal mandate. In fact, Title III allows for both parties to be held "jointly and severally liable." Thus, even if the facility fails to provide appropriate architectural access, the sponsoring organization bears some legal responsibility, as well.

Private individuals may bring lawsuits in which they can obtain court orders to stop discrimination. Individuals may also file complaints with the Attorney General, who is authorized to bring lawsuits in cases of general public importance or where a pattern or practice of discrimination is alleged. In these cases, the Attorney General may seek monetary damages and civil penalties. Civil penalties may not exceed $55,000 for a first violation or $110,000 for any subsequent violation.

Every meeting contract should contain provisions that clearly define the responsibilities of the meeting facility and the meeting sponsor, and a hold harmless clause to protect each in the event of failure by the other to meet these responsibilities. The facility should assume the responsibility for ensuring that it meets the ADA Accessibility Guidelines. The contract should also state that the meeting sponsor is responsible for advising the facility if any special accommodations are needed. The meeting sponsor should also bear the responsibility for ensuring that meeting areas over which it has control are in compliance and/or provide the accommodations needed by those attendees who notify the meeting sponsor of their special needs.

Be aware that some non-profit organizations and places of worship are exempt from the requirements of the ADA; however, these requirements are very limited. Thus, when making the decision to hold an event in a facility owned by such entities, the meeting manager is responsible for taking into account any accommodations needed by the attendees. For example, a historic building that has accessibility problems and is owned by a non-profit organization might not be a proper venue if several potential attendees are denied access to the event.

DEFINITIONS OF DISABILITY AND COMPLIANCE

By law, a person with a disability is anyone with a physical or mental impairment that substantially limits one or more activities of daily life. More than 50 million people in the United States fit this definition. This includes people who are blind or visually impaired, deaf or hearing impaired, or those who are mobility impaired. Individuals with psychological disabilities, chronic health impairments, learning disabilities, or cognitive limitations are also included in the definition.

The ADA mandates that reasonable accommodation must be made to enable a person with a disability to participate in a meeting. Meeting managers may find defining what is *not* considered reasonable under the law easier than defining the full scope of reasonable accommodations. Therefore, the meeting manager may assume that if a requested accommodation is not unreasonable, it must be a reasonable request.

It is not a reasonable accommodation if:

- Making the accommodation poses a direct threat to the health or safety of others
- Making the accommodation means making a substantial alteration in the manner in which business is conducted
- Making the accommodation represents an undue financial or administrative hardship

When looking at whether a requested accommodation represents a direct threat, remember that this refers to a threat to others. Under the law, an individual has the right to choose to assume a risk to himself or herself. Wheelchair users, for example, cannot be told they may not use the swimming pool unless another person is with them when the sign posted above the pool reads: "Swim at your own risk." However, wheelchair users can be told not to sit in a certain place if their wheelchairs are blocking a fire aisle or an emergency exit.

An organization is not required to make a substantial alteration in the manner in which services are delivered. Providing shower chairs or visual alarm systems in hotel rooms is not a substantial alteration in the mode of operation. Hotels are in the business of providing lodging in exchange for payment and must now provide additional support to allow the individual with a disability to receive full use of that lodging. On the other hand, being asked to provide an attendant to assist with dressing or eating is not a reasonable request. Neither the meeting manager nor the hotel is providing personal care for other attendees; that is not part of what the organization or the facility setout to do in offering a meeting.

Undue financial and administrative burdens are two circumstances under which accommodations need not be made. However, the ADA holds that these costs must be compared to overall financial assets—not just those within one or two departments.[1] The Department of Justice has made very clear that in assessing whether something is an undue financial burden. The overall cost of (in this case) providing the meeting is considered, not the relative benefit gained from having the individual with a disability in attendance. For example, if a deaf individual requests sign language, and providing interpreters will cost $650 over the course of three days, while the registration fee the individual is paying is only $375, the organization may think the request represents an undue financial burden. However, if the overall budget for the meeting is $140,000, the federal government is not going to find adding $650 an undue burden.

While the ADA requires a person's preferences to be considered, complete acceptance of that request is not mandatory. Participation by individuals is the goal.[2] The federal government does not require an organization to do the impossible (or nearly impossible). For example, if an attendee requests a room close to the elevator as a disability-related accommodation (to decrease the distance he or she must walk), blocking that attendee into such a room is a reasonable accommodation, even if attendees are not usually assigned to specific rooms (other than the wheelchair-accessible rooms). If, on the other hand, someone with multiple chemical sensitivities requests that no one on the staff or in attendance at the meeting be wearing scented personal care products, the organization has the right to say this is an undue administrative burden. No one can demand that staff and guests avoid scented products, and such a ban could not be reasonably enforced if someone did try to establish it.

IMPLICATIONS FOR MEETINGS

ADA compliance requires that meeting managers and facility staff understand their responsibilities for making programs and facilities accessible. In theory, this translates to the need for meeting managers to ensure that the program is accessible, and for facilities to ensure that the building and appropriate spaces are accessible. In reality, all parties must work together to determine the best accommodations for all attendees with disabilities. Written instructions concerning any special requirements of attendees should be provided to all staff.

These accommodations will affect the meeting budget. Right from the start, include ADA compliance as a budget line item. It will serve as a reminder of the organization's responsibilities, as well as the first piece of documentation showing "good faith effort" in the event of any litigation.

The amount budgeted for program accommodations will depend upon attendees' projected needs. For example, budgeting for alternate media (large print, audiotape, Braille, and computer disk) requires less money than budgeting for sign language interpreters. Know the attendees well. Do not assume that all attendees with disabilities will remember to ask for accommodations. Also, do not assume that a non-disabled attendee will bring only non-disabled guests and family members. Guest and children's programming must also be accessible.

The ADA applies only to meetings held within the United States. When planning a meeting in another country, research the host country's regulations regarding attendees with disabilities and make every effort to ensure that the meeting is accessible.

> ### Put It Into Practice
>
> Check for the number of sleeping rooms in the hotel that can accommodate people in wheelchairs. Be sure the hotel and meeting registration form includes a section for accommodation requests.

ACCOMMODATING PEOPLE WITH DISABILITIES

The key to providing accommodations for a person with a disability is direct communication, with the utmost sensitivity for that person's needs. Representatives from the property and the organization must allow the person with a disability to identify himself or herself and to request reasonable accommodations. Someone from the organization must coordinate requests and confirm the individual's preferences.[3]

Hotel and meeting registration forms should include a section for attendees with disabilities to identify themselves and describe their needs prior to the meeting. Personal followup with individuals with special needs is advisable. Document the outcome of your communication to ensure the accommodations requested are provided.

The meeting manager may be called upon to provide the following:

Accommodations for Wheelchair Users

Most hotels and convention centers have taken the steps necessary to bring their facilities into compliance with the ADA. An organization called the U.S. Access Board has issued ADA Accessibility Guidelines to be followed by entities that are places of accommodation and subject to the provisions of the ADA. These Guidelines have been adopted by the Department of Justice as Appendix A to its rules implementing Title III of the ADA. The Guidelines are very specific and define exactly what must be done in order for a facility to be in compliance with the law.

Meeting room setups are an important consideration for meeting managers. When deciding on room setups, remember that if there are a large number of attendees who use wheelchairs, approximately 10% of the room's seating capacity will be lost. A theater-style setup, for example, should allow wheelchair users a choice of seating throughout the room.

Accommodations for the Deaf or Hearing Impaired

Each individual's functional limitations determine the accommodations necessary for attendees who are hearing impaired. For example, several different types of sign language exist. Contact the people who request this service to be certain the correct version is provided. People who are not deaf, but hearing impaired, may require assistive listening devices, preferential seating, or oral interpreters. Another possible accommodation is real-time captioning. This option should be discussed with the individuals involved as they might prefer an interpreter.

Other considerations for accommodating deaf or hearing impaired attendees include the following options:

- Have pens or pencils and pads of paper available at registration desks and, if necessary, use written notes to communicate.
- Text telephones should be available from the front desk for private use, as well as for use at public phone locations.

Fast Facts

Required Accommodations

- Wheelchair users
- Deaf or hearing impaired
- Blind or visually impaired
- Other disabilities

- Operators should know which rooms are occupied by deaf or hearing-impaired guests, so that written telephone messages are provided instead of voice mail service.
- Crisis management plans should include instructions on how to alert deaf guests to evacuate the facility.

Accommodations for the Blind or Visually Impaired

Facility managers should inspect corridors, lobbies, and other public areas to minimize the number of obstructions for people who have visual impairments. Elevators should be equipped with audible signals, as well as floor numbers and emergency instructions in Braille. Meeting room, restroom, and other room signs should be available in large print and in Braille.

Areas should be available close to the property for guide dog relief. Hotel/facility information and menus should be available in large print and in Braille. Checkout procedures should include an alternative to the express check-out via in-room television. Message delivery systems should provide an alternative for people with visual impairments who cannot see flashing red lights on the telephone and might not find an envelope that is slipped under the door, let alone be able to read it.

Other considerations for accommodating blind or visually impaired attendees include the following items:

- Purchase a hand Brailler/labeler to make labels for items in guest rooms.
- Provide bowls of water for guide dogs during breaks.
- Instruct bell staff on how to orient blind or visually impaired attendees to guest rooms and meeting rooms.

The meeting manager is responsible for ensuring that all print materials (e.g., registration forms, programs, handouts) are available in alternate media. Options include Braille, large print, audiotape, and computer disk. Talk with each individual with a disability about which medium will best meet his or her needs. Request speakers to provide handouts in alternate formats if not arranging for handout reproduction.

Exhibit hall managers should provide a guide for attendees who are blind or visually impaired. Expect requests for tactile maps, especially if the show is large. Aisle width is another important consideration. If a fair number of people with disabilities is expected (especially visually impaired attendees and wheelchair users), the aisles must be wider to facilitate movement. This will affect booth availability and, therefore, the budget. Be sure to plan accordingly.

Put It Into Perspective

The Widget Manufacturers Association ("WMA") was hosting its annual meeting at the Burning Privy Resort and Conference Center. Prior to the meeting, WMA received two requests for accommodations from persons with disabilities. The first request was made by a deaf person who advised WMA that she needed a sign language interpreter to accompany her to each session, to all networking functions, and to the trade show. The second request was made by a blind person. He requested that he be permitted to have his guide dog accompany him to all sessions, networking functions, and the trade show. He also requested that all handout materials and collateral materials distributed at the trade show be printed in Braille. Both individuals requested disability-compliant hotel rooms. Discuss the respective responsibilities of WMA and the hotel and WMA's strategy for addressing such requested accommodations.

Put It Into Perspective

Before the ADA, it was very unusual to see persons with disabilities at a number of events. Now we routinely see people in wheelchairs and sign language interpreters at meetings.

Other considerations for making accommodations on the show floor include the following items:

- Place a Braille index card at the corner of exhibitors' tables. Blind attendees will be able to identify the booth at a touch.
- Send disks with the conference program to attendees with visual impairments at least two weeks ahead of time. Many people have the technology to download the information to a portable assistive device or make their own Braille copy.
- Hire an orientation and mobility specialist to ensure that attendees with visual impairments receive a professional guide through the property and exhibit area.

Accommodations for People with Other Disabilities

- Many chronic health conditions require a smoke-free environment. People who request a non-smoking room due to a disabling condition take priority over those whose request is preferential.
- People on certain medications may need access to an in-room refrigerator.
- For an attendee with special dietary needs, the meeting manager may need to facilitate a conversation between that individual and the chef.
- People with learning disabilities may request accommodations similar to those requested by attendees who are blind or visually impaired.
- Someone who is easily fatigued should be assigned a room close to the elevators.

WHERE TO GET HELP

Each person with a disability is an individual, and each is the best expert as to his or her particular functional limitations and the accommodations needed to fully participate in the meeting or event. Communicate with the person requesting accommodation. For example, although an attendee uses a wheelchair, he or she may manage in a regular guest room with a shower bench. Or, a deaf attendee may need an oral interpreter, not a sign language interpreter.

The Office on the Americans with Disabilities Act, Civil Rights Division, U.S. Department of Justice, provides information on the ADA, standards, resources, and technical assistance. Information may be accessed on the Internet (www.usdoj.gov/crt/ada/adahom1.htm) or by telephone at (800) 514-0301.

Another excellent resource would be the disability service office at a local college or university. These professionals have been working with architectural and program accommodations for decades.

Seek legal advice to determine the reasonableness of an accommodation and whether contract language in facility agreements properly protects the organization.

SUMMARY

The Americans with Disabilities Act was designed to provide equal opportunities for people with disabilities. A disability is any physical or mental impairment that substantially limits one or more activities of daily life. To be in compliance with the ADA means providing reasonable accommodations that address the functional limitations of people with disabilities and enable them to participate in an event in the same way as attendees who are not disabled.

Meeting managers need a general knowledge of their responsibilities under Title III of the ADA. Communication is critical to compliance, as each individual with a disability is the expert on his or her particular needs and functional limitations. People with disabilities must have the opportunity to indicate their accommodation needs. The organization must make a good faith effort to accommodate those needs.

Accommodations may include both barrier-free meeting space and the provision of the auxiliary aids and services necessary for individuals with disabilities to have equal access.

REFERENCES

1. 42 U.S.C. § 12101 et seq.

KEY TERMS

Alternate media	Compliance	Public accommodation
Americans with Disabilities Act (ADA)	Disabilities	Reasonable accommodation
	Good faith effort	
Auxiliary aids and services		

COMPELLING QUESTIONS FOR CONSIDERATION

1. What is the purpose of the Americans with Disabilities Act?

2. What are some of the types of disabilities covered by the ADA?

3. List some of the accommodations a meeting sponsor might be called upon to provide.

4. What sources of information and assistance are available regarding ADA compliance?

CHAPTER 44

RISK PLANNING AND EMERGENCY MANAGEMENT

Tyra W. Hilliard, JD, CMP

ASSOCIATE PROFESSOR

DEPARTMENT OF TOURISM AND CONVENTION ADMINISTRATION

UNIVERSITY OF NEVADA, LAS VEGAS

LEARNER OUTCOMES

When the reader has completed reading this chapter, he/she should be able to . . .

1 Assess the risks for a specific meeting, facility, or organization.

2 Analyze the risks for a specific meeting, facility, or organization.

3 Distinguish between the concepts of risk, emergency, crisis, disaster, and business continuity and how each may manifest itself differently.

4 Apply the risk management model to create a specific risk management plan for different meetings and meeting-related services.

5 Evaluate existing risk management plans and tools in order to improve them in the future.

> There are risks and costs to a program of action. But they are far less than the long-range risks and costs of comfortable inaction.
>
> *John F. Kennedy (1917–1963)*

OVERVIEW

Studies have shown that safety and security concerns are among the very most important factors for meeting effectiveness to both meeting managers and meeting participants.[1] For this reason, risk management is an essential part of the process of planning and managing meetings, conventions, exhibitions, and events. Emergencies, crises, and disasters can adversely affect the meeting organizer, the meeting venue, the meeting destination, and may delay or disrupt the provision of services or delivery of goods essential to meeting management. Failing to have an official risk management plan in place for meetings can leave the meeting manager and his/her organization vulnerable at a time when decisions have to be made quickly and responses can mean the difference between success and failure, even life or death. Examples of just a few realized risks that have affected the meeting and hospitality industries in recent history:

- November 2005—Suicide bombers walk into three hotels in Amman, Jordan, Radisson SAS, Grand Hyatt, and Days Inn. Fifty-seven people are killed and 110 more are wounded[2] ("Suicide bombers," 2005).
- September 2005—A food service worker at a major convention center is found to be a carrier of hepatitis A virus shortly after serving ice cream to an undetermined number of the 26,000 people attending a convention at the convention center.[3]
- August 2005—Hurricane Katrina, a Category 4 hurricane, tears through New Orleans. Many groups are forced to cancel or reschedule conventions. Recovery and rebuilding take many months.

Unfortunately, these are only a few of the many instances of realized risk that have affected the meetings industry. Waiting until a risk has been realized to organize a plan and put it into action is too late. The prepared meeting manager will have a risk team in place and trained to assess and analyze the risks specific to his/her organization and meetings and to plan for likely risks before anything even occurs. In this way, the meeting manager can be prepared to act immediately when an emergency, crisis, or disaster strikes.

Although often used interchangeably, the words risk, emergency, crisis, and disaster are different in meaning and scope. For purposes of this chapter, *risk* means the potential for exposure to loss[4] or the possibility that something may happen that will adversely affect a meeting. An *emergency* is an unexpected actual or impending situation that may cause injury, loss of life, destruction of property or cause the interference, loss or disruption of an organization's normal business operations to such an extent that it poses a threat.[4] A *crisis* is a critical event, which, if not handled in an appropriate manner, may dramatically impact an organization's profitability, reputation, or ability to operate.[4] A *disaster* is a sudden, unplanned calamitous event causing great damage or loss as defined or determined by a risk assessment or any event that creates an inability on an organization's part to provide the critical business functions for some predetermined period of time.[4] Although the planning process is similar for emergencies, crises, and disasters, the response to and recovery from each may be different since they may be considered different levels of realized risk.

FORMING A RISK TEAM

Every organization that holds or supports meetings should have a risk team in place. The composition and nature of the risk team may vary based on the nature of the organization. For example, hotels and convention centers may already have risk teams in place spearheaded by security or loss prevention directors. One of the challenges in applying typical risk management strategies to meetings is that the risks are not limited to the physical facility (for example, the building in which the organization is headquartered). In fact, for meetings, the physical facility may often change. That is, a meeting may be held in a hotel in San Francisco one year, but in a convention center in Washington, D.C., the next year. For a specific meeting with essentially the same attendees, the risks are different each time the location or even the dates are changed. For this reason, commonly accepted risk management and business continuity strategies have to be modified for the ever-changing nature of meetings.

In the *Emergency Management Guide for Business and Industry*,[5] the Federal Emergency Management Agency (FEMA) indicates that an individual or group must be in charge of developing an emergency management plan. The risk team is responsible for creating the emergency management plan, reviewing it periodically, revising it as necessary, and may serve as the point team when emergency response is required.

Although the composition of this team may vary for different types of organizations, FEMA offers the following general guidelines for forming the team:

- *Team members*—Choose people who can be active members of the team and who can serve in an advisory capacity. Even if one or two people will be doing most of the work, the team needs input from all functional areas including executive, meetings, accounting, marketing, and legal.

- *Management support*—To give credibility to the risk team, management should give explicit authority to the group to take the steps necessary to develop a plan. Ideally, the group should be led by a top executive of the organization or, if it is a meeting-specific risk management plan, by a top meeting department executive.

- *Mission statement*—The risk team leader, supported by the top executive of the organization, should issue a mission statement regarding the organization's commitment to emergency management. The statement should define the purpose of the plan, specify that the plan will involve the entire organization, and clarify the authority and structure of the risk team.[5]

RISK ASSESSMENT

No organization can plan for all possible risks. In order to make an informed decision about which risks to plan for, a meeting organizer needs to conduct a risk assessment to determine which risks are most likely to affect a specific meeting and which risks may have the worst consequences if they occur. The National Fire Protection Association (NFPA) recommends, at a minimum, considering the impact of both natural hazards (including geological, meteorological, and biological) and human-caused events (including both accidental and intentional).[6]

The risk management plan should be created only after an organization has brainstormed a list of possible risks and determined what impact realized risks would have:

- Health and safety of meeting attendees, organization staff, and volunteers (including possible death or injury)
- Continuity of operations (e.g., can the organization continue to operate without interruption if _____ happens?)
- Property, facilities, and infrastructure (e.g., will the occurrence affect the hotel, convention center, the organization's headquarters?)
- Delivery of services (e.g., can the hotel, convention center, or vendor continue to provide services needed for the meeting? Can the association continue to provide services to its members if _____ happens?)
- The environment

- Economic and financial condition
- Regulatory and contractual obligations (e.g., will the force majeure clause allow termination of the contract without liability if _____ happens?)
- Reputation of the organization[6]

Internal Risk Assessment

Typically, risk assessment would include a review of internal plans and policies such as evacuation plans, fire protection plans, and security procedures.[5] Because many of these plans are the responsibility of the facility in which a meeting may be held, the risk management plan for a meeting organizer may include an action step requiring the meeting manager to request information from the meeting facilities about these types of internal plans. The risk team would still want to review its own internal policies related to insurance, finance and purchasing, employee manuals, and meeting registration policies and procedures relating to the collection and storage of emergency contact information for meeting attendees.[5]

Internal risk assessment for meetings also means brainstorming the possible risks associated specifically with a meeting program or the nature of attendees. Again, these may vary with each meeting. Some examples of each of these types of risks include the following:

- *Program Risk*
  - A pharmaceutical launch is dependent on the U.S. Food & Drug Administration (FDA) approval of the new drug.
  - High-level political speakers are being invited to speak at the meeting which may draw protestors.

- *Attendee Risk*
  - The meeting is being attended by a large number of persons with disabilities.
  - The meeting is being attended by a large number of military or reserve military attendees, so a military action by the United States may cause a drastic drop in numbers.

External Risk Assessment

In addition to evaluating internal risks, the meeting organizer must evaluate external risks associated with the meeting destination or the meeting facility. Some examples of each of these types of risks include the following:

- *Destination Risk*
  - An international meeting is being held in an area that has some history of political unrest or terrorism.
  - A winter meeting is scheduled in a destination that gets a great deal of snow, causing an increased risk of flight cancellations or delays and power outages.

- *Facility Risk*
  - The meeting has been booked into a facility that is still under construction and the expected completion date is within weeks of the meeting dates.
  - A meeting facility is chosen that is known to be a target for terrorist activity.

To properly evaluate external risks and risk management strategies, the meeting manager and risk team need to be aware of events that may affect the meeting. Most meeting managers consider things like travel warnings issued by the U.S. Department of State (http://www.travel.state.gov) for international cities, but the connection is not always made between something more remote to the meeting itself, like a threatened strike by transportation or sanitation workers. In addition to using general sources like the American Red Cross (www.redcross.org), the National Weather Service (www.nws.noaa.gov), and trade press to stay aware of broad impact issues, the meeting manager and risk team can evaluate external risks specific to a meeting destination by establishing and maintaining contact with the destination's convention and visitors bureau (CVB), the community emergency management office, and the destination's fire and police departments. The contact information (phone number and web site) for all of these entities should be compiled and included in the written risk plan.

RISK ANALYSIS

Although risk assessment includes creating a brainstormed list of all potential risks that may occur, no meeting organizer has the time or resources to plan for all of the things that might possibly happen. Instead, the risk team needs to estimate through risk analysis (1) the probability that a specific risk may occur and (2) the consequences if the specific risk does occur.[5] FEMA recommends listing all possible types of emergencies or risks on a vulnerability analysis chart (see Figure 44.1) and following these steps for each possible emergency:

1. Estimate the probability that each emergency may occur on a scale of 5 (highest probability) to 1 (lowest probability).
2. Assess the potential impact on humans, property, and business on a scale of 5 (highest impact) to 1 (lowest impact).
3. Assign a score to internal resources that reflects your confidence in the resources and their ability to respond if the given emergency happens.
4. Assign a score to external resources that reflects your confidence in the resources and their ability to respond if the given emergency happens.
5. Add the columns. Those items with a high score should be priorities in the risk management plan.

RISK PLANNING

The risk plan should be compiled in such a way that the written document is actually usable and useful in the event of a realized risk. If the only copy of the risk management plan is kept in a 4-inch thick binder locked in the bottom file cabinet drawer of the executive director's file cabinet, then the plan probably will not be used as intended. The plan should be manageable enough in length and content to actually provide guidance in a stressful time of emergency, crisis, or disaster. If the plan does not fit in a 1- to 2-inch binder, pare it down until it does. The actual risk plan should include the following sections:

1. *Overview*
   - The purpose of the plan
   - A contact list of members of the risk team
   - A contact list of response team members, including each person's emergency management role and responsibility
     - Response team members are those people who will take action in the case of an actual emergency, crisis, or disaster; these may include members of the risk team, but may include others as well
     - In the case of multiple meetings or a citywide meeting housed in multiple facilities, there may be multiple response teams so that there is a team in place in each facility or at each meeting
   - A listing of the types of emergencies, crises, and disasters included in the plan[5]

Fast Facts

Risk Plan

- Overview
- Emergency Response Procedures
- Supporting Documents

TYPE OF EMERGENCY	Probability	Human Impact	Property Impact	Business Impact	Internal Resources	External Resources	Total
	High Low 5 ←→ 1	High Impact 5 ←——→ 1 Low Impact			Weak Resources 5 ←→ 1 Strong Resources		

The lower the score the better

FIGURE 44.1
Vulnerability Assessment Chart

2. *Emergency Response Procedures*

General sections should be set forth for emergencies, crises, and disasters, organized from broad categories to more narrow specific categories for which response procedures are listed. Emergencies, crises, and disasters for which the response is similar (e.g., emergencies requiring immediate evacuation) should be included in the same section rather than repeating response information separately. For example, a plan may include a list like the following (although the list should be customized for each organization and each meeting):

- Natural disasters and emergencies
  - Hurricane, tornado
  - Flood
  - Earthquake
- Accidents
  - Serious injury or medical emergency
  - Damage to or loss of essential program materials or information
- Intentional human-caused events
  - Acts of terrorism, bombings
  - Strikes, picketing, boycotts
  - Assault

- Technological events
  - Utility outage in facility or city
  - Computer crash, including loss of registration or other private data[6]

This list is not intended to be comprehensive, but only to provide an example of the types of emergencies, crises, and disasters that might be included. The meeting manager must consider which major and minor categories to include and customize the plan to the specific needs and nature of his or her organization and meeting.

Emergency responses for each major and sub-category should be included in the plan. These responses should include specifying the actions necessary to:

- Assess the situation
- Protect staff, volunteers, attendees, registration and program materials, equipment, and other vital records and assets
- Determine whether to hold, continue, or cancel a meeting

3. *Supporting Documents*

Because the occurrence of any emergency, crisis, or disaster may have a serious effect on the meeting, the organization holding the meeting, and the facility hosting the meeting, a good written risk management plan has all of the elements necessary to make quick but well-informed decisions. Documents that may be needed in the event of an emergency, crisis, or disaster that affects a meeting or meeting attendees may include:

- Emergency contact lists
  - Staff and support for the organization holding the meeting (staff, lawyer, accountant, insurance agent, etc.)
  - Meeting facility, vendor, and supplier contacts
  - Attendee emergency contact information
  - Emergency personnel within city (police, fire, hospital, etc.)
- Facility floor plans including emergency exits and location of emergency equipment and personnel
- Facility evacuation and shelter-in-place plans
- Facility and destination safety and security checklists (ideally completed at the time of site inspection)
- Listing of any attendees or staff with special needs
- Listing of all staff with special skills (certified in CPR, paramedic, language skills, etc.)
- Resource lists[5]

OTHER RISK MANAGEMENT TOOLS

In addition to having a risk team in place to plan for possible risks and respond to realized risks, other risk management tools are available that meeting managers should use to reduce the probability of risks or to mitigate the consequences of realized risks that cannot be prevented.

Information

Information is power and the wise meeting manager will use information to protect both attendees and the meeting organizer from the effects of realized risks. For example, the meeting organizer should collect emergency contact information from attendees. This can be done in advance on the registration form and

---

Fast Facts

Other Risk Management Tools

- Information
- Site inspections
- Security
- Exhibit security
- Badges
- Contracts
- Insurance

maintained in a database, as well as a printed list, that can be used in case of a power outage or data loss. For meetings where advance registration is not collected, collecting emergency contact information from attendees can be as simple as putting spaces on the on-site registration form and the back of name badges for attendees to write this information themselves.

Likewise, meeting managers should be prepared to provide information to meeting attendees to help the attendees minimize personal risks. For example, the U.S. Department of State's "Tips for Traveling Abroad" could be included in advance registration materials or registration confirmations for people attending international meetings.[7] These "tips" include passport and visa information, and the U.S. Department of State Bureau of Consular Affairs web site (www.travel.state.gov) also includes helpful information about health issues, safety issues, children and family issues, and U.S. embassies and consulates in other countries.

Meeting management or the organization should distribute a map to all staff, exhibitors, and official service providers in advance and on-site, with instructions on what to do in case of fire or other emergencies (e.g., bomb threat, power failure). Key staff should be trained before the event in what to do in case of emergency. Instructional safety signs should be posted for exhibitors and attendees if not adequately displayed by the facility.

Site Inspections

Using due diligence in choosing a safe meeting destination, facility, and services is a legal and ethical responsibility for meeting managers. The site inspection and request for proposals (RFP) process is an ideal time to collect information about the safety and security of a given destination, facility, or vendor. Ideally, the meeting manager should not sign a contract with the facility or vendor until he/she is confident that the facility or vendor meets his/her stringent standards of safety and security. One way to accomplish this is to include a checklist or disclosure form that the facility or vendor must fill out, along with other details about goods and services offered. Although the types of questions asked will be different for facilities and vendors, and will vary with the nature and needs of the organization and the meeting, questions should be asked about things like security personnel (e.g., number, training, hours of coverage), permits and licenses, fire safety equipment, emergency medical equipment on-site (e.g., automated external defibrillators), location and estimated response time of fire, police, and paramedics, processes and procedures, and so on. The local police department can also be a good source of information about the relative safety of an area.

Security

Planning for security should begin during an early site-inspection trip. Security needs vary for each meeting. Check the security staff in meeting facilities to see if there is a need for additional security personnel.

Many facilities require security. Obtain a copy of the rules and regulations to determine particular requirements for security and other services, and ask if the facility manager will provide a list of exclusive, preferred, or recommended security companies. In giving instructions to the security company, include not only the number of security personnel needed and when, but also information on each security officer's specific responsibilities. If guards will be checking badges, provide badge samples and recommendations for handling problems. Qualities to look for in a good security company include the flexibility they have in making personnel changes and additions on-site, and the extent of on-site supervision provided. Superior companies have ongoing training programs for their personnel. The ideal security staff person is polite, personable but firm, tactful, alert, and knowledgeable.

Obtain references and ask other meeting managers about the characteristics of the company's personnel and their dependability and punctuality. If possible, attend a show at which the security company is working in order to observe them and ask questions. Determine the hourly rate for security officers, supervisors, relief officers, and any other costs to be included. Ask what minimum rates will be in effect, as well as details on overtime charges and how they are applied. On-site personnel may use cellular phones, pagers, walkie-talkies, etc., to stay in constant communication with one another. Require a description or photograph of the uniforms worn by guards and supervisors.

Discuss security with facility personnel who can advise which entrances and exits can or cannot be locked and assist in identifying other areas that need attention. In the case of a large trade show, indicate on a floor plan the specific duty location for each officer and indicate if the officer is to be stationary or is to move between certain points. Review your security plan in advance with the convention center or hotel security director. Your security company should coordinate its efforts directly with the facility's security staff.

Monitor the performance of security personnel as frequently as possible, observing the alertness and courtesy with which they fulfill their responsibilities. Knowing if the organization is getting its money's worth in the case of evening security may be difficult. If possible, a different person should pay a surprise visit at a different hour each evening.

Ask bidding security companies to recommend the amount of security based on the nature of the event and the floor plan. Compare their recommendations with the advice of the facility's security staff and review all requirements outlined by the facility. Use the floor plan as a vehicle for negotiations.

Exhibit Security

Exhibitor security needs have increased significantly with the increased usage of audiovisual and technical equipment, which is now used by many exhibitors on the show floor.

The show manager should present a final floor plan in advance to the convention center or hotel security staff and discuss the characteristics of the show and the type of equipment that will be on the floor. These experts know their facilities and can recommend the amount of staff needed in order to provide adequate security.

Contact all suppliers who will need to enter the hall (e.g., florist, cleaning, caterers, computer rental, furniture). Compile a list of the number of employees, and names (if possible), and give the list to security staff. A duplicate list should be kept in the meeting office. Have adequate roving security when the number of suppliers is greater than what stationary officers can handle. For example, cleaning crews often consist of a large number of workers all arriving at one time, and stationary officers at a few doors cannot possibly protect exhibitor booths.

With such a wide range of individuals involved in the production of a meeting, especially a trade show, the potential for theft and tampering is high. The most crucial times for security are the move-in and move-out periods, and after the exhibit area is closed each day. Vulnerable hours for theft to occur are the time spans between the delivery of equipment and its display, and from the close of the show until merchandise and equipment are packed for shipment. If possible, the booth should not be left unattended during these periods. If the exhibitor's budget permits, hiring booth security is an effective measure.

Encourage all exhibitors to remove small items of value. The exhibition manager may provide lockable, guarded security rooms, or the facility or contractor may have security cages available for this purpose. Unauthorized removal of items from the exhibit area can be controlled by several methods—merchandise removal passes on which the trade show manager's signature is required, a business card with matching photograph and ID, and/or restricting the removal of any merchandise until the conclusion of the trade show.

Shortly before the event, send a special mailing to exhibitors with exhibitor security tips. Encourage all exhibitors to have their own security plan to protect their booth and product. Video cameras and bar code security measures are recommended.

Include these tips:

- Do not pack until security staff is on duty. (The exhibition manager should provide exhibitors with a schedule of the starting and ending times for security during the show.)
- Pack immediately after the show is over.
- Do not leave purses, briefcases, flat-screens, laptops, computers, or other electronic devices unattended. Give someone the responsibility of protecting such important assets.
- Do not leave any samples out.
- Report thefts to show security immediately.
- Do not label the contents of crates that hold valuables (e.g., computers, VCRs).

Badges

Issuing badges to participants is another good security measure. Badges may be simple or more complex photo badges or radio frequency identification (RFID) badges encoded with identifying information. The level of security for your event will determine what type of badge to use. Meeting attendees should be encouraged to recycle badges and not to throw them away in trash cans where someone else could find and use them.

If badges are to be checked for certain sessions, some meeting managers utilize college students, interns, or other volunteers. Most CVBs have personnel who can assist for an hourly wage. However, meeting managers should always utilize professional security staff in areas where safety and money are involved.

Contracts

Contracts are covered more fully in another chapter of this book. These are risk management tools. Because the consequences of realized risks may include legal and financial consequences, contracts must be considered in their risk management context. Cancellation clauses, attrition clauses, and force majeure clauses are but a few of the clauses that should be carefully reviewed for their role in the overall risk assessment and emergency management strategy. In the aftermath of recent emergencies, crises, and disasters, disputes have arisen around the issue of whether the emergency, crisis, or disaster truly constituted a force majeure (allowing a group to terminate a contract without liability) or a cancellation (meaning a group might have to pay monetary contract damages if they failed to hold the meeting). The difference can mean the difference between walking away amicably and having a legal dispute over thousands of dollars.

Insurance

Having insurance does not prevent a possible risk from occurring, but it can provide financial support for losses and expenses that an organization incurs in the event of an emergency, crisis, or disaster that impacts a meeting. Consider the following coverages.

Commercial General Liability (CGL) Insurance

Most organizations have commercial general liability (CGL) insurance (or are self-insured) to protect the organization's assets, including coverage to protect the organization if someone else suffers injury or damage of property and sues the organization. Many facilities require proof of this type of insurance coverage in specific amounts. Meeting professionals should check contract terms carefully to ensure that they are aware of the facility's requirement.

Event Cancellation Insurance

Event cancellation insurance compensates the organization for revenue lost as a result of cancellation or business interruption of the event caused by any unexpected occurrence from covered peril beyond the control of the organization. Poor planning or inadequate registrations do not constitute a cause beyond the control of the organization. The common convention cancellation policy also covers physical loss to personal property. All property owned, leased, rented, or otherwise the responsibility of the insured is covered while in transit to or from the event or during use at the event. Additionally, most cancellation insurance policies cover the loss of money collected on-site for registration or tickets.

As new emergencies, crises, and disasters occur, insurance programs adjust their coverage. After September 11, 2001, insurers excluded terrorism from coverage until the Terrorism Risk Insurance Act (TRIA) was enacted in November 2002. TRIA was a short-term measure designed to help insurance companies help the insured by offering terrorism insurance. This coverage remained extremely expensive. When something new like major power outages or labor disputes occur, meeting managers should check their insurance policies to ensure that no underwriting changes are being made that will affect their expected coverage. Work most closely with knowledgeable insurance brokers to determine the kinds of risks that will be covered and excluded. Read and understand the various limitations and exclusions of the policy before signing the policy.

Worker's Compensation

Worker's compensation is a no-fault coverage protecting employees who suffer an injury or illness arising out of and in the course of business. Meeting sponsors must have coverage for their employees and make sure suppliers have such coverage for their employees. Contracts with independent contractors should explicitly state that the independent contractor is responsible for its own worker's compensation coverage.

Additional Coverage

Each organization has its own insurance needs, depending on the type of meeting, the location, and the liability requirements imposed by the facility and suppliers. Protection may be provided in the organization's commercial general liability policy or through separate policies for such eventualities as fire, malpractice, burglary or robbery, and accidental death or dismemberment.

PLANNING AND RESPONDING TO SPECIFIC EMERGENCIES

Medical Emergencies

Most medical emergencies at a meeting are accidental injuries, but the likelihood of heart ailment, stroke, and other life-threatening illnesses and how to deal with them deserves serious consideration and planning. In evaluating the probability of the occurrence of medical emergencies, meeting managers should factor in attendee demographics, history of occurrences at previous and similar meetings, weather conditions, and program schedule and elements. Of course, a change in diet, liquor consumption, and fatigue can make any attendee physically vulnerable to illness or injury. They can also be emotionally vulnerable due to their reaction to unfamiliar surroundings, separation from the usual personal support systems, and a break from routine.

Local attendees, the facility, and the convention and the CVB can assist in setting up an effective medical emergency plan in the city in which your meeting is being held. The written risk management plan should include contact information for a hospital, an ambulance service, and appropriate medical and dental specialists who will be available during the time of the meeting. Inform all staff and publish emergency telephone numbers in the program and in other meeting materials.

If the meeting is held in a convention center, the convention center license agreement or insurance agreement may require that the organization hire a nurse or paramedic to be on-site whenever the facility is being used. Some convention centers have a first-aid room and can arrange staffing. The first-aid room/station typically must be staffed during all scheduled hours of the meeting.

Demonstrations and Confrontations

Major meetings or conventions may provide an enticing target for a demonstration or confrontation. The term demonstration is usually applied to events that are organized to picket or protest the organization with signs, literature, songs, and shouts. Sometimes the demonstrators have a grievance against the facility and use your meeting as a backdrop for their cause. Understand where the demonstration can be held, and where the authority of the convention facility begins and ends. If properly handled, these activities need not be a major disruption to the meeting itself.

A confrontation, on the other hand, is an effort on the part of the dissident group to interrupt the meeting. As a result, the protest itself may become the dominant theme. Both demonstrations and confrontations represent crises that often require the participation of meeting staff and facility officials to resolve. A critical factor to keep in mind is who has the authority to remove disruptive individuals from the property.

If a demonstration or confrontation seems imminent, take the steps necessary to minimize the disturbance. If a demonstration is anticipated, discuss the matter with local police officials to ensure their cooperation and involvement. This may prevent an overreaction on the part of the police, which can magnify the problem and stimulate unnecessary publicity. The meeting organizer's efforts should be to ensure that the demonstration is peaceful and does not unduly inconvenience or threaten meeting attendees. If a demonstration or confrontation is likely to occur, advise meeting participants beforehand to reduce the element of surprise.

The goal of the protesting group expects to make organization officials angry and uncomfortable. If the protesting group has an identified leader, suggest a conference with the leadership of the organization. A demonstration should not escalate to the level of a confrontation.

One of the most effective techniques to reduce the degree of hostility is to provide controlled opportunities for the dissident group to express its opinions. One method is to provide the group with a table in a designated area to display its literature. To avoid a serious disruption of the meeting, consider providing a room and a time for the dissidents to have a forum to discuss their issues with interested (or curious) attendees. In each of these methods, you retain essential control without fostering increased antagonism.

Did You Know?

A person can survive

- Four minutes without air
- Four hours without heat
- Four days without water
- Four weeks without food[9]

Over 80% of fire deaths occur in the places people sleep, such as houses, motels, hotels, condominiums, mobile homes, and apartments.[9]

You Can't Plan for Everything...

On January 15, 1919, 2 million gallons of molasses flooded the streets of Boston when a holding tank ruptured. The molasses killed 21 people.[10]

The biggest killers by continent in the last decade (excluding conflict- and disease-related deaths) were:

- Africa—transport accidents (49% of all those killed)
- The Americas—floods (46% of all those killed)
- Asia and Oceania—earthquakes and tsunamis (42% and 67%, respectively, of all those killed)
- Europe—extreme temperatures (51% of all those killed)[11]

When the issues involved attract the attention of the press, identify one staff member as responsible for press contacts to be certain that the position of the organization is made clear. A press conference can be called to articulate the organization's position. A prepared position statement should be carefully crafted by the sponsor's public relations department. Have speakers available who are willing to be interviewed on behalf of the organization, should the occasion arise.

WEATHER

Predictable weather problems should always be a consideration when a site for the meeting is selected. Even if a warm climate was selected, however, a snowstorm in some other area may interfere with travel to the meeting destination. When weather affects arrival and departure patterns, all you can do is modify the meeting arrangements to accommodate a small registration and wait until afterwards to balance the budget.

If bad weather interferes with participants returning home at the conclusion of the meeting, you may be able to negotiate longer stays with the hotels. In this situation, the hotels are having just as much trouble with delayed arrivals as they are with delayed departures, so it may not be difficult to arrange for extended stays. If some of the participants are stranded, consider turning the misfortune into a memorable event by having an impromptu party. A "Blizzard Bash" can be the highlight of the attendees' experience and keep them occupied during the weather emergency.

In case of severe weather such as a hurricane, you and your staff must be familiar with evacuation procedures in the area so you can provide needed guidance to your attendees. Follow the facility's evacuation plan and coordinate ground transportation out of the area, if possible.

STRIKES, STOPPAGES, AND SHORTAGES

A sudden interruption in services to the meeting can be devastating. In the early stage of site selection, investigate the current and projected labor situation. If a major union contract is to be negotiated at the time of the meeting, it could seriously affect the decision or the agreements made with suppliers. Wildcat strikes

Put It Into Practice

You are the director of meetings for an organization that is having their convention in coastal community. Your meeting is about 5,000 rooms on peak night and about 15,000 people are expected to attend. Your meeting is scheduled in August.

You know your meeting is taking place during hurricane season and you want to be prepared. What can you do to prepare yourself, your organization, and the meeting attendees should a hurricane approach your meeting destination? You understand that being prepared will require you to take a look at various situations and that you will need to react should any one of the situations arise.

Scenario 1

It is 2 weeks prior to your convention's opening day and you are scheduled to leave in 5 days to start the set up the meeting. A weather report indicates a hurricane is tracking in the direction of your meeting destination. What steps would you take at this time?

Scenario 2

You are on-site 5 days before your convention's opening day and the weather reports indicates a hurricane is tracking in the direction of your meeting destination. Should the hurricane continue on its projected path, it will arrive on the third day of your 4-day convention. What do you do to prepare?

1. What would you require from the following?
   - convention center facility
   - headquarters hotel and overflow hotels in your contracted block
   - local government
   - convention and visitors bureau
2. What emergency plans would you have in place?
3. What communication plans would you have in place?
4. Is there anything you can do in advance to prepare the organization, meeting attendees, and yourself should a disaster occur prior to your meeting dates or should a disaster occur while you are on-site?

Contributed by: Donna R. Karl, CMP, Vice President of Client Relations, New Orleans Convention and Visitors Bureau.

---

and stoppages cannot be anticipated, but timing for renewal of union contracts is a known entity.

When the unforeseen labor crisis occurs, the meeting is in jeopardy, and the time for recrimination is past. The first task is to identify which functions of the meeting will be most affected. Next, consider innovative strategies to keep as much of the program intact as possible. If exhibits cannot be delivered, arrange for table-top displays of literature, or a reception to give exhibitors an opportunity to meet and talk to the attendees. If hotel personnel are involved, management can be expected to fill in some of the gaps. However, you may need to change a sit-down luncheon to a buffet, or to ask attendees to make their own beds. The meeting staff will probably find that some of their assignments have changed, and some attendees will be willing to help.

Transportation strikes are particularly difficult for the meeting manager. If alternative transportation can be arranged, a travel desk at the convention headquarters is essential. If all transportation is stopped, treat it like the weather or some other natural disaster.

FIRE

Every meeting participant should be aware of survival techniques in the event of a fire. Panic and smoke, rather than the fire itself, are often the ultimate cause of fire deaths. Many hotels inform their guests of the steps to take in such an emergency, but your role is to ensure that the participants are protected and have adequate information available to them. Many organizations have developed fire safety brochures that are included in registration packets. Some hotels have a safety and security video that plays on the televisions in guest rooms. Speakers should be encouraged to find and announce all fire exits at the beginning of sessions. These small efforts can save lives. During the preliminary site inspection, particularly of multi-story hotels, become familiar with the safety features available. The following checklist covers safety features that are easily observable, even to the unpracticed eye:

- Is there an automatic fire extinguishing system (sprinklers)?
- Where are the sprinklers located—corridors, sleeping rooms, public areas, kitchens?
- If the building does not have an automatic fire extinguishing system, are there smoke detectors throughout?
- Are there two remote fire exits on every floor of the building?
- Do fire exits lead directly to the outside of the building?
- Are exit signs visible and well illuminated?
- Are there directional signs at the elevators directing guests to use the stairways in case of fire?
- Look at the tag on a fire extinguisher. Has it been checked on a regular monthly basis?
- Are there manual fire alarms in reasonable locations on every floor?

Using this checklist will not qualify you as a bona fide safety engineer. However, it will help you to recognize some of the more important basic safety features. Taking the time and the trouble to prepare for the unlikely emergency may seem tedious and unnecessary. Remember that saving one life or avoiding one calamity will make it all worthwhile.

BOMB THREATS OR TERRORIST ACTIVITY

Bomb threats and terrorist activity are harsh realities in today's world, especially following the events of September 11, 2001. The U.S. Bureau of Alcohol, Tobacco and Firearms (ATF) provides detailed instructions for preparing for and responding to bomb threats in its online publication "Bomb Threats and Physical Security Planning."[8] Additionally, many organizations have implemented terrorist response plans.

Bomb threats are delivered in a variety of ways. The majority of threats are called in to the target by someone who either has definite knowledge or believes that an explosive device has been or will be placed in the facility and wants to minimize personal injury or property damage; or someone who wants to create an atmosphere of anxiety and panic that will, in turn, result in a disruption of the normal activities at the facility where the device is purportedly placed.[8] Likewise, terrorist activity or threatened activity may disrupt operations and result in injury, panic, or property damage. Planning for bomb threats and terrorist activities means coordinating carefully with the meeting facility, as facility security are most likely to be contacted regarding a threat and will be the most likely to have the equipment, personnel, and processes for immediate response to such a threat, including channels for contacting local law enforcement (see Figure 44.2).

Evacuation

The most serious of all decisions to be made by management in the event of a threat is whether to evacuate the building. You have

FIGURE 44.2
September 18, 2001: The Millenium Hotel was located only a block from the World Trade Center 9/11 attacks in New York.

Photo by Michael Rieger / FEMA News Photo

three alternatives: Ignore the threat, evacuate immediately, or search and evacuate if warranted.

Ignoring the threat completely has obvious consequences if the threat is real. Also, if the caller feels ignored, he/she may go beyond the threat and actually plant a bomb or instigate an attack. Evacuating immediately is an alternative that, on face value, appears to be the preferred approach. However, immediate evaluation is disruptive, and a bomber wishing to cause personal injuries could place a bomb near an exit normally used to evacuate and then call in the threat. Initiating a search after a threat is received and evacuating a building if a suspicious package or device is found is usually the best approach. If a device is found, the evacuation can be accomplished expeditiously while at the same time avoiding the potential danger areas of the bomb.

An evacuation unit consisting of management personnel should be trained in how to evacuate the building during a bomb threat. You should consider priority of evacuation (e.g., evacuation by floor level). Evacuate the floor levels above and below the danger area to remove those persons from danger as quickly as possible. Training in this type of evacuation is usually available from police, fire or other units within the community.

You may also train the evacuation unit in search techniques, or you may establish a separate search unit. Consult with the appropriate authority regarding search techniques and measures to take in the event that a suspicious object is located.

MEDIA MANAGEMENT

In the event of an emergency, crisis, or disaster big enough to draw media attention, the meeting organizer and facility must be prepared to answer questions immediately. Because of the immediate dissemination of information over television, radio, and Internet, the media has great power over people's perceptions. A destination, a facility, or a meeting manager may get a reaction of sympathy or scorn based solely on the media's initial coverage of an emergency, crisis, or disaster. For this reason, someone within the organization must be trained to handle the media appropriately.

Some tips for establishing a crisis communication plan include:

1. Before a Crisis
   - Maintain trustworthy, credible relationships with the media all of the time. If you do, the media will be less suspicious and more cooperative in the midst of a crisis.
   - In addition to the media representations you deal with regularly, take time to learn the names and contact information for key media representatives in your host city.
   - Have a contact list for crisis management team members, including office, home, and cell or mobile phone numbers. Also have copies of their biographies. In a crisis, the press may want to know the backgrounds of those dealing with it.
   - Give designated spokespersons training in dealing with the media.
   - Determine the message, target, and media outlets that could be used in various crisis plans.
   - Have a plan for setting up a media crisis center. This should cover such items as desks, chairs, phones, parking, electrical outlets, placement of satellite trucks, copy machines, and even coffee. You also need to think about how to keep an office secure, particularly for your own staff.
   - Practice crisis communication before you experience a crisis.

2. During a Crisis
   - When a crisis hits, immediately get the word to the press. Otherwise, the media will get their information through other means.
   - Set up a 24-hour crisis and media center at a central place from which news is released, rumors dealt with, facts gathered, and briefings held.
   - Immediately "go public" with a trained spokesperson at the scene to conduct press briefings. Let the media—and therefore the public—know that you are dealing with the situation.
   - Say what you know and *only* what you know. Do not speculate. Don't be bullied into saying anything based on rumor. If you do not know something, admit it. Saying "the matter is under investigation" may be the best response.
   - Gather information as quickly as possible. Determine the basic who, what, when, where, and how. You might not get the "why" until later.
   - Summon the organization's leader and other top management to the crisis center. Cancel other plans. People want to see the leader, not just the public affairs staff. Having top management in front of the press during a crisis lends credibility and shows that the organization is not treating the situation lightly.
   - Inform your internal audiences—the staff, members, and meeting attendees—at the same time you inform the press. If the press is the only source of information for the staff and attendees, morale can be damaged and employees and members can become confused and hurt, especially if the incident is reported inaccurately in the press. Because of where they work, the staff will be viewed as sources of information, and they can be the origin of leaks and rumors. Be sure they have current and correct information.

Put It Into Perspective

Although all meeting managers should integrate risk management into hotel site inspection, site selection, and contract language, government meeting managers have special risk management requirements for government meetings. The Hotel and Motel Fire Safety Act of 1990 (Public Law 101-391) was enacted to promote fire safety in hotels, motels, and other places of public accommodation. The law requires that all properties be equipped with:

1. *Hard-wired, single-station smoke detectors in each guestroom in accordance with the National Fire Protection Association (NFPA) standard 72*
2. *An automatic sprinkler system, with a sprinkler head in each guest room in compliance with NFPA standards 13 or 13R. Properties three stories or lower in height are exempt from the sprinkler requirement[12]*

Government meeting managers must be particularly aware of this law in site inspections because Section 6(a) of the Hotel and Motel Fire Safety Act (1990) forbids the use of federal funds to "sponsor or fund in whole or in part a meeting, convention, conference or training seminar" in a facility which does not comply with the law. Thus, government meeting managers need to know whether a hotel they are considering is compliant with the Hotel and Motel Fire Safety Act. This can be accomplished by asking the question of the hotel and also putting language in the meeting contract requiring the hotel to warrant that it is in compliance and will continue to be in compliance over the meeting dates. Because U.S. federal government travelers are required to stay in hotels that are compliant with the Hotel and Motel Fire Safety Act when on official travel, the U.S Fire Administration maintains a *Hotel/Motel Fire-Safe List* that lists over 35,0000 hotel properties that are compliant with the terms of the Hotel and Motel Fire Safety Act (United States Fire Administration, 2006).[13] This site is publicly available on the U.S. Fire Administration web site.

Meeting planners for any type of entity should ask about fire safety during site inspections and choose hotels that are compliant with the Hotel and Motel Fire Safety Act. However, meeting managers should also realize that the Hotel and Motel Fire Safety Act is a minimum regulatory fire safety law, and not a guarantee of fire safety.

- Communicate with your internal audiences by email, if available, or through press releases and statements delivered to each office. If the staff is small enough, call a meeting at which members of the crisis team are available to answer staff questions.
- Maintain a calm, gracious, and helpful presence. Avoid appearing flustered or overwhelmed.
- Pre-empt negative publicity and communicate the actions being taken to solve the crisis. Verify news before releasing it.
- Arrange for media access to the scene of the crisis, if at all possible. Television wants pictures. If you have space constraints, use press pool reports, with a representative of each type of media—wire service, newspaper, TV, radio, magazine, and photography—at the scene, writing a report and taking pictures for their colleagues. No one may use these reports, including those in the pool, until they have been distributed to everyone.
- Take care of the practical needs of the press, such as parking, phones, electrical outlets, desks, and chairs.
- Keep a log of reporters who have called, what they asked, their deadlines, what you promised, and to whom it was delegated.
- Always return phone calls. If you do not, reporters will look elsewhere for information. Stories will be written with or without your assistance. Being nonresponsive takes control of a story away from the organization.
- Simple sympathetic gestures can help rebuild the public's confidence. Offer reassurance. Tell what actions are being taken to solve the problem, to help those affected, and to return things to normal.
- Make sure the press spokesperson is involved with senior management in every decision and policy made. Every decision has a public ramification, whether management recognizes it or not.
- Avoid fixing blame—That can be done after an investigation.
- Appeal to third-party endorsements for your efforts. Get credible people who have been through similar experiences and command the public's attention to speak on your behalf.
- Update information frequently and regularly. Announce when your next update will be.
- Monitor media reports and correct errors immediately.
- Establish a web site to inform people about the status of the situation. Put all news releases, statements, fact sheets, and links to other information on the site.

3. After the crisis
- Remove outdated information regarding the crisis from your web site as soon as possible.
- Interview or survey all key participants following the crisis to assess how risk management and crisis communication processes worked during the event. Share this information with the assessment group.
- Update your crisis plans.
- Practice before the next crisis occurs.
- Remember: openness and responsiveness during a crisis enhances your respect and credibility with the media. It can help you in the long run.[6]

SUMMARY

The meeting manager must assess and analyze the risks for a specific meeting, facility, or organization. This planning can be facilitated by putting in place a risk team. Once a risk team is formed, the group goes through the steps of risk assessment, risk analysis, and risk planning to create a written risk management plan. Although the plan will have a core of common information, this plan may have to be modified for each meeting. Response to emergencies, crises, and disasters will be guided by the risk management plan.

However, the risk team cannot possibly plan for every conceivable risk, so the risk team must use internal and external factors of the meeting and the organization to brainstorm a list of risks that are of concern. Once risks have been assessed, the risk team has to determine, based on probability and consequences, which of the risks to include in the risk management plan. A risk team and meeting manager should distinguish between the concepts of risk, emergency, crisis, disaster, and business continuity and how each may manifest itself differently.

Risk is the possibility that something may happen to adversely affect a meeting, whereas realized risks may be categorized as emergencies (causes injury, loss of life, destruction or property, or disruption of business). A crisis is a critical event that may dramatically impact an organization or a meeting, whereas a disaster is a calamitous event causing great damage or loss and disrupting business operations for some period of time. Meeting managers must apply the risk management model to create a specific risk management plan for different meetings and meeting-related services, which includes evaluating existing risk management plans and tools in order to improve them in the future.

Just as the written risk management plan is information about risk management for internal staff and volunteers, risk management information should be distributed to meeting attendees. In addition to reviewing the written risk management plan at least annually, meeting managers should conduct site inspections with risk management in mind. Contracts and insurance policies should also be considered valuable risk management tools. Risk management planning should include media management, which involves critical action before, during, and after a crisis.

References

1. Enz, C. A., & Taylor, M. S. (2002). The safety and security of U.S. hotels: A post-September-11 report. *Cornell hotel and restaurant administration quarterly, 43*(5), 119–136; Hinkin, T. R., & Tracey, J. B. (2003a). The service imperative: Factors driving meeting effectiveness. *Cornell hotel and restaurant administration quarterly, 44*(5/6), 17–26; Hinkin, T. R., & Tracey, J. B. (2003b). Continued relevance of "factors driving meeting effectiveness." *Cornell hotel and restaurant administration quarterly, 44*(5/6), 27–30.

2. Suicide bombers attack three Jordanian hotels. (2005, November 9). *Meeting News*. Retrieved on November 10, 2005, from http://www.mimegasite.com/mimegasite/search/article_display.jsp?vnu_content_id=1001477089.

3. Harasim, P. (2005). Alert targets 26,000 at expo. *Las Vegas review-journal*, A1.

4. Disaster Recovery Journal Editorial Board. (n.d.). *Business continuity glossary.* Retrieved December 19, 2005, from http://www.drj.com/glossary/drjglossary.html

5. Federal Emergency Management Association (FEMA). (1993). *Emergency management guide for business and industry.* (FEMA 141). Washington, DC: Author.

6. National Fire Protection Association (NFPA). (2004). *NFPA 1600 standard on disaster/emergency management and business continuity programs (2004 Edition).* (NFPA 1600). Quincy, MA: Author.

7. U.S. Department of State. (n.d.a). *Tips for traveling abroad.* Retrieved December 20, 2005, from http://www.travel.state.gov/travel/tips/tips_1232.html; U.S. Department of State. (n.d.a). *International information programs: Crisis communications.* Retrieved December 20, 2005, from http://usinfo.state.gov/products/pubs/pressoffice/crisis.htm

8. U.S. Department of Treasury. (1987). *Bomb threats and physical security planning*. (ATF P 7550.2). Washington, DC: Author.

9. Region of Peel. (n.d.). *Emergency facts and figures*. Retrieved on December 21, 2005, from http://www.region.peel.on.ca/prep/whatis_facts.htm

10. Hotfact. (2005). *Disaster trivia*. Retrieved December 12, 2005, from http://www.hotfact.com/disaster-trivia.html.

11. Reuters Foundation. (2005). *Factbox: World disaster facts and figures*. Retrieved on December 12, 2005, from http://www.alertnet.org/thefacts/reliefresources/112849951172.htm.

12. SafePlace. (2005). *Safety tips for meeting planners and corporate travel managers*. Retrieved on December 20, 2005, from http://www.safeplace.com/meeting_planner.html.

13. Hotel and Motel Fire Safety Act, Public Law 101–391 (1990).

Key Terms

Commercial general liability (CGL) insurance

Crisis

Crisis Communication Plan

Disaster event cancellation insurance

Emergency

Federal Emergency Management Agency (FEMA)

Media management

Realized risks

Response team

Radio frequency identification (RFID)

Risk

Risk analysis

Risk assessment

Risk team

Safety

Security

Worker's compensation

Compelling Questions For Consideration

1. How might the risks for a non-profit association meeting in a major U.S. city differ from those of a corporate meeting being held in Asia? Add other factors (such as time of year, nature of program, type of attendees) and go through the process of risk assessment.

2. Using one of the meetings above or another actual meeting, analyze the risks listed using the vulnerability assessment chart provided in Figure 44.1.

3. Who would be the best candidates to be on the risk team in your current organization? Why?

4. If you are holding a meeting in a city that suddenly suffers a widespread power outage, is this most likely an emergency, crisis, or disaster? Under what circumstances might a power outage escalate to the level of a crisis or disaster?

5. Think about recent emergencies, crises, or disasters that have occurred anywhere in the world. Discuss how any of these would affect your meeting if it was being held in one of these destinations and how you can plan to minimize the impact of an emergency, crisis, or disaster like this in the future.

CHAPTER 45

DETERMINE THE SUCCESS OF YOUR MEETING THROUGH EVALUATION

Monica Myhill, CMP
President
Meeting Returns

Jack Phillips, PhD
Chairman
ROI Institute, Inc.

LEARNER OUTCOMES

When the reader has completed reading this chapter, he/she should be able to . . .

1 Discuss the purposes and benefits of evaluating a meeting or event.

2 Explain the six levels of evaluation and the data collected within each level.

3 Identify possible data sources and data collection methods.

4 Formulate questions for data collection instruments.

5 Apply methods to increase response rates.

There is no failure.
Only feedback.

Robert G. Allen

OVERVIEW

Evaluation is a "systematic process to determine the worth, value, or meaning of an activity or process."[1] An evaluation of a meeting or events helps determine whether the objectives of a meeting or event were met and to what degree.

The evaluation process begins ideally when the needs assessment is conducted prior to a meeting or event and continues through the life cycle of a meeting. A thorough evaluation not only provides you with information about a past event, but also guidance on the planning of future meetings and the needs of your meeting stakeholders.

Six levels of measurement form a helpful framework when planning an evaluation. These levels start with the most basic data on attendance and budgetary figures and statistics and progress to more business minded data such as return on investment (ROI) calculations.

Feedback on a meeting, its application, and results come from a variety of sources and are gathered through numerous data collection methods. The most popular method to evaluate a meeting is through a questionnaire distributed to meeting attendees.

Once an evaluation has been conducted, it is essential to report the results to key stakeholders. Through communication and action, the results can be utilized to improve future meetings and the meeting management process. This chapter will identify the stages of the evaluation process, methods to gather information, strategies for improving response rates, and how the results of the process should be reported.

WHY EVALUATE?

In today's environment, meeting managers are struggling to meet demands from management for profit contributions, from participants who want a meeting that produces results, and from shareholders that demand accountability. Only through a thorough evaluation process can one determine whether a meeting was successful and achieved the meeting's objectives. There are eight purposes or benefits of meeting evaluation, including:

1. *To determine success in accomplishing meeting objectives.* Every meeting should have measurable, specific, and realistic objectives. Evaluation determines if objectives were met and to what extent. For more information on creating meeting objectives (see Chapter 2).

2. *To identify the strengths and weaknesses in the meeting management and design process.* Probably the most common purpose of evaluation is to determine the effectiveness of the various elements and components. These components include, but are not limited to, methods of presentation, learning environment, meeting content, networking events, learning aids, schedule, presenters, and logistics of the meeting. Each component can make a difference in the meeting and must be evaluated in order to make improvements.

3. *To compare the meeting costs to the benefits.* With today's business focus on the bottom line, determining a meeting's cost-effectiveness is crucial. Evaluation can compare the cost of a meeting to its usefulness or value, measured in monetary benefits. A meeting's return on investment is commonly used to express this comparison. ROI calculations provide management with information needed to eliminate unproductive meetings, increase support for meetings that yield a high payoff, or to make adjustments to meetings in order to increase benefits.

Fast Facts

Purpose of Evaluation

1. Determine success
2. Identify strengths and weaknesses
3. Compare costs to benefits
4. Decide on participants
5. Identify most successful participants
6. Reinforce major points
7. Gather data
8. Determine appropriate solutions

4. *To decide who should participate in future meetings.* Sometimes evaluation provides information to help prospective participants decide if they should be involved in a meeting or trade show. Communicating these results to other potential attendees can help them decide about future meeting participation.

5. *To identify which participants were the most successful with the meeting content.* An evaluation may identify which participants excelled or were unsuccessful at learning and implementing skills, knowledge, or professional contacts from the meeting. It may point out which attendee types, membership classifications, or customer groups enjoy the greatest success with the meeting content and thus gain the most benefits from the meeting.

6. *To reinforce major points made to the participant.* A followup evaluation can reinforce the information covered in a meeting measuring the results achieved by participants. The evaluation reminds participants what they should have applied on the job and the subsequent results that should be realized. This followup evaluation reinforces to participants the actions they should be taking.

7. *To gather data to assist in marketing future meetings.* In many situations, meeting managers are interested in knowing why participants attend a specific meeting, particularly when many meetings are offered and available. An evaluation can provide information to develop the marketing strategy for future meetings by determining why participants attended the meeting, who made the decision to attend, how participants found out about the meeting, and if participants would recommend the meeting to others.

8. *To determine if the meeting was the appropriate solution for the specific need.* Sometimes evaluation can determine if the original problem needed a meeting solution. Too often, a meeting is conducted to correct problems that cannot be corrected by a meeting. There may be other reasons for performance deficiencies, such as procedures, workflow, or the quality of supervision. An evaluation may yield insight into whether or not the meeting was necessary, and possibly even point leadership toward the source of the problem.

LEVELS OF EVALUATION

In the 1970s, Phillips created multiple levels of evaluation to determine the return on investment (ROI) for training and development programs and subsequently developed an ROI methodology, which was refined through application and use in the 1980s and implemented globally during the 1990s. To satisfy the needs of meeting managers, an additional level, featuring data on meeting statistics, scope, and volume, was added to the Phillips levels of evaluation.

Currently over 2,000 organizations worldwide are using this Phillips methodology within training and development, human resources, performance improvement, technology initiatives and now meetings and events to evaluate and calculate the ROI of these efforts. Over 15 books have been published on the ROI methodology and its application and over 100 ROI case studies have published in books, journals, and industry publications.

This conceptual framework of six levels is used to create meeting objectives and the subsequent evaluation strategy and measurement plan for the meeting.

Level 0—Statistics, Scope, and Volume collects data on meeting statistics as well as the scope and volume of meeting attendance, exhibitors, marketing efforts, press coverage, budgetary measures, web site traffic, and so on. Much of this information can be found in an organization's records, upon review of an organization's balance sheet, or through a scan of media coverage.

Fast Facts

Levels of Evaluation

- Level 0—Statistics, Scope, and Volume
- Level 1—Reaction, Satisfaction, and Planned Action
- Level 2—Learning
- Level 3—Application
- Level 4—Business Impact
- Level 5—ROI

When gathering Level 0 data, consider asking meeting attendees demographic questions about:

- Organization for which they work
- Industry in which they work
- Number of years in industry in which they currently work
- Position, title, and/or role within company
- Number of persons that report to them
- City, county, state, and/or country in which they live and work
- Length of membership in association organizing the meeting
- Age group
- Gender
- Professional designations
- Education level

When analyzing the results, you may notice that some demographic groups had greater satisfaction levels or were more likely to complete and return the questionnaire. Make sure to review and examine this info before making assumptions about the larger group.

Level 1—Reaction, Satisfaction, and Planned Action evaluation collects reactions to the meeting or event and can indicate the planned actions of the participants following the meeting. More specifically, this level of measurements gathers info on what stakeholders thought of the planning process, marketing efforts, the meeting itself, meeting materials, presenters, facilities, content, and so on.

Also at this level, the attendee, exhibitor, sponsor, and/or other meeting stakeholders indicate what they will do with the meeting content, professional contacts, or sales leads following the meeting.

When gathering Level 1 data, consider asking meeting attendees questions about:

- Importance and relevance of meeting or event to their job, organization, interests, and career path
- Effectiveness of speakers and facilitators
- Usefulness of marketing materials, on-site programs, handouts, and so on
- Recommendation of meeting to others
- Comments on how to improve the meeting, what topics/speakers should be offered in the future, and so on
- Intention of stakeholder to use what they learned or acquired at the meeting

Ask on-site staff, program committee members, and volunteers about the planning process, execution of the meeting, and specifically:

- Deadlines for submitting materials, documents, and plans
- Communication of essential information about the meeting and its requirements/deadlines
- Organization and execution of marketing, registration, transportation, housing, and so on
- Process and deadlines for completing meeting management steps
- Effectiveness and responsiveness of staff

Some specific meeting components to evaluate at this level include:

- Pre-meeting marketing, registration, travel arrangements, and information
- Meeting location, facilities, venues, and meeting rooms

- Food and beverage functions
- Meeting content and messages
- Program schedule and timing
- Speakers, facilitators, and entertainment
- Networking opportunities
- Vendors and suppliers servicing the meeting
- Transportation
- Trade show and its exhibitors

Participant reaction is sometimes useful in identifying trends, pinpointing problems in the meeting's design, and making improvements to the meeting logistics. Yet, making decisions on future meeting content and whether to cancel or continue a meeting based only on Level 1 data can be unwise.

Level 2—Learning evaluation is concerned with measuring the extent to which principles, facts, techniques, skills, and professional contacts have been acquired during the meeting. There are many different measures of learning, including paper-and-pencil tests, skill practices, case studies, job simulations, participant feedback, and facilitator observations.

Level 3—Application is measured to determine the extent to which skills, knowledge, and professional contacts learned or acquired at the meeting were utilized or applied on the job or in the personal life of the attendee. Evaluations in this category may include before meeting and after meeting comparisons, observations from the participant's superiors, subordinates, peers, and self-assessments.

The barriers or enablers that support or hinder the application of the meeting content and professional contacts should also be explored at this stage in the evaluation process. Barriers for the attendee may include lack of supervisor support, lack of time to apply the new knowledge and skills, no confidence to apply the new knowledge, or the meeting content is not essential or necessary to the attendee's success in the workplace. Common enablers for attendees are supervisor support, confidence to apply the new knowledge, and opportunities to utilize the skills, knowledge, and professional contacts.

When gathering Level 3 data, ask meeting attendees questions about:

- Effectiveness in applying knowledge, skills, and professional contacts from the meeting back in the workplace
- Frequency that knowledge, skills, opinions, and professional contacts have been applied in the workplace
- Barriers and enablers to applying the meeting content

Level 4—Business Impacts evaluation involves monitoring organizational improvement of business measures such as increased sales, cost savings, work output changes, and quality changes. For more information on possible business measures, see the box that follows. This data can be obtained from performance monitoring of organizational records, participant questionnaires, and action plans. Depending upon the perspective being evaluated, these business results could be for the meeting host, attendees, attendees' employers, exhibitors, sponsors, and so on.

Level 5—ROI evaluation addresses the return on investment for stakeholders such as the meeting host, attendees, exhibitors and sponsors. The ROI calculation compares the net meeting benefits with the fully loaded costs of the meeting. ROI can be expressed as a benefit/cost ratio (BCR) or an ROI percentage. For more information on ROI, see Chapter 46.

Fast Facts

Criteria For Selecting Meetings and Events for Level 3 Evaluation

- Meeting content is significantly important to customer satisfaction and service goals of the corporation holding the meeting or of meeting attendees
- Meeting content is significantly important to success of the meeting host or attendee's strategic goals and objectives
- Significant gaps in performance suspected
- Safety and health of attendees at risk
- Pilot meeting or similar meeting previously held and evaluated

Put It Into Perspective

Business Measures Impacted by Meetings and Events

OUTPUT

Units produced
Items assembled
Revenue
Items sold
Forms processed
Inventory turnover
Output per hour
Productivity
New accounts generated

COSTS

Budget variances
Unit costs
Cost by account
Variable costs
Fixed costs
Overhead cost
Operating costs
Number of cost reductions
Project cost savings
Accident costs
Sales expense

CUSTOMER SERVICE

Customer satisfaction survey
Customer satisfaction index
Customer complaints
Customer comments
Customer defection
Customer retention

WORK HABITS

Absenteeism
Tardiness
First aid treatments
Violations of safety rules

TIME

Equipment downtime
Overtime
On-time shipments
Time to project completion
Processing time
Cycle time
Supervisory time
Training time
Repair time
Efficiency

Order response
Lost time days

QUALITY

Scrap
Waste
Rejects
Error rates
Rework
Shortages
Product defects
Deviation from standard
Product failures
Inventory adjustments
Number of Accidents

WORK CLIMATE

Number of grievances
Number of discrimination charges
Employee complaints
Job satisfaction
Organizational commitment
Employee turnover
Reduced litigation

EVALUATION PLANNING

Evaluation is a team effort that involves many resources, both internal and external to the organization. For example, in an association, the membership department provides the mailing lists to promote the meeting and may want specific attendee demographics collected. The creative services department designs and produces the evaluation instrument. The education department needs to know if the meeting content met the desired educational objectives. They must also uncover the attendees' future educational needs and desires. Staff support may be required to handle the physical distribution of the evaluation and assist in data entry. External resources, such as a professional evaluation firm, can be brought in to assist with evaluation planning, data collection, analysis, and report generation.

The most successful evaluations are planned at the beginning of the needs assessment process, when the questions that will shape the meeting are asked. The evaluation planning stage can take days, weeks, or even months to complete. Regardless of the length or size of the meeting, careful consideration should be given to each stage of the planning process.

Before a meeting evaluation plan is developed, several key questions must be answered to ensure the evaluation progresses logically.

- *What is the purpose of the evaluation?* Evaluation purposes should be considered prior to developing the evaluation plan because the purposes will often determine the scope of the evaluation, the types of instruments used, and the type of data collected. For many meetings, multiple evaluation purposes will be pursued.

- *What data will be collected?* The meeting objectives guide you in making decisions on what data to collect. Depending upon the purpose of the evaluation, hard data, covering specific costs, output, time and quality, may be needed along with soft data featuring opinions, reactions, and attitudes. What data will your stakeholders easily be able to provide?

- *Data can be collected at one or more levels of evaluation.* If an ROI analysis is planned, data should be collected at Levels 1, 2, 3, and 4 to ensure that the chain of impact occurs as participants react to the meeting, learn the skills/knowledge, apply them on-the-job, and obtain business results.

- *When will the data be collected?* Data can be collected before, during and after a meeting. The timing of data collection depends on the type of data you require and your ultimate level of measurement.

- *How will the data be collected?* A variety of data collection instruments can be used and should be selected in the evaluation planning stage. The instruments most familiar to the culture of the organization and appropriate for the setting and evaluation requirements should be used in the data collection process. The two most popular methods for collecting data are questionnaires and focus groups.

- *Who will collect the data?* An organization's staff, volunteers, or an evaluation company can collect data.

- *Who will analyze the data?* Data are usually collected to be tabulated, summarized, and reported to others. The planned analyses, including the statistical comparisons, should be considered during the evaluation planning stage. It is often best to have a third-party or a person or department separate from the meetings staff analyze the data to ensure that the results are unbiased.

- *Who will utilize and receive the results or final report?* There may be one or more target audiences for the results. Who needs the data and results in order to make decisions on future meetings? Who will review the data in its raw state or in a summary? Who will read the full report? How will the report be used?

STAGES OF THE EVALUATION PROCESS

The Phillips Evaluation and ROI process shown in Figure 45.1 on the following page illustrates a complete meeting evaluation process model for measuring the success of Level 0 through Level 5 objectives. Depending upon the ultimate level of evaluation pursued, some of the steps can be skipped. For example, it is only necessary to isolate the effects of the meeting, convert data to monetary value and tabulate the cost of the meeting when a Level 5—ROI Evaluation is pursued.

DATA SOURCES

When considering possible sources of data to provide input on the success of a meeting or event, there are six major categories, including:

1. *Meeting Attendees*—One of the best sources of data is from those that attended or participated in the meeting or event. These participants are a rich source of data for Level 1, 2, 3, and 4 objectives. In some cases, obtaining attendee feedback may be the only way to measure the success of Level 3, 4, and 5 objectives.

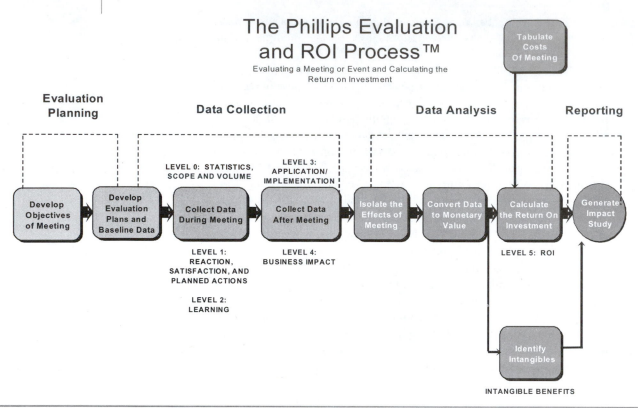

FIGURE 45.1
Phillips Evaluation and ROI Process™

2. *Internal and External Stakeholders Essential to the Delivery of the Meeting*—Staff feedback can be insightful to the success of Level 1—Reaction and Satisfaction objectives since they will often see first-hand the reactions of attendees to various meeting components. If the educational content of the program was developed by a committee, follow up with committee members about the mechanics of preparing the program, and what did and did not work. The meeting facility staff, service contractors, speakers, and suppliers should also be asked for feedback. Ask what they thought of the meeting's organization, attendees, the program, and so on. Ask for constructive criticism and listen carefully. Examining the planning process, noting problems, and requesting solutions will result in better planning processes in the future. Additionally, speakers and facilitators may provide input on the attendees' success at attaining the skills and knowledge (Level 2—Learning objectives) acquired in their session or workshop.

3. *Organizational Performance Records*—The most useful and credible sources of evaluation data are the organization's records and reports. Registration summaries and balance sheets are helpful in determining the success of Level 0 objectives. Performance records for an individual, work unit, department, division, region, or company overall can be used to measure Level 4 objectives. Sometimes there may be a difficulty in locating this data when an organization has been inconsistent in record keeping or if an attendee does not have easy access to this data.

4. *Supervisors of Meeting Attendees*—Those individuals who directly supervise meeting attendees are another important source of data. These supervisors may have a vested interest in the evaluation process and results since they most likely approved the meeting expense and/or the attendee's time

away from the office. Often, supervisors will have observed the meeting attendees as they attempt to use the knowledge and skills acquired at the meeting in the workplace.

5. *Subordinates of Meeting Attendees*—In some cases, the subordinates of meeting attendees can provide info about changes in the meeting attendee's behavior since the meeting. Input from subordinates is best for Level 3 data; yet, be careful of data potential biases from this group.

6. *Team Members or Peer Group of Meeting Attendees*—Peer group members or professional colleagues can provide input on the change in the attendee's behavior after a meeting. Using this source of data is most appropriate when this individual, in addition to the meeting attendee, has participated in the meeting and is reporting on changes in behavior following the meeting.

DATA COLLECTION METHODS

It is most appropriate to select a data collection method when the evaluation strategy is being developed, rather than after the meeting has taken place. The challenge is to select the data collection method or methods appropriate for the setting, the specific meeting, and the time and budget constraints of the organization. Data are collected using a variety of methods including the following:

1. *Data Collection Instruments*—Questionnaires, interviews, focus groups, observations, and action plans are evaluation instruments that serve as a data-gathering devices administered at appropriate timeframes to one or more stakeholders of the meeting.

   • *Questionnaires* are the most common and preferred data collection method and are used to capture Level 0, 1, 2, 3, and 4 data. They can be administered via telephone survey; distributed in paper form to attendees by a workshop monitor or other on-site staff; available to meeting attendees through an on-site computer kiosk; delivered to participants through a session's audience response equipment; sent to an attendee through email; or provided as a web link to an online questionnaire. A questionnaire asks meeting attendees to provide responses to a variety of open-ended and close-ended questions. Typically, completed questionnaires should be submitted anonymously in order to ensure honest feedback.

Put It Into Perspective

Paper Versus Online Questionnaires

Depending upon the preferred communication preferences of your stakeholders, select the questionnaire delivery method (paper or online) that will result in the highest number of returned and completed questionnaires called a response rate. Some of your stakeholders may prefer online or web-based evaluation forms while others may not have access to email or the Internet and thus prefer paper evaluation forms which are either given to them in person, mailed, or faxed.

If you have a limited evaluation budget, consider creating, scanning, and processing your own paper-based forms. For example with Principia Product's Remark Office OMR (www.principialproducts.com), you can create questionnaires in Microsoft Word, make your own copies of the questionnaire, scan the completed forms, and process the data.

Online or web-based questionnaires will often produce higher response rates, generate quicker results, reduce the need for data entry by staff, and shorten the analysis time. There are numerous Internet survey tools available that allow you to cheaply and easily create and distribute questionnaires. For a listing of popular providers, see References (this chapter).

Annual Meeting Evaluation

(Date, Location)

SESSION EVALUATION FORM

Your feedback is important to us. Please complete the information below and drop this completed evaluation form in any session evaluation box throughout the Convention Center. Answer all questions by shading the circle. Example: ● Yes O No

Session Number: Session Title:

Date and Time:

IMPORTANT: Please write in your Badge I.D.#:

What is your membership category?

- O Professional/ Assoc. Professional
- O Supplier Partner/ Assoc. Supplier Partner
- O Faculty
- O Student
- O Non-member

Number of years in the industry:

- O Less than 1 yr.
- O 1-4 yrs.
- O 5-8 yrs.
- O More than 8 yrs.

LEARNING EXPERIENCE / SESSION EVALUATION

Please rate the following:	Strongly agree	Agree	Disagree	Strongly Disagree	Don't Know/NA
The program design effectively blended speakers and attendee knowledge	O	O	O	O	O
The content and experience matched the promotional materials	O	O	O	O	O
The stated learner outcomes were achieved	O	O	O	O	O
I obtained information and ideas that will be useful in my work	O	O	O	O	O
The program content was presented at the correct level	O	O	O	O	O
A sufficient amount of time was allocated for delivery of the program content	O	O	O	O	O
Overall I am satisfied with the value I received with this learning experience	O	O	O	O	O

If you responded with "Don't know/NA", "Disagree", or "Strongly disagree" to any of the statements listed above, we would value your comments to help us learn how the session could be improved:

PRESENTER(S) EVALUATION

	Knowledge of Subject					Presentation & Facilitation Skills					Organization & Clarity of Content					Content Relevance to Learning Objectives				
The following presenter(s) provided value/usefulness for the categories shown:	Strongly agree	Agree	Disagree	Strongly Disagree	Don't Know/NA	Strongly agree	Agree	Disagree	Strongly Disagree	Don't Know/NA	Strongly agree	Agree	Disagree	Strongly Disagree	Don't Know/NA	Strongly agree	Agree	Disagree	Strongly Disagree	Don't Know/NA
	O	O	O	O	O	O	O	O	O	O	O	O	O	O	O	O	O	O	O	O
	O	O	O	O	O	O	O	O	O	O	O	O	O	O	O	O	O	O	O	O
	O	O	O	O	O	O	O	O	O	O	O	O	O	O	O	O	O	O	O	O
	O	O	O	O	O	O	O	O	O	O	O	O	O	O	O	O	O	O	O	O
	O	O	O	O	O	O	O	O	O	O	O	O	O	O	O	O	O	O	O	O
	O	O	O	O	O	O	O	O	O	O	O	O	O	O	O	O	O	O	O	O

COMMENTS REGARDING THIS SESSION/ PRESENTERS

What is the most significant takeaway from this session, the idea or insight you definitely won't forget and are likely to share with others?

Additional topics or presenters you would recommend for future programs:

FIGURE 45.2
Session Evaluation Example

- On-the-job *observations* capture actual skill application and are used to measure the success of Level 3 objectives. Observations are particularly useful in customer service training meetings and are most effective when the observer is either invisible or transparent. Secret shoppers can be utilized to evaluate at this level.
- *Interviews* can be conducted with meeting stakeholders before, during and after meetings and events. During a personal interview, a trained interviewer solicits responses to forced close-ended or open-ended questions. Interviews can be used to collect needs assessment data, satisfaction feedback, extent to which meeting content has been utilized on-the-job, and the business measures impacted due to the meeting.

  Face-to-face or phone interviews allow for probing to uncover specific applications and are most appropriate for collecting Level 3 and 4 data.
- *Focus groups* can be conducted before, during, and after a meeting for the same purposes as interviews. Focus groups are small group interviews of 6 to 10 persons led by a facilitator. The responses are typically recorded by

video and/or audio tape and analyzed later. The facilitator helps keep the interaction going, keeps the discussion focused on the subject, and ensures that no one person dominates the conversation.

- *Focus groups* are most appropriate for determining the degree to which a group of attendees have applied the info, skills, messages, and/or professional contacts of the meeting to the workplace or personal situations (Level 3 data).
- *Action plans* are developed at the meeting and are implemented on the job after the meeting is completed. Action plans gathered during a meeting or shortly after can indicate the planned actions of the attendees as well as expected intangible benefits from the meeting. Within 2 to 6 months of the meetings, check back with attendees and report back on the status and success of their action plans (Levels 3 and 4 data).

2. *Other Data Collection Methods* include meeting assignments, performance contracts, and performance monitoring.

- *Meeting assignments* are useful for simple short-term projects. Participants complete the assignment on-the-job, utilizing skills or knowledge learned in the meeting. Completed assignments can often contain both Level 3 and 4 data.

Fast Facts
Data Collection During the Meeting

	Level 0	Level 1	Level 2
Audience response equipment	✓	✓	✓
Action plans		✓	
Focus groups		✓	✓
Observations			✓
Questionnaires	✓	✓	✓
Tests			✓

Put It Into Practice
Data Collection After the Meeting

	Level 0: Meeting Statistics	Level 1: Reaction	Level 2: Learning	Level 3: Application	Level 4: Business Impact
Action plans		✓		✓	✓
Assignments				✓	✓
Focus groups		✓	✓	✓	✓
Followup session				✓	✓
Interviews				✓	✓
Observation on the job				✓	
Performance contracting				✓	✓
Performance records monitoring	✓			✓	✓
Questionnaires	✓	✓	✓	✓	✓

- *Performance contracts* are developed in advance of a meeting when the attendee and his/her supervisor, agree on specific outcomes from the meeting. Performance contracts are appropriate for both Level 3 and 4 data.
- A *followup session* to a meeting is utilized to capture evaluation data, present additional information and messages, and reinforce the content of the meeting. In the followup session, participants discuss their success with the meeting. Followup sessions are appropriate for both Level 3 and 4 data.
- *Performance monitoring* is useful where various performance records and operational data are examined for improvement. This method is particularly useful for Level 0 and 4 data.

Put It Into Practice

Corporate Team Building Meeting

Case Study

The Florida Gas, Water and Electric Company (Florida GWE) held a team-building meeting for 32 team leaders over various operations areas. The 3-day meeting consisted of a keynote, workshops, outdoor team-building event, and networking activities.

This meeting was designed to energize the team leaders in order to improve team performance and build five essential core skills. The following results were attained:

LEVEL OF MEASUREMENT		MEETING OBJECTIVE	RESULTS
0	**Meeting Statistics**	• Have 35 team leaders attend team-building meeting. • Fill 90% or more of the room block. • Meeting expenses will be 5% less than budgeted.	Thirty-two team leaders attended. The contracted room block was 100% filled. The cost per attendee was $2,500. The meeting came under budget by 10%.
1	**Reaction, satisfaction, and planned action**	• Attendees will rate the meeting experience an average of 4.0 out of 5.0. • Participants will rate the relevance of the meeting to their job success an average of 4.5 out of 5.0. • All attendees will complete and submit an action plan during the meeting.	Meeting feedback was very positive. On an emailed questionnaire sent immediately following the meeting, attendees rated it 4.2 out of 5.0 in an overall assessment. They indicated that the meeting content was relevant to their jobs and essential to their job success. Thirty managers completed and submitted an action plan on-site which covered steps to apply the meeting content to the jobs in the 4 months following the meeting.
2	**Learning**	• Through skill practice activities during the workshop, effectively demonstrate the five core team leadership skills. • Score 75 or better out of 100 on a test covering the meeting content.	Meeting attendees learned new team leadership and team-building skills. The workshop facilitator observed that participants were able to perform the five core team leadership skills during workshop skill practices. Participants took a multiple-choice test on the content covered and all scored a 75 out of 100 or better.

(continued)

Put It Into Practice, continued

	LEVEL OF MEASUREMENT	MEETING OBJECTIVE	RESULTS
3	Application	• Seventy-five percent of attendees will successfully utilize at least 4 of the five core team leadership skills within 3 months of the meeting. • Seventy-five percent of attendees will implement 80% or more steps within their action plans.	Meeting attendees applied the learned knowledge and skills to their jobs. Eighty percent of the attendees completed 75% or better of their action plan steps. On a followup questionnaire, team leaders reported high levels of use of the five core team leadership skills. Also, they identified several barriers and enablers to the transfer of the knowledge/skills to their job.
4	Business impact	• Improve productivity, quality and efficiency by 10% within 6 months of meeting.	Six months following the meeting, performance records indicated the following: • For productivity measures, a 23% improvement • For quality measure, a 18% improvement • For efficiency measures, a 14.5% improvement In focus groups, meeting attendees were asked to isolate the effects of the meeting on these improvements. They indicated that there were several other company initiatives and changes in work processes that could have impacted these measures. Thus, these improvements were adjusted to reflect the attendee's estimate of the meeting's impact along with their confidence level of the information to: • In productivity measures, an 11.3% improvement • In quality measures, a 5% improvement • In efficiency measures, an 8.4% improvement
5	ROI	• Achieve a 25% or better return on investment using first year benefits.	The fully-loaded costs of the meeting totaled $80,000. When the business measure improvements were converted to monetary values using standard values available through Florida GWE, the total meeting benefits equaled $400,000. The ROI of this meeting for Florida GWE was 400%. $$\text{ROI} = \frac{\$400,000 - \$80,000}{\$80,000} \times 100 = 400\%$$

ASKING THE RIGHT QUESTIONS

There are numerous ways to create questions for evaluation instruments. Questions are either close-ended, meaning the response choices are provided, or open-ended so that respondents can provide their own response or feedback. All questions should be simple and straightforward to prevent confusing the respondent or leading him/her to a desired response. Unfamiliar terms or acronyms should be avoided or explained.

One of the most common formats used with close-ended questions is Likert scaling or scaled rating. In this question format, the respondent is presented with a question or statement and is asked to select one response in a scale of possible choices. Some common rating scales include:

- Strongly Agree, Agree, Neither Agree nor Disagree, Disagree, Strongly Disagree
- Excellent, Good, Fair, Not Good, Poor
- Very Interested, Interested, Somewhat Interested, Not At All Interested
- No Opportunity to Apply, No Change, Some Change, Moderate Change, Significant Change, Very Significant Change
- Not Useful, Useful, Very Useful

You may add "No Opinion," "Don't' Know," "Don't Care," "Does Not Apply," or "No Opportunity to Apply or Conduct" to these scales, but place that choice apart from the rating scale. Do not assign these response options any point value when calculating an average score for the question.

- Please rate the following. Mark like this: ●   Not like this: ∅ ⍉ ⍉

	Strongly Agree	Agree	Neutral	Disagree	Strongly Disagree
The speaker was prepared.	O	O	O	O	O
I learned new knowledge/ skills from this meeting.	O	O	O	O	O
I learned new knowledge/ skills from my fellow attendees.	O	O	O	O	O

- Listed below are the objectives from the Leadership Development Meeting. After reflecting on the meeting, please indicate your degree of success in achieving these objectives. Please check the appropriate response beside each item.

Skill/Behavior	No Success	Very Little Success	Limited Success	Generally Successful	Completely Successful
Apply the 11-step goal-setting process	O	O	O	O	O

Another form of a close-ended question is a checklist question, which features a list of items of which the respondent selects one of more choices.

- By applying the skills, knowledge, and professional contacts acquired at the meeting, which measures were you able to positively influence? *(please check all that apply)*

O Customer satisfaction   O Sales
O Employee satisfaction   O Cost
O Productivity   O Time
O Quality   O Do not know

Two-way questions have alternate responses such as yes/no or other possibilities.

- Did you recommend the Annual Conference to others?
  O Yes
  O No

In multiple-choice questions, the respondent has several choices and is asked to select the most correct or best one.

- I was able to apply what I learned at the Annual Conference to my job *(please check only one answer)*:
  O Immediately upon returning to my job
  O Within 1 month of the conference
  O Within 2 to 5 months of the conference
  O I haven't applied what I learned but plan to in the future.
  O I haven't applied what I learned and most likely will not in the future.

Ranking scale questions require the respondent to rank a list of items.

- The following list contains factors that influenced your decision to attend this Annual Conference. Place a one (1) by the item that most influenced you, a two (2) by the item that was second in importance, and so on. The item ranked six (6) had the least influence on your decision.

  Networking opportunities   _____
  Educational opportunities   _____
  Cost to attend   _____
  Location of conference   _____
  Time of the year   _____
  Colleague recommendation _____

An open-ended question allows respondents to provide their own answer to a question. These responses can be further analyzed for trends or re-occurring answers. The most common open-ended question is utilized to obtain respondent comments.

- Please note any ways in which your conference experience could be improved.
- As a result of this meeting, what will you do differently?

It is possible to provide an open-ended response area for checklist or multiple-choice type questions as well.

- What helped or supported you in applying the knowledge and skills learned from this meeting? Check all that apply.
  O I had one or more opportunities to use the skills/knowledge.
  O My supervisor / manager supports my use of the skills/knowledge.

   O My work environment (peers, colleagues, systems, processes, etc.) supports my use of the skills/knowledge.

   O I have the confidence to apply the skills/knowledge because of having sufficient knowledge and practice.

   O Other—please specify:

After the questions are created, they should be tested with a small group of meeting attendees to ensure that they are clear, free of grammatical or spelling errors, and easy to answer. Collect as much input and criticism as possible and revise as necessary. It is better to catch mistakes now before the instrument is distributed to the larger attendee group.

SELECTING A SAMPLE

It can be difficult, if not impossible, to collect data from a large group of attendees. Sampling, or the process of selecting a percentage of all meeting attendees at random, is an acceptable method of generalizing data from a smaller group (sample) to a larger population (all meeting attendees).

Sampling is cheaper, faster, and can produce reliable results. Two major concerns must be addressed before establishing a sample group: who will participate in the sample group and the size of the sample group in comparison to the population or entire attendee group.

With simple random sampling, participants are selected on a random basis which eliminates any prejudice or unevenness in the selected sample group. Each meeting attendee has an equal chance of being included in the sample. For example, if you want to select a sample of 20 people from a meeting of 100 attendees, each attendee would have a one in five chance of being selected.

When multiple demographic groups or attendee types are represented at your meeting, it may be necessary to utilize a stratified random sample. In this method, attendees are divided into smaller groupings and a random sample is drawn from each subgroup to provide an overall sample. For example, if an association's membership can be separated into three distinct groups such as active members, affiliate members, and student members, random samples can be drawn from each of these groups.

There are numerous and complicated factors that can influence the appropriate sample size. These factors include size of the total population, variation in the data being collected, desired accuracy of the data, and the desired level of confidence in the results. In summary, decisions on sample size can be a complex process. Basically, it is best to utilize a sample that is as large as possible and a size that is convincing to the meeting's key stakeholders. For more information on this topic, it is best to consult an expert in this area.

INCREASING RESPONSE RATES

At one time or another, everyone has less than ideal response rates to questionnaires. Strive for the highest return rate possible in order to have the most statistically valid results. Ways to increase return rates fall into seven categories:

1. *Questionnaire Design*
   - When designing a questionnaire, make sure questions are clear, brief, and easy to answer.
   - Keep the questionnaire short and ask only the most pertinent questions. Attendees may be pressed for time and may not complete, or may even ignore, your questionnaire if they think it will take too long to complete.

- Pilot test the instrument with a group of attendees to insure the questions make sense, are easy to answer and are free of errors.
- Directions, questions, and response options should be clear and concise. The respondent should not have to interpret anything or guess the meaning of a question.
- Try to place open-ended questions at the end of a questionnaire. This way you may get answers to the close-ended questions even if respondents do not answer the open-ended ones.
- Design the questionnaire with a professional format.

2. *Leadership Support*
- Early in the evaluation planning stage, ask managers, supervisors, senior executives, and/or association leadership to support the evaluation process. Ask them to distribute questionnaires, show support for the evaluation process, and encourage meeting attendees to complete and return the questionnaires. A couple of verbal or written comments by a senior executive about the importance of attendee feedback can be vital to an evaluation's success.

3. *Delivery and Collection Timing*
- Distribute questionnaire to a captive audience. Consider giving participants a questionnaire during a formal session and providing them with time to complete it within the session.
- Sending out an emailed questionnaire immediately following a meeting may generate a higher response rate since attendees may have very specific suggestions for improvement or still be on a high from the meeting.
- Provide enough time for respondent to complete the evaluation instrument. A time crunch can cause problems if attendees are in a hurry to leave a workshop room or the meeting itself. Some business impact data may require the respondent to collect organizational reports or figures, thus necessitating the need for additional response time.
- Give a deadline time and/or date for returning the questionnaire and then send out reminders prior to the deadline.

4. *Communications*
- Clearly communicate the why, when, what, and who. Provide the reasons and purpose for the evaluation, when participants will be asked to complete the questionnaire, what will happen with the results, and who will see and take action on the results.
- Provide a copy of the evaluation instrument in advance. For lengthy forms covering meetings that span several days, it is helpful to distribute a copy of the form in the registration packet or early in the meeting so participants can familiarize themselves with the questions.
- Provide one or two followup reminders using a different medium for each.
- Send a summary of results to attendees and other key stakeholders.
- Review the questionnaire at the end of a formal session.
- Add emotional appeal to the request to complete the evaluation.

5. *Incentives*
- A gift or chance of a prize may encourage some attendees to submit their completed questionnaire. Enclosing a pen, coffee gift certificate, discount coupon for a future meeting, or other token of value often helps to increase response rates.

6. *Confidentiality*
- Maintain respondent confidentiality. If an attendee is concerned about being identified with his/her responses, the likelihood of truthful feedback is diminished.

Fast Facts

Increase Response Rates
1. Questionnaire design
2. Leadership support
3. Delivery and collection timing
4. Communications
5. Incentives
6. Confidentiality
7. Submitting questionnaires

- Consider hiring an outside evaluation company to gather the necessary data as many attendees may be more willing to share their responses if they are sure they can do so anonymously.

7. *Submitting Questionnaires*
   - If evaluations are to be collected on-site, place clearly marked receptacles in convenient locations.
   - On-site have staff or volunteers collect evaluations as attendees exit meeting rooms.
   - For online questionnaires, allow meeting participants to save their responses and return at a later time to complete them.
   - If evaluations are to be returned by mail, provide a self-addressed, postage-paid envelope.
   - Provide multiple ways to respond (collected at a meeting, submitted through email, faxed, or mailed).

REPORTING THE RESULTS OF YOUR MEETINGS

If you take the time to gather and analyze evaluation data, share the results with stakeholders. Communicating results is as important as achieving them.

Customize the meeting results to the interests and needs of your various stakeholders. By determining the most effective report format for each stakeholder group, you can increase the likelihood that it will be read. For example, prepare an executive summary for senior executives that cover the business impacts of the meeting instead of whether attendees liked meal functions. Yet, your convention services manager will appreciate feedback on how attendees felt about their facility, service levels, and meals.

Results can be shared in face-to-face meetings, memos, newsletters, company intranet, email blasts, or articles. Results should be communicated as soon as they are available.

When results indicate that one or more elements of the meeting did not go well or could be improved in the future, use these negative or average results as

Fast Facts

Target Audience for Evaluation Results	Reason for Sharing Results
Top executives and organization leadership	Secure approval for meeting, build credibility for the meeting staff, and stimulate interest in meetings
Attendee managers and supervisors	Gain support for the meeting and enhance reinforcement of the meeting content
Participants	Enhance results of future meetings
All employees or association members	Demonstrate accountability for meeting expenditures
Prospective meeting attendees and association members	Market future meetings

an opportunity to recommend changes to future meetings or to the meeting management process. If you seek greater respect or recognition from senior management, use the results as a chance to demonstrate strategic thinking and provide ways the meeting can have a greater impact next time.

SUMMARY

The purposes and benefits of evaluating a meeting are numerous. The two most important reasons to evaluate a meeting are to determine whether the meeting objectives were met and to what degree and to identify ways the meeting can be improved in the future.

This chapter presented the model developed by Phillips, which describes six levels of evaluation and the data collected within each level. These levels start with the most basic data on attendance and budgetary figures and statistics and progress to more business minded data such as ROI calculations.

There are six major categories of data sources with meeting attendees and organizational performance records serving as the primary sources. A meeting or event can utilize multiple data collection methods depending upon the meeting objectives. The most common data collection methods feature questionnaires and focus groups.

When formulating questions for data collection instruments, questions are either close-ended, meaning the response choices are provided, or open-ended so that respondents can provide their own response or feedback. Close-ended questions can be in the form of a Likert-type scale, checklist, multiple-choice, or two-way question. Open-ended questions typically solicit comments or recommendations for future meetings.

It is vitally important that the data collected has validity and represents reality therefore, it is important that sufficient data is collected from your meeting population. Response rates to evaluation instruments can be improved by proper questionnaire design, leadership support of the evaluation process, thoughtful timing of the delivery and collection of instruments, communication about the evaluation plan, use of incentives, ensured confidentiality of responses, and easy submission methods.

REFERENCES

1. Phillips, J. J. (1997). *Handbook of training evaluation and measurement methods.* (3rd Ed.) Woburn, MA: Butterworth-Heinemann.

2. Convention Industry Council. (2005). The APEX post-event report template. Retrieved December 15, 2005, from http://www.conventionindustry.org/apex/acceptedpractices/posteventreport.doc

KEY TERMS

Action plan	Hard data	Sample
Audience response	Learning environment	Sampling
equipment	Observation	Secret shoppers
Balance sheet	Open-ended question	Simple random sampling
Benefit/cost ratio	Population	Simulation
Case study	Questionnaire	Soft data
Close-ended questions	Response rate	Stratified random sample
Evaluation	Return on investment	Survey
Focus group	(ROI)	Web link

Fast Facts

Ways to Report Results:

- Articles
- Brief report
- Brochure
- Complete report
- Executive summary
- Face-to-face meeting
- Memos
- Newsletter
- One page summary
- Web site

COMPELLING QUESTIONS FOR CONSIDERATION

1. What levels of evaluation data are most important to your stakeholders?

2. What data collection methods work best in your organization?

3. What would you include in a final report to your meeting stakeholders on the success of a meeting?

CHAPTER 46

RETURN ON INVESTMENT FOR MEETINGS AND EVENTS

Monica Myhill, CMP
PRESIDENT
MEETING RETURNS

Jack Phillips, PhD
CHAIRMAN
ROI INSTITUTE, INC.

LEARNER OUTCOMES

When the reader has completed reading this chapter, he/she should be able to . . .

1 Identify the reasons for calculating the return on investment on meetings and events.

2 Describe the criteria for an effective return on investment process.

3 Compare and contrast techniques to isolate the effects of meetings and events.

4 List the methods used to convert meeting benefits to monetary value.

> Action is the foundational
> key to all success.
>
> *Pablo Picasso*

OVERVIEW

There has been much debate on the issue of measuring the return on investment (ROI) in meetings and events. It is rare for a topic to stir up emotions to the degree that the ROI issue seems to generate. Some people characterize any ROI measurement as seriously flawed and inappropriate. Others passionately characterize ROI as the answer to their accountability woes. The truth probably lies somewhere in between these two extreme viewpoints. The important point is to understand the drivers for the ROI process and the inherent weaknesses and advantages of measuring ROI. Then it is possible to take a rational approach to the issue and implement an appropriate mix of evaluation strategies, including the ROI.

As long as there is a need for accountability of meeting, event, and trade show expenditures and the concept of an investment payoff is desired, an ROI calculation will be used to evaluate major investments in meetings and events. This ROI measurement is calculated by dividing the net meeting benefits by the fully loaded meeting costs.

In order to arrive at an ROI calculation, six levels of evaluation must be pursued to observe a chain of impact and to ensure that it was the meeting that caused the change or improvement. It is also necessary to isolate the effects of the meeting and then convert data to monetary values to arrive at the ROI.

For an ROI process to be useful, it must balance many issues, such as feasibility, simplicity, credibility, and soundness. In addition, meeting managers, senior executives, and key meeting stakeholders must be satisfied with the ROI process to find it credible and utilize it.

Communicating the results of an ROI impact study is the final critical step in the ROI process. It is not only important to communicate achieved results once the study is complete, it is also important to share results throughout the process.

KEY ROI ISSUES

ROI Will Not Go Away

One thing is certain in the debate on ROI: *ROI is not a fad. It is here to stay.* As long as there is a need for accountability of meeting, event, and trade show expenditures and the concept of an investment payoff is desired, the ROI will be used to evaluate major investments in meetings and events. A fad is a new idea or approach or a new spin on an old approach. The concept of ROI has been used for centuries. The 75th anniversary issue of the Harvard Business Review (HBR) traced the tools used to measure results in organizations.[1] In the early issues of HBR, during the 1920s, the ROI was the emerging tool to place a value on the payoff of investments. In recent years, the application of the concept has been expanded to all types of investments, including training, change initiatives, technology, and meetings. With increased adoption and use, it appears that ROI is here to stay.

The Ultimate Level of Evaluation: ROI

The ROI process is based on six levels of measurement, a concept that is both helpful and instructive in understanding how the return on investment is calculated. Table 46.1 shows the six level measurement framework. For more information on meeting evaluation and these six levels, see Chapter 45.

At Level 0, *Meeting Statistics, Scope and Volume* type measures are reported. These key indicators are selected based on issues critical to the meeting host organization, senior executives, organization leadership, and/or other key stakeholder groups. Some indicators at this level include meeting participation statis-

TABLE 46.1
Six Levels of Evaluation

Level		Measurement Focus
0	Statistics, Scope, and Volume	Measures meeting statistics as well as the scope and volume of meeting attendance, press coverage, budgetary measures, and so on.
1	Reaction, Satisfaction, and Planned Action	Measures participant satisfaction with the meeting and captures planned action.
2	Learning	Measures changes in knowledge, skills, attitudes, and professional contacts due to the meeting.
3	Application	Measures changes in behavior following the meeting.
4	Business Results	Measures changes in business-impact variables.
5	Return on Investment	Compares meeting benefits to meeting costs.

tics and figures, budgetary measures, press coverage or media impressions, and contracted sleeping room block pickup numbers. Contrary to some opinions, attainment of Level 0 objectives is not a gauge of a meeting's true success.

At Level 1, *Reaction, Satisfaction, and Planned Action*, satisfaction from meeting participants is measured along with how they planned to apply what they have learned. Almost all organizations evaluate at Level 1, usually with a generic, end-of-program questionnaire. While this level of evaluation is important as a customer satisfaction measure, a favorable reaction does not ensure that attendees acquired new learned new skills or knowledge.

At Level 2, *Learning* measurements focus on what participants learned during the meeting using tests, skill practices, role-plays, simulations, group evaluations, and other assessment tools. A learning check is helpful to ensure that participants have absorbed the meeting material or messages and know how to use or apply them properly. This level also measures the number of new professional contacts and the extent to which existing contacts were strengthened. However, a positive measure at this level is no guarantee that what was learned or the contacts acquired will be used on the job. The literature is laced with studies that show the failure of learning to be transferred to the job.[2]

At Level 3, *Application*, a variety of follow-up methods are used to determine if meeting attendees applied the skills, knowledge, or professional contacts from the meeting to their job or back in their personal lives. The frequency and use of these skills, knowledge, and contacts are important measures at Level 3. While Level 3 evaluations are important to gauge the success of the application of the meeting, they still do not guarantee that there will be a positive business impact for the organization or meeting attendee.

At Level 4, *Business Results*, the measurement focuses on the actual results achieved by meeting participants as they successfully apply the meeting material, messages, or contacts. Typical Level 4 measures include output, sales, quality, costs, time, and customer satisfaction. Although the meeting may produce a measurable business impact, there is still a concern that the meeting may cost too much.

At Level 5, the ultimate level of evaluation, *Return on Investment*, the measurement compares the monetary benefits from the meeting with the meeting costs. Although the ROI can be expressed in several ways, it is usually presented as a percent or cost benefit ratio. The evaluation chain is not complete until the Level 5 evaluation is conducted.

While most associations and corporations conduct evaluations to measure the level of satisfaction with their meetings and events, very few actually conduct evaluations at the ROI level. Perhaps the best explanation for this situation is that ROI evaluation is often characterized as a difficult and expensive process. When business results and ROI are desired, it is also very important to evaluate the other levels. A chain of impact (see Figure 46.1) should occur through the levels as the skills and acquired knowledge (Level 2) are applied on the job (Level 3) to produce business results (Level 4). If measurements are not taken at each level, it is difficult to conclude that the results achieved were actually caused by the program. Because of this, it is recommended that evaluation be conducted at all levels when a Level 5 evaluation is planned. For the training and development industry, this practice is consistent with the practices of the benchmarking forum members of the American Society for Training and Development.[3]

Why ROI?

There are some good reasons why return on investment has become a hot topic. Although the viewpoints and explanations may vary, some things are very clear. First, many organizations' meeting budgets grew until 9/11 occurred, and then experienced a downturn due to the economy's reaction to the event. In this ever-demanding economy, accountability and proof of value become more critical issues, often prompting the need to determine ROI.

Second, total quality management, continuous process improvement, balanced scorecards, and procurement's role in meetings have focused increased attention on measurement issues. Organizations now measure processes and outputs that were not previously measured, monitored, and reported. This measurement focus has placed increased pressure on meetings and events to develop measures of successes.

Third, internal restructuring, the threat of outsourcing, and procurement initiatives have caused many meeting managers to focus more clearly and directly on bottom-line issues. Many meetings and events have been reengineered so that they are more closely aligned with business needs and to ensure that maximum efficiencies are achieved in the meeting management cycle. These change

Chain of Impact is Critical!

1. **Participants react favorably to the meeting**

2. **Participants learn new skills or enhance knowledge as they explore their role in the meeting**

3. **Participants apply new skills and implement the program/issues discussed in the meeting in their jobs**

4. **The consequences of implementation are captured as business impact measures, linked to the meeting**

5. **A return on investment is generated**

FIGURE 46.1
Chain of Impact

processes have brought more attention to evaluation issues and resulted in measuring the contribution of specific meetings. The threat of outsourcing has forced some meeting managers to more closely align programs to organizational objectives and to measure successes so that management can understand their contribution to the organization.

Fourth, the business management mindset of many current meeting managers causes them to place more emphasis on economic issues within their function. The meeting manager of today is more aware of bottom-line issues in the organization and is more knowledgeable of operational and financial areas. This new "enlightened" manager often takes a business approach to meetings and events and the ROI issue is a part of this strategy.

Fifth, there has been a persistent trend toward accountability in organizations all over the globe. Shareholders, clients, members, and the general public are demanding an increasing level of accountability from corporations, nonprofit organizations, professional associations, and government entities. This can be witnessed in the United States' Sarbanes-Oxley Act of 2002, one of the most comprehensive changes ever to the rules and regulations that govern public company financial reporting and internal operations.

Every support function is attempting to show its worth by capturing the value that it adds to the organization. From the accountability perspective, meetings and events should be no different from the other functions. It must show its contribution.

Sixth, top executives and sponsors are now demanding ROI calculations in organizations where previously they were not required. For years, meeting managers have felt that meetings and events cannot be measured, at least at the level desired by executives. Yet, many of the executives are now finding out that ROI on events *can and is* being measured in many organizations, thanks in part to articles in publications aimed at top executives.[4]

After becoming aware that ROI on meetings can be done, top executives are subsequently demanding the same accountability in their organizations. In some extremes, organizations such as IBM are being asked to show the return of their training meetings or face significant budget cuts.[5] Others are just asking for results. The chief operating officer for a global telecommunications company recently described it this way: "For years we have evaluated training with variables such as number of participants, number of programs, length of programs, cost of programs, and content of programs. These are input focused measures. Now, we must show what these programs are doing for our company and speak in terms that we can understand. We need output focused measures."[6] These no nonsense comments are being repeated throughout major organizations.

BUILDING A FEASIBLE ROI PROCESS

Concerns with ROI

Although much progress has been made, the ROI process is not without its share of problems and drawbacks. The mere presence of the process creates a dilemma for many organizations. When an organization embraces the concept and implements the process, the management team is usually anxiously waiting the results, only to be disappointed when they are not quantifiable. For an ROI process to be useful, it must balance many issues, such as feasibility, simplicity, credibility, and soundness. More specifically, three major audiences must be pleased with the ROI process in order for it to be accepted and used in an organization.

Meeting Managers—With this perceived complexity, meeting managers could visualize the tremendous efforts required for data collection and analysis, and more importantly, the increased cost necessary to make the process work. Because of these concerns, these managers are seeking an ROI process that is simple and easy to understand so that they can easily implement the steps and strategies. Also, they need a process that will not take an excessive time frame to implement and will not consume too much precious staff time. Finally, meeting managers need a process that is not too expensive. With competition for financial resources, they need a process that will not command a significant portion of the budget. In summary, from the perspective of the meeting manager, the ROI process must be user friendly, save time, and be cost efficient.

Senior Executives—Executives, who must approve meeting, event, and trade show budgets, request programs, or cope with the results of meetings, have a strong interest in developing the ROI. They want a process that provides quantifiable results, using a method similar to the ROI formula applied to other types of investments. Senior executives have a never-ending desire to have it all come down to an ROI calculation, reflected as a percentage. And, like meeting managers, they also want a process that is simple and easy to understand. The assumptions made in the calculation and the methodology used in the process must reflect their point of reference, experience, and level of understanding. They do not want, or need, a string of formulas, charts, and complicated models. Instead, they need a process that they can explain to others, if necessary. More importantly, they need a process with which they can identify; one that is sound and realistic enough to earn their confidence.

Meeting Stakeholders—Finally, stakeholders will support only a process that measures up to their scrutiny and close examination. Stakeholders will insist that models, formulas, assumptions, and theories are sound and based on commonly accepted practices. Also, they want a process that produces accurate values and consistent outcomes. If estimates are necessary, stakeholders want a process that provides the most accuracy within the constraints of the situation, recognizing that adjustments need to be made when there is uncertainty in the process.

The challenge is to develop acceptable requirements for an ROI process that will satisfy stakeholders and, at the same time, please meeting managers and senior executives.

Criteria for an Effective ROI Process

To satisfy the needs of the three critical groups described above, the ROI process must meet several requirements. Ten essential criteria for an effective ROI process are outlined below.[7]

1. The ROI process must be *simple*. It must be void of complex formulas, lengthy equations, and complicated methodologies. Most ROI attempts have failed to meet this requirement. In an attempt to obtain statistical perfection and use too many theories, several ROI models and processes have become too complex to understand and use. Consequently, they have not been implemented.

2. The ROI process must be *economical,* with the ability to be implemented easily. The process should have the capability to become a routine part of meetings and events without requiring significant additional resources. Sampling for ROI calculations and early planning for ROI are often necessary to make progress without adding new staff.

3. The assumptions, methodology, and outcomes must be *credible*. Logical, methodical steps are needed to earn the respect of practitioners, senior executives, and stakeholders. This requires a very practical approach to the process.

Fast Facts

ROI Criteria

1. Simple
2. Economical
3. Credible
4. Sound
5. Variable
6. Applicable
7. Flexible
8. Operable
9. Financial
10. Track Record

4. From a research perspective, the ROI process must be *theoretically sound* and based on generally accepted practices. Unfortunately, this requirement can lead to an extensive, complicated process. Ideally, the process must strike a balance between maintaining a practical and sensible approach and a sound and theoretical basis for the procedures. This is perhaps one of the greatest challenges to those who have developed models for the ROI process.

5. An ROI process must *account for other factors* that have influenced output variables. One of the most often overlooked issues, isolating the influence of a meeting, is necessary to build credibility and accuracy within the process. The ROI process should pinpoint the contribution of the meeting or event when compared to other influences.

6. The ROI process must be appropriate for a *variety of meetings and events*. Ideally, the process must be applicable to all types of meetings and events, such as association annual conferences, corporate customer events, and incentive travel programs.

7. The ROI process must have the *flexibility* to be applied on a pre-meeting basis as well as on a post-meeting basis. In some situations, an estimate of the ROI is required before the actual meeting is developed. Ideally, the process should be able to adjust to a range of potential time frames for calculating the ROI.

8. The ROI process must be *applicable with all types of data*, including hard data, which is typically represented as sales, output, quality, costs, and time; and soft data, which include job satisfaction, customer satisfaction, absenteeism, turnover, grievances, and complaints.

9. The ROI process must *include the costs* of the meeting or event. The ultimate level of evaluation compares the benefits with costs. Although the term ROI has been loosely used to express any benefit of the meeting or event, an acceptable ROI formula must include costs. Omitting or understating costs will only destroy the credibility of the ROI values.

10. Finally, the ROI process must have a successful *track record* in a variety of applications. In far too many situations, models are created but never successfully applied. An effective ROI process should withstand the wear and tear of implementation and prove valuable to users.

Because these criteria are considered essential, an ROI process should meet the vast majority, if not all, of the criteria. The bad news is that most ROI processes do not meet these criteria. The good news is that the ROI process presented below meets all ten of the criteria.

A PRACTICAL MODEL FOR THE ROI PROCESS

The evaluation of meetings and events and the calculation of ROI begin with the basic model (see Figure 46.2). The ROI process model provides a systematic approach to evaluation and ROI calculation.

This step-by-step approach helps to keep the process manageable so that users can tackle one issue at a time. The model also emphasizes the fact that this is a logical, systematic process that flows from one step to another. Applying the model provides consistency from one ROI calculation to another.

For more information on the evaluation planning, data collection, and reporting steps, see Chapter 45.

Isolating the Effects of the Meeting or Event

An often-overlooked step in most attempts to calculate ROI is the process that is used to isolate the effects of the meeting or event. In this step of the process,

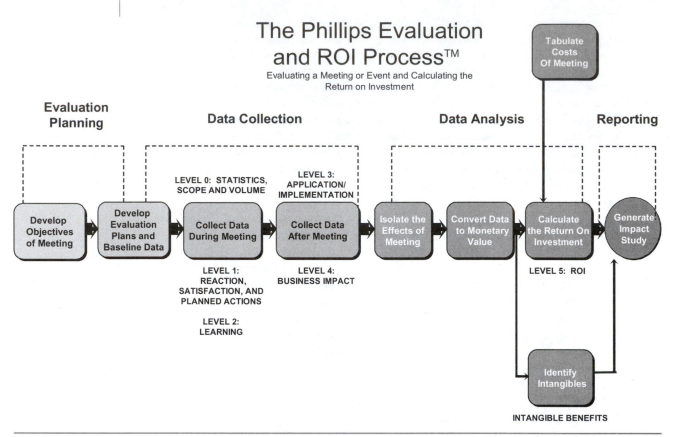

FIGURE 46.2
A Systematic ROI Process Model[8]

specific strategies are explored that determine the amount of performance output that is directly related to the meeting. This step is essential because there are many factors that will influence performance data after meetings and events have been conducted. There are specific strategies at this step that will pinpoint the amount of improvement that is directly related to the meeting. The result is increased accuracy and credibility of the ROI calculation. The following strategies have been utilized by organizations to tackle this important issue.[8]

- A *control group* arrangement can be used to isolate impact. With this strategy, one group participates in the meeting while another similar group does not. The difference in the performance of the two groups is attributed to the meeting. When properly set up and implemented, the control group management is the most effective way to isolate the effects of meetings and events.

- *Trend lines* are used to project the value of specific output variables, if the meeting had not been undertaken. The projection is compared to the actual data after the meeting and the difference represents the estimate of the impact. Under certain conditions this strategy can be an accurate way to isolate the impact of meetings and events.

- When mathematical relationships between input and output variables are known, a *forecasting* model is used to isolate the effects of a meeting. With this approach, the output variable is predicted using the forecasting model with the assumption that the meeting is not conducted. The actual performance of the variable after the meeting is then compared with the forecasted value to estimate the impact of meetings and events.

- *Participants estimate* the amount of improvement related to meetings and events. With this approach, participants are provided with the total amount of improvement, on a pre- and post-meeting basis, and are asked to indicate the percent of the improvement that is actually related to the meeting.

- *Supervisors of participants estimate* the impact of meeting and events on the output variables. With this approach, supervisors of participants are presented with the total amount of improvement and are asked to indicate the percent that is related to the meeting.

- *Senior managers estimate* the impact of meetings and events. In these cases, managers provide an estimate or "adjustment" to reflect the portion of the improvement that is related to the meeting. While perhaps inaccurate, there are some advantages to having senior management involved in this process, such as senior management ownership of the results.

- *Experts provide estimates* of the impact of meetings and events on the performance variables. Because the estimates are based on previous experience, the experts must be familiar with the type of meeting and the specific situation.

- In supervisory and management type meetings, the *subordinates of participants* identify changes in the work climate that could influence the output variables. With this approach, the subordinates of the supervisors who attended the meeting determine if other variables changed in the work climate that could have influenced output performance.

- When feasible, *other influencing factors are identified and the impact is estimated or calculated,* leaving the remaining unexplained improvement attributed to meetings and events. In this case, the influence of all of the other factors is developed and the meeting remains the one variable that is not accounted for in the analysis. The unexplained portion of the output is then attributed to the meeting.

- In some situations, *customers or meeting attendees provide input on the extent to which the meeting or event has influenced their decision* to use a product or service. Although this strategy has limited applications, it can be quite useful in marketing events, user group meetings, and other customer meetings and events.

Collectively, these strategies provide a comprehensive set of tools to tackle the important and critical issue of isolating the effects of meetings and events.

Converting Data to Monetary Values

To calculate the return on investment, data collected in a Level 4 evaluation are converted to monetary values to compare to meeting costs. This calculation requires a value to be placed on each unit of data connected with the meeting. Ten strategies are available to convert data to monetary values. The specific strategy selected usually depends on the type of data and the situation.[9]

- *Output data are converted to profit contributions or cost savings.* With this strategy, increases in output are converted to monetary value based on their unit contribution to profit or cost reduction. These values are readily available in most organizations.

- The *cost of quality is calculated* and quality improvements are directly converted to cost savings. These values are available in many organizations.

- For programs where employee time is saved, the participants' *wages and benefits are used for the value of time.* Because a variety of meetings focus on improving the time required to complete projects, processes, or daily activities, the value of time becomes an important and necessary issue.

Fast Facts

Ways to Isolate the Effects of the Meeting

- Use of control groups
- Trend line analysis
- Forecasting methods
- Participants' estimate of impact
- Supervisors' estimate of impact
- Management's estimate of impact
- Use of experts
- Subordinates' reports of other factors
- Calculating/Estimating the impact of other factors
- Customer input

Fast Facts

Ways to Convert Data to Monetary Value

- Converting output to contribution
- Converting the cost of quality
- Converting employees' time
- Using historical costs
- Using internal and external experts
- Using data from external databases
- Using participants' estimates
- Linking with other measures
- Using supervisors' and managers' estimates
- Using learning staff estimates

- *Historical costs and current records* are used when they are available for a specific variable. In this case, the improvement.
- *Supervisors of participants* provide estimates when they are both willing and capable of assigning values to the organizational cost data are utilized to establish the specific value of an improvement.
- When available, *internal and external experts* may be used to estimate a value for an improvement. In this situation, the credibility of the estimate hinges on the expertise and reputation of the individual.
- *External databases* are sometimes available to estimate the value or cost of data items. Research, government, and industry databases can provide important information for these values. The difficulty lies in finding a specific database related to the situation.
- *Participants estimate* the value of the data item. For this approach to be effective, participants must be capable of providing a value for improvement. This approach is especially useful when participants are not fully capable of providing this input or in situations where supervisors need to confirm or adjust the participant's estimate.
- *Senior management provides estimates* on the value of an improvement when they are willing to offer estimates. This approach is particularly helpful to establish values for performance measures that are very important to senior management.
- *Meeting staff estimates* may be used to determine the value of an output data item. In these cases it is essential for the estimates to be provided on an unbiased basis.

This step in the ROI model is very important and is absolutely necessary to determine the monetary benefits from meetings and events. The process is challenging, particularly with soft data, but can be methodically accomplished using one or more of the strategies described above.

Put It Into Perspective

ROI calculations can be done from the perspective of multiple stakeholder groups. This multiple perspective option is most appropriate for associations, nonprofit organizations, and government entities to consider. For associations, the best meetings and events on which to conduct ROI impact studies are:

- Annual conferences from the attendee, exhibitor, and sponsor perspectives
- Trade shows from the exhibitor perspective
- New member recruitment events from the association perspective
- Specialty or in-depth member training or certification programs from the participant perspective
- Trade show booths promoting membership in the association, from the association perspective

Corporations may want to consider conducting ROI impact studies not only from their own perspective, but also from the perspective of the meeting attendees. For example, financial planning and insurance companies can assess the ROI of independent agents attending their conferences and training meetings. Likewise, a franchisor company can calculate the ROI for franchise owners participating in meetings and events.

Corporations should consider conducting a Level 5 ROI evaluation on a variety of meetings and events, such as:

- User, customer, client, independent agent, and franchisee owner group conferences
- Product roll-out meetings and events
- Marketing events
- Team-building meetings and events
- Training meetings
- Corporate sponsorship of civic, charitable, professional, and industry meetings and events
- Management meetings
- Annual sales kick-off meetings
- Customer or client appreciation events
- Incentive programs and meetings

Tabulating Meeting/Event Costs

The other part of the equation on a benefit/cost analysis is the cost of the meeting or event. Tabulating the costs involves monitoring or developing all of the related costs of the meeting targeted for the ROI calculation. The cost components that may be included, depending upon the ROI perspective, are:

- The cost to *design and develop the meeting/event*, possibly prorated over the expected life of the meeting or event
- The cost of all *meeting materials*—such as participant handouts, signage, decoration, and so on
- The cost of the *speakers, instructors, and/or facilitators*, including preparation time and delivery time
- The cost of the *facilities* for the meeting
- *Travel, housing and food and beverage* costs for the participants
- *Salaries plus employee benefits* of the participants and staff to attend the meeting
- *The administrative and overhead costs* of the meeting management function, allocated in some convenient way to the meeting or event

In addition, specific costs related to the needs assessment and evaluation should be included, if appropriate. The conservative approach is to include all of these costs so that the total is fully loaded.

Calculating the ROI

The return on investment is calculated using the meeting benefits and costs. The benefit/cost ratio (BCR) is the meeting benefits divided by cost. In formula form it is:

$$BCR = \frac{\text{Net Meeting Benefits}}{\text{Meeting Costs}}$$

The return on investment uses the net benefits divided by meeting costs. The net benefits are the meeting benefits minus the costs. In formula form, the ROI becomes:

$$ROI\,(\%) = \frac{\text{Net Meeting Benefits}}{\text{Meeting Costs}} \times 100$$

This is the same basic formula used in evaluating other investments where, traditionally, the ROI is reported as earnings divided by investment.

Identifying Intangible Benefits

In addition to tangible, monetary benefits, most meetings and events will have intangible non-monetary benefits. The ROI calculation is based on converting both hard and soft data to monetary values. Intangible benefits are results or data items that are not converted to monetary values and include items such as:

- Increased job satisfaction
- Increased organizational commitment
- Improved teamwork
- Improved customer service
- Reduced complaints
- Reduced conflicts

During data analysis, every attempt is made to convert all data to monetary values. All hard data, such as output, quality, and time, are converted to monetary values. The conversion of soft data is attempted for each data item. However, if the process used for conversion is too subjective or inaccurate and the resulting values lose credibility in the process, then the data are listed as an intangible benefit with the appropriate explanation. For some meetings, intangible, non-monetary benefits are extremely valuable, often carrying as much influence as the hard data items.

Best Meetings and Events for ROI Measurements

Not all meetings are candidates for ROI measurement. Together, these factors make a meeting a good candidate for an ROI impact study:

• Long life cycle of the meeting
• Linkage of the meeting to operational goals and issues
• Importance of the meeting to strategic objectives
• High meeting costs
• Significant visibility of the meeting
• High number of meeting participants
• Considerable investment of time on the part of the meeting organizer or the meeting attendees
• Comprehensive needs assessment has been conducted prior to designing and planning the meeting
• Senior executives are interested in the ROI measurement

Guiding Principles

Through the years, a set of guiding principles has been established in order to keep the ROI process as credible as possible.

1. When a higher level evaluation is conducted, data must be collected at lower levels.
2. When an evaluation is planned for a higher level, the previous level of evaluation does not have to be comprehensive.
3. When collecting and analyzing data, use only the most credible sources.
4. When analyzing data, choose the most conservative among alternatives.
5. At least one method must be used to isolate the effects of the meeting.
6. If no improvement data are available, it is assumed that little or no improvement has occurred.
7. Estimates of improvement should be adjusted for the potential error of the estimate.
8. Extreme data items and unsupported claims should not be used in ROI calculations.
9. Only the first year of benefits should be used in the ROI analysis of short-term projects.
10. Meeting costs should be fully loaded for ROI analysis.
11. Intangible measures are defined as measures that are purposely not converted to monetary value.
12. The results from the ROI methodology must be communicated to all key stakeholders.

REPORTING ROI RESULTS

Communicating the results of an ROI impact study is a critical step in the ROI process. It is not only important to communicate achieved results once the study is complete, it is also important to share results throughout the process. As with any evaluation or measurement results, it is essential that the results be shared with key stakeholders so that they are aware of the results and can take necessary steps to act results. With an initial ROI impact study, take care not to release the ROI calculation without a through explanation of the ROI methodology and process. Communicating evaluation results, especially those pertaining to business impacts and ROI, can quickly become confusing for event the most sophisticated audiences.

SUMMARY

ROI calculations are being developed by hundreds of organizations to meet the demands of a variety of influential stakeholders. The result is a process that shows the value added by meetings and events in a format desired by many senior administrators, executives, attendees, and sponsors. However, this chapter has demonstrated that the ROI process represents a significant and challenging dilemma for most organizations. While there are many drivers for the tremendous interest in, and need for, the ROI process, some question its appropriateness, accuracy, and necessity. The important point is that ROI calculations can be developed reliably and accurately for almost any type of meeting or event. To accomplish this, the process must be approached with careful planning, methodical procedures, and logical and practical analyses. Above all, the steps, techniques, assumptions, and issues must follow a conservative approach to build the credibility needed for acceptance of the process.

As long as there is a need for and pressure from stakeholders for accountability of meeting, event, and trade show expenditures and the concept of an investment payoff is desired, ROI calculations will be used to evaluate major investments in meetings and events.

To satisfy the needs of meeting managers, senior executives, and meeting stakeholders, the ROI process must meet 10 essential criteria ranging from simple, economical, and credible to appropriate from the standpoint of a variety of meetings and events.

When calculating ROI, the step of isolating the effect of a meeting or event is often overlooked. Yet it is an essential step in the ROI process and lends credibility to the final ROI calculation. Depending upon the meeting type and the business measure it impacts, one or more techniques can be used to isolate these effects. The most credible means is through the use of a control group, yet the most often used is the meeting participant's estimate.

Ten strategies are available to convert data collected in a Level 4 evaluation to a monetary value for the ROI calculation. The specific strategy selected typically depends on the type of data and the situation. The most credible methods are to covert output data to a profit contribution, cost savings, or hourly time value for one or more employees.

Only about 5% of an organization's meetings and events should even be taken to an ROI calculation. The best meetings to evaluate for ROI are those that link to the strategic objectives of the host organization or meeting participant and incur significant costs and/or time for the host or participant.

REFERENCES

1. Sibbet, D. (1998). *Harvard business review, 75 years of management ideas and practice 1922–1997*. Boston: Graduate School of Business Administration, Harvard University.

2. Broad, M.L., & Newstrom, J.W. (1992). *Transfer of training*. Reading, MA: Addison-Wesley.

Fast Facts

ROI Target Options

- Set at break even, 0% (typical for associations)
- Set the value as with other investments, e.g., 15%
- Set slightly above other investments, e.g., 25%
- Set higher than achieved ROI from previous meeting

3. Kimmerling, G. (1993). Gathering best practices. *Training & development, 47(3)*, p. 28–36.

4. William and Mary Business Review. (1995). *Corporate training: Does it pay off?*, Williamsburg, VA: William and Mary Business Review.

5. Geber, B. (February, 1994). A clean break for education at IBM. *Training*, 33–36.

6. Based on an interview with the author.

7. Phillips, J.J. (1997) *Return on investment in training and performance improvement programs*. Houston, TX: Gulf Publishing.

8. Phillips, J.J. (1996). Was it the training? *Training & development, 50(3)*, 28–32.

9. Phillips, J.J. (1996). How much is the training worth? *Training & development, 50(4)*, 20–24.

KEY TERMS

Benefit/Cost ratio (BCR)	Forecasting model	Return on investment
Control group	Intangible benefits	(ROI)
		Trend line

COMPELLING QUESTIONS FOR CONSIDERATION

1. Which of your next meetings and events would be best for an ROI impact study?

2. Which method for isolating the effects of a meeting would your stakeholders view as most credible?

What Is a Professional Meeting Manager?

While some still see meeting planning as primarily focused on logistics, professional meeting managers understand that logistics execution is just one aspect of the overall contributions they make to individual event and overall organizational success. This section examines what it means to be a good professional including an exploration of professional ethics, interpersonal and organizational leadership, and ongoing professional development and skills enhancement.

CHAPTER 47

THE PROFESSIONAL MEETING MANAGER

Joan L. Eisenstodt
CHIEF STRATEGIST
EISENSTODT ASSOCIATES, LLC

Mitchell Beer, CMM
PRESIDENT
THE CONFERENCE PUBLISHERS, INC.

LEARNER OUTCOMES

When the reader has completed reading this chapter, he/she should be able to . . .

1 Identify the attributes of the meetings over the last 25 years.

2 Evaluate the future of meetings and the meetings manager.

3 Define the skills and attributes needed by meeting managers of the future.

4 Determine the role that meeting managers will be expected to plan in the future of the meetings industry.

> Be curious always. For knowledge will not acquire you; you must acquire it.
>
> *Sudie Back*

Overview

The early twenty-first century is a period of transition for meetings and events, and for all of the professions and disciplines involved in shaping them. Meeting managers and the industry as a whole are scrambling to live up to an old set of expectations, even as they assume a wider, more strategic position that would have been unimaginable to past generations of planners and suppliers.

This duality is reflected in the working lives of meeting managers, and in the organizations they serve. Many associations still expect their in-house meeting managers to fulfill the purely logistical job description that was the state of the art as recently as the late-1980s. Increasingly, however, employers and clients have higher expectations of the people who plan and execute their meetings—they are looking for more measurable results for all stakeholders. More and more meeting managers are deliberately stepping up to that role, and away from the purely logistical function.

The chapters in this book have identified many of today's best practices that enable meeting managers to position themselves as both masterful logisticians and strategic partners in the meetings industry. Additionally, topics have also included some of the new methods of delivering educational content—on-site and at a distance. Gaining the most from this book will come if read with the future of the industry in mind.

This chapter will help define the role of the meeting manager in the future of the meetings industry. It explores the future of meetings and the professions that support them, and defines the skills and attributes that meeting managers will need in the twenty-first century. Finally, it provides resources for meeting managers to access, assess, and build their own skills in the areas that will matter most as the profession enters its second century.

Where Meeting Management Began

Where did meeting management begin? Look back far enough, and you will find colleagues who trace the earliest days of the profession to the planners who helped organize Noah, "Mrs. Noah," and the animals to vacate a disaster area. Even then, the focus was on logistics, albeit on a large enough scale to accommodate elephants and giraffes.

In the 1960s and 1970s, a meeting manager's responsibilities were still purely tactical, dealing with logistics versus strategy. Meeting managers were the logisticians who made sure there were enough coffee cups for a 15-minute break. They ensured that the pastries were cut in half (to save money), and that enough chairs were set in straight, unbroken rows to accommodate the right number of participants. Standard meeting technology was overhead and slide projectors and videotape recording was the state of the art and very expensive.

Industry manuals said little or nothing about issues as basic as contract negotiations or attrition. They reflected a vision of women's roles that was largely limited to the spouses' program. Meeting participants were mostly male and white, and so were the people who planned the events. The few women who made it into the meetings industry came from secretarial positions, or were likely to have served as volunteers for civic or religious organizations.

The limited, linear composition of the average meeting also found its parallel in the delivery of the on-site educational program:

- Rooms were set for the standard lectures that many of us remembered—with varying degrees of fondness or dread—from school. For example, straight rows of chairs, or "classroom style" with tables set in straight rows, all far from the speaker.

- The vast majority of session time was devoted to subject matter experts (SMEs) who rarely adapted their content or presentation formats to the variety of adult learning styles in the audience.
- The question and answer period was limited to the last 10 minutes, and could easily be dropped if a speaker ran out of time.
- Handouts were held to the very end, on the assumption that shuffling papers would distract from the prepared presentation.
- Breaks were kept to the absolute minimum; with little or no thought given to the informal networking and learning that takes place between organized sessions.

Anything that had to do with learners and learning—the different ways in which people acquire and retain knowledge, the educational impact of different room set-ups, the design of the broader learning environment, the use of learning environments outside a standard classroom or meeting room, the comfort of the participants who would spend several days in that environment—all of that was seen as futuristic thinking, if it was seen at all.

That future is now within reach. As the meeting management profession and those in it have matured, the role of meeting managers has continued to evolve as well. While this evolution has not gone as far as some would like and the process has been more slow than many would prefer, the profession is progressing in directions that largely bode well for meetings and events, and for the people who attend, organize, host, and sponsor them.

WHERE MEETING MANAGEMENT IS GOING

As the meetings management profession moves to a new level of sophistication, the future will belong to managers and suppliers who have the knowledge, experience, and perspective to:

- Understand the specific purpose behind every meeting and event in which they are involved
- Design every element of a meeting or event to reflect and respect participants' learning needs and styles
- Maximize participants' pre-meeting and on-site experiences to spark their interest in learning
- Organize venues and deliver services in ways that better meet the strategic and educational objectives behind an event

So, who is this meeting manager of the future? What traits, characteristics, and skills will that person possess? And how do we begin building and refining that knowledge base and skill set today?

HOW TO GET THERE

Moving ahead, the meeting manager may want to consider internalizing and introspection through assessment of personal strengths, shifting your perspective of how you approach your job, building networks for communication, and learning and expanding your skills.

Assess Your Strengths

Knowing yourself—understanding your strengths, and recognizing gaps in your knowledge and experience—is the first step to meeting the challenges of the future. The field of vocational counselling offers a wide variety of insights and

---

Fast Facts

Some things that meeting managers do today that they did not do 10 years ago:

- Establish or help their organizations/clients establish meeting goals and objectives
- Knowledgeable about nutrition and its impact on learning
- Define aspects of risk and plan for contingencies and catastrophes
- Identify and learn about global issues impacting their organizations/clients

self-help materials, beginning with *Now, Discover Your Strengths.* As the authors of that book, Buckingham and Clifton, write: "The great organization must not only accommodate the fact that each employee is different, *it must capitalize on these difference.*"[1] Meeting managers could do far worse than to organize every event from the same starting point.

Shift Your Perspective

In shifting from sheer logistics to a more strategic focus, meeting managers are broadening their view to encompass the significance of a meeting or event to all its stakeholders: the sponsoring organization, meeting participants, vendors, and the venue in which it is held. They can and should do the same with the educational content presented on-site. According to Pink, author of *A Whole New Mind: Moving from the Information Age to the Conceptual Age*, the best uses of information will be high concept and high touch.[2]

> In his book, Pink explains that high concept involves the capacity to detect patterns and opportunities, create artistic and emotional beauty, craft a satisfying narrative, and combine seemingly unrelated ideas into something new. Moreover, high touch involves the ability to empathize with others, to understand the subtleties of human interaction, to find joy in one's self and elicit it in others, and stretch beyond the quotidian in pursuit of purpose and meaning.

Build Your Networks

Business and professional networking is widely recognized as the lifeblood of the meetings industry. At its best, networking is about bringing colleagues and professional partners together to share information, ideas, and opportunities, secure in the knowledge that if the substance is sound, commercial success will follow.

In *The Tipping Point*, author Gladwell describes Connectors as those who seem to know everyone—just because they genuinely enjoy building connections with the people in their lives.[3]

> All of us know someone like this. But I don't think that we spend a lot of time thinking about the importance of these kinds of people. I'm not even sure that most of us really believe that the kind of person who knows everyone really knows everyone. But they do.

Gladwell's research supports that in a variety of social, educational, and income groups, there are subsets of people who are excellent, relentless networkers. "Sprinkled among every walk of life…are a handful of people with a truly extraordinary knack of making friends and acquaintances. These are the Connectors."

Expand Your Skills

The perspective that working professionals in the meetings industry must continuously expand their skills is relatively new to the meeting management profession. Yet this is an essential building block for the future professional's success. As meeting managers strive to position themselves as experts in the creation of unique adult learning opportunities, they must become committed adult learners themselves—dedicated to the continuous pursuit of the latest knowledge, ideas, techniques, and strategies within their direct industry and outside it. The content of that new learning will continue to shift, but it certainly will include:

- A broader, more inclusive understanding of different languages and cultures
- A more welcoming approach to varied learning styles
- An understanding of the new and emerging facilitation techniques that are bringing the best of adult education into the meetings arena, including open space meetings
- A focus on the substance of every meeting, and on ways of capturing content as a strategic resource
- An ability and eagerness to adapt and improvise, to take advantage of learning opportunities as they arise through the process of managing a meeting

THE NEW NORMAL

"The future ain't what it used to be."

—*Yogi Berra*

A new career profile is emerging for meeting managers, and the transition will almost certainly require successful professionals to continually evaluate the value that they provide their organization throughout their working lives.

The industry's professional associations, sponsoring organizations, and meeting managers themselves are leading these changes. It is reflected in the growing number and sophistication of post-secondary programs in meeting and event management. It is mirrored in the way many event managers see and perform their own work, and in the level and quality of professional development they expect and demand at the local, regional, national, and international levels.

The end objective is as ambitious as it is essential. To set and attain new standards for professionalism, accountability, ethics, and strategic focus, thereby positioning meeting managers to:

- Organize better, more effective meetings with more lasting, measurable results.
- Earn the recognition and senior standing that go along with the results they produce for their organizations.

The transition is extremely timely. Organizations of all kinds are searching for ways to improve the products and services they deliver to their members, shareholders, and other stakeholders, including employees. Meetings are seen, quite rightly, as a part of the solution. For meeting managers, the "new normal" is defined by a set of demands that were unimaginable—and, quite likely, unattainable—in the recent past:

- *High stakes*—in an environment where time and resources will be taken away from events (or any other initiatives within an organization) that fail to deliver on their objectives
- *High expectations*—leading to a better understanding of measurement tools and their application to meetings and events
- *Increased use of technology*—creating opportunities for managers to streamline their events and challenging them to keep up with the latest innovations
- *A bottom-line focus*—with organizations paying closer attention to meeting expenditures and expecting more revenue at the end of the project

- *Shorter planning horizons*—requiring meeting managers to fall back on their own flexibility, resourcefulness, and peer networks to deliver solid results

These trends have emerged quickly. They are not, however, unique to the meeting management profession. Not too long ago, procurement officers were seen as purchasing agents, and human resource professionals were relegated to the role of payroll clerk. Practitioners in both of these occupational groups have transformed and elevated themselves to more senior, responsible positions in their organizations.

In meetings, there will always be a place for people who are interested in the purely logistical functions that once defined the profession. But those practitioners will quickly become the minority, and the job market of the future will almost certainly perceive and compensate them as junior to mid-level administrators.

The higher ground—and, by far, the more interesting and rewarding work—will belong to seasoned, committed meeting managers with the skills, experience, confidence, determination, and network of qualified colleagues to take charge of a major event and deliver a meaningful return on investment to *all* stakeholders. New standards for the "independent planner" will gradually extend beyond a principal focus on site selection to embrace the range and quality of advisory services that organizations expect from a trusted internal or external consultant.

Through the Convention Industry Council (www.conventionindustry.org), PCMA has joined with other industry associations to support the Accepted Practices Exchange (APEX), an initiative to define and put into practice many of the key functions on which a successful meeting depends. According to the Convention Industry Council web site:

> …accepted practices will make the industry more efficient, freeing up valuable time to devote collaborative energies to broader, more pressing industry issues. Can you imagine what you would do with more time to think creatively, less repetitive work to complete, and better relationships with your customers and suppliers?[4]

For many meeting managers, APEX is an opportunity wrapped in a challenge. The profession will be able to embrace a more thoughtful, strategic future only when it is fully in control of the front-line logistics that are essential to any event. By the same token, APEX creates new expectations for practitioners who are satisfied with a role that is purely tactical. APEX creates a further challenge, as well, by allowing anyone with Internet access and a modicum of English to provide the services of a logistician from afar. Outsourcing will continue, and may increase, in our industry. The future truly *is not* what it used to be, and the industry is challenging all its members to move forward to a more conceptual role.

Moreover, while APEX is an important and timely initiative, it may only be the first step. For the meeting manager of the future, success will be a matter of combining state-of-the-art industry knowledge with new insights from disciplines as diverse as adult education, demographics, nutrition, and emergency planning.

The Business of Meetings

The first wave of change in the North American meetings industry has focused largely on the business-related aspects of meetings and events. While many of these trends are being defined and tracked by managers who work in corporate settings, the same expectations are beginning to emerge in other sectors, and will soon be standard for managers and suppliers across the profession.

Here are some of the key emerging issues the industry has identified in recent years:

- *Procurement and strategic sourcing*—Competitive forces are requiring organizations to manage expenditures better and meetings have been identified as a major controllable expense. Meeting managers will be expected to track their event budgets more precisely, consolidate spending with a smaller number of preferred vendors, maximize the volume discounts and efficiencies that are built into a single, global contract, and make the case for value-added services that deliver better results—even if they cost more on paper.

- *ROI and measurement*—Beyond the "happy sheet" evaluations that ask questions about the temperature of the room and the taste of the coffee, meeting managers are learning to measure the results of every event against the objectives set by all of the stakeholders. Those objectives might come from participants, sponsors, exhibitors, speakers, senior management—or, most likely, all of the above. The most effective managers and suppliers are proficient at understanding the unique goals and objectives behind every meeting and event and measuring results accordingly.

- *Relationships that last*—The relationships that shape the meetings profession are often forged between buyers and sellers. The most successful of these relationships evolve into partnerships that extend far beyond a single project, a short-term promotion, or a quarterly sales report. As the industry and the profession continue to evolve, the best relationships will be based on an ever-deepening understanding of clients' needs and objectives. At that point, the actual sale is almost secondary—it is simply the logical end point of a professional dialogue about the services a client needs and the most effective way to deliver them.

- *Outsourcing*—In an increasingly global society, where access to the Internet is assured, English is the language of business, and costs must be kept to a minimum, the logistical jobs in the meetings industry will be those most easily outsourced. In *A Whole New Mind*, Daniel Pink states that "mastery of design, empathy, play and other seemingly 'soft' aptitudes is now the main way for individuals and firms to stand out in a crowded marketplace."[3] This will be the way for those in the meetings industry to stand out and move ahead.

- *Contingency planning and emergency preparedness*—The most experienced meeting managers conduct a risk assessment and develop a comprehensive emergency plan for every meeting and event which begins with site and vendor selection, extends to contracts, and culminates in actual site management. This practice is rapidly, and necessarily, becoming an industry norm. The best contingency and emergency plans address the factors a meeting manager can reasonably control, seek to anticipate, and prevent. For years, many meeting managers said that what they did was not "brain surgery." They have learned, some of them the hard way, that it is: The meeting manager's role in ensuring the safety and security of people, places, and assets is growing as we learn the consequences of a lack of preparedness.

- *Ethics in practice*—The advent in the United States of the Sarbanes-Oxley (SOX) law put ethics into law. The industry professional of today and the future will look at each transaction with an eye to what is right and what is ethical, understanding that long-term relationships and business will rely on what is done today for tomorrow.

The Heart of the Business

The associations that support and represent the meeting management profession are quite rightly challenging their members to shift focus from "the meetings business" to "the business of meetings." There is no doubt that tomorrow's meeting management professional will have to understand the issues and language that drive their organizations, whether they work for associations, corporations, government agencies, or a combination of all of them.

But meetings and events are fundamentally about knowledge and learning. Meeting managers will deprive their organizations of an essential resource—and lose the heart and soul of the industry—if they fail to maximize the adult education opportunities built into every conference, and into every opportunity that they have, as individuals and as a profession. The character of those opportunities will vary widely. That is all the more reason to embrace the full range of skills and resources that can help them deliver a more powerful educational experience, targeting the full range of adult learning styles and resources.

The front lines of that effort are constantly shifting. Here are some of the elements that savvy meeting managers must keep in mind.

- *Site selection and session design for learning*—The design of a session agenda, the degree and sequencing of audience participation, the opportunity for discussion in small breakout groups or table groups, the availability of unconventional learning tools, the set-up of the meeting room, the decision to hold an educational session outside a formal meeting space, and the atmosphere in which the learning takes place: these are all elements of a learner-centered approach to education. Adult educators have assembled a wealth of knowledge on the learning styles, experiences, needs, and limitations that learners bring into a conference session. These insights have the potential to change our assumptions, rewrite our logistics, and transform our events. Tomorrow's best meeting managers will position themselves as knowledge and learning specialists, while retaining the ability to organize and supply an event that any adult educator would find stimulating.

- *Content and delivery that make a difference*—The best educational sessions stand or fall on the quality of their content and the format of the delivery. For the meeting managers of the future, a focus on strategic outcomes will extend to the mix of learning delivery methods, including the balance between learning facilitators and more formal lectures. The "right" answer will almost certainly change from one meeting to the next; it will invariably mean delivering content in the format, style, and level of detail that reflect participants' learning objectives and needs.

- *So many ways to meet*—Beginning in 1983, there was a sense that learning would happen using new technologies—in that era, that meant teleconferencing. Since 2001, we have seen a rapid increase in the use of teleconferences, videoconferences, online discussions, and a variety of other e-learning/virtual alternatives to face-to-face meetings. Despite dire predictions in the early years of the new century, the demise of face-to-face (F2F) meetings has been exaggerated. In some cases, virtual meetings save time and money and may be effective as delivery and collaboration tools. In others, they may enhance F2F meetings. To date, there is no method that replaces the higher impact of face-to-face contact, or the informal networking and peer-to-peer learning opportunities that go with a live event. By becoming familiar with all the new ways to meet, meeting managers can position themselves as in-house or external consultants on the best options for achieving a given set of objectives for an event.

- *Greener learning environments*—There is no shortage of good reasons to locate events at green meeting facilities. It makes sound business sense to align the profession with the future of the planet, using the convening power of the global meetings industry to help point the way to a more environmentally sustainable future. The bottom line for adult learners is that a well-designed green facility is a more comfortable learning environment, featuring bright, natural light and better air circulation than its conventional counterpart. As green facilities gradually become the norm, educational outcomes are sure to benefit. As the meetings industry moves toward wanting to help sustain the planet, managers can "green" their meetings inside and outside green facilities by adopting smart practices as simple as recycling materials and printing on both sides of a page.

- *Changing demographics*—In a global society, with more generations in the workplace than ever before, meetings must be geared to, and meeting managers must be savvy about, the needs of people of different races, religions, nationalities, genders and transgenders, sexual orientation, abilities, ages, and other differences. To plan a meeting, or to host a meeting in one's facility, it is crucial to know the makeup of the group and plan for participants' unique needs.

SUMMARY

The meetings industry, which has been for a very long time is in the midst of an exciting transition. Current meeting managers are adapting to these changes while working to fulfill today's expectations. Professional and academic organizations that support the industry are creating the structure and educational content that will help shape tomorrow's reality.

No longer will the viewpoint of the meeting manager as a purely tactical position be common. More and more organizations are beginning to recognize their in-house or contract meeting managers as full-fledged professionals, with access to an established body of knowledge and a tested network of colleagues and supplier partners. The meeting manager of the future will be seen as part adult educator, part creative consultant, and part orchestra conductor for an ever-widening range of specialty services that bring a meeting to life.

REFERENCES

1. Buckingham, M. & Clifton, D. (2001). *Now, discover your strengths*. New York: Free Press.

2. Gladwell, M. (2000). *The tipping point*. Boston, MA: Little, Brown and Co.

3. Pink, D. (2005). *A whole new mind: Moving from the information age to the conceptual age*. New York: Penguin.

4. APEX Initiative. Convention Industry Council. Retrieved March, 27, 2006 from http://www.conventionindustry.org/apex/apex.htm.

KEY TERMS

Accepted Practices Exchange (APEX)	Face-to-face meeting (F2F)	High concept
Connector	Green meeting facility	High touch
		Subject matter expert (SME)

COMPELLING QUESTIONS FOR CONSIDERATION

1. What will the industry look like in five years? 10 years? 20 years?

2. Who will attend meetings?

3. In what way will facilities support learning?

4. What global issues will impact meetings and those who attend them?

5. If meetings are no longer relevant, what skills will you have that are transferable?

6. How will you adapt to changes in society?

RESOURCES

The resources identified in this appendix represent author suggestion to obtain further information. Not all authors provided additional reference materials.

CHAPTER 2

Convention Industry Council, Accepted Practices Exchange (APEX). (n.d.). Retrieved April 27, 2006 from http://www.conventionindustry.org/apex/apex.htm

Phillips, J. J. (1997). *Handbook of training and evaluation and measurement methods* (3rd ed.). Houston, TX: Gulf Publishing.

Phillips, J. J., & Phillips, P. P. (2005). *Return on investment (ROI) basics*. Washington, DC: ASTD Press.

Phillips, J. J., & Phillips, P. P. (2005). *ROI at work: Best-practice case studies from the real world*. Washington, DC: ASTD Press.

Phillips, J. J., & Stone, R. D. (2002) *How to measure training results: A practical guide to tracking the six key indicators*. New York, NY: McGraw-Hill.

Phillips, J. J. (2003). *Return on investment in training and performance improvement programs* (2nd ed.). Burlington, MA: Butterworth-Heinemann.

Phillips, P. P. (2002). *The bottomline on ROI*. Atlanta, GA: CEP Press.

CHAPTER 3

Corbin Ball Associates, used courtesy of James Spellos, MeetingU. (n.d.). *Attrition data*. Retrieved April 27, 2006 from http://www.corbinball.com/assets/forms/xl-attrition.xls

Corbin Ball Associates. (n.d.). *Catering estimate worksheet*. Retrieved April 27, 2006 from http://www.corbinball.com/assets/forms/xl-catering.xls

Corbin Ball Associates. (n.d.). *Meeting expense worksheet*. Retrieved April 27, 2006 from http://www.corbinball.com/assets/forms/xl-budgetconsolidation.xls

Corbin Ball Associates. (n.d.). *Budget worksheet*. Retrieved April 27, 2006 from http://www.eventageous.com/planning_guides/budgetcalc.htm

CHAPTER 7

Books

Weiss, A. (2005). *Million dollar consulting: The professional's guide to growing a practice*. New York, NY : McGraw-Hill Corporation.

Weiss, A. (2002). *Value-based fees: How to charge—and get—what you're worth*. San Francisco: Jossey-Bass/Pfeiffer.

The Internet

Small Business Administration. (n.d.). Retrieved April 27, 2006 from http://www.sba.gov/

Internet Search Terms

"Independent contractor" • "Independent consultant"

CHAPTER 8

Mina, E. (2000). *The complete handbook of business meetings*. New York: American Management Association.

International Association of Conference Centers. (n.d.). Retrieved April 28, 2006 from http://www.iacconline.org/

CHAPTER 9

Books

Little, H. (1999). *Volunteers—How to get them, how to keep them: An essential guide for volunteer leaders and staff of professional, trade and charitable nonprofit organizations.* Naperville, IL: Paneca Press.

Ellis, S.J. (1996). *From the top down: The executive role in volunteer program success.* Revised edition. Philadelphia: Energize Books.

Campbell, K.N., & Ellis, S.J. (1995). *The (HELP!) I-don't-have-enough-time guide to volunteer management.* Philadelphia: Energize Books.

Conners, T.D. (1995). *The volunteer management handbook.* New York: John Wiley & Sons.

Kuric, C., & Koll, S. (2000). *A roadmap to managing volunteer systems — From grassroots to national.* Washington, DC: National Health Council.

Lynch, R., & McCurley, S. (1998). *Essential volunteer management* (2nd ed.). Downers Grove, IL: Heritage Arts Press.

Scheier, I. (1993). *Building staff/volunteer relations.* Philadelphia: Energize Books.

Vineyard, S., & McCurley, S. (2001). *Best practices for volunteer programs.* Downers Grove, IL: Heritage Arts.

Web Sites

Energize Inc. (n.d.). Retrieved on April 27, 2006 from www.energizeinc.com

e-Volunteerism: The Electronic Journal of the Volunteer Community. (n.d.). Retrieved April 27, 2006 from http://www.e-volunteerism.com/

Volunteer Today: The Electronic Gazette for Volunteerism. (n.d.). Retrieved April 27, 2006 from http://www.volunteertoday.com/

CHAPTER 16

Convention Industry Council (CIC). (n.d.). Retrieved April 27, 2006 from http://www.conventionindustry.org/

Destination Marketing Association International (DMAI). (n.d.). Retrieved April 27, 2006 from http://www.destinationmarketing.org/

International Association of Professional Conference Organisers (IAPCO). (n.d.). Retrieved April 27, 2006 from http://www.iapco.org/

International Congress and Convention Association (ICCA). (n.d.). Retrieved April 27, 2006 from http://www.congresscity.com/

International Association of Congress Centers. (n.d.). Retrieved April 27, 2006 from http://www.aipc.org/

US State Department. Visa requirements and travel warnings (n.d.). Retrieved April 27, 2006 from http://www.state.gov/

Centers for Disease Control. International traveler information. (n.d.). Retrieved April 27, 2006 from http://www.cdc.gov/

International currency converter. (n.d.). Retrieved April 27, 2006 from http://www.xe.com/

Computer translation (free). (n.d.). Retrieved April 27, 2006 from http://www.altavista.com/

International times and dates. (n.d.). Retrieved April 28, 2006 from http://www.timeanddate.com/

The Weather Channel, International Weather. (n.d.). Retrieved April 27, 2006 from http://www.weather.com/

CultureGrams, 4-page briefings on greetings, dining, courtesies, gestures, lifestyles, and attitudes of a nation's people; available for 175 countries, updated annually. (n.d.). Retrieved April 27, 2006 from http://www.culturgrams.com/

MeetingsNet. (n.d.). *2005 Beyond Borders Resource Guide.* Retrieved April 27, 2006 http://meetingsnet.com/international/meetings_beyond_borders_resource_4/

CHAPTER 23

Web Sites

Professional Convention Management Association, PCMA Space Verification Program. (n.d.). Retrieved April 27, 2006 from http://www.pcma.org/resources/industry/space-verification/default.asp

MeetingMatrix International. (n.d.). Retrieved April 27, 2006 from http://www.meetingmatrix.com/

Newmarket's Delphi Diagrams. (n.d.). Retrieved April 27, 2006 from http://www.newmarketinc.com/products/diagrams.html

Hilton Hotels, Space Design Software. (n.d.). Retrieved April 27, 2006 from http://www.optimumsettings.com/hhc.html

Vivien, 3D Space Rendering Software. (n.d.). Retrieved April 27, 2006 from http://www.cast-soft.com/cast/software/home.jsp

Timesaver Software, Room Viewer. (n.d.). Retrieved April 27, 2006 from http://www.timesaverssoftware.com

Generic Room Capacity Calculator. (n.d.). Retrieved April 27, 2006 from http://www.webcalc.net/calc/0449.php

CHAPTER 26

Online Resources

BizBash. (n.d.). Retrieved April 27, 2006 from http://www.bizbash.com/

National Association of Catering Executives. (n.d.). Retrieved April 27, 2006 from http://www.nace.net/

International Special Events Society. (n.d.). Retrieved April 27, 2006 from http://www.ises.com/

Special Events Magazine. (n.d.). Retrieved April 27, 2006 from http://www.specialevents.com/

Event Solutions Magazine. (n.d.). Retrieved April 27, 2006 from http://www.event-solutions.com/

Floral Directory. (n.d.). Retrieved April 28, 2006 from http://www.hlla.com/reference/floral/floral gloss1.html

Food Network. (n.d.). Retrieved April 27, 2006 from http://www.foodtv.com/

Epicurious. (n.d.). Retrieved April 27, 2006 from http://www.epicurious.com/

The Wine Lovers Page, Wine Lexicon, Wine Label Decoder and Food and Wine Matching Engine. (n.d.). Retrieved April 27, 2006 from http://www.wine-lovers-page.com/.

Diabetic Gourmet. (n.d.). Retrieved April 27, 2006 from http://diabeticgourmet.com/

GourmetSpot, Newspaper Food Sections. (n.d.). Retrieved April 27, 2006 from http://www.gourmetspot.com/newspapers.htm

GourmetSpot, Food Magazines. (n.d.). Retrieved April 27, 2006 from http://www.gourmetspot.com/magazines.htm

CHAPTER 28

Lynch, D. (1960). *The image of the city.* Cambridge, MA: The MIT Press.

Symonds North America Inc. (n.d.) Retrieved November 28, 2005, from http://www.symondsna.com/crowd-dynamics.htm

Hoffman, P. Usability Interface, Accommodating Color Blindness. Retrieved December 12, 2006 from http://www.stcsig.org/usability/newsletter/9910-color-blindness.html. Reprinted from *Usability Interface*, Vol 6, No. 2, October 1999. Verified April 27, 2006.

Causes of Vision Impairment. (1978). Estimates reported from National Society to Prevent Blindness, 1980. Retrieved December 12, 2005 from http://www.visionconnection.org/Content/Research/EpidemiologyandStatistics/ Statistics/CausesofVisionImpairment/default.htm?cookie%5Ftest=1#cat

CHAPTER 30
Web Sites

America's Second Harvest. (n.d.). Retrieved April 27, 2006 from http://www.secondharvest.org/

BlueGreen Meetings. (n.d.). Retrieved April 27, 2006 from http://www.bluegreenmeetings.org/
This is a good basic green meeting web site for planners and suppliers.

Blue Ocean Institute. (n.d.). Retrieved April 27, 2006 from http://www.blueoceaninstitute.org
This site provides a mini-guide for environmentally responsible seafood choices.

Ceres Green Hotel Initiative. (n.d.). Retrieved April 27, 2006 from http://www.ceres.org/pub/publication.php?pid=61
This site offers tools to assist planners in selecting a green hotel.

Chef's Collaborative. (n.d.). Retrieved April 27, 2006 from http://www.chefscollaborative.org/
This web site is for a national network of more than 1,000 members of the food community who promote sustainable cuisine.

Climate Trust. (n.d.). Retrieved April 27, 2006 from http://www.carboncounter.org/
This organization offers an online carbon-offset calculator.

Convention Industry Council. (n.d.). Retrieved April 27, 2006 from http://www.conventionindustry.org/projects/green_meetings_report.pdf
The Convention Industry Council (CIC) is an organization of over 30 members that facilitates the exchange of information and develops programs to promote professionalism within the industry and educate the public. Green guidelines provided on Web site.

Consumers Union. (n.d.). Retrieved April 27, 2006 from http://www.eco-labels.org/home.cfm
Consumers Union, publishers of Consumer Reports, *has a Web guide to environmental labels.*

EcoLogical Solutions, Inc. (n.d.). Retrieved April 27, 2006 from http://www.ecological-solutions.net/
This group assists hotels with economic and environmental savings.

Give instead of take – The Socially Responsible Incentive Initiative. c/o Diltheystrasse 48, 41239 Mönchengladbach, Germany, info@give-instead-of-take.com, http://www.give-instead-of-take.com

Gifts in Kind. (n.d.). Retrieved April 27, 2006 from http://www.giftsinkind.org/
The network provides a conduit for products to be given to charity and is one of the most cost-effective charities in the world.

Green Globe 21. (n.d.). Retrieved April 27, 2006 from http://www.greenglobe21.com/
A worldwide benchmarking and certification program which facilitates sustainable travel and tourism for consumers, companies and communities.

Green Meeting Industry Council. (n.d.). Retrieved April 27, 2006 from http://www.greenmeetings.info/
The Council is dedicated to promoting environmentally responsible practices within the meetings industry.

Green Seal, Green Seal Certification Program. (n.d.). Retrieved April 27, 2006 from http://www.greenseal.org/greeninglodge.htm

Habitat for Humanity. (n.d.). Retrieved April 27, 2006 from
http://www.habitatforhumanity.org/
This organization is dedicated to providing shelter for needy families. They appreciate donations of building materials from trade shows as well as service projects.

Husbandry Institute. (n.d.). Retrieved April 27, 2006 from
http://www.husbandryinstitute.org/
The Institute is a nonprofit creating consumer demand for and developing farm networks to provide livestock raised humanely by family farmers, on land managed in an environmentally responsible way.

Leonardo Academy. (n.d.). Retrieved April 27, 2006 from
http://www.leonardoacademy.org/
This web site offers a Cleaner and Greener Event Certification to offset greenhouse gas emissions.

Meeting Strategies Worldwide. (n.d.). Retrieved April 27, 2006 from
http://www.meetingstrategiesworldwide.com/
Case studies of environmentally responsible conferences available here.

Oceans Alive. (n.d.). *Seafood Selector*. Retrieved April 27, 2006 from
http://www.oceansalive.org/eat.cfm
Oceans Alive is part of the nonprofit Environmental Defense. The Web site includes what it calls the "Eco-Best" and "Eco-Worst" fish, as well as this downloadable, pocket-sized "Seafood Selector."

Professional Convention Management Association (PCMA). Information about the Bill Emerson Good Samaritan Food Donation Act. (n.d.). Retrieved April 27, 2006 from http://www.pcma.org/source/community/network/usa/how/billemerson.asp

The Programmes of Purpose Award recognizes outstanding programs which demonstrate an effort to benefit a charitable cause. Louise Hall Reider, CITEE. lhr@lhrco.com.

Terra Choice Environmental Services, Inc. (n.d.). Retrieved April 28, 2006 from
http://www.terrachoice.ca
This organization is dedicated to working with the marketplace to improve the environment by assisting organizations in turning their environmental challenges into opportunities.

U.S. Dept. of Agriculture, The National Organic Program. (n.d.). Retrieved April 28, 2006 from http://www.ams.usda.gov/nop/indexIE.htm

U.S. Dept. of Agriculture. (n.d.). *Food recovery and gleaning initiative*. Retrieved April 28, 2006 from http://www.usda.gov/news/pubs/gleaning/content.htm
This is a comprehensive guide to food donation laws, including links to state Good Samaritan Laws and resource lists and information on food recovery.

U.S. Environmental Protection Agency. (n.d.). *Comprehensive manual on greening meetings.* Retrieved April 28, 2006 from http://www.epa.gov/oppt/greenmeetings/

World Centric – Fair Trade and Eco Store.Online. (n.d.) Retrieved April 27, 2006 from http://www.worldcentric.org/store/index.htm
This is an online store with several serviceware products that are biodegradable and compostable.

CHAPTER 38
Web Sites

The American Society of Composers, Authors and Publishers. (n.d.). Retrieved April 27, 2006 from http://www.ascap.com

BMI. (n.d.). Retrieved April 27, 2006 from http://www.bmi.com

SESAC. (n.d.). Retrieved April 27, 2006 from http://sesac.com

Convention Industry Council. (n.d.). Retrieved April 27, 2006 from http://www.conventionindustry.org

CHAPTER 40

Web Sites

For research on an organization:

Hoovers. (n.d.). Retrieved April 27, 2006 from http://www.hoovers.com

Yahoo! Finance. (n.d.). Retrieved April 28, 2006 from http://finance.yahoo.com

Destination Marketing Association International. (n.d.). Retrieved April 27, 2006 from http://www.dmai.org

Sites about negotiations and/or conflict management:

Beyond Intractability. (n.d.). Retrieved April 27, 2006 from http://www.beyondintractability.org

Technology Meetings. (n.d.). Retrieved April 27, 2006 from http://technologymeetings.com/ar/meetings_convention_center_negotiations

The Regents of the University of California Agricultural Issues Center. (2001). *Conflict Management Resolution*. Retrieved April 27, 2006 from http://www.cnr.berkeley.edu/ucce50/ag-labor/7labor/13.htm

International Association for Conflict Management. (n.d.). Retrieved April 27, 2006 from http://www.iacm-conflict.org

CHAPTER 42

Convention Industry Council, Accepted Practices Exchange (APEX). (n.d.). Retrieved April 27, 2006 from http://www.conventionindustry.org/apex/apex.htm

Ball, C. (n.d.). *Application service providers (ASPs) – 88 key questions to ask before you buy*. Retrieved April 27, 2006 from http://www.corbinball.com/articles/art-ASP.htm

Meetings Industry Forum. (n.d.). Retrieved on April 26, 2006 from www.mim.com

Mpoint. (n.d.). Retrieved April 27, 2006 from www.mpoint.com

Global Meetings Industry Portal. (n.d.). Retrieved April 26, 2006 from http://www.conworld.net

Trade Show News Network—The Ultimate Trade Show Directory. (n.d.). Retrieved April 27, 2006 from www.tsnn.com

Meetings Industry Megasite. (n.d.). Retrieved April 27, 2006 from http://www.mimegasite.com

CHAPTER 45

Popular Internet Survey Providers

SurveyMonkey.com. (n.d.). Retrieved April 27, 2006 from www.surveymonkey.com

Zoomerang. (n.d.). Retrieved April 27, 2006 from info.zoomerang.com

See Chapter 2 citations for additional resources.

CHAPTER 46

See Chapter 2 citations for additional resources.

Appendix B

ABOUT THE EDITORS

EXECUTIVE EDITOR
Glen C. Ramsborg, PhD

Dr. Ramsborg is Senior Director, Education at the Professional Convention Management Association and has been a member for over 20 years. He has been a frequent author for PCMA's *Convene* magazine, authored the book titled, *Objectives to Outcomes: Your Contract with the Learner,* and wrote the introductory chapter to *Professional Meeting Management,* 3rd edition. He has served on PCMA's education and *Convene* editorial advisory committees. Dr. Ramsborg received the MPI-CAC President's Award in 1990 and PCMA's Educator of the Year Award in 2002. Dr. Ramsborg is a certified registered nurse anesthetist, is prepared at the master's level in curriculum and instruction and at the doctorate level in education policy and administration. He is a retired colonel from the United States Air Force.

LEAD EDITOR
Brian Miller, EdD

Dr. Miller is Assistant Professor of Hospitality Informational Technology at the University of Delaware. Dr. Miller holds a doctorate degree from the University of Massachusetts, Amherst in Curriculum Development where his dissertation was "Technology and Learning in the Undergraduate Classroom." Published research articles include the use of technology to increase student learning and satisfaction, students' perceptions of the use of simulations in the classroom, building e-loyalty with lodging brand web sites, and the effects of tipping on employee organizational and occupational commitment. His research has been presented at academic and industry conferences in the United States, Europe, Jamaica, and the Middle East. Dr. Miller served as the chair of the Core Competencies Task Force for PCMA and received PCMA's Educator of the Year award in 2005.

CONTENT EDITORS

Deborah Breiter, PhD

Dr. Breiter is the Department Chair for Tourism, Events, and Attractions at the Rosen College of Hospitality Management at the University of Central Florida in Orlando. She also holds an endowed position in Convention and Conference Management. She teaches convention management and trade show management. Her research has covered topics such as exhibitors' and attendees' perceptions of convention centers, attrition, and attendees' motivations for attending trade shows. She recently spearheaded the introduction of the first Bachelor of Science in Event Management in the United States. Dr. Breiter has been an active member of PCMA since 1998 and advises the student chapter at the Rosen College.

B. J. Reed, EdD, APR, CMP

Dr. Reed has held various positions in the meetings industry. She spent several years as an association meeting planner, then moved to the supply side as the executive director for a convention and visitors bureau. Five years later, she moved back to the meeting management arena as an independent planner. Through all of these positions, Dr. Reed was intent on teaching in the industry and completed four degrees in related fields. She joined PCMA in 1987 and earned her CMP in 1991. She began teaching full time in 1997. Currently, she teaches public relations and communication courses to undergraduate and graduate students at the University of Wisconsin-Platteville.

Amanda Rushing, CMP

Ms. Rushing is Director, Conferences and Meeting Services at the American Society of Civil Engineers in Reston, Virginia. Ms. Rushing has over 18 years of association management experience and has almost ten years as a full-time meeting manager and received her CMP in 1998. Ms. Rushing has published industry-related articles, and frequently speaks at industry events. She is an active PCMA volunteer, serving on numerous committees at the local and national levels; and, currently she serves as a PCMA Capital Chapter Board Member. She is a PCMA CMP study course facilitator and is the lead facilitator and instructor for teaching the CMP curriculum at the Capital Chapter CMP Study Weekends.

MEETING MANAGEMENT BY THE BOOK

Professional Meeting Management Turns 20

Sara Torrence, CMP
PRESIDENT, SARA TORRENCE AND ASSOCIATES
CONTRIBUTING EDITOR, *CONVENE*

Professional Convention Management Association (PCMA) celebrates yet another anniversary along with its 50th annual meeting. Professional Meeting Management (PMM), the venerable text that has become a standard in the meetings industry, was first published 20 years ago by PCMA. In many ways, the evolution of the book—from the first edition published in 1985, to the 5th edition, scheduled to be published in mid-2006—parallels that of the meetings industry, and of PCMA as an organization, casting light on the changes and growth in the industry during the past 20 years.

FIRST EDITION, 1985

All children must have a mother to bring them into the world. So it was with *PMM*; that "mother" was Barbara Nichols, at the time the director of meetings for the Federation of American Societies of Experimental Biology (FASEB). An active PCMA volunteer, Nichols sat on the education committee. "The Education Foundation was being formed, and the committee members were discussing what we could do to contribute to education in the meetings industry. There were no formal college or university courses at the time for meeting managers. So, I suggested a 'how-to' book, since I was writing a 'how-to' column for *Meeting News* at the time," she remembered.

Nichols prepared an outline for the committee's consideration, based on the steps meeting managers must take to organize a meeting. She and the committee subsequently selected writers for each of the chapters, based on their knowledge in the subject(s) covered.

In the middle of the production, Nichols moved to the American College of Cardiology (ACC) as director of meeting services. "Both FASEB and ACC were very supportive of my involvement. When I said I couldn't possibly take on the enormous task of editing this book without a personal computer, the ACC executive director, William Nelligan, got me one. Can you believe I was the only person to have a PC on my desk at the time?" she exclaimed. "Back then, the authors of each chapter were their own reviewers. There were no photos in the first printing," she recalled. However, the book proved to be a blockbuster in the industry, and became required reading for the newly initiated Certified Meeting Professional (CMP) examination.

SECOND EDITION, 1989

The second edition built on the strengths of the first edition. However, Nichols worked hard to edit it so that the chapters read "with one voice," she recalled. "Peter Shure, for whom I had written at *Meeting News,* taught me how to write in a more positive voice. Therefore, I used this knowledge to the advantage of PMM," she said. (Shure later became editor-in-chief and associate publisher of *Convene.*) "We also added photos and pen drawings to make the book more visually attractive," she recalled. And, important to the budding meetings industry classrooms, the book was published as a paperback, so that it could be more affordable for students. "We also made the text cleaner, with bullet points, and checklists. This improved its usefulness to the readers," Nichols said.

She recalled Roy Evans, CAE, PCMA's executive vice president at the time, as being "really visionary about the book. He could see the book's effectiveness in growing the organization—PCMA and the Education Foundation."

THIRD EDITION, 1996

By the time the third edition was published, PCMA student chapters had been established, and meetings management was an ever-growing curriculum in colleges and universities. "The driving force for the third edition was to design a resource that could be used more successfully as a textbook," said Ed Polivka, the third edition's editor, who was senior vice president of PCMA at the time of publication. "There were more colleges that were offering meeting management courses than there were campuses with PCMA student chapters. We were responding to a faculty need," he said. Polivka had himself been a college instructor and had offered one of the earliest meeting management courses at Northeastern State University in Oklahoma.

The book began with a chapter on the adult learner, authored by Glen Ramsborg, Ph.D. (who is currently senior director of education at PCMA and executive editor of the upcoming fifth edition). It is a subject that was being emphasized in meeting management education at the time. "Did you know that more adults *learn* at educational sessions of meetings than on college and university campuses?" Polivka pointed out. The volume was published in soft cover, again to make it affordable to students at a lower price.

"All chapters were reviewed carefully to make the volume relevant to state-of-the-art meeting management. We wanted a book that was as current as possible," Polivka remembered. There were hundreds of reviewers and authors, representing every aspect of the meetings industry. "Virtually every chapter was rewritten in some way," Polivka said. "Each chapter began with objectives, or expected reader outcomes, and ended with key terms and discussion questions. Endnotes, citing references, were also added," he said. This edition included an easy-to-use index and glossary for the first time.

In addition, Polivka acknowledged the importance of technology, and the changes it had brought to meeting management, as well as the growth of the profession. This was the first edition that focused on "modern meeting issues" such as technology, green meetings, and the meeting manager profession.

Polivka is quick to point out that this edition could not have been accomplished without Curtis Love, Ph.D., PCMA director of education at the time. "It was *his* baby," he said.

FOURTH EDITION, 2002

Technology and its effect on the meetings industry was once again a reason for the publication of the fourth edition of *PMM*. Technology had changed rapidly. Cell phones had become commonplace and electronic mail (e-mail), which had once been used mostly for internal office correspondence, was transforming the way the industry communicated. "I think the association sector used e-mail first, and the hotels followed," remembered Barbara Connell, CAE, CMP, executive editor of the fourth edition, and PCMA's executive director of the PCMA foundation and senior vice president of education at the time.

Connell said the next consideration was to take into account the "thought changes in the legal aspects of the industry." Representatives of meeting facilities became more realistic in their attitude about legal contracts, realizing that planners had issues, too. "Reciprocity was making contracts more even-handed—not just benefiting the facility. Hoteliers were beginning to consult with planners if they needed to change meeting space assignments. Planners and suppliers alike were working more as a team," Connell added.

The third driving force was the growing realization of the impact disasters and disturbances could have on meetings. "Planners and facility managers were coming to the realization of what meetings meant to the bottom line of their organizations. They were also starting to feel that they were *personally* responsible for the meeting's outcome. The position of meeting manager within the organization had assumed a higher level of responsibility—actually upper management—and was more integrated into the fabric of the association from a global perspective, both fiscally and operationally. CEOs began to understand the importance of the meeting professional as an integral part of the management team of the association."

The tragedy of September 11, 2001 made an emphasis on emergency preparedness all the more important, "but the subject was already in the pipeline," Connell said. "In the fourth edition we had already addressed bomb threats and terrorist activity [before September 11, 2001 took place]. But we also covered medical emergencies, demonstrations and confrontations, weather and fire emergencies, as well as strikes, work stoppages and shortages."

The production of *PMM* also changed. PCMA hired professional editors to work on the fourth edition. "At first, the editors and I reviewed the third edition and they made recommendations for formatting, and moving various subjects, such as audiovisual technology, to other chapters," Connell said. (For example, AV was moved to the learning environment chapter.) "We also involved the meetings industry as a whole," she said. If the editors could find the original author(s) of a chapter, it was sent to that author and at least three other meeting professionals for review. "No one knew who else was looking at a chapter," she emphasized. They also looked outside of the "usual suspects," including business, legal, and technical experts as authors and reviewers.

FIFTH EDITION, 2006

"The minute the fifth edition is published, it will probably be outdated, because of technology and the number of changes occurring daily in our industry," observed Ramsborg. "However, we will have a text that is as cutting-edge as possible," he added. To determine content, e-mail surveys were sent to the entire membership and an outside faculty list.

The Accepted Practices Exchange (APEX)-accepted practices, an initiative of the Convention Industry Council (CIC), will be integrated into each chapter as appropriate. The CIC APEX glossary will be used for all key terms. The role of convention service managers will be included throughout chapters where relevant, emphasizing how they contribute to the success of a meeting. Independent meeting managers and other third parties will also be featured. Additional chapters will cover many of the issues that face meeting planners in today's world, such as room block management, sponsorships, procurement, security, and risk management. Convention centers will be featured in a separate chapter. Recognizing the changing face of conference audiences, content will also focus on multigenerational and multicultural issues, and international protocol, i.e., when dealing with other cultures, will also be featured.

The book will feature photographs, graphs, and charts, to make it visually attractive. Each chapter will end with a bulleted, easy-to-read summary, thought-provoking questions for further consideration, simple facts related to the content area, and references. An important addition will be a "put it into practice" section for each chapter, which will offer case studies or best practices from real-life experiences. There will also be a "put it into perspective" feature that will outline how practices might vary for the association, corporate, government, or independent planner. The author (and co-author) of each chapter will be acknowledged in that chapter.

In direct response to requests from professors and instructors, faculty and student guides will be created as companion resources to the textbook, for use in colleges and universities as well as additional resources for industry certified programs. "Faculty overwhelmingly wanted these aides, and we listened," Ramsborg said.

More than 90 industry representatives—at least four per chapter—have reviewed the fourth edition and provided feedback on the greatest strengths and weaknesses of each chapter and the overall content. They have also addressed the topics covered and organization, the writing style, the approach to a topic, the accuracy and currency of the material, and if applications are appropriate in today's world. This feedback is intended to guide authors as they revise, rewrite, or update each chapter.

"We have changed this edition to be responsive to meeting professionals' concerns in this ever changing world. We realize a printed volume cannot be as up-to-date as today's news. However, by surveying the industry, and responding to industry concerns, we hope to have a book that will have a shelf life of at least 3 years," Ramsborg said.

This article appeared in the December 2005 issue of *Convene*. Reprinted with permission of *Convene*, the magazine of the Professional Convention Management Association. ©2005. www.pcma.org

PAST CONTRIBUTORS

The following individuals have contributed to previous editions of *Professional Meeting Management*. Some served as authors, others as reviewers, while others had a part in the production aspect of the book. To each and everyone, we owe a debt of gratitude. (Editor's note: There is always a risk when listing names that someone was unintentionally overlooked. If this has happened, it is with a sincere apology.)

Holly R. Albert—3
James E. Anderson—3, 4
William T. Applegate—1
Pat Apter—3
Lea Arbesu—3
Janet Astner—3
April Autrey—3
Debra A. Bachman-Zabloudil—4
Kimberly Casper Baker—3, 4
Corbin Ball—4
Dana Barnett—3
Mike Barns—1, 2
Jerry M. Barshop—1, 2
Earl J. Bauer—1, 2
Eric J. Bean—1, 2
Ellen J. Beckert—1, 2
Sue Beggs—3
Laurie Behncke—3, 4
Deborah Bender—3
Renèe Bentel—3
Vicky A. Betzig—3, 4
Lisa Block—3
Kaye K. Boyer—4
Pam Boyles—3
Janet Brackett—3
James L. Breeling—1, 2
Ruthann Brettell—3
Bruce Brennan—1, 2
Warren Breaux—3
Nancy Brewer—3
Catherine A. Brown—3
Harold W. Brunn—1
Kathleen D. Bryan—1, 2
Wendy Buhrley—3
Julie F. Burford—3
Karen K. Burke—1, 2
Kathleen M. Butcosk—3
Francine Butler—1, 2, 3
Mac F. Cahal—1, 2
Karlotta Caldwell—3
Kathleen K. Callendar—4
Barbara Campbell—3
David O. Campbell—1, 2

Jerry J. Campbell—1, 2
Linda Campbell—1, 2
Delia M. Chang—3
Margaret Channel—2
Cathy Chatfield-Taylor—4
Wade Childress—3
Karen Lewis Clarke—3
Bradford W. Claxton—1, 2
Diane Claytor—1, 2
Judith A. Collier-Reid—4
Martha C. Collins—4
Barbara Connell—3, 4
H. Conway—1, 2
John Conway—1, 2
Bonnie L. Cunningham—3
Karen Cuviello—4
James R. Daggett—3, 4
Peggy Daidakis—3
Diane Dale—1, 2
Darline D. Daley—3
Larry Darlington—1, 2
Amy Davis—1
Sharon D. DelaBarre—4
Trisha Delozier—3
Dennis Denkeler—1, 2
Ted Deutsch—1, 2
Ted de Werd—1, 2
Jim Dillbeck—3
Maryalice Ditzler—1, 2
Richard L. Dobson—1
James S. Dolph—3
Colleen M. Donohoe—4
Robert J. Donovan—3
Cheryl A. Doss—3
Penny C. Dotson—3
Dawn Dreyer—3
Sandy Driscoll—1, 2
Theodore G. Driscoll, Jr.—1, 2
David A. DuBois—3
Douglas L. Ducate—3
Barbara Dunlavey—4
Jack Edelman—3
Roxanne Edsall—2

Joan L. Eisenstodt—3
Robert E. Elam—3
Nancy L. Elder—4
Mark W. Erickson—1, 2
David R. Evans—1
Roy B. Evans, Jr.—1, 2, 3
Tom Fallon—3
James A. Fausel—3
Susan G. Feingold—1, 2
Michele S. Fetsko—4
Laurie Fitzgerald—4
Carol Fojtik—3
John Folks—4
John S. Foster—4
Cindy Fowler—1, 2
Kelly M. Fox—4
Frank Fredericks—3
Barbara A. Freel—1, 2
Debra G. Friedman—3
Walter E. Galanty, Jr.—3
Richard Gartrell—1, 2
Paul G. Gebhard—1, 2
Thomas J. Gillen—1, 2
Brian J. Glasgow—4
Margaret Glos—1, 2
Ruth M. Glynn—4
Marisa W. Goldberg—4
Nolan I. Goldsmith—3
Geri P. Goodenough—1, 2
Edward T. Goodman, Jr.—1, 2
Pamela Graham—4
Anetha Grant—3
Shelley Graves—2
Dan Graveline—1, 2
Joy Greene—1, 2
Rickie Hall—1, 2, 3
Jacy R. Hanson—4
Bruce W. Harris—3
E. Alun Harris—3
Edward Harris—1, 2
R. Dobby Harris—3
Lisa Heaton—2
Kimberly Hill—3

William N. Hilliard—1, 2
Robert E. Hobart III—1, 2
Noel Hoekstra—1, 2
Jo Ann Hoffman—3
Heinz U. Hofmann—1, 2
Jonathan T. Howe—1, 2, 4
Andrea Brown Hubbert—4
Terri Hurst—3
Lindsey R. Iacovino—1, 2
Janet Jakobsen—3
Jane E. Jarrow—3
William Jenkinson—1, 2
Eric Johnson—3
Brenda Jones-Little—2
Robin Joyner—3
Jackie Jungemann—3
William H. Just—1, 2, 3, 4
Donna R. Karl—4
James Karson—3
Susan R. Katz—4
Gretchen Kihm—3
H. Jeffrey Kincaid - 4
George D. Kirkland—1, 2
Maribeth Kraus—3
Robert E. Kristofco—3, 4
Roberta Kulp—1, 2
Bev Kulyk—3
Anne-Marie Laderoute—4
Amy A. Ledoux—4
Nicholas Leever—3
Denise J. Lodrige—3
Dave Long—1, 2
Shirley Long—1, 2
Curtis Love—3
Rosalyn Lowe-Gershell—1, 2
Jerry Lowery—1, 2
Jim Luce—3
Amy Cates Lyle—3
Diane B. Lyons—4
Cynthia J. Macklin—3
Don MacLaurin—3
Debbie Mann—3
Victor Marchessault—1
Mike Marcian—2
John V. Marenzana—3
Stephen T. Martin—3
Bill Masheter—1, 2
Barbara Mason—3
Ann Matthews—3
Kelly Maynord—2, 3
Allan A. McCune—1, 2
Patricia A. McLaughlin—4
Wilbert McNamara—1, 2
Michael T. McQuade—3
Pamela McQueen—3

Martha J. Moores—3
Tony Melis—4
Dale C. Mers—1, 2
John Metcalfe—1, 2
Evelyn Miller—1
Helen Mitchell—3
Stephen A. Mirsky—2, 3
James C. Monroe—4
Roxanne Morgan—3
Sandra L. Morrow—4
Margaret Coffey Mullen—1
James R. Mulligan—1, 2
William J. Myers—3
Ardyce Myhre—3
LaVerne Neeley—2
Barbara C. Nichols—1, 2
Edward Nielsen—4
Felix P. Niespodziewanski—1, 2
David J. Noonan—1, 2
Cheryl K. Nordstedt—1, 2
Sara Norton—1, 2
Beverly Nykiel—3
Laura Odell—3
Michael I. O'Connor—1, 2
Jean A. O'Donnell—4
John Oliver—2, 3
Ciritta B. Park—3
Dennis L. Park—1, 2
Lori Parker—3
John Patronski—4
Deneen Pennington—3
Dean Petersen—3
Susan Petrus—3
Maureen S. Pickell—3
Melinda Piper—3
Ronald M. Pobuda—2
Louise A. Pochelski—4
Edward G. Polivka—3
Bonnie Polvinale—4
Terri Posey—2
Aimee Potts—3
Julie T. Prazmark—3
Christine P. Pruitt—3
Elisa D. Putman—3
Bill Quain—4
Patrick E. Raleigh—1
Glen C. Ramsborg—3
Jeffrey W. Rasco—4
Michael E. Reed—1, 2
Verbraunia Rhodes—1, 2
Jerre Riffle—1, 2
Kathy F. Rivera—4
Bruce E. Robinson—1
Tammie Roegelein—3

Terri Rojas—4
Marcia Rosenthal—1
Sylvia A. Rottman—1, 2, 3
Carey A. Rountree—3 ·
Lillian Sablack—1, 2
Gerri A. Salvatore—4
Mickey Schaefer—3
Shirley E. Schlessinger—1, 2
Anthony Schopp—3
Nancy Selvey—1, 2
Ian K. Sequeira—4
Patti J. Shock—3
Peter Shure—3
EJ Siwek—4
David H. Slaughter—1, 2
LaTrelle Smart—3
Catherine Smith—3
Craig Smith—1, 2
Christy Smith—3
Lee Smitherman—3
Jerry Smolka—1, 2
Fred C. Spillman—1, 2
Charlotte St. Martin—3
Sheila Stampfli—3
Frank Stasiowski—3
William E. Stone—1, 2
Lois Stratemeier—1, 2
Anver Suleiman—1, 2
Valerie M. Sumner—3
James H. Sweeney—4
Gregg H. Talley—3, 4
Robert K. Talley—1, 2
Terry L. Tannery—3
Nannette Tucker—1, 2
Roger Tusken—1, 2
Michael Uminowicz—1
Sylvia van Laar—3
John T. Vance—1, 2
Casey B. Wall—1, 2
Dobby Wall—3
Bob Walker—4
Dena Walter—1, 2
Daniel E. Weber—3
Edward W. Weimer—1, 2
Elizabeth White—3
David E. Whitney—4
L. Hadley Williams—1
Samantha Williams—3
Ruth Williams—1, 2
Leigh Wintz—3
Laurie Wong—3
Deborah A. Woodcock—1, 2
Eleanor Woods—3
Karen Zimmerman—3

This glossary uses the terminology and definitions of the Accepted Practice Exchange (APEX) Glossary of Terms as its standard. APEX definitions are annotated by an asterisk (*) following the entry. The APEX Glossary of Terms is published by the Convention Industry Council (CIC) and has been used with permission. When using this glossary, the number(s) following each definition indicates the primary chapter(s) of reference within this book. However, every occurrence of the term is not necessarily listed. For additional occurrences, please refer to the book index. Throughout the glossary, references to synonyms or other related terms will be suggested but may not be included in this glossary. In this instance, refer to the online CIC APEX Glossary of Terms (www.conventionindustry.org) for definitions.

abstract—written summaries of speeches or papers, generally between 200-500 words; a brief statement of content. *19**

Accepted Practices Exchange (APEX)—an initiative of the meetings, conventions, and exhibitions industry managed by the Convention Industry Council (CIC); develops and manages the implementation of accepted industry practices (voluntary standards). *10, 30, 38, 47**

accessibility—airline lift into and out of a destination; capable of being used by people with physical challenges and disabilities, an important aspect of the United States' Americans with Disabilities Act (ADA). *23, 32**

accrual accounting—an accounting method that records income and expenses at the time of contract versus when payment is received or expenses incurred (cash accounting); a system in which revenue and expenses are accounted for as soon as they are committed. *3**

acknowledgments—written notice sent to a guest that a room reservation request has been received and is being processed. *25**

Act of God clause —part of a contract that releases both parties from liability in the event that something happens that is out of their control (hurricane, tornado, war, etc.). *41*

action plan—a detailed plan describing the actions and steps to be implemented following a meeting or event due to the skills, knowledge, and professional contacts acquired at a meeting or event. *45*

actual budget—current budget that exists in fact. *3*

addendum—an addition to a completed written document; must be signed by all parties to become part of a legally binding contract. *41, 42*

adult learner—an adult who is usually pursuing education to attain a specific, practical goal. *18, 19, 20*

advance deposit—amount of money paid in advance to secure a room, facility, or service. *3*

advance registration—allows attendees to register for an event before it actually takes place; done by mail, phone, fax, e-mail, or online. Synonym: pre-registration. *3, 24, 25*

advertising—information about an event that the organizer pays to have printed or announced in various forms of media, e.g., press, TV, radio, cinema, outdoor. *4, 5**

advisory board—a group that offers advice or counsel to an event organizer, event management, or other organization on strategic options such as conference content, exhibitor matters, contracting policies or other issues. *9**

affinity group—group sharing common interests, usually people who are members of an organization. *19**

agenda—a list, outline, or plan of items to be done or considered at an event or during a specific time block. May include time schedule. *8, 19**

airport hotel—hotel located near a major airport; usually does not have a lot of recreational facilities. *11**

alternate media—alternatives to print materials, e.g., Braille, large print, etc., provided to assist people with disabilities in achieving full participation. *43**

alternative dispute resolution—method for resolving disputes without going to court. *42*

ambient light—level of illumination from natural lighting sources already existing in an environment; uncontrolled and unintended illumination. *23**

amenity, amenities—complimentary items in sleeping rooms such as writing supplies,

---

* denotes APEX definition

bathrobes, fruit baskets, shower caps, shampoo, or shoeshine mitt provided by a facility for guests. *34, 40**

American plan (AP)—a type of hotel rate that includes the price of the room and all meals. See also inclusive rate, Bermuda plan, continental plan, demi-pension, European plan, modified American plan. *11**

Americans with Disabilities Act (ADA)— U.S. legislation passed in 1992 requiring public buildings (offices, hotels, restaurants, etc.) to make adjustments meeting minimum standards to make their facilities accessible to individuals with physical disabilities. *43**

anchor—a data point that serves to fix a negotiation and affect the final deal. *40*

ancillary center—event facility that is typically part of a larger hospitality complex. *15**

ancillary services or activities—all event-related support services within a facility that generate revenue; activities that may be arranged and/or promoted by the meeting manager that complement the meeting, but are not considered essential meeting components (e.g., local tours before or after the meeting). *14, 35*

andragogy—the art and science of helping adults learn, as opposed to pedagogy, which is the science of helping children learn. *18**

APEX—See Accepted Practices Exchange. *10, 30, 38, 47**

application service provider (ASP)—a company that manages and distributes software-based solutions to customers across a wide area network from a central data center. *10, 24, 25**

arbitration—a procedure devised to resolve a dispute outside of the court system. *41*

arrival/departure pattern—a description of arrival and departure activities of an event's attendees. This information should be included in the event specifications guide for an event. *25**

asset—something of value that is owned by an organization or individual. *4**

asset valuation—the value, or determining the value, of something that is owned by an organization. *4*

attendance—total number of people at an event. *17**

attendee—an individual who is registered for or participating in an event. Includes delegates, exhibitors, media, speakers, and guests. *2, 42**

attendee data—demographic information on each attendee. *24*

attrition—difference between the actual number of sleeping rooms picked-up (or food and beverage covers or revenue projections) and

the number or formulas agreed to in the terms of the facility's contract. Usually a certain shortfall is allowed before damages are assessed. *16, 17, 25, 35**

attrition clause—contract wording that outlines potential damages or fees that a party may be required to pay in the event that it does not fulfill minimum commitments in the contract. *25**

audience polling—computer application that enables voting and then collects and displays the results, simplifying decision-making among event participants. *13**

audience response system (ARS)—hand held devices connected to a computer application that enable individual meeting participants to vote or respond to questions and then see the results or answers from the entire group. *10, 45*

audioconference—a conference using only voice transmissions between two or more sites. *13**

audiovisual (A/V)—equipment, materials, and teaching aids used in sound and visual presentations, such as television monitors, video, sound equipment, etc. *42, 29**

auditorium set-up—seating arrangement where chairs are arranged in rows facing head table, stage, or speaker. Variations include semi-circular and V-shaped. See theater set-up. *23**

auditory learners—learners who prefer to hear content, rather than reading content or experimenting to access content. *18*

authorized signature—signature from a person with the legal power and influence to make a decision; required on all written contracts. *41*

autograph table—traditionally, a table where a speaker autographs books after a speaking engagement. Many speakers currently use the term to mean the table at the back of the room from which they sell their products. *23**

auxiliary aids and services—contracted services, e.g., stewards, technicians, interpreters, tour guides, that provide support for an event; the use of adaptive equipment or assistance to ensure accessibility for people with disabilities. *43**

auxiliary business—business that is brought to the facility because of, or in conjunction with, an event. See also in conjunction with (ICW). *26**

back light—a light source that illuminates any transparent or translucent material from behind; a lighting instrument used behind and above a presenter to give more depth and better image when video taping or using image-magnification. *23**

---

* denotes APEX definition

backbone—a permanently installed series of cables comprising of copper wire cable and/or fiber optic cable, utilized as the main thoroughfare in a building to transmit voice and data signals in or out of the facility. *13**

backup material—actual receipts and other documents concerning charges made to the master account; these should accompany the final invoice. *38*

badge—identifying sign, tag, or emblem worn by event participants; sometimes called a nametag. *24**

balance sheet—a statement of financial status at a given time (includes liabilities, assets, etc.). *3, 45*

bandwidth—amount of information that can be transmitted in an information channel such as a telephone line, ISDN, or ethernet. Higher bandwidth means that images and sound will load more quickly for use in videoconferences or on the Internet. Usually expressed in bits per second. *13**

banquet—an elaborate, and often ceremonious, meal for numerous people, often in honor of a person or persons. *8, 10, 26, 34, 36*

banquet event order (BEO)—a form most often used by hotels or other facilities to provide details to personnel concerned with a specific food and beverage function or event room set-up. See also function sheet. *8, 10, 34, 36**

barndoor—movable hinged flap used on stage lights to control light spill. *29*

base currency—currency in which all official business transactions will take place. *16, 35**

BATNA—best alternative to a negotiated agreement. *40*

benchmarking—data points that should be reached by a specified time/date to assess progress toward stated goals and objectives; marketing system based on assessing progress toward stated goals and objectives by comparison to competitors; accounting process of comparing the financial status of a company to other selected companies, typically in the same industry or based on identified, logical parameters. *5*

benefit /cost ratio (BCR)— a ratio which identifies the relationship between the cost and benefits of a project, meeting, or event. *2, 45, 46**

bid—a statement of what one will give or take in return for something else (a price); proposal submitted by a convention and visitors bureau and/or hotel(s) to an event organizer that includes defined dates and room blocks. *11, 12*

bill of lading—a document that establishes the terms of a contract between a shipper and a transportation company under which freight is to be moved between specified points for a specified charge. Usually prepared by the shipper on forms issued by the carrier, it serves as a document of title, a contract of carriage, and a receipt of goods. *34**

biodegradable—Capable of being broken down by natural processes, such as bacterial action. *30*

bit—a unit of measurement that represents one figure or character of data. A bit is the smallest unit of storage in a computer. Bit multiples are called bytes. *13**

blacklist—a list that indicates selected items on the basis of negative history. In some cases, it may be illegal. *10*

blind commission—a commission that is paid by a hotel to a third party that reimburses for services and comes out of the hotel sleeping room rate, but is not disclosed to the guests or the event organizer. Such commissions may fall within commercial bribery laws and, if involving use of interstate commerce, may be federal law violation. *7**

blog, web log—web-based publication of periodic writings; may be hosted by an organization or specific author. *5, 10*

Bluetooth—industrial for the personal area network (PAN), providing wireless convergence of cell phones, computers, personal digital assistants (PDAs), etc. *10, 13**

board of directors—a governing group consisting of elected or appointed members to oversee the operations of an organization; typically these are strategic decision makers, rather than personnel who attend to day-to-day operations. *2*

boardroom set-up—seating arrangement in which a rectangle or oval table is set up with chairs on both sides and ends. Often confused with hollow-square or hollow-rectangle set-ups. *23**

booking—an arrangement with a company for use of facilities, goods, or services. *25**

booking policy—guidelines by which a convention center (or other venue) prioritizes reservations; may correspond to hotel rooms the event will use in the area. *12, 14*

booth—one or more standard units of exhibit space. In the United States, a standard unit is generally a 10' x 10' space (one standard booth/stand unit, equaling 100 net sq. ft.). However, if an exhibitor purchases multiple units side-by-side or back-to-back, the combined space is also still referred to as a booth; specific area assigned by management to exhibitor under contractual agreement. See also stand. *27**

---

* denotes APEX definition

brand identity—a trademark or distinctive name identifying a product, service, or organization; the qualities that differentiate a product, service, or organization from its competitors. *5*

break—short interval between sessions at which time coffee, tea, and/or other refreshments are served. *19**

break-even analysis—determining the point at which income covers expenses. *3*

breakout session—small group sessions, panels, workshops, or presentations, offered concurrently within the event, formed to focus on specific subjects. The event is apart from the general session, but within the event format, formed to focus on specific subjects. These sessions can be arranged by basic, intermediate, or advanced, or divided by interest areas or industry segment. *19**

broadband—high-speed data transmission, commonly used to refer to T-1 line rate (1.5 mbps) and above. *13, 29*

budget—a statement of estimated revenues and expenditures for a specified period of time; divided into subject categories and arranged by principal areas of revenue and expense. *3, 7**

budget handbook—detailed book containing quotes and figures used to determine line items in the functional budget. *3*

buffet—assortment of foods, offered on a table, self-served. *26**

business plan—a document that provides the development plans for an enterprise; typically includes background information, feasibility studies, audience identification, marketing plans, budgetary guidelines, and other resources. *7*

butler service—servers offer a variety of both hot and cold hors d'oeuvres on platters to guests at receptions; a style of table service where guests serve themselves from platters presented by the server; specialized in-room service offered by a hotel. *26**

cabaret set-up—room arrangement with cocktail tables with chairs and a stage. *23**

cabaret table—small round table, 15-30 inches in diameter (38-76 centimeters) used for cocktail type parties; also called cocktail table. *23**

cafeteria service—a food service operation in which customers carry their own trays and select food from a display counter or counters. It is similar to a buffet, but food is served by attendants. *26**

camera-ready—type and/or artwork materials ready for photographic reproduction or printing production. *5*

cancellation clause—provision in a contract which outlines damages to be paid to the non-canceling party if cancellation occurs due the canceling party's breach of the contract. *21**

carbon offset—a way of counteracting the carbon emitted when the use of fossil fuel causes greenhouse gas emissions. Offsets commonly involve investing in projects such as renewable energy, tree planting, and energy efficient projects. *30*

cart-style service—a style of French service for small events where guests are seated, heating and garnishing of food is done table-side, and an assembled plate is served to the guest by a server. *26*

case study—an analysis of a particular case or situation used for the purpose of gaining depth of understanding into the issues being investigated. *19, 45**

cash bar—private room bar set-up where guests pay for drinks individually. *26**

cash flow—transfer of monies into and out of an enterprise. *7**

cash-based accounting—an accounting method that enters income and expenses into the books at the time when payment is received or expenses incurred. *3**

category cable—unshielded twisted pair (UTP) cable. Usually referred to as Cat. 1, 2, 3, 4, or 5 cable. Cat. 5 transmits data the fastest. Fast ethernet requires enhanced Cat. 5 cable or Cat. 5 to operate at its full potential. *13**

catering manager—person at the facility who is responsible for catering events. *32*

Compact Disk-Read Only Memory (CD-ROM)—a disk that can hold many times the data of a traditional floppy disk. *5*

ceiling height—maximum height of ceiling of an exhibition hall or event room. Dimensions quoted by halls and hotels often do not take into account any light fixtures hanging from the ceiling. *23**

Certified Meeting Professional (CMP)—certification program offered by the Convention Industry Council; the designation certifies competency in 27 areas of meeting management through application and examination.

chart of accounts—a numbering system used to identify each line item of the budget by account number, allowing deposits and expenditures to be posted in the correct account. *3*

charter—exclusive use of all or some space on an airplane, bus, ship, or other vehicle for a special period of time and for a specific

---

* denotes APEX definition

itinerary; to create a new association, organization, or subgroup of an association or organization. *33**

chat—a real time synchronous electronic discussion forum where participants can communicate with instructors, mentors, and peers to simulate the classroom environment. *13**

chef's table—the opportunity to sample a menu in advance of the event, usually in the company of the chef; also refers to a food event held in the kitchen where the attendees interact with the chef and kitchen staff. *14**

chevron set-up—seating arrangement in which chairs are arranged in rows slanted in a V-shape and separated by a center aisle. They face the head table or speaker. See also herringbone set-up and V-shape set-up. *23**

citywide meeting (event)—an event that requires the use of a convention center or event complex, as well as multiple hotels in the host city. *12, 33, 35**

classroom style—seating arrangement in which rows of tables face the presenter and each person has a space for writing. Synonym: schoolroom style. *23*

classroom table—rectangular table, often narrower than regular tables 30-inches high. Can be 6' or 8' long and 18- or 24-inches wide. *23**

climate neutral—climate neutral products or services reduce and offset the greenhouse gases generated at each stage of their life-cycle on a cradle-to-cradle basis; the sourcing of their materials, their manufacturing or production, their distribution, use, and ultimate end-of-life disposition. *30**

close-ended questions—type of question format in which the respondent must make a forced choice between given options. *45**

CODEC—Compression/Decompression or Coder/Decoder. Videoconferencing standard, included in hardware and/or software, used to compress or code video, audio, and data signals for transmission and decompress or decode the signal at the other end of the transmission. *13**

colloquium—an informal meeting for the purpose of discussion; usually of an academic or research nature and in order to ascertain areas of mutual interest through exchange of ideas. Conducted as and when convenient, but with little regularity. *19**

co-location—to hold two related events at the same time and in the same place. See also in conjunction with (ICW). *17**

commission—a payment to a sales representative for meeting or exceeding a sales revenue goal; a payment made to an individual or organization for bringing business to another individual or organization. *37**

committable rooms—rooms available for contract (room block) purposes from a specific hotel. *25*

committee notebook—distributed to volunteer committee members, with background materials and resource information they need to fulfill their duties and make informed decisions. *9*

complete meeting package—an all-inclusive plan offered by conference centers; includes lodging, all meals, and support services. *8, 15*

complimentary—provided free as a courtesy or favor, at no charge; often a reflection of how many units (rooms or tickets) were actually sold to meeting attendees. *33*

concierge—facility staff which provides special services such as tickets to local events, transportation, and tour arrangements; designated area in facility providing special amenities and services to guests. *15, 31*

concurrent sessions—multiple sessions scheduled at the same time. Programs on different themes or subjects offered simultaneously. *2, 19**

conference—participatory meeting designed for discussion, fact-finding, problem solving and consultation; an event used by any organization to meet and exchange views, convey a message, open a debate, or give publicity to some area of opinion on a specific issue. No tradition, continuity, or periodicity is required to convene a conference. Although not generally limited in time, conferences are usually of short duration with specific objectives. Conferences are generally on a smaller scale than congresses. See also congress, convention. *2**

conference call—telephone or video connection between three or more persons. *21**

conference center—a facility that provides a dedicated environment for events, especially small events. May be certified by the International Association of Conference Centers. *11, 15*

conference service coordinator—primary contact person assigned to an event in a convention center. *35, 37**

confirmations—oral or written agreement by a facility to accept a request for accommodation; to be binding the agreement must state the intent of the parties, the particular date, the rate, type of

---

* denotes APEX definition

accommodations, and the number to be accommodated; oral agreement may require a credit card number. See also confirmed reservation. *24, 25**

conflict-of-interest statement—written document requiring individuals to disclose any conflicts of interest that may be created by their involvement with an organization. *21**

consular information—information provided by the U.S. State Department regarding travel warnings and other matters involving foreign countries; (Consular Declaration) a formal statement, made to the consul of a country, describing goods to be shipped. *16, 35*

consultant—individual who provides counsel and assistance to a client on specific assignments. For very large projects, a consulting firm may be retained rather than a individual. *2**

Consumer Price Index (CPI) rate—an index of prices used to measure the change in the cost of basic goods and services in comparison with a fixed-base period. *40*

content—the educational component of an event. See also conference. *2, 19**

continental breakfast—light morning meal consisting of pastries, juices, and hot beverages. Usually served buffet style. *26**

continuing education—Structured educational and training experiences for personal or professional development. *2**

Continuing Education Unit (CEU)—requirement of many professional groups by which members must certify participation in formal educational programs designed to maintain their level of ability beyond their original certification date. CEUs are non-academic credit. One CEU is awarded for each 10 contact hours in an accredited program. *2**

contracted service—service for which the meeting manager bargains or negotiates a formal contract. *37*

control group—in research, this group either receives no treatment or receives neutral treatment. The results provide a baseline comparison with the experimental group (the group that does receive treatment). *46*

controversy panel—to stimulate interest and debate, arrange for two or three views of a controversial issue to be presented. *19**

convention—an event where the primary activity of the attendees is to attend educational sessions, participate in meetings/discussions, socialize, or attend other organized events. There is a secondary exhibit component. See also meeting, exhibition, trade show, consumer show. *17**

convention and visitor bureau (CVB)—CVBs are not-for-profit organizations charged with representing a specific destination and helping the long-term development of communities through a travel and tourism strategy. CVBs are usually membership organizations bringing together businesses that rely on tourism and events for revenue. For visitors, CVBs are like a key to the city. As an unbiased resource, CVBs can serve as a broker or an official point of contact for convention and event planners, tour operators, and visitors. They assist planners with event preparation and encourage business travelers and visitors alike to visit local historic, cultural, and recreational sites. *12, 14, 25, 35*

convention center—facility that combines an exhibition space with a substantial number of smaller event spaces. The purpose of these buildings is to host trade shows, public shows, conventions, large food functions and other functions related to the convention industry. They may be purpose built or converted and municipally or privately owned. See also exhibition center, facility, hall. *11, 14, 17**

convention services manager (CSM)—a professional at a hotel, convention center, or convention bureau who is responsible for event operations management on all levels. *35, 36, 37**

copy—all original material being prepared for reproduction; reproduction of original material; text. *5**

copyediting—checking material (usually text) for mistakes and inconsistencies before it is printed; also called proofreading. *5*

copyright—the exclusive legal right to reproduce, publish, or sell literary, musical, or artistic work and ideas. *21, 41*

copyright waiver—written authorization from a speaker that an organization may record a presentation for sale or future use. *21*

corporate meeting—gathering of employees or representatives of a commercial organization. Usually, attendance is required and travel, room, and most meal expenses are paid for by the organization. *2**

crescent round set-up—seating style that uses round tables with seating on two-thirds or three-quarters of each table and no seating with backs to the speaker or head table. *23*

crisis—a critical event which may dramatically impact an organization's profitability, reputation, or ability to operate. *44*

---

* denotes APEX definition

cross-cultural communication—written, oral, or non-verbal communication that occurs between representatives of two or more cultures. *22*

crowd dynamics—the study of how crowds form, function, and behave; the process of controlling crowds for movement, function, behavior, and safety. *28*

culture—an integrated collection of learned behaviors, attitudes, and beliefs shared by members of a specific society. *22*

customer relationship management (CRM)—all aspects of interaction an organization has with its customer, whether sales or service related; using CRM, organizations can personalize electronic marketing campaigns and the online experience for customers. *5*

customs—the governmental authorities designated to collect duties levied by a country on imports and exports. The term also applies to the procedures involved in such collection; practices common to many of a particular group. *16, 35**

customs brokers—an individual or company which provides customs clearing services to shippers of goods to and from another country. Licensing and requirements vary from country to country. In the United States, a customs broker must be licensed by the Treasury Department and pass a government examination covering a broad range of knowledge, including all phases of import regulations, rates of duties, and customs law. *16, 35**

cut-off date—deadline for holding a number of rooms or ticket guarantees at the group rate; due date for a decision on a contract or proposal. *24*

cyber café—a network of computers, connected to the Internet, giving meeting attendees access to e-mail, web sites, and event-specific information. *13*

dais—raised platform usually above the floor of a hall or large room. See also podium, riser. *23**

deadlock—a stalemate in which both sides either threaten to or actually do leave the negotiation table. *40*

debt service—regular payments required to keep a loan current. *14**

decorator—an individual or company providing installation & dismantle and booth/stand and hall dressing services for a trade show and/or its exhibitors. Decorator services may be provided by carpenters, sign painters, or others depending upon union jurisdiction. Term applies to both contractor and skilled craftsperson. See also general services contractor (GSC). *42**

delegate—person who attends an event primarily to visit exhibits or attend meetings and/or conference sessions. This excludes exhibitors, media, speakers, and companions; registered meeting participant; voting representative at a meeting. *2**

demographic(s)—characteristics that help create a profile of exhibitors and attendees. May include gender, age, company location, job function, purchase budget, purchase intentions, etc. *2, 27, 31, 42**

demonstration—the act of showing how to do something; a group of individuals organized to picket or protest against a group using placards, literature, songs, shouts and, sometimes, marches or sit-ins. *19**

design—artist's concept or visualization of how a printed piece should look. Also called graphic design. *1**

desktop publishing—using a personal computer to prepare materials for printing. *5**

destination management company (DMC)—local supplier who can arrange, manage, and/or plan any function or service for a meeting at the destination. See also Professional Congress Organizer (PCO), ground operator. *12, 31*

destination marketing—communication strategies targeted at promoting a particular location as a meeting site and/or a tourist attraction. *5*

developmental learning—learning that occurs during the first half of life when education is directed at building a personal life, a career, and a future. *18*

digital light projection (DLP)—high-end projector most commonly used for very large screen and large room applications; has extremely high light output (up to 15,000 lumens) and high scan output. *29*

digital signs—signage at meeting facilities that are electronic displays, rather than printed signs. *28*

digital subscriber line (DSL)—provides high-speed access to the Internet via copper wire telephone lines; upstream data transmission at rates of up to 1 Mbps; downstream data transmission at rates of up to 32 Mbps; DSL service requires a DSL modem. *13*

direct billing—accounts receivable made available to individuals or firms with established credit. *8**

direct mail—a marketing technique in which material is mailed directly to individuals in a target audience. *5**

directional signs—meeting signs placed to assist attendees in finding event locations. *28, 34*

---

* denotes APEX definition

disability —a physical or mental impairment limiting normal life functions. *43*

dispatcher—person responsible for scheduling and routing freight, labor, shuttle busses, etc. *33**

distance learning—a type of education where students work on their own at home or from an office, and communicate with faculty and other students via email, electronic forums, chat, web conferencing, and other forms of online communication. Includes correspondence courses, audio, video, and Internet delivery. Meeting and event web sites can facilitate distance learning by offering online educational programs. *9, 18, 22**

double room—a sleeping room occupied by two persons. The room may have one or more beds of any type in it. *25**

double/double—sleeping room, intended for at least two people, with two beds which are double size. *25**

dram shop laws—a legal term, in the United States, for laws covering the liability of people serving alcoholic beverages. Under dram shop laws, a party injured by an intoxicated person can sue establishments contributing to that person's intoxication. Many dram shop laws also cover serving alcohol to a minor. *26**

drayage—delivery of exhibit materials from the dock to an assigned exhibit space, removing empty crates, returning crates at the end of the event for recreating, and delivering materials back to dock for carrier loading. *27, 37, 42**

DS3—see T-3 line. *13*

dual projection—the projection of two images at the same time using two separate projectors and two screens. *29*

dueling menus—split (dual) entrées, e.g., surf & turf. *26**

dummy—mock-up of printed pieces as they should appear in the final form, made up of the correct size and number of pages, showing the position of the various text elements and illustrations. *5**

duoserve property—a hotel property in which logistics are handled by the convention services manager (CSM), with catering handled by a separate manager. *35**

duty—fee levied on imported and exported goods. Duties are generally based on the value of the goods (ad valorem duties), some other factors such as weight or quantity (specific duties), or a combination of value and other factors (compound duties). See ad valorem tax. *16, 35**

ecological footprint—the measure of area needed to supply national populations with the resources and area needed to absorb their wastes. *30*

ecology—the system of relationships between organisms and their environments. *30*

ecosystem—a community of living organisms interacting with themselves and with their environment. *30*

ecotourism—tourism that respects the culture, natural history, and environment of destinations and seeks to minimize the negative impact of travel on the environment. *30*

electronic contract—an electronic document with valid electronic signatures that all parties agree is legally binding. *41*

electronic signature—a sound, symbol, or process attached to or logically associated with a contract or other record and executed or adopted by a person with the intent to sign the record. *41*

electronic whiteboard—computer input device that allows the user to convert handwritten notes on a whiteboard into text on a computer; input variations include computerized pens. *10, 13*

ellipsoidal spotlight—type of adjustable spotlight formerly known as a klieg light. It is used to light lecterns, signs, and areas that need a tightly focused pool of light. See also lekos. *23**

email newsletter—a newsletter distributed to a subscriber list via email. Often referred to as opt-in or permission marketing because subscribers choose to receive the information. *10**

e-marketing —a marketing campaign implemented via the Internet using email and/or a web site. *10*

emergency—an unexpected actual or impending situation that may cause injury, loss of life, destruction of property, or the interference, loss, or disruption of an organization's normal business operations. *44*

emotional factors—emotions brought to class by adult learners that may help or hinder their learning. *18**

energy star equipment —a voluntary labeling program of the U.S. Environmental Protection agency (EPA) and the U.S. Department of Energy that identifies energy efficient products. Qualified products exceed minimum federal standards for energy consumption by a certain amount, or, where no federal standards exist, have certain energy saving features. Such products may display the Energy Star label. *30*

---

* denotes APEX definition

English breakfast—a large, hearty breakfast that can include juice, hot cereal, eggs, meat (often fish), pastries with jellies and preserves, and hot beverages. *26**

enterprise wide—procedure and/or technology that is implemented throughout the entire organization or business. *10*

escoffier dish—serving containers for chafing dishes. *26**

European plan (EP)—a room rate that does not include meals. See also American plan, Bermuda plan, continental plan, demi-pension, modified American plan. *15, 16, 35**

European Union—Since 1993, the European Union is the block of European countries formerly known as the European Economic Community (EEC) or the European Community (EC). *16, 35*

evaluation—critiquing and rating the overall success of an event; developing an event profile from accurate event statistics; a systematic process to determine the worth, value, or meaning of an activity or process. *2, 45**

evaluative learning method—tests whether attendees learned what was expected, and if they can use the information effectively. *19**

event—an organized occasion such as a meeting, convention, exhibition, special event, gala dinner, etc. An event is often composed of several different yet related functions. *2**

event specifications guide (ESG)—the industry preferred term for a comprehensive document that outlines the complete requirements and instructions for an event. This document is typically authored by the event planner and is shared with all appropriate vendors as a vehicle to communicate the expectations of services for a project. The industry accepted practice is to use the APEX Event Specifications Guide. Sometimes called spec guide, staging guide, résumé. *8, 34, 35, 38**

exchange rate—the relative value of two different currencies at a specific time. *16, 35**

exclusive contract—contract between a facility and a service provider designating that provider as the only provider of a specific service in that facility. *14, 37, 41, 42*

exclusive contracts/contractors—contract between a facility and a service provider designating that provider as the only provider of a specific service or products in that facility. *14, 37, 40**

executive committee—a committee of the Board of Directors that acts between meetings of the board to determine organizational policy. *9**

exhibit—a booth at an exhibition for marketing, demonstration, or sale of products or services; the process of showcasing a product or service at a show designed for this purpose. *17, 27*

exhibit hall—area within facility where exhibitions are located. *17, 27**

exhibition—an event at which products and services are displayed. The primary activity of attendees is visiting exhibits on the show floor. These events focus primarily on business-to-business (B2B) relationships; display of products or promotional material for the purposes of public relations, sales, and/or marketing. See also trade show, consumer show, gate show, public show. *17, 27**

exhibition service contractor—supplier of booth/stand equipment, rental furnishings, floor coverings, labor, drayage, and signs for exhibitions and trade shows. See also general services contractor. *16, 35**

exhibitor—person or firm that displays its products or services at an event; event attendee whose primary purpose for attending the event is to staff a booth/stand. *2, 42**

exhibitor advisory committee—representatives of an event's exhibiting companies who act as advisers to show management on rules and procedures, and also update show management on industry trends and issues. *27**

exhibitor appointed contractors (EACs)—any company other than the designated official contractor providing a service to an exhibitor. Can refer to an install & dismantle company (I&D house), photographer, florist, or any other type of contractor. *14, 42**

exhibitor prospectus—direct mail promotional materials sent to current and prospective exhibitors to encourage participation and promote the benefits of exhibiting in a specific show. Contains information about technical points, cost of exhibition space, floor plan of the exhibition, and application for participation. *27, 37**

exit visas—an endorsement made on a passport denoting that a person may leave the country. *16, 35**

exposition—see exhibition. *17, 27**

expository learning—instructor presents to the learners and the learners remain passive and watch or listen. *19**

extensible markup language (XML)—an organizational markup language that describes text in a digital document. *10**

---

* denotes APEX definition

facilitator—an individual who guides discussion and/or decision making. *2, 8**

facility—a structure that is built, installed, or established to serve a particular purpose. See also convention center, hall. *11**

fair—exhibition of products or services in a specific area of activity held with the objective of promoting business. *17**

familiarization (FAM) trip—offered to potential buyers of a venue, a program designed to acquaint participants with specific destinations or services and to stimulate the booking of an event. Often offered in groups, but sometimes on an individual basis. See also site inspection. *39**

fast-fold screen—brand name for a large screen with a frame which folds down into a small case for storage. The legs of this screen are attached at the sides of the screen, or the screen may be flown from above. *29**

feedback—regeneration of sound from audio speakers back through a microphone causing a squealing sound; response about an activity, policy, or idea. *38**

fiberoptic cable—a cable that is made up of tiny glass strands that are wrapped and bundled together to make up a cable. Fiber can transmit voice, data, and video at gigabyte speed, or, 1 billion bytes per second, with less signal loss than copper wire because the signal is carried by light rather than electricity. *13**

file transfer protocol (FTP)—process of uploading or downloading web sites or other data. *13**

finger food—food at a reception that does not require a knife, fork or spoon. *26**

firewall—a software or hardware solution that restricts or blocks outside access to a computer or network. *13*

fixed expense (fixed cost)—expense incurred regardless of the number of event attendees. *3**

flat rate—a hotel or motel agrees to offer any of its available sleeping rooms (with the exception of suites) to a group. Final assignment of rooms is at the discretion of the hotel. See also run-of-the-house rate. *40*

floor load—maximum amount of weight per square foot/meter a floor can support; may also refer to the maximum amount of power available from floor outlets and ports. *27**

floor manager—person retained by event management to supervise the installation, dismantling, and operation of the exhibit area. *27**

floor microphone—microphone mounted on a stationary floor stand. *29*

floor plan—schematic drawing of an exhibit hall including dimensions, design, shape, entrances, aisles, numbered exhibit booth/stands, lounges, concession areas, restrooms, electrical/plumbing accessibility, etc.; scale plan of the floor area of a hotel's event space; schematic drawing of a function room with specific requirements (dais, tables, chairs, etc.) drawn to scale. *27**

fluorescent—light using high-intensity discharge electric arcs combined with phosphors to produce bright light throughout the room; incapable of dimming. *23*

focus group—method of doing research using a small group led by a facilitator. *2, 45**

font—alphabet of type in a specific style. See also typeface. *5**

force majeure clause—a clause in a contract that excuses a party from liability if some greater force or event beyond the control of that party prevents completion of the contract obligation. *41*

foreign exchange currency risk—risk that an organization takes when dealing with foreign currency due to exchange rates fluctuating over time. *16, 35**

French service - banquet and cart style—French service cart style involves the use of serving pieces (usually silver), heating and garnishing of food table-side by a captain, and plated entrees are served to the guest by a server; for French service, banquet style, service platters of food are prepared in the kitchen, each food item is served by a server from platters onto individual plates; any course can be "Frenched" by having the dressing put on the salad or the sauce added to a dessert after it is in front of the guest. *26*

fresnel—lens which produces a soft edged beam of light; theatrical fixture with adjustable lens 150W through 1500W. *29*

front projection—projection of an image onto the front surface of a light reflecting screen from a projector placed within or behind the audience. *29*

fulfillment—provision of a service that has been ordered and paid for in advance, usually through subscription. *4*

full American plan (FAP)—see American plan (AP). *16, 35**

full breakfast—breakfast menu that includes meats, eggs, breads and pastries, potatoes, cereals, fruit, and beverages. *26*

function sheet—a collection of all details relative to a meeting's needs (including sleeping rooms, billing arrangements, contractor information, etc.); this document is circulated to all key personnel in the facility and organization. Synonyms: event order,

---

* denotes APEX definition

meeting résumé, function order. See also event specifications guide (ESG), banquet event order (BEO). *34*

function space—area in a facility which can be reserved by a individual or entity to hold events. *23**

function ticket—a ticket for admission to an event that is part of the planned meeting activities. *24*

fundraising event—an event that requires a registration fee, ticket, or cover charge, or where donations are sought to raise funds for the host organization or a cause identified by the host organization. *32*

gala—primary social function of an event, usually in the evening, including entertainment or speeches after a formal meal. *32**

ganging menus—when two or more groups in facility have the same menu. *26**

gel—theatrical color filter used in conjunction with theatrical projection fixtures and spotlights. *29**

general services contractor (GSC)—an organization that provides event management and exhibitors with a wide range of services, sometimes including, but not limited to, installation & dismantle, creating and hanging signage and banners, laying carpet, drayage, and providing booth/stand furniture. See also decorator. *27, 37, 42**

generic signs—signs printed without specific dates that can be used for future meetings. *38*

gigabit—1,000 megabits, or one billion bits of data. *13*

glass-beaded surface—projection screen with a very reflective surface made of tiny glass beads; this type of screen has a narrow viewing angle. *29*

gobo—a pre-cut, etched pattern fabricated from metal or glass that fits in the focal plane of a lighting instrument to form projected light into a shape (logo, graphic, or even scenery). Templates can form light images on ceilings and walls. The pattern or template can be used in a projection type spotlight, to project decorative patterns on the walls. The bat image from Batman is an example. *32**

good faith effort—a true and honest effort to uphold the law or a contract. *43**

gratuity—a voluntary payment added to a bill (e.g. a restaurant check), to signify good service. See also service charge. *26, 38**

green room—a room, stocked with refreshments, for artists, featured speakers, and entourage to meet guests and media

representatives. See also holding room, speakers' ready room. *23**

group history—facts and figures detailing a group's past events. *25*

group rate—confirmed rate extended to attendees booking their sleeping room accommodations as part of a group room block. *40**

guarantee—a promise or commitment to provide a minimum amount of sleeping rooms, food and beverage, or other revenues. Usually there is financial liability if the commitment is not met. The final number of persons to be served is usually required at least 48 hours in advance of a food and beverage event. *25**

guaranteed reservation—hotel room reservation for which the first night's fee is paid in advance. *26*

guest program—educational and/or social events planned for spouses and guests of event participants. *23**

half-round—a semi-circular table. *23*

hands-on participation—demonstration of a product or service in which people actively participate with the product or service. *19**

hard costs or gains—those factors that can be easily and quantifiably measured numerically such as dollars or time. *40*

hard currency—a currency that can be traded outside its native country. *16, 35*

hard data—objective, rational, undisputed facts that are easily accumulated and usually quantifiable. *45**

hardwall—a type of exhibit construction in which the walls are of solid material, rather than fabric. *16, 35, 37**

head count—actual number of people attending a catered function. See also audience count, covers. *26**

head table—table used to seat VIPs, speakers, and other dignitaries, often elevated on a dais or stage. See also dais, very important person (VIP). *23**

headquarters—facility, as the center of operations, where registration, general sessions, and conference staff office are located. *40**

headquarter hotel—one hotel in a multiple-hotel meeting where VIPs stay and official functions are held. *34*

health warning—decree issued by the World Health Organization warning travelers of the outbreak of a communicable disease in a given area. *16, 35**

herringbone set-up—seating arrangement in which chairs are arranged in rows slanted in a V-shape and separated by a center aisle. They face the head table or speaker. See also chevron set-up, V-shape set-up. *23**

high season—period when the demand for a supplier's product or service is highest. Prices generally increase in high season. Also called peak season. See also low season. *8, 14**

hold all space—blanket hold on all available space in a facility without specific meeting or function room names. *40*

hold harmless—a type of indemnity clause that requires one party to fully protect the other from a claim asserted. This would include the payment of costs or attorney fees. *42**

hollow square set-up—seating arrangement of tables set in a square (or rectangle) with chairs placed around the outside of the table. Center (inside) table is hollow. *23**

home radio frequency (homeRF)—designed for wireless networks in homes, in contrast to IEEE 802.11, which was created for use in businesses; uses radio frequency waves for the transmission of voice and data within a range of up to 150 feet. *13*

horizontal show—an exhibition at which the products or services being displayed represent all segments of an industry or profession. See also exhibition, vertical show. *17**

hors d'oeuvres—small appetizers; hot and/or cold finger foods served at a reception. *26**

horseshoe set-up—tables set up in rounded U-shape with chairs placed outside. Chairs may be placed inside, if needed. See also U-shape set-up. *23**

hospitality program—plan for receiving and entertaining guests in a friendly and generous manner. *15, 31**

hospitality suite—room or suite of rooms used to entertain guests; an event in the United States usually separate from the exhibit, in which refreshments are served and exhibitor personnel and visitors socialize. *11**

host—on a network, any computer that is a repository for services available to other computers on the network; person assigned to assist a speaker before, during, and after a presentation; organization that manages a meeting or event, usually called the host organization; sponsor. *21, 26**

hotel/motel room tax (room or bed tax)—see transient occupancy tax. *14**

housekeeping—facility department charged with maintaining and cleaning a venue. *34**

houseman—service-staff member who handles function room set-up and tear down. See banquet set-up. *23**

housing—shelter or lodging. *12, 45**

housing bureau, service, or vendor—third-party agency capable of managing reservations of sleeping space for a meeting, based on a housing list provided by the meeting manager or by individual requests from attendees. *25*

housing list—a list of all guests provided by the meeting manager; details room requirements, special guests, payment method, etc. *25*

housing report—document detailing housing utilization (reservations, pick-up, etc.). *12, 25**

hypertext—text that links to another file and can be selected (clicked on) to go to another document, image, or FTP (download/upload) site. *5**

identification sign—exhibit booth/stand identification sign. *28**

IEEE 802.11b—a local wireless networking protocol or standard allowing transmissions at a rate of 11 Mbps; also known as wireless fidelity or Wi-Fi. *13*

image magnification (i-mag)—technology by which a presenter's image is projected onto a large screen, allowing large audiences to see details from the stage. *29**

in conjunction with (ICW)—an event or function that occurs because of another event. *26, 40**

incentive event—a reward event intended to showcase persons who meet or exceed sales or production goals. *2**

incidentals—expenses other than room and tax, billed to a guest's account (e.g., phone, room service, etc.). *25**

income statement—a statement of revenues and expenses. also known as a profit and loss statement. *3**

indemnification clause—a contract clause in which one party agrees to pay damages or claims that the other party may be required to pay to another. For example, if a hotel is sued by an attendee that is injured at an event due to the fault of the group, an indemnification clause might require the group to pay back the hotel. Sometimes the law requires one party to indemnify another even without a specific clause. Generally, the terms of the clause will be followed over the state law. See also hold harmless. *42**

independent contractor/planner—person contractually retained by another (other than as an employer) to perform specific tasks. The other person has no control over the independent contractor other than as provided in the contract. In the context of group travel, a tour manager or tour brochure

---

* denotes APEX definition

designer/writer might be retained in this capacity. *7**

indirect expenses (indirect costs)—also called overhead or administrative costs, these are expenses not directly related to the event. They can include salaries, rent, and building and equipment maintenance. *3**

individualized learning patterns—learning activities that the learner completes by him/herself. *18**

inducement—marketing tools or programs used to influence buying patterns and build customer loyalty. *37**

information desk (kiosk)—stand at which an official gives information. *36**

in-house contractor—contractor retained by a facility to be on-site and provide services as needed. In some cases, planners are not required to use their services, but may be charged a surcharge or facility fee for bringing in an outside contractor for the same service. See also exclusive contractor. *37**

in-kind—sponsors that do not pay in cash but rather in services that reduce the organization's costs. *4*

inline booth—exhibit space with exhibit booths on either side and back. See also inside booth/stand. *27**

installation and dismantle (I & D)—the set-up and teardown of exhibits; firm that does I & D work. See also erection. *27, 42**

insurance—legal agreement by which one party guarantees to undertake loss suffered by the other under specific circumstances. *42*

integrated marketing—marketing activities with a common focus on the marketplace or a customer segment. The execution of each individual piece of the integrated marketing plan is consistent with, and supportive of, each of the other pieces of the plan. *5**

integrated services digital network (ISDN)—a set of protocol and interface standards that make up an integrated (voice, data, video) telephone network; supports data transfer rates of up to 64 kbps. *13*

intelligent lighting—lighting instruments that can be computer controlled to move light around the room, and project color and patterns on screens, scenery, walls or floor. *29*

interactive learning—learning activities in which learners participate together. *18**

international freight forwarders—an independent business which handles export shipments for compensation. At the request of the shipper, the forwarder makes the actual arrangements and provides the necessary services for expediting the shipment to its overseas destination. The forwarder takes care of all documentation needed to move the shipment from origin to destination, making up and assembling the necessary documentation for submission to the bank in the exporter's name. The forwarder arranges for cargo insurance, makes the necessary overseas communications, and advises the shipper on overseas requirements of marking and labeling. The forwarder operates on a fee basis paid by the exporter and often receives an additional percentage of the freight charge from the common carrier. In the United States, an export freight forwarder must be licensed by the Federal Maritime Commission to handle ocean freight and by the International Air Transport Association (IATA) to handle air freight. An ocean freight forwarder dispatches shipments from the United States via common carriers, books or arranges space for the shipments, and handles the shipping documentation. See also freight forwarder, customs broker. *35**

international meeting—any event that includes participants from three or more countries. *16, 35*

internet protocol address (IP address)—a numeric value unique to an individual computer that allows a signal to find that computer on a network. The IP address is assigned through an Internet service provider (ISP) or network administrator. *10**

internet service provider (ISP)—service that provides access to the Internet. *13, 37**

interpretation—the process of explaining or translating. See also consecutive interpretation, interpretation in relay, simultaneous interpretation, translation, whispered interpretation, wireless infrared interpreting system. *16, 35**

interview technique—method of directly questioning registrants instead of having them complete a form independently during on-site registration. *24*

island booth—booth/stand space with aisles on all four sides. *27**

joint agreement—union contract covering more than one employer and a union, more than one union and an employer, or a number of employees and a number of unions. *37**

jurisdiction—the jobs that may be performed by a specific labor union; the locality where a contractual dispute is decided; in law, the ability of a court to hear and decide a matter brought before it. *42**

---

* denotes APEX definition

kbps—kilobits per second. A rate of data transmission over a computer network. *13**

keynote—opening remarks or presentation at a meeting that sets the tone or theme of the event and motivates attendees. *2, 19, 21**

keynote speaker—speaker whose presentation establishes the theme or tone of the event. *19**

kilobit—1,000 bits of data. *13*

kilowatt hour—1,000 watts of electricity used for one hour. *30*

labor union—workforce organization requiting various rules to be followed by the employing facility advocating the well-being of the workers. *37**

large-group patterns—learning activities that require the participation of a large group of learners. *18**

last-seat availability—agreement whereby an attendee is allowed to purchase a ticket at the reduced fare and on the official airline (if seats are open at the time of travel) regardless of its yield-management rate. *33*

lavaliere microphone—a wired or wireless microphone that hooks around the neck or is clipped to clothing. Sometimes called a necklace, lapel, or pendant microphone. *29*

LCD projector—self-contained unit with a LCD (liquid crystal display) panel, light source, and lens that works with both PC and Mac computers and duplicates the image being shown on the monitor without any need for special software or complex setting up. *29*

lead—(rhymes with seed) according to the Destination Management Association International (DMAI), when an inquiry by a corporation/association/ organization/independent event organizer that includes a request for a minimum of 10 sleeping rooms over a specific set/range of dates is forwarded by the CVB sales staff only to those hotels that meet the event organizer's event criteria. A lead is more formalized than just exchanging/ forwarding business cards to hotels. For convention center events, if the CVB sends a lead first to the convention center for date availability and then to the hotels for room blocks as a matter of policy, this process should be counted as one (1) lead for reporting purposes; customer; amount of space between lines of type (rhymes with dead). See also sales lead. *12**

lead retrieval—the process whereby exhibitors receive a potential customer's contact information in a standardized manner. A system for capturing and following up on leads generated at an exhibition. *10**

lead time—time between when arrangements are made and when an event occurs, etc. *33**

leadership in energy and environmental design (LEED)—a Green Building Rating System® is a voluntary, consensus-based national standard for developing high-performance, sustainable buildings developed by the United States Green Building Council. *30*

learning environment—the physical, emotional, psychological, physiological, and social factors surrounding the learning experience. *18, 23, 45**

learning style—the way a person learns new skills or gains new knowledge; the three basic learning styles are visual (learning through seeing), auditory (learning through hearing), and kinesthetic (learning through activity). *18*

lectern—a stand upon which a speaker may rest notes or books. May be standing, which rests on the floor, or table-top which is placed on a table. Often confused with podium. *23**

legacy issues—those factors that create expectations of current and future negotiations based upon past negotiations. *10, 40*

lekos—type of adjustable spotlight used to light lecterns, signs, and areas that need a tightly focused pool of light. See also ellipsoidal spotlight, lectern. *29*

letter of agreement—contract; document outlining proposed services, space, or products which becomes binding upon signature by authorized representatives of both parties. It lists services, foods, beverages, and so forth. *11, 40, 42**

liability disclaimer—legal statement releasing the organization from responsibility for any arrangements made by attendees with services listed by the organization (e.g., child care). *31**

license—written permission granted by an authority to engage in a specific action or business. *7**

lifelong learning—an ongoing process in which an individual actively seeks to understand and contribute to change. *18**

lift—number of airplane seats available on flights to a destination. *33**

light emitting diode (LED)—a solid-state diode rectifier whose atomic properties cause it to emit light when electric current is passed through it. Current LED technology allows the emission of light from infrared through green

---

* denotes APEX definition

frequencies, and visible light LEDs are available in colors from deep red to green. *29*

limited consumption bar—host establishes the maximum dollar amount to be spent at an open bar. Bar is closed or converted to cash when limit is reached. *26**

linear display—linear exhibits are generally 10' deep. They are offered in 10' or 15' widths and can be combined to create an exhibit of almost any length. *27**

liquid crystal display (LCD)—display composed of mobile crystals in liquid suspension which align themselves and polarize light in response to a small electric charge. The crystals are manufactured in pockets within the display which correspond to areas of dark on light background. *29*

loading dock—area on premises where goods are received. Usually a raised area that back loading trucks can back up to and offload freight easily. *27*

local area network (LAN)—a computer network limited to the immediate area, often the same building or floor of a building. *13*

local sponsorship—the practice of enlisting local organizations (or branches) to endorse holding a meeting in their area. *16, 35*

low season—period when the demand for a supplier's product or service is lowest. Prices general decrease in low season. Also called value season; compare with high season. *8, 14**

market segment—categorization of people, organizations or businesses by professional discipline or primary areas of interest for the purposes of sales analysis or assignment. *5**

marketing—a process of identifying human wants and needs, and developing a plan to meet those wants and needs. Refers to everything involved with convincing an attendee to come to the event. Also refers to providing information to support the exhibit sales function. *2, 5*

mass learning patterns—learning activities delivered through mass communication media. *18**

master account—a record of transactions during an event where the resulting balance is paid directly by the group. May include room, tax, incidentals, food and beverage, audiovisual equipment, decor, etc. Also called master bill. *3, 8, 35, 37, 38**

material handling—services performed by general services contractor (GSC); includes delivery of exhibit materials from the dock to assigned space, removing empty crates, returning crates at the end of the event for re-crating, and delivering materials back to the dock for carrier loading. It is a two-way charge, incoming and outgoing. Formerly known as drayage. *37**

mbps—megabits (millions of bits) per second; a rate of data transmission over a computer network. *13**

media kit—packet of information that is supplied to the media; contains all the details of an event that are required to attract media attention and attendees. *5**

meet and greet—service for meeting and greeting a person upon arrival in a city, usually at the airport, pier or rail station and assisting him or her with entrance formalities, collecting baggage, and obtaining transportation. *33**

meeting—an event where the primary activity of the attendees is to attend educational sessions, participate in meetings/discussions, socialize, or attend other organized events. There is no exhibit component to this event. Compare with convention, exhibition, trade show, consumer show. *2**

meeting history—facts and details from previous meetings. *19, 40*

meeting industry network (MINT)—formerly known as CINET or Convention Industry Network; online information network tracking historical and future site/booking information. MINT is provided by Destination Management Association International (DMAI). *12**

meeting manager—person whose job it is to arrange every aspect of planning and conducting a meeting or convention. See also planner. *1, 2*

meeting profile—a written report outlining statistics of previous events, anticipated use of all services, profile of attendees, hotel occupancy patterns, etc. *2, 11, 40**

message center—a place where mail and messages are kept or transmitted. *36**

metropolitan hotel—hotel located in the downtown area of a large city; usually close to shopping and other points of interest. *11**

microphone—instrument which converts sound into electrical signals for transmitting or recording sound. *29*

minutes—formal written record of a meeting. *19**

mixer—console with separate channels to control volume and sound quality produced by each microphone; sometimes called a sound board or mixing board. *29*

moderator—person who presides over panel discussions and forums. *19**

---

* denotes APEX definition

modified American plan (MAP)—a type of room rate that includes breakfast and one other meal (usually dinner). See also American plan, Bermuda plan, continental plan, European plan. *11, 16, 35**

move-in—dates set for installation. See also set-up. *27**

move-out—dates set for dismantling. See also tear down. *27**

multiple life experiences—the experience that adult learners bring to the learning environment that may help or hinder their learning. *18**

multi-point meeting —a real-time gathering of people in two or more distant locations for the exchange of ideas and information through the use of technology, such as audio-, video- or web-conferencing. *13*

negotiation goal—overarching objective of a negotiation, such as building relationships through your negotiations and moving beyond win-win. *40*

negotiation plan—the analytical tool that helps to guide the analysis of an upcoming negotiation. *40*

networking—the exchange of information or services among individuals, groups, or institutions. *7, 31*

non-residential conference centers—facility equipped for meetings, but without sleeping accommodations. *15*

no-show—reservation made, but not kept. Any person, group, or exhibitor who fails to appear to claim a meal reservation, exhibit space, or ordered service. Participant did not attend, nor cancel according to cancellation guidelines; an exhibitor that does not show up to claim booth/stand space; a hotel guest who does not honor a reservation; a speaker/entertainer who does not arrive. *12**

not-for-profit—an organization that exists with the intention of providing a service for its members. *12**

observation—the act of noting and recording a behavior or skill through the use of instruments. *45**

occupancy rate—in the hotel/motel industry, the percentage of total number of available sleeping rooms actually occupied. Derived by dividing the total number of rooms occupied during a given time period (night, week, year) by the total number of rooms available for occupancy during that same period; measurement of building use, usually expressed as an annual percentage rate comparing potential facility capacity to actual usage. See also exhibition occupancy. *40**

offer—a promise, proposal, or other expression of willingness to make and carry out a contract under proposed terms with another party which has the ability to accept it upon receiving it. Space and rent proposal from a facility. It may be in the form of a contract or license agreement. *11**

office suite—similar to a hospitality suite, but geared more exclusively toward typical office communications services (i.e. phone, fax, computer, copier). *36**

official airline—airline contracted by the sponsor of an event to provide special deals or amenities to attendees. *33**

official language—language in which an organization states that it will conduct all of its business. *16, 35**

off-season—see low season. *40**

off-site event—event held at a location other than the host facility. *32*

omni-directional—microphone that picks up sound from all directions. *29*

online registration—registration made via the web. *10, 24, 25**

on-site office—organizations' temporary headquarters office that is set up on-site to handle business during the event. *36**

on-site registration—process of signing up for an event on the day of, or at the site of, the event. *24**

open bar—private room bar set up where guests do not pay for drinks. See also host bar, sponsored bar. *26**

open seating—guests can sit anywhere; extra banquet tables are placed, but not fully set; these can be prepared quickly if there are more guests than expected. *26**

open space session—breakout facilitation where topics for conversation emerge from the group. People who want to lead a conversation post discussion topics during a morning news gathering. Then, participants split up and go to discuss the topic area they want to discuss. Everyone is asked to go to the topic that they have the most passion and interest around. The underlying assumption is that whoever shows up to the topic are the right people to be there. No assignments are made. Each group is asked to take notes so that they can share back or publish their ideas. Some people may decide to be butterflies moving from group to group over the course of the conversation time. If no one shows up it means that there is no interest in that topic. People can make more of a difference and have a greater impact on things that they are passionate about. *8**

---

* denotes APEX definition

open-ended questions—type of question format in which respondents are asked to communicate a response in their own words. *8, 45**

opt-in—an email marketing campaign that only sends messages to users who have requested (or opted-in) to receive specific types of information. Email conference reminders and newsletters are examples of opt-in email marketing campaigns based upon permission marketing. See also permission marketing. *5**

opt-out—see permission marketing. *5*

organic foods—grown without chemicals that can harm the land, water, or human health; organic certification of food can be through an independent organization or government program. *30*

outside vendor—supplier who is not directly associated with the facility. *40**

outsourcing—hiring an outside firm or individual to perform the task instead of using in-house staff; to subcontract a task or responsibility to a third party. *7, 37**

overhead projector—equipment which projects an image on a screen by passing light through a transparent slide or other transparency. *29*

P+1—parlor suite with one connecting room identified as single, double, or double/double. *25*

P+2—parlor suite with two connecting rooms identified as singles, doubles, or double/double. *25*

paid-out—in-house facility form authorizing cash withdrawal to be charged to master account or individual guest. *38**

panel discussion—instructional technique using a group of people chosen to discuss a topic in the presence of an audience. *2, 19, 23**

par—common term for sealed beam spot or flood lamp with self-contained lens surfaced glass. *29*

parlor suite—hotel living room, usually with a hide-a-bed sofa, connected to an adjoining sleeping room. *25**

participant—a person who takes part in an event; compare with attendee. *2**

participatory learning—occurs when the participants share knowledge, experience, and work together to learn. *19**

passport—a government issued document that allows the citizen of one country to travel into other countries. Required for all international travel. *16, 17, 35**

pavilion—a designated area within the event highlighting a special product category for marketing and exposure; a group presentation of different companies for the purpose of generating collected impact. *35**

peak night—referring to the night during an event when the most rooms are occupied by those in attendance. *14, 25**

peninsula booth—an exhibit with aisles on three sides. *27**

percentage of change formula—formula used to establish the variability in cost for future facility services. *40**

perimeter booth (perimeter wall booth)—exhibit space located on an outside wall. See also backwall, booth/stand. *27**

perimeter seating—seating arrangement in which chairs are placed around the walls of a room. The chairs are often meant for spectators to observe an activity or event in the center of the room. *23**

permission marketing—an email marketing campaign that only sends messages to users who have requested (or opted-in) to receive specific types of information. Email conference reminders and newsletters are examples of opt-in email marketing campaigns based upon permission marketing. See opt-in. *5**

personal digital assistant (PDA)—a handheld device that combines a personal organizer, cell phone, email messaging, and/or wireless web browser. *10, 13, 30, 36*

physical factors—the architectural design, furnishing, temperature, and other such factors that impact the learning environment. *18**

physiological factors—factors related to age, memory span, etc, that impact how an adult learns. *18**

pick-up—number of facility guest rooms actually used out of a room block. *12, 40**

pipe and drape—materials used to physically construct booths at an exhibition. *25*

place card—card placed on the banquet table, inscribed with the name of the person designated to sit at that place. *26**

planner—person whose job it is to oversee and arrange every aspect of an event. Person can be an employee or hired ad hoc by large companies, professional associations, or trade associations to plan, organize, implement, and control meetings, conventions, and other events. *2, 7**

planning matrix—a grid used to plan meeting formats and finalize subject areas, topics, and assignments. *19**

plated buffet—selection of preplated foods and entrees set on a buffet table. Can also be set on a roll-in cart. *26**

---

* denotes APEX definition

plenary session—general assembly for all participants. *19**

point-to-point—a videoconference between two distinct sites. *13*

population—the total of any kind of unit under consideration in an evaluation. *45**

portals—a web site or service that offers a broad array of resources and services, such as email, forums, search engines, and online shopping malls to attract and retain a large audience. *10**

post-consumer material—an end product that has completed its lifecycle as a consumer item and would otherwise have been disposed of as solid waste. Post-consumer materials include recyclables collected in commercial and residential recycling programs, such as office paper, cardboard, aluminum cans, plastics, and metals. *30*

post-consumer waste—post-consumer waste is recycled material collected after people have tossed it in the blue bin. Office recycling programs and household recycling programs are the main source of post-consumer waste. *30*

post-conference meeting (post-con meeting)—meeting at the primary facility at which an event occurred just after it has ended. Attendees generally include the primary event organizer, representatives of the event organizer/host organization, department heads at the facility, other facility staff as appropriate, and contractors. The agenda focuses on evaluating the implementation of the event and completing the APEX post event report. It often includes a final review of bills with accounts payable. Compare with pre-con meeting. *3, 35, 36, 37, 38*

poster session—display of reports and papers, usually scientific, accompanied by authors or researchers; a session dedicated to the discussion of the posters shown inside the meeting area. When this discussion is not held in a special session, it can take place directly between the person presenting the poster and interested delegate(s). See also abstract board. *19**

pre-conference meeting (pre-con meeting)—a meeting at the primary facility at which an event will take place just prior to the event beginning. Attendees generally include the primary event organizer, representatives of the event organizer/host organization, department heads at the facility, other facility staff as appropriate, and contractors. The agenda focuses on reviewing the purpose and details of the event and making final adjustments as needed. Compare with post-con meeting. *3, 33, 34, 35, 36**

preplated items—food placed on plates in the kitchen prior to being served. *26**

presenter—person explaining a given topic in an informational session. *21**

presenter-discussant format—A panel of three or four experts in certain subject areas are identified, with each giving a brief presentation. After each lecture the other panelists become discussants of the material just offered. At the conclusion of the presentations, the audience is given an opportunity to ask questions of the entire panel. *19**

preset service—placing plated foods on banquet tables prior to seating guests. *26**

press conference—event held to communicate information to media representatives. *5**

press release—a prepared statement released to the news media. Can be for immediate release, or at a specified time or date; an article intended for use by the media about a company, product, service, individual, or show. Also called news release. *5**

press room—a room where members of the media may obtain exhibitor press kits, conduct interviews, or relax. Larger press rooms contain typewriters, computers, phones, and fax machines for use by the press in filing their stories. *5**

pricing—decision making process of ascertaining what price to charge for a given service or activity once total costs are known. Involves determining the mark-up, studying the completion, and evaluating the tour value for the price to be charged. Usually a management function. *4**

priority point system—system of assigning points to exhibiting companies to determine which firms will receive priority in selecting booth/stand space for the next event. Also called priority rating system. *27**

problem-solving orientation—adult learner's tendency to seek education in order to solve a problem or fulfill a need. *18*

procurement—process of obtaining the necessary goods and services to conduct the business of the organization. In the past, it was often referred to as "purchasing." *6, 41*

productivity tickets—complimentary tickets awarded by the official airline after the event according to the number of attendees who used the airline. *33**

professional congress organizer (PCO)—a type of company, often in Europe, that is comparable to a destination management

---

* denotes APEX definition

company (DMC) in the United States. Local supplier who can arrange, manage, and/or plan any function or service for an event. See also ground operator. *12, 16, 35**

professional speaker—a speaker who is paid a fee for performances and makes a living from presenting information to various organizations. *21**

profile of attendees—data concerning attendees, including their average age, spending habits, etc. A profile of event participants. *2, 11, 40*

program committee—a volunteer committee charged with responsibility for planning, organizing, and delivering the meeting or conference content. *9, 19*

program design—structure of event program elements to achieve specific goals and objectives. *2, 19**

program development—planning that takes place before an event regarding its specific content and fabric. *2**

proofing—checking preliminary printed materials for errors before the final printing. *5**

proposal—plan put forth for consideration or acceptance; communication sent by a supplier to a potential customer detailing the supplier's offerings and prices. *11**

props—stage furniture, set dressing, and all articles used by actors or entertainers. *32**

protocol—customs and regulations dealing with diplomatic formality, precedence, and etiquette; a formal description of message formats and the rules two computers must follow to exchange messages. *16, 22, 35**

proxemics—addresses how different cultures use space. *22*

public accommodation—a private entity that owns, rents, or leases a public facility. *43**

public relations—presentation of an event via the media or other outlets, stressing the benefits and desirability of such event. *5**

publicity—a media campaign, normally consisting of a series of public notices and advertising activities, aimed at ensuring maximum attendance by focusing attention on an event. See also marketing, promotion. *5**

quad—room with two or more beds for four persons. *25**

questionnaire—a formalized set of questions for obtaining information from respondents. *2, 45**

rack rate—facility's standard, pre-established guest room rates. *40**

radio frequency identification tags (RFID)—devices that share information between a receiver and small transponder. *10, 44*

rear projection—movie, slide, or computer image presentation where the screen is between the viewer and the projector. Often used in terms of a front projection screen which is translucent to images being projected from the rear and can be viewed from the front. *29*

reasonable accommodation—any provision that aids the participation of a person with a disability, as long as it does not create a hazard to others; a major disruption in business, or an undue financial or administrative burden. *43**

rebate—a return of part of a payment. *37**

receiving fees—arbitrary fees sometimes imposed by a host government to officially recognize an event. *16, 35**

reception—stand-up social function where beverages and light foods are served. Foods may be presented on small buffet tables or passed by servers. May precede a meal function. *32**

recycled paper—according to U.S. government standards, uncoated paper with at least 30% post-consumer waste and coated paper with at least 10% post-consumer waste can be called recycled paper. *30*

recycling—the collection of waste materials and reprocessing them into new materials or products, which are then sold again. *30*

referral child care—when an event host organization publishes a list of child care service providers available. Attendees then make their own arrangements with these services. *31**

refund policy—rules and regulations which determine allowable reasons and timelines under which fees for a meeting or event will be refunded in whole or in part. *24**

registrant—individual who has submitted a registration form and attends an event. *24**

registration—process by which an individual indicates his/her intent to attend a conference or stay at a property; a method of booking and payment; the process of recording data about an attendee (or exhibitor), sending a confirmation, and creating a badge used on-site. *24**

registration area—designated area where event registration takes place. *23, 24**

registration form—form used by an event attendee to sign up to attend an event. It is used to collect important information about

---

* denotes APEX definition

the attendee and his/her intended participation in the event. *24**

reimbursement policy—statement of procedures that speakers and personnel must follow in order to have their expenses reimbursed. *38**

request for proposal (RFP)—a document that stipulates what services the organization wants from an outside contractor and requests a bid to perform such services. Synonyms: bid, manual specifications. *2, 10, 11, 12, 25, 37, 42*

resort—regions associated with recreation and leisure, such as the mountains, seashore, or natural or man-made attractions. A resort hotel or motel offers, or is located near facilities for sports and recreational activities such as tennis, swimming, sailing, etc. *11**

resort conference centers—a conference facility with at least one major amenity. *15**

resource workbook—usually a loose-leaf binder in which additions and deletions are made as the program develops. *19**

response rate—the number or percentage of persons in a sample who complete and return an evaluation instrument. *45**

résumé—See event specifications guide. *10, 35, 37, 38**

return on investment (ROI)—earnings divided by the investment; or, net profit divided by net worth. In context of calculating the ROI for a meeting or event, the earning become the net benefits from the meeting (monetary benefits minus the costs), and the investment is the meeting cost; a financial ratio indicating the degree of profitability. *2, 3, 7, 8, 11, 17, 28, 38, 45, 46*

rider—an additional clause in artist's contract stipulating special requirements such as travel, dressing rooms, technical equipment, etc. *32**

right to work state—where joining a union is not a condition of employment. *37**

right-of-first-refusal—a courtesy a facility extends to a previously booked party to approve or disapprove a concurrent booking or to keep uncontracted space for the previously booked party for program growth. *14**

riser—raised platform. See also dais, podium, cyclorama. *23**

risk—the potential for exposure to loss; possibility that something may happen that will adversely affect a meeting. *44*

risk assessment—determines the risks that are most likely to affect a specific meeting and which risks may have the worst consequences, should they occur. *44*

risk management—recognizing the possibility of injury, damage, or loss, and having a means to prevent it or provide insurance. *32, 44**

risk team—group of individuals responsible for creating an emergency management plan. *44*

room block—total number of sleeping rooms that are utilized and attributable to one event. *25**

room capacity—number of people that can function safely and comfortably in a room. *23**

room gap analysis—evaluating the difference between the total number of attendees and the number of hotel rooms used on peak night. *40*

room nights—number of rooms blocked or occupied multiplied by number of nights each room is reserved or occupied. *40**

room occupancy pattern—number of single and double rooms used. *40**

room rate—the amount charged for the occupancy of a room. *40**

rounded hollow square set-up—hollow square room set-up with corners replaced by serpentine or half-round tables. *23*

rounds—banquet tables, usually 60 inches (152 centimeters) in diameter. Also available in 66- and 72-inch (168- and 183-centimeter) diameters. A round for 8 is a banquet table at which 8 place settings should be set. Another common configuration is a round for 10. Commonly, a 60-inch (152 cm) round is used to seat 8, a 66-inch (168 cm) round seats 9, and a 72-inch (183 cm) round seats 10. *23**

roundtable—a group of experts who meet on an equal basis to review and discuss specialized, professional matters, either in closed session or, more frequently, before an audience. *19, 23*

run-of-the-house rate—rooms given at random according to availability when the reservations are made; flat rate for which a hotel or motel agrees to offer any of its available rooms (with the exception of suites) to a group. Final assignment of rooms is at the discretion of the hotel. See also flat rate. *40**

Russian service—the food is fully prepared in the kitchen. All courses are served either from platters or an escoffier dish. Tureens are used for soup and special bowls for salad. The server places the proper plate in front of the guest. After the plates are placed, the server returns with a tray of food and, moving counter-clockwise around the table, serves the food from the guest's left with the right hand. With this style of service, the

---

* denotes APEX definition

server controls the amount served to each guest. See also butler service. *26**

sales leads—names and contact information of potential customers. Attendee lists are often provided as sales leads to exhibitors as an incentive to participate in an exhibition. *2, 27**

sample—any portion of a population selected for an evaluation study. *45**

sampling—a way to obtain information about a population by examining a smaller, randomly chosen selection (the sample) of the population. If the sampling is conducted correctly, the results will be representative of the sampling population as a whole. *45**

Sarbanes-Oxley Act of 2002—a federal law which makes corporate accountability mandatory for public corporations. Abbreviated SOX. *39, 42*

schedule(s)—table(s) of time and location for all functions related to an event. This information should be included in the event specifications guide (ESG) for an event. *19, 33**

schoolroom set-up—see classroom set-up. *23*

scope of work—a detailed list of services to be provided. *42*

secret shopper—someone employed to test or evaluate the skills of an employee or the service in a shop or business by pretending to be a normal customer. *45**

security—a system of protecting people or property against crime, attack, or danger. Security is often in place for events to protect exhibits and can include guards, surveillance cameras, etc. See also security cage, security contractor, security guard, security service. *36, 44**

self-direction—acceptance and assumption of responsibility for one's own life; a characteristic of adult learners. *18**

serpentine—curved, S-shape tables that when placed together make a snake form. *23**

serpentine queue—line formation of people going to the same area; line feeds off into several different service stations. *23, 24**

service charge—a mandatory and automatic amount added to standard food and beverage charges, usually used to defray the cost of labor, such as housemen, servers, technicians, etc., and the facility receives a portion of the charge. In return, the guest is relieved the responsibility for tipping; a fee charged to a client by a travel agent in addition to the commissions paid to him or her by his or her principals. See also gratuity. *26, 40**

set-up—way in which a function room is arranged; erecting displays, installation, or, articles in their assembled condition; mixers, fruit, and glassware accompanying a liquor order. See also floor plan. *23, 36**

set-up drawings—the plans from which the exhibit components are assembled. *23**

set-up personnel—exhibit or function room equipment installers. *23**

set-up plan—See floor plan. *23**

set-up time—the period necessary for the preparation of the conference and exhibition venue before the arrival of delegates and exhibitors. *23**

shade grown coffee—coffee that is grown in the traditional manner, with coffee plants interspersed under a canopy of trees. End result: more habitat for birds, less need for chemical inputs, and the forest is not disrupted. *30*

shipping agent—third-party hired to handle the shipping of goods to and from an event. Also called shipper. *38**

shoulder season—period when the demand for a supplier's product or service is neither high nor low. See also high season, low season. *8, 40**

show daily—a newspaper published each day during the run of an event or conference. It includes articles about the exhibits and events, and often, advertising. *27**

show directory—a listing, with booth/stand numbers, of all the exhibitors in an event and a map showing booth/stand locations. *27**

shuttle—a vehicle, usually a bus, contracted to transport event attendees between facilities during a certain time period. *33**

sightseeing tour—an outing to points of interest, often by bus or van. *31**

signage—informational and directional signs and placards at an event. *28, 34, 36**

simple random sampling—method of sampling in which each member of the population has an equal chance of being included in the sample. *45**

simulation—a mode of instruction that relies on imitating or estimating how an event, process, skill or behavior might occur in a real situation. *45**

simulation encounter—interactive instructional technique in which an individual simulates certain behavior which can then be examined, studied and discussed by the attendees. *19**

single room—sleeping room occupied by one person. The room may have one or more beds in it. *25**

---

* denotes APEX definition

site inspection—in-person, on-site review and evaluation of a venue or location for an event. See familiarization (FAM) trip. *11, 12**

site selection—Choosing a venue for an event. *2, 11, 12**

slide projector—apparatus used for projecting photographic slides onto a screen. It will often have a remote (either wired or wireless) that can be used to advance the slides. *29*

slippage—reduction in the number of rooms used from the original reserved block. *40**

small group learning patterns—a learning activity that is dependent on the participation of a small group of people. *18**

smart card—a plastic credit card with an embedded integrated circuit chip that can store up to 16,000 bits of data for lead retrieval and other functions. *13**

social/cultural factors—factors related to interaction with other learners that affect the way a person learns. *18**

soft costs or gains—those that are qualitative or not easily measurable such as relational issues, hassles, or morale. *40*

soft data—information collected in the areas of attitude, motivation, satisfaction, and skill usage; is often subjective and difficult to measure. *45**

speaker—the presenter of a program. Types of speakers include keynote, general session, seminar leader, trainer, workshop leader, and change of pace speakers such as humorists and entertainers; device for sound output. *2**

speaker (bureau)—a booking or sales company that sells the services of multiple speakers. *21**

speaker ready room—see ready room. *21, 23**

special event—one time event staged for the purpose of celebration; unique activity. *32**

sponsor—person(s) or company(s) underwriting all or part of the costs of an event. Sponsors may or may not participate in any of the profit from the event; an individual who assumed all or part of the financial responsibility for an event. A commercial sponsor that provides financial backing for an aspect of an event and who in return receives visibility, advertising, or other remuneration in lieu of cash. *2, 4**

sponsorship—donated financial or material support, usually in exchange for recognition; paid opportunity for an entity or an exhibitor to increase its visibility at the event. *4, 27**

spotlight—strong focused light thrown upon a particular person or object, such as on a stage. *29*

spreadsheet—a listing of expected revenue and expenses to analyze cash flow on a monthly basis. *3*

stakeholders—all individuals who are invested in a project or event such as the sponsors, attendees, vendors, media, and others. *2**

standard booth—a basic 10- by 10-foot (3.05- by-3.05-meter) booth designed to stand back-to-back with an opposite row of booths. Synonyms: linear booth, in-line booth. *27*

standing committee—committee, defined by organizational bylaws, which meets for a specific purpose. *9**

statistics—quantitative details of an event, e.g., number of attendees, sleeping rooms, etc. *2, 40**

steering committee—select group which sets policies and makes basic decisions relative to a group or an event. *9**

strategic relationships—an agreement between two or more enterprises to conduct specified business processes in a joint manner. Usually related to technology development and/or marketing and distribution efforts. *4**

stratified random sample—a population is divided into demographic groups and each group is then randomly selected to participate in a sample. *45**

streaming media—a method for delivering audio, video, and animated content over the web. Streaming refers to the ability of web site visitors to access multimedia content without having to download an entire file first. *10**

structured question(s)—prepare eight or ten questions per one hour presentation to be distributed in advance of the session to selected attendees. Following each major presentation, attendees ask questions from the list. *19**

style sheet—a list of special spellings, terms, and style points to be used consistently in publications related to an event. *5**

sub-blocks—any group of rooms that is classified or separated differently than the general attendee block within the event-contracted block (ECB). See also event-contracted block. *25**

suburban hotel—hotel on the outskirts of a large city, which may or may not be near local attractions. *11**

supplier—purveyor, provider, vendor, contractor offering facilities, products and/or services. *2**

survey—a formalized set of questions for obtaining information from respondents. *45**

---

* denotes APEX definition

symposium—a meeting of a number of experts in a particular field, at which papers are presented and discussed by specialists on particular subjects with a view to making recommendations concerning the problems under discussion. *19**

T-1 Line—transmitting data at speeds of up to 1.544 Mbps, operates at a much higher capacity than an ISDN line and can be split to accommodate several users at one time; known as a fractional T-1. See also T-3 line. *13**

T-3 Line—transmitting data at speeds of up to 44.184 Mbps, is faster than a T-1 line, allowing performance of more tasks simultaneously at a greater speed. See also T-1 line. *13**

tablet chairs—chairs with attached writing surfaces. See also writing chairs. *23**

tagline—an often-repeated phrase associated with an individual, organization, or commercial product; describes the entity's overall goal or mission. *5*

talk show set-up—seating arrangement, often used for panel discussions, in which a desk, for the moderator/facilitator, is set perpendicular to arm chairs for the panelists. *23**

target audience—group to which you direct your marketing efforts. *5, 32*

tariffs—a schedule of duties imposed by a government on imported and exported goods; published list of fares or rates and conditions of service from a supplier. *35**

team building—a structured group activity designed to facilitate a closer professional relationship between members of a company or organization. *32*

teaser—promotional piece designed to build interest in an event. *5*

teaser copy—copy written to get attention and entice the reader to open and read a promotional piece. *5*

technological factors—factors related to equipment used in the learning environment that affect the way a person learns. *18**

temps—temporary workers used for registration and other duties. *9**

theater semicircular set-up—seating arrangement in which seats are in semicircular rows facing the stage area; no tables. *23**

theme party—event at which all foods, beverages, decorations, and entertainment relate to a single theme. *32**

third party—a person other than the principals. *7**

third-party provider—any service provider that is compensated by acting as an agent for another supplier; this role can encompass facilitating, recommending, and/or contracting services on behalf of an end user. *14, 37*

ticket exchange—banquet-control procedure whereby guests exchange an event coupon from their registration packet for an actual event ticket and seat assignment; increases control; tends to reduce the number of no-shows to provide more accurate guarantees. *26**

time agenda—an outlined program of events and time of commencement that is tailored to the needs of an event; also known as sequence of events. *2**

time lines—includes each task to be accomplished and is the core of the program plan. *8**

tip—a voluntary and selective amount of money, given at will, for special or excellent service. *26, 38**

tour(s)—any prearranged journey to one or more destinations and back to the point of origin; a recreational trip or activity provided to event attendees and/or accompanying persons as a scheduled portion of the event program. Also called excursion. *33**

trade show—an exhibition of products and/or services held for members of a common or related industry. Not open to the general public. See also exhibition. Compare with gate show, public show, consumer show. *2, 17**

trade-out—a type of barter. The exchange of goods and services instead of using money. *5**

traffic density—how crowded the aisles are at an event. *17**

traffic flow—movement of people through an area; a supposed or directed path that attendees will take through an exhibition. *2**

transformative learning—learning that occurs during the second half of life which is directed at attaining a new consciousness and self-understanding. *18**

transient—momentary amplitude peak in program source. A pop from a switch or scratched record may form signal transients. Musical transients occur as a result of such things as percussion instruments, piano, and guitar. Normal musical transients may have amplitude peaks as high as 40dB above the average program levels, requiring headroom in the circuits and equipment used to reproduce them. *12**

transient occupancy tax (TOT)—tax placed on hotel/motel room rentals; generally all or part of revenues thus generated is used in

---

* denotes APEX definition

financing the operation of convention facilities. Also called bed tax, room tax, hotel tax. *12**

translation—the rendering of one language into another of something written or spoken. See also consecutive interpretation, interpretation, whispered interpretation, wireless infrared interpreting system. *35**

transparency—audiovisual material designed to be shown on an overhead projector; also called an overhead. *29*

triple room—three people occupying a double/double room. *25*

tripod screen—portable projection screen, usually not larger than 10-12 feet, with three folding legs and a pull-up surface supported by a rod on the back. *29*

T-shape set-up—series of tables set up in the shape of the block-T with chairs set all around except at the head table. *23**

turnover—breaking down and resetting a function room with a different set-up; a pastry that usually has a fruit filling. *23**

underground hospitality suite—hospitality suite that is not hosted by an official sponsoring organization; liability risk. *26**

unidirectional microphone—microphone used for speeches that is designed to pick up sound from only one direction. *29*

uniform resource locator (URL)—Internet address for a web site; starts with http://. *5**

union house—facility in which workers are governed and regulated by an organized union; often maintain exclusive contractors. *40**

uniserve property—a hotel property in which the convention services manager (CSM) handles all aspects of the event, including catering. *35, 36**

uplink—the station used to transmit signals from earth to a satellite; videoconferencing. *13**

U-shape set-up—series of tables set up in the shape of the letter U, with chairs set all around on one or both sides. *23**

value added tax (VAT)—a tax that is added to a product at each step of the manufacturing and marketing process reflecting value which has been added to the product by processing; applies to all European Community countries, Switzerland, and other countries around the world. A tax on the estimated market value added to any product at each stage of its manufacture or distribution, ultimately passed on to the consumer. The percentage applies to CIF value and duties and the percentage differs from one country to another. Local VAT on forwarding/handling

services is not charged between EC companies with a registered VAT number, or to non-EC exhibitors on condition the local forwarder executes customs clearance and transport. *3, 16, 35**

variable expenses (variable costs)—expenses that vary based upon various factors, such as the number of attendees. *3**

vegans—an individual who eats no meat, and does not use other animal products and by-products such as eggs, dairy products, honey, leather, fur, silk, wool, cosmetics, and soaps derived from animal products. See also vegetarian. *26**

vendor—one who sells services or goods. *2**

venue—site or destination of a meeting, event, or show; location of a performance such as hall, ballroom, auditorium, etc. *17, 35**

vertical show—an exhibition at which the products or services being displayed represent one element of an industry or profession. See also exhibition, horizontal show. *17**

very important person (VIP)—person who has a special function at the event (speaker, dignitary, etc.) and should be treated with special care and attention. *40**

videoconference—a meeting between two or more people or groups across a distance, including video, audio, and potentially other data, utilizing telecommunications or communications satellites for transmission of the signal. See also teleconference. *13**

videographers—professionals hired to develop videotape that can be used to promote an event. *36**

viral marketing—a strategy that encourages individuals to pass on a marketing message to others, creating the potential for rapid multiplication of the message's exposure and influence. *5*

virtual private network (VPN)—a private network that is constructed using the Internet to transmit data between computing devices. *13*

virtual trade show—exhibit of products or services that can be viewed over the Internet. *10**

visa—permit, recorded in a passport, to enter a country for a specific purpose and period of time. *10, 35**

visitor—an attendee and/or a potential customer; according to the World Tourism Organization; visitor refers to any person traveling to a place other than that of his/her usual environment for less than 12 consecutive months and whose main purpose of trip is other than the exercise of an

---

* denotes APEX definition

activity remunerated from within the place visited. *2**

volunteer speaker—speaker (usually a member of the organization) who volunteers their skills as a presenter for a meeting. *21**

voucher plan—hotel plan whereby the daily rate covers the room cost and provides a set amount that can be applied to food and beverage items. *16, 35**

V-shape set-up—seating arrangement in which chairs are arranged in rows slanted in a V-shape and separated by a center aisle. They face the head table or speaker. See also herringbone set-up, chevron set-up. *23**

walk and talk—slang for a reception without seating. *23**

walkie-talkie—wireless radio that transmits and receives oral communications. *36**

wash light—colored light that softly illuminates an area. *23, 29**

wayfinding—addresses the evolving response to the human need to find our way; the use of visual cues which allow people to form personal mental maps of orientation. *28*

web browser—a software program that helps a user navigate the World Wide Web, access specific sites, and search for sites on a particular topic. *13*

web cast—an event that broadcasts the audio and/or video portion of a keynote presentation or other educational sessions over the web in real-time or on-demand. *13, 27**

web conference—web browser-based videoconferencing. *13**

web link—a web site address that points to a web page or other file (image, video, PDF, etc.) on a web server. Links reside on web pages, in email messages and in word processing documents as well as any other document type that supports hypertext and URL addressing. *45**

web page—a single page of information on a web site, often connected to other web pages by hyperlinks. *5*

web site—a location or address on the World Wide Web; may contain several web pages of related information. *5*

white boarding—a feature of videoconferencing systems which allows the placement of shared documents on an on-screen shared space or whiteboard. Participants can edit and mark up the document just as on a physical whiteboard. *13**

wide area network (WAN)—any Internet or network that covers an area larger than a single building or campus; it spans multiple geographic distances. *13**

win-win situation—negotiable concept in which all parties benefit from the contract. *7, 40**

wireless application protocol (WAP)—a secure specification that allows users to access information instantly via handheld wireless devices such as mobile phones, pagers, two-way radios, and personal digital assistants; WAP supports most wireless networks. *13*

wireless microphones—microphones that operate by transmitting a signal to a receiver. *29*

wireless network—a system of computers or other devices using the airwaves rather than cables to send and receive information; may be connected to other wireless or cabled networks. *13*

working program—timetable of conference content. *2**

workshop—meeting of several persons for intensive discussion. The workshop concept has been developed to compensate for diverging views in a particular discipline or on a particular subject; informal and public session of free discussion organized to take place between formal plenary sessions or commissions of a congress or of a conference, either on a subject chosen by the participants themselves or else on a special problem suggested by the organizers; training session in which participants, often through exercises, develop skills and knowledge in a given field. *2, 19**

World Wide Web (www)—the fastest-growing segment of the Internet; called the web because each site is connected by hyperlinks that allow a user to travel from site to site. *13*

yield management system—computer program that uses variable pricing models to maximize the return on a fixed (perishable) inventory, such as hotel rooms, based on supply-and-demand theory. Also referred to as revenue management. *10**

zero-based budgeting—the process of building a budget without benefit of a previous year's budget. *3**

zone fare—unpublished rates offered from particular areas of the United States and Canada to specified event destinations; they do not require a Saturday night stay over. *33**

zone of possible agreement (ZOPA)—the area where it is better for the individuals or organizations involved to reach a deal rather than walk away. *40*

---

* denotes APEX definition

PCMA Membership—Join Today!

The Education and Resource Center for the Meetings Industry™

The high-quality education and sense of community offered by PCMA is unmatched by any other similar organization. Just take a look at what our members are saying…

"PCMA means…a chance to be with our people in the meetings industry, to share in their experiences and ideas…to get excited about new ideas, to get my battery charged through top notch speakers and motivators."

> Norman Burkhalter
> Director, National Events
> Boy Scouts of America

"I get immediate interaction and specific details about how other planners are dealing with the same issues. This type of networking is invaluable."

> Sherry Romello, CMP
> Director, Meetings & Conventions
> National Association of Convenience Stores

"Membership in PCMA is a necessity for anyone in the meeting and conventions industry…PCMA membership provides the needed education and networking opportunities crucial to success within our industry"

> David W. Giger
> Director, Sales & Industry Relations
> Hilton Hotels Corporation

"Networking with professionals is the most valuable benefit as a student member. There are numerous opportunities…where networking leads to mentors, job shadowing, internships or job opportunities."

> Katie Steigerwalt
> University of Delaware

"There's never been a more exciting time to be a PCMA member than right now!"

> Leigh Wintz, CAE
> 2006 PCMA Chairman of the Board

Join over 5,000 leading meeting professionals and become part of the Professional Convention Management Association community today. Visit www.pcma.org or call 312.423.7262 and learn why membership in PCMA is one of the best investments you can make in your career!